Lecture Notes in Computer Science   13692

More information about this series at https://link.springer.com/bookseries/558

Shai Avidan · Gabriel Brostow ·
Moustapha Cissé · Giovanni Maria Farinella ·
Tal Hassner (Eds.)

Computer Vision – ECCV 2022

17th European Conference
Tel Aviv, Israel, October 23–27, 2022
Proceedings, Part XXXII

Springer

Editors
Shai Avidan
Tel Aviv University
Tel Aviv, Israel

Gabriel Brostow (iD)
University College London
London, UK

Moustapha Cissé
Google AI
Accra, Ghana

Giovanni Maria Farinella (iD)
University of Catania
Catania, Italy

Tal Hassner (iD)
Facebook (United States)
Menlo Park, CA, USA

ISSN 0302-9743   ISSN 1611-3349 (electronic)
Lecture Notes in Computer Science
ISBN 978-3-031-19823-6   ISBN 978-3-031-19824-3 (eBook)
https://doi.org/10.1007/978-3-031-19824-3

This Springer imprint is published by the registered company Springer Nature Switzerland AG
The registered company address is: Gewerbestrasse 11, 6330 Cham, Switzerland

Foreword

Organizing the European Conference on Computer Vision (ECCV 2022) in Tel-Aviv during a global pandemic was no easy feat. The uncertainty level was extremely high, and decisions had to be postponed to the last minute. Still, we managed to plan things just in time for ECCV 2022 to be held in person. Participation in physical events is crucial to stimulating collaborations and nurturing the culture of the Computer Vision community.

There were many people who worked hard to ensure attendees enjoyed the best science at the 16th edition of ECCV. We are grateful to the Program Chairs Gabriel Brostow and Tal Hassner, who went above and beyond to ensure the ECCV reviewing process ran smoothly. The scientific program includes dozens of workshops and tutorials in addition to the main conference and we would like to thank Leonid Karlinsky and Tomer Michaeli for their hard work. Finally, special thanks to the web chairs Lorenzo Baraldi and Kosta Derpanis, who put in extra hours to transfer information fast and efficiently to the ECCV community.

We would like to express gratitude to our generous sponsors and the Industry Chairs, Dimosthenis Karatzas and Chen Sagiv, who oversaw industry relations and proposed new ways for academia-industry collaboration and technology transfer. It's great to see so much industrial interest in what we're doing!

Authors' draft versions of the papers appeared online with open access on both the Computer Vision Foundation (CVF) and the European Computer Vision Association (ECVA) websites as with previous ECCVs. Springer, the publisher of the proceedings, has arranged for archival publication. The final version of the papers is hosted by SpringerLink, with active references and supplementary materials. It benefits all potential readers that we offer both a free and citeable version for all researchers, as well as an authoritative, citeable version for SpringerLink readers. Our thanks go to Ronan Nugent from Springer, who helped us negotiate this agreement. Last but not least, we wish to thank Eric Mortensen, our publication chair, whose expertise made the process smooth.

October 2022

Rita Cucchiara
Jiří Matas
Amnon Shashua
Lihi Zelnik-Manor

Preface

Welcome to the proceedings of the European Conference on Computer Vision (ECCV 2022). This was a hybrid edition of ECCV as we made our way out of the COVID-19 pandemic. The conference received 5804 valid paper submissions, compared to 5150 submissions to ECCV 2020 (a 12.7% increase) and 2439 in ECCV 2018. 1645 submissions were accepted for publication (28%) and, of those, 157 (2.7% overall) as orals.

846 of the submissions were desk-rejected for various reasons. Many of them because they revealed author identity, thus violating the double-blind policy. This violation came in many forms: some had author names with the title, others added acknowledgments to specific grants, yet others had links to their github account where their name was visible. Tampering with the LaTeX template was another reason for automatic desk rejection.

ECCV 2022 used the traditional CMT system to manage the entire double-blind reviewing process. Authors did not know the names of the reviewers and vice versa. Each paper received at least 3 reviews (except 6 papers that received only 2 reviews), totalling more than 15,000 reviews.

Handling the review process at this scale was a significant challenge. To ensure that each submission received as fair and high-quality reviews as possible, we recruited more than 4719 reviewers (in the end, 4719 reviewers did at least one review). Similarly we recruited more than 276 area chairs (eventually, only 276 area chairs handled a batch of papers). The area chairs were selected based on their technical expertise and reputation, largely among people who served as area chairs in previous top computer vision and machine learning conferences (ECCV, ICCV, CVPR, NeurIPS, etc.).

Reviewers were similarly invited from previous conferences, and also from the pool of authors. We also encouraged experienced area chairs to suggest additional chairs and reviewers in the initial phase of recruiting. The median reviewer load was five papers per reviewer, while the average load was about four papers, because of the emergency reviewers. The area chair load was 35 papers, on average.

Conflicts of interest between authors, area chairs, and reviewers were handled largely automatically by the CMT platform, with some manual help from the Program Chairs. Reviewers were allowed to describe themselves as senior reviewer (load of 8 papers to review) or junior reviewers (load of 4 papers). Papers were matched to area chairs based on a subject-area affinity score computed in CMT and an affinity score computed by the Toronto Paper Matching System (TPMS). TPMS is based on the paper's full text. An area chair handling each submission would bid for preferred expert reviewers, and we balanced load and prevented conflicts.

The assignment of submissions to area chairs was relatively smooth, as was the assignment of submissions to reviewers. A small percentage of reviewers were not happy with their assignments in terms of subjects and self-reported expertise. This is an area for improvement, although it's interesting that many of these cases were reviewers hand-picked by AC's. We made a later round of reviewer recruiting, targeted at the list of authors of papers submitted to the conference, and had an excellent response which helped provide enough emergency reviewers. In the end, all but six papers received at least 3 reviews.

The challenges of the reviewing process are in line with past experiences at ECCV 2020. As the community grows, and the number of submissions increases, it becomes ever more challenging to recruit enough reviewers and ensure a high enough quality of reviews. Enlisting authors by default as reviewers might be one step to address this challenge.

Authors were given a week to rebut the initial reviews, and address reviewers' concerns. Each rebuttal was limited to a single pdf page with a fixed template.

The Area Chairs then led discussions with the reviewers on the merits of each submission. The goal was to reach consensus, but, ultimately, it was up to the Area Chair to make a decision. The decision was then discussed with a buddy Area Chair to make sure decisions were fair and informative. The entire process was conducted virtually with no in-person meetings taking place.

The Program Chairs were informed in cases where the Area Chairs overturned a decisive consensus reached by the reviewers, and pushed for the meta-reviews to contain details that explained the reasoning for such decisions. Obviously these were the most contentious cases, where reviewer inexperience was the most common reported factor.

Once the list of accepted papers was finalized and released, we went through the laborious process of plagiarism (including self-plagiarism) detection. A total of 4 accepted papers were rejected because of that.

Finally, we would like to thank our Technical Program Chair, Pavel Lifshits, who did tremendous work behind the scenes, and we thank the tireless CMT team.

October 2022

Gabriel Brostow
Giovanni Maria Farinella
Moustapha Cissé
Shai Avidan
Tal Hassner

Organization

General Chairs

Rita Cucchiara	University of Modena and Reggio Emilia, Italy
Jiří Matas	Czech Technical University in Prague, Czech Republic
Amnon Shashua	Hebrew University of Jerusalem, Israel
Lihi Zelnik-Manor	Technion – Israel Institute of Technology, Israel

Program Chairs

Shai Avidan	Tel-Aviv University, Israel
Gabriel Brostow	University College London, UK
Moustapha Cissé	Google AI, Ghana
Giovanni Maria Farinella	University of Catania, Italy
Tal Hassner	Facebook AI, USA

Program Technical Chair

Pavel Lifshits	Technion – Israel Institute of Technology, Israel

Workshops Chairs

Leonid Karlinsky	IBM Research, Israel
Tomer Michaeli	Technion – Israel Institute of Technology, Israel
Ko Nishino	Kyoto University, Japan

Tutorial Chairs

Thomas Pock	Graz University of Technology, Austria
Natalia Neverova	Facebook AI Research, UK

Demo Chair

Bohyung Han	Seoul National University, Korea

Social and Student Activities Chairs

Tatiana Tommasi   Italian Institute of Technology, Italy
Sagie Benaim   University of Copenhagen, Denmark

Diversity and Inclusion Chairs

Xi Yin   Facebook AI Research, USA
Bryan Russell   Adobe, USA

Communications Chairs

Lorenzo Baraldi   University of Modena and Reggio Emilia, Italy
Kosta Derpanis   York University & Samsung AI Centre Toronto,
                                Canada

Industrial Liaison Chairs

Dimosthenis Karatzas   Universitat Autònoma de Barcelona, Spain
Chen Sagiv   SagivTech, Israel

Finance Chair

Gerard Medioni   University of Southern California & Amazon,
                                USA

Publication Chair

Eric Mortensen   MiCROTEC, USA

Area Chairs

Lourdes Agapito   University College London, UK
Zeynep Akata   University of Tübingen, Germany
Naveed Akhtar   University of Western Australia, Australia
Karteek Alahari   Inria Grenoble Rhône-Alpes, France
Alexandre Alahi   École polytechnique fédérale de Lausanne,
                                Switzerland
Pablo Arbelaez   Universidad de Los Andes, Columbia
Antonis A. Argyros   University of Crete & Foundation for Research
                                and Technology-Hellas, Crete
Yuki M. Asano   University of Amsterdam, The Netherlands
Kalle Åström   Lund University, Sweden
Hadar Averbuch-Elor   Cornell University, USA

Matthijs Douze	Facebook AI Research, USA
Mohamed Elhoseiny	King Abdullah University of Science and Technology, Saudi Arabia
Sergio Escalera	University of Barcelona, Spain
Yi Fang	New York University, USA
Ryan Farrell	Brigham Young University, USA
Alireza Fathi	Google, USA
Christoph Feichtenhofer	Facebook AI Research, USA
Basura Fernando	Agency for Science, Technology and Research (A*STAR), Singapore
Vittorio Ferrari	Google Research, Switzerland
Andrew W. Fitzgibbon	Graphcore, UK
David J. Fleet	University of Toronto, Canada
David Forsyth	University of Illinois at Urbana-Champaign, USA
David Fouhey	University of Michigan, USA
Katerina Fragkiadaki	Carnegie Mellon University, USA
Friedrich Fraundorfer	Graz University of Technology, Austria
Oren Freifeld	Ben-Gurion University, Israel
Thomas Funkhouser	Google Research & Princeton University, USA
Yasutaka Furukawa	Simon Fraser University, Canada
Fabio Galasso	Sapienza University of Rome, Italy
Jürgen Gall	University of Bonn, Germany
Chuang Gan	Massachusetts Institute of Technology, USA
Zhe Gan	Microsoft, USA
Animesh Garg	University of Toronto, Vector Institute, Nvidia, Canada
Efstratios Gavves	University of Amsterdam, The Netherlands
Peter Gehler	Amazon, Germany
Theo Gevers	University of Amsterdam, The Netherlands
Bernard Ghanem	King Abdullah University of Science and Technology, Saudi Arabia
Ross B. Girshick	Facebook AI Research, USA
Georgia Gkioxari	Facebook AI Research, USA
Albert Gordo	Facebook, USA
Stephen Gould	Australian National University, Australia
Venu Madhav Govindu	Indian Institute of Science, India
Kristen Grauman	Facebook AI Research & UT Austin, USA
Abhinav Gupta	Carnegie Mellon University & Facebook AI Research, USA
Mohit Gupta	University of Wisconsin-Madison, USA
Hu Han	Institute of Computing Technology, Chinese Academy of Sciences, China

Bohyung Han   Seoul National University, Korea
Tian Han   Stevens Institute of Technology, USA
Emily Hand   University of Nevada, Reno, USA
Bharath Hariharan   Cornell University, USA
Ran He   Institute of Automation, Chinese Academy of
                            Sciences, China
Otmar Hilliges   ETH Zurich, Switzerland
Adrian Hilton   University of Surrey, UK
Minh Hoai   Stony Brook University, USA
Yedid Hoshen   Hebrew University of Jerusalem, Israel
Timothy Hospedales   University of Edinburgh, UK
Gang Hua   Wormpex AI Research, USA
Di Huang   Beihang University, China
Jing Huang   Facebook, USA
Jia-Bin Huang   Facebook, USA
Nathan Jacobs   Washington University in St. Louis, USA
C. V. Jawahar   International Institute of Information Technology,
                            Hyderabad, India
Herve Jegou   Facebook AI Research, France
Neel Joshi   Microsoft Research, USA
Armand Joulin   Facebook AI Research, France
Frederic Jurie   University of Caen Normandie, France
Fredrik Kahl   Chalmers University of Technology, Sweden
Yannis Kalantidis   NAVER LABS Europe, France
Evangelos Kalogerakis   University of Massachusetts, Amherst, USA
Sing Bing Kang   Zillow Group, USA
Yosi Keller   Bar Ilan University, Israel
Margret Keuper   University of Mannheim, Germany
Tae-Kyun Kim   Imperial College London, UK
Benjamin Kimia   Brown University, USA
Alexander Kirillov   Facebook AI Research, USA
Kris Kitani   Carnegie Mellon University, USA
Iasonas Kokkinos   Snap Inc. & University College London, UK
Vladlen Koltun   Apple, USA
Nikos Komodakis   University of Crete, Crete
Piotr Koniusz   Australian National University, Australia
Philipp Kraehenbuehl   University of Texas at Austin, USA
Dilip Krishnan   Google, USA
Ajay Kumar   Hong Kong Polytechnic University, Hong Kong,
                            China
Junseok Kwon   Chung-Ang University, Korea
Jean-Francois Lalonde   Université Laval, Canada

Ivan Laptev	Inria Paris, France
Laura Leal-Taixé	Technical University of Munich, Germany
Erik Learned-Miller	University of Massachusetts, Amherst, USA
Gim Hee Lee	National University of Singapore, Singapore
Seungyong Lee	Pohang University of Science and Technology, Korea
Zhen Lei	Institute of Automation, Chinese Academy of Sciences, China
Bastian Leibe	RWTH Aachen University, Germany
Hongdong Li	Australian National University, Australia
Fuxin Li	Oregon State University, USA
Bo Li	University of Illinois at Urbana-Champaign, USA
Yin Li	University of Wisconsin-Madison, USA
Ser-Nam Lim	Meta AI Research, USA
Joseph Lim	University of Southern California, USA
Stephen Lin	Microsoft Research Asia, China
Dahua Lin	The Chinese University of Hong Kong, Hong Kong, China
Si Liu	Beihang University, China
Xiaoming Liu	Michigan State University, USA
Ce Liu	Microsoft, USA
Zicheng Liu	Microsoft, USA
Yanxi Liu	Pennsylvania State University, USA
Feng Liu	Portland State University, USA
Yebin Liu	Tsinghua University, China
Chen Change Loy	Nanyang Technological University, Singapore
Huchuan Lu	Dalian University of Technology, China
Cewu Lu	Shanghai Jiao Tong University, China
Oisin Mac Aodha	University of Edinburgh, UK
Dhruv Mahajan	Facebook, USA
Subhransu Maji	University of Massachusetts, Amherst, USA
Atsuto Maki	KTH Royal Institute of Technology, Sweden
Arun Mallya	NVIDIA, USA
R. Manmatha	Amazon, USA
Iacopo Masi	Sapienza University of Rome, Italy
Dimitris N. Metaxas	Rutgers University, USA
Ajmal Mian	University of Western Australia, Australia
Christian Micheloni	University of Udine, Italy
Krystian Mikolajczyk	Imperial College London, UK
Anurag Mittal	Indian Institute of Technology, Madras, India
Philippos Mordohai	Stevens Institute of Technology, USA
Greg Mori	Simon Fraser University & Borealis AI, Canada

Vittorio Murino   Istituto Italiano di Tecnologia, Italy
P. J. Narayanan   International Institute of Information Technology,
                                    Hyderabad, India
Ram Nevatia   University of Southern California, USA
Natalia Neverova   Facebook AI Research, UK
Richard Newcombe   Facebook, USA
Cuong V. Nguyen   Florida International University, USA
Bingbing Ni   Shanghai Jiao Tong University, China
Juan Carlos Niebles   Salesforce & Stanford University, USA
Ko Nishino   Kyoto University, Japan
Jean-Marc Odobez   Idiap Research Institute, École polytechnique
                                    fédérale de Lausanne, Switzerland
Francesca Odone   University of Genova, Italy
Takayuki Okatani   Tohoku University & RIKEN Center for
                                    Advanced Intelligence Project, Japan
Manohar Paluri   Facebook, USA
Guan Pang   Facebook, USA
Maja Pantic   Imperial College London, UK
Sylvain Paris   Adobe Research, USA
Jaesik Park   Pohang University of Science and Technology,
                                    Korea
Hyun Soo Park   The University of Minnesota, USA
Omkar M. Parkhi   Facebook, USA
Deepak Pathak   Carnegie Mellon University, USA
Georgios Pavlakos   University of California, Berkeley, USA
Marcello Pelillo   University of Venice, Italy
Marc Pollefeys   ETH Zurich & Microsoft, Switzerland
Jean Ponce   Inria, France
Gerard Pons-Moll   University of Tübingen, Germany
Fatih Porikli   Qualcomm, USA
Victor Adrian Prisacariu   University of Oxford, UK
Petia Radeva   University of Barcelona, Spain
Ravi Ramamoorthi   University of California, San Diego, USA
Deva Ramanan   Carnegie Mellon University, USA
Vignesh Ramanathan   Facebook, USA
Nalini Ratha   State University of New York at Buffalo, USA
Tammy Riklin Raviv   Ben-Gurion University, Israel
Tobias Ritschel   University College London, UK
Emanuele Rodola   Sapienza University of Rome, Italy
Amit K. Roy-Chowdhury   University of California, Riverside, USA
Michael Rubinstein   Google, USA
Olga Russakovsky   Princeton University, USA

James Tompkin	Brown University, USA
Lorenzo Torresani	Dartmouth College, USA
Alexander Toshev	Apple, USA
Du Tran	Facebook AI Research, USA
Anh T. Tran	VinAI, Vietnam
Zhuowen Tu	University of California, San Diego, USA
Georgios Tzimiropoulos	Queen Mary University of London, UK
Jasper Uijlings	Google Research, Switzerland
Jan C. van Gemert	Delft University of Technology, The Netherlands
Gul Varol	Ecole des Ponts ParisTech, France
Nuno Vasconcelos	University of California, San Diego, USA
Mayank Vatsa	Indian Institute of Technology Jodhpur, India
Ashok Veeraraghavan	Rice University, USA
Jakob Verbeek	Facebook AI Research, France
Carl Vondrick	Columbia University, USA
Ruiping Wang	Institute of Computing Technology, Chinese Academy of Sciences, China
Xinchao Wang	National University of Singapore, Singapore
Liwei Wang	The Chinese University of Hong Kong, Hong Kong, China
Chaohui Wang	Université Paris-Est, France
Xiaolong Wang	University of California, San Diego, USA
Christian Wolf	NAVER LABS Europe, France
Tao Xiang	University of Surrey, UK
Saining Xie	Facebook AI Research, USA
Cihang Xie	University of California, Santa Cruz, USA
Zeki Yalniz	Facebook, USA
Ming-Hsuan Yang	University of California, Merced, USA
Angela Yao	National University of Singapore, Singapore
Shaodi You	University of Amsterdam, The Netherlands
Stella X. Yu	University of California, Berkeley, USA
Junsong Yuan	State University of New York at Buffalo, USA
Stefanos Zafeiriou	Imperial College London, UK
Amir Zamir	École polytechnique fédérale de Lausanne, Switzerland
Lei Zhang	Alibaba & Hong Kong Polytechnic University, Hong Kong, China
Lei Zhang	International Digital Economy Academy (IDEA), China
Pengchuan Zhang	Meta AI, USA
Bolei Zhou	University of California, Los Angeles, USA
Yuke Zhu	University of Texas at Austin, USA

Todd Zickler   Harvard University, USA
Wangmeng Zuo   Harbin Institute of Technology, China

Technical Program Committee

Davide Abati
Soroush Abbasi
  Koohpayegani
Amos L. Abbott
Rameen Abdal
Rabab Abdelfattah
Sahar Abdelnabi
Hassan Abu Alhaija
Abulikemu Abuduweili
Ron Abutbul
Hanno Ackermann
Aikaterini Adam
Kamil Adamczewski
Ehsan Adeli
Vida Adeli
Donald Adjeroh
Arman Afrasiyabi
Akshay Agarwal
Sameer Agarwal
Abhinav Agarwalla
Vaibhav Aggarwal
Sara Aghajanzadeh
Susmit Agrawal
Antonio Agudo
Touqeer Ahmad
Sk Miraj Ahmed
Chaitanya Ahuja
Nilesh A. Ahuja
Abhishek Aich
Shubhra Aich
Noam Aigerman
Arash Akbarinia
Peri Akiva
Derya Akkaynak
Emre Aksan
Arjun R. Akula
Yuval Alaluf
Stephan Alaniz
Paul Albert
Cenek Albl

Filippo Aleotti
Konstantinos P.
  Alexandridis
Motasem Alfarra
Mohsen Ali
Thiemo Alldieck
Hadi Alzayer
Liang An
Shan An
Yi An
Zhulin An
Dongsheng An
Jie An
Xiang An
Saket Anand
Cosmin Ancuti
Juan Andrade-Cetto
Alexander Andreopoulos
Bjoern Andres
Jerone T. A. Andrews
Shivangi Aneja
Anelia Angelova
Dragomir Anguelov
Rushil Anirudh
Oron Anschel
Rao Muhammad Anwer
Djamila Aouada
Evlampios Apostolidis
Srikar Appalaraju
Nikita Araslanov
Andre Araujo
Eric Arazo
Dawit Mureja Argaw
Anurag Arnab
Aditya Arora
Chetan Arora
Sunpreet S. Arora
Alexey Artemov
Muhammad Asad
Kumar Ashutosh

Sinem Aslan
Vishal Asnani
Mahmoud Assran
Amir Atapour-Abarghouei
Nikos Athanasiou
Ali Athar
ShahRukh Athar
Sara Atito
Souhaib Attaiki
Matan Atzmon
Mathieu Aubry
Nicolas Audebert
Tristan T.
  Aumentado-Armstrong
Melinos Averkiou
Yannis Avrithis
Stephane Ayache
Mehmet Aygün
Seyed Mehdi
  Ayyoubzadeh
Hossein Azizpour
George Azzopardi
Mallikarjun B. R.
Yunhao Ba
Abhishek Badki
Seung-Hwan Bae
Seung-Hwan Baek
Seungryul Baek
Piyush Nitin Bagad
Shai Bagon
Gaetan Bahl
Shikhar Bahl
Sherwin Bahmani
Haoran Bai
Lei Bai
Jiawang Bai
Haoyue Bai
Jinbin Bai
Xiang Bai
Xuyang Bai

Yang Bai
Yuanchao Bai
Ziqian Bai
Sungyong Baik
Kevin Bailly
Max Bain
Federico Baldassarre
Wele Gedara Chaminda
    Bandara
Biplab Banerjee
Pratyay Banerjee
Sandipan Banerjee
Jihwan Bang
Antyanta Bangunharcana
Aayush Bansal
Ankan Bansal
Siddhant Bansal
Wentao Bao
Zhipeng Bao
Amir Bar
Manel Baradad Jurjo
Lorenzo Baraldi
Danny Barash
Daniel Barath
Connelly Barnes
Ioan Andrei Bârsan
Steven Basart
Dina Bashkirova
Chaim Baskin
Peyman Bateni
Anil Batra
Sebastiano Battiato
Ardhendu Behera
Harkirat Behl
Jens Behley
Vasileios Belagiannis
Boulbaba Ben Amor
Emanuel Ben Baruch
Abdessamad Ben Hamza
Gil Ben-Artzi
Assia Benbihi
Fabian Benitez-Quiroz
Guy Ben-Yosef
Philipp Benz
Alexander W. Bergman

Urs Bergmann
Jesus Bermudez-Cameo
Stefano Berretti
Gedas Bertasius
Zachary Bessinger
Petra Bevandić
Matthew Beveridge
Lucas Beyer
Yash Bhalgat
Suvaansh Bhambri
Samarth Bharadwaj
Gaurav Bharaj
Aparna Bharati
Bharat Lal Bhatnagar
Uttaran Bhattacharya
Apratim Bhattacharyya
Brojeshwar Bhowmick
Ankan Kumar Bhunia
Ayan Kumar Bhunia
Qi Bi
Sai Bi
Michael Bi Mi
Gui-Bin Bian
Jia-Wang Bian
Shaojun Bian
Pia Bideau
Mario Bijelic
Hakan Bilen
Guillaume-Alexandre
    Bilodeau
Alexander Binder
Tolga Birdal
Vighnesh N. Birodkar
Sandika Biswas
Andreas Blattmann
Janusz Bobulski
Giuseppe Boccignone
Vishnu Boddeti
Navaneeth Bodla
Moritz Böhle
Aleksei Bokhovkin
Sam Bond-Taylor
Vivek Boominathan
Shubhankar Borse
Mark Boss

Andrea Bottino
Adnane Boukhayma
Fadi Boutros
Nicolas C. Boutry
Richard S. Bowen
Ivaylo Boyadzhiev
Aidan Boyd
Yuri Boykov
Aljaz Bozic
Behzad Bozorgtabar
Eric Brachmann
Samarth Brahmbhatt
Gustav Bredell
Francois Bremond
Joel Brogan
Andrew Brown
Thomas Brox
Marcus A. Brubaker
Robert-Jan Bruintjes
Yuqi Bu
Anders G. Buch
Himanshu Buckchash
Mateusz Buda
Ignas Budvytis
José M. Buenaposada
Marcel C. Bühler
Tu Bui
Adrian Bulat
Hannah Bull
Evgeny Burnaev
Andrei Bursuc
Benjamin Busam
Sergey N. Buzykanov
Wonmin Byeon
Fabian Caba
Martin Cadik
Guanyu Cai
Minjie Cai
Qing Cai
Zhongang Cai
Qi Cai
Yancheng Cai
Shen Cai
Han Cai
Jiarui Cai

Bowen Cai
Mu Cai
Qin Cai
Ruojin Cai
Weidong Cai
Weiwei Cai
Yi Cai
Yujun Cai
Zhiping Cai
Akin Caliskan
Lilian Calvet
Baris Can Cam
Necati Cihan Camgoz
Tommaso Campari
Dylan Campbell
Ziang Cao
Ang Cao
Xu Cao
Zhiwen Cao
Shengcao Cao
Song Cao
Weipeng Cao
Xiangyong Cao
Xiaochun Cao
Yue Cao
Yunhao Cao
Zhangjie Cao
Jiale Cao
Yang Cao
Jiajiong Cao
Jie Cao
Jinkun Cao
Lele Cao
Yulong Cao
Zhiguo Cao
Chen Cao
Razvan Caramalau
Marlène Careil
Gustavo Carneiro
Joao Carreira
Dan Casas
Paola Cascante-Bonilla
Angela Castillo
Francisco M. Castro
Pedro Castro

Luca Cavalli
George J. Cazenavette
Oya Celiktutan
Hakan Cevikalp
Sri Harsha C. H.
Sungmin Cha
Geonho Cha
Menglei Chai
Lucy Chai
Yuning Chai
Zenghao Chai
Anirban Chakraborty
Deep Chakraborty
Rudrasis Chakraborty
Souradeep Chakraborty
Kelvin C. K. Chan
Chee Seng Chan
Paramanand Chandramouli
Arjun Chandrasekaran
Kenneth Chaney
Dongliang Chang
Huiwen Chang
Peng Chang
Xiaojun Chang
Jia-Ren Chang
Hyung Jin Chang
Hyun Sung Chang
Ju Yong Chang
Li-Jen Chang
Qi Chang
Wei-Yi Chang
Yi Chang
Nadine Chang
Hanqing Chao
Pradyumna Chari
Dibyadip Chatterjee
Chiranjoy Chattopadhyay
Siddhartha Chaudhuri
Zhengping Che
Gal Chechik
Lianggangxu Chen
Qi Alfred Chen
Brian Chen
Bor-Chun Chen
Bo-Hao Chen

Bohong Chen
Bin Chen
Ziliang Chen
Cheng Chen
Chen Chen
Chaofeng Chen
Xi Chen
Haoyu Chen
Xuanhong Chen
Wei Chen
Qiang Chen
Shi Chen
Xianyu Chen
Chang Chen
Changhuai Chen
Hao Chen
Jie Chen
Jianbo Chen
Jingjing Chen
Jun Chen
Kejiang Chen
Mingcai Chen
Nenglun Chen
Qifeng Chen
Ruoyu Chen
Shu-Yu Chen
Weidong Chen
Weijie Chen
Weikai Chen
Xiang Chen
Xiuyi Chen
Xingyu Chen
Yaofo Chen
Yueting Chen
Yu Chen
Yunjin Chen
Yuntao Chen
Yun Chen
Zhenfang Chen
Zhuangzhuang Chen
Chu-Song Chen
Xiangyu Chen
Zhuo Chen
Chaoqi Chen
Shizhe Chen

Xiaotong Chen
Xiaozhi Chen
Dian Chen
Defang Chen
Dingfan Chen
Ding-Jie Chen
Ee Heng Chen
Tao Chen
Yixin Chen
Wei-Ting Chen
Lin Chen
Guang Chen
Guangyi Chen
Guanying Chen
Guangyao Chen
Hwann-Tzong Chen
Junwen Chen
Jiacheng Chen
Jianxu Chen
Hui Chen
Kai Chen
Kan Chen
Kevin Chen
Kuan-Wen Chen
Weihua Chen
Zhang Chen
Liang-Chieh Chen
Lele Chen
Liang Chen
Fanglin Chen
Zehui Chen
Minghui Chen
Minghao Chen
Xiaokang Chen
Qian Chen
Jun-Cheng Chen
Qi Chen
Qingcai Chen
Richard J. Chen
Runnan Chen
Rui Chen
Shuo Chen
Sentao Chen
Shaoyu Chen
Shixing Chen

Shuai Chen
Shuya Chen
Sizhe Chen
Simin Chen
Shaoxiang Chen
Zitian Chen
Tianlong Chen
Tianshui Chen
Min-Hung Chen
Xiangning Chen
Xin Chen
Xinghao Chen
Xuejin Chen
Xu Chen
Xuxi Chen
Yunlu Chen
Yanbei Chen
Yuxiao Chen
Yun-Chun Chen
Yi-Ting Chen
Yi-Wen Chen
Yinbo Chen
Yiran Chen
Yuanhong Chen
Yubei Chen
Yuefeng Chen
Yuhua Chen
Yukang Chen
Zerui Chen
Zhaoyu Chen
Zhen Chen
Zhenyu Chen
Zhi Chen
Zhiwei Chen
Zhixiang Chen
Long Chen
Bowen Cheng
Jun Cheng
Yi Cheng
Jingchun Cheng
Lechao Cheng
Xi Cheng
Yuan Cheng
Ho Kei Cheng
Kevin Ho Man Cheng

Jiacheng Cheng
Kelvin B. Cheng
Li Cheng
Mengjun Cheng
Zhen Cheng
Qingrong Cheng
Tianheng Cheng
Harry Cheng
Yihua Cheng
Yu Cheng
Ziheng Cheng
Soon Yau Cheong
Anoop Cherian
Manuela Chessa
Zhixiang Chi
Naoki Chiba
Julian Chibane
Kashyap Chitta
Tai-Yin Chiu
Hsu-kuang Chiu
Wei-Chen Chiu
Sungmin Cho
Donghyeon Cho
Hyeon Cho
Yooshin Cho
Gyusang Cho
Jang Hyun Cho
Seungju Cho
Nam Ik Cho
Sunghyun Cho
Hanbyel Cho
Jaesung Choe
Jooyoung Choi
Chiho Choi
Changwoon Choi
Jongwon Choi
Myungsub Choi
Dooseop Choi
Jonghyun Choi
Jinwoo Choi
Jun Won Choi
Min-Kook Choi
Hongsuk Choi
Janghoon Choi
Yoon-Ho Choi

Yukyung Choi
Jaegul Choo
Ayush Chopra
Siddharth Choudhary
Subhabrata Choudhury
Vasileios Choutas
Ka-Ho Chow
Pinaki Nath Chowdhury
Sammy Christen
Anders Christensen
Grigorios Chrysos
Hang Chu
Wen-Hsuan Chu
Peng Chu
Qi Chu
Ruihang Chu
Wei-Ta Chu
Yung-Yu Chuang
Sanghyuk Chun
Se Young Chun
Antonio Cinà
Ramazan Gokberk Cinbis
Javier Civera
Albert Clapés
Ronald Clark
Brian S. Clipp
Felipe Codevilla
Daniel Coelho de Castro
Niv Cohen
Forrester Cole
Maxwell D. Collins
Robert T. Collins
Marc Comino Trinidad
Runmin Cong
Wenyan Cong
Maxime Cordy
Marcella Cornia
Enric Corona
Huseyin Coskun
Luca Cosmo
Dragos Costea
Davide Cozzolino
Arun C. S. Kumar
Aiyu Cui
Qiongjie Cui

Quan Cui
Shuhao Cui
Yiming Cui
Ying Cui
Zijun Cui
Jiali Cui
Jiequan Cui
Yawen Cui
Zhen Cui
Zhaopeng Cui
Jack Culpepper
Xiaodong Cun
Ross Cutler
Adam Czajka
Ali Dabouei
Konstantinos M. Dafnis
Manuel Dahnert
Tao Dai
Yuchao Dai
Bo Dai
Mengyu Dai
Hang Dai
Haixing Dai
Peng Dai
Pingyang Dai
Qi Dai
Qiyu Dai
Yutong Dai
Naser Damer
Zhiyuan Dang
Mohamed Daoudi
Ayan Das
Abir Das
Debasmit Das
Deepayan Das
Partha Das
Sagnik Das
Soumi Das
Srijan Das
Swagatam Das
Avijit Dasgupta
Jim Davis
Adrian K. Davison
Homa Davoudi
Laura Daza

Matthias De Lange
Shalini De Mello
Marco De Nadai
Christophe De
    Vleeschouwer
Alp Dener
Boyang Deng
Congyue Deng
Bailin Deng
Yong Deng
Ye Deng
Zhuo Deng
Zhijie Deng
Xiaoming Deng
Jiankang Deng
Jinhong Deng
Jingjing Deng
Liang-Jian Deng
Siqi Deng
Xiang Deng
Xueqing Deng
Zhongying Deng
Karan Desai
Jean-Emmanuel Deschaud
Aniket Anand Deshmukh
Neel Dey
Helisa Dhamo
Prithviraj Dhar
Amaya Dharmasiri
Yan Di
Xing Di
Ousmane A. Dia
Haiwen Diao
Xiaolei Diao
Gonçalo José Dias Pais
Abdallah Dib
Anastasios Dimou
Changxing Ding
Henghui Ding
Guodong Ding
Yaqing Ding
Shuangrui Ding
Yuhang Ding
Yikang Ding
Shouhong Ding

Haisong Ding
Hui Ding
Jiahao Ding
Jian Ding
Jian-Jiun Ding
Shuxiao Ding
Tianyu Ding
Wenhao Ding
Yuqi Ding
Yi Ding
Yuzhen Ding
Zhengming Ding
Tan Minh Dinh
Vu Dinh
Christos Diou
Mandar Dixit
Bao Gia Doan
Khoa D. Doan
Dzung Anh Doan
Debi Prosad Dogra
Nehal Doiphode
Chengdong Dong
Bowen Dong
Zhenxing Dong
Hang Dong
Xiaoyi Dong
Haoye Dong
Jiangxin Dong
Shichao Dong
Xuan Dong
Zhen Dong
Shuting Dong
Jing Dong
Li Dong
Ming Dong
Nanqing Dong
Qiulei Dong
Runpei Dong
Siyan Dong
Tian Dong
Wei Dong
Xiaomeng Dong
Xin Dong
Xingbo Dong
Yuan Dong

Samuel Dooley
Gianfranco Doretto
Michael Dorkenwald
Keval Doshi
Zhaopeng Dou
Xiaotian Dou
Hazel Doughty
Ahmad Droby
Iddo Drori
Jie Du
Yong Du
Dawei Du
Dong Du
Ruoyi Du
Yuntao Du
Xuefeng Du
Yilun Du
Yuming Du
Radhika Dua
Haodong Duan
Jiafei Duan
Kaiwen Duan
Peiqi Duan
Ye Duan
Haoran Duan
Jiali Duan
Amanda Duarte
Abhimanyu Dubey
Shiv Ram Dubey
Florian Dubost
Lukasz Dudziak
Shivam Duggal
Justin M. Dulay
Matteo Dunnhofer
Chi Nhan Duong
Thibaut Durand
Mihai Dusmanu
Ujjal Kr Dutta
Debidatta Dwibedi
Isht Dwivedi
Sai Kumar Dwivedi
Takeharu Eda
Mark Edmonds
Alexei A. Efros
Thibaud Ehret

Max Ehrlich
Mahsa Ehsanpour
Iván Eichhardt
Farshad Einabadi
Marvin Eisenberger
Hazim Kemal Ekenel
Mohamed El Banani
Ismail Elezi
Moshe Eliasof
Alaa El-Nouby
Ian Endres
Francis Engelmann
Deniz Engin
Chanho Eom
Dave Epstein
Maria C. Escobar
Victor A. Escorcia
Carlos Esteves
Sungmin Eum
Bernard J. E. Evans
Ivan Evtimov
Fevziye Irem Eyiokur
    Yaman
Matteo Fabbri
Sébastien Fabbro
Gabriele Facciolo
Masud Fahim
Bin Fan
Hehe Fan
Deng-Ping Fan
Aoxiang Fan
Chen-Chen Fan
Qi Fan
Zhaoxin Fan
Haoqi Fan
Heng Fan
Hongyi Fan
Linxi Fan
Baojie Fan
Jiayuan Fan
Lei Fan
Quanfu Fan
Yonghui Fan
Yingruo Fan
Zhiwen Fan

Zicong Fan
Sean Fanello
Jiansheng Fang
Chaowei Fang
Yuming Fang
Jianwu Fang
Jin Fang
Qi Fang
Shancheng Fang
Tian Fang
Xianyong Fang
Gongfan Fang
Zhen Fang
Hui Fang
Jiemin Fang
Le Fang
Pengfei Fang
Xiaolin Fang
Yuxin Fang
Zhaoyuan Fang
Ammarah Farooq
Azade Farshad
Zhengcong Fei
Michael Felsberg
Wei Feng
Chen Feng
Fan Feng
Andrew Feng
Xin Feng
Zheyun Feng
Ruicheng Feng
Mingtao Feng
Qianyu Feng
Shangbin Feng
Chun-Mei Feng
Zunlei Feng
Zhiyong Feng
Martin Fergie
Mustansar Fiaz
Marco Fiorucci
Michael Firman
Hamed Firooz
Volker Fischer
Corneliu O. Florea
Georgios Floros

Wolfgang Foerstner
Gianni Franchi
Jean-Sebastien Franco
Simone Frintrop
Anna Fruehstueck
Changhong Fu
Chaoyou Fu
Cheng-Yang Fu
Chi-Wing Fu
Deqing Fu
Huan Fu
Jun Fu
Kexue Fu
Ying Fu
Jianlong Fu
Jingjing Fu
Qichen Fu
Tsu-Jui Fu
Xueyang Fu
Yang Fu
Yanwei Fu
Yonggan Fu
Wolfgang Fuhl
Yasuhisa Fujii
Kent Fujiwara
Marco Fumero
Takuya Funatomi
Isabel Funke
Dario Fuoli
Antonino Furnari
Matheus A. Gadelha
Akshay Gadi Patil
Adrian Galdran
Guillermo Gallego
Silvano Galliani
Orazio Gallo
Leonardo Galteri
Matteo Gamba
Yiming Gan
Sujoy Ganguly
Harald Ganster
Boyan Gao
Changxin Gao
Daiheng Gao
Difei Gao

Chen Gao
Fei Gao
Lin Gao
Wei Gao
Yiming Gao
Junyu Gao
Guangyu Ryan Gao
Haichang Gao
Hongchang Gao
Jialin Gao
Jin Gao
Jun Gao
Katelyn Gao
Mingchen Gao
Mingfei Gao
Pan Gao
Shangqian Gao
Shanghua Gao
Xitong Gao
Yunhe Gao
Zhanning Gao
Elena Garces
Nuno Cruz Garcia
Noa Garcia
Guillermo
    Garcia-Hernando
Isha Garg
Rahul Garg
Sourav Garg
Quentin Garrido
Stefano Gasperini
Kent Gauen
Chandan Gautam
Shivam Gautam
Paul Gay
Chunjiang Ge
Shiming Ge
Wenhang Ge
Yanhao Ge
Zheng Ge
Songwei Ge
Weifeng Ge
Yixiao Ge
Yuying Ge
Shijie Geng

Zhengyang Geng
Kyle A. Genova
Georgios Georgakis
Markos Georgopoulos
Marcel Geppert
Shabnam Ghadar
Mina Ghadimi Atigh
Deepti Ghadiyaram
Maani Ghaffari Jadidi
Sedigh Ghamari
Zahra Gharaee
Michaël Gharbi
Golnaz Ghiasi
Reza Ghoddoosian
Soumya Suvra Ghosal
Adhiraj Ghosh
Arthita Ghosh
Pallabi Ghosh
Soumyadeep Ghosh
Andrew Gilbert
Igor Gilitschenski
Jhony H. Giraldo
Andreu Girbau Xalabarder
Rohit Girdhar
Sharath Girish
Xavier Giro-i-Nieto
Raja Giryes
Thomas Gittings
Nikolaos Gkanatsios
Ioannis Gkioulekas
Abhiram
   Gnanasambandam
Aurele T. Gnanha
Clement L. J. C. Godard
Arushi Goel
Vidit Goel
Shubham Goel
Zan Gojcic
Aaron K. Gokaslan
Tejas Gokhale
S. Alireza Golestaneh
Thiago L. Gomes
Nuno Goncalves
Boqing Gong
Chen Gong

Yuanhao Gong
Guoqiang Gong
Jingyu Gong
Rui Gong
Yu Gong
Mingming Gong
Neil Zhenqiang Gong
Xun Gong
Yunye Gong
Yihong Gong
Cristina I. González
Nithin Gopalakrishnan
   Nair
Gaurav Goswami
Jianping Gou
Shreyank N. Gowda
Ankit Goyal
Helmut Grabner
Patrick L. Grady
Ben Graham
Eric Granger
Douglas R. Gray
Matej Grcić
David Griffiths
Jinjin Gu
Yun Gu
Shuyang Gu
Jianyang Gu
Fuqiang Gu
Jiatao Gu
Jindong Gu
Jiaqi Gu
Jinwei Gu
Jiaxin Gu
Geonmo Gu
Xiao Gu
Xinqian Gu
Xiuye Gu
Yuming Gu
Zhangxuan Gu
Dayan Guan
Junfeng Guan
Qingji Guan
Tianrui Guan
Shanyan Guan

Denis A. Gudovskiy
Ricardo Guerrero
Pierre-Louis Guhur
Jie Gui
Liangyan Gui
Liangke Gui
Benoit Guillard
Erhan Gundogdu
Manuel Günther
Jingcai Guo
Yuanfang Guo
Junfeng Guo
Chenqi Guo
Dan Guo
Hongji Guo
Jia Guo
Jie Guo
Minghao Guo
Shi Guo
Yanhui Guo
Yangyang Guo
Yuan-Chen Guo
Yilu Guo
Yiluan Guo
Yong Guo
Guangyu Guo
Haiyun Guo
Jinyang Guo
Jianyuan Guo
Pengsheng Guo
Pengfei Guo
Shuxuan Guo
Song Guo
Tianyu Guo
Qing Guo
Qiushan Guo
Wen Guo
Xiefan Guo
Xiaohu Guo
Xiaoqing Guo
Yufei Guo
Yuhui Guo
Yuliang Guo
Yunhui Guo
Yanwen Guo

Akshita Gupta
Ankush Gupta
Kamal Gupta
Kartik Gupta
Ritwik Gupta
Rohit Gupta
Siddharth Gururani
Fredrik K. Gustafsson
Abner Guzman Rivera
Vladimir Guzov
Matthew A. Gwilliam
Jung-Woo Ha
Marc Habermann
Isma Hadji
Christian Haene
Martin Hahner
Levente Hajder
Alexandros Haliassos
Emanuela Haller
Bumsub Ham
Abdullah J. Hamdi
Shreyas Hampali
Dongyoon Han
Chunrui Han
Dong-Jun Han
Dong-Sig Han
Guangxing Han
Zhizhong Han
Ruize Han
Jiaming Han
Jin Han
Ligong Han
Xian-Hua Han
Xiaoguang Han
Yizeng Han
Zhi Han
Zhenjun Han
Zhongyi Han
Jungong Han
Junlin Han
Kai Han
Kun Han
Sungwon Han
Songfang Han
Wei Han

Xiao Han
Xintong Han
Xinzhe Han
Yahong Han
Yan Han
Zongbo Han
Nicolai Hani
Rana Hanocka
Niklas Hanselmann
Nicklas A. Hansen
Hong Hanyu
Fusheng Hao
Yanbin Hao
Shijie Hao
Udith Haputhanthri
Mehrtash Harandi
Josh Harguess
Adam Harley
David M. Hart
Atsushi Hashimoto
Ali Hassani
Mohammed Hassanin
Yana Hasson
Joakim Bruslund Haurum
Bo He
Kun He
Chen He
Xin He
Fazhi He
Gaoqi He
Hao He
Haoyu He
Jiangpeng He
Hongliang He
Qian He
Xiangteng He
Xuming He
Yannan He
Yuhang He
Yang He
Xiangyu He
Nanjun He
Pan He
Sen He
Shengfeng He

Songtao He
Tao He
Tong He
Wei He
Xuehai He
Xiaoxiao He
Ying He
Yisheng He
Ziwen He
Peter Hedman
Felix Heide
Yacov Hel-Or
Paul Henderson
Philipp Henzler
Byeongho Heo
Jae-Pil Heo
Miran Heo
Sachini A. Herath
Stephane Herbin
Pedro Hermosilla Casajus
Monica Hernandez
Charles Herrmann
Roei Herzig
Mauricio Hess-Flores
Carlos Hinojosa
Tobias Hinz
Tsubasa Hirakawa
Chih-Hui Ho
Lam Si Tung Ho
Jennifer Hobbs
Derek Hoiem
Yannick Hold-Geoffroy
Aleksander Holynski
Cheeun Hong
Fa-Ting Hong
Hanbin Hong
Guan Zhe Hong
Danfeng Hong
Lanqing Hong
Xiaopeng Hong
Xin Hong
Jie Hong
Seungbum Hong
Cheng-Yao Hong
Seunghoon Hong

Yi Hong
Yuan Hong
Yuchen Hong
Anthony Hoogs
Maxwell C. Horton
Kazuhiro Hotta
Qibin Hou
Tingbo Hou
Junhui Hou
Ji Hou
Qiqi Hou
Rui Hou
Ruibing Hou
Zhi Hou
Henry Howard-Jenkins
Lukas Hoyer
Wei-Lin Hsiao
Chiou-Ting Hsu
Anthony Hu
Brian Hu
Yusong Hu
Hexiang Hu
Haoji Hu
Di Hu
Hengtong Hu
Haigen Hu
Lianyu Hu
Hanzhe Hu
Jie Hu
Junlin Hu
Shizhe Hu
Jian Hu
Zhiming Hu
Juhua Hu
Peng Hu
Ping Hu
Ronghang Hu
MengShun Hu
Tao Hu
Vincent Tao Hu
Xiaoling Hu
Xinting Hu
Xiaolin Hu
Xuefeng Hu
Xiaowei Hu

Yang Hu
Yueyu Hu
Zeyu Hu
Zhongyun Hu
Binh-Son Hua
Guoliang Hua
Yi Hua
Linzhi Huang
Qiusheng Huang
Bo Huang
Chen Huang
Hsin-Ping Huang
Ye Huang
Shuangping Huang
Zeng Huang
Buzhen Huang
Cong Huang
Heng Huang
Hao Huang
Qidong Huang
Huaibo Huang
Chaoqin Huang
Feihu Huang
Jiahui Huang
Jingjia Huang
Kun Huang
Lei Huang
Sheng Huang
Shuaiyi Huang
Siyu Huang
Xiaoshui Huang
Xiaoyang Huang
Yan Huang
Yihao Huang
Ying Huang
Ziling Huang
Xiaoke Huang
Yifei Huang
Haiyang Huang
Zhewei Huang
Jin Huang
Haibin Huang
Jiaxing Huang
Junjie Huang
Keli Huang

Lang Huang
Lin Huang
Luojie Huang
Mingzhen Huang
Shijia Huang
Shengyu Huang
Siyuan Huang
He Huang
Xiuyu Huang
Lianghua Huang
Yue Huang
Yaping Huang
Yuge Huang
Zehao Huang
Zeyi Huang
Zhiqi Huang
Zhongzhan Huang
Zilong Huang
Ziyuan Huang
Tianrui Hui
Zhuo Hui
Le Hui
Jing Huo
Junhwa Hur
Shehzeen S. Hussain
Chuong Minh Huynh
Seunghyun Hwang
Jaehui Hwang
Jyh-Jing Hwang
Sukjun Hwang
Soonmin Hwang
Wonjun Hwang
Rakib Hyder
Sangeek Hyun
Sarah Ibrahimi
Tomoki Ichikawa
Yerlan Idelbayev
A. S. M. Iftekhar
Masaaki Iiyama
Satoshi Ikehata
Sunghoon Im
Atul N. Ingle
Eldar Insafutdinov
Yani A. Ioannou
Radu Tudor Ionescu

Umar Iqbal
Go Irie
Muhammad Zubair Irshad
Ahmet Iscen
Berivan Isik
Ashraful Islam
Md Amirul Islam
Syed Islam
Mariko Isogawa
Vamsi Krishna K. Ithapu
Boris Ivanovic
Darshan Iyer
Sarah Jabbour
Ayush Jain
Nishant Jain
Samyak Jain
Vidit Jain
Vineet Jain
Priyank Jaini
Tomas Jakab
Mohammad A. A. K.
    Jalwana
Muhammad Abdullah
    Jamal
Hadi Jamali-Rad
Stuart James
Varun Jampani
Young Kyun Jang
YeongJun Jang
Yunseok Jang
Ronnachai Jaroensri
Bhavan Jasani
Krishna Murthy
    Jatavallabhula
Mojan Javaheripi
Syed A. Javed
Guillaume Jeanneret
Pranav Jeevan
Herve Jegou
Rohit Jena
Tomas Jenicek
Porter Jenkins
Simon Jenni
Hae-Gon Jeon
Sangryul Jeon

Boseung Jeong
Yoonwoo Jeong
Seong-Gyun Jeong
Jisoo Jeong
Allan D. Jepson
Ankit Jha
Sumit K. Jha
I-Hong Jhuo
Ge-Peng Ji
Chaonan Ji
Deyi Ji
Jingwei Ji
Wei Ji
Zhong Ji
Jiayi Ji
Pengliang Ji
Hui Ji
Mingi Ji
Xiaopeng Ji
Yuzhu Ji
Baoxiong Jia
Songhao Jia
Dan Jia
Shan Jia
Xiaojun Jia
Xiuyi Jia
Xu Jia
Menglin Jia
Wenqi Jia
Boyuan Jiang
Wenhao Jiang
Huaizu Jiang
Hanwen Jiang
Haiyong Jiang
Hao Jiang
Huajie Jiang
Huiqin Jiang
Haojun Jiang
Haobo Jiang
Junjun Jiang
Xingyu Jiang
Yangbangyan Jiang
Yu Jiang
Jianmin Jiang
Jiaxi Jiang

Jing Jiang
Kui Jiang
Li Jiang
Liming Jiang
Chiyu Jiang
Meirui Jiang
Chen Jiang
Peng Jiang
Tai-Xiang Jiang
Wen Jiang
Xinyang Jiang
Yifan Jiang
Yuming Jiang
Yingying Jiang
Zeren Jiang
ZhengKai Jiang
Zhenyu Jiang
Shuming Jiao
Jianbo Jiao
Licheng Jiao
Dongkwon Jin
Yeying Jin
Cheng Jin
Linyi Jin
Qing Jin
Taisong Jin
Xiao Jin
Xin Jin
Sheng Jin
Kyong Hwan Jin
Ruibing Jin
SouYoung Jin
Yueming Jin
Chenchen Jing
Longlong Jing
Taotao Jing
Yongcheng Jing
Younghyun Jo
Joakim Johnander
Jeff Johnson
Michael J. Jones
R. Kenny Jones
Rico Jonschkowski
Ameya Joshi
Sunghun Joung

Felix Juefei-Xu
Claudio R. Jung
Steffen Jung
Hari Chandana K.
Rahul Vigneswaran K.
Prajwal K. R.
Abhishek Kadian
Jhony Kaesemodel Pontes
Kumara Kahatapitiya
Anmol Kalia
Sinan Kalkan
Tarun Kalluri
Jaewon Kam
Sandesh Kamath
Meina Kan
Menelaos Kanakis
Takuhiro Kaneko
Di Kang
Guoliang Kang
Hao Kang
Jaeyeon Kang
Kyoungkook Kang
Li-Wei Kang
MinGuk Kang
Suk-Ju Kang
Zhao Kang
Yash Mukund Kant
Yueying Kao
Aupendu Kar
Konstantinos Karantzalos
Sezer Karaoglu
Navid Kardan
Sanjay Kariyappa
Leonid Karlinsky
Animesh Karnewar
Shyamgopal Karthik
Hirak J. Kashyap
Marc A. Kastner
Hirokatsu Kataoka
Angelos Katharopoulos
Hiroharu Kato
Kai Katsumata
Manuel Kaufmann
Chaitanya Kaul
Prakhar Kaushik

Yuki Kawana
Lei Ke
Lipeng Ke
Tsung-Wei Ke
Wei Ke
Petr Kellnhofer
Aniruddha Kembhavi
John Kender
Corentin Kervadec
Leonid Keselman
Daniel Keysers
Nima Khademi Kalantari
Taras Khakhulin
Samir Khaki
Muhammad Haris Khan
Qadeer Khan
Salman Khan
Subash Khanal
Vaishnavi M. Khindkar
Rawal Khirodkar
Saeed Khorram
Pirazh Khorramshahi
Kourosh Khoshelham
Ansh Khurana
Benjamin Kiefer
Jae Myung Kim
Junho Kim
Boah Kim
Hyeonseong Kim
Dong-Jin Kim
Dongwan Kim
Donghyun Kim
Doyeon Kim
Yonghyun Kim
Hyung-Il Kim
Hyunwoo Kim
Hyeongwoo Kim
Hyo Jin Kim
Hyunwoo J. Kim
Taehoon Kim
Jaeha Kim
Jiwon Kim
Jung Uk Kim
Kangyeol Kim
Eunji Kim

Daeha Kim
Dongwon Kim
Kunhee Kim
Kyungmin Kim
Junsik Kim
Min H. Kim
Namil Kim
Kookhoi Kim
Sanghyun Kim
Seongyeop Kim
Seungryong Kim
Saehoon Kim
Euyoung Kim
Guisik Kim
Sungyeon Kim
Sunnie S. Y. Kim
Taehun Kim
Tae Oh Kim
Won Hwa Kim
Seungwook Kim
YoungBin Kim
Youngeun Kim
Akisato Kimura
Furkan Osman Kınlı
Zsolt Kira
Hedvig Kjellström
Florian Kleber
Jan P. Klopp
Florian Kluger
Laurent Kneip
Byungsoo Ko
Muhammed Kocabas
A. Sophia Koepke
Kevin Koeser
Nick Kolkin
Nikos Kolotouros
Wai-Kin Adams Kong
Deying Kong
Caihua Kong
Youyong Kong
Shuyu Kong
Shu Kong
Tao Kong
Yajing Kong
Yu Kong

Zishang Kong
Theodora Kontogianni
Anton S. Konushin
Julian F. P. Kooij
Bruno Korbar
Giorgos Kordopatis-Zilos
Jari Korhonen
Adam Kortylewski
Denis Korzhenkov
Divya Kothandaraman
Suraj Kothawade
Iuliia Kotseruba
Satwik Kottur
Shashank Kotyan
Alexandros Kouris
Petros Koutras
Anna Kreshuk
Ranjay Krishna
Dilip Krishnan
Andrey Kuehlkamp
Hilde Kuehne
Jason Kuen
David Kügler
Arjan Kuijper
Anna Kukleva
Sumith Kulal
Viveka Kulharia
Akshay R. Kulkarni
Nilesh Kulkarni
Dominik Kulon
Abhinav Kumar
Akash Kumar
Suryansh Kumar
B. V. K. Vijaya Kumar
Pulkit Kumar
Ratnesh Kumar
Sateesh Kumar
Satish Kumar
Vijay Kumar B. G.
Nupur Kumari
Sudhakar Kumawat
Jogendra Nath Kundu
Hsien-Kai Kuo
Meng-Yu Jennifer Kuo
Vinod Kumar Kurmi

Yusuke Kurose
Keerthy Kusumam
Alina Kuznetsova
Henry Kvinge
Ho Man Kwan
Hyeokjun Kweon
Heeseung Kwon
Gihyun Kwon
Myung-Joon Kwon
Taesung Kwon
YoungJoong Kwon
Christos Kyrkou
Jorma Laaksonen
Yann Labbe
Zorah Laehner
Florent Lafarge
Hamid Laga
Manuel Lagunas
Shenqi Lai
Jian-Huang Lai
Zihang Lai
Mohamed I. Lakhal
Mohit Lamba
Meng Lan
Loic Landrieu
Zhiqiang Lang
Natalie Lang
Dong Lao
Yizhen Lao
Yingjie Lao
Issam Hadj Laradji
Gustav Larsson
Viktor Larsson
Zakaria Laskar
Stéphane Lathuilière
Chun Pong Lau
Rynson W. H. Lau
Hei Law
Justin Lazarow
Verica Lazova
Eric-Tuan Le
Hieu Le
Trung-Nghia Le
Mathias Lechner
Byeong-Uk Lee

Chen-Yu Lee
Che-Rung Lee
Chul Lee
Hong Joo Lee
Dongsoo Lee
Jiyoung Lee
Eugene Eu Tzuan Lee
Daeun Lee
Saehyung Lee
Jewook Lee
Hyungtae Lee
Hyunmin Lee
Jungbeom Lee
Joon-Young Lee
Jong-Seok Lee
Joonseok Lee
Junha Lee
Kibok Lee
Byung-Kwan Lee
Jangwon Lee
Jinho Lee
Jongmin Lee
Seunghyun Lee
Sohyun Lee
Minsik Lee
Dogyoon Lee
Seungmin Lee
Min Jun Lee
Sangho Lee
Sangmin Lee
Seungeun Lee
Seon-Ho Lee
Sungmin Lee
Sungho Lee
Sangyoun Lee
Vincent C. S. S. Lee
Jaeseong Lee
Yong Jae Lee
Chenyang Lei
Chenyi Lei
Jiahui Lei
Xinyu Lei
Yinjie Lei
Jiaxu Leng
Luziwei Leng

Jan E. Lenssen
Vincent Lepetit
Thomas Leung
María Leyva-Vallina
Xin Li
Yikang Li
Baoxin Li
Bin Li
Bing Li
Bowen Li
Changlin Li
Chao Li
Chongyi Li
Guanyue Li
Shuai Li
Jin Li
Dingquan Li
Dongxu Li
Yiting Li
Gang Li
Dian Li
Guohao Li
Haoang Li
Haoliang Li
Haoran Li
Hengduo Li
Huafeng Li
Xiaoming Li
Hanao Li
Hongwei Li
Ziqiang Li
Jisheng Li
Jiacheng Li
Jia Li
Jiachen Li
Jiahao Li
Jianwei Li
Jiazhi Li
Jie Li
Jing Li
Jingjing Li
Jingtao Li
Jun Li
Junxuan Li
Kai Li

Kailin Li
Kenneth Li
Kun Li
Kunpeng Li
Aoxue Li
Chenglong Li
Chenglin Li
Changsheng Li
Zhichao Li
Qiang Li
Yanyu Li
Zuoyue Li
Xiang Li
Xuelong Li
Fangda Li
Ailin Li
Liang Li
Chun-Guang Li
Daiqing Li
Dong Li
Guanbin Li
Guorong Li
Haifeng Li
Jianan Li
Jianing Li
Jiaxin Li
Ke Li
Lei Li
Lincheng Li
Liulei Li
Lujun Li
Linjie Li
Lin Li
Pengyu Li
Ping Li
Qiufu Li
Qingyong Li
Rui Li
Siyuan Li
Wei Li
Wenbin Li
Xiangyang Li
Xinyu Li
Xiujun Li
Xiu Li

Xu Li
Ya-Li Li
Yao Li
Yongjie Li
Yijun Li
Yiming Li
Yuezun Li
Yu Li
Yunheng Li
Yuqi Li
Zhe Li
Zeming Li
Zhen Li
Zhengqin Li
Zhimin Li
Jiefeng Li
Jinpeng Li
Chengze Li
Jianwu Li
Lerenhan Li
Shan Li
Suichan Li
Xiangtai Li
Yanjie Li
Yandong Li
Zhuoling Li
Zhenqiang Li
Manyi Li
Maosen Li
Ji Li
Minjun Li
Mingrui Li
Mengtian Li
Junyi Li
Nianyi Li
Bo Li
Xiao Li
Peihua Li
Peike Li
Peizhao Li
Peiliang Li
Qi Li
Ren Li
Runze Li
Shile Li

Sheng Li
Shigang Li
Shiyu Li
Shuang Li
Shasha Li
Shichao Li
Tianye Li
Yuexiang Li
Wei-Hong Li
Wanhua Li
Weihao Li
Weiming Li
Weixin Li
Wenbo Li
Wenshuo Li
Weijian Li
Yunan Li
Xirong Li
Xianhang Li
Xiaoyu Li
Xueqian Li
Xuanlin Li
Xianzhi Li
Yunqiang Li
Yanjing Li
Yansheng Li
Yawei Li
Yi Li
Yong Li
Yong-Lu Li
Yuhang Li
Yu-Jhe Li
Yuxi Li
Yunsheng Li
Yanwei Li
Zechao Li
Zejian Li
Zeju Li
Zekun Li
Zhaowen Li
Zheng Li
Zhenyu Li
Zhiheng Li
Zhi Li
Zhong Li

Zhuowei Li
Zhuowan Li
Zhuohang Li
Zizhang Li
Chen Li
Yuan-Fang Li
Dongze Lian
Xiaochen Lian
Zhouhui Lian
Long Lian
Qing Lian
Jin Lianbao
Jinxiu S. Liang
Dingkang Liang
Jiahao Liang
Jianming Liang
Jingyun Liang
Kevin J. Liang
Kaizhao Liang
Chen Liang
Jie Liang
Senwei Liang
Ding Liang
Jiajun Liang
Jian Liang
Kongming Liang
Siyuan Liang
Yuanzhi Liang
Zhengfa Liang
Mingfu Liang
Xiaodan Liang
Xuefeng Liang
Yuxuan Liang
Kang Liao
Liang Liao
Hong-Yuan Mark Liao
Wentong Liao
Haofu Liao
Yue Liao
Minghui Liao
Shengcai Liao
Ting-Hsuan Liao
Xin Liao
Yinghong Liao
Teck Yian Lim

Che-Tsung Lin
Chung-Ching Lin
Chen-Hsuan Lin
Cheng Lin
Chuming Lin
Chunyu Lin
Duhua Lin
Wei Lin
Zheng Lin
Huaijia Lin
Jason Lin
Jierui Lin
Jiaying Lin
Jie Lin
Kai-En Lin
Kevin Lin
Guangfeng Lin
Jiehong Lin
Feng Lin
Hang Lin
Kwan-Yee Lin
Ke Lin
Luojun Lin
Qinghong Lin
Xiangbo Lin
Yi Lin
Zudi Lin
Shijie Lin
Yiqun Lin
Tzu-Heng Lin
Ming Lin
Shaohui Lin
SongNan Lin
Ji Lin
Tsung-Yu Lin
Xudong Lin
Yancong Lin
Yen-Chen Lin
Yiming Lin
Yuewei Lin
Zhiqiu Lin
Zinan Lin
Zhe Lin
David B. Lindell
Zhixin Ling

Zhan Ling
Alexander Liniger
Venice Erin B. Liong
Joey Litalien
Or Litany
Roee Litman
Ron Litman
Jim Little
Dor Litvak
Shaoteng Liu
Shuaicheng Liu
Andrew Liu
Xian Liu
Shaohui Liu
Bei Liu
Bo Liu
Yong Liu
Ming Liu
Yanbin Liu
Chenxi Liu
Daqi Liu
Di Liu
Difan Liu
Dong Liu
Dongfang Liu
Daizong Liu
Xiao Liu
Fangyi Liu
Fengbei Liu
Fenglin Liu
Bin Liu
Yuang Liu
Ao Liu
Hong Liu
Hongfu Liu
Huidong Liu
Ziyi Liu
Feng Liu
Hao Liu
Jie Liu
Jialun Liu
Jiang Liu
Jing Liu
Jingya Liu
Jiaming Liu

Jun Liu
Juncheng Liu
Jiawei Liu
Hongyu Liu
Chuanbin Liu
Haotian Liu
Lingqiao Liu
Chang Liu
Han Liu
Liu Liu
Min Liu
Yingqi Liu
Aishan Liu
Bingyu Liu
Benlin Liu
Boxiao Liu
Chenchen Liu
Chuanjian Liu
Daqing Liu
Huan Liu
Haozhe Liu
Jiaheng Liu
Wei Liu
Jingzhou Liu
Jiyuan Liu
Lingbo Liu
Nian Liu
Peiye Liu
Qiankun Liu
Shenglan Liu
Shilong Liu
Wen Liu
Wenyu Liu
Weifeng Liu
Wu Liu
Xiaolong Liu
Yang Liu
Yanwei Liu
Yingcheng Liu
Yongfei Liu
Yihao Liu
Yu Liu
Yunze Liu
Ze Liu
Zhenhua Liu

Zhenguang Liu
Lin Liu
Lihao Liu
Pengju Liu
Xinhai Liu
Yunfei Liu
Meng Liu
Minghua Liu
Mingyuan Liu
Miao Liu
Peirong Liu
Ping Liu
Qingjie Liu
Ruoshi Liu
Risheng Liu
Songtao Liu
Xing Liu
Shikun Liu
Shuming Liu
Sheng Liu
Songhua Liu
Tongliang Liu
Weibo Liu
Weide Liu
Weizhe Liu
Wenxi Liu
Weiyang Liu
Xin Liu
Xiaobin Liu
Xudong Liu
Xiaoyi Liu
Xihui Liu
Xinchen Liu
Xingtong Liu
Xinpeng Liu
Xinyu Liu
Xianpeng Liu
Xu Liu
Xingyu Liu
Yongtuo Liu
Yahui Liu
Yangxin Liu
Yaoyao Liu
Yaojie Liu
Yuliang Liu

Yongcheng Liu
Yuan Liu
Yufan Liu
Yu-Lun Liu
Yun Liu
Yunfan Liu
Yuanzhong Liu
Zhuoran Liu
Zhen Liu
Zheng Liu
Zhijian Liu
Zhisong Liu
Ziquan Liu
Ziyu Liu
Zhihua Liu
Zechun Liu
Zhaoyang Liu
Zhengzhe Liu
Stephan Liwicki
Shao-Yuan Lo
Sylvain Lobry
Suhas Lohit
Vishnu Suresh Lokhande
Vincenzo Lomonaco
Chengjiang Long
Guodong Long
Fuchen Long
Shangbang Long
Yang Long
Zijun Long
Vasco Lopes
Antonio M. Lopez
Roberto Javier
    Lopez-Sastre
Tobias Lorenz
Javier Lorenzo-Navarro
Yujing Lou
Qian Lou
Xiankai Lu
Changsheng Lu
Huimin Lu
Yongxi Lu
Hao Lu
Hong Lu
Jiasen Lu

Juwei Lu
Fan Lu
Guangming Lu
Jiwen Lu
Shun Lu
Tao Lu
Xiaonan Lu
Yang Lu
Yao Lu
Yongchun Lu
Zhiwu Lu
Cheng Lu
Liying Lu
Guo Lu
Xuequan Lu
Yanye Lu
Yantao Lu
Yuhang Lu
Fujun Luan
Jonathon Luiten
Jovita Lukasik
Alan Lukezic
Jonathan Samuel Lumentut
Mayank Lunayach
Ao Luo
Canjie Luo
Chong Luo
Xu Luo
Grace Luo
Jun Luo
Katie Z. Luo
Tao Luo
Cheng Luo
Fangzhou Luo
Gen Luo
Lei Luo
Sihui Luo
Weixin Luo
Yan Luo
Xiaoyan Luo
Yong Luo
Yadan Luo
Hao Luo
Ruotian Luo
Mi Luo

Tiange Luo
Wenjie Luo
Wenhan Luo
Xiao Luo
Zhiming Luo
Zhipeng Luo
Zhongyi Luo
Diogo C. Luvizon
Zhaoyang Lv
Gengyu Lyu
Lingjuan Lyu
Jun Lyu
Yuanyuan Lyu
Youwei Lyu
Yueming Lyu
Bingpeng Ma
Chao Ma
Chongyang Ma
Congbo Ma
Chih-Yao Ma
Fan Ma
Lin Ma
Haoyu Ma
Hengbo Ma
Jianqi Ma
Jiawei Ma
Jiayi Ma
Kede Ma
Kai Ma
Lingni Ma
Lei Ma
Xu Ma
Ning Ma
Benteng Ma
Cheng Ma
Andy J. Ma
Long Ma
Zhanyu Ma
Zhiheng Ma
Qianli Ma
Shiqiang Ma
Sizhuo Ma
Shiqing Ma
Xiaolong Ma
Xinzhu Ma

Gautam B. Machiraju
Spandan Madan
Mathew Magimai-Doss
Luca Magri
Behrooz Mahasseni
Upal Mahbub
Siddharth Mahendran
Paridhi Maheshwari
Rishabh Maheshwary
Mohammed Mahmoud
Shishira R. R. Maiya
Sylwia Majchrowska
Arjun Majumdar
Puspita Majumdar
Orchid Majumder
Sagnik Majumder
Ilya Makarov
Farkhod F.
   Makhmudkhujaev
Yasushi Makihara
Ankur Mali
Mateusz Malinowski
Utkarsh Mall
Srikanth Malla
Clement Mallet
Dimitrios Mallis
Yunze Man
Dipu Manandhar
Massimiliano Mancini
Murari Mandal
Raunak Manekar
Karttikeya Mangalam
Puneet Mangla
Fabian Manhardt
Sivabalan Manivasagam
Fahim Mannan
Chengzhi Mao
Hanzi Mao
Jiayuan Mao
Junhua Mao
Zhiyuan Mao
Jiageng Mao
Yunyao Mao
Zhendong Mao
Alberto Marchisio

Diego Marcos
Riccardo Marin
Aram Markosyan
Renaud Marlet
Ricardo Marques
Miquel Martí i Rabadán
Diego Martin Arroyo
Niki Martinel
Brais Martinez
Julieta Martinez
Marc Masana
Tomohiro Mashita
Timothée Masquelier
Minesh Mathew
Tetsu Matsukawa
Marwan Mattar
Bruce A. Maxwell
Christoph Mayer
Mantas Mazeika
Pratik Mazumder
Scott McCloskey
Steven McDonagh
Ishit Mehta
Jie Mei
Kangfu Mei
Jieru Mei
Xiaoguang Mei
Givi Meishvili
Luke Melas-Kyriazi
Iaroslav Melekhov
Andres Mendez-Vazquez
Heydi Mendez-Vazquez
Matias Mendieta
Ricardo A. Mendoza-León
Chenlin Meng
Depu Meng
Rang Meng
Zibo Meng
Qingjie Meng
Qier Meng
Yanda Meng
Zihang Meng
Thomas Mensink
Fabian Mentzer
Christopher Metzler

Gregory P. Meyer
Vasileios Mezaris
Liang Mi
Lu Mi
Bo Miao
Changtao Miao
Zichen Miao
Qiguang Miao
Xin Miao
Zhongqi Miao
Frank Michel
Simone Milani
Ben Mildenhall
Roy V. Miles
Juhong Min
Kyle Min
Hyun-Seok Min
Weiqing Min
Yuecong Min
Zhixiang Min
Qi Ming
David Minnen
Aymen Mir
Deepak Mishra
Anand Mishra
Shlok K. Mishra
Niluthpol Mithun
Gaurav Mittal
Trisha Mittal
Daisuke Miyazaki
Kaichun Mo
Hong Mo
Zhipeng Mo
Davide Modolo
Abduallah A. Mohamed
Mohamed Afham
   Mohamed Aflal
Ron Mokady
Pavlo Molchanov
Davide Moltisanti
Liliane Momeni
Gianluca Monaci
Pascal Monasse
Ajoy Mondal
Tom Monnier

Aron Monszpart
Gyeongsik Moon
Suhong Moon
Taesup Moon
Sean Moran
Daniel Moreira
Pietro Morerio
Alexandre Morgand
Lia Morra
Ali Mosleh
Inbar Mosseri
Sayed Mohammad
    Mostafavi Isfahani
Saman Motamed
Ramy A. Mounir
Fangzhou Mu
Jiteng Mu
Norman Mu
Yasuhiro Mukaigawa
Ryan Mukherjee
Tanmoy Mukherjee
Yusuke Mukuta
Ravi Teja Mullapudi
Lea Müller
Matthias Müller
Martin Mundt
Nils Murrugarra-Llerena
Damien Muselet
Armin Mustafa
Muhammad Ferjad Naeem
Sauradip Nag
Hajime Nagahara
Pravin Nagar
Rajendra Nagar
Naveen Shankar Nagaraja
Varun Nagaraja
Tushar Nagarajan
Seungjun Nah
Gaku Nakano
Yuta Nakashima
Giljoo Nam
Seonghyeon Nam
Liangliang Nan
Yuesong Nan
Yeshwanth Napolean

Dinesh Reddy
    Narapureddy
Medhini Narasimhan
Supreeth
    Narasimhaswamy
Sriram Narayanan
Erickson R. Nascimento
Varun Nasery
K. L. Navaneet
Pablo Navarrete Michelini
Shant Navasardyan
Shah Nawaz
Nihal Nayak
Farhood Negin
Lukáš Neumann
Alejandro Newell
Evonne Ng
Kam Woh Ng
Tony Ng
Anh Nguyen
Tuan Anh Nguyen
Cuong Cao Nguyen
Ngoc Cuong Nguyen
Thanh Nguyen
Khoi Nguyen
Phi Le Nguyen
Phong Ha Nguyen
Tam Nguyen
Truong Nguyen
Anh Tuan Nguyen
Rang Nguyen
Thao Thi Phuong Nguyen
Van Nguyen Nguyen
Zhen-Liang Ni
Yao Ni
Shijie Nie
Xuecheng Nie
Yongwei Nie
Weizhi Nie
Ying Nie
Yinyu Nie
Kshitij N. Nikhal
Simon Niklaus
Xuefei Ning
Jifeng Ning

Yotam Nitzan
Di Niu
Shuaicheng Niu
Li Niu
Wei Niu
Yulei Niu
Zhenxing Niu
Albert No
Shohei Nobuhara
Nicoletta Noceti
Junhyug Noh
Sotiris Nousias
Slawomir Nowaczyk
Ewa M. Nowara
Valsamis Ntouskos
Gilberto Ochoa-Ruiz
Ferda Ofli
Jihyong Oh
Sangyun Oh
Youngtaek Oh
Hiroki Ohashi
Takahiro Okabe
Kemal Oksuz
Fumio Okura
Daniel Olmeda Reino
Matthew Olson
Carl Olsson
Roy Or-El
Alessandro Ortis
Guillermo Ortiz-Jimenez
Magnus Oskarsson
Ahmed A. A. Osman
Martin R. Oswald
Mayu Otani
Naima Otberdout
Cheng Ouyang
Jiahong Ouyang
Wanli Ouyang
Andrew Owens
Poojan B. Oza
Mete Ozay
A. Cengiz Oztireli
Gautam Pai
Tomas Pajdla
Umapada Pal

Simone Palazzo
Luca Palmieri
Bowen Pan
Hao Pan
Lili Pan
Tai-Yu Pan
Liang Pan
Chengwei Pan
Yingwei Pan
Xuran Pan
Jinshan Pan
Xinyu Pan
Liyuan Pan
Xingang Pan
Xingjia Pan
Zhihong Pan
Zizheng Pan
Priyadarshini Panda
Rameswar Panda
Rohit Pandey
Kaiyue Pang
Bo Pang
Guansong Pang
Jiangmiao Pang
Meng Pang
Tianyu Pang
Ziqi Pang
Omiros Pantazis
Andreas Panteli
Maja Pantic
Marina Paolanti
Joao P. Papa
Samuele Papa
Mike Papadakis
Dim P. Papadopoulos
George Papandreou
Constantin Pape
Toufiq Parag
Chethan Parameshwara
Shaifali Parashar
Alejandro Pardo
Rishubh Parihar
Sarah Parisot
JaeYoo Park
Gyeong-Moon Park

Hyojin Park
Hyoungseob Park
Jongchan Park
Jae Sung Park
Kiru Park
Chunghyun Park
Kwanyong Park
Sunghyun Park
Sungrae Park
Seongsik Park
Sanghyun Park
Sungjune Park
Taesung Park
Gaurav Parmar
Paritosh Parmar
Alvaro Parra
Despoina Paschalidou
Or Patashnik
Shivansh Patel
Pushpak Pati
Prashant W. Patil
Vaishakh Patil
Suvam Patra
Jay Patravali
Badri Narayana Patro
Angshuman Paul
Sudipta Paul
Rémi Pautrat
Nick E. Pears
Adithya Pediredla
Wenjie Pei
Shmuel Peleg
Latha Pemula
Bo Peng
Houwen Peng
Yue Peng
Liangzu Peng
Baoyun Peng
Jun Peng
Pai Peng
Sida Peng
Xi Peng
Yuxin Peng
Songyou Peng
Wei Peng

Weiqi Peng
Wen-Hsiao Peng
Pramuditha Perera
Juan C. Perez
Eduardo Pérez Pellitero
Juan-Manuel Perez-Rua
Federico Pernici
Marco Pesavento
Stavros Petridis
Ilya A. Petrov
Vladan Petrovic
Mathis Petrovich
Suzanne Petryk
Hieu Pham
Quang Pham
Khoi Pham
Tung Pham
Huy Phan
Stephen Phillips
Cheng Perng Phoo
David Picard
Marco Piccirilli
Georg Pichler
A. J. Piergiovanni
Vipin Pillai
Silvia L. Pintea
Giovanni Pintore
Robinson Piramuthu
Fiora Pirri
Theodoros Pissas
Fabio Pizzati
Benjamin Planche
Bryan Plummer
Matteo Poggi
Ashwini Pokle
Georgy E. Ponimatkin
Adrian Popescu
Stefan Popov
Nikola Popović
Ronald Poppe
Angelo Porrello
Michael Potter
Charalambos Poullis
Hadi Pouransari
Omid Poursaeed

Shraman Pramanick
Mantini Pranav
Dilip K. Prasad
Meghshyam Prasad
B. H. Pawan Prasad
Shitala Prasad
Prateek Prasanna
Ekta Prashnani
Derek S. Prijatelj
Luke Y. Prince
Véronique Prinet
Victor Adrian Prisacariu
James Pritts
Thomas Probst
Sergey Prokudin
Rita Pucci
Chi-Man Pun
Matthew Purri
Haozhi Qi
Lu Qi
Lei Qi
Xianbiao Qi
Yonggang Qi
Yuankai Qi
Siyuan Qi
Guocheng Qian
Hangwei Qian
Qi Qian
Deheng Qian
Shengsheng Qian
Wen Qian
Rui Qian
Yiming Qian
Shengju Qian
Shengyi Qian
Xuelin Qian
Zhenxing Qian
Nan Qiao
Xiaotian Qiao
Jing Qin
Can Qin
Siyang Qin
Hongwei Qin
Jie Qin
Minghai Qin

Yipeng Qin
Yongqiang Qin
Wenda Qin
Xuebin Qin
Yuzhe Qin
Yao Qin
Zhenyue Qiu
Zhiwu Qing
Heqian Qiu
Jiayan Qiu
Jielin Qiu
Yue Qiu
Jiaxiong Qiu
Zhongxi Qiu
Shi Qiu
Zhaofan Qiu
Zhongnan Qu
Yanyun Qu
Kha Gia Quach
Yuhui Quan
Ruijie Quan
Mike Rabbat
Rahul Shekhar Rade
Filip Radenovic
Gorjan Radevski
Bogdan Raducanu
Francesco Ragusa
Shafin Rahman
Md Mahfuzur Rahman
    Siddiquee
Hossein Rahmani
Kiran Raja
Sivaramakrishnan
    Rajaraman
Jathushan Rajasegaran
Adnan Siraj Rakin
Michaël Ramamonjisoa
Chirag A. Raman
Shanmuganathan Raman
Vignesh Ramanathan
Vasili Ramanishka
Vikram V. Ramaswamy
Merey Ramazanova
Jason Rambach
Sai Saketh Rambhatla

Clément Rambour
Ashwin Ramesh Babu
Adín Ramírez Rivera
Arianna Rampini
Haoxi Ran
Aakanksha Rana
Aayush Jung Bahadur
    Rana
Kanchana N. Ranasinghe
Aneesh Rangnekar
Samrudhdhi B. Rangrej
Harsh Rangwani
Viresh Ranjan
Anyi Rao
Yongming Rao
Carolina Raposo
Michalis Raptis
Amir Rasouli
Vivek Rathod
Adepu Ravi Sankar
Avinash Ravichandran
Bharadwaj Ravichandran
Dripta S. Raychaudhuri
Adria Recasens
Simon Reiß
Davis Rempe
Daxuan Ren
Jiawei Ren
Jimmy Ren
Sucheng Ren
Dayong Ren
Zhile Ren
Dongwei Ren
Qibing Ren
Pengfei Ren
Zhenwen Ren
Xuqian Ren
Yixuan Ren
Zhongzheng Ren
Ambareesh Revanur
Hamed Rezazadegan
    Tavakoli
Rafael S. Rezende
Wonjong Rhee
Alexander Richard

Christian Richardt
Stephan R. Richter
Benjamin Riggan
Dominik Rivoir
Mamshad Nayeem Rizve
Joshua D. Robinson
Joseph Robinson
Chris Rockwell
Ranga Rodrigo
Andres C. Rodriguez
Carlos Rodriguez-Pardo
Marcus Rohrbach
Gemma Roig
Yu Rong
David A. Ross
Mohammad Rostami
Edward Rosten
Karsten Roth
Anirban Roy
Debaditya Roy
Shuvendu Roy
Ahana Roy Choudhury
Aruni Roy Chowdhury
Denys Rozumnyi
Shulan Ruan
Wenjie Ruan
Patrick Ruhkamp
Danila Rukhovich
Anian Ruoss
Chris Russell
Dan Ruta
Dawid Damian Rymarczyk
DongHun Ryu
Hyeonggon Ryu
Kwonyoung Ryu
Balasubramanian S.
Alexandre Sablayrolles
Mohammad Sabokrou
Arka Sadhu
Aniruddha Saha
Oindrila Saha
Pritish Sahu
Aneeshan Sain
Nirat Saini
Saurabh Saini

Takeshi Saitoh
Christos Sakaridis
Fumihiko Sakaue
Dimitrios Sakkos
Ken Sakurada
Parikshit V. Sakurikar
Rohit Saluja
Nermin Samet
Leo Sampaio Ferraz
  Ribeiro
Jorge Sanchez
Enrique Sanchez
Shengtian Sang
Anush Sankaran
Soubhik Sanyal
Nikolaos Sarafianos
Vishwanath Saragadam
István Sárándi
Saquib Sarfraz
Mert Bulent Sariyildiz
Anindya Sarkar
Pritam Sarkar
Paul-Edouard Sarlin
Hiroshi Sasaki
Takami Sato
Torsten Sattler
Ravi Kumar Satzoda
Axel Sauer
Stefano Savian
Artem Savkin
Manolis Savva
Gerald Schaefer
Simone Schaub-Meyer
Yoni Schirris
Samuel Schulter
Katja Schwarz
Jesse Scott
Sinisa Segvic
Constantin Marc Seibold
Lorenzo Seidenari
Matan Sela
Fadime Sener
Paul Hongsuck Seo
Kwanggyoon Seo
Hongje Seong

Dario Serez
Francesco Setti
Bryan Seybold
Mohamad Shahbazi
Shima Shahfar
Xinxin Shan
Caifeng Shan
Dandan Shan
Shawn Shan
Wei Shang
Jinghuan Shang
Jiaxiang Shang
Lei Shang
Sukrit Shankar
Ken Shao
Rui Shao
Jie Shao
Mingwen Shao
Aashish Sharma
Gaurav Sharma
Vivek Sharma
Abhishek Sharma
Yoli Shavit
Shashank Shekhar
Sumit Shekhar
Zhijie Shen
Fengyi Shen
Furao Shen
Jialie Shen
Jingjing Shen
Ziyi Shen
Linlin Shen
Guangyu Shen
Biluo Shen
Falong Shen
Jiajun Shen
Qiu Shen
Qiuhong Shen
Shuai Shen
Wang Shen
Yiqing Shen
Yunhang Shen
Siqi Shen
Bin Shen
Tianwei Shen

Xi Shen
Yilin Shen
Yuming Shen
Yucong Shen
Zhiqiang Shen
Lu Sheng
Yichen Shong
Shivanand Venkanna
    Sheshappanavar
Shelly Sheynin
Baifeng Shi
Ruoxi Shi
Botian Shi
Hailin Shi
Jia Shi
Jing Shi
Shaoshuai Shi
Baoguang Shi
Boxin Shi
Hengcan Shi
Tianyang Shi
Xiaodan Shi
Yongjie Shi
Zhensheng Shi
Yinghuan Shi
Weiqi Shi
Wu Shi
Xuepeng Shi
Xiaoshuang Shi
Yujiao Shi
Zenglin Shi
Zhenmei Shi
Takashi Shibata
Meng-Li Shih
Yichang Shih
Hyunjung Shim
Dongseok Shim
Soshi Shimada
Inkyu Shin
Jinwoo Shin
Seungjoo Shin
Seungjae Shin
Koichi Shinoda
Suprosanna Shit

Palaiahnakote
    Shivakumara
Eli Shlizerman
Gaurav Shrivastava
Xiao Shu
Xiangbo Shu
Xinjun Shu
Yang Shu
Tianmin Shu
Jun Shu
Zhixin Shu
Bing Shuai
Maria Shugrina
Ivan Shugurov
Satya Narayan Shukla
Pranjay Shyam
Jianlou Si
Yawar Siddiqui
Alberto Signoroni
Pedro Silva
Jae-Young Sim
Oriane Siméoni
Martin Simon
Andrea Simonelli
Abhishek Singh
Ashish Singh
Dinesh Singh
Gurkirt Singh
Krishna Kumar Singh
Mannat Singh
Pravendra Singh
Rajat Vikram Singh
Utkarsh Singhal
Dipika Singhania
Vasu Singla
Harsh Sinha
Sudipta Sinha
Josef Sivic
Elena Sizikova
Geri Skenderi
Ivan Skorokhodov
Dmitriy Smirnov
Cameron Y. Smith
James S. Smith
Patrick Snape

Mattia Soldan
Hyeongseok Son
Sanghyun Son
Chuanbiao Song
Chen Song
Chunfeng Song
Dan Song
Dongjin Song
Hwanjun Song
Guoxian Song
Jiaming Song
Jie Song
Liangchen Song
Ran Song
Luchuan Song
Xibin Song
Li Song
Fenglong Song
Guoli Song
Guanglu Song
Zhenbo Song
Lin Song
Xinhang Song
Yang Song
Yibing Song
Rajiv Soundararajan
Hossein Souri
Cristovao Sousa
Riccardo Spezialetti
Leonidas Spinoulas
Michael W. Spratling
Deepak Sridhar
Srinath Sridhar
Gaurang Sriramanan
Vinkle Kumar Srivastav
Themos Stafylakis
Serban Stan
Anastasis Stathopoulos
Markus Steinberger
Jan Steinbrener
Sinisa Stekovic
Alexandros Stergiou
Gleb Sterkin
Rainer Stiefelhagen
Pierre Stock

Ombretta Strafforello	Shanlin Sun	Zichang Tan
Julian Straub	Yu Sun	Zhentao Tan
Yannick Strümpler	Zhun Sun	Kenichiro Tanaka
Joerg Stueckler	Che Sun	Masayuki Tanaka
Hang Su	Lin Sun	Yushun Tang
Weijie Su	Tao Sun	Hao Tang
Jong-Chyi Su	Yiyou Sun	Jingqun Tang
Bing Su	Chunyi Sun	Jinhui Tang
Haisheng Su	Chong Sun	Kaihua Tang
Jinming Su	Weiwei Sun	Luming Tang
Yiyang Su	Weixuan Sun	Lv Tang
Yukun Su	Xiuyu Sun	Sheyang Tang
Yuxin Su	Yanan Sun	Shitao Tang
Zhuo Su	Zeren Sun	Siliang Tang
Zhaoqi Su	Zhaodong Sun	Shixiang Tang
Xiu Su	Zhiqing Sun	Yansong Tang
Yu-Chuan Su	Minhyuk Sung	Keke Tang
Zhixun Su	Jinli Suo	Chang Tang
Arulkumar Subramaniam	Simon Suo	Chenwei Tang
Akshayvarun Subramanya	Abhijit Suprem	Jie Tang
A. Subramanyam	Anshuman Suri	Junshu Tang
Swathikiran Sudhakaran	Saksham Suri	Ming Tang
Yusuke Sugano	Joshua M. Susskind	Peng Tang
Masanori Suganuma	Roman Suvorov	Xu Tang
Yumin Suh	Gurumurthy Swaminathan	Yao Tang
Yang Sui	Robin Swanson	Chen Tang
Baochen Sun	Paul Swoboda	Fan Tang
Cheng Sun	Tabish A. Syed	Haoran Tang
Long Sun	Richard Szeliski	Shengeng Tang
Guolei Sun	Fariborz Taherkhani	Yehui Tang
Haoliang Sun	Yu-Wing Tai	Zhipeng Tang
Haomiao Sun	Keita Takahashi	Ugo Tanielian
He Sun	Walter Talbott	Chaofan Tao
Hanqing Sun	Gary Tam	Jiale Tao
Hao Sun	Masato Tamura	Junli Tao
Lichao Sun	Feitong Tan	Renshuai Tao
Jiachen Sun	Fuwen Tan	An Tao
Jiaming Sun	Shuhan Tan	Guanhong Tao
Jian Sun	Andong Tan	Zhiqiang Tao
Jin Sun	Bin Tan	Makarand Tapaswi
Jennifer J. Sun	Cheng Tan	Jean-Philippe G. Tarel
Tiancheng Sun	Jianchao Tan	Juan J. Tarrio
Libo Sun	Lei Tan	Enzo Tartaglione
Peize Sun	Mingxing Tan	Keisuke Tateno
Qianru Sun	Xin Tan	Zachary Teed

Ajinkya B. Tejankar
Bugra Tekin
Purva Tendulkar
Damien Teney
Minggui Teng
Chris Tensmeyer
Andrew Beng Jin Teoh
Philipp Terhörst
Kartik Thakral
Nupur Thakur
Kevin Thandiackal
Spyridon Thermos
Diego Thomas
William Thong
Yuesong Tian
Guanzhong Tian
Lin Tian
Shiqi Tian
Kai Tian
Meng Tian
Tai-Peng Tian
Zhuotao Tian
Shangxuan Tian
Tian Tian
Yapeng Tian
Yu Tian
Yuxin Tian
Leslie Ching Ow Tiong
Praveen Tirupattur
Garvita Tiwari
George Toderici
Antoine Toisoul
Aysim Toker
Tatiana Tommasi
Zhan Tong
Alessio Tonioni
Alessandro Torcinovich
Fabio Tosi
Matteo Toso
Hugo Touvron
Quan Hung Tran
Son Tran
Hung Tran
Ngoc-Trung Tran
Vinh Tran

Phong Tran
Giovanni Trappolini
Edith Tretschk
Subarna Tripathi
Shubhendu Trivedi
Eduard Trulls
Prune Truong
Thanh-Dat Truong
Tomasz Trzcinski
Sam Tsai
Yi-Hsuan Tsai
Ethan Tseng
Yu-Chee Tseng
Shahar Tsiper
Stavros Tsogkas
Shikui Tu
Zhigang Tu
Zhengzhong Tu
Richard Tucker
Sergey Tulyakov
Cigdem Turan
Daniyar Turmukhambetov
Victor G. Turrisi da Costa
Bartlomiej Twardowski
Christopher D. Twigg
Radim Tylecek
Mostofa Rafid Uddin
Md. Zasim Uddin
Kohei Uehara
Nicolas Ugrinovic
Youngjung Uh
Norimichi Ukita
Anwaar Ulhaq
Devesh Upadhyay
Paul Upchurch
Yoshitaka Ushiku
Yuzuko Utsumi
Mikaela Angelina Uy
Mohit Vaishnav
Pratik Vaishnavi
Jeya Maria Jose Valanarasu
Matias A. Valdenegro Toro
Diego Valsesia
Wouter Van Gansbeke
Nanne van Noord

Simon Vandenhende
Farshid Varno
Cristina Vasconcelos
Francisco Vasconcelos
Alex Vasilescu
Subeesh Vasu
Arun Balajee Vasudevan
Kanav Vats
Vaibhav S. Vavilala
Sagar Vaze
Javier Vazquez-Corral
Andrea Vedaldi
Olga Veksler
Andreas Velten
Sai H. Vemprala
Raviteja Vemulapalli
Shashanka
  Venkataramanan
Dor Verbin
Luisa Verdoliva
Manisha Verma
Yashaswi Verma
Constantin Vertan
Eli Verwimp
Deepak Vijaykeerthy
Pablo Villanueva
Ruben Villegas
Markus Vincze
Vibhav Vineet
Minh P. Vo
Huy V. Vo
Duc Minh Vo
Tomas Vojir
Igor Vozniak
Nicholas Vretos
Vibashan VS
Tuan-Anh Vu
Thang Vu
Mårten Wadenbäck
Neal Wadhwa
Aaron T. Walsman
Steven Walton
Jin Wan
Alvin Wan
Jia Wan

Jun Wan

Xiaoyue Wan

Fang Wan

Guowei Wan

Renjie Wan

Zhiqiang Wan

Ziyu Wan

Bastian Wandt

Dongdong Wang

Limin Wang

Haiyang Wang

Xiaobing Wang

Angtian Wang

Angelina Wang

Bing Wang

Bo Wang

Boyu Wang

Binghui Wang

Chen Wang

Chien-Yi Wang

Congli Wang

Qi Wang

Chengrui Wang

Rui Wang

Yiqun Wang

Cong Wang

Wenjing Wang

Dongkai Wang

Di Wang

Xiaogang Wang

Kai Wang

Zhizhong Wang

Fangjinhua Wang

Feng Wang

Hang Wang

Gaoang Wang

Guoqing Wang

Guangcong Wang

Guangzhi Wang

Hanqing Wang

Hao Wang

Haohan Wang

Haoran Wang

Hong Wang

Haotao Wang

Hu Wang

Huan Wang

Hua Wang

Hui-Po Wang

Hengli Wang

Hanyu Wang

Hongxing Wang

Jingwen Wang

Jialiang Wang

Jian Wang

Jianyi Wang

Jiashun Wang

Jiahao Wang

Tsun-Hsuan Wang

Xiaoqian Wang

Jinqiao Wang

Jun Wang

Jianzong Wang

Kaihong Wang

Ke Wang

Lei Wang

Lingjing Wang

Linnan Wang

Lin Wang

Liansheng Wang

Mengjiao Wang

Manning Wang

Nannan Wang

Peihao Wang

Jiayun Wang

Pu Wang

Qiang Wang

Qiufeng Wang

Qilong Wang

Qiangchang Wang

Qin Wang

Qing Wang

Ruocheng Wang

Ruibin Wang

Ruisheng Wang

Ruizhe Wang

Runqi Wang

Runzhong Wang

Wenxuan Wang

Sen Wang

Shangfei Wang

Shaofei Wang

Shijie Wang

Shiqi Wang

Zhibo Wang

Song Wang

Xinjiang Wang

Tai Wang

Tao Wang

Teng Wang

Xiang Wang

Tianren Wang

Tiantian Wang

Tianyi Wang

Fengjiao Wang

Wei Wang

Miaohui Wang

Suchen Wang

Siyue Wang

Yaoming Wang

Xiao Wang

Ze Wang

Biao Wang

Chaofei Wang

Dong Wang

Gu Wang

Guangrun Wang

Guangming Wang

Guo-Hua Wang

Haoqing Wang

Hesheng Wang

Huafeng Wang

Jinghua Wang

Jingdong Wang

Jingjing Wang

Jingya Wang

Jingkang Wang

Jiakai Wang

Junke Wang

Kuo Wang

Lichen Wang

Lizhi Wang

Longguang Wang

Mang Wang

Mei Wang

Min Wang
Peng-Shuai Wang
Run Wang
Shaoru Wang
Shuhui Wang
Tan Wang
Tiancai Wang
Tianqi Wang
Wenhai Wang
Wenzhe Wang
Xiaobo Wang
Xiudong Wang
Xu Wang
Yajie Wang
Yan Wang
Yuan-Gen Wang
Yingqian Wang
Yizhi Wang
Yulin Wang
Yu Wang
Yujie Wang
Yunhe Wang
Yuxi Wang
Yaowei Wang
Yiwei Wang
Zezheng Wang
Hongzhi Wang
Zhiqiang Wang
Ziteng Wang
Ziwei Wang
Zheng Wang
Zhenyu Wang
Binglu Wang
Zhongdao Wang
Ce Wang
Weining Wang
Weiyao Wang
Wenbin Wang
Wenguan Wang
Guangting Wang
Haolin Wang
Haiyan Wang
Huiyu Wang
Naiyan Wang
Jingbo Wang

Jinpeng Wang
Jiaqi Wang
Liyuan Wang
Lizhen Wang
Ning Wang
Wenqian Wang
Sheng-Yu Wang
Weimin Wang
Xiaohan Wang
Yifan Wang
Yi Wang
Yongtao Wang
Yizhou Wang
Zhuo Wang
Zhe Wang
Xudong Wang
Xiaofang Wang
Xinggang Wang
Xiaosen Wang
Xiaosong Wang
Xiaoyang Wang
Lijun Wang
Xinlong Wang
Xuan Wang
Xue Wang
Yangang Wang
Yaohui Wang
Yu-Chiang Frank Wang
Yida Wang
Yilin Wang
Yi Ru Wang
Yali Wang
Yinglong Wang
Yufu Wang
Yujiang Wang
Yuwang Wang
Yuting Wang
Yang Wang
Yu-Xiong Wang
Yixu Wang
Ziqi Wang
Zhicheng Wang
Zeyu Wang
Zhaowen Wang
Zhenyi Wang

Zhenzhi Wang
Zhijie Wang
Zhiyong Wang
Zhongling Wang
Zhuowei Wang
Zian Wang
Zifu Wang
Zihao Wang
Zirui Wang
Ziyan Wang
Wenxiao Wang
Zhen Wang
Zhepeng Wang
Zi Wang
Zihao W. Wang
Steven L. Waslander
Olivia Watkins
Daniel Watson
Silvan Weder
Dongyoon Wee
Dongming Wei
Tianyi Wei
Jia Wei
Dong Wei
Fangyun Wei
Longhui Wei
Mingqiang Wei
Xinyue Wei
Chen Wei
Donglai Wei
Pengxu Wei
Xing Wei
Xiu-Shen Wei
Wenqi Wei
Guoqiang Wei
Wei Wei
XingKui Wei
Xian Wei
Xingxing Wei
Yake Wei
Yuxiang Wei
Yi Wei
Luca Weihs
Michael Weinmann
Martin Weinmann

Congcong Wen
Chuan Wen
Jie Wen
Sijia Wen
Song Wen
Chao Wen
Xiang Wen
Zeyi Wen
Xin Wen
Yilin Wen
Yijia Weng
Shuchen Weng
Junwu Weng
Wenming Weng
Renliang Weng
Zhenyu Weng
Xinshuo Weng
Nicholas J. Westlake
Gordon Wetzstein
Lena M. Widin Klasén
Rick Wildes
Bryan M. Williams
William Williem
Ole Winther
Scott Wisdom
Alex Wong
Chau-Wai Wong
Kwan-Yee K. Wong
Yongkang Wong
Scott Workman
Marcel Worring
Michael Wray
Safwan Wshah
Xiang Wu
Aming Wu
Chongruo Wu
Cho-Ying Wu
Chunpeng Wu
Chenyan Wu
Ziyi Wu
Fuxiang Wu
Gang Wu
Haiping Wu
Huisi Wu
Jane Wu

Jialian Wu
Jing Wu
Jinjian Wu
Jianlong Wu
Xian Wu
Lifang Wu
Lifan Wu
Minye Wu
Qianyi Wu
Rongliang Wu
Rui Wu
Shiqian Wu
Shuzhe Wu
Shangzhe Wu
Tsung-Han Wu
Tz-Ying Wu
Ting-Wei Wu
Jiannan Wu
Zhiliang Wu
Yu Wu
Chenyun Wu
Dayan Wu
Dongxian Wu
Fei Wu
Hefeng Wu
Jianxin Wu
Weibin Wu
Wenxuan Wu
Wenhao Wu
Xiao Wu
Yicheng Wu
Yuanwei Wu
Yu-Huan Wu
Zhenxin Wu
Zhenyu Wu
Wei Wu
Peng Wu
Xiaohe Wu
Xindi Wu
Xinxing Wu
Xinyi Wu
Xingjiao Wu
Xiongwei Wu
Yangzheng Wu
Yanzhao Wu

Yawen Wu
Yong Wu
Yi Wu
Ying Nian Wu
Zhenyao Wu
Zhonghua Wu
Zongze Wu
Zuxuan Wu
Stefanie Wuhrer
Teng Xi
Jianing Xi
Fei Xia
Haifeng Xia
Menghan Xia
Yuanqing Xia
Zhihua Xia
Xiaobo Xia
Weihao Xia
Shihong Xia
Yan Xia
Yong Xia
Zhaoyang Xia
Zhihao Xia
Chuhua Xian
Yongqin Xian
Wangmeng Xiang
Fanbo Xiang
Tiange Xiang
Tao Xiang
Liuyu Xiang
Xiaoyu Xiang
Zhiyu Xiang
Aoran Xiao
Chunxia Xiao
Fanyi Xiao
Jimin Xiao
Jun Xiao
Taihong Xiao
Anqi Xiao
Junfei Xiao
Jing Xiao
Liang Xiao
Yang Xiao
Yuting Xiao
Yijun Xiao

Yao Xiao
Zeyu Xiao
Zhisheng Xiao
Zihao Xiao
Binhui Xie
Christopher Xie
Haozhe Xie
Jin Xie
Guo-Sen Xie
Hongtao Xie
Ming-Kun Xie
Tingting Xie
Chaohao Xie
Weicheng Xie
Xudong Xie
Jiyang Xie
Xiaohua Xie
Yuan Xie
Zhenyu Xie
Ning Xie
Xianghui Xie
Xiufeng Xie
You Xie
Yutong Xie
Fuyong Xing
Yifan Xing
Zhen Xing
Yuanjun Xiong
Jinhui Xiong
Weihua Xiong
Hongkai Xiong
Zhitong Xiong
Yuanhao Xiong
Yunyang Xiong
Yuwen Xiong
Zhiwei Xiong
Yuliang Xiu
An Xu
Chang Xu
Chenliang Xu
Chengming Xu
Chenshu Xu
Xiang Xu
Huijuan Xu
Zhe Xu

Jie Xu
Jingyi Xu
Jiarui Xu
Yinghao Xu
Kele Xu
Ke Xu
Li Xu
Linchuan Xu
Linning Xu
Mengde Xu
Mengmeng Frost Xu
Min Xu
Mingye Xu
Jun Xu
Ning Xu
Peng Xu
Runsheng Xu
Sheng Xu
Wenqiang Xu
Xiaogang Xu
Renzhe Xu
Kaidi Xu
Yi Xu
Chi Xu
Qiuling Xu
Baobei Xu
Feng Xu
Haohang Xu
Haofei Xu
Lan Xu
Mingze Xu
Songcen Xu
Weipeng Xu
Wenjia Xu
Wenju Xu
Xiangyu Xu
Xin Xu
Yinshuang Xu
Yixing Xu
Yuting Xu
Yanyu Xu
Zhenbo Xu
Zhiliang Xu
Zhiyuan Xu
Xiaohao Xu

Yanwu Xu
Yan Xu
Yiran Xu
Yifan Xu
Yufei Xu
Yong Xu
Zichuan Xu
Zenglin Xu
Zexiang Xu
Zhan Xu
Zheng Xu
Zhiwei Xu
Ziyue Xu
Shiyu Xuan
Hanyu Xuan
Fei Xue
Jianru Xue
Mingfu Xue
Qinghan Xue
Tianfan Xue
Chao Xue
Chuhui Xue
Nan Xue
Zhou Xue
Xiangyang Xue
Yuan Xue
Abhay Yadav
Ravindra Yadav
Kota Yamaguchi
Toshihiko Yamasaki
Kohei Yamashita
Chaochao Yan
Feng Yan
Kun Yan
Qingsen Yan
Qixin Yan
Rui Yan
Siming Yan
Xinchen Yan
Yaping Yan
Bin Yan
Qingan Yan
Shen Yan
Shipeng Yan
Xu Yan

Yan Yan	Yang Yang	Xiaolong Yang
Yichao Yan	Muli Yang	Xue Yang
Zhaoyi Yan	Le Yang	Yubin Yang
Zike Yan	Qiushi Yang	Ze Yang
Zhiqiang Yan	Ren Yang	Ziyi Yang
Hongliang Yan	Ruihan Yang	Yi Yang
Zizheng Yan	Shuang Yang	Linjie Yang
Jiewen Yang	Siyuan Yang	Yuzhe Yang
Anqi Joyce Yang	Su Yang	Yiding Yang
Shan Yang	Shiqi Yang	Zhenpei Yang
Anqi Yang	Taojiannan Yang	Zhaohui Yang
Antoine Yang	Tianyu Yang	Zhengyuan Yang
Bo Yang	Lei Yang	Zhibo Yang
Baoyao Yang	Wanzhao Yang	Zongxin Yang
Chenhongyi Yang	Shuai Yang	Hantao Yao
Dingkang Yang	William Yang	Mingde Yao
De-Nian Yang	Wei Yang	Rui Yao
Dong Yang	Xiaofeng Yang	Taiping Yao
David Yang	Xiaoshan Yang	Ting Yao
Fan Yang	Xin Yang	Cong Yao
Fengyu Yang	Xuan Yang	Qingsong Yao
Fengting Yang	Xu Yang	Quanming Yao
Fei Yang	Xingyi Yang	Xu Yao
Gengshan Yang	Xitong Yang	Yuan Yao
Heng Yang	Jing Yang	Yao Yao
Han Yang	Yanchao Yang	Yazhou Yao
Huan Yang	Wenming Yang	Jiawen Yao
Yibo Yang	Yujiu Yang	Shunyu Yao
Jiancheng Yang	Herb Yang	Pew-Thian Yap
Jihan Yang	Jianfei Yang	Sudhir Yarram
Jiawei Yang	Jinhui Yang	Rajeev Yasarla
Jiayu Yang	Chuanguang Yang	Peng Ye
Jie Yang	Guanglei Yang	Botao Ye
Jinfa Yang	Haitao Yang	Mao Ye
Jingkang Yang	Kewei Yang	Fei Ye
Jinyu Yang	Linlin Yang	Hanrong Ye
Cheng-Fu Yang	Lijin Yang	Jingwen Ye
Ji Yang	Longrong Yang	Jinwei Ye
Jianyu Yang	Meng Yang	Jiarong Ye
Kailun Yang	MingKun Yang	Mang Ye
Tian Yang	Sibei Yang	Meng Ye
Luyu Yang	Shicai Yang	Qi Ye
Liang Yang	Tong Yang	Qian Ye
Li Yang	Wen Yang	Qixiang Ye
Michael Ying Yang	Xi Yang	Junjie Ye

Sheng Ye
Nanyang Ye
Yufei Ye
Xiaoqing Ye
Ruolin Ye
Yousef Yeganeh
Chun-Hsiao Yeh
Raymond A. Yeh
Yu-Ying Yeh
Kai Yi
Chang Yi
Renjiao Yi
Xinping Yi
Peng Yi
Alper Yilmaz
Junho Yim
Hui Yin
Bangjie Yin
Jia-Li Yin
Miao Yin
Wenzhe Yin
Xuwang Yin
Ming Yin
Yu Yin
Aoxiong Yin
Kangxue Yin
Tianwei Yin
Wei Yin
Xianghua Ying
Rio Yokota
Tatsuya Yokota
Naoto Yokoya
Ryo Yonetani
Ki Yoon Yoo
Jinsu Yoo
Sunjae Yoon
Jae Shin Yoon
Jihun Yoon
Sung-Hoon Yoon
Ryota Yoshihashi
Yusuke Yoshiyasu
Chenyu You
Haoran You
Haoxuan You
Yang You

Quanzeng You
Tackgeun You
Kaichao You
Shan You
Xinge You
Yurong You
Baosheng Yu
Bei Yu
Haichao Yu
Hao Yu
Chaohui Yu
Fisher Yu
Jin-Gang Yu
Jiyang Yu
Jason J. Yu
Jiashuo Yu
Hong-Xing Yu
Lei Yu
Mulin Yu
Ning Yu
Peilin Yu
Qi Yu
Qian Yu
Rui Yu
Shuzhi Yu
Gang Yu
Tan Yu
Weijiang Yu
Xin Yu
Bingyao Yu
Ye Yu
Hanchao Yu
Yingchen Yu
Tao Yu
Xiaotian Yu
Qing Yu
Houjian Yu
Changqian Yu
Jing Yu
Jun Yu
Shujian Yu
Xiang Yu
Zhaofei Yu
Zhenbo Yu
Yinfeng Yu

Zhuoran Yu
Zitong Yu
Bo Yuan
Jiangbo Yuan
Liangzhe Yuan
Weihao Yuan
Jianbo Yuan
Xiaoyun Yuan
Ye Yuan
Li Yuan
Geng Yuan
Jialin Yuan
Maoxun Yuan
Peng Yuan
Xin Yuan
Yuan Yuan
Yuhui Yuan
Yixuan Yuan
Zheng Yuan
Mehmet Kerim Yücel
Kaiyu Yue
Haixiao Yue
Heeseung Yun
Sangdoo Yun
Tian Yun
Mahmut Yurt
Ekim Yurtsever
Ahmet Yüzügüler
Edouard Yvinec
Eloi Zablocki
Christopher Zach
Muhammad Zaigham
    Zaheer
Pierluigi Zama Ramirez
Yuhang Zang
Pietro Zanuttigh
Alexey Zaytsev
Bernhard Zeisl
Haitian Zeng
Pengpeng Zeng
Jiabei Zeng
Runhao Zeng
Wei Zeng
Yawen Zeng
Yi Zeng

Yiming Zeng	Hengrui Zhang	Tao Zhang
Tieyong Zeng	Hongming Zhang	Wenwei Zhang
Huanqiang Zeng	Mingfang Zhang	Wenqiang Zhang
Dan Zeng	Jianpeng Zhang	Wen Zhang
Yu Zeng	Jiaming Zhang	Xiaolin Zhang
Wei Zhai	Jichao Zhang	Xingchen Zhang
Yuanhao Zhai	Jie Zhang	Xingxuan Zhang
Fangneng Zhan	Jingfeng Zhang	Xiuming Zhang
Kun Zhan	Jingyi Zhang	Xiaoshuai Zhang
Xiong Zhang	Jinnian Zhang	Xuanmeng Zhang
Jingdong Zhang	David Junhao Zhang	Xuanyang Zhang
Jiangning Zhang	Junjie Zhang	Xucong Zhang
Zhilu Zhang	Junzhe Zhang	Xingxing Zhang
Gengwei Zhang	Jiawan Zhang	Xikun Zhang
Dongsu Zhang	Jingyang Zhang	Xiaohan Zhang
Hui Zhang	Kai Zhang	Yahui Zhang
Binjie Zhang	Lei Zhang	Yunhua Zhang
Bo Zhang	Lihua Zhang	Yan Zhang
Tianhao Zhang	Lu Zhang	Yanghao Zhang
Cecilia Zhang	Miao Zhang	Yifei Zhang
Jing Zhang	Minjia Zhang	Yifan Zhang
Chaoning Zhang	Mingjin Zhang	Yi-Fan Zhang
Chenxu Zhang	Qi Zhang	Yihao Zhang
Chi Zhang	Qian Zhang	Yingliang Zhang
Chris Zhang	Qilong Zhang	Youshan Zhang
Yabin Zhang	Qiming Zhang	Yulun Zhang
Zhao Zhang	Qiang Zhang	Yushu Zhang
Rufeng Zhang	Richard Zhang	Yixiao Zhang
Chaoyi Zhang	Ruimao Zhang	Yide Zhang
Zheng Zhang	Ruisi Zhang	Zhongwen Zhang
Da Zhang	Ruixin Zhang	Bowen Zhang
Yi Zhang	Runze Zhang	Chen-Lin Zhang
Edward Zhang	Qilin Zhang	Zehua Zhang
Xin Zhang	Shan Zhang	Zekun Zhang
Feifei Zhang	Shanshan Zhang	Zeyu Zhang
Feilong Zhang	Xi Sheryl Zhang	Xiaowei Zhang
Yuqi Zhang	Song-Hai Zhang	Yifeng Zhang
GuiXuan Zhang	Chongyang Zhang	Cheng Zhang
Hanlin Zhang	Kaihao Zhang	Hongguang Zhang
Hanwang Zhang	Songyang Zhang	Yuexi Zhang
Hanzhen Zhang	Shu Zhang	Fa Zhang
Haotian Zhang	Siwei Zhang	Guofeng Zhang
He Zhang	Shujian Zhang	Hao Zhang
Haokui Zhang	Tianyun Zhang	Haofeng Zhang
Hongyuan Zhang	Tong Zhang	Hongwen Zhang

Hua Zhang
Jiaxin Zhang
Zhenyu Zhang
Jian Zhang
Jianfeng Zhang
Jiao Zhang
Jinkni Zhang
Lefei Zhang
Le Zhang
Mi Zhang
Min Zhang
Ning Zhang
Pan Zhang
Pu Zhang
Qing Zhang
Renrui Zhang
Shifeng Zhang
Shuo Zhang
Shaoxiong Zhang
Weizhong Zhang
Xi Zhang
Xiaomei Zhang
Xinyu Zhang
Yin Zhang
Zicheng Zhang
Zihao Zhang
Ziqi Zhang
Zhaoxiang Zhang
Zhen Zhang
Zhipeng Zhang
Zhixing Zhang
Zhizheng Zhang
Jiawei Zhang
Zhong Zhang
Pingping Zhang
Yixin Zhang
Kui Zhang
Lingzhi Zhang
Huaiwen Zhang
Quanshi Zhang
Zhoutong Zhang
Yuhang Zhang
Yuting Zhang
Zhang Zhang
Ziming Zhang

Zhizhong Zhang
Qilong Zhangli
Bingyin Zhao
Bin Zhao
Chenglong Zhao
Lei Zhao
Feng Zhao
Gangming Zhao
Haiyan Zhao
Hao Zhao
Handong Zhao
Hengshuang Zhao
Yinan Zhao
Jiaojiao Zhao
Jiaqi Zhao
Jing Zhao
Kaili Zhao
Haojie Zhao
Yucheng Zhao
Longjiao Zhao
Long Zhao
Qingsong Zhao
Qingyu Zhao
Rui Zhao
Rui-Wei Zhao
Sicheng Zhao
Shuang Zhao
Siyan Zhao
Zelin Zhao
Shiyu Zhao
Wang Zhao
Tiesong Zhao
Qian Zhao
Wangbo Zhao
Xi-Le Zhao
Xu Zhao
Yajie Zhao
Yang Zhao
Ying Zhao
Yin Zhao
Yizhou Zhao
Yunhan Zhao
Yuyang Zhao
Yue Zhao
Yuzhi Zhao

Bowen Zhao
Pu Zhao
Bingchen Zhao
Borui Zhao
Fuqiang Zhao
Hanbin Zhao
Jiun Zhao
Mingyang Zhao
Na Zhao
Rongchang Zhao
Ruiqi Zhao
Shuai Zhao
Wenda Zhao
Wenliang Zhao
Xiangyun Zhao
Yifan Zhao
Yaping Zhao
Zhou Zhao
He Zhao
Jie Zhao
Xibin Zhao
Xiaoqi Zhao
Zhengyu Zhao
Jin Zhe
Chuanxia Zheng
Huan Zheng
Hao Zheng
Jia Zheng
Jian-Qing Zheng
Shuai Zheng
Meng Zheng
Mingkai Zheng
Qian Zheng
Qi Zheng
Wu Zheng
Yinqiang Zheng
Yufeng Zheng
Yutong Zheng
Yalin Zheng
Yu Zheng
Feng Zheng
Zhaoheng Zheng
Haitian Zheng
Kang Zheng
Bolun Zheng

Haiyong Zheng
Mingwu Zheng
Sipeng Zheng
Tu Zheng
Wenzhao Zheng
Xiawu Zheng
Yinglin Zheng
Zhuo Zheng
Zilong Zheng
Kecheng Zheng
Zerong Zheng
Shuaifeng Zhi
Tiancheng Zhi
Jia-Xing Zhong
Yiwu Zhong
Fangwei Zhong
Zhihang Zhong
Yaoyao Zhong
Yiran Zhong
Zhun Zhong
Zichun Zhong
Bo Zhou
Boyao Zhou
Brady Zhou
Mo Zhou
Chunluan Zhou
Dingfu Zhou
Fan Zhou
Jingkai Zhou
Honglu Zhou
Jiaming Zhou
Jiahuan Zhou
Jun Zhou
Kaiyang Zhou
Keyang Zhou
Kuangqi Zhou
Lei Zhou
Lihua Zhou
Man Zhou
Mingyi Zhou
Mingyuan Zhou
Ning Zhou
Peng Zhou
Penghao Zhou
Qianyi Zhou

Shuigeng Zhou
Shangchen Zhou
Huayi Zhou
Zhize Zhou
Sanping Zhou
Qin Zhou
Tao Zhou
Wenbo Zhou
Xiangdong Zhou
Xiao-Yun Zhou
Xiao Zhou
Yang Zhou
Yipin Zhou
Zhenyu Zhou
Hao Zhou
Chu Zhou
Daquan Zhou
Da-Wei Zhou
Hang Zhou
Kang Zhou
Qianyu Zhou
Sheng Zhou
Wenhui Zhou
Xingyi Zhou
Yan-Jie Zhou
Yiyi Zhou
Yu Zhou
Yuan Zhou
Yuqian Zhou
Yuxuan Zhou
Zixiang Zhou
Wengang Zhou
Shuchang Zhou
Tianfei Zhou
Yichao Zhou
Alex Zhu
Chenchen Zhu
Deyao Zhu
Xiatian Zhu
Guibo Zhu
Haidong Zhu
Hao Zhu
Hongzi Zhu
Rui Zhu
Jing Zhu

Jianke Zhu
Junchen Zhu
Lei Zhu
Lingyu Zhu
Luyang Zhu
Menglong Zhu
Peihao Zhu
Hui Zhu
Xiaofeng Zhu
Tyler (Lixuan) Zhu
Wentao Zhu
Xiangyu Zhu
Xinqi Zhu
Xinxin Zhu
Xinliang Zhu
Yangguang Zhu
Yichen Zhu
Yixin Zhu
Yanjun Zhu
Yousong Zhu
Yuhao Zhu
Ye Zhu
Feng Zhu
Zhen Zhu
Fangrui Zhu
Jinjing Zhu
Linchao Zhu
Pengfei Zhu
Sijie Zhu
Xiaobin Zhu
Xiaoguang Zhu
Zezhou Zhu
Zhenyao Zhu
Kai Zhu
Pengkai Zhu
Bingbing Zhuang
Chengyuan Zhuang
Liansheng Zhuang
Peiye Zhuang
Yixin Zhuang
Yihong Zhuang
Junbao Zhuo
Andrea Ziani
Bartosz Zieliński
Primo Zingaretti

Nikolaos Zioulis
Andrew Zisserman
Yael Ziv
Liu Ziyin
Xingxing Zou
Danping Zou
Qi Zou

Shihao Zou
Xueyan Zou
Yang Zou
Yuliang Zou
Zihang Zou
Chuhang Zou
Dongqing Zou

Xu Zou
Zhiming Zou
Maria A. Zuluaga
Xinxin Zuo
Zhiwen Zuo
Reyer Zwiggelaar

Contents – Part XXXII

ARAH: Animatable Volume Rendering of Articulated Human SDFs

Shaofei Wang[1]([✉]), Katja Schwarz[2,3], Andreas Geiger[2,3], and Siyu Tang[1]

[1] ETH Zürich, Zürich, Switzerland
shaofei.wang@inf.ethz.ch
[2] Max Planck Institute for Intelligent Systems, Tübingen, Germany
[3] University of Tübingen, Tübingen, Germany

Abstract. Combining human body models with differentiable rendering has recently enabled animatable avatars of clothed humans from sparse sets of multi-view RGB videos. While state-of-the-art approaches achieve a realistic appearance with neural radiance fields (NeRF), the inferred geometry often lacks detail due to missing geometric constraints. Further, animating avatars in out-of-distribution poses is not yet possible because the mapping from observation space to canonical space does not generalize faithfully to unseen poses. In this work, we address these shortcomings and propose a model to create animatable clothed human avatars with detailed geometry that generalize well to out-of-distribution poses. To achieve detailed geometry, we combine an articulated implicit surface representation with volume rendering. For generalization, we propose a novel joint root-finding algorithm for simultaneous ray-surface intersection search and correspondence search. Our algorithm enables efficient point sampling and accurate point canonicalization while generalizing well to unseen poses. We demonstrate that our proposed pipeline can generate clothed avatars with high-quality pose-dependent geometry and appearance from a sparse set of multi-view RGB videos. Our method achieves state-of-the-art performance on geometry and appearance reconstruction while creating animatable avatars that generalize well to out-of-distribution poses beyond the small number of training poses.

Keywords: 3D computer vision · Clothed human modeling · Cloth modeling · Neural rendering · Neural implicit functions

1 Introduction

Reconstruction and animation of clothed human avatars is a rising topic in computer vision research. It is of particular interest for various applications in AR/VR and the future metaverse. Various sensors can be used to create clothed human avatars, ranging from 4D scanners over depth sensors to simple RGB

Supplementary Information The online version contains supplementary material available at https://doi.org/10.1007/978-3-031-19824-3_1.

Inputs:	Output:	Our Results on	Existing Works
Sparse Multi-view Videos	Animatable Avatar	Out-of-distribution Poses	(Neural Body, Ani-NeRF)
(Observation Space)	(Canonical Space)		

Fig. 1. Detailed Geometry and Generalization to Extreme Poses. Given sparse multi-view videos with SMPL fittings and foreground masks, our approach synthesizes animatable clothed avatars with realistic pose-dependent geometry and appearance. While existing works, *e.g.* Neural Body [56] and Ani-NeRF [54], struggle with generalizing to unseen poses, our approach enables avatars that can be animated in extreme out-of-distribution poses.

cameras. Among these data sources, RGB videos are by far the most accessible and user-friendly choice. However, they also provide the least supervision, making this setup the most challenging for the reconstruction and animation of clothed humans.

Traditional works in clothed human modeling use explicit mesh [1,2,6,7,17, 18,29,33,52,63,68,78,83] or truncated signed distance fields (TSDFs) of fixed grid resolution [34,35,66,76,81] to represent the geometry of humans. Textures are often represented by vertex colors or UV-maps. With the recent success of neural implicit representations, significant progress has been made towards modeling articulated clothed humans. PIFu [60] and PIFuHD [61] are among the first works that propose to model clothed humans as continuous neural implicit functions. ARCH [24] extends this idea and develops animatable clothed human avatars from monocular images. However, this line of works does not handle dynamic pose-dependent cloth deformations. Further, they require ground-truth geometry for training. Such ground-truth data is expensive to acquire, limiting the generalization of these methods.

Another line of works removes the need for ground-truth geometry by utilizing differentiable neural rendering. These methods aim to reconstruct humans from a sparse set of multi-view videos with only image supervision. Many of them use NeRF [46] as the underlying representation and achieve impressive visual fidelity on novel view synthesis tasks. However, there are two fundamental drawbacks of these existing approaches: (1) the NeRF-based representation lacks proper geometric regularization, leading to inaccurate geometry. This is particularly detrimental in a sparse multi-view setup and often results in artifacts in the form of erroneous color blobs under novel views or poses. (2) Existing approaches condition their NeRF networks [56] or canonicalization networks [54] on inputs in observation space. Thus, they cannot generalize to unseen out-of-distribution poses.

In this work, we address these two major drawbacks of existing approaches. (1) We improve geometry by building an articulated signed-distance-field (SDF) representation for clothed human bodies to better capture the geometry of clothed humans and improve the rendering quality. (2) In order to render the

SDF, we develop an efficient joint root-finding algorithm for the conversion from observation space to canonical space. Specifically, we represent clothed human avatars as a combination of a forward linear blend skinning (LBS) network, an implicit SDF network, and a color network, all defined in canonical space and do not condition on inputs in observation space. Given these networks and camera rays in observation space, we apply our novel joint root-finding algorithm that can efficiently find the iso-surface points in observation space and their correspondences in canonical space. This enables us to perform efficient sampling on camera rays around the iso-surface. All network modules can be trained with a photometric loss in image space and regularization losses in canonical space.

We validate our approach on the ZJU-MoCap [56] and the H36M [25] dataset. Our approach generalizes well to unseen poses, enabling robust animation of clothed avatars even under out-of-distribution poses where existing works fail, as shown in Fig. 1. We achieve significant improvements over state-of-the-arts for novel pose synthesis and geometry reconstruction, while also outperforming state-of-the-arts in the novel view synthesis task on training poses. Code and data are available at https://neuralbodies.github.io/arah/.

2   Related Works

Clothed Human Modeling with Explicit Representations: Many explicit mesh-based approaches represent cloth deformations as deformation layers [1,2, 6–8] added to minimally clothed parametric human body models [5,20,27,37,50, 53,75]. Such approaches enjoy compatibility with parametric human body models but have difficulties in modeling large garment deformations. Other mesh-based approaches model garments as separate meshes [17,18,29,33,52,63,68,78, 83] in order to represent more detailed and physically plausible cloth deformations. However, such methods often require accurate 3D-surface registration, synthetic 3D data or dense multi-view images for training and the garment meshes need to be pre-defined for each cloth type. More recently, point-cloud-based explicit methods [38,39,82] also showed promising results in modeling clothed humans. However, they still require explicit 3D or depth supervision for training, while our goal is to train using sparse multi-view RGB supervision alone.

Clothed Humans as Implicit Functions: Neural implicit functions [12,41,42, 51,57] have been used to model clothed humans from various sensor inputs including monocular images [21,22,24,31,59–61,65,73,86], multi-view videos [28,36, 48,54,56,74], sparse point clouds [6,13,15,70,71,87], or 3D meshes [10,11,14,44, 45,62,67]. Among the image-based methods, [4,22,24] obtain animatable reconstructions of clothed humans from a single image. However, they do not model pose-dependent cloth deformations and require ground-truth geometry for training. [28] learns generalizable NeRF models for human performance capture and only requires multi-view images as supervision. But it needs images as inputs for synthesizing novel poses. [36,48,54,56,74] take multi-view videos as inputs and do not need ground-truth geometry during training. These methods generate personalized per-subject avatars and only need 2D supervision. Our approach follows this line of work and also learns a personalized avatar for each subject.

Neural Rendering of Animatable Clothed Humans: Differentiable neural rendering has been extended to model animatable human bodies by a number of recent works [48,54,56,58,65,74]. Neural Body [56] proposes to diffuse latent per-vertex codes associated with SMPL meshes in observation space and condition NeRF [46] on such latent codes. However, the conditional inputs of Neural Body are in the observation space. Therefore, it does not generalize well to out-of-distribution poses. Several recent works [48,54,65] propose to model the radiance field in canonical space and use a pre-defined or learned backward mapping to map query points from observation space to this canonical space. A-NeRF [65] uses a deterministic backward mapping defined by piecewise rigid bone transformations. This mapping is very coarse and the model has to use a complicated bone-relative embedding to compensate for that. Ani-NeRF [54] trains a backward LBS network that does not generalize well to out-of-distribution poses, even when fine-tuned with a cycle consistency loss for its backward LBS network for each test pose. Further, all aforementioned methods utilize a volumetric radiance representation and hence suffer from noisy geometry [49,69,79,80]. In contrast to these works, we improve geometry by combining an implicit surface representation with volume rendering and improve pose generalization via iterative root-finding. H-NeRF [74] achieves large improvements in geometric reconstruction by co-training SDF and NeRF networks. However, code and models of H-NeRF are not publicly available. Furthermore, H-NeRF's canonicalization process relies on imGHUM [3] to predict an accurate signed distance in *observation space*. Therefore, imGHUM needs to be trained on a large corpus of posed human scans and it is unclear whether the learned signed distance fields generalize to out-of-distribution poses beyond the training set. In contrast, our approach does not need to be trained on any posed scans and it can generalize to extreme out-of-distribution poses.

Concurrent Works: Several concurrent works extend NeRF-based articulated models to improve novel view synthesis, geometry reconstruction, or animation quality [9,23,26,30,43,55,64,72,77,85]. [85] proposes to jointly learn forward blending weights, a canonical occupancy network, and a canonical color network using differentiable surface rendering for head-avatars. In contrast to human heads, human bodies show much more articulation. Abrupt changes in depth also occur more frequently when rendering human bodies, which is difficult to capture with surface rendering [69]. Furthermore, [85] uses the secant method to find surface points. For each secant step, this needs to solve a root-finding problem from scratch. Instead, we use volume rendering of SDFs and formulate the surface-finding task of articulated SDFs as a joint root-finding problem that only needs to be solved once per ray. We remark that [26] proposes to formulate surface-finding and correspondence search as a joint root-finding problem to tackle geometry reconstruction from photometric and mask losses. However, they use pre-defined skinning fields and surface rendering. They also require estimated normals from PIFuHD [61] while our approach achieves detailed geometry reconstructions without such supervision.

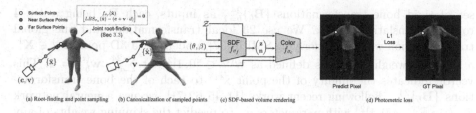

(a) Root-finding and point sampling   (b) Canonicalization of sampled points   (c) SDF-based volume rendering   (d) Photometric loss

Fig. 2. Overview of Our Pipeline. (a) Given a ray $(\mathbf{c}, \mathbf{v})$ with camera center $\mathbf{c}$ and ray direction $\mathbf{v}$ in observation space, we jointly search for its intersection with the SDF iso-surface and the correspondence of the intersection point via a novel joint root-finding algorithm (Sect. 3.3). We then sample near/far surface points $\{\bar{\mathbf{x}}\}$. (b) The sampled points are mapped into canonical space as $\{\hat{\mathbf{x}}\}$ via root-finding. (c) In canonical space, we run an SDF-based volume rendering with canonicalized points $\{\hat{\mathbf{x}}\}$, local body poses and shape (θ, β), an SDF network feature $\mathbf{z}$, surface normals $\mathbf{n}$, and a per-frame latent code $\mathcal{Z}$ to predict the corresponding pixel value of the input ray (Sect. 3.4). (d) All network modules, including the forward LBS network LBS_{σ_w}, the canonical SDF network f_{σ_f}, and the canonical color network f_{σ_c}, are trained end-to-end with a photometric loss in image space and regularization losses in canonical space (Sect. 3.5).

3 Method

Our pipeline is illustrated in Fig. 2. Our model consists of a forward linear blend skinning (LBS) network (Sect. 3.1), a canonical SDF network, and a canonical color network (Sect. 3.2). When rendering a specific pixel of the image in observation space, we first find the intersection of the corresponding camera ray and the observation-space SDF iso-surface. Since we model a canonical SDF and a forward LBS, we propose a novel joint root-finding algorithm that can simultaneously search for the ray-surface intersection and the canonical correspondence of the intersection point (Sect. 3.3). Such a formulation does not condition the networks on observations in observation space. Consequently, it can generalize to unseen poses. Once the ray-surface intersection is found, we sample near/far surface points on the camera ray and find their canonical correspondences via forward LBS root-finding. The canonicalized points are used for volume rendering to compose the final RGB value at the pixel (Sect. 3.4). The predicted pixel color is then compared to the observation using a photometric loss (Sect. 3.5). The model is trained end-to-end using the photometric loss and regularization losses. The learned networks represent a personalized animatable avatar that can robustly synthesize new geometries and appearances under novel poses (Sect. 4.1).

3.1 Neural Linear Blend Skinning

Traditional parametric human body models [5,20,37,50,53,75] often use linear blend skinning (LBS) to deform a template model according to rigid bone transformations and skinning weights. We follow the notations of [71] to describe LBS. Given a set of N points in canonical space, $\hat{\mathbf{X}} = \{\hat{\mathbf{x}}^{(i)}\}_{i=1}^{N}$, LBS takes a set of rigid bone transformations $\{\mathbf{B}_b\}_{b=1}^{24}$ as inputs, each $\mathbf{B}_b$ being a 4×4 rotation-translation matrix. We use 23 local transformations and one global transformation with an underlying SMPL [37] model. For a 3D point $\hat{\mathbf{x}}^{(i)} \in \hat{\mathbf{X}}^1$, a skinning weight vector is defined as $\mathbf{w}^{(i)} \in [0, 1]^{24}$, s.t. $\sum_{b=1}^{24} \mathbf{w}_b^{(i)} = 1$. This vector indicates the affinity of the point $\hat{\mathbf{x}}^{(i)}$ to each of the bone transformations $\{\mathbf{B}_b\}_{b=1}^{24}$. Following recent works [11,45,62,71], we use a neural network $f_{\sigma_w}(\cdot) \cdot \mathbb{R}^3 \mapsto [0, 1]^{24}$ with parameters σ_w to predict the skinning weights of any point in space. The set of transformed points $\bar{\mathbf{X}} = \{\bar{\mathbf{x}}^{(i)}\}_{i=1}^N$ is related to $\hat{\mathbf{X}}$ via:

$$\bar{\mathbf{x}}^{(i)} = LBS_{\sigma_w}\left(\hat{\mathbf{x}}^{(i)}, \{\mathbf{B}_b\}\right), \quad \forall i = 1, \dots, N$$

$$\Longleftrightarrow \bar{\mathbf{x}}^{(i)} = \left(\sum_{b=1}^{24} f_{\sigma_w}(\hat{\mathbf{x}}^{(i)})_b \mathbf{B}_b\right) \hat{\mathbf{x}}^{(i)}, \quad \forall i = 1, \dots, N \qquad (1)$$

where Eq. (1) is referred to as the forward LBS function. The process of applying Eq. (1) to all points in $\hat{\mathbf{X}}$ is often referred to as *forward skinning*. For brevity, for the remainder of the paper, we drop $\{\mathbf{B}_b\}$ from the LBS function and write $LBS_{\sigma_w}(\hat{\mathbf{x}}^{(i)}, \{\mathbf{B}_b\})$ as $LBS_{\sigma_w}(\hat{\mathbf{x}}^{(i)})$.

3.2 Canonical SDF and Color Networks

We model an articulated human as a neural SDF $f_{\sigma_f}(\hat{\mathbf{x}}, \theta, \beta, \mathcal{Z})$ with parameters σ_f in canonical space, where $\hat{\mathbf{x}}$ denotes the canonical query point, θ and β denote local poses and body shape of the human which capture pose-dependent cloth deformations, and $\mathcal{Z}$ denotes a per-frame optimizable latent code which compensates for time-dependent dynamic cloth deformations. For brevity, we write this neural SDF as $f_{\sigma_f}(\hat{\mathbf{x}})$ in the remainder of the paper.

Similar to the canonical SDF network, we define a canonical color network with parameters σ_c as $f_{\sigma_c}(\hat{\mathbf{x}}, \mathbf{n}, \mathbf{v}, \mathbf{z}, \mathcal{Z})$: $\mathbb{R}^{9+|\mathbf{z}|+|\mathcal{Z}|} \mapsto \mathbb{R}^3$. Here, $\mathbf{n}$ denotes a normal vector in the observation space. $\mathbf{n}$ is computed by transforming the canonical normal vectors using the rotational part of forward transformations $\sum_{b=1}^{24} f_{\sigma_w}(\hat{\mathbf{x}}^{(i)})_b \mathbf{B}_b$ (Eq. (1)). $\mathbf{v}$ denotes viewing direction. Similar to [69,79,80], $\mathbf{z}$ denotes an SDF feature which is extracted from the output of the second-last layer of the neural SDF. $\mathcal{Z}$ denotes a per-frame latent code which is shared with the SDF network. It compensates for time-dependent dynamic lighting effects. The outputs of f_{σ_c} are RGB color values in the range $[0, 1]$.

3.3 Joint Root-Finding

While surface rendering [47,80] could be used to learn the network parameters introduced in Sects. 3.1 and 3.2, it cannot handle abrupt changes in depth, as demonstrated in [69]. We also observe severe geometric artifacts when applying surface rendering to our setup, we refer readers to the Supp. Mat. for such an

---

[1] With slight abuse of notation, we also use $\hat{\mathbf{x}}$ to represent points in homogeneous coordinates when necessary.

ablation. On the other hand, volume rendering can better handle abrupt depth changes in articulated human rendering. However, volume rendering requires multi-step dense sampling on camera rays [69,79], which, when combined naively with the iterative root-finding algorithm [11], requires significantly more memory and becomes prohibitively slow to train and test. We thus employ a hybrid method similar to [49]. We first search the ray-surface intersection and then sample near/far surface points on the ray. In practice, we initialize our SDF network with [71]. Thus, we fix the sampling depth interval around the surface to $[-5\,\mathrm{cm}, +5\,\mathrm{cm}]$.

A naive way of finding the ray-surface intersection is to use sphere tracing [19] and map each point to canonical space via root-finding [11]. In this case, we need to solve the costly root-finding problem during each step of the sphere tracing. This becomes prohibitively expensive when the number of rays is large. Thus, we propose an alternative solution. We leverage the skinning weights of the nearest neighbor on the registered SMPL mesh to the query point $\bar{\mathbf{x}}$ and use the inverse of the linearly combined forward bone transforms to map $\bar{\mathbf{x}}$ to its rough canonical correspondence. Combining this approximate backward mapping with sphere tracing, we obtain rough estimations of intersection points. Then, starting from these rough estimations, we apply a novel joint root-finding algorithm to search the precise intersection points and their correspondences in canonical space. In practice, we found that using a single initialization for our joint root-finding works well already. Adding more initializations incurs drastic memory and runtime overhead while not achieving any noticeable improvements. We hypothesize that this is due to the fact that our initialization is obtained using inverse transformations with SMPL skinning weights rather than rigid bone transformations (as was done in [11]).

Formally, we define a camera ray as $\mathbf{r} = (\mathbf{c}, \mathbf{v})$ where $\mathbf{c}$ is the camera center and $\mathbf{v}$ is a unit vector that defines the direction of this camera ray. Any point on the camera ray can be expressed as $\mathbf{c} + \mathbf{v} \cdot d$ with $d >= 0$. The joint root-finding aims to find canonical point $\hat{\mathbf{x}}$ and depth d on the ray in observation space, such that:

$$f_{\sigma_f}(\hat{\mathbf{x}}) = 0$$
$$LBS_{\sigma_\omega}(\hat{\mathbf{x}}) - (\mathbf{c} + \mathbf{v} \cdot d) = \mathbf{0} \tag{2}$$

in which $\mathbf{c}, \mathbf{v}$ are constants per ray. Denoting the joint vector-valued function as $g_{\sigma_f, \sigma_\omega}(\hat{\mathbf{x}}, d)$ and the joint root-finding problem as:

$$g_{\sigma_f, \sigma_\omega}(\hat{\mathbf{x}}, d) = \begin{bmatrix} f_{\sigma_f}(\hat{\mathbf{x}}) \\ LBS_{\sigma_\omega}(\hat{\mathbf{x}}) - (\mathbf{c} + \mathbf{v} \cdot d) \end{bmatrix} = \mathbf{0} \tag{3}$$

we can then solve it via Newton's method

$$\begin{bmatrix} \hat{\mathbf{x}}_{k+1} \\ d_{k+1} \end{bmatrix} = \begin{bmatrix} \hat{\mathbf{x}}_k \\ d_k \end{bmatrix} - \mathbf{J}_k^{-1} \cdot g_{\sigma_f, \sigma_\omega}(\hat{\mathbf{x}}_k, d_k) \tag{4}$$

where:

$$J_k = \begin{bmatrix} \frac{\partial f_{\sigma_f}}{\partial \hat{x}}(\hat{\mathbf{x}}_k) & 0 \\ \frac{\partial LBS_{\sigma_w}}{\partial \hat{x}}(\hat{\mathbf{x}}_k) & -\mathbf{v} \end{bmatrix} \tag{5}$$

Following [11], we use Broyden's method to avoid computing J_k at each iteration.

Amortized Complexity: Given the number of sphere-tracing steps as N and the number of root-finding steps as M, the amortized complexity for joint root-finding is $O(M)$ while naive alternation between sphere-tracing and root-finding is $O(MN)$. In practice, this results in about 5× speed up of joint root-finding compared to the naive alternation between sphere-tracing and root-finding. We also note that from a theoretical perspective, our proposed joint root-finding converges quadratically while the secant-method-based root-finding in the concurrent work [85] converges only superlinearly.

We describe how to compute implicit gradients wrt. the canonical SDF and the forward LBS in the Supp. Mat. In the main paper, we use volume rendering which does not need to compute implicit gradients wrt. the canonical SDF.

3.4   Differentiable Volume Rendering

We employ a recently proposed SDF-based volume rendering formulation [79]. Specifically, we convert SDF values into density values σ using the scaled CDF of the Laplace distribution with the negated SDF values as input

$$\sigma(\hat{\mathbf{x}}) = \frac{1}{b}\left(\frac{1}{2} + \frac{1}{2}\text{sign}(-f_{\sigma_f}(\hat{\mathbf{x}}))\left(1 - \exp(-\frac{|-f_{\sigma_f}(\hat{\mathbf{x}})|}{b})\right)\right) \tag{6}$$

where b is a learnable parameter. Given the surface point found via solving Eq. (3), we sample 16 points around the surface points and another 16 points between the near scene bound and the surface point, and map them to canonical space along with the surface point. For rays that do not intersect with any surface, we uniformly sample 64 points for volume rendering. With N sampled points on a ray $\mathbf{r} = (\mathbf{c}, \mathbf{v})$, we use standard volume rendering [46] to render the pixel color

$$\hat{C}(\mathbf{r}) = \sum_{i=1}^{N} T^{(i)}\left(1 - \exp(-\sigma(\hat{\mathbf{x}}^{(i)})\delta^{(i)})\right) f_{c_\sigma}(\hat{\mathbf{x}}^{(i)}, \mathbf{n}^{(i)}, \mathbf{v}, \mathbf{z}, \mathcal{Z}) \tag{7}$$

$$T^{(i)} = \exp\left(-\sum_{j<i}\sigma(\hat{\mathbf{x}}^{(j)})\delta^{(j)}\right) \tag{8}$$

where $\delta^{(i)} = |d^{(i+1)} - d^{(i)}|$.

3.5   Loss Function

Our loss consists of a photometric loss in observation space and multiple regularizers in canonical space

$$\mathcal{L} = \lambda_C \cdot \mathcal{L}_C + \lambda_E \cdot \mathcal{L}_E + \lambda_O \cdot \mathcal{L}_O + \lambda_I \cdot \mathcal{L}_I + \lambda_S \cdot \mathcal{L}_S \qquad (9)$$

$\mathcal{L}_C$ is the L1 loss for color predictions. $\mathcal{L}_E$ is the Eikonal regularization [16]. $\mathcal{L}_O$ is an off-surface point loss, encouraging points far away from the SMPL mesh to have positive SDF values. Similarly, $\mathcal{L}_I$ regularizes points inside the canonical SMPL mesh to have negative SDF values. $\mathcal{L}_S$ encourages the forward LBS network to predict similar skinning weights to the canonical SMPL mesh. Different from [26,74,80], we do not use an explicit silhouette loss. Instead, we utilize foreground masks and set all background pixel values to zero. In practice, this encourages the SDF network to predict positive SDF values for points on rays that do not intersect with foreground masks. For detailed definitions of loss terms and model architectures, please refer to the Supp. Mat.

4   Experiments

We validate the generalization ability and reconstruction quality of our proposed method against several recent baselines [54,56,65]. As was done in [56], we consider a setup with 4 cameras positioned equally spaced around the human subject. For an ablation study on different design choices of our model, including ray sampling strategy, LBS networks, and number of initializations for root-finding, we refer readers to the Supp. Mat.

Datasets: We use the ZJU-MoCap [56] dataset as our primary testbed because its setup includes 23 cameras which allows us to extract pseudo-ground-truth geometry to evaluate our model. More specifically, the dataset consists of 9 sequences captured with 23 calibrated cameras. We use the training/testing splits from Neural Body [56] for both the cameras and the poses. As one of our goals is learn to detailed geometry, we collect pseudo-ground-truth geometry for the training poses. We use all 23 cameras and apply NeuS with a background NeRF model [69], a state-of-the-art method for multi-view reconstruction. Note that we refrain from using the masks provided by Neural Body [56] as these masks are noisy and insufficient for accurate static scene reconstruction. We observe that geometry reconstruction with NeuS [69] fails when subjects wear black clothes or the environmental light is not bright enough. Therefore, we manually exclude bad reconstructions and discard sequences with less than 3 valid reconstructions. For completeness, we also tested our approach on the H36M dataset [25] and report a quantitative comparison to [48,54] in the Supp. Mat.

Baselines: We compare against three major baselines: Neural Body [56](NB), Ani-NeRF [54](AniN), and A-NeRF [65](AN). Neural Body diffuses per-SMPL-vertex latent codes into observation space as additional conditioning for NeRF models to achieve state-of-the-art novel view synthesis results on training poses.

Ani-NeRF learns a canonical NeRF model and a backward LBS network which predicts residuals to the deterministic SMPL-based backward LBS. Consequently, the LBS network needs to be re-trained for each test sequence. A-NeRF employs a deterministic backward mapping with bone-relative embeddings for query points and only uses keypoints and joint rotations instead of surface models (*i.e.* SMPL surface). For the detailed setups of these baselines, please refer to the Supp. Mat.

Benchmark Tasks: We benchmark our approach on three tasks: generalization to unseen poses, geometry reconstruction, and novel-view synthesis. To analyze generalization ability, we evaluate the trained models on unseen testing poses. Due to the stochastic nature of cloth deformations, we quantify performance via perceptual similarity to the ground-truth images with the LPIPS [84] metric. We report PSNR and SSIM in the Supp. Mat. We also encourage readers to check out qualitative comparison videos at https://neuralbodies.github.io/arah/.

For geometry reconstruction, we evaluate our method and baselines on the training poses. We report point-based L2 Chamfer distance (CD) and normal consistency (NC) wrt. the pseudo-ground-truth geometry. During the evaluation, we only keep the largest connected component of the reconstructed meshes. Note that is in favor of the baselines as they are more prone to producing floating blob artifacts. We also remove any ground-truth or predicted mesh points that are below an estimated ground plane to exclude outliers from the ground plane from the evaluation. For completeness, we also evaluate novel-view synthesis with PSNR, SSIM, and LPIPS using the poses from the training split.

Table 1. Generalization to Unseen Poses. We report LPIPS [84] on synthesized images under unseen poses from the testset of the ZJU-MoCap dataset [56] (*i.e.* all views except 0, 6, 12, and 18). Our approach consistently outperforms the baselines by a large margin. We report PSNR and SSIM in the Supp. Mat.

Sequence	Metric	NB	AniN	AN	Ours
313	LPIPS ↓	0.126	0.115	0.209	**0.092**
315	LPIPS ↓	0.152	0.167	0.232	**0.105**
377	LPIPS ↓	0.119	0.153	0.165	**0.093**
386	LPIPS ↓	0.171	0.187	0.241	**0.127**
387	LPIPS ↓	0.135	0.145	0.162	**0.099**
390	LPIPS ↓	0.163	0.173	0.226	**0.126**
392	LPIPS ↓	0.135	0.169	0.183	**0.106**
393	LPIPS ↓	0.132	0.155	0.175	**0.104**
394	LPIPS ↓	0.150	0.171	0.199	**0.111**

Table 2. Geometry Reconstruction. We report L2 Chamfer Distance (CD) and Normal Consistency (NC) on the training poses of the ZJU-MoCap dataset [56]. Note that AniN and AN occasionally produce large background blobs that are connected to the body resulting in large deviations from the ground truth.

Sequence	Metric	NB	AniN	AN	Ours
313	CD ↓	1.258	1.242	9.174	**0.707**
	NC ↑	0.700	0.599	0.691	**0.809**
315	CD ↓	2.167	2.860	1.524	**0.779**
	NC ↑	0.636	0.450	0.610	**0.753**
377	CD ↓	1.062	1.649	1.008	**0.840**
	NC ↑	0.672	0.541	0.682	**0.786**
386	CD ↓	2.938	23.53	3.632	**2.880**
	NC ↑	0.607	0.325	0.596	**0.741**
393	CD ↓	1.753	3.252	1.696	**1.342**
	NC ↑	0.600	0.481	0.605	**0.739**
394	CD ↓	1.510	2.813	558.8	**1.177**
	NC ↑	0.628	0.540	0.639	**0.762**

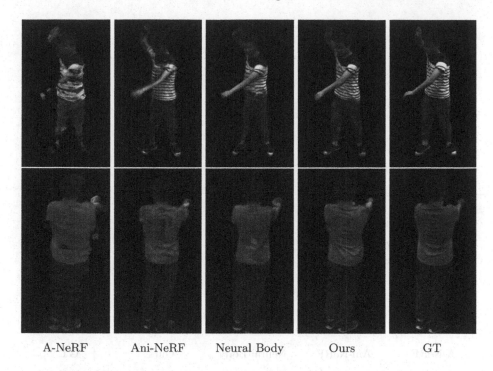

A-NeRF   Ani-NeRF   Neural Body   Ours   GT

Fig. 3. Generalization to Unseen Poses on the testing poses of ZJU-MoCap. A-NeRF struggles with unseen poses due to the limited training poses and the lack of a SMPL surface prior. Ani-NeRF produces noisy images as it uses an inaccurate backward mapping function. Neural Body loses details, e.g. wrinkles, because its conditional NeRF is learned in observation space. Our approach generalizes well to unseen poses and can model fine details like wrinkles.

4.1 Generalization to Unseen Poses

We first analyze the generalization ability of our approach in comparison to the baselines. Given a trained model and a pose from the test set, we render images of the human subject in the given pose. We show qualitative results in Fig. 3 and quantitative results in Table 1. We significantly outperform the baselines both qualitatively and quantitatively. The training poses of the ZJU-MoCap dataset are extremely limited, usually comprising just 60–300 frames of repetitive motion. This limited training data results in severe overfitting for the baselines. In contrast, our method generalizes well to unseen poses, even when training data is limited.

We additionally animate our models trained on the ZJU-MoCap dataset using extreme out-of-distribution poses from the AMASS [40] and AIST++ [32] datasets. As shown in Fig. 5, even under extreme pose variation our approach produces plausible geometry and rendering results while all baselines show severe artifacts. We attribute the large improvement on unseen poses to our root-finding-based backward skinning, as the learned forward skinning weights are

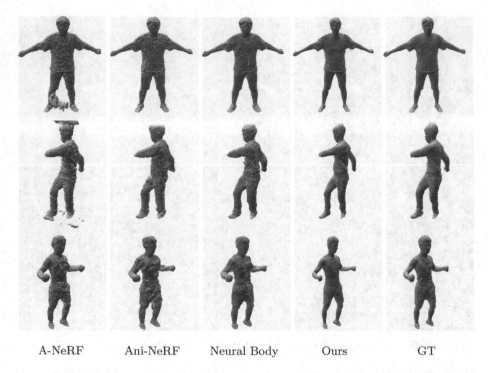

A-NeRF   Ani-NeRF   Neural Body   Ours   GT

Fig. 4. Geometry Reconstruction. Our approach reconstructs more fine-grained geometry than the baselines while preserving high-frequency details such as wrinkles. Note that we remove an estimated ground plane from all meshes.

constants per subject, while root-finding is a deterministic optimization process that does not rely on learned neural networks that condition on inputs from the observation space. More comparisons can be found in the Supp. Mat.

4.2   Geometry Reconstruction on Training Poses

Next, we analyze the geometry reconstructed with our approach against reconstructions from the baselines. We compare to the pseudo-ground-truth obtained from NeuS [69]. We show qualitative results in Fig. 4 and quantitative results in Table 2. Our approach consistently outperforms existing NeRF-based human models on geometry reconstruction. As evidenced in Fig. 4, the geometry obtained with our approach is much cleaner compared to NeRF-based baselines, while preserving high-frequency details such as wrinkles.

Table 3. Novel View Synthesis. We report PSNR, SSIM, and LPIPS [84] for novel views of training poses of the ZJU-MoCap dataset [56]. Due to better geometry, our approach produces more consistent rendering results across novel views than the baselines. We include qualitative comparisons in the Supp. Mat. Note that we crop slightly larger bounding boxes than Neural Body [56] to better capture loose clothes, *e.g.* sequence 387 and 390. Therefore, the reported numbers vary slightly from their evaluation.

	313			315			377		
Method	PSNR ↑	SSIM ↑	LPIPS ↓	PSNR ↑	SSIM ↑	LPIPS ↓	PSNR ↑	SSIM ↑	LPIPS ↓
NB	30.5	0.967	0.068	26.4	0.958	0.079	**28.1**	**0.956**	0.080
Ani-N	29.8	0.963	0.075	23.1	0.917	0.138	24.2	0.925	0.124
A-NeRF	29.2	0.954	0.075	25.1	0.948	0.087	27.2	0.951	0.080
Ours	**31.6**	**0.973**	**0.050**	**27.0**	**0.965**	**0.058**	27.8	**0.956**	**0.071**
	386			387			390		
Method	PSNR ↑	SSIM ↑	LPIPS ↓	PSNR ↑	SSIM ↑	LPIPS ↓	PSNR ↑	SSIM ↑	LPIPS ↓
NB	29.0	**0.935**	0.112	26.7	0.942	0.101	**27.9**	0.928	0.112
Ani-N	25.6	0.878	0.199	25.4	0.926	0.131	26.0	0.912	0.148
A-NeRF	28.5	0.928	0.127	26.3	0.937	0.100	27.0	0.914	0.126
Ours	**29.2**	0.934	**0.105**	**27.0**	**0.945**	**0.079**	27.9	**0.929**	**0.102**
	392			393			394		
Method	PSNR ↑	SSIM ↑	LPIPS ↓	PSNR ↑	SSIM ↑	LPIPS ↓	PSNR ↑	SSIM ↑	LPIPS ↓
NB	**29.7**	**0.949**	0.101	**27.7**	0.939	0.105	28.7	0.942	0.098
Ani-N	28.0	0.931	0.151	26.1	0.916	0.151	27.5	0.924	0.142
A-NeRF	28.7	0.942	0.106	26.8	0.931	0.113	28.1	0.936	0.103
Ours	29.5	0.948	**0.090**	**27.7**	**0.940**	**0.093**	28.9	0.945	**0.084**

4.3   Novel View Synthesis on Training Poses

Lastly, we analyze our approach for novel view synthesis on training poses. Table 3 provides a quantitative comparison to the baselines. While not the main focus of this work, our approach also outperforms existing methods on novel view synthesis. This suggests that more faithful modeling of geometry is also beneficial for the visual fidelity of novel views. Particularly when few training views are available, NeRF-based methods produce blob/cloud artifacts. By removing such artifacts, our approach achieves high image fidelity and better consistency across novel views. Due to space limitations, we include further qualitative results on novel view synthesis in the Supp. Mat.

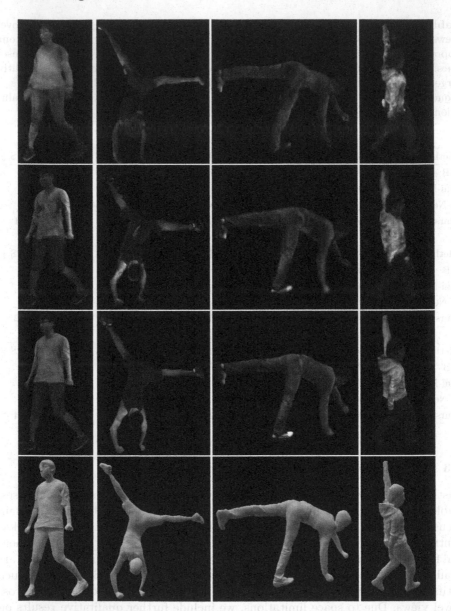

Fig. 5. Qualitative Results on Out-of-distribution Poses from the AMASS [40] and AIST++ [32] datasets. From top to bottom row: Neural Body, Ani-NeRF, our rendering, and our geometry. Note that Ani-NeRF requires re-training their backward LBS network on novel pose sequence. We did not show A-NeRF results as it already produces severe overfitting effects on ZJU-MoCap test poses. For more qualitative comparisons, please refer to the Supp. Mat.

5   Conclusion

We propose a new approach to create animatable avatars from sparse multi-view videos. We largely improve geometry reconstruction over existing approaches by modeling the geometry as articulated SDFs. Further, our novel joint root-finding algorithm enables generalization to extreme out-of-distribution poses. We discuss limitations of our approach in the Supp. Mat.

Acknowledgement. Shaofei Wang and Siyu Tang acknowledge the SNF grant 200021 204840. Katja Schwarz was supported by the BMWi in the project KI Delta Learning (project number 19A19013O). Andreas Geiger was supported by the ERC Starting Grant LEGO-3D (850533) and the DFG EXC number 2064/1 - project number 390727645.

References

1. Alldieck, T., Magnor, M., Bhatnagar, B.L., Theobalt, C., Pons-Moll, G.: Learning to reconstruct people in clothing from a single RGB camera. In: Proceedings of CVPR (2019)
2. Alldieck, T., Magnor, M., Xu, W., Theobalt, C., Pons-Moll, G.: Video based reconstruction of 3d people models. In: Proceedings of CVPR (2018)
3. Alldieck, T., Xu, H., Sminchisescu, C.: imGHUM: implicit generative models of 3d human shape and articulated pose. In: Proceedings of CVPR (2021)
4. Alldieck, T., Zanfir, M., Sminchisescu, C.: Photorealistic monocular 3d reconstruction of humans wearing clothing. In Proceedings of CVPR (2022)
5. Anguelov, D., Srinivasan, P., Koller, D., Thrun, S., Rodgers, J., Davis, J.: Scape: shape completion and animation of people. In: ACM Transasctions Graphics, vol. 24 (2005)
6. Bhatnagar, B.L., Sminchisescu, C., Theobalt, C., Pons-Moll, G.: Combining implicit function learning and parametric models for 3d human reconstruction. In: proceedings of ECCV (2020)
7. Bhatnagar, B.L., Sminchisescu, C., Theobalt, C., Pons-Moll, G.: LoopReg: self-supervised learning of implicit surface correspondences, pose and shape for 3d human mesh registration. In: Proceedings of NeurIPS (2020)
8. Burov, A., Nießner, M., Thies, J.: Dynamic surface function networks for clothed human bodies. In: proceedings of ICCV (2021)
9. Chen, J., et al.: Animatable neural radiance fields from monocular RGB videos. arXiv preprint arXiv:2106.13629 (2021)
10. Chen, X., et al.: gDNA: towards generative detailed neural avatars. In: Proceedings of CVPR (2022)
11. Chen, X., Zheng, Y., Black, M., Hilliges, O., Geiger, A.: Snarf: differentiable forward skinning for animating non-rigid neural implicit shapes. In: Proceedings of ICCV (2021)
12. Chen, Z., Zhang, H.: Learning implicit fields for generative shape modeling. In: Proceedings of CVPR (2019)
13. Chibane, J., Alldieck, T., Pons-Moll, G.: Implicit functions in feature space for 3d shape reconstruction and completion. In: Proceedings of CVPR (2020)

14. Corona, E., Pumarola, A., Alenyà, G., Pons-Moll, G., Moreno-Noguer, F.: SMPLicit: topology-aware generative model for clothed people. In: Proceedings of CVPR (2021)
15. Dong, Z., Guo, C., Song, J., Chen, X., Geiger, A., Hilliges, O.: Pina: Learning a personalized implicit neural avatar from a single RGB-D video sequence. In: In Proceedings of of CVPR (2022)
16. Gropp, A., Yariv, L., Haim, N., Atzmon, M., Lipman, Y.: Implicit geometric regularization for learning shapes. In: Proceedings of of ICML (2020)
17. Guan, P., Reiss, L., Hirshberg, D.A., Weiss, E., Black, M.J.: Drape: dressing any person. ACM Trans. Graph. 31(4), 1–10 (2012)
18. Gundogdu, E., Constantin, V., Seifoddini, A., Dang, M., Salzmann, M., Fua, P.: Garnet: a two-stream network for fast and accurate 3d cloth draping. In: Proceedings of of ICCV (2019)
19. Hart, J.C.: Sphere tracing: a geometric method for the antialiased ray tracing of implicit surfaces. Vis. Comput. 12(10), 527–545 (1995)
20. Hasler, N., Stoll, C., Sunkel, M., Rosenhahn, B., Seidel, H.P.: A statistical model of human pose and body shape. Comput. Graph. Forum 28, 337–346 (2009)
21. He, T., Collomosse, J., Jin, H., Soatto, S.: Geo-PIFu: geometry and pixel aligned implicit functions for single-view human reconstruction. In: Proceedings of of NeurIPS (2020)
22. He, T., Xu, Y., Saito, S., Soatto, S., Tung, T.: Arch++: animation-ready clothed human reconstruction revisited. In: Proceedings of of ICCV (2021)
23. Hu, T., Yu, T., Zheng, Z., Zhang, H., Liu, Y., Zwicker, M.: HVTR: hybrid volumetric-textural rendering for human avatars. arXiv preprint arXiv:2112.10203 (2021)
24. Huang, Z., Xu, Y., Lassner, C., Li, H., Tung, T.: ARCH: animatable reconstruction of Clothed Humans. In: Proceedings of CVPR (2020)
25. Ionescu, C., Papava, D., Olaru, V., Sminchisescu, C.: Human3.6 m: large scale datasets and predictive methods for 3d human sensing in natural environments. IEEE Trans. Pattern Anal. Mach. Intell. 36(7), 1325–1339 (2014)
26. Jiang, B., Hong, Y., Bao, H., Zhang, J.: SelfRecon: self reconstruction your digital avatar from monocular video. In: Proceedings of CVPR (2022)
27. Joo, H., Simon, T., Sheikh, Y.: Total capture: A 3d deformation model for tracking faces, hands, and bodies. In: Proceedings of CVPR (2018)
28. Kwon, Y., Kim, D., Ceylan, D., Fuchs, H.: Neural human performer: Learning generalizable radiance fields for human performance rendering. In: Proceedings of NeurIPS (2021)
29. Lähner, Z., Cremers, D., Tung, T.: DeepWrinkles: accurate and realistic clothing modeling. In: Proceedings of ECCV (2018)
30. Li, R., et al.: TAVA: template-free animatable volumetric actors. In: Proceedings of ECCV (2022)
31. Li, R., Xiu, Y., Saito, S., Huang, Z., Olszewski, K., Li, H.: Monocular real-time volumetric performance capture. In: Proceedings of ECCV (2020)
32. Li, R., Yang, S., Ross, D.A., Kanazawa, A.: Ai choreographer: music conditioned 3d dance generation with aist++. In: Proceedings of ICCV (2021)
33. Li, Y., Habermann, M., Thomaszewski, B., Coros, S., Beeler, T., Theobalt, C.: Deep physics-aware inference of cloth deformation for monocular human performance capture. In: Proceedings of 3DV (2021)
34. Li, Z., Yu, T., Pan, C., Zheng, Z., Liu, Y.: Robust 3d self-portraits in seconds. In: Proceedings of CVPR (2020)

35. Li, Z., Yu, T., Zheng, Z., Guo, K., Liu, Y.: POSEFusion: pose-guided selective fusion for single-view human volumetric capture. In: Proceedings of CVPR (2021)
36. Liu, L., Habermann, M., Rudnev, V., Sarkar, K., Gu, J., Theobalt, C.: Neural actor: neural free-view synthesis of human actors with pose control. ACM Trans. Graph. (ACM SIGGRAPH Asia) **40**(6), 1–16 (2021)
37. Loper, M., Mahmood, N., Romero, J., Pons-Moll, G., Black, M.J.: SMPL: a skinned multi-person linear model. ACM Trans. Graph. **34**(6), 1–16 (2015)
38. Ma, Q., Saito, S., Yang, J., Tang, S., Black, M.J.: SCALE: modeling clothed humans with a surface codec of articulated local elements. In: Proceedings of CVPR (2021)
39. Ma, Q., Yang, J., Tang, S., Black, M.J.: The power of points for modeling humans in clothing. In: Proceedings of ICCV (2021)
40. Mahmood, N., Ghorbani, N., Troje, N.F., Pons-Moll, G., Black, M.J.: AMASS: archive of motion capture as surface shapes. In: Proceedings of ICCV (2019)
41. Mescheder, L., Oechsle, M., Niemeyer, M., Nowozin, S., Geiger, A.: Occupancy networks: Learning 3d reconstruction in function space. In: Proceedings of CVPR (2019)
42. Michalkiewicz, M., Pontes, J.K., Jack, D., Baktashmotlagh, M., Eriksson, A.: Implicit surface representations as layers in neural networks. In: Proceedings of ICCV (2019)
43. Mihajlovic, M., Bansal, A., Zollhoefer, M., Tang, S., Saito, S.: KeypointNeRF: generalizing image-based volumetric avatars using relative spatial encoding of keypoints. In: Proceedings of ECCV (2022)
44. Mihajlovic, M., Saito, S., Bansal, A., Zollhoefer, M., Tang, S.: COAP: compositional articulated occupancy of people. In: Proceedings of CVPR (2022)
45. Mihajlovic, M., Zhang, Y., Black, M.J., Tang, S.: LEAP: learning articulated occupancy of people. In: Proceedings of CVPR (2021)
46. Mildenhall, B., Srinivasan, P.P., Tancik, M., Barron, J.T., Ramamoorthi, R., Ng, R.: Nerf: representing scenes as neural radiance fields for view synthesis. In: Proceedings of ECCV (2020)
47. Niemeyer, M., Mescheder, L., Oechsle, M., Geiger, A.: Differentiable volumetric rendering: learning implicit 3d representations without 3d supervision. In: Proceedings of CVPR (2020)
48. Noguchi, A., Sun, X., Lin, S., Harada, T.: Neural articulated radiance field. In: Proceedings of ICCV (2021)
49. Oechsle, M., Peng, S., Geiger, A.: UNISURF: unifying neural implicit surfaces and radiance fields for multi-view reconstruction. In: Proceedings of ICCV (2021)
50. Osman, A.A.A., Bolkart, T., Black, M.J.: Star: Sparse trained articulated human body regressor. In: Proceedings of ECCV (2020)
51. Park, J.J., Florence, P., Straub, J., Newcombe, R., Lovegrove, S.: DeepSDF: learning continuous signed distance functions for shape representation. In: Proceedings of CVPR (2019)
52. Patel, C., Liao, Z., Pons-Moll, G.: TailorNet: predicting clothing in 3d as a function of human pose, shape and garment style. In: Proceedings of CVPR (2020)
53. Pavlakos, G., et al.: Expressive body capture: 3d hands, face, and body from a single image. In: Proceedings of CVPR (2019)
54. Peng, S., et al.: Animatable neural radiance fields for modeling dynamic human bodies. In: Proceedings of ICCV (2021)
55. Peng, S., et al.: Animatable neural implicit surfaces for creating avatars from videos. arXiv preprint arXiv:2203.08133 (2022)

56. Peng, S., et al.: Neural body: Implicit neural representations with structured latent codes for novel view synthesis of dynamic humans. In: Proceedings of CVPR (2021)
57. Peng, S., et al.: Shape as points: a differentiable poisson solver. In: Proceedings of NeurIPS (2021)
58. Prokudin, S., Black, M.J., Romero, J.: SMPLpix: neural avatars from 3D human models. In: Proceedings WACV (2021)
59. Raj, A., Tanke, J., Hays, J., Vo, M., Stoll, C., Lassner, C.: Anr-articulated neural rendering for virtual avatars. In: Proceedings of CVPR (2021)
60. Saito, S., Huang, Z., Natsume, R., Morishima, S., Kanazawa, A., Li, H.: PIFu: pixel-aligned implicit function for high-resolution clothed human digitization. In: Proceedings of ICCV (2019)
61. Saito, S., Simon, T., Saragih, J., Joo, H.: PIFuHD: multi-level pixel-aligned implicit function for high-resolution 3d human digitization. In: Proceedings of CVPR (2020)
62. Saito, S., Yang, J., Ma, Q., Black, M.J.: SCANimate: Weakly supervised learning of skinned clothed avatar networks. In: Proceedings of CVPR (2021)
63. Santesteban, I., Thuerey, N., Otaduy, M.A., Casas, D.: Self-Supervised Collision Handling via Generative 3D Garment Models for Virtual Try-On. In: Proceedings of CVPR (2021)
64. Su, S.Y., Bagautdinov, T., Rhodin, H.: DANBO: disentangled articulated neural body representations via graph neural networks. In: Proceedings of ECCV (2022)
65. Su, S.Y., Yu, F., Zollhoefer, M., Rhodin, H.: A-neRF: articulated neural radiance fields for learning human shape, appearance, and pose. In: Proceedings of NeurIPS (2021)
66. Su, Z., Xu, L., Zheng, Z., Yu, T., Liu, Y., Fang, L.: RobustFusion: human volumetric capture with data-driven visual cues using a RGBD camera. In: Vedaldi, A., Bischof, H., Brox, T., Frahm, J.-M. (eds.) ECCV 2020. LNCS, vol. 12349, pp. 246–264. Springer, Cham (2020). https://doi.org/10.1007/978-3-030-58548-8_15
67. Tiwari, G., Sarafianos, N., Tung, T., Pons-Moll, G.: Neural-GIF: neural generalized implicit functions for animating people in clothing. In: Proceedings of ICCV (2021)
68. Tiwari, L., Bhowmick, B.: DeepDraper: fast and accurate 3d garment draping over a 3d human body. In: Proceedings of the IEEE/CVF International Conference on Computer Vision (ICCV) Workshops (2021)
69. Wang, P., Liu, L., Liu, Y., Theobalt, C., Komura, T., Wang, W.: NeuS: learning neural implicit surfaces by volume rendering for multi-view reconstruction. In: Proceedings NeurIPS (2021)
70. Wang, S., Geiger, A., Tang, S.: Locally aware piecewise transformation fields for 3d human mesh registration. In: In Proceedings of CVPR (2021)
71. Wang, S., Mihajlovic, M., Ma, Q., Geiger, A., Tang, S.: MetaAvatar: learning animatable clothed human models from few depth images. In: Proceedings of NeurIPS (2021)
72. Weng, C.Y., Curless, B., Srinivasan, P.P., Barron, J.T., Kemelmacher-Shlizerman, I.: HumanNeRF: free-viewpoint rendering of moving people from monocular video. In: Proceedings CVPR (2022)
73. Xiu, Y., Yang, J., Tzionas, D., Black, M.J.: ICON: implicit clothed humans obtained from Normals. In: Proceedings of CVPR (2022)
74. Xu, H., Alldieck, T., Sminchisescu, C.: H-neRF: neural radiance fields for rendering and temporal reconstruction of humans in motion. In: Proceedings of NeurIPS (2021)
75. Xu, H., Bazavan, E.G., Zanfir, A., Freeman, W.T., Sukthankar, R., Sminchisescu, C.: GHUM & GHUML: generative 3d human shape and articulated pose models. In: Proceedings of CVPR (2020)

76. Xu, L., Su, Z., Han, L., Yu, T., Liu, Y., Fang, L.: UnstructuredFusion: real-time 4d geometry and texture reconstruction using commercial RGBD cameras. IEEE Trans. Pattern Anal. Mach. Intell. **42**(10), 2508–2522 (2020)
77. Xu, T., Fujita, Y., Matsumoto, E.: Surface-aligned neural radiance fields for controllable 3d human synthesis. In: CVPR (2022)
78. Yang, J., Franco, J.S., Hétroy-Wheeler, F., Wuhrer, S.: Analyzing clothing layer deformation statistics of 3d human motions. In: Proceedings of ECCV (2018)
79. Yariv, L., Gu, J., Kasten, Y., Lipman, Y.: Volume rendering of neural implicit surfaces. In: Proceedings of NeurIPS (2021)
80. Yariv, L., et al.: Multiview neural surface reconstruction by disentangling geometry and appearance. In: Proceedings of NeurIPS (2020)
81. Yu, T., et al.: DoubleFusion: real-time capture of human performances with inner body shapes from a single depth sensor. In: Proceedings of CVPR (2018)
82. Zakharkin, I., Mazur, K., Grigorev, A., Lempitsky, V.: Point-based modeling of human clothing. In: Proceedings of ICCV (2021)
83. Zhang, C., Pujades, S., Black, M.J., Pons-Moll, G.: Detailed, accurate, human shape estimation from clothed 3d scan sequences. In: Proceedings of CVPR (2017)
84. Zhang, R., Isola, P., Efros, A.A., Shechtman, E., Wang, O.: The unreasonable effectiveness of deep features as a perceptual metric. In: Proceedings of CVPR (2018)
85. Zheng, Y., Abrevaya, V.F., Bühler, M.C., Chen, X., Black, M.J., Hilliges, O.: I M Avatar: implicit morphable head avatars from videos. In: Proceedings of CVPR (2022)
86. Zheng, Z., Yu, T., Liu, Y., Dai, Q.: Pamir: parametric model-conditioned implicit representation for image-based human reconstruction. IEEE Trans. Pattern Anal. Mach. Intell. 1 (2021). https://doi.org/10.1109/TPAMI.2021.3050505
87. Zuo, X., Wang, S., Sun, Q., Gong, M., Cheng, L.: Self-supervised 3d human mesh recovery from noisy point clouds. arXiv preprint arXiv:2107.07539 (2021)

ASpanFormer: Detector-Free Image Matching with Adaptive Span Transformer

Hongkai Chen[2(✉)], Zixin Luo[1], Lei Zhou[1], Yurun Tian[1], Mingmin Zhen[1], Tian Fang[1], David McKinnon[1], Yanghai Tsin[1], and Long Quan[1]

[1] Apple Inc., Cupertino, USA
{zixin_luo,zhou_lei,tian_ray,mingmin.zhen,fangtian,dmckinnon,ytsin, quan.long}@apple.com
[2] HKUST, Hong Kong, People's Republic of China
hchencf@cse.ust.hk

Abstract. Generating robust and reliable correspondences across images is a fundamental task for a diversity of applications. To capture context at both global and local granularity, we propose ASpanFormer, a Transformer-based detector-free matcher that is built on hierarchical attention structure, adopting a novel attention operation which is capable of adjusting attention span in a self-adaptive manner. To achieve this goal, first, flow maps are regressed in each cross attention phase to locate the center of search region. Next, a sampling grid is generated around the center, whose size, instead of being empirically configured as fixed, is adaptively computed from a pixel uncertainty estimated along with the flow map. Finally, attention is computed across two images within derived regions, referred to as attention span. By these means, we are able to not only maintain long-range dependencies, but also enable fine-grained attention among pixels of high relevance that compensates essential locality and piece-wise smoothness in matching tasks. State-of-the-art accuracy on a wide range of evaluation benchmarks validates the strong matching capability of our method.

Keywords: Image matching · Visual localization · Pose estimation · Transformer

1 Introduction

Image matching lays the foundation for various geometric computer vision tasks, including Structure from Motion (SfM) [1,2], visual localization [3], and Simultaneous Localization And Mapping (SLAM) [4,5]. As a widely accepted pipeline for

---

Supplementary Information The online version contains supplementary material available at https://doi.org/10.1007/978-3-031-19824-3_2.

Fig. 1. An illustration of the proposed adaptive attention span (top row) and final dense matching results (bottom row). Particularly, in the top row, a rectangle with 8×8 uniform sampling grid is drawn to explain the position and size of adaptive attention span. In addition, three typical types of correspondences are visualized. Easy match in green with rich texture, which can be well localized and matched with small local contexts. Hard match in yellow with little texture, which requires larger contexts to guide matching. Impossible match in red in non-overlapping or occluded region, which has a very large attention span to avoid falsely fitting to certain regions. With this design, we enable Transformer to adaptively capture necessary context according to matching difficulty. (Color figure online)

image matching, cross-image correspondences are usually established by matching a set of detected and described sparse keypoints, such as SIFT [6], ORB [7], or their learning-based counterparts [8–12]. Despite its general effectiveness, this detector-based matching pipeline struggles in extreme situations, including large view point changes and textureless areas, due to the reliance on keypoint detector and context loss in feature description.

Concurrent with detector-based matching, another line of works [13–22] focus on generating correspondences directly from raw images, where richer context can be leveraged while keypoint detection step can be eschewed. Earlier works [16–18] in detector-free matching often rely on iterative convolution upon correlation or cost volume to discover potential neighbourhood consensus. Recently, some works [13,14,22] base their methods on Transformer [23,24] backbone for better modeling of long-range dependencies. As a representative work, LoFTR utilizes self and cross attention blocks to update cross-view features, where Linear Transformer [25] is adopted to replace global full attention in order to achieve manageable computation cost. Although proven effective, a concern about LoFTR is the lack of fine-level local interaction among pixel tokens, which could limit its capability to extract highly accurate and well-localized correspondences. This concern is deepened by the findings [22] of Tang et al., which reveals that the cross attention map generated by LoFTR's Linear

Transformer tends to diffuse among large areas instead of sharply focusing on actual corresponding regions.

To capture both global context and local details, we propose a Transformer-based detector-free matcher, equipped with a hierarchical attention framework. Our foundation processing blocks, referred to as Global-Local Attention (GLA) block, performs a coarse-level global attention at low resolution to acquire long-range dependencies, meanwhile, conducts fine-level local attention at high resolution within only a concentrated region around a current correspondence found through dense flow prediction.

The key challenge for fine-level local attention is to determine the size of the attention span. A naive approach is to regard its size as a fixed hyper parameter, which, however, neglects the intrinsic matchability of different regions where the dependency of context varies. As shown in Fig. 1, regions in rich texture areas can be easily matched within a small neighbourhood, while the textureless areas are more uncertain about their correspondences and require larger context for matching, not to mention areas that lie out of overlapping regions and are impossible to be matched. To mitigate this issue, we introduce an adaptive attention span driven by probabilistic modelling, which can be adjusted for different locations based on underlying matching difficulty. We summarize our contributions in three aspects:

- A hierarchical attention framework is proposed for feature matching, where attention operations are performed at different scales to enable both global context awareness and fine-grained matching.
- A novel uncertainty-driven scheme, based on probabilistic modelling of flow prediction, is proposed to adaptively adjust local attention span. Through this design, our network assigns varying size of contexts to different locations according to their essential matchability and context richness.
- State-of-the-arts results on extensive set of benchmarks are achieved. Our method outperforms both detector-free and detector-based matching baselines in two-view pose estimation. Further experiments on challenging visual localization also proves our method's potential to be integrated into c omplicated down-stream applications.

2 Related Works

2.1 Detector-Free Image Matching

Differing from detector-based matching methods, which typical involve detecting [8–11], describing [12, 26–29] and matching [30–36] a set of keypoints, detector-free matching consumes a pair of images and output correspondences in one shot. Thanks to the removal of keypoint detection stage, detector-free matching is able to capture richer contexts from original images, thus exhibits strong potential to match in extreme situations, such as low texture areas and repetitive patterns.

Despite the potential merits of detector-free matching, its popularity hardly outperforms detector-based methods during early deep learning times due to the intrinsic difficulties in robust and distinctive features. Recently, with the help of deep neural network, possibility is explored to build high performance detector-free matching frameworks based on deep features, which can roughly be classified into two categories: cost volume-based methods [15–19,37] and Transformer-based methods [13,14,22]. Both kinds of methods leverage strong signals in deep features' correlation, either in form of correlation layer or cross attention, to guide correspondence search and feature update. Our method follows works on Transformer-based methods and employs multilevel cross attention for mutual feature update, encoding two-view contexts into original features for both global and local consensus.

2.2   Global-Local Structure

Balancing receptive field and interaction granularity is a long-standing issue for both cost volume-based and Transformer-based matching. To ensure global receptive field, cost volume based methods are often designed to perform convolution on large global correlation volume, while Transformer-based methods need to conduct attention among all pixel tokens in image pairs. Due to the high cost of global interaction, the input features are usually downsampled into coarse resolution [14,18,19] or being projected into low rank [13], which to some degree limits the networks' capability for fined grained feature update.

Complementary to global interaction, some methods propose to perform local interaction only within a certain region instead of a global field, enabling to process fine level features given a limited computation budget. This practice is especially common in cost volume based methods and are referred to as local correlation layer [15,19,38,39], where the cost volumes/vectors are only constructed around neighbourhood of each correspondence estimation. Intuitively, the idea of complementary global-local interaction can also be introduced to Transformer-based matcher. In our method, a global-local attention block is proposed for message passing across images, ensuring both global receptive field and fine level feature processing. Specially, instead of fixing span for local attention, we design an adaptive mechanism to determine the size of area that each pixel should attend to.

2.3   Flow Regression and Uncertainty Modeling

Flow maps depicts correspondence coordinates, which can either be absolute or relative, for each location in an image. Predicting correspondence coordinates from an image pair has been intensively investigated by works in optical flow estimation [38–41] and general dense image matching [15,19,37]. In these works, the flow maps are regressed from structured correlation volumes which are implicitly position-aware. Recently, a Transformer-based method, COTR [14], proves that flows can also be retrieved from positional-embedded features after several turns of attention update.

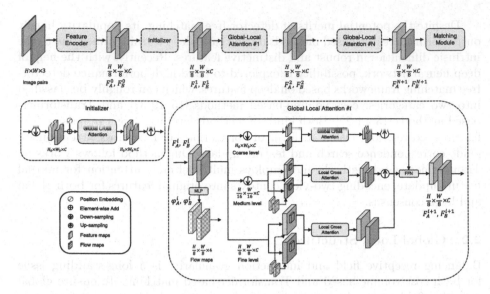

Fig. 2. We use CNN backbone to extract initial features. After initialization, the features are fed into iterative GLA blocks for updating. A matching module is used to determine final matches.

Naturally, the reliability of flow estimation in each location is not equal and predicting associated confidence scores is essential for many scenarios. As an elegant framework for uncertainty prediction, some works [15,42–45] propose to use probabilistic model to jointly explain both flows estimations and their confidence. Inspired by above works, we propose a network that regresses a flow map for each attention block to guide local attention region and adjust the attention span adaptively based on uncertainty prediction.

3   Methodology

We present an overview of our network structure in Fig. 2. Taking an image pair I_A, I_B as input, our network produces reliable correspondences across images. The matching process starts with a CNN-based encoder to extract initial features F_A^0, F_B^0 for both images separately. After initialization, these features are turned into F_A^1, F_B^1 and fed into the proposed Adaptive Span Transformer (ASpanFormer) module for updating, which is composed of iterative global-local attention (**GLA**) blocks with hierarchical structure. Particularly, for each GLA block, we regress auxiliary flow maps ϕ_A, ϕ_B describing correspondence coordinates (flows) and their uncertainty. Instead of adopting these flow maps as our correspondence output, we use them to guide local cross attention, enabling adaptive local attention span according to matching uncertainty. After N GLA blocks, the updated features $F_A^{(N+1)}, F_B^{(N+1)}$ are use to construct coarse level matches, which will be further refined into final correspondences.

In the following part, we demonstrate the details of each individual block as well as the underlying insights.

3.1 Preliminary

Before introducing the structure of our network, we first clarify necessary notations and concepts.

Attention. As the key operation in Vision Transformer, attention is defined over a set of query (Q), key (K) and value (V) vectors as

$$M = \text{Att}(Q, K, V) = \text{softmax}(QK^T)V, \tag{1}$$

where Q, K, V are linear projections of upstream features F and M is retrieved message. More specially, in the context of cross attention, Q are derived from source features F_s and K, V vectors are derived from target features F_t. M is used to update source features F_s through a feed forward network (FFN), which involves concatenation, layer normalization and linear layers.

$$F_s^{i+1} = \mathbf{FFN}(F_S^i, M). \tag{2}$$

Typically, in each pass, the position of source/target features can be switched and cross attention is performed symmetrically.

Flow Map. Flow maps $\phi_A, \phi_B \in R^{H \times W \times 2}$ depict the correspondence relationship between an image pair $I_A, I_B \in R^{H \times W}$, such that for any location (i, j) in an image, $I_A[i, j] \leftrightarrow I_B[\phi_A[i, j]], I_B[i, j] \leftrightarrow I_A[\phi_B[i, j]]$. Here, $\leftrightarrow$ denotes that the points on two sides are correspondences.

Instead of depicting simple correspondences, a stream of works [15, 42–45] proposes to model flow field with a probabilistic framework. Following these works, we model the flow field as a Gaussian distribution defined by a set of parameters. More specifically, assuming conditional independence among pixels, two flow maps $\phi_A, \phi_B \in R^{H, W, 4}$ are predicted, such that $\phi[i, j] = [u_x^{ij}, u_y^{ij}, \sigma_x^{ij}, \sigma_y^{ij}]$, where (u_x^{ij}, u_y^{ij}) are estimated correspondence coordinates and $(\sigma_x^{ij}, \sigma_y^{ij})$ are standard deviations. The probability for $I_A[i, j] \leftrightarrow I_B[x, y]$ is given by

$$P(x, y | \phi_A[i, j]) = \frac{1}{2\pi \sigma_x^{ij} \sigma_y^{ij}} \exp\left(-\frac{(x - u_x^{ij})^2}{2\sigma_x^{ij^2}} - \frac{(y - u_y^{ij})^2}{2\sigma_y^{ij^2}}\right) \tag{3}$$

Instead of thresholding flow estimation with uncertainty, we use it to adjust the search region for subsequent network interaction, as described in later sections.

3.2 Feature Extractor

As the first part of our network, a convolutional neural network (CNN) is used to extract $1/8$ down-sampled initial features $F_A, F_B \in R^{\frac{H}{8} \times \frac{W}{8}}$ for each image. As is shown in previous works [8–10,12,26–29], CNN exhibits strong capability to capture local context and generates high-level features, which can be directly used to perform nearest neighbour matching. However, since these features are processed independently for each image and critical cross view contexts are missed. To enrich features with long range and cross view contexts, the initial features are further fed into our proposed Transformer module for updating.

3.3 Initialization

Our Transformer-module starts with a fast initialization block, which conducts (1) positional encoding and (2) two-view contexts initialization.

Positional Encoding. As validated in Transformer networks [13,14,30], positional encoding is critical in maintaining spatial information for the flattened tokens. Following the same formulation in LoFTR [13], 2D sinusoidal signals in different frequencies are used to encode position information and are added to initial features. Specially, we apply normalization when testing resolution differs from training resolution. We provide more details in Appendix A.5.

Two-View Contexts Initialization. At each local attention phase, our network requires regressing an auxiliary flow map as guidance, which requires cross view contexts. To this end, we pass positional embedded features to a light-weight cross attention block. More specifically, These features are downsampled to low resolution H_0, W_0 and two global cross attention blocks are used for feature processing. After initialization, the features are upsampled back to original input resolution, denoted as F_A^1, F_B^1, and sent to iterative global-local attention blocks for further processing.

3.4 Global-Local Attention Block

The basic structure of our Transformer network is global-local attention (**GLA**) block. As is shown in Fig. 2, for each GLA block, attention is performed upon a 3-level coarse-to-fine feature pyramid built by strided average pooling.

For the i-th GLA block, **global attention** is conducted on coarsest downsampled features in resolution $[H_0, W_0]$, while **local attention** with adaptive span is used to pass message between medium-resolution features in resolution $[\frac{H}{16}, \frac{W}{16}]$ and fine level features in resolution $[\frac{H}{8}, \frac{W}{8}]$. Note that we keep the coarsest resolution as a constant, making the complexity of global full attention unaffected by input size. Retrieved messages M^c, M^m, M^f from coarse/medium/fine level are upsampled to same $[\frac{H}{8}, \frac{W}{8}]$ resolution, concatenated and fused with an MLP to update source features.

$$M = \mathbf{MLP}(M^c || M^m || M^f), \qquad (4)$$

$$F^{i+1} = \mathbf{FFN}(M, F^i). \qquad (5)$$

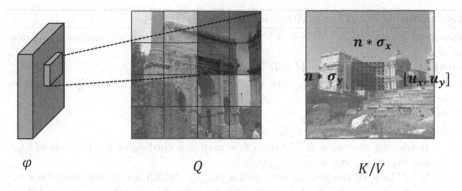

$$\varphi \qquad\qquad Q \qquad\qquad K/V$$

Fig. 3. Illustration Local cross attention. Query map Q are partitioned into cells in size $S \times S(S = 2$ in this case), retrieving prediction from flow map ϕ and generate attention span. Here we only show attention span for one cell (marked in red). (Color figure online)

The FFN in our network is defined as

$$\mathbf{FFN}(M, F) = F + \mathbf{LN}(\mathbf{Conv}_3(F||M)). \qquad (6)$$

LN stands for layer normalization. Specially, we adopt a 3×3 convolution **Conv**$_3$ in FFN for locality modeling, which compensate for the absence of self attention within each feature map. Empirically, we find 3×3 convolution in FFN works better than the combination of linear projection FFN and self attention, more details can be found in Appendix A.5.

Local Cross Attention with Adaptive Attention Span. To facilitate fine-grained attention with modest cost, we adopt local attention on medium and fine level feature maps, where attention span focuses on the neighbourhood regions around current correspondences estimation.

A key problem for local attention is how to define the size of neighbour-hood region. A naive approach is to define neighbourhood with a fixed radius r for all pixels, neglecting the fact that the optimal attention span for different regions varies. For instance, it is sufficient to match regions with distinctive features using small contexts, while regions that are harder to match require larger contexts. Instead of using fixed attention span for all pixels, we propose to adaptively adjust the attention span according to the uncertainty of flow estimation. This design lets each area balance their local receptive fields with uncertainty awareness. Regions with high confidence in flow estimation can sharply focus on a small region for fine level matching, while larger contexts are extracted in low confidence areas for better convergence.

Formally, for the i-th GLA block, we first regress flow maps ϕ_A^i, ϕ_B^i from input features F_A^i, F_B^i in fine level with an MLP, while the medium level flow map are obtained by strided average pooling. For each scale level, we partition the corresponding query map Q into cells with size $S \times S$. For each cell, we

---

Algorithm 1. Local Cross Attention

Input: $Q, K, V \in R^{H \times W \times C}, \phi \in R^{H \times 4}$, span coefficient n, sample number w, window size S

Output: Retrieved message $M \in R^{H \times W \times C}$

1: Partition Q into cells set Q_p with window size $S \times S$, there will be $\frac{H}{S} \times \frac{W}{S}$ cells in total

2: $M = [\,]$

3: **for** each cell $Q_{pi} \in R^{S^2 \times C}$ in Q_p **do in parallel**

4:     Retrieving flow $\phi_p \in R^{S^2 \times 4}$ from flow map ϕ according to the location of Q_{pi}

5:     Let $[u_x, u_y, \sigma_x, \sigma_y] = \overline{\phi_p} = \sum_j \phi_p[j,:]$

6:     Let Γ be a rectangle area with center $[u_x, u_y]$, width $n * \sigma_x$ and height $n * \sigma_y$

7:     Uniformly sample w^2 tokens in Γ region from K, V, denoted as $K_\Gamma, V_\Gamma \in R^{w^2 \times C}$

8:     Attention $m_i = \text{Att}(Q_{pi}, K_\Gamma, V_\Gamma)$

9:     Append m_i to M

10: Reshaping M into $R^{H \times W \times C}$

11: **return** M

---

use the mean flow estimation to generate a rectangle region upon K, V map and uniformly sample a fixed number of tokens. Attention is performed between each cell and the sampled tokens. The detailed process is defined in Algorithm 1. An illustration for local attention is given in Fig. 3. Since number of sampled tokens for each location is fixed, the whole process retains linear complexity.

3.5   Matches Determination

We inherit the scheme in LoFTR [13] to generate final correspondences, including a coarse matching stage and a sub-pixel refinement stage.

After being updated by N GLA blocks, we flatten the output features into $\tilde{F}_A \in R^{n \times c}, \tilde{F}_B \in R^{m \times c}$ and construct correlation matrix $C = \tau \tilde{F}_A \tilde{F}_B^T \in R^{n \times m}$, where τ is a temperature parameter and n, m are feature numbers of two images. By applying dual-direction softmax in both column/row dimensions, a score matrix is given by $S = \text{softmax}_{row}(C) \cdot \text{softmax}_{col}(C)$, from which we retain coarse-level matches M_c by mutual nearest neighbour (MNN) and filtering scores below a certain threshold θ. The coarse matches M_c are further fed into a correlation-based refinement block, which is the same with LoFTR [13], to obtain the final matching results.

3.6   Loss Formulation

We formulate the final loss from three parts, (1) coarse matches loss L_c, (2) fine-level loss L_f and (3) flow estimation loss L_{flow}

$$L = L_c + L_f + \alpha L_{flow}. \tag{7}$$

For coarse level loss L_c, the ground truth matches M_{gt} is determined by reprojection using depth and camera poses in datasets. We supervise the dual-softmax score matrix S with cross entropy loss

$$L_c = -\frac{1}{|M_{gt}|} \sum_{(i,j) \in M_{gt}} \log(S(i,j)). \tag{8}$$

The fine-level loss is supervised directly with L2-distance between each refined coordinates $M_f(i,j)$ and ground truth reprojection coordinates, which are further normalized by the coordinate variance.

For flow estimation supervision, we minimize the log-likelihood for each estimated distribution. Formally, given flow estimation Φ from each layer and ground truth flow D^{gt}, L_{flow} is defined as

$$L_{flow} = -\frac{1}{|D^{gt}|} \sum_{ij} log(P(D^{gt}_{ij}|\Phi_{ij})). \tag{9}$$

In our implementation, this log-likelihood formulation can be further substituted and decomposed into a more compact form, which is elaborated in Appendix B.

3.7 Implementation Details

Our network shares the same ResNet-18 [46] CNN feature extractor with LoFTR. After feature extraction and flow initialization, we use 4 GLA blocks for updating. For adaptive attention span, we set $n = 5$, meaning that using 5 standard deviation to crop local neighbourhood region for each token. We uniformly sample 8×8 features in each cropped local region.

We train two different models specified for indoor and outdoor scenes respectively. Both models are optimized using Adam with learning rate 1×10^{-3} for 30 epochs on 8 V-100 GPUs. Indoor model is trained on ScanNet [47] dataset with batch size 24, where the training consumes 5 d. Outdoor model is trained on MegaDepth [48] with batch size 8, taking 2 d to converge. More details about implementation are introduced in Appendix A.3.

4 Experiments

In this section, we demonstrate the performance of our method on two-view pose estimation and visual localization tasks, among both indoor and outdoor scenes. Besides, we conduct ablation study to validate the effectiveness of key design components of our method.

4.1 Two-View Pose Estimation

We resort to two popular datasets, ScanNet [47] and MegaDepth [48], introduced below, to demonstrate the matching ability of our method in indoor scenes and outdoor scenes, respectively. We also provide additional results on YFCC100M [49] and Image Matching Challenge(IMC) 2022 in Appendix C.

Fig. 4. Qualitative results of dense matching in different scenarios.

Indoor Two-View Matching Dataset. ScanNet dataset [47] is composed of 1613 sequences, each of which contains RGB images exposing large view changes and repetitive or textureless patterns, with ground-truth depth maps and camera poses associated. For fair comparison, we follow the same training and testing protocols used by SuperGlue [30] and LoFTR [13], where 230 M and 1.5K image pairs are sampled for training and testing, respectively. In congruent with LoFTR, we resize all test images to 480 × 640.

Outdoor Two-View Matching Dataset. MegaDepth [48] consists of 196 3D reconstructions from 1M Internet images, whose camera poses and depth maps are initially computed from COLMAP [1] and then refined as ground-truth. We perform two view pose estimation on 1.5k testing pairs. All test images are resized so that their longest dimension is 1152.

Evaluation Protocols. Following previous works [13,30], we train and evaluate our method separately on the two datasets. Two-view pose is recovered by solving essential matrix from correspondences produced, while pose accuracy is measured by AUC at multiple error thresholds (5°, 10° and 20°). A pose is only considered accurate if both its angular rotation error and translation error is under a certain threshold compared with ground-truth poses.

Comparative Methods. We compare the proposed method with 1) detector-based approaches, including SuperGlue [30] and SGMNet [31] that are equipped with SuperPoint(SP) [9] as local feature extractor, 2) detector-free approaches, including DRC-Net [18], PDC-Net [15,50], LoFTR [13], QuadTree Attention [22], MatchFormer [51] and DKM [52].

Results. As presented in Table 1 and Table 2, our method consistently achieves the best accuracy in both indoor and outdoor scenes. Visualization in Fig. 4 qualitatively demonstrates our method performance against other matches. More visualizations are provided in Appendix D.

4.2 Visual Localization

Apart from evaluation on two-view pose estimation task, we further integrate our network into a visual localization pipeline, and use two popular datasets,

Table 1. Two-view pose estimation results on ScanNet dataset [47] in indoor scenes.

Method	Pose estimation AUC		
	@5°	@10°	@20°
SP [9]+SuperGlue [30]	16.2	33.8	51.8
SP [9]+SGMNet [31]	15.4	32.1	48.3
DRC-Net [18]	7.7	17.9	30.5
PDC-Net+(H) [50]	20.2	39.4	57.1
LoFTR [13]	22.0	40.8	57.6
QuadTree [22]	24.9	44.7	61.8
MatchFormer [51]	24.3	43.9	61.4
DKM [52]	24.8	44.4	61.9
Ours	**25.6**	**46.0**	**63.3**

Table 2. Two-view pose estimation results on MegaDepth dataset [48] in outdoor scenes.

Method	Pose estimation AUC		
	@5°	@10°	@20°
SP [9]+SuperGlue [30]	42.2	61.2	75.9
SP [9]+SGMNet [31]	40.5	59.0	73.6
DRC-Net [18]	27.0	42.9	58.3
PDC-Net+(H) [50]	43.1	61.9	76.1
LoFTR [13]	52.8	69.2	81.2
QuadTree [22]	54.6	70.5	82.2
MatchFormer [51]	53.3	69.7	81.8
DKM [52]	54.5	70.7	82.3
Ours	**55.3**	**71.5**	**83.1**

InLoc [53] and Aachen Day-Night v1.1 [3,54,55] datasets, to demonstrate performance on multi-view matching in indoor scenes and outdoor scenes, respectively.

Indoor Localization Dataset. InLoc dataset [53] contains a database of 9, 972 RGBD indoor images that are geometrically registered to form the reference scene model, while 329 RGB query images are provided for visual localization, annotated with manually verified camera poses. Great challenge is posed in matching textureless or repetitive patterns under large perspective differences.

Outdoor Localization Dataset. Aachen Day-Night v1.1 dataset [54] depicts a city whose reference scene model is built upon 6, 697 day-time images. For visual localization, the dataset provides another 824 day-time images and 191 night-time images as queries. Great challenge is posed in identifying correspondences from, in particular, night-time images under extremely large illumination changes.

Evaluation Protocols. We follow the instructions from Long-Term Visual Localization Benchmark [56] to compute query poses. For both datasets, we use pre-trained HLoc [57] to retrieve candidate pairs, and recover camera poses with the model trained on MegaDepth dataset following SuperGlue [30] and LoFTR [13]. More details on localization pipeline are elaborated in Appendix A.4.

Results. On InLoc dataset, as shown in Table 3, our methods achieves overall best results compared with multiple comparative methods. On Aachen V1.1, as shown in Table 4, our method outperforms all other methods except SuperGlue. We partially ascribe this to the fact that we use only coarse matches for database reconstruction (see Appendix A.4.), causing localization error that harms pose estimation. In general, our method generalizes well in practical pipelines.

Table 3. Visual localization results on InLoc dataset [53].

Method	DUC1	DUC2
	(0.25 m,2°)/(0.5 m,5°) / (1 m,10°)	
HLoc [57] + SP [9]+SuperGlue [30]	49.0/68.7/80.8	53.4/**77.1**/82.4
HLoc [57] + LoFTR [13]	47.5/72.2/84.8	54.2/74.8/**85.5**
HLoc [57] + Ours	**51.5**/**73.7**/**86.4**	**55.0**/74.0/81.7

Table 4. Visual localization results on Aachen V1.1 dataset [54].

Method	Day	Night
	(0.25 m,2°)/(0.5 m,5°)/(1 m,10°)	
Localization with matching pairs provided in dataset		
R2D2 [8] + NN	–	71.2/86.9/98.9
ASLFeat [10] + NN	–	72.3/86.4/97.9
SP [9]+SuperGlue [30]	–	73.3/88.0/98.4
SP [9]+SGMNet [01]	–	72.3/85.3/97.9
Localization with matching pairs generated by HLoc		
SP [9]+SuperGlue [30]	**89.8**/**96.1**/**99.4**	77.0/90.6/**100.0**
LoFTR [13]	88.7/95.6/99.0	**78.5** 90.6/99.0
Ours	89.4/95.6/99.0	77.5/**91.6**/99.5

4.3 Ablation Study

To validate the effectiveness of different design components of our method, we conduct ablation experiments on ScanNet dataset [47] following the same setting in Sect. 4.1. Specifically, we compare three designs of attention structure:

- *Single-Level Attn.*: A design with only global attention at coarsest feature maps without the need of flow estimation. In this design, global context is well captured, whereas essential locality in motion smoothness is omitted and fine-grained message exchange becomes difficult.
- *Multi-Level Attn.*: A design with the hierarchical attention framework proposed in this paper, except that the size of local attention span is fixed to 13 px, i.e., the statistical mean of the adaptive attention span used in our network.
- *Adaptive Span Attn.*: Our full design that enables hierarchical attention with adaptive attention span. By this means, the need of context for different pixels is dynamically decided regarding different matchability.

As presented in Table 5, both hierarchical global-local attention and adaptive attention span improve overall performance by a considerable margin, validating the essentiality of our network designs.

Table 5. Ablation study on ScanNet dataset [47].

Method	Pose estimation AUC		
	@5°	@10°	@20°
Single-Level Attn.	22.65	40.72	59.06
Multi-Level Attn.	24.85	44.86	62.71
Adaptive Span Attn.	**25.61**	**46.04**	**63.33**

Table 6. Flow estimation accuracy.

Stage	<6px (%)	5σ (px)		
		Matchable	Unmatchable	Total
Iter#1	69.1	9.2	19.4	13.4
Iter#2	71.2	8.2	20.2	12.5
Iter#3	72.0	7.8	23.8	12.6
Iter#4	72.3	7.7	27.1	13.3

Left image overlayed with uncertainty map v.s. right image

Fig. 5. Visualization of uncertainty map which is predicted along with flows, warmer color indicates smaller uncertainties.

4.4 Understanding ASpanFormer

Flow Estimation. We analyze the flow estimation through multiple iterations. As shown in Table 6, precision of flow regression is gradually improved as attention iterations are performed and converges after four iterations.

As for uncertainty estimation, we split all pixels into two categories, matchable and unmatchable pixels, identified by ground-truth camera poses and depths, and report their mean standard deviation (σ). On one hand, mean σ decreases with iterations for matchable pixels, as the network becomes more certain about its flow prediction in later stages. On the other hand, the network gradually increases uncertainty values of unmatchable pixels to prevent over-confidence to a certain region.

Uncertainty map. In Fig. 5, we provide visualization of uncertainty map of flow prediction. Overlapping and non-overlapping regions are firstly distinguished, while uncertainty values in textureless regions are usually larger, indicating context of larger size is required during cross attention.

Runtime Evaluation. We evaluate the runtime of proposed method and compare it with LoFTR [13] where both methods apply Transformer backend. The runtime speed is tested on 100 randomly sampled ScanNet image pairs (640×480) with a NVIDIA V100 GPU. Runtime differs only on *Attention Module* compared with LoFTR, as we adopt the same Local Feature *CNN* backbone and coarse-to-fine matching module. As shown in Table 7, the proposed method is overall slightly slower than LoFTR due to the more complicated attention operation.

Table 7. Runtime speed evaluated on 640×480 images.

Stage	Runtime (ms)	
	LoFTR	Ours
Local Feature CNN	32.2	32.2
Attention Module	24.6	40.5
Matching	40.9	40.8
Total	97.7	113.5

5 Conclusion

In this paper, we have proposed a novel Transformer framework based on feature hierarchy, whose attention span is adaptively decided so as to acquire capabilities to capture both long-term dependencies as well as fine-grained details in local regions. State-of-the-art results validates the effectiveness of our method. With more engineering optimizations, we are looking forward to wider application of our method in real use.

References

1. Schonberger, J.L., Frahm, J.M.: Structure-from-motion revisited. In: CVPR (2016)
2. Widya, A.R., Torii, A., Okutomi, M.: Structure from motion using dense CNN features with keypoint relocalization. IPSJ Trans. Comput. Vis. Appl. **10**(1), 1–7 (2018). https://doi.org/10.1186/s41074-018-0042-y
3. Sattler, T., Weyand, T., Leibe, B., Kobbelt, L.: Image retrieval for image-based localization revisited. In: BMVC (2012)
4. Mur-Artal, R., Montiel, J.M.M., Tardos, J.D.: ORB-SLAM: a versatile and accurate monocular slam system. IEEE Trans. Robot. **31**(5), 1147–1163 (2015)
5. Mur-Artal, R., Tardos, J.: ORB-SLAM2: an open-source slam system for monocular, stereo and RGB-D cameras. IEEE Trans. Robot. **33**(5), 1255–1262 (2016)
6. Lowe, D.G.: Distinctive image features from scale-invariant keypoints. In: IJCV (2004)
7. Rublee, E., Rabaud, V., Konolige, K., Bradski, G.R.: ORB: an efficient alternative to sift or surf. In: ICCV (2011)
8. Revaud, J., et al.: R2D2: repeatable and reliable detector and descriptor. In: NeurIPS (2019)
9. DeTone, D., Malisiewicz, T., Rabinovich, A.: SuperPoint: self-supervised interest point detection and description. In: CVPRW (2018)
10. Luo, Z., et al.: ASLFeat: learning local features of accurate shape and localization. In: CVPR (2020)
11. Dusmanu, M., et al.: D2-net: a trainable CNN for joint description and detection of local features. In: CVPR (2019)
12. Luo, Z., et al.: ContextDesc: local descriptor augmentation with cross-modality context. In: CVPR (2019)
13. Sun, J., Shen, Z., Wang, Y., Bao, H., Zhou, X.: LoFTR: detector-free local feature matching with transformers. In: CVPR (2021)

14. Jiang, W., Trulls, E., Hosang, J., Tagliasacchi, A., Yi, K.M.: COTR: correspondence transformer for matching across images. In: CVPR (2021)
15. Truong, P., Danelljan, M., Gool, L.V., Timofte, R.: Learning accurate dense correspondences and when to trust them. In: CVPR (2021)
16. Rocco, I., Cimpoi, M., Arandjelovi, R., Torii, A., Pajdla, T., Sivic, J.: Neighbourhood consensus networks. In: NeurIPS (2018)
17. Rocco, I., Arandjelović, R., Sivic, J.: Efficient neighbourhood consensus networks via submanifold sparse convolutions. In: ECCV (2020)
18. Li, X., Han, K., Li, S., Prisacariu, V.: Dual-resolution correspondence networks. In: NeurIPS (2020)
19. Truong, P., Danelljan, M., Timofte, R.: GLU-Net: global-local universal network for dense flow and correspondences. In: CVPR (2020)
20. Min, J., Cho, M.: Convolutional hough matching networks. In: CVPR (2021)
21. Shen, X., Darmon, F., Efros, A., Aubry, M.: Ransac-flow: generic two-stage image alignment. In: ECCV (2020)
22. Tang, S., Zhang, J., Zhu, S., Tan, P.: Quadtree attention for vision transformers. In: ICLR (2021)
23. Vaswani, A., et al.: Attention is all you need. In: NeurIPS (2017)
24. Dosovitskiy, A., et al.: An image is worth 16 x 16 words: transformers for image recognition at scale. In: ICLR (2020)
25. Katharopoulos, A., Vyas, A., Pappas, N., Fleuret, F.: Transformers are RNNs: fast autoregressive transformers with linear attention. In: ICML (2020)
26. Mishchuk, A., Mishkin, D., Radenović, F., Matas, J.: Working hard to know your neighbor's margins: local descriptor learning loss. In: NeurIPS (2017)
27. Tian, Y., Fan, B., Wu, F.: L2-net: deep learning of discriminative patch descriptor in Euclidean space. In: CVPR (2017)
28. Luo, Z., et al.: GeoDesc: learning local descriptors by integrating geometry constraints. In: ECCV (2018)
29. Wang, Q., Zhou, X., Hariharan, B., Snavely, N.: Learning feature descriptors using camera pose supervision. In: ECCV (2020)
30. Sarlin, P.E., DeTone, D., Malisiewicz, T., Rabinovich, A.: Superglue: learning feature matching with graph neural networks. In: CVPR (2020)
31. Chen, H., et al.: Learning to match features with seeded graph matching network. In: ICCV (2021)
32. Zhang, J., et al.: Learning two-view correspondences and geometry using order-aware network. In: ICCV (2019)
33. Yi*, K.M., Trulls*, E., Ono, Y., Lepetit, V., Salzmann, M., Fua, P.: Learning to find good correspondences. In: CVPR (2018)
34. Sun, W., Jiang, W., Tagliasacchi, A., Trulls, E., Yi, K.M.: Attentive context normalization for robust permutation-equivariant learning. In: CVPR (2020)
35. Cavalli, L., Larsson, V., Oswald, M.R., Sattler, T., Pollefeys, M.: Handcrafted outlier detection revisited. In: ECCV (2020)
36. Bian, J., et al.: GMS: grid-based motion statistics for fast, ultra-robust feature correspondence. In: IJCV (2020)
37. Truong, P., Danelljan, M., Gool, L., Timofte, R.: Gocor: bringing globally optimized correspondence volumes into your neural network. In: NeurIPS (2020)
38. Ilg, E., Mayer, N., Saikia, T., Keuper, M., Dosovitskiy, A., Brox, T.: Flownet 2.0: evolution of optical flow estimation with deep networks. In: CVPR (2017)
39. Teed, Z., Deng, J.: Raft: recurrent all-pairs field transforms for optical flow. In: ECCV (2020)

40. Fischer, P., et al.: FlowNet: learning optical flow with convolutional networks. In: ICCV (2015)
41. Yin, Z., Shi, J.: Geonet: unsupervised learning of dense depth, optical flow and camera pose. In: CVPR (2018)
42. Zhou, L., et al.: Kfnet: learning temporal camera relocalization using kalman filtering. In: CVPR (2020)
43. Gast, J., Roth, S.: Lightweight probabilistic deep networks. In: CVPR (2018)
44. Ilg, E., et al.: Uncertainty estimates and multi hypotheses networks for optical flow. In: ECCV (2018)
45. Danelljan, M., Gool, L., Timofte, R.: Probabilistic regression for visual tracking. In: CVPR (2020)
46. He, K., Zhang, X., Ren, S., Sun, J.: Deep residual learning for image recognition. In: CVPR (2016)
47. Dai, A., Chang, A.X., Savva, M., Halber, M., Funkhouser, T., Nießner, M.: ScanNet: richly-annotated 3d reconstructions of indoor scenes. In: CVPR (2017)
48. Li, Z., Snavely, N.: MegaDepth: learning single-view depth prediction from internet photos. In: CVPR (2018)
49. Thomee, B., et al.: YFCC100M: the new data in multimedia research. Commun. ACM 59(2), 64–73 (2016)
50. Truong, P., Danelljan, M., Timofte, R., Van Gool, L.: PDC-Net+: enhanced probabilistic dense correspondence network (2021)
51. Wang, Q., Zhang, J., Yang, K., Peng, K., Stiefelhagen, R.: Matchformer: interleaving attention in transformers for feature matching (2022)
52. Edstedt, J., Wadenbäck, M., Felsberg, M.: Deep kernelized dense geometric matching (2022)
53. Taira, H., et al.: InLoc: indoor visual localization with dense matching and view synthesis. In: CVPR (2018)
54. Zhang, Z., Sattler, T., Scaramuzza, D.: Reference pose generation for long-term visual localization via learned features and view synthesis. In: IJCV (2021)
55. Sattler, T., et al.: Benchmarking 6DOF outdoor visual localization in changing conditions. In: CVPR (2018)
56. Toft, C., et al.: Long-term visual localization revisited. In: TPAMI (2020)
57. Sarlin, P.E., Cadena, C., Siegwart, R., Dymczyk, M.: From coarse to fine: robust hierarchical localization at large scale. In: CVPR (2019)

NDF: Neural Deformable Fields
for Dynamic Human Modelling

Ruiqi Zhang🆔 and Jie Chen(✉)🆔

Department of Computer Science, Hong Kong Baptist University, Hong Kong,
People's Republic of China
{csrqzhang,chenjie}@comp.hkbu.edu.hk

Abstract. We propose Neural Deformable Fields (NDF), a new representation for dynamic human digitization from a multi-view video. Recent works proposed to represent a dynamic human body with shared canonical neural radiance fields which links to the observation space with deformation fields estimations. However, the learned canonical representation is static and the current design of the deformation fields is not able to represent large movements or detailed geometry changes. In this paper, we propose to learn a neural deformable field wrapped around a fitted parametric body model to represent the dynamic human. The NDF is spatially aligned by the underlying reference surface. A neural network is then learned to map pose to the dynamics of NDF. The proposed NDF representation can synthesize the digitized performer with novel views and novel poses with a detailed and reasonable dynamic appearance. Experiments show that our method significantly outperforms recent human synthesis methods.

Keywords: Neural implicit representation · Volumetric rendering · Novel view synthesis · Dynamic motion · Human shape and appearance modelling

1 Introduction

Vision-based human performance capture has seen great progress in recent years due to fast development in both hardware and reconstruction algorithms like novel learning-based representation. It enables a wide variety of applications such as tele-presence, sportscast, and mixed reality. The enduring pandemic restricts our travel and public activities, which makes human performance digitization a research topic with great social and economic implications.

Human performance digitization can be roughly divided into human performance capture and human animation. Traditionally, to achieve high-fidelity human performance capture including geometry and texture reconstruction,

---

Supplementary Information The online version contains supplementary material available at https://doi.org/10.1007/978-3-031-19824-3_3.

dense camera rigs [5,8,9] and controlled lighting conditions [2,6] are required. These systems are extremely bulky and expensive, which limits their popularity. Nevertheless, these conventional capture systems could still fail under multi-person scenarios due to severe occlusion, which leads to ambiguity in appearance, pose, and motion sampling. After performance capture, human animation requires skilled artists to manually create a skeleton suitable for the human model and carefully design skinning weights [11] to achieve realistic animation, which requires countless human labor.

This paper aims to reduce the cost and improve the flexibility of human performance digitization. Many recent works have investigated the potential of neural implicit fields in novel view synthesis. NeRF [20] proposed a neural implicit representation that can be effectively learned from multi-view images. The neural implicit representation is rendered to realistic images from novel views with volume rendering. However, NeRF has a high requirement for the camera numbers and it can only model a static scene which does not apply to multi-view videos of dynamic humans. To extend NeRF to dynamic scenes, an effective idea is to aggregate all observations over different video frames [12,22–24,26]. D-NeRF [26] and Nerfies [22] decompose a reconstruction into a canonical neural radiance field and a set of deformation fields that transform points in observation space to canonical space. To further simplify the learning of the deformation fields, Animatable NeRF [24] resorts to a parametric human body model as a strong geometry prior to the deformation fields. However, we claim that the current design of a shared canonical space and deformation fields prevents these methods from learning large movements and detailed geometry changes such as wrinkles of clothes as shown in the experiment.

To solve the above problems, rather than learning shared canonical neural radiance fields from multi-view videos, we use Neural Deformable Fields (NDF) to represent a dynamic scene. Specifically, we unwrap observation space to NDF space using the surface of a parametric body model as reference. NDF space is automatically aligned across frames and we further adopt the skeletal pose as posterior condition to model the dynamic changes. As a result, NDF space is more compact than the original observation space and it can model the dynamic changes caused by different poses. After training, we are able to animate the performer to different views and poses with a high degree of realism.

We evaluate our method on ZJU-MoCap [25] and DynaCap [7] datasets that capture dynamic humans in complex motions with synchronized cameras. The results show that our method can achieve high-fidelity reconstructions, especially for realistic dynamic changes in novel pose synthesis. The code is avaliable at https://github.com/HKBU-VSComputing/2022_ECCV_NDF.

In summary, the contributions of this paper are following:

– We propose a compact novel representation called NDF, which can model the dynamic changes caused by different poses.
– The experiment results demonstrate significant improvement on the novel pose synthesis task, especially the detailed and realistic dynamic changes caused by different poses.

2   Related Works

Learning-Based Scene Representations. According to the dimensionality of representation, several paradigms have been investigated for 3D content embedding in the context of image-based novel view synthesis. Multiplane image (MPI) [19,31], voxels [16,28], point cloud [1,3], and neural radiance fields [4,13,18,20,30] have all been under intense research focus recently. MPI learns scene representation in the form of fronto-parallel color and α planes, and novel views are rendered via homography-wraping. Sitzmann ct al. [28] proposed to learn a deepvoxel representation by dividing the 3D space into discrete 3D units that embed learned features, which was further replaced with a continuous learnable function [29]. Mildenhall et al. [20] proposed to represent the scene as a neural radiance field (NeRF) by directly mapping a continuous 5D coordinate to the volume density and view-dependent emitted radiance. NeRF has special advantages in that it can represent a continuous scene in arbitrary resolution and it can be effectively learned from multi-view images. Our method follows NeRF to reconstruct scenes from images and further extends it to dynamic scenes.

Neural Implicit Representation for Human. Habermann et al. [7] leverage a 3D scanned person-specific template to learn motion-dependent geometry as well as motion- and view-dependent dynamic textures from multi-view videos. The requirement of a high-quality 3D scanning restricted its use. Several recent works resort to learning a shared representation via deformable functions (in the form of NeRF [21,22,26,27]). Restricted by the design choice of the function, it is difficult for these methods to model relatively large movements efficiently and they show limited generalizability to novel poses. Liu et al. [15] learns a person-specific embedding of the actor's appearance given a monocular video and a textured mesh template of the actor. Neural Body [25] learns neural representations over the same set of latent codes anchored to the deformable human model SMPL [17], and naturally integrate observations across frames. The sparsity allows it to effectively aggregate observations across frames but the result shows it losses details like wrinkles of clothes. Neural Actor [14] learns an unposed implicit human model via inverse linear blend skinning functions (LBS). The model cannot handle surface dynamics and certain geometric information has been lost during the generation of 2D texture maps. Animatable NeRF [24] can animate the performer to novel poses however it requires fine-tuning on the novel pose frames. This would be impossible when applied to a completely novel pose that the performer has never done. Our method does not require fine-tuning and can be directly applied to completely novel poses after training.

3   Proposed Method

Problem Setup. Given a training set of T-frame multi-view video of a dynamic human target over a sparse set of K synchronized and calibrated cameras: $\mathcal{I} = \{I_t^k\}$ ($t = 1 \ldots T, k = 1 \ldots K$), our goal is to digitize this performer using the proposed Neural Deformable Field (NDF) representation for both novel-view synthesis (NVS) and novel pose synthesis (NPS). Specifically, in the NVS task,

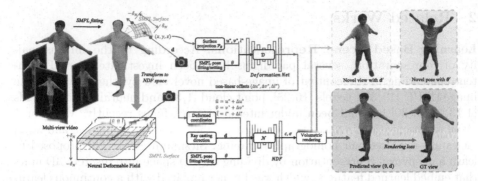

Fig. 1. Overview of proposed method. We query points in observation space, infer their densities and colors in NDF space and adopt volume rendering technique to synthesize images. For a given point $\mathbf{x} = (x, y, z)$ in observation space, we project it to NDF space with surface projection $\mathcal{P}_\theta$ and further adopt deformation net $\mathcal{D}$ to slightly adjust the projection point $\tilde{\mathbf{u}} = (\tilde{u}, \tilde{v}, \tilde{l})$ in NDF space. A radiance field is then learned to predict the color $\mathbf{c}$ and density σ for the point $\tilde{\mathbf{u}}$ in the unwrapped NDF space. The predicted color $\mathbf{c}$ and density σ is then assigned back to the observation-space point $\mathbf{x}$. Finally, volume rendering is used to synthesize an image in the observation space.

we synthesize free-viewpoint renderings of the performance with novel camera angles. In the NPS task, we synthesize renderings with novel, unseen poses.

We build the NDF representation based on the state-of-the-art volumetric rendering model - Neural Radiance Field (NeRF) [20], which predicts the color $\mathbf{c}$ and density σ at spatial location $\mathbf{x} \in \mathbb{R}^3$ and view direction $\mathbf{d} \in \mathbb{S}^2$ via a neural network $\mathcal{F}: (\mathbf{x}, \mathbf{d}) \mapsto (\mathbf{c}, \sigma)$. Subsequently, volumetric rendering functions are used to render the final pixel color. The differentiable rendering process enables optimization via comparing the output image with ground truth without 3D supervision. However, there are mainly two challenges in this setting. First, in our problem setup, only $K = 4$ cameras are used, which is much less than what is sufficient to train a NeRF network. Second, due to the dynamic property of the human target, directly training a NeRF with all the frames will always cause artifacts and produce a coarse result.

To address these challenges, NDF fits a parametric human body model SMPL to associate 3D points among different video frames and learns a neural implicit field wrapped around and driven by the SMPL surface:

$$\mathcal{N} : (\mathcal{D}(\mathcal{P}_\theta(\mathbf{x})), \mathbf{d}, \theta) \mapsto (\mathbf{c}, \sigma), \tag{1}$$

where $\mathcal{P}_\theta$ is a projection function which projects a point's spatial location $\mathbf{x}$ to NDF space conditioned on the posed SMPL model with parameter θ. $\mathcal{D}$ is a non-linear deformation function which keeps the surface continuity in the projection process. With the spatial alignment reference provided by the SMPL surface, NDF efficiently accumulates visual observations from the multi-view video frames; and given the strong geometry prior, NDF learns a geometry-guided field instead of a volume, which greatly reduces the learning complexity, leading to a much higher modelling efficiency. The details of each module will be introduced in this section.

3.1   SMPL as Projection Reference with Non-linear Deformation

To decrease NeRF's high requirement of camera numbers, a typical solution is to learn a deformation function $\Phi_t(\mathbf{x}) : \mathbb{R}^3 \mapsto \mathbb{R}^3$ to map sample points $\mathbf{x}$ in frame t to a shared canonical space [24, 26]. However, restricted by current design, these methods cannot deal with large movements or detailed geometry changes such as clothes wrinkles. To overcome these drawbacks, we resort to the texture map of SMPL as a reference to align 3D points across different frames and jointly train an integral NeRF model.

SMPL [17] is a skinned vertex-based model, which is defined as a function of shape parameters β, pose parameters θ and a rigid transformation $\mathbf{W}$ using Linear Blending Skinning (LBS). The template model $\bar{\mathbf{T}}$ includes pre-defined 6890 vertices and their connections. With the pose-blend shape $B_P(\theta)$ and shape-blend shape $B_S(\beta)$, the posed mesh $M(\theta, \beta)$ is got from the following equation:

$$M(\theta, \beta) = \mathbf{W}(\bar{\mathbf{T}} + B_S(\beta) + B_P(\theta)). \tag{2}$$

In this paper, we assume the posed mesh is pre-computed from the multi-view video and use the texture map of this mesh to conduct the projection function $\mathcal{P}_\theta$ from observation space to NDF space.

Coordinates Projection. As shown in Fig. 1, a 3D point $\mathbf{x} = (x, y, z)$ is projected to a point $\mathbf{u}^* = (u^*, v^*, l^*)$ in the *unwrapped* Neural Deformable Fields (NDF) space with the projection function $\mathcal{P}_\theta : \mathbf{x} \mapsto \mathbf{u}^*$. $\mathcal{P}_\theta$ first projects the point $\mathbf{x}$ to the closest point $\mathbf{x}' \in \mathbb{R}^3$ on the fitted SMPL surface. $\mathbf{x}'$ has a 2D texel coordinate (u^*, v^*) which is defined over SMPL's texture map and is calculated via:

$$(u^*, v^*, f^*) = \arg\min_{u,v,f} \|\mathbf{x} - B_{u,v}(\mathcal{V}_{[\mathcal{F}(f)]})\|_2^2, \tag{3}$$

where $f \in \{1 \ldots N_F\}$ is the triangle index, $\mathcal{V}_{[\mathcal{F}(f)]}$ is the three vertices of triangle $\mathcal{F}(f)$, $(u, v) : u, v \in [0, 1]$ are the texel coordinates on the texture map and $B_{u,v}(\cdot)$ is the barycentric interpolation function. SMPL is designed for modelling skinned human body and cannot capture surface dynamic changes. To model the dynamic geometry that deviates from the SMPL surface, we extend NDF to 3 dimensions with the euclidean distance l^* between $\mathbf{x}$ and $\mathbf{x}'$ being the third dimension.

Non-linear Deformation. We have projected an observation-space point $\mathbf{x}$ to $\mathbf{u}^*$ in NDF space using the UV coordinate of its nearest point on the SMPL surface as a reference. However, the continuous real surface will become discontinuous after projection. As shown in Fig. 2(b), the two yellow points located on the continuous real surface in observation space will be closest to the same vertex on the SMPL surface if they locate in the same intersection of surface normals. After projection, the two yellow points will have the same u^*, v^* but different l^* in the NDF space. This will cause discontinuity at (u^*, v^*) and hinder the

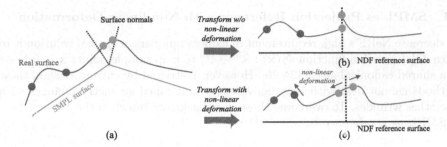

Fig. 2. A simplified 2D demonstration of transformation from the (x, y, z) camera coordinates (a) to the (u, v, l) NDF coordinates with and without non-linear deformation in (c) and (b), respectively.

learning of neural radiance fields. To solve this problem, we adopt a deformation net to slightly adjust the projection coordinate. As shown in Fig. 2(c), this non-linear deformation can unwrap the surface fragment between the surface normal interval and the continuity of the real surface can be maintained. Formally, the deformed projection location $\tilde{\mathbf{u}} = (\tilde{u}, \tilde{v}, \tilde{l})$ is described as following:

$$\triangle u^*, \triangle v^*, \triangle l^* = \mathcal{D}(\gamma_u(u^*, v^*, l^*), \theta), \quad (4)$$

$$\tilde{u}, \tilde{v}, \tilde{l} = u^* + \triangle u^*, v^* + \triangle v^*, l^* + \triangle l^*, \quad (5)$$

where $\mathcal{D}(\cdot)$ is the deformation net and $\gamma_u(\cdot)$ is the position embedding of $\mathbf{u}^*$. Note that the deformation aims to maintain the surface continuity in projection, but not to align points to a shared canonical space as in D-NeRF [26] and Nerfies [22].

3.2 Neural Deformable Fields

Rendering. For a given 3D spatial location $\mathbf{x}$ along the target camera's tracing ray direction $\mathbf{d}$, a point $\tilde{\mathbf{u}}$ will be found in the NDF space via projection and non-linear deformation as described above. The density for the point $\mathbf{x}$ will be estimated using an MLP M_σ: $\sigma(\mathbf{x}) = M_\sigma(\gamma_u(\tilde{\mathbf{u}}), \theta)$. The color will be estimated with another MLP M_c: $c(\mathbf{x}) = M_c(\gamma_u(\tilde{\mathbf{u}}), \gamma_d(\mathbf{d}), \theta)$, with an additional embedding $\gamma_d(\mathbf{d})$ for viewing direction, which ensures view-dependent effects.

The final image will be rendered via volumetric rendering [10] using numerical quadrature with N consecutive samples $\{x_1, \ldots, x_N\}$ along the tracing ray:

$$I_{out} = \sum_{n=1}^{N} (\prod_{m=1}^{n-1} e^{-\sigma(\mathbf{x_m}) \cdot \delta_m}) \cdot (1 - e^{-\sigma_n \cdot \delta_n}) \cdot c(\mathbf{x_n}). \quad (6)$$

Here $\delta_n = \|\mathbf{x_n} - \mathbf{x_{n-1}}\|_2$ denotes the quadrature segment along the ray.

Geometry-guided Sampling Strategy. To further facilitate the learning process of NDF, we use the fitted SMPL as geometry guidance to sample points more effectively and cancel the hierarchical sampling adopted in the original NeRF. Specifically, as shown in Fig. 1, we take uniform samples but only accept samples if the projection distance l^* is smaller than a hyper-parameter δ_N.

Remark. NDF representation is lightweight, detailed, and intuitive. As compared with volumetric representations, its underlying geometrical linkage is well-defined by posed SMPL, resulting in reduced dimensionality for geometry reasoning, therefore significantly reducing model complexity and is much easier to train. The feature space of NDF span the whole UV dimension, which records much more details compared with Neural Body [25], where shared canonical features are only located at SMPL vertices. By learning neural radiance fields conditioned on the pose, NDF can recover more intuitive dynamics related to changing pose rather than having to learn how to change query position in the canonical space through a per-frame deformation field like in Neural Actor [14].

3.3 Deformable Fields for Novel Pose Synthesis

Pose-driven NeRF. By projecting points from the observation space to the NDF space, we are able to jointly learn a shared neural radiance field across frames. However, this representation would be only capable to capture a static geometry though it can be deformed to different poses. To model the dynamic change of human body geometry, we resort to the skeletal pose of SMPL as the posterior to infer the dynamic changes, i.e. we change the model from simply learning $\mathcal{N} : (\mathcal{D}(\mathcal{P}_\theta(\mathbf{x})), \mathbf{d}) \mapsto (\mathbf{c}, \sigma)$ to learning $\mathcal{N} : (\mathcal{D}(\mathcal{P}_\theta(\mathbf{x})), \mathbf{d}, \theta) \mapsto (\mathbf{c}, \sigma)$, where θ is the pose parameters of SMPL. In SMPL, the pose parameters θ is the axis-angle representation of the relative rotation of part k with respect to its parent in the kinematic tree. Besides being used for changing pose, θ is also used to generate a pose-blend shape that describes the shape deformation caused by different poses. Inspired by this, we infer from pose θ the dynamics of the scene. In practice, we apply an additional feature extractor to extract high-level features of pose parameters which contain significantly more information than the pure pose parameters. The extracted pose features are then concatenated with the position embedding of $\tilde{\mathbf{u}}$ and fed into the following neural networks.

Animation. After training, NDF can be generalized to novel views or poses that do not occur in the training data $\mathcal{I}$. Specifically, given a viewing direction $\mathbf{d}$, a shape parameter β and a skeletal pose θ got from a motion capture system or designed by hand, we calculate the mesh vertices through Eq. 2. Then we sample points around the SMPL surface and render an image viewing from $\mathbf{d}$ with Eq. 6.

Remark. NDF does not need to be fine-tuned on novel pose images compared with Animatable NeRF [25] and can be applied to only sparse cameras compared with Neural Actor [14], where dense cameras are needed to pre-compute a realistic texture map. This animation ability only from sparse cameras would have a wide range of potential applications in VR or the metaverse.

4 Experiment

4.1 Dataset and Metrics

ZJU-MoCap. [25] records multi-view videos with 21 synchronous cameras and collects the shape parameters of SMPL as well as the global translation and the SMPL's pose parameters with an off-the-shelf SMPL tracking system [32]. Following [25], we choose 0 sequences and 4 uniformly distributed cameras are used for training and the remaining cameras for testing. The video clips for evaluating novel view synthesis and novel pose synthesis are also the same with [25].

DynaCap. To further evaluate the generalization ability of our method, we select two sequences D1 and D2 from the DynaCap dataset [7]. These two sequences record a performer with over 50 synchronous cameras. We fit neutral SMPL to these cameras using [32] and uniformly select 10 cameras for training and 5 cameras for testing.

Metrics. Following typical protocols [20] and works most related to us [24] [25], we evaluate our method on image synthesis using two metrics: peak signal-to-noise ratio (PSNR) and structural similarity index (SSIM).

4.2 Performance on NVS and NPS

We compare our method with state-of-the-art view synthesis methods [24,25] that also use SMPL models and can handle dynamic scenes. Neural Body [25] represents the dynamic scene with an implicit field conditioned on a shared set of latent codes anchored on the vertices of SMPL and renders the images using volume rendering. Animatable NeRF [24] predicts the blend weights for each sample point and aggregates observations across frames to a shared canonical representation and further improves on novel pose synthesis by fine-tuning on novel pose images. All methods train a separate network for each scene.

Evaluation on Novel View Synthesis. Table 1 shows the comparison of our method with Neural Body [25] and Animatable NeRF [24] on ZJU-MoCap dataset. Our method outperforms Animatable NeRF [24] by a margin of 0.49 in terms of the PSNR metric and 0.01 in terms of the SSIM metric. It also performs close to Neural Body. Moreover, our method maintains its superiority when applied to DynaCap dataset as shown in Table 3.

Figure 3 presents the qualitative comparison of our method with [24,25] on the ZJU-MoCap dataset. Both [25] and [24] have difficulty in recovering fine details of the dynamic scene. Neural Body [25] turns to over-smooth the result as shown in the third person and the fourth person of Fig. 3. The clothes seam of the third person almost disappears and the small wrinkles on the clothes of the fourth person also disappear. Animatable NeRF [24] shows more artifacts as the blur of the first person's face and the second person's clothes. In contrast, our method can always recover realistic details like the hem of the third person.

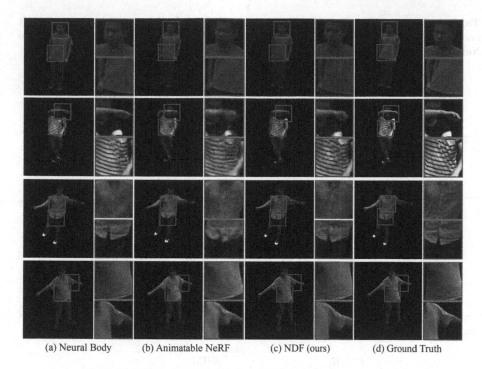

(a) Neural Body   (b) Animatable NeRF   (c) NDF (ours)   (d) Ground Truth

Fig. 3. Qualitative results of novel view synthesis on the ZJU-MoCap dataset.

Figure 5 further presents the qualitative comparison on the DynaCap dataset. For the first two rows of novel view synthesis, our method can always recover realistic details. For the second row, Neural Body [25] losses wrinkles on the back and Animatable NeRF [24] suffers from artifacts. While our method can reproduce high-quality wrinkles on the back.

Evaluation on Novel Pose Synthesis. Table 2 shows the comparison of our method with Neural Body [25] and Animatable NeRF [24] on novel pose synthesis. The result shows that our method outperforms compared method on most of the sequences and performs best for the average metrics. Note that Animatable NeRF [24] needs to be fine-tuned on novel pose images while our method can be directly applied to novel pose synthesis.

The qualitative results are shown in Fig. 4. Neural Body [25] learns latent codes for training frames and does not model the dynamic change with respect to poses, thus it always suffers from artifacts when applied to novel pose synthesis. Though fine-tuned on novel pose images, Animatable NeRF [24] has difficulty in modelling large movements and also leads to blur result. Our method is able to recover details such as the hem of clothes for the third person even when applied to novel pose synthesis.

The bottom 2 rows of Fig. 5 show the qualitative comparison on the DynaCap dataset. Neural Body [25] fails to recover the face of the second person and

46   R. Zhang and J. Chen

Table 1. Results of novel view synthesis on the ZJU-MoCap dataset in terms of PSNR and SSIM (higher is better). "NB" means Neural Body. "AN" means Animatable NeRF. The best and the second best results are highlighted in red and blue, respectively.

	PSNR			SSIM		
	NB [25]	AN [24]	OURS	NB [25]	AN [24]	OURS
313	30.39	29.27	29.84	0.970	0.962	0.969
315	26.53	24.22	25.71	0.964	0.033	0.040
377	27.49	26.63	26.85	0.950	0.941	0.946
386	28.66	26.78	28.21	0.928	0.891	0.923
387	25.52	24.75	24.52	0.922	0.913	0.911
390	27.25	26.19	26.33	0.920	0.915	0.913
392	29.41	27.79	28.40	0.944	0.928	0.937
393	27.41	26.06	26.73	0.934	0.916	0.926
394	28.65	27.53	27.98	0.939	0.925	0.932
Average	27.92	26.58	27.17	0.940	0.924	0.934

Table 2. Results of novel pose synthesis on the ZJU-MoCap dataset in terms of PSNR and SSIM (higher is better)

	PSNR			SSIM		
	NB [25]	AN [24]	OURS	NB [25]	AN [24]	OURS
313	23.49	23.61	23.29	0.898	0.908	0.903
315	19.38	19.45	19.50	0.847	0.854	0.857
377	23.89	25.03	25.18	0.914	0.927	0.928
386	25.63	25.14	26.33	0.877	0.878	0.893
387	21.75	22.94	22.41	0.865	0.892	0.880
390	23.81	24.51	24.11	0.868	0.889	0.881
392	25.66	24.15	25.62	0.908	0.900	0.914
393	23.30	23.97	24.03	0.891	0.899	0.902
394	23.76	24.29	24.29	0.876	0.893	0.890
Average	23.41	23.68	23.86	0.883	0.893	0.894

Animatable NeRF produces severe artifacts on the face and hands, while our method can produce reliable realistic face and hands for the second person.

4.3 Temporal Consistency

NDF uses pose as condition which changes continuously and smoothly over time, while Neural Body and Animatable NeRF separately learn appearance codes for different frames. This endows NDF with better temporal consistency as can be seen from Fig. 6. The red circles point out the flickering part of previous methods while NDF always shows better temporal consistency.

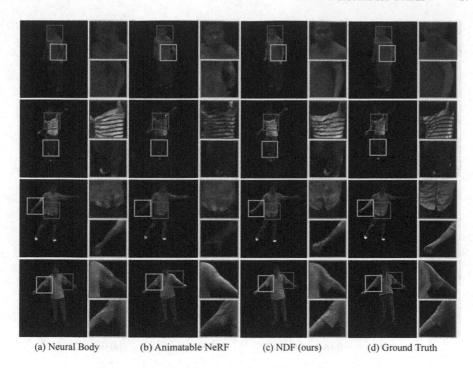

(a) Neural Body   (b) Animatable NeRF   (c) NDF (ours)   (d) Ground Truth

Fig. 4. Qualitative results of novel pose synthesis on the ZJU-MoCap dataset.

4.4 Ablation Study

We conduct ablation studies on one subject (313) of the ZJU-MoCap [25] dataset in terms of the novel view synthesis and novel pose synthesis performance. We test the impact of the surface distance $\tilde{l}$, the impact of using pose as the condition to model dynamic change, the impact of projection from observation space to NDF space, the impact of deformation net, and the reliance of specific reference surface to show the effectiveness of our choice.

Impact of the Surface Distance $\tilde{l}$ in NDF Rendering. To capture the dynamic geometry that cannot be captured by naked SMPL surface, we adopt the distance from a query point to its closest point on SMPL as the third dimension to model the NDF space as a field rather than a naked SMPL surface. To test the impact of this design, we only sample points on the SMPL surface thus the $\tilde{l}$ for projected points are all 0. As shown in the first column of Fig. 7 and Table 4, modelling the NDF space as naked SMPL surface causes severe artifacts, especially for clothes that cannot be captured by SMPL surface.

Using Pose as Condition to Model Dynamic Change. In this experiment, we cancel using pose as the condition and jointly learn a shared canonical NDF for all frames. As shown in the second column of Fig. 7, the model cannot handle dynamic changes and produces blur rendering at dynamic regions.

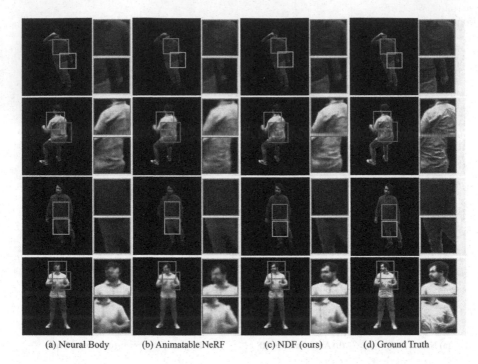

(a) Neural Body   (b) Animatable NeRF   (c) NDF (ours)   (d) Ground Truth

Fig. 5. Qualitative results of novel view synthesis and novel pose synthesis on the DynaCap dataset. Top 2 rows: novel view synthesis. Bottom 2 rows: novel pose synthesis.

Impact of Projection from Observation Space to NDF Space. In this experiment, we directly use the observation-space coordinates (x, y, z) as input to the neural network. The model needs to learn the mapping from pose to the whole 3D volume however it is severely difficult. As shown in the third column of Fig. 7, though the model can synthesize novel views of the performer, it totally fails on novel pose synthesis.

Impact of Deformation Net. The deformation net aims to maintain the surface continuity after projection as claimed in Fig. 2. As shown in the fourth column of Fig. 7, the face and shoes become slightly noisier and we infer this is because the triangle surfaces of SMPL are small and dense on the face and feet. The result confirms the effectiveness of our design of the deformation net.

Reliance of Specific Reference Surface. NDF does not rely on a specific texture map as the reference surface. To validate this, we replace the default texture map of SMPL with a self-designed texture map which can be found in the supplementary material. We cut the seam of the SMPL mesh in Blender and unwrap the mesh into one piece in the UV space. As shown in the fifth column of Fig. 7 and Table 4, with the 1-piece texture map as reference surface, the face

Table 3. Results of novel view synthesis and novel pose synthesis on the DynaCap dataset in terms of PSNR and SSIM (higher is better).

	PSNR			SSIM		
	NB [25]	AN [24]	OURS	NB [25]	AN [24]	OURS
Novel view	23.96	22.99	24.73	0.889	0.872	0.904
Novel pose	21.19	20.98	21.42	0.828	0.828	0.841

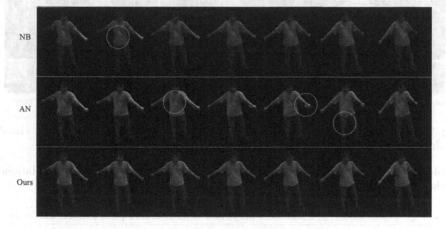

Fig. 6. Qualitative results of continuous frames to show temporal consistency. The red circles point out the flickering part of previous methods. (Color figure online)

becomes slightly blurred but the whole effect is still robust. This is because the UV region corresponding to the face occurs to be much smaller than in the default texture map of SMPL. The result shows that our method does not rely on a specific texture map and a self-designed texture map can also be used to unwrap points from observation space to NDF space.

5   Limitations and Future Works

Learning neural radiance fields conditioned on pose in NDF space enables us to obtain impressive performances on human digitization. However, our method has a few limitations. 1) Currently our method has a high requirement for the fitting effect of SMPL. Hopefully, in the future, we can integrate the fitting of SMPL in the pipeline and make the fitting and rendering benefit from each other. 2) In more complex scenes, the dynamic content depends both on pose and temporal information. A potential solution is to train the model with an auto-regressive way to model the relationship to temporal information.

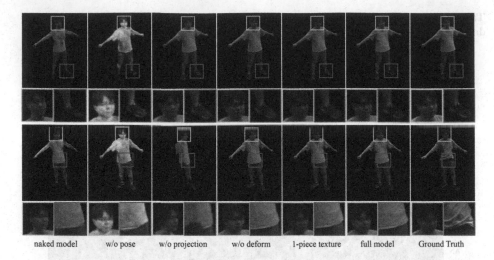

| naked model | w/o pose | w/o projection | w/o deform | 1-piece texture | full model | Ground Truth |

Fig. 7. Qualitative results of ablations. The first row and second row show the visual results for novel view synthesis and novel pose synthesis, respectively.

Table 4. PSNR results of novel view synthesis and novel pose synthesis of ablations (higher is better).

	Naked model	w/o pose	w/o projection	w/o deform	1-piece texture	Full model
Novel view	23.65	21.98	29.73	29.72	29.93	29.75
Novel pose	21.71	20.43	18.42	23.35	23.38	23.41

6   Conclusions

We propose a novel representation of Neural Deformable Fields (NDF) to model dynamic humans. We unwrap observation space to NDF space using a parametric body model as a reference. Then a neural radiance field conditioned on skeletal pose is learned and volume rendering is used to render the pixel color. After training from multi-view videos, our method can synthesize the performer with arbitrary view direction and pose. Extensive experiments on ZJU-MoCap and DynaCap demonstrated that our method outperforms the state-of-the-art in terms of rendering quality and produces faithful pose-dependent appearance changes and wrinkle patterns.

Acknowledgments. The research was supported by the Theme-based Research Scheme, Research Grants Council of Hong Kong (T45-205/21-N).

References

1. Aliev, K.A., Sevastopolsky, A., Kolos, M., Ulyanov, D., Lempitsky, V.: Neural point-based graphics. In: European Conferenc on Computer Vision, pp. 696–712 (2020)

2. Collet, A., et al.: High-quality streamable free-viewpoint video. ACM Trans. Graph. **34**(4), 1–13 (2015)
3. Dai, P., Zhang, Y., Li, Z., Liu, S., Zeng, B.: Neural point cloud rendering via multi-plane projection. In: Proceedings of the IEEE/CVF Conference on Computer Vision and Pattern Recognition, pp. 7830–7839 (2020)
4. Garbin, S.J., Kowalski, M., Johnson, M., Shotton, J., Valentin, J.: FastNeRF: high-fidelity neural rendering at 200fps. In: Proceedings of the IEEE/CVF International Conference on Computer Vision, pp. 14346–14355 (2021)
5. Gortler, S.J., Grzeszczuk, R., Szeliski, R., Cohen, M.F.: The lumigraph. In: Proceedings of the 23rd Annual Conference on Computer Graphics and Interactive Techniques, pp. 43–54 (1996)
6. Guo, K., et al.: The relightables: volumetric performance capture of humans with realistic relighting. ACM Trans. Graph. **38**(6), 1–19 (2019)
7. Habermann, M., Liu, L., Xu, W., Zollhoefer, M., Pons-Moll, G., Theobalt, C.: Real-time deep dynamic characters. ACM Trans. Graph. **40**(4), 1–16 (2021)
8. Hedman, P., Philip, J., Price, T., Frahm, J.M., Drettakis, G., Brostow, G.: Deep blending for free-viewpoint image-based rendering. ACM Trans. Graph. **37**(6), 1–15 (2018)
9. Joo, H., Simon, T., Sheikh, Y.: Total capture: A 3d deformation model for tracking faces, hands, and bodies. In: Proceedings of the IEEE Conference on Computer Vision and Pattern Recognition, pp. 8320–8329 (2018)
10. Kajiya, J.T., Von Herzen, B.P.: Ray tracing volume densities. ACM SIGGRAPH Comput. Graph. **18**(3), 165–174 (1984)
11. Lewis, J.P., Cordner, M., Fong, N.: Pose space deformation: a unified approach to shape interpolation and skeleton-driven deformation. In: Proceedings of the 27th Annual Conference on Computer Graphics and Interactive Techniques, pp. 165–172 (2000)
12. Li, Z., Niklaus, S., Snavely, N., Wang, O.: Neural scene flow fields for space-time view synthesis of dynamic scenes. In: Proceedings of the IEEE/CVF Conference on Computer Vision and Pattern Recognition, pp. 6498–6508 (2021)
13. Liu, L., Gu, J., Zaw Lin, K., Chua, T.S., Theobalt, C.: Neural sparse voxel fields. Adv. Neural Inf. Process. Syst. **33**, 15651–15663 (2020)
14. Liu, L., Habermann, M., Rudnev, V., Sarkar, K., Gu, J., Theobalt, C.: Neural actor: neural free-view synthesis of human actors with pose control. ACM Trans. Graph. **40**(6), 1–6 (2021)
15. Liu, L., e al.: Neural human video rendering by learning dynamic textures and rendering-to-video translation. IEEE Trans. Vis. Comput. Graph. 1 (2020)
16. Lombardi, S., Simon, T., Saragih, J., Schwartz, G., Lehrmann, A., Sheikh, Y.: Neural volumes: learning dynamic renderable volumes from images. ACM Trans. Graph. **38**(4), 65:1–65:14 (2019)
17. Loper, M., Mahmood, N., Romero, J., Pons-Moll, G., Black, M.J.: SMPL: a skinned multi-person linear model. ACM Trans. Graph. **34**(6), 1–16 (2015)
18. Martin-Brualla, R., Radwan, N., Sajjadi, M.S., Barron, J.T., Dosovitskiy, A., Duckworth, D.: Nerf in the wild: Neural radiance fields for unconstrained photo collections. In: Proceedings of the IEEE/CVF Conference on Computer Vision and Pattern Recognition, pp. 7210–7219 (2021)
19. Mildenhall, B., et al.: Local light field fusion: practical view synthesis with prescriptive sampling guidelines. ACM Trans. Graph. **38**(4), 1–14 (2019)
20. Mildenhall, B., Srinivasan, P.P., Tancik, M., Barron, J.T., Ramamoorthi, R., Ng, R.: NERF: representing scenes as neural radiance fields for view synthesis. In: European Conference on Computer Vision, pp. 405–421 (2020)

21. Noguchi, A., Sun, X., Lin, S., Harada, T.: Neural articulated radiance field. In: Proceedings of the IEEE/CVF International Conference on Computer Vision, pp. 5762–5772 (2021)
22. Park, K., et al.: Nerfies: deformable neural radiance fields. In: IEEE International Conference on Computer Vision, pp. 5865–5874 (2021)
23. Park, K., et al.: HyperNeRF: a higher-dimensional representation for topologically varying neural radiance fields. ACM Trans. Graph. **40**(6) (2021)
24. Peng, S., et al.: Animatable neural radiance fields for modeling dynamic human bodies. In: Proceedings of the IEEE/CVF International Conference on Computer Vision, pp. 14314–14323 (2021)
25. Peng, S., et al.: Neural body: Implicit neural representations with structured latent codes for novel view synthesis of dynamic humans. In: IEEE Conference on Computer Vision and Pattern Recognition, pp. 9054–9063 (2021)
26. Pumarola, A., Corona, E., Pons-Moll, G., Moreno-Noguer, F.: D-nerf: neural radiance fields for dynamic scenes. In: Proceedings of the IEEE/CVF Conference on Computer Vision and Pattern Recognition, pp. 10318–10327 (2021)
27. Shao, R., et al.: DoubleField: bridging the neural surface and radiance fields for high-fidelity human reconstruction and rendering. In: Proceedings of the IEEE/CVF Conference on Computer Vision and Pattern Recognition, pp. 15872–15882 (2022)
28. Sitzmann, V., Thies, J., Heide, F., Nießner, M., Wetzstein, G., Zollhofer, M.: DeepVoxels: learning persistent 3d feature embeddings. In: IEEE Conference on Computer Vision and Pattern Recognition, pp. 2437–2446 (2019)
29. Sitzmann, V., Zollhoefer, M., Wetzstein, G.: Scene representation networks: continuous 3d-structure-aware neural scene representations. Adv. Neural Inf. Process. Syst. **32**, 1121–1132 (2019)
30. Yu, A., Ye, V., Tancik, M., Kanazawa, A.: pixelNeRF: neural radiance fields from one or few images. In: Proceedings of the IEEE/CVF Conference on Computer Vision and Pattern Recognition, pp. 4578–4587 (2021)
31. Zhou, T., Tucker, R., Flynn, J., Fyffe, G., Snavely, N.: Stereo magnification: learning view synthesis using multiplane images. ACM Trans. Graph. **37**(4), 1–12 (2018)
32. zju3dv: Easymocap. http://github.com/zju3dv/EasyMocap (2021)

Neural Density-Distance Fields

Itsuki Ueda[1]([✉]) , Yoshihiro Fukuhara[2] , Hirokatsu Kataoka[3] ,
Hiroaki Aizawa[4] , Hidehiko Shishido[1] , and Itaru Kitahara[1]

[1] University of Tsukuba, Tsukuba 3058577, Japan
{ueda.itsuki,shishido.hidehiko,kitahara.itaru}@image.iit.tsukuba.ac.jp
[2] Waseda University, Tokyo 1698050, Japan
f_yoshi@ruri.waseda.jp
[3] National Institute of Advanced Industrial Science and Technology (AIST),
Tsukuba 3058560, Japan
hirokatsu.kataoka@aist.go.jp
[4] Hiroshima University, Higashihiroshima 7398511, Japan
hiroaki-aizawa@hiroshima-u.ac.jp

Abstract. The success of neural fields for 3D vision tasks is now indisputable. Following this trend, several methods aiming for visual localization (e.g., SLAM) have been proposed to estimate distance or density fields using neural fields. However, it is difficult to achieve high localization performance by only density fields-based methods such as Neural Radiance Field (NeRF) since they do not provide density gradient in most empty regions. On the other hand, distance field-based methods such as Neural Implicit Surface (NeuS) have limitations in objects' surface shapes. This paper proposes Neural Distance-Density Field (NeDDF), a novel 3D representation that reciprocally constrains the distance and density fields. We extend distance field formulation to shapes with no explicit boundary surface, such as fur or smoke, which enable explicit conversion from distance field to density field. Consistent distance and density fields realized by explicit conversion enable both robustness to initial values and high-quality registration. Furthermore, the consistency between fields allows fast convergence from sparse point clouds. Experiments show that NeDDF can achieve high localization performance while providing comparable results to NeRF on novel view synthesis. The code is available at https:// github.com/ueda0319/neddf.

1 Introduction

Representing 3D shapes using coordinate-based neural networks, also known as neural fields [25] have recently attracted attention as an alternative to using point clouds, voxels, meshes, and others [3,13,17–19,21,23]. Neural Radiance Fields (NeRF) [13], in particular, have shown impressive quality for tasks such as novel view-synthesis. However, since NeRF has limited regions with smooth spatial density and color, many conventional methods still require good initial

---

Supplementary Information The online version contains supplementary material available at https://doi.org/10.1007/978-3-031-19824-3_4.

S. Avidan et al. (Eds.): ECCV 2022, LNCS 13692, pp. 53–68, 2022.
https://doi.org/10.1007/978-3-031-19824-3_4

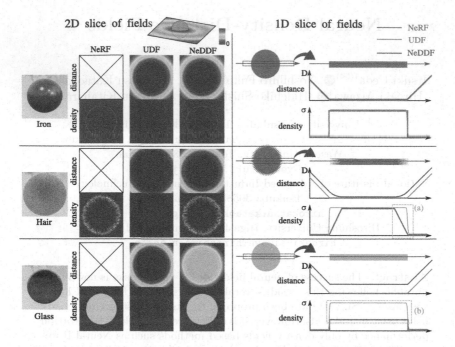

Fig. 1. (left) Visualization of the 2D slice for each field with iron, hair, and glass spheres as examples. (right) Plots of 1D slices for each field. NeRF provides no distance information. Unsigned Distance Field (UDF) cannot handle some cases correctly, such as (a) ambiguous density changes such as a hairball or (b) low densities such as a glass ball. Proposed NeDDF can represent both cases properly.

values for registration and localization tasks. This paper proposes a distance field representation that is reciprocally constrained to the density field, named Neural Density Distance Field (NeDDF). NeDDF achieves robust localization with distance fields while providing object reconstruction quality comparable to NeRF.

As shown in Fig. 1, there are two main types of 3D shape representation in neural fields: density field used in NeRF [13] and distance field used in NeuS [23]. Density field has high expressiveness for translucent objects, such as smoke and water, and high-frequency shapes, such as hair. However, in most areas except the boundary, the gradient of the field is zero. This makes it difficult to set up a convex objective function in a problem setting such as registration, as shown in Fig. 2. Distance field provides the gradient over a wide range even after the optimization converges. Thus, we can establish objective functions with high convexity in registration. The field can be learned from the image via volume rendering by defining a conversion equation from distance to density. For example, NeuS assumes that the density follows a logistic distribution close to the object surface. On the other hand, since we assume explicit boundaries, the convertible density field is tightly restricted.

As shown in Fig. 3 (a), we focus on the Unsigned Distance Field (UDF), which ignores surface direction inside objects and can distinguish between the

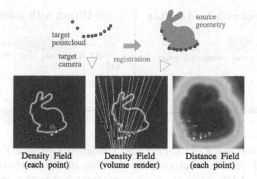

Fig. 2. Registration following in each representation: white and black points (small circles) denote the points where the gradient direction is available or not, respectively. In the density field (left), point-by-point gradients cannot be obtained in most regions except for the boundary. In volume rendering of the density field (center), it is impossible to obtain the gradient component in the vertical direction of view. In the distance field (right), we can obtain both the gradient direction and the residuals for each point.

inside and outside objects not only by the sign of distance D but also by the magnitude of its gradient. We extend the distance field to be able to recover arbitrary density distributions by interpreting D by the depth derived from the volume rendering equation and fitting the density information of translucent objects to the mid-level gradient magnitude, as shown in Fig. 3 (b). This method eliminates the need for constraints on the density, as in NeuS, when learning the distance field from images. In other words, when learning the density field, we can simultaneously obtain a consistent distance field where the shape and camera pose have the same optimal values. As shown in Fig. 4, the NeDDF has a network that inputs a position and outputs the distance and its gradient, and a converter that explicitly calculates the density. NeDDF enables both high expressiveness of the density field and good registration of the associated distance field.

The present paper provides the following three contributions: (1) Extending the distance field to be definable for arbitrary density distributions. (2) Proposing a method to recover the corresponding density from independent points using the distance field and gradient information. (3) Providing an implementation to alleviate the instability of the distance gradient caused by cusp points and sampling frequency. Furthermore, the effectiveness of the proposed method in terms of both expressiveness and registration performance is evaluated through experiments.

2 Related Work

2.1 Neural Fields

The traditional way of representing volumes is to discretize the density or distance from the surface at each position into voxels [5,8–10,14,15]. Since voxels require data complexity that is cubic in resolution, it is difficult to increase

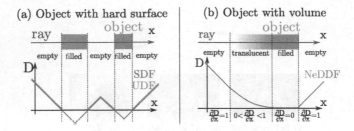

Fig. 3. (a) Signed Distance Field (SDF) and Unsigned Distance Field (UDF) distinguish the inside and outside of objects by the sign of the distance field ($D > 0$ or $D = 0$). In addition, UDF does not have a gradient inside the object, but can distinguish between inside and outside of objects by the magnitude of the gradient. (b) NeDDF assigns semitransparent density information to the distance gradient from 0 to 1.

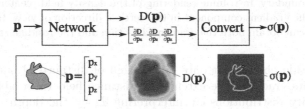

Fig. 4. Flow of proposed model: created network takes the position **p** as input and outputs the distance D and its gradient. Differentiable conversion formula for the network output gives the density of position $\sigma(\mathbf{p})$.

the spatial resolution. In recent years, memory-efficient representations such as octree [2,7] or hash table [16] have been proposed. However, these grid structures cannot represent the geometry information with higher frequencies than the Nyquist frequency. With advances in geometric deep learning following Atlas-Net [6] and Foldingnet [26], some studies have focused on handling irregular non-grid structures such as point clouds and meshes. While these methods can handle detailed geometry information efficiently, they are limited to interpolation due to their spatially discrete representations based on the coordinates of each point and vertex.

In recent years, the methods called neural fields [25] which directly represent continuous signals by embedding implicit surfaces with neural networks, has been attracting significant interest in the research community. Given sufficient parameters, fully connected neural networks can encode continuous signals over arbitrary dimensions. Since a neural field automatically adapts the expressiveness of the network to high frequency regions, it is possible to obtain a shape representation with high resolution using a significantly smaller number of parameters than conventional discrete representation based methods. Furthermore, since neural fields are continuous representation, we can expand the input and output dimensions without increasing the model capacity. It is also possible to model topological changes by considering the density field as a three-dimensional slice of high dimensional space and embed time-series information by adding a multi-dimensional deformation code to the input [20].

By using a smooth activation function in the neural networks, neural fields can be regarded as a continuously differentiable field. Modeling using gradient information has been proposed, such as divergence in Non-Rigid-NeRF [22] and elasticity constraints using the Jacobian matrix of the deformation field in Nerfies [19]. Inspired by the ideas behind these approaches, we have developed a model in which the gradient of the distance field describes the density information. The proposed model outputs a distance field and a density field that are explicitly consistent with each other. Since an optimization-based penalty term does not constrain the model, it can be optimized reciprocally from an objective function that is appropriate for each field.

2.2 Density Field

The density field outputs the volume density for the input of the 3D position. Many methods, such as NeRF, use the density field together with the color field, thus enabling volume rendering. The density field is characterized by high expressiveness. For example, a low value of the density field can describe a semi-transparent object such as glass or smoke to represent proportional light transmission. For spatially high-frequency shapes such as fur, for which the boundary surface is complex, the field can describe a scene by considering the light interaction at an arbitrary point as a function of density, ray direction, and color. In particular, combining this with the color field makes it possible to model specular reflections, including viewing angle dependency.

Although NeRF can describe complex scenes, it has a substantial limitation in that the camera pose should be known for the observed image and the scene should be static, making it challenging to capture a usable set of images with unknown camera poses. Therefore, many NeRF-based methods for estimation of camera pose and registration of object deformation have been proposed [12,29]. However, since blank areas with a density value of 0 have uncertain gradient directions, camera pose tracking is only valid with initial values such that most of the object area overlaps. NeRF−− [24] optimizes camera parameters directly with backpropagation but is limited to camera configurations close to the line of sight. NSFF [11] requires the optical flow to follow the deformation. D-NeRF is limited to CG images with no background and low-frequency texture. Nerfies [19] adds warmup to positional embedding and delays learning of high-frequency components to ensure registration but is limited to camera configurations with close view directions.

NeDDF provides a consistent distance field while retaining the expressiveness of the density field. By providing gradients where no objects are present, we can improve registration performance from a rough initial camera poses.

2.3 Distance Field

A distance field takes a 3D position as input and outputs the distance to the nearest neighbor boundary. SDF is widely used in fusion and registration because it can provide stable bounding surfaces and normal vectors. SDF also provides residuals and gradient directions, enabling fast-fitting of two shapes by the Gauss-Newton method without corresponding point matching [5,8–10,14,15]. A typical example is KinectFusion [15], which performs localization and shape integration from a depth map of unknown viewpoints for a static scene. DynamicFusion [14] constructs a sparse deformation field called WarpField to describe the deformation amount and performs registration for non-rigid scenes.

In addition, several studies have proposed methods by which to handle distance fields by neural fields. DeepSDF [18] proposes a generative model for the continuous SDFs based on the auto-decoder model. SAL [1] enables the neural field to learn the shapes of boundary surfaces directly from raw unsigned data such as point clouds. UDF [3] makes the unsigned distance field continuous and shows its suitability for unclosed surfaces and complex shapes. Since density fields such as NeRF are noisy in surface reconstruction by level sets, several methods have been proposed to handle distance fields in neural fields that can present boundary surfaces and assume a static density distribution for the signed distance. IDR [28] introduces differentiable surface rendering to learn the neural field from multi-view images. However, unlike volume rendering, calculating a single surface intersection for each ray makes shape reconstruction unstable for complex shapes that cause abrupt depth changes in the image. UNISURF [17] enables a combination of surface and volume rendering with a neural field that describes occupancy. Several studies attempt to optimize the SDF with differentiable volume rendering by modeling the transform equation from the distance to the density field with the hypothesis on the shape of the density distribution. VolSDF [27] interprets the volume density as Laplace's cumulative distribution function for SDF. NeuS [23] assumes a density distribution over the signed distance using the learnable variance values. However, these distance fields assume the existence of a boundary surface, which limits the kind of shape that can be represented. This study extends the distance field to correspond to various density distributions from depth values derived from volume rendering. The present extends the distance field to correspond to various density distributions from depth values derived from volume rendering.

3 Method

In this section, we consider reciprocally constrained distance and density fields. Section 3.1 redefines the distance field to interpret arbitrary density fields, including boundaryless scenes. Section 3.2 introduces a conversion formula to obtain the density of independent points from the distance and the gradient of the distance value in the redefined distance field.

3.1 Distance Field from Density Field

The distance field in boundary surfaces $D_b(\mathbf{p})$ describes the distance to the nearest surface for location $\mathbf{p} \in \mathbb{R}^3$. We can interpret $D_b(\mathbf{p})$ as the minimum of the depth value $d_b(\mathbf{p}, \mathbf{v})$ over the viewing direction $\mathbf{v} \in \mathcal{S}^2$ (see Fig. 5):

$$D_b(\mathbf{p}) := \min_{\mathbf{v} \in S^2}[d_b(\mathbf{p}, \mathbf{v})]. \tag{1}$$

We extend the distance field to be defined for arbitrary density distributions by replacing the depth value $d_b(\mathbf{p}, \mathbf{v})$ with the depth value derived from the volume rendering equation (see Fig. 6).

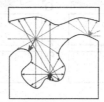

Fig. 5. The distance field uses depth for the nearest surface.

Assuming that the density distribution $\sigma(\mathbf{p})$ is known, we can calculate the depth value $d(\mathbf{p}, \mathbf{v})$ for a viewpoint position $\mathbf{p}$ and a viewing direction $\mathbf{v}$. Equation 2 is the volume rendering formula in NeRF [13]. For a point on the ray $\mathbf{r}(t) = \mathbf{p} + t\mathbf{v}$ with the visible range $[t_n, t_f]$, the color of each ray $\mathbf{C}(\mathbf{r})$ is obtained through the integral of each color $\mathbf{c}(\mathbf{r}(t), \mathbf{v})$ multiplied by transmission rate $T(t) = \exp\left(-\int_{t_n}^{t} \sigma(\mathbf{r}(s))ds\right)$:

$$C(\mathbf{r}) := \int_{t_n}^{t_f} T(t)\sigma(\mathbf{r}(t))\mathbf{c}(\mathbf{r}(t), \mathbf{v})dt. \tag{2}$$

Similarly, the depth $d(\mathbf{p}, \mathbf{v})$ is defined to be an integral of the depths at each point, as follows:

$$d(\mathbf{p}, \mathbf{v}) := t_n + \int_{t_n}^{t_f} tT(t)\sigma(\mathbf{r}(t))dt. \tag{3}$$

Here, $d(\mathbf{p})$ takes the same value for the depth value $d_b(\mathbf{p})$ in the presence of a boundary surface by taking the density $\sigma(\mathbf{p})$ to be 0 outside ($0 < t < d_b$) and ∞ inside ($d_b \leq t$).

In practice, calculating the depths over all directions is computationally expensive, so we use a distance field that removes the dependence on the viewing direction $\mathbf{v}$. We define the distance field $D(\mathbf{p}) := \min_{\mathbf{v} \in S^2}[d(\mathbf{p}, \mathbf{v})]$, for adopting the shortest depth for each position as in the bounding surface model. Assuming continuity in the adopted view direction $\mathbf{v}_n = \operatorname*{argmin}_{\mathbf{v} \in S^2}[d(\mathbf{p}, \mathbf{v})]$, we can restore this quantity from the tangent plane using the gradient of the distance field $\nabla D(\mathbf{p})$ as follows:

$$\mathbf{v}_n = \frac{-\nabla D(\mathbf{p})}{\|\nabla D(\mathbf{p})\|_2}, \tag{4}$$

$$\nabla D(\mathbf{p}) = \left[\frac{\partial D(\mathbf{p})}{\partial p_x} \frac{\partial D(\mathbf{p})}{\partial p_y} \frac{\partial D(\mathbf{p})}{\partial p_z}\right]. \tag{5}$$

In practice, $\mathbf{v}_n$ has discontinuities which makes this calculation difficult. In the next section, we will discuss some strategies to alleviate this.

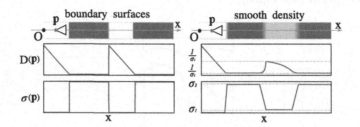

Fig. 6. Depth of volume rendering in case camera is on the x-axis. In a translucent region of density σ, the upper bound of the depth value becomes $1/\sigma$. When σ takes ∞ inside the object, the depth value takes 0, corresponding to the conventional hard surface model.

3.2 Density from Distance Field

In Sect. 3.1, we extended the distance field to shapes with no explicit boundary surface but with a known density field. In this section, we derive the corresponding density field when the distance field is known.

For the distance field around position $\mathbf{p}$, we consider $D(\mathbf{r}(t)), \mathbf{r}(t) = \mathbf{p} + t\mathbf{v}$, which is sliced in the gradient direction v. Calculating the derivative of the distance field in the direction of the gradient, $\frac{\partial D(\mathbf{r}(t))}{\partial t}$, we can derive an expression for σ as follows: (the derivation is given in supplementary material)

$$\frac{\partial D(\mathbf{r}(t))}{\partial t}\Big|_{t=0} = \lim_{\Delta t \to 0} \frac{d(\mathbf{r}(\Delta t), \mathbf{v}) - d(\mathbf{r}(0), \mathbf{v})}{\Delta t} \tag{6}$$

$$= -1 + (D(\mathbf{p}) - t_n)\sigma(\mathbf{p} + t_n\mathbf{v}). \tag{7}$$

We can also express $\frac{\partial D(\mathbf{r}(t))}{\partial t}$ using the gradient vector of the distance field $\nabla D(\mathbf{p})$ as follows:

$$\frac{\partial D(\mathbf{r}(t))}{\partial t} = \frac{\partial D}{\partial p_x}\frac{\partial p_x}{\partial t} + \frac{\partial D}{\partial p_y}\frac{\partial p_y}{\partial t} + \frac{\partial D}{\partial p_z}\frac{\partial p_z}{\partial t} \tag{8}$$

$$= \nabla D(\mathbf{p}) \cdot \mathbf{v} \tag{9}$$

$$= -\|\nabla D(\mathbf{p})\|_2. \tag{10}$$

From Eqs. 7 and 10, the density σ can be obtained as follows:

$$\sigma(\mathbf{p}) = \frac{1 - \|\nabla D(\mathbf{p} - t_n \mathbf{v})\|_2}{D(\mathbf{p} - t_n \mathbf{v}) - t_n}. \tag{11}$$

From Eq. 3, t_n is the interval in which the transmittance $T(t_n) = 1$, which is the lower limit of D. While it is natural for t_n to take the value 0, the density is undefined for $D \sim 0$ as a numerical problem. Assuming t_n is sufficiently small, by introducing the approximations in Eqs. 12, 13, σ can be calculated as in Eq. 14:

$$D(\mathbf{p} - t_n \mathbf{v}) \simeq D(\mathbf{p}) + t_n, \tag{12}$$

$$\nabla D(\mathbf{p} - t_n \mathbf{v}) \simeq \nabla D(\mathbf{p}), \tag{13}$$

$$\sigma(\mathbf{p}) \simeq \frac{1 - \|\nabla D(\mathbf{p})\|_2}{D(\mathbf{p})}. \tag{14}$$

The differentiability of the network allows us to determine the distance $D(\mathbf{p}_i)$ and gradient vector $\nabla D(\mathbf{p}_i)$ with independent sampling points $\mathbf{p}_i$ as input to the neural fields, such as regressing a distance field. Equation 14 allows us to compute the density $\sigma(\mathbf{p}_i)$ with a differentiable conversion formula. In other words, it is possible to learn mutually constrained distance and density fields. Note that from $t_n > 0$, the density is limited to $\sigma(\mathbf{p}) < \frac{1}{t_n}$.

3.3 Removing Cusps

The distance to density conversion by Eq. 14 assumed that the distance field is first-order differentiable. However, a distance field is not differentiable at the cusps where the minimum distance direction switches. In practice, although the distance field around the cups is smoothly connected due to the continuity of the neural field, small gradient values around the cups are still converted to false densities that should not exist by Eq. 14 (see Fig. 7). To alleviate this problem at the caps, we extend the domain of the distance field from a 3-dimensional space to a 4-dimensional hyperspace $[x, y, z, w]$ with an auxiliary gradient axis (w-axis) and consider the slice at $w = 0$ of the hyperspace to be the distance field. The gradient components $\frac{\partial D}{\partial w}$ are distributed so that the gradient ∇D satisfies the Eq. 14 in the vicinity of the cusp to suppress spurious densities.

When the auxiliary gradient also describes the density outside the cusp region, the shape of the global distance field is compromised. Therefore, we constrain the shape of the auxiliary gradient and use a penalty term to induce convergence to the optimal form. In this study, when $\frac{\partial D}{\partial t} > 0$, we use the following heuristic constraint:

$$\frac{\partial^2 D}{\partial t \partial w} = \alpha \frac{1}{D} \frac{\partial D}{\partial w}. \tag{15}$$

Note that α is a hyperparameter that determines the scale of the gradient. The shape of the auxiliary gradient for each α is shown in appendix. Since the Eq. 15

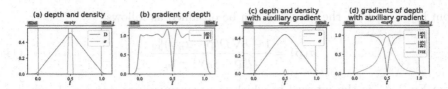

Fig. 7. A visualization of each field in the toy model with $0 \leq t \leq 1$ as object exterior.

is a constraint other than $\frac{\partial D}{\partial t} = 0$, and since it becomes unstable around $D = 0$ and $\frac{\partial D}{\partial w} = 0$, we introduce the following weight coefficient β:

$$\beta = D \left(\frac{\partial D}{\partial t} \right)^2 \frac{\partial D}{\partial w}. \tag{16}$$

Note that since β is a value for discriminating the target point, it is separated from the calculation graph during training like stop-gradient operator. For M sampling points $\mathcal{P}$, the objective function L_{const} for the shape constraint of the auxiliary gradient is set as:

$$L_{\text{const}} = \frac{\lambda_{\text{const}}}{M} \sum_{\mathbf{p} \in \mathcal{P}} \beta \left[\frac{\partial^2 D}{\partial t \partial w} - \frac{\alpha}{D(\mathbf{p})} \frac{\partial D}{\partial w} \right]^2. \tag{17}$$

Note that λ_{const} is a hyperparameter.

4   Reprojection Error for Volume Rendering

Previous NeRF-based localization such as iNeRF [29] uses photometric error, the residual $\|\mathbf{C}(\mathbf{q}) - \hat{\mathbf{C}}(\mathbf{q})\|_2$ from the observed color $\mathbf{C}(\mathbf{q})$, and the estimated color $\hat{\mathbf{C}}(\mathbf{q})$ aggregated by volume rendering for selected pixel $\mathbf{q}$. While photometric error can follow objects without hard surfaces, it can only follow local regions with smooth color changes. NeDDF provides the object's direction and approximate distance from a sampling point. Therefore, we can calculate the pseudo-correspondence point and estimate the camera pose using the reprojection error. This section describes a method that uses color information to calculate the correspondence points as a simple example.

When training the network, the objective function with volume rendering has no constraints about the color field in the blank region. We record the same color in the gradient direction of the distance field by penalizing the color change in the distance gradient direction for a blank region. For a point $\mathbf{p}_i$, camera depth t_i and a viewing direction $\mathbf{v}$, let the output be color $\mathbf{c}_i$, distance D_i, and distance gradient ∇D_i. The penalty takes $L_{\text{blank}} = \sum_i \|\nabla \mathbf{c}_i (\nabla D_i)^T\|_2$. Since $\|\nabla D_i\|_2$ takes small values inside the object, this penalty becomes active for regions outside the object. Training the network by introducing this penalty

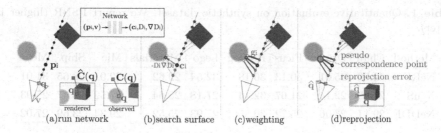

Fig. 8. Localization by reprojection error: (a) Network execution outputs the color and distance of each sampling point. Network provides the color c_i, distance D_i and its gradient ∇D_i for the sampling point p_i. (b) Network output gives the points near the surface. (c) Weight g_i takes the value that emphasizes sampling points with similar colors or smaller distances. (d) Pseudo-correspondence points synthesized from the weights produce the reprojection error.

makes it possible to obtain the nearest neighbor object's color, direction, and distance from sampling points outside the object.

In estimating camera poses, finding the pseudo-correspondence points for each ray provides the calculation of the reprojection error, as shown in the Fig. 8. The network output for sampling point p_i leads to the near-surface point of color c_i at position $p_i - D_i(\nabla D_i)$. We calculate the pseudo-correspondence points for each ray by selecting points closer to $C(q)$ than $\hat{C}(q)$ with combining near-surface points by focusing weights closer to the color and the distance between them. The weight g_i of sampling point p_i is calculated as follows:

$$g_i = \text{softmax}(-\lambda_D \frac{D_i\|\nabla D_i \times v\|_2}{t_i} - \lambda_c\|C(q) - c_i\|_2). \tag{18}$$

Note that λ_D and λ_c are hyperparameters, softmax aggregates for axis with index i. The reprojection error measures the distance $\|q - \hat{q}\|_2$ between the pixel coordinates of the ray q and the projected pseudo-correspondence point $\hat{q}$.

5   Experiments

5.1   Experimental Setup

(a) Quality of Novel View Synthesis. We confirm that NeDDF retains the comparable quality of novel view synthesis as NeRF. We use the NeRF synthetic dataset which contains CG images of the eight scenes rendered from camera positions placed on a hemispherical surface. Using NeRF and NeuS as baselines, we compare the quality of the new viewpoint images using PSNR.

(b) Accuracy of Localization. In NeDDF, the pseudo correspondence points enable estimation of camera pose using reprojection error. We confirm that the use of reprojection error improves the accuracy of localization from only using

Table 1. Quantitative evaluation on synthetic dataset. We report PSNR (higher is better).

Method	Chair	Drums	Ficus	Hotdog	Lego	Materials	Mic	Ship	Mean
NeRF	33.00	25.01	30.13	36.18	32.54	29.62	32.91	28.65	31.01
NeuS	27.69	22.14	21.67	32.14	27.18	25.64	27.52	23.47	25.93
NeDDF	29.11	23.96	25.72	30.85	27.93	25.52	29.34	23.69	27.02

photometric error under poor initial camera poses. The experiment uses 200 test viewpoints of the Lego scene in the NeRF synthetic Dataset. Each camera takes the initial pose given by random rotations and translations applied to the ground truth values of the test viewpoint. We evaluate the camera position and angle errors for three cases: optimizing the camera pose for 300 iterations by photometric error, 300 iterations by reprojection error, and 100 iterations by reprojection error plus 200 iterations by photometric error. The localization flows follow similar practices to iNeRF. The optimization uses the gradient of the camera pose as a 6D parameter of SE(3) and sets the increment by Adam [4] with exponential decay. In each iterations, interest region sampling [29] selects 256 rays for optimization.

5.2 Results

(a) **Quality of Novel View Synthesis.** Table 1 shows the PSNR for each scene and each method for evaluating the quality of the generated images The NeDDF results retain the comparable quality of the state-of-the-art methods in novel view synthesis, although the PSNR comparison is slightly inferior. Figure 9 shows visualizations of Drums and Ficus as examples of scenes with transparency and delicate shapes, where conventional distance-field-based methods are weak. For the Drum scene, NeuS could not represent the transparent parts of the drums and colored the transparent surfaces. In contrast, NeDDF reproduces the transparent parts and obtains the metal parts on the back through. The NeuS results show blurred images for the Ficus scene since it fails to assign the appropriate density distributions due to the difficulty of understanding the model for thin surfaces such as leaves. NeDDF provides comparatively high-quality image restoration even for delicate shapes such as leaves. NeDDF allows for the reconstruction of thinner surfaces than the sampling interval by interpreting their occupancy as a lower density.

(b) **Accuracy of Localization.** Figure 10 shows a plot of the camera attitude estimation results. Optimization by photometric error works very accurately when the initial value of the position error is approximately 0.5 [m] or less, and the initial value of the angular error is 10 [deg] or less, while the error increases when the initial value of the error is significant. Since photometric error only provides reasonable gradient directions in smooth color changing,

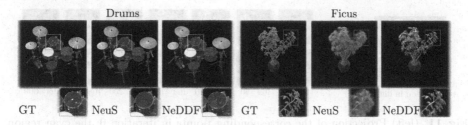

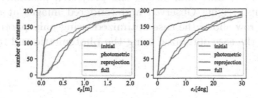

Fig. 9. Comparisons on test-set views for scenes from NeRF synthetic dataset generated with a volume renderer.

Fig. 10. Quantitative evaluation of camera poses estimation accuracy. The horizontal axis represents the position and angle error, and the vertical axis represents the number of cameras recovered under the errors.

significant initial value errors may lead to erroneous local solutions. Optimization by reprojection error does not improve camera posture residuals much on its own. This is because the correspondence point calculation based on color similarity lacks uniqueness, which leads to many mismatches in the correspondence points. On the other hand, optimization by reprojection error can roughly estimate the camera pose such that regions with close colors overlap. Using this as a preprocessing step for optimization by photometric error can significantly expand the range of initial values for highly accurate estimation.

Figure 11 shows the localization process with large initial value errors. The left figure shows the projected positions of the sampling points and the calculated correspondence points at iter=0. The figure shows that even when the sampling points are far from the object, as in the lower-left region, we can obtain the corresponding points in the object region. On the other hand, in the upper left area of the bucket, the model selects the wrong correspondence points. We can reduce the impact of such rays by reducing the weights or calculating the corresponding points using features with higher uniqueness instead of color. The figure on the right shows the overlaid rendered and observed images at each optimization iteration. The overlapped object area between the rendered and observed images is small for iter=0. Optimization using only photometric error gives little progress since it cannot provide a reasonable gradient. Rough alignment using the reprojection error by the 100th iteration enables the use of photometric error with an effective gradient, which provides highly accurate localization.

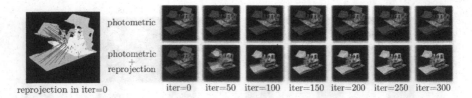

Fig. 11. (left) Projection of the corresponding points in iteration 0. the cyan region is the rendered object region of the observed image, and the yellow region is the rendered object region estimated from the current camera attitude. The red dots denote sampling points, and the blue dots denote the projected positions of the calculated correspondence points. (right) Observed and rendered images at each optimization iteration: the upper row shows the case optimized using only photometric error, and the lower row shows the case optimized using the photometric and reprojection errors. (Color figure online)

6   Conclusions

This study proposed NeDDF to represent reciprocally constrained distance and density fields. We extended the distance field to a formulation that can adapt to any density field. We also derived the conversion formula between distance and density using the distance and its gradient, enabling learning the these fields while constraining each other. We also alleviate the problem of discontinuity points by introducing the auxiliary gradient. The visualization experiments demonstrated that NeDDF could acquire the properties of both the conventional density field and the distance field. The quantitative evaluation showed that NeDDF could provide competitive quality of novel view synthesis, more stable meshes, and a more comprehensive range of following camera poses than NeRF.

One limitation of our method is the lack of information about the distance field inside the objects. Since NeDDF is based on UDF, it cannot provide helpful gradient directions in the interior object region. NeDDF also has the same limitations as the original NeRF [13], such as time-consuming optimization and rendering. However, since NeDDF provides a differentiable density field and retains the same formulation as NeRF, many of the latest advances in improving NeRF, such as speedup and stabilization, may apply to NeDDF. In addition, we calculated the pseudo correspondence points from the colors in the localization as a simple example of obtaining the reprojection error. We believe that using information with higher uniqueness, such as semantic segmentation, will increase the usefulness of the reprojection error.

Acknowledgments. This work was supported by JSPS KAKENHI Grant Number JP19H00806, JP21KK0070 and JP22H01580. We would like to thank Mr. Towaki Takikawa, Mr. Naoya Chiba, and Mr. Ryota Suzuki for their helpful discussions.

References

1. Atzmon, M., Lipman, Y.: Sal: sign agnostic learning of shapes from raw data. In: Proceedings of the IEEE Conference on Computer Vision and Pattern Recognition (CVPR), pp. 2565–2574 (2020)
2. Chen, H.H., Huang, T.S.: A survey of construction and manipulation of octrees. Comput. Vis. Graph. Image Process. **43**(3), 409–431 (1988)
3. Chibane, J., Mir, A., Pons-Moll, G.: Neural unsigned distance fields for implicit function learning. In: Advances in Neural Information Processing Systems (NeurIPS), pp. 21638–21652 (2020)
4. Diederik P. Kingma, J.B.: Adam: a method for stochastic optimization. In: International Conference on Learning Representations (2015)
5. Ge, L., Liang, H., Yuan, J., Thalmann, D.: 3d convolutional neural networks for efficient and robust hand pose estimation from single depth images. In: Proceedings of the IEEE Conference on Computer Vision and Pattern Recognition (CVPR), pp. 1991–2000 (2017)
6. Groueix, T., Fisher, M., Kim, V.G., Russell, B., Aubry, M.: AtlasNet: a papier-Mâché Approach to Learning 3D Surface Generation. In: Proceedings of the IEEE Conference on Computer Vision and Pattern Recognition (CVPR), pp. 216–224 (2018)
7. Laine, S., Karras, T.: Efficient sparse voxel octrees. IEEE Trans. Vis. Comput. Graph. **17**(8), 1048–1059 (2010)
8. Lee, J.H., Ha, H., Dong, Y., Tong, X., Kim, M.H.: TextureFusion: high-quality texture acquisition for real-time RGB-D scanning. In: Proceedings of the IEEE Conference on Computer Vision and Pattern Recognition (CVPR), pp. 1272–1280 (2020)
9. Li, Y., Bozic, A., Zhang, T., Ji, Y., Harada, T., Nießner, M.: Learning to optimize non-rigid tracking. In: Proceedings of the IEEE Conference on Computer Vision and Pattern Recognition (CVPR), pp. 4910–4918 (2020)
10. Li, Y., Zhang, T., Nakamura, Y., Harada, T.: Splitfusion: simultaneous tracking and mapping for non-rigid scenes. In: IROS, pp. 5128–5134 (2020)
11. Li, Z., Niklaus, S., Snavely, N., Wang, O.: Neural scene flow fields for space-time view synthesis of dynamic scenes. In: Proceedings of the IEEE Conference on Computer Vision and Pattern Recognition (CVPR). pp. 6498–6508 (2021)
12. Lin, C.H., Ma, W.C., Torralba, A., Lucey, S.: Barf: bundle-adjusting neural radiance fields. In: Proceedings of the IEEE International Conference on Computer Vision (ICCV), pp. 5741–5751 (2021)
13. Mildenhall, B., Srinivasan, P.P., Tancik, M., Barron, J.T., Ramamoorthi, R., Ng, R.: Nerf: representing scenes as neural radiance fields for view synthesis. In: Proceedings of the European Conference on Computer Vision (ECCV), pp. 405–421 (2020)
14. Newcombe, R.A., Fox, D., Seitz, S.M.: DynamicFusion: reconstruction and tracking of non-rigid scenes in real-time. In: Proceedings of the IEEE Conference on Computer Vision and Pattern Recognition (CVPR), pp. 343–352 (2015)
15. Newcombe, R.A., et al.: KinectFusion: real-time dense surface mapping and tracking. In: 10th IEEE International Symposium on Mixed and Augmented Reality (ISMAR), pp. 127–136 (2011)
16. Nießner, M., Zollhöfer, M., Izadi, S., Stamminger, M.: Real-time 3d reconstruction at scale using voxel hashing. ACM Trans. Graph. (ToG) **32**(6), 1–11 (2013)

17. Oechsle, M., Peng, S., Geiger, A.: UNISURF: unifying neural implicit surfaces and radiance fields for multi-view reconstruction. In: Proceedings of the IEEE International Conference on Computer Vision (ICCV), pp. 5589–5599 (2021)
18. Park, J.J., Florence, P., Straub, J., Newcombe, R., Lovegrove, S.: DeepSDF: learning continuous signed distance functions for shape representation. In: Proceedings of the IEEE Conference on Computer Vision and Pattern Recognition (CVPR), pp. 165–174 (2019)
19. Park, K., et al.: Nerfies: deformable neural radiance fields. In: Proceedings of the IEEE International Conference on Computer Vision (ICCV), pp. 5865–5874 (2021)
20. Park, K., et al.: HyperNeRF: a higher-dimensional representation for topologically varying neural radiance fields. ACM Trans. Graph. (ToG) **40**(6), 1–12 (2021)
21. Pumarola, A., Corona, E., Pons-Moll, G., Moreno-Noguer, F.: D-nerf: neural radiance fields for dynamic scenes. In: Proceedings of the IEEE Conference on Computer Vision and Pattern Recognition (CVPR), pp. 10318–10327 (2021)
22. Tretschk, E., Tewari, A., Golyanik, V., Zollhöfer, M., Lassner, C., Theobalt, C.: Non-rigid neural radiance fields: reconstruction and novel view synthesis of a dynamic scene from monocular video. In: Proceedings of the IEEE International Conference on Computer Vision (ICCV), pp. 12959–12970 (2021)
23. Wang, P., Liu, L., Liu, Y., Theobalt, C., Komura, T., Wang, W.: NeuS: learning neural implicit surfaces by volume rendering for multi-view reconstruction. In: Advances in Neural Information Processing Systems (NeurIPS) (2021)
24. Wang, Z., Wu, S., Xie, W., Chen, M., Prisacariu, V.A.: NeRF−−: neural radiance fields without known camera parameters. arXiv preprint arXiv: 2102.07064 (2021)
25. Xie, Y., et al.: Neural fields in visual computing and beyond. arXiv preprint arXiv: 2111.11426 (2021)
26. Yang, Y., Feng, C., Shen, Y., Tian, D.: FoldingNet: point cloud auto-encoder via deep grid deformation. In: Proceedings of the IEEE Conference on Computer Vision and Pattern Recognition (CVPR), pp. 206–215 (2018)
27. Yariv, L., Gu, J., Kasten, Y., Lipman, Y.: Volume rendering of neural implicit surfaces. In: Advances in Neural Information Processing Systems (NeurIPS) (2021)
28. Yariv, L., et al.: Multiview neural surface reconstruction by disentangling geometry and appearance. In: Advances in Neural Information Processing Systems (NeurIPS), vol. 33 (2020)
29. Yen-Chen, L., Florence, P., Barron, J.T., Rodriguez, A., Isola, P., Lin, T.Y.: iNeRF: inverting neural radiance fields for pose estimation. In: Proceedings of the IEEE/RSJ Conference on Intelligent Robots and Systems (IROS), pp. 1323–1330 (2021)

NeXT: Towards High Quality Neural Radiance Fields via Multi-skip Transformer

Yunxiao Wang[1], Yanjie Li[1], Peidong Liu[1], Tao Dai[2(✉)], and Shu-Tao Xia[1,3]

[1] Tsinghua Shenzhen International Graduate School, Tsinghua University, Beijing, China
{wang-yx20,lyj20,lpd19}@mails.tsinghua.edu.cn
[2] College of Computer Science and Software Engineering, Shenzhen University, Shenzhen, China
daitao.edu@gmail.com
[3] Research Center of Artificial Intelligence, Peng Cheng Laboratory, Shenzhen, China
xiast@sz.tsinghua.edu.cn

Abstract. Neural Radiance Fields (NeRF) methods show impressive performance for novel view synthesis by representing a scene via a neural network. However, most existing NeRF based methods, including its variants, treat each sample point individually as input, while ignoring the inherent relationships between adjacent sample points from the corresponding rays, thus hindering the reconstruction performance. To address this issue, we explore a brand new scheme, namely *NeXT*, introducing a multi-skip transformer to capture the rich relationships between various sample points in a ray-level query. Specifically, ray tokenization is proposed to represent each ray as a sequence of point embeddings which is taken as input of our proposed NeXT. In this way, relationships between sample points are captured via the built-in self-attention mechanism to promote the reconstruction. Besides, our proposed NeXT can be easily combined with other NeRF based methods to improve their rendering quality. Extensive experiments conducted on three datasets demonstrate that NeXT significantly outperforms all previous state-of-the-art work by a large margin. In particular, the proposed NeXT surpasses the strong NeRF baseline by **2.74** dB of PSNR on Blender dataset. The code is available at https://github.com/Crishawy/NeXT.

Keywords: View synthesis · Neural representation · Scene representation · 3D deep learning

1 Introduction

Novel View Synthesis (NVS) aims to render a scene from unobserved viewpoints with a set of images and camera poses as input. Recently, Neural Radiance

---

Y Wang and Y Li—Equal contribution.

Supplementary Information The online version contains supplementary material available at https://doi.org/10.1007/978-3-031-19824-3_5.

S. Avidan et al. (Eds.): ECCV 2022, LNCS 13692, pp. 69–86, 2022.
https://doi.org/10.1007/978-3-031-19824-3_5

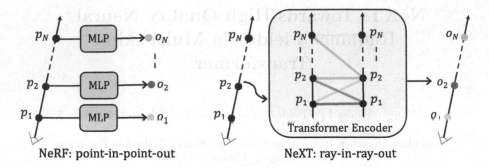

Fig. 1. NeRF (left) renders scenes by individually point-level query of a MLP, *i.e.*, one point in and one point out, which ignores the relations between sample points. NeXT (right) regards the entire ray as network input to make ray-level query, *i.e.*, one ray in and one ray out, to capture the intrinsic dependencies between sample points via self-attention mechanism built-in Transformer encoder.

Field (NeRF) [31] and its variants have demonstrated compelling performance in this task by representing a scene's geometry and appearance with a Multi-Layer Perceptron (MLP). To render each pixel in an output image, NeRF adopts volume rendering to combine the RGB colors and volume densities from many points sampled along the corresponding 3D ray.

Despite the success of NeRF based methods in novel view synthesis, most existing methods adopt MLP as the function approximator to render scenes in a point-level way. As shown in Fig. 1 (left), NeRF queries the MLP network with one sample point from the corresponding 3D ray. However, such point-level query ignores the *inherent relations* in sample points from the same rays, which deeply imprisons the potential of NeRF.

To exploit such relations among sample points, we attempt to explore a transformer-based paradigm, named NeXT, to achieve ray-level query. The proposed NeXT regards an individual ray, *i.e.*, the whole sampled points set, as the network input, as shown in Fig. 1 (right). In this way, the intrinsic relations between sampled points are captured by self-attention mechanism built in transformer, which help enrich the scene properties information for rendering. To further improve the performance, we propose a multi-skip connection module to better utilize the position information of the sampled points. The network architecture of our proposed NeXT is illustrated in Fig. 2.

In contrast to the previous NeRF-based methods, the proposed NeXT has several benefits for novel view synthesis. **First**, our method renders pixels in a ray-level way to exploit the relations among sample points. **Second**, benefiting from the ray-level query and the captured relationships between sample points, our approach shows much less dependence on the two-stage coarse-to-fine sampling. Even with only one-stage coarse sampling, our approach achieves competitive results compared to the two-stage NeRF. **Third**, the proposed NeXT significantly benefits from scaling up the model capacity, which may provide a promising path towards high quality view synthesis.

The main contributions can be summarized as follows:

- We propose a novel transformer-based paradigm, called NeXT, to realize ray-level query for novel view synthesis. Benefiting from that, inherent relations between sample points along a ray are captured to promote reconstruction.
- We propose a multi-skip connection module to improve the model performance, which enriches the original positional information from sample points.
- Comprehensive experiments conducted over Blender [31], DeepVoxels [46], and multiscale Blender [2] demonstrate that our proposed NeXT outperforms all previous state-of-the-art methods by a large margin.

2   Related Work

Scene Representations for View Synthesis The view synthesis task aims to represent a scene using a set of observed images and camera poses for rendering novel photorealistic images from unobserved viewpoints. With densely captured images, methods based on light field interpolation [11,20,24] tackle this task without reconstructing an intermediate representation of the scene. By contrast, when images of the scene are sparsely-captured, explicit representations of the scene's 3D geometry and appearance usually tend to be reconstructed. A line of popular view synthesis methods use mesh-based representations along with either diffuse [56] or view-dependent appearance [6,12,59], consisting of classical [6,12,56] and learning-based [42,43] ones. Mesh-based methods demonstrate advantage in storage and compatibility with graphics rendering pipelines. Nevertheless, gradient-based mesh representation methods are typically hard due to local minima or the poor conditioning of loss landscape.

Another line of methods consider volumetric representations for view synthesis. In the early stage, volumetric methods directly color voxel grids given some observed images [45]. More recent approaches tend to train deep neural networks for the purpose of predicting voxel representations of scenes [16,29,30,46,49,67]. Different from mesh-based methods, adopting gradient-based learning to optimize volumetric approaches is natural and well-suited. In addition, volumetric approaches can realistically represent complex shapes and materials, yield less artifacts, thus become increasing popular. While discrete voxel-based methods have demonstrate impressive performance for novel view synthesis, they are typically restricted at higher resolutions.

A promising trend is to adopt neural function representations to alleviate the limitation of discrete voxel grids [31,34,47,62]. Among those, volumetric NeRF [31] representation has recently raised dramatically increasing attention, which uses a continuous function parameterized by MLP to map 3D coordinates and viewing directions to volumetric densities and color values. NeRF has inspired various subsequent extensions under varying settings, including dynamic scenes [26,35,37], limited training views [18,22,38,41,51,54,57,64], generative modeling [8,33,44], non-rigidly deforming objects [17,36], speed-up [19,21,27,28,32,39,40,63] and reflectance modeling for relighting [3,4,48].

Despite the success of NeRF and its follow-ups, little attention has been paid to exploit the relations between sample points along rays. NeRF renders a scene by point-level query, which lacks of consideration about the inherent relationships thus leads to suboptimal results. NeXT addresses this issue, enabling ray-level query and points relationships modeling by introducing a novel multi-skip Transformer-based paradigm for novel view synthesis.

Transformers. Transformers [55] were first proposed for machine translation, and have since revolutionized many natural language processing tasks [10,14,55]. Very recently, Transformer-based methods make impressive strides in computer vision tasks [7,9,15,25,50,53,60,61,65,66,68], including image classification [15, 53,65], semantic segmentation [50,60] and object detection [7,9,68].

As far as we know, Transformer in NeRF is explored in NeRF-ID [1] and IBRNet [57]. NeRF-ID aims to learn to propose samples via a differentiable module (e.g., Transformer, Pool, MLPMix [52]), while still remains point-level query. IBRNet [57] focuses on learning a generic view interpolation function that generalizes to novel scenes, where a CNN is critical and color prediction follows point-level query. By contrast, NeXT is a pure Transformer-based paradigm to predict both color and density via ray-level query, proposing multi-skip connection to enrich position information for high quality renderings.

3 Method

Our proposed method is built upon NeRF [13,31], and can be easily expanded to other follow-ups. In this section, we first revisit the original design of NeRF, and then describe the details of proposed NeXT.

3.1 Background

NeRF [31] represents a scene by an Multilayer Perceptron (MLP), which takes as input a 3D position $\mathbf{x}$ and viewing direction $\mathbf{d}$ and output the corresponding color $\mathbf{c}$ and density σ. To promote the learning of high-frequency details, $\mathbf{x}$ and $\mathbf{d}$ are transformed via a positional encoding γ as the pre-processing.

In NeRF, a pixel is rendered by querying an MLP of n sample points $\mathbf{x}_1, ..., \mathbf{x}_n$ along a ray which connects the camera center with the target pixel. The query process is operated point by point. After that, a set of color values $\mathbf{c}_i$ and density values σ_i is obtained. The final pixel color $\hat{\mathbf{c}}$ can be calculated by:

$$\hat{\mathbf{c}} = \sum_{i=1}^{n} T_i(1 - \exp(-\sigma_i \delta_i))\mathbf{c}_i, \text{ where } T_i = \exp(-\sum_{j=1}^{i-1} \sigma_j \delta_j), \qquad (1)$$

where $\delta_i = ||\mathbf{x}_{i+1} - \mathbf{x}_i||$ is the distance between adjacent samples and T_i represents the transmittance along the ray.

To improve the sampling efficiency, NeRF propose a coarse-to-fine strategy. In the coarse stage, NeRF obtains N_c evenly-spaced random points with stratified

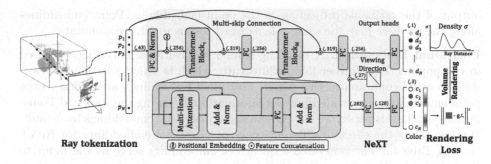

Fig. 2. Overall framework of the proposed NeXT, which consists of three components, *i.e.*, Transformer blocks, multi-skip connection module and output heads for generating density σ and color RGB **c**. First, NeXT uses *ray tokenization* to generate a set of point embeddings from N sample points along the ray. The obtained embeddings are then fed into the subsequent M *Transformer blocks* to learn relationships between points via self-attention. Note that the *multi-skip connection* is adopted to enrich the original positional information after each Transformer block. Finally, the N output point representations are utilized to yield the scene properties by *output heads* and L_2 reconstruction loss between groundtruth and rendered pixels is adopted for network training.

sampling. Given the output of "coarse" network, a piece-constant PDF along the ray is then produced to describe the distribution of the visible scene content. In the fine stage, N_f new points are then obtained based on the PDF using inverse transform sampling. Consequently, the resulting union of these $N_c + N_f$ sample points are sorted and passed to the "fine" network to yield final rendered pixel color. This hierarchical sampling allocates more samples to informative regions.

To render an image with $W \times H$ pixels, the MLP in NeRF is queried $W \times H \times n$ times. The network parameters are optimized by minimizing an L_2 reconstruction loss between the ground-truth and corresponding rendered pixels. For more details, readers may refer to the original NeRF paper [31].

3.2 NeXT

Different from NeRF [31], NeXT aims to capture the inherent relationships between sample points along the same ray and provides a ray-level query paradigm, which is accomplished by the proposed multi-skip Transformer-based network. An overview of our method is shown in Fig. 2.

Ray Tokenization. To achieve ray-level query, we first expand the vanilla Transformer to serve as the function approximator instead of MLP used in NeRF. To handle a ray, N points are sampled, resulting in an input sequence length of N for the Transformer. The 3D position information of these points are transformed to a higher dimension space using high frequency functions in [31], and then mapped to D dimensions with a learnable linear projection. In addition, D is also the latent vector sizer of Transformer layer. In this paper, we refer the output of this trainable projection as the point embeddings. Point embeddings along the ray here play the same role as word tokens in NLP community.

Positional Embedding. A mapping similar to positional encoding γ is used in the popular Transformer [55] architecture, which is called *positional embedding* to avoid confusion in this paper. Positional embeddings are added to the point embeddings to provide the order information, following the standard Transformer [55]. In this paper, we use 1D sinusoidal positional embeddings by default. We also study the effect of different types of positional embeddings for NeXT later in Table 4a. The generated sequence of embeddings serve as the input to the subsequent Transformer encoder.

Query Network. To achieve ray-level rendering, NeXT adopts the Transformer encoder as the query network to represent a scene. Specifically, the encoder learns point feature representation by stacking M blocks, given the 1D point token embeddings sequence as input. Each Transformer block consists of a multi-head self-attention (MSA) module and a multilayer perception (MLP) module. Self-attention is the core mechanism of Transformer and adopted in this work for capturing relationships between sample points along the same ray.

Local-Window Self-attention. To alleviate the computation cost of self-attention, we divide the point embeddings $\mathbf{X} \in \mathbb{R}^{N \times D}$ into a set of non-overlapping small windows: $\mathbf{X} \rightarrow \{\mathbf{X}_1, \mathbf{X}_2, ..., \mathbf{X}_W\}$. Each window covers L points in order. Then the multi-head self-attention is performed within each window independently. The multi-head self-attention within the i-th window is calculated as:

$$\text{MSA}(\mathbf{X}_i) = \text{SA}(\mathbf{X}_i)_1 \oplus \text{SA}(\mathbf{X}_i)_2 \oplus ... \oplus \text{SA}(\mathbf{X}_i)_H, \tag{2}$$

$$\text{SA}(\mathbf{X}_i)_h = \text{Softmax}[\frac{(\mathbf{X}_i \mathbf{W}_q^h)(\mathbf{X}_i \mathbf{W}_k^h)^\text{T}}{\sqrt{D/H}}]\mathbf{X}_i \mathbf{W}_v^h, \tag{3}$$

where $\mathbf{W}_q^h \in \mathbb{R}^{\frac{D}{H} \times D}$, $\mathbf{W}_k^h \in \mathbb{R}^{\frac{D}{H} \times D}$, $\mathbf{W}_v^h \in \mathbb{R}^{\frac{D}{H} \times D}$ for $h \in \{1, ..., H\}$ are learnable parameters of three linear projection layers. H represents the number of heads and $\oplus$ means concatenation. Compared to global self-attention, local-window reduces the computational complexity from $O(N^2)$ to $O(LN)$, which is of linear complexity with the number of sample points.

Multi-skip Connection. Vanilla Transformer performs unsatisfactorily for rendering. Inspired by NeRF, we propose a multi-skip connection module to strengthen the utilization of position information from the sample points, which is shown in Fig. 2. Consequently, the input of j-th Transformer Block is obtained by:

$$\mathbf{X}_{in}^j = \text{FC}(\mathbf{X}_{out}^{j-1} \oplus \gamma(\mathbf{X}^0)), \text{ where } j = 2, ..., M, \tag{4}$$

where $\mathbf{X}_{out}^{j-1}$ is the output of $(j-1)$-th block, FC means a fully-connected layer to map the input to D dimensions, $\mathbf{X}^0$ is the original 3D positions of sample points, γ is the positional encoding pre-processing.

Output Heads. The output of the Transformer encoder serves as feature representations to yield the final network output, *i.e.*, the scene properties of samples. To output the density σ and RGB color $\mathbf{c}$, a single linear layer and a two-layers MLP are attached as heads, respectively. It's worth noting that the color head takes as input both of feature representations and the viewing direction vectors.

Architecture Variants. We introduce our small model with parameters similar to NeRF, denoted as NeXT-S. To achieve high quality rendering results, we further scale up the model and build NeXT-B and NeXT-L, which are variants of about 1.7× and 3.3× model size, respectively. Note that the number of heads is $H = 8$ by default. The architecture hyper-parameters of these three variants are: $D = 192, 256, 256$, $M = 2, 2, 4$ for NeXT-S, NeXT-B and NeXT-L, respectively.

Compared to the MLP in NeRF, the Transformer in NeXT is only queried $W \times H$ times to render an image with $W \times H$ pixels. And L_2 reconstruction loss is also adopted for network training, following NeRF [31].

3.3   Integration with NeRF Methods

The proposed NeXT serves as the function approximator to achieve ray-level query and relationships modeling for novel view synthesis task, which can be regarded as a substitute of MLP used by NeRF and most follow-ups. Given its simplicity and effectiveness, it's easy and convenient to improve various existing NeRF methods by our proposed NeXT. In this paper, the original NeRF and the previous state-of-the-art Mip-NeRF [2] are chosen as the examples to show the superiority of proposed NeXT.

4   Experiment

Note that the proposed NeXT can be easily incorporated into various NeRF methods to serve as the query network, achieving higher quality rendering results. In this section, we show the examples of integrating NeXT with the original NeRF on Blender as well as DeepVoxels dataset, and Mip-NeRF on multiscale Blender dataset, respectively. The key lies in replacing their query strategy by our proposed NeXT. Our implementation is built based on JAX [5].

4.1   Setup

To verify the effectiveness of proposed method, comprehensive experiments are conducted on three popular datasets, *i.e.*, Blender [31], DeepVoxels [46] and multiscale Blender dataset [2]. We report the average peak signal-to-noise ratio (PSNR) and structural similarity (SSIM) [58] metric, which is widely used by NeRF-based methods [1,2,31,40]. Following NeRF [31] and Mip-NeRF [2], our method is trained with batch size 4096 for 1 million iterations. The Adam [23] optimizer with cosine learning rate decay from 5×10^{-4} to 5×10^{-6} is used for optimization. We set $N_c = 128$ and $N_f = 128$ for coarse and fine stage,

Table 1. PSNR comparisons on Blender dataset. "*" means adopting center pixel [2] which generates rays through the center of each pixel. NeXT variants surpass previous state-of-the-art methods.

	#Params	Chair	Drums	Ficus	Hotdog	Lego	Materials	Mic	Ship	Avg.
SRN [47]	-	26.96	17.18	20.73	26.81	20.85	18.09	26.85	20.60	22.26
NV [29]	-	28.33	22.58	24.79	30.71	26.08	24.22	27.78	23.93	26.05
LLFF [30]	-	28.72	21.13	21.79	31.41	24.54	20.72	27.48	23.22	24.88
NSVF [28]	3.2M-16M	33.19	25.18	31.23	37.14	32.29	32.68	34.27	27.93	31.74
NeRF [31]	1,191K	33.00	25.01	30.13	36.18	32.54	29.62	32.91	28.65	31.01
NeRF (JAX) [13]	1,191K	34.06	25.13	30.48	36.87	33.33	29.94	34.66	28.77	31.66
Vanilla Trans	1,889K	33.59	24.97	30.31	36.25	33.38	31.92	33.13	27.99	31.44
NeXT-S	1,232K	33.75	25.34	32.62	37.42	34.52	32.09	33.74	29.25	32.34
NeXT-B	2,152K	34.70	25.79	33.77	38.10	35.67	32.48	34.46	30.07	33.13
NeXT-L	4,062K	36.05	26.32	35.30	38.27	36.78	34.06	35.19	30.35	34.04
NeXT-L*	4,062K	**36.37**	**26.49**	**35.67**	**38.46**	**37.39**	**34.16**	**35.96**	**30.73**	**34.40**

Table 2. Comparisons on DeepVoxels dataset. "*" means adopting center pixel [2]. "NA" represents that the results fail to converge after repeating experiments over five times. By contrast, NeXT converges stably and quantitatively outperforms previous state-of-the-art methods over all scenes by a large margin.

	Chair PSNR/SSIM	Pedestal PSNR/SSIM	Cube PSNR/SSIM	Vase PSNR/SSIM	Avg. PSNR/SSIM
DeepVoxels [46]	33.45/0.99	32.35/0.97	28.42/0.97	27.99/0.96	30.55/0.97
SRN [47]	36.67/0.982	35.91/0.957	28.74/0.944	31.46/0.969	33.20/0.963
NV [29]	35.15/0.980	36.47/0.963	26.48/0.916	20.39/0.857	29.62/0.929
LLFF [30]	36.11/0.992	35.87/0.983	32.58/0.983	32.97/0.983	34.38/0.985
NeRF [31]	42.65/0.991	41.44/0.986	39.19/0.996	37.32/0.992	40.15/0.991
NeRF (JAX) [13]	44.97/0.994	43.74/0.992	42.43/0.998	NA/NA	NA/NA
NeXT-S	47.53/0.995	45.57/0.994	47.98/0.999	42.72/0.997	45.95/0.996
NeXT-B	48.20/0.996	47.04/0.995	48.44/0.999	44.61/0.998	47.07/0.997
NeXT-L	48.73/0.997	48.81/0.997	49.23/0.999	44.98/0.998	47.94/0.998
NeXT-L*	**50.43/0.998**	**50.60/0.998**	**51.55/0.999**	**46.36/0.999**	**49.74/0.999**

respectively. We adopt local-window self-attention with $L = 64$ for Blender and multiscale Blender dataset, and global self-attention for DeepVoxels dataset. Besides, we reimplement NeRF based on JAX as a stronger baseline.

4.2 Quantitative Experiments

Blender Dataset. Table 1 shows the PSNR results of our proposed NeXT, and SSIM results are shown in the appendix. Compared to NeRF, our NeXT-S obtains **0.68** PSNR gain with similar parameters. Our methods remarkably benefit from increasing the model capacity. NeXT-L significantly outperforms NeRF by **2.38** PSNR. Especially, when adopting center pixel [2], our NeXT-L* achieves a new state-of-the-art result, crossing **34** average PSNR threshold on

Table 3. Comparisons on multiscale Blender dataset. NeXT boosts Mip-NeRF by a clear margin, especially on low resolution scenes.

	#Params	Full Res. PSNR/SSIM	$1/2$ Res PSNR/SSIM	$1/4$ Res PSNR/SSIM	$1/8$ Res PSNR/SSIM
NeRF (JAX) [13]	1,191K	31.20/0.950	30.65/0.956	26.25/0.930	22.53/0.871
Mip-NeRF [2]	612K	32.63/0.958	34.34/0.970	35.47/0.979	35.60/0.983
NeXT-S	616K	32.18/0.954	34.32/0.969	36.43/0.980	37.57/0.987
NeXT-B	1,076K	32.92/0.959	35.06/0.973	36.99/0.982	38.05/0.988
NeXT-L	2,031K	**34.38/0.968**	**36.47/0.979**	**38.19/0.986**	**39.29/0.991**

Blender dataset for the first time. It's worth noting that vanilla Transformer performs worse ($\downarrow$0.20 PSNR) even with more parameters than NeRF.

DeepVoxels Dataset. Table 2 presents the results of our method and other state-of-the-art methods on DeepVoxels dataset, which has about 5× more number of training images than Blender dataset (479 for training and 1000 for testing). As Table 2 shown, all of our NeXT variants outperform previous top-performed methods by a large margin. We also reimplement NeRF based on JAX to serve as a stronger baseline, which brings consistent improvement over the original NeRF for most scenes yet fail to converge for "Vase". By contrast, the proposed NeXT converges stably and achieves best performance on all scenes. In particular, our best model NeXT-L* achieves new state-of-the-art results ($\uparrow$**9.59** PSNR compared to NeRF) on DeepVoxels dataset.

Multiscale Blender Dataset. Multi-scale Blender dataset [2] is designed to better probe accuracy on multi-resolution scenes, which is much more challenging than NeRF's Blender dataset [31]. Mip-NeRF [2] shows impressing superiority over NeRF and previously serves as the state-of-the-art method in this dataset. Hence, we choose Mip-NeRF as the baseline and replace its query network by NeXT. As shown in Table 3, with similar parameters, our NeXT-S boosts Mip-NeRF by **0.62** PSNR gain on average. By further increasing the model capacity, our NeXT-L shows consistent improvement on all resolution scenes and surpasses the previous best-performed Mip-NeRF by a clear margin ($\uparrow$**2.57** PSNR). Note that the model sizes of our variants are cut in half here by following Mip-NeRF.

4.3   Ablation Studies

Model Scaling. A natural question is that whether the original NeRF can benefit from model scaling like our proposed NeXT? To answer this question, we conduct comparison experiments between NeRF and NeXT under different model parameters and GFLOPs as shown in Fig. 3. The MLP used in the original NeRF has 8 fully-connected layers with 256 channels per layer. To explore its potential, we increase the model size of MLP by making it deeper and wider. Figure 3 shows that NeRF does benefit from increasing network capacity yet the

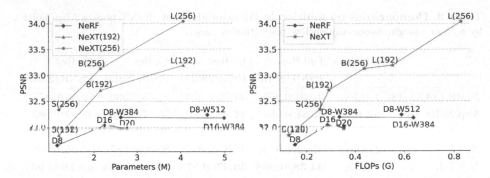

Fig. 3. Model scaling. PSNR results are achieved by NeRF and NeXT under different model parameters and FLOPs on Blender dataset. D and W indicate the depth and width of the MLP network in NeRF. The value in the parentheses denotes $N_c + N_f$ and are set to 192 for NeRF by default. NeXT variants show strong scalability of model capacity and significantly benefit from the increase of sample points. Note that FLOPs is calculated to measure the computation cost of rendering a pixel via the query network.

gain is limited and overfitting tend to occur. (i) As the MLP goes deeper, the performance of NeRF increases first and then drops when has 20 layers. (ii) As the MLP becomes deeper and wider, it seems that saturation occurs: NeRF-D16-W384 with 4,988K parameters brings no gain than that NeRF-D8-W384 with 2,624K parameters. By contrast, our proposed NeXT variants show strong scalability, *i.e.*, tendency of saturation is not observed by increasing model capacity from NeXT-S to NeXT-L (↑**1.34** PSNR). When increasing the number of sample points from 192 to 256, NeXT-L achieves further improvement with **0.85** PSNR gain. Besides, our NeXT variants show consistent improvement compared to NeRF with similar FLOPs.

Positional Embedding in Transformer. To illustrate the effect of positional embedding, we conduct experiments with different positional embedding types (*i.e.*, no positional embedding, 1D sinusoidal and learnable positional embedding) on Blender dataset. As Table 4a shown, employing 1D sinusoidal positional embedding significantly improves the performance by 0.53 PSNR at most.

Local-Window Self-attention. The computation cost of global attention increase squarely with enlarging the number of sample points along a ray. Hence, it's of significance to introduce local-window self-attention to alleviate the computation burden. Table 4b shows the results of NeXT with different local window size, which demonstrates that employing local-window self-attention achieves competitive performances compared to using global attention mechanism.

Multi-skip Connection. Table 4c shows both NeRF and NeXT benefit from the utilization of multi-skip connection, which demonstrates that the enhancement of position information is vital for novel view synthesis. For example, multi-skip connection brings **0.24** and **1.00** PSNR gains to NeRF and NeXT, respectively.

Table 4. Ablation studies. If not otherwise specified, all the ablation studies are performed on NeXT-B on Blender dataset. "LWSA" denotes local-window self-attention. N_c/N_f refer to the number of sample points in coarse/fine stage.

(a) **Positional embedding in Transformer.**
The 1D sinusoidal positional embedding strategy performs better.

Positional Embed.	PSNR	SSIM
✗	32.19	0.955
Learnable	32.44	0.956
Sinusoid	**32.72**	**0.958**

(b) **Attention design.** NeXT with LWSA reduces computational complexity and maintains competitive performance.

Method	Window Size	PSNR	SSIM
w/o LWSA	-	32.25	0.955
w/ LWSA	64	**32.34**	**0.955**
	32	32.26	0.954

(c) **Multi-skip connection.** Multi-skip connection boosts both the proposed NeXT and original NeRF.

Method	Skip Layer	PSNR	SSIM
NeRF (JAX)	4	31.66	0.953
NeRF (JAX)	2,4,6	31.90	0.955
NeXT	-	31.44	0.949
NeXT	1	31.83	0.951
NeXT	1,2	**32.44**	**0.956**

(d) **Hierarchical sampling.** NeXT benefits from more sample points and shows less dependence on coarse-to-fine sampling.

Method	N_c	N_f	PSNR	SSIM
NeRF (JAX)	128	128	31.76	0.954
NeRF (JAX)	64	128	31.66	0.953
NeRF (JAX)	192	0	29.97	0.938
NeXT	128	128	**32.94**	**0.959**
NeXT	64	128	32.44	0.956
NeXT	192	0	32.12	0.953

Hierarchical Sampling. We conduct experiments on the hierarchical sampling shown in Table 4d and draw conclusions as follows. First, the proposed NeXT relies much less on the two-stage coarse-to-fine sampling compared to NeRF. When only adopts coarse sampling, *i.e.*, $N_f = 0$, the resulted performance degradation is ↓0.32 vs. ↓1.69 PSNR (NeXT vs. NeRF). Second, our approach prominently benefits from more sample points. Increasing the total number of sample points from $N_c + N_f = 192$ to 256 brings ↑0.50 PSNR gains for NeXT yet only ↑0.10 PSNR gains for NeRF.

4.4 Visualization

What is Learnt? Sample points along a ray contribute differently to the final rendered pixel. For example, points in the free space or occluded regions barely affect the rendered image. In the light of that the proposed NeXT renders a pixel via a ray-level query, it's expected that NeXT can learn the relative importance of each point via the built-in self-attention mechanism. To investigate what is learnt in NeXT, we first refer to the average received attention scores of each point as "attention weights". Given the multi-head attention scores matrix $\mathbf{AW} \in \mathbb{R}^{H \times N \times N}$, the average attention weight $\mathbf{A\hat{W}} \in \mathbb{R}^N$ is calculated by:

$$\mathbf{A\hat{W}} = \text{Softmax}(\frac{1}{H}\sum_{h}^{H}\sum_{i}^{N}\mathbf{AW}_{h,i,:}), \tag{5}$$

where H and N is the number of attention head and sample points respectively.

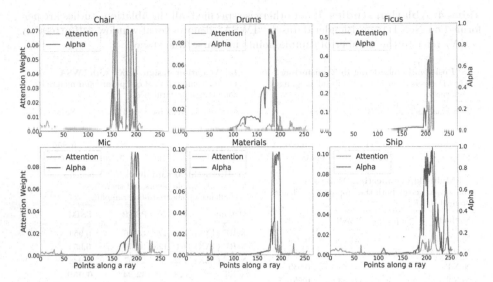

Fig. 4. Visualization of average attention weight and alpha values of sample points for rendering scenes on Blender dataset. The attention weight curve show some similar trends to alpha curve.

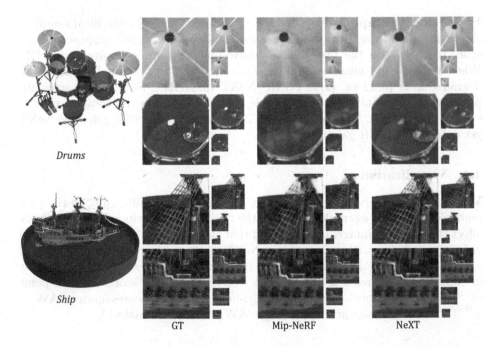

Fig. 5. Visualization of renderings of NeXT-L compared to the groundtruth and Mip-NeRF on two scenes of multiscale Blender dataset. We visualize the cropped regions in four different scales. NeXT qualitatively outperforms Mip-NeRF with more fine details (*e.g.*, the gloss on the drum).

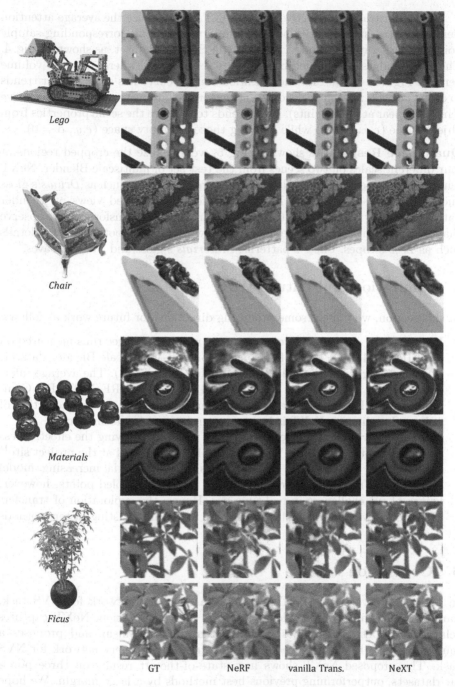

GT   NeRF   vanilla Trans.   NeXT

Fig. 6. Visualization of synthesized views of NeXT-L* versus the groundtruth, NeRF and vanilla Transformer. Cropped regions on four scenes of Blender dataset are presented. NeXT remarkably outperforms NeRF, particularly on objects with rich texture details such as *Chair's* patterns and *Ficus's* leaves.

To demonstrate the effectiveness of NeXT, we visualize the average attention weight in the last NeXT-B block and alpha values of all corresponding sample points along a ray when rendering scenes in Blender dataset, as shown in Fig. 4. The alpha values is obtained by $\alpha_i = 1 - \exp(-\sigma_i \delta_i)$, where σ_i is the volume density. Figure 4 shows that the attention weight curve has some similar trends to alpha curve (*e.g.*, the peaks of the attention weight curve and the alpha curve tend to appear at close points). NeXT tends to capture the scene properties from object space (*e.g.*, $\alpha > 0$) while ignoring those of empty space (*e.g.*, $\alpha = 0$).

Qualitative Results. As shown in Fig. 5, we visualize the cropped regions at four different scales on two scenes from the test set of multiscale Blender. NeXT remarkably outperforms Mip-NeRF with more fine details such as *Drums*'s gloss and *Ship*'s nets. In addition, Fig. 6 shows four synthesized views on Blender dataset of NeXT versus groundtruth, NeRF and vanilla Transformer. We observe that NeXT qualitatively outperforms prior work with smooth and fine details such as *Lego*'s ropes, *Chair*'s patterns, *Materials*'s gloss and *Ficus*'s leaves.

5 Limitation and Future Work

In this section, we present some promising directions for future work as follows:

- **Lightweight design.** We report average runtime of three runs measured on 8 NVIDIA V100 GPUs for fair comparisons on Multi-scale Blender dataset. Total training time: 17.07/43.31 h (Mip-NeRF/NeXT-B). The average inference time for rendering an image: 2.45/4.01 s (Mip-NeRF/NeXT-B). Compared to NeRF methods, NeXT has higher runtime due to the interaction of points. Speeding up NeXT is important and promising future work.
- **Real Forward-Facing Scenes.** We also work on verifying the effectiveness of NeXT on other datasets. The results will be presented at the project site[1].
- **Knowledge distillation.** NeXT boosts renderings via increasing model capacity and modeling interdependencies between sampled points, however, brings about challenges in real-time use. Hence, the exploration of transferring the knowledge encoded in NeXT for improving existing faster methods is expected.

6 Conclusion

In this paper, we explore a Transformer-based query network for NVS task, namely NeXT, achieving ray-level query by ray tokenization. NeXT captures relationships between samples via self-attention mechanism, and proposes a multi-skip module to further adapt Transformer-based query network for NVS task. The proposed NeXT shows new state-of-the-art results on three popular datasets, outperforming previous best methods by a large margin. We hope that the general query network presented in this paper will be valuable to other researchers and provide a potential path towards high quality renderings.

---

[1] https://github.com/Crishawy/NeXT.

Acknowledgements. This work is supported in part by the National Natural Science Foundation of China under Grant 62171248, and the PCNL KEY project (PCL2021A07).

References

1. Arandjelović, R., Zisserman, A.: Nerf in detail: learning to sample for view synthesis. arXiv preprint arXiv:2106.05264 (2021)
2. Barron, J.T., Mildenhall, B., Tancik, M., Hedman, P., Martin-Brualla, R., Srinivasan, P.P.: Mip-NeRF: a multiscale representation for anti-aliasing neural radiance fields. In: Proceedings of the IEEE/CVF International Conference on Computer Vision, pp. 5855–5864 (2021)
3. Bi, S., et al.: Neural reflectance fields for appearance acquisition. arXiv preprint arXiv:2008.03824 (2020)
4. Boss, M., Braun, R., Jampani, V., Barron, J.T., Liu, C., Lensch, H.: Nerd: neural reflectance decomposition from image collections. In: Proceedings of the IEEE/CVF International Conference on Computer Vision, pp. 12684–12694 (2021)
5. Bradbury, J., et al.: Jax: composable transformations of python+ numpy programs 2018. http://github.com/google/jax 4, 16 (2020)
6. Buehler, C., Bosse, M., McMillan, L., Gortler, S., Cohen, M.: Unstructured lumigraph rendering. In: Proceedings of the 28th Annual Conference on Computer Graphics and Interactive Techniques, pp. 425–432 (2001)
7. Carion, N., Massa, F., Synnaeve, G., Usunier, N., Kirillov, A., Zagoruyko, S.: End-to-end object detection with transformers. In: Vedaldi, A., Bischof, H., Brox, T., Frahm, J.-M. (eds.) ECCV 2020. LNCS, vol. 12346, pp. 213–229. Springer, Cham (2020). https://doi.org/10.1007/978-3-030-58452-8_13
8. Chan, E.R., Monteiro, M., Kellnhofer, P., Wu, J., Wetzstein, G.: Pi-GAN: periodic implicit generative adversarial networks for 3d-aware image synthesis. In: Proceedings of the IEEE/CVF Conference on Computer Vision and Pattern Recognition, pp. 5799–5809 (2021)
9. Dai, Z., Cai, B., Lin, Y., Chen, J.: UP-DETR: unsupervised pre-training for object detection with transformers. In: Proceedings of the IEEE/CVF Conference on Computer Vision and Pattern Recognition, pp. 1601–1610 (2021)
10. Dai, Z., Yang, Z., Yang, Y., Carbonell, J., Le, Q.V., Salakhutdinov, R.: Transformer-xl: attentive language models beyond a fixed-length context. arXiv preprint arXiv:1901.02860 (2019)
11. Davis, A., Levoy, M., Durand, F.: Unstructured light fields. In: Computer Graphics Forum, vol. 31, pp. 305–314. Wiley Online Library (2012)
12. Debevec, P.E., Taylor, C.J., Malik, J.: Modeling and rendering architecture from photographs: a hybrid geometry-and image-based approach. In: Proceedings of the 23rd annual conference on Computer Graphics and Interactive Techniques, pp. 11–20 (1996)
13. Deng, B., Barron, J.T., Srinivasan, P.P.: JaxNeRF: an efficient JAX implementation of NeRF (2020)
14. Devlin, J., Chang, M.W., Lee, K., Toutanova, K.: Bert: pre-training of deep bidirectional transformers for language understanding. arXiv preprint arXiv:1810.04805 (2018)
15. Dosovitskiy, A., et al.: An image is worth 16 x 16 words: transformers for image recognition at scale. arXiv preprint arXiv:2010.11929 (2020)

16. Flynn, J., et al.: DeepView: view synthesis with learned gradient descent. In: Proceedings of the IEEE/CVF Conference on Computer Vision and Pattern Recognition, pp. 2367–2376 (2019)
17. Gafni, G., Thies, J., Zollhofer, M., Nießner, M.: Dynamic neural radiance fields for monocular 4d facial avatar reconstruction. In: Proceedings of the IEEE/CVF Conference on Computer Vision and Pattern Recognition, pp. 8649–8658 (2021)
18. Gao, C., Shih, Y., Lai, W.S., Liang, C.K., Huang, J.B.: Portrait neural radiance fields from a single image. arXiv preprint arXiv:2012.05903 (2020)
19. Garbin, S.J., Kowalski, M., Johnson, M., Shotton, J., Valentin, J.: FastNeRF: high-fidelity neural rendering at 200fps. In: Proceedings of the IEEE/CVF International Conference on Computer Vision, pp. 14346–14355 (2021)
20. Gortler, S.J., Grzeszczuk, R., Szeliski, R., Cohen, M.F.: The lumigraph. In: Proceedings of the 23rd Annual Conference on Computer Graphics and Interactive Techniques, pp. 43–54 (1996)
21. Hedman, P., Srinivasan, P.P., Mildenhall, B., Barron, J.T., Debevec, P.: Baking neural radiance fields for real-time view synthesis. In: Proceedings of the IEEE/CVF International Conference on Computer Vision, pp. 5875–5884 (2021)
22. Jain, A., Tancik, M., Abbeel, P.: Putting nerf on a diet: semantically consistent few-shot view synthesis. In: Proceedings of the IEEE/CVF International Conference on Computer Vision, pp. 5885–5894 (2021)
23. Kingma, D.P., Ba, J.: Adam: a method for stochastic optimization. arXiv preprint arXiv:1412.6980 (2014)
24. Levoy, M., Hanrahan, P.: Light field rendering. In: Proceedings of the 23rd Annual Conference on Computer Graphics and Interactive Techniques, pp. 31–42 (1996)
25. Li, Y., et al.: TokenPose: learning keypoint tokens for human pose estimation. In: Proceedings of the IEEE/CVF International Conference on Computer Vision, pp. 11313–11322 (2021)
26. Li, Z., Niklaus, S., Snavely, N., Wang, O.: Neural scene flow fields for space-time view synthesis of dynamic scenes. In: Proceedings of the IEEE/CVF Conference on Computer Vision and Pattern Recognition, pp. 6498–6508 (2021)
27. Lindell, D.B., Martel, J.N., Wetzstein, G.: AutoInt: automatic integration for fast neural volume rendering. In: Proceedings of the IEEE/CVF Conference on Computer Vision and Pattern Recognition, pp. 14556–14565 (2021)
28. Liu, L., Gu, J., Zaw Lin, K., Chua, T.S., Theobalt, C.: Neural sparse voxel fields. Adv. Neural Inf. Process. Syst. 33, 15651–15663 (2020)
29. Lombardi, S., Simon, T., Saragih, J., Schwartz, G., Lehrmann, A., Sheikh, Y.: Neural volumes: learning dynamic renderable volumes from images. arXiv preprint arXiv:1906.07751 (2019)
30. Mildenhall, B., et al.: Local light field fusion: practical view synthesis with prescriptive sampling guidelines. ACM Trans. Graph. (TOG) 38(4), 1–14 (2019)
31. Mildenhall, B., Srinivasan, P.P., Tancik, M., Barron, J.T., Ramamoorthi, R., Ng, R.: NeRF: representing scenes as neural radiance fields for view synthesis. In: Vedaldi, A., Bischof, H., Brox, T., Frahm, J.-M. (eds.) ECCV 2020. LNCS, vol. 12346, pp. 405–421. Springer, Cham (2020). https://doi.org/10.1007/978-3-030-58452-8_24
32. Neff, T., et al.: Donerf: towards real-time rendering of neural radiance fields using depth oracle networks. arXiv e-prints pp. arXiv-2103 (2021)
33. Niemeyer, M., Geiger, A.: Giraffe: representing scenes as compositional generative neural feature fields. In: Proceedings of the IEEE/CVF Conference on Computer Vision and Pattern Recognition, pp. 11453–11464 (2021)

34. Niemeyer, M., Mescheder, L., Oechsle, M., Geiger, A.: Differentiable volumetric rendering: Learning implicit 3d representations without 3d supervision. In: Proceedings of the IEEE/CVF Conference on Computer Vision and Pattern Recognition, pp. 3504–3515 (2020)

35. Ost, J., Mannan, F., Thuerey, N., Knodt, J., Heide, F.: Neural scene graphs for dynamic scenes. In: Proceedings of the IEEE/CVF Conference on Computer Vision and Pattern Recognition, pp. 2856–2865 (2021)

36. Park, K., et al.: Nerfies: Deformable neural radiance fields. In: Proceedings of the IEEE/CVF International Conference on Computer Vision, pp. 5865–5874 (2021)

37. Pumarola, A., Corona, E., Pons-Moll, G., Moreno-Noguer, F.: D-nerf: neural radiance fields for dynamic scenes. In: Proceedings of the IEEE/CVF Conference on Computer Vision and Pattern Recognition, pp. 10318–10327 (2021)

38. Raj, A., et al.: Pva: pixel-aligned volumetric avatars. arXiv preprint arXiv:2101.02697 (2021)

39. Rebain, D., Jiang, W., Yazdani, S., Li, K., Yi, K.M., Tagliasacchi, A.: Derf: decomposed radiance fields. In: Proceedings of the IEEE/CVF Conference on Computer Vision and Pattern Recognition, pp. 14153–14161 (2021)

40. Reiser, C., Peng, S., Liao, Y., Geiger, A.: KiloNeRF: speeding up neural radiance fields with thousands of tiny MLPs. In: Proceedings of the IEEE/CVF International Conference on Computer Vision, pp. 14335–14345 (2021)

41. Rematas, K., Martin-Brualla, R., Ferrari, V.: ShaRF: shape-conditioned radiance fields from a single view. arXiv preprint arXiv:2102.08860 (2021)

42. Riegler, G., Koltun, V.: Free view synthesis. In: Vedaldi, A., Bischof, H., Brox, T., Frahm, J.-M. (eds.) ECCV 2020. LNCS, vol. 12364, pp. 623–640. Springer, Cham (2020). https://doi.org/10.1007/978-3-030-58529-7_37

43. Riegler, G., Koltun, V.: Stable view synthesis. In: Proceedings of the IEEE/CVF Conference on Computer Vision and Pattern Recognition, pp. 12216–12225 (2021)

44. Schwarz, K., Liao, Y., Niemeyer, M., Geiger, A.: Graf: Generative radiance fields for 3d-aware image synthesis. Adv. Neural Inf. Process. Syst. **33**, 20154–20166 (2020)

45. Seitz, S.M., Dyer, C.R.: Photorealistic scene reconstruction by voxel coloring. Int. J. Comput. Vision **35**(2), 151–173 (1999)

46. Sitzmann, V., Thies, J., Heide, F., Nießner, M., Wetzstein, G., Zollhofer, M.: DeepVoxels: learning persistent 3d feature embeddings. In: Proceedings of the IEEE/CVF Conference on Computer Vision and Pattern Recognition, pp. 2437–2446 (2019)

47. Sitzmann, V., Zollhöfer, M., Wetzstein, G.: Scene representation networks: continuous 3d-structure-aware neural scene representations. In: Advances in Neural Information Processing Systems, vol. 32 (2019)

48. Srinivasan, P.P., Deng, B., Zhang, X., Tancik, M., Mildenhall, B., Barron, J.T.: NeRV: neural reflectance and visibility fields for relighting and view synthesis. In: Proceedings of the IEEE/CVF Conference on Computer Vision and Pattern Recognition, pp. 7495–7504 (2021)

49. Srinivasan, P.P., Tucker, R., Barron, J.T., Ramamoorthi, R., Ng, R., Snavely, N.: Pushing the boundaries of view extrapolation with multiplane images. In: Proceedings of the IEEE/CVF Conference on Computer Vision and Pattern Recognition, pp. 175–184 (2019)

50. Strudel, R., Garcia, R., Laptev, I., Schmid, C.: Segmenter: transformer for semantic segmentation. In: Proceedings of the IEEE/CVF International Conference on Computer Vision, pp. 7262–7272 (2021)

51. Tancik, M., et al.: Learned initializations for optimizing coordinate-based neural representations. In: Proceedings of the IEEE/CVF Conference on Computer Vision and Pattern Recognition, pp. 2846–2855 (2021)
52. Tolstikhin, I.O., et al.: MLP-Mixer: an all-MLP architecture for vision. In: Advances in Neural Information Processing Systems, vol. 34 (2021)
53. Touvron, H., Cord, M., Douze, M., Massa, F., Sablayrolles, A., Jégou, H.: Training data-efficient image transformers & distillation through attention. In: International Conference on Machine Learning, pp. 10347–10357. PMLR (2021)
54. Trevithick, A., Yang, B.: GRF: learning a general radiance field for 3d representation and rendering. In: Proceedings of the IEEE/CVF International Conference on Computer Vision, pp. 15182–15192 (2021)
55. Vaswani, A., et al.: Attention is all you need. In: Advances in Neural Information Processing systems vol. 30 (2017)
56. Waechter, M., Moehrle, N., Goesele, M.: Let there be color! large-scale texturing of 3d reconstructions. In: Fleet, D., Pajdla, T., Schiele, B., Tuytelaars, T. (eds.) Computer Vision - ECCV 2014, ECCV 2014. Lecture Notes in Computer Science, vol. 8693, pp. 836–850. Springer, Cham (2014). https://doi.org/10.1007/978-3-319-10602-1_54
57. Wang, Q., et al.: IBRNet: learning multi-view image-based rendering. In: Proceedings of the IEEE/CVF Conference on Computer Vision and Pattern Recognition, pp. 4690–4699 (2021)
58. Wang, Z., Bovik, A.C., Sheikh, H.R., Simoncelli, E.P.: Image quality assessment: from error visibility to structural similarity. IEEE Trans. Image Process. **13**(4), 600–612 (2004)
59. Wood, D.N., et al.: Surface light fields for 3d photography. In: Proceedings of the 27th Annual Conference on Computer Graphics and Interactive Techniques, pp. 287–296 (2000)
60. Xie, E., Wang, W., Yu, Z., Anandkumar, A., Alvarez, J.M., Luo, P.: SegFormer: simple and efficient design for semantic segmentation with transformers. In: Advances in Neural Information Processing Systems, vol. 34 (2021)
61. Yang, S., Quan, Z., Nie, M., Yang, W.: Transpose: towards explainable human pose estimation by transformer. arXiv e-prints pp. arXiv-2012 (2020)
62. Yariv, L., et al.: Multiview neural surface reconstruction by disentangling geometry and appearance. Adv. Neural Inf. Process. Syst. **33**, 2492–2502 (2020)
63. Yu, A., Li, R., Tancik, M., Li, H., Ng, R., Kanazawa, A.: Plenoctrees for real-time rendering of neural radiance fields. In: Proceedings of the IEEE/CVF International Conference on Computer Vision, pp. 5752–5761 (2021)
64. Yu, A., Ye, V., Tancik, M., Kanazawa, A.: pixelNeRF: neural radiance fields from one or few images. In: Proceedings of the IEEE/CVF Conference on Computer Vision and Pattern Recognition, pp. 4578–4587 (2021)
65. Yuan, L., et al.: Tokens-to-Token ViT: training vision transformers from scratch on ImageNet. In: Proceedings of the IEEE/CVF International Conference on Computer Vision, pp. 558–567 (2021)
66. Yuan, Y., et al.: HRformer: high-resolution transformer for dense prediction. arXiv preprint arXiv:2110.09408 (2021)
67. Zhou, T., Tucker, R., Flynn, J., Fyffe, G., Snavely, N.: Stereo magnification: learning view synthesis using multiplane images. arXiv preprint arXiv:1805.09817 (2018)
68. Zhu, X., Su, W., Lu, L., Li, B., Wang, X., Dai, J.: Deformable DETR: deformable transformers for end-to-end object detection. arXiv preprint arXiv:2010.04159 (2020)

Learning Online Multi-sensor Depth Fusion

Erik Sandström[1(✉)], Martin R. Oswald[1,2], Suryansh Kumar[1], Silvan Weder[1], Fisher Yu[1], Cristian Sminchisescu[3,5], and Luc Van Gool[1,4]

[1] ETH Zürich, Zürich, Switzerland
esandstroem@ee.ethz.ch
[2] University of Amsterdam, Amsterdam, Netherlands
[3] Lund University, Lund, Sweden
[4] KU Leuven, Leuven, Belgium
[5] Google Research, Sunnyvale, USA

Abstract. Many hand-held or mixed reality devices are used with a single sensor for 3D reconstruction, although they often comprise multiple sensors. Multi-sensor depth fusion is able to substantially improve the robustness and accuracy of 3D reconstruction methods, but existing techniques are not robust enough to handle sensors which operate with diverse value ranges as well as noise and outlier statistics. To this end, we introduce SenFuNet,- a depth fusion approach that learns sensor-specific noise and outlier statistics and combines the data streams of depth frames from different sensors in an online fashion. Our method fuses multi-sensor depth streams regardless of time synchronization and calibration and generalizes well with little training data. We conduct experiments with various sensor combinations on the real-world CoRBS and Scene3D datasets, as well as the Replica dataset. Experiments demonstrate that our fusion strategy outperforms traditional and recent online depth fusion approaches. In addition, the combination of multiple sensors yields more robust outlier handling and more precise surface reconstruction than the use of a single sensor. The source code and data are available at https://github.com/tfy14esa/SenFuNet.

1 Introduction

Real-time online 3D reconstruction has become increasingly important with the rise of applications like mixed reality, autonomous driving, robotics, or live 3D content creation via scanning. The majority of 3D reconstruction hardware platforms like phones, tablets, or mixed reality headsets contain a multitude of sensors, but few algorithms leverage them jointly to increase their accuracy, robustness, and reliability. For instance, the HoloLens2 has four tracking cameras and a depth camera for mapping. Neither is its depth camera used for tracking, nor are the tracking cameras used for mapping. Fusing the data from multiple sensors

Supplementary Information The online version contains supplementary material available at https://doi.org/10.1007/978-3-031-19824-3_6.

S. Avidan et al. (Eds.): ECCV 2022, LNCS 13692, pp. 87–105, 2022.
https://doi.org/10.1007/978-3-031-19824-3_6

88   E. Sandström et al.

ToF   MVS[46]   TSDF Fusion[11] RoutedFusion[54]   Ours   Ground Truth

Fig. 1. Online multi-sensor depth map fusion. We fuse depth streams from a time-of-flight (ToF) camera and multi-view stereo (MVS) depth. Compared to competitive depth fusion methods such as TSDF Fusion and RoutedFusion, our learning-based approach can handle multiple depth sensors and significantly reduces the amount of outliers without loss of completeness.

is challenging since different sensors typically operate in different domains, have diverse value ranges as well as noise and outlier statistics. This diversity is, however, what motivates sensor fusion. For example, RGB stereo cameras typically have a larger field of view and higher resolution than time-of-flight (ToF) cameras, but typically struggle on homogeneously textured surfaces. ToF cameras perform well regardless of texture, but show performance drops around edges. Fig. 1 shows the online fusion result of a ToF camera and a multi-view stereo (MVS) depth sensor. Both traditional and recent learning-based techniques such as TSDF Fusion [11] and RoutedFusion [54] respectively, reveal a high degree of noise and outliers when fusing multi-sensor depth. Although other recent works tackle depth map fusion [23,50,55,56] with learning techniques, there is yet no work that considers multiple sensors for online dense reconstruction.

In this paper, we present an approach for sensor fusion (SenFuNet) which jointly learns (1) the iterative online fusion of depth maps from a single sensor and (2) the effective fusion of depth data from multiple different sensors. During training, our method learns relevant sensor properties which impact the reconstruction accuracy to locally emphasize the better sensor for particular input and geometry configurations (see Fig. 1). We demonstrate with multiple sensor combinations that the learned sensor weighting is generic and can also be used as an expert system, e.g. for fusing the results of different stereo methods. In this case, our method predicts which algorithm performs better on which part of the scene. Since our approach handles time asynchronous sensor inputs, it is also applicable to collaborative multi-agent reconstruction. Our contributions are:

- Our approach learns location-dependent fusion weights for the individual sensor contributions according to learned sensor statistics. For various sensor combinations our method extracts multi-sensor results that are consistently better than those obtained from the individual sensors.
- Our pipeline is end-to-end trained in an online manner, is light-weight, real-time capable and generalizes well even for small amounts of training data.
- In contrast to early fusion approaches which directly fuse depth values and thus generally assume a time synchronized sensor setup, our approach is flexible and can fuse the recovered scene reconstruction from asynchronous sensors. Our system is therefore more robust (compared to early fusion) to sensor differences such as sampling frequency, pose and resolution differences.

2   Related Work

In this section, we discuss dense online 3D reconstruction, multi-sensor depth fusion and multi-sensor dense 3D reconstruction.

Dense Online 3D Scene Reconstruction. The foundation for many volumetric online 3D reconstruction methods via truncated signed distance functions (TSDF) was laid by Curless and Levoy [11]. Popular extensions of this seminal work are KinectFusion [24] and scalable generalizations with voxel hashing [25,38,39], octrees [48], or increased pose robustness via sparse image features [5]. Further extensions include tracking for Simultaneous Localization and Mapping (SLAM) [37,47,50,60] which potentially also handle loop closures, *e.g.* BundleFusion [12]. To account for greater depth noise, RoutedFusion [54] learns online updates of the volumetric grid. NeuralFusion [55] extends this idea by additionally learning the scene representation which significantly improves robustness to outliers. DI-Fusion [23], similarly to [55], learns the scene representation, but additionally decodes a confidence of the signed distance per voxel. Continual Neural Mapping [56] learns a continuous scene representation through a neural network from sequential depth maps. Several recent works do not require depth input and instead perform online reconstruction from RGB-cameras such as Atlas [35], VolumeFusion [9], TransformerFusion [4] and NeuralRecon [51]. None of these approaches consider multiple sensors and their extensions to sensor-aware data fusion is often by no means straightforward. Nevertheless, by treating all sensors equally, they can be used as baseline methods.

The majority of the aforementioned traditional methods do not properly account for varying noise and outlier levels for different depth values, which are better handled by probabilistic fusion methods [15–17,28]. Cao *et al.* [7] introduced a probabilistic framework via a Gaussian mixture model into a surfel-based reconstruction framework to account for uncertainties in the observed depth. For a recent survey on online RGB-D 3D scene reconstruction, readers are referred to [61]. Overall, none of the state-of-the-art methods for dense online 3D scene reconstruction consider multiple sensors.

Multi-sensor Depth Fusion. The task of fusing depth maps from diverse sensors has been studied extensively. Many works study the fusion of a specific set of sensors. For example, RGB stereo and time-of-flight (ToF) [1,2,10,13,14,18,33,52], RGB stereo and Lidar [31], RGB and Lidar [40,41,44], RGB stereo and monocular depth [34] and the fusion of multiple RGB stereo algorithms [42]. All these methods only study a specific set of sensors, while we do not enforce such a limitation. Few works study the fusion of arbitrary depth sensors [43]. Contrary to our method, all methods performing depth map fusion assume time synchronized sensors, which is hard, if not impossible, to achieve with realistic multi-sensor equipment.

Multi-sensor Dense 3D Reconstruction. Some works consider the problem of offline multi-sensor dense 3D reconstruction. For example, depth map fusion for semantic 3D reconstruction [45], combining multi-view stereo with a ToF sensor in a probabilistic framework [27], the combination of a depth sensor

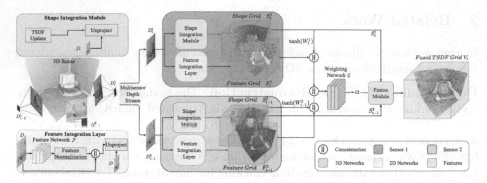

Fig. 2. SenFuNet Architecture. Given a depth stream D_t^i, with known camera poses, our method fuses each frame at time t from sensor i into global sensor-specific shape S_t^i and feature F_t^i grids. The **Shape Integration Module** fuses the frames into $S_t^i = \{V_t^i, W_t^i\}$ consisting of a TSDF grid V_t^i and a weight counter grid W_t^i. In parallel, the **Feature Integration Layer** extracts features from the depth maps using a 2D Feature Network $\mathcal{F}^i$ and integrates them into the feature grid F_t^i. Next, S_t^i and F_t^i are combined and decoded through a 3D **Weighting Network** $\mathcal{G}$ into a sensor weighting $\alpha \in [0,1]$. Together with S_t^i and α, the **Fusion Module** computes the fused grid V_t at each voxel location.

with photometric stereo [6] and large scene reconstruction using unsynchronized RGBD cameras mounted on an indoor robot [57]. These offline methods do not address the online problem setting that we are concerned with. Some works use sensor fusion to achieve robust pose estimation in an online setting [20,58]. In contrast to our method, these works do not leverage sensor fusion for mapping. Ali *et al.* [3] present an online framework which perhaps is most closely related to our work. They take Lidar and stereo depth maps as input and fuse the TSDF signals of both sensors with a linear average before updating the global grid using TSDF Fusion [11]. To reduce noise further, they optimize a least squares problem which encourages surface smoothing. Contrary to our method, no learning is used and their system is only designed to fuse stereo depth with Lidar.

3   Method

Overview. Given multiple noisy depth streams $D_t^i : \mathbb{R}^2 \rightarrow \mathbb{R}$ from different sensors with known camera calibration, *i.e.* extrinsics $P_t^i \in \mathbb{SE}(3)$ and intrinsics $K^i \in \mathbb{R}^{3 \times 3}$, our method integrates each depth frame at time $t \in \mathbb{N}$ from sensor $i \in \{1, 2\}$ into a globally consistent shape S_t^i and feature F_t^i grid. Through a series of operations, we then decode S_t^i and F_t^i into a fused TSDF grid $V_t \in \mathbb{R}^{X \times Y \times Z}$, which can be converted into a mesh with marching cubes [29]. Our overall framework can be split into four components (see Fig. 2). First, the **Shape Integration Module** integrates depth frames D_t^i successively into the zero-initialized shape representation $S_t^i = \{V_t^i, W_t^i\}$. S_t^i consists of a TSDF grid $V_t^i \in \mathbb{R}^{X \times Y \times Z}$ and a corresponding weight grid $W_t^i \in \mathbb{N}^{X \times Y \times Z}$, which keeps track of the number of updates to each voxel. In parallel, the **Feature Integration Layer** extracts features from the depth maps using a 2D feature network $\mathcal{F}^i$: $D_t^i \in \mathbb{R}^{W \times H \times 1} \rightarrow f_t^i \in \mathbb{R}^{W \times H \times n}$, with n being the feature dimension. We use separate feature networks per sensor to learn sensor-specific depth dependent statistics such as shape and edge information. The extracted features f_t^i are then integrated into the zero-initialized feature grid $F_t^i \in \mathbb{R}^{X \times Y \times Z \times n}$. Next, S_t^i and F_t^i are combined and decoded through a 3D **Weighting Network** $\mathcal{G}$ into a location-dependent sensor weighting $\alpha \in [0, 1]$. Together with S_t^i and α, the **Fusion Module** fuses the information into V_t at each voxel location. Key to our approach is the separation of per sensor information into different representations along with the successive aggregation of shapes and features in the 3D domain. This strategy enables $\mathcal{G}$ to learn a fusion strategy of the incoming multi-sensor depth stream. Our method is able to fuse the sensors in a spatially dependent manner from a smooth combination to a hard selection as illustrated in Fig. 3. Our scheme hence avoids the need to perform post-outlier filtering by thresholding with the weight W_t^i, which is difficult to tune and is prone to reduce scene completion [54]. Another popular outlier filtering technique is free-space carving[1], but this can be computationally expensive and is not required by our method. Instead, we use the learned α as part of an outlier filter at test time, requiring no manual tuning. Next, we describe each component in detail.

(a) Shape Integration Module. For each depth map D_t^i and pixel, a full perspective unprojection of the depth into the world coordinate frame yields a 3D point $\mathbf{x}_w \in \mathbb{R}^3$. Along each ray from the camera center, centered at $\mathbf{x}_w$, we sample T points uniformly over a predetermined distance l. The coordinates are then converted to the voxel space and a local shape grid $S_{t-1}^{i,*}$ is extracted from S_{t-1}^i through nearest neighbor extraction. To incrementally update the local shape grid, we follow the moving average update scheme of TSDF Fusion [11]. For numerical stability, the weights are clipped at a maximum weight $\omega_{\max}$. For more details, see the suppl. material.

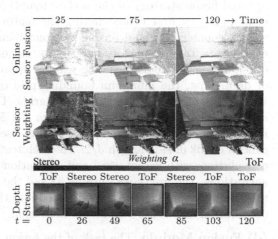

Fig. 3. Overview. Left to right: Sequential fusion of a multi-sensor noisy depth stream. Our method integrates each depth frame at time t and produces a sensor weighting which fuses the sensors in a spatially dependent manner. For example, areas in yellow denote high trust of the ToF sensor.

---

[1] Enforcing free space for voxels along the ray from the camera to the surface [36]. Note that outliers behind surfaces are not removed with this technique.

(b) **Feature Integration Layer.** Each depth map D_t^i is passed through a 2D network $\mathcal{F}^i$ to extract context information f_t^i, which can be useful during the sensor fusion process. When fusing sensors based on the stereo matching principle, we provide the RGB frame as additional input channels to $\mathcal{F}^i$. The network is fully convolutional and comprises 7 network blocks, each consisting of the following operations, 1) a 3×3 convolution with zero padding 1 and input channel dimension 4 and output dimension 4 (except the first block which takes 1 channel as input when only depth is provided), 2) a tanh activation, 3) another 3×3 convolution with zero padding 1 outputting 4 channels and 4) a tanh activation. The output of the first six blocks is added to the output of the next block via residual connections. Finally, we normalize the feature vectors at each pixel location and concatenate the input depth.

Next, we repeat the features T times along the direction of the viewing ray from the camera, $f_t^i \xrightarrow[\text{T times}]{\text{Repeat}} f_t^{i,T} \in \mathbb{R}^{W \times H \times T \times n}$. The local feature grid $F_{t-1}^{i,*}$ is then updated using the precomputed update indices from the Shape Integration Module with a moving average update: $F_t^{i,*} = \frac{W_{t-1}^{i,*} F_{t-1}^{i,*} + f_t^{i,T}}{W_{t-1}^{i,*}+1}$. For all update locations the grid F_t^i is replaced with $F_t^{i,*}$.

(c) **Weighting Network.** The task of the weighting network $\mathcal{G}$ is to predict the optimal fusion strategy of the surface hypotheses V_t^i. The input to the network is prepared by first concatenating the features F_t^i and the tanh-transformed weight counters W_t^i and second by concatenating the resulting vectors across the sensors. Due to memory constraints, the entire scene cannot be fit onto the GPU, and hence we use a sliding-window approach at test time to feed $\mathcal{G}$ chunks of data. First, the minimum bounding grid of the measured scene (i.e. where $W_t^i > 0$) is extracted from the global grids. Then, the extracted grid is parsed using chunks of size $d \times d \times d$ through $\mathcal{G} : \mathbb{R}^{d \times d \times d \times 2(n+1)} \rightarrow \alpha \in \mathbb{R}^{d \times d \times d \times 1}$ into $\alpha \in [0,1]$. To avoid edge effects, we use a stride of $d/2$ and update the central chunk of side length $d/2$. The architecture of $\mathcal{G}$ combines 2 layers of 3D-convolutions with kernel size 3 and replication padding 1 interleaved with ReLU activations. The first layer outputs 32 and the second layer 16 channels. Finally, the 16-dimensional features are decoded into the sensor weighting α by a $1 \times 1 \times 1$ convolution followed by a sigmoid activation.

(d) **Fusion Module.** The task of the fusion module is to combine α with the shapes S_t^i. In the following, we define the set of voxels where only sensor 1 integrates as $C^1 = \{W_t^1 > 0, W_{t-1}^2 = 0\}$, the set where only sensor 2 integrates as $C^2 = \{W_t^1 = 0, W_{t-1}^2 > 0\}$ and the set where both sensors integrate as $C^{12} = \{W_t^1 > 0, W_{t-1}^2 > 0\}$. Let us also introduce $\alpha_1 = \alpha$ and $\alpha_2 = 1 - \alpha$. The fusion module computes the fused grid V_t as

$$V_t = \begin{cases} \alpha_1 V_t^1 + \alpha_2 V_{t-1}^2 & \text{if } C^{12} \\ V_t^1 & \text{if } C^1 \\ V_{t-1}^2 & \text{if } C^2. \end{cases} \tag{1}$$

Depending on the voxel set, V_t is computed either as a weighted average of the two surface hypotheses or by selecting one of them. With only one sensor observation, a weighted average would corrupt the result. Hence, the single observed surface is selected. At test time, we additionally apply a learned **Outlier Filter** which utilizes α_i and W_t^i. The filter is formulated for sensors 1 and 2 as

$$\hat{W}_t^1 = \mathbb{1}_{\{C^1,\ \alpha_1>0.5\}} W_t^1, \quad \hat{W}_{t-1}^2 = \mathbb{1}_{\{C^2,\ \alpha_2>0.5\}} W_{t-1}^2, \tag{2}$$

where $\mathbb{1}_{\{.\}}$ denotes the indicator function[2]. When only one sensor is observed at a certain voxel, we remove the observation if α_i, which could be interpreted as a confidence, is below 0.5. This is done by setting the weight counter to 0.

Loss Function. The full pipeline is trained end-to-end using the overall loss

$$\mathcal{L} = \mathcal{L}_f + \lambda_1 \sum_{i=1}^{2} \mathcal{L}_{C^i}^{in} + \lambda_2 \sum_{i=1}^{2} \mathcal{L}_{C^i}^{out}. \tag{3}$$

The term $\mathcal{L}_f$ computes the mean L_1 error to the ground truth TSDF masked by C^{12} (4). To supervise the voxel sets C^1 and C^2, we introduce two additional terms, which penalize L_1 deviations from the optimal α. The purpose of these terms is to provide a training signal for the outlier filter. If the L_1 TSDF error is smaller than some threshold η, the observation is deemed to be an inlier, and the corresponding confidence α_i should be 1, otherwise 0. The loss is computed as the mean L_1 error to the optimal α:

$$\mathcal{L}_f = \frac{1}{N_{C^{12}}} \sum \mathbb{1}_{\{C^{12}\}} |V_t - V^{GT}|_1, \quad \mathcal{L}_{C^i}^{in} = \frac{1}{N_{C^i}^{in}} \sum \mathbb{1}_{\{C^i,\ |V_t-V^{GT}|_1<\eta\}} |\alpha_i - 1|_1,$$

$$\mathcal{L}_{C^i}^{out} = \frac{1}{N_{C^i}^{out}} \sum \mathbb{1}_{\{C^i,\ |V_t-V^{GT}|_1>\eta\}} |\alpha_i|_1, \tag{4}$$

where the normalization factors are defined as

$$N_{C^{12}} = \sum \mathbb{1}_{\{C^{12}\}}, \quad N_{C^i}^{in} = \sum \mathbb{1}_{\{C^i,\ |V_t-V^{GT}|_1<\eta\}},$$

$$N_{C^i}^{out} = \sum \mathbb{1}_{\{C^i,\ |V_t-V^{GT}|_1>\eta\}}. \tag{5}$$

Training Forward Pass. After the integration of a new depth frame D_t^i into the shape and feature grids, the update indices from the Shape Integration Module are used to compute the minimum bounding box of update voxels in S_t^i and F_t^i. The update box varies in size between frames and cannot always fit on the GPU. Due to this and for the sake of training efficiency, we extract a $d \times d \times d$ chunk from within the box volume. The chunk location is randomly selected using a uniform distribution along each axis of the bounding box. If the bounding box volume is smaller along any dimension than d, the chunk shrinks to the minimum size along the affected dimension. To maximize the number of voxels that are used to train the networks F^i, we sample a chunk until we find one with at least 2000

---

[2] See supplementary material for a definition.

update indices. At most, we make 600 attempts. If not enough valid indices are found, the next frame is integrated. The update indices in the chunk are finally used to mask the loss. We randomly reset the shape and feature grids with a probability of 0.01 at each frame integration to improve training robustness.

4   Experiments

We first describe our experimental setup and then evaluate our method against state-of-the-art online depth fusion methods on Replica, the real-world CoRBS and the Scene3D datasets. All reported results are averages over the respective test scenes. Further experiments and details are in the supplementary material.

Implementation Details. We use $\omega_{max} = 500$ and extract $T = 11$ points along the update band $l = 0.1$ m. We store $n = 5$ features at each voxel location and use a chunk side length of $d = 64$. For the loss (3) $\lambda_1 = 1/60$, $\lambda_2 = 1/600$ and $\eta = 0.04$ m. In total, the networks of our model comprise 27.7K parameters, where 24.3K are designated to $\mathcal{G}$ and the remaining parameters are split equally between $\mathcal{F}^1$ and $\mathcal{F}^2$. For our method and all baselines, the image size is $W = H = 256$, the voxel size is 0.01 m and we mask the 10 pixel border of all depth maps to avoid edge artifacts, *i.e.* pixels belonging to the mask are not integrated into 3D. Since our TSDF updates cannot be larger than 0.05 m, we truncate the ground truth TSDF grid at $l/2 = 0.05$ m.

Evaluation Metrics. The TSDF grids are evaluated using the Mean Absolute Distance (MAD), Mean Squared Error (MSE), Intersection over Union (IoU) and Accuracy (Acc.). The meshes, produced by marching cubes [29] from the TSDF grids, are evaluated using the F-score which is the harmonic mean of the Precision (P) and Recall (R).

Baseline Methods. Since there is no other multi-sensor online 3D reconstruction method that addresses the same problem, we define our own baselines by generalizing single sensor fusion pipelines to multiple sensors. TSDF Fusion [11] is the gold standard for fast, dense mapping of posed depth maps. It generalizes to the multi-sensor setting effortlessly by integrating all depth frames into the same TSDF grid at runtime. RoutedFusion [54] extends TSDF Fusion by learning the TSDF mapping. We generalize RoutedFusion to multiple sensors by feeding all depth frames into the same TSDF grid, but each sensor is assigned a separate fusion network to account for sensor-dependent noise[3]. NeuralFusion [55] extends RoutedFusion for better outlier handling, but despite efforts and help from the authors, the network did not converge during training due to heavy loss oscillations caused by integrating different sensors. DI-Fusion [23] learns the scene representation and predicts the signed distance value as well as the uncertainty σ per voxel. We use the provided model from the authors and integrate all frames from both sensors into the same volumetric grid. In the following, we refer

---

[3] Additionally, we tweak the original implementation to get rid of outliers. See supplementary material.

to each multi-sensor baseline by using the corresponding single sensor name. For additional comparison, when time synchronized sensors with ground truth depth are available, we train a so-called "Early Fusion" baseline by fusing the 2D depth frames of both sensors. The fusion is performed with a modified version of the 2D denoising network proposed by Weder *et al.* [54] followed by TSDF Fusion to attain the 3D model (see supplementary material). This baseline should be interpreted as a light-weight alternative to our proposed SenFuNet, but assumes synchronized sensors, which SenFuNet does not. Finally, for the single-sensor results, we evaluate the TSDF grids V_t^i. To make the comparisons fair, we do not use weight counter thresholding as post-outlier filter for any method. For DI-Fusion, we filter outliers by thresholding the learned voxel uncertainty. The default value provided in the implementation is used.

Table 1. Replica Dataset. ToF+PSMNet Fusion. (a) Our method outperforms the baselines as well as both of the sensor inputs and sets a new state-of-the-art for multi-sensor online depth fusion. (b) The denoising network mitigates outliers along planar regions, compare to Table 1a. Our method even outperforms the Early Fusion baseline, which assumes synchronized sensors.

Model \ Metric	MSE↓ *e-04	MAD↓ *e-02	IoU↑ [0,1]	Acc.↑ [%]	F↑ [%]	P↑ [%]	R↑ [%]
Single Sensor							
PSMNet [8]	7.30	1.95	0.664	83.23	56.20	43.10	81.34
ToF [21]	7.48	1.99	0.664	83.65	58.52	45.84	84.85
Multi-Sensor Fusion							
TSDF Fusion [11]	8.20	2.11	0.669	84.09	49.58	35.33	**85.44**
RoutedFusion [54]	5.62	1.66	0.735	87.22	61.08	49.51	79.92
DI-Fusion [23] σ=0.15	-	-	-	-	48.39	34.24	85.29
SenFuNet (Ours)	**4.65**	**1.54**	**0.753**	**88.05**	**69.29**	**62.05**	79.81

(a) Without depth denoising.

Model \ Metric	MSE↓ *e-04	MAD↓ *e-02	IoU↑ [0,1]	Acc.↑ [%]	F↑ [%]	P↑ [%]	R↑ [%]
Single Sensor							
PSMNet [8]	6.35	1.77	0.673	84.54	60.28	48.26	80.41
ToF [21]	5.08	1.58	0.709	87.32	68.93	59.01	83.08
Multi-Sensor Fusion							
TSDF Fusion [11]	6.40	1.80	0.681	85.31	52.93	38.95	**84.60**
RoutedFusion [54]	6.04	1.68	0.644	85.10	62.67	51.75	79.52
Early Fusion	6.40	1.40	0.760	89.02	74.60	67.46	83.47
DI-Fusion [23] σ=0.15	-	-	-	-	55.66	41.49	85.33
SenFuNet (Ours)	**3.49**	**1.31**	**0.761**	**89.61**	**76.47**	**73.58**	79.77

(b) With depth denoising

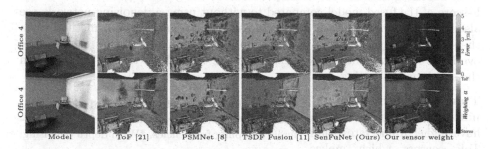

Model   ToF [21]   PSMNet [8]   TSDF Fusion [11]   SenFuNet (Ours)   Our sensor weight

Fig. 4. Replica Dataset. Our method fuses the sensors consistently better than the baselines. Concretely, our method learns to detect and remove outliers much more effectively (best viewed on screen). **Top row:** ToF+PSMNet Fusion without denoising. See also Table 1a. **Bottom row:** ToF+PSMNet Fusion with denoising. See also Table 1b.

4.1 Experiments on the Replica Dataset

The Replica dataset [49] comprises high-quality 3D reconstructions of a variety of indoor scenes. We collect data from Replica to create a multi-sensor dataset suitable for depth map fusion. To prepare ground truth signed distance grids, we first make the 3D meshes watertight using screened Poisson surface reconstruction [26]. The meshes are then converted to signed distance grids using a modified version of mesh-to-sdf[4] to accommodate non-cubic voxel grids. Ground truth depth and an RGB stereo pair are extracted using AI Habitat [32] along random trajectories. In total, we collected 92698 frames. We use 7 training and 3 test scenes. We simulate a depth sensor by adding noise to the GT depth of the left stereo view. Correspondingly, from the RGB stereo pairs a left stereo view depth map can be predicted using (optionally multi-view) stereo algorithms. In the following, we construct two sensor combinations and evaluate our model.

ToF+PSMNet Fusion. We simulate a ToF sensor by adding realistic noise to the ground truth depth maps[5] [21]. To balance the two sensors, we increase the noise level by a factor 5 compared to the original implementation. We simulate another depth sensor from the RGB stereo pair using PSMNet [8]. We train the network on the Replica train set and keep it fixed while training our pipeline. Table 1a shows that our method outperforms both TSDF Fusion, RoutedFusion and DI-Fusion on all metrics except Recall with at least 13% on the F-score. Additionally, the F-score improves with a minimum of 18% compared to the input sensors. Specifically, note the absence of outliers (colored yellow) in Fig. 4 *Top row* when comparing our method to TSDF Fusion. Also note the sensor weighting *e.g.* we find lots of noise on the right wall of the ToF scene and thus, our method puts more weight on the stereo sensor in this region.

Weder *et al.* [54] showed that a 2D denoising network (called routing network in the paper) that preprocesses the depth maps can improve performance when noise is present in planar regions. To this end, we train our own denoising network on the Replica train set and train a new model which applies a fixed denoising network. According to Table 1, this yields a gain of 10% on the F-score of the fused model compared to without using a denoising network, see also Fig. 4 *Bottom row*. Early Fusion is a strong alternative to our method when the sensors are synchronized. We want to highlight, however, that the resource overhead of our method is worthwhile since we outperform Early Fusion even in the synchronized setting.

Time Asynchronous Evaluation. RGB cameras often have higher frame rates than ToF sensors which makes Early Fusion more challenging as one sensor might lack new data. We simulate this setting by giving the PSMNet sensor twice the sampling rate

Table 2. Time Asynchronous Evaluation. SenFuNet outperforms Early Fusion for sensors with different sampling frequencies. *With depth denoising.

| | Metric | MSE↓ | MAD↓ | IoU↑ | Acc.↑ | F↑ | P↑ | R↑ |
Model		*e-04	*e-02	[0,1]	[%]	%	[%]	[%]
Early Fusion		7.66	1.99	0.642	84.65	61.34	48.47	**83.63**
SenFuNet (Ours)		4.21	1.45	0.755	88.26	73.04	69.13	78.43
SenFuNet (Ours)*		**3.15**	**1.23**	**0.760**	**89.52**	**79.26**	**79.91**	78.79

of the ToF sensor, *i.e.* we drop every second ToF frame. To provide a correspond-

[4] https://github.com/marian42/mesh_to_sdf.
[5] http://redwood-data.org/indoor/dataset.html.

ing ToF frame for Early Fusion, we reproject the latest observed ToF frame into the current view of the PSMNet sensor. As demonstrated in Table 2 the gap between our SenFuNet late fusion approach and Early Fusion becomes even larger (cf. Table 1 (b)).

Table 3. Replica Dataset. SGM+PSMNet Fusion. Our method does not assume a particular sensor pairing and works well for all tested sensors. The gain from the denoising network is marginal with a 2% F-score improvement since there are few outliers on planar regions of the stereo depth maps and the denoising network over-smooths the depth along discontinuities. Our method outperforms Early Fusion (which generally assumes synchronized sensors) on most metrics even without depth denoising.

Metric / Model	MSE↓ *e-04	MAD↓ *e-02	IoU↑ [0,1]	Acc.↑ [%]	F↑ [%]	P↑ [%]	R↑ [%]
Single Sensor							
PSMNet [8]	7.30	1.95	0.664	83.23	56.20	43.10	81.34
SGM [22]	8.90	2.17	0.610	81.48	57.71	44.40	84.08
Multi-Sensor Fusion							
TSDF Fusion [11]	9.17	2.24	0.634	82.62	47.75	33.39	85.10
RoutedFusion [54]	7.11	1.82	0.671	84.63	60.31	48.47	80.21
DI-Fusion [23] $\sigma=0.15$	-	-	-	-	47.29	32.92	**85.14**
SenFuNet (Ours)	**4.77**	**1.56**	**0.738**	**87.62**	**69.83**	**63.20**	79.12

(a) Without depth denoising

Metric / Model	MSE↓ *e-04	MAD↓ *e-02	IoU↑ [0,1]	Acc.↑ [%]	F↑ [%]	P↑ [%]	R↑ [%]
Single Sensor							
PSMNet [8]	6.35	1.77	0.673	84.54	60.28	48.26	80.41
SGM [22]	6.60	1.80	0.659	84.29	60.79	49.78	78.13
Multi-Sensor Fusion							
TSDF Fusion [11]	7.28	1.93	0.669	84.74	54.09	40.45	81.65
RoutedFusion [54]	8.09	2.05	0.580	80.18	59.88	47.13	82.12
Early Fusion	4.99	1.51	0.707	86.99	69.40	61.07	80.36
DI-Fusion [23] $\sigma=0.15$	-	-	-	-	52.65	38.50	**83.62**
SenFuNet (Ours)	**4.04**	**1.41**	**0.737**	**88.11**	**71.18**	**66.81**	76.27

(b) With depth denoising

SGM+PSMNet Fusion. Our method does not assume a particular sensor pairing. We show this, by replacing the ToF sensor with a stereo sensor acquired using semi-global matching [22]. In Table 3, we show state-of-the-art sensor fusion performance both with and without a denoising network. The denoising network tends to over-smooth depth discontinuities, which negatively affects performance when few outliers exist. Additionally, even without using a denoising network, we outperform Early Fusion on most metrics. TSDF Fusion, RoutedFusion and DI-Fusion aggregate outliers across the sensors leading to worse performance than the single sensor results.

4.2   Experiments on the CoRBS Dataset

The real-world CoRBS dataset [53] provides a selection of reconstructed objects with very accurate ground truth 3D and camera trajectories along with a consumer-grade RGBD camera. We apply our method to the dataset by training a model on the desk scene and testing it on the human scene. The procedure to create the ground truth signed distance grids is identical to the Replica dataset. We create an additional depth sensor along the ToF depth using MVS with COLMAP [46][6]. Fig. 5 shows that our model can fuse very imbalanced sensors while the baseline methods fail severely. Even if one sensor (MVS) is significantly worse, our method still improves on most metrics. This confirms that our method learns to meaningfully fuse the sensors even if one sensor adds very little.

---

[6] Unfortunately, no suitable public real 3D dataset exists, which comprises binocular stereo pairs, and an active depth sensor, as well as ground truth geometry.

4.3   Experiments on the Scene3D Dataset

We demonstrate that our framework can fuse imbalanced sensors on room-sized real-world scenes using the RGBD Scene3D dataset [59]. The Scene3D dataset comprises a collection of 3D models of indoor and outdoor scenes. We train our model on the stonewall scene and test it on the copy room scene. To create the ground truth training grid, we follow the steps outlined previously except that it was not necessary to make the mesh watertight. We fuse every 10th frame during train and test time. Equivalent to the study on CoRBS, we create an MVS depth sensor using COLMAP and perform ToF and MVS fusion. We only integrate MVS depth in the interval [0.5, 3.0] m. Table 4a along with Fig. 6 *Top row* shows that our method yields a fused result better than the individual input sensors and the baseline methods. Further, Fig. 1 shows our method in comparison with TSDF Fusion [11] and RoutedFusion [54] on the lounge scene.

Model	Metric	MSE↓ *e-04	MAD↓ *e-02	IoU↑ [0,1]	Acc.↑ [%]	F↑ [%]	P↑ [%]	R↑ [%]
Single Sensor								
MVS [46]		15.39	3.25	0.263	74.84	17.73	9.77	95.96
ToF		7.11	1.52	0.486	83.13	72.98	57.85	98.82
Multi-Sensor Fusion								
TSDF Fusion [11]		15.09	3.15	0.290	75.96	18.13	9.98	99.19
RoutedFusion [54]		23.09	4.40	0.222	49.42	2.36	1.27	16.43
DI-Fusion [23] r=0.15		-	-	-	-	28.19	16.71	90.15
SenFuNet (Ours)		6.53	1.55	0.510	84.88	74.56	59.74	99.16

(a)

(b)

Fig. 5. CoRBS Dataset. ToF+MVS Fusion. Our model can find synergies between very imbalanced sensors. (a) The numerical results show that our fused model is better than the individual depth sensor inputs and significantly better than any of the baseline methods. (b) Contrary to our method, the baseline methods cannot handle the high degree of outliers from the MVS sensor.

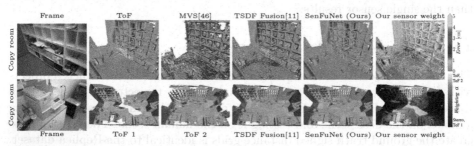

Fig. 6. Top row: Our method effectively fuses the ToF and MVS sensors. Note specifically the absence of yellow outliers in the corner of the bookshelf. See also Table 4a. **Bottom row:** Multi-Agent ToF Reconstruction. Our method is flexible and can perform Multi-Agent reconstruction. Note that our model learns where to trust each agent at different spatial locations for maximum completeness, while also being noise aware. See for instance the left bottom corner of the bookshelf where both agents integrate, but the noise-free agent is given a higher weighting. The above scene is taken from the Scene3D Dataset [59] (best viewed on screen). See also Table 4b.

Multi-agent ToF Fusion. Our method is not exclusively applicable to sensor fusion, but more flexible. We demonstrate this by formulating a Multi-Agent reconstruction problem, which assumes that two identical ToF sensors with different camera trajectories are provided. The task is to fuse the reconstructions from the two agents. This requires an understanding of

Table 4. Scene3D Dataset. (a) ToF+MVS Fusion. Our method outperforms the baselines on real-world data on a room-sized scene. (b) **Multi-Agent ToF Reconstruction.** Our method is flexible and can perform collaborative sensor fusion from multiple sensors with different camera trajectories.

Model	F↑ [%]	P↑ [%]	R↑ [%]	Model	F↑ [%]	P↑ [%]	R↑ [%]
Single Sensor				*Single Sensor*			
MVS [46]	44.26	32.08	71.33	ToF 1	84.68	89.92	80.01
ToF	90.73	85.53	96.61	ToF 2	77.77	79.65	75.97
Multi-Sensor Fusion				*Multi-Sensor Fusion*			
TSDF Fusion [11]	54.77	38.11	97.29	TSDF Fusion [11]	90.73	85.53	96.61
RoutedFusion [54]	53.98	37.73	94.86	RoutedFusion [54]	84.11	74.16	97.14
DI-Fusion [23] σ=0.15	48.84	32.50	**98.24**	DI-Fusion [23] σ=0.15	86.31	77.27	**97.74**
SenFuNet (Ours)	**93.39**	**91.28**	95.60	SenFuNet (Ours)	**93.73**	**91.56**	96.00
(a)				(b)			

when to perform sensor selection for increased completeness and smooth fusion when both sensors have registered observations. Note that this formulation is different from typical works on collaborative 3D reconstruction *e.g.* [19] where the goal is to align 3D reconstruction fragments to produce a complete model. In our Multi-Agent setting, the alignment is given and the task is instead to perform data fusion on the 3D fragments. No modification of our method is required to perform this task. We set $\lambda_1 = 1/1200$ and $\lambda_2 = 1/12000$ and split the original trajectory into 100 frame chunks that are divided between the agents. Table 4b and Fig. 6 *Bottom row* show that our method effectively fuses the incoming data streams and yields a 4% F-score gain on the TSDF Fusion baseline.

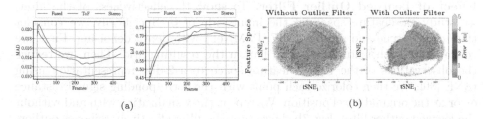

(a)   (b)

Fig. 7. (a) Performance over Camera Trajectory. Our fused output outperforms the single sensor reconstructions (V_t^i) for all frames along the camera trajectory. The above results are evaluated on the Replica *office 0* scene using {ToF, PSMNet} with depth denoising. Note that the results get slightly worse after 300 frames. This is due to additional noise from the depth sensors when viewing the scene from further away. **(b) Effect of Learned Outlier Filter.** The learned filter is crucial for robust outlier handling. Erroneous outlier predictions shown in yellow are effectively removed by our approach while keeping the correct green-colored predictions. (Color figure online)

4.4 More Statistical Analysis

Performance over Camera Trajectory. To show that our fused output is not only better at the end of the fusion process, we visualize the quantitative performance across the accumulated trajectory. In Fig. 7a, we evaluate the office

0 scene on the sensors {ToF, PSMNet} with depth denoising. Our fused model consistently improves on the inputs.

Architecture Ablation. We perform a network ablation on the Replica dataset with the sensors {SGM, PSMNet} without depth denoising. In Table 5, we investigate the number of layers with kernel size 3 in the Weighting Network $\mathcal{G}$. Two layers yield optimal performance which amounts to a receptive field of $9 \times 9 \times 9$. This is realistic given that the

Table 5. Architecture Ablation. We vary the number of 3D convolutional layers with kernel size 3. Performance is optimal at 2 layers, equivalent to a receptive field of 9^3.

# Layers	0	1	2	3	4
F1	48.57	68.47	**69.86**	69.45	68.21

support for a specific sensor is local by nature.

Generalization Capability. Table 6 shows our model's generalization ability for {SGM, PSMNet} fusion when evaluated against a model trained and tested on the *office 0* scene. Our model generalizes well and performs almost on par with one which is only trained on the

Table 6. Generalization Capability. Our model generalizes well when evaluated on the *office 0* scene. We conclude this by training a model only on *office 0*.

Train Set	MSE↓ *e-04	MAD↓ *e-02	IoU↑ [0,1]	Acc.↑ [%]	F↑ %	P↑ [%]	R↑ [%]
Full Train Set	**4.51**	1.54	0.748	87.78	68.70	**59.49**	81.28
Office 0	4.54	**1.53**	**0.752**	**87.97**	**69.23**	59.45	**82.86**

office 0 scene. The generalization capability is not surprising since $\mathcal{G}$ has a limited receptive field of $9 \times 9 \times 9$.

Effect of Learned Outlier Filter. To show the effectiveness of the filter, we study the feature space on the input side of $\mathcal{G}$. Specifically, we consider the *hotel 0* scene and sensors {ToF, PSMNet} with depth denoising. First, we concatenate both feature grids and flatten the resulting grid. Then, we reduce the observations of the 12-dim feature space to a 2-dim representation using tSNE [30]. We then colorize each point with the corresponding signed distance error at the original voxel position. We repeat the visualization with and without the learned outlier filter. Fig. 7b shows that the filter effectively removes outliers while keeping good predictions.

Loss Ablation. Table 7 shows the performance difference when the model is trained only with the term $\mathcal{L}_f$ compared to the full loss (3). We perform {SGM, PSMNet} fusion on the Replica dataset. The extra terms of the full loss clearly help improve overall performance and specifically to filter outliers.

Table 7. Loss Ablation. When only the term $\mathcal{L}_f$ is used, we observe a significant performance drop compared to the full loss. Note, however, that only with the term $\mathcal{L}_f$, our model still improves on the single sensor input metrics compared to Table 3a.

Loss $\mathcal{L}$	MSE↓ *e-04	MAD↓ *e-02	IoU↑ [0,1]	Acc.↑ [%]	F↑ [%]	P↑ [%]	R↑ [%]
Only $\mathcal{L}_f$	6.04	1.78	0.710	86.20	62.65	50.88	**82.17**
Full Loss	**4.77**	**1.56**	**0.738**	**87.62**	**69.83**	**63.20**	79.12

Limitations. Our framework currently supports two sensors. Its extension to a k-sensor setting is straightforward, but the memory footprint grows linearly with the number of sensors. However, few devices have more than two or three depth sensors. While our method generates better results on average, some local regions may not improve and our method struggles with overlapping outliers from both sensors. For qualitative examples, see the supplementary material. Ideally, outliers can be filtered and the data fused with a learned scene representation as in [55], but our efforts to make [55] work with multiple sensors suggests that this is a harder learning problem which deserves attention in future work.

5   Conclusion

We propose a machine learning approach for online multi-sensor 3D reconstruction using depth maps. We show that a fusion decision on 3D features rather than directly on 2D depth maps generally improves surface accuracy and outlier robustness. This also holds when 2D fusion is straightforward, *i.e.* for time synchronized sensors, equal sensor resolution and calibration. The experiments demonstrate that our model handles various sensors, can scale to room-sized real-world scenes and produce a fused result that is quantitatively and qualitatively better than the single sensor inputs and the compared baselines methods.

Acknowledgements. This work was supported by the Google Focused Research Award 2019-HE-318, 2019-HE-323, 2020-FS-351, 2020-HS-411, as well as by research grants from FIFA and Toshiba. We further thank Hugo Sellerberg for helping with video editing.

References

1. Agresti, G., Minto, L., Marin, G., Zanuttigh, P.: Deep learning for confidence information in stereo and ToF data fusion. In: Proceedings of the IEEE International Conference on Computer Vision, pp. 697–705 (2017)
2. Agresti, G., Minto, L., Marin, G., Zanuttigh, P.: Stereo and ToF data fusion by learning from synthetic data. Inf. Fusion **49**, 161–173 (2019)
3. Ali, M.K., Rajput, A., Shahzad, M., Khan, F., Akhtar, F., Börner, A.: Multi-sensor depth fusion framework for real-time 3d reconstruction. IEEE Access **7**, 136471–136480 (2019)
4. Božič, A., Palafox, P., Thies, J., Dai, A., Nießner, M.: Transformerfusion: monocular RGB scene reconstruction using transformers. arXiv preprint arXiv:2107.02191 (2021)
5. Bylow, E., Olsson, C., Kahl, F.: Robust online 3d reconstruction combining a depth sensor and sparse feature points. In: 2016 23rd International Conference on Pattern Recognition (ICPR), pp. 3709–3714 (2016)
6. Bylow, E., Maier, R., Kahl, F., Olsson, C.: Combining depth fusion and photometric stereo for fine-detailed 3d models. In: Felsberg, M., Forssén, P.-E., Sintorn, I.-M., Unger, J. (eds.) SCIA 2019. LNCS, vol. 11482, pp. 261–274. Springer, Cham (2019). https://doi.org/10.1007/978-3-030-20205-7_22
7. Cao, Y.P., Kobbelt, L., Hu, S.M.: Real-time high-accuracy three-dimensional reconstruction with consumer RGB-D cameras. ACM Trans. Graph. (TOG) **37**(5), 1–16 (2018)

8. Chang, J.R., Chen, Y.S.: Pyramid stereo matching network. In: Proceedings of the IEEE Conference on Computer Vision and Pattern Recognition, pp. 5410–5418 (2018)
9. Choe, J., Im, S., Rameau, F., Kang, M., Kweon, I.S.: VolumeFusion: deep depth fusion for 3d scene reconstruction. In: Proceedings of the IEEE/CVF International Conference on Computer Vision (ICCV), pp. 16086–16095, October 2021
10. Choi, O., Lee, S.: Fusion of time-of-flight and stereo for disambiguation of depth measurements. In: Lee, K.M., Matsushita, Y., Rehg, J.M., Hu, Z. (eds.) ACCV 2012. LNCS, vol. 7727, pp. 640–653. Springer, Heidelberg (2013). https://doi.org/10.1007/978-3-642-37447-0_49
11. Curless, B., Levoy, M.: A volumetric method for building complex models from range images. In: Proceedings of the 23rd Annual Conference on Computer Graphics and Interactive Techniques, pp. 303–312 (1996)
12. Dai, A., Nießner, M., Zollhöfer, M., Izadi, S., Theobalt, C.: BundleFusion: real-time globally consistent 3d reconstruction using on-the-fly surface reintegration. ACM Trans. Graph. (ToG) 36(4), 1 (2017)
13. Dal Mutto, C., Zanuttigh, P., Cortelazzo, G.M.: Probabilistic TOF and stereo data fusion based on mixed pixels measurement models. IEEE Trans. Pattern Anal. Mach. Intell. 37(11), 2260–2272 (2015)
14. Deng, Y., Xiao, J., Zhou, S.Z.: TOF and stereo data fusion using dynamic search range stereo matching. IEEE Trans. Multimedia 24, 2739–2751 (2021)
15. Dong, W., Wang, Q., Wang, X., Zha, H.: PSDF fusion: probabilistic signed distance function for on-the-fly 3d data fusion and scene reconstruction. In: Proceedings of the European Conference on Computer Vision (ECCV), pp. 701–717 (2018)
16. Duan, Y., Pei, M., Wang, Y.: Probabilistic depth map fusion of kinect and stereo in real-time. In: 2012 IEEE International Conference on Robotics and Biomimetics (ROBIO), pp. 2317–2322. IEEE (2012)
17. Duan, Y., Pei, M., Wang, Y., Yang, M., Qin, I., Jia, Y.: A unified probabilistic framework for real-time depth map fusion. J. Inf. Sci. Eng. 31(4), 1309–1327 (2015)
18. Evangelidis, G.D., Hansard, M., Horaud, R.: Fusion of range and stereo data for high-resolution scene-modeling. IEEE Trans. Pattern Anal. Mach. Intell. 37(11), 2178–2192 (2015)
19. Golodetz, S., Cavallari, T., Lord, N.A., Prisacariu, V.A., Murray, D.W., Torr, P.H.: Collaborative large-scale dense 3d reconstruction with online inter-agent pose optimisation. IEEE Trans. Visual. Comput. Graph. 24(11), 2895–2905 (2018)
20. Gu, P., et al.: A 3d reconstruction method using multisensor fusion in large-scale indoor scenes. Complexity 2020 (2020)
21. Handa, A., Whelan, T., McDonald, J., Davison, A.J.: A benchmark for RGB-D visual odometry, 3d reconstruction and slam. In: 2014 IEEE International Conference on Robotics and Automation (ICRA), pp. 1524–1531. IEEE (2014)
22. Hirschmuller, H.: Stereo processing by semiglobal matching and mutual information. IEEE Trans. Pattern Anal. Mach. Intell. 30(2), 328–341 (2007)
23. Huang, J., Huang, S.S., Song, H., Hu, S.M.: Di-fusion: online implicit 3d reconstruction with deep priors. In: Proceedings of the IEEE/CVF Conference on Computer Vision and Pattern Recognition, pp. 8932–8941 (2021)
24. Izadi, S., et al.: KinectFusion: real-time 3d reconstruction and interaction using a moving depth camera. In: Proceedings of the 24th annual ACM Symposium on User Interface Software and Technology, pp. 559–568. ACM (2011)
25. Kähler, O., Prisacariu, V.A., Ren, C.Y., Sun, X., Torr, P.H.S., Murray, D.W.: Very high frame rate volumetric integration of depth images on mobile devices. IEEE Trans. Vis. Comput. Graph. 21(11), 1241–1250 (2015)

26. Kazhdan, M., Hoppe, H.: Screened poisson surface reconstruction. ACM Trans. Graph. (ToG) **32**(3), 1–13 (2013)
27. Kim, Y.M., Theobalt, C., Diebel, J., Kosecka, J., Miscusik, B., Thrun, S.: Multi-view image and TOF sensor fusion for dense 3d reconstruction. In: 2009 IEEE 12th International Conference on Computer Vision Workshops, ICCV workshops, pp. 1542–1549. IEEE (2009)
28. Lefloch, D., Weyrich, T., Kolb, A.: Anisotropic point-based fusion. In: 2015 18th International Conference on Information Fusion (Fusion), pp. 2121–2128. IEEE (2015)
29. Lorensen, W.E., Cline, H.E.: Marching cubes: a high resolution 3d surface construction algorithm. ACM siggraph Comput. Graph. **21**(4), 163–169 (1987)
30. Van der Maaten, L., Hinton, G.: Visualizing data using t-sne. J. Mach. Learn. Res. **9**(11), 2579–2605 (2008)
31. Maddern, W., Newman, P.: Real-time probabilistic fusion of sparse 3d lidar and dense stereo. In: 2016 IEEE/RSJ International Conference on Intelligent Robots and Systems (IROS), pp. 2181–2188. IEEE (2016)
32. Savva, M., et al.: Habitat: a platform for embodied AI Research. In: Proceedings of the IEEE/CVF International Conference on Computer Vision (ICCV) (2019)
33. Marin, G., Zanuttigh, P., Mattoccia, S.: Reliable fusion of ToF and stereo depth driven by confidence measures. In: Leibe, B., Matas, J., Sebe, N., Welling, M. (eds.) ECCV 2016. LNCS, vol. 9911, pp. 386–401. Springer, Cham (2016). https://doi.org/10.1007/978-3-319-46478-7_24
34. Martins, D., Van Hecke, K., De Croon, G.: Fusion of stereo and still monocular depth estimates in a self-supervised learning context. In: 2018 IEEE International Conference on Robotics and Automation (ICRA), pp. 849–856. IEEE (2018)
35. Murez, Z., van As, T., Bartolozzi, J., Sinha, A., Badrinarayanan, V., Rabinovich, A.: Atlas: end-to-end 3D scene reconstruction from posed images. In: Vedaldi, A., Bischof, H., Brox, T., Frahm, J.-M. (eds.) ECCV 2020. LNCS, vol. 12352, pp. 414–431. Springer, Cham (2020). https://doi.org/10.1007/978-3-030-58571-6_25
36. Newcombe, R.A., et al.: KinectFusion: real-time dense surface mapping and tracking. In: ISMAR, vol. 11, pp. 127–136 (2011)
37. Newcombe, R.A., Lovegrove, S.J., Davison, A.J.: DTAM: dense tracking and mapping in real-time. In: ICCV (2011)
38. Nießner, M., Zollhöfer, M., Izadi, S., Stamminger, M.: Real-time 3d reconstruction at scale using voxel hashing. ACM Trans. Graph. (TOG) **32** (2013). https://doi.org/10.1145/2508363.2508374
39. Oleynikova, H., Taylor, Z., Fehr, M., Siegwart, R., Nieto, J.I.: Voxblox: incremental 3d euclidean signed distance fields for on-board MAV planning. In: 2017 IEEE/RSJ International Conference on Intelligent Robots and Systems, IROS 2017, Vancouver, BC, Canada, 24–28 September 2017, pp. 1366–1373. IEEE (2017). https://doi.org/10.1109/IROS.2017.8202315
40. Park, K., Kim, S., Sohn, K.: High-precision depth estimation with the 3d lidar and stereo fusion. In: 2018 IEEE International Conference on Robotics and Automation (ICRA), pp. 2156–2163. IEEE (2018)
41. Patil, V., Van Gansbeke, W., Dai, D., Van Gool, L.: Don't forget the past: Recurrent depth estimation from monocular video. IEEE Robot. Autom. Lett. **5**(4), 6813–6820 (2020)
42. Poggi, M., Mattoccia, S.: Deep stereo fusion: combining multiple disparity hypotheses with deep-learning. In: 2016 Fourth International Conference on 3D Vision (3DV), pp. 138–147. IEEE (2016)

43. Pu, C., Song, R., Tylecek, R., Li, N., Fisher, R.B.: SDF-MAN: semi-supervised disparity fusion with multi-scale adversarial networks. Remote Sens. **11**(5), 487 (2019)
44. Qiu, J., et al.: Deeplidar: deep surface normal guided depth prediction for outdoor scene from sparse lidar data and single color image. In: IEEE Conference on Computer Vision and Pattern Recognition, CVPR 2019, Long Beach, CA, USA, 16–20 June 2019, pp. 3313–3322. Computer Vision Foundation/IEEE (2019). https://doi.org/10.1109/CVPR.2019.00343, https://openaccess.thecvf. com/content_CVPR_2019/html/Qiu_DeepLiDAR_Deep_Surface_Normal_Guided_ Depth_Prediction_for_Outdoor_Scene_CVPR_2019_paper.html
45. Rozumnyi, D., Cherabier, I., Pollefeys, M., Oswald, M.R.: Learned semantic multi-sensor depth map fusion. In: International Conference on Computer Vision Workshop (ICCVW), Workshop on 3D Reconstruction in the Wild, 2019. Seoul, South Korea (2019)
46. Schönberger, J.L., Zheng, E., Frahm, J.-M., Pollefeys, M.: Pixelwise view selection for unstructured multi-view stereo. In: Leibe, B., Matas, J., Sebe, N., Welling, M. (eds.) ECCV 2016. LNCS, vol. 9907, pp. 501–518. Springer, Cham (2016). https:// doi.org/10.1007/978-3-319-46487-9_31
47. Schops, T., Sattler, T., Pollefeys, M.: BAD SLAM: bundle adjusted direct RGB-D SLAM. In: CVPR (2019)
48. Steinbrucker, F., Kerl, C., Cremers, D., Sturm, J.: Large-scale multi-resolution surface reconstruction from RGB-D sequences. In: 2013 IEEE International Conference on Computer Vision, pp. 3264–3271 (2013)
49. Straub, J., et al.: The replica dataset: a digital replica of indoor spaces. arXiv preprint arXiv:1906.05797 (2019)
50. Sucar, E., Liu, S., Ortiz, J., Davison, A.: iMAP: implicit mapping and positioning in real-time. In: Proceedings of the IEEE International Conference on Computer Vision (2021)
51. Sun, J., Xie, Y., Chen, L., Zhou, X., Bao, H.: NeuralRecon: real-time coherent 3d reconstruction from monocular video. In: Proceedings of the IEEE/CVF Conference on Computer Vision and Pattern Recognition, pp. 15598–15607 (2021)
52. Van Baar, J., Beardsley, P., Pollefeys, M., Gross, M.: Sensor fusion for depth estimation, including TOF and thermal sensors. In: 2012 Second International Conference on 3D Imaging, Modeling, Processing, Visualization & Transmission, pp. 472–478. IEEE (2012)
53. Wasenmüller, O., Meyer, M., Stricker, D.: Corbs: comprehensive RGB-D benchmark for slam using kinect v2. In: 2016 IEEE Winter Conference on Applications of Computer Vision (WACV), pp. 1–7. IEEE (2016)
54. Weder, S., Schönberger, J.L., Pollefeys, M., Oswald, M.R.: RoutedFusion: learning real-time depth map fusion. ArXiv abs/2001.04388 (2020)
55. Weder, S., Schonberger, J.L., Pollefeys, M., Oswald, M.R.: NeuralFusion: online depth fusion in latent space. In: Proceedings of the IEEE/CVF Conference on Computer Vision and Pattern Recognition, pp. 3162–3172 (2021)
56. Yan, Z., Tian, Y., Shi, X., Guo, P., Wang, P., Zha, H.: Continual neural mapping: learning an implicit scene representation from sequential observations. In: Proceedings of the IEEE/CVF International Conference on Computer Vision (ICCV), pp. 15782–15792, October 2021
57. Yang, S., et al.: Noise-resilient reconstruction of panoramas and 3d scenes using robot-mounted unsynchronized commodity RGB-D cameras. ACM Trans. Graph. (TOG) **39**(5), 1–15 (2020)

58. Yang, S., Li, B., Liu, M., Lai, Y.K., Kobbelt, L., Hu, S.M.: HeteroFusion: dense scene reconstruction integrating multi-sensors. IEEE Trans. Visual. Comput. Graph. **26**(11), 3217–3230 (2019)
59. Zhou, Q.Y., Koltun, V.: Dense scene reconstruction with points of interest. ACM Trans. Graph. (ToG) **32**(4), 1–8 (2013)
60. Zhu, Z., et al.: Nice-slam: neural implicit scalable encoding for slam. In: Proceedings of the IEEE/CVF Conference on Computer Vision and Pattern Recognition, pp. 12786–12796 (2022)
61. Zollhöfer, M., et al.: State of the art on 3d reconstruction with RGB-D cameras. In: Computer Graphics Forum, vol. 37, pp. 625–652. Wiley Online Library (2018)

BungeeNeRF: Progressive Neural Radiance Field for Extreme Multi-scale Scene Rendering

Yuanbo Xiangli[1], Linning Xu[1], Xingang Pan[2], Nanxuan Zhao[1,3], Anyi Rao[1], Christian Theobalt[2], Bo Dai[4(✉)], and Dahua Lin[1,4]

[1] The Chinese University of Hong Kong, Shenzhen, China
{xy019,xl020,ra018,dhlin}@ie.cuhk.edu.hk
[2] Max Planck Institute for Informatics, Saarbrucken, Germany
{xpan,theobalt}@mpi-inf.mpg.de
[3] University of Bath, Bath, UK
[4] Shanghai Artificial Intelligence Laboratory, Shanghai, China
daibo@pjlab.org.cn

Abstract. Neural radiance fields (NeRF) has achieved outstanding performance in modeling 3D objects and controlled scenes, usually under a single scale. In this work, we focus on multi-scale cases where large changes in imagery are observed at drastically different scales. This scenario vastly exists in real-world 3D environments, such as city scenes, with views ranging from satellite level that captures the overview of a city, to ground level imagery showing complex details of an architecture; and can also be commonly identified in landscape and delicate minecraft 3D models. The wide span of viewing positions within these scenes yields multi-scale renderings with very different levels of detail, which poses great challenges to neural radiance field and biases it towards compromised results. To address these issues, we introduce BungeeNeRF, a progressive neural radiance field that achieves level-of-detail rendering across drastically varied scales. Starting from fitting distant views with a shallow base block, as training progresses, new blocks are appended to accommodate the emerging details in the increasingly closer views. The strategy progressively activates high-frequency channels in NeRF's positional encoding inputs and successively unfolds more complex details as the training proceeds. We demonstrate the superiority of BungeeNeRF in modeling diverse multi-scale scenes with drastically varying views on multiple data sources (city models, synthetic, and drone captured data) and its support for high-quality rendering in different levels of detail.

1 Introduction

Neural volumetric representations [15,16,21,22,24,37] have demonstrated remarkable capability in representing 3D objects and scenes from images.

Y. Xiangli and L. Xu—Equal contribution.

Supplementary Information The online version contains supplementary material available at https://doi.org/10.1007/978-3-031-19824-3_7.

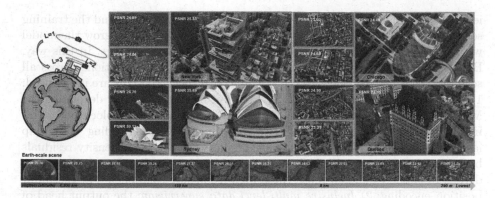

Fig. 1. BungeeNeRF is capable of packing extreme multi-scale city scenes into a unified model, which preserves high-quality details across scales varying from satellite-level to ground-level. *Top:* We use the edge colors to denote three scales from the most remote to the closest, with PSNR values displayed at the top-left corner of each rendered image. *Bottom:* BungeeNeRF can even accommodate variations at *earth-scale*. (src: *New York, Chicago, Sydney,* and *Quebec* scenes ©2022 Google).

Neural radiance fields (NeRF) [22] encodes a 3D scene with a continuous volumetric function parameterized by a multilayer perceptron (MLP), and maps a 5D coordinate (position and viewing direction) to the corresponding color and volume density in a scene. While NeRF has been shown effective in controlled environments with a bounded and single-scale setting, the "single-scale" assumption can easily be violated in real-world scenarios. Despite early attempts on representing multi-scale 3D scenes have been made in [2,3,14], it remains unclear how well a neural radiance field can handle scenarios at drastically varied scales.

In this work, we are interested in offering high-quality renderings of scenes under such extreme scale variations. One typical scenario is our living city, which is essentially large- and multi-scale with adequate variety in components. A direct observation on capturing city scenes is that, the large span of allowed viewing positions within the scene can induce significant visual changes: as the camera ascends, the imagery of ground objects exhibit less geometric detail and lower texture resolution; meanwhile, new objects from peripheral regions are getting streamingly included into the view with growing spatial coverage, as shown in Fig. 1. As the result, the variation in levels of detail and linear field of view raises a tension among scales when learning to model such scenes with neural representations. It poses great challenges on NeRF and its derivatives which treat all pixel signals indiscriminately regardless of their scales. With limited model capacity, the rendered close views always have blurry textures and shapes, and remote views tend to be incomplete with artifacts in peripheral scene areas. Other than city scenes, such challenges also commonly exist in synthetic scenes, for example in minecraft model and delicate 3D objects.

Targeting the above challenges, we propose BungeeNeRF, a progressive neural radiance field that enables level-of-detail rendering across the drastically varied scales. Starting from the most remote scale, we gradually expand the training set by one closer scale at each training stage, and synchronously grow the model with multiple output heads for different level-of-detail renderings. In this way, BungeeNeRF robustly learns a hierarchy of radiance representations across all scales of the scene. To facilitate the learning, two special designs are introduced: 1) *Growing model with residual block structure*: instead of naively deepening the MLP network, we grow the model by appending an additional block per training stage. Each block is re-exposed to the input position encoding via a skip layer, and has its own output head that predicts the color and density residuals between successive stages, which encourages the block to focus on the emerging details in closer views and reuse these high-frequency components in the input position encoding; 2) *Inclusive multi-level data supervision*: the output head of each block is supervised by the union of images from the most remote scale up to its corresponding scale. In other words, the last block receives supervision from all training images while the earliest block is only exposed to the images of the coarsest scale. With such design, each block module is able to fully utilize its capacity to model the increasingly complex details in closer views with the input Fourier position encoding features, and guarantees a consistent rendering quality between scales.

Extensive experiments show that, in the presence of multi-scale scenes with large-scale changes, BungeeNeRF is able to construct more complete remote views and brings out significantly more details in close views, as shown in Fig. 1, whereas baseline NeRF/Mip-NeRF trained under vanilla scheme constantly fail. Specifically, our model effectively preserves scene features learnt on remote views, and actively access higher frequency Fourier features in the positional encoding to construct finer details for close views. Furthermore, BungeeNeRF allows views to be rendered by different output heads from shallow to deep blocks, providing additional flexibility of viewing results in a level-of-detail manner.

2   Related Work

NeRF and Beyond. NeRF has inspired many subsequent works that extend its continuous neural volumetric representation for more practical scenarios beyond simple static scenes, including unbounded scenes [3,42], dynamic scenes [12,41], nonrigidly deforming objects [25–27,38], phototourism settings with changing illumination and occluders [19,28], etc. In this work, we deal with a more extreme scenario in terms of the spatial span, and aim to bring neural radiance fields with an unprecedented multi-scale capability, such as that in a city scenario where images can be captured from satellite-level all the way down to the ground.

While this extreme multi-scale characteristic is often compounded with the "large scale" characteristic, such as delivering an entire city model containing hundreds of city blocks, in this project, we separate the large scenes in single-scale cases [35,39] from our study focus. Orthogonal to these works which focus on dealing with the large horizontal span of urban data with proposed division and blending solutions using multiple NeRF models, we try to enlarge NeRF's capability in representing multi-scale scenes under a new training paradigm.

Multi-scale Representations in 3D Scenes. The adoption of position encoding in NeRF enables the multilayer perceptron (MLP) to learn high-frequency functions from the low-dimensional coordinate input [36]. A line of works have been proposed to tackle the multi-scale issue or coarse-to-fine learning problem by adjusting this position encoding. In particular, Mip-NeRF [2] uses integrated positional encoding (IPE) that replaces NeRF's point-casting with cone-casting, which allows the model to explicitly reason about 3D volumes. [13,25,26] alternatively adopt windowed positional encoding to aid learning dynamic shapes via a coarse-to-fine training. BACON [14] differs from these works by designing multi-scale architecture that achieves mult-iscale outputs via Multiplicative Filter Networks [6]. While these approaches have shown multi-scale properties on common objects and small scenes, their generalization to drastic scale changes (*e.g.* city scenes) remain unexplored, and often caught unstable training in practice.

In image processing, many techniques relies on image pyramid [30] to represent images at multiple resolutions. A related concept to multi-scale representation in computer graphics is *level-of-detail* (LOD) [4,17], which refers to the complexity of a 3D model representation, in terms of metrics such as geometric detail and texture resolution. The hierarchical representation learnt by BungeeNeRF can be seen as an analogue to this concept, where features learnt at different blocks represent geometries and textures of different complexity. [34] proposed to represent implicit surfaces using an octree-based feature volume which adaptively fits shapes with multiple discrete LODs. [18] used a multi-scale block-coordinate decomposition approach that is optimized during training. Recently, [23] propose a multiresolution structure with hash tables storing trainable feature vectors that achieves a combined speedup of several orders of magnitude. These approaches work under the assumption of bounded scenes, where the covered 3D volume can be divided into multi-granularity grids or cells, whose vertices store scene features at different scales. Unlike these feature-based multi-scale representations, we take an alternative approach to represent multi-scale information with a dynamic model grown in blocks, which allows representing scenes of arbitrary size, instead of relying on pre-learnt features on vertices within a bounded scene.

3   BungeeNeRF

In this paper, we aim at representing extreme multi-scale application scenarios with a progressive neural radiance field, where scenes are captured by cameras of very different distances towards the target. For intuitive demonstration, our methodology is majorly elaborated in the context of city scenes. Figure 1 illustrates that, the drastic span in camera distance brings extreme multi-scale characteristic in renderings, induced by large-scale change in levels of detail and linear field of view.

In the following sections, Sect. 3.1 gives the necessary background for NeRF and Mip-NeRF. Section 3.2 discusses the challenges of representing scenes under the drastic multi-scale condition with neural radiance field. Our proposed progressive network growing and training scheme is elaborated in Sect. 3.3.

Fig. 2. Observed artifacts on modeling multi-scale scenes with neural radiance fields [2]: (a) jointly train on all scales and (b) separately on each scale. Artifacts on rendered images are highlighted by solid boxes, with ground truth patches (GT) displayed on the side. Joint training on all scales results in blurry texture in close views and incomplete geometry in remote views; while separate training on each scale yields inconsistent renderings between successive scales, where an additional fusion step is generally required.

3.1 Preliminaries on NeRF and Mip-NeRF

NeRF [22] parameterizes the volumetric density and color as a function of input coordinates, using the weights of a MLP. For each pixel on the image, a ray $\mathbf{r}(t)$ is emitted from the camera's center of projection and passes through the pixel. For any query point $\mathbf{r}(t_k)$ on the ray, the MLP takes in its Fourier transformed features, *i.e.* position encoding (PE), and outputs the per-point density and color. Mip-NeRF [2] treats rays as cones and extends NeRF's point-based input to volumetric frustums, which remedies NeRF's aliasing issue when rendering at varying resolution. For each interval $T_k = [t_k, t_{k+1})$ along the ray, the conical frustum is represented by its mean and covariance $(\mu, \Sigma) = \mathbf{r}(T_k)$ which is further transformed to Fourier features with integrated positional encoding (IPE):

$$\gamma(\mu, \Sigma) = \left\{ \begin{bmatrix} \sin(2^m \mu) \exp(-2^{2m-1} \operatorname{diag}(\Sigma)) \\ \cos(2^m \mu) \exp(-2^{2m-1} \operatorname{diag}(\Sigma)) \end{bmatrix} \right\}_{m=0}^{M-1},$$

based on a Gaussian approximation over the conical frustum. The MLP is then optimized abiding by the classical volume rendering, where the estimated densities and colors for all the sampled points $\mathbf{r}(t_k)$ are used to approximate the volume rendering integral using numerical quadrature [20]:

$$\mathbf{C}(\mathbf{r}; \mathbf{t}) = \sum_k T_k \left(1 - \exp\left(-\tau_k \left(t_{k+1} - t_k\right)\right)\right) \mathbf{c}_k, \quad T_k = \exp\left(-\sum_{k' < k} \tau_{k'} \left(t_{k'+1} - t_{k'}\right)\right),$$

where $\mathbf{C}(\mathbf{r}; \mathbf{t})$ is the final predicted color of the pixel. The final loss is the total squared error between the rendered and ground truth colors for the collection of sampled rays within a batch.

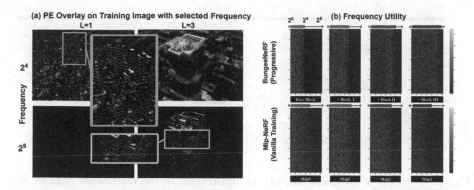

Fig. 3. (a) Imagery at different scales requires different Fourier feature frequencies in positional encoding to recover corresponding details. For example, rendering close views ($L = 3$) requires higher-frequency components with $m = 10$, while lower-frequency components with $m = 5$ are sufficient for remote views ($L = 1$). (b) BungeeNeRF's progressive neural radiance field effectively activates higher-frequency Fourier features in position encoding at deeper blocks, whereas MipNeRF trained under the vanilla scheme is biased to use only lower-frequency Fourier features, even at the deepest skip connection.

3.2 Challenges

The challenges brought by drastic multi-scale scene rendering are manifold. Firstly, the regions observed by close cameras is a subspace of remote cameras, whilst remote cameras captures significant parts of the scene that are not covered by close ones. This results in inconsistent quality within rendered images, as illustrated in Fig. 2(a). In contrast, training each scale separately eliminates such inconsistency but sacrifices the communication between successive scales, leading to significant discrepancies as shown in Fig. 2(b), which requires further fusion steps to blend the results.

It is noted that the *effective frequency channels* in PE and IPE differ from one scale to another. As depicted in Fig. 3(a)[1], for a close view ($L = 3$) showing complex details of a rooftop, the low-frequency Fourier feature appears to be insufficient, while a higher-frequency Fourier feature is activated to better align with such details. In contrast, the remote view ($L = 1$) can be well represented by the low-frequency Fourier feature, hence the high-frequency one is dampened. Subsequently, the high-frequency channels in PE are only activated in close views. However, due to the limited amount of close views in the training data, NeRF/MipNeRF trained on all scales as a whole tend to overlook these high-frequency scene components, leading to compromised solutions that are biased to utilize low-frequency features only.

---

[1] The visualizations are acquired by inferring point weights from a trained Mip-NeRF, and accumulate only the selected frequency channel values, following a similar approach of Eq. 3.1 by replacing $\mathbf{c}_k$ with the selected channel value for each point.

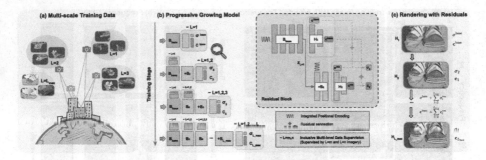

Fig. 4. Overview of BungeeNeRF. (a) An illustration of the multi-scale data in city scenes, where we use $L \in \{1, 2, 3, ...\}$ to denote scales. At each stage, our model grows in synchronization with the training set. (b) New residual blocks are appended to the network as the training proceeds, supervised by the union of samples from the most remote scale up to the current scale. The paradigm of a residual block is shown in the dashed box. (c) LOD rendering results obtained at different residual blocks. From shallow to deep, details are added bit by bit. (src: *Sydney* scene ©2022 Google)

3.3   Progressive Model with Multi-level Supervision

The large-scale data change induced by the drastic multi-scale characteristic implies varying learning difficulty and focus. We therefore propose to build and train the model in a progressive manner, with the aim to encourage the division of works among network layers, and unleash the power of the full frequency band in PE. Moreover, insights from curriculum learning [5,7–10,33,44] tell that training models in a meaningful order may ease the training on difficult tasks with model weights initialized on easy samples. This further underpins our motivation to adopt a progressive training strategy. The overall paradigm of BungeeNeRF is presented in Fig. 4.

In our framework, the training data and the model are grown in a synchronized multi-stage fashion. We denote L_{max} as the total number of training stages pre-determined for a captured scene, which also discretizes the continuous distance between the camera and the scene. In experiments, we partition the training data according to the camera distance, approximating a hierarchy of resolutions of objects in the scene abide by projective geometry. We regard the closest view as at full resolution. A new scale is set when the camera zooms out by a factor of $\{2^1, 2^2, 2^3, ...\}$.[2] Each image is then assigned with a stage indicator I_l that is shared among all its pixels and the sampling points along casted rays, with $\{I_l = L\}$ denoting the set of images belong to the scale L.[3]

---

[2] In general cases where the distance/depth information are not accessible, I_l can be approximated by the spatial size of textures in the image. The choice of L_{max} is relatively flexible since it is natural to interpolate results obtained from successive blocks and achieve smooth LOD transition.

[3] Per-pixel assigned scale is also possible and is likely to gain improvements if depth value is available. For our experiments, image-wise assignment already suffices.

Start from remote views ($L{=}1$), as the training progresses, views from one closer scale $L + 1$ are incorporated at each training stage. Such data feeding scheme remedies the bias in sample distribution by allowing the model to put more effort on peripheral regions at the early training stage. Meanwhile, a rough scene layout can be constructed, which naturally serves as a foundation for closer views in subsequent training stages. Along with the expansion of the training set, the model grows by appending new blocks. As illustrated in Fig. 4, each block is paired with an output head to predict the color and density *residuals* of scene contents viewed at successively closer scales. The most remote views are allowed to exit from the shallow block with only base color, while close-up views have to be processed by deeper blocks and rendered with progressively added residual colors. PE is injected to each block via a skip connection to capture the emerging complex details in scene components. All layers in the network remain trainable throughout the training process.

Residual Block Structure. It can be observed that remote views usually exhibit less complex details, making it a relatively easier task to start with. We adopt a shallow MLP to be our *base block*, denoted as B_{base}, with $D_{base}{=}4$ hidden layers and $W{=}256$ hidden units each to fit the most remote scale $\{I_l = 1\}$. A skip connection is not included as the base block is shallow. The output head for color and density follows the original NeRF paper.

When we proceed to the next training stage, a block B_L consisting of $D_{res}{=}2$ layers of non-linear mappings is appended to the model. A skip connection is added to forward the positional encoding $\gamma(\mathbf{x})$ to the block. The intuition is that, since shallow layers are fitted on remote views, the features are learnt to match with low level of detail, hence only low-frequency channels in PE are activated. However, the new layers need to access the high-frequency channels in PE to construct the emerging details in closer views. As verified in Fig. 3(b), our progressive training strategy is able to resort to higher-frequency Fourier features at a deeper block. In contrast, the matching baseline (*i.e.* Mip-NeRF-full) is incapable of activating high-frequency channels in PE even after the deepest skip layer, thus failing to represent more complex details.

The additive block B_L outputs residual colors and densities based on the latent features $\mathbf{z}_{L-1}$ obtained from the last mapping layer of the previous block:

$$(\mathbf{c}_L^{res}, \sigma_L^{res}) = f_L^{res}(\mathbf{z}_{L-1}, \mathbf{x}, \mathbf{d}). \tag{1}$$

The output exit from head H_L is then aggregated as

$$\mathbf{c}_L = \mathbf{c}^{base} + \sum_{l=2}^{L} \mathbf{c}_l^{res}, \quad \sigma_L = \sigma^{base} + \sum_{l=2}^{L} \sigma_l^{res}. \tag{2}$$

The design with residuals has mutual benefits for all scales. Firstly, it encourages intermediate blocks to concentrate on the missing details and take advance of the high-frequency Fourier features supplied via skip connection. Furthermore, it enables gradients obtained from latter blocks to smoothly flow back to earlier blocks and enhance the shallow features with the supervision from closer views.

Inclusive Multi-level Supervision. To guarantee a consistent rendering quality across all scales, at training stage L, the output head H_L is supervised by the union of images from previous scales, *i.e.* $\{I_l \leq L\}$. The loss at stage L is aggregated over all previous output heads from H_1 to H_L:

$$\mathcal{L}_L = \sum_{l=1}^{L} \sum_{r \in \mathcal{R}_l} \left(\left\| \hat{C}(\mathbf{r}) - C(\mathbf{r}) \right\|_2^2 \right), \tag{3}$$

where $\mathcal{R}_l$ is the set of rays with stage indicator up to stage l, and $C(\mathbf{r}), \hat{C}(\mathbf{r})$ are the ground truth and predicted RGB.

The design of multi-level supervision embeds the idea of *level-of-detail*, with deeper output heads providing more complex details in the rendered views. Compared to traditional mipmapping [40] which requires a pyramid of pre-defined models at each scale, this strategy unifies different levels of detail into a single model and can be controlled with L.

4   Experiment

We train BungeeNeRF on multi-scale city data acquired from Google Earth Studio [1] and evaluate the quality of reconstructed views and synthesized novel views. More experiments are also conducted on landscape scenes, real-world UAV captured scenes, and Blender-synthetic scenes. We compare our method to NeRF [22], NeRF with windowed positional encoding (NeRF w/WPE) [25], and Mip-NeRF [2]. The effects of the progressive strategy, and the block design with skip layer and residual connection are further analyzed in the ablation study.

Data Collection. Google Earth Studio [1] is used as the main data source for our experiments, considering their easy capturing of multi-scale city imagery by specifying camera positions, with sufficient data quality and rich functionalities to mimic the challenges in real world. We test our model and compare it against baselines on twelve city scenes across the world. When collecting data, we move the camera in a circular motion and gradually elevate the camera from a low altitude ($\sim$ ground-level) to a high altitude ($\sim$ satellite-level). The radius of the orbit trajectory is expanded during camera ascent to ensure a large enough spatial coverage. Statistics of the collected scenes are listed in Table 1. Additional data sources are introduced and experimented in Sect. 4.3.

Metrics. We report all metrics on the results exit from the last output head in BungeeNeRF. For quantitative comparison, results are evaluated on low-level full reference metrics, including PSNR and SSIM [32]. Perceptually, we use LPIPS [43] which utilizes a pre-trained VGG encoder [31]. Since the scenes are captured across different scales, a single mean metric averaged from all rendering results cannot fairly reflect quality considering the varied detail complexity across scales. We additionally report the mean PSNR obtained at each scale.

Implementation. We set $L_{max}=4$ for BungeeNeRF, hence the model at the final training stage has 10 layers of 256 hidden units, with skip connections at

Table 1. Twelve city scenes captured in Google Earth Studio.

	Main experiments		Extra tests: used for various illustrations throughout the paper and additional comparisons in Supplementary								
City Scene	New York	San Francisco	Sydney	Seattle	Chicago	Quebec	Amsterdam	Barcelona	Rome	Los Angeles	Bilbao	Paris
Alt (m)	56 Leonard	Transamerica	Opera House	Space Needle	Pritzker Pavilion	Château Frontenac	New Church	Sagrada Família	Colosseum	Hollywood	Guggenheim	Pompidou
Lowest	290	326	115	271	365	166	95	299	130	660	163	159
Highest	3,389	2,962	2,136	18,091	6,511	3,390	2,3509	8,524	8,225	12,642	7,260	2,710
# Images	463	455	220									

Table 2. Quantitative comparison on *56 Leonard* and *Transamerica* scenes. *D* denotes model depth and *Skip* indicates which layer(s) the skip connection is inserted to. Better performance can be achieved if each stage is trained until convergence. (**best**/2nd best)

	56 Leonard (PSNR ↑)				Transamerica (PSNR ↑)				56 Leonard (Avg.)			Transamerica (Avg.)		
	Stage I	Stage II	Stage III	Stage IV	Stage I	Stage II	Stage III	Stage IV	PSNR ↑	LPIPS ↓	SSIM ↑	PSNR ↑	LPIPS ↓	SSIM ↑
NeRF (D = 8, Skip = 4)	21.279	22.053	22.100	21.853	22.711	22.811	_22.976_	_21.581_	21.702	0.320	0.636	22.642	0.318	0.690
NeRF w/ WPE (D = 8, Skip = 4)	22.022	22.097	21.799	21.439	_23.382_	_23.171_	22.450	20.806	21.672	0.365	0.633	22.352	0.331	0.680
Mip-NeRF-small (D = 8, Skip = 4)	21.899	22.179	22.045	21.763	23.346	23.030	22.645	20.937	21.975	0.344	0.648	22.692	0.327	0.687
Mip-NeRF-large (D = 10, Skip = 4)	22.020	22.403	22.277	21.975	23.196	22.900	22.439	20.743	22.227	0.318	0.666	22.525	0.330	0.686
Mip-NeRF-full (D = 10, Skip = 4,6,8)	_22.043_	_22.484_	_22.690_	_22.355_	23.377	23.156	22.854	21.152	_22.312_	_0.266_	_0.689_	_22.828_	_0.314_	_0.699_
BungeeNeRF (same iter as baselines)	**23.145**	**23.548**	**23.744**	**23.015**	**24.259**	**23.911**	**23.507**	**22.942**	**23.481**	**0.235**	**0.739**	**23.606**	**0.265**	**0.749**
BungeeNeRF (until convergence)	**24.120**	**24.345**	**25.382**	**25.112**	**24.608**	**24.350**	**24.357**	**24.608**	**24.513**	**0.160**	**0.815**	**24.415**	**0.192**	**0.801**

the 4, 6, 8-th layer. For a fair comparison, the best baseline model with the same configuration is also implemented. Mip-NeRF's IPE [2] is adopted in BungeeN-eRF as we found it consistently outperforms the vanilla PE in multi-scale scenes. For all methods, the highest frequency is set to $M=10$, with 128 sample queries per ray. We train BungeeNeRF for $100k$ iterations per stage and the baselines till converge. All models are optimized using Adam [11] with a learning rate decayed exponentially from $5e^{-4}$ and a batch size of $2,048$. The optimizer is reset at each training stage for BungeeNeRF.

4.1 Experiment Results

Table 2 shows our experiment results obtained at the final training phase on two populated city scenes. Extras scenes listed in Table 1 serve as various illustrations throughout the paper, with qualitative results provided in Supplementary. In general, BungeeNeRF achieves PSNR gains of 0.5–5 B compared to MipNeRF, especially at close scales rich in geometry details. Figure 5 shows the rendered novel views with BungeeNeRF and baseline methods on *New York* scene.

We show that naively deepening the network cannot resolve the problems arisen from different levels of detail and spatial coverage among scales, where remote views still suffer from blurry artifacts at edges. On the other hand, BungeeNeRF attains a superior visual quality both on the entire dataset and *at each scale* on all metrics, with a notable improvement in remote scales, where peripheral areas in the rendered views appear to be clearer and more complete compared to jointly training on all images. When approaching the central target as the camera descends, BungeeNeRF continuously brings more details to the scene components, whereas baseline methods always result in blurry background.

Figure 3(b) visualizes the network weights associated with each channel of PE, where a clear shift towards the higher frequency portion indicates that the

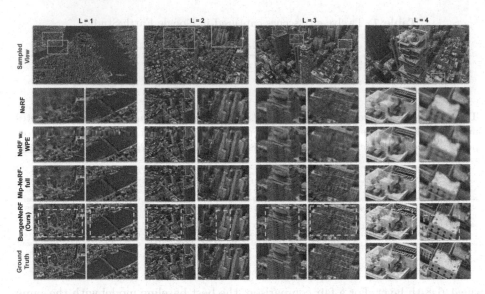

Fig. 5. Qualitative comparisons between NeRF [22], NeRF w/WPE [25], Mip-NeRF-full [2], and BungeeNeRF. BungeeNeRF consistently outperforms baseline methods across all scales with reliably constructed details. We strongly encourage readers for more results on diverse scenes in supplementary. (src: *New York* scene ©2022 Google)

Fig. 6. Rendering results from different output heads. BungeeNeRF allows flexible exits from different residual blocks with controllable LOD. Green box: remote views can exit from earlier heads with sufficient image details, and close views can get finer details when exiting from latter blocks. (src: *Amsterdam* scene ©2022 Google) (Color figure online)

model is able to leverage these parts of the information to construct details in the view. It is also noted that manually truncating PE for different blocks was experimentally found inferior than letting the model learn to choose from all frequencies in our experiments with large-scale changes.

Figure 6 qualitatively shows the rendering results from different output heads. It can be noticed that H_2 produces the coarsest visual results, which omits a significant amount of details when zooming in to closer views, but appears to be plausible for the set of remote views. The latter output heads gradually add more

Table 3. Ablation studies on *56 Leonard* and *Transamerica Pyramid* scene. The first set ablates the progressive strategy and the second set ablates residual block designs.

	56 Leonard (PSNR ↑)				Transamerica (PSNR ↑)				56 Leonard (Avg.)			Transamerica (Avg.)		
	Stage I	Stage II	Stage III	Stage IV	Stage I	Stage II	Stage III	Stage IV	PSNR ↑	LPIPS ↓	SSIM ↑	PSNR ↑	LPIPS ↓	SSIM ↑
Full BungeeNeRF	**23.145**	**23.548**	**23.744**	**23.015**	**24.259**	**23.911**	**23.507**	**22.942**	**23.481**	**0.235**	**0.739**	**23.606**	**0.265**	**0.749**
- inclusive supervision	22.570	22.475	23.300	23.188	23.623	23.039	22.508	21.294	22.773	0.298	0.700	22.789	0.309	0.696
- data feeding scheme	22.268	22.660	22.380	21.949	23.563	23.355	23.015	21.366	22.340	0.324	0.679	23.015	0.310	0.711
- model growing	22.826	22.121	21.471	20.972	24.026	23.560	22.554	20.503	22.139	0.326	0.666	23.055	0.317	0.706
- skip layer	23.046	23.364	23.317	22.746	24.232	23.696	22.950	22.151	23.159	0.259	0.730	23.235	0.283	0.725
- residual	23.104	23.325	23.228	22.786	24.091	23.608	23.236	22.796	23.139	0.257	0.729	23.364	0.272	0.735

complex geometric and texture details to the coarse output from previous stages, while maintaining the features learnt at shallower layers meaningful to earlier output heads. In practice, one may consider using earlier heads for rendering remote views for the sake of storage and time consumption.

4.2 Ablation Study

Effectiveness of Progressive Strategy. The effectiveness of progressive learning strategy is analyzed through the corresponding three ablation studies: 1) Ablate the inclusive multi-level data supervision, *i.e.* replacing the output head supervision $\{I_l \leq L\}$ with $\{I_l = L\}$; 2) Ablate the progressive data feeding schedule with fixed model size $L=4$, *i.e.* trained on all scales simultaneously, with different scales predicted by different output heads. 3) Ablate model progression and only use the output head H_4 of the final block. Note we still adopt the progressive data feeding schedule for this case. Results are listed in Table 3.

It is observed that: 1) Without the inclusive multi-level data supervision, the model achieves a slightly higher PSNR at the closest scale ($L = 4$), but the performances at remote scales degrade drastically. This is because deeper blocks are solely trained on close views, and are not responsible for constructing remote views. As the result, the additive blocks might deviate to better fit the close views, whilst shallow layers just maintain their status and ignore the extra information from deeper layers. 2) Without the progressive data feeding strategy, the results are even inferior than baselines. Firstly, due to the residual connection, the suboptimal results from remote views set a less ideal foundation for the modeling of closer views. Secondly, with all data being fitted simultaneously, the effective channels in PE still can not be distinguished between scales. On top of this, regularizing shallow features with remote views puts more restrictions on model capacity, which further harms the performance. 3) Without appending new layers, it is difficult for the model to accommodate the newly involved high-frequency information from closer scales, where the model has already been well fitted on distant scales. As the result, it achieves decent performance on the most remote scale ($L=1$) but becomes worse at closer scales.

Effectiveness of Model Design. To determine the effectiveness of the residual connection and the skip connection in our newly introduced block structure for neural radiance fields, we run ablations on: 1) Discarding the residual connection

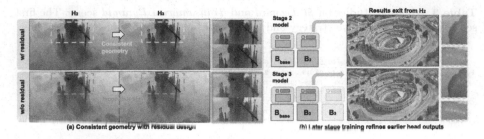

(a) Consistent geometry with residual design   (b) Later stage training refines earlier head outputs

Fig. 7. The residual connection enables supervisions from latter blocks to help refine the outputs from earlier heads (Fig.(b)), yielding more accurate geometries with consistent depths across scales (Fig.(a)). It also helps BungeeNeRF to focus on the missing details between the results rendered by shallower blocks and ground truth, leading to sharper visuals. (src: *Barcelona* and *Rome* scenes ©2022 Google)

when growing the network; 2) Inserting a skip connection at the same position as the original NeRF and discarding the rest in the additive blocks.

Table 3 shows that, without the skip layer or the residual connection, performance at each scale slightly degenerates but still outperforms baselines. 1) It can be observed that, the influence of skip layer is more notable on closer scales. In particular, on *Transamerica* scene, the absence of skip connection severely harms the performance at scale $L=4$, which could be ascribed to the fact that its remote views are much easier than close views. 2) Residual connections help form a better scene feature at remote scales for shallow output heads, by leveraging the supervision from deeper blocks to help correct the errors in early training phases, as shown in Fig. 7. Consequently, rendering results of lower LOD are more accurate, which in turn benefit latter training phases on closer views. Furthermore, we found that as the training proceeds, BungeeNeRF with residual gains an increasing advantage compared to the counterpart without residual. The additive nature of residual densities and colors enforces the model to emphasize the errors between the images rendered by previous stages and the ground truth, guiding the deeper blocks to recover the missing details using the newly introduced frequency information. Meanwhile, it also improves the predictions from previous output heads, yielding better base geometries and colors.

4.3   Extensions

Apart from city scenes, experiments are also conducted on landscape (in supplementary) and Blender-synthetic scenes (Fig. 10). BungeeNeRF can also represent scale changes expanding earth-level scenes as shown in Fig. 1. Additional to single dive-in and -out camera trajectory, Fig. 9 shows results obtained on a scene with multi-dive flying pattern, where BungeeNeRF effectively recovers details of multiple targets. Besides synthetic scenes, we also tested on UAV captured real-world scene where camera poses are estimated by COLMAP [29] (Fig. 8).

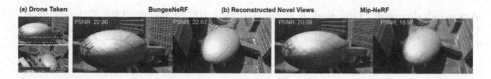

Fig. 8. Results on UAV captured scenes. (a) Recorded camera information shows the wide range of camera altitude changes (24~76m). (b) Novel views rendered with BungeeNeRF (a simpilied $L=2$ setting) demonstrate the superior performance compared to Mip-NeRF, which suggests its practical usage in real-world applications.

Fig. 9. BungeeNeRF (trained with $L=3$ stages) successfully recovers the fine details in a multi-dive city scene. (src: *Ellis Island, NY*©2022 Google)

Fig. 10. Results on Blender Synthetic data showing four scales. From left to right are Mip-NeRF, BungeeNeRF (trained with $L=4$ stages), and ground truth images.

5 Discussion and Conclusion

In this work, we propose BungeeNeRF, a progressive neural radiance field, to model scenes under a drastic multi-scale setting, with large-scale variation in level of detail and linear field of view, where a NeRF/Mip-NeRF trained under normal scheme has difficulty in accommodating such extreme data change. BungeeNeRF adopts a novel progressive training paradigm that synchronously grows the model and training set to learn a hierarchy of scene representations from coarse to fine, which demonstrates superior results on various scenes compared to baselines with ensured high-quality rendering across all scales.

While BungeeNeRF functions as a good building block for modeling large-scale 3D scenes in real world which is naturally rich in multi-scale observations, it is natural to consider its combined use with orthogonal advanced neural rendering techniques to bring more high-quality renderings results. Facing such needs, a comprehensive neural rendering system with integrated merits on multiple characteristics (*e.g.*, large-scale, photorealistic, dynamic, editable, etc.) with accurate control could be a promising and interesting research direction in the future.

Acknowledgment. This work is supported by GRF 14205719, TRS T41-603/20-R, Centre for Perceptual and Interactive Intelligence, and CUHK Interdisciplinary AI Research Institute.

References

1. Google earth studio. https://earth.google.com/studio/
2. Barron, J.T., Mildenhall, B., Tancik, M., Hedman, P., Martin-Brualla, R., Srinivasan, P.P.: Mip-NeRF: a multiscale representation for anti-aliasing neural radiance fields. arXiv preprint arXiv:2103.13415 (2021)
3. Barron, J.T., Mildenhall, B., Verbin, D., Srinivasan, P.P., Hedman, P.: Mip-NeRF 360: unbounded anti-aliased neural radiance fields. In: Proceedings of the IEEE/CVF Conference on Computer Vision and Pattern Recognition, pp. 5470–5479 (2022)
4. Clark, J.H.: Hierarchical geometric models for visible surface algorithms. Commun. ACM **19**(10), 547–554 (1976)
5. Dai, X., Chen, D., Liu, M., Chen, Y., Yuan, L.: DA-NAS: data adapted pruning for efficient neural architecture search. ArXiv abs/2003.12563 (2020)
6. Fathony, R., Sahu, A.K., Willmott, D., Kolter, J.Z.: Multiplicative filter networks. In: International Conference on Learning Representations (2020)
7. Guo, S., Huang, W., Zhang, H., Zhuang, C., Dong, D., Scott, M.R., Huang, D.: CurriculumNet: weakly supervised learning from large-scale web images. ArXiv abs/1808.01097 (2018)
8. Guo, Y., et al.: Breaking the curse of space explosion: towards efficient NAS with curriculum search. ArXiv abs/2007.07197 (2020)
9. Karras, T., Aila, T., Laine, S., Lehtinen, J.: Progressive growing of GANs for improved quality, stability, and variation. arXiv preprint arXiv:1710.10196 (2017)
10. Karras, T., Laine, S., Aittala, M., Hellsten, J., Lehtinen, J., Aila, T.: Analyzing and improving the image quality of styleGAN. In: 2020 IEEE/CVF Conference on Computer Vision and Pattern Recognition (CVPR), pp. 8107–8116 (2020)
11. Kingma, D.P., Ba, J.: Adam: a method for stochastic optimization. arXiv preprint arXiv:1412.6980 (2014)
12. Li, Z., Niklaus, S., Snavely, N., Wang, O.: Neural scene flow fields for space-time view synthesis of dynamic scenes. In: Proceedings of the IEEE/CVF Conference on Computer Vision and Pattern Recognition, pp. 6498–6508 (2021)
13. Lin, C.H., Ma, W.C., Torralba, A., Lucey, S.: BARF: bundle-adjusting neural radiance fields. arXiv preprint arXiv:2104.06405 (2021)
14. Lindell, D.B., Van Veen, D., Park, J.J., Wetzstein, G.: BACON: band-limited coordinate networks for multiscale scene representation. arXiv preprint arXiv:2112.04645 (2021)
15. Liu, L., Gu, J., Lin, K.Z., Chua, T.S., Theobalt, C.: Neural sparse voxel fields. ArXiv abs/2007.11571 (2020)
16. Lombardi, S., Simon, T., Saragih, J.M., Schwartz, G., Lehrmann, A.M., Sheikh, Y.: Neural volumes. ACM Trans. Graph. **38**, 1–14 (2019)
17. Luebke, D., Reddy, M., Cohen, J.D., Varshney, A., Watson, B., Huebner, R.: Level of Detail for 3D Graphics. Morgan Kaufmann, San Francisco (2003)
18. Martel, J.N., Lindell, D.B., Lin, C.Z., Chan, E.R., Monteiro, M., Wetzstein, G.: ACORN: adaptive coordinate networks for neural scene representation. arXiv preprint arXiv:2105.02788 (2021)

19. Martin-Brualla, R., Radwan, N., Sajjadi, M.S., Barron, J.T., Dosovitskiy, A., Duckworth, D.: Nerf in the wild: Neural radiance fields for unconstrained photo collections. In: Proceedings of the IEEE/CVF Conference on Computer Vision and Pattern Recognition, pp. 7210–7219 (2021)

20. Max, N.: Optical models for direct volume rendering. IEEE Trans. Visual. Ccoput. Graph. **1**, 99–108 (1995)

21. Mescheder, L.M., Oechsle, M., Niemeyer, M., Nowozin, S., Geiger, A.: Occupancy networks: learning 3d reconstruction in function space. 2019 IEEE/CVF Conference on Computer Vision and Pattern Recognition (CVPR), pp. 4455–4465 (2019)

22. Mildenhall, Ben, Srinivasan, Pratul P.., Tancik, Matthew, Barron, Jonathan T.., Ramamoorthi, Ravi, Ng, Ren: NeRF: representing scenes as neural radiance fields for view synthesis. In: Vedaldi, Andrea, Bischof, Horst, Brox, Thomas, Frahm, Jan-Michael. (eds.) ECCV 2020. LNCS, vol. 12346, pp. 405–421. Springer, Cham (2020). https://doi.org/10.1007/978-3-030-58452-8_24

23. Müller, T., Evans, A., Schied, C., Keller, A.: Instant neural graphics primitives with a multiresolution hash encoding. arXiv preprint arXiv:2201.05989 (2022)

24. Park, J.J., Florence, P.R., Straub, J., Newcombe, R.A., Lovegrove, S.: Deepsdf: Learning continuous signed distance functions for shape representation. In: 2019 IEEE/CVF Conference on Computer Vision and Pattern Recognition (CVPR), pp. 165–174 (2019)

25. Park, K., et al.: NerFies: deformable neural radiance fields. In: Proceedings of the IEEE/CVF International Conference on Computer Vision, pp. 5865–5874 (2021)

26. Park, K., et al.: HyperNerf: a higher-dimensional representation for topologically varying neural radiance fields. arXiv preprint arXiv:2106.13228 (2021)

27. Pumarola, A., Corona, E., Pons-Moll, G., Moreno-Noguer, F.: D-NeRF: neural radiance fields for dynamic scenes. In: Proceedings of the IEEE/CVF Conference on Computer Vision and Pattern Recognition, pp. 10318–10327 (2021)

28. Rematas, K., et al.: Urban radiance fields. arXiv preprint arXiv:2111.14643 (2021)

29. Schonberger, J.L., Frahm, J.M.: Structure-from-motion revisited. In: Proceedings of the IEEE Conference on Computer Vision and Pattern Recognition, pp. 4104–4113 (2016)

30. Simoncelli, E.P., Freeman, W.T.: The steerable pyramid: a flexible architecture for multi-scale derivative computation. In: Proceedings of the International Conference on Image Processing, vol. 3, pp. 444–447 (1995)

31. Simonyan, K., Zisserman, A.: Very deep convolutional networks for large-scale image recognition. CoRR abs/1409.1556 (2015)

32. Sitzmann, V., Zollhoefer, M., Wetzstein, G.: Scene representation networks: continuous 3D-structure-aware neural scene representations. ArXiv abs/1906.01618 (2019)

33. Soviany, P., Ionescu, R.T., Rota, P., Sebe, N.: Curriculum learning: a survey. arXiv preprint arXiv:2101.10382 (2021)

34. Takikawa, T., et al.: Neural geometric level of detail: real-time rendering with implicit 3d shapes. In: Proceedings of the IEEE/CVF Conference on Computer Vision and Pattern Recognition, pp. 11358–11367 (2021)

35. Tancik, M., et al.: Block-NeRF: scalable large scene neural view synthesis. arXiv preprint arXiv:2202.05263 (2022)

36. Tancik, M., et al.: Fourier features let networks learn high frequency functions in low dimensional domains. arXiv preprint arXiv:2006.10739 (2020)

37. Tewari, A., et al.: Advances in neural rendering. arXiv preprint arXiv:2111.05849 (2021)

38. Tretschk, E., Tewari, A., Golyanik, V., Zollhofer, M., Lassner, C., Theobalt, C.: Non-rigid neural radiance fields: Reconstruction and novel view synthesis of a dynamic scene from monocular video. In: Proceedings of the IEEE/CVF International Conference on Computer Vision, pp. 12959–12970 (2021)
39. Turki, H., Ramanan, D., Satyanarayanan, M.: Mega-NeRF: scalable construction of large-scale nerfs for virtual fly-throughs. arXiv preprint arXiv:2112.10703 (2021)
40. Williams, L.: Pyramidal parametrics. In: Proceedings of the 10th Annual Conference on Computer Graphics and Interactive Techniques, pp. 1–11 (1983)
41. Xian, W., Huang, J.B., Kopf, J., Kim, C.: Space-time neural irradiance fields for free-viewpoint video. In: Proceedings of the IEEE/CVF Conference on Computer Vision and Pattern Recognition, pp. 9421–9431 (2021)
42. Zhang, K., Riegler, G., Snavely, N., Koltun, V.: Nerf++: analyzing and improving neural radiance fields. arXiv preprint arXiv:2010.07492 (2020)
43. Zhang, K., Riegler, G., Snavely, N., Koltun, V.: Nerf++: analyzing and improving neural radiance fields. arXiv preprint arXiv:2010.07492 (2020)
44. Zhou, T., Wang, S., Bilmes, J.A.: Robust curriculum learning: from clean label detection to noisy label self-correction. In: ICLR (2021)

Decomposing the Tangent of Occluding Boundaries According to Curvatures and Torsions

Huizong Yang$^{(\boxtimes)}$ and Anthony Yezzi

Georgia Institute of Technology, Atlanta, USA
huizong.yang@gatech.edu, anthony.yezzi@ece.gatech.edu

Abstract. This paper develops new insight into the local structure of occluding boundaries on 3D surfaces. Prior literature has addressed the relationship between 3D occluding boundaries and their 2D image projections by radial curvature, planar curvature, and Gaussian curvature. Occluding boundaries have also been studied implicitly as intersections of level surfaces, avoiding their explicit description in terms of local surface geometry. In contrast, this work studies and characterizes the local structure of occluding curves explicitly in terms of the local geometry of the surface. We show how the first order structure of the occluding curve (its tangent) can be extracted from the second order structure of the surface purely along the viewing direction, without the need to consider curvatures or torsions in other directions. We derive a theorem to show that the tangent vector of the occluding boundary exhibits a strikingly elegant decomposition along the viewing direction and its orthogonal tangent, where the decomposition weights precisely match the geodesic torsion and the normal curvature of the surface respectively only along the line-of-sight! Though the focus of this paper is an enhanced theoretical understanding of the occluding curve in the continuum, we nevertheless demonstrate its potential numerical utility in a straight-forward marching method to explicitly trace out the occluding curve. We also present mathematical analysis to show the relevance of this theory to computer vision and how it might be leveraged in more accurate future algorithms for 2D/3D registration and/or multiview stereo reconstruction.

Keywords: Occluding boundaries · Differential geometry · Radial curves

1 Introduction

Occluding boundaries constitute one of the most important features of 3D surfaces with respect to a given viewpoint. They convey fruitful information such

Supplementary Information The online version contains supplementary material available at https://doi.org/10.1007/978-3-031-19824-3_8.

as silhouettes, topology, occlusions, etc., and have been intensively studied in both computer vision and computer graphics. One of the most beautiful mathematical properties, first published by Koenderink [15], is the elegant relationship between the radial 3D curvature of the occluding boundary, the 2D curvature of their perspective projection, and the 3D Gaussian curvature of the underlying surface. Less attention, however, has been directed toward understanding the local geometry of the 3D occluding boundaries themselves (without reference to the geometry of their 2D projections), which would have special relevance in formulating variational methods involving perspective projections of 3D shapes.

As such, we study the local behavior of the 3D occluding boundary curve itself, motivated by the goal to capture properties that can be conveniently computed on the surface for future use in numerical algorithms. Understanding the geometrical properties of occluding boundaries is not only important for classical 3D computer vision problems such as camera pose estimation, but can also guide the design of data-driven methods [33]. We will develop a theorem which shows that the first order structure of the occluding boundary curve can be determined entirely by second order properties of the underlying surface just along the viewing direction, greatly simplifying its future exploitation in numerical algorithms by obviating the need to estimate principal curvatures and directions.

1.1   Relationship to Prior Work

Marr [24] first analyzed occluding contours and related them to projections from various types of 3D solid shapes. While numerous useful conclusions were derived, a major point of insight was developed by Koenderink [15], showing that inflection correspondences between occluding contours and boundary curves are related by a specific property that the Gaussian curvature of the occlusion point (3D) is the product of its apparent curvature (2D) and radial curvature (3D). Lazbenik etc. [20], Hebert and Ponce [25] later extended Koenderink's work into pure projective geometry and enriched the understanding of solid shapes. A point to note about Koenderink's results that it did not invoke properties along the occluding tangent direction but rather along the radial (viewing) direction.

Numerous methods utilize occluding boundary cues to recover 3D shape [11, 12,31,32]. Specifically, Ikeuchi and Horn [12] attempted to determine the self-shadow boundary of objects but presumed the boundary curve to be laid on a plane, which is generally not the case. In addition to 3D shape inference, occluding boundary curves can also serve to accomplish recognition tasks [14]. Still, computing space curves satisfying certain conditions is not an easy task.

Recently, Fabbri and Kimia [9] developed a comprehensive theory on multiview differential occluding boundary curves, classified as non stationary curves in their frame work where these curves move as the view point changes. They derive differential equations to describe the evolution of points on the occluding curve with respect to a moving viewpoint, whereas our complementary focus will be to study the structure of a static occluding curve (fixed viewpoint).

More generic, yet closely related work is found in the computer graphics community [1,3,7,8,17,18,23,34] for calculating the intersection between two surfaces. In [18], Kriegman and Ponce represented space curves as the intersection of two implicit surface functions (alternatively approximated by polynomial functions). Occluding boundary curves could fit into this framework as a special case. Given an initial point [2], Kriegman and Ponce directly solved these equations numerically through looking for the next closest projection on a 2D subspace spanned by constant basis, then correcting it back to the intersection with Newton's method. Ye and Maekawa [34], furthermore, focused on computing the differential properties of the intersection curves by two implicit surfaces, including the tangent vectors of these curves. They also analyzed the singularities of different types of intersections, and gave the analytical expressions for these tangent vectors with respect to the normals of two surfaces. Düldül and Çalişkan also analyzed the curvatures and torsions of the intersection curves. Abdel-All [1] extended to characterizing the singularities of the intersection curves. They also gave necessary and sufficient conditions for those curves to be straight, planar, helical, and helix circular. While analytical solutions were studied and present in aforementioned works, calculations are restricted to pairs of implicit functions while the theorem we develop gives the solution in terms of the local geometric properties of the observed surface alone, independently of its representation.

1.2 Contributions of this Paper

While algorithms already exist to compute occluding boundaries as the intersections between the object surfaces and visibility hulls via surface intersection methods [3, 29], the relationship between the boundaries and the local surface patch has not been unveiled. This is the primary goal of this paper, and specifically to do so invoking only properties along the radial (viewing) direction. The resulting occluding tangent decomposition theorem is therefore the only intended contribution of this work, allowing numerical schemes in future algorithms to directly compute the occluding tangent from the surface and without calculating principal curvatures nor the principal directions along the surface, which become ill-defined at umbilical points and unstable to compute at near-umbilical points.

To validate the theorem numerically and illustrate how it may be exploited practically, we will demonstrate a new explicit tracing algorithm which leverages the results of the theorem in a very direct and obvious manner. More sophisticated and mature strategies can clearly be developed, and although our simple illustrative approach turned out surprisingly well, it is not our intent to claim any premature contribution in actual curve extraction algorithms here. Rather, the goal of our numerical experiments is to reinforce the theory numerically and demonstrate how it might be used for practical benefit.

1.3 Outline of Paper

The rest is structured as follows: we cover some preliminaries and derive the main theorem (Theorem 1) and contribution of this paper in Sect. 2. We follow with computational experiments in Sect. 3 to validate its numerical applicability by leveraging the theorem in an explicit rim tracing strategy. For both simple and more complicated geometries, we show how the decomposition in this Theorem can be used to directly trace out the occluding boundary (considering only local, not yet global, occlusion conditions thus far) by taking small steps in the resulting tangent direction from an arbitrarily detected starting point.

We follow this numerical validation of the theorem by further mathematical analysis, in Sect. 4, relating the variation of the projected 2D curve to that of the 3D occluding boundary curve, revealing the explicit appearance of the 3D tangent vector and thereby illustrating the relevance of this theory to the future design of improved variational methods in computer vision problems such as silhouette matching, 2D/3D registration, and multiview stereo reconstruction.

2   Occluding Tangent Decomposition

Occluding tangents are the tangent vectors to a space curve that divides the exterior of orientable surfaces into visible and invisible parts from certain view points (shown in Fig. 1). Formally we define the *local* occluding curve as

$$\mathcal{S}^* : \{X : \mathbf{n} \cdot (X - P) = 0, \ X \in \mathcal{S}\}$$

where $\mathbf{n}$ denotes the surface normal at point X, P the view point. Note that $\mathcal{S}^*$ is a superset of the *global* occluding rim $\mathcal{S}^{**}$ that projects to the silhouette boundary as self occlusions can make portions $\mathcal{S}^*$ project inside the silhouette.

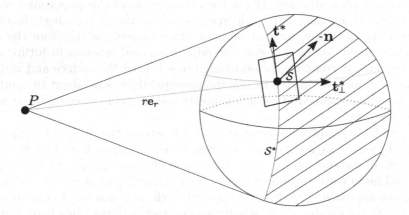

Fig. 1. Illustration of the occluding boundary curve $\mathcal{S}^*$ (blue) of a sphere. The red curve on the sphere is the *radial curve* and the grey straight dotted lines the lines of sight that touch the upper and the lower bound of the occluding boundary. P represents the view point, $\mathbf{e}_r$ the unit view direction and r the distance from view point to the surface point S.

2.1   Occluding Boundary Curve

If we consider a fixed viewpoint $P \in \mathbb{R}^3$ which is off the surface, we may construct a local parameterization of the surface by a radial distance $r = \|S - P\|$ and a radial unit vector $\mathbf{e}_r = (S - P)/r$ along the viewing direction

$$S(u,v) = P + r(u,v)\,\mathbf{e}_r(u,v)$$

where (u,v) denote the local surface parameters. We define the tangent vectors

$$\mathbf{t}_r = \mathbf{e}_r - (\mathbf{e}_r \cdot \mathbf{n})\mathbf{n}, \qquad \mathbf{t}_{r\perp} = \mathbf{n} \times \mathbf{t}_r \tag{1}$$

where $\mathbf{t}_r$ is the projection of $\mathbf{e}_r$ onto the tangent plane of S and where $\mathbf{t}_{r\perp}$ points in the orthogonal transverse direction. The resulting 3D frame $\mathbf{t}_r$, $\mathbf{t}_{r\perp}$, $\mathbf{n}$ becomes degenerate at any front-to-parallel point where $\mathbf{e}_r = \pm\mathbf{n}$ (such points in an angular sense, however, are maximally distant from occluding boundaries).

Accordingly, the occluding boundary curve $\mathcal{S}^*$ is pre-classified by the condition $\mathbf{t}_r = \mathbf{e}_r$ (recalling that $\mathcal{S}^*$ is a superset of the actual global occluding rim $\mathcal{S}^{**}$). We may equivalently express $\mathcal{S}^*$ by the zero level set of the following local occlusion function $g : \mathcal{S} \to \mathbb{R}$ along the surface.

$$g(S) \doteq \underbrace{(S - P)}_{r\,\mathbf{e}_r} \cdot \mathbf{n} \tag{2}$$

We will use the $*$ superscript notation to denote the restriction of any entity to/on the zero level set of g. Along the occluding boundary $\mathcal{S}^*$ the radial and transverse tangent vectors become unit vectors $\mathbf{t}_r^* = \mathbf{e}_r^*$ and $\mathbf{t}_{r\perp}^* = \mathbf{n}^* \times \mathbf{e}_r^*$.

Using the convention of an *inward-pointing normal* $\mathbf{n}$ (so that positive curvature indicates convexity and negative curvature concavity), a point on the surface is visible only if $g(S) > 0$ and is occluded if $g(S) < 0$. The occluding boundary curve therefore travels along the sign transition, and based on our sign convention, the intrinsic gradient $\nabla_S\, g(\mathcal{S}^*)$ along the occluding boundary will point *inward toward* the potentially visible subset of S.

2.2   Decomposition

Given the function g defined in (2), the surface tangent vector $\mathbf{t}_\perp^*$ pointing to the visible side of the surface can be found by taking the intrinsic gradient of g at $\mathcal{S}^*$. Rotating this tangent vector by $\pi/2$ around the unit normal yields the tangent $\mathbf{t}^*$ of the occluding curve.

If we seek an occluding tangent vector $\mathbf{t}^*$ which follows the occluding boundary $\mathcal{S}^*$ in the counterclockwise direction when seen from the viewpoint P, then its counterclockwise rotation around the *inward unit normal* (the convention for $\mathbf{n}$ where positive curvature indicates convexity) will point *away from* the visible subset of S (where $g(S) < 0$) which is in the opposite direction of $\nabla_S g$. By looking at both the covariant and contravariant components of the shape operator in this direction, we may prove the formal theorem below (see complete proof in the appendix).

Theorem 1. *Letting $\mathbf{e}_r$, κ_r, τ_r, denote the radial direction, radial curvature, and radial torsions respectively at a point S^* on the occluding boundary, we may construct the (unnormalized) occluding tangent vector $\mathbf{t}^*$ and its orthogonal complement $\mathbf{t}^*_\perp$ in terms of $\mathbf{e}_r$ and $\mathbf{n} \times \mathbf{e}_r$ as follows.*

$$\mathbf{t}^*_\perp = \kappa_r\, \mathbf{e}_r + \tau_r\, (\mathbf{n} \times \mathbf{e}_r) \tag{3}$$

$$\mathbf{t}^* = \begin{cases} \kappa_r\, (\mathbf{e}_r \times \mathbf{n}) + \tau_r\, \mathbf{e}_r, & \text{for inward } \mathbf{n} \\ \kappa_r\, (\mathbf{n} \times \mathbf{e}_r) + \tau_r\, \mathbf{e}_r & \text{for outward } \mathbf{n} \end{cases} \tag{4}$$

What is particularly appealing about this decomposition is that the second order properties of the surface need be computed only along the radial (line-of-sight) direction to determine the direction of the occluding boundary. Its two degrees of freedom within the tangent plane are captured by two second order pieces of information, the normal curvature and geodesic torsion in a single direction. Said in another way, the direction of the occluding boundary can therefore be determined purely from the geodesic along the radial direction (i.e. by examining its curvature and torsion).

3   Numerical Demonstration

In this section we demonstrate experiments that contain two synthetic shapes (a sphere and a torus) and a bunny example [22], in order to validate the computational feasibility of our proposed theorem by both the qualitative and quantitative results. Note that the achievement on the best accuracy is not our main purpose for it depends on implementations and data representations. For validation purpose, we utilize the implicit representation defined on voxel grid and take a simple curves extraction strategy shown to be able to achieve decent accuracy later. Implementation details and calculations of the coefficients for this implicit representation are included in the supplementary material.

Now that the occluding tangent direction is known to each point on the occluding boundaries, straightforwardly following the tangent direction produces the curves. As such, an intuitive algorithm (the marching method) is: to move the point along the normalized tangent direction $\mathbf{t}^*$ for a small step followed by recomputing the unit tangent vector at the new point and moving it again to trace out the curve. The error accumulates without any surprises, resulting a drifting problem. However, the drift can be easily addressed by solving a system that makes sure the point is both on the object surface and the visibility hull.

In computer graphics, 3D objects like these are commonly represented as triangle meshes consisting of vertices and edges. This data representation enables one to evaluate the function g mentioned in Sect. 2.1 at each vertex of a mesh, and to extract the zero level [30] set as a comparison. We evaluate the discrepancy in the metric of voxel length by averaging all the closest distance from the estimated occluding points to the references curves. Note that for synthetic examples, we compute the errors among the estimated curves to the analytical occluding boundaries with the same distance measurement.

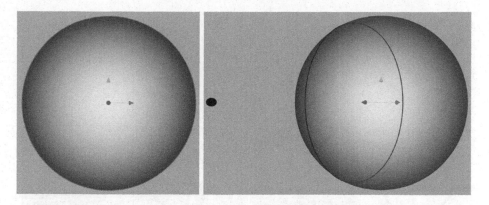

Fig. 2. Occluding boundary extraction of a sphere whose opacity is set such that one can observe invisible areas from other angles. The black dot represents the view point. The right image is viewed from a tilted angle, the left viewed from the black dot.

3.1   Sphere Case

A simple case starts with a sphere. If the view point is set in the exterior space of this object, neither self-occlusion nor multiple occluding boundary curves occur due to the convexity of the whole shape. Specifically, exactly one curve appears.

Figure 2 shows the occluding boundary curve found by our tracing algorithm and the reference curve, displayed as the thin blue line and the red thick band, respectively. The curve generated by the simple marching algorithm is able to match the analytical ground truth with an average error 0.03% of the voxel length. Additionally, the estimated curve (blue) differs from the reference curve (red) by 0.6% of the voxel length, a discrepancy level hard to perceive (Fig. 2).

3.2   Torus Case

In order to examine whether our proposed algorithm manages to extract the occluding boundaries under varying curvatures, we also demonstrate a more sophisticated 3D object, a torus, on which self-occlusion might occur from certain views and curvatures vary. Different from the sphere example, at least one curve exists and exactly two candidate curves compose the local occluding boundaries.

Three cases are tested at different view points. Among them are three categories of occlusion for the inner part–no occlusion, half occlusion and full occlusion. The easiest situation is illustrated from the top row of Fig. 3. Clearly, homogeneous curvatures along the occluding boundaries and zero torsions prevent the method from numerical issues. The third row of Fig. 3 indicates the results of full occlusion case, wherein varying curvatures and torsions makes the task harder but we can still benefit from the fronto-parallel voxel grid. Moreover, only one occluding curve (i.e. the outer rim) should occur, while two are displayed because invisible points rejection has not been taken. We may nevertheless observe from the zoomed in figures that the predicted occluding boundary curves align with

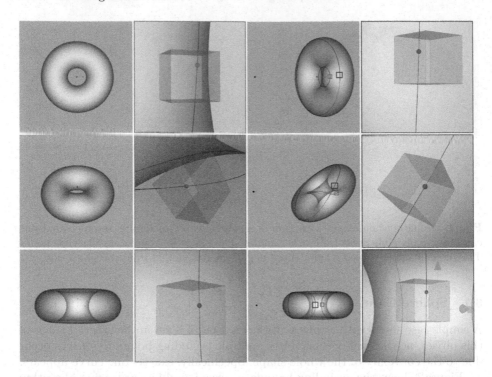

Fig. 3. Torus example. The torus is set to be relatively transparent in order to visualize the invisible areas. The columns from left to right are: view from the view point (black dot), zoomed-in details (marked by a green box) of occluded curve for the inner part, view from a tilted angle, zoomed-in details (marked by a dark blue box) of the visible curve (the outer part). Red curves are the reference superset of occluding boundaries and blue ones the predicted set by our theorem. A voxel is overlaid at the zoomed-in figures to qualitatively demonstrate the error. (Color figure online)

the reference curves pretty well. We do not zoom in heavily as the relevant scale to the voxel would become imperceptible. The average distance difference is less than 0.6% of the voxel length while the error to the analytical ground truth remains around 0.04%.

Being the most complex case, the slanted view point not only brings up different curvatures of the occluding curves as well, but aslo makes the voxel grid non-fronto-parallel with potential numerical issues. In fact, it turns out that our theorem with the simple method yields 0.06% mean error to the analytical ground truth. The estimated curves only differs from the reference curves by an average of 0.7% of the voxel length.

3.3 Bunny Case

We also demonstrate the numerical feasibility on real data, Stanford bunny [22], instead of purely on synthetic data. Real data is more challenging as the surface curvatures have a wider range that could cause numerical issues. We show in Fig. 4 that our theorem manages to handle the real data. The average discrepancy to the reference curves for this example is 7% of the voxel length. As shown from the previous synthetic examples, reference curves can deviate from the real occluding boundaries for the normal calculation in the marching cube method has inaccuracy especially around highly bent regions. Hence, the reference curves cannot guarantee to be the most accurate ones, and we can still conclude the numerical feasibility of our theorem given the acceptable discrepancy.

Fig. 4. Real data demonstration. We omitted the view point rendering to make the second image as the same size with the others. The first image is rendered from the viewpoint, the second from a rotated view and the third from the side view. Discrepancies around the tail region are perceptible.

From the experiments we show that a simple and naive strategy can also bring significant accuracy without suffering from numerical problems. We believe more sophisticated methods to perform even better.

4   Discussion for Potential Applications

4.1   Occluding Curve and Tangent in 3D Pose Estimation

To illustrate the relevance of the new theorem 1 in practical computer vision problems, we show how the occluding curve (and its tangent) play an important role in variational approaches to 2D/3D registration. While the contribution of this paper is theoretical, we feel it is nevertheless important to outline how its introduction to the computer vision community might drive upcoming research in this community, particularly mathematical approaches that require grounding in solid geometric theory. A few existing methods [5,26] within the 2D/3D registration area, which we believe to be the most promising area for future benefits from the knowledge of the occluding curve structure relayed by the theorem.

Silhouette Matching (the Simplest Case). Given a known 3D shape but with unknown pose with respect to a viewing camera, a simple region based method to estimate the camera pose parameters is to minimize the area-mismatch M between the projected silhouette of the shape (which depends upon each pose parameter λ) and a binary mask B representing a segmented/labeled region corresponding to the detected object within the domain Ω of the camera image. We may express this mismatch in integral form

$$M = \int_\Omega |\chi_S - B| \, d\mathbf{x}$$

where χ_S denotes the characteristic function of the 2D silhouette within the domain Ω of the camera image. Most minimization strategies require calculation of the derivative of the mismatch with respect to each pose parameter λ, which can be expressed in terms of the normal derivative of the projected silhouette 2D boundary contour $\mathbf{c}$ with respect to λ as follows.

$$\frac{\partial M}{\partial \lambda} = \int_{\mathbf{c}} \underbrace{(1 - 2B)}_{\substack{\text{signed} \\ \text{mismatch}}} \underbrace{\left\langle \frac{\partial \mathbf{c}}{\partial \lambda}, \hat{\mathbf{n}} \right\rangle}_{\substack{\text{normal} \\ \text{sensitivity}}} \underbrace{\left\| \frac{\partial \mathbf{c}}{\partial s} \right\| ds}_{\text{arclength}} \tag{5}$$

where s denotes an arbitrary contour parameter and $\hat{\mathbf{n}}$ the 2D unit normal.

However, direct computation of the derivative $\frac{\partial \mathbf{c}}{\partial \lambda}$ is not possible using only the structure of the silhouette boundary $\mathbf{c}$ itself. Rather, it depends on the differential structure of the back-projected 3D occluding curve $\mathbf{C}$ as follows[1]

$$\left\langle \frac{\partial \mathbf{c}}{\partial \lambda}, \hat{\mathbf{n}} \right\rangle \left\| \frac{\partial \mathbf{c}}{\partial s} \right\| = -\frac{L_h L_v}{Z^3} \left\langle \frac{\partial \mathbf{C}}{\partial s}, \mathbf{C} \times \frac{\partial \mathbf{C}}{\partial \lambda} \right\rangle \tag{6}$$

where $\mathbf{C} = (X, Y, Z)$ denotes the corresponding 3D occluding curve in camera frame coordinates (which depend on each camera pose parameter λ) and where L_h and L_v denote the horizontal and vertical focal scales of the camera (first two diagonal elements of the intrinsic matrix). Since s is an arbitrary contour parameter which parameterizes both the projected 2D silhouette boundary $\mathbf{c}$ as well as its originating 3D occluding curve $\mathbf{C}$, it may be conveniently chosen in reference to $\mathbf{C}$, by plugging (6) into (5) to obtain the following expression for the mismatch derivative as an integral along the occluding 3D curve

$$\frac{\partial M}{\partial \lambda} = -L_h L_v \int_{\mathbf{C}} \frac{1 - 2B}{Z^3} \left\langle \underbrace{\frac{\partial \mathbf{C}}{\partial s}}_{\substack{\text{occluding} \\ \text{3D tangent}}}, \mathbf{C} \times \frac{\partial \mathbf{C}}{\partial \lambda} \right\rangle ds \tag{7}$$

---

[1] This assumes no radial/tangential lens distortion, otherwise we must also multiply the right hand side of (6) by the determinant of the distortion model's Jacobian.

where the derivative $\frac{\partial \mathbf{C}}{\partial \lambda}$ of the camera coordinates $\mathbf{C} = (X, Y, Z)$ of each occluding 3D point with respect to the camera pose parameter λ is now straightforward. Detailed derivation can be found in [5].

Note that the integral (7) leverages not only the extracted occluding curve points, illustrating the usefulness for but also makes explicit use of the occluding tangent vector $\frac{\partial \mathbf{C}}{\partial s}$ at each point as well. As such, not only does (7) illustrate an important application in modern computer vision for occluding curve extraction, but it also suggests that extraction algorithms based on the explicit representation of the occluding tangent developed in this paper are likely to yield numerically superior estimates pose derivatives compared to algorithms which construct the tangent afterwards more coarsely based on differences between nearby extracted points. Tangent estimates using the decomposition Theorem 1 would provide a more direct numerical link to the second order structure of the underlying 3D surface, thus further compensating the loss of information via discretization by the use of additional "off curve" sample points needed for the numerical second derivative calculations.

More Complex 2D/3D Registration with Appearance Models. While the importance of the occluding curve, including the explicit use of its tangent estimate in (7), is immediately evident for the simplest case of silhouette matching, it is equally relevant for more complicated silhouette matching strategies which pair the geometry of a known 3D shape together with an appearance model. In such cases the derivative of the more sophisticating matching criterion with respect to any pose parameter λ will consist of a region based integral inside the silhouette, which will evaluate the residual error between the image (or image features) and the appearance model, together with a contour integral along the silhouette boundary which will once again involve the normal sensitivity (6) of the silhouette boundary with respect to the pose parameter λ. Due to the problem of computing this sensitivity, several modern schemes either ignore this integral component [16], or are formulated purely around point features [4,13,19], rather than region based properties, in order to avoid this all together [27]. For example, some works [26] embed curves or surfaces into a level set function and bypass computing the normal sensitivity by adding an approximated Heaviside function with accuracy however sacrificed. The theorem 1 presented here now reveals a practically exploitable structure about the occluding curve, around which tractable and accurate numerical schemes can be developed to better estimate this boundary-based contribution to the pose-gradients of blended geometric and appearance based models.

4.2 Variational Approaches to 3D Reconstruction

Finally, we note that in various generative model based approaches to 3D stereo reconstruction, ranging from shape-from-silhouettes to more sophisticated appearance matching methods [10,27,28], the normal sensitivity (6) of the silhouette boundary once again arises, whether with respect to a pose parameter

λ, or a more general shape parameter in its place. Once again, new strategies which leverage the decomposition Theorem 1 to numerically compute the occluding tangent can, in turn, exploit expression (6) to more accurately compute such sensitivities. While we assume this gain in accuracy is probably less important for early iterates in these reconstruction techniques, the gain in accuracy is likely to become more important and noticeable near convergence in the later iterates with these techniques.

5   Conclusion and Discussion

We have derived in details the tangent of occluding boundary curves in terms of local geometric properties only along radial directions. In particular, we decompose the tangent into the radial direction and its orthogonal complement weighted by the radial curvatures and geodesic torsions along the line-of-sight. The theorem 1, as shown by itself, does not depend on the representations of the surface. In addition to the pioneer work from Koenderink [15], who formally gave an elegant formula between the surface curvatures, apparent curvature, we provide a new perspective of understanding the occluding tangent along the radial and its orthogonal tangent directions.

We also undertake three experiments to validate the numerical feasibility of this theorem from a simple strategy and demonstrate the trivial error. While the formula does not suffice to extract the global occluding boundary curves, additional visibility test [6,18,21] can be applied to reject invisible parts and segments whose projections fall within silhouettes for retrieving global occluding boundaries.

Although we mainly focus on the theoretical contribution in this work, we also provide the explicit connections between the Theorem 1 and three computer vision applications. We hope this new theorem to invoke improvements on more vision tasks.

A   Appendices

A.1   Intrinsic Gradient

If $f : \mathcal{S} \rightarrow \mathbb{R}$ is a differentiable function defined on $\mathcal{S}$, the "intrinsic gradient" would naturally correspond to the projection onto the tangent plane of the standard $\mathbb{R}^3$ gradient of any local differentiable extension $\hat{f} : \mathbb{R}^3 \rightarrow \mathbb{R}$, where $\hat{f}(S) = f(S)$.

$$\nabla_S f = \nabla \hat{f} - \left(\nabla \hat{f} \cdot \mathbf{n} \right) \mathbf{n}$$

However, we can intrinsically define the gradient of f, without reference to any extension function $\hat{f}$, as the unique tangent vector $\nabla_S f$ which satisfies the equality $\partial_{\mathbf{t}} f = \nabla_S f \cdot \mathbf{t}$ for any tangent vector $\mathbf{t}$ (where $\partial_{\mathbf{t}} f$ denotes the directional derivative of f along the vector $\mathbf{t}$). We can solve for this vector using the first fundamental form coefficients E, F, G together with the partial derivatives of f with respect to the surface parameters u, v as follows.

$$\nabla_s f = \begin{bmatrix} \frac{\partial S}{\partial u} & \frac{\partial S}{\partial v} \end{bmatrix} \begin{bmatrix} E & F \\ F & G \end{bmatrix}^{-1} \begin{bmatrix} \frac{\partial f}{\partial u} \\ \frac{\partial f}{\partial v} \end{bmatrix}$$

A.2   Orthogonal Decomposition of the Shape Operator

We first orthogonally decompose the shape operator (which actually generalizes Theorem 1) to see both its covariant action and its contravariant action which is ignored in classical differential geometry but highly relevant to our exploration.

Lemma 1. *The action of the shape operator $\mathbb{S}$ on any tangent vector $\mathbf{t} \in \mathbb{R}^3$ can be decomposed into a covariant component parallel to its argument $\mathbf{t}$ and a contravariant component along the perpendicular tangent direction $\mathbf{t}_\perp = \mathbf{n} \times \mathbf{t}$*

$$\mathbb{S}(\mathbf{t}) = \kappa(\mathbf{t})\,\mathbf{t} + \tau(\mathbf{t})\,\mathbf{t}_\perp$$

where $\kappa(\mathbf{t})$ is the normal curvature (by definition) in the direction of $\mathbf{t}$ and where $\tau(\mathbf{t})$ matches the geodesic torsion in the direction of $\mathbf{t}$.

Proof. As an operator from the tangent space back to the tangent space, we may decompose the action of the shape operator into two orthogonal directions within the tangent plane, one parallel to its argument $\mathbf{t}$ and the other along the perpendicular tangent direction $\mathbf{t}_\perp$ as follows,

$$
\begin{aligned}
\mathbb{S}(\mathbf{t}) &= \left(\mathbb{S}(\mathbf{t}) \cdot \frac{\mathbf{t}}{\|\mathbf{t}\|}\right)\frac{\mathbf{t}}{\|\mathbf{t}\|} + \left(\mathbb{S}(\mathbf{t}) \cdot \frac{\mathbf{t}_\perp}{\|\mathbf{t}\|}\right)\frac{\mathbf{t}_\perp}{\|\mathbf{t}\|} \\
&= \underbrace{\left(\mathbb{S}\left(\frac{\mathbf{t}}{\|\mathbf{t}\|}\right) \cdot \frac{\mathbf{t}}{\|\mathbf{t}\|}\right)}_{\kappa(\mathbf{t})}\mathbf{t} + \underbrace{\left(\mathbb{S}\left(\frac{\mathbf{t}}{\|\mathbf{t}\|}\right) \cdot \frac{\mathbf{t}_\perp}{\|\mathbf{t}\|}\right)}_{\tau(\mathbf{t})}\mathbf{t}_\perp \\
&= \kappa(\mathbf{t})\mathbf{t} + \tau(\mathbf{t})\mathbf{t}_\perp
\end{aligned}
\tag{8}
$$

A.3   Proof for Theorem 1

Proof. We first compute the intrinsic gradient of the local occlusion function g.

$$
\begin{aligned}
\nabla_s g &= \begin{bmatrix} \frac{\partial S}{\partial u} & \frac{\partial S}{\partial v} \end{bmatrix} \begin{bmatrix} E & F \\ F & G \end{bmatrix}^{-1} \nabla_{u,v}\left((S-P)\cdot\mathbf{n}\right) \\
&= \begin{bmatrix} \frac{\partial S}{\partial u} & \frac{\partial S}{\partial v} \end{bmatrix} \begin{bmatrix} E & F \\ F & G \end{bmatrix}^{-1} \begin{bmatrix} \underbrace{\frac{\partial S}{\partial u}\cdot\mathbf{n}}_{0} + \underbrace{(S-P)\cdot\frac{\partial N}{\partial u}}_{re_r} \\ \underbrace{\frac{\partial S}{\partial v}\cdot\mathbf{n}}_{0} + \underbrace{(S-P)\cdot\frac{\partial N}{\partial v}}_{re_r} \end{bmatrix} \\
&= r\begin{bmatrix} \frac{\partial S}{\partial u} & \frac{\partial S}{\partial v} \end{bmatrix} \begin{bmatrix} E & F \\ F & G \end{bmatrix}^{-1} \begin{bmatrix} \frac{\partial N}{\partial u}\cdot\mathbf{e}_r \\ \frac{\partial N}{\partial v}\cdot\mathbf{e}_r \end{bmatrix}
\end{aligned}
$$

Notice that

$$\frac{\partial N}{\partial u} \cdot \mathbf{t}_r = \frac{\partial N}{\partial u} \cdot (\mathbf{e}_r - (\mathbf{e}_r \cdot \mathbf{n})\mathbf{n}) = \frac{\partial N}{\partial u} \cdot \mathbf{e}_r - (\mathbf{e}_r \cdot \mathbf{n}) \underbrace{\frac{\partial N}{\partial u} \cdot \mathbf{n}}_{0}$$

$$\frac{\partial N}{\partial v} \cdot \mathbf{t}_r = \frac{\partial N}{\partial v} \cdot (\mathbf{e}_r - (\mathbf{e}_r \cdot \mathbf{n})\mathbf{n}) = \frac{\partial N}{\partial v} \cdot \mathbf{e}_r - (\mathbf{e}_r \cdot \mathbf{n}) \underbrace{\frac{\partial N}{\partial u} \cdot \mathbf{n}}_{0}$$

which allows us to substitute $\mathbf{e}_r$ with $\mathbf{t}_r = \begin{bmatrix} \frac{\partial S}{\partial u} & \frac{\partial S}{\partial v} \end{bmatrix} t_r$, where t_r denotes the 2D intrinsic representation of $\mathbf{t}_r$ in the basis $\frac{\partial S}{\partial u}$ and $\frac{\partial S}{\partial v}$

$$\nabla_s g = r \begin{bmatrix} \frac{\partial S}{\partial u} & \frac{\partial S}{\partial v} \end{bmatrix} \begin{bmatrix} E & F \\ F & G \end{bmatrix}^{-1} \begin{bmatrix} \frac{\partial N}{\partial u} & \frac{\partial N}{\partial v} \end{bmatrix}^T \begin{bmatrix} \frac{\partial S}{\partial u} & \frac{\partial S}{\partial v} \end{bmatrix} t_r$$

$$= -r \underbrace{\begin{bmatrix} \frac{\partial S}{\partial u} & \frac{\partial S}{\partial v} \end{bmatrix} \begin{bmatrix} E & F \\ F & G \end{bmatrix}^{-1} \begin{bmatrix} e & f \\ f & g \end{bmatrix} t_r}_{\text{Weingarten}}$$

where e, f, g are the coefficients of second fundamental form **II**. The appearance of the Weingarten formulas allows us to recognize this part of the expression as the shape operator $\mathbb{S}$ applied to the radial tangent vector $\mathbf{t}_r$ and therefore write

$$\frac{\nabla_s g}{r} = -\mathbb{S}(\mathbf{t}_r) \qquad (9)$$

Since we define in Lemma 1 the direction of $\mathbf{t}_\perp^*$ opposite to direction of $\nabla_s g$, we may then write

$$\mathbf{t}_\perp^* = -\frac{\nabla_s g}{r} = \mathbb{S}(\mathbf{t}_r) = \kappa_r \mathbf{t}_r + \tau_r \mathbf{t}_{r\perp}$$

Subsequently, the occluding tangent is computed as follows,

$$\mathbf{t}^* = -\mathbf{n} \times \mathbf{t}_\perp^* = -\kappa_r \mathbf{n} \times \mathbf{e}_r - \tau_r \mathbf{n} \times (\mathbf{n} \times \mathbf{e}_r)$$

$$= -\kappa_r \mathbf{n} \times \mathbf{e}_r - \tau_r \left(\mathbf{n} \underbrace{(\mathbf{n} \cdot \mathbf{e}_r)}_{\frac{g(S)}{r}=0} - \mathbf{e}_r \underbrace{(\mathbf{n} \cdot \mathbf{n})}_{1} \right) = -\kappa_r \mathbf{n} \times \mathbf{e}_r + \tau_r \mathbf{e}_r$$

For the *outward unit normal* $\mathbf{n}$, we negate $\mathbf{n}$ in the equations above. Therefore, we have

$$\mathbf{t}^* = \begin{cases} \kappa_r (\mathbf{e}_r \times \mathbf{n}) + \tau_r \mathbf{e}_r, & \text{for inward } \mathbf{n} \\ \kappa_r (\mathbf{n} \times \mathbf{e}_r) + \tau_r \mathbf{e}_r & \text{for outward } \mathbf{n} \end{cases}$$

References

1. Abdel-All, N.H., Badr, S.A.N., Soliman, M., Hassan, S.A.: Intersection curves of two implicit surfaces in r3. J. Math. Comput. Sci. **2**(2), 152–171 (2012)

2. Abdel-Malek, K., Yeh, H.J.: On the determination of starting points for parametric surface intersections. Comput. Aided Des. **29**(1), 21–35 (1997)
3. Bajaj, C.L., Hoffmann, C.M., Lynch, R.E., Hopcroft, J.: Tracing surface intersections. Comput. Aided Geomet. Des. **5**(4), 285–307 (1988)
4. Chen, H.C., et al.: Model-based measurement of food portion size for image-based dietary assessment using 3D/2D registration. Meas. Sci. Technol. **24**(10), 105701 (2013)
5. Dambreville, S., Sandhu, R., Yezzi, A., Tannenbaum, A.: Robust 3D Pose estimation and efficient 2D region-based segmentation from a 3D shape prior. In: Forsyth, D., Torr, P., Zisserman, A. (eds.) ECCV 2008. LNCS, vol. 5303, pp. 169–182. Springer, Heidelberg (2008). https://doi.org/10.1007/978-3-540-88688-4_13
6. De Vivo, F., Battipede, M., Gili, P.: Occlusion points identification algorithm. Comput. Aided Des. **91**, 75–83 (2017)
7. DeCarlo, D., Finkelstein, A., Rusinkiewicz, S., Santella, A.: Suggestive contours for conveying shape. In: ACM SIGGRAPH 2003 Papers. pp. 848–855 (2003)
8. Düldül, B.U., Çalişkan, M.: The geodesic curvature and geodesic torsion of the intersection curve of two surfaces. Acta Universitatis Apulensis. Math. Informat **24**, 161–172 (2010)
9. Fabbri, R., Kimia, B.B.: Multiview differential geometry of curves. Int. J. Comput. Vision **120**(3), 324–346 (2016)
10. Faugeras, O., Keriven, R.: Variational principles, surface evolution, PDE's, level set methods and the stereo problem. IEEE Trans. Image Process. **7**, 336–344 (2002)
11. Giblin, P.: Reconstruction of surfaces from profiles. In: Proceedings of 1st International Conference on Computer Vision, London, 1987 (1987)
12. Ikeuchi, K., Horn, B.K.: Numerical shape from shading and occluding boundaries. Artif. Intell. **17**(1–3), 141–184 (1981)
13. Kaptein, B., Valstar, E., Stoel, B., Rozing, P., Reiber, J.: A new model-based RSA method validated using cad models and models from reversed engineering. J. Biomech. **36**(6), 873–882 (2003)
14. Kehtarnavaz, N., Defigueiredo, R.: Recognition of 3D curves based on curvature and torsion. In: Digital and Optical Shape Representation and Pattern Recognition. vol. 938, pp. 357–364. International Society for Optics and Photonics (1988)
15. Koenderink, J.J.: What does the occluding contour tell us about solid shape? Perception **13**(3), 321–330 (1984)
16. Kolev, K., Klodt, M., Brox, T., Cremers, D.: Continuous global optimization in multiview 3D reconstruction. Int. J. Comput. Vision **84**(1), 80–96 (2009)
17. Kriegman, D.J., Ponce, J.: A new curve tracing algorithm and some applications. In: Curves and Surfaces, pp. 267–270. Elsevier, Philadelphia (1991)
18. Kriegman, D.J., Ponce, J.: Geometric modeling for computer vision. In: Curves and Surfaces in Computer Vision and Graphics II, vol. 1610, pp. 250–260. International Society for Optics and Photonics (1992)
19. Lamecker, H., Wenckebach, T.H., Hege, H.C.: Atlas-based 3D-shape reconstruction from X-ray images. In: 18th International Conference on Pattern Recognition (ICPR 2006), vol. 1, pp. 371–374. IEEE (2006)
20. Lazebnik, S., Ponce, J.: The local projective shape of smooth surfaces and their outlines. Int. J. Comput. Vision **63**(1), 65–83 (2005)
21. Li, T.M., Aittala, M., Durand, F., Lehtinen, J.: Differentiable monte CARLO ray tracing through edge sampling. ACM Trans. Graph. **37**(6), 1–11 (2018)
22. Lindstrom, P., Turk, G.: Fast and memory efficient polygonal simplification. In: Proceedings Visualization'98 (Cat. No. 98CB36276,. pp. 279–286. IEEE (1998)

23. Lone, M.S., Shahid, M.H., Sharma, S.: A new approach towards transversal inter-section curves of two surfaces in $\mathbb{R}^3$. Geom. Imag. Comput. **3**(3), 81–99 (2016)
24. Marr, D.: Analysis of occluding contour. Proc. R. Soc. Lond. Ser. B. Biol. Sci. **197**(1129), 441–475 (1977)
25. Ponce, J., Hebert, M.: On image contours of projective shapes. In: Fleet, D., Pajdla, T., Schiele, B., Tuytelaars, T. (eds.) ECCV 2014. LNCS, vol. 8692, pp. 736–749. Springer, Cham (2014). https://doi.org/10.1007/978-3-319-10593-2_48
26. Prisacariu, V.A., Reid, I.D.: PWP3D: real-time segmentation and tracking of 3D objects. Int. J. Comput. Vis. **98**(3), 335–354 (2012)
27. Runz, M., et al.: Frodo: From detections to 3D objects. In: Proceedings of the IEEE/CVF Conference on Computer Vision and Pattern Recognition, pp. 14720–14729 (2020)
28. Sandhu, R., Dambreville, S., Yezzi, A., Tannenbaum, A.: A nonrigid kernel-based framework for 2D–3D pose estimation and 2D image segmentation. IEEE Trans. Pattern Anal. Mach. Intell. **33**(6), 1098–1115 (2010)
29. Soliman, M.A.L., Abdel-All, N.H., Hassan, S.A., Badr, S.A.N., et al.: Intersection curves of implicit and parametric surfaces in r 3. Appl. Math. **2**(08), 1019 (2011)
30. Thirion, J.P., Gourdon, A.: The 3D marching lines algorithm. Graph. Models Image Process. **58**(6), 503–509 (1996)
31. Vaillant, R.: Using occluding contours for 3D object modeling. In: Faugeras, O. (ed.) ECCV 1990. LNCS, vol. 427, pp. 454–464. Springer, Heidelberg (1990). https://doi.org/10.1007/BFb0014895
32. Vaillant, R., Faugeras, O.D.: Using extremal boundaries for 3-d object modeling. IEEE Trans. Pattern Anal. Mach. Intell. **14**(02), 157–173 (1992)
33. Wang, C., Fu, H., Tao, D., Black, M.: Occlusion boundary: A formal definition & its detection via deep exploration of context. IEEE Trans. Pattern Anal. Mach. Intell. **44**, 2641–2656 (2020)
34. Ye, X., Maekawa, T.: Differential geometry of intersection curves of two surfaces. Comput. Aided Geomet. Des. **16**(8), 767–788 (1999)

NeuRIS: Neural Reconstruction of Indoor Scenes Using Normal Priors

Jiepeng Wang[1], Peng Wang[1], Xiaoxiao Long[1], Christian Theobalt[2],
Taku Komura[1], Lingjie Liu[2], and Wenping Wang[3(✉)]

[1] The University of Hong Kong, Hong Kong, China
{jpwang,pwang3,xxlong,taku}@cs.hku.hk
[2] Max Planck Institute for Informatics, Saarbrücken, Germany
{theobalt,lliu}@mpi-inf.mpg.de
[3] Texas A&M University, College Station, USA
wenping@tamu.edu

Abstract. Reconstructing 3D indoor scenes from 2D images is an important task in many computer vision and graphics applications. A main challenge in this task is that large texture-less areas in typical indoor scenes make existing methods struggle to produce satisfactory reconstruction results. We propose a new method, named *NeuRIS*, for high-quality reconstruction of indoor scenes. The key idea of *NeuRIS* is to integrate estimated normal of indoor scenes as a prior in a neural rendering framework for reconstructing large texture-less shapes and, importantly, to do this in an adaptive manner to also enable the reconstruction of irregular shapes with fine details. Specifically, we evaluate the faithfulness of the normal priors on-the-fly by checking the multi-view consistency of reconstruction during the optimization process. Only the normal priors accepted as faithful will be utilized for 3D reconstruction, which typically happens in the regions of smooth shapes possibly with weak texture. However, for those regions with small objects or thin structures, for which the normal priors are usually unreliable, we will only rely on visual features of the input images, since such regions typically contain relatively rich visual features (e.g., shade changes and boundary contours). Extensive experiments show that *NeuRIS* significantly outperforms the state-of-the-art methods in terms of reconstruction quality. Our project page: https://jiepengwang.github.io/NeuRIS/.

Keywords: Indoor reconstruction · Neural volume rendering · Adaptive prior

1 Introduction

Reconstructing 3D indoor scenes from multiple input images is an important and challenging task in many practical applications, such as robotic navigation, vir-

Supplementary Information The online version contains supplementary material available at https://doi.org/10.1007/978-3-031-19824-3_9.

S. Avidan et al. (Eds.): ECCV 2022, LNCS 13692, pp. 139–155, 2022.
https://doi.org/10.1007/978-3-031-19824-3_9

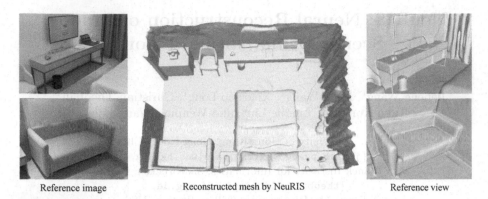

Reference image   Reconstructed mesh by NeuRIS   Reference view

Fig. 1. Room-scale indoor reconstruction. Given a set of images equally sampled from a video (captured by iPhone 11), NeuRIS succeeds in reconstructing smooth surfaces with fine details. Note the large-area flat regions (like the floor, the sofa) and the delicate structures (like the chair legs and the desk) in our reconstructed mesh.

tual reality and path planning. Indoor scenes usually contain many large texture-less areas and repetitive patterns, such as white walls, floors, and reflecting surfaces, which is challenging for applying conventional matching-based dense reconstruction algorithms [28,29,44] that heavily rely on the correspondence of distinct visual features, leading to poor reconstruction results. With the success of deep neural networks, data-driven (depth-based and TSDF-based) methods [10,17,22,31,33,34] have proven effective in alleviating the texture-less problem by exploiting various geometric priors learned from a large amount of data. However, these methods struggle to produce high-quality reconstruction of indoor scenes with geometry details. For example, depth-based methods [10,33] usually estimate depth maps individually, which causes lack of coherence and scale ambiguities across frames, as well as noisy surface and floating outliers in reconstruction. TSDF-based methods [22,31] suffer from high memory consumption due to their usage of the explicit 3D volumetric representation; as the memory requirement grows prohibitively large when the resolution is high, they cannot be applied at a level where the fine details can be reconstructed (Fig. 1).

Recently, neural scene representations, along with the inverse rendering techniques [20,24,36,40,41] have shown impressive results on geometry reconstruction, by encoding the volume density, occupancy, or signed distance in a compact and differentiable representation. However, most neural methods fail to reconstruct indoor scenes with large texture-less regions that do not contain sufficient visual features needed for pixel-level optimization. To address this issue, NerfingMVS [38] integrates depth priors to guide the sampling of points in NeRF's framework [20] to reduce shape-radiance ambiguity. Although it can predict better depth maps than the original NeRF's estimation, the fused geometry of its output depth maps still has limited surface quality.

We present a novel neural surface reconstruction method, called *NeuRIS*, that is specialized for indoor scenes. Our key idea is to leverage learned normal priors in an adaptive manner to facilitate the learning of the neural surface representation, where the normal priors provide more globally consistent geometric constraints to guide the optimization process. Specifically, we first estimate the normal maps of the input images using an existing monocular normal estimation network. Then, besides the appearance supervision provided by the input images, the normal priors are used to provide additional constraints to mitigate the geometry ambiguity issue at texture-less regions, which typically consist of smooth or regular shapes.

Note that the normal priors may be inaccurate in the regions with small objects, complex shapes, or thin structures, impeding high-quality reconstruction. Hence, for such regions, we propose to use the normal priors in an adaptive manner. To this end, we develop a mechanism to evaluate the faithfulness of the normal priors on-the-fly, based on multi-view photography consistency across the input images. For the regions where the multi-view consistency is not satisfied, the normal constraint will be removed and only the appearance information is utilized for optimization. We observe that the regions where the normal priors are not faithful typically consist of sharp features or irregular shapes with relatively rich visual features in the input images, which are often sufficient for reconstructing high quality surfaces by appearance supervision from the images. This adaptive strategy of utilizing the normal priors makes the reconstruction process more robust for general indoor scenes. As a result, NeuRIS achieves high-quality reconstruction of complex indoor scenes with rich geometric details.

To summarize, NeuRIS has the following advantages:

– We advocate the use of normal priors because they are invariant to translation and scaling, and exhibit better multi-view consistency than the depth prior used in prior methods. The normal priors provide globally consistent geometric constraints across input images, leading to significant improvement of reconstruction quality in texture-less regions of large smooth objects, typically present in indoor scenes.
– We apply the normal priors in an adaptive manner, which is achieved by evaluating the faithfulness of the normal priors on-the-fly. This strategy enables complex shapes with geometric details in indoor scenes to be faithfully reconstructed.

Extensive validations and comparisons are presented to show that NeuRIS achieves superior results on ScanNet [4] and significantly outperforms the state-of-the-art methods in terms of the reconstruction quality of indoor scenes.

2   Related Works

2.1   Indoor Scene Reconstruction

Traditional multi-view stereo methods [28,29,44] can produce plausible geometry of textured surfaces, but struggle with texture-less regions such as those in indoor scenes. Recently, learning-based MVS methods achieve promising results for tackling texture-less surfaces. Such methods can be divided into two categories: depth based methods [10, 15–18, 33] and TSDF (truncated signed distance function) based methods [22, 31]. The depth based methods first estimate depth maps of images individually, and then leverage extra filtering and fusion procedures to reconstruct the scene. Such methods often suffer from incompleteness, noisy surfaces and scale ambiguities, due to the inconsistency caused by individual estimation of depth maps. To alleviate these problems, some methods [22, 31] directly regress input images to TSDF. Atlas [22] proposes a volumetric design to regress a 3D global feature volume constructed from a sequence of images to TSDF. Constrained by its global design and computational resources, Atlas can only process a limited number of images, and its reconstruction results lack details. To reduce the computational burden, unlike Atlas that processes the whole image sequences at once, NeuralRecon [31] proposes a coarse-to-fine framework, that reconstructs the whole scene by processing local fragments incrementally. However, due to its local estimation design, it is challenging for NeuralRecon to obtain a global reconstruction with fine details.

2.2   Neural Volume Rendering and Prior Guided Optimization

Recently, coordinate-based neural representations, that encode a field by regressing the 3D coordinates to outputting values by Multi-Layer Perceptrons (MLPs), have become a popular way to represent scenes for their compactness and flexibility. Neural fields have achieved remarkable results on encoding images [3, 26, 30], shapes [1, 7, 19, 25, 30], and 3D scenes [20, 24, 36, 39–41]. In this paper we mainly focus on neural 3D scene representation and its inverse rendering techniques. Different types of fields are chosen for different goals. Neural Radiance Fields [20], which encodes the scene geometry by volume density, is suitable for the tasks of novel view synthesis by volume rendering. However, volume density cannot represent high-fidelity surfaces due to the lack of surface constraints. A better reconstruction of surface geometry can be achieved by using occupancy and signed distances; they can be optimized by both surface rendering [23, 41] and volume rendering [24, 36, 40] from the supervision of reference images. In order to further improve the reconstruction accuracy, a concurrent work NeuralWarp [5] proposes a warping-based loss term of image patches to improve the reconstruction accuracy. However, these methods perform poorly on indoor scenes because of the lack of textures in indoor scenes. Thus, some methods try to introduce geometric priors to guide the optimization process.

Depth Priors. Some methods [14, 38] use depth priors to supervise the training process and/or to guide the sampling process of NeRF [20] for indoor scene rendering to alleviate the shape ambiguity problem. Although they can predict better depth maps than those rendered from NeRF, the inherent problems of depth-based methods described in Sect. 2.1 still remain, and they cannot produce smooth geometries even after post-processing the data by filtering and fusion. Similarly, Roessle et al. [27] utilize dense depth priors in NeRF's optimization framework for novel view synthesis with sparse input views. They construct a depth completion network to get dense depth priors from sparse point cloud of SfM. However, the framework is designed for novel view synthesis but not for geometry reconstruction.

Normal Priors. Surface normal is important for 3D scene understanding [42, 43] and recently single view normal estimation has made great progress with high accuracy [2,6,9,37]. We observe that the estimated normal priors show high consistency in planar regions and across input views, and also provide obvious clues of underlying geometry, as shown in Fig. 6. For the good properties of normal priors, and also in order to avoid the problems brought by depth priors as mentioned above, we choose to integrate normal priors into the volume rendering framework for improving the optimization of the surface representation.

3   Method

Given a set of calibrated RGB images $\{\mathcal{I}_k\}$ of an indoor scene, our goal is to accurately reconstruct the scene geometry with fine details. To this end, we adopt a global neural surface representation and optimize it with the supervision of RGB images. To reconstruct high-fidelity indoor scenes that contain both large texture-less regions and irregular shapes with fine details, we propose an adaptive, prior-guided optimization method. Specifically, we incorporate normal priors learned from a large dataset of indoor scenes into a neural rendering framework for 3D reconstruction. Noting that normal priors tend to be inaccurate in regions with irregular shapes and thin structures, we propose to use normal priors in an adaptive manner. This is achieved by evaluating the multi-view consistency of the normal priors, so that they are only applied for reconstructing smooth and regular shapes, but not for objects with intricate geometries.

Our pipeline has two phases. In the first phase, we use the normal priors predicted by a monocular method [6] to provide constraints on the normals rendered with the neural volume rendering framework. Note that the evaluation of the normal prior is not invoked in this phase (Sect. 3.1). What we obtain in the first phase is a coarse shape with fairly good depth estimations, but lacks local fine details. At this stage, large flat shapes are reconstructed in reasonably good quality, thanks to the use of the normal prior, but inaccurate gross shapes are produced for thin structures or small objects with irregular shape features, since the normal priors are not reliable for such areas.

Hence, in the second phase, we introduce a scheme to evaluate the faithfulness of the normal priors by evaluating the multi-view photometric consistency induced by the currently estimated normals and depths. Only those normal priors whose resulting corresponding geometry passes the photometric-consistency test will be considered reliable and are used for supervision in the following optimization steps. For those unreliable normal priors, we will remove them from the supervision and only rely on the color information for the following optimization steps. This scheme improves the quality of regions where there are sharp geometry features with relatively more visual features (Sect. 3.2). Figure 2 shows an overview of our approach.

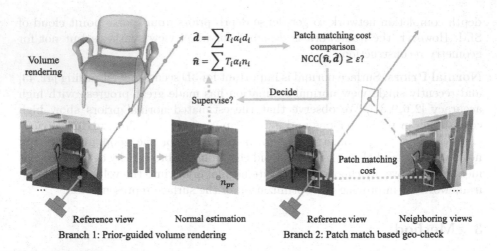

$$\hat{\mathbf{d}} = \sum T_i \alpha_i d_i$$

$$\hat{\mathbf{n}} = \sum T_i \alpha_i n_i$$

Patch matching cost comparison
$\text{NCC}(\hat{\mathbf{n}}, \hat{\mathbf{d}}) \geq \varepsilon?$

Volume rendering

Supervise? ◄— Decide

Patch matching cost

n_{pr}

Reference view   Normal estimation   Reference view   Neighboring views

Branch 1: Prior-guided volume rendering   Branch 2: Patch match based geo-check

Fig. 2. Method overview. Our training process is composed by two phases. In the first phase, we train a coarse model to fit both the multi-view images and the estimated normal maps by volume rendering (Sect. 3.1), without any filtering strategy. In the second phase, we adaptively impose the supervision from normal priors, where two branches are performed simultaneously: in one branch we conduct a geometric quality evaluation by computing multi-view visual consistency; in the other branch, only those prior normals that pass the geometric check are accepted as proper supervisions to the rendered normals.

3.1 Prior-Guided Volume Rendering

Scene Representation. Similar to NeuS [36], a 3D indoor scene is represented by two Multi-layer Perceptrons (MLPs): geometry network $f_{\theta_g} : \mathbb{R}^3 \to \mathbb{R}$ to encode the signed distance function (SDF), and color network $c_{\theta_c} : \mathbb{R}^3 \times \mathbb{R}^3 \to \mathbb{R}^3$ to encode the colors associated by a spatial position and view direction. The surface $\mathcal{S}$ is then defined as the zero level-set of the SDF, that is,

$$\mathcal{S} = \{\mathbf{x} | f_{\theta_g}(\mathbf{x}) = 0\}. \tag{1}$$

Volume Rendering. To enable robust supervision using the 2D image observations, we adopt the volume rendering technique, which is proven powerful in NeRF and its variants. Specifically, for each pixel we sample a set of points along the corresponding emitted ray, denoted as $\mathbf{p}_i = \mathbf{o} + d_i \mathbf{v}$, where $\mathbf{p}_i$ are the sampled points, $\mathbf{o}$ is the camera center and $\mathbf{v}$ is the direction of this ray. Then the color is accumulated along the ray through Eq. 2.

$$\hat{\mathbf{c}} = \sum_{i=1}^{n} T_i \alpha_i c(\mathbf{p}_i, \mathbf{v}), \tag{2}$$

where $T_i = \prod_{j=1}^{i-1}(1 - \alpha_j)$ denotes the *accumulated transmittance*, $\alpha_i = 1 - \exp(-\int_{t_i}^{t_{i+1}} \rho(t)dt)$ is the discrete opacity, and the opaque density $\rho(t)$ follows the original definition in NeuS [36]. Since the rendering procedure is fully differentiable, we can learn the weights of f_{θ_g} and c_{θ_c} by minimizing the difference between the rendering results and reference images.

However, as shown in our experiments (Sect. 4.2), due to the lack of texture, the pixel-wise colors do not provide sufficient information, thus simply using supervision by the input images would lead to noisy results at texture-less regions.

Prior-Guided Optimization. A key observation is that the above volume rendering scheme can generate not only appearance, but also geometric properties such as depth and normal vectors. That is, we can approximate the surface normal and depth observed from a viewpoint using the volume accumulation along this ray by

$$\hat{\mathbf{n}} = \sum_{i=1}^{n} T_i \alpha_i \mathbf{n}_i, \quad \hat{d} = \sum_{i=1}^{n} T_i \alpha_i d_i, \tag{3}$$

where $\mathbf{n}_i = \nabla f(\mathbf{p}_i)$ is the spatial gradient of SDF at $\mathbf{p}_i$ and d_i is the corresponding depth.

Given the geometric priors represented by normal maps $\{\mathcal{N}_k\}$ predicted from RGB images $\{\mathcal{I}_k\}$, we supervise the rendered normal $\hat{\mathbf{n}}$ by comparing it with the corresponding estimation from $\mathcal{N}_k$. We use a pre-trained single view normal estimation network [6] to generate the reference normal maps as supervision. Although the direct use of normal priors without any filtering helps reconstruct complete surfaces, the results still lack fine details. This is because the estimated normal maps are usually over-smoothed, inaccurate even grossly on some delicate structures, such as chair legs, curtains, etc. This motivates us to develop a filtering scheme to use the normal priors in an adaptive manner for reconstructing more accurate surface geometry.

3.2 Adaptive Check of Normal Priors

In this section, we introduce a checking method for evaluating the normal quality and adaptively imposing the prior supervision in the optimization process. Our method is developed over a crucial observation: the predicted normal maps are overly smooth in regions where there are sharp geometric details. Moreover, such regions usually have rich visual features, which provide useful clues for validating the accuracy of the normals by evaluating the photometric consistency, i.e., by projecting the reconstructed shape to input images and computing the visual differences across the multi-view images. Based on this observation, we propose a check scheme based on the patch match technique for evaluating the multi-view consistency from rendered depth and normal vectors (Eq. 3). This multi-view consistency evaluation can help NeuRIS identify whether the current geometry is well reconstructed or not. If not, the normal priors would be regarded as unreliable and not used for further refinement of reconstruction.

Specifically, consider evaluating the visual consistency of the surface observed from a pixel q on a reference image $\mathcal{I}_i$, a local 3D plane $\{\mathbf{p}|\mathbf{p}^{\mathsf{T}}\mathbf{n} = d\mathbf{v}^{\mathsf{T}}\mathbf{n}\}$ is defined in the reference camera space associated from q, where $\mathbf{v}$ is the view direction, d and $\mathbf{n}$ are the distance and the normal estimation from q. We then find a set of neighboring images, and say one of the neighboring images is $\mathcal{I}_j$. The homography transformation from $\mathcal{I}_i$ to $\mathcal{I}_j$ can be computed by Eq. 4.

$$H_{\mathbf{n},d} = K_j (R_j R_i^{-1} - \frac{(\mathbf{t}_i - \mathbf{t}_j)\mathbf{n}^{\mathsf{T}}}{d\mathbf{v}^T \mathbf{n}}) K_i^{-1}. \tag{4}$$

Here $\{K_*, R_*, \mathbf{t}_*\}$ are the camera parameters denoting intrinsic matrices, rotations and translations.

Then for pixel q in $\mathcal{I}_i$, we find a squared patch P centered at it and warp this patch to its neighbor view $\mathcal{I}_j$ with the calculated homography matrix. The visual consistency of $(\mathbf{n}, d)$ is evaluated with the Normalized Cross Correlation (NCC) following the conventional patch-match techniques [28] by

$$\mathrm{NCC}_j(P, \mathbf{n}, d) = \frac{\sum_{q \in P} \hat{\mathcal{I}}_i(q) \hat{\mathcal{I}}_j(H_{\mathbf{n},d}(q))}{\sqrt{\sum_{q \in P} \hat{\mathcal{I}}_i(q)^2 \sum_{q \in P} \hat{\mathcal{I}}_j(H_{\mathbf{n},d}(q))^2}}, \tag{5}$$

where $\hat{\mathcal{I}}_*(q) = \mathcal{I}_*(q) - \overline{\mathcal{I}}_*(q)$ denotes the result subtracted by the mean value of the local patch.

During the training process, the sampled pixel q along with the patch P in the reference image is associated with the plane by its accumulated depth $\hat{d}$ and normal $\hat{\mathbf{n}}$ in volume rendering. If the reconstructed geometry is not accurate at the sampled pixel, it will fail to satisfy multi-view photometric consistency, which means that its associated normal prior has failed to provide help for the reconstruction process. By comparing the NCC at the sampled patch to a robust threshold ϵ, we can adaptively decide the training weight of normal priors, using the indicator function:

$$\Omega_q(\hat{\mathbf{n}}, \hat{d}) = \begin{cases} 1 & \text{if } \sum_j \mathrm{NCC}_j(P, \hat{\mathbf{n}}, \hat{d}) \geq \epsilon \\ 0 & \text{if } \sum_j \mathrm{NCC}_j(P, \hat{\mathbf{n}}, \hat{d}) < \epsilon. \end{cases} \tag{6}$$

Only when $\Omega_q(\hat{\mathbf{n}}, \hat{d})$ equals 1 the normal prior will be used for supervision. And once the normal priors are judged as unfaithful, they will not be used in the subsequent optimization process.

3.3 Training

In the training stage, we sample a batch of pixels and adaptively minimize the difference of the color and normal estimations and the corresponding references. Specifically, during training, in each iteration we sample m pixels $\{q_k\}$ and their corresponding reference colors $\{\mathcal{I}(q_k)\}$ and normals $\{\mathcal{N}(q_k)\}$. For each pixel we sample n points along its corresponding ray in the world space. The overall loss is defined as

$$\mathcal{L} = \lambda_c \mathcal{L}_c + \lambda_p \mathcal{L}_p + \lambda_{eik} \mathcal{L}_{eik}. \tag{7}$$

Here the color loss $\mathcal{L}_c$ is defined as

$$\mathcal{L}_c = \frac{1}{m} \sum_k \|\mathcal{I}(q_k) - \hat{\mathbf{c}}(q_k)\|_1, \tag{8}$$

where $\hat{\mathbf{c}}(q_k)$ is the predicted pixel colors by volume rendering. The normal prior loss is denoted by

$$\mathcal{L}_p = \frac{1}{m} \sum_k \|\mathcal{N}(q_k) - \hat{\mathbf{n}}(q_k)\|_1 \cdot \Omega_{q_k}(\hat{\mathbf{n}}(q_k), \hat{d}(q_k)). \tag{9}$$

Note that there are two phases in the whole training process and at the first phase, there is no geometric check. Thus, the indicator $\Omega_{q_k}(\hat{\mathbf{n}}(q_k), \hat{d}(q_k))$ is always equal to 1 at the first phase while it follows Eq. 6 at the second phase.

The Eikonal loss [8] to regularize the SDF is defined as

$$\mathcal{L}_{eik} = \frac{1}{nm} \sum_{k,i} (\|\nabla f(\mathbf{p}_{k,i})\|_2 - 1)^2. \tag{10}$$

$\lambda_c, \lambda_p, \lambda_{eik}$ are hyperparameters for weighting color loss, prior loss and Eikonal loss, respectively.

4 Experiments

4.1 Implementation Details

Architecture. We adopt the same network architecture of NeuS [36], where the signed distance function and color function are modeled by an MLP with 8 and 6 hidden layers respectively. Positional encoding [20] and sphere initialization [1] are applied to the network. For the normal priors, we adopt the recent method [6] and re-train its network with our training/test splits to predict the normals of input images instead of using its officially pretrained model. We sample 512 rays for each batch to train the model. And we first train the model for 60k iterations with normal priors and then continue to train the full model for another 100k iterations, which takes about 10 h in total on a single NVIDIA RTX2080Ti GPU. More details can be found in the supplementary.

Dataset. We test the performance of our algorithm on ScanNet [4]. ScanNet is a large-scale dataset consisting of 1613 indoor scenes with ground truth camera intrinsics, camera poses and surface reconstructions. Following NerfingMVS [38], we randomly select 8 scenes and all images are resized in 640×480 resolution. Different from NerfingMVS [38] using images covering a local region in a room, we aim to perform room-scale reconstruction. For each scene, a set of equally-spaced images (about 150–600 images) is sampled from the corresponding video, thus the number of sampled images is proportional to the video length.

Baselines. We compare our method with the following methods: (1) Depth-based method: DeepV2D [33]; (2) TSDF based methods: NeuralRecon [31] and

Atlas [22]; (3) Neural volume rendering methods: NeRF [20], NerfingMVS [38], NeuS [36] and VolSDF [40]; and (4) Traditional MVS reconstruction method COLMAP [28]. For the depth based method DeepV2D, to address the scale ambiguity issue of it, we re-scale every predicted depth map according to the ground truth depth map using the median scale strategy [45] and then fuse its predicted depth maps following NeuralRecon [31] to construct global surface geometry. For COLMAP, we use ground truth poses to reconstruct point cloud and then use Screened Poisson Surface Reconstruction [11] to get a mesh.

Evaluation Metrics. For complete quantitative comparisons, we evaluate the 3D surface geometry results, following the metrics defined in NeuralRecon [31]. Among those metrics, F-score is usually considered as the most suitable metric to evaluate geometry quality [31]. The definitions of those metrics can be found in the supplementary. Because of the smoothness property of SDF, even the not observed areas can be reconstructed, which are usually out of the scope of the ground truth (GT) mesh. In order to guarantee a fair comparison, for the predicted mesh, we remove faces in the areas that can not be observed in the GT mesh. Refer to the supplementary for more details.

4.2 Comparisons

3D Reconstruction. Table 1 shows the quantitative results compared with the state-of-the-art methods. Note that for the data-driven methods [22,31,33], we use the official pre-trained models. As shown in Table 1, our method can significantly surpass existing methods, especially when compared with neural volume rendering methods. For the metric Comp. (Completeness), NeuRIS is slightly worse than DeepV2D. This is because we scale each depth map of DeepV2D to the GT depth map, and thus after the fusion of the depth maps, there are sufficient points near the GT mesh (i.e., a low Comp. error), but also many points are still far away from the GT mesh (i.e., a high Accuracy error). For NeRF, we use the level set 20 to extract surfaces, where the level set is carefully selected (See the supplementary). Figure 3 shows the qualitative comparisons. Our method is visually much better than other methods with fine details. We remark that our method can produce much complete and smooth results and fill the holes that exist in the ground truth surface, which is mainly caused by occlusions and incomplete scans [22]. Refer to the supplementary for more qualitative results.

Normal Predictions. Except for accurate geometry reconstruction, our method can also achieve more accurate normal predictions than [6]. For the monocular normal estimation method [6], the estimated normal maps may contain wrong predictions when there are severe occlusions or ambiguities. For example, when a wall is observed too locally, it's hard to utilize the global information for precise normal estimations. Thanks to the proposed adaptive normal guided optimization, our method can improve the global consistency of normal maps across views and correct the wrong estimations from [6]. Figure 4 clearly shows

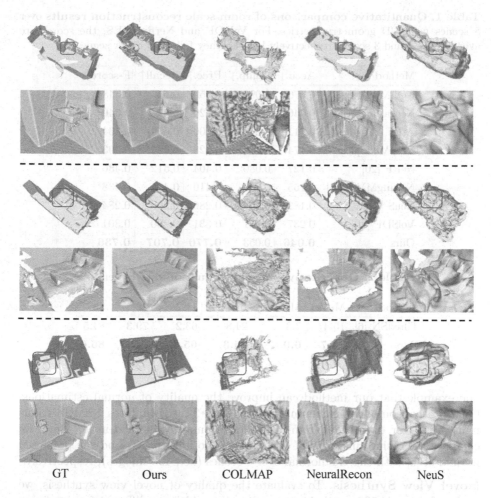

| GT | Ours | COLMAP | NeuralRecon | NeuS |

Fig. 3. Qualitative geometry comparisons. For each block, the first row is the top view of the whole room and the second row is the zoom-in view of the marked area. Our method can produce more accurate and complete reconstruction results and preserve fine details of the scenes.

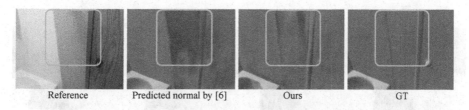

| Reference | Predicted normal by [6] | Ours | GT |

Fig. 4. Qualitative normal comparisons. When the wall is observed too locally, the normal estimation of [6] in the marked area is not accurate while it can be improved by leveraging multi-view information with better observations in our method.

Table 1. Quantitative comparisons of room-scale reconstruction results over 8 scenes using 3D geometry metrics. For VolSDF and NerfingMVS, the scores are averaged on 5 and 3 scenes respectively because they failed on other scenes.

Method	Accu.↓	Comp.↓	Prec.↑	Recall↑	F-score↑
COLMAP [28]	0.076	0.096	0.559	0.545	0.548
NeuralRecon [31]	0.046	0.081	0.720	0.577	0.640
Atlas [22]	0.211	0.070	0.500	0.659	0.564
DeepV2D [33]	0.174	**0.049**	0.528	0.682	0.593
NeRF [20]	0.127	0.080	0.404	0.512	0.436
NerfingMVS [38]	0.155	0.087	0.410	0.471	0.438
NeuS [36]	0.183	0.152	0.286	0.290	0.284
VolSDF [40]	0.237	0.171	0.331	0.280	0.301
Ours	**0.046**	0.053	**0.770**	**0.707**	**0.736**

Table 2. Quantitative normal evaluation over 8 scenes.

Method	Mean↓	Median↓	RMSE↓	11.25°↑	22.5°↑	30°↑
TiltedSN [6]	15.4	7.3	24.8	63.2	79.3	84.5
Ours	**14.7**	**6.9**	**24.3**	**65.4**	**81.1**	**86.0**

one example that our method can improve the quality of normal estimations. Quantitative comparisons summarized in Table 2 also validates NeuRIS's normals are better than those from [6], using the metrics defined in [6]. Here, we compare the cosine similarity of our rendered normal (Eq. 3) and the predicted normal of [6] with the GT normal over 8 scenes (i.e., 493 images), respectively.

Novel View Synthesis. To evaluate the quality of novel view synthesis, we uniformly sample 500 novel views over 8 scenes, which are different from training images. Our rendering quality is better than those of NeRF and NeuS, benefitting from our high-quality geometry. The average PSNR of NeRF, NeuS and ours are 23.3, 22.7 and 24.4, respectively. Figure 5 shows one sample of qualitative comparisons and refer to the supplementary for more results.

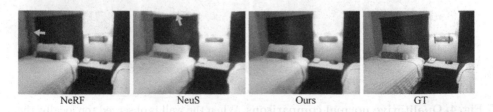

NeRF	NeuS	Ours	GT

Fig. 5. Novel view synthesis results. Our method can produce much better rendering results than the baseline methods NeRF and NeuS.

4.3   Ablation Studies

In order to evaluate the effectiveness of our proposed components, we conduct experiments in three different settings: (1) NeuS with the default setting; (2) NeuS with normal priors; (3) Ours: NeuS with normal priors and geometric check. Table 3 shows that integrating normal priors significantly improves the reconstruction quality because it reduces ambiguities caused by lack of texture. With geometry-check, we can remove the wrongly estimated normals and further improve geometry quality. Moreover, as shown in Fig. 6, adopting all normal priors naively in NeuS can reconstruct the wall and floor but fail to reconstruct the chair leg. For the pixels corresponding to the chair leg, their multi-view consistency constraints are not satisfied and the normal priors at this area should be removed during the training process. Finally with our geometry check the chair leg can be successfully reconstructed. This demonstrates that our geometry-check can remove wrongly estimated normals.

Table 3. Ablation studies of each component of our method over 8 scenes.

NeuS	Prior	Geo	Accu.↓	Comp.↓	Prec.↑	Recall↑	F-score↑
✓			0.183	0.152	0.286	0.290	0.284
✓	✓		0.050	0.053	0.749	0.701	0.724
✓	✓	✓	**0.046**	**0.053**	**0.770**	**0.707**	**0.736**

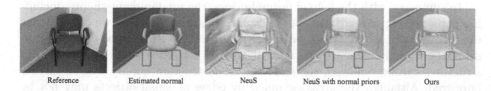

Reference   Estimated normal   NeuS   NeuS with normal priors   Ours

Fig. 6. Ablation study. The estimated normal priors of reference images show high fidelity at planar regions but they are not correct at chair legs. Naively using all normal priors as supervision can help reconstruct the planar regions but fail to reconstruct the chair legs, while our method can reconstruct them all in high quality.

We also show the reconstruction results of a challenging thin structure put at a desk corner, given a set of images sampled from a video sequence. Figure 7 shows that NeuS can reconstruct the thin structure but there are artifacts, including wrongly reconstructed desk surfaces and redundant surfaces indicated by the red arrow. NeuS with normal priors can reconstruct the background desk surface well but still fail to reconstruct some parts of the thin structure well (blue arrows). As for our method, both the background desk surfaces and foreground thin structures can be well reconstructed. Moreover, different from the methods [12,13,32,35] which only focus on thin structure reconstruction, our method does not need foreground extraction for each input image as preprocessing and can handle hybrid scenes which contain both thin structures and general objects.

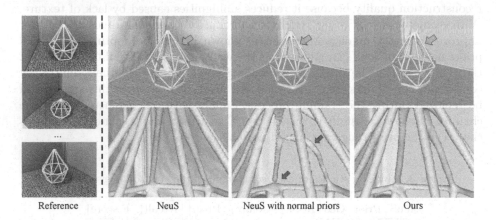

| Reference | NeuS | NeuS with normal priors | Ours |

Fig. 7. Reconstruction of a thin structure and desk corner. The left part shows the reference images. The right part shows the reconstruction results under 3 different settings, where the first row shows the overview of reconstruction results and the second row shows the zoom-in view of the area indicated by yellow arrows. (Color figure online)

In summary, with the help of normal priors, the predominant shapes, including planar or regular surfaces, can be well reconstructed. Thus, we can see that the reconstruction quality can be greatly improved. With the geo-check mechanism, the wrongly estimated normals at areas of relatively small objects or thin structures can be removed, therefore the reconstruction quality can be further improved. Although the areas occupied by edges or small objects may not be large in a room, the accurate reconstruction of them is critical to the overall success of reconstruction in terms of perceptual quality.

5   Conclusion and Future Work

In this work, we propose a novel prior-guided optimization framework of neural volume rendering with geometric constraints, which can adaptively integrate normal priors into neural volume rendering efficiently and accurately. This way enables the network to utilize prior knowledge at texture-less areas and maintain the capacity to reconstruct fine details of small objects with relatively more texture. This method has practical uses in VR/AR or other applications that require precise indoor geometry. Currently, our method requires per-scene optimization for several hours, which hinders our method from reconstructing scenes at a large scale. In the future, we will try to integrate some hybrid neural representations such as the multi-resolution hash encoding [21] into our model to speed up the training process and try to adaptively integrate other kinds of priors into our framework, such as depth priors, to get better reconstruction quality.

Acknowlegements. We thank Yuan Liu and Nenglun Chen for the help with experiments. Christian Theobalt was supported by ERC Consolidator Grant 770784. Lingjie Liu was supported by Lise Meitner Postdoctoral Fellowship. Computational resources are mainly provided by HKU GPU Farm.

References

1. Atzmon, M., Lipman, Y.: SAL: sign agnostic learning of shapes from raw data. In: Proceedings of the IEEE/CVF Conference on Computer Vision and Pattern Recognition, pp. 2565–2574 (2020)
2. Bae, G., Budvytis, I., Cipolla, R.: Estimating and exploiting the aleatoric uncertainty in surface normal estimation. In: International Conference on Computer Vision (ICCV) (2021)
3. Chen, Y., Liu, S., Wang, X.: Learning continuous image representation with local implicit image function. In: Proceedings of the IEEE/CVF Conference on Computer Vision and Pattern Recognition, pp. 8628–8638 (2021)
4. Dai, A., Chang, A.X., Savva, M., Halber, M., Funkhouser, T., Nießner, M.: ScanNet: richly-annotated 3D reconstructions of indoor scenes. In: Proceedings of the Computer Vision and Pattern Recognition (CVPR). IEEE (2017)
5. Darmon, F., Bascle, B., Devaux, J.C., Monasse, P., Aubry, M.: Improving neural implicit surfaces geometry with patch warping. arXiv preprint arXiv:2112.09648 (2021)
6. Do, T., Vuong, K., Roumeliotis, S.I., Park, H.S.: Surface normal estimation of *Tilted* images via spatial rectifier. In: Vedaldi, A., Bischof, H., Brox, T., Frahm, J.-M. (eds.) ECCV 2020. LNCS, vol. 12349, pp. 265–280. Springer, Cham (2020). https://doi.org/10.1007/978-3-030-58548-8_16
7. Gropp, A., Yariv, L., Haim, N., Atzmon, M., Lipman, Y.: Implicit geometric regularization for learning shapes. arXiv preprint arXiv:2002.10099 (2020)
8. Gropp, A., Yariv, L., Haim, N., Atzmon, M., Lipman, Y.: Implicit geometric regularization for learning shapes. In: 2020 Proceedings of Machine Learning and Systems, pp. 3569–3579 (2020)
9. Huang, J., Zhou, Y., Funkhouser, T., Guibas, L.J.: FrameNet: learning local canonical frames of 3D surfaces from a single RGB image. In: Proceedings of the IEEE/CVF International Conference on Computer Vision, pp. 8638–8647 (2019)
10. Im, S., Jeon, H.G., Lin, S., Kweon, I.S.: DPSNET: end-to-end deep plane sweep stereo. arXiv preprint arXiv:1905.00538 (2019)
11. Kazhdan, M., Hoppe, H.: Screened poisson surface reconstruction. ACM Trans. Graph. (ToG) **32**(3), 1–13 (2013)
12. Liu, L., Ceylan, D., Lin, C., Wang, W., Mitra, N.J.: Image-based reconstruction of wire art. ACM Trans. Graph. (ToG) **36**(4), 1–11 (2017)
13. Liu, L., Chen, N., Ceylan, D., Theobalt, C., Wang, W., Mitra, N.J.: CurveFusion: reconstructing thin structures from RGBD sequences **37**(6) (2018)
14. Liu, L., Gu, J., Lin, K.Z., Chua, T.S., Theobalt, C.: Neural sparse voxel fields. In: NeurIPS (2020)

154   J. Wang et al.

15. Long, X., et al.: Adaptive surface normal constraint for depth estimation. In: ICCV (2021)
16. Long, X., Liu, L., Li, W., Theobalt, C., Wang, W.: Multi-view depth estimation using epipolar spatio-temporal network. In: CVPR (2021)
17. Long, X., Liu, L., Theobalt, C., Wang, W.: Occlusion-aware depth estimation with adaptive normal constraints. In: Vedaldi, A., Bischof, H., Brox, T., Frahm, J.-M. (eds.) ECCV 2020. LNCS, vol. 12354, pp. 640–657. Springer, Cham (2020). https://doi.org/10.1007/978-3-030-58545-7_37
18. Luo, X., Huang, J., Szeliski, R., Matzen, K., Kopf, J.: Consistent video depth estimation. ACM Trans. Graph. (ToG) **39**(4), 71:1–71:13 (2020)
19. Mescheder, L., Oechsle, M., Niemeyer, M., Nowozin, S., Geiger, A.: Occupancy networks: learning 3D reconstruction in function space. In: Proceedings of the IEEE/CVF Conference on Computer Vision and Pattern Recognition, pp. 4460–4470 (2019)
20. Mildenhall, B., Srinivasan, P.P., Tancik, M., Barron, J.T., Ramamoorthi, R., Ng, R.: NeRF: representing scenes as neural radiance fields for view synthesis. In: Vedaldi, A., Bischof, H., Brox, T., Frahm, J.-M. (eds.) ECCV 2020. LNCS, vol. 12346, pp. 405–421. Springer, Cham (2020). https://doi.org/10.1007/978-3-030-58452-8_24
21. Müller, T., Evans, A., Schied, C., Keller, A.: Instant neural graphics primitives with a multiresolution hash encoding. arXiv:2201.05989 (2022)
22. Murez, Z., van As, T., Bartolozzi, J., Sinha, A., Badrinarayanan, V., Rabinovich, A.: Atlas: end-to-end 3D scene reconstruction from posed images. In: Vedaldi, A., Bischof, H., Brox, T., Frahm, J.-M. (eds.) ECCV 2020. LNCS, vol. 12352, pp. 414–431. Springer, Cham (2020). https://doi.org/10.1007/978-3-030-58571-6_25
23. Niemeyer, M., Mescheder, L., Oechsle, M., Geiger, A.: Differentiable volumetric rendering: learning implicit 3D representations without 3D supervision. In: Proceedings of the IEEE/CVF Conference on Computer Vision and Pattern Recognition, pp. 3504–3515 (2020)
24. Oechsle, M., Peng, S., Geiger, A.: UNISURF: unifying neural implicit surfaces and radiance fields for multi-view reconstruction. In: International Conference on Computer Vision (ICCV) (2021)
25. Park, J.J., Florence, P., Straub, J., Newcombe, R., Lovegrove, S.: DeepSDF: learning continuous signed distance functions for shape representation. In: Proceedings of the IEEE/CVF Conference on Computer Vision and Pattern Recognition, pp. 165–174 (2019)
26. Ramasinghe, S., Lucey, S.: Beyond periodicity: towards a unifying framework for activations in coordinate-MLPs. arXiv preprint arXiv:2111.15135 (2021)
27. Roessle, B., Barron, J.T., Mildenhall, B., Srinivasan, P.P., Nießner, M.: Dense depth priors for neural radiance fields from sparse input views. arXiv preprint arXiv:2112.03288 (2021)
28. Schönberger, J.L., Zheng, E., Frahm, J.-M., Pollefeys, M.: Pixelwise view selection for unstructured multi-view stereo. In: Leibe, B., Matas, J., Sebe, N., Welling, M. (eds.) ECCV 2016. LNCS, vol. 9907, pp. 501–518. Springer, Cham (2016). https://doi.org/10.1007/978-3-319-46487-9_31
29. Shen, S.: Accurate multiple view 3D reconstruction using patch-based stereo for large-scale scenes. IEEE Trans. Image Process. **22**(5), 1901–1914 (2013)
30. Sitzmann, V., Martel, J.N., Bergman, A.W., Lindell, D.B., Wetzstein, G.: Implicit neural representations with periodic activation functions. arXiv preprint arXiv:2006.09661 (2020)

31. Sun, J., Xie, Y., Chen, L., Zhou, X., Bao, H.: NeuralRecon: real-time coherent 3D reconstruction from monocular video. In: CVPR (2021)
32. Tabb, A.: Shape from silhouette probability maps: reconstruction of thin objects in the presence of silhouette extraction and calibration error, pp. 161–168, June 2013. https://doi.org/10.1109/CVPR.2013.28
33. Teed, Z., Deng, J.: DeepV2D: video to depth with differentiable structure from motion. arXiv preprint arXiv:1812.04605 (2018)
34. Wang, K., Shen, S.: MVDepthNet: real-time multiview depth estimation neural network. In: International Conference on 3D Vision (3DV) (2018)
35. Wang, P., Liu, L., Chen, N., Chu, H.K., Theobalt, C., Wang, W.: Vid2Curve: simultaneous camera motion estimation and thin structure reconstruction from an RGB video. ACM Trans. Graph. **39**(4), 1–12 (2020)
36. Wang, P., Liu, L., Liu, Y., Theobalt, C., Komura, T., Wang, W.: NeuS: learning neural implicit surfaces by volume rendering for multi-view reconstruction. arXiv preprint arXiv:2106.10689 (2021)
37. Wang, R., Geraghty, D., Matzen, K., Szeliski, R., Frahm, J.M.: VPLNet: deep single view normal estimation with vanishing points and lines. In: Proceedings of the IEEE/CVF Conference on Computer Vision and Pattern Recognition, pp. 689–698 (2020)
38. Wei, Y., Liu, S., Rao, Y., Zhao, W., Lu, J., Zhou, J.: NerfingMVS: guided optimization of neural radiance fields for indoor multi-view stereo. In: ICCV (2021)
39. Xiangli, Y., et al.: CityNeRF: building NeRF at city scale. arXiv preprint arXiv:2112.05504 (2021)
40. Yariv, L., Gu, J., Kasten, Y., Lipman, Y.: Volume rendering of neural implicit surfaces. In: Advances in Neural Information Processing Systems, vol. 34 (2021)
41. Yariv, L., et al.: Multiview neural surface reconstruction by disentangling geometry and appearance. In: Advances in Neural Information Processing Systems, vol. 33 (2020)
42. Yin, W., Liu, Y., Shen, C., Yan, Y.: Enforcing geometric constraints of virtual normal for depth prediction. In: Proceedings of the IEEE/CVF International Conference on Computer Vision, pp. 5684–5693 (2019)
43. Zhao, W., Liu, S., Wei, Y., Guo, H., Liu, Y.J.: A confidence-based iterative solver of depths and surface normals for deep multi-view stereo. In: Proceedings of the IEEE/CVF International Conference on Computer Vision, pp. 6168–6177 (2021)
44. Zheng, E., Dunn, E., Jojic, V., Frahm, J.M.: PatchMatch based joint view selection and depthmap estimation. In: Proceedings of the IEEE Conference on Computer Vision and Pattern Recognition, pp. 1510–1517 (2014)
45. Zhou, T., Brown, M., Snavely, N., Lowe, D.G.: Unsupervised learning of depth and ego-motion from video. In: Proceedings of the IEEE Conference on Computer Vision and Pattern Recognition, pp. 1851–1858 (2017)

Generalizable Patch-Based Neural Rendering

Mohammed Suhail[1](✉), Carlos Esteves[4], Leonid Sigal[1,2,3],
and Ameesh Makadia[4]

[1] University of British Columbia, Vancouver, Canada
{suhail33,lsigal}@cs.ubc.ca
[2] Vector Institute for AI, Toronto, Canada
[3] Canada CIFAR AI Chair, Vancouver, Canada
[4] Google, Vancouver, Canada
{machc,makadia}@google.com

Abstract. Neural rendering has received tremendous attention since the advent of Neural Radiance Fields (NeRF), and has pushed the state-of-the-art on novel-view synthesis considerably. The recent focus has been on models that overfit to a single scene, and the few attempts to learn models that can synthesize novel views of unseen scenes mostly consist of combining deep convolutional features with a NeRF-like model. We propose a different paradigm, where no deep visual features and no NeRF-like volume rendering are needed. Our method is capable of predicting the color of a target ray in a novel scene directly, just from a collection of patches sampled from the scene. We first leverage epipolar geometry to extract patches along the epipolar lines of each reference view. Each patch is linearly projected into a 1D feature vector and a sequence of transformers process the collection. For positional encoding, we parameterize rays as in a light field representation, with the crucial difference that the coordinates are canonicalized with respect to the target ray, which makes our method independent of the reference frame and improves generalization. We show that our approach outperforms the state-of-the-art on novel view synthesis of unseen scenes even when being trained with considerably less data than prior work. Our code is available at https://mohammedsuhail.net/gen_patch_neural_rendering/.

1 Introduction

Synthesizing novel views of a scene from a set of images obtained from different viewpoints is a long-standing problem in computer graphics and computer vision. Recent advances in this problem [63] employ neural networks to learn scene representations (neural scene representations), combined with classical volume rendering to produce a novel view from any desired viewpoint, an idea spearheaded by NeRF [36]. Most of these methods are trained by overfitting to a single scene

---

Supplementary Information The online version contains supplementary material available at https://doi.org/10.1007/978-3-031-19824-3_10.

Fig. 1. Motivation overview. Our goal is to predict the color of a target ray, given only the reference images and camera poses. Consider the patches along each epipolar line, which correspond to samples of increasing depth along the target ray. If there are many matching patches at some depth, there is a high chance that the patch around the target ray also matches. In this example, the matching patches contain the flower, which is where the target ray hits. This motivates our three-stage architecture, that first exchanges information along views at each depth (yellow), then aggregates information along depths for each view (green), and finally aggregates information among reference views to predict the ray color (blue). The figure shows only 2 reference views with 15 sampled patches each, but in practice we use a larger number of views and samples. (Color figure online)

in order to produce arbitrary novel views of that same scene. While capable of producing high-quality photorealistic images, the need for retraining on each new scene limits their practical application.

In this paper, we consider the more difficult task of training a single model that is capable of generating novel views of unseen scenes. There are a few notable efforts in this direction [8,68,77]. One key idea of these methods is to augment NeRF inputs with deep convolutional features, which include both local and global context. However, these methods still rely on scene-specific inputs such as 3D positions and directions, which are not reliable on unseen scenes. We also hypothesize that using feature extractors that have large receptive fields such as UNet [49] or Feature Pyramid Networks [27] is harmful when generalizing to scenes visually far from the training distribution.

We propose a different approach that takes only local linear patch embeddings as input, eschewing deep convolutional networks. Moreover, our method does not require the ubiquitous volume rendering from NeRF; it produces the color of a target pixel directly from a set of reference view patches.

We are inspired by both classical and recent works. Classical computer vision tasks such as optical flow and image feature matching for 3D reconstruction were historically dominated by techniques operating on local patches [18,31, 33,56]. In fact, for some tasks the classical methods still outperform modern deep learning ones [52]. Another example is COLMAP [53,54] which is a widely popular method for 3D reconstruction and typically used to generate camera poses (and sometimes depth maps) that are inputs to modern neural rendering.

Our decision to focus on local patches and to avoid convolutional features is supported by the recent success of the Vision Transformers (ViT) [13], which we employ. A second reason to use transformers [66] is that our input is effectively a set of patches, and self-attention is a powerful mechanism to learn from sets without making any assumption about the order of the elements. We show that transformers can effectively replace both the convolutional features and the volume rendering typically employed in the tasks we consider.

Our key contribution is to leverage the structure of the patch collection to build a multiview representation that is further refined along epipolar lines and reference views to predict the final color. Figure 1 explains the idea. Another unique aspect of our method is the canonicalized positional encoding of rays, depths, and camera poses, which is independent of the frame of reference, enabling superior generalization performance.

Contributions: Our contributions can be summarized as follows,

- We introduce a model that renders target rays in unseen scenes directly from a collection of patches sampled along epipolar lines of reference views.
- To exploit the structure of the patch collection, we design an architecture with stacked transformers operating over different subsets of the collection such that features are learned, combined, and aggregated in principled ways.
- To improve generalization to unseen scenes, we introduce canonicalized positional encodings of rays, depths, and camera poses such that all inputs to the model are independent of the scene's frame of reference.
- Our model outperforms previous baselines in multiple train and evaluation datasets, while using as little as 11% of training data in certain cases.

2   Related Work

2.1   Neural Scene Representations

Our method is in the broad category known as neural rendering, where neural networks are used to represent a scene and/or directly render views [63]. Neural fields [71] are also closely related. The majority of recent methods employ neural scene representations coupled with classical rendering methods, as popularized by NeRF [36]. These works can be broadly classified into models that represent the scene using a *surface* or *volumetric* representation [63]. Surface representation methods either explicitly represent the scene as point clouds [1,25,43,50,69,74], meshes [4,21,64], or implicitly using signed distance function [10,24,42,62,73]. Volumetric representations on the other hand typically use voxel grids [39,60], octrees [28,76], multi-plane [70,78], implicitly using a neural network [16,29, 40] or a coordinate-based network as in NeRF [36] and its variants [3,34,37]. Recently, works such as Vol-SDF [72], NeuS [67] and UNISURF [41] propose to use volumetric rendering methods to extract a surface representation.

Our method differs from these because there is no structured neural scene representation and no volume rendering – the target pixel color is obtained directly by learning weights to blend reference pixels, taking only a set of patches around the reference pixels as input. Thus, our approach fits into the category of image-based rendering.

Moreover, our model can be trained once on a set of scenes and applied to novel scenes, which can be more efficient than re-training scene-specific models for every new scene as is common. Concurrent work has achieved impressive results on accelerating NeRFs [38,75], providing a reasonable alternative when efficiency is important and re-training for every scene is not a hindrance.

2.2 Image-Based Rendering

Image-based rendering methods [57,58] typically construct novel views of a scene by warping and compositing a set of reference images. Shum and Kang [57] classified most of these works into categories that use *no* geometry, *explicit* geometry or *implicit* geometry. Methods that do not model the geometry rely on the characterization of the plenoptic function. Light field rendering [26] is one such method that used 4D light field plenoptic function to render novel views by interpolating a set of input samples. Light field rendering, however, requires a dense sampling of input views to be accurate. Follow-up works such as Lumigraph [17] incorporate approximate geometry to overcome the dense sampling requirement. Explicit geometry based methods [19,20,46,47] generate a geometric reconstruction of the scene in the form of a 3D mesh. However, explicit 3D reconstruction without 3D supervision is a hard learning problem, and undesirable artifacts in the reconstructed geometry impact rendering quality. Implicit geometry methods [9,55] rely on aggregating multiple input views to synthesize a novel view. Recently, LFNR [61] proposed to use epipolar geometry in conjunction with light field ray representations to model view-dependent effects. Other works [2,14,59] similarly have explored neural representations for light field rendering. Part of our architecture is similar to LFNR; however, our method is aimed at generalizing to unseen scenes as opposed to overfitting on a single scene, which avoids expensive retraining for each new scene.

Stereo Radiance Fields [12] has a focus on efficiency and was one of the first methods tackling generalization to novel scenes. PixelNeRF [77] conditions a NeRF [36] on deep convolutional visual features of the reference views, enabling generalization to new scenes; however, it uses absolute positions and directions as inputs to the NeRF, which generalize poorly across scenes. Similarly, IBR-Net [68] also uses deep features and NeRF-like volume rendering, but it learns to blend colors from neighboring views for each point along a ray. IBRNet uses the difference between view directions as MLP inputs; while this is superior to absolute coordinates, the relative view directions still depend on a global reference frame which is scene-specific. MVSNeRF [8] constructs a cost volume from deep visual features. The voxel features are then concatenated to the usual NeRF inputs including absolute positions and directions for rendering novel views.

In contrast with these works, our method 1) does not require deep convolutional features, operating directly on linear projections of local patches, similarly to ViT [13]; 2) does not require volume rendering, producing the final colors directly from a reference set of patches; and 3) is independent of the input frame of reference, leveraging canonicalized ray, point and camera representations, which improves its generalization ability. Concurrent work on neural rendering generalizable to unseen scenes include GeoNeRF [23] and NeuRay [30], but both require at least partial depth maps during training.

2.3 Transformers in Vision

Popularized by Vaswani *et al.* [66], transformers are sequence-to-sequence models that use an attention mechanism to incorporate contextual information from relevant parts of the input. Initially developed for NLP tasks [11], transformer-based models have also achieved state-of-the-art on a variety of vision problems [6,7,13,32,61].

Recently, Robin *et al.* [48] proposed the use of transformers to generate novel views from a single image without explicit geometric modeling. Scene representation transformers [51] similarly presented a model for novel view synthesis using self-supervision from images. Their experiments, however, are limited to low resolution images (maximum size of 178 × 128 pixels). Slightly more related to our approach are IBRNet [68], which employs a ray-transformer module to estimate densities via self-attention over samples along the ray, and NerFormer [44], which alternates self-attention over views and rays, but is object-based and aims to generalize only to new instances of the same object category.

Our use of transformers differs greatly from such works because (i) we use transformers in all stages, from the patch embedding to final target ray color prediction, not requiring deep convolutional features nor volume rendering, and (ii) we design a unique architecture with three different transformers operating along and collapsing different dimensions.

3 Approach

Given a set of scenes with a collection of images and their corresponding camera poses, we aim to learn a generic rendering model that is capable of rendering novel views of a scene without training on it. At the core of our model is a reference-frame-agnostic rendering network that relies only on local patches observed from nearby reference cameras. Figure 2 provides a visual overview. We present our approach in the following order: first we introduce light field representations; then we discuss the construction and embedding of reference patches; and finally we detail our transformer-based rendering network that maps a target light field and reference patches to radiance.

3.1 Light Field Representation

The light field characterizes the radiance through points in space. It can be described by a five-dimensional function on $\mathbb{R}^3 \times S^2$, mapping each direction through each point to its radiance. In free space, the radiance along a ray remains constant, thus allowing to parametrize the light field as a $4D$ function [26].

Depending on the camera configuration, different light field representations can be used. For example, for a scene with forward-facing camera configuration,

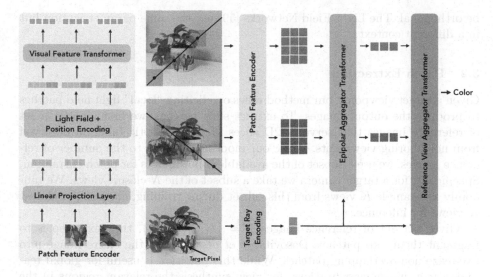

Fig. 2. Model Overview. Our model consists of three stages, with a different transformer per stage. First, patches along epipolar lines are extracted, linearly projected, and arranged in a grid of K reference views by M sampled depths. The first transformer takes a sequence of views and is repeated for each depth, returning another $K \times M$ grid. The second transformer takes a sequence of depths and is repeated for each view; it collapses features along the depth dimension, returning K view features. The third transformer aggregates the K view features. Attention weights extracted from the second and third transformers are used to blend colors over views and epipolar lines and make the final prediction. A canonicalized positional encoding of rays, depths and cameras is appended to the transformer inputs.

the rays can be parametrized by their intersections with two planes perpendicular to the forward direction, a representation known as the light slab [26]. The entries of the $4D$ vector are the coordinates of the intersections on each plane's $2D$ coordinate system. An alternative representation suitable for bounded scenes observed from all directions is known as the two-sphere [5], and represents rays by their two intersections with a sphere bounding the scene. Prior works such as LFNR [61] exploit the camera configuration information of the scene to decide the underlying parametrization. They use light slab parametrization for forward-facing-scenes and two-sphere parametrization for 360° scenes.

In this work, the ray representations are used as positional encoding in the transformers. Since we wish to generalize to new scenes and therefore cannot make assumptions about the camera configurations, we use Plücker coordinates as the choice of parametrization. Given a ray through a point o (the ray origin) with direction v, the Plücker coordinates can be obtained as $r = (v, o \times v)$. The representation is six-dimensional, however it has only four degrees of freedom since it is defined up to a scale factor and the two vectors that compose it must be orthogonal. The Light Field Networks [59] use the same parametrization but in a different context.

3.2 Patch Extraction

Given a target viewpoint, our method relies on eliciting "local" light field patches to produce the output images. To extract such patches, we first identify a set of reference images that serve as 2D slices of the plenoptic function observed from neighboring viewpoints. While our model is agnostic to the number of reference images, we use a subset of the available input images for patch extraction. Specifically, for a target camera we take a subset of the N closest views. We randomly sub-sample K views from this subset during training, and use the closest K views for inference.

Given the set of reference images $\mathcal{I} = \{I_1, I_2, ..., I_K\}$, the next step is to fragment them into patches. Dosovitskiy et al. [13] split the entire image into fixed-size non-overlapping patches. While this partition is useful for global reasoning (e.g. image classification), for view synthesis the relevant regions in the image can isolated by exploiting the epipolar geometry between views. For a given image in the reference set $\mathcal{I}$, we compute the epipolar line corresponding to the target pixel. We sample M points along this epipolar line such that their 3D re-projections on the target ray are spaced linearly in depth. We then extract square patches around each of the M points, and this process is repeated for all reference images. The resulting reference patch set is indexed by view and depth: $\mathcal{P} = \{P_k^m \mid 1 \leq k \leq K, 1 \leq m \leq M\}$.

3.3 Patch Embedding and Positional Encoding

The inputs to the transformers are patch embeddings which we generate we generate by linearly projecting flattened input patches The patch features for the m-th sample along the epipolar line on view k is denoted p_k^m.

Since transformers are agnostic to the position of each element in the input sequence, typically a positional encoding is added to the features to represent the spatial relationship between elements. Unlike prior works [13], since the location and source of patches do not remain the same across batches, we cannot include a learnable embedding into the sequence. Instead, we extract the geometric information associated with each patch and append them to the flattened patch feature vectors.

We use three forms of positional encoding:

1. To retain the reference patch position in space, we use the light field encoding of the rays emanating from the reference camera as described in Sect. 3.1. We represent the m-th ray along the epipolar line of view k by r_k^m.
2. To retain the position of the patch in the sequence of patches along the epipolar line, we encode the distance along the target ray corresponding to the patch center using a sinusoidal positional encoding that follows NeRF [36]. The encoded distance for the m-th sample is represented by d^m.

3. To retain geometry between target and reference cameras, we also append the relative camera pose as a flattened rotation matrix and a 3D translation, which is shared among all patches associated to the same camera and denoted by c_k for camera k.

3.4 Canonicalized Ray Representation

Structure-from-Motion (SfM) methods that are used to estimate camera extrinsics can only reconstruct scenes up to an arbitrary similarity transformation – rotation, translation and scaling. Prior works [8,68,77] use such estimations to compute scene specific coordinates such as view directions and $3D$ coordinates of points.

We hypothesize that for best generalization to unseen scenes, the inputs to the model should be invariant to similarity transformations. This means that model should produce the same result upon a change of reference frame or rescaling of the input camera poses. IBRNet [68] takes a step towards this idea by using the difference between reference and target direction vectors instead of absolute directions, but the difference is still a 3D vector that is not independent of the frame of reference, and so are the 3D positions of points along the target ray.

The positional encoding of relative camera poses and distance values, as described in Sect. 3.3, are made invariant to similarities by simply scaling the camera positions by the maximum depth of the scene output by SfM.

The encoding of rays in the light field, however, need to be canonicalized. Our key idea is to define a local frame centered on each ray (not camera). For a target pixel $x \in \mathbf{RP}^2$ in the target camera with extrinsics $[R \mid t]$ and intrinsics C, we first obtain the corresponding ray direction $v = R^{\top} C^{-1} x$. We use v and the camera y axis to determine the local frame. Specifically, we use the Gram-Schmidt orthonormalization process. Let $v' = v/\|v\|$ and $y' = y - (y \cdot v')v'$. The canonicalizing transformation is then

$$R_c = \left[\frac{y'}{\|y'\|} \times v' \quad \frac{y'}{\|y'\|} \quad v' \right] \tag{1}$$

$$T = [R_c^{\top} \mid -R_c^{\top} t] \tag{2}$$

where $T \in \mathbf{SE}(3)$. We apply T to every camera pose, which results in the target ray having origin $(0,0,0)$ and direction $(0,0,1)$, and all other ray representations computed from the canonicalized camera poses will be invariant to similarities. We show the benefit of such canonicalization in Sect. 4.2.

3.5 Rendering Network

Given the patch embeddings and positional encodings of a target ray, as described in Sects. 3.3 and 3.4, our rendering network predicts the ray color.

We argue that predicting the target ray color is deeply related to finding correspondences to the target ray in the reference images. Take, for example, LFNR [61]. Its first stage aggregates features along each epipolar line, which is essentially finding correspondences to the target ray. Since LFNR overfits to a single scene, the model can learn the structure of the scene and use it to estimate correspondences based only on ray coordinates.

However, the LFNR [61] approach cannot generalize to novel scenes, since, given just an epipolar line, it is impossible to know which point corresponds to a target ray without knowing the structure of the scene.

Our main contribution is to provide visual features for a similar epipolar transformer, such that the correspondence is solved visually (see Fig 1 for illus tration), which is advantageous because the visual features can be extracted from novel scenes in a single forward step starting from small local patches. Crucially, such features cannot come from a single epipolar line. It is the combination of visual features from different epipolar lines cast by the same target ray that allows correspondences to be established. To learn this combination, we propose to use a transformer.

Thus, our model consists of three transformers. The first, which we call "Visual Feature Transformer", learns visual features by combining information from patches along different reference views. The second and third are similar to the ones in LFNR [61], with the major differences that the positional encodings of rays, depths and cameras are canonicalized as described in Sect. 3.4 and that the final color is predicted by directly blending pixel colors from reference views, instead of using learned features; both changes greatly improve the generalization performance.

Each transformer follows the ViT [13] architecture, which uses residual connections to interleave layer normalization (LN), self-attention (SA), and multilayer perceptron (MLP). Each layer consists of LN → SA → LN → MLP.

Visual Feature Transformer. This stage exchanges visual information between potentially corresponding patches on different reference images, leading to visual features with multi-view awareness. The input to this stage is the set of patch linear embeddings and positional encoding vectors p_k^m, r_k^m, d^m, c_k, indexed by the view k and the m-th sampled depth, as described in Sect. 3.3. We first define the feature concatenation at layer zero (the input) as

$$f_0^{k,m} = [p_k^m \parallel r_k^m \parallel d^m \parallel c_k]. \tag{3}$$

This stage is repeated for each depth sample, therefore it operates on sequences of K views. Formally, it repeats

$$f_1^m = T_1 \left(\left\{ f_0^{k,m} \mid 1 \leq k \leq K \right\} \right) \tag{4}$$

for $1 \leq m \leq M$, where T_1 is a transformer written as a set to set map. This stage takes a (K, M, C_0) tensor of C_0-dimensional features of K views sampled at M depths, and returns a (K, M, C_1) tensor of C_1-dimensional features.

Epipolar Aggregator Transformer. This stage aggregates information along each epipolar line, resulting in per reference view features. The input to this stage is the set $f_1 = \{f_1^m \mid 1 \leq m \leq M\}$, concatenated with positional encodings. We refer to the features corresponding to view k in the set f_1^m as $f_1^{k,m}$. The transformer is repeated for each view, therefore operating along the sequence of M epipolar line samples. Formally, we first compute

$$f_2^k = T_2\left(\{r^0\} \bigcup \left\{\left[f_1^{k,m} \,\|\, r_k^m \,\|\, d^m \,\|\, c_k\right] \mid 1 \leq m \leq M\right\}\right),\qquad(5)$$

for $1 \leq k \leq K$, where r^0 is a special token to represent the target ray. We then apply a learned weighted sum along the M epipolar line samples as follows,

$$\alpha_k^m = \frac{\exp\left(W_1 \left[f_2^{k,0} \,\|\, f_2^{k,m}\right]\right)}{\sum\limits_{m'=1}^{M} \exp\left(W_1 \left[f_2^{k,0} \,\|\, f_2^{k,m'}\right]\right)},\qquad(6)$$

$$f_{2'}^k = \sum_{m=1}^{M} \alpha_k^m f_2^{k,m},\qquad(7)$$

for $1 \leq k \leq K$, resulting in a feature vector per view k, where W_1 are learnable weights and $f_2^{k,0}$ is the output corresponding to the target ray token.

Dimension-wise, this stage takes a (K, M, C_1) tensor and returns a (K, C_2) tensor of C_2-dimensional features per reference view.

Reference View Aggregator Transformer. This final transformer aggregates the features over reference views and predicts the color of the target ray. Its input is the set of per reference view features $f_{2'} = \{f_{2'}^k \mid 1 \leq k \leq K\}$, concatenated with the camera relative positional encoding. Formally, we compute

$$f_3 = T_3\left(\{r^0\} \bigcup \left\{\left[f_{2'}^k \,\|\, c_k\right] \mid 1 \leq k \leq K\right\}\right).\qquad(8)$$

Similarly to the previous stage, we compute the blending weights

$$\beta_k = \frac{\exp\left(W_2 \left[f_3^0 \,\|\, f_3^k\right]\right)}{\sum\limits_{k'=1}^{K} \exp\left(W_2 \left[f_3^0 \,\|\, f_3^k\right]\right)},\qquad(9)$$

which are used in conjunction with the weights from the previous stage to estimate the color of the target ray by blending colors along each epipolar line sample at each reference view,

$$\mathfrak{c} = \sum_{k=1}^{K} \beta_k \left(\sum_{m=1}^{M} \alpha_k^m \mathfrak{c}_k^m\right),\qquad(10)$$

where $\mathfrak{c}_k^m$ is the pixel color at the m-th sample along the epipolar line of view k. Our approach here differs from the last stage of LFNR, which does the aggregation on feature space using only the weights β_k, and linearly projects the resulting feature to predict the color. We argue that using the input pixel values from reference views instead helps generalization, which we confirm experimentally (see appendix). This is possible by using the two sets of attention weights α_k^m (Eq. (6)) and β_k (Eq. (9)), which allow blending colors from all epipolar line samples and all reference views.

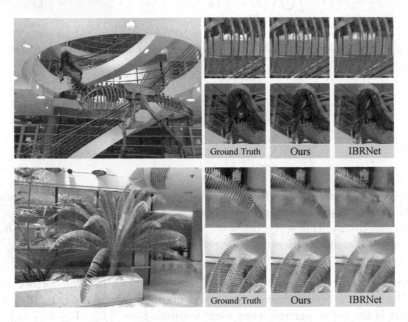

Fig. 3. Qualitative results on RFF (setting 1). We show our method and the baseline on the *T-Rex* and *Fern* scenes from the real forward-facing dataset. Compared with IBRNet [68], our method produce sharper details and less blurring at boundaries. For example, the top row in the *Fern* scene shows that the baseline methods either fail to reconstruct the leaves or produce inconsistent shapes. Our method is able to retain the shape boundaries accurately along with majority of the texture details.

4 Experiments

4.1 Implementation Details

Each of the three transformers in our model consist of 8 blocks each with a feature dimension of 256. We select reference views using $K = 10$ and $N = 20$ (see Sect. 3.2). We use a batch size of 4096 rays and train for $250k$ iterations with a Adam optimizer and initial learning rate of $3 \cdot 10^{-4}$. We use a linear learning rate warm-up for $5k$ iterations and cosine decay afterwards. Training our model takes $\sim$24 h on 32 TPUs. We report the average PSNR (peak signal-to-noise ratio), SSIM (structural similarity index measure) and LPIPS (learned perceptual image patch similarity) for all our experiments.

Table 1. Results for setting 1. Our model outperforms the baselines even when training with strictly less data. IBRNet uses three datasets that are not part of our training set, while GeoNeRF uses one extra dataset and also leverages input depth maps during training. IBRNet* was trained using the same training set as our method; in this fair comparison, our advantage in accuracy widens.

Method	Real forward-facing			Shiny-6			Blender		
	PSNR	SSIM	LPIPS	PSNR	SSIM	LPIPS	PSNR	SSIM	LPIPS
LLFF [35]	24.13	0.798	0.212	–	–	–	24.88	0.911	0.114
IBRNet [68]	25.13	0.817	0.205	23.60	0.785	0.180	25.49	0.916	0.100
GeoNeRF [23]	25.44	0.839	0.180	–	–	–	28.33	0.938	0.087
IBRNet*	24.33	0.801	0.213	23.37	0.784	0.181	21.32	0.888	0.131
Ours	25.72	0.880	0.175	24.12	0.860	0.170	26.48	0.944	0.091

4.2 Results

There is no standard training and evaluation procedure for generalizable neural rendering. IBRNet [68] trains on the LLFF dataset [35], renderings of Google scanned objects [45], Spaces dataset [15], RealEstate10K dataset [78] and on their own scenes. They evaluate on the real forward-facing (RFF) dataset [36], which comprises held-out LLFF scenes, Blender (consisting of 360° scenes) [36], and Diffuse Synthetic 360° [60]. Contrastingly, MVSNeRF [8] trains on DTU [22] and tests on held out DTU scenes, real forward-facing dataset (RFF) [36], and Blender [36]. Various other works [23,30,65] have explored different experimental setups. In this work, in an attempt to fairly evaluate against prior works, we use two experimental settings.

Setting 1. In the first setting, we train on a strict subset of the IBRNet training set, comprised of 37 LLFF scenes and 131 IBRNet collected scenes (amounting to 11% of the training set used by IBRNet). We then evaluate on the real forward-facing, Shiny [70] and Blender datasets. On Shiny, we compute the results for IBRNet using their publicly available pretrained weights. Table 1 reports quantitative while Figs. 3 and 4 show qualitative results. IBRNet and GeoNeRF (a concurrent work) use a larger training set than ours, and GeoNeRF uses depth maps during training, but our method shows the best performance in most metrics regardless. Additionally, IBRNet is trained on 360° scenes whereas our method is trained only on forward-facing scenes. Nonetheless, our model achieves superior performance on Blender as compared to IBRNet.

Setting 2. Here, we train our model on DTU, following the MVSNeRF [8] procedure, and evaluate on the held-out DTU scenes and the Blender dataset. For training on DTU, we follow the same split as PixelNeRF [77] and MVSNeRF. We partition the dataset into 88 scenes for training and 16 scenes for testing, each containing images of resolution 512×640. Table 2 shows quantitative results. MVSNeRF is trained with 3 reference views while our method performs best with 10. We evaluated MVSNeRF with 10 views, which did not improve their performance; Table 2, thus, compares the best number of views for each model. Our model consistently outperforms across all three metrics.

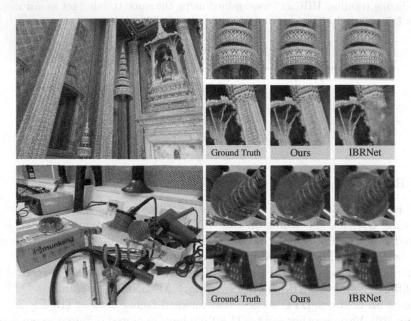

Fig. 4. Qualitative results on Shiny [70] **(setting 1).** While still consisting of forward facing scenes, Shiny scenes have scale and view density that differ from the usual in setting 1, which makes it more challenging than LLFF. IBRNet [70] produces noticeable artifacts that are not present in our method's renderings.

Ablation. To investigate the effectiveness of our contributions, we perform various ablations experiments. We train the model on 504×378 resolution images of LLFF and IBRNet scenes and test on the real forward-facing dataset at the same resolution. We start with a "base model" that does not use the visual feature transformer or the coordinate canonicalization. We then incrementally add components of our proposed approach. Table 3 reports the ablation results. We observe that the "base" model generalized poorly to unseen scenes. Incorporating the visual feature transformer improves the performance significantly. For the canonicalization ablation, we split the component into two, (1) ray canonicalization, where the light field ray representation is computed independent of the frame of reference, and (2) coordinate canonicalization where the $3D$ samples along the target ray are canonicalized. We observe that both forms of canonicalization help improve the accuracy.

Table 2. Results for setting 2. All models are trained on DTU and evaluated on either the DTU held-out set or Blender. Our approach outperforms the baselines.

Method	DTU			Blender		
	PSNR	SSIM	LPIPS	PSNR	SSIM	LPIPS
PixelNeRF [77]	19.31	0.789	0.671	7.39	0.658	0.411
IBRNet [68]	26.04	0.917	0.190	22.44	0.874	0.195
MVSNeRF [8]	26.63	0.931	0.168	23.62	0.897	0.176
Ours	28.50	0.932	0.167	24.10	0.933	0.097

Table 3. Ablations. Ablation study for model trained on LLFF and IBRNet scenes and tested on RFF with a resolution of 504×378. Results show that our main contributions – the visual feature transformer and the canonicalized positional encoding – lead to superior generalization performance.

Visual transformer	Ray canonicalization	Coordinate canonicalization	PSNR	SSIM	LPIPS
✗	✗	✗	22.62	0.763	0.313
✓	✗	✗	25.42	0.879	0.154
✓	✓	✗	25.86	0.885	0.142
✓	✓	✓	26.42	0.896	0.129

5 Limitations

One limitation of our model is that since it operates on small local patches to aid generalization, it relies on a large number of views to produce meaningful features. In the comparison against MVSNeRF [8] in Table 2, while our method is more accurate by significant margins, it also requires 10 reference views while MVSNeRF only uses 3. Rendering novel scenes with our approach is fast since it consists only of forward steps, but training is slow, comparable with LFNR [61]. The appendix shows a quantitative timing evaluation.

6 Conclusion

This paper introduced a method to generate novel views from unseen scenes that predicts the color of an arbitrary ray directly from a collection of small local patches sampled from reference views according to epipolar constraints. Our model departs from the common combination of using deep visual features and NeRF-like volume rendering for this task. We introduced a three-stage transformer architecture, coupled with canonicalized positional encodings, which operates on local patches – all these properties aid in generalizing to unseen scenes. This is demonstrated by our outperforming of the current state-of-the-art while using only 11% of the amount of training data.

We include more details and results in the appendix, including more ablation experiments, timing evaluation, other combinations of train and evaluation sets, and more qualitative results.

References

1. Aliev, K.-A., Sevastopolsky, A., Kolos, M., Ulyanov, D., Lempitsky, V.: Neural point-based graphics. In: Vedaldi, A., Bischof, H., Brox, T., Frahm, J.-M. (eds.) ECCV 2020. LNCS, vol. 12367, pp. 696–712. Springer, Cham (2020). https://doi.org/10.1007/978-3-030-58542-6_42
2. Attal, B., Huang, J.B., Zollhöfer, M., Kopf, J., Kim, C.: Learning neural light fields with ray-space embedding. In: Proceedings of the IEEE/CVF Conference on Computer Vision and Pattern Recognition, pp. 19819–19829 (2022)
3. Barron, J.T., Mildenhall, B., Tancik, M., Hedman, P., Martin-Brualla, R., Srinivasan, P.P.: Mip-NeRF: a multiscale representation for anti-aliasing neural radiance fields. In: IEEE/CVF International Conference on Computer Vision (ICCV), pp. 5855–5864 (2021)
4. Burov, A., Nießner, M., Thies, J.: Dynamic surface function networks for clothed human bodies. In: IEEE/CVF International Conference on Computer Vision (ICCV), pp. 10754–10764 (2021)
5. Camahort, E., Lerios, A., Fussell, D.: Uniformly sampled light fields. In: Drettakis, G., Max, N. (eds.) EGSR 1998. E, pp. 117–130. Springer, Vienna (1998). https://doi.org/10.1007/978-3-7091-6453-2_11
6. Carion, N., Massa, F., Synnaeve, G., Usunier, N., Kirillov, A., Zagoruyko, S.: End-to-end object detection with transformers. In: Vedaldi, A., Bischof, H., Brox, T., Frahm, J.-M. (eds.) ECCV 2020. LNCS, vol. 12346, pp. 213–229. Springer, Cham (2020). https://doi.org/10.1007/978-3-030-58452-8_13
7. Chang, H., Zhang, H., Jiang, L., Liu, C., Freeman, W.T.: MaskGIT: masked generative image transformer. arXiv preprint arXiv:2202.04200 (2022)
8. Chen, A., et al.: MVSNeRF: fast generalizable radiance field reconstruction from multi-view stereo. In: IEEE/CVF International Conference on Computer Vision (ICCV), pp. 14124–14133 (2021)
9. Chen, S.E., Williams, L.: View interpolation for image synthesis. In: Proceedings of the 20th Annual Conference on Computer Graphics and Interactive Techniques, SIGGRAPH 1993, pp. 279–288. Association for Computing Machinery (1993)
10. Chen, Z., Zhang, H.: Learning implicit fields for generative shape modeling. In: IEEE/CVF Conference on Computer Vision and Pattern Recognition (CVPR), pp. 5939–5948 (2019)
11. Chernyavskiy, A., Ilvovsky, D., Nakov, P.: Transformers: "the end of history" for NLP? arXiv preprint arXiv:2105.00813 (2021)
12. Chibane, J., Bansal, A., Lazova, V., Pons-Moll, G.: Stereo radiance fields (SRF): learning view synthesis for sparse views of novel scenes. In: IEEE/CVF Conference on Computer Vision and Pattern Recognition (CVPR), pp. 7911–7920 (2021)
13. Dosovitskiy, A., et al.: An image is worth 16×16 words: transformers for image recognition at scale. arXiv preprint arXiv:2010.11929 (2020)
14. Feng, B.Y., Varshney, A.: SIGNET: efficient neural representation for light fields. In: Proceedings of the IEEE/CVF International Conference on Computer Vision, pp. 14224–14233 (2021)
15. Flynn, J., et al.: DeepView: view synthesis with learned gradient descent. In: IEEE/CVF Conference on Computer Vision and Pattern Recognition (CVPR), pp. 2367–2376 (2019)
16. Genova, K., Cole, F., Vlasic, D., Sarna, A., Freeman, W.T., Funkhouser, T.: Learning shape templates with structured implicit functions. In: IEEE/CVF International Conference on Computer Vision (ICCV), pp. 7154–7164 (2019)

17. Gortler, S.J., Grzeszczuk, R., Szeliski, R., Cohen, M.F.: The lumigraph. In: Proceedings of the 23rd Annual Conference on Computer Graphics and Interactive Techniques, pp. 43–54 (1996)
18. Harris, C., Stephens, M.: A combined corner and edge detector. In: Proceedings of Fourth Alvey Vision Conference, pp. 147–151 (1988)
19. Hedman, P., Alsisan, S., Szeliski, R., Kopf, J.: Casual 3D photography. ACM Trans. Graph. (TOG) **36**(6), 1–15 (2017)
20. Hedman, P., Kopf, J.: Instant 3D photography. ACM Trans. Graph. (TOG) **37**(4), 1–12 (2018)
21. Hu, R., Ravi, N., Berg, A.C., Pathak, D.: Worldsheet: wrapping the world in a 3D sheet for view synthesis from a single image. In: IEEE/CVF International Conference on Computer Vision (ICCV), pp. 12528–12537 (2021)
22. Jensen, R., Dahl, A., Vogiatzis, G., Tola, E., Aanæs, H.: Large scale multi-view stereopsis evaluation. In: IEEE Conference on Computer Vision and Pattern Recognition (CVPR), pp. 406–413 (2014)
23. Johari, M.M., Lepoittevin, Y., Fleuret, F.: GeoNeRF: generalizing nerf with geometry priors. arXiv preprint arXiv:2111.13539 (2021)
24. Kellnhofer, P., Jebe, L.C., Jones, A., Spicer, R., Pulli, K., Wetzstein, G.: Neural lumigraph rendering. In: IEEE/CVF Conference on Computer Vision and Pattern Recognition (CVPR), pp. 4287–4297 (2021)
25. Lassner, C., Zollhofer, M.: Pulsar: efficient sphere-based neural rendering. In: IEEE/CVF Conference on Computer Vision and Pattern Recognition (CVPR), pp. 1440–1449 (2021)
26. Levoy, M., Hanrahan, P.: Light field rendering. In: Proceedings of the 23rd Annual Conference on Computer Graphics and Interactive Techniques, pp. 31–42 (1996)
27. Lin, T.Y., Dollár, P., Girshick, R., He, K., Hariharan, B., Belongie, S.: Feature pyramid networks for object detection. In: IEEE Conference on Computer Vision and Pattern Recognition (CVPR), pp. 2117–2125 (2017)
28. Liu, L., Gu, J., Zaw Lin, K., Chua, T.S., Theobalt, C.: Neural sparse voxel fields. In: Advances in Neural Information Processing Systems, vol. 33, pp. 15651–15663 (2020)
29. Liu, S., Zhang, Y., Peng, S., Shi, B., Pollefeys, M., Cui, Z.: DIST: rendering deep implicit signed distance function with differentiable sphere tracing. In: IEEE/CVF Conference on Computer Vision and Pattern Recognition (CVPR), pp. 2019–2028 (2020)
30. Liu, Y., et al.: Neural rays for occlusion-aware image-based rendering. arXiv preprint arXiv:2107.13421 (2021)
31. Lowe, D.G.: Distinctive image features from scale-invariant keypoints. Int. J. Comput. Vis. **60**(2), 91–110 (2004). https://doi.org/10.1023/B:VISI.0000029664.99615.94
32. Lu, J., Batra, D., Parikh, D., Lee, S.: ViLBERT: pretraining task-agnostic visiolinguistic representations for vision-and-language tasks. In: Advances in Neural Information Processing Systems, vol. 32 (2019)
33. Lucas, B.D., Kanade, T.: An iterative image registration technique with an application to stereo vision. In: Proceedings of the 7th International Joint Conference on Artificial Intelligence, IJCAI 1981, San Francisco, CA, USA, vol. 2, pp. 674–679. Morgan Kaufmann Publishers Inc. (1981)
34. Mildenhall, B., Hedman, P., Martin-Brualla, R., Srinivasan, P., Barron, J.T.: NeRF in the dark: high dynamic range view synthesis from noisy raw images. arXiv preprint arXiv:2111.13679 (2021)

35. Mildenhall, B., et al.: Local light field fusion: practical view synthesis with prescriptive sampling guidelines. ACM Trans. Graph. (TOG) **38**(4), 1–14 (2019)
36. Mildenhall, B., Srinivasan, P.P., Tancik, M., Barron, J.T., Ramamoorthi, R., Ng, R.: NeRF: representing scenes as neural radiance fields for view synthesis. In: Vedaldi, A., Bischof, H., Brox, T., Frahm, J.-M. (eds.) ECCV 2020. LNCS, vol. 12346, pp. 405–421. Springer, Cham (2020). https://doi.org/10.1007/978-3-030-58452-8_24
37. Müller, T., Evans, A., Schied, C., Keller, A.: Instant neural graphics primitives with a multiresolution hash encoding. arXiv preprint arXiv:2201.05989 (2022)
38. Müller, T., Evans, A., Schied, C., Keller, A.: Instant neural graphics primitives with a multiresolution hash encoding. CoRR (2022). http://arxiv.org/abs/2201.05989v1
39. Nguyen-Phuoc, T., Li, C., Theis, L., Richardt, C., Yang, Y.L.: HoloGAN: unsupervised learning of 3D representations from natural images. In: IEEE/CVF International Conference on Computer Vision (ICCV), pp. 7588–7597 (2019)
40. Niemeyer, M., Mescheder, L., Oechsle, M., Geiger, A.: Differentiable volumetric rendering: learning implicit 3D representations without 3D supervision. In: IEEE/CVF Conference on Computer Vision and Pattern Recognition (CVPR), pp. 3504–3515 (2020)
41. Oechsle, M., Peng, S., Geiger, A.: UNISURF: unifying neural implicit surfaces and radiance fields for multi-view reconstruction. In: IEEE/CVF International Conference on Computer Vision (ICCV), pp. 5589–5599 (2021)
42. Park, J.J., Florence, P., Straub, J., Newcombe, R., Lovegrove, S.: DeepSDF: learning continuous signed distance functions for shape representation. In: IEEE/CVF Conference on Computer Vision and Pattern Recognition (CVPR), pp. 165–174 (2019)
43. Pfister, H., Zwicker, M., Van Baar, J., Gross, M.: Surfels: surface elements as rendering primitives. In: Proceedings of the 27th Annual Conference on Computer Graphics and Interactive Techniques, pp. 335–342 (2000)
44. Reizenstein, J., Shapovalov, R., Henzler, P., Sbordone, L., Labatut, P., Novotny, D.: Common objects in 3D: large-scale learning and evaluation of real-life 3D category reconstruction. In: International Conference on Computer Vision (2021)
45. Google Research: Google scanned objects. https://app.ignitionrobotics.org/GoogleResearch/fuel/collections/GoogleScannedObjects
46. Riegler, G., Koltun, V.: Free view synthesis. In: Vedaldi, A., Bischof, H., Brox, T., Frahm, J.-M. (eds.) ECCV 2020. LNCS, vol. 12364, pp. 623–640. Springer, Cham (2020). https://doi.org/10.1007/978-3-030-58529-7_37
47. Riegler, G., Koltun, V.: Stable view synthesis. In: IEEE/CVF Conference on Computer Vision and Pattern Recognition (CVPR), pp. 12216–12225 (2021)
48. Rombach, R., Esser, P., Ommer, B.: Geometry-free view synthesis: transformers and no 3D priors. In: IEEE/CVF International Conference on Computer Vision (ICCV), pp. 14356–14366 (2021)
49. Ronneberger, O., Fischer, P., Brox, T.: U-Net: convolutional networks for biomedical image segmentation. In: Navab, N., Hornegger, J., Wells, W.M., Frangi, A.F. (eds.) MICCAI 2015. LNCS, vol. 9351, pp. 234–241. Springer, Cham (2015). https://doi.org/10.1007/978-3-319-24574-4_28
50. Rückert, D., Franke, L., Stamminger, M.: ADOP: approximate differentiable one-pixel point rendering. arXiv preprint arXiv:2110.06635 (2021)
51. Sajjadi, M.S., et al.: Scene representation transformer: geometry-free novel view synthesis through set-latent scene representations. arXiv preprint arXiv:2111.13152 (2021)

52. Schönberger, J.L., Hardmeier, H., Sattler, T., Pollefeys, M.: Comparative evaluation of hand-crafted and learned local features. In: 2017 IEEE Conference on Computer Vision and Pattern Recognition (CVPR), pp. 6959–6968 (2017)
53. Schönberger, J.L., Frahm, J.M.: Structure-from-motion revisited. In: Conference on Computer Vision and Pattern Recognition (CVPR) (2016)
54. Schönberger, J.L., Zheng, E., Frahm, J.-M., Pollefeys, M.: Pixelwise view selection for unstructured multi-view stereo. In: Leibe, B., Matas, J., Sebe, N., Welling, M. (eds.) ECCV 2016. LNCS, vol. 9907, pp. 501–518. Springer, Cham (2016). https://doi.org/10.1007/978-3-319-46487-9_31
55. Seitz, S.M., Dyer, C.R.: View morphing. In: Proceedings of the 23rd Annual Conference on Computer Graphics and Interactive Techniques, SIGGRAPH 1996, pp. 21–30. Association for Computing Machinery, New York (1996). https://doi.org/10.1145/237170.237196
56. Shi, J., Tomasi: Good features to track. In: IEEE Conference on Computer Vision and Pattern Recognition (CVPR), pp. 593–600 (1994)
57. Shum, H., Kang, S.B.: Review of image-based rendering techniques. In: Visual Communications and Image Processing 2000, vol. 4067, pp. 2–13. SPIE (2000)
58. Shum, H.Y., Chan, S.C., Kang, S.B.: Image-Based Rendering. Springer, New York (2007). https://doi.org/10.1007/978-0-387-32668-9
59. Sitzmann, V., Rezchikov, S., Freeman, W.T., Tenenbaum, J.B., Durand, F.: Light field networks: neural scene representations with single-evaluation rendering. In: Advances in Neural Information Processing Systems (NeurIPS) (2021)
60. Sitzmann, V., Thies, J., Heide, F., Nießner, M., Wetzstein, G., Zollhofer, M.: DeepVoxels: learning persistent 3D feature embeddings. In: IEEE/CVF Conference on Computer Vision and Pattern Recognition (CVPR), pp. 2437–2446 (2019)
61. Suhail, M., Esteves, C., Sigal, L., Makadia, A.: Light field neural rendering. CoRR (2021). http://arxiv.org/abs/2112.09687v1
62. Takikawa, T., et al.: Neural geometric level of detail: real-time rendering with implicit 3D shapes. In: IEEE/CVF Conference on Computer Vision and Pattern Recognition (CVPR), pp. 11358–11367 (2021)
63. Tewari, A., et al.: Advances in neural rendering. arXiv preprint arXiv:2111.05849 (2021)
64. Thies, J., Zollhöfer, M., Nießner, M.: Deferred neural rendering: image synthesis using neural textures. ACM Trans. Graph. (TOG) 38(4), 1–12 (2019)
65. Trevithick, A., Yang, B.: GRF: learning a general radiance field for 3D representation and rendering. In: IEEE/CVF International Conference on Computer Vision (ICCV), pp. 15182–15192 (2021)
66. Vaswani, A., et al.: Attention is all you need. In: Advances in Neural Information Processing Systems, vol. 30 (2017)
67. Wang, P., Liu, L., Liu, Y., Theobalt, C., Komura, T., Wang, W.: NeuS: learning neural implicit surfaces by volume rendering for multi-view reconstruction. arXiv preprint arXiv:2106.10689 (2021)
68. Wang, Q., et al.: IBRNet: learning multi-view image-based rendering. In: IEEE/CVF Conference on Computer Vision and Pattern Recognition (CVPR), pp. 4690–4699 (2021)
69. Wiles, O., Gkioxari, G., Szeliski, R., Johnson, J.: SynSin: end-to-end view synthesis from a single image. In: IEEE/CVF Conference on Computer Vision and Pattern Recognition (CVPR) (2020)
70. Wizadwongsa, S., Phongthawee, P., Yenphraphai, J., Suwajanakorn, S.: NeX: real-time view synthesis with neural basis expansion. In: IEEE/CVF Conference on Computer Vision and Pattern Recognition (CVPR), pp. 8534–8543 (2021)

71. Xie, Y., et al.: Neural fields in visual computing and beyond (2021). https://neuralfields.cs.brown.edu/
72. Yariv, L., Gu, J., Kasten, Y., Lipman, Y.: Volume rendering of neural implicit surfaces. In: Advances in Neural Information Processing Systems, vol. 34 (2021)
73. Yenamandra, T., et al.: i3DMM: deep implicit 3D morphable model of human heads. In: IEEE/CVF Conference on Computer Vision and Pattern Recognition (CVPR), pp. 12803–12813 (2021)
74. Yifan, W., Serena, F., Wu, S., Öztireli, C., Sorkine-Hornung, O.: Differentiable surface splatting for point-based geometry processing. ACM Trans. Graph. (TOG) **38**(6), 1–14 (2019)
75. Yu, A., Fridovich-Keil, S., Tancik, M., Chen, Q., Recht, B., Kanazawa, A.: Plenoxels: radiance fields without neural networks. CoRR (2021). http://arxiv.org/abs/2112.05131v1
76. Yu, A., Li, R., Tancik, M., Li, H., Ng, R., Kanazawa, A.: PlenOctrees for real-time rendering of neural radiance fields. In: IEEE/CVF International Conference on Computer Vision (ICCV), pp. 5752–5761 (2021)
77. Yu, A., Ye, V., Tancik, M., Kanazawa, A.: pixelNeRF: neural radiance fields from one or few images. In: IEEE/CVF Conference on Computer Vision and Pattern Recognition (CVPR), pp. 4578–4587 (2021)
78. Zhou, T., Tucker, R., Flynn, J., Fyffe, G., Snavely, N.: Stereo magnification: learning view synthesis using multiplane images. arXiv preprint arXiv:1805.09817 (2018)

Improving RGB-D Point Cloud Registration by Learning Multi-scale Local Linear Transformation

Ziming Wang[1], Xiaoliang Huo[1], Zhenghao Chen[2], Jing Zhang[1],
Lu Sheng[1(✉)], and Dong Xu[3]

[1] School of Software, Beihang University, Beijing, China
{by1906050,huoxiaoliangchn,lsheng}@buaa.edu.cn
[2] School of Electrical and Information Engineering, The University of Sydney,
Camperdown, Australia
[3] Department of Computer Science, The University of Hong Kong, Hong Kong, China

Abstract. Point cloud registration aims at estimating the geometric transformation between two point cloud scans, in which point-wise correspondence estimation is the key to its success. In addition to previous methods that seek correspondences by hand-crafted or learnt geometric features, recent point cloud registration methods have tried to apply RGB-D data to achieve more accurate correspondence. However, it is not trivial to effectively fuse the geometric and visual information from these two distinctive modalities, especially for the registration problem. In this work, we propose a new Geometry-Aware Visual Feature Extractor (GAVE) that employs multi-scale local linear transformation to progressively fuse these two modalities, where the geometric features from the depth data act as the geometry-dependent convolution kernels to transform the visual features from the RGB data. The resultant visual-geometric features are in canonical feature spaces with alleviated visual dissimilarity caused by geometric changes, by which more reliable correspondence can be achieved. The proposed GAVE module can be readily plugged into recent RGB-D point cloud registration framework. Extensive experiments on 3D Match and ScanNet demonstrate that our method outperforms the state-of-the-art point cloud registration methods even without correspondence or pose supervision.

Keywords: Point cloud registration · Geometric-visual feature extractor · Local linear transformation

---

Z. Wang and X. Huo–Equal contributions.

© The Author(s), under exclusive license to Springer Nature Switzerland AG 2022
S. Avidan et al. (Eds.): ECCV 2022, LNCS 13692, pp. 175–191, 2022.
https://doi.org/10.1007/978-3-031-19824-3_11

1   Introduction

Point cloud registration [1,3,5,8,15,19,21,38] is a task to estimate geometric transformation, such as rotation and translation, between two point clouds. By applying the geometric transformation, we can merge the partial scans from two views of the same 3D scene or object into a complete 3D point cloud, which is a key component of numerous tasks in the community of robotics and AR/VR and also plays an essential role on understanding the whole environment.

The common approach to point cloud registration relies on two processes: (1) correspondence extraction and (2) geometric model fitting, where accurate correspondence is the key for reliable model fitting. The recent 3D deep learning techniques [8–10,12,15,16,19,39] outperform the traditional methods [5,31] by finding more accurate correspondence based on learnable geometric features [10,16], or further combining the model fitting process into an end-to-end learning framework [8,15,16,19]. However, the geometric features from 3D points are still less discriminative in comparison to visual features from the RGB images. Thanks to the rapid popularization of RGB-D cameras, it becomes promising to collect the RGB-D data for extracting more reliable correspondence, such that both geometric and visual consistencies can be well examined between two views. A couple of learning based works [15,16] belong to this line of work, which achieve superior registration performance even without ground-truth poses or correspondence as their supervision information. However, UR&R [15] just uses RGB images for correspondence estimation, while BYOC [16] relies on pseudo-correspondence from RGB images to train the geometric correspondence. Thus both methods [15,16] do not fully leverage the complementary visual and geometric information. Moreover, according to our experiments (see Sect. 4), we can only achieve marginal gains by simply concatenating RGB-D data as the input for correspondence estimation in UR&R [15]. A possible explanation that it is hard to fully exploit the geometry clues by using the CNN networks due to the intrinsic difference between the geometric and visual features.

To this end, we propose a Geometry-Aware Visual Feature Extractor (GAVE) that can generate distinctive but comprehensive geometric-visual features from RGB-D images, which facilitates reliable correspondence estimation for better point cloud registration. This module can be readily used to replace the feature extractor in UR&R [15], and significantly improve the point cloud registration performance even trained in an unsupervised manner[1]. To be specific, in the GAVE module, we propose a Local Linear Transformation (LLT) module, where the geometric features (extracted from the geometric feature extractor) act as the guided signal and are converted as point-wise linear coefficients to enhance the visual features (extracted from the visual feature extractor), through point-wise linear transformation. Moreover, to enhance the content awareness of the transformation with respect to the input depth image, we borrow the idea from the edge-aware image enhancement method [17], which employs the Bilateral

---

[1] As shown in the ablation study, GAVE module can also be applied into the supervised pipelines.

Grid and an edge-aware guidance map (both are estimated from the depth image) to generate our content-aware linear coefficients. Note that this LLT module is applied in the GAVE module in a multi-scale fashion, which thus enriches the scale awareness of the generated visual-geometric features.

More specifically, the proposed LLT module can be viewed as multi-scale dynamic convolutions over visual features that are guided by the geometric clues, which offers more descriptive and complementary combination between visual and geometric features than the common used operations such as concatenation, summation or product. Since the geometric feature can represent local geometric structure and indicate local orientations, it is easier for dynamic convolution-based fusion network to learn how to better project visual features into the new feature space where the projected features are robust to geometric changes, which is crucial for registration. To our best knowledge, it is the first work that applies a dynamic convolution-based fusion strategy in RGB-D point cloud registration, whose design is tailored to the nature of this particular task.

Our Geometry-Aware Visual Feature Extractor is trained in an end-to-end manner together with the subsequent correspondence estimation and differentiable geometric model fitting modules, e.g., those from UR&R [15]. The state-of-the-art results are achieved on the standard point cloud registration benchmark dataset ScanNet [11] with the models respectively trained based on the Scan-Net [11] and 3D Match [39] datasets, which clearly outperform the existing point cloud-based supervised baselines and RGB-D-based unsupervised methods.

2   Related Work

2.1   3D Feature Extractors

To extract the useful 3D features for various 3D vision tasks, early methods adopted the hand-crafted statistic-based strategies [4,5,27,32] to discover local 3D geometries. With the recent success of deep learning techniques, many learning-based 3D feature extraction methods [6,9,10,12,15,16] have been proposed. While some of them are proposed for extracting the features from point clouds [2,9,10,30], our methods are inspired more from those methods that extract the features from RGB-D images/videos [11,29,33,34,39]. However, most existing geometric-visual feature extractors just simply combine the features respectively from RGB images and depth maps without carefully considering how to exploit their correlation.

2.2   Bilateral Feature Fusion

Several methods [7,17,18,22,36,37] have conducted feature fusion in a bilateral manner. Particularly, the works [17,36,37] produce the edge-aware affine color transformation by using the Bilateral Grid. Inspired by those methods, we also develop the content-aware local linear coefficients through the Bilateral Grid, which act as the geometry-guided convolution kernels to transform the visual features.

2.3   3D Point Cloud Registration

The earlier 3D point cloud registration methods extracted point cloud features and then align them with robust model fitting technologies [4,10,13,14,24,27, 32]. Some learning-based methods [8,10,19] leverage the extra ground-truth poses to learn better geometric features from point clouds. However, it is not trivial to collect such ground-truth annotations. Recently, the unsupervised learning methods, such as UR&R [15] and BYOC [16], enforce cross-view geometric and visual consistency to implicitly supervise the training of registration. But the features used for correspondence extraction are either directly based on the RGB data [15] or trained by the pseudo-correspondence labels from the visual correspondences [15], where the extraction of visual and geometric clues are usually independent without effectively exploiting their correlation. Our work is inspired by [15,16], but would like to explore more reliable geometry-aware visual features for more robust registration. In contrast to those existing methods adopting the fusion operations such as concatenation, summation and attention [35], our newly proposed LLT module explores the correlation between visual and geometric information by using multi-scale dynamic convolutions over visual features, whose kernels are guided by the geometric clues.

3   Methodology

In this work, we propose a Geometry-Aware Visual Feature Extractor (GAVE) to learn distinctive and comprehensive geometric-visual features. Specifically, given each RGB-D image, the GAVE module extracts the visual features and geometric features in a parallel way, and then we densely apply the newly proposed Local Linear Transformation (LLT) module in a multi-scale fashion to progressively fuse the features from these two modalities. Therefore, a pair of RGB-D images $\{I_R, I_T\}$ (I_R as the reference RGB-D image, I_T as the target RGB-D image) can be encoded as a pair of geometric-visual features $\{F_R, F_T\}$, which are then inputted into a correspondence estimation module to calculate the correspondence. The set of captured correspondence is finally used in a geometric model fitting module (e.g., a differentiable alignment module in UR&R [15]), together with the point clouds $\mathcal{P}_R$ and $\mathcal{P}_T$ converted from I_R and I_T, to produce the rotation matrix $R_{R \to T} \in \mathbb{R}^{3 \times 3}$ and the translation vector $t_{R \to T} \in \mathbb{R}^{3 \times 1}$ from the reference RGB-D image to the target RGB-D image. In our work, we adopt the correspondence estimation and differentiable alignment modules from UR&R [15] in addition to our GAVE module, thus the whole registration framework can be trained in an end-to-end unsupervised learning manner. The overall framework is shown in Fig. 1.

3.1   Overview of Our Geometry-Aware Visual Feature Extractor

In our Geometry-Aware Visual feature Extractor, we have two parallel subnetworks, namely a visual feature extractor and a geometric feature extractor

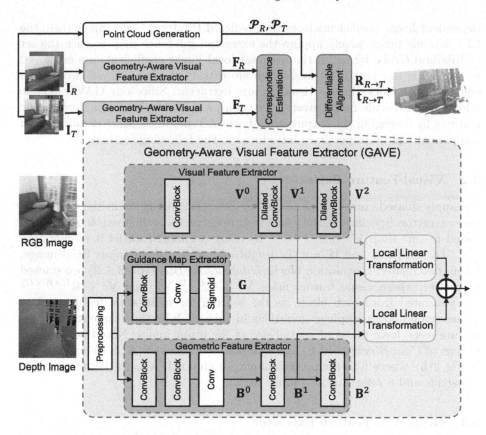

Fig. 1. The overview of our Geometry-Aware Visual Feature Extractor (GAVE) based framework. We first generate the multi-scale visual features, multi-scale geometric features and the guidance map, respectively. Then, we fuse the extracted visual and geometric features by using our proposed Local Linear Transformation (LLT) modules with the learned guidance map to produce the intermediate visual-geometric features. The intermediate features from two different scales are then averaged to generate the final visual-geometric features. Once we obtain the pair of the visual-geometric features $(\mathbf{F}_R, \mathbf{F}_T)$ from the reference RGB-D image and the target RGB-D image, we can then perform the matching and registration operations to produce the rotation matrix and the translation vector by using the correspondence generation and the differentiable alignment module in [15]. The details of our proposed LLT module and the basic *ConvBlock* and *DilatedConvBlock* modules will be illustrated in Fig. 2.

respectively, to extract the visual and geometric features from a RGB-D image. The visual feature extractor contains 2 dilated convolution blocks to enlarge the receptive fields that describes the visual contents. The geometric features after the last 2 convolution blocks are converted into a set of Bilateral Grids [17], which act as the source of the local linear coefficients for the proposed Local Linear Transformation modules. In addition, based on depth image, we also produce an edge-aware guidance map that further helps to interpolate geometry-dependent linear coefficients from the predicted Bilateral Grids. Since then, the LLT module progressively applies the extracted guidance map to slice the set of Bilateral Grids, by which the resultant local linear coefficients are employed to transform the visual features, which are extracted after the last two dilated convolutional blocks in the visual feature extractor. Since our GAVE module adopts a multi-scale fusion strategy, we can produce the final visual-geometric features by averaging the outputs from both LLT modules. More details of each component will be respectively introduced in the following sections.

3.2   Visual Feature Extractor

We apply dilated convolutions to enlarge the receptive fields in the visual feature extractor. Specifically, the visual feature extractor at first extracts an initial visual feature map $\mathbf{V}^0 \in \mathbb{R}^{H \times W \times D_c}$ by using a $ConvBlock(64, 3, 1)$ operation (*i.e.*, $D_c = 64$). H and W are the height and width of the input RGB image. Then, two dilated convolution blocks $DilatedConvBlock(64, 3, 1, 2)$ are stacked thereafter, where visual feature maps $\mathbf{V}^1 \in \mathbb{R}^{H \times W \times D_c}$ and $\mathbf{V}^2 \in \mathbb{R}^{H \times W \times D_c}$ are generated from each block, as the sources for multi-scale feature fusion. There are no downsampling operations in this module, thus the output visual feature maps have the same spatial size as the input image. Note that the definitions of $ConvBlock(N, K, S)$ and $DilatedConvBlock(N, K, S, d)$ are depicted in Fig. 2(b), where N is the number of output channel, K is the kernel size, S is the stride and d refers to the dilation factor.

3.3   Geometric Feature Extractor

The input depth image is at first normalized to $[0, 1)$ through some linear normalization operations with a `sigmoid` function. Since raw depth image may contain holes due to sensor's systematic errors, thus in the pre-processing step, we also apply the Joint Bilateral Filtering (JBF) method [26] to fill the depth holes with the aid of the corresponding RGB image.

Once we produce the normalized depth map, we first encode it by using a stack of convolution operations (*i.e.*, $ConvBlock(32, 3, 2)$, $ConvBlock(256, 3, 2)$ and $Conv(768, 3, 2)^2$) to generate an initial down-scaled geometric feature map $\mathbf{B}^0 \in \mathbb{R}^{(H/8) \times (W/8) \times D_d}$ (we use $D_d = 768$ in this work, so as to match the size of the visual features, which will be explained in Sect. 3.5). Since then, we use two $ConvBlock(768, 3, 1)$ modules to respectively generate two geometric feature maps representing two different scales. Each Bilateral Grid is reshaped from each geometric feature map as $\mathbf{B}^i \in \mathbb{R}^{(H/8) \times (W/8) \times (D_d/n_{grid}) \times n_{grid}}$, where $i = 1, 2$, and n_{grid} is the depth of the Bilateral Grid (in this work we set $n_{grid} = 3$ for balancing the efficiency and effectiveness). Please refer to [17] for more details about Bilateral Grid.

---

[2] $Conv(N, K, S)$ is a standard convolution operation with the output channel N, the kernel size K and the stride size S.

3.4 Guidance Map Extractor

In order to provide the content-structural information when generating the local linear coefficients, we define a guidance map by using a point-wise nonlinear transformation on the depth map. Specifically, we input the normalized and hole-filled depth map and then directly employ several convolution operations (*i.e.*, $ConvBlock(3, 3, 1)$ and $Conv(1, 3, 1)$) and a `sigmoid` activation function to produce a learned guidance map $\mathbf{G} \in \mathbb{R}^{H \times W \times 1}$, which preserves the piece-wise smoothness as well as discontinuity presented in the depth image.

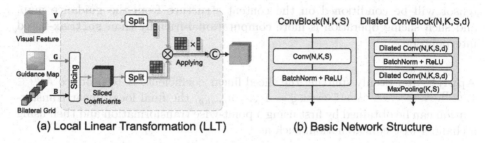

(a) Local Linear Transformation (LLT)   (b) Basic Network Structure

Fig. 2. For our "Local Linear Transformation" in (a), we first produce the sliced coefficients from the guidance map and Bilateral Grid by using the slicing operation in [17]. Then, at each position, the sliced coefficient matrix will be split in to group-wise coefficient matrix. To produce the transformed feature at each group, we then perform the applying operation (*i.e.*, the linear transformation) between each group-wise coefficient and each group-wise visual feature, which is also split from the previously learned visual feature. Finally, we generate the final output feature by using the channel-wise concatenation operation on these transformed features from all groups. The basic module is shown in (b) "Basic Network Structure". "$Conv(N, K, S)$" represents the convolution operation with the output channel, the kernel size and the stride as N, $K \times K$ and S, respectively. "d" in "$DilatedConv(N, K, S, d)$" refers to the dilation parameter of the dilated convolution operation.

3.5 Multi-scale Local Linear Transformation

In order to effectively fuse the visual and geometric clues, we progressively apply the local linear transformation to learn the visual-geometric features in a multi-scale manner. To be specific, in each LLT module, we would like to *slice* the generated Bilateral Grids to produce the content-aware local linear coefficients, and then *apply* the sliced coefficients to transform the visual features. For the sake of efficiency, we also split the local linear transformation into several groups evenly along the channel dimension, and then concatenate these group-wise outputs as the final visual-geometric features.

Slicing. The slicing operation is performed between a Bilateral Grid $\mathbf{B}$ (*i.e.*, $\mathbf{B}^1$ or $\mathbf{B}^2$) and the guidance map $\mathbf{G}$. At each spatial location in the guidance map, we use its spatial coordinates and the value at that location to sample nearest points in the Bilateral Grid, and then bilinearly interpolate the sampled coefficients to eventually generate the sliced linear coefficients. Therefore, the sliced coefficients become a tensor $\tilde{\mathbf{A}} \in \mathbb{R}^{H \times W \times (D_d/n_{grid})}$. Note that we split the local linear transformation into n_{group} ($n_{group} = 16$ in this work) groups, namely the sliced coefficients $\check{\mathbf{A}}$ can be reshaped as $\mathbf{A} \subset \mathbb{R}^{H \times W \times D_o \times (D_c/n_{group})}$. Note that when $D_c = 64$ and $D_d = 768$, $n_{grid} = 3$ and $n_{group} = 16$, $\tilde{\mathbf{A}}$ and $\mathbf{A}$ have the same number of elements. In this way, the context of the sliced coefficient tensor will be conditioned on the content structure from the guidance map, and such slicing operation is more computational-friendly than `softmax`-based interpolation.

Apply. After evenly splitting the sliced linear coefficients $\mathbf{A}$ to produce $\mathbf{A}^{(g)} \in \mathbb{R}^{H \times W \times (D_c/n_{group}) \times (D_c/n_{group})}$, $g = 1, \ldots, n_{group}$, the final local linear transformation can be obtained by first using a point-wise transformation and then using a channel-wise concatenation, such as

$$\mathbf{F} = \overset{n_{group}}{\underset{g=1}{\|}} \mathbf{A}^{(g)} \otimes \mathbf{V}^{(g)} \qquad (1)$$

where $\overset{n_{group}}{\underset{g=1}{\|}}$ means channel-wise concatenation among n_{group} linearly transformed group-wise features, $\otimes$ indicates the matrix multiplication operation at every spatial position. $\mathbf{V}^{(g)} \in \mathbb{R}^{H \times W \times (D_c/n_{group})}$ is the g-th group of $\mathbf{V}$, which is evenly split from $\mathbf{V}$ along the channel dimension. Moreover, $\mathbf{F} \in \mathbb{R}^{H \times W \times D_c}$ has the same size as the visual feature $\mathbf{V}$. Note that we take the LLT module from one scale as an example for better illustration. We omit the superscript i (*i.e.*, the scale index) in $\mathbf{V}$, $\mathbf{V}^{(g)}$ and $\mathbf{F}$ for brevity, as the LLT module from each scale shares the same process. Thus, our local linear transformation-based fusion method inherently takes advantage of both modalities and provide a more flexible fusion strategy than simple concatenation or summation operations.

Multi-scale Fusion. The fused visual-geometric features $\mathbf{F}^i \in \mathbb{R}^{H \times W \times D_c}$, $i = 1, 2$ in both scales are then averaged at the end of the GAVE module, so as to fulfill the multi-scale awareness of the features, which is essential for correspondence estimation in point cloud registration.

3.6   Correspondence, Registration and Objective Functions

Correspondence and Registration. After feeding two RGB-D images $(\mathbf{I}_R, \mathbf{I}_T)$ to our GAVE extractor to produce the visual-geometric feature pairs $(\mathbf{F}_R, \mathbf{F}_T)$, we can then perform the following correspondence estimation and differentiable alignment operations. Specifically, we first follow the work in [15] to compute the top-k (we set $k = 400$ in this work) correspondence pairs and then employ such correspondence pairs to estimate the rotation matrix $\mathbf{R}_{R \rightarrow T}$ and the translation vector $\mathbf{t}_{R \rightarrow T}$ by using the differentiable alignment module [15].

Objective Function. As proposed by UR&R [15], we also apply the photometric, depth and correspondence consistencies to train the whole RGB-D point cloud registration framework. The photometric consistency is measured by comparing the target image with the differentiably rendered reference image, according to the estimated rotation and translation parameters. The depth consistency is similar to the photometric consistency, but it compares the depth value instead. Correspondence consistency directly measures the matching errors between the corresponded points. Please refer to [15] for more details.

Table 1. Pairwise registration errors on the ScanNet [11] dataset. We report the mean and median errors in terms of rotation error (°), translation error (mm), and Chamfer distance (cm). Features for correspondence estimation may come from visual or geometric/3D modality. The training set can be 3D Match [39] or ScanNet [11]. "Sup" means training with ground-truth pose supervision.

Methods	Train set	Sup	Features		Rotation		Translation		Chamfer		FMR
			Visual	3D	Mean	Med.	Mean	Med.	Mean	Med.	
SIFT [27]	N/A		✓		18.6	4.3	26.5	11.2	42.6	1.7	–
SuperPoint [14]	N/A		✓		8.9	3.6	16.1	9.7	19.2	1.2	–
FCGF [10]	N/A			✓	9.5	3.3	23.6	8.3	24.4	0.9	–
BYOC [16]	3D match		✓	✓	7.4	3.3	16.0	8.2	9.5	0.9	–
DGR [8]	3D match	✓		✓	9.4	1.8	18.4	4.5	13.7	0.4	–
3D MV Reg [19]	3D match	✓		✓	6.0	1.2	11.7	2.9	10.2	0.2	–
UR&R [15]	3D match		✓		4.3	1.0	9.5	2.8	7.2	0.2	0.78
UR&R (RGB-D)	3D match		✓	✓	3.8	1.1	8.5	3.0	6.5	0.2	0.78
Ours	3D match		✓	✓	**3.0**	**0.9**	**6.4**	**2.4**	**5.3**	**0.1**	**0.87**
BYOC [16]	ScanNet		✓	✓	3.8	1.7	8.7	4.3	5.6	0.3	–
UR&R [15]	ScanNet		✓		3.4	0.8	7.3	2.3	5.9	0.1	0.85
UR&R (RGB-D)	ScanNet		✓	✓	2.6	0.8	5.9	2.3	5.0	0.1	0.91
Ours	ScanNet		✓	✓	**2.5**	**0.8**	**5.5**	**2.2**	**4.6**	**0.1**	**0.94**

4 Experiments

4.1 Datasets and Experimental Setup

Datasets. We follow UR&R [15] and adopt the large-scale indoor RGB-D dataset ScanNet [11] for evaluating our proposed GAVE module. Specifically, there are 1513 scenes in the ScanNet dataset [11] and each scene contains both RGB-D images and their ground-truth camera poses. We use its original training/testing split, which respectively contain 1045 and 312 scenes. In addition, as in [15], we also provide more evaluation results, in which we train our model based on another smaller point cloud dataset 3D Match [39] with 101 real-world indoor scenes and then evaluate the learnt model on the ScanNet dataset. Each scene in 3D Match also provides RGB-D images and point clouds data.

Table 2. Pairwise registration accuracies on the ScanNet [11] dataset. We report the rotation accuracy with different angles (*i.e.*, 5°, 10° and 45°), the translation accuracy with different lengths (*i.e.*, 5 cm, 10 cm and 25 cm) and the Chamfer accuracy with different metric distances (*i.e.*, 1 mm, 5 mm and 10 mm).

Methods	Train set	Sup	Features		Rotation			Translation			Chamfer		
			Visual	3D	5	10	45	5	10	25	1	5	10
SIFT [27]	N/A		✓		55.2	75.7	89.2	17.7	44.5	79.8	38.1	70.6	78.3
SuperPoint [14]	N/A		✓		65.5	86.9	96.6	21.2	51.7	88.0	45.7	81.1	88.2
FCGF [10]	N/A			✓	70.2	87.7	96.2	27.5	58.3	82.9	52.0	78.0	83.7
BYOC [16]	3D match		✓	✓	66.5	85.2	97.8	30.7	57.6	88.9	54.1	82.8	89.5
DGR [8]	3D match	✓		✓	81.1	89.3	94.8	54.5	76.2	88.7	70.5	85.5	89.0
3D MV Reg [19]	3D match	✓		✓	87.7	93.2	97.0	69.0	83.1	91.8	78.9	89.2	91.8
UR&R [15]	3D match		✓		87.6	93.1	98.3	69.2	84.0	93.8	79.7	91.3	94.0
UR&R (RGB-D) [15]	3D match		✓	✓	87.6	93.7	98.8	67.5	83.8	94.6	78.6	91.7	94.6
Ours	3D match		✓	✓	**93.4**	**96.5**	**98.8**	**76.9**	**90.2**	**96.7**	**86.4**	**95.1**	**96.8**
BYOC [16]	ScanNet		✓	✓	86.5	95.2	99.1	56.4	80.6	96.3	78.1	93.9	86.4
UR&R [15]	ScanNet		✓		92.7	95.8	98.5	77.2	89.6	96.1	86.0	94.6	96.1
UR&R (RGB-D) [15]	ScanNet		✓	✓	94.1	97.0	99.1	78.4	91.1	97.3	87.3	95.6	97.2
Ours	ScanNet		✓	✓	**95.5**	**97.6**	**99.1**	**80.4**	**92.2**	**97.6**	**88.9**	**96.4**	**97.6**

Evaluation Metrics. We adopt the evaluation metrics, *i.e.*, the rotation error, the translation error and the Chamfer distance, as used in UR&R [15]. We report both the mean and the median values for these three error metrics in Sect. 4.2 and Sect. 4.3. In addition, we report the registration accuracy, *i.e.*, the rotation accuracy within three thresholds of angles, the translation accuracy within three thresholds of lengths and the Chamfer accuracy within three thresholds of metric distances, as introduced in UR&R [15]. We also include FMR [10,12] to directly compare the extracted correspondence with the reference methods, in which we use rigorous thresholds $\tau_1 = 0.05$ and $\tau_2 = 0.5$.

Baseline Methods. We compare our work with the conventional registration methods, which extract 3D features by SIFT [27], SuperPoint [14] and FCGF [10], and then estimate the geometric transformation via RANSAC. Moreover, we compare with the learning-based registration approaches, such as DGR [8] and 3D MV Reg [19] as the supervised approaches, and UR&R [15], BYOC [16] as the unsupervised approaches. The results of these methods are borrowed from [15,16]. Last, we also use the RGB-D images as the input for correspondence estimation in UR&R [15] (*i.e.*, UR&R (RGB-D)), as another important baseline method.

Training Details. For fair comparison, we follow the same training scheme as in [15]. Specifically, we train our model based on the 3D Match dataset for only 14 epochs with the learning rate of 1e−4. We also train our model based on the ScanNet dataset for only 1 epoch with the learning rate 1e−4. All models are trained on the machine with one NVIDIA Tesla V100 GPU. The batch size is 8. We use Adam Optimizer [25] with epsilon 1e−4 and momentum 0.9.

4.2   Experimental Results

We provide our experimental results, *i.e.*, registration errors in Table 1 and registration accuracies in Table 2. It is observed that our newly proposed method not only outperforms UR&R (RGB-D), but also achieves significant improvement over the baseline methods [10, 14–16, 19, 20, 27]. Specifically, our method trained on the 3D Match dataset achieves much better results than all other end-to-end optimized methods that are also trained on the 3D Match dataset. For example, when compared to the most recent unsupervised point cloud registration method UR&R [15], we respectively reduce 21.1% mean rotation error, 24.7% mean translation error, and 18.5% mean Chamfer distance. We also increase the FMR performance for about 11.54%, which directly validates the superior correspondence estimation performance of our method. With respect to registration accuracies, we also achieve significant gains at the strictest thresholds. These results demonstrate that our proposed network has universal registration ability, because significant gains can be achieved on the large-scale ScanNet dataset by simply training the network in a smaller 3D Match dataset.

We have similar observations when compared with these methods trained on the ScanNet dataset. But without any domain gap between training & testing data, the baseline methods can achieve almost saturated performance (over 90% in terms of most metrics for UR&R). While it is non-trivial to achieve further gains in this case, our method still reduces up to 23.7%/9.3%/12.6% relative error rate over the baselines in terms of rotation/translation/Chamfer distance.

Table 3. Comparision between our complete method (*i.e.*, the 4th row) and three alternative methods, which directly adopt the concatenation of RGB images and depth maps for generating the intermediate feature. "MS" means multi-scale strategy, "DC" means dilated convolutions in the visual feature extractor, and "LLT" is the local linear transformation module. All models are trained based on the 3D Match dataset.

MS	DC	LLT	Rotation					Translation					Chamfer				
			Accuracy			Error		Accuracy			Error		Accuracy			Error	
			5	10	45	Mean	Med.	5	10	25	Mean	Med.	1	5	10	Mean	Med.
			88.4	94.2	98.6	3.8	1.1	67.3	83.8	94.5	8.5	3.0	78.9	91.7	94.6	6.5	0.2
✓			88.5	94.4	98.6	3.8	1.1	68.1	84.5	94.8	8.3	3.0	79.5	92.1	94.9	6.3	0.2
✓	✓		90.4	95.0	98.6	3.6	1.0	70.8	86.5	95.3	8.1	2.8	81.8	93.1	95.4	6.2	0.2
✓	✓	✓	**93.4**	**96.5**	**98.8**	**3.0**	**0.9**	**76.9**	**90.2**	**96.7**	**6.4**	**2.4**	**86.4**	**95.1**	**96.8**	**5.3**	**0.1**

Table 4. Comparision between our complete method and four variants, which are (1) the method without adopting the fusion mechanism at all (*i.e.*, the 3th row in Table 3), (2) the method without the guidance map, and (3) the method that replaces LLT by the affine transformation. (4) the method that replaces LLT by multi-head cross-attention (MHCA). All models are trained on the 3D Match dataset.

Fusion strategies	Rotation					Translation					Chamfer				
	Accuracy			Error		Accuracy			Error		Accuracy			Error	
	3	10	45	Mean	Med	5	10	25	Mean	Med.	1	5	10	Mean	Med.
No fusion	90.4	95.0	98.6	3.6	1.0	70.8	86.5	95.3	8.1	2.8	81.8	93.1	95.4	6.2	0.2
LLT w/o guidance map	92.3	95.9	98.8	3.2	0.9	74.7	88.7	96.3	7.0	2.5	84.6	94.4	96.2	5.4	0.1
Affine transformation	92.3	96.0	98.8	3.1	0.9	75.3	89.0	96.3	6.7	2.5	85.2	94.5	96.3	5.4	0.1
MHCA	91.3	95.1	98.4	3.8	0.9	73.5	87.6	95.2	8.4	2.6	83.4	93.3	95.4	6.5	0.2
LLT (ours)	**93.4**	**96.5**	**98.8**	**3.0**	**0.9**	**76.9**	**90.2**	**96.7**	**6.4**	**2.4**	**86.4**	**95.1**	**96.8**	**5.3**	**0.1**

Table 5. Comparision between our method and UR&R (RGB-D) when trained based on ground truth camera poses. All models are trained on the 3D Match dataset.

Methods	Rotation					Translation					Chamfer				
	Accuracy			Error		Accuracy			Error		Accuracy			Error	
	5	10	45	Mean	Med.	5	10	25	Mean	Med.	1	5	10	Mean	Med.
UR&R (RGB-D)	92.3	95.3	98.2	3.8	0.8	77.6	89.4	95.5	7.8	2.3	86.1	94.0	95.6	6.7	0.1
Ours	**96.5**	**97.8**	**98.8**	**2.7**	**0.8**	**83.8**	**93.8**	**97.6**	**5.8**	**2.0**	**91.2**	**96.7**	**97.6**	**4.8**	**0.1**

4.3   Ablation Study and Analysis

Analysis of Each Component. In Table 3, we analyse the effectiveness of each proposed component, *i.e.*, the local linear transformation (LLT) module, the multi-scale (MS) fusion strategy and dilated convolution (DC), by comparing our complete method to three alternative methods. We train all models based on the 3D Match dataset. The first variant in the 1st row replaces the dilation convolutions with regular convolutions, and does not adopt either multi-scale fusion strategy or the LLT module. The second variant in the 2nd row introduces the multi-scale fusion strategy upon the first alternative, and the third variant in the 3rd row further includes dilated convolution in the visual feature extractor. The first variant achieves the worst registration performance, while the second one reduces 2.4% mean translation error and 3.1% mean Chamfer distance when compared to the first variant. The third variant further reduces 7.6% mean rotation error, 2.4% mean translation error and 1.6% mean Chamfer distance when compared to the second alternative method. Note that our complete method in the 4th row after using the LLT module can bring the most significant gains.

Different Fusion Strategies. In Table 4, we further compare our LLT based fusion module with the other alternatives. We train these models on the 3D Match dataset. The first variant in the 1st row does not adopt the fusion mechanism at all, which achieves the worst registration performance. The second one in the 2nd row directly uses the Bilateral Grid without using the guidance map, while the third variant in the 3rd row replaces the linear transformation by the affine transformation. It is observed that both the second and the third variants can intuitively bring some performance improvements. In contrast, our proposed LLT module in the 5th row can bring the most significant gains. It is interesting that the variant using affine transformation is worse than that using the linear transformation. A possible explanation is that the bias term in the affine transformation indicates another summation operation between the geometric features and the visual features, which may deteriorate the feature representation if two modalities are quite different. Last, in the 4th row, we adopt the fast multi-head cross attention (MHCA) mechanism of Linear Transformer [23] to replace the LLT module. Here, we do not apply vanilla MHCA [35] to avoid huge memory and computational costs. The results show that LLT is better than this variant in terms of all evaluation metrics.

Fig. 3. Visualization of pairwise matching results by UR&R (RGB-D) [15] and our method (trained on the 3D Match dataset [39]). We show the positive correspondence (*i.e.*, the matching error < 10 cm) and the negative correspondence (*i.e.*, the matching error ≥ 10 cm) as the green lines and the red lines, respectively. Best viewed on screen. (Color figure online)

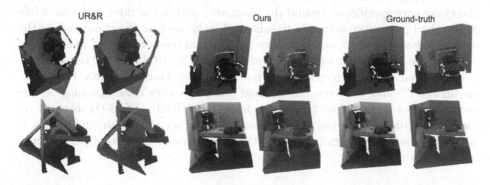

Fig. 4. Visualization of point cloud registration results from UR&R (RGB-D) [15] and our method (trained on the 3D Match dataset [39]). In the 1st, the 3rd and the 5th columns, we show the stitched 3D scenes; while we use the purple and yellow points to represent the point clouds from the target and reference viewpoints (see the 2nd, the 4th and the 6th columns). Best viewed on screen. (Color figure online)

Supervised Learning. In Table 5, our proposed feature extractor can be trained under the supervised learning setting. Specifically, as in [8], we adopt the camera pose data as the ground-truth labels during the training procedure, for both our method and our baseline UR&R (RGB-D). The results show that our method is much better than UR&R (RGB-D) in terms of all metrics.

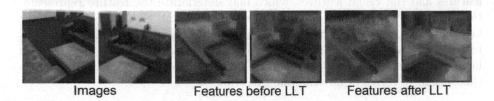

Images   Features before LLT   Features after LLT

Fig. 5. The 3rd and the 4th columns represent the projected 3D features, which are the input to our LLT, while the 5th and the 6th columns represent the projected 3D features, which are the output from our LLT. We use t-SNE [28] for visualization, in which each 3D feature is mapped to the corresponding color.

4.4 Qualitative Results

Visual Comparison About Correspondence Estimation and Registration. In Fig. 3, we visualize the matching results for both UR&R [15] (RGB-D) and our proposed method, in which we use the models trained on 3D Match. It is observed that our method provides more accurate matching results across two views. Taking the results in the left of Fig. 3 as an example, UR&R (RGB-D) finds false correspondence around the plain area within the floor and wall, while our method pays more attention to salient objects, such as the chairs, where the correspondence can be found in a more reliable and repeatable way. In Fig. 4, we visualize the registration results for both UR&R [15] (RGB-D) and our method. It is observed that our method achieves better registration results. For example, in the 1st and 4th rows, our method generates very close stitching results to the ground-truth, while the results from the UR&R (RGB-D) method are completely failed. As we can already produce more accurate matching results, it is not surprised that we can achieve better point cloud registration performance than UR&R (RGB-D).

Feature Visualization. In Fig. 5, the 3rd and 4th columns and the 5th and 6th columns are the projected 3D features from left and right images by using t-SNE, before and after using the LLT module. We observe that the learnt features (e.g. within the table area) after using our LLT are more likely to follow the geometric structure, and have become more consistent across two views.

5 Conclusion

In this work, we have proposed a new geometric-aware visual feature extractor (GAVE) to effectively learn visual-geometric features, in which we propose multi-scale local linear transformation to progressively fuse the geometric and visual features. Our proposed GAVE module can be easily plugged into different end-to-end point cloud registration pipelines like [15] (as already discussed in this work), which significantly enhances the point cloud registration performance. Extensive experiments not only show our method outperforms the existing registration methods, but also indicate the effectiveness of our newly proposed LLT module and multi-scale fusion strategy. It is possible to further extend and apply our proposed GAVE feature extractor for more RGB-D based 3D computer vision tasks, such as recognition, tracking, reconstruction and *etc.*, which will be studied in our future work.

Acknowledgement. This work was partially supported by the National Natural Science Foundation of China (No. 61906012, No. 62132001, No. 62006012).

References

1. Ao, S., Hu, Q., Yang, B., Markham, A., Guo, Y.: SpinNet: learning a general surface descriptor for 3D point cloud registration. In: Proceedings of the IEEE/CVF Conference on Computer Vision and Pattern Recognition, pp. 11753–11762 (2021)
2. Aoki, Y., Goforth, H., Srivatsan, R.A., Lucey, S.: PointNetLK: robust and efficient point cloud registration using PointNet. In: Proceedings of the IEEE/CVF Conference on Computer Vision and Pattern Recognition, pp. 7163–7172 (2019)
3. Bai, X., et al.: PointDSC: robust point cloud registration using deep spatial consistency. In: Proceedings of the IEEE/CVF Conference on Computer Vision and Pattern Recognition, pp. 15859–15869 (2021)
4. Bay, H., Tuytelaars, T., Van Gool, L.: SURF: speeded up robust features. In: Leonardis, A., Bischof, H., Pinz, A. (eds.) ECCV 2006. LNCS, vol. 3951, pp. 404–417. Springer, Heidelberg (2006). https://doi.org/10.1007/11744023_32
5. Besl, P.J., Mckay, H.D.: A method for registration of 3-D shapes. IEEE Trans. Pattern Anal. Mach. Intell. **14**(2), 239–256 (1992)
6. Chen, Z., Gu, S., Lu, G., Xu, D.: Exploiting intra-slice and inter-slice redundancy for learning-based lossless volumetric image compression. IEEE Trans. Image Process. **31**, 1697–1707 (2022)
7. Chen, Z., Lu, G., Hu, Z., Liu, S., Jiang, W., Xu, D.: LSVC: a learning-based stereo video compression framework. In: Proceedings of the IEEE/CVF Conference on Computer Vision and Pattern Recognition, pp. 6073–6082 (2022)
8. Choy, C., Dong, W., Koltun, V.: Deep global registration. In: Proceedings of the IEEE/CVF Conference on Computer Vision and Pattern Recognition, pp. 2514–2523 (2020)
9. Choy, C., Gwak, J., Savarese, S.: 4D spatio-temporal convnets: minkowski convolutional neural networks. In: Proceedings of the IEEE/CVF Conference on Computer Vision and Pattern Recognition, pp. 3075–3084 (2019)
10. Choy, C., Park, J., Koltun, V.: Fully convolutional geometric features. In: Proceedings of the IEEE/CVF International Conference on Computer Vision, pp. 8958–8966 (2019)

11. Dai, A., Chang, A.X., Savva, M., Halber, M., Funkhouser, T., Nießner, M.: Scan-Net: richly-annotated 3D reconstructions of indoor scenes. In: Proceedings of the IEEE Conference on Computer Vision and Pattern Recognition, pp. 5828–5839 (2017)
12. Deng, H., Birdal, T., Ilic, S.: PPFNet: global context aware local features for robust 3D point matching. IEEE (2018)
13. Derpanis, K.G.: The Harris corner detector. York University **2** (2004)
14. DeTone, D., Malisiewicz, T., Rabinovich, A.: SuperPoint: self-supervised interest point detection and description. In: Proceedings of the IEEE Conference on Computer Vision and Pattern Recognition Workshops, pp. 224–236 (2018)
15. El Banani, M., Gao, L., Johnson, J.: UnsupervisedR&R: unsupervised point cloud registration via differentiable rendering. In: Proceedings of the IEEE/CVF Conference on Computer Vision and Pattern Recognition, pp. 7129–7139 (2021)
16. El Banani, M., Johnson, J.: Bootstrap your own correspondences. In: Proceedings of the IEEE/CVF International Conference on Computer Vision, pp. 6433–6442 (2021)
17. Gharbi, M., Chen, J., Barron, J.T., Hasinoff, S.W., Durand, F.: Deep bilateral learning for real-time image enhancement. ACM Trans. Graph. (TOG) **36**(4), 1–12 (2017)
18. Gharbi, M., Chen, J., Barron, J.T., Hasinoff, S.W., Durand, F.: Deep bilateral learning for real-time image enhancement. ACM Trans. Graph. **36**(4), 118 (2017)
19. Gojcic, Z., Zhou, C., Wegner, J.D., Guibas, L.J., Birdal, T.: Learning multiview 3D point cloud registration. In: Proceedings of the IEEE/CVF Conference on Computer Vision and Pattern Recognition, pp. 1759–1769 (2020)
20. Guo, Y., Wang, H., Hu, Q., Liu, H., Bennamoun, M.: Deep learning for 3D point clouds: a survey. IEEE Trans. Pattern Anal. Mach. Intell. **43**, 4338–4364 (2020)
21. Huang, S., Gojcic, Z., Usvyatsov, M., Wieser, A., Schindler, K.: PREDATOR: registration of 3D point clouds with low overlap. In: Proceedings of the IEEE/CVF Conference on computer vision and pattern recognition, pp. 4267–4276 (2021)
22. Hui, T., Ngan, K.N.: Depth enhancement using RGB-D guided filtering, pp. 3832–3836 (2014)
23. Katharopoulos, A., Vyas, A., Pappas, N., Fleuret, F.: Transformers are RNNs: fast autoregressive transformers with linear attention. In: International Conference on Machine Learning, pp. 5156–5165. PMLR (2020)
24. Ke, Y.: PCA-SIFT: a more distinctive representation for local image descriptors. In: 2004 Proceedings of the CVPR International Conference on Computer Vision and Pattern Recognition (2004)
25. Kingma, D., Ba, J.: Adam: a method for stochastic optimization. Comput. Sci. (2014)
26. Kopf, J., Cohen, M.F., Lischinski, D., Uyttendaele, M.: Joint bilateral upsampling. ACM Trans. Graph. (ToG) **26**(3), 96-es (2007)
27. Lowe, D.G.: Distinctive image features from scale-invariant keypoints. Int. J. Comput. Vis. **60**(2), 91–110 (2004). https://doi.org/10.1023/B:VISI.0000029664.99615.94
28. van der Maaten, L., Hinton, G.: Visualizing data using t-SNE. J. Mach. Learn. Res. **9**, 2579–2605 (2008)
29. Silberman, N., Hoiem, D., Kohli, P., Fergus, R.: Indoor segmentation and support inference from RGBD images. In: Fitzgibbon, A., Lazebnik, S., Perona, P., Sato, Y., Schmid, C. (eds.) ECCV 2012. LNCS, vol. 7576, pp. 746–760. Springer, Heidelberg (2012). https://doi.org/10.1007/978-3-642-33715-4_54

30. Qi, C.R., Su, H., Mo, K., Guibas, L.J.: PointNet: deep learning on point sets for 3D classification and segmentation. In: 2017 IEEE Conference on Computer Vision and Pattern Recognition (CVPR) (2017)

31. Rister, B., Horowitz, M.A., Rubin, D.L.: Volumetric image registration from invariant keypoints. IEEE Trans. Image Process. **26**(10), 4900–4910 (2017)

32. Rublee, E., Rabaud, V., Konolige, K., Bradski, G.R.: ORB: an efficient alternative to SIFT or SURF. In: 2011 IEEE International Conference on Computer Vision, ICCV 2011, Barcelona, Spain, 6–13 November 2011 (2011)

33. Song, S., Lichtenberg, S.P., Xiao, J.: SUN RGB-D: a RGB-D scene understanding benchmark suite. In: IEEE Conference on Computer Vision & Pattern Recognition, pp. 567–576 (2015)

34. Sturm, J., Engelhard, N., Endres, F., Burgard, W., Cremers, D.: A benchmark for the evaluation of RGB-D slam systems. In: Proceedings of the International Conference on Intelligent Robot Systems (IROS), October 2012

35. Vaswani, A., et al.: Attention is all you need. In: Advances in Neural Information Processing Systems, vol. 30 (2017)

36. Xia, X., et al.: Joint bilateral learning for real-time universal photorealistic style transfer. In: Vedaldi, A., Bischof, H., Brox, T., Frahm, J.-M. (eds.) ECCV 2020. LNCS, vol. 12353, pp. 327–342. Springer, Cham (2020). https://doi.org/10.1007/978-3-030-58598-3_20

37. Xu, B., Xu, Y., Yang, X., Jia, W., Guo, Y.: Bilateral grid learning for stereo matching networks. In: Proceedings of the IEEE/CVF Conference on Computer Vision and Pattern Recognition, pp. 12497–12506 (2021)

38. Yu, H., Li, F., Saleh, M., Busam, B., Ilic, S.: CoFiNet: reliable coarse-to-fine correspondences for robust pointcloud registration. In: Advances in Neural Information Processing Systems, vol. 34, pp. 23872–23884 (2021)

39. Zeng, A., Song, S., Nießner, M., Fisher, M., Xiao, J., Funkhouser, T.: 3DMatch: learning local geometric descriptors from RGB-D reconstructions. In: Proceedings of the IEEE Conference on Computer Vision and Pattern Recognition, pp. 1802–1811 (2017)

Real-Time Neural Character Rendering with Pose-Guided Multiplane Images

Hao Ouyang[1], Bo Zhang[2], Pan Zhang[2], Hao Yang[2], Jiaolong Yang[2],
Dong Chen[2], Qifeng Chen[1(✉)], and Fang Wen[2]

[1] Hong Kong University of Science and Technology, Hong Kong, China
cqf@ust.hk
[2] Microsoft Research Asia, Beijing, China

Abstract. We propose pose-guided multiplane image (MPI) synthesis
which can render an animatable character in real scenes with photorealistic quality. We use a portable camera rig to capture the multi-view images
along with the driving signal for the moving subject. Our method generalizes the image-to-image translation paradigm, which translates the
human pose to a 3D scene representation—MPIs that can be rendered in
free viewpoints, using the multi-views captures as supervision. To fully
cultivate the potential of MPI, we propose depth-adaptive MPI which
can be learned using variable exposure images while being robust to
inaccurate camera registration. Our method demonstrates advantageous
novel-view synthesis quality over the state-of-the-art approaches for characters with challenging motions. Moreover, the proposed method is generalizable to novel combinations of training poses and can be explicitly
controlled. Our method achieves such expressive and animatable character rendering all in real time, serving as a promising solution for practical
applications.

1 Introduction

Using a *handy camera rig* for data capturing, can we synthesize a photorealistic
character with *controllable viewpoints and body poses* in *real-time*? Such a technique would democratize personalized, photorealistic avatars and enable various
intriguing applications such as telepresence, where people will feel the virtual
character of a remote person as a real person talking in real time.

Traditionally, free-viewpoint rendering of a moving person is approached by
capturing a high-fidelity 3D human model in a specialized studio [5,6,8,11],
which is a costly and brittle process and is not accessible to common users.
Recently, researchers use data-driven methods [3,12,18–20,44,46] to expedite
this process. These methods focus on rendering and animating human actors
but do not address the interactions between human and real scenes (*e.g.*, a

---

Supplementary Information The online version contains supplementary material
available at https://doi.org/10.1007/978-3-031-19824-3_12.

S. Avidan et al. (Eds.): ECCV 2022, LNCS 13692, pp. 192–209, 2022.
https://doi.org/10.1007/978-3-031-19824-3_12

(a) Input images   (b) Pose guided   (c) Motion transfer
novel view synthesis

Fig. 1. Using images from a handy capture device, our method renders a photo-realistic character in real time. The character is animatable through motion transfer.

person sitting on a couch with arms on a table). Moreover, they cannot handle challenging motions such as finger movements. Recently, deformable NeRF methods [27,28,32,40] have been proposed to model the person and the scene by learning an implicit deformation field along with a canonical radiance field that serves as the template. However, these methods can only handle small deformations as it is hard to model complex human motions with a single canonical representation. Besides, the expensive volumetric rendering process prohibits real-time video synthesis.

For character modeling in unconstrained environments, we propose a novel capture setup that comprises a portable capture rig and a fixed driving camera. Synchronized mobile phone cameras are mounted on the rig, and the videographer slightly moves the camera rig to capture the light field of the scene. The fixed camera is used to extract the driving keypoints that users can manipulate for character retargeting. With this handy setup, we strike the desired balance between 3D sensing accuracy and hardware affordability since the rig movement greatly reduces the number of cameras needed.

We also introduce *pose-guided multiplane images* for fast and controllable character rendering with high fidelity. The multiplane image (MPI) representation [49] uses a set of parallel semi-transparent planes to approximate the light field and has shown compelling quality for complex scene modeling. Rather than performing optimization directly upon MPI [9,25,45,49], we propose to use a neural network to produce the planes with pose conditioning, and the whole framework is essentially a pose-to-MPI translation network. We use 2D keypoints on the image plane of the driving camera to define the pose, and predict the multiplane images in the frustum of the same camera. Hence, the two representations are spatially aligned and compatible for network processing. During inference, the keypoints serve as the driving signal, and one can obtain the corresponding character in novel views by rendering the predicted MPI from the target viewpoint.

Our method brings several benefits. 1) Since we do not assume a human model or a canonical template but learn character modeling purely in a data-driven manner, our method offers improved flexibility to characterize the subject as well as complex interactions with the scene. In particular, we observe substantial improvement for gesture modeling, which is challenging for prior arts. 2) Taking advantage of the inductive bias of convolutional neural networks, our method demonstrates improved generalization ability. Instead of memorizing the scene, the network trained with large data can hallucinate plausible outputs for diverse poses. 3) The MPI rendering is blazingly fast, and our network can synthesize videos of 640×360 resolution in real time.

We further propose several techniques to achieve better MPI synthesis. As opposed to evenly placing the planes in disparity space, we propose adaptive planes whose positions are jointly optimized during training, which considerably improves the modeling quality because the planes are now densely placed near the real surfaces of the scene. To compensate for the exposure mismatch among different cameras, we also introduce a learnable exposure code for each camera. Moreover, when dealing with long video sequences (e.g., >4k frames), we observe unsatisfactory camera pose estimation using conventional structure-from-motion (SfM) pipeline [34], which leads to blurry results. To solve this, we refine the camera poses during training using the gradients of the static background pixels.

We demonstrate that our pose-guided MPI quantitatively and qualitatively outperforms state-of-the-art approaches including Video-NeRF [17], Nerfies [27], HyperNeRF [28], and NeX [45] on novel view synthesis for characters with complex motion. Moreover, the character rendered by our method can be explicitly controlled, and we achieve photorealistic results of character reenactment, as illustrated in Fig. 1. The whole rendering framework runs in real time and is scalable to high resolutions.

2   Related Work

Neural Character Rendering. Traditional graphics pipelines [5,6,8,11] require a well-orchestrated studio with a dense array of cameras to build the mesh for the characters. In the past years, deep generative neural networks have been introduced to synthesize photorealistic characters [38,39]. A popular synthesis paradigm is image-to-image translation [14,43], which learns the mapping from certain representations, such as joint heatmap [2,4,23,48,50], rendered skeleton [7,31,35,36,42], and depth map [24], to real images of the character. These works have certain generalization ability to novel poses and have shown compelling rendering quality even for complex clothing and in-the-wild scenes. However, they cannot guarantee view consistency as they learn the generation in 2D screen space. More recent methods attempt to solve this by leveraging a human model, e.g., SMPL model [21]. One line of works [3,19,33] unwraps the body mesh to 2D UV space where the network learns texture synthesis and then translates the rendered textured mesh to images. Meanwhile, another line of works improves view consistency by learning the deformation to a canonical

3D space enforced by the SMPL model [12]. In comparison, our method does not assume an explicit human model and hence can model complicated finger motions as well as the character's interactions with the scene. Our method generalizes the image translation but the output representation we adopt ensures multi-view consistency.

Neural Scene Representation. Instead of rendering with a black-box image translation process, recent works turn to using neural networks to model some intrinsic aspects of the scene followed by a physics-based differentiable renderer. One recent notable work is to model the scene as a neural radiance field (NeRF) whose color and volumetric density across the continuous coordinates are parameterized by the multilayer perceptron (MLP). The NeRF representation ensures that the images rendered at different views have coherent geometry, and the volumetric rendering is able to produce realistic outputs with stunning details.

Several NeRF variants [10,17,27,28,32,40] have been proposed to handle dynamic scenes. One category of these works is deformation-based [27,28,32,40] which optimizes a deformation field that warps each observed point to a canonical NeRF. These approaches have shown impressive quality even for in-the-wild scenes, but only simple deformation can be modeled as it is difficult to find a template that accounts for all the observations. To render characters with NeRF [18,29,44,46], there are works that use the SMPL model to enforce the canonical NeRF, but they may suffer from the limited modeling capability of the parametric human model. Some methods modulate NeRF with additional conditioning [17,47] and achieve enhanced expressivity to model dramatic topology change. Nonetheless, the majority of these methods are designed for replaying the dynamic scene, and it is hard to generalize to novel character poses. This is because the point-wise MLPs in NeRF models do not leverage a larger context for generative modeling. In contrast, we employ a convolutional neural network which leverages a large image context for hallucination, and thus our method is more amenable to animation and generalizes better. Moreover, our method renders characters much faster than NeRF-based approaches.

Multiplane Images Representation. The MPI representation uses a stack of RGBα layers arranged at various depths to approximate the light field. Initially, the MPI is used for the stereo magnification problem [49] where an MPI is predicted from a CNN given a stereo pair input. Later, a few works extend the MPI for view synthesis where images from a variable number of viewpoints can be accessed [9,16,25,37,41,45]. The multiplane images can be optimized in three ways: direct optimization [25,37,45], using a CNN to learn gradient updates upon MPI [9] or directly predicting the MPI using CNN [16,41]. The main drawback of MPI methods is that the rendered view range is limited by the number of planes. To solve this, [25] proposes to use multiple MPIs to account for local light fields, which are further blended for the final output. MPI-based approaches have limited power for handling non-Lambertian surfaces and wide viewing angles, and they are outshined by the recent advances of NeRF-based methods. Very recently, NeX [45] tackles view-dependent modeling by representing the pixel color of MPI as a combination of spherical basis functions, and it excels over NeRF in visual quality with much faster rendering speed. However, no existing method ever studies the controllability of such a representation. Our approach is motivated by the recent success of MPI, and we demonstrate the great potential of this representation for animatable character rendering.

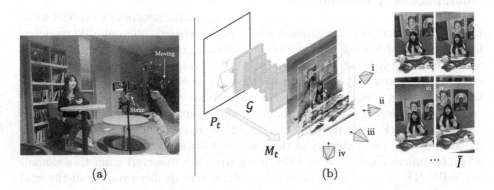

(a)   (b)

Fig. 2. Overview of our method. (a) The device we use to capture data for building an animatable character in a real scene. (b) The built character is controllable. Given any pose $\mathbf{P}_t$ at time step t, we feed its pose image into a pre-trained network $\mathcal{G}_\theta$ to acquire a 3D character represented in MPI ($\mathbf{M}_t$). The character has the same pose with $\mathbf{P}_t$, and can also be efficiently rendered in free views.

3   Approach

We aim to render an animatable character that can be controlled by a driving input. To this end, we devise a portable data capture setup to ease the multi-view capture in open scenes (Sect. 3.1). Once we finish the data capture for the moving character, we train a neural network conditioned on character poses to predict the multiplane images that explain the multi-view observations (Sect. 3.2). During inference, we can render realistic characters given a driving input (Sect. 3.3). Next, we elaborate on these three parts respectively.

3.1   Data Capture

In our design, data capturing should meet the following requirements. First, the capture device should be portable, lightweight, and low-cost to benefit as many users as possible for their character creation. Second, the captured images for the moving subject should resolve most motion ambiguity. Otherwise, the character reconstruction from sparse views is highly ill-posed. Third, we need to use some driving signal handy for user control, and such signal should be readily obtained from the same capture setup.

Taking these into consideration, we propose a novel character capture setup as shown in Fig. 2(a), which consists of a moving camera rig along with a static camera fixed on a tripod. We mount four smartphone cameras on the capture rig, which the videographer can hold and move to capture the subject. Such capturing manner is motivated by Nerfies [27] that uses a single moving camera for selfies. In our early attempts, we find a single camera does not suffice to resolve the ambiguity for complex non-rigid motion, whereas adding a few more cameras significantly improves the modeling quality. Also, the rig motion makes the capture to cover various combinations of viewpoints and character poses, which helps to reduce the number of multi-view cameras by requiring longer sequence capturing. On the other hand, we propose to use body keypoints as the driving signal for character animation. We believe manipulating 2D keypoints is easy for most users since people can extract such keypoints from their monocular videos to drive the virtual character. Hence, we also require a fixed camera, or "driving camera", which is used to extract the driving keypoints. Compared to a specialized lab, it is much cheaper to build this capture setup. Once we capture the data, we use audio to synchronize the multi-view videos with the driving camera and run COLMAP [34] to estimate the camera poses for each frame.

3.2 Conditional MPI Representation

Our method builds on the multiplane image (MPI) scene representation, which consists of D fronto-parallel planes, each with an associated $H \times W \times 4$ RGBα image. As illustrated in Fig. 2(b), the multiplane images are scaled and positioned at different depths $d_1, ..., d_D$ within the view frustum of the driving camera. Typically, the planes are placed equally in the depth space (for the bounded scene) or in the disparity space (for the unbounded scene).

While MPI-based methods have shown impressive quality in modeling static scenes from sparse views, its ability to model a moving character, especially those with complex motions, remains underexplored. To accomplish this, we formulate the character rendering by pose-guided MPI synthesis framework, which is illustrated in Fig. 2(b). Given the pose image $\mathbf{P}_t$ extracted from the driving camera at time t, we train a convolutional neural network $\mathcal{G}_\theta$ to translate this input to multiplane images $\mathbf{M}_t = \mathcal{G}_\theta(\mathbf{P}_t)$, using the supervision of the multi-view observations $\{\mathbf{I}_t^n\}_{n=1}^N$. Here, N denotes the number of cameras we use for data capture. During training, we extract rich character pose information using [22], which includes facial landmarks, body keypoints, and finger keypoints that are extracted from the driving frames. Note that both $\mathbf{P}_t$ and $\mathbf{M}_t$ are spatially aligned as they are viewed from the same driving camera; hence their mapping is naturally suitable for the CNN learning.

The synthesized MPI can be rendered in the target view by compositing the colors along the rays. The implementation is efficient: the image planes are first warped towards the target view and then alpha-blended. Specifically, we refer to the RGB channels of the MPI as $\mathbf{C} = \{c_1, ..., c_D\}$ and the corresponding alpha channels as $\mathbf{A} = \{\alpha_1, ..., \alpha_D\}$. The MPI rendering can be formulated as

$$\tilde{\mathbf{I}} = \mathcal{O}\big(\mathcal{W}(C), \mathcal{W}(A)\big), \tag{1}$$

where the warping operator $\mathcal{W}$ warps the images via a homography function [49] depending on the relative rotation $\mathbf{R}$ and translation $\mathbf{t}$ from the target to the source view and the layer depth d_i. Formally, the warping matrix is

$$\mathbf{K}_s(\mathbf{R} - \frac{\mathbf{tn}^T}{d_i})\mathbf{K}_t^{-1}, \tag{2}$$

where $\mathbf{n}$ is the normal vector; $\mathbf{K}_s$ and $\mathbf{K}_t$ respectively are intrinsic matrix of source camera and target camera. Besides, $\mathcal{O}$ in Eq. 1 denotes the composition [30] of the warped images (c_i' and α_i') from back to front, i.e.,

$$\mathcal{O}(C, A) = \sum_{i=1}^{D} \Big(c_i' \alpha_i' \prod_{j=i+1}^{D} (1 - \alpha_j') \Big). \tag{3}$$

The above rendering process is fully differentiable, so the MPI synthesis network can be trained end-to-end using 2D supervision.

This pose-guided MPI enjoys many features of CNNs and shows various advantages over implicit approaches. First of all, we do not explicitly model the geometry of the scene or assume a template for all the character motions, so our model is more expressive and can better fit challenging motions and delicate details, as proved in our view synthesis experiments. Second, compared to implicit neural representation, our method can generalize better thanks to the inductive bias of CNNs. Intuitively, it seems that our approach is good at hallucinating plausible outputs, even for unseen poses. Third, manipulating the keypoints is more straightforward for character animation instead of using latent code or body parameters. Finally, the MPI is inferred with a single feed-forward pass of the network, and its rendering is also fast.

To cultivate the full potential of the above framework and achieve state-of-the-art quality, we introduce the following key components.

Depth-Adaptive MPI. We argue that manually placing the multiplane images at fixed depth may not be optimal. Ideally, the planes should be distributed more densely around the real scene surfaces. Otherwise, some planes are wasted for modeling the vacant space. More importantly, in our scenario the bound of the scene cannot be reliably estimated because we have to mask out the moving foreground when computing the COLMAP. As a result, the MPIs initialized with a mistaken depth range may lead to scene clipping modeling.

In view of this, we propose to make the MPI depth as learnable parameters so that MPIs positions can be adaptive to the scene content. Formally, we refer to the initialized depth as d_i^{init}. During training, we learn the residual δ_i which is initialized with zeros, so the refined depth becomes $d_i = d_i^{init} + \delta_i$. As we know, the homography warping $\mathcal{W}$ in Eq. 1 is the function of d_i; hence the gradient can be back-propagated to update the depth as the training proceeds.

However, one may notice that the depth refinement may alter the plane orderings, which will mislead the alpha composition (Eq. 3) that renders the planes from back to front. Therefore, we need to enforce the depth order to be unchanged in the depth refinement. To achieve this, we clamp the value of δ_i once we find the plane shift causes the crossing over the adjacent planes. During training, the depth refinement uses $0.1\times$ learning rate compared to the network.

Learning with Variable Exposure Images. There always exist exposure and color differences among cameras even if we employ cameras of the same type and manually choose the ISO and exposure time. To use different exposed images for our training, we assume that the MPI rendering models the true light intensity of the scene but we introduce learnable exposure coefficients to account for the exposure variance among cameras. Specifically, we adopt a linear exposure model [1,26] which outputs the image as

$$\hat{\mathbf{I}} = clamp((\tilde{\mathbf{I}} + \beta) \circ \gamma), \tag{4}$$

where $clamp(\cdot) = \min(\max(\cdot, 0), 1)$ whereas $\beta \in \mathbb{R}^3$ and $\gamma \in \mathbb{R}^3$ are learnable exposure coefficients associated with each camera. Here, γ accounts for the exposure time whereas β is for compensating the shift of black level.

Learnable Camera Poses. In our experiments, the model sometimes fails to reconstruct the static background because of the inaccurate camera pose estimation from SfM. The problem becomes even worse when dealing with long video sequences to capture more diverse character poses.

To improve the robustness of inaccurate camera registration, we jointly refine the camera poses during training. The gradient through the homography warping can be used to update the camera poses for each frame. Note that the pose refinement can only leverage the gradient of a static background, whereas the MPI synthesis is updated using the whole image. Therefore, the optimization follows an alternative manner: we take two consecutive training steps to alternatively optimize the MPI synthesis network and the camera pose, with the loss computing over the whole image and the background, respectively. Since this may slow down the training speed, we only apply this strategy for sequences with blurry background reconstruction.

Sharing Textures for Compact MPI. It is known that a large number of RGBA layers are helpful for high-fidelity modeling, but this brings huge memory costs when directly using the network for the MPI synthesis. To make the MPI more compact, we follow the strategy of NeX [45] and share the RGB textures for every K layers. In this way, we reduce the output channels from $4D$ to $(D + 3D/K)$ without obvious degradation in visual quality.

Losses. To optimize our model, we feed input pose to generate the MPI and render an output image $\hat{\mathbf{I}}$ using the camera pose of the ground-truth image $\mathbf{I}$. We use three losses for reconstruction: mean square error between $\mathbf{I}$ and $\hat{\mathbf{I}}$ as $\mathcal{L}2$: $||\mathbf{I} - \hat{\mathbf{I}}||^2$, gradient difference along the width and height dimension as $\mathcal{L}_{grad}$: $||\nabla \mathbf{I} - \nabla\hat{\mathbf{I}}||^2$ and the perceptual loss of the difference between VGG features: $\mathcal{L}_{perceptual}$: $||VGG_F(\mathbf{I}) - VGG_F(\hat{\mathbf{I}})||_1$. In total we optimize:

$$\min_{\theta, d, R, t, \beta, \gamma} \mathcal{L}_2 + \lambda_1 \mathcal{L}_{grad} + \lambda_2 \mathcal{L}_{perceptual}. \tag{5}$$

Note that for $\mathcal{L}_2$ loss and the $\mathcal{L}_{grad}$, we apply a $10\times$ weight on the foreground person using the object mask detected by [13].

3.3 Motion Transfer

Our pose-to-MPI translation network learns to generate 3D representation with a conditional pose. Given a trained model of a character, we can transfer the motion from the driving character and generate novel views. Since characters differ in height, limb length and body shape, it is not suitable to transfer the absolute pose directly from the driving character to the source character built by our method. Relative motion transfer, which keeps the physical characteristics of the source character, is desired. Our input pose comprises face keypoints, body keypoints, and finger keypoints. Denote the face landmarks of the driving character by t and that of the source character by s. To transfer the relative motion, we find the landmarks t' most similar to s in the driving video. Thus, the transferred pose for the source character becomes $s + t - t'$. We treat the body landmarks as a tree structure for body motion transfer. We generate the transferred body keypoints by keeping the same limb length as the source body while utilizing the limb direction of the driving body. The tree root is the midpoint of the left shoulder and right shoulder. Finger motion transfer is similar to body transfer, except that the tree root is changed to the wrist. Please refer to the supplementary material for more details.

4   Experiments

4.1   Implementation Details

The output MPI is composed of 192 alpha layers, with every 12 alpha layers sharing the same RGB texture layer, which leads to $192/12 = 16$ RGB texture layers. The total number of channels to output thus becomes $192 + 16 \times 3 = 240$. Our video sequences are all captured in 1080p resolution. The temporal length of each captured sequence lies between 1 to 3 min. For each sequence, 1/16 frames are selected as a validation set with the rest for training. We down-sample each video frame to 360×640 for fast inference. However, the resolution of each output MPI layer is larger than this to support rendering with wider view angles: it is equal to padding 180 pixels to all four sides of the 360×640 frame. We train the model using Adam [15] optimizer and decay the learning rate from $1e-3$ to $1e-4$ in 500 epochs. The training takes 12 h with four Tesla V100 GPUs.

4.2 Evaluation

Both quantitative and qualitative analysis is conducted to evaluate our methods thoroughly w.r.t the following two aspects: (i) the ability to synthesize novel views (ii) the ability to generalize to novel poses. We highly recommend the readers to watch our video for a more comprehensive evaluation.

Table 1. Quantitative comparisons on different datasets in terms of PNSR↑, SSIM↑, and LPIPS↓. The best results are highlighted in **bold**.

	Sequence 1 (755 images)			Sequence 2 (755 images)			Sequence 3 (755 images)			Mean		
	PSNR	SSIM	LPIPS	PSNR	SSIM	LPIPS	PSNR	SSIM	LPIPS	PSNR	SSIM	LPIPS
NeX [45]	24.05	0.919	0.168	22.63	0.921	0.197	24.26	0.908	0.225	23.65	0.916	0.197
Video-Nerf [17]	27.74	0.940	0.189	26.94	0.932	0.230	27.20	0.931	0.221	27.30	0.934	0.213
Nerfies [27]	27.91	0.938	0.180	26.90	0.922	0.180	26.84	0.932	0.191	27.22	0.931	0.187
HyperNerf [28]	28.10	0.946	0.162	**27.13**	0.942	0.178	**27.23**	0.939	0.193	**27.48**	0.942	0.178
Ours	**28.20**	**0.954**	**0.062**	26.72	**0.957**	**0.082**	26.95	**0.945**	**0.092**	27.29	**0.952**	**0.079**

Table 2. Quantitative ablation results. The best results are highlighted in **bold**.

	Sequence 3 (755 images)			Sequence 4 (755 images)			Sequence 5 (5000 images)			Mean		
	PSNR	SSIM	LPIPS	PSNR	SSIM	LPIPS	PSNR	SSIM	LPIPS	PSNR	SSIM	LPIPS
Ours w/o AD	18.00	0.793	0.314	23.27	0.918	0.110	20.34	0.812	0.205	20.54	0.841	0.210
Ours w/o EC	26.70	0.940	0.092	26.53	0.922	0.078	21.82	0.822	0.187	25.02	0.895	0.119
Ours-s	26.88	0.940	0.103	26.21	0.928	0.090	21.22	0.817	0.190	24.77	0.895	0.128
Ours	26.95	**0.945**	0.092	**26.63**	**0.932**	**0.077**	21.92	0.823	0.186	25.17	0.900	0.118
Ours w/LCP	**27.01**	0.943	**0.091**	26.48	0.920	0.084	**23.12**	**0.845**	**0.162**	**25.54**	**0.902**	**0.112**

Novel View Synthesis. We compare our approach with four other scene representation methods. Among them, NeX [45] is the state-of-the-art MPI-based method. It is proposed to represent only static scenes. The other three are NeRF-variants, which comprise different extensions to handle dynamic scenes. In specific, Video-NeRF [17] conditions NeRF functions on an extra time-variant latent

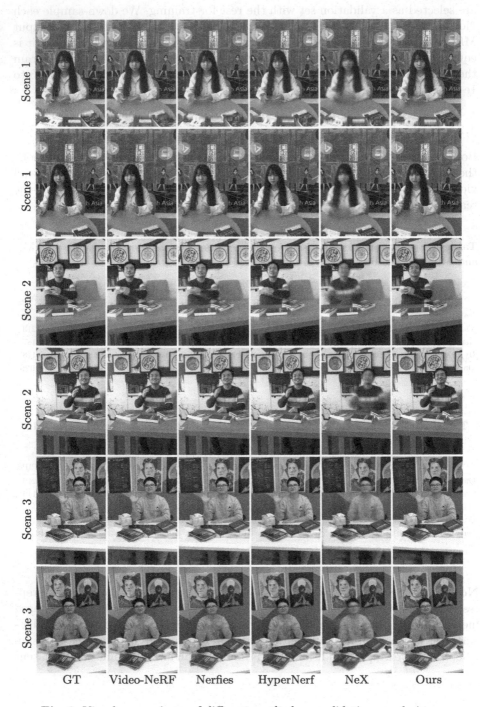

Fig. 3. Visual comparisons of different methods on validation novel views.

code; Nerfies [27] introduces dynamic deformations into NeRF; HyperNeRF [28], on the other hand, combines both the latent code and the deformation into NeRF representation and achieves better performance. Moreover, we also introduce weighted sampling to emphasize the foreground training. Some dataset-specific settings are adopted for the baselines to ensure a fair comparison. We also make sure that images with the same timestamp share the same learned latent code and images from the same camera share the same appearance code. During training, we raise the sampling probability of foreground rays to be 10× of the sampling probability corresponding to background. We find that employing these settings generally improves the results of baseline methods.

We illustrate visual comparisons in Fig. 3. Without a dynamic modeling capability, NeX fails to capture motions and generates only blurry bodies and faces. As for Video-NeRF, Nerfies, and Hyper-NeRF, they hardly capture the complex motion of hands since their conditioning input is latent vectors, which are too compressed to represent a detailed pose of a character. In comparison, our method well handles the challenging motions with delicate details.

We also conduct a quantitative comparison using three metrics: LPIPS, MS-SSIM, and PSNR. We report scores on three testing sequences in Table 1. Our method achieves better SSIM and LPIPS on all sequences but relatively inferior PSNR on Sequences 2 and 3. We agree with [27] that PSNR is very sensitive to small misalignments between prediction and ground truth hence it might not well reflect real perceptual quality under these cases. Moreover, we report the inference time of all these methods in Table 3. NeRF-base methods rely on a densely sampling procedure, both time and memory-consuming. Instead, our results is inferred with a single forward pass of a CNN, which leads to hundreds of times of acceleration over all the other baseline methods.

Fig. 4. Qualitative results for the ablation study.

Table 3. Inference speed comparison. The performance is measured on images with 360×640 resolution using a single Tesla V100 GPU.

Method	NeX	VideoNerf	Nerfies	HyperNerf	Ours	Ours-s
Inference time (s)	3.232	12.315	18.661	19.676	0.049	**0.031**
FPS	0.309	0.081	0.053	0.051	20.41	**32.26**

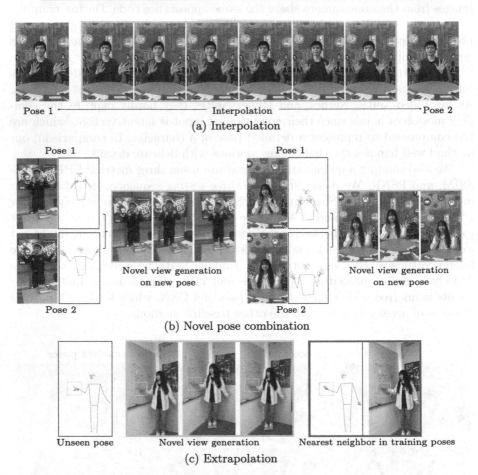

(a) Interpolation

(b) Novel pose combination

(c) Extrapolation

Fig. 5. Generalization study. Our approach performs well on motion interpolation and novel pose combination, and allows pose extrapolation to some extent.

Novel Poses. As shown in Fig. 5, we introduce three settings to illustrate the capability of our method in handling novel poses. *Interpolation*: unseen poses are smoothly interpolated between two given poses. As shown by Fig. 5(a), our method can generate a character that smoothly acts following the interpolated poses. *Novel combination*: unseen poses are generated by combining different parts of given poses. As shown by Fig. 5(b), the 3D character generated from

Fig. 6. The generated character (rightmost results) can be driven by the subject with photorealistic quality.

our method faithfully combines the two poses, *e.g.* the tilted-head man with thumb-up gestures, the girl with both hands waving to the same side. These poses are never observed in the training dataset. *Small extrapolation*: As shown by Fig. 5(c), our framework can also handle small extrapolation as the trained network is essentially a generative model for a single person. Please refer to our supplemental material for more results on novel poses.

Ablation Study. We conduct an ablation study to evaluate the effectiveness of each proposed design. We report scores in Table 2, with results visualized in Fig. 4. AD stands for the "adaptive depth", EC means to use the "exposure coefficients", while LCP stands for the "learnable camera poses". We have the following findings: (i) Without the adaptive plane depth, the learning process is sensitive to the initial plane depth assignment and fails to represent the details of some objects, *e.g.* the book. (ii) In cases where the initial camera registration is inaccurate, the learnable pose adjusts the initial camera poses and leads to obvious improvement in generating clearer faces. (iii) Besides, the exposure code helps adjust the global luminance level, which results in slight improvements in quantitative metrics. (iv) We also test our method with smaller U-Nets (Ours-s in Table 2) with fewer channels and only observe minor quality degradation.

Applications. As a straightforward application, our framework can synchronize different 3D characters with the same pose, as shown by Fig. 6. With the learned representation of a 3D character, we extract a 2D pose motion from the driving character and transfer it to the character. The 3D character can be controllable by any given 2D poses and rendered to novel views in real time.

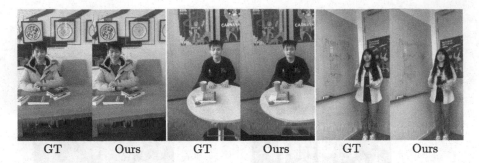

GT   Ours   GT   Ours   GT   Ours

Fig. 7. Failure cases. Our model fails to generate the reflection effects and may present undesired layered textures. The quality also degrades for large extrapolated motions.

5 Limitations and Conclusion

This work studies a controllable representation of a real-scene 3D character based on a pose-guided MPI. Extensive experiments show that our approach is able to represent a 3D character in real scenes with unprecedented quality, which can be not only rendered into novel views in real-time speed but also be controllably guided by different human poses. Still, our method suffers from some artifacts as shown in Fig. 7. Our MPI representation only outputs diffuse colors, and the rendered images thus cannot handle view-dependent effects such as the reflections. Our method also suffers from typical MPI artifacts, such as the layered section exposed near the boundary. Even though our framework can generalize to some new unseen poses fairly well, the quality of synthesis would still degrade, especially when the new pose deviates too far away from the training data. The proposed method is promising to serve as a practical solution for character rendering and we expect further works to solve the remaining issues.

References

1. Abdelhamed, A., Lin, S., Brown, M.S.: A high-quality denoising dataset for smartphone cameras. In: Proceedings of the IEEE Conference on Computer Vision and Pattern Recognition, pp. 1692–1700 (2018)
2. Aberman, K., Shi, M., Liao, J., Lischinski, D., Chen, B., Cohen-Or, D.: Deep video-based performance cloning. In: Computer Graphics Forum, vol. 38, pp. 219–233. Wiley Online Library (2019)
3. Bagautdinov, T., et al.: Driving-signal aware full-body avatars. ACM Trans. Graph. (TOG) **40**(4), 1–17 (2021)
4. Balakrishnan, G., Zhao, A., Dalca, A.V., Durand, F., Guttag, J.: Synthesizing images of humans in unseen poses. In: Proceedings of the IEEE Conference on Computer Vision and Pattern Recognition, pp. 8340–8348 (2018)
5. Carranza, J., Theobalt, C., Magnor, M.A., Seidel, H.P.: Free-viewpoint video of human actors. ACM Trans. Graph. (TOG) **22**(3), 569–577 (2003)
6. Casas, D., Volino, M., Collomosse, J., Hilton, A.: 4D video textures for interactive character appearance. In: Computer Graphics Forum, vol. 33, pp. 371–380. Wiley Online Library (2014)

7. Chan, C., Ginosar, S., Zhou, T., Efros, A.A.: Everybody dance now. In: Proceedings of the IEEE/CVF International Conference on Computer Vision, pp. 5933–5942 (2019)
8. Collet, A., et al.: High-quality streamable free-viewpoint video. ACM Trans. Graph. (ToG) **34**(4), 1–13 (2015)
9. Flynn, J., et al.: DeepView: view synthesis with learned gradient descent. In: Proceedings of the IEEE/CVF Conference on Computer Vision and Pattern Recognition, pp. 2367–2376 (2019)
10. Gao, C., Saraf, A., Kopf, J., Huang, J.B.: Dynamic view synthesis from dynamic monocular video. In: Proceedings of the IEEE/CVF International Conference on Computer Vision, pp. 5712–5721 (2021)
11. Guo, K., et al.: The relightables: volumetric performance capture of humans with realistic relighting. ACM Trans. Graph. (ToG) **38**(6), 1–19 (2019)
12. Habermann, M., Liu, L., Xu, W., Zollhoefer, M., Pons-Moll, G., Theobalt, C.: Real-time deep dynamic characters. ACM Trans. Graph. (TOG) **40**(4), 1–16 (2021)
13. He, K., Zhang, X., Ren, S., Sun, J.: Deep residual learning for image recognition. In: Proceedings of the IEEE Conference on Computer Vision and Pattern Recognition, pp. 770–778 (2016)
14. Isola, P., Zhu, J.Y., Zhou, T., Efros, A.A.: Image-to-image translation with conditional adversarial networks. In: Proceedings of the IEEE Conference on Computer Vision and Pattern Recognition, pp. 1125–1134 (2017)
15. Kingma, D.P., Ba, J.: Adam: a method for stochastic optimization. arXiv preprint arXiv:1412.6980 (2014)
16. Li, J., Feng, Z., She, Q., Ding, H., Wang, C., Lee, G.H.: MINE: towards continuous depth MPI with NeRF for novel view synthesis. In: Proceedings of the IEEE/CVF International Conference on Computer Vision, pp. 12578–12588 (2021)
17. Li, T., et al.: Neural 3D video synthesis. arXiv preprint arXiv:2103.02597 (2021)
18. Liu, L., Habermann, M., Rudnev, V., Sarkar, K., Gu, J., Theobalt, C.: Neural actor: neural free-view synthesis of human actors with pose control. ACM Trans. Graph. (TOG) **40**(6), 1–16 (2021)
19. Liu, L., et al.: Neural human video rendering by learning dynamic textures and rendering-to-video translation. arXiv preprint arXiv:2001.04947 (2020)
20. Lombardi, S., Saragih, J., Simon, T., Sheikh, Y.: Deep appearance models for face rendering. ACM Trans. Graph. (ToG) **37**(4), 1–13 (2018)
21. Loper, M., Mahmood, N., Romero, J., Pons-Moll, G., Black, M.J.: SMPL: a skinned multi-person linear model. ACM Trans. Graph. (TOG) **34**(6), 1–16 (2015)
22. Lugaresi, C., et al.: MediaPipe: a framework for building perception pipelines. arXiv preprint arXiv:1906.08172 (2019)
23. Ma, L., Jia, X., Sun, Q., Schiele, B., Tuytelaars, T., Van Gool, L.: Pose guided person image generation. In: Advances in Neural Information Processing Systems, vol. 30 (2017)
24. Martin-Brualla, R., et al.: LookinGood: enhancing performance capture with real-time neural re-rendering. arXiv preprint arXiv:1811.05029 (2018)
25. Mildenhall, B., et al.: Local light field fusion: practical view synthesis with prescriptive sampling guidelines. ACM Trans. Graph. (TOG) **38**(4), 1–14 (2019)
26. Ouyang, H., Shi, Z., Lei, C., Law, K.L., Chen, Q.: Neural camera simulators. In: Proceedings of the IEEE/CVF Conference on Computer Vision and Pattern Recognition, pp. 7700–7709 (2021)
27. Park, K., et al.: Nerfies: deformable neural radiance fields. In: Proceedings of the IEEE/CVF International Conference on Computer Vision, pp. 5865–5874 (2021)

28. Park, K., et al.: HyperNeRF: a higher-dimensional representation for topologically varying neural radiance fields. arXiv preprint arXiv:2106.13228 (2021)
29. Peng, S., et al.: Animatable neural radiance fields for human body modeling. arXiv e-prints, arXiv-2105 (2021)
30. Porter, T., Duff, T.: Compositing digital images. In: Proceedings of the 11th Annual Conference on Computer Graphics and Interactive Techniques, pp. 253–259 (1984)
31. Pumarola, A., Agudo, A., Sanfeliu, A., Moreno-Noguer, F.: Unsupervised person image synthesis in arbitrary poses. In: Proceedings of the IEEE Conference on Computer Vision and Pattern Recognition, pp. 8620–8628 (2018)
32. Pumarola, A., Corona, E., Pons-Moll, G., Moreno-Noguer, F.: D-NeRF: neural radiance fields for dynamic scenes. In: Proceedings of the IEEE/CVF Conference on Computer Vision and Pattern Recognition, pp. 10318–10327 (2021)
33. Sarkar, K., Mehta, D., Xu, W., Golyanik, V., Theobalt, C.: Neural re-rendering of humans from a single image. In: Vedaldi, A., Bischof, H., Brox, T., Frahm, J.-M. (eds.) ECCV 2020. LNCS, vol. 12356, pp. 596–613. Springer, Cham (2020). https://doi.org/10.1007/978-3-030-58621-8_35
34. Schonberger, J.L., Frahm, J.M.: Structure-from-motion revisited. In: Proceedings of the IEEE Conference on Computer Vision and Pattern Recognition, pp. 4104–4113 (2016)
35. Shysheya, A., et al.: Textured neural avatars. In: Proceedings of the IEEE/CVF Conference on Computer Vision and Pattern Recognition, pp. 2387–2397 (2019)
36. Si, C., Wang, W., Wang, L., Tan, T.: Multistage adversarial losses for pose-based human image synthesis. In: Proceedings of the IEEE Conference on Computer Vision and Pattern Recognition, pp. 118–126 (2018)
37. Srinivasan, P.P., Tucker, R., Barron, J.T., Ramamoorthi, R., Ng, R., Snavely, N.: Pushing the boundaries of view extrapolation with multiplane images. In: Proceedings of the IEEE/CVF Conference on Computer Vision and Pattern Recognition, pp. 175–184 (2019)
38. Tewari, A., et al.: State of the art on neural rendering. In: Computer Graphics Forum, vol. 39, pp. 701–727. Wiley Online Library (2020)
39. Tewari, A., et al.: Advances in neural rendering. arXiv preprint arXiv:2111.05849 (2021)
40. Tretschk, E., Tewari, A., Golyanik, V., Zollhöfer, M., Lassner, C., Theobalt, C.: Non-rigid neural radiance fields: reconstruction and novel view synthesis of a dynamic scene from monocular video. In: Proceedings of the IEEE/CVF International Conference on Computer Vision, pp. 12959–12970 (2021)
41. Tucker, R., Snavely, N.: Single-view view synthesis with multiplane images. In: Proceedings of the IEEE/CVF Conference on Computer Vision and Pattern Recognition, pp. 551–560 (2020)
42. Wang, T.C., et al.: Video-to-video synthesis. arXiv preprint arXiv:1808.06601 (2018)
43. Wang, T.C., Liu, M.Y., Zhu, J.Y., Tao, A., Kautz, J., Catanzaro, B.: High-resolution image synthesis and semantic manipulation with conditional GANs. In: Proceedings of the IEEE Conference on Computer Vision and Pattern Recognition, pp. 8798–8807 (2018)
44. Weng, C.Y., Curless, B., Srinivasan, P.P., Barron, J.T., Kemelmacher-Shlizerman, I.: HumanNeRF: free-viewpoint rendering of moving people from monocular video. arXiv preprint arXiv:2201.04127 (2022)
45. Wizadwongsa, S., Phongthawee, P., Yenphraphai, J., Suwajanakorn, S.: NeX: real-time view synthesis with neural basis expansion. In: Proceedings of the IEEE/CVF Conference on Computer Vision and Pattern Recognition, pp. 8534–8543 (2021)

46. Xu, H., Alldieck, T., Sminchisescu, C.: H-NeRF: neural radiance fields for rendering and temporal reconstruction of humans in motion. In: Advances in Neural Information Processing Systems, vol. 34 (2021)
47. Zhang, J., et al.: Editable free-viewpoint video using a layered neural representation. ACM Trans. Graph. (TOG) 40(4), 1–18 (2021)
48. Zhang, P., Zhang, B., Chen, D., Yuan, L., Wen, F.: Cross-domain correspondence learning for exemplar-based image translation. In: Proceedings of the IEEE/CVF Conference on Computer Vision and Pattern Recognition, pp. 5143–5153 (2020)
49. Zhou, T., Tucker, R., Flynn, J., Fyffe, G., Snavely, N.: Stereo magnification: learning view synthesis using multiplane images. arXiv preprint arXiv:1805.09817 (2018)
50. Zhou, X., et al.: CoCosNet v2: full-resolution correspondence learning for image translation. In: Proceedings of the IEEE/CVF Conference on Computer Vision and Pattern Recognition, pp. 11465–11475 (2021)

SparseNeuS: Fast Generalizable Neural Surface Reconstruction from Sparse Views

Xiaoxiao Long[1], Cheng Lin[2], Peng Wang[1], Taku Komura[1], and Wenping Wang[3(✉)]

[1] The University of Hong Kong, Pok Fu Lam, Hong Kong
[2] Tencent Games, Shenzhen, China
[3] Texas A&M University, College Station, USA
wenping@tamu.edu

Abstract. We introduce *SparseNeuS*, a novel neural rendering based method for the task of surface reconstruction from multi-view images. This task becomes more difficult when only sparse images are provided as input, a scenario where existing neural reconstruction approaches usually produce incomplete or distorted results. Moreover, their inability of generalizing to unseen new scenes impedes their application in practice. Contrarily, *SparseNeuS* can generalize to new scenes and work well with sparse images (as few as 2 or 3). *SparseNeuS* adopts signed distance function (SDF) as the surface representation, and learns generalizable priors from image features by introducing *geometry encoding* volumes for generic surface prediction. Moreover, several strategies are introduced to effectively leverage sparse views for high-quality reconstruction, including 1) a multi-level geometry reasoning framework to recover the surfaces in a coarse-to-fine manner; 2) a multi-scale color blending scheme for more reliable color prediction; 3) a consistency-aware fine-tuning scheme to control the inconsistent regions caused by occlusion and noise. Extensive experiments demonstrate that our approach not only outperforms the state-of-the-art methods, but also exhibits good efficiency, generalizability, and flexibility (Visit our project page: https://www.xxlong.site/SparseNeuS).

Keywords: Reconstruction · Volume rendering · Sparse views

1 Introduction

Reconstructing 3D geometry from multi-view images is a fundamental problem in computer vision and has been extensively researched for decades. Conventional methods for multi-view stereo [2,7,8,18,19,36,37] reconstruct 3D geometry from

Supplementary Information The online version contains supplementary material available at https://doi.org/10.1007/978-3-031-19824-3_13.

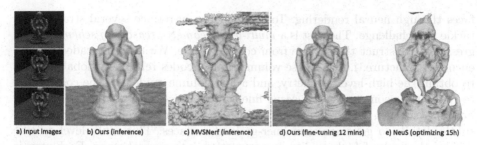

a) Input Images   b) Ours (inference)   c) MVSNerf (inference)   d) Ours (fine-tuning 12 mins)   e) NeuS (optimizing 15h)

Fig. 1. Our method can generalize across diverse scenes, and reconstruct neural surfaces from only three input images (a) via fast network inference (b). The reconstruction quality of the fast inference step is more accurate and faithful than the result of MVSNerf [3] (c). Our inference result can be further improved by a per-scene fine-tuning process. Compared to NeuS [44] (e), our per-scene optimization result (d) not only achieves noticeably better reconstruction quality, but also takes much less time to converge (12 min v.s. 15 h).

input images by finding corresponding matches across the input images. However, when only a sparse set of images are available as input, image noises, weak textures and reflections make it difficult for these methods to build dense and complete matches (Fig. 1).

With the recent advances in neural implicit representations, neural surface reconstruction methods [32,44,49,50] leverage neural rendering to jointly optimize the implicit geometry and the radiance field by minimizing the difference of rendered views and ground truth views. Although the methods can produce plausible geometry and photorealistic novel views, they suffer from two major limitations. First, existing methods heavily depend on a large number of input views, i.e. dense views, that are often not available in practice. Second, they require time-consuming per-scene optimization for reconstruction, thus incapable of generalizing to new scenes. The limitations need to be resolved for making such reconstruction methods relevant and useful for practical application.

We propose *SparseNeuS*, a novel multi-view surface reconstruction method with two distinct advantages: 1) it generalizes well to new scenes; 2) it needs only a sparse set of images (as few as 2 or 3 images) for successful reconstruction. *SparseNeuS* achieves these goals by learning generalizable priors from image features and hierarchically leverages the information encoded in the sparse input.

To learn generalizable priors, following MVSNerf [3], we construct a *geometry encoding* volume which aggregates the 2D image features from multi-view input, and use these informative latent features to infer 3D geometry. Consequently, our surface prediction network takes a hybrid representation as input, i.e., xyz coordinates and the corresponding features from the geometry encoding volume, to predict the network-encoded signed distance function (SDF) for the reconstructed surface.

The most crucial part of our pipeline is in how to effectively incorporate the limited information from sparse input images to obtain high-quality surfaces through neural rendering. To this end, we introduce several strategies to tackle this challenge. The first is a *multi-level geometry reasoning scheme* to progressively construct the surface from coarse to fine. We use a cascaded volume encoding structure, i.e., a coarse volume that encodes relatively global features to obtain the high-level geometry, and a fine volume guided by the coarse level to refine the geometry. A per-scene fine-tuning process is further incorporated into this scheme, which is conditioned on the inferred geometry to construct subtle details to generate even finer-grained surfaces. This multi level scheme divides the task of high-quality reconstruction into several steps. Each step is based upon the geometry from the preceding step and focuses on constructing a finer level of details. Besides, due to the hierarchical nature of the scheme, the reconstruction efficiency is significantly boosted, because numerous samples far from the coarse surface can be discarded, so as not to burden the computation in the fine-level geometry reasoning.

The second important strategy that we propose is a *multi-scale color blending scheme* for novel view synthesis. Given the limited information in the sparse images, the network would struggle to directly regress accurate colors for rendering novel views. Thus, we mitigate this issue by predicting the linear blending weights of the input image pixels to derive colors. Specifically, we adopt both pixel-based and patch-based blending to jointly evaluate local and contextual radiance consistency. This multi-scale blending scheme yields more reliable color predictions when the input is sparse.

Another challenge in multi-view 3D reconstruction is that 3D surface points often do not have consistent projections across different views, due to occlusion or image noises. With only a small number of input views, the dependence of geometry reasoning on each image further increases, which aggravates the problem and results in distorted geometry. To tackle this challenge, we propose a *consistency-aware fine-tuning scheme* in the fine-tuning stage. This scheme automatically detects regions that lack consistent projections, and excludes these regions in the optimization. This strategy proves effective in making the fine-tuned surface less susceptible to occlusion and noises, thus more accurate and cleaner, contributing to a high-quality reconstruction.

We evaluated our method on the DTU [11] and BlendedMVS [48] datasets, and show that our method outperforms the state-of-the-art unsupervised neural implicit surface reconstruction methods both quantitatively and qualitatively.

In summary, our main contributions are:

- We propose a new surface reconstruction method based on neural rendering. Our method learns generalizable priors across scenes and thus can generalize to new scenes for 3D reconstruction with high-quality geometry.
- Our method is capable of high-quality reconstruction from a sparse set of images, as few as 2 or 3 images. This is achieved by effectively inferring 3D surfaces from sparse input images using three novel strategies: a) multi-level geometry reasoning; b) multi-scale color blending; and c) consistency-aware fine-tuning.

– Our method outperforms the state-of-the-arts in both reconstruction quality and computational efficiency.

2   Related Work

2.1   Multi-view Stereo (MVS)

Classical MVS methods utilize various 3D representations for reconstruction such as: voxel grids based [12,13,15,18,37,40], 3D point clouds based [7,19], and depth maps based [2,8,10,25–27,36,42,46,47]. Compared with voxel grids and 3D point clouds, depth maps are much more flexible and appropriate for parallel computation, so depth map based methods are most common, like the well-known method COLMAP [36]. Depth map based methods first estimate the depth map of each image, and then utilize filtering operations to fuse the depth maps together into a global point cloud, which can be further processed using a meshing algorithm like Screened Poisson surface reconstruction [16]. These methods achieve promising results with densely captured images. However, with a limited number of images, these methods become more sensitive to image noises, weak textures and reflections, making it difficult for these methods to produce complete reconstructions.

2.2   Neural Surface Reconstruction

Recently, neural implicit representations of 3D geometry are successfully applied in shape modeling [1,4,9,28,29,33], novel view synthesis [21,24,30,34,38,38,39, 43] and mutli-view 3D reconstruction [6,14,17,22,31,32,44,49,50,52]. For the task of multi-view reconstruction, the 3D geometry is represented by a neural network which outputs either occupancy field or Signed Distance Function (SDF). Some methods utilize surface rendering [31] for multi-view reconstruction, but they always need extra object masks [31,50] or depth priors [52], which is inefficient for practical applications. To avoid extra masks or depth priors, some methods [6,32,44,49] leverage volume rendering for reconstruction. However, they also heavily depend on a large number of images to perform a time-consuming per-scene optimization, thus incapable of generalizing to new scenes.

In terms of generalization, there are some successful attempts [3,5,23,45, 51] for neural rendering. These methods take sparse views as input and make use of the radiance information of the images to generate novel views, and can generalize to unseen scenes. Although they can generate plausible synthesized images, the extracted geometries from these methods always suffer from noises, incompleteness and distortion.

3   Method

Given a few (i.e., three) views with known camera parameters, we present a novel method that hierarchically recovers surfaces and generalizes across scenes. As

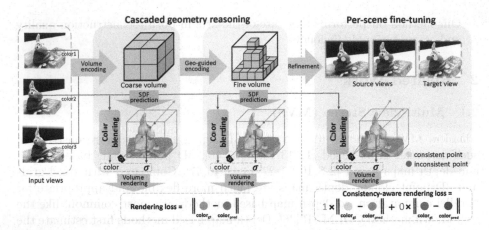

Fig. 2. The overview of *SparseNeuS*. The cascaded geometry reasoning scheme first constructs a coarse volume that encodes relatively global features to obtain the fundamental geometry, and then constructs a fine volume guided by the coarse level to refine the geometry. Finally, a consistency-aware fine-tuning strategy is used to add subtle geometry details, thus yielding high-quality reconstructions with fine-grained surfaces. Specially, a multi-scale color blending module is leveraged for more reliable color prediction.

illustrated in Fig. 2, our pipeline can be divided into three parts: (1) **Geometry reasoning**. *SparseNeuS* first constructs cascaded *geometry encoding* volumes that encode local geometry surface information, and recover surfaces from the volumes in a coarse-to-fine manner (see Sect. 3.1). (2) **Appearance prediction**. *SparseNeuS* leverages a multi-scale color blending module to predict colors by aggregating information from input images, and then combines the estimated geometry with predicted colors to render synthesized views using volume rendering (see Sect. 3.2). (3) **Per-scene fine-tuning**. Finally, a consistency-aware fine-tuning scheme is proposed to further improve the obtained geometry with fine-grained details (see Sect. 3.3).

3.1   Geometry Reasoning

SparseNeuS constructs cascaded *geometry encoding* volumes of two different resolutions for geometry reasoning, which aggregates image features to encode the information of local geometry. Specially, the coarse geometry is first extracted from a *geometry encoding* volume of low resolution, and then it is used to guide the geometry reasoning of the fine level.

Geometry Encoding Volume. For the scene captured by N input images $\{I_i\}_{i=0}^{N-1}$, we first estimate a bounding box which can cover the region of interests. The bounding box is defined in the camera coordinate system of the centered input image, and then grided into regular voxels. To construct a *geometry encoding* volume M, 2D feature maps $\{F_i\}_{i=0}^{N-1}$ are extracted from the input images

$\{I_i\}_{i=0}^{N-1}$ by a 2D feature extraction network. Next, with the camera parameters of one image I_i, we project each vertex v of the bounding box to each feature map F_i and obtain its features $F_i(\pi_i(v))$ by interpolation, where $\pi_i(v)$ denotes the projected pixel location of v on the feature map F_i. For simplicity, we abbreviate $F_i(\pi_i(v))$ as $F_i(v)$.

The *geometry encoding* volume M is constructed using all the projected features $\{F_i(v)\}_{i=0}^{N-1}$ of each vertex. Following prior methods [3,46], we first calculate the variance of all the projected features of a vertex to build a cost volume B, and then apply a sparse 3D CNN Ψ to aggregate the cost volume B to obtain the *geometry encoding* volume M:

$$M = \psi(B), \quad B(v) = \mathrm{Var}\left(\{F_i(v)\}_{i=0}^{N-1}\right), \tag{1}$$

where Var is the variance operation, which computes the variance of all the projected features $\{F_i(v)\}_{i=0}^{N-1}$ of each vertex v.

Surface Extraction. Given an arbitrary 3D location q, an MLP network f_θ takes the combination of the 3D coordinate and its corresponding interpolated features of *geometry encoding* volume $M(q)$ as input, to predict the Signed Distance Function (SDF) $s(q)$ for surface representation. Specially, positional encoding PE is applied on its 3D coordinates, and the surface extraction operation is expressed as: $s(q) = f_\theta(\mathrm{PE}(q), M(q))$.

Cascaded Volumes Scheme. For balancing the computational efficiency and reconstruction accuracy, *SparseNeuS* constructs cascaded *geometry encoding* volumes of two resolutions to perform geometry reasoning in a coarse-to-fine manner. A coarse *geometry encoding* volume is first constructed to infer the fundamental geometry, which presents the global structure of the scene but is relatively less accurate due to limited volume resolution. Guided by the obtained coarse geometry, a fine level *geometry encoding* volume is constructed to further refine the surface details. Numerous vertices far from the coarse surfaces can be discarded in the fine-level volume, which significantly reduces the computational memory burden and improves efficiency.

3.2 Appearance Prediction

Given an arbitrary 3D location q on a ray with direction d, we predict its color by aggregating appearance information from the input images. Given limited information in the sparse input images, it is difficult for a network to directly regress color values for rendering novel views. Unlike prior works [3,51], *SparseNeuS* predicts blending weights of the input images to generate new colors. A location q is first projected to the input images to obtain the corresponding colors $\{I_i(q)\}_{i=0}^{N-1}$. Then the colors from different views are blended together as the predicted color of q using the estimated blending weights.

Blending Weights. The key of generating the blending weights $\{w_i^q\}_{i=0}^{N-1}$ is to consider the photography consistency of the input images. We project q onto the feature maps $\{F_i\}_{i=0}^{N-1}$ to extract the corresponding features $\{F_i(q)\}_{i=0}^{N-1}$ using bilinear interpolation. Moreover, we calculate the mean and variance of the features $\{F_i(q)\}_{i=0}^{N-1}$ from different views to capture the global photographic consistency information. Each feature $F_i(q)$ is concatenated with the mean and variance together, and then fed into a tiny MLP network to generate a new feature $F_i'(q)$. Next, we feed the new feature $F_i'(q)$, the viewing direction of the query ray relative to the viewing direction of the i_{th} input image $\Delta d_i = d - d_i$, and the trilinearly interpolated volume encoding feature $M(q)$ into an MLP network f_c to generate blending weight: $w_i^q = f_c(F_i'(q), M(q), \Delta d_i)$. Finally, blending weights $\{w_i^q\}_{i=0}^{N-1}$ are normalized using a Softmax operator.

Pixel-Based Color Blending. With the obtained blending weights, the color c_q of a 3D location q is predicted as the weighted sum of its projected colors $\{I_i(q)\}_{i=0}^{N-1}$ on the input images. To render the color of the query ray, we first predict the color and SDF values of 3D points sampled on the ray. The color and SDF values of the sampled points are aggregated to obtain the final colors of the ray using SDF based volume rendering [44]. Since the color of a query ray corresponds to a pixel of the synthesized image, we name this operation pixel-based blending. Although supervision on the colors rendered by pixel-based blending already induces effective geometry reasoning, the information of a pixel is local and lacks contextual information, thus usually leading to inconsistent surface patches when input is sparse.

Patch-Based Color Blending. Inspired by classical patch matching, we consider enforcing the synthesized colors and ground truth colors to be contextually consistent; that is, not only in pixel level but also in patch level. To render the colors of a patch with size $k \times k$, a naive implementation is to query the colors of k^2 rays using volume rendering, which causes a huge amount of computation. We, therefore, leverage local surface plane assumption and homography transformation to achieve a more efficient implementation.

The key idea is to estimate a local plane of a sampled point to efficiently derive the local patch. Given a sampled point q, we leverage the property of the SDF network $s(q)$ to estimate the normal direction n_q by computing the spatial gradient, i.e., $n_q = \nabla s(q)$. Then, we sample a set of points on the local plane (q, n_q), project the sampled points to each view, and obtain the colors by interpolation on each input image. All the points on the local plane share the same blending weights with q, and thus only one query of the blending weights is needed. Using local plane assumption, we consider the neighboring geometric information of a query 3D position, which encodes contextual information of local patches and enforces better geometric consistency. By adopting patch-based volume rendering, synthesized regions contain more global information than single pixels, thus producing more informative and consistent shape context, especially in the regions with weak texture and changing intensity.

Volume Rendering. To rendering the pixel-based color $C(r)$ or patch-based color $P(r)$ of a ray r passing through the scene, we query the pixel-based colors c_i, patch-based colors p_i and sdf values s_i of M samples on the ray, and then utilize [44] to convert sdf values s_i into densities σ_i. Finally, the densities are used to accumulate pixel-based and patch-based colors along the ray:

$$U(r) = \sum_{i=1}^{M} T_i \left(1 - \exp\left(-\sigma_i\right)\right) u_i, \quad \text{where} \quad T_i = \exp\left(-\sum_{j=1}^{i-1} \sigma_j\right). \quad (2)$$

Here $U(r)$ denotes $C(r)$ or $P(r)$, while u_i denotes the pixel-based color c_i or patch-based color p_i of the i_{th} sample on the ray.

3.3 Per-scene Fine-Tuning

With the generalizable priors and effective geometry reasoning framework, given sparse images from a new scene, *SparseNeuS* can already recover geometry surfaces via fast network inference. However, due to the limited information in the sparse input views and the high diversity and complexity of different scenes, the geometry obtained by the generic model may contain inaccurate outliers and lack subtle details. Therefore, we propose a novel fine-tuning scheme, which is conditioned on the inferred geometry, to reconstruct subtle details and generate finer-grained surfaces. Thanks to the initialization given by the network inference, the per-scene optimization can fast converge to a high-quality surface.

Fine-Tuning Networks. In the fine-tuning, we directly optimize the obtained fine-level *geometry encoding* volume and the signed distance function (SDF) network f_θ, while the 2D feature extraction network and 3D sparse CNN networks are discarded. Moreover, the CNN based blending network used in the generic setting is replaced by a tiny MLP network. Although the CNN based network can be also used in per-scene fine-tuning, by experiments, we found that a new tiny MLP can speed up the fine-tuning without loss of performance since the MLP is much smaller than the CNN based network. The MLP network still outputs blending weights $\{w_i^q\}_{i=0}^{N-1}$ of a query 3D position q, but it takes the input as the combination of 3D coordinate q, the surface normal n_q, the ray direction d, the predicted SDF $s(q)$, and the interpolated feature of the *geometry encoding* volume $M(q)$. Specially, positional encoding PE is applied on the 3D position q and the ray direction d. The MLP network f_c' is defined as : $\{w_i^q\}_{i=0}^{N-1} = f_c'(\text{PE}(q), \text{PE}(d), n_q, s(q), M(q))$, where $\{w_i^q\}_{i=0}^{N-1}$ are the predicted blending weights, and N is the number of input images.

Consistency-Aware Color Loss. We observe that in multi-view stereo, 3D surface points often do not have consistent projections across different views, since the projections may be occluded or contaminated by image noises. As a result, the errors of these regions suffer from sub-optima, and the predicted surfaces of the regions are always inaccurate and distorted. To tackle this problem, we propose a consistency-aware color loss to automatically detect the regions lacking consistent projections and exclude these regions in the optimization:

$$\mathcal{L}_{color} = \sum_{r \in \mathbb{R}} O\left(r\right) \cdot \mathcal{D}_{pix} \left(C\left(r\right), \tilde{C}\left(r\right)\right) + \sum_{r \in \mathbb{R}} O\left(r\right) \cdot \mathcal{D}_{pat} \left(P\left(r\right), \tilde{P}\left(r\right)\right)$$
$$+ \lambda_0 \sum_{r \in \mathbb{R}} log\left(O\left(r\right)\right) + \lambda_1 \sum_{r \in \mathbb{R}} log\left(1 - O\left(r\right)\right), \tag{3}$$

where r is a query ray, $\mathbb{R}$ is the set of all query rays, $O\left(r\right)$ is the sum of accumulated weights along the ray r obtained by volume rendering. From Eq. 2, we can easily derive $O\left(r\right) = \sum_{i=1}^{M} T_i\left(1 - exp\left(-\upsilon_i\right)\right)$. $C\left(r\right)$ and $\tilde{C}\left(r\right)$ are the rendered and ground truth pixel-based colors of the query ray respectively, $P\left(r\right)$ and $\tilde{P}\left(r\right)$ are the rendered and ground truth patch-based colors of the query ray respectively, and $\mathcal{D}_{pix}$ and $\mathcal{D}_{pat}$ are the loss metrics of the rendered pixel color and rendered patch colors respectively. Empirically, we choose $\mathcal{D}_{pix}$ as L1 loss and $\mathcal{D}_{pat}$ as Normalized Cross Correlation (NCC) loss.

The rationale behind this formulation is, the points with inconsistent projections always have relatively large color errors that cannot be minimized in the optimization. Therefore, if the color errors are difficult to be minimized in optimization, we force the sum of the accumulated weights $O\left(r\right)$ to be zero, such that the inconsistent regions will be excluded in the optimization. To control the level of consistency, we introduce two logistic regularization terms: decreasing the ratio λ_0/λ_1 will lead to more regions being kept; otherwise, more regions are excluded and the surfaces are cleaner.

3.4   Training Loss

By enforcing the consistency of the synthesized colors and ground truth colors, the training of *SparseNeuS* does not rely on 3D ground-truth shapes. The overall loss function is defined as a weighted sum of the three loss terms:

$$\mathcal{L} = \mathcal{L}_{color} + \alpha \mathcal{L}_{eik} + \beta \mathcal{L}_{sparse}. \tag{4}$$

We note that, in the early stage of generic training, the estimated geometry is relatively inaccurate, and 3D surface points may have large errors, where the errors do not provide clear clues on whether the regions are radiance consistent or not. We utilize consistency-aware color loss in the per-scene fine-tuning, and remove the last two consistence-aware logistic terms of Eq. 3 in the training of the generic model.

An Eikonal term [9] is applied on the sampled points to regularize the SDF values derived from the surface prediction network f_θ:

$$\mathcal{L}_{eik} = \frac{1}{\|\mathbb{Q}\|} \sum_{q \in \mathbb{Q}} \left(\|\nabla f_\theta\left(q\right)\|_2 - 1\right)^2, \tag{5}$$

where q is a sampled 3D point, $\mathbb{Q}$ is the set of all sampled points, $\nabla f_\theta\left(q\right)$ is the gradient of network f_θ relatively to sampled point q, and $\|\cdot\|_2$ is l_2 norm. The Eikonal term enforces the network f_θ to have unit l_2 norm gradient, which encourages f_θ to generate smooth surfaces.

Table 1. Evaluation on DTU [11] dataset.

Scan	24	37	40	55	63	65	69	83	97	105	106	110	114	118	122	Mean
PixelNerf [51]	5.13	8.07	5.85	4.40	7.11	4.64	5.68	6.76	9.05	6.11	3.95	5.92	6.26	6.89	6.93	6.28
IBRNet [45]	2.29	3.70	2.66	1.83	3.02	2.83	1.77	2.28	2.73	1.96	1.87	2.13	1.58	2.05	2.09	2.32
MVSNerf [3]	1.96	3.27	2.54	1.93	2.57	2.71	1.82	1.72	2.29	1.75	1.72	1.47	1.29	2.09	2.26	2.09
Ours	**1.68**	**3.06**	**2.25**	**1.10**	**2.37**	**2.18**	**1.28**	**1.47**	**1.80**	**1.23**	**1.19**	**1.17**	**0.75**	**1.56**	**1.55**	**1.64**
IDR† [50]	4.01	6.40	3.52	1.91	3.96	2.36	4.85	1.62	6.37	5.97	1.23	4.73	0.91	1.72	1.26	3.39
VolSdf [49]	4.03	4.21	6.12	0.91	8.24	1.73	2.74	1.82	5.14	3.09	2.08	4.81	0.60	3.51	2.18	3.41
UniSurf [32]	5.08	7.18	3.96	5.30	4.61	2.24	3.94	3.14	5.63	3.40	5.09	6.38	2.98	4.05	2.81	4.39
Neus [44]	4.57	4.49	3.97	4.32	4.63	1.95	4.68	3.83	4.15	2.50	1.52	6.47	1.26	5.57	6.11	4.00
IBRNet-ft [45]	1.67	2.97	2.26	1.56	2.52	2.30	1.50	2.05	2.02	1.73	1.66	1.63	1.17	1.84	1.61	1.90
Colmap [35]	**0.90**	2.89	1.63	1.08	2.18	1.94	1.61	1.30	2.34	1.28	1.10	1.42	0.76	1.17	**1.14**	1.52
Ours-ft	1.29	**2.27**	**1.57**	**0.88**	**1.61**	1.86	**1.06**	1.27	**1.42**	**1.07**	**0.99**	**0.87**	**0.54**	**1.15**	1.18	**1.27**

† Optimization using extra object masks.

Besides, due to the property of accumulated transmittance in volume rendering, the invisible query samples behind the visible surfaces lack supervision, which causes uncontrollable free surfaces behind the visible surfaces. To enable our framework to generate compact geometry surfaces, we adopt a sparseness regularization term to penalize the uncontrollable free surfaces:

$$\mathcal{L}_{sparse} = \frac{1}{\|\mathbb{Q}\|} \sum_{q \in \mathbb{Q}} \exp\left(-\tau \cdot |s(q)|\right), \tag{6}$$

where $|s(q)|$ is the absolute SDF value of sampled point q, τ is a hyperparameter to rescale the SDF value. This term will encourage the SDF values of the points behind the visible surfaces to be far from 0. When extracting 0-level set SDF to generate mesh, this term can avoid uncontrollable free surfaces.

4 Datasets and Implementation

Datasets. We train our framework on the DTU [11] dataset to learn a generalizable network. We use 15 scenes for testing, same as those used in IDR [50], and the remaining non-overlapping 75 scenes for training. All the evaluation results on the testing scenes are generated using three views with a resolution of 600 × 800, and each scene contains two sets of three images. The foreground masks provided by IDR [50] are used for evaluating the testing scenes. For memory efficiency, we use the center cropped images with resolution of 512 × 640 for training. We observe that the images of DTU dataset contain large black backgrounds and the regions have considerable image noises, so we utilize a simple threshold based denoising strategy to alleviate the noises of such regions in the training images. Optionally, the black backgrounds with zero RGB values can be used as a simple dataset prior to encourage the geometry predictions of such regions to be empty. We further tested on 7 challenging scenes from the BlendedMVS [48] dataset. For each scene, we select one set of three images with

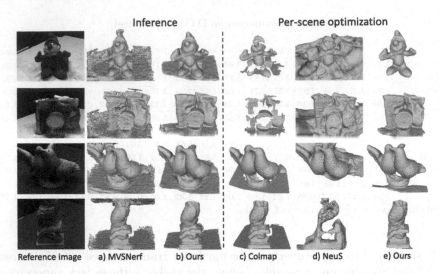

Fig. 3. Visual comparisons on DTU [11] dataset.

a resolution of 768 × 576 as input. Note that, in the per-scene fine-tuning stage, we still use the three images for optimization without any new images.

Implementation Details. Feature Pyramid Network [20] is used as the image feature extraction network to extract multi-scale features from input images. We implement the sparse 3D CNN networks using a U-Net like architecture, and use torchsparse [41] as the implementation of 3D sparse convolution. The resolutions of the coarse level and fine level *geometry encoding* volumes are 96 × 96 × 96 and 192 × 192 × 192 respectively. The patch size used in patch-based blending is 5 × 5. We adopt a two-stage training strategy to train our generic model: in the first stage, the networks of coarse level are first trained for 150k iterations; in the second stage, the networks of fine level are trained for another 150k iterations while the networks of coarse level are fixed. We train our model on two RTX 2080Ti GPUs with a batch size of 512 rays.

5   Experiments

We compare our method with the state-of-the-art approaches from three classes: 1) generic neural rendering methods, including PixelNerf [51], IBRNet [45] and MVSNerf [3], where we use a density threshold to extract meshes from the learned implicit field; 2) per-scene optimization based neural surface reconstruction methods, including IDR [50], NeuS [44], VolSDF [49], and UniSurf [32]; 3) a widely used classic MVS method COLMAP [35], where we reconstruct a mesh from the output point cloud of COLMAP with Screened Poisson Surface Reconstruction [16]. All the methods take three images as input.

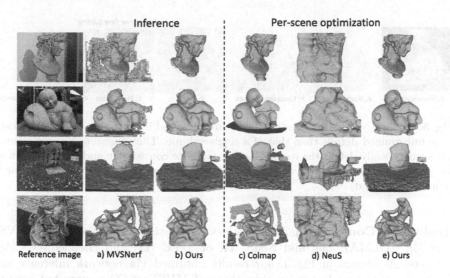

Fig. 4. Visual comparisons on BlendedMVS [48] dataset.

Table 2. Ablation studies on DTU dataset.

Scheme	Setting	Chamfer dist.
Single volume	Generic	1.80
Cas. volumes		1.56
Single volume	Fine-tuning	1.32
Cas. volumes		1.21

(a) The usefulness of Cascaded volumes in both generic and fine-tuning settings.

Pixel	Patch	Consistency	Chamfer dist.
✓	✗	✗	1.39
✓	✓	✗	1.28
✓	✓	✓	1.21

(b) The usefulness of Pixel-based and Patch-based blending, and Consistency-aware scheme in per-scene fine-tuning.

5.1 Comparisons

Quantitative Comparisons. We perform quantitative comparisons with the SOTA methods on DTU dataset. We measure the Chamfer Distances of the predicted meshes with ground truth point clouds, and report the results in Table 1. The results show that our method outperforms the SOTA methods by a large margin in both generic setting and per-scene optimization setting. Our results obtained by a per-scene fine-tuning with 10k iterations (20 min) shows remarkable improvements than those of per-scene optimization methods. Note that IDR [50] needs extra object masks for per-scene optimization while others do not need object masks, and we provide the results of IDR for reference.

We further perform a fine-tuning with 10k iterations for IBRNet and MVS-Nerf with the three input images. With the fine-tuning, the results of IBRNet are improved compared with its generic setting but still worse than our fine-tuned results. MVSNerf fails to perform a fine-tuning with the three input images, therefore, no meaningful geometries are extracted. Furthermore, we observe that MVSNerf usually needs more than 10 images to perform a successful fine-tuning, and thus the failure might be caused by the radiance ambiguity problem.

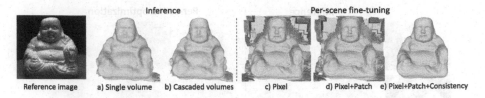

Fig. 5. Qualitative ablation studies. The result obtained by cascaded volumes presents more fine-grained details than that of a single volume. The consistency-aware scheme can automatically detect the regions lacking radiance consistency and exclude them in the fine-tuning, thus yielding cleaner result (e) than the results without consistency-aware scheme (c, d).

Qualitative Comparisons. We conduct qualitative comparisons with MVS-Nerf [3], COLMAP [35] and NeuS [44] on DTU [11] and BlendedMVS [48] datasets. As shown in Fig. 3, our results obtained via network inference are much smoother and less noisy than those of MVSNerf. The extracted meshes of MVSNerf are noisy since its representation of density implicit field does not have sufficient constraint on level sets of 3D geometry surfaces.

After a short-time per-scene fine-tuning, our results are largely improved with fine-grained details and become more accurate and cleaner. Compared with the results of COLMAP, our results are more complete, especially for the objects with weak textures. With only three input images, NeuS suffers from the radiance ambiguity problem and its geometry surfaces are distorted and incomplete.

To validate the generalizability and robustness of our method, we further perform cross dataset evaluation on BlendedMVS dataset. As shown in Fig. 4, although our method is not trained on BlendedMVS, our generic model shows strong generalizability and produces cleaner and more complete results than those of MVSNerf. Take the fourth scene in Fig. 4 as an example, our method successfully recovers subtle details like the hose, while COLMAP misses the fine-grained geometry. For the scenes with weak textures, NeuS can only produces rough shapes and struggles to recover the details of geometry.

5.2   Ablations and Analysis

Ablation Studies. We conduct ablation studies (Table 2 and Fig. 5) to investigate the individual contribution of the important designs of our method. The ablation studies are evaluated on one set of three images of the 15 testing scenes. The first key module is a *multi-level geometry reasoning scheme* for progressively constructing the surface from coarse to fine. Specially, a cascaded volume scheme is proposed, a coarse volume to generate coarse but high-level geometry, a fine volume guided by the coarse level to refine the geometry. As shown in (a) of Table 2, the cascaded volumes scheme considerably boosts the performance of our method than single volume scheme. In Fig. 5, we can see the geometry obtained by cascaded volumes contains more detailed geometry than that of a single volume.

The second important design is a multi-scale color blending strategy, which can enforce the local and contextual radiance consistency of rendered colors and ground truth colors. As shown in (b) of Table 2, the combination of pixel-based and patch-based blending is better than solely using the pixel-based blending. Another important strategy is a consistency-aware scheme that automatically detects the regions lacking photographic consistency and excludes these regions in fine-tuning. As shown in (b) of Table 2 and Fig. 5, result using consistency-aware scheme is noticeably better than those that do not, which is cleaner and gets rid of distorted geometries.

Per-scene Optimization With or Without Priors. Owing to the good initialization provided by the learned priors, the per-scene optimization of our method converges much faster and avoids sub-optimal caused by the radiance ambiguity problem. To validate the effectiveness of the learned priors, we directly perform an optimization without using the learned priors. As shown in Fig. 6, the Chamfer Distance of the result with priors is 1.65 while that without prior-based

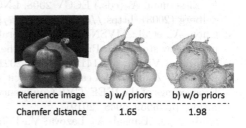

Reference image	a) w/ priors	b) w/o priors
Chamfer distance	1.65	1.98

Fig. 6. Per-scene optimization with priors or without priors.

initialization is 1.98. Obviously, the result with learned priors is more complete and smooth, which shows a stark contrast to the direct optimization.

6 Conclusions

We propose *SparseNeuS*, a novel neural rendering based surface reconstruction method to recover surfaces from multi-view images. Our method generalizes to new scenes and produces high-quality reconstructions with sparse images, which prior works [32,44,49] struggle with. To make our method generalize to new scenes, we therefore introduce *geometry encoding* volumes to encode geometry information for generic geometry reasoning. Moreover, a series of strategies are proposed to handle the difficult sparse views setting. First, we propose a multi-level geometry reasoning framework to recover the surfaces in a coarse-to-fine manner. Second, we adopt a multi-scale color blending scheme, which jointly evaluates local and contextual radiance consistency for more reliable color prediction. Third, a consistency-aware fine-tuning scheme is used to control the inconsistent regions caused by occlusion and image noises, yielding accurate and clean reconstruction. Experiments show our method achieve better performance than the state-of-the-arts in both reconstruction quality and computational efficiency. Due to signed distance field adopted, our method can only produce closed-surfaces reconstructions. Possible future directions include utilizing other representations like unsigned distance field to reconstruct open-surfaces objects.

Acknowledgements. We thank the valuable feedbacks of reviewers. Xiaoxiao Long is supported by Hong Kong PhD Fellowship Scheme.

References

1. Atzmon, M., Lipman, Y.: SAL: sign agnostic learning of shapes from raw data. In: Proceedings of the IEEE/CVF Conference on Computer Vision and Pattern Recognition, pp. 2565–2574 (2020)
2. Campbell, N.D.F., Vogiatzis, G., Hernández, C., Cipolla, R.: Using multiple hypotheses to improve depth-maps for multi-view stereo. In: Forsyth, D., Torr, P., Zisserman, A. (eds.) ECCV 2008. LNCS, vol. 5302, pp. 766–779. Springer, Heidelberg (2008). https://doi.org/10.1007/978-3-540-88682-2_58
3. Chen, A., et al.: MVSNeRF: fast generalizable radiance field reconstruction from multi-view stereo. In: Proceedings of the IEEE/CVF International Conference on Computer Vision, pp. 14124–14133 (2021)
4. Chen, Z., Zhang, H.: Learning implicit fields for generative shape modeling. In: Proceedings of the IEEE/CVF Conference on Computer Vision and Pattern Recognition, pp. 5939–5948 (2019)
5. Chibane, J., Bansal, A., Lazova, V., Pons-Moll, G.: Stereo radiance fields (SRF): learning view synthesis for sparse views of novel scenes. In: Proceedings of the IEEE/CVF Conference on Computer Vision and Pattern Recognition, pp. 7911–7920 (2021)
6. Darmon, F., Bascle, B., Devaux, J.C., Monasse, P., Aubry, M.: Improving neural implicit surfaces geometry with patch warping. arXiv preprint arXiv:2112.09648 (2021)
7. Furukawa, Y., Ponce, J.: Accurate, dense, and robust multiview stereopsis. IEEE Trans. Pattern Anal. Mach. Intell. **32**(8), 1362–1376 (2009)
8. Galliani, S., Lasinger, K., Schindler, K.: Massively parallel multiview stereopsis by surface normal diffusion. In: Proceedings of the IEEE International Conference on Computer Vision, pp. 873–881 (2015)
9. Gropp, A., Yariv, L., Haim, N., Atzmon, M., Lipman, Y.: Implicit geometric regularization for learning shapes. arXiv preprint arXiv:2002.10099 (2020)
10. Gu, X., Fan, Z., Zhu, S., Dai, Z., Tan, F., Tan, P.: Cascade cost volume for high-resolution multi-view stereo and stereo matching. In: Proceedings of the IEEE/CVF Conference on Computer Vision and Pattern Recognition, pp. 2495–2504 (2020)
11. Jensen, R., Dahl, A., Vogiatzis, G., Tola, E., Aanæs, H.: Large scale multi-view stereopsis evaluation. In: Proceedings of the IEEE Conference on Computer Vision and Pattern Recognition, pp. 406–413 (2014)
12. Ji, M., Gall, J., Zheng, H., Liu, Y., Fang, L.: SurfaceNet: an end-to-end 3d neural network for multiview stereopsis. In: Proceedings of the IEEE International Conference on Computer Vision, pp. 2307–2315 (2017)
13. Ji, M., Zhang, J., Dai, Q., Fang, L.: SurfaceNet+: an end-to-end 3d neural network for very sparse multi-view stereopsis. IEEE Trans. Pattern Anal. Mach. Intell. **43**(11), 4078–4093 (2020)
14. Jiang, Y., Ji, D., Han, Z., Zwicker, M.: SDFDiff: differentiable rendering of signed distance fields for 3d shape optimization. In: Proceedings of the IEEE/CVF Conference on Computer Vision and Pattern Recognition, pp. 1251–1261 (2020)
15. Kar, A., Häne, C., Malik, J.: Learning a multi-view stereo machine. In: Advances in Neural Information Processing Systems, vol. 30 (2017)

16. Kazhdan, M., Hoppe, H.: Screened poisson surface reconstruction. ACM Trans. Graph. (ToG) **32**(3), 1–13 (2013)
17. Kellnhofer, P., Jebe, L.C., Jones, A., Spicer, R., Pulli, K., Wetzstein, G.: Neural lumigraph rendering. In: Proceedings of the IEEE/CVF Conference on Computer Vision and Pattern Recognition, pp. 4287–4297 (2021)
18. Kutulakos, K.N., Seitz, S.M.: A theory of shape by space carving. Int. J. Comput. Vision **38**(3), 199–218 (2000)
19. Lhuillier, M., Quan, L.: A quasi-dense approach to surface reconstruction from uncalibrated images. IEEE Trans. Pattern Anal. Mach. Intell. **27**(3), 418–433 (2005)
20. Lin, T.Y., Dollár, P., Girshick, R., He, K., Hariharan, B., Belongie, S.: Feature pyramid networks for object detection. In: Proceedings of the IEEE Conference on Computer Vision and Pattern Recognition, pp. 2117–2125 (2017)
21. Liu, L., Gu, J., Zaw Lin, K., Chua, T.S., Theobalt, C.: Neural sparse voxel fields. Adv. Neural. Inf. Process. Syst. **33**, 15651–15663 (2020)
22. Liu, S., Zhang, Y., Peng, S., Shi, B., Pollefeys, M., Cui, Z.: DIST: rendering deep implicit signed distance function with differentiable sphere tracing. In: Proceedings of the IEEE/CVF Conference on Computer Vision and Pattern Recognition, pp. 2019–2028 (2020)
23. Liu, Y., et al.: Neural rays for occlusion-aware image-based rendering. arXiv preprint arXiv:2107.13421 (2021)
24. Lombardi, S., Simon, T., Saragih, J., Schwartz, G., Lehrmann, A., Sheikh, Y.: Neural volumes: learning dynamic renderable volumes from images. arXiv preprint arXiv:1906.07751 (2019)
25. Long, X., et al.: Adaptive surface normal constraint for depth estimation. In: Proceedings of the IEEE/CVF International Conference on Computer Vision, pp. 12849–12858 (2021)
26. Long, X., Liu, L., Li, W., Theobalt, C., Wang, W.: Multi-view depth estimation using epipolar spatio-temporal networks. In: Proceedings of the IEEE/CVF Conference on Computer Vision and Pattern Recognition, pp. 8258–8267 (2021)
27. Long, X., Liu, L., Theobalt, C., Wang, W.: Occlusion-aware depth estimation with adaptive normal constraints. In: Vedaldi, A., Bischof, H., Brox, T., Frahm, J.-M. (eds.) ECCV 2020. LNCS, vol. 12354, pp. 640–657. Springer, Cham (2020). https://doi.org/10.1007/978-3-030-58545-7_37
28. Mescheder, L., Oechsle, M., Niemeyer, M., Nowozin, S., Geiger, A.: Occupancy networks: learning 3d reconstruction in function space. In: Proceedings of the IEEE/CVF Conference on Computer Vision and Pattern Recognition, pp. 4460–4470 (2019)
29. Michalkiewicz, M., Pontes, J.K., Jack, D., Baktashmotlagh, M., Eriksson, A.: Implicit surface representations as layers in neural networks. In: Proceedings of the IEEE/CVF International Conference on Computer Vision, pp. 4743–4752 (2019)
30. Mildenhall, B., Srinivasan, P.P., Tancik, M., Barron, J.T., Ramamoorthi, R., Ng, R.: NeRF: representing scenes as neural radiance fields for view synthesis. In: Vedaldi, A., Bischof, H., Brox, T., Frahm, J.-M. (eds.) ECCV 2020. LNCS, vol. 12346, pp. 405–421. Springer, Cham (2020). https://doi.org/10.1007/978-3-030-58452-8_24
31. Niemeyer, M., Mescheder, L., Oechsle, M., Geiger, A.: Differentiable volumetric rendering: Learning implicit 3d representations without 3d supervision. In: Proceedings of the IEEE/CVF Conference on Computer Vision and Pattern Recognition, pp. 3504–3515 (2020)

32. Oechsle, M., Peng, S., Geiger, A.: UNISURF: unifying neural implicit surfaces and radiance fields for multi-view reconstruction. In: Proceedings of the IEEE/CVF International Conference on Computer Vision, pp. 5589–5599 (2021)

33. Park, J.J., Florence, P., Straub, J., Newcombe, R., Lovegrove, S.: DeepSDF: learning continuous signed distance functions for shape representation. In: Proceedings of the IEEE/CVF Conference on Computer Vision and Pattern Recognition, pp. 165–174 (2019)

34. Saito, S., Huang, Z., Natsume, R., Morishima, S., Kanazawa, A., Li, H.: PIFu: pixel-aligned implicit function for high-resolution clothed human digitization In: Proceedings of the IEEE/CVF International Conference on Computer Vision, pp. 2304–2314 (2019)

35. Schonberger, J.L., Frahm, J.M.: Structure-from-motion revisited. In: Proceedings of the IEEE Conference on Computer Vision and Pattern Recognition, pp. 4104–4113 (2016)

36. Schönberger, J.L., Zheng, E., Frahm, J.-M., Pollefeys, M.: Pixelwise view selection for unstructured multi-view stereo. In: Leibe, B., Matas, J., Sebe, N., Welling, M. (eds.) ECCV 2016. LNCS, vol. 9907, pp. 501–518. Springer, Cham (2016). https://doi.org/10.1007/978-3-319-46487-9_31

37. Seitz, S.M., Dyer, C.R.: Photorealistic scene reconstruction by voxel coloring. Int. J. Comput. Vision **35**(2), 151–173 (1999)

38. Sitzmann, V., Thies, J., Heide, F., Nießner, M., Wetzstein, G., Zollhofer, M.: DeepVoxels: learning persistent 3d feature embeddings. In: Proceedings of the IEEE/CVF Conference on Computer Vision and Pattern Recognition, pp. 2437–2446 (2019)

39. Sitzmann, V., Zollhöfer, M., Wetzstein, G.: Scene representation networks: continuous 3d-structure-aware neural scene representations. In: Advances in Neural Information Processing Systems, vol. 32 (2019)

40. Sun, J., Xie, Y., Chen, L., Zhou, X., Bao, H.: NeuralRecon: real-time coherent 3d reconstruction from monocular video. In: Proceedings of the IEEE/CVF Conference on Computer Vision and Pattern Recognition, pp. 15598–15607 (2021)

41. Tang, H., et al.: Searching efficient 3D architectures with sparse point-voxel convolution. In: Vedaldi, A., Bischof, H., Brox, T., Frahm, J.-M. (eds.) ECCV 2020. LNCS, vol. 12373, pp. 685–702. Springer, Cham (2020). https://doi.org/10.1007/978-3-030-58604-1_41

42. Tola, E., Strecha, C., Fua, P.: Efficient large-scale multi-view stereo for ultra high-resolution image sets. Mach. Vis. Appl. **23**(5), 903–920 (2012)

43. Trevithick, A., Yang, B.: GRF: learning a general radiance field for 3d representation and rendering. In: Proceedings of the IEEE/CVF International Conference on Computer Vision, pp. 15182–15192 (2021)

44. Wang, P., Liu, L., Liu, Y., Theobalt, C., Komura, T., Wang, W.: NeuS: learning neural implicit surfaces by volume rendering for multi-view reconstruction. In: Advances in Neural Information Processing Systems, vol. 34 (2021)

45. Wang, Q., et al.: IBRNet: learning multi-view image-based rendering. In: Proceedings of the IEEE/CVF Conference on Computer Vision and Pattern Recognition, pp. 4690–4699 (2021)

46. Yao, Y., Luo, Z., Li, S., Fang, T., Quan, L.: MVSNet: depth inference for unstructured multi-view stereo. In: Ferrari, V., Hebert, M., Sminchisescu, C., Weiss, Y. (eds.) ECCV 2018. LNCS, vol. 11212, pp. 785–801. Springer, Cham (2018). https://doi.org/10.1007/978-3-030-01237-3_47

47. Yao, Y., Luo, Z., Li, S., Shen, T., Fang, T., Quan, L.: Recurrent MVSNet for high-resolution multi-view stereo depth inference. In: Proceedings of the IEEE/CVF Conference on Computer Vision and Pattern Recognition, pp. 5525–5534 (2019)
48. Yao, Y., et al.: BlendedMVS: a large-scale dataset for generalized multi-view stereo networks. In: Proceedings of the IEEE/CVF Conference on Computer Vision and Pattern Recognition, pp. 1790–1799 (2020)
49. Yariv, L., Gu, J., Kasten, Y., Lipman, Y.: Volume rendering of neural implicit surfaces. In: Advances in Neural Information Processing Systems, vol. 34 (2021)
50. Yariv, L., et al.: Multiview neural surface reconstruction by disentangling geometry and appearance. Adv. Neural. Inf. Process. Syst. **33**, 2492–2502 (2020)
51. Yu, A., Ye, V., Tancik, M., Kanazawa, A.: pixelNeRF: neural radiance fields from one or few images. In: Proceedings of the IEEE/CVF Conference on Computer Vision and Pattern Recognition, pp. 4578–4587 (2021)
52. Zhang, J., Yao, Y., Quan, L.: Learning signed distance field for multi-view surface reconstruction. In: Proceedings of the IEEE/CVF International Conference on Computer Vision, pp. 6525–6534 (2021)

Disentangling Object Motion and Occlusion for Unsupervised Multi-frame Monocular Depth

Ziyue Feng[1] , Liang Yang[2(✉)], Longlong Jing[2], Haiyan Wang[2], YingLi Tian[2], and Bing Li[1(✉)]

[1] Clemson University, Clemson, USA
bli4@clemson.edu
[2] City University of New York, New York, USA
lyang1@ccny.cuny.edu

Abstract. Conventional self-supervised monocular depth prediction methods are based on a static environment assumption, which leads to accuracy degradation in dynamic scenes due to the mismatch and occlusion problems introduced by object motions. Existing dynamic-object-focused methods only partially solved the mismatch problem at the training loss level. In this paper, we accordingly propose a novel multi-frame monocular depth prediction method to solve these problems at both the prediction and supervision loss levels. Our method, called DynamicDepth, is a new framework trained via a self-supervised cycle consistent learning scheme. A Dynamic Object Motion Disentanglement (DOMD) module is proposed to disentangle object motions to solve the mismatch problem. Moreover, novel occlusion-aware Cost Volume and Re-projection Loss are designed to alleviate the occlusion effects of object motions. Extensive analyses and experiments on the Cityscapes and KITTI datasets show that our method significantly outperforms the state-of-the-art monocular depth prediction methods, especially in the areas of dynamic objects. Code is available at https://github.com/AutoAILab/DynamicDepth

1 Introduction

3D environmental information is crucial for autonomous vehicles, robots, and AR/VR applications. Self-supervised monocular depth prediction [8,9,11,29] provides an efficient solution to retrieve 3D information from a single camera without requiring expensive sensors or labeled data. In recent years these methods are getting more and more popular in both the research and industry communities.

Supplementary Information The online version contains supplementary material available at https://doi.org/10.1007/978-3-031-19824-3_14.

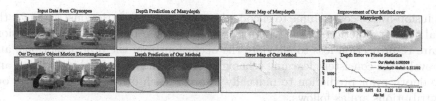

Fig. 1. Conventional monocular depth prediction methods like manydepth [35] makes severe mistakes on dynamic object areas due to mismatch and occlusion problems introduced by object motions. Our method achieved significant improvement with our proposed dynamic object motion disentanglement and occlusion alleviation.

Conventional self-supervised monocular depth prediction methods [8,9,11] take a single image as input and predicts the dense depth map. They generally use a re-projection loss which constraints the geometric consistency between adjacent frames in the training loss level, but they are not capable of geometric reasoning through temporal frames in the network prediction level, which limits their overall performance (Fig. 1).

Temporal and spatially continuous images are available in most real-world scenarios like autonomous vehicles [3,24] or smart devices [13,16]. Recent years multi-frame monocular depth prediction methods [4,26,33,35–37] are proposed to utilize the temporal image sequences to improve the depth prediction accuracy. Cost-volume-based methods [35,36] adopted the cost volume from stereo match tasks to enable the geometric reasoning through temporal image sequences in the network prediction level, and achieved overall state-of-the-art depth prediction accuracy while not requiring time-consuming recurrent networks.

However, both the re-projection loss function and the cost volume construction are based on the static environment assumption, which does not hold for most real-world scenarios. Object motion will violate this assumption and cause re-projection mismatch and occlusion problems. The cost volume and loss values in the dynamic object areas are unable to reflect the quality of depth hypothesis and prediction, which will mislead the model training. Recent work [9,18,19,22] attempted to optimize depth prediction of dynamic object areas and achieved noticeable improvements, but they still have several drawbacks. (1) They only solve the mismatch problem at the loss function level, still cannot reason geometric constraints through temporal frames for dynamic objects, which limits its accuracy potential. (2) The occlusion problem introduced by object motions is still unsolved. (3) Redundant object motion prediction networks increased the model complexity and does not work for the motions of non-rigid objects.

Pursuing accurate and generic depth prediction, we propose DynamicDepth, a self-supervised temporal depth prediction framework that disentangles the dynamic object motions. First, we predict a depth prior from the target frame and project to the reference frames for an implicit estimation of object motion without rigidity assumption, which is later disentangled by our Dynamic Object Motion Disentanglement (DOMD) module. We then build a multi-frame occlusion-aware cost volume to encode the temporal geometric constraints for the final depth prediction. In the training level, we further propose a novel occlusion-aware re-projection loss to alleviate the occlusion from the object motions, and a novel cycle consistent learning scheme to enable the final depth prediction and the depth prior prediction to mutually improve each other. To summarize, our contributions are as follows:

- We propose a novel Dynamic Object Motion Disentanglement (DOMD) module which leverages an initial depth prior prediction to solve the object motion mismatch problem in the final depth prediction.
- We devise a Dynamic Object Cycle Consistent training scheme to mutually reinforce the Prior Depth and the Final Depth prediction.
- We design an Occlusion-aware Cost Volume to enable geometric reasoning across temporal frames even in object motion occluded areas, and a novel Occlusion-aware Re-projection Loss to alleviate the motion occlusion problem in training supervision.
- Our method significantly outperforms existing state-of-the-art methods on the Cityscapes [3] and KITTI [24] datasets.

2   Related Work

In this section, we review self-supervised depth prediction approaches relevant to our proposed method in the following three categories: (1) single-frame, (2) multi-frame, (3) dynamic-objects-optimized.

Self-supervised Single-Frame Monocular Depth Prediction: Due to the limited availability of labeled depth data, self-supervised monocular depth prediction methods [1,8,9,11,21,29] have become more and more popular. Mon-odepth2 [9] set a benchmark for robust monocular depth, FeatDepth [29] tried to improve the low-texture area depth prediction, and PackNet [11] explored a more effective network backbone. These self-supervised depth models generally take a single frame as input and predict the dense depth map. In the training stage, the temporally neighboring frames are projected to the current image plane by the predicted depth map. If the prediction is accurate, the re-projected images are supposed to be identical to the actual current frame image. The training is based on enforcing the re-projection photo-metric [34] consistency.

These methods provided a successful paradigm to learn the depth prediction without labeled data, but they have a major and common problem with dynamic objects: the re-projection loss function assumes the environment is static, which does not hold for real-world applications. When objects are moving, even if the prediction is perfect, the re-projected reference image will still not match the target frame image. The loss signal from the dynamic object areas will generate misleading gradients to degrade the model performance. In contrast, our proposed Dynamic Object Motion Disentanglement solves this mismatch problem and achieves superior accuracy, especially in the dynamic object areas.

Multi-frame Monocular Depth Prediction: The above mentioned re-projection loss only uses temporal constraints at the training loss function level. The model itself does not take any temporal information as input for reasoning, which limits its performance. One promising way to improve self-supervised monocular depth prediction is to leverage the temporal information in the input and prediction stage. Early works [4,26,33,37] explored recurrent networks to process image sequences for monocular depth prediction. These recurrent models are computationally expensive and do not explicitly encode and reason geometric constraints in their prediction. Recently, Manydepth [35] and MonoRec [36] adopt the cost volumes from stereo matching tasks to enable the geometric-based reasoning during inference. They project the reference frame feature map to the current image plane with multiple pre-defined depth hypothesises, whose difference to the current frame feature maps are stacked to form the cost volume. Hypothesises which are closer to the actual depth are supposed to have a lower value in the cost volume, while the entire cost volume is supposed to encode the inverse probability distribution of the actual depth value. With this integrated cost volume, they achieve great overall performance improvement while preserving real-time efficiency.

However, the construction of the cost volume relies on the static environment assumption as well, which leads to catastrophic failure in the dynamic object area. They either circumvent this problem [36] or simply use a $L1$ loss [35] to mimic the prediction of the single-frame model, which makes less severe mistakes for dynamic objects. This $L1$ loss alleviates but does not actually solve the problem. Our proposed Dynamic Object Motion Disentanglement, Occlusion-aware Cost Volume, and Re-projection Loss solve the mismatch and occlusion problem at both the reasoning and the training loss levels and outperform all other methods, especially in the dynamic object areas.

Dynamic Objects in Self-supervised Depth Prediction: The research community has attempted to solve the above-mentioned ill-posed re-projection geometry for dynamic objects. SGDepth [18] tried to exclude the moving objects from the loss function, Li *et al.* [22] proposed to build a dataset only containing non-moving dynamic-category objects. The latest state-of-the-art methods [1,7, 10,19–21] tried to predict pixel-level or object-level translation and incorporate it into the loss function re-projection geometry.

However, these methods still have several drawbacks. First, their single frame input did not enable the model to reason from the temporal domain. Second, explicitly predicting object motions requires redundant models and increased complexity. Third, they only focused on the re-projection mismatch, the occlusion problem introduced by object motions is still unsolved. Our proposed Dynamic Object Motion Disentanglement works at both the cost volume and the loss function levels, solving the re-projection mismatch problem while enabling the geometric reasoning through temporal frames in the inference stage, without additional explicit object motion prediction. Furthermore, we propose Occlusion-aware Cost Volume and Occlusion-aware Re-projection Loss to solve the occlusion problem introduced by object motion.

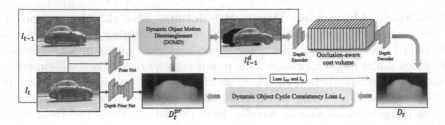

Fig. 2. DynamicDepth Architecture: The inputs are images I_{t-1} and I_t, from which dynamic-object-disentangled frame I_{t-1}^d is generated by the DOMD module for the final depth prediction D_t. The occlusion-aware cost volume is constructed to facilitate geometric reasoning and the dynamic object cycle consistency loss is devised for mutual reinforcement between D_t and D_t^{pr}. Green arrows indicates knowledge flow. (Color figure online)

3 Method

3.1 Overview

Given two images $I_{t-1} \in R^{W \times H \times 3}$ and $I_t \in R^{W \times H \times 3}$ of a target scene, our purpose is to estimate a dense depth map D_t of I_t by taking advantage of two views' observations while solving the mismatch and occlusion problems introduced by object motions.

As shown in Fig. 2, our model contains three major innovations: We first use a Depth Prior Net θ_{DPN} and Pose Net θ_p to predict an initial depth prior D_t^{pr} and ego-motion, which is sent to the (1) Dynamic Object Motion Disentanglement (DOMD) to solve the object motion mismatch problem (see Sect. 3.2). The disentangled frame I_{t-1}^d and the current frame I_t are encoded by the Depth Encoder to construct the (2) Occlusion-aware Cost Volume for reasoning through temporal frames while diminishing the motion occlusion problem (see Sect. 3.3). The final depth prediction D_t is generated by the Depth Decoder from our cost volume. During training, our (3) Dynamic Object Cycle Consistency Loss L_c enables the mutual improvement of the depth prior D_t^{pr} and the final depth prediction D_t, while our Occlusion-aware Re-projection Loss L_{or} solved the object motion occlusion problem (see Sect. 3.4).

3.2 Dynamic Object Motion Disentanglement (DOMD)

There is an observation [1,9] that single-frame monocular depth prediction models suffer from dynamic objects, which cause even more severe problems in multi-frame methods [35,36]. This is because the static environment assumption does not hold for dynamic objects, which introduce mismatch and occlusion problems. Here, we describe our DOMD to solve the mismatch problem.

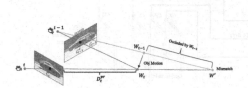 

Fig. 3. Dynamic Object Motion Disentanglement: A dynamic object moves from W_{t-1} to W_t, C_{t-1} and C_t are corresponding image patches. D_t^{pr} is our depth prior prediction. Conventional methods tend to mismatch at W'. We re-project C_t to C_{t-1}^d with depth prior D_t^{pr} to replace C_{t-1} to disentangle the object motion. This solves the mismatch problem, making our cost volume and re-projection loss correctly converge at W_t.

Fig. 4. Dynamic object motion disentangled image: Left is the I_{t-1}^d when depth prior is accurate. The right blue image patch shows the re-projected C_{t-1}^d with inaccurate depth prior. (Color figure online)

Why the Cost Volume and Self-supervision Mismatch on Dynamic Objects: Either in the cost volume or re-projection loss function, the current frame feature map F_t or image I_t is projected to the 3D space and re-projected back to the reference frame $t-1$ by the depth hypothesis or predictions. We illustrate the re-projection geometry in Fig. 3. The dynamic object moves from W_{t-1} to W_t, its corresponding image patches are C_{t-1} and C_t respectively. Conventional methods suppose the photo-metric difference between C_{t-1} and the re-projected C_t is lowest when the depth prediction or hypothesis is correctly close to W_t. However, due to the object motions, image or feature patches tend to mismatch at W' instead: $E(C_{t-1}, \pi_{t-1}(W')) < E(C_{t-1}, \pi_{t-1}(W_t))$, π is the projection operator. This mismatch misleads the reasoning in the cost volume and the supervision in the re-projection loss.

Dynamic Object Motion Disentanglement: Our DOMD module M_o takes two image frames (I_{t-1}, I_t) with its dynamic category (*e.g.*,vehicle, people, bike) segmentation masks (S_{t-1}, S_t) as input to generate the disentangled image I_{t-1}^d.

$$M_o : (I_t, I_{t-1}, S_{t-1}, S_t) \mapsto I_{t-1}^d. \quad (1)$$

We first use a single-frame depth prior network θ_{DPN} to predict an initial depth prior D_t^{pr}. As shown in Fig. 3, the D_t^{pr} is used to re-project the dynamic object image patch C_t to C_{t-1}^d, which indicates the $t-1$ camera perspective of the dynamic object at location W_t. Finally, we replace the C_{t-1} with C_{t-1}^d to form the dynamic object motion disentangled image I_{t-1}^d. Note that we do not require the rigidity of the dynamic object.

$$C_a = I_a \cdot S_a, \quad C_{t-1}^d = \pi_{t-1}(\pi_t^{-1}(C_t, D_t^{pr})), \quad I_{t-1}^d = I_{t-1}(C_{t-1} \rightarrow C_{t-1}^d). \quad (2)$$

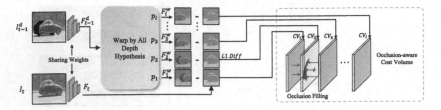

Fig. 5. Occlusion-aware Cost Volume: Feature map F_{t-1}^d of the I_{t-1}^d is warped to the I_t plane with multiple pre-defined depth hypothesizes P_i to construct the cost volume. The black area in the cost volume indicates the noise from object motion occlusion, which is replaced with the nearby non-occluded area to avoid polluting the cost distribution. (Color figure online)

Our Multi-frame model θ_{MF} then construct the geometric constraint in the cost volume with the disentangled image frame I_{t-1}^d and current image frame I_t to predict the final depth D_t.

We further propose a Dynamic Object Cycle Consistency Loss L_c (Details in Sect. 3.4 and Sect. 4.4.) to enable the D_t to backward supervise the D_t^{pr} training. Both the D_t^{pr} and D_t could be greatly improved with our cycle consistent learning. Our θ_{DPN} already outperforms the existing dynamic-object-focused state-of-the-art methods such as InstaDM [19] with joint and cycle consistent learning.

Why Final Depth Improves Over Depth Prior: As shown in Fig. 4, when the depth prior prediction is inaccurate, the re-projected image patch C_{t-1}^d will occlude some background pixels which are visible at time t. Those pixels will generate a higher photometric error in the re-projection loss. To minimize it, the network will manage to decode the error of depth prior from the disentangled image I_{t-1}^d to predict a better final depth to improve the depth prior prediction by our later introduced cycle-consistency loss.

3.3 Occlusion-Aware Cost Volume

To encode the geometric constraints through the temporal frames while solving the occlusion problem introduced by dynamic objects motions, we propose an Occlusion-aware Cost Volume $CV^{occ} \in R^{|P| \times W \times H \times C}$, where $P = \{p_1, p_2, ..., p_{|P|}\}$ is the pre-defined depth hypothesis, C is the channel number.

As shown in Fig. 5, we warp the feature map F_{t-1}^d of the dynamic object disentangled image I_{t-1}^d to the current frame image plane with all pre-defined depth hypothesis P. The cost volume layer CV_i is the $L1$ difference between the warped feature map F_i^w and the current frame feature map F_t. We obtain the cost volume CV by stacking all the layers. For each pixel, the cost value is supposed to be lower when the corresponding depth hypothesis is closer to the actual depth. The cost values over different depth hypotheses are supposed to encode the inverse probability distribution of the actual depth.

$$CV_i = |F_t - F_i^w|_1, \qquad F_i^w = \pi_t(\pi_{t-1}^{-1}(F_{t-1}^d, p_i)). \qquad (3)$$

In Fig. 5, the black area in the image I_{t-1}^d corresponds to the backgrounds which may be visible at time t but are occluded by the dynamic object at time $t-1$. The $L1$ difference between the feature of backgrounds at time t and the feature of black pixels is meaningless, which pollutes the distribution of the cost volume. We propose to replace these values with non-occluded area cost values from neighboring depth hypothesis p'. This preserves the global cost distribution and leads the training gradients flow to the nearby non-occluded areas. Our ablation study in Sect. 4 confirms the effectiveness of our design.

$$CV_{p,w,h}^{occ} = \begin{cases} CV_{p,w,h}, & \text{if } F_{p,w,h}^w \in V, \\ CV_{p',w,h}, & \text{if } F_{p,w,h}^w \in O, F_{p',w,h}^w \in V, p' \in r, \end{cases} \qquad (4)$$

where O/V are the set of occluded/visible areas in F^w, r is the neighbors of p.

3.4 Loss Functions

During the training of our framework, our proposed Occlusion-aware Re-projection Loss L_{or} enforces the re-projection consistency between adjacent frames while alleviating the influence of the object-motion-caused occlusion problem. Our joint learning and novel Dynamic Object Cycle Consistency Loss L_c further enables the depth prior prediction D_t^{pr} and final depth prediction D_t to mutually reinforce each other to achieve the best performance.

Dynamic Object Cycle Consistency Loss: As shown in Fig. 2, during the self-supervised learning, our initial depth prior prediction D_t^{pr} is used in our Dynamic Object Motion Disentanglement (DOMD) module to produce the motion disentangled reference frame I_{t-1}^d which is later encoded in our Occlusion-aware Cost Volume to guide the final depth prediction D_t. To enable the multi-frame final depth D_t to backward guide the learning of single-frame depth prior D_t^{pr} to achieve a mutual reinforcement scheme, we propose a novel Dynamic Object Cycle Consistency Loss L_c to enforce the consistency between D_t and D_t^{pr}.

Since only the dynamic objects area of D_t^{pr} are employed in our DOMD module, we only apply the Dynamic Object Cycle Consistency Loss L_c at these areas and only active when the inconsistency is large enough:

$$A = \{i \in I_t | \frac{\left|D_t^i - D_t^{pr,i}\right|_1}{\min\{D_t^i, D_t^{pr,i}\}} > 1\}, \qquad (5)$$

$$L_c = \frac{1}{|A \cap S|} \sum_{i \in (A \cap S)} \left|D_t^i - D_t^{pr,i}\right|_1. \qquad (6)$$

where S is the semantic segmentation mask of dynamic category objects.

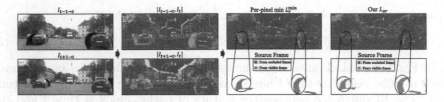

Fig. 0. Occlusion-aware Re-projection Loss: Using the non-occluded source pixels for the re-projection loss could avoid most occlusions. The widely-used [9,20,35] per-pixel minimum L_r^{min} fails when the occluded pixels do not have lower photo-metric error. We propose Occlusion-aware Re-projection Loss L_{or} to solve this problem.

Occlusion-Aware Re-projection Loss: In self-supervised monocular depth prediction, the image from reference frames (I_{t-1}, I_{t+1}) are warped to the current image plane with the predicted depth map D_t. If the depth prediction is correct, the conventional re-projection loss L_r supposes the warped image $(I_{t-1 \to t}, I_{t+1 \to t})$ to be identical with the current frame image I_t. They penalize the photo-metric error E between them.

$$\hat{E}_a = E(I_t, I_{a \to t}), \qquad L_r = \frac{1}{2}(\hat{E}_{t-1} + \hat{E}_{t+1}). \tag{7}$$

As mentioned above, the dynamic object motions break the static environment assumption and lead to the mismatch problem in this re-projection geometry. Our Dynamic Object Motion Disentanglement (DOMD) module M_o could solve this mismatch problem but the background pixels occluded by the dynamic object at reference time $(t-1, t+1)$ are still missing. As shown in Fig. 6, using the photo-metric error E between these occluded pixels in the warped image $((I_{t-1 \to t}, I_{t+1 \to t}))$ and visible background pixels in I_t as training loss only introduces noise and misleads the model learning.

Fortunately, object motions are normally consistent in a short time window, which means the backgrounds occluded at time $t-1$ are usually visible at time $t+1$ and vise-versa. It is possible to switch the source frame between $t-1$ and $t+1$ for each pixel to avoid the occlusion. The widely used per-pixel minimum re-projection loss [9] L_r^{min} assumes the visible source pixels will have lower photo-metric error than the occluded ones, they thus proposed to choose the minimum error source frame for each pixel: $L_r^{min} = \frac{1}{|I_t|} \sum_{i \in I_t} min(\hat{E}_{t-1}^i, \hat{E}_{t+1}^i)$.

However, in practice, as shown in the right columns of Fig. 6 we observe that around half of the visible source pixels do not have a lower photo-metric error than the occluded source. Since we can obtain the exact occlusion mask O and visible mask V from our DOMD module M_o, we propose Occlusion-aware Re-projection Loss L_{or}, which always choose the non-occluded source frame pixels for photo-metric error. More details are in the supplementary materials.

Following [8,38], a combination of L1 norm and SSIM [34] with coefficient γ is used as our photo-metric error E_p. The SSIM takes the pixels within a local window into account for error computation. In $I_{t-1 \to t}$ and $I_{t+1 \to t}$ the occluded

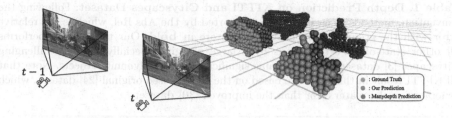

Fig. 7. Error Visualization: In the left $t-1$ image, red image patch is the original data used by the Manydepth [35] while the blue patch is generated by the DOMD module for our prediction. We project the dynamic object depths into point clouds. Our prediction matches the ground truth better. (Color figure online)

pixels thus influence the neighboring non-occluded pixel's SSIM error. We propose Occlusion Masking M_a, which paints the corresponding pixels in target frame I_t to be black when calculating the SSIM error with reference frames. This neutralizes the influence of the occlusion areas on neighboring pixels in SSIM. The ablation study in Sect. 4.4 confirms applying our source pixel switching and occlusion masking mechanisms together makes the best improvement in the depth prediction quality.

$$E_p[I_a, I_b] = \frac{\gamma}{2}(1 - \text{SSIM}(I_a, I_b)) + (1-\gamma)|I_a - I_b|_1 \,. \tag{8}$$

$$EO_{t'} = E_p[M_a(I_t), I_{t' \to t}], \tag{9}$$

We further adopt the edge-aware metric from [31] into our smoothness loss L_s to make it invariant to output scale, which is formulated as:

$$L_s = |\partial_x d_t^*| e^{-|\partial_x I_t|} + |\partial_y d_t^*| e^{-|\partial_y I_t|}, \tag{10}$$

where $d_t^* = d_t/\overline{d_t}$ is the mean-normalized inverse depth, ∂ is the image gradient.

Our final loss L is the sum of our Dynamic Object Cycle Consistency Loss L_c, Occlusion-aware Re-projection Loss L_{or}, and smoothness loss L_s:

$$L = L_c + L_{or} + 1e^{-3} \cdot L_s. \tag{11}$$

4 Experiments

The experiments are mainly focused on the challenging Cityscapes [3] dataset, which contains many dynamic objects. To comprehensively compare with more state-of-the-art methods, we also report the performance on the widely-used KITTI [24] dataset. Since our method is mainly focused on the dynamic objects, we further conduct additional evaluation on the depth errors of the dynamic objects areas, which clearly demonstrate the effectiveness of our method. The design decision and the effectiveness of our proposed framework is evaluated by an extensive ablation study.

Table 1. Depth Prediction on KITTI and Cityscapes Dataset. Following the convention, methods in each category are sorted by the Abs Rel, which is the relative error with the ground truth. Best methods are in **bold**. Our method out-performs all other state-of-the-art methods by a large margin especially on the challenging Cityscapes [3] dataset, which contains significantly more dynamic objects. Note that all KITTI result in this table are based on the widely-used original [24] dataset, which generates much greater error than the improved [30] dataset.

	Method	Test frames	WxH	The lower the better				The higher the better		
				Abs Rel	Sq Rel	RMSE	RMSE log	$\delta < 1.25$	$\delta < 1.25^2$	$\delta < 1.25^3$
KITTI	Ranjan et al.[28]	1	832 x 256	0.148	1.149	5.464	0.226	0.815	0.935	0.973
	EPC++ [23]	1	832 x 256	0.141	1.029	5.350	0.216	0.816	0.941	0.976
	Struct2depth (M) [1]	1	416 x 128	0.141	1.026	5.291	0.215	0.816	0.945	0.979
	Li et al.[21]	1	416 x 128	0.130	0.950	5.138	0.209	0.843	0.948	0.978
	Videos in the wild [10]	1	416 x 128	0.128	0.959	5.230	0.212	0.845	0.947	0.976
	Monodepth2 [9]	1	640 x 192	0.115	0.903	4.863	0.193	0.877	0.959	0.981
	Lee et al. [20]	1	832 x 256	0.114	0.876	4.715	0.191	0.872	0.955	0.981
	InstaDM [19]	1	832 x 256	0.112	0.777	4.772	0.191	0.872	0.959	0.982
	Packnet-SFM [11]	1	640 x 192	0.111	0.785	4.601	0.189	0.878	0.960	0.982
	Johnston et al. [15]	1	640 x 192	0.106	0.861	4.699	0.185	0.889	0.962	0.982
	Guizilini et al.[12]	1	640 x 192	0.102	0.698	4.381	0.178	0.896	0.964	0.984
	Patil et al.[26]	N	640 x 192	0.111	0.821	4.650	0.187	0.883	0.961	0.982
	Wang et al.[32]	2 (-1, 0)	640 x 192	0.106	0.799	4.662	0.187	0.889	0.961	0.982
	ManyDepth [35]	2 (-1, 0)	640 x 192	0.098	0.770	4.459	0.176	**0.900**	**0.965**	0.983
	DynamicDepth	2 (-1, 0)	640 x 192	**0.096**	**0.720**	**4.458**	**0.175**	0.897	0.964	**0.984**
Cityscapes	Pilzer et al.[27]	1	512 x 256	0.240	4.264	8.049	0.334	0.710	0.871	0.937
	Struct2Depth 2 [2]	1	416 x 128	0.145	1.737	7.280	0.205	0.813	0.942	0.976
	Monodepth2 [9]	1	416 x 128	0.129	1.569	6.876	0.187	0.849	0.957	0.983
	Videos in the Wild [10]	1	416 x 128	0.127	1.330	6.960	0.195	0.830	0.947	0.981
	Li et al.[21]	1	416 x 128	0.119	1.290	6.980	0.190	0.846	0.952	0.982
	Lee et al. [20]	1	832 x 256	0.116	1.213	6.695	0.186	0.852	0.951	0.982
	InstaDM [19]	1	832 x 256	0.111	1.158	6.437	0.182	0.868	0.961	0.983
	Struct2Depth 2 [2]	3 (-1, 0, +1)	416 x 128	0.151	2.492	7.024	0.202	0.826	0.937	0.972
	ManyDepth [35]	2 (-1, 0)	416 x 128	0.114	1.193	6.223	0.170	0.875	0.967	0.989
	DynamicDepth	2 (-1, 0)	416 x 128	**0.103**	**1.000**	**5.867**	**0.157**	**0.895**	**0.974**	**0.991**

4.1 Implementation Details:

We use frames $\{I_{t-1}, I_t, I_{t+1}\}$ for training and $\{I_{t-1}, I_t\}$ for testing. All dynamic objects is this paper are determined by an off-the-shelf semantic segmentation model EffcientPS [25]. Note that we do not need instance-level masks and inter-frame correspondences, all dynamic category pixels are projected together at once. All network modules including the depth prior net θ_{DPN} are trained together from scratch or ImageNet [5] pre-training. ResNet18 [14] is used as the backbone. We use the Adam [17] optimizer with a learning rate of 10^{-4} to train for 10 epochs, which takes about 10 hours on a single Nvidia A100 GPU.

4.2 Cityscapes Results

Cityscapes [3] is a challenging dataset with significant amount of dynamic objects. It contains $5,000$ videos each with 30 frames, totaling $150,000$ image frames. We exclude the first, last, and static-camera frames in each video for

Table 2. Depth Error on Dynamic Objects. We evaluate the depth prediction errors of dynamic objects (*e.g.*,Vehicles, Person, Bike) on KITTI [24] and Cityscapes [3] datasets. The best results are in **bold**, second best are underlined. Our depth prior prediction D_t^{pr} already outperform the state-of-the-art method InstaDM [19] using the same single frame input, while our final depth prediction D_t sets a new benchmark.

<table>
<thead>
<tr><th rowspan="2"></th><th rowspan="2">Method</th><th rowspan="2">WxH</th><th colspan="4">The lower the better</th><th colspan="3">The higher the better</th></tr>
<tr><th>Abs Rel</th><th>Sq Rel</th><th>RMSE</th><th>RMSE log</th><th>$\delta < 1.25$</th><th>$\delta < 1.25^2$</th><th>$\delta < 1.25^3$</th></tr>
</thead>
<tbody>
<tr><td rowspan="5">KITTI</td><td>Monodepth2 [9]</td><td>640 x 192</td><td>0.169</td><td>1.878</td><td>5.711</td><td>0.271</td><td>0.805</td><td>0.909</td><td>0.944</td></tr>
<tr><td>InstaDM [19]</td><td>832 x 256</td><td><u>0.151</u></td><td><u>1.314</u></td><td>5.546</td><td>0.271</td><td>0.805</td><td>0.905</td><td>0.946</td></tr>
<tr><td>ManyDepth [35]</td><td>640 x 192</td><td>0.175</td><td>2.000</td><td>5.830</td><td>0.278</td><td>0.776</td><td>0.895</td><td>0.943</td></tr>
<tr><td>**Our Depth Prior**</td><td>640 x 192</td><td>0.155</td><td>1.317</td><td><u>5.253</u></td><td><u>0.269</u></td><td>0.805</td><td><u>0.908</u></td><td><u>0.946</u></td></tr>
<tr><td>**DynamicDepth**</td><td>640 x 192</td><td>**0.150**</td><td>**1.313**</td><td>**5.146**</td><td>**0.264**</td><td>**0.807**</td><td>**0.915**</td><td>**0.949**</td></tr>
<tr><td rowspan="5">Cityscapes</td><td>Monodepth2 [9]</td><td>416 x 128</td><td>0.159</td><td>1.937</td><td>6.363</td><td>0.201</td><td>0.816</td><td>0.950</td><td>0.981</td></tr>
<tr><td>InstaDM [19]</td><td>832 x 256</td><td>0.139</td><td>1.698</td><td>5.760</td><td>0.181</td><td><u>0.859</u></td><td>0.959</td><td>0.982</td></tr>
<tr><td>ManyDepth [35]</td><td>416 x 128</td><td>0.169</td><td>2.175</td><td>6.634</td><td>0.218</td><td>0.789</td><td>0.921</td><td>0.969</td></tr>
<tr><td>**Our Depth Prior**</td><td>416 x 128</td><td><u>0.137</u></td><td><u>1.285</u></td><td><u>4.674</u></td><td><u>0.174</u></td><td>0.852</td><td><u>0.961</u></td><td><u>0.985</u></td></tr>
<tr><td>**DynamicDepth**</td><td>416 x 128</td><td>**0.129**</td><td>**1.273**</td><td>**4.626**</td><td>**0.168**</td><td>**0.862**</td><td>**0.965**</td><td>**0.986**</td></tr>
</tbody>
</table>

training, resulting in 58, 335 frames training data. The official testing set contains 1, 525 image frames.

Table 1 shows the depth prediction results on the Cityscapes [3] testing set. Following the convention, we rank all methods based on the absolute-relative-errors. Since the Cityscapes dataset contains significant amount of dynamic objects, the object-motion-optimized method InstaDM [19] achieved the best accuracy among all the existing methods. With the help of our proposed Dynamic Object Motion Disentanglement (DOMD), Dynamic Object Cycle Consistency Loss, Occlusion-aware Cost Volume and the Occlusion-aware Re-projection Loss, our method outperforms the InstaDM [19] by a large margin in all of the metrics using a lower resolution and more concise architecture (we do not require the explicit per-object-motion network, instance level segmentation prior and inter-frame correspondences). Qualitative visualizations are in Fig. 8.

Table 2 shows the depth errors in the dynamic objects area. Our Depth Prior Network θ_{DPN} shares a similar architecture with the Monodepth2 [9] while trained jointly with our multi-frame model θ_{MF} using Dynamic Object Cycle Consistency Loss L_c. It outperforms all the existing methods including Monodepth2 [9] and InstaDM [19]. Manydepth [35] suffers catastrophic failure on the dynamic objects due to the aforementioned mismatch and occlusion problems. They employed an separate single-frame model as a teacher for dynamic objects area. However, since it does not actually solve the mismatch and occlusion problems, it still makes severe mistakes on dynamic objects. In contrast, with our proposed innovations, our multi-frame model θ_{MF} boosts up the accuracy even higher, achieves superior advantages on all the metrics, showing its significant effectiveness. We show a qualitative visualization in Fig. 7.

Table 3. Ablation Study: Evaluating the effects for our proposed Dynamic Object Motion Disentanglement, Cycle Consistent Training, Occlusion-aware Cost Volume and Re-projection Loss on the Cityscapes [3] dataset.

Dynamic Object Motion Disentanglement	Dynamic Object Cycle Consistency	Occlusion-aware Cost Volume	Occlusion-aware Loss Switching	Masking	The Lower the Better Abs Rel	Sq Rel	RMSE	RMSE$_{log}$
			Evaluating Dynamic Object Motion Disentanglement					
					0.114	1.193	6.223	0.170
✓					0.110	1.172	6.220	0.166
			Evaluating Occlusion-aware CV and Loss					
✓					0.110	1.172	6.220	0.166
✓			✓		0.110	1.168	6.223	0.166
✓				✓	0.110	1.167	6.210	0.167
✓			✓	✓	0.108	1.139	5.992	0.163
✓		✓			0.108	1.131	5.994	0.162
			Evaluating Dynamic Object Cycle Consistent Training					
✓		✓	✓	✓	0.107	1.121	5.924	0.160
✓	✓	✓	✓	✓	**0.103**	**1.000**	**5.867**	**0.157**

4.3 KITTI Results

Our proposed framework is further evaluated on the widely-used KITTI [24] dataset Eigen [6] split, which contains $39,810$ training images, $4,424$ validation images, and 697 testing images. According to our statistic, only 0.34% of the pixels in the KITTI [24] dataset are dynamic category objects (*e.g.,*Vehicle, Person, Bike), and most of the vehicles are not moving.

The comparison of our method with the state-of-the-art single-frame models [1,9,11,21], multi-frame models [26,32,35], and dynamic-objects-optimized models [19,20] is summarized in Table 1. Unsurprisingly dynamic-objects-focused methods [1,7,10,19–21] showed a minor advantage on this dataset. Our method only achieve 2% improvement over the existing state-of-the-art method Many-depth [35]. However, when we only focus on dynamic objects as in Table 2, our method achieve a much more significant 14.3% improvement.

4.4 Ablation Study

To comprehensively understand the effectiveness of our proposed modules and prove our design decision, we perform an extensive ablation study on the challenging Cityscapes [3] dataset. As shown in Table 3, our experiments fall into three groups, evaluating Dynamic Object Motion Disentanglement, Occlusion-aware Cost Volume and Loss, and Cycle Consistent Training.

Dynamic Object Motion Disentanglement: In the first group of the Table 3, we evaluate our proposed Dynamic Object Motion Disentanglement (DOMD) module. When the DOMD is enabled, the cost volume and the re-projection loss is based on the disentangled I_{t-1}^d image instead of the original I_{t-1} image. The Abs Rel Error reduced by 4%, confirms its effectiveness.

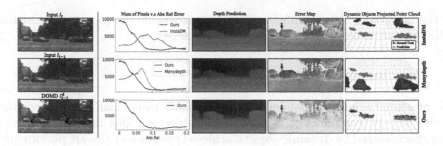

Fig. 8. Qualitative Visualization: The left column shows the input image frames and our disentangled image I_{t-1}^d, later columns show the comparison with other state-of-the-art methods. In the Histograms, most pixels of our method has lower depth error. In the error map, our method has lighter red color which indicates lower depth errors. We project the dynamic object area depths to 3D point clouds and compare them with ground truth point clouds in the last column. Our prediction matches the ground truth significantly better. More comparisons are provided in the supplementary document. (Color figure online)

Occlusion-Aware Cost Volume and Loss: The second group of the Table 3 shows the effectiveness of the proposed Occlusion-aware Cost Volume CV^{occ} and Occlusion-aware Re-projection Loss L_{or}. Our innovation in the Occlusion-aware Re-projection Loss includes two operations: the switching and masking. Solely using either the switching or masking mechanism does not improve the accuracy. These results meet our expectation. The re-projection loss switching mechanism is designed to switch the re-projection source between two reference frames I_{t-1}^d and I_{t+1}^d to avoid occlusion areas, and the masking mechanism is designed to neutralize the influence on the photo-metric error [34] from occlusion areas to neighboring non-occluded areas. Only avoiding the occlusion area while ignoring its influence on the neighboring areas or vise-versa could not solve the problem. Applying both mechanisms together can significantly improve the depth accuracy. As for the Occlusion-aware Cost Volume, our occlusion-filling mechanism replaces the noisy occluded cost voxels with neighboring non-occluded voxel values to recover the distribution of the costs and guide the training gradients. Experiments confirm the effectiveness of our design.

Cycle Consistent Training: The depth prior prediction D_t^{pr} from θ_{DPN} is used in our DOMD module to disentangle the dynamic objects motion, which is further encoded with geometric constraints in the cost volume to predict the final depth D_t. The proposed Dynamic Object Cycle Consistency Loss L_c enables the final depth D_t to backwards supervise the training of the depth prior prediction D_t^{pr} and forms a closed-loop mutual reinforcement. In the first row of the Table 3 third group, we first train the Depth Prior Net θ_{DPN} separately, then freeze it and train the later multi-frame model to cut off the backwards supervision. In this experiment, θ_{DPN} performs similar as normal single-frame model Monodepth2 [9] and the final depth prediction only shows limited performance.

In the last row, when we unfreeze the θ_{DPN} to enable the joint and consistent training, our model achieves the best performance.

5   Conclusions

We presented a novel self-supervised multi-frame monocular depth prediction model, namely DynamicDepth. It disentangle object motions and diminish occlusion effects caused by dynamic objects, achieved the state-of-the-art performance especially at the dynamic object areas on the Cityscapes [3] and KITTI [24] datasets.

Acknowledgement. This work was partially supported by the U.S. Department of Transportation (DOT) Center for Connected Multimodal Mobility grant # No. 69A3551747117-2024230, and National Science Foundation (NSF) grant # No. IIS-2041307.

References

1. Casser, V., Pirk, S., Mahjourian, R., Angelova, A.: Depth prediction without the sensors: leveraging structure for unsupervised learning from monocular videos. In: AAAI (2019)
2. Casser, V., Pirk, S., Mahjourian, R., Angelova, A.: Unsupervised monocular depth and ego-motion learning with structure and semantics. In: CVPR Workshops (2019)
3. Cordts, M., et al.: The cityscapes dataset for semantic urban scene understanding. In: Proceedings of the IEEE Conference on Computer Vision and Pattern Recognition (CVPR) (2016)
4. CS Kumar, A., Bhandarkar, S.M., Prasad, M.: Depthnet: a recurrent neural network architecture for monocular depth prediction. In: Proceedings of the IEEE Conference on Computer Vision and Pattern Recognition Workshops, pp. 283–291 (2018)
5. Deng, J., Dong, W., Socher, R., Li, L.J., Li, K., Fei-Fei, L.: Imagenet: a large-scale hierarchical image database. In: 2009 IEEE Conference on Computer Vision and Pattern Recognition, pp. 248–255. IEEE (2009)
6. Eigen, D., Fergus, R.: Predicting depth, surface normals and semantic labels with a common multi-scale convolutional architecture. In: Proceedings of the IEEE International Conference on Computer Vision, pp. 2650–2658 (2015)
7. Gao, F., Yu, J., Shen, H., Wang, Y., Yang, H.: Attentional separation-and-aggregation network for self-supervised depth-pose learning in dynamic scenes. arXiv preprint arXiv:2011.09369 (2020)
8. Godard, C., Mac Aodha, O., Brostow, G.J.: Unsupervised monocular depth estimation with left-right consistency. In: Proceedings of the IEEE Conference on Computer Vision and Pattern Recognition, pp. 270–279 (2017)
9. Godard, C., Mac Aodha, O., Firman, M., Brostow, G.J.: Digging into self-supervised monocular depth estimation. In: Proceedings of the IEEE/CVF International Conference on Computer Vision, pp. 3828–3838 (2019)
10. Gordon, A., Li, H., Jonschkowski, R., Angelova, A.: Depth from videos in the wild: unsupervised monocular depth learning from unknown cameras. In: ICCV (2019)

11. Guizilini, V., Ambrus, R., Pillai, S., Raventos, A., Gaidon, A.: 3D packing for self-supervised monocular depth estimation. In: CVPR (2020)
12. Guizilini, V., Hou, R., Li, J., Ambrus, R., Gaidon, A.: Semantically-guided representation learning for self-supervised monocular depth. In: ICLR (2020)
13. Ha, H., Im, S., Park, J., Jeon, H.G., Kweon, I.S.: High-quality depth from uncalibrated small motion clip. In: Proceedings of the IEEE Conference on Computer Vision and Pattern Recognition, pp. 5413–5421 (2016)
14. He, K., Zhang, X., Ren, S., Sun, J.: Deep residual learning for image recognition. In: Proceedings of the IEEE Conference on Computer Vision and Pattern Recognition, pp. 770–778 (2016)
15. Johnston, A., Carneiro, G.: Self-supervised monocular trained depth estimation using self-attention and discrete disparity volume. In: CVPR (2020)
16. Joshi, N., Zitnick, C.L.: Micro-baseline stereo. Microsoft Research Technical Report (2014)
17. Kingma, D.P., Ba, J.: Adam: a method for stochastic optimization. arXiv preprint arXiv:1412.6980 (2014)
18. Klingner, M., Termöhlen, J.-A., Mikolajczyk, J., Fingscheidt, T.: Self-supervised monocular depth estimation: solving the dynamic object problem by semantic guidance. In: Vedaldi, A., Bischof, H., Brox, T., Frahm, J.-M. (eds.) ECCV 2020. LNCS, vol. 12365, pp. 582–600. Springer, Cham (2020). https://doi.org/10.1007/978-3-030-58565-5_35
19. Lee, S., Im, S., Lin, S., Kweon, I.S.: Learning monocular depth in dynamic scenes via instance-aware projection consistency. In: 35th AAAI Conference on Artificial Intelligence/33rd Conference on Innovative Applications of Artificial Intelligence/11th Symposium on Educational Advances in Artificial Intelligence, pp. 1863–1872. Assoc Advancement Artificial Intelligence (2021)
20. Lee, S., Rameau, F., Pan, F., Kweon, I.S.: Attentive and contrastive learning for joint depth and motion field estimation. In: Proceedings of the IEEE/CVF International Conference on Computer Vision, pp. 4862–4871 (2021)
21. Li, H., Gordon, A., Zhao, H., Casser, V., Angelova, A.: Unsupervised monocular depth learning in dynamic scenes. In: CoRL (2020)
22. Li, Z., et al.: Learning the depths of moving people by watching frozen people. In: Proceedings of the IEEE/CVF Conference on Computer Vision and Pattern Recognition, pp. 4521–4530 (2019)
23. Luo, C., et al.: Every pixel counts++: joint learning of geometry and motion with 3D holistic understanding. PAMI (2019)
24. Menze, M., Geiger, A.: Object scene flow for autonomous vehicles. In: Conference on Computer Vision and Pattern Recognition (CVPR) (2015)
25. Mohan, R., Valada, A.: Efficientps: efficient panoptic segmentation. Int. J. Comput. Vis. **129**(5), 1551–1579 (2021)
26. Patil, V., Van Gansbeke, W., Dai, D., Van Gool, L.: Don't forget the past: recurrent depth estimation from monocular video. IEEE Robot. Autom. Lett. **5**(4), 6813–6820 (2020)
27. Pilzer, A., Xu, D., Puscas, M.M., Ricci, E., Sebe, N.: Unsupervised adversarial depth estimation using cycled generative networks. In: 3DV (2018)
28. Ranjan, A., Jampani, V., Kim, K., Sun, D., Wulff, J., Black, M.J.: Competitive collaboration: Joint unsupervised learning of depth, camera motion, optical flow and motion segmentation. In: CVPR (2019)
29. Shu, C., Yu, K., Duan, Z., Yang, K.: Feature-Metric Loss for Self-supervised Learning of Depth and Egomotion. In: Vedaldi, A., Bischof, H., Brox, T., Frahm, J-M.

(eds.) ECCV 2020. LNCS, vol. 12364, pp. 572–588. Springer, Cham (2020). https://doi.org/10.1007/978-3-030-58529-7_34

30. Uhrig, J., Schneider, N., Schneider, L., Franke, U., Brox, T., Geiger, A.: Sparsity invariant CNNS. In: International Conference on 3D Vision (3DV) (2017)

31. Wang, C., Buenaposada, J.M., Zhu, R., Lucey, S.: Learning depth from monocular videos using direct methods. In: Proceedings of the IEEE Conference on Computer Vision and Pattern Recognition, pp. 2022–2030 (2018)

32. Wang, J., Zhang, G., Wu, Z., Li, X., Liu, L.: Self-supervised joint learning framework of depth estimation via implicit cues. arXiv:2006.09876 (2020)

33. Wang, R., Pizer, S.M., Frahm, J.M.: Recurrent neural network for (un-) supervised learning of monocular video visual odometry and depth. In: Proceedings of the IEEE/CVF Conference on Computer Vision and Pattern Recognition, pp. 5555–5564 (2019)

34. Wang, Z., Bovik, A.C., Sheikh, H.R., Simoncelli, E.P.: Image quality assessment: from error visibility to structural similarity. IEEE Trans. image Process. **13**(4), 600–612 (2004)

35. Watson, J., Mac Aodha, O., Prisacariu, V., Brostow, G., Firman, M.: The temporal opportunist: self-supervised multi-frame monocular depth. In: Proceedings of the IEEE/CVF Conference on Computer Vision and Pattern Recognition, pp. 1164–1174 (2021)

36. Wimbauer, F., Yang, N., Von Stumberg, L., Zeller, N., Cremers, D.: Monorec: semi-supervised dense reconstruction in dynamic environments from a single moving camera. In: Proceedings of the IEEE/CVF Conference on Computer Vision and Pattern Recognition, pp. 6112–6122 (2021)

37. Zhang, H., Shen, C., Li, Y., Cao, Y., Liu, Y., Yan, Y.: Exploiting temporal consistency for real-time video depth estimation. In: Proceedings of the IEEE/CVF International Conference on Computer Vision, pp. 1725–1734 (2019)

38. Zhao, H., Gallo, O., Frosio, I., Kautz, J.: Loss functions for image restoration with neural networks. IEEE Trans. Comput. Imaging **3**(1), 47–57 (2016)

Depth Field Networks For Generalizable Multi-view Scene Representation

Vitor Guizilini[1]([✉]), Igor Vasiljevic[1], Jiading Fang[2], Rareş Ambruş[1], Greg Shakhnarovich[2], Matthew R. Walter[2], and Adrien Gaidon[1]

[1] Toyota Research Institute, Los Altos, CA, USA
vitor.guizilini@tri.global
[2] Toyota Technological Institute at Chicago, Chicago, IL, USA

Abstract. Modern 3D computer vision leverages learning to boost geometric reasoning, mapping image data to classical structures such as cost volumes or epipolar constraints to improve matching. These architectures are specialized according to the particular problem, and thus require significant task-specific tuning, often leading to poor domain generalization performance.Recently, generalist Transformer architectures have achieved impressive results in tasks such as optical flow and depth estimation by encoding geometric priors as inputs rather than as enforced constraints.In this paper, we extend this idea and propose to learn an implicit, multi-view consistent scene representation, introducing a series of 3D data augmentation techniques as a geometric inductive prior to increase view diversity. We also show that introducing view synthesis as an auxiliary task further improves depth estimation. Our Depth Field Networks (DeFiNe) achieve state-of-the-art results in stereo and video depth estimation without explicit geometric constraints, and improve on zero-shot domain generalization by a wide margin. Project page: https://sites.google.com/view/tri-define.

Keywords: Multi-view depth estimation · Representation learning

1 Introduction

Estimating 3D structure from a pair of images is a cornerstone problem of computer vision. Traditionally, this is treated as a correspondence problem, whereby one applies a homography to stereo-rectify the images and then matches pixels (or patches) along epipolar lines to obtain disparity estimates. Contemporary approaches to stereo are specialized variants of classical methods, relying on correspondences to compute cost volumes, epipolar losses, bundle adjustment objectives, or projective multi-view constraints, among others. These are either baked directly into the model architecture or enforced as part of the loss function (Fig. 1).

V. Guizilini, I. Vasiljevic, and J. Fang—Denotes equal contribution.

Supplementary Information The online version contains supplementary material available at https://doi.org/10.1007/978-3-031-19824-3_15.

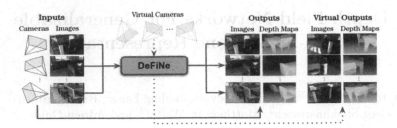

Fig. 1. Our **Depth Field Networks (DeFiNe)** achieve state of the art in multi-view depth estimation, while also enabling predictions from arbitrary viewpoints.

Applying the principles of classical vision in this way has given rise to architectures that achieve state-of-the-art results on tasks such as stereo depth estimation [18,24], optical flow [46], and multi-view depth [45]. However, this success comes at a cost: each architecture is specialized and purpose-built for a single task. Great strides have been made to alleviate the dependence on strong geometric assumptions [12,50], and two recent trends allow us to *decouple* the task from the architecture: (i) implicit representations and (ii) generalist networks. Our work draws upon both of these directions.

Implicit representations of geometry and coordinate-based networks have recently achieved incredible popularity in the vision community. This direction is pioneered by work on neural radiance fields (NeRF) [29,54], where a point- and ray-based parameterization along with a volume rendering objective allow simple MLP-based networks to achieve state-of-the-art view synthesis results. Follow-up works extend this coordinate-based representation to the pixel domain [57], allowing predicted views to be conditioned on image features. The second trend in computer vision has been the use of generalist architectures, pioneered by Vision Transformers [5]. Emerging as an attention-based architecture for NLP, Transformers have been used for a diverse set of tasks, including depth estimation [23,32], optical flow [16], and image generation [8]. Transformers have also been applied to geometry-free view synthesis [35], demonstrating that attention can learn long-range correspondence between views for 2D-3D tasks. Representation Transformers (SRT) [36] use the Transformer encoder-decoder model to learn scene representations for view synthesis from sparse, high-baseline data with no geometric constraints. However, owing to the quadratic scaling of the self-attention module, experiments are limited to low-resolution images and require very long training periods.

To alleviate the quadratic complexity of self-attention, the Perceiver architecture [17] disentangles the dimensionality of the latent representation from that of the inputs by fixing the size of the latent representation. Perceiver IO [16] extends this architecture to allow for arbitrary outputs, with results on optical flow estimation that outperform traditional cost-volume based methods. Similarly, the recent Input-level Inductive Bias (IIB) architecture [56] uses image features and camera information as input to Perceiver IO to directly regress stereo depth, outperforming baselines that use explicit geometric constraints. Building upon these works, we propose to learn a *geometric scene representation* for depth synthesis from novel viewpoints, including estimation, interpolation, and extrapolation. We expand the

IIB framework to the scene representation setting, taking sequences of images and predicting a consistent multi-view latent representation suitable for different down-stream tasks. Taking advantage of the query-based nature of the Perceiver IO architecture, we propose a series of 3D augmentations that increase viewpoint density and diversity during training, thus encouraging (rather than enforcing) multi-view consistency. Furthermore, we show that the introduction of view synthesis as an auxiliary task, decoded from the same latent representation, improves depth estimation without additional ground truth.

We test our model on the popular ScanNet benchmark [3], achieving state-of-the-art real-time results for stereo depth estimation and competitive results for video depth estimation, without relying on memory- or compute-intensive operations such as cost volume aggregation and test-time optimization. We show that our 3D augmentations lead to significant improvements over baselines that are limited to the viewpoint diversity of training data. Furthermore, our zero-shot transfer results from ScanNet to 7-Scenes [40] improve the state-of-the-art by a large margin, demonstrating that our method generalizes better than specialized architectures, which suffer from poor performance on out-of-domain data. Our contributions are summarized as follows:

- We use a generalist Transformer-based architecture to learn a depth estimator from an arbitrary number of posed images. In this setting, we (i) **propose a series of 3D augmentations** that improve the geometric consistency of our learned latent representation; and (ii) show that **jointly learning view synthesis as an auxiliary task improves depth estimation**.
- Our Depth Field Networks (DeFiNe) not only achieve **state-of-the-art stereo depth estimation results** on the widely used ScanNet dataset, but also exhibit superior generalization properties with **state-of-the-art results on zero-shot transfer to 7-Scenes.**
- DeFiNe also **enables depth estimation from arbitrary viewpoints.** We evaluate this novel generalization capability in the context of *interpolation* (between timesteps), and *extrapolation* (future timesteps).

2   Related Work

Monocular Depth Estimation. Supervised depth estimation—the task of estimating per-pixel depth given an RGB image and a corresponding ground-truth depth map—dates back to the pioneering work of Saxena et al. [37]. Since then, deep learning-based architectures designed for supervised monocular depth estimation have become increasingly sophisticated [6,7,9,21,22], generally offering improvements over the standard encoder-decoder convolutional architecture. Self-supervised methods provide an alternative to those that rely on ground-truth depth maps at training time, and are able to take advantage of the new availability of large-scale video datasets. Early self-supervised methods relied on stereo data [10], and then progressed to fully monocular video sequences [59], with increasingly sophisticated losses [41] and architectures [11,13,52].

Multi-view Stereo. Traditional multi-view stereo approaches have dominated even in the deep learning era. COLMAP [38] remains the standard framework for structure-from-motion, incorporating sophisticated bundle adjustment and keypoint refinement procedures, at the cost of speed. With the goal of producing closer to real-time estimates, multi-view stereo learning approaches adapt traditional cost volume-based approaches to stereo [2,18] and multi-view [15,55] depth estimation, often relying on known extrinsics to warp views into the frame of the reference camera. Recently, iterative refinement approaches that employ recurrent neural networks have made impressive strides in optical flow estimation [46]. Follow-on work applies this general recurrent correspondence architecture to stereo depth [24], scene-flow [48], and even SLAM [47]. While their results are impressive, recurrent neural networks can be difficult to train, and test-time optimization increases inference time over a single forward pass.

Recently, Transformer-based architectures [51] have replaced CNNs in many geometric estimation tasks. The Stereo Transformer [23] architecture replaces cost volumes with a correspondence approach inspired by sequence-to-sequence modeling. The Perceiver IO [16] architecture constitutes a large departure from cost volumes and geometric losses. For the task of optical flow, Perceiver IO feeds positionally encoded images through a Transformer [17], rather than using a cost volume for processing. IIB [56] adapts the Perceiver IO architecture to generalized stereo estimation, proposing a novel epipolar parameterization as an additional input-level inductive bias. Building upon this baseline, we propose a series of geometry-preserving 3D data augmentation techniques designed to promote the learning of a *geometrically-consistent latent scene representation*. We also introduce novel view synthesis as an auxiliary task to depth estimation, decoded from the same latent space. Our video-based representation (aided by our 3D augmentations) allows us to generalize to novel viewpoints, rather than be restricted to the stereo setting.

Video Depth Estimation. Video and stereo depth estimation methods generally produce monocular depth estimates at test time. ManyDepth [52] combines a monocular depth framework with multi-view stereo, aggregating predictions in a cost volume and thus enabling multi-frame inference at test-time. Recent methods accumulate predictions at train and test time, either with generalized stereo [49] or with sequence data [58]. DeepV2D [45] incorporates a cost-volume based multi-view stereo approach with an incremental pose estimator to iteratively improve depth and pose estimates at train and test time.

Another line of work draws on the availability of monocular depth networks that perform accurate but *multi-view inconsistent* estimates at test time [28]. In this setting, additional geometric constraints are enforced to finetune the network and improve multi-view consistency through epipolar constraints. Consistent Video Depth Estimation [28] refines COLMAP [38] results with a monocular depth network constrained to be multi-view consistent. Subsequent work jointly optimizes depth and pose for added robustness to challenging scenarios with poor calibration [19]. A recent framework incorporates many architectural elements

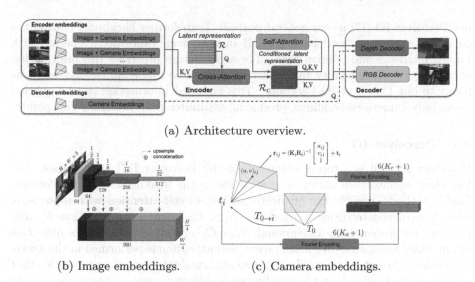

(a) Architecture overview.

(b) Image embeddings.   (c) Camera embeddings.

Fig. 2. Overview of our proposed DeFiNe architecture, and the embeddings used to encode and decode information for depth and view synthesis.

of prior work into a Transformer-based architecture that takes video data as input for multi-view depth [26]. NeuralRecon [43] moves beyond depth-based architectures to learn Truncated Signed Distance Field (TSDF) volumes as a way to improve surface consistency.

Novel View Synthesis. Since the emergence of neural radiance fields [29], implicit representations and volume rendering have emerged as the *de facto* standard for view synthesis. They parameterize viewing rays and points with positional encoding, and need to be re-trained on a scene-by-scene basis. Many recent improvements leverage depth supervision to improve view synthesis in a volume rendering framework [1,4,34,53,60]. An alternative approach replaces volume rendering with a directly learned light field network [42], predicting color values directly from viewing rays. This is the approach we take when estimating the auxiliary view synthesis loss, due to its computational simplicity. Other works attempt to extend the NeRF approach beyond single scene models by incorporating learned *features*, enabling few-shot volume rendering [57]. Feature-based methods have also treated view synthesis as a sequence-learning task, such as the Scene Representation Transformer (SRT) architecture [36].

3   The DeFiNe Architecture

Our proposed DeFiNe architecture (Fig. 2a) is designed with flexibility in mind, so data from different sources can be used as input and different output tasks can be estimated from the same latent space. Similar to Yifan et al. [56], we use Perceiver IO [17] as our general-purpose Transformer backbone. During the encoding stage, our model takes RGB images from calibrated cameras, with known intrinsics and relative poses. The architecture processes this information according to the modality into different pixel-wise embeddings that serve as input to our Perceiver IO backbone. This encoded information can be queried using only camera embeddings, producing estimates from arbitrary viewpoints.

3.1   Perceiver IO

Perceiver IO [16] is a recent extension of the Perceiver [17] architecture. The Perceiver architecture alleviates one of the main weaknesses of Transformer-based methods, namely the quadratic scaling of self-attention with input size. This is achieved by using a fixed-size $N_l \times C_l$ latent representation $\mathcal{R}$, and learning to project high-dimensional $N_e \times C_e$ encoding embeddings onto this latent space using cross-attention layers. Self-attention is performed in the lower-dimensional latent space, producing a *conditioned latent representation* $\mathcal{R}_c$ that can be queried using $N_d \times C_d$ decoding embeddings to generate estimates, again using cross-attention layers.

3.2   Input-Level Embeddings

Image Embeddings (Fig. 2b). Input $3 \times H \times W$ images are processed using a ResNet18 [14] encoder, producing a list of features maps at increasingly lower resolutions and higher dimensionality. Feature maps at $1/4$ the original resolution are concatenated with lower-resolution feature maps, after upsampling using bilinear interpolation. The resulting image embeddings are of shape $H/4 \times W/4 \times 960$, and are used in combination with the camera embeddings from each corresponding pixel (see below) to encode visual information.

Camera Embeddings (Fig. 2c). These embeddings capture multi-view scene geometry (e.g., camera intrinsics and extrinsics) as additional inputs during the learning process. Let $\mathbf{x}_{ij} = (u, v)$ be an image coordinate corresponding to pixel i in camera j, with assumed known pinhole 3×3 intrinsics $\mathbf{K}_j$ and 4×4 transformation matrix $T_j = \begin{bmatrix} \mathbf{R}_j & \mathbf{t}_j \\ \mathbf{0} & 1 \end{bmatrix}$ relative to a canonical camera T_0. Its origin $\mathbf{o}_j$ and direction $\mathbf{r}_{ij}$ are given by:

$$\mathbf{o}_j = -\mathbf{R}_j \mathbf{t}_j \quad , \quad \mathbf{r}_{ij} = \left(\mathbf{K}_j \mathbf{R}_j\right)^{-1} [u_{ij}, v_{ij}, 1]^T + \mathbf{t}_j \tag{1}$$

Note that this formulation differs from the standard convention [29], which does not consider the camera translation $\mathbf{t}_j$ when generating viewing rays $\mathbf{r}_{ij}$. We ablate this variation in Table 1, showing that it leads to better performance for the task of depth estimation. These two vectors are then Fourier-encoded dimension-wise to produce higher-dimensional vectors, with a mapping of:

$$x \mapsto \left[x, \sin(f_1 \pi x), \cos(f_1 \pi x), \ldots, \sin(f_K \pi x), \cos(f_K \pi x)\right]^\top \tag{2}$$

where K is the number of Fourier frequencies used (K_o for the origin and K_r for the ray directions), equally spaced in the interval $[1, \frac{\mu}{2}]$. The resulting camera

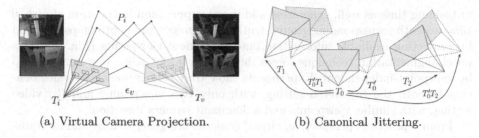

(a) Virtual Camera Projection.   (b) Canonical Jittering.

Fig. 3. Geometric augmentations. (a) Information from camera i is projected onto a virtual camera at T_v, creating additional supervision from other viewpoints. (b) Noise T_0' is introduced to the canonical camera at T_0, and then propagated to other cameras to preserve relative scene geometry.

embedding is of dimensionality $2\big(3(K_o+1)+3(K_r+1)\big) = 6\,(K_o + K_r + 2)$. During the encoding stage, camera embeddings are produced per-pixel assuming a camera with $1/4$ the original input resolution, resulting in a total of $\frac{HW}{16}$ vectors. During the decoding stage, embeddings from cameras with arbitrary calibration (i.e., intrinsics and extrinsics) can be queried to produce virtual estimates.

3.3 Geometric 3D Augmentations

Data augmentation is a core component of deep learning pipelines [39] that improves model robustness by applying transformations to the training data consistent with the data distribution in order to introduce desired equivariant properties. In computer vision and depth estimation in particular, standard data augmentation techniques are usually constrained to the 2D space and include color jittering, flipping, rotation, cropping, and resizing [11,56]. Recent works have started looking into 3D augmentations [36] to improve robustness to errors in scene geometry in terms of camera localization (i.e., extrinsics) and parameters (i.e., intrinsics). Conversely, we are interested in *encoding* scene geometry at the input-level, so our architecture can learn a multi-view-consistent geometric latent scene representation. Therefore, in this section we propose a series of 3D augmentations to increase the number and diversity of training views while maintaining the spatial relationship between cameras, thus enforcing desired equivariant properties within this setting.

Virtual Camera Projection. One of the key properties of our architecture is that it enables querying from arbitrary viewpoints, since only camera information (viewing rays) is required at the decoding stage. When generating predictions from these novel viewpoints, the network creates *virtual* information consistent with the implicit structure of the learned latent scene representation, conditioned on information from the encoded views. We evaluate this capability in Sect. 4.5, showing superior performance relative to the explicit projection of information from encoded views. Here, we propose to leverage this property at training time as well, generating additional supervision in the form of *virtual cameras* with corresponding ground-truth RGB images and depth maps obtained by projecting available information onto these new viewpoints (Fig. 3a). This novel augmentation technique forces the learned latent scene representation to be viewpoint-independent. Experiments show that this approach provides benefits in both the (a) stereo setting, with only two viewpoints; and (b) video setting, with similar viewpoints and a dominant camera direction.

From a practical perspective, virtual cameras are generated by adding translation noise $\epsilon_v = [\epsilon_x, \epsilon_y, \epsilon_z]_v \sim \mathcal{N}(0, \sigma_v)$ to the pose of a camera i. The viewing angle is set to point towards the center c_i of the pointcloud P_i generated by unprojecting information from the selected camera, which is also perturbed by $\epsilon_c = [\epsilon_x, \epsilon_y, \epsilon_z]_c \sim \mathcal{N}(0, \sigma_v)$. When generating ground-truth information, we project the combined pointcloud from all available cameras onto these new viewpoints as a way to preserve full scene geometry. Furthermore, because the resulting RGB image and depth map will be sparse, we can improve efficiency by only querying at these specific locations.

Canonical Jittering. When operating in a multi-camera setting, it is standard practice to select one camera to be the *reference* camera, and position all other cameras relative to it [15]. One drawback of this convention is that one camera will always be at the same location (the origin of its own coordinate system) and will therefore produce the same camera embeddings, leading to overfitting. Intuitively, scene geometry should be invariant to the translation and rotation of the entire sensor suite. To enforce this property on our learned latent scene representation, we propose to inject some amount of noise to the canonical pose itself, so it is not located at the origin of the coordinate system. Note that this is different from methods that inject per-camera noise [31] with the goal of increasing robustness to localization errors. We only inject noise *once*, on the canonical camera, and propagate it to other cameras, so relative scene geometry is preserved within a translation and rotation offset (Fig. 3a). However, this offset is reflected on the input-level embeddings produced by each camera, and thus forces the latent representation to be invariant to these transformations.

In order to perform canonical jittering, we randomly sample translation $\epsilon_t = [\epsilon_x, \epsilon_y, \epsilon_z]^\top \sim \mathcal{N}(0, \sigma_t)$ and rotation $\epsilon_r = [\epsilon_\phi, \epsilon_\theta, \epsilon_\psi]^\top \sim \mathcal{N}(0, \sigma_r)$ errors from zero-mean normal distributions with pre-determined standard deviations. Represented as Euler angles, we convert each set of rotation errors to a 3×3 rotation matrix $\mathbf{R}_r$. We then use the rotation matrix and translation error to create a jittered canonical transformation matrix $T_0' = \begin{bmatrix} \mathbf{R}_r & \epsilon_t \\ \mathbf{0} & 1 \end{bmatrix}$ that is then propagated to all other N cameras, such that $T_i' = T_0' \cdot T_i, \forall i \in \{1, \ldots, N-1\}$.

Canonical Randomization. As an extension to canonical jittering, we also introduce canonical randomization to encourage generalization to different relative camera configurations, while still preserving scene geometry. Assuming N cameras, we randomly select $o \in \{0, \ldots, N-1\}$ as the canonical index. We then compute the relative transformation matrix T_i' given world-frame transformation matrix T_i as $T_i' = T_i \cdot T_o^{-1} \; \forall i \in \{0, \ldots, N-1\}$.

3.4 Decoders

We use task-specific decoders, each consisting of one cross-attention layer between the $N_d \times C_d$ queries and the $N_l \times C_l$ conditioned latent representation $\mathcal{R}_c$, followed by a linear layer that creates an output of size $N_d \times C_o$, and a sigmoid activation function $\sigma(x) = \frac{1}{1+e^{-x}}$ to produce values in the interval $[0, 1]$. We set $C_o^d = 1$ for depth estimation and $C_o^s = 3$ for view synthesis. Depth estimates are scaled to lie within the range $[d_{\min}, d_{\max}]$. Note that other decoders can be incorporated with DeFiNe without any modification to the underlying architecture, enabling the generation of multi-task estimates from arbitrary viewpoints.

3.5 Losses

We use an L1-log loss $\mathcal{L}_d = \|\log(d_{ij}) - \log(\hat{d}_{ij})\|_1$ to supervise depth estimation, where $\hat{d}_{ij}$ and d_{ij} are depth estimates and ground truth, respectively, for pixel j at camera i. For view synthesis, we use an L2 loss $\mathcal{L}_s = \|\mathbf{p}_{ij} - \hat{\mathbf{p}}_{ij}\|^2$, where $\hat{\mathbf{p}}_{ij}$ and $\mathbf{p}_{ij}$ are RGB estimates and ground truth, respectively, for pixel j at camera i. We use a weight coefficient λ_s to balance these two losses, and another λ_v to balance losses from available and virtual cameras. The final loss is of the form:

$$\mathcal{L} = \mathcal{L}_d + \lambda_s \mathcal{L}_s + \lambda_v \big(\mathcal{L}_{d,v} + \lambda_s (\mathcal{L}_{s,v}) \big) \tag{3}$$

Note that because our architecture enables querying at specific image coordinates, we can improve efficiency at training time by not computing estimates for pixels without ground truth (e.g., sparse depth maps or virtual cameras).

4 Experiments

4.1 Datasets

ScanNet [3]. We evaluate our DeFiNe for both *stereo* and *video* depth estimation using ScanNet, an RGB-D video dataset that contains 2.5 million views from around 1500 scenes. For the stereo experiments, we follow the same setting as Kusupati et al. [20]: we downsample scenes by a factor of 20 and use a custom split to create stereo pairs, resulting in 94212 training and 7517 test samples. For the video experiments, we follow the evaluation protocol of Teed et al. [45], with a total of 1405 scenes for training. For the test set, we use a custom split to select 2000 samples from 90 scenes not covered in the training set. Each training sample includes a target frame and a context of $[-3, 3]$ frames with stride 3. Each test sample includes a pair of frames, with a context of $[-3, 3]$ relative to the first frame of the pair with stride 3.

7-Scenes [40]. We also evaluate on the test split of 7-Scenes to measure zero-shot cross-dataset performance. Collected using KinectFusion [30], the dataset consists of 640 × 480 images in 7 settings, with a variable number of scenes in each setting. There are 500–1000 images in each scene. We follow the evaluation protocol of Sun et al. [43], median-scaling predictions using ground-truth information before evaluation.

4.2 Stereo Depth Estimation

To test the benefits our proposed geometric 3D augmentation procedures over the IIB [56] baseline, we first evaluate DeFiNe on the task of stereo depth estimation. Here, because each sample provides minimal information about the scene (i.e., only two frames), the introduction of additional virtual supervision should have the largest effect. We report our results in Fig. 4a and visualize examples of reconstructed pointclouds in Fig. 5. DeFiNe significantly outperforms other methods on this dataset, including IIB. Our virtual view augmentations lead to a large (20%) relative improvement, showing that DeFiNe benefits from a scene representation that encourages multi-view consistency.

Method	Abs.Rel↓	RMSE↓	$\delta_{1.25}$↑
DPSNet [15]	0.126	0.314	—
NAS [20]	0.107	0.281	—
IIB [56]	0.116	0.281	0.908
DeFiNe (128 × 192)	0.093	0.246	0.911
DeFiNe (240 × 320)	**0.089**	**0.232**	**0.915**

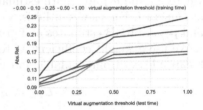

(a) Depth estimation results.   (b) Virtual depth estimation results.

Fig. 4. Depth estimation results on ScanNet-Stereo. (a) We outperform contemporary methods by a large margin. (b) Depth estimation results on virtual cameras using different values for σ_v at training and test time.

Table 1. Ablation study for ScanNet-Stereo, using different variations.

Variation		Lower is better ↓			Higher is better ↑		
		Abs. Rel	Sq. Rel	RMSE	$\delta_{1.25}$	$\delta_{1.25^2}$	$\delta_{1.25^3}$
1	Depth-Only	0.098	0.046	0.257	0.902	0.972	0.990
2	w/ Conv. RGB encoder [16]	0.114	0.058	0.294	0.866	0.961	0.982
3	w/ 64-dim R18 RGB encoder	0.104	0.049	0.270	0.883	0.966	0.985
4	w/o camera information	0.229	0.157	0.473	0.661	0.874	0.955
5	w/o global rays encoding	0.097	0.047	0.261	0.897	0.962	0.988
6	w/ equal loss weights	0.095	0.047	0.259	0.908	0.968	0.990
7	w/ epipolar cues [56]	0.094	0.048	0.254	0.905	0.972	0.990
8	w/o Augmentations	0.117	0.060	0.291	0.870	0.959	0.981
9	w/o Virtual Cameras	0.104	0.058	0.268	0.891	0.965	0.986
10	w/o Canonical Jittering	0.099	0.046	0.261	0.897	0.970	0.988
11	w/o Canonical Randomization	0.096	0.044	0.253	0.905	0.971	0.989
	DeFiNe	**0.093**	**0.042**	**0.246**	**0.911**	**0.974**	**0.991**

4.3   Ablation Study

We perform a detailed ablation study to evaluate the effectiveness of each component in our proposed architecture, with results shown in Table 1. Firstly, we evaluate performance when (Table 1:1) learning only depth estimation, and see that the joint learning of view synthesis as an auxiliary task leads to significant improvements. The claim that depth estimation improves view synthesis has been noted before [4,53], and is attributed to the well-known fact that multi-view consistency facilitates the generation of images from novel viewpoints. However, our experiments also show the inverse: view synthesis improves depth estimation. Our hypothesis is that appearance is required to learn multi-view consistency since it enables visual correlation across frames. By introducing view synthesis as an additional task, we are also encoding appearance-based information into our latent representation. This leads to improvements in depth estimation even though no explicit feature matching is performed at an architecture or loss level.

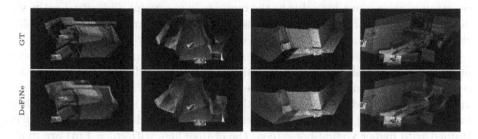

Fig. 5. Reconstructed two-view pointclouds, from ScanNet-Stereo. DeFiNe point-clouds are generated using both depth maps and RGB images queried from our learned latent representation.

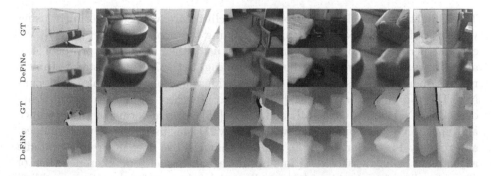

Fig. 6. Depth estimation and view synthesis results on ScanNet. Although view synthesis is not our primary goal, it can be achieved with minimal modifications, and we show that it improves depth estimation performance.

We also ablate different variations of our RGB encoder for the generation of image embeddings and show that (Table 1:2) our proposed multi-level feature map concatenation (Fig. 2b) leads to the best results relative to the standard single convolutional layer, or (Table 1:3) using 1/4-resolution ResNet18 64-dimensional feature maps. Similarly, we also ablate some of our design choices, namely (Table 1:4) the use of camera embeddings instead of positional encodings; (Table 1:5) global viewing rays (Sect. 3.2) instead of traditional relative viewing rays; (Table 1:6) the use of $\lambda_s = 1$ in the loss calculation (Eq. 3) such that both depth and view synthesis tasks have equal weights; and (Table 1:7) the use of epipolar cues as additional geometric embeddings, as proposed by IIB [56]. As expected, camera embeddings are crucial for multi-view consistency and global viewing rays improve over the standard relative formulation. Interestingly, using a smaller λ_s degrades depth estimation performance, providing further evidence that the joint learning of view synthesis is beneficial for multi-view consistency. We did not observe meaningful improvements when incorporating the epipolar cues from IIB [56], indicating that DeFiNe is capable of directly capturing these constraints at an input-level due to the increase in viewpoint diversity. Lastly, we ablate the impact of our various proposed geometric augmentations (Sect. 3.3), showing that they are key to our reported state-of-the-art performance.

Lastly, we evaluate depth estimation from virtual cameras, using different noise levels σ_v at test time. We also train models using different noise levels and report the results in Fig. 4b. From these results, we can see that the optimal virtual noise level, when evaluating at the target location, is $\sigma_v = 0.25\,\mathrm{m}$ (yellow line), relative to the baseline without virtual noise (blue line). However, models trained with higher virtual noise (e.g., the orange line, with $\sigma_v = 1\,\mathrm{m}$) are more robust to larger deviations from the target location.

4.4 Video Depth Estimation

To highlight the flexibility of our proposed architecture, we also experiment using video data from ScanNet following the training protocol of Tang et al. [44]. We evaluate performance on both ScanNet itself, using their evaluation protocol [44], as well as zero-shot transfer (without fine-tuning) to the 7-Scenes dataset. Table 2 reports quantitative results, while Fig. 6 provides qualitative examples. On Scan-Net, DeFiNe outperforms most published approaches, significantly improving over DeMoN [49], BA-Net [44], and CVD [28] both in terms of performance and speed. We are competitive with DeepV2D [45] in terms of performance, and roughly 14× faster, owing to the fact that DeFiNe does not require bundle adjustment or any sort of test-time optimization. In fact, our inference time of 49 ms can be split into 44 ms for encoding and only 5 ms for decoding, enabling very efficient generation of depth maps after information has been encoded once. The only method that outperforms DeFiNe in terms of speed is NeuralRecon [43], which uses a sophisticated TSDF integration strategy. Performance-wise, we are also competitive with NeuralRecon, improving over their reported results in one of the three metrics (Sq. Rel).

Next, we evaluate zero-shot transfer from ScanNet to 7-Scenes, which is a popular test of generalization for video depth estimation. In this setting, DeFiNe significantly improves over all other methods, including DeepV2D (which fails to generalize) and NeuralRecon (~40% improvement). We attribute this large gain to the highly intricate and specialized nature of these other architectures. In contrast, our method has no specialized module and instead learns a geometrically-consistent multi-view latent representation.

In summary, we achieve competitive results on ScanNet and significantly improve the state-of-the-art for video depth generalization, as evidenced by the large gap between DeFiNe and the best-performing methods on 7-Scenes.

4.5 Depth From Novel Viewpoints

We previously discussed the strong performance that DeFiNe achieves on traditional depth estimation benchmarks, and showed how it improves out-of-domain generalization by a wide margin. Here, we explore another aspect of generalization that our architecture enables: viewpoint generalization. This is possible because, in addition to traditional depth estimation from RGB images, DeFiNe can also generate depth maps from arbitrary viewpoints since it only requires

Table 2. Depth estimation results on ScanNet and 7-Scenes. DeFiNe is competitive with other state-of-the-art methods on ScanNet, and outperforms all published methods in zero-shot transfer to 7-Scenes by a large margin.

Method	Abs. Rel↓	Sq. Rel↓	RMSE↓	Speed (ms)↓
ScanNet test split [44]				
DeMoN [49]	0.231	0.520	0.761	110
MiDas-v2 [33]	0.208	0.318	0.742	–
BA-Net [44]	0.091	0.058	0.223	95
CVD [28]	0.073	0.037	0.217	2400
DeepV2D [45]	0.057	**0.010**	<u>0.168</u>	690
NeuralRecon [43]	**0.047**	0.024	**0.164**	**30**
DeFiNe (128 × 192)	0.059	0.022	0.184	<u>49</u>
DeFiNe (240 × 320)	<u>0.056</u>	<u>0.019</u>	0.176	78
Zero-shot transfer to 7-Scenes [40]				
DeMoN [49]	0.389	0.420	0.855	110
NeuralRGBD [25]	0.176	0.112	0.441	202
DPSNet [15]	0.199	0.142	0.438	322
DeepV2D [45]	0.437	0.553	0.869	347
CNMNet [27]	0.161	0.083	0.361	80
NeuralRecon [43]	0.155	0.104	0.347	**30**
EST [56]	<u>0.118</u>	<u>0.052</u>	<u>0.298</u>	71
DeFiNe (128 × 192)	**0.100**	**0.039**	**0.253**	<u>49</u>

camera embeddings to decode estimates. We explore this capability in two different ways: *interpolation* and *extrapolation*. When interpolating, we encode frames at $\{t - 5, t + 5\}$, and decode virtual depth maps at locations $\{t - 4, \ldots, t + 4\}$. When extrapolating, we encode frames at $\{t - 5, \ldots, t - 1\}$, and decode virtual depth maps at locations $\{t, \ldots, t + 8\}$. We use the same training and test splits as in our stereo experiments, with a downsampling factor of 20 to encourage smaller overlaps between frames. As baselines for comparison, we consider the explicit projection of 3D information from encoded frames onto those new viewpoints. We evaluate both standard depth estimation networks [11,13,22] as well as DeFiNe itself, that can be used to either explicitly project information from encoded frames onto new viewpoints (projection), or query from the latent representation at that same location (query).

Figure 7 reports results in terms of root mean squared error (RMSE) considering only valid projected pixels. Of particular note, our multi-frame depth estimation architecture significantly outperforms other single-frame baselines. However, and most importantly, results obtained by implicit querying consistently outperform those obtained via explicit projection. This indicates that our model is able to improve upon available encoded information via the learned latent representation. Furthermore, we also generate geometrically consistent estimates for areas without valid explicit projections (Fig. 7c). As the camera tilts to the right, the floor is smoothly recreated in unobserved areas, as well as

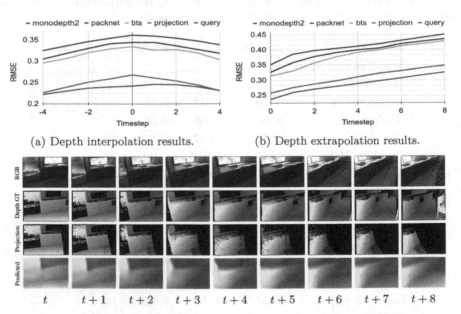

(a) Depth interpolation results.   (b) Depth extrapolation results.

(c) Depth extrapolation to future timesteps. Images and ground-truth depth maps are displayed only for comparison. DeFiNe can complete unseen portions of the scene in a geometrically-consistent way, generating dense depth maps from novel viewpoints.

Fig. 7. Depth estimation results from novel viewpoints.

the partially observed bench. Interestingly, the chair at the extreme right was not recreated, which could be seen as a failure case. However, because the chair was never observed in the first place, it is reasonable for the model to assume the area is empty, and recreate it as a continuation of the floor.

5   Conclusion

We introduced Depth Field Networks (DeFiNe), a generalist framework for training multi-view consistent depth estimators. Rather than explicitly enforcing geometric constraints at an architecture or loss level, we use geometric embeddings to condition network inputs, alongside visual information. To learn a geometrically-consistent latent representation, we propose a series of 3D augmentations designed to promote viewpoint, rotation, and translation equivariance. We also show that the introduction of view synthesis as an auxiliary task improves depth estimation without requiring additional ground truth. We achieve state-of-the-art results on the popular ScanNet stereo benchmark, and competitive results on the ScanNet video benchmark with no iterative refinement or explicit geometry modeling. We also demonstrate strong generalization properties by achieving state-of-the-art results on zero-shot transfer from ScanNet to 7-Scenes. The general nature of our framework enables many exciting avenues for future work, including additional tasks such as optical flow, extension to dynamic scenes, spatio-temporal representations, and uncertainty estimation.

References

1. Azinović, D., Martin-Brualla, R., Goldman, D.B., Nießner, M., Thies, J.: Neural RGB-D surface reconstruction. arXiv preprint arXiv:2104.04532 (2021)
2. Chang, J.R., Chen, Y.S.: Pyramid stereo matching network. In: Proceedings of the IEEE Conference on Computer Vision and Pattern Recognition (CVPR), pp. 5410–5418 (2018)
3. Dai, A., Chang, A.X., Savva, M., Halber, M., Funkhouser, T., Nießner, M.: Scan-Net: richly-annotated 3D reconstructions of indoor scenes. In: Proceedings of the IEEE Conference on Computer Vision and Pattern Recognition (CVPR), pp. 5828–5839 (2017)
4. Deng, K., Liu, A., Zhu, J.Y., Ramanan, D.: Depth-supervised NeRF: fewer views and faster training for free. arXiv preprint arXiv:2107.02791 (2021)
5. Dosovitskiy, A., et al.: An image is worth 16x16 words: transformers for image recognition at scale. arXiv preprint arXiv:2010.11929 (2020)
6. Eigen, D., Fergus, R.: Predicting depth, surface normals and semantic labels with a common multi-scale convolutional architecture. In: Proceedings of the International Conference on Computer Vision (ICCV), pp. 2650–2658 (2015)
7. Eigen, D., Puhrsch, C., Fergus, R.: Depth map prediction from a single image using a multi-scale deep network. In: Advances in Neural Information Processing Systems (NeurIPS) (2014)
8. Esser, P., Rombach, R., Ommer, B.: Taming transformers for high-resolution image synthesis. In: Proceedings of the IEEE/CVF Conference on Computer Vision and Pattern Recognition, pp. 12873–12883 (2021)

9. Fu, H., Gong, M., Wang, C., Batmanghelich, K., Tao, D.: Deep ordinal regression network for monocular depth estimation. In: Proceedings of the IEEE Conference on Computer Vision and Pattern Recognition (CVPR), pp. 2002–2011 (2018)

10. Godard, C., Mac Aodha, O., Brostow, G.J.: Unsupervised monocular depth estimation with left-right consistency. In: Proceedings of the IEEE Conference on Computer Vision and Pattern Recognition (CVPR), pp. 270–279 (2017)

11. Godard, C., Mac Aodha, O., Firman, M., Brostow, G.J.: Digging into self-supervised monocular depth prediction. In: Proceedings of the International Conference on Computer Vision (ICCV) (2019)

12. Gordon, A., Li, H., Jonschkowski, R., Angelova, A.: Depth from videos in the wild: Unsupervised monocular depth learning from unknown cameras. In: Proceedings of the IEEE Conference on Computer Vision and Pattern Recognition (CVPR) (2019)

13. Guizilini, V., Ambrus, R., Pillai, S., Raventos, A., Gaidon, A.: 3D packing for self-supervised monocular depth estimation. In: Proceedings of the IEEE Conference on Computer Vision and Pattern Recognition (CVPR) (2020)

14. He, K., Zhang, X., Ren, S., Sun, J.: Deep residual learning for image recognition. In: Proceedings of the IEEE Conference on Computer Vision and Pattern Recognition (CVPR), pp. 770–778 (2016)

15. Im, S., Jeon, H.G., Lin, S., Kweon, I.S.: DPSNet: End-to-end deep plane sweep stereo. In: Proceedings of the International Conference on Learning Representations (ICLR) (2019)

16. Jaegle, A., et al.: Perceiver IO: a general architecture for structured inputs & outputs. arXiv preprint arXiv:2107.14795 (2021)

17. Jaegle, A., Gimeno, F., Brock, A., Vinyals, O., Zisserman, A., Carreira, J.: Perceiver: General perception with iterative attention. In: Proceedings of the International Conference on Machine Learning (ICML), pp. 4651–4664 (2021)

18. Kendall, A., et al.: End-to-end learning of geometry and context for deep stereo regression. In: Proceedings of the International Conference on Computer Vision (ICCV), pp. 66–75 (2017)

19. Kopf, J., Rong, X., Huang, J.B.: Robust consistent video depth estimation. In: Proceedings of the IEEE Conference on Computer Vision and Pattern Recognition (CVPR), pp. 1611–1621 (2021)

20. Kusupati, U., Cheng, S., Chen, R., Su, H.: Normal assisted stereo depth estimation. In: Proceedings of the IEEE Conference on Computer Vision and Pattern Recognition (CVPR), pp. 2189–2199 (2020)

21. Laina, I., Rupprecht, C., Belagiannis, V., Tombari, F., Navab, N.: Deeper depth prediction with fully convolutional residual networks. In: Proceedings of the International Conference on 3D Vision (3DV), pp. 239–248 (2016)

22. Lee, J.H., Han, M.K., Ko, D.W., Suh, I.H.: From big to small: multi-scale local planar guidance for monocular depth estimation. arXiv:1907.10326 (2019)

23. Li, Z., et al.: Revisiting stereo depth estimation from a sequence-to-sequence perspective with transformers. In: Proceedings of the IEEE/CVF International Conference on Computer Vision, pp. 6197–6206 (2021)

24. Lipson, L., Teed, Z., Deng, J.: RAFT-Stereo: multilevel recurrent field transforms for stereo matching. In: Proceedings of the International Conference on 3D Vision (3DV), pp. 218–227 (2021)

25. Liu, C., Gu, J., Kim, K., Narasimhan, S.G., Kautz, J.: Neural RGB → D sensing: Depth and uncertainty from a video camera. In: Proceedings of the IEEE Conference on Computer Vision and Pattern Recognition (CVPR), pp. 10986–10995 (2019)

26. Long, X., Liu, L., Li, W., Theobalt, C., Wang, W.: Multi-view depth estimation using epipolar spatio-temporal networks. In: Proceedings of the IEEE Conference on Computer Vision and Pattern Recognition (CVPR), pp. 8258–8267 (2021)
27. Long, X., Liu, L., Theobalt, C., Wang, W.: Occlusion-aware depth estimation with adaptive normal constraints. In: Proceedings of the European Conference on Computer Vision (ECCV), pp. 640–657 (2020)
28. Luo, X., Huang, J.B., Szeliski, R., Matzen, K., Kopf, J.: Consistent video depth estimation. ACM Trans. Graphics (TOG) **39**(4) (2020)
29. Mildenhall, B., Srinivasan, P.P., Tancik, M., Barron, J.T., Ramamoorthi, R., Ng, R.: NeRF: representing scenes as neural radiance fields for view synthesis. In: Proceedings of the European Conference on Computer Vision (ECCV), pp. 405–421 (2020)
30. Newcombe, R.A., et al.: KinectFusion: real-time dense surface mapping and tracking. In: Proceedings of the IEEE International Symposium on Mixed and Augmented Reality (ISMAR) (2011)
31. Novotny, D., Larlus, D., Vedaldi, A.: Learning 3D object categories by looking around them. In: Proceedings of the International Conference on Computer Vision (ICCV), pp. 5218–5227 (2017)
32. Ranftl, R., Bochkovskiy, A., Koltun, V.: Vision transformers for dense prediction. In: Proceedings of the IEEE/CVF International Conference on Computer Vision, pp. 12179–12188 (2021)
33. Ranftl, R., Lasinger, K., Hafner, D., Schindler, K., Koltun, V.: Towards robust monocular depth estimation: Mixing datasets for zero-shot cross-dataset transfer. IEEE Trans. Patt. Anal. Mach. Intell. **44**, 1623–1637 (2020)
34. Rematas, K., et al.: Urban radiance fields. arXiv preprint arXiv:2111.14643 (2021)
35. Rombach, R., Esser, P., Ommer, B.: Geometry-free view synthesis: transformers and no 3D priors. In: Proceedings of the International Conference on Computer Vision (ICCV), pp. 14356–14366 (2021)
36. Sajjadi, M.S., et al..: Scene representation transformer: Geometry-free novel view synthesis through set-latent scene representations. arXiv preprint arXiv:2111.13152 (2021)
37. Saxena, A., Chung, S., Ng, A.: Learning depth from single monocular images. In: Advances in Neural Information Processing Systems (NeurIPS) (2005)
38. Schonberger, J.L., Frahm, J.M.: Structure-from-motion revisited. In: Proceedings of the IEEE Conference on Computer Vision and Pattern Recognition (CVPR), pp. 4104–4113 (2016)
39. Shorten, C., Khoshgoftaar, T.M.: A survey on image data augmentation for deep learning. J. Big Data **6**(1), 1–48 (2019)
40. Shotton, J., Glocker, B., Zach, C., Izadi, S., Criminisi, A., Fitzgibbon, A.: Scene coordinate regression forests for camera relocalization in RGB-D images. In: Proceedings of the IEEE Conference on Computer Vision and Pattern Recognition (CVPR), pp. 2930–2937 (2013)
41. Shu, C., Yu, K., Duan, Z., Yang, K.: Feature-metric loss for self-supervised learning of depth and egomotion. In: Proceedings of the European Conference on Computer Vision (ECCV), pp. 572–588 (2020)
42. Sitzmann, V., Rezchikov, S., Freeman, B., Tenenbaum, J., Durand, F.: Light field networks: neural scene representations with single-evaluation rendering. In: Advances in Neural Information Processing Systems (NeurIPS) (2021)
43. Sun, J., Xie, Y., Chen, L., Zhou, X., Bao, H.: NeuralRecon: real-time coherent 3D reconstruction from monocular video. In: Proceedings of the IEEE Conference on Computer Vision and Pattern Recognition (CVPR), pp. 15598–15607 (2021)

44. Tang, C., Tan, P.: BA-Net: Dense bundle adjustment network. arXiv preprint arXiv:1806.04807 (2018)
45. Teed, Z., Deng, J.: DeepV2D: video to depth with differentiable structure from motion. In: Proceedings of the International Conference on Learning Representations (ICLR) (2020)
46. Teed, Z., Deng, J.: RAFT: recurrent all-pairs field transforms for optical flow. In: Proceedings of the European Conference on Computer Vision (ECCV) (2020)
47. Teed, Z., Deng, J.: DROID-SLAM: deep visual SLAM for monocular, stereo, and RGB-D cameras. In: Advances in Neural Information Processing Systems (NeurIPS) (2021)
48. Teed, Z., Deng, J.: Raft-3D: Scene flow using rigid-motion embeddings. In: Proceedings of the IEEE Conference on Computer Vision and Pattern Recognition (CVPR), pp. 8375–8384 (2021)
49. Ummenhofer, B., et al.: DeMoN: depth and motion network for learning monocular stereo. In: Proceedings of the IEEE Conference on Computer Vision and Pattern Recognition (CVPR), pp. 5038–5047 (2017)
50. Vasiljevic, I., et al.: Neural ray surfaces for self-supervised learning of depth and ego-motion. In: Proceedings of the International Conference on 3D Vision (3DV) (2020)
51. Vaswani, A., et al.: Attention is all you need. In: Advances in Neural Information Processing Systems (NeurIPS) (2017)
52. Watson, J., Mac Aodha, O., Prisacariu, V., Brostow, G., Firman, M.: The temporal opportunist: Self-supervised multi-frame monocular depth. In: Proceedings of the IEEE Conference on Computer Vision and Pattern Recognition (CVPR), pp. 1164–1174 (2021)
53. Wei, Y., Liu, S., Rao, Y., Zhao, W., Lu, J., Zhou, J.: NerfingMVS: guided optimization of neural radiance fields for indoor multi-view stereo. In: Proceedings of the International Conference on Computer Vision (ICCV) (2021)
54. Xie, Y., et al.: Neural fields in visual computing and beyond. arXiv preprint arXiv:2111.11426 (2021)
55. Yao, Y., Luo, Z., Li, S., Fang, T., Quan, L.: MVSNet: depth inference for unstructured multi-view stereo. In: Proceedings of the European Conference on Computer Vision (ECCV), pp. 767–783 (2018)
56. Yifan, W., Doersch, C., Arandjelović, R., Carreira, J., Zisserman, A.: Input-level inductive biases for 3D reconstruction. arXiv preprint arXiv:2112.03243 (2021)
57. Yu, A., Ye, V., Tancik, M., Kanazawa, A.: pixelNeRF: neural radiance fields from one or few images. In: Proceedings of the IEEE Conference on Computer Vision and Pattern Recognition (CVPR) (2021)
58. Zhou, H., Ummenhofer, B., Brox, T.: DeepTAM: deep tracking and mapping. In: Proceedings of the European Conference on Computer Vision (ECCV), pp. 822–838 (2018)
59. Zhou, T., Brown, M., Snavely, N., Lowe, D.G.: Unsupervised learning of depth and ego-motion from video. In: Proceedings of the IEEE Conference on Computer Vision and Pattern Recognition (CVPR) (2017)
60. Zhu, Z., et al.: NICE-SLAM: neural implicit scalable encoding for SLAM. arXiv preprint arXiv:2112.12130 (2021)

Context-Enhanced Stereo Transformer

Weiyu Guo[1,2](✉)(iD), Zhaoshuo Li[3](✉)(iD), Yongkui Yang[1](✉)(iD),
Zheng Wang[1](✉)(iD), Russell H. Taylor[3], Mathias Unberath[3], Alan Yuille[3],
and Yingwei Li[3](✉)(iD)

[1] Shenzhen Institute of Advanced Technology, Chinese Academy of Sciences,
Shenzhen, China
{wy.guo,yk.yang,zheng.wang}@siat.ac.cn
[2] University of Chinese Academy of Sciences, Beijing, China
[3] Johns Hopkins University, Baltimore, USA
{zli122,yingwei.li}@jhu.edu

Abstract. Stereo depth estimation is of great interest for computer
vision research. However, existing methods struggles to generalize and
predict reliably in hazardous regions, such as large uniform regions.
To overcome these limitations, we propose Context Enhanced Path
(CEP). CEP improves the generalization and robustness against common failure cases in existing solutions by capturing the long-range global
information. We construct our stereo depth estimation model, Context
Enhanced Stereo Transformer (CSTR), by plugging CEP into the state-
of-the-art stereo depth estimation method Stereo Transformer. CSTR is
examined on distinct public datasets, such as Scene Flow, Middlebury-
2014, KITTI-2015, and MPI-Sintel. We find CSTR outperforms prior
approaches by a large margin. For example, in the zero-shot synthetic-
to-real setting, CSTR outperforms the best competing approaches on
Middlebury-2014 dataset by 11%. Our extensive experiments demonstrate that the long-range information is critical for stereo matching
task and CEP successfully captures such information([1]Code available
at: github.com/guoweiyu/Context-Enhanced-Stereo-Transformer).

Keywords: Stereo depth estimation · Transformer · Context
extraction

1 Introduction

Stereo depth estimation is a critical task in computer vision that has been widely
used in various fields, such as robotics [27], autonomous driving [24], and 3D
scene reconstruction [29]. Recent developments in learning-based stereo disparity estimation algorithms generally use using techniques restricted to local information for matching the feature patterns between the left and right images. For
example, prior works [2,8,36] construct a cost volume with pre-defined disparity
range and use 3D convolutions to process the cost volume, limiting themselves
to the receptive field of convolution kernel. Xu *et al.*[32] proposed to instead
process the cost volume using 2D convolutions, however, facing the same challenge. Recently, approaches that attempt to capture more global information

© The Author(s), under exclusive license to Springer Nature Switzerland AG 2022
S. Avidan et al. (Eds.): ECCV 2022, LNCS 13692, pp. 263–279, 2022.
https://doi.org/10.1007/978-3-031-19824-3_16

have been proposed. For example, STTR [17] and RAFT-Stereo [19] computes attention or correlation between all pixels of the left and right images on the same epipolar lines. However, they all fail to take advantage of cross-epipolar line information, which is a critical component of global information processing. Thus, as shown in Fig. 1, these methods cannot address hazardous regions like textureless, large uniform regions, specularity, and transparency [15,37], which are particularly challenging for stereo algorithms to produce reliable estimates. The features of left and right frames in these regions are often similar or misleading, which makes the feature matching ambiguous [37]. If disparities of these regions cannot be reliably predicted, downstream applications, such as 3D object detection [28], may be severely impacted due to missing or wrong predictions. Therefore, in this paper, we seek to answer this critical question: how to guide the stereo models properly handle those hazardous regions.

To address this question, we hypothesize that the long-range contextual information help to improve the predictions on hazardous regions. For example, as shown in Fig. 1(a), previous work performs unreliably in large white wall. However, if we could use the global information (e.g., orientation, edge information) of the house, the prediction can be improved. Such global context information in theory will inform the model about the geometry on a global scale and guide the model to resolve the ambiguity in prediction. To this end, we proposed a plug-in module, called Context Enhanced Path (CEP), which helps stereo matching models to better understand the global structure of the hazardous regions. Compared to existing methods, CEP offers the following three unique advantages: (1) strong generalization ability, compared with previous methods [2,17], CEP shows strong results on unseened real-world data even if only training on synthetic data; (2) robustness against hazardous, thanks to modeling the long-range contextual information.(3) generic, unlike [9,14,34], our method serves as a plug-in that can be potentially applied to most of stereo matching methods.

We construct our stereo depth estimation model based on CEP, namely Context Enhanced Stereo Transformer (CSTR). We have examined CSTR on several popular and diverse datasets, such as, Middlebury-2014 [26], KITTI-2015 [24], and MPI sintel [1]. Our extensive experiments demonstrate that (1) the long-range information is critical for stereo depth estimation, (2) CSTR attains strong generalization ability, and (3) more importantly, CSTR can better handle hazardous regions, such as texturelessness and disparity jumps (shown in Fig. 1 and Table 3). This result is attributed to our simple yet powerful observation: using long-range contextual information to better understand the global structure of the image can significantly help stereo depth estimation especially for those hazardous area. This result suggests that modeling long-range context information is critical for building a robust and generalizable stereo depth estimation algorithm.

To summarize, our contributions are 3-fold: (1) we found global contextual information is critical for stereo depth estimation; (2) we design a plug-in module, Context Enhanced Path (CEP), for generic stereo depth estimation models; (3) we integrate our plug-in module and build a stereo matching model named Context Enhanced Stereo Transformer (CSTR), which achieves the state-of-the-

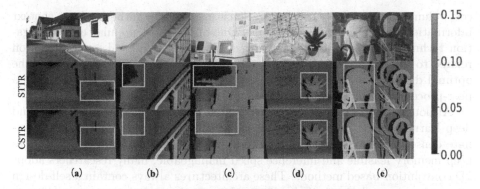

Fig. 1. Sample visualizations of hazardous regions taken from KITTI-2015 and Middlebury-2014 datasets. First row is the input left images. Second row is the disparity predicted by Stereo Transformer (STTR) [17]. Third row is the disparity predicted by our proposed Context Enhanced Stereo Transformer (CSTR). The color map shown on the right is based on the disparity value relative to the image width.

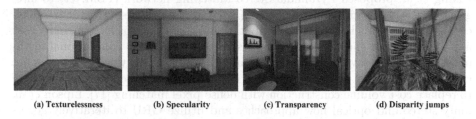

(a) Texturelessness   (b) Specularity   (c) Transparency   (d) Disparity jumps

Fig. 2. Examples of hazardous regions including: (a) Texturelessness: the wall and the ceiling in the room a (b) Specularity: the screen of a TV (c) Transparency: the sliding door (d) Disparity jumps: objects such as bamboos, fences and plants give frequent disparity discontinuities. Images are from Zhang *et al.* [37].

art generalisation results on several popular datasets, including Middlebury-2014-2014 [26], KITTI-2015 [24], and MPI-sintel [1].

2   Related Work

Rectified stereo depth estimation obtains per-pixel depth from the left and right frames provided by the binocular camera. It has a wide range of applications in robotics, autonomous driving, scene understanding, 3D modeling, *etc.* In contrast to the success of deep learning in many high-level vision problems, low-level deep learning algorithms for vision tasks are still in their early stages [15]. In the field of stereo depth estimation, many works aim to improve a single step of the classical pipeline by replacing it with a deep learning module [15,38], where the quality of cost volume directly determines the accuracy of the disparity map. Chen *et al.* proposed Deep Embed to learn a cost function from different windows by processing multi-patches at different resolutions [4]. After cost volume computation, cost aggregation is essential for gathering large context information from the huge cost volume. One of the most popular cost aggregation techniques is Semiglobal Matching (SGM) [12]. A global energy function related to the disparity map is set to minimize this energy function to solve the optimal disparity of each pixel. The raw disparity map should be refined by a post-processing algorithm.

Although there are still several remaining challenges, recently, end-to-end deep learning begin to be used in binocular stereo depth estimation and dominate dense disparity estimation in several well-known benchmarks. In order to keep memory feasible and inference speed manageable, many researchers adopt 2D convolution-based methods. These architectures always contain a self-design layer namely correlation layer in charge of computing correlation scores between left and right features. Mayer *et al.* proposed an encoder-decoder architecture based on U-net named DispNet [23]. Some researchers adopt 3D convolutions in stereo matching which take a 4D tensor (disparity range, height, weight, feature) as the input and directly process a matching volume-like representation. Chang *et al.* proposed Pyramidal Stereo Matching network (PSMNet) to integrate Spatial Pyramidal Pooling layers (SPP) in the feature extractor [2]. However, these methods lead to large computational costs, such as huge memory cost and low inference speed. Besides, the disparity range of the conventional methods are limited, preventing them to be used in many cases when the scenes are close to the camera. Recently, Li *et al.* use a sequence-to-sequence perspective to replace cost volume construction with dense pixel matching [17]. Lipson *et al.* unify stereo and optical flow approaches and utilize GRU to iteratively generate the final disparity map [19]. Others [16,18] exploit auxiliary information for detph estimation. However, stereo depth estimation is still limited by difficulties like textureless surfaces, disparity jumps, and occlusions.

Hazardous Regions. Most of stereo algorithms rely on the following basic assumptions [37]: (1) well-textured local surface for feature extraction without large homogeneous regions; (2) single image layer assumption with only Lambertian surface; (3) the disparity varies slowly and smoothly in space without sudden jumps. However, as shown in Fig. 2, these assumptions can easily be broken in many real world scenarios. For example, textureless regions like large wall are commonly seen and specular surfaces will create multiple image layers. Furthermore, disparity jumps can break the local smoothness assumption. The aforementioned regions are called hazardous regions [35]. In this work, we specifically study these commonly seen yet challenging scenarios for more robust stereo depth estimation.

Efficient Attention. Attention has a good ability to capture correspondence between two sequences and solves the problem that RNN cannot be calculated in parallel [30]. There are many successful applications that adopt attention to encode long-range sequences [3]. Recently, attention has been applied to extract non-local features in computer vision and led to SOTA performance for

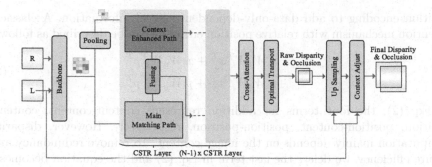

Fig. 3. CSTR consists of two main components:(1) Context Enhanced Path that extracts long-range context information in low resolution feature. (2) Main Matching Path that use Axial-Attention to enhance context and Cross-Attention to compute raw disparity. Then a learnable Up Sampling block up restore the original scale of disparity and Context Adjustment block refines the disparity with context information across epipolar lines conditioned on the left image.

many vision tasks [7]. However, it is computational expensive when the input of attention module is large. In order to reduce its complexity, efficient attention approaches have been proposed. Yang *et al.*incorporate coarse-grained global attention and fine-grained local attentions depending on the distance to the token [33].

Axial Attention. Wang *et al.* factorize 2D self-attention into two 1D self-attentions to propose Axial-Attention [31]. In this paper, we adopt Axial-Attention to enhance context of feature before pixel matching. Most previous works proposed efficient attention by adding various local constraints. However, these constraints always sacrifice the global context and limit the attention's receptive field.

To ensure both efficient computation and global context, Wang et al. employ two Axial-Attention layers consecutively for the height-axis and width-axis, respectively [31]. A width-axis attention layer can be described as:

$$y_i = \sum_{j \in N_{(W*1)}(i)} S(q_i^T k_i + q_i^T r_{j-i})(v_j) \tag{1}$$

where $N_{w*1}(i)$ is the $w * h$ scale 1D region around i stands for relative position encoding, and q, k, v, S denote query, key, value, soft-max, respectively. In practice, $w * h$ is much smaller than the full feature shape.

Compared with local constraints attention, width-Axial-Attention computes the attention line by line with weight sharing. W is equal to the width of input. Height-axis attention is the same as width-Axial-Attention besides computing the attention column by column.

Furthermore, positional information is critical for pixel matching, especially in large textureless regions. Due to shift-invariance in an image, we adopt relative position encoding to add data-only-dependent spatial information. A classical attention mechanism with relative position encoding can be described as follows.

$$
\begin{aligned}
a_{i,j} = {} & x_i W_q W_k^T x_j^T + x_i W_q W_k^T p_j^T \\
& + p_i W_q W_k^T x_j^T + p_i W_q W_k^T p_j^T
\end{aligned}
\tag{2}
$$

In Eq. (2), the four terms for addition represent content-content, content-position, position-content, position-position, respectively. However, disparity computation mainly depends on the image content. To remove redundancy and ensure efficiency, we delete the last term in Eq. (2) and the equation becomes:

$$
a_{i,j} = x_i W_q W_k^T x_j^T + x_i W_q W_k^T p_j^T + p_i W_q W_k^T x_j^T
\tag{3}
$$

In the field of NLP, a similar design is adopted in DeBERT [11] and it is found that most tasks only require relative position information.

3 Context Enhanced Path

We propose a plug-in module, Context Enhanced Path (CEP), that provides additional context information to help stereo matching model to better understand the global structure of the input images. The goal of CEP is to maintain the context features for left and right images, and provide the context features to the Main Matching Path as additional complementary information. The detailed structure of the CEP is shown in Fig. 4. As a layer-by-layer module, CEP first obtains the context feature from the previous CEP layer. Then, the Axial-Attention layer and the Cross-Attention layer are applied to further process the context features. The processed context features are served as the complementary information used for fusing with the Main Matching Path. Finally, we generate the context features as the input of the next CEP layer with 3 different strategies (M_1, M_2, M_3). From M_1 to M_3, the enhancement of the context information extraction increases sequentially. In the M_1, we only use low-level features to extract context information. Specifically, the features output by backbone only go through one layer of Axial-Attention and one layer of Cross-Attention before fusing with the main matching path. Compared to M_1, M_2 extract higher-level context information. In the M_2, the features output by backbone go through L layers of Axial-Attention and one layer of Cross-Attention before being fused to the L-th layer of the main matching path. In the M_3, the features output by backbone go through L layers of Axial-Attention and L layers of Cross-Attention before the fusion.

4 Context Enhanced Stereo Transformer

Based on our proposed Context Enhanced Path, we further propose a transformer-based stereo depth estimation model, Context Enhanced Stereo Transformer (CSTR). We will first introduce the architecture of CSTR, and then introduce each component in detail.

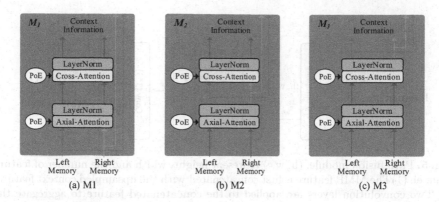

Fig. 4. Three different design choices for Context Enhanced Path (CEP). All strategies are composed of Axial-Attention and Cross-Attention, but the feature fed to next layer is different.

4.1 Pipeline

The architecture of CSTR is shown in Fig. 3. The whole pipeline is mainly following the architecture of STTR [17] but the context information is enhanced. Given the pair of left (L) and right (R) input images, a convolution-based backbone is used to extract the left and right features separately. The pair of left and right features then processed by several CSTR layers to obtain the disparity map with a coarse-to-fine manner. In each CSTR layer, there are 3 critical modules (Context Enhanced Path, Main Matching Path, and the path fusion module) that helps to incorporate the context information for generating better disparity map. The Context Enhanced Path is discussed in Sect. 3, the other two modules, Main Matching Path and the path fusion module, will be explained in detail in the rest part of this section. Finally, we apply several post-processing modules (*e.g.*, optimal transport layer, upsampling layer, and context adjust layer) to obtain the final disparity.

4.2 Main Matching Path

Main Matching Path is similar to the Transformer module from STTR [17], which includes a self-attention module followed by a Cross-Attention module as shown in Fig. 6(a). The self-attention module is used to aggregate the information in the same image, while the Cross-Attention module is used to compute the similarity of pixels from the different images. Note that the self-attention module only computes attention between pixels along the *same* epipolar line in the same image, leading to difficulty to collection contextual information from other epipolar lines.

To help the model gather more context information, as shown in Fig. 6(b), we replace the original self-attention layer to an Axial-Attention layer, including a horizontal Axial-Attention module and a vertical Axial-Attention module, to collect the context information from both horizontal and vertical axials.

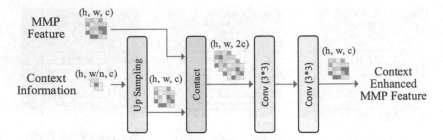

Fig. 5. Path fusion module. (h, w,c) represent height, width and the number of feature channel. (1)The MMP feature is first concatenated with the upsampled context feature. (2) Two convolution layers are applied to the concatenated feature to aggregate the context information to the Main Matching Path(MMP) features. (3) We use the fused feature as the input of the next MMP module

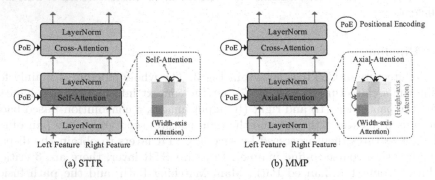

Fig. 6. (a) Overview of the Matching Path in STTR. (b) Overview of the Main Matching Path with alternating Axial-Attention and Cross-Attention in CSTR.

4.3   Path Fusion Module

The path fusion module aims to fuse the context feature from the Context Enhanced Path (CEP) to the main matching features in the Main Matching Path (MMP). This will keep the main matching path capturing long-range context from low-resolution features. The architecture is shown in Fig. 5. Specifically, the MMP feature is first concatenated with the upsampled context feature. Then, two convolution layers are applied to the concatenated feature to aggregate the context information to the main features. Finally, we use the fused feature as the input of the next main matching path module.

4.4 Other Important Modules

This section discuss other important modules in our pipeline, including Attention Mask, Optimal Transport, Raw Disparity and Occlusion Computation. Other details are illustrated in Sect. 5.2.

Attention Mask and Optimal Transport. We further compress the pixels' matching space based on the following two observations.

First, when a point in the physical world is imaged by a binocular camera, the imaging position in the left image will be more to the left than the imaging position in the right image. Let us denote the P_L, P_R as the imaging point of a real point in the left and right image. Then the following formula always holds:

$$P_L - P_R <= 0 \tag{4}$$

Therefore, the point at P_L in the left image should just match the candidate point at $P > P_L$ in the right image.

Second, every pixel in the left image can only match one pixel in the right image which is called uniqueness constraint. We adopt entropy-regularized optimal transport [5] to implement such constraints in a soft way. Entropy-regularized optimal transport is proposed to improve the network performance in a similar task of semantic correspondence matching [21]. In the following section, we denote the optimal transport assignment matrix as T which contains a correlation score of pixels in two images.

Raw Disparity and Occlusion Computation. In order to improve the model robustness in multi-modal distributions, we use a small number of candidate disparity in a local region rather than use all candidate disparity. First, we compute raw disparity by finding the location(S_h) of the highest correlation score. Then, a 3 px window $N_{3x3}(S_h)$ is built around S_h in matrix T to regress raw disparity. t is used to represent correlation score in $N_{3x3}(S_h)$. The raw disparity regression can be described as:

$$\sum_{i \in N_{3*3}(S_h)} t_i = 1, i \in N_{3*3}(S_h) \tag{5}$$

$$\overline{t_i} = \frac{t_i}{\sum_{i \in N_{3*3}(S_h)}}, i \in N_{3*3}(S_h) \tag{6}$$

$$\overline{d_{raw}}(S_h) = \sum_{i \in N_{3*3}(S_h)} d_i \overline{t_i} \tag{7}$$

where $\overline{d_{raw}}$ represents regressed raw disparity and d_i denotes the raw disparity in $N_{3*3}(S_h)$. Occlusion probability($p_{occ}(S_h)$) can be interpreted as the probability that one pixel has no matching pixel in another image. Thus it can be described as (Fig. 7):

$$p_{occ}(S_h) = 1 - \sum_{i \in N_{3*3}(S_h)} t_i \tag{8}$$

Fig. 7. Results on KITTI-2015, Middlebury-2014, MPI Sintel in zero-shot synthetic-to-real setting. Black represent occlusion. The color map is the image width × 0.2 and is shown on the right which used to visualize disparity. (Color figure online)

5   Experiments

5.1   Experimental Settings

Datasets. We evaluate CSTR on four popular but diverse datasets: Scene Flow [23], KITTI-2015 [24], Middlebury [26], and MPI Sintel [1]. These datasets contain random objects, real street scene, indoor scene, and realistic artifacts, respectively. Scene Flow is a synthetic dataset of random object with many subset. We use FlyingThings3D subset with 21818 training samples (960 × 540) in the experiment. KITTI-2015 contains stereo videos of road scenes from a calibrated pair of cameras mounted on a car with 200 training samples (1242 × 375). MPI Sintel contains sufficiently realistic scenes including natural image degradations such as fog and motion blur with 1064 training samples (1024 × 436).

Evaluation Metric. We use both EPE (end-point-error) and 3 px Error (percentage of EPE > 3) as evaluation metrics. we use Intersection over Union (IOU) to evaluate occlusion estimation. In the rest of this Section, we report the results for the non-occluded regions.

5.2   Implementation Details

CSTR is implemented in Pytorch [25] and is trained using one Tesla A100 GPU. During training, we use the AdamW [22] optimizer with weight decay of 1e–4. We pre-train on Scene Flow for 17 epochs using a fixed learning rate of 1e–4 for the CSTR layer and backbone, and 2e–4 for the context adjustment layer.

Feature Extractor. In order to efficiently extract both global and local context information, we adopt an hourglass-shaped feature extractor composed of encoding and decoding paths. The encoding path is based on spatial pyramid pooling [2] modules and residual blocks [10] while the decoding path consists of dens-blocks [13], transposed convolution layer, a final average pooling layer

Fig. 8. KITTI-2015's ground truth is missing part of occlusion. However CSTR can accurately give this part of the missing occlusion. First row are left image and ground truth. Second row are right image and our predicted disparity.

for generating multi-scale features. The scale of feature map output by transposed convolution layer is at 1/4 resolution as the input image. For an input like (H,W), we generate a multi-scale feature$(H,W/2K)$ with repeating average pooling of the width dimension, where K is the down sample rate.

Supervision. Motivated by Relative Response loss L_{rr} [20], we split assignment matrix T to matched pixel sets M and unmatched pixel sets U. The loss can be described as:

$$t_i^* = LinerInterp(T_i, p_i - d_{gt,i}) \tag{9}$$

$$L_{rr} = \frac{1}{N_M} \sum_{i \in M} -log(t_i^*) + \frac{1}{N_U} \sum_{i \in M} -log(t_{i,\Phi}) \tag{10}$$

where t_i stands for i-th matching probability and $d_{gt,i}$ represents i-th ground truth disparity. To accelerate the convergence of the model, we adopt smooth L1 [6] on both raw and final disparities. Furthermore, we use a binary-entropy loss to supervise the occlusion map. The total loss L is computed as:

$$\begin{aligned} L = w_1 L_{rr,raw} + w_2 L_{d1,raw} + \\ w_3 L_{d1,final} + w_4 L_{be,final} \end{aligned} \tag{11}$$

where $L_{rr,raw}$, $L_{d1,raw}$, $L_{d1,final}$, $L_{be,final}$ represent Relative Response loss on raw disparity, L1 loss on raw disparity, L1 loss on final disparity,binary-entropy loss on final occlusion, respectively.

Hyperparameters. In our experiments, we use 6 CSTR layers with feature of 128 channels. We use multi-head attention with 4 heads. The resolution of feature in MMP is set to 1/4 of full resolution. Sinkhorn algorithm is run for 10 iterations [5].

Baselines. In this work, we compare CSTR with prior work based on different learning-based stereo depth paradigms: **PSMNet** [2] is a 3D convolution-based model consists two main modules—spatial pyramid pooling and 3D CNN; **AANet** [32] is a correlation-based model which is proposed to replace 3D

Table 1. Generalization experiment. The models are only trained on Scene Flow without fine-tuning on MPI Sintel, KITTI-2015, Middlebury-2014 dataset. **Bold** is the best result.

	Middlebury 2014(varies)			MPI Sintel† (1024 * 436)			KITTI-2015 (1242 * 375)		
	3px Error ↓	EPE ↓	Occ IOU ↑	3px Error ↓	EPE ↓	Occ IOU ↑	3px Error ↓	EPE ↓	Occ IOU ↑
AANet	6.29	2.24	Null	9.57	**1.71**	Null	7.06	1.31	Null
PSMNet	7.93	3.70	Null	10.24	2.02	Null	7.43	1.39	Null
GwcNet-g	5.83	1.32	Null	6.60	1.95	Null	6.75	1.59	Null
RAFT-Stereo	7.57	1.21	Null	13.02	17.36	Null	5.00	1.10	Null
STTR	6.19	2.33	0.95	5.75	3.01	0.86	6.74	1.50	0.98
CSTR (Ours)	**5.16**	**1.16**	**0.95**	**5.51**	2.58	**0.92**	5.78	1.43	**0.98**

convolutions to realize fast inference speed while ensure comparable accuracy; **GwcNet-g** [8] is a correlation and 3D convolution hybrid approach which constructs the cost volume by group-wise correlation; **STTR** [17] is a transformer-based model which revisits the problem from a sequence-to-sequence correspondence perspective to replace cost volume construction; **RAFT-stereo** [19] is a state-of-the-art recurrent model on Middlebury-2014 and Scene Flow datasets using iterative refinement to compute disparity.

5.3 Zero-Shot Generalization

We compare the zero-shot generalization ability between our proposed CSTR and previous popular stereo depth estimation methods. Specifically, the models are trained on the SceneFlow synthetic dataset, and then test on real data such as KITTI-2015 (real outdoor scene), Middlebury-2014 (real indoor scene), and MPI Sintel (Synthesized complex game scenes).

The results are shown in Table 1. Our model CSTR is better than our baseline method STTR [17] on all datasets and on all different metrics. For example, compared with the STTR baseline, the 3px error on Middlebury dataset is improved from 6.19 to 5.16. These improvement shows that the design of context extraction of our network facilitates generalization.

Besides, our model achieves the best results on both Middlebury 2014 and MPI Sintel datasets compared with previous methods. The quantitative results on KITTI-2015 dataset is not as good as RAFT-Stereo. Compared with RAFT-Stereo, the 3px error is dropped from 5.68 to 5.78. However, by visualizing and comparing the ground-truth label and the output of CSTR, we observe that our predicted results are even more precise than the grounding truth in the occlusion areas. See Fig. 8 for more details.

5.4 Ablations

In Table 2, we provide quantitative results for the effects of the Axial-Attention and three different context extraction strategies. All ablated models are trained on FlyingThings of Scene Flow. Below we describe each of the experiments in more detail.

Table 2. Ablation generalization experiments.The model only trained on Scene Flow without fine-tune. Following prior work, we validate on the Scene Flow test set. STTR: Stereo Transformer; MMP: Main Matching Path with Aixal-Attention; M_1, M_1, M_1 are three different Context Enhanced Path.

Experiment					Scene flow			Middlebury-2014		
STTR	MMP	M_1	M_2	M_3	3px Err	EPE	IOU	3px Err	EPE	IOU
✓					1.54	0.50	0.97	6.93	2.24	0.95
✓	✓				1.28	0.43	0.98	5.55	2.03	0.95
✓	✓	✓			**1.18**	0.42	0.98	5.47	1.44	0.95
✓	✓		✓		1.20	0.42	0.98	5.38	1.60	0.95
✓	✓			✓	1.20	**0.42**	**0.98**	**5.13**	**1.16**	**0.95**

Main Matching Path. Main Matching Path adopt Axial-Attention which factorizing 2D self-attention into two 1D self-attentions rather than the stand-alone self attention. This allows performing attention in a larger region to extract context information with acceptable computation cost. As shown in Table 2, comparing with STTR which adopt 1D attention on epipolar, Main Matching Path have better EPE and 3px Err. Especially, it reduce EPE by 17% and reduce 3px Err by 14% on Scene Flow. This improvement shows that the global information extracted by Axial-Attention is benefit to stereo matching.

Three Context Enhanced Path Strategies. We design three different context enhanced strategies(M_1, M_2, M_3) that extract the context from low resolution features to enhanced the Main Matching Path. M_1, M_2, M_3 improve the result of EPE and 3px Error on Scene Flow, especially, M_3 achieves an EPE 7% reduction. As it has been approved, these context enhanced strategies of CEP further impove the stereo matching performance. The result on Scene FLow of three strategies are verly similar, we will further compare their real-world generalization performance and robustness in following Section.

Real World Generalization Experiment. We evaluate the generalization performance of MMP and three CEP on Middlebury-2014. The model only trained on FlyingThings of Scene Flow. As listed in Table 2, the MMP significantly outperform the baseline setting STTR which only has 1D self-attentions epipolar. The Axial-Attention for global information extraction reduce the EPE and the 3px Err by 20% and 9% on Middlebury-2014. This shows the global information is critical for model's generalization.

All three context enhanced strategies outperform the MMP. It shows that the context information provided by CET facilitates generalization. M_3 achieves the best results on both EPE and 3px Err. For example, compared with MMP, M_3 reduce the 3px error by 7% and even reduce the EPE by 42%. This proves that the design of our CEP is important for enhancing generalization performance.

Table 3. EPE results of Ablation and Rubostness experiments. The model only trained on Scene Flow without fine-tune. Hazardous Data is a dataset that label the hazardous regions in KITTI-2015 [37]; SPL: Specularity; TEL:Texturelessness; TRS:Transparency.

Experiment					Hazardous data			
STTR	MMP	M_1	M_2	M_3	SPL	TEL	TRS	AVG
✓					5.43	10.42	7.03	7.63
✓	✓				4.98	8.59	6.8	6.79
✓	✓	✓			4.75	10.74	7.64	7.71
✓	✓		✓		**3.68**	11.28	7.01	7.32
✓	✓			✓	4.54	**8.21**	**6.01**	**6.25**

Finally, compared with STTR, the best setting of CSTR with Axial-Attention and CEP of M_3 reduce the 3px error by 26% and even reduce the EPE by 48%.

Robustness Against Hazardous Regions. The images regions like texturelessness, transparency, specularity are likely to cause the failure of an algorithm, namely hazardous regions [35]. Zhang *et al.* [37] lable the hazardous regions in KITTI-2015 and we use it to provide quantitative results for the effects of the MMP, three CEP strategies summarized in Table 3. Using Axial-Attention instead of stand alone self-attention can effectively improve average EPE of harzardous regions in with 11%, especially on Textureless regions with 17%. Using M_1 or M_2, which memory feature just past one Cross-Attention layer, lead to a decrease in average EPE. However, M_3 which are used in our final CSTR, can bring additional 8 % improvement in average EPE compared with MMP. This may be because M_3 uses the same number of Cross-Attention layers as MMP, which is beneficial for MMP to better integrate context information.

6   Conclusions

Current stereo depth estimation models usually fail to handle the hazardous regions. In this paper, we found using global context information mitigate this issue. Therefore, we proposed a plug-in module, Context Enhanced Path. Based on CEP, we then built a stereo depth estimation model, Context Enhanced Stereo Transformer. According to our experimental results, our method achieves strong cross dataset generalization ability, handles hazardous regions robustly, and provides accurate occlusion prediction.

Acknowledgments. This paper is supported by Key-Area Research and Development Program of Guangdong Province (Grant No. 2019B010155003), Guangdong Basic and Applied Basic Research Foundation (Grant No. 2020B1515120044, 2020A1515110495), Johns Hopkins University internal funds, ONR award N00014-21-1-2812, and NIH award K08DC019708.

References

1. Butler, D.J., Wulff, J., Stanley, G.B., Black, M.J.: A naturalistic open source movie for optical flow evaluation. In: Fitzgibbon, A., Lazebnik, S., Perona, P., Sato, Y., Schmid, C. (eds.) ECCV 2012. LNCS, vol. 7577, pp. 611–625. Springer, Heidelberg (2012). https://doi.org/10.1007/978-3-642-33783-3_44

2. Chang, J.R., Chen, Y.S.: Pyramid stereo matching network. In: Proceedings of the IEEE Conference on Computer Vision and Pattern Recognition, pp. 5410–5418 (2018)

3. Chaudhari, S., Mithal, V., Polatkan, G., Ramanath, R.: An attentive survey of attention models. ACM Trans. Intell. Syst. Technol. 12(5), 1–32 (2021)

4. Chen, Z., Sun, X., Wang, L., Yu, Y., Huang, C.: A deep visual correspondence embedding model for stereo matching costs. In: Proceedings of the IEEE International Conference on Computer Vision, pp. 972–980 (2015)

5. Cuturi, M.: Sinkhorn distances: lightspeed computation of optimal transport. Adv, Neural Inform. Process. Syst. 26 (2013)

6. Girshick, R.: Fast R-CNN. In: Proceedings of the IEEE International Conference on Computer Vision, pp. 1440–1448 (2015)

7. Guo, M.H., et al.: Attention mechanisms in computer vision: a survey. arXiv preprint arXiv:2111.07624 (2021)

8. Guo, X., Yang, K., Yang, W., Wang, X., Li, H.: Group-wise correlation stereo network. In: Proceedings of the IEEE/CVF Conference on Computer Vision and Pattern Recognition, pp. 3273–3282 (2019)

9. Hartmann, W., Galliani, S., Havlena, M., Gool, L.V., Schindler, K.: Learned multi-patch similarity. In: 2017 IEEE International Conference on Computer Vision (ICCV) (2017)

10. He, K., Zhang, X., Ren, S., Sun, J.: Deep residual learning for image recognition. IEEE (2016)

11. He, P., Liu, X., Gao, J., Chen, W.: Deberta: decoding-enhanced bert with disentangled attention. arXiv (2020)

12. Hirschmuller, H.: Stereo processing by semiglobal matching and mutual information. IEEE Trans. Patt. Anal. Mach. Intell. 30(2), 328–341 (2007)

13. Huang, G., Liu, Z., Laurens, V., Weinberger, K.Q.: Densely connected convolutional networks. IEEE Computer Society (2016)

14. Huang, P.H., Matzen, K., Kopf, J., Ahuja, N., Huang, J.B.: Deepmvs: learning multi-view stereopsis. IEEE (2018)

15. Laga, H., Jospin, L.V., Boussaid, F., Bennamoun, M.: A survey on deep learning techniques for stereo-based depth estimation. IEEE Trans. Patt. Anal. Mach. Intell. 44, 1738–1764 (2020)

16. Li, Z., Drenkow, N., et al.: On the sins of image synthesis loss for self-supervised depth estimation. arXiv preprint arXiv:2109.06163 (2021)

17. Li, Z., et al.: Revisiting stereo depth estimation from a sequence-to-sequence perspective with transformers. In: 2021 IEEE International Conference on Computer Vision (ICCV) (2021)

18. Li, Z., et al.: Temporally consistent online depth estimation in dynamic scenes. arXiv preprint arXiv:2111.09337 (2021)

19. Lipson, L., Teed, Z., Deng, J.: Raft-stereo: multilevel recurrent field transforms for stereo matching. In: 2021 International Conference on 3D Vision (3DV), pp. 218–227. IEEE (2021)

20. Liu, X., et al.: Extremely dense point correspondences using a learned feature descriptor. In: Proceedings of the IEEE/CVF Conference on Computer Vision and Pattern Recognition, pp. 4847–4856 (2020)
21. Liu, Y., Zhu, L., Yamada, M., Yang, Y.: Semantic correspondence as an optimal transport problem. In: Proceedings of the IEEE/CVF Conference on Computer Vision and Pattern Recognition, pp. 4463–4472 (2020)
22. Loshchilov, I., Hutter, F.: Decoupled weight decay regularization. arXiv preprint arXiv:1711.05101 (2017)
23. Mayer, N., et al.: A large dataset to train convolutional networks for disparity, optical flow, and scene flow estimation. In: Proceedings of the IEEE Conference on Computer Vision and Pattern Recognition, pp. 4040–4048 (2016)
24. Menze, M., Geiger, A.: Object scene flow for autonomous vehicles. In: Proceedings of the IEEE Conference on Computer Vision and Pattern Recognition, pp. 3061–3070 (2015)
25. Paszke, A., et al.: Pytorch: An imperative style, high-performance deep learning library. Adv. Neural Inf. Process. Syst. **32** (2019)
26. Scharstein, D., et al.: High-Resolution Stereo Datasets with Subpixel-Accurate Ground Truth. In: Jiang, X., Hornegger, J., Koch, R. (eds.) GCPR 2014. LNCS, vol. 8753, pp. 31–42. Springer, Cham (2014). https://doi.org/10.1007/978-3-319-11752-2_3
27. Schmid, K., Tomic, T., Ruess, F., Hirschmüller, H., Suppa, M.: Stereo vision based indoor/outdoor navigation for flying robots. In: 2013 IEEE/RSJ International Conference on Intelligent Robots and Systems, pp. 3955–3962. IEEE (2013)
28. Sun, J., et al.: DISP R-CNN: Stereo 3d object detection via shape prior guided instance disparity estimation. In: Proceedings of the IEEE/CVF Conference on Computer Vision and Pattern Recognition, pp. 10548–10557 (2020)
29. Tomono, M.: Robust 3d slam with a stereo camera based on an edge-point ICP algorithm. In: 2009 IEEE International Conference on Robotics and Automation, pp. 4306–4311. IEEE (2009)
30. Vaswani, A., et al.: Attention is all you need. Adv. Neural Inf. Process. Syst. 30 (2017)
31. Wang, H., Zhu, Y., Green, B., Adam, H., Yuille, A., Chen, L.C.: Axial-DeepLab: stand-Alone Axial-Attention for Panoptic Segmentation. In: Vedaldi, A., Bischof, H., Brox, T., Frahm, J.-M. (eds.) ECCV 2020. LNCS, vol. 12349, pp. 108–126. Springer, Cham (2020). https://doi.org/10.1007/978-3-030-58548-8_7
32. Xu, H., Zhang, J.: Aanet: adaptive aggregation network for efficient stereo matching. In: Proceedings of the IEEE/CVF Conference on Computer Vision and Pattern Recognition, pp. 1959–1968 (2020)
33. Yang, J., et al.: Focal self-attention for local-global interactions in vision transformers. arXiv preprint arXiv:2107.00641 (2021)
34. Yao, C., Jia, Y., Di, H., Li, P., Wu, Y.: A decomposition model for stereo matching. In: Proceedings of the IEEE/CVF Conference on Computer Vision and Pattern Recognition, pp. 6091–6100 (2021)
35. Zendel, O., Murschitz, M., Humenberger, M., Herzner, W.: Cv-hazop: introducing test data validation for computer vision. In: Proceedings of the IEEE International Conference on Computer Vision, pp. 2066–2074 (2015)
36. Zhang, F., Prisacariu, V., Yang, R., Torr, P.H.: Ga-net: guided aggregation net for end-to-end stereo matching. In: Proceedings of the IEEE/CVF Conference on Computer Vision and Pattern Recognition, pp. 185–194 (2019)

37. Zhang, Y., Qiu, W., Chen, Q., Hu, X., Yuille, A.: Unrealstereo: controlling hazardous factors to analyze stereo vision. In: 2018 International Conference on 3D Vision (3DV), pp. 228–237. IEEE (2018)
38. Zhao, C., Sun, Q., Zhang, C., Tang, Y., Qian, F.: Monocular depth estimation based on deep learning: an overview. Sci. China Technol. Sci. **63**(9), 1612–1627 (2020)

PCW-Net: Pyramid Combination and Warping Cost Volume for Stereo Matching

Zhelun Shen[1], Yuchao Dai[2(✉)], Xibin Song[1(✉)], Zhibo Rao[2], Dingfu Zhou[1], and Liangjun Zhang[1]

[1] Robotics and Autonomous Driving Lab, Baidu Research, Beijing, China
song.sducg@gmail.com, zhangliangjun@baidu.com
[2] Northwestern Polytechnical University, Xi'an, China
daiyuchao@nwpu.edu.cn

Abstract. Existing deep learning based stereo matching methods either focus on achieving optimal performances on the target dataset while with poor generalization for other datasets or focus on handling the cross-domain generalization by suppressing the domain sensitive features which results in a significant sacrifice on the performance. To tackle these problems, we propose PCW-Net, a **P**yramid **C**ombination and **W**arping cost volume-based network to achieve good performance on both cross-domain generalization and stereo matching accuracy on various benchmarks. In particular, our PCW-Net is designed for two purposes. First, we construct combination volumes on the upper levels of the pyramid and develop a cost volume fusion module to integrate them for initial disparity estimation. Multi-scale receptive fields can be covered by fusing multi-scale combination volumes, thus, domain-invariant features can be extracted. Second, we construct the warping volume at the last level of the pyramid for disparity refinement. The proposed warping volume can narrow down the residue searching range from the initial disparity searching range to a fine-grained one, which can dramatically alleviate the difficulty of the network to find the correct residue in an unconstrained residue searching space. When training on synthetic datasets and generalizing to unseen real datasets, our method shows strong cross-domain generalization and outperforms existing state-of-the-arts with a large margin. After fine-tuning on the real datasets, our method ranks 1st on KITTI 2012, 2nd on KITTI 2015, and 1st on the Argoverse among all published methods as of 7, March 2022.

Keywords: Stereo matching · Pyramid cost volume · Cross-domain generalization

1 Introduction

Stereo matching aims to estimate the disparity map between a rectified image pair, which contributes to various applications, such as autonomous driving [3]

Supplementary Information The online version contains supplementary material available at https://doi.org/10.1007/978-3-031-19824-3_17.

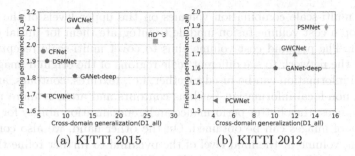

(a) KITTI 2015   (b) KITTI 2012

Fig. 1. Model generalization ability vs fine-tuning performance on KITTI 2012&2015 datasets. X-axis: all methods are trained on synthetic datasets and then tested on KITTI training sets to evaluate the cross-domain generalization. Y-axis: all methods are finetuned on the KITTI training sets and then tested on KITTI testing sets to evaluate the fine-tuning performance. D1_all is used for evaluation (the lower the better) and PCWNet is our method, which achieves the best overall performance.

and robotics navigation [1]. Benefiting from the unprecedented development of deep learning technologies, remarkable progress has been achieved in solving the task of stereo matching.

To achieve remarkable stereo matching performance, approaches [21] are usually trained on large-scale synthetic datasets (e.g., SceneFlow [16]) first and then fine-tuned on limited target dataset collected from the real scenarios such as KITTI [8], Middlebury [23], and ETH3D [24]. By extracting representative features [2,19] and constructing powerful cost volume [11,13], these methods achieve state-of-the-art performances on most of the standard stereo matching benchmarks. However, their performance decreases dramatically on unseen real-world scenes due to the large domain gaps across different datasets. Furthermore, these methods even cannot achieve consistent fine-tuning performances on different real-world datasets from similar scenarios. For example, some methods [2,34] perform well on the KITTI datasets [8,17], while having limited performances on the Argoverse benchmark [29] with high image resolutions though both of them are collected by a driving vehicle in the traffic environment.

Meanwhile, many approaches [25,28,35] are also specifically designed to handle domain generalization issues in stereo matching which aims to improve the generalization of the network to unseen scenes. By incorporating geometry priors and extracting domain-invariant features, these methods show strong cross-domain generalization when trained on synthetic datasets and generalized to unseen real datasets. However, such methods [35] normally need a significant sacrifice on accuracy to improve the cross-domain generalization due to the filtration of domain-sensitive features. Thus, a key problem for further research is designing a framework that can achieve excellent performances on the target dataset and also have satisfactory generalization ability to novel scenarios.

To relieve the issue mentioned above, we introduce the PCW-Net to construct a **P**yramid **C**ombination and **W**arping cost volume to hit two birds with one stone for achieving both generalization ability and good performance. Specifically, we use the pyramid cost volumes for two purposes. On one hand, we construct multi-scale combination volumes on the upper levels of the pyramid and develop a cost volume fusion module to integrate them for initial disparity estimation. The pyramid cost volume aims to cover multi-scale receptive fields and boost the network to see different scale regions of the original image. Thus, multi-level information can be fused together, i.e., textures, contours, and areas. Typically, non-local information (such as contours and area) is more robust to domain changes, thus better performance and generalization ability for different resolutions of images can be obtained. On the other hand, we also construct a 3D warping volume at the final level of the pyramid to further refine the initial disparity map. With the constructed 3D warping volume, we can narrow down the residue searching range from an initial disparity searching range to a fine-grained one, which can dramatically alleviate the difficulty of the network to find the correct residue in an unconstrained residue searching space.

To prove the effectiveness of the proposed PCW-Net, we perform extensive experimental evaluations on various benchmarks to verify its fine-tuning performance and generalization ability. When trained on synthetic datasets and generalized to unseen real-world datasets, PCW-Net shows strong cross-domain generalization and outperforms best prior work [25] by a noteworthy margin. After fine-tuning on the real dataset, our method can achieve consistent SOTA performance across diverse datasets. Specifically, it ranked first on KITTI 2012 leaderboard[1], second on KITTI 2015 leaderboard, and first on Argoverse leaderboard[2] [29] among all published methods as of 6 March 2021. As demonstrated in Fig. 1, our method can achieve the best overall performance when considering both the fine-tuning accuracy and cross-domain generalization on the KITTI 2015 benchmark.

Our main contributions can be summarized as:

- An effective framework, i.e., PCW-Net, is proposed which achieves remarkable generalization ability from synthetic dataset to real dataset while also excellent performances on the various target benchmarks after model fine-tuning.
- A novel multi-scale cost volume fusion module is proposed to cover multi-scale receptive fields and extract domain-invariant structural cues, thus better stereo matching performance of different resolutions of images is achieved.
- An efficient warping volume-based disparity refinement module is proposed to narrow down the unconstrained residue searching space to a fine-grained one, which can dramatically alleviate the difficulty of the network to find the correct residue in an unconstrained residue searching space.
- The proposed PCW-Net set new SOTA performance on both KITTI 2012 and Argoverse leaderboards among all the methods with publications, while it also achieves the 2nd on the KITTI 2015 benchmark.

2   Related Work

Cost Volume based Deep Stereo Matching. DispNet [16] first introduces the concept of cost volume (correlation volume) into end-to-end stereo matching

---

[1] http://www.cvlibs.net/datasets/kitti.

[2] https://eval.ai/web/challenges/challenge-page/917/leaderboard/2412.

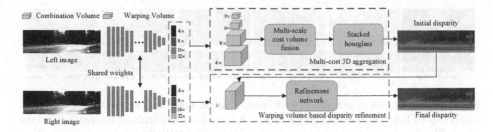

Fig. 2. General Structure of the proposed PCW-Net, which consists of three main modules as multi-scale feature extraction, multi-scale combination volume based cost aggregation, and warping volume based disparity refinement.

methods. Following this work, GCNet [13] proposes to construct concatenation volume and regularize it with 3D convolution layers and GwcNet [11] introduces group-wise correlation to provide better similarity measures. For all these prior works, cost volume construction has been placed in an extremely important position and deserves further exploration.

Deep Stereo Matching with Disparity Refinement. Recently, many researchers [7,14,20,26,27,36,38] attempt to integrate the disparity refinement step into an end-to-end model. [20] introduces a two-stage network called CRL in which the first stage extends DispNet [16] to get an initial disparity map and the second stage refines the initial disparity map in a residual manner. MCV-MFC [14] proposes to calculate reconstruction error in feature space rather than color space and share features between disparity estimation network and refinement network. PWCNet [26] proposes a context network, which is based on dilated convolutions to refine flow. However, existing methods mainly depend on the fitting capabilities of the networks to directly regress a residue with context information. Different from these works [14,20], here we introduce the warping volume to guide the disparity refinement. Specifically, the warping volume is constructed by warped right image features and left image features according to a pre-defined residue range. That is the warping volume narrows down the residue searching space from initial disparity searching space to a fine-grained one, which makes the network easier to find the corresponding pixel-level residue.

Multi-scale-Based Deep Stereo Matching. Multi-scale information has been widely employed in deep stereo matching methods. These methods can be roughly categorized into two types: (1) The first category [2,14,19] usually employs a multi-scale feature extraction network to generate feature maps at different scales and then fuse them to construct a single volume at a fixed resolution. That is these methods mainly use multi-scale features rather than multi-scale cost volumes. (2) The second category [4,10,15,32] proposes to construct cascade pyramid cost volume and progressively regress a high-quality disparity map from the coarsest cost volume. That is these methods employ each scale cost volume to estimate disparity maps separately. Different from the former two categories, our work selects to directly fuse multi-scale combination volumes to capture

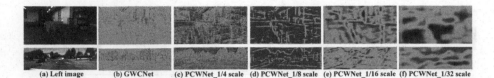

(a) Left image   (b) GWCNet   (c) PCWNet_1/4 scale   (d) PCWNet_1/8 scale   (e) PCWNet_1/16 scale   (f) PCWNet_1/32 scale

Fig. 3. Visualization of extracted multi-scale feature maps on two real-world datasets (from top to bottom: ETH3D and KITTI). All methods are trained on synthetic data (SceneFlow) and tested on unseen real scenes. Note that GWCNet only extracts feature maps at 1/4 scale for following single-scale cost volume construction while our method extracts multi-scale feature maps for pyramid cost volume construction.

a more robust feature representation for initial disparity estimation. Then, we employ warping volume to further refine the initial disparity. More related to our work is SSPCV [30], which also proposes a cost volume fusion module. However, SSPCV just fuses the pyramid cost volume by constantly employing 3D hourglass modules to regularize the upsampled cost volume. Such operation is time-consuming and GPU memory-unfriendly.

3   Proposed Approach

We propose a PCW cost volume to effectively exploit the multi-scale cues for accurate and robust disparity estimation. The architecture of our network is illustrated in Fig. 2, which consists of three parts: multi-scale feature extraction, multi-scale combination volume based cost aggregation, and warping volume based disparity refinement. Specifically, the extracted multi-scale features are first employed to construct a pyramid cost volume. Then, the pyramid volumes have been used for two purposes. Firstly, we construct combination volumes on the upper levels of the pyramid and develop a cost volume fusion module to integrate them for initial disparity estimation. Secondly, we construct the warping volume at the last level of the pyramid for disparity refinement. Details of each module will be introduced as follows.

3.1   Multi-scale Features Extraction

As shown in Fig. 2, given an image pair, following the Resnet-like network proposed in [2,11], we use three convolution layers with 3×3 kernels, four basic residual blocks, and a $\times 2$ dilated block to get the unary feature map at the first level (1/4 of the original input image size). Then three residual blocks with stride 2 are employed to obtain the feature maps at the other three levels with $\frac{1}{8}$, $\frac{1}{16}$ and $\frac{1}{32}$ of the original input image size. With the extracted features, a series of pyramid cost volumes can be constructed at different levels.

3.2   Combination Volume Based 3D Aggregation

We propose to construct multi-scale combination volumes and develop a cost volume fusion module for initial disparity estimation. Previous work [35] observes that the limited effective receptive field of current deep stereo matching methods will drive the network to learn domain-sensitive local features. Instead, our method can cover multi-scale receptive fields and boost the network to see different scale regions of the original image by fusing multi-scale cost volumes. As shown in the Fig. 3, we visualize the extracted multi-scale feature map on various real datasets. It can be seen from Fig. 3. (b) that GWCNet [11] only extracts 1/4 scale features of the input image, which only contains local information such as textures, thus the performance is limited. On the contrary, our method extracts features with multi-scales, which contain much more high-level information (sub-figs (c)-(f)), i.e., textures (c), contours (d,e), and areas (f). Typically, non-local information (such as contours and area) is more robust to domain changes and that is why our method achieves better generalization ability. Moreover, sub-figs (a) shows that the used two real datasets have significant domain shifts, e.g., indoors vs outdoors and color vs gray. However, our method can still extract domain-invariant contours (sub-figs (d)-(e)) and areas (sub-figs (f)) information from two real datasets, which further verifies the effectiveness of the proposed method. In addition, high-level information, i.e., contours and area can drive the network to better learn the affiliation between an object and its sub-region, e.g., textureless regions and repeated patterns such as car window is a part of the car, thus, better performance and generalization ability for different resolutions (high and low resolutions) of images can be obtained.

Multi-scale Combination Volume Construction. The combination volume is constructed at 4 pyramid levels and for each level i, the combination volume V_{comb}^i is a 4D volume with the size of $H^i \times W^i \times D^i \times C$ which includes concatenation volume V_{concat}^i and group-wise correlation volume V_{corr}^i [11], where (H^i, W^i) is the spatial size. Assuming the extracted feature at level i is f^i, the combination volume V_{comb}^i can be computed as:

$$
\begin{aligned}
V_{comb}^i &= V_{concat}^i \parallel V_{corr}^i, \\
V_{concat}^i(d, x, y) &= \delta_1(f_L^i(x, y)) \parallel \delta_1(f_R^i(x - d, y)) \\
V_{corr}^i(d, x, y, g) &= \frac{1}{N_c^i/N_g} \left\langle \delta_2(f_L^{ig}(x, y)), \delta_2(f_R^{ig}(x - d, y)) \right\rangle
\end{aligned}
\tag{1}
$$

where $\parallel$ denotes concatenation operation at the feature axis and f_L^i, f_R^i are extracted features at left and right images respectively. f^{ig} are grouped features, which are evenly divided from the extracted feature f^i according to the number of group N_g. d denotes all disparity levels in $(0, D_{\max}^i)$, N_c is the channels of f^i and $\langle, \rangle$ represents the inner product. Different with gwcnet [11], during the construction of combination volume, we add one more convolution layer without activation function and batch normalization (named as normalization layer δ) to make the two terms of feature (f^i and f^{ig}) share the same data distribution. Experimental results show that this simple while efficient operation can optimize the two terms of cost volume complementary to each other and thus promote the final performance. Then the multi-scale combination volume will be fused together to predict the initial disparity map.

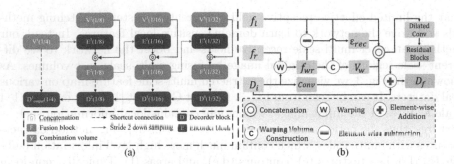

Fig. 4. (a) Structure of multi-scale cost volume fusion module. (b) Structure of warping volume-based refinement network. D_f denotes the final disparity estimation.

Multi-scale Cost Volumes Fusion. The multi-scale cost volume fusion module is shown in Fig. 4 (a), where the combination volumes, encoder blocks, fusion blocks, and decoder blocks are denoted as V^i, E^i, F^i, D^i, respectively, ($i \in \{1, 2, 3, 4\}$ denotes different levels). The final output fused cost volume is D^1_{output}. Then we use three stacked 3D hourglass networks to further process the fused cost volume and generate the initial disparity map d_i.

Fusion Blocks. The proposed fusion blocks have two main inputs. i) The encoder blocks, which characterize the information of higher resolution cost volume. ii) The combination volume, which directly measures the similarity between the left feature and the corresponding right feature according to a coarser disparity index. By employing the fusion blocks, we can integrate multi-scale cost volume and boost the network to evaluate the similarity of the left feature and candidate matching right feature at different scale disparity plane intervals, e.g., each disparity index represents 4 pixels interval at scale one while 32 pixels interval at scale four. Specifically, the fusion process can be formulated as:

$$F^i = \text{Conv}(V^i || E^i), \tag{2}$$

where $||$ denotes the concatenation operation at the feature axis and $\text{Conv}()$ refers to the 3D convolution layer.

Encoder Block. Encoder block is downsampled from the previous scale fusion block by a 3D convolution with stride 2, except for E^1, which is directly downsampled from the first scale combination volume.

Decoder Blocks. Decoder blocks comprise two main components. i) The main data flow, which continually upsamples different scale decoder blocks from D^4 to D^1. ii) The shortcut connection, which combines scale-matching fusion (encoder blocks at scale one) and decoder blocks by element-wise addition. By employing the shortcut connection, we can control the contribution of the last scale decoder block and thus balance the information flowing between upsampled decoder blocks and corresponding fusion blocks. Specifically, the decoder process can be formulated as:

$$D^i = \begin{cases} \text{Conv}^T(D^{i+1}) + S(F^i) & if \quad i = 2, 3, 4 \\ \text{Conv}^T(D^{i+1}) + S(V^i) & if \quad i = 1 \end{cases} \tag{3}$$

where $\text{Conv}^T()$ denotes the 3D transposed convolution. $S()$ refers to the shortcut connection, which is implemented by $1 \times 1 \times 1$ 3D convolution.

3.3 Warping Volume-Based Disparity Refinement

As an essential step in typical stereo matching algorithms, disparity refinement has been widely used in deep learning-based methods. Different from previous stereo matching methods [14,20] which learn the residual disparity value directly by the network, a multi-modal input is introduced to help our network more purposefully learn the residue. Specifically, our multi-modal input consists of the 3D warping volume, initial disparity map, left features, and reconstructed error, where the 3D warping volume is at the core. By employing the 3D warping volume, we can define a fine-grained residue searching range and alleviate the difficulty of the network to find the correct residue in an unconstrained residue searching space. Below we will describe each input in more detail.

3D Warping Volume. We employ the left feature and warped right feature to construct the warping volume at the last level of the pyramid. Other than the right features we used in the combination volume, we select to warp the right features according to the estimated initial disparity D_i. In this case, we can narrow down the residue searching range from initial disparity searching range $(0, D_{\max}^i)$ to a fine-grained one $(D_i - d_{res}, D_i + d_{res})$. Intuitively, the residual disparity is small. Hence, a small residue searching range d_{res} is enough to correct the wrong correspondences. Specifically, the warping volume is computed as:

$$V_w(d_{res}, x, y) = \tfrac{1}{N_c} \langle f_l(x, y), f_{wr}(x - d_{res}, y) \rangle,$$
$$f_{wr} = \text{warping}(f_r, D_i), \tag{4}$$

where f_l and f_r are upsampled from the first level feature to the original image size, d denotes all residue levels in $(D_i - d_{res}, D_i + d_{res})$ and $\langle \, , \, \rangle$ represents the inner product.

Besides, the warping operation is implemented differentially by bilinear sampling [12]. Note that the proposed warping volume measures the similarities between left features and warped right features at each residue level which guides the network to output the optimal residual disparity with the most similarity. Moreover, we construct 3D warping volume ($H \times W \times D \times 1$) by inner product to avoid 3D convolutions which can significantly decrease the computational complexity and memory consumption.

Reconstructed Error. We introduce the reconstructed error to identify inaccurate regions of initial disparity estimation, which can be computed as:

$$\mathcal{E}_{rec} = f_l(x, y) - f_{wr}(x, y). \tag{5}$$

The definition of our reconstruction error is inspired by the typical left-right consistency check, while we select to construct it at the feature level rather than the image level. By employing the reconstructed error to indicate the incorrect regions of initial disparity, our refinement network can better identify the pixels that should be further optimized.

Left Image Feature and Initial Disparity. Left image features and initial disparity map are the other two inputs of our refinement network. The initial disparity map provides the network a base estimation for further optimization and the left image feature contains the context informing for residual learning. To balance the weight of multi-model input, the one-channel initial disparity map is regularized by a convolution layer to generate a 32-channel feature map.

Warping Volume-Based Refinement Network. In summary, the warping volume, initial disparity map, left image features, and reconstructed error are the input of our refinement network. The detailed architecture of the refinement network is given in Fig. 4 (b). A dilated convolution [33] based network is employed to enlarge the receptive field which can enhance the network to give a better estimation in low-texture and occluded regions. Specifically, it has 5 convolution layers and three basic residual blocks with different dilation constants. The dilation constants are 1, 1, 2, 4, 8, 16, 1, and 1 from top to bottom.

3.4 Loss Function

Inspired by previous work [2,11], we employ smooth L_1 loss function [9] to train our network in an end-to-end way. For each cost volume fusion module and stacked hourglass network in cost aggregation, the same output module and soft argmin operation are used to get intermediate disparity map [11]. In total, we get six disparity maps $d_0, d_1, d_2, d_3, d_4, d_5$ and the loss function is described as:

$$\mathcal{L} = \sum_{j=0}^{j=5} w_j \cdot \mathcal{L}_{\text{smooth-L1}}(d_j - \hat{d}), \tag{6}$$

$\mathcal{L}_{\text{smooth-L1}}$ represents the $smooth - L1$ loss and $\hat{d}$ represents the ground-truth disparity and w_j is the weight of the jth estimation of disparity map.

4   Experimental Results

We evaluate our PCW-Net on various of benchmarks, including: Scene Flow [16], ETH3D [24], KITTI 2012&2015 [8,17], and Argoverse [29].

4.1 Datasets

(1). **SceneFlow:** is a large synthetic dataset with 35,454 training and 4,370 test images of size 960 × 540. It includes "Flyingthings3D", "Driving", and "Monkaa" with dense and accurate ground-truth for training. Here, we use the Finalpass of the Scene Flow datasets for pre-training. (2). **ETH3D:** is a grayscale image dataset with both indoor and outdoor scenes. The 27 training image pairs of ETH3D are employed to verify the generalization of different approaches. (3). **Middlebury:** is an indoor dataset with 15 training image pairs and 15 testing image pairs with full, half, and quarter resolutions. We select half-resolution training image pairs to evaluate the generalization of different approaches. (4). **KITTI 2015 & KITTI 2012:** are collected from the real world with a driving car. KITTI 2015 contains 200 training and 200 testing image pairs while KITTI 2012 provides 194 training and 195 testing image pairs, respectively. For each dataset, we select 180 image pairs from the training split for training and the rest image pairs are taken as the validation set. (5). **Argoverse:** is a high-resolution real-world dataset collected from a driving car. It provides 5530 training images and 1094 testing images of size 2056×2464. We use it to evaluate the performance of our method on high-resolution datasets, e.g., 10 times higher than KITTI.

Table 1. (a) Evaluation Results on the KITTI 2012&2015 benchmark and all pixels in occluded and non-occluded areas are evaluated. (b) Evaluation Results on the Argoverse stereo benchmark. For a clear comparison, we highlight the best result in **bold** and the second-best result in blue for each column. All metrics are the lower the better.

Methods	KITTI 2015			KITTI 2012			
	D1-bg	D1-fg	D1-all	2 px	3 px	4 px	5 px
CSPN [5]	1.51	**2.88**	1.74	2.27	1.53	1.19	0.98
GANet-deep [34]	1.48	3.46	1.81	2.50	1.60	1.23	1.02
ACFNet [37]	1.51	3.80	1.89	2.35	1.54	1.21	1.01
GWCNet [11]	1.74	3.93	2.11	2.71	1.70	1.27	1.03
SSPCVNet [30]	1.75	3.89	2.11	3.09	1.90	1.41	1.14
PSMNet [2]	1.86	4.62	2.32	3.01	1.89	1.42	1.15
LEAStereo [6]	1.40	2.91	**1.65**	2.39	1.45	1.08	0.88
Our PCW-Net	**1.37**	3.16	1.67	**2.18**	**1.37**	**1.01**	**0.81**

(a)

Mehtod	10 px(%)			5 px(%)			3 px(%)		
	All	Fg	Bg	All	Fg	Bg	All	Fg	Bg
4Fun	1.79	2.20	1.62	3.39	3.07	3.52	6.92	4.41	7.95
SMD-Stereo	1.90	2.26	1.75	3.62	3.15	3.81	7.32	4.48	8.49
Cicero-stereo	1.99	2.29	1.87	3.68	3.13	3.90	6.37	4.13	7.29
NLCANet [22]	2.00	2.38	1.85	3.69	3.31	3.84	7.44	4.60	8.59
GANet-refine [34]	2.17	2.23	2.15	3.73	3.09	3.99	7.35	4.43	8.55
CFNet [25]	2.38	3.70	1.80	4.05	4.72	3.78	7.60	6.18	8.18
PSMNet [2]	3.05	3.81	2.75	4.85	4.98	4.79	8.51	6.20	9.45
Our PCW-Net	**1.64**	**1.98**	**1.49**	**3.17**	**2.89**	**3.28**	7.05	4.29	8.18

(b)

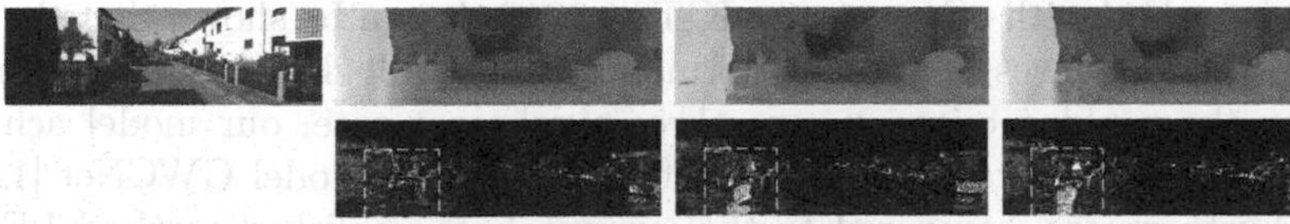

(a) left image   (b) PCW-Net   (c) GANet-deep   (d) GWCNet

Fig. 5. Visualization results on KITTI 2012 testset. The left panel shows the left input image of the stereo image pair, and for each example, the first row shows the predicted colorized disparity map and the second row shows the error map.

4.2   Implementation Details

The proposed framework is implemented using Pytorch and trained in an end-to-end manner with Adam optimizer ($\beta_1 = 0.9, \beta_2 = 0.999$). Inspired by HSM-Net [31], we employ asymmetric chromatic augmentation and asymmetric occlusion for data augmentation. Moreover, we proposed a *switch training strategy* to train our model for better network parameters. Specifically, it can be realized in three steps. First, the *Relu* activation function is employed to train our network from scratch on the SceneFlow dataset for the first 20 epochs. We set the initial learning rate as 0.001 and down-scale it by 2 times after epoch 12, 16, and 18, respectively. Then, *Mish* [18] is used to prolong the pre-training process on the SceneFlow dataset for another 15 epochs. Finally, the pre-trained models are fine-tuned on KITTI 2015 and KITTI 2012 for another 400 epochs. The learning rate of this process begins at 0.001 and decreases to 0.0001 after epoch 200. Similar to other approaches, we only use the training images of KITTI 2012 for the fine-tuning process on KITTI 2012 benchmark while we merge the training images of both datasets for the training of KITTI 2015 benchmark. For all the experiments, the batch size is set to 4 for training on 2 NVIDIA V100 GPUs and the weights of six outputs are 0.5, 0.5, 0.5, 0.7, 1.0, and 1.3. The inherent principle of the proposed switch training strategy will be discussed in the supplementary materials.

4.3   Fine-Tuning Performance Evaluation

In this section, we conduct experiments on various benchmarks to verify our claim in Sec. 1 that the proposed method can achieve consistent SOTA fine-tuning performance on diverse real-world datasets with different proprieties. Specifically, Argoverse [29] and KITTI 2012&2015 [8,17] are used for evaluation. Below we describe each dataset's result in more detail.

Results on KITTI 2012&2015. We train our model on the SceneFlow dataset first and then fine-tune it on the KITTI dataset. Here, we compare our fine-tuned model with other existing state-of-the-art methods. All results are obtained from the official KITTI evaluation website. Table 1(a) illustrates the comparison of the proposed method with others on the KITTI-2012. It can be shown that the proposed method achieves the best performances across all the pixels error thresholds. For the ranking criterion e.g., three-pixel-error rate, our model achieves a 1.37% overall error rate which outperforms our base model GWCNet [11] by 19.4%. Furthermore, compared to the current best-published method LEAStereo [6], our method can also achieve a 5.5% error reduction on the overall three-pixel-error rate.

The comparison with other state-of-the-art approaches on the KITTI-2015 benchmark is given in Table 1(a). From this table, generally, we can easily find that the proposed method achieves 1 first-place and 1 s-places among all the three categories. Specifically, our method achieves a 1.67% overall three-pixel-error rate, which surpasses the base model GWCNet by 20.85%. Compared to

LEAStereo [6], we can obtain very similar results, especially for the ranking criterion "D1-all" category (1.65 vs 1.67).

Qualitative comparison results on the KITTI 2012 benchmark are shown in Fig. 5, and we can see that our method shows significant improvement in ill-posed regions and fence regions (see dash boxes in the picture). The visualization results further support our claim that employing multi-scale cost volumes can guide the network to learn the affiliation between an object and its sub-region, thus promoting the estimation of the textureless region and repeated pattern. More qualitative results are given in the supplementary materials.

Results on Argoverse. Argoverse is a high-resolution real-world dataset collected from a driving car. In comparison to KITTI, it has 10 times the resolution and 16 times as many training frames, making it a more robust and challenging dataset. Similar to the KITTI, we train our model on the SceneFlow dataset first and then fine-tuning it on the Argoverse dataset. Here, we compare our fine-tuned model with other existing state-of-the-art methods in Table 1(b). All results are obtained from the official Argoverse evaluation website. To be clear, *the 10-pixel error* is taken as the *official evaluation metric* in this benchmark due to its high image resolution. From this table, we can easily find that existing state-of-the-art stereo matching methods [2,22,25,34] cannot achieve consistent finetuning performance on the Argoverse dataset. This is likely caused by the different proprieties between KITTI and Argoverse, e.g., high-resolution vs low-resolution and large-scale dataset vs small-scale dataset. Instead, as shown in Table 1(b), we can easily find that the proposed method achieves 6 first places among all the nine categories, which further verifies our claim that the proposed method can achieve consistent performance on diverse datasets. We attribute this result to the proposed multi-scale cost volume fusion module, which can cover multi-scale receptive fields and boost the network to see different scale regions

Table 2. Cross-domain generalization evaluation on four real datasets. For a fair comparison, all methods are only trained on the SceneFlow training set and tested on four real datasets. We highlight the best result in **bold** and the second-best result in blue for each column. All the metrics are the lower the better. Half resolution training sets of Middlebury is employed for evaluation.

Method	KITTI2012 D1_all(%)	KITTI2015 D1_all(%)	Middlebury(half) bad 2.0(%)	ETH3D bad 1.0(%)	time (s)
HD^3	23.6	26.5	37.9	54.2	**0.14**
PSMNet	15.1	16.3	25.1	23.8	0.41
GWCNet	12.0	12.2	24.1	11.0	0.32
GANet	10.1	11.7	20.3	14.1	1.8
DSMNet	6.2	6.5	**13.8**	6.2	1.5
CFNet	**4.7**	**5.8**	19.5	**5.8**	0.22
Our PC-Net	4.5	5.8	19.00	5.4	0.33
Our PCW-Net	**4.2**	**5.6**	**15.77**	**5.2**	0.44

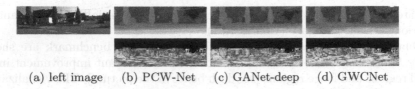

(a) left image   (b) PCW-Net   (c) GANet-deep   (d) GWCNet

Fig. 6. Cross-domain generalization comparison on KITTI2012 trainset. All methods are trained on the synthetic dataset and tested on KITTI2012 trainsets. The left panel shows the left input image of stereo image pairs, and for each example, the first row shows the predicted colorized disparity map and the second row shows the error map.

of the original image. Such an operation is well suited for both low-resolution and high-resolution images. Specifically, our method outperforms state-of-the-art approaches on overall ten-pixel-error and five-pixel-error rates with 1.64% and 3.17%. Cicero-stereo is the best method on the three-pixel-error rate and our method can achieve comparable results with it, especially for the ranking criterion "fg" category (4.29% vs 4.13%). Note that the evaluation images in Argoverse Dataset are with high resolution (2056 × 2464). Thus, ten-pixel-error and five-pixel-error are the main evaluation metrics. All in all, our method ranks 1st on the Argoverse leaderboard and sets a new SOTA performance.

4.4 Cross-Domain Generalization Evaluation

In this section, we conduct experiments to verify our claim in Sec. 1 that the proposed PCWNet can achieve strong cross-domain generalization. Specifically, we design an experiment by training the model on the synthetic data only and testing it on four real datasets such as KITTI 2012, KITTI 2015, ETH3D, and Middlebury. To make a fair comparison, all the methods are trained only on the Scene Flow dataset (without any other synthetic or real data will be used, e.g., Carla [35]). The comparison with other approaches is given in Table 2. From this table, we can find that our method outperforms the baseline model *gwcnet* on all four datasets with a large margin. Compared to the second-best method CFNet [25], our proposed PCNet (refers to the network without the warping volume based disparity refinement) has achieved comparable performance and the proposed PCWNet can further surpass it on all four datasets. Specifically, the error rate on KITTI 2012, KITTI 2015, ETH3D, and Middlebury has been decreased by 10.64%, 3.45%, 10.34%, and 19.13%, respectively compared to CFNet. Most importantly, both CFNet and DSMNet are specially designed for cross-domain generalization and will make a significant compromise on finetuning performance, e.g., the D1_all error rate of CFNet [25] on the KITTI 2015 benchmark is 1.88%, which is 10.11% higher than ours. In summary, the comparison between these domain-generalization methods further shows that our PCW-Net can make a good balance between performance and generalization.

In addition, we compare the generalization results of our method with some state-of-the-art methods in Fig. 6. From this figure, we can clearly see that most existing dataset-specific methods [11,34] generalize poorly to unseen real scenes while our method can correct most errors and generate a reasonable result. More qualitative results on other datasets will be given in the supplementary materials.

4.5 Ablation Studies

To verify the effectiveness of different modules, we set a series of experiments in this section. For efficient evaluation, only the KITTI 2015 dataset (without pre-training from Scene Flow) has been used for training and evaluation. Generally, four types of experiments have been executed here.

Multi-scale Cost Volume Fusion. The proposed multi-scale cost volume fusion module consists of the combination volumes, encoder blocks, fusion blocks, and decoder blocks. Here, we verify the impact of removing the fusion blocks, which means that the multi-scale combination volume information is ignored. As shown in the $Multi - scale\ Cost\ Volume\ Fusion$ section of Table 3, the D1_all error rate increase from 1.97% (D+E+F(ours)) to 2.09% (D+E) after removing the fusion blocks, which further verifies the necessity of including multi-scale information.

Cost Volume Construction. The proposed combination volume consists of concatenation volume and group-wise correlation volume. Here, We test the impact of using different cost volumes. As shown in Table 3, the proposed combination volume achieves the best result. Moreover, the performance of combination volume without the normalization layer δ is even worse than the usage of single cost volume. Thus, it's essential to add this layer to make the two cost volumes share the same data distribution.

Multi-modal Input Evaluation. In the disparity refinement module, we employ multi-modal input to help our network learn the residue more purposefully. Here, we test the impact of each input individually. As shown in the $Multi$-$modal\ input$ section of Table 3, each input is indispensable and the 3D warping volume is at the core. Specifically, the improvements of each part are: 0.29% for V_w, 0.08% for $\mathcal{E}_{rec}$, 0.02% for f_i and D_i, respectively. The result verifies all the multi-modal inputs work positively to improve the performance and compared with other inputs, the 3D warping volume V_w achieves the largest gain.

Model Generalization. Moreover, to further verify the generalization of the proposed method, we conduct two more ablation studies. In this setting, all the frameworks are trained on the SceneFlow dataset and evaluated on the Scene-Flow testing set and KITTI 2015 training set without finetuning. The comparison results are given in Table 4 (a). From the table, we can find that the proposed multi-scale cost volume fusion(MSCVF) and warping volume based disparity refinement (WVBDF) can both promote the generalization ability on KITTI as

Table 3. Ablation Study of the proposed method on the KITTI2015 dataset. V_w, $\mathcal{E}_{rec}$, f_l, D_i denote the 3D warping volume, reconstructed Error, left features, and initial disparity map, respectively. D, E, and F represent decoder blocks, encoder blocks, and fusion blocks, respectively. D1_all is used for evaluation (the lower the better). We test a component of our method individually in each section of the table and the approach which is used in our final model is underlined.

Experiment	Method	KITTI D1_all
Multi-scale Cost Volume Fusion	D+E	2.09
	D+E+F (ours)	**1.97**
Cost volume	concatenation volume	2.04
	group-wise correlation volume	2.13
	combination volume without C_r	2.14
	combination volume (ours)	**1.97**
Multi-modal input	Multi-modal input without V_w	2.26
	Multi-modal input without $\mathcal{E}_{rec}$	2.05
	Multi-modal input without f_l and D_i	1.99
	Multi-modal input (ours)	**1.97**

Table 4. (a) Ablation study of model generalization. (b) Sub-module generalization analysis on three real datasets. All methods are only trained on the synthetic dataset and tested on three real datasets. MSCVF and WVBDF denote the multi-scale cost volume fusion module and warping volume based disparity refinement module, respectively. Raw disparity refers to the disparity estimation result before cost volume fusion.

Method	SceneFlow EPE (px)	KITTI 2015 (w/o finetuning) D1_all (%)
No WVBDF + MSCVF	0.8578	6.18
No WVBDF	0.8387	5.81
PCWNet	**0.7868**	**5.55**

(a)

Different operations	KITTI 2012 D1_all (%)	KITTI 2015 D1_all (%)	ETH3D bad 1.0 (%)
Raw disparity	8.60	8.57	16.44
MSCVF	5.62 (**-2.98**)	6.5 (**-2.07**)	9.96 (**-6.48**)
Stacked hourglass	4.49 (-1.13)	5.84 (-0.66)	6.57 (-3.39)
WVBDF	4.23 (-0.26)	5.55 (-0.29)	5.2 (-1.37)

(b)

well as finetuning performance on SceneFlow. The error on the KITTI dataset has been decreased from 6.18% to 5.55%. Moreover, we further analyze the effect of each module on generalization in Table 4 (b). As shown, each module works positively for better generalization, and the multi-scale cost volume fusion module (MSCVF) is at the core, which contributes 68.19%, 68.54%, 57.65% error reduction on KITTI2012, KITTI2015, and ETH3D, respectively.

5 Conclusion

In this paper, we have proposed a pyramid combination and warping cost volume based network, i.e., PCW-Net, for accurate and robust stereo matching. Our pyramid cost volume can be divided into two parts. First, we construct combination volumes on the upper levels of the pyramid and develop a cost volume fusion module to integrate them for initial disparity estimation. Second, we construct the warping volume on the last level of the pyramid and employ it to refine the initial disparity. Experimental results show the superiority of PCW-Net across a diverse range of datasets. Specifically, PCW-Net achieves state-of-the-art performance and strong cross-domain generalization at the same time.

Acknowledgements. This research was supported by National Key Research and Development Program of China (2018AAA0102803) and NSFC (61871325).

References

1. Biswas, J., Veloso, M.: Depth camera based localization and navigation for indoor mobile robots. In: IEEE International Coference on Robtics and Automation (ICRA), pp. 1697–1702 (2011)
2. Chang, J.R., Chen, Y.S.: Pyramid stereo matching network. In: IEEE/CVF Conference on Computer Vision and Pattern Recognition (CVPR), pp. 5410–5418 (2018)
3. Chen, C., Seff, A., Kornhauser, A., Xiao, J.: DeepDriving: learning affordance for direct perception in autonomous driving. In: IEEE/CVF International Conference on Computer Vision (ICCV), pp. 2722–2730 (2015)
4. Cheng, S., et al.: Deep stereo using adaptive thin volume representation with uncertainty awareness. In: IEEE/CVF Conference on Computer Vision and Pattern Recognition (CVPR), pp. 2524–2534 (2019)
5. Cheng, X., Wang, P., Yang, R.: Learning depth with convolutional spatial propagation network. IEEE Trans. Pattern Anal. Mach. Intell. (TPAMI) **42**(10), 2361–2379 (2019)
6. Cheng, X., et al.: Hierarchical neural architecture search for deep stereo matching. In: Advances in Neural Information Processing Systems (NIPS), pp. 22158–22169 (2020)
7. Duggal, S., Wang, S., Ma, W.C., Hu, R., Urtasun, R.: DeepPruner: learning efficient stereo matching via differentiable patchmatch. In: IEEE/CVF International Conference on Computer Vision (ICCV), pp. 4384–4393 (2019)
8. Geiger, A., Lenz, P., Urtasun, R.: Are we ready for autonomous driving? The KITTI vision benchmark suite. In: IEEE/CVF Conference on Computer Vision and Pattern Recognition (CVPR), pp. 3354–3361. IEEE (2012)
9. Girshick, R.: Fast R-CNN. In: IEEE/CVF International Conference on Computer Vision (ICCV), pp. 1440–1448 (2015)
10. Gu, X., Fan, Z., Zhu, S., Dai, Z., Tan, F., Tan, P.: Cascade cost volume for high-resolution multi-view stereo and stereo matching. In: IEEE/CVF Conference on Computer Vision and Pattern Recognition (CVPR), pp. 2495–2504 (2020)
11. Guo, X., Yang, K., Yang, W., Wang, X., Li, H.: Group-wise correlation stereo network. In: IEEE/CVF Conference on Computer Vision and Pattern Recognition (CVPR), pp. 3273–3282 (2019)
12. Jaderberg, M., Simonyan, K., Zisserman, A., et al.: Spatial transformer networks. In: Advances in Neural Information Processing Systems (NIPS), pp. 2017–2025 (2015)
13. Kendall, A., et al.: End-to-end learning of geometry and context for deep stereo regression. In: IEEE/CVF International Conference on Computer Vision (ICCV), pp. 66–75 (2017)
14. Liang, Z., et al.: Stereo matching using multi-level cost volume and multi-scale feature constancy. IEEE Trans. Pattern Anal. Mach. Intell. (TPAMI) **43**, 300–315 (2019)

15. Mao, Y., et al.: UASNet: Uncertainty adaptive sampling network for deep stereo matching. In: Proceedings of the IEEE/CVF International Conference on Computer Vision, pp. 6311–6319 (2021)
16. Mayer, N., et al.: A large dataset to train convolutional networks for disparity, optical flow, and scene flow estimation. In: IEEE/CVF Conference on Computer Vision and Pattern Recognition (CVPR), pp. 4040–4048 (2016)
17. Menze, M., Heipke, C., Geiger, A.: Object scene flow. ISPRS J. Photogramm. Remote Sens. 140, 60–76 (2018)
18. Misra, D.: Mish: A self regularized non-monotonic neural activation function. arXiv preprint arXiv:1908.08681 (2019)
19. Nie, G.Y., et al.: Multi-level context ultra-aggregation for stereo matching. In: IEEE/CVF Conference on Computer Vision and Pattern Recognition (CVPR), pp. 3283–3291 (2019)
20. Pang, J., Sun, W., Ren, J.S., Yang, C., Yan, Q.: Cascade residual learning: a two-stage convolutional neural network for stereo matching. In: IEEE/CVF International Conference on Computer Vision workshop (ICCV workshop), pp. 887–895 (2017)
21. Rao, Z., Dai, Y., Shen, Z., He, R.: Rethinking training strategy in stereo matching. IEEE Trans. Neural Netw. Learn. Syst. (2022)
22. Rao, Z., et al.: NLCA-Net: a non-local context attention network for stereo matching. APSIPA Trans. Signal Inf. Process. 9, e18 (2020)
23. Scharstein, D., Szeliski, R.: A taxonomy and evaluation of dense two-frame stereo correspondence algorithms. Int. J. Comput. Vis. (IJCV) 47(1), 7–42 (2002)
24. Schops, T.,et al.: A multi-view stereo benchmark with high-resolution images and multi-camera videos. In: IEEE/CVF Conference on Computer Vision and Pattern Recognition (CVPR), pp. 3260–3269 (2017)
25. Shen, Z., Dai, Y., Rao, Z.: CFNet: cascade and fused cost volume for robust stereo matching. In: IEEE/CVF Conference on Computer Vision and Pattern Recognition (CVPR), pp. 13906–13915 (2021)
26. Sun, D., Yang, X., Liu, M.Y., Kautz, J.: PWC-Net: CNNs for optical flow using pyramid, warping, and cost volume. In: IEEE/CVF Conference on Computer Vision and Pattern Recognition (CVPR), pp. 8934–8943 (2018)
27. Tonioni, A., Tosi, F., Poggi, M., Mattoccia, S., Stefano, L.D.: Real-time self-adaptive deep stereo. In: IEEE/CVF Conference on Computer Vision and Pattern Recognition (CVPR), pp. 195–204 (2019)
28. Wang, J., Jampani, V., Sun, D., Loop, C., Birchfield, S., Kautz, J.: Improving deep stereo network generalization with geometric priors. arXiv preprint arXiv:2008.11098 (2020)
29. Wilson, B.,et al.: Argoverse 2.0: Next generation datasets for self-driving perception and forecasting. In: Advances in Neural Information Processing Systems Datasets and Benchmarks Track (Round 2) (2021)
30. Wu, Z., Wu, X., Zhang, X., Wang, S., Ju, L.: Semantic stereo matching with pyramid cost volumes. In: IEEE/CVF International Conference on Computer Vision (ICCV), pp. 7484–7493 (2019)
31. Yang, G., Manela, J., Happold, M., Ramanan, D.: Hierarchical deep stereo matching on high-resolution images. In: IEEE/CVF Conference on Computer Vision and Pattern Recognition (CVPR), pp. 5515–5524 (2019)
32. Yang, J., Mao, W., Alvarez, J.M., Liu, M.: Cost volume pyramid based depth inference for multi-view stereo. In: IEEE/CVF Conference on Computer Vision and Pattern Recognition (CVPR), pp. 4877–4886 (2020)

33. Yu, F., Koltun, V.: Multi-scale context aggregation by dilated convolutions. In: International Conference on Learning Representations (ICLR) (2016)
34. Zhang, F., Prisacariu, V., Yang, R., Torr, P.H.: GA-Net: guided aggregation net for end-to-end stereo matching. In: IEEE/CVF Conference on Computer Vision and Pattern Recognition (CVPR), pp. 185–194 (2019)
35. Zhang, F., Qi, X., Yang, R., Prisacariu, V., Wah, B., Torr, P.: Domain-invariant stereo matching networks. In: the Europe Conference on Computer Vision (ECCV), pp. 420–439 (2020)
36. Zhang, S., Wang, Z., Wang, Q., Zhang, J., Wei, G., Chu, X.: EDNet: efficient disparity estimation with cost volume combination and attention-based spatial residual. In: IEEE/CVF Conference on Computer Vision and Pattern Recognition (CVPR), pp. 5433–5442 (2021)
37. Zhang, Y.,et al.: Adaptive unimodal cost volume filtering for deep stereo matching, pp. 12926–12934 (2020)
38. Zhong, Y., et al.: Displacement-invariant cost computation for stereo matching. Int. J. Comput. Vis. **130**(5), 1196–1209 (2022)

Gen6D: Generalizable Model-Free 6-DoF Object Pose Estimation from RGB Images

Yuan Liu[1], Yilin Wen[1], Sida Peng[2], Cheng Lin[3], Xiaoxiao Long[1], Taku Komura[1], and Wenping Wang[4]($\boxtimes$)

[1] The University of Hong Kong, Hong Kong, China
[2] Zhejiang University, Hangzhou, China
[3] Tencent, Shenzhen, China
[4] Texas A&M University, College Station, USA
wenping@tamu.edu

Abstract. In this paper, we present a generalizable model-free 6-DoF object pose estimator called Gen6D. Existing generalizable pose estimators either need the high-quality object models or require additional depth maps or object masks in test time, which significantly limits their application scope. In contrast, our pose estimator only requires some posed images of the unseen object and is able to accurately predict poses of the object in arbitrary environments. Gen6D consists of an object detector, a viewpoint selector and a pose refiner, all of which do not require the 3D object model and can generalize to unseen objects. Experiments show that Gen6D achieves state-of-the-art results on two model-free datasets: the MOPED dataset and a new GenMOP dataset. In addition, on the LINEMOD dataset, Gen6D achieves competitive results compared with instance-specific pose estimators. Project page: https://liuyuan-pal.github.io/Gen6D/.

Keywords: 6-Dof object pose estimation · Camera pose estimation

1 Introduction

Estimating the orientation and location of an object in 3D space is a preliminary and necessary step for many tasks involving interaction with the object. In the last decade, 3D vision has witnessed tremendous development ranging from robotics, games, to VR/AR. These applications raise new demands for the 6-DoF object pose estimation, requiring a pose estimator to be generalizable, flexible, and easy-to-use. However, existing methods suffer from several restrictive conditions. Most methods [28,63,69] can only be used for a specific object or category same as the training data. Some methods [29,41,43,56,71–73] can generalize to unseen objects, but they rely on high-quality target 3D models [29,43,56,71,73], or additional depth maps [41] and masks [41,72] at test time. These requirements severely limit the practical applications of the existing pose estimators.

Supplementary Information The online version contains supplementary material available at https://doi.org/10.1007/978-3-031-19824-3_18.

S. Avidan et al. (Eds.): ECCV 2022, LNCS 13692, pp. 298–315, 2022.
https://doi.org/10.1007/978-3-031-19824-3_18

(a) Reference Images   (b) Query Images   (c) Object poses

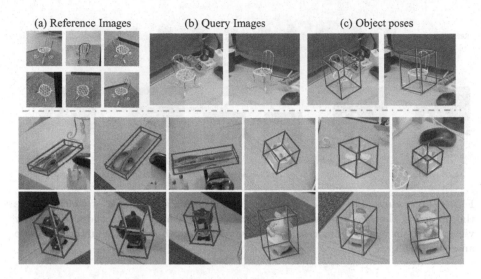

Fig. 1. Given (a) reference images of an object with known poses and (b) query images containing the same object with unknown poses, our pose estimator is able to accurately estimate (c) their object poses in the query images, where green color means ground-truth and blue color means estimation. **Note that all objects are unseen in the training set and the same estimator is applied for all objects**. (Color figure online)

To meet demands in practical applications, we argue that such a pose estimator should have the following properties. 1) **Generalizable**. The pose estimator can be applied on an arbitrary object without training on the object or its category. 2) **Model-free**. When generalizing to an unseen object, the estimator only needs some reference images of this object with known poses to define the object reference coordinate system, as shown in Fig. 1 (a), but does not rely on a 3D model of the object. 3) **Simple inputs**. When estimating object poses, the estimator only takes RGB images as inputs without requiring additional object masks or depth maps.

To the best of our knowledge, there is no existing pose estimator satisfying all the above three properties simultaneously. Thus, in this paper, we propose a simple but effective pose estimator, called **Gen6D**, which possesses the three properties above. Given input reference images of an arbitrary object with known poses, Gen6D is able to directly predict its object pose in any query images, as shown in Fig. 1. In general, an object pose can be estimated by directly predicting rotation/translation by regression [27,58,69], solving a Perspective-n-Points (PnP) problem [42,47] or matching images with known poses [56,57,68]. Direct prediction of rotation and translation by regression is mostly limited to a specific instance or category, which has difficulty in generalizing to unseen objects. Meanwhile, due to the lack of 3D models, PnP-based methods do not have 3D keypoints to build 2D-3D correspondences so that they are incompatible with model-free setting. Hence, we apply image-matching in our framework for pose estimation, which can generalize to unseen objects by learning a general image similarity metric.

In Gen6D, we propose a novel image-matching based framework to estimate the object pose in a coarse-to-fine manner. The framework consists of an object

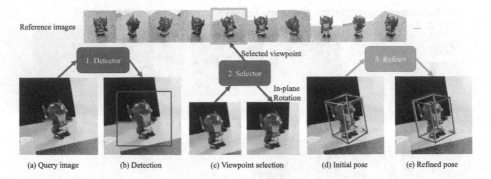

(a) Query image   (b) Detection   (c) Viewpoint selection   (d) Initial pose   (e) Refined pose

Fig. 2. Overview. The proposed pose estimator consists of a detector which detects the object in the query image, a viewpoint selector which selects the most similar viewpoint from reference images, and a pose refiner which refines the initial pose into an accurate object pose.

detector, a viewpoint selector and a pose refiner, as shown in Fig. 2. Given reference images and a query image, an object detector first detects the object regions by correlating the reference images with the query image, which is similar to [1]. Then, a viewpoint selector matches the query image against the reference images to produce a coarse initial pose. Finally, the initial pose is further refined by a pose refiner to search for an accurate object pose.

A challenge is how to design a viewpoint selector when the reference images are sparse and contain cluttered background. Existing image-matching methods [2,22,56,57,68] have difficulty in handling this problem due to two problems. First, these image-matching methods embed images into feature vectors and compute similarities using distances of feature vectors, in which cluttered background interferes the embedded feature vectors and thus severely degenerates the accuracy. Second, given a query image, there may not be a reference image with exactly the same viewpoint as the query image. In this case, there will be multiple plausible reference images and the selector has to select the one with the nearest viewpoint as the query image, which usually are very ambiguous as shown in Fig. 3.

To address these problems in viewpoint selection, we propose to use neural networks to pixel-wisely compare the query image with every reference image to produce similarity scores and select the reference image with highest similarity score. This pixel-wise comparison enables our selector to concentrate on object regions and reduces the influence of cluttered background. Furthermore, we add global normalization layers and self-attention layers to share similarity information across different reference images. These two kinds of layers enable every reference images to commute with each other, which provides context information for the selector to select the most similar reference image.

The main challenge of developing our pose refiner is the unavailability of the object model. Existing pose refiners [29,73] are based on rendering-and-comparison, which render an image on the input pose and then match the ren-

Query   Nearest   2nd Nearest   Query   Nearest   2nd Nearest

Fig. 3. Query images and reference images have cluttered background. The reference image with the nearest viewpoint looks very similar as the one with second nearest viewpoint, which brings challenges for the selector to correctly select the nearest one.

dered image with the query image to refine the input pose. However, without the object model, rendering high-quality images on arbitrary poses is difficult, which makes these refinement methods infeasible in the model-free setting.

To address this problem, we propose a novel 3D volume-based pose refinement method. Given a query image and an input pose, we find several reference images that are near to the input pose. These reference images are projected back into 3D space to construct a feature volume. Then, the constructed feature volume is matched against the features projected from the query image by a 3D CNN to refine the input pose. In comparison with previous pose refiners [29,73], our pose refiner avoids rendering any new images. Meanwhile, the constructed 3D feature volume enables our method to infer the 3D pose refinement in the 3D space. In contrast, previous pose refiners [29,73] only rely on 2D image features to regress a 3D relative pose, which are less accurate especially for unseen objects.

To validate the effectiveness of our generalizable model-free pose estimator, we introduce a new dataset, called General Model-free Object Pose Dataset (GenMOP), which contains video sequences of objects in different environments and lighting conditions. We choose one sequence as reference images and the rest sequences of the same object as test query images. Experiments show that without training on these objects, our method still outperforms instance-specific estimator PVNet [42] on the GenMOP dataset and another model-free MOPED [41] dataset. We also evaluate our method on the LINEMOD dataset [23], on which our generalizable pose estimator achieves comparable results as instance-specific estimators which needs to be trained with excessive rendered images.

2 Related Works

2.1 Specific Object Pose Estimator

Most object pose estimators [14, 24–28, 34, 42, 45, 46, 53, 54, 57, 62, 67, 69] are instance-specific, which cannot generalize to unseen objects and usually require a 3D model of the object to render extensive images for training. Recent instance-specific pose estimators [6, 33, 40] reconstruct the object model implicitly in the pipeline so that they are model-free. Category-specific pose estimators [8–11, 13, 15, 16, 30, 31, 59, 63, 66] can generalize to objects in the same category and also do not require the object model. However, they are still unable to predict poses for objects in unseen categories. In comparison, Gen6D is generalizable, which makes no assumption of the category or the instance of the object and also does not need the 3D model of the object.

2.2 Generalizable Object Pose Estimator

Generalizable pose estimators mostly require an object model either for shape embedding [12,43,44,71] or template matching [2,21,22,37,56,68,74] or rendering-and-comparison [4,18,29,38,56,73]. To avoid using 3D models, recent works [41,72] utilize the advanced neural rendering techniques [36] to directly render from posed images for pose estimation. However, current rendering methods are only able to render images under exactly the same appearance like lighting conditions, which degenerates the accuracy under varying appearance. To remedy this, these methods have to resort to additional depth maps [41] or object masks [41,72] to achieve robustness. There are also some works focusing on estimating poses of unseen objects using RGBD sequences [5,17,20,38,51,65]. In contrast to these methods, Gen6D is model-free and does not require depth maps or masks. There are also concurrent works [50,55] of generalizable pose estimation.

2.3 Instance Detection

Instance detection aims to detect a given object with some images of the object [1,19,35,39]. There are some instance detection methods which also estimate viewpoints [3,70] for novel category in one- or few-shot setting. The detector of Gen6D is inspired by [1], which uses correlation to find the object region. The target of Gen6D is to estimate the 6-DoF object pose, which is different from these methods for detection or category-level viewpoint estimation.

3 Method

Given N_r images of an object with known camera poses, called **reference images**, our target is to predict the pose of the object in a **query image**. The object pose here means a translation $\mathbf{t}$ and a rotation $\mathbf{R}$ that transform the object coordinate $\mathbf{x}_{obj}$ to the camera coordinate $\mathbf{x}_{cam} = \mathbf{R}\mathbf{x}_{obj} + \mathbf{t}$. All the intrinsics parameters of images are already known.

Data Normalization . For every object, we can estimate a rough size of the object by triangulating points from reference images or simply unprojecting reference images to find an intersection. The center of triangulated points or the center of the 3D intersection region is regarded as the object center. Then, the object coordinate system is normalized so that the object center locates at the origin and the object size is 1, which means the whole object resides inside a unit sphere at the origin. This data normalization ensures the feature volume constructed by our pose refiner in Sect. 3.3 will contain the target object. More details about the normalization can be found in the supplementary materials.

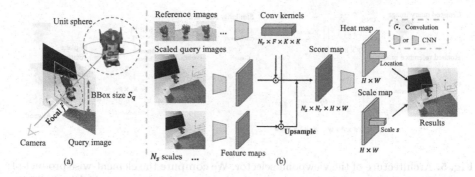

Fig. 4. (a) Detection outputs. Depth can be computed from the bounding box size S_q, which along with the 2D projection of the object center determine the location of the object center. (b) Architecture of the detector. We use features of reference images as kernels to convolve features of multi-scale query images to get score maps. Score maps are further processed by a CNN to produce a heat map about the object center and a scale map to determine the bounding box size.

Overview . As shown in Fig. 2, the proposed Gen6D pose estimator consists of an object detector, a view selector and a pose refiner. The object detector crops the object region and estimates an initial translation (Sect. 3.1). The view selector finds an initial rotation by selecting the most similar reference image and estimating an in-plane rotation (Sect. 3.2). The initial translation and rotation are used in the pose refiner to iteratively estimate an accurate pose (Sect. 3.3).

3.1   Detection

The query image is usually very large and the object only occupies a small region on the query image. To focus on the object, we apply a correlation-based instance detector similar to [1]. We decompose the detection problem into two parts, i.e. finding the 2D projection q of the object center and estimating a compact square bounding box size S_q that encloses the unit sphere. As shown in Fig. 4 (a), such a compact bounding box size is used in computing the depth of the object center by $d = 2\tilde{f}/S_q$, where 2 is the diameter of the unit sphere and $\tilde{f}$ is a virtual focal length by changing the principle point to the estimated projection q. The projection q and the depth d will determine the location of the object center, which provides an initial translation for the object pose.

The design of our detector is shown in Fig. 4 (b). We extract feature maps on both the reference images and the query image by a VGG [52]-11 network. Then, the feature maps of all reference images are regarded as convolution kernels to convolve with the feature map of the query image to get score maps. To account for scale differences, we conduct such convolution at N_s predefined scales by resizing the query images to different scales. Based on the multi-scale score maps, we regress a heat map and a scale map. We select the location with the max value on the heat map as the 2D projection of the object center and use the scale value s at the same location on the scale map to compute the bounding box size $S_q = S_r * s$, where S_r is the size of reference images.

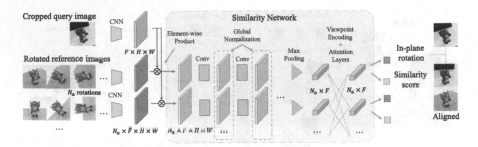

Fig. 5. Architecture of the viewpoint selector. We compute the element-wise product of every reference image with the query image to get a score map, on which a similarity network is applied to compute an in-plane rotation and a similarity score for this reference image. Note that in the similarity network, we use global normalization layers and a transformer to share information across reference images.

With the detected 2D projections and scales, we compute the initial 3D translations and crop the object regions for subsequent processing. More details about architecture and training of detector networks can be found in the supplementary materials.

3.2 Viewpoint Selection

Viewpoint selection aims to select a reference image whose viewpoint is the nearest to the query image. Meanwhile, we will estimate an in-plane rotation between the query image and the selected reference image. We approximately regard the viewpoint of the selected reference image as the viewpoint of the query image, which along with the estimated in-plane rotation forms an initial rotation for the object pose.

As shown in Fig. 5, we design a viewpoint selector to compare the query image with every reference image to compute similarity scores. Specifically, we first extract feature maps by applying a VGG [52]-11 on reference images and the query image. Then, for every feature map of reference images, we compute its element-wise product with the feature map of the query image to produce a correlation score map. Finally, the correlation score map is processed by a similarity network to produce a similarity score and a relative in-plane rotation to align the query image with the reference image. In our viewpoint selector, we have three special designs.

In-Plane Rotation . To account for in-plane rotations, every reference image is rotated by N_a predefined angles and all rotated versions are used in the element-wise product with the query image.

Global Normalization . For every feature map produced by the similarity network, we normalize it with the mean and variance computed from all feature maps of reference images. Such a global normalization helps our selector select the relatively most similar reference image because it allows the distribution of feature maps to encode the context similarity and amplifies the similarity differences among different reference images. For every reference image, max-pooling is applied on its feature map to produce a similarity feature vector.

Reference View Transformer . We apply a transformer on the similarity feature vectors of all reference images, which includes the positional encoding of their viewpoints and attention layers over all similarity feature vectors. Such a transformer lets feature vectors communicate with each other to encode contextual information [48,60,64], which is helpful to determine the most similar reference image. The outputs of reference view transformer will be used to regress a similarity score and an in-plane rotation angle for each reference image. The viewpoint of the reference image with highest score will be selected.

With the selected viewpoint and the estimated in-plane rotation, we estimated an initial rotation for the object pose, which will be refined by the pose refiner. More details about the network and training can be found in the supplementary materials.

3.3   Pose Refinement

Combining the translation estimated by the object detector and the rotation estimated by the viewpoint selector, we get an initial coarse object pose. This initial pose is further refined by a 3D volume-based pose refiner.

Specifically, since the objects are already normalized inside an unit sphere at the origin, we build a volume within the unit cube at the origin with $S_v^3 = 32^3$ vertices. As shown in Fig. 6 (a), to construct the features on these vertices, we first select $N_n = 6$ reference images that are near to the input pose. We extract feature maps on these selected reference images by a 2D CNN. Then, these feature maps are unprojected into the 3D volume and we compute the mean and variance of features among all reference images as features for volume vertices. For the query image, we also extract its feature map by the same 2D CNN, unproject feature map into the 3D volume using the input pose and concatenate the unprojected query features with the mean and variance of reference image features. Finally, we apply a 3D CNN on the concatenated features of the volume to predict a pose residual to update the input pose.

Similarity Approximation . Instead of regressing the rigid pose residual directly, we approximate it with a similarity transformation, as shown in Fig. 6 (b). The approximate similarity transformation consists of a 2D in-plane offset, a scale factor and a residual 3D rotation. The reason of using this approximation is that it avoids direct regression of the 3D translation from the red circle to the solid green circle in Fig. 6, which is out of the scope of the feature volume. Instead, we regress a similarity transformation from red circle to dotted green circle, which can be easily inferred from the features defined in the volume. More details can be found in the supplementary materials. In our implementation, we apply the refiner iteratively 3 times by default.

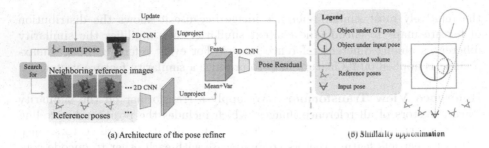

(a) Architecture of the pose refiner   (b) Similarity approximation

Fig. 6. (a) Architecture of our pose refiner. (b) A 2D diagram to illustrate the similarity transformation approximation. Though the ground-truth pose residual from the input object pose (solid red circle) to the ground-truth object pose (solid green circle) is a rigid transformation, we can approximate this rigid transformation by a similarity transformation inside the feature volume. Our pose refiner predicts the similarity transformation, which transforms the input red circle to the dotted greed circle. Then, the similarity transformation can be converted to a rigid transformation. (Color figure online)

Discussion . The key difference between our volume-based refiner and other pose refiners [29,56,73] is that our pose refiner does not require rendering an image on the input pose, which thus is more suitable for the model-free pose estimation. Meanwhile, since the 3D volume is constructed by multiple reference images with different poses, our volume-based refiner is able to know the image features under different poses and infer how pose changes affect the image features for unseen objects. In comparison, previous pose refiners [29,56,73] only compare a rendered image with the input query image to compute a pose residual. Such a 2D image does not provide enough 3D structure information to infer how pose changes affect image patterns, especially for unseen objects. Thus, it is hard for these methods to predict correct pose residuals for unseen objects.

4   Experiments

4.1   GenMOP Dataset

To validate the effectiveness of the proposed method, we collect a dataset called General Model-free Object Pose Dataset (GenMOP). GenMOP dataset consists of 10 objects ranging from flatten objects like "scissors" to thin structure objects like "chair" as shown in Fig. 7. For each object, two video sequences of the same object are collected in different environments like backgrounds and lighting conditions. Every video sequence is split into ∼200 images. For each sequence, we apply COLMAP [49] to reconstruct the camera poses in each sequences separately and manually label keypoints on the object for cross-sequence alignment. More details about the GenMOP dataset can be found in the supplementary.

Chair Piggy PlugEN Scissors TFormer Cup Knife Love PlugCN Miffy

Fig. 7. Objects in the GenMOP dataset. The first 5 objects are used in test and the last 5 objects are used in training.

4.2 Protocol

We evaluate Gen6D pose estimator on the GenMOP dataset, the LINEMOD [23] dataset and the MOPED [41] dataset.

GenMOP . On the GenMOP dataset, we select one video sequence as reference images and the other video sequence in a different environment as test query images, both of which contain ∼200 images.

LINEMOD . The LINEMOD [23] dataset is a widely-used dataset for object pose estimation. On the LINEMOD dataset, we follow the commonly-used train-test split as [58]. We select the training images (∼180) as reference images and all the rest ∼1000 test images as query images for evaluation.

MOPED . The MOPED [41] dataset is intended for model-free object pose estimation. Since the MOPED dataset is generated automatically by depth fusion and point cloud registration, object poses in some sequences are not very accurate. Thus, we manually select reliable subsets from 5 objects for evaluation. For each object, there are 200–600 reference images and 100–300 query images.

Training Datasets . The training dataset of Gen6D estimator consists of: 1) Rendered images from ∼2000 ShapeNet [7] models, 2) Google Scanned Object dataset rendered by [64] with 1023 objects, 3) 5 objects from the Gen-MOP dataset and 4) 5 objects (ape/can/holepuncher/iron/phone) from the LINEMOD dataset. Note we only train a single model and test its performance on the unseen objects on GenMOP, LINEMOD and MOPED dataset.

Metrics . We adopt the widely-used Average Distance (ADD) [23] and the projection error as metrics. On the ADD, we compute the recall rate with 10% of the object diameter (ADD-0.1d) and the AUC in 0–10cm (ADD-AUC). On the projection error, we compute the recall rate at 5 pixels (Prj-5).

4.3 Results on GenMOP

For comparison, we choose the generalizable image-matching based ObjDesc [68] and two instance-specific estimators PVNet [42] and RLLG [6] as baseline methods. Quantitative results are shown in Table 1 and some qualitative results are shown in Fig. 1. More qualitative results are in the supplementary.

Table 1. Performance on the GenMOP dataset. "General" means generalizable or not. "Ours w/o Ref." means not using the pose refiner in the Gen6D estimator.

Metrics	Method	General	Object Name					Avg.
			Chair	PlugEN	Piggy	Scissors	TFormer	
ADD-0.1d	PVNet [42]	✗	49.50	2.33	**77.89**	**44.40**	19.84	38.79
	RLLG [6]	✗	0.70	1.28	1.01	3.45	0.79	2.71
	ObjDesc [68]	✓	3.50	5.14	14.07	1.25	7.54	8.55
	Ours w/o Ref	✓	14.00	7.48	00.70	16.81	11.51	17.90
	Ours	✓	**61.50**	**19.63**	75.38	32.76	**62.70**	**50.39**
Prj-5	PVNet [42]	✗	15.00	30.37	83.42	**96.55**	59.52	56.97
	RLLG [6]	✗	2.00	4.67	17.59	35.78	7.94	13.59
	ObjDesc [68]	✓	4.00	10.75	4.52	18.53	8.33	9.23
	Ours w/o Ref	✓	11.50	40.65	33.17	34.05	64.29	36.73
	Ours	✓	**55.00**	**72.90**	**92.96**	93.53	**98.81**	**82.64**

Baseline Implementation . For the generalizable template-matching ObjDesc [68], we use the same training dataset as Gen6D. In testing, we crop the object region by our object detector and then use ObjDesc to select the most similar reference image to the query image. The pose of the selected reference image is regarded as the pose of the query image. All objects used in evaluation are unseen for Gen6D and ObjDesc in training. For instance-specific estimators PVNet [42] and RLLG [6], we have to train different models for different objects separately. On every test object, the reference images for Gen6D are used as training set for PVNet and RLLG. However, only ~200 reference images are not enough to produce reasonable results so we additionally label the object masks on these reference images and cut the object to randomly paste on backgrounds from COCO [32] to enlarge their training set. For PVNet, we use its 8 corners of the 3D bounding box as keypoints for voting because no model is available.

Comparison with Baselines . 1) Both ObjDesc [68] and "Ours w/o Ref" select the most similar reference image to estimate the object pose. The results show that our viewpoint selector is able to select more accurate viewpoint than ObjDesc. However, only selecting the best reference viewpoint is not enough for predicting accurate poses because the reference images do not cover all possible viewpoints. 2) With further pose refinement, our Gen6D estimator is able to produce better results than the instance-specific methods PVNet and RLLG on average. The main reason is that for PVNet and RLLG, these reference images are not enough for training a very accurate pose estimator. In contrast, Gen6D well adapts into this setting with limited reference images of a novel object. Our pose refiner is able to learn generalizable features for accurate pose refinement.

4.4   Results on LINEMOD [23]

We further report results in ADD-0.1d on the LINEMOD [23] dataset in Table 2 and show qualitative results in Fig. 8. For baselines, we include the instance-specific pose estimators [6,29,42,57,61,69,73] and a generalizable estimator

Table 2. ADD-0.1d on LINEMOD [23] dataset. "Training" means what kind of training set is used. "Synthetic" means the model only uses synthetic data of the given object for training; "Real" means the model is trained on both the synthetic images and real images of the given model; "No" means the model is not trained on any data of the test object. "GT-BBox" means a model uses the ground-truth bounding box or not to produce its performance. "Refine" means the pose refiner.

Training	Name	GT-BBox	Refine	Object name						Avg.
				cat	Duck	Bvise	Cam	Driller	Lamp	
Synthetic	AAE [57]	✗	No	17.90	4.86	20.92	30.47	23.99	60.47	26.44
	Self6D [61]	✗	No	57.90	19.60	75.20	36.90	67.00	68.20	54.13
	DPOD [73]	✗	No	32.36	26.12	66.76	24.22	66.60	57.26	45.55
	DPOD [73]	✗	DPOD [73]	65.10	50.04	72.69	34.76	73.32	74.27	61.70
Real	PFS [71]	✓	DeepIM [29]	54.10	48.60	63.80	40.00	75.30	55.30	56.18
	PVNet [42]	✗	No	79.34	52.58	99.90	86.86	96.43	99.33	85.74
	PoseCNN [69]	✗	DeepIM [29]	82.10	77.70	97.40	93.50	95.00	96.84	95.19
	DPOD [73]	✗	DPOD [73]	94.71	86.29	98.45	96.07	98.80	97.50	90.53
Gen	PFS [71]	✓	No	15.40	8.20	25.10	12.10	18.60	6.50	14.32
	Ours	✓	No	94.11	81.31	99.52	94.31	96.33	93.38	93.16
	Ours	✗	No	15.97	7.89	25.48	22.06	17.24	35.80	20.74
	Ours	✗	Volume	60.68	40.47	77.03	66.67	67.39	89.83	67.01

Pose-From-Shape (PFS) [71]. The instance-specific estimators are either trained on the synthetic data of the object ("synthetic training") [57,61,73] or trained on both the synthetic and real data of the object ("real training") [42,69,73]. PFS [71] is trained on ShapeNet [7], which embeds an object shape into a feature vector and applies the embedded feature vector on a query image to predict an object pose. For [69,71,73], we also include their reported performance using pose refiners DeepIM [29] or DPOD [73], both of which are trained on the synthetic data or real data of the test object. Ground-truth bounding box is used in PFS to crop the object region for the pose estimation. For baselines, we use the performance reported in their paper for comparison.

The results in Table 2 show that: 1) In comparison with the generalizable pose estimator PFS [71], Gen6D outperforms PFS [71] with or without subsequent pose refinement. Note the PFS [71] uses the DeepIM [29] refiner which actually is trained on the synthetic data of the test object while our volume-based refiner is not trained on the test object at all. 2) In comparison with instance-specific estimators [57,61,73] with synthetic training on the test object, Gen6D clearly outperforms all these methods. 3) However, Gen6D performs worse than instance-specific estimators [42,69,73] with real training. The main reason is the inaccurate estimation of the depth. Since the object is usually very far away from the camera and small scale difference (1–2 pixels) will result in a huge offset in the depth direction. Without training on the object, Gen6D cannot perceive such subtle scale changes, which results in worse performance. 4) With ground-truth bounding box, Gen6D achieves comparable results as the instance-specific estimators [42,69,73] with real training because such ground-truth bounding boxes provide correct depths.

Table 3. ADD-AUC on the MOPED dataset with threshold 0–10cm. "LF" means Latent-Fusion [41]. "General" means the pose estimator is trained on the specific object or not. "Input" means the required type of query images at test time.

Method	General	Input	Object name					Avg.
			B.Drill	D.Dude	V.Mug	T.Plane	R.Aid	
LF [41]	✓	RGBD	**74.11**	**75.40**	38.27	54.95	62.97	61.14
PVNet [42]	✗	RGD	10.49	43.30	**67.78**	48.61	**72.92**	56.42
Ours	✓	RGB	64.87	59.23	50.95	**69.83**	72.03	**63.38**

Fig. 8. Qualitative results on the LINEMOD [23] dataset. Ground-truth poses are drawn in green while predicted poses of Gen6D are drawn in blue.

4.5   Results on MOPED [41]

On the MOPED dataset, we compare Gen6D with Latent-Fusion [41] and PVNet [42]. Latent-Fusion [41] is also a generalizable pose estimator which does not require training on the test object but needs depth and object masks on query images. We use the official codes and the pretrained weights of Latent-Fusion [41] for evaluation. For training PVNet [42], we apply the same strategy as used on the GenMOP dataset. Table 3 reports ADD-AUC on the MOPED dataset, which shows that Gen6D outperforms both baselines on average while Gen6D only uses simple RGB inputs and does not require training on the object.

4.6   Analysis

Ablation Study on the Viewpoint Selector. To demonstrate the designs in the viewpoint selector, we conduct ablation studies on the GenMOP dataset and results are shown in Table 4. Without global normalization and reference view transformer, our viewpoint selector already outperforms the baseline image embedding method ObjDesc [68] by a large margin because our selector pixel-wisely compare the query image with reference images to compute similarity scores, which is more robust to clutter backgrounds. Meanwhile, adding the global normalization or the reference view transformer further improves the results because they exchange information between reference images to help the selector choose the relatively most similar reference image.

Analysis on the Pose Refiner. To demonstrate the advantage of our volume-based refiner on unseen objects over other rendering-and-comparison

Table 4. Ablations on the GenMOP dataset. "GN" means the global normalization used in view selector. "RVT" means the reference view transformer. "+ DeepIM Ref." means using the refiner DeepIM [29] to refine the pose for one step. "+Volume Ref." means refinement with our volume-base refiner for one step.

Metrics	Method	Object name					Avg.
		Chair	PlugEN	Piggy	Scissors	TFormer	
ADD-0.1d	ObjDesc [68]	3.50	5.14	14.07	1.25	7.54	8.55
	W/o GN and RVT	8.50	13.08	36.18	14.66	1.98	14.88
	W/o RVT	14.50	10.75	36.18	14.22	11.51	17.43
	Full selector	14.00	7.48	39.70	16.81	11.51	17.90
	+ DeepIM Ref	12.50	6.54	29.15	18.10	31.35	19.53
	+ Volume Ref	50.50	9.81	55.28	24.57	52.78	38.59
Prj-5	ObjDesc [68]	4.00	10.75	4.52	18.53	8.33	9.23
	W/o GN and RVT	7.00	40.19	20.60	28.88	54.76	30.28
	W/o RVT	16.00	46.73	31.66	24.57	55.16	34.82
	Full selector	11.50	40.65	33.17	34.05	64.29	36.73
	+ DeepIM Ref	4.50	5.23	18.50	61.64	73.81	42.16
	+ Volume Ref	44.00	71.03	92.96	84.48	95.24	77.54

based refiners [29,56,73], we report results on the GenMOP in Table 4. For the baseline refiner DeepIM [29], we regard the reference image selected by our selector as the rendered image and use DeepIM to match it with the query image to update the pose, i.e. one step refinement. Note further refinement with more steps using DeepIM are infeasible because there is no object model to render a new image on the updated pose. The DeepIM refiner is trained on the same training data as our volume-based refiner. The results show that our volume-based refiner has better generalization ability on unseen objects than DeepIM.

More Analysis . We provide more analysis about reference image number, comparison with finetuned DeepIM [29], refinement iterations, ablation on training data and symmetric objects in the supplementary material.

Limitations . The generalization ability of Gen6D mainly comes from matching image patterns in the viewpoint selection and the pose refinement. Thus, Gen6D requires enough diverse training data to learn general image matching for accurate pose estimation and it performs worse with limited training data. Meanwhile, Gen6D is not specially designed to handle occlusions and the performance may degenerate when severe occlusions exist.

Running Time . To process an image of size 540×960, Gen6D estimator costs ~0.64 s in total on a 2080Ti GPU, in which the object detector costs ~0.1 s, the viewpoint selector costs ~0.04 s and the refiner with 3 times refinement costs ~0.5 s.

5   Conclusion

In this paper, we propose an easy-to-use 6-DoF pose estimator Gen6D for unseen objects. To predict poses for unseen objects, Gen6D does not require the object model but only needs some posed images of the object to predict its pose in arbitrary environments. In Gen6D, we design a novel viewpoint selector and a novel volume-based pose refiner. Experiments demonstrate the superior performance of Gen6D estimator in predicting poses for unseen objects in the model-free setting.

References

1. Ammirato, P., Fu, C.Y., Shvets, M., Kosecka, J., Berg, A.C.: Target driven instance detection. arXiv preprint arXiv:1803.04610 (2018)
2. Balntas, V., Doumanoglou, A., Sahin, C., Sock, J., Kouskouridas, R., Kim, T.K.: Pose guided RGBD feature learning for 3D object pose estimation. In: ICCV (2017)
3. Banani, M.E., Corso, J.J., Fouhey, D.F.: Novel object viewpoint estimation through reconstruction alignment. In: CVPR (2020)
4. Busam, B., Jung, H.J., Navab, N.: I like to move it: 6D pose estimation as an action decision process. arXiv preprint arXiv:2009.12678 (2020)
5. Cai, D., Heikkilä, J., Rahtu, E.: OVE6D: object viewpoint encoding for depth-based 6D object pose estimation. In: CVPR (2022)
6. Cai, M., Reid, I.: Reconstruct locally, localize globally: a model free method for object pose estimation. In: CVPR (2020)
7. Chang, A.X., et al.: ShapeNet: an information-rich 3D model repository. arXiv preprint arXiv:1512.03012 (2015)
8. Chen, D., Li, J., Wang, Z., Xu, K.: Learning canonical shape space for category-level 6D object pose and size estimation. In: CVPR (2020)
9. Chen, K., Dou, Q.: SGPA: structure-guided prior adaptation for category-level 6D object pose estimation. In: ICCV (2021)
10. Chen, W., Jia, X., Chang, H.J., Duan, J., Shen, L., Leonardis, A.: FS-Net: fast shape-based network for category-level 6D object pose estimation with decoupled rotation mechanism. In: CVPR (2021)
11. Chen, X., Dong, Z., Song, J., Geiger, A., Hilliges, O.: Category level object pose estimation via neural analysis-by-synthesis. In: ECCV (2020)
12. Dani, M., Narain, K., Hebbalaguppe, R.: 3DPoselite: a compact 3D pose estimation using node embeddings. In: WACV (2021)
13. Deng, X., Geng, J., Bretl, T., Xiang, Y., Fox, D.: iCaps: iterative category-level object pose and shape estimation. IEEE Robot. Autom. Lett. **7**, 1784–1791 (2022)
14. Di, Y., Manhardt, F., Wang, G., Ji, X., Navab, N., Tombari, F.: So-Pose: exploiting self-occlusion for direct 6D pose estimation. In: CVPR (2021)
15. Di, Y., et al.: GPV-Pose: category-level object pose estimation via geometry-guided point-wise voting. arXiv preprint arXiv:2203.07918 (2022)
16. Goodwin, W., Vaze, S., Havoutis, I., Posner, I.: Zero-shot category-level object pose estimation. arXiv preprint arXiv:2204.03635 (2022)
17. Gou, M., Pan, H., Fang, H.S., Liu, Z., Lu, C., Tan, P.: Unseen object 6D pose estimation: a benchmark and baselines. arXiv preprint arXiv:2206.11808 (2022)
18. Grabner, A., et al.: Geometric correspondence fields: learned differentiable rendering for 3D pose refinement in the wild. In: ECCV (2020)

19. Gu, Q., Okorn, B., Held, D.: OSSID: online self-supervised instance detection by (and for) pose estimation. IEEE Robot. Autom. Lett. **7**, 3022–3029 (2022)

20. He, Y., Wang, Y., Fan, H., Sun, J., Chen, Q.: FS6D: few-shot 6D pose estimation of novel objects. In: CVPR (2022)

21. Hinterstoisser, S., et al.: Gradient response maps for real-time detection of texture-less objects. T-PAMI **34**(5), 876–888 (2011)

22. Hinterstoisser, S., et al.: Multimodal templates for real-time detection of texture-less objects in heavily cluttered scenes. In: ICCV (2011)

23. Hinterstoisser, S., et al.: Model based training, detection and pose estimation of texture-less 3D objects in heavily cluttered scenes. In: ACCV (2012)

24. Hodan, T., Barath, D., Matas, J.: EPOS: estimating 6D pose of objects with symmetries. In: CVPR (2020)

25. Hodan, T., et al.: BOP: benchmark for 6D object pose estimation. In: ECCV (2018)

26. Hodaň, T., et al.: Bop challenge 2020 on 6D object localization. In: ECCV (2020)

27. Hu, Y., Fua, P., Wang, W., Salzmann, M.: Single-stage 6D object pose estimation. In: CVPR (2020)

28. Labbé, Y., Carpentier, J., Aubry, M., Sivic, J.: CosyPose: consistent multi-view multi-object 6D pose estimation. In: ECCV (2020)

29. Li, Y., Wang, G., Ji, X., Xiang, Y., Fox, D.: DeepIM: deep iterative matching for 6D pose estimation. In: ECCV (2018)

30. Lin, J., Li, H., Chen, K., Lu, J., Jia, K.: Sparse steerable convolutions: an efficient learning of se (3)-equivariant features for estimation and tracking of object poses in 3D space. NeurIPS (2021)

31. Lin, J., Wei, Z., Li, Z., Xu, S., Jia, K., Li, Y.: DualPoseNet: category-level 6D object pose and size estimation using dual pose network with refined learning of pose consistency. In: ICCV (2021)

32. Lin, T.-Y., et al.: Microsoft COCO: common objects in context. In: Fleet, D., Pajdla, T., Schiele, B., Tuytelaars, T. (eds.) ECCV 2014. LNCS, vol. 8693, pp. 740–755. Springer, Cham (2014). https://doi.org/10.1007/978-3-319-10602-1_48

33. Liu, X., Iwase, S., Kitani, K.M.: StereOBJ-1M: large-scale stereo image dataset for 6D object pose estimation. In: CVPR (2021)

34. Liu, X., Jonschkowski, R., Angelova, A., Konolige, K.: KeyPose: multi-view 3D labeling and keypoint estimation for transparent objects. In: CVPR (2020)

35. Mercier, J.P., Garon, M., Giguere, P., Lalonde, J.F.: Deep template-based object instance detection. In: WACV (2021)

36. Mildenhall, B., Srinivasan, P.P., Tancik, M., Barron, J.T., Ramamoorthi, R., Ng, R.: NeRF: representing scenes as neural radiance fields for view synthesis. In: ECCV (2020)

37. Nguyen, V.N., Hu, Y., Xiao, Y., Salzmann, M., Lepetit, V.: Templates for 3D object pose estimation revisited: generalization to new objects and robustness to occlusions. In: CVPR (2022)

38. Okorn, B., Gu, Q., Hebert, M., Held, D.: ZePHyR: zero-shot pose hypothesis rating. In: ICRA (2021)

39. Osokin, A., Sumin, D., Lomakin, V.: OS2D: one-stage one-shot object detection by matching anchor features. In: ECCV (2020)

40. Park, J., Cho, N.I.: DProST: 6-DoF object pose estimation using space carving and dynamic projective spatial transformer. arXiv preprint arXiv:2112.08775 (2021)

41. Park, K., Mousavian, A., Xiang, Y., Fox, D.: LatentFusion: end-to-end differentiable reconstruction and rendering for unseen object pose estimation. In: CVPR (2020)

42. Peng, S., Liu, Y., Huang, Q., Zhou, X., Bao, H.: PVNet: pixel-wise voting network for 6-DoF pose estimation. In: CVPR (2019)
43. Pitteri, G., Bugeau, A., Ilic, S., Lepetit, V.: 3D object detection and pose estimation of unseen objects in color images with local surface embeddings. In: ACCV (2020)
44. Pitteri, G., Ilic, S., Lepetit, V.: CorNet: generic 3D corners for 6D pose estimation of new objects without retraining. In: ICCVW (2019)
45. Pitteri, G., Ramamonjisoa, M., Ilic, S., Lepetit, V.: On object symmetries and 6D pose estimation from images. In: 3DV (2019)
46. Ponimatkin, G., Labbé, Y., Russell, B., Aubry, M., Sivic, J.: Focal length and object pose estimation via render and compare. In: CVPR (2022)
47. Rad, M., Lepetit, V.: BB8: a scalable, accurate, robust to partial occlusion method for predicting the 3D poses of challenging objects without using depth. In: CVPR (2017)
48. Sarlin, P.E., DeTone, D., Malisiewicz, T., Rabinovich, A.: SuperGlue: learning feature matching with graph neural networks. In: CVPR (2020)
49. Schönberger, J.L., Frahm, J.M.: Structure-from-motion revisited. In: CVPR (2016)
50. Shugurov, I., Li, F., Busam, B., Ilic, S.: OSOP: a multi-stage one shot object pose estimation framework. In: CVPR (2022)
51. Simeonov, A., et al.: Neural descriptor fields: Se (3)-equivariant object representations for manipulation. arXiv preprint arXiv:2112.05124 (2021)
52. Simonyan, K., Zisserman, A.: Very deep convolutional networks for large-scale image recognition. arXiv preprint arXiv:1409.1556 (2014)
53. Song, C., Song, J., Huang, Q.: HybridPose: 6D object pose estimation under hybrid representations. In: CVPR (2020)
54. Su, Y., et al.: ZebraPose: coarse to fine surface encoding for 6DoF object pose estimation. In: CVPR (2022)
55. Sun, J., et al.: OnePose: one-shot object pose estimation without CAD models. CVPR (2022)
56. Sundermeyer, M., et al.: Multi-path learning for object pose estimation across domains. In: CVPR (2020)
57. Sundermeyer, M., Marton, Z.C., Durner, M., Brucker, M., Triebel, R.: Implicit 3D orientation learning for 6D object detection from RGB images. In: ECCV (2018)
58. Tekin, B., Sinha, S.N., Fua, P.: Real-time seamless single shot 6D object pose prediction. In: CVPR (2018)
59. Tian, M., Ang, M.H., Lee, G.H.: Shape prior deformation for categorical 6D object pose and size estimation. In: ECCV (2020)
60. Vaswani, A., et al.: Attention is all you need. In: NeurIPS (2017)
61. Wang, G., Manhardt, F., Shao, J., Ji, X., Navab, N., Tombari, F.: Self6D: self-supervised monocular 6D object pose estimation. In: ECCV (2020)
62. Wang, G., Manhardt, F., Tombari, F., Ji, X.: GDR-Net: geometry-guided direct regression network for monocular 6D object pose estimation. In: CVPR (2021)
63. Wang, H., Sridhar, S., Huang, J., Valentin, J., Song, S., Guibas, L.J.: Normalized object coordinate space for category-level 6D object pose and size estimation. In: CVPR (2019)
64. Wang, Q., et al.: IBRNet: learning multi-view image-based rendering. In: CVPR (2021)
65. Wen, B., Bekris, K.: BundleTrack: 6D pose tracking for novel objects without instance or category-level 3D models. In: IROS (2021)
66. Wen, Y., et al.: Disentangled implicit shape and pose learning for scalable 6D pose estimation. arXiv preprint arXiv:2107.12549 (2021)

67. Wen, Y., Pan, H., Yang, L., Wang, W.: Edge enhanced implicit orientation learning with geometric prior for 6D pose estimation. In: IROS (2020)
68. Wohlhart, P., Lepetit, V.: Learning descriptors for object recognition and 3D pose estimation. In: CVPR (2015)
69. Xiang, Y., Schmidt, T., Narayanan, V., Fox, D.: PoseCNN: a convolutional neural network for 6D object pose estimation in cluttered scenes. Robot.: Sci. Syst. (2018)
70. Xiao, Y., Marlet, R.: Few-shot object detection and viewpoint estimation for objects in the wild. In: ECCV (2020)
71. Xiao, Y., Qiu, X., Langlois, P.A., Aubry, M., Marlet, R.: Pose from Shape: deep pose estimation for arbitrary 3D objects. In: BMVC (2019)
72. Yen-Chen, L., Florence, P., Barron, J.T., Rodriguez, A., Isola, P., Lin, T.Y.: INeRF: inverting neural radiance fields for pose estimation. In: IROS (2021)
73. Zakharov, S., Shugurov, I., Ilic, S.: DPOD: 6D pose object detector and refiner. In: ICCV (2019)
74. Zhao, C., Hu, Y., Salzmann, M.: Fusing local similarities for retrieval-based 3D orientation estimation of unseen objects. arXiv preprint arXiv:2203.08472 (2022)

Latency-Aware Collaborative Perception

Zixing Lei[1], Shunli Ren[1], Yue Hu[1], Wenjun Zhang[1], and Siheng Chen[1,2(✉)]

[1] Cooperative Medianet Innovation Center, Shanghai Jiao Tong University,
Shanghai, China
{chezacarss,renshunli,10071120361,zhangwenjun,sihengc}@sjtu.edu.cn
[2] Shanghai AI Laboratory, Shanghai, China

Abstract. Collaborative perception has recently shown great potential to improve perception capabilities over single-agent perception. Existing collaborative perception methods usually consider an ideal communication environment. However, in practice, the communication system inevitably suffers from latency issues, causing potential performance degradation and high risks in safety-critical applications, such as autonomous driving. To mitigate the effect caused by the inevitable latency, from a machine learning perspective, we present the first latency-aware collaborative perception system, which actively adapts asynchronous perceptual features from multiple agents to the same time stamp, promoting the robustness and effectiveness of collaboration. To achieve such a feature-level synchronization, we propose a novel latency compensation module, called *SyncNet*, which leverages feature-attention symbiotic estimation and time modulation techniques. Experiments results show that the proposed latency aware collaborative perception system with *SyncNet* can outperforms the state-of-the-art collaborative perception method by 15.6% in the communication latency scenario and keep collaborative perception being superior to single agent perception under severe latency.

1 Introduction

Collaborative perception considers a multi-agent system to perceive a scene, where multiple agents collaborate through a communication network [4, 6, 8, 15–17, 27, 34, 35, 37–40]. With the observation from multiple agents, collaborative perception can fundamentally overcome the physical limits of single-agent perception, such as over-the-horizon and occlusion. Such collaborative perception models can be widely applied to practical applications, such as autonomous driving and robotics mapping. Previous collaborative perception methods [15–17, 27] have achieved remarkable success in multiple perception tasks, including 2D/3D object detection [21, 22, 36], and semantic segmentation [5, 20, 33, 41]. [16, 17] focus on semantic segmentation for drones and [15, 27] discuss the 3D object detection based on the vehicle-to-vehicle-communication-aided autonomous driving. Considering the trade-off between communication bandwidth and perception performance, previous works achieve the collaboration in the intermediate-feature space and leverage attentive mechanisms to fuse the collaboration features.

Code is available at: https://github.com/MediaBrain-SJTU/SyncNet

S. Avidan et al. (Eds.): ECCV 2022, LNCS 13692, pp. 316–332, 2022.
https://doi.org/10.1007/978-3-031-19824-3_19

(a) Collaboration without latency (b) Collaboration with 1s latency   (c) Single-agent perception

Fig. 1. Collaborative 3D detection. Red: *Detected*, green: *Ground truth*. Collaboration without considering latency could be even worse than no collaboration. (Color figure online)

However, none of these previous collaborative perception methods consider a realistic communication setting where latency is inevitable. As stated in [13], in a real-time LTE-V2X communication system, the latency time is up to an average of (498 communication periods) + 131.30 ms. Besides, the varying latency times of various communication channels would cause severe time asynchronous issues. Experimentally, latency issue severely damages the collaborative perception system, resulting in even worse performance than single-agent perception. From Fig. 1, we see that: i) the detected vehicles in the purple box in (a) with collaboration is missed in the (b); ii) the correctly detected vehicles in the blue box in (c) are incorrect in (b). The reason is that the received collaborative data with latency represents the situation 1s ago, it misleads the detector to output boxes with significant deviation. This motivates us to consider a collaborative perception system robust to the inevitable communication latency.

To tackle the latency issue, from a machine learning perspective, we propose the first latency-aware collaborative perception system, which actively adapts asynchronous perceptual features from multiple agents to the same time stamp, promoting the robustness and effectiveness of collaboration. As shown in Fig. 2, our latency-aware collaborative perception system follows the intermediate collaboration framework [15] and consists of five components: i) encoding module, extracting perceptual features from the raw data; ii) communication module, transmitting the perceptual features across agents under varying communication latency; iii) latency compensation module, synchronizing multiple agents' features to the same time stamp; iv) fusion module, aggregating all the synchronized features and producing the fusion feature; v) decoding module, adopting the fusion feature to get the final perception output. The main advantage of our latency-aware collaborative perception system is that it's able to synchronize the collaboration features before aggregation, mitigating the effect caused by latency instead of directly aggregate the received asynchronous features.

The key component of the proposed system is the latency compensation module, aiming to achieve feature-level synchronization. To realize this, we propose a novel *SyncNet*, which leverages historical collaboration information to simultaneously estimate the current feature and the corresponding collaboration attention, both of which are unknown due to latency. As the attention weight between two agents during collaboration, the proposed collaboration attention

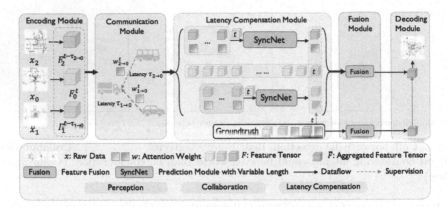

Fig. 2. Overview of the proposed latency-aware collaborative perception system: The key module is latency compensation module. To realize this, we propose SyncNet, which leverages historical collaboration information to synchronize the asynchronized information from multiple agents caused by the latency issue.

has the same spatial resolution with the features and indicates the informative level of each spatial region in the features. It thus provides informative hints for the collaboration partner about how to exploit the collaboration features. Intuitively, the feature and the corresponding collaboration attention are coupling together. Based on this design rationale, the proposed SyncNet leverages a feature-attention symbiotic estimation, which simultaneously infers the collaboration features and the corresponding collaboration attention unknown due to latency, mutually enhancing each other and avoiding the cascading error;

Compared with common time-series prediction methods, the proposed SyncNet has two main differences: i) feature-level estimation, instead of output-level prediction; ii) estimation of coupling features and the associated collaboration attention, instead of predicting a single output.

We extensively evaluate the novel latency-aware collaborative perception system with SyncNet on V2X-Sim dataset [14] on collaborative 3D object detection for autonomous driving. The results verify the robustness of our system and show substantial improvements over state-of-the-art approaches. With SyncNet, our latency-aware collaborative perception system significantly and consistently outperforms single-agent perception under varying communication latency.

To summarize, our contributions are as follows:

- We formulate the communication latency challenge in collaborative perception for the first time and propose a novel latency-aware collaborative perception system, which promotes robust multi-agents perception by mitigating the effect of inevitable communication latency.
- We propose a novel latency compensation module, termed *SyncNet*, to achieve feature-level synchronization. It achieves symbiotic estimation of two types of critical collaboration information, including intermediate features and collaboration attention, mutually enhancing each other.

- We conduct comprehensive experiments to show that our proposed SyncNet achieves huge performance improvement in latency scenarios compared with the previous method and keeps collaborative perception being superior to single-agent perception under severe latency.

2   Related Work

2.1   V2V Communication

V2V communication has two major protocols: IEEE 802.11p protocol and cellular network standards [18]. In IEEE 802.11p protocol, there is a Wireless Access in Vehicular Environment mode to allow users to skip a Basic Service Set, which reduces the overhead in connection setup [11]. In the cellular network, the Long Term Evolution(LTE) standard has derived LTE-V2X [1]. Though the achieved progress in the V2V network, the communication latency issues are still far from perfect and extremely risky for collaborative perception, the latency time is up to an average of (498 communication periods) + 131.30 ms [13]. Instead of avoiding latency from the communication perspective, we aim to mitigate the effect caused by inevitable communication latency from a machine learning perspective, leading to a novel latency-aware collaborative perception system.

2.2   Collaborative Perception

Collaborative perception enables agents to share perceived information through the communication network, fundamentally upgrades perception capabilities over single-agent perception. [16,17] uses a handshake mechanism to determine which two agents should communicate; [27] introduces a multi-round message passing graph neural networks; [15] proposes a graph-based collaborative perception system with knowledge distillation to balance the communication cost and perception performance. Most previous works focus on the collaboration strategy learning under ideal scenarios. Recently, more realistic scenarios are considered. [25] exploits a pose error regression module to correct errors in the received noisy posture. However, none of the previous works consider the realistic imperfect communication in the collaboration system. To fill this gap, we address the unavoidable communication latency issue, which is extremely risky to the collaboration system, and build a latency-aware collaborative perception system to mitigate the effect caused by latency.

2.3   Time-Series Prediction

Time-series prediction targets to predict the future signal according to the historical data. [23] proposes a conv-LSTM architecture in precipitation nowcasting. Video prediction, a universal and representative time-series type, has been actively studied [19,24,28–31]. By leveraging prediction techniques, our work recovers the missing information due to latency from historical collaboration information. However, unlike standard prediction, our goal is to maximize the final perception performance, instead of precisely estimating the current state.

3   Methodology

To tackle the latency issue, we propose a latency-aware collaborative perception system in Sect. 3.1. As the key of the entire system, the latency compensation module is realized by the proposed SyncNet; see Sect. 3.2. Finally, Sect. 3.3 introduces the loss function for training supervision.

3.1   Latency-Aware Collaborative Perception System

Collaborative perception enables multiple agents to perceive a scene together by sharing the perceived data through a communication network. Since communication latency is inevitable in a realistic communication system, here we focus on a latency-aware collaborative perception system; that is, given a non-ideal communication channel with uncontrollable latency, we aim to optimize the perception ability of each agent by mitigating the effect of latency.

We consider that there are N agents perceiving the environment in a scene. Let $\mathbf{X}_i^{(t)}$, $\mathbf{F}_i^{(t)}$ and $\widetilde{\mathbf{Y}}_i^{(t)}$, be the raw observation, the perceptual feature, and the final perception output of the ith agent at time stamp t, respectively; $\tau_{j \to i}^{(t)}$ be the time delay (latency) to transmit data from the jth agent to the ith agent; $\mathbf{W}_{j \to i}^{(t)}$ be the collaboration attention between agent j and agent i at time stamp t. The collaboration attention is calculated by learnable network, $f_{\text{attention}}\left(\mathbf{F}_i^{(t)}, \mathbf{F}_j^{(t)}\right)$ to point-wisely assign the attention among all the collaboration features in collaborative perception system. Note that i) the latency value $\tau_{j \to i}^{(t)}$ is *time-varying* and we omit its superscript t just for notation simplicity from now on; and ii) this work considers the collaboration happens at discrete time stamps and τ is discrete as each agent has a certain sampling rate of observation. Experimental results also validate that when discretizing the continuous time with reasonably small time interval, the resulting mismatch is minor. Then, the proposed latency-aware collaborative perception is formulated as:

$$\mathbf{F}_i^{(t)} = f_{\text{encoder}}\left(\mathbf{X}_i^{(t)}\right), \tag{1a}$$

$$\mathbf{F}_j^{(t-\tau_{j \to i})} = f_{\text{encoder}}\left(\mathbf{X}_j^{(t-\tau_{j \to i})}\right), \tag{1b}$$

$$\widetilde{\mathbf{F}}_j^{(t)}, \widetilde{\mathbf{W}}_{j \to i}^{(t)} = c\left(\tau_{j \to i}, \mathbf{F}_i^{(t)}, \left\{\mathbf{F}_j^{(t-\tau_{j \to i}-k)}\right\}_{k=0,1,\dots,N}\right), \tag{1c}$$

$$\widetilde{\mathbf{H}}_i^{(t)} = \sum_{j \in \mathcal{N}_i} \widetilde{\mathbf{W}}_{j \to i}^{(t)} \odot \widetilde{\mathbf{F}}_j^{(t)} + \mathbf{F}_i^{(t)} \odot \widetilde{\mathbf{W}}_i^{(t)}, \tag{1d}$$

$$\widetilde{\mathbf{Y}}_i^{(t)} = f_{\text{decoder}}\left(\widetilde{\mathbf{H}}_i^{(t)}\right), \tag{1e}$$

where $\widetilde{\mathbf{F}}_j^{(t)}$ is the estimated feature of the jth agent at time stamp t after synchronization, $\widetilde{\mathbf{W}}_{j \to i}^{(t)}$ is the estimated collaboration attention between the ith agent and the nth agent at time stamp t, $\widetilde{\mathbf{H}}_i^{(t)}$ is the estimated feature of the ith agent at time stamp t after aggregating estimated collaboration information.

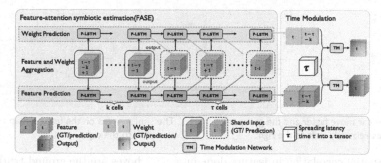

Fig. 3. SyncNet architecture: SyncNet includes feature-attention symbiotic estimation (**FASE**), a dual-branch pyramid LSTM(P-LSTM in the figure) network which shares the same input, this is, the aggregation of feature and attention, and **Time-Modulation module** to allocate time domain attention between the estimated features with the received asynchronous feature.

Step (1a) considers perceptual feature extraction from observation data, where $f_{\text{encoder}}(\cdot)$ is the encoding network. In Step (1b), we receive perceptual features from other agents with varying latency times. To compensate for latency, Step (1c) estimates the feature and collaborative attention at time stamp t by leveraging historical features from the same agent and the real-time feature perceived by ego agent i, where $c(\cdot)$ denotes the estimation network. Here we assume that each agent can store k frames of historical features in memory. Step (1d) fuses all the estimated collaboration information. Finally, Step (1e) outputs the final perceptual output, where $f_{\text{decoder}}(\cdot)$ is the decoder network. To correspond to Fig. 2, Steps (1a) and (1b) contribute to the encoding module; Steps (1c) contribute to the latency compensation module; Step (1d) contribute to the latency fusion module; and Step (1e) contribute to the decoding module.

The proposed latency-aware system has four advantages: **i)** we explicitly include the communication latency into the design of a collaborative perception system, which has never been done in previous works; see (1b) (1c); **ii)** we mitigate the effect of latency by estimating missing information from historical collaboration information; see (1c). Instead of synchronizing the perceptual output, we consider feature-level synchronization, because it allows an end-to-end learning framework with more learning flexibility; **iii)** In (1c), we estimate the coupling collaboration feature and attention simultaneously. If we only estimate the features, we would need to calculate the collaboration attention based on the estimated features. This would amplify the estimation error, causing cascading failures; and **iv)** we adopt the attention-based estimation, which leverages the collaboration attention in (1c) to promote more precise estimation on more perceptual-sensitive area; see (1d).

3.2 SyncNet: Latency Compensation Module

Since the latency compensation module is the key of the latency-aware collaborative perception system, we specifically design the estimation networks $c_F(\cdot)$

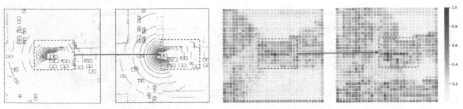

Center car move faster and the group of vehicles relatively shift to the right

The similar areas on the feature map are also shift to the right

Fig. 4. Spatial correlation in feature domain. Green boxes are the ground truth. The heatmap is the feature map $\mathbf{F} \in \mathbb{R}^{H \times W \times C}$ summed over channel dimension. (Color figure online)

and $c_W (\cdot)$ in (1c), and propose the novel SyncNet. Its functionality is to leverage historical information to achieve latency compensation. SyncNet includes two parts: feature-attention symbiotic estimation, which adopts a dual-branch pyramid LSTM to estimate the real-time features and collaboration attention simultaneously, and time modulation, which uses the latency time to adaptively adjust the final estimation of the collaboration features.

Feature-Attention Symbiotic Estimation. Feature-attention symbiotic estimation (FASE) simultaneously estimates the feature and its corresponding collaboration attention by leveraging a novel dual-branch architecture, including feature estimation branch and attention estimation branch. Both branches of the dual-LSTM network share the same input including real-time features perceived by the ego-agent i and k frames of the historical features perceived by its collaborator j. Each branch is implemented by a pyramid LSTM, which models the series of historical collaborative information and estimates the current state. Pyramid LSTM is specifically designed to capture spatially correlated collaboration features. As shown in Fig. 4, when the vehicle group in the red box relatively moves to the right compared with the central vehicle, the same movements occur in similar areas on the feature. The fact shows that the spatial information is significant for our estimation task. We modify the matrix multiplication in LSTM [10] to a multi-scale convolution architecture; see details in Fig. 5a. The main differences between the proposed pyramid LSTM and the ordinary ones are that LSTM [10] does not specifically consider extracting spatial features; conv-LSTM [23] extracts spatial features at a single scale; while the proposed pyramid LSTM is designed to capture local-to-global features at multiple scales.

The feature estimation branch aims to obtain the most informative features for collaboration at current time. To achieve this, the feature estimation branch should be attention-aware. And the attention estimation branch aims to find the most informative areas for collaboration at current time, besides, it has to suppress the areas with large estimation errors. To achieve this, the attention estimation branch should be feature-aware. To allow the estimation of feature and the corresponding attention be aware of each other, we recurrently leverage both the estimated feature map and collaboration attention from the previous time stamp to be the input of the following time stamp for either branch.

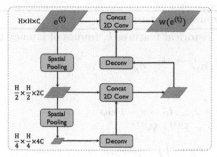

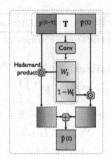

(a) Multi-resolution spatial convolution.   (b) Time modulation

Fig. 5. (a) shows multi resolution spatial convolution in pyramid LSTM. Both $w\,(\cdot)$ and $u\,(\cdot)$ functions can be represented by this figure. (b) shows time modulation and final estimation feature is $\widetilde{\mathbf{F}}^{(t)}$.

The entire process is shown in Algorithm 1, where τ is the latency time, k be the historical frames, t_0 be the current time, $\mathbf{W}_j^{(t)}$ and $\mathbf{F}_j^{(t)}$ are the collaboration attention and feature from jth agent to ith agent at time stamp t, respectively, $\widetilde{\mathbf{F}}_j^{(t)}$ and $\widetilde{\mathbf{W}}_j^{(t)}$ are the estimation of collaboration attention and feature at time stamp t, respectively, $\mathbf{e}^{(t)}$ is the input of pyramid LSTM at time stamp t, $\mathbf{h}_F^{(t)}$, $\mathbf{c}_F^{(t)}$, $\mathbf{h}_W^{(t)}$ and $\mathbf{c}_W^{(t)}$ are the the hidden states and cell states of the pyramid LSTM in each branch, respectively.

The proposed feature-attention symbiotic estimation has three characteristics: i) the dual-branch structure simultaneously infers the collaboration features and the corresponding collaboration attention, keeping independent and eliminating the cascaded failure; ii) the estimation networks take the collaboration attention as input so that to focus on more informative areas, promoting more effective estimation; iii) the learnable attention estimation network obtains the information of the feature and gets supervision from attention and fusion feature under ideal collaboration. During the end-to-end optimization, it can not only imitate the weight distribution calculated without latency, but also actively learn to reduce the attention of the spatial position with large noise in features.

Time Modulation. Although FASE achieves the basic functionality of $c_F\,(\cdot)$ and $c_W\,(\cdot)$, we find, when latency is low, the performance degradation caused by latency is relatively minor than the estimation noise led by FASE. To handle this, we propose time modulation, it attentively fuses the raw (working well at low latency) and estimated (working well at high latency) features conditioned on the latency time, generating more comprehensive and reliable estimation.

Let $\mathbf{M}_F^{(t)}, \mathbf{M}_W^{(t)} \in \mathbb{R}^{H \times W}$ be a confidence matrix to reflect the estimation uncertainty level of each spatial region, $\mathbf{T}_F \in \mathbb{R}^{H \times W \times C}$ and $\mathbf{T}_W \in \mathbb{R}^{H \times W}$ be the latency tensor obtained from the expansion of latency time $\tau \in \mathbb{R}$ with the same shape as $\widehat{\mathbf{F}}^{(t)}$ and $\widehat{\mathbf{W}}^{(t)}$, respectively. Time modulation works as

$$\mathbf{M}_F^{(t)} = m_F\left(\widetilde{\mathbf{F}}^{(t)} \mid \mathbf{F}^{(t-\tau)} \mid \mathbf{T}_W\right), \mathbf{M}_W^{(t)} = m_W\left(\widetilde{\mathbf{W}}^{(t)} \mid \mathbf{W}^{(t-\tau)} \mid \mathbf{T}_F\right), \qquad (2a)$$

Algorithm 1: Feature-attention symbiotic estimation

Parameters: Frames of numbers of historical features k, frames of latency time τ

Initialization: $\mathbf{h}_W^{(t_0-\tau-k)}$, $\mathbf{c}_W^{(t_0-\tau-k)}$, $\mathbf{h}_F^{(t_0-\tau-k)}$, $\mathbf{c}_F^{(t_0-\tau-k)}$.

1 **Input:** $\mathbf{F}_i^{(t_0)}$, $\left\{ \mathbf{F}_j^{(t')} \right\}_{t'=t-\tau-k+1,...,t-\tau}$:

2 $\quad$ **for** $t = t_0 - \tau - k + 1, t_0 - \tau - k + 2, ..., t_0 - \tau - 1$ **do**

3 $\quad\quad$ $\mathbf{W}^{(t)} = f_{\text{attention}}(\mathbf{F}_i^{t_0}, \mathbf{F}_j^t)$, $\mathbf{e}^{(t)} = \mathbf{F}_j^{(t)} \mid \mathbf{W}_j^{(t)}$

4 $\quad\quad$ $\left(\mathbf{h}_F^{(t)}, \mathbf{c}_F^{(t)} \right) = p_F \left(\mathbf{e}^{(t)}, \left(\mathbf{h}_F^{(t-1)}, \mathbf{c}_F^{(t-1)} \right) \right)$

5 $\quad\quad$ $\left(\mathbf{h}_W^{(t)}, \mathbf{c}_W^{(t)} \right) = p_W \left(\mathbf{e}_W^{(t)}, \left(\mathbf{h}_W^{(t-1)}, \mathbf{c}_W^{(t-1)} \right) \right)$

6 $\quad$ **end**

7 $\quad$ **for** $t = t_0 - \tau + 1, t_0 - \tau + 2, ..., t_0 - 1$ **do**

8 $\quad\quad$ $\widetilde{\mathbf{F}}_j^{(t)} = d_F(\mathbf{h}_F^{(t-1)})$ $\quad\quad\quad\quad$ $\leftarrow$ **Estimation of the feature at** t

9 $\quad\quad$ $\widetilde{\mathbf{W}}_j^{(t)} = d_W(\mathbf{h}_W^{(t-1)})$ $\quad\quad\quad\quad$ $\leftarrow$ **Estimation of the attention at** t

10 $\quad\quad$ $\mathbf{e}^{(t)} = \widetilde{\mathbf{F}}_j^{(t)} \mid \widetilde{\mathbf{W}}_j^{(t)}$

11 $\quad\quad$ $\left(\mathbf{h}_F^{(t)}, \mathbf{c}_F^{(t)} \right) = p_F \left(\mathbf{e}^{(t)}, \left(\mathbf{h}_F^{(t-1)}, \mathbf{c}_F^{(t-1)} \right) \right)$

12 $\quad\quad$ $\left(\mathbf{h}_W^{(t)}, \mathbf{c}_W^{(t)} \right) = p_W \left(\mathbf{e}_W^{(t)}, \left(\mathbf{h}_W^{(t-1)}, \mathbf{c}_W^{(t-1)} \right) \right)$

13 $\quad$ **end**

14 $\quad$ $\widetilde{\mathbf{F}}_j^{(t_0)} = d_F(\mathbf{h}_F^{(t_0-1)})$, $\widetilde{\mathbf{W}}_j^{(t_0)} = d_W(\mathbf{h}_W^{(t_0-1)})$

$$\widetilde{\widetilde{\mathbf{F}}}^{(t)} = \widetilde{\mathbf{F}}^{(t)} \odot \mathbf{M}_F^{(t)} + \mathbf{F}^{(t-\tau)} \odot (1 - \mathbf{M}_F^{(t)}), \quad \widetilde{\widetilde{\mathbf{W}}}^{(t)} = \widetilde{\mathbf{W}}^{(t)} \odot \mathbf{M}_W^{(t)} + \mathbf{W}^{(t-\tau)} \odot (1 - \mathbf{M}_W^{(t)}), \quad (2b)$$

where $m_F(\cdot)$ and $m_W(\cdot)$ are both the lightweight convolution neural network with a sigmoid activation function, $\mathbf{1} \in \mathbb{R}^{H \times W}$ is a matrix in which all elements are 1. Step (2a) respectively obtains the confidence level of the feature estimation at each spatial region by leveraging the concatenation of the estimated collaborative feature/attention by FASE, the latest asynchronous feature/attention, and the latency tensor. According to the confidence matrix, Step (2b) respectively combines the estimated feature/attention and the latest asynchronous feature/attention. We expect when the latency is high, the confidence matrix would have higher weights and the estimated feature/attention would contribute more to the final estimation; also see the process in Fig. 5b.

3.3 Loss Function

Let $\mathbf{Y}_i^{(t)}$ be the ground truth of final perception output of the ith agent at time stamp t, $\mathbf{H}_i^{(t)}$ be the ground truth feature of the ith agent at time stamp t after aggregating real-time collaboration information, $\mathbf{F}_i^{(t)}$ be the ground truth feature map of the ith agent at time stamp t, and $\mathbf{W}_{j \to i}^{(t)}$ be the ground truth collaboration attention from the jth agent to the ith at time stamp t. We consider minimizing the following objective to optimize the overall latency-aware collaborative perception system:

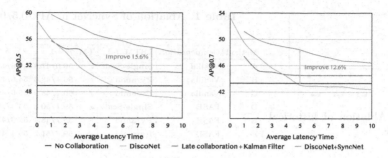

Fig. 6. Comparison of the performance of No Collaboration, DiscoNet [15], late collaboration with Kalman Filter, DiscoNet + SyncNet in latency of 1–10 frames.

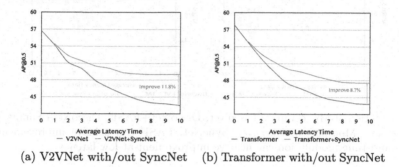

(a) V2VNet with/out SyncNet   (b) Transformer with/out SyncNet

Fig. 7. SyncNet integrated with different fusion frameworks in AP 0.5.

$$\mathcal{L} = \lambda_o \ell_{\text{output}}\left(\mathbf{Y}_i^{(t)}, \widetilde{\mathbf{Y}}_i^{(t)}\right) + \lambda_f \ell_{\text{fusion}}\left(\mathbf{H}_i^{(t)}, \widetilde{\mathbf{H}}_i^{(t)}\right) +$$
$$\lambda_f \ell_{\text{feature}}\left(\mathbf{F}_i^{(t)}, \widetilde{\mathbf{F}}_i^{(t)}\right) + \lambda_w \ell_{\text{weight}}\left(\mathbf{W}_{j\rightarrow i}^{(t)}, \widetilde{\mathbf{W}}_{j\rightarrow i}^{(t)}\right),$$

where λ denotes the weight of each item, $\ell_{\text{output}}(\cdot)$ is the ultimate perception loss, $\ell_{\text{fusion}}(\cdot), \ell_{\text{feature}}(\cdot), \ell_{\text{weight}}(\cdot)$ are losses for fused feature, intermediate estimated feature and estimated collaborative attention, respectively. The first term supervises the perception output and the second term supervises the estimated fusion feature. The third and fourth terms provide more supervision on intermediate feature maps and collaborative attentions to promote faster convergence.

4   Experiments

4.1   Multi-agent 3D Object Detection Dataset

We validate our SyncNet on LIDAR-based 3D object detection task [3,9] with a multi-agent dataset, V2X-Sim [14]. V2X-Sim is built with the co-simulation of SUMO [12] and CARLA [7]. V2X-Sim includes 80 scenes in the training set

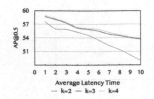

Fig. 8. Ablation of historical frames k.

Table 1. Ablation of SyncNet in AP@0.5/0.7.

Method	Compensation	LSTM	TM	$\tau = 1$	$\tau = 5$
A	Vanilla	Single-Scale	✓	56.0/47.8	54.6/44.2
B	Vanilla	Pyramid		56.1/48.3	54.6/44.2
C	Vanilla	Pyramid	✓	60.1/48.9	55.6/45.1
D	FASE	Single-Scale	✓	59.1/50.8	55.3/48.8
E	FASE	Pyramid		55.7/48.4	54.3/47.6
F	FASE	Pyramid	✓	59.7/51.2	56.1/48.8

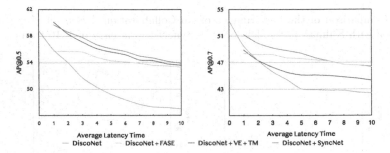

Fig. 9. Ablation study: compare DiscoNet, DiscoNet+FASE, DiscoNet+Vanilla Estimation+Time Modulation, DiscoNet+SyncNet. FASE can achieve improvement for AP@0.7 and time modulation can achieve improvement at low latency.

and 11 scenes in the test set. Each sample contains 2.67 agents on average and includes 3D point clouds input and 3D bounding box annotations. The 3D point clouds are generated by a LIDAR with 32 channels and 70 m max range, 20 Hz rotation frequency, 5 Hz recorded frequency. To simulate collaborative perception under a latency scenario, we load data in asynchronous time stamps, and the latency time τ is randomly generated from an exponential distribution.

4.2 Implementation Details

Experimental Setting. We crop the point clouds which locate in the region of $[-32\,\text{m}, 32\,\text{m}] \times [-32\,\text{m}, 32\,\text{m}] \times [0, 5\,\text{m}]$ defined in the ego-vehicle Cartesian coordinate system. We set the size of each voxel as $0.25\,\text{m} \times 0.25\,\text{m} \times 0.4\,\text{m}$. After crop and voxelization, we get a Bird's-Eyes view map with dimension $256 \times 256 \times 13$. The encoded features to be transmitted has a dimension of $32 \times 32 \times 256$. The latency between two agents can be a fixed or random number generated by exponential distribution rounded to an integer. We train our model using NVIDIA RTX 3090 GPU with Pytorch. The evaluation metric is the Average Precision(AP) metric at Intersection-over-Union threshold of 0.5 and 0.7.

Baselines. Our proposed latency-aware collaborative perception system adopts one of the state-of-the-art collaborative perception frameworks, DiscoNet [15], and leverages the proposed SyncNet as the latency compensation module to han-

Latency-Aware Collaborative Perception   327

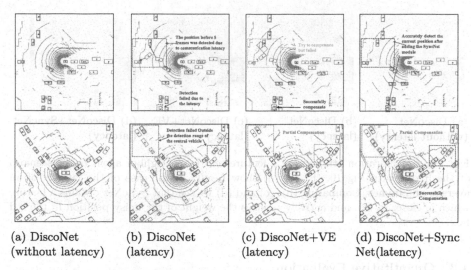

(a) DiscoNet   (b) DiscoNet   (c) DiscoNet+VE   (d) DiscoNet+Sync
(without latency)   (latency)   (latency)   Net(latency)

Fig. 10. FASE architecture qualitatively improves the performance under communication latency. (a) shows the detection results of DiscoNet [15] without communication latency. (b) (c) (d) show results in the case of the latency of an average of 5 frames.

dle various latency settings. To validate our latency-aware collaborative perception system, *DiscoNet+SyncNet*, we compare with three baselines: i) single-agent perception system, *No Collaboration*; ii) latency-unaware collaborative perception, *DiscoNet* [15]; iii) naive latency-aware late-fusion-based collaborative perception by using Kalman filter [32], *Late collaboration+Kalman Filter*. Note that SyncNet can also work as a plugin latency compensation module for other intermediate collaborative perception methods, such as V2VNet [27]. SyncNet is equivalent to feature-attention symbiotic estimation (FASE) + time modulation(TM). Corresponding to FASE with the dual-branch structure, a simplified variation is Vanilla Estimation(VE), which adopts a single-branch LSTM to estimate collaborative features only. In ablation study, we will compare the performances of *DiscoNet*, *DiscoNet+FASE*, *DiscoNet+VE* and *DiscoNet+SyncNet*.

Training Strategy. We use a curriculum learning [2] strategy in the training stage. Curriculum learning starts with easy samples and then gradually increases the difficulty. To handle the flexible latency time, we train the model under various latency settings. However, the training loss sharply increasing with the latency time causes an unstable and vulnerable training process. To tackle this issue, we employ the curriculum learning technology and gradually increase the latency time by 1 every 10 epochs until 10. Afterward, we randomly sample the latency time with an exponential distribution averaging 5 to further upgrade the model to accommodate the flexible communication latency.

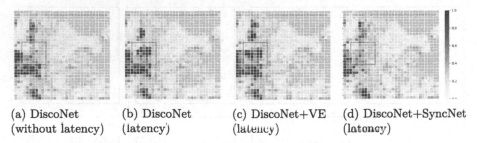

(a) DiscoNet   (b) DiscoNet   (c) DiscoNet+VE   (d) DiscoNet+SyncNet
(without latency)   (latency)   (latency)   (latency)

Fig. 11. Collaboration attention of a feature sent by a neighbor agent in the scenario of the first row in Fig. 10. (b) (c) (d) show results in the case of the latency of an average of 5 frames. Comparing (b), (c) and (d) we see that SyncNet obtains a feature which is closer to (a), and actively reduces the weight of the noisy position in the red box.

4.3 Quantitative Evaluation

Figure 6 compares the detection performances among our latency-aware collaborative perception system, no collaboration, DiscoNet without latency compensation, and late collaboration with a Kalman filter as a function of latency time. We see that: i) *DiscoNet* is vulnerable to latency, whose performance is even lower than *No Collaboration* at high latency; ii) our *DiscoNet+SyncNet* is robust to latency and outperforms *No Collaboration* even in a terrible communication condition with a communication latency of up to 10 frames; iii) our *DiscoNet+SyncNet* consistently outperforms *DiscoNet* under varying communication latency, and improves performance in AP@0.5/0.7 by up to 15.6%/12.6%.

Figure 7 shows the performances of other frameworks, including V2VNet and a transformer-based fusion module, with and without SyncNet. The transformer-based fusion module deploys a multi-head attention architecture [26] to fuse the collaborative features at each spatial position. The SyncNet module improves the performance up to 11.8%/8.7% in AP@0.5, respectively. It shows that various collaborative perception models are vulnerable to latency and the proposed compensation module consistently and significantly benefits those frameworks.

4.4 Ablation Study

We first study the effect of historical frames k in Fig. 8. We see that, $k = 3$ significantly outperforms $k = 2$, but $k = 4$ only brings marginal benefit. The default choice in the paper is $k = 3$, achieving a reasonable balance between computation efficiency and performance. We further validate the effectiveness of the two major components of our proposed latency compensation module (SyncNet): FASE and TM. Vanilla Estimation(VE) adopts a single-branch structure only estimating collaborative features. Figure 9 compares *DiscoNet*, *DiscoNet + FASE*, *DiscoNet + VE* and *DiscoNet + SyncNet* as a function of latency time. We see that: i) comparing green line with blue line, our latency-aware collaborative perception system only needs a vanilla LSTM compensation module to achieve significant performance improvement in latency scenarios. ii) comparing red line with blue line, FASE architecture can improve performance in AP@0.7 metric; iii) comparing red line with yellow line, TM can improve performance when latency is low. Table 1 further discusses the effectiveness of the compensation model, multi-scale convolution and time modulation module at low($\tau = 1$) and high latency($\tau = 5$). We see that: i) D surpasses A, E surpasses B, F surpasses C, reflecting FASE is consistently effective in AP@0.7 metric; ii) C surpasses B, F surpasses E, reflecting TM is consistently effective when latency is high.

4.5   Qualitative Evaluation

Figure 10 shows the detection results of *DiscoNet* without latency, *DiscoNet* with latency, *DiscoNet+VE* and *DiscoNet + SyncNet*. Comparing (a) with (b), we see that the correctly detected vehicles in the purple box in (a) are missed or incorrectly detected in (b) due to the latency. (c) shows that the vanilla estimation (without FASE) partially compensates latency error in the blue box but fails to achieve accurate estimation in the orange box, while our SyncNet could precisely recover the true position of both vehicles, shown in purple box of (d). Plot (d) shows that SyncNet achieves the best compensation and precisely recovers the true position of vehicles.

Figure 11 shows the attention weight of the collaboration feature from the neighbor agent in the example shown in the first row of Fig. 10. We can see that: (b), (c) both have a similar large weights in the red box, which introduce noise into the collaboration, and (d) has a small weight like (a), here to capture the truly informative area and avoid the cascading errors caused by the inaccurate feature estimation because the attention estimation branch in SyncNet under the supervision of the ground truth of collaboration attention. These qualitative results suggests the effectiveness of SyncNet.

5   Conclusions

We introduce latency-aware collaborative perception and propose a novel latency compensation module, SyncNet, for time-domain synchronization, which fits in existing intermediate collaboration methods. SyncNet adopts a novel symbiotic estimation architecture, which jointly estimates intermediate features and attention weights, as well as the time modulation, which significantly improves the overall performance at low-latency range. Comprehensive quantitative and qualitative experiments show that the proposed SyncNet can improve the perception performance in the communication latency scenario and effectively address the latency issue in the collaborative perception.

Acknowledgements. This research is partially supported by the National Key R&D Program of China under Grant 2021ZD0112801, National Natural Science Foundation of China under Grant 62171276, the Science and Technology Commission of Shanghai Municipal under Grant 21511100900 and CALT Grant 2021–01.

References

1. Araniti, G., Campolo, C., Condoluci, M., Iera, A., Molinaro, A.: LTE for vehicular networking: a survey. IEEE Commun. Mag. **51**, 148–157 (2013)
2. Bengio, Y., Louradour, J., Collobert, R., Weston, J.: Curriculum learning. In: Proceedings of the 26th Annual International Conference on Machine Learning, pp. 41–48 (2009)
3. Chen, S., Liu, B., Feng, C., Vallespi-Gonzalez, C., Wellington, C.: 3D point cloud processing and learning for autonomous driving: impacting map creation, localization, and perception. IEEE Signal Process. Mag. **38**(1), 68–86 (2021). https://doi.org/10.1109/MSP.2020.2984780
4. Chen, W., Xu, R., Xiang, H., Liu, L., Ma, J.: Model-agnostic multi-agent perception framework. arXiv preprint arXiv:2203.13168 (2022)
5. Choy, C., Gwak, J., Savarese, S.: 4D Spatio-Temporal ConvNets: Minkowski convolutional neural networks. In: Proceedings of the IEEE/CVF Conference on Computer Vision and Pattern Recognition, pp. 3075–3084 (2019)
6. Cui, J., Qiu, H., Chen, D., Stone, P., Zhu, Y.: Coopernaut: end-to-end driving with cooperative perception for networked vehicles. In: Proceedings of the IEEE/CVF Conference on Computer Vision and Pattern Recognition, pp. 17252–17262 (2022)
7. Dosovitskiy, A., Ros, G., Codevilla, F., Lopez, A., Koltun, V.: CARLA: an open urban driving simulator. In: Conference on robot learning, pp. 1–16. PMLR (2017)
8. Glaser, N., Liu, Y.C., Tian, J., Kira, Z.: Overcoming obstructions via bandwidth-limited multi-agent spatial handshaking. In: 2021 IEEE/RSJ International Conference on Intelligent Robots and Systems (IROS), pp. 2406–2413. IEEE (2021)
9. Guo, Y., Wang, H., Hu, Q., Liu, H., Liu, L., Bennamoun, M.: Deep learning for 3D point clouds: a survey. IEEE Trans. Pattern Anal. Mach. Intell. **43**(12), 4338–4364 (2020)
10. Hochreiter, S., Schmidhuber, J.: Long short-term memory. Neural Comput. **9**(8), 1735–1780 (1997)
11. Jiang, D., Delgrossi, L.: IEEE 802.11p: towards an international standard for wireless access in vehicular environments. VTC Spring 2008 - IEEE Vehicular Technology Conference, pp. 2036–2040 (2008)
12. Krajzewicz, D., Erdmann, J., Behrisch, M., Bieker, L.: Recent Development and Applications of SUMO-simulation of Urban MObility. Int. J. Adv. Syst. Meas. **5**(3,4) (2012)
13. Lee, K., Kim, J., Park, Y., Wang, H., Hong, D.: Latency of cellular-based V2X: perspectives on TTI-proportional latency and TTI-independent latency. IEEE Access **5**, 15800–15809 (2017). https://doi.org/10.1109/ACCESS.2017.2731777
14. Li, Y., An, Z., Wang, Z., Zhong, Y., Chen, S., Feng, C.: V2X-Sim: a virtual collaborative perception dataset for autonomous driving. IEEE Robot. Autom. Lett. (2022)
15. Li, Y., Ren, S., Wu, P., Chen, S., Feng, C., Zhang, W.: Learning distilled collaboration graph for multi-agent perception. In: Advances in Neural Information Processing Systems 34 (2021)
16. Liu, Y.C., Tian, J., Glaser, N., Kira, Z.: When2com: multi-agent perception via communication graph grouping. In: Proceedings of the IEEE/CVF Conference on Computer Vision and Pattern Recognition, pp. 4106–4115 (2020)
17. Liu, Y.C., Tian, J., Ma, C.Y., Glaser, N., Kuo, C.W., Kira, Z.: Who2com: collaborative perception via learnable handshake communication. In: 2020 IEEE International Conference on Robotics and Automation (ICRA), pp. 6876–6883. IEEE (2020)

18. Mei, J., Zheng, K., Zhao, L., Teng, Y., Wang, X.: A latency and reliability guaranteed resource allocation scheme for LTE v2v communication systems. IEEE Trans. Wireless Commun. **17**, 3850–3860 (2018)
19. Oliu, M., Selva, J., Escalera, S.: Folded recurrent neural networks for future video prediction. In: Proceedings of the European Conference on Computer Vision (ECCV), pp. 716–731 (2018). https://doi.org/10.1007/978-3-031-19839-7
20. Qi, C.R., Yi, L., Su, H., Guibas, L.J.: PointNet++: deep hierarchical feature learning on point sets in a metric space. In: Advances in Neural Information Processing Systems 30 (2017)
21. Shi, S., et al.: PV-RCNN: point-voxel feature set abstraction for 3D object detection. In: Proceedings of the IEEE/CVF Conference on Computer Vision and Pattern Recognition, pp. 10529–10538 (2020)
22. Shi, S., Wang, X., Li, H.: PointRCNN: 3D object proposal generation and detection from point cloud. In: Proceedings of the IEEE/CVF Conference on Computer Vision and Pattern Recognition, pp. 770–779 (2019)
23. Shi, X., Chen, Z., Wang, H., Yeung, D.Y., Wong, W.K., Woo, W.C.: Convolutional LSTM network: a machine learning approach for precipitation nowcasting. In: Advances in Neural Information Processing Systems 28 (2015)
24. Su, J., Byeon, W., Kossaifi, J., Huang, F., Kautz, J., Anandkumar, A.: Convolutional Tensor-train LSTM for Spatio-temporal learning. Adv. Neural. Inf. Process. Syst. **33**, 13714–13726 (2020)
25. Vadivelu, N., Ren, M., Tu, J., Wang, J., Urtasun, R.: Learning to communicate and correct pose errors. In: Conference on Robot Learning, pp. 1195–1210. PMLR (2021)
26. Vaswani, A., et al.: Attention is all you need. In: Guyon, I., et al. (eds.) Advances in Neural Information Processing Systems, vol. 30. Curran Associates, Inc. (2017)
27. Wang, T.-H., Manivasagam, S., Liang, M., Yang, B., Zeng, W., Urtasun, R.: V2VNet: vehicle-to-vehicle communication for joint perception and prediction. In: Vedaldi, A., Bischof, H., Brox, T., Frahm, J.-M. (eds.) ECCV 2020. LNCS, vol. 12347, pp. 605–621. Springer, Cham (2020). https://doi.org/10.1007/978-3-030-58536-5_36
28. Wang, Y., Gao, Z., Long, M., Wang, J., Philip, S.Y.: PredRNN++: towards a resolution of the deep-in-time dilemma in spatiotemporal predictive learning. In: International Conference on Machine Learning, pp. 5123–5132. PMLR (2018)
29. Wang, Y., Jiang, L., Yang, M.H., Li, L.J., Long, M., Fei-Fei, L.: Eidetic 3D LSTM: a model for video prediction and beyond. In: ICLR (2019)
30. Wang, Y., Long, M., Wang, J., Gao, Z., Yu, P.S.: PredRNN: recurrent neural networks for predictive learning using spatiotemporal LSTMs. In: Advances in Neural Information Processing Systems 30 (2017)
31. Wang, Y., Zhang, J., Zhu, H., Long, M., Wang, J., Yu, P.S.: Memory in memory: a predictive neural network for learning higher-order non-stationarity from spatiotemporal dynamics. In: Proceedings of the IEEE/CVF Conference on Computer Vision and Pattern Recognition, pp. 9154–9162 (2019)
32. Welch, G., Bishop, G., et al.: An introduction to the Kalman filter (1995)
33. Wu, P., Chen, S., Metaxas, D.N.: MotionNet: joint perception and motion prediction for autonomous driving based on bird's eye view maps. In: Proceedings of the IEEE/CVF Conference on Computer Vision and Pattern Recognition, pp. 11385–11395 (2020)
34. Xu, R., Xiang, H., Tu, Z., Xia, X., Yang, M.H., Ma, J.: V2X-ViT: vehicle-to-everything cooperative perception with vision transformer. arXiv preprint arXiv:2203.10638 (2022)

35. Xu, R., Xiang, H., Xia, X., Han, X., Li, J., Ma, J.: OPV2V: an open benchmark dataset and fusion pipeline for perception with vehicle-to-vehicle communication. In: 2022 International Conference on Robotics and Automation (ICRA), pp. 2583–2589. IEEE (2022)

36. Yin, T., Zhou, X., Krahenbuhl, P.: Center-based 3D object detection and tracking. In: Proceedings of the IEEE/CVF Conference on Computer Vision and Pattern Recognition, pp. 11784–11793 (2021)

37. Yu, H., et al.: DAIR-V2X: A large-scale dataset for vehicle-infrastructure cooperative 3D object detection. In: Proceedings of the IEEE/CVF Conference on Computer Vision and Pattern Recognition, pp. 21361–21370 (2022)

38. Yuan, Y., Sester, M.: Comap: a synthetic dataset for collective multi-agent perception of autonomous driving. Int. Arc. Photogramm. Remote Sens. Spat. Inf. Sci. **43**, 255–263 (2021)

39. Yuan, Y., Cheng, H., Sester, M.: Keypoints-based deep feature fusion for cooperative vehicle detection of autonomous driving. IEEE Rob. Autom. Lett. **7**(2), 3054–3061 (2022)

40. Zhang, X., et al.: EMP: edge-assisted multi-vehicle perception. In: Proceedings of the 27th Annual International Conference on Mobile Computing and Networking, pp. 545–558 (2021)

41. Zhao, H., Jiang, L., Jia, J., Torr, P.H., Koltun, V.: Point transformer. In: Proceedings of the IEEE/CVF International Conference on Computer Vision, pp. 16259–16268 (2021)

TensoRF: Tensorial Radiance Fields

Anpei Chen[1](✉), Zexiang Xu[2], Andreas Geiger[3], Jingyi Yu[1], and Hao Su[4]

[1] ShanghaiTech University, Shanghai, China
anpei.chen@inf.ethz.ch
[2] Adobe Research, San Jose, USA
[3] University of Tübingen and MPI-IS, Tübingen, Germany
[4] UC San Diego, San Diego, USA
https://apchenstu.github.io/TensoRF/

Abstract. We present TensoRF, a novel approach to model and reconstruct radiance fields. Unlike NeRF that purely uses MLPs, we model the radiance field of a scene as a 4D tensor, which represents a 3D voxel grid with per-voxel multi-channel features. Our central idea is to factorize the 4D scene tensor into multiple compact low-rank tensor components. We demonstrate that applying traditional CANDECOMP/PARAFAC (CP) decomposition – that factorizes tensors into rank-one components with compact vectors – in our framework leads to improvements over vanilla NeRF. To further boost performance, we introduce a novel vector-matrix (VM) decomposition that relaxes the low-rank constraints for two modes of a tensor and factorizes tensors into compact vector and matrix factors. Beyond superior rendering quality, our models with CP and VM decompositions lead to a significantly lower memory footprint in comparison to previous and concurrent works that directly optimize per-voxel features. Experimentally, we demonstrate that TensoRF with CP decomposition achieves fast reconstruction (< 30 min) with better rendering quality and even a smaller model size (< 4 MB) compared to NeRF. Moreover, TensoRF with VM decomposition further boosts rendering quality and outperforms previous state-of-the-art methods, while reducing the reconstruction time (< 10 min) and retaining a compact model size (< 75 MB).

1 Introduction

Modeling and reconstructing 3D scenes as representations that support high-quality image synthesis is crucial for computer vision and graphics with various applications in visual effects, e-commerce, virtual and augmented reality, and robotics. Recently, NeRF [37] and its many follow-up works [31,69] have shown success on modeling a scene as a radiance field and enabled photo-realistic rendering of scenes with highly complex geometry and view-dependent appearance

---

A. Chen and Z. Xu—Equal Contribution.
Research done when Anpei Chen was in a remote internship with UCSD.

Supplementary Information The online version contains supplementary material available at https://doi.org/10.1007/978-3-031-19824-3_20.

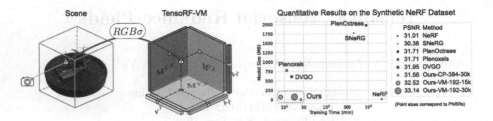

Fig. 1. Left: We model a scene as a tensorial radiance field using a set of vectors ($\mathbf{v}$) and matrices ($\mathbf{M}$) that describe scene appearance and geometry along their corresponding axes. These vector/matrix factors are used to compute volume density σ and view-dependent RGB color via vector-matrix outer products for realistic volume rendering. Right: In comparison with previous and concurrent methods, our TensoRF models can achieve the best rendering quality and are the only methods that can simultaneously achieve fast reconstruction and high compactness. (Our models are denoted with their decomposition techniques, number of components, and training steps.) (Color figure online)

effects. Despite the fact that (purely MLP-based) NeRF models require small memory, they take a long time (hours or days) to train. In this work, we pursue a novel approach that is both *efficient in training time* and *compact in memory footprint*, and at the same time achieves *state-of-the-art* rendering quality.

To do so, we propose TensoRF, a novel radiance field representation that is highly compact and also fast to reconstruct, enabling efficient scene reconstruction and modeling. Unlike coordinate-based MLPs used in NeRF, we represent radiance fields as an explicit voxel grid of features. Note that it is *unclear* whether voxel grid representation can benefit the efficiency of reconstruction: While previous work has used feature grids [20,31,67], they require large GPU memory to store the voxels whose size grows cubically with resolution, and some even require pre-computing a NeRF for distillation, leading to very long reconstruction time.

Our work addresses the inefficiency of voxel grid representations in a principled framework, leading to a family of simple yet effective methods. We leverage the fact that a feature grid can naturally be seen as a 4D tensor, where three of its modes correspond to the XYZ axes of the grid and the fourth mode represents the feature channel dimension. This opens the possibility of exploiting classical tensor decomposition techniques – which have been widely applied to high-dimensional data analysis and compression in various fields [27] – for radiance field modeling. We, therefore, propose to factorize the tensor of radiance fields into multiple *low-rank* tensor components, leading to an accurate and compact scene representation. Note that our central idea of tensorizing radiance fields is general and can be potentially adopted to any tensor decomposition technique.

In this work, we first attempt the classic CANDECOMP/PARAFAC (CP) decomposition [7]. We show that TensoRF with CP decomposition can already achieve photo-realistic rendering and lead to a more compact model than NeRF that is purely MLP based (see Fig. 1 and Table 1). However, experimentally, to further push reconstruction quality for complex scenes, we have to use more component factors, which undesirably increases training time.

Therefore, we present a novel vector-matrix (VM) decomposition technique that effectively reduces the number of components required for the same expression capacity, leading to faster reconstruction and better rendering. In particular, inspired by the CP and block term decomposition [13], we propose to factorize the full tensor of a radiance field into multiple vector and matrix factors per tensor component. Unlike the sum of outer products of pure vectors in CP decomposition, we consider the sum of vector-matrix outer products (see Fig. 2). In essence, we relax the ranks of two modes of each component by jointly modeling two modes in a matrix factor. While this increases the model size compared to pure vector-based factorization in CP, we enable each component to express more complex tensor data of higher ranks, thus significantly reducing the required number of components in radiance field modeling.

With CP/VM decomposition, our approach compactly encodes spatially varying features in the voxel grid. Volume density and view-dependent color can be decoded from the features, supporting volumetric radiance field rendering. Because a tensor expresses discrete data, we also enable efficient trilinear interpolation for our representation to model a continuous field. Our representation supports various types of per-voxel features with different decoding functions, including neural features – depending on an MLP to regress view-dependent colors from the features – and spherical harmonics (SH) features (coefficients) – allowing for simple color computation from the fixed SH functions and leading to a representation without neural networks.

Our tensorial radiance fields can be effectively reconstructed from multi-view images and enable realistic novel view synthesis. In contrast to previous works that directly reconstruct voxels, our tensor factorization reduces space complexity from $\mathcal{O}(n^3)$ to $\mathcal{O}(n)$ (with CP) or $\mathcal{O}(n^2)$ (with VM), significantly lowering memory footprint. Note that, although we leverage tensor decomposition, we are not addressing a decomposition/compression problem, but a reconstruction problem based on gradient decent, since the feature grid/tensor is unknown. In essence, our CP/VM decomposition offers low-rank regularization in the optimization, leading to high rendering quality. We present extensive evaluation of our approach with various settings, covering both CP and VM models, different numbers of components and grid resolutions. We demonstrate that all models are able to achieve realistic novel view synthesis results that are on par or better than previous state-of-the-art methods (see Fig. 1 and Table 1). More importantly, our approach is of high computation and memory efficiency. All TensoRF models can reconstruct high-quality radiance fields in 30 min; our fastest model with VM decomposition takes less than 10 min, which is significantly faster (about 100x) than NeRF and many other methods, while requiring substantially less memory than previous and concurrent voxel-based methods. Note that, unlike concurrent works [38,49] that require unique data structures and customized CUDA kernels, our model's efficiency gains are obtained using a standard PyTorch implementation. As far as we know, our work is the first that views radiance field modeling from a tensorial perspective and pose the problem of radiance field reconstruction as one of low-rank tensor reconstructions.

2 Related Work

Tensor Decomposition. Tensor decomposition [27] has been studied for decades with diverse applications in vision, graphics, machine learning, and other fields [1,14,23,24,42,58]. In general, the most widely used decompositions are Tucker decomposition [57] and CP decomposition [7,19], both of which can be seen as generalizations of the matrix singular value decomposition (SVD). CP decomposition can also be seen as a special Tucker decomposition whose core tensor is diagonal. By combining CP and Tucker decomposition, block term decomposition (BTD) has been proposed with its many variants [13] and used in many vision and learning tasks [2,65,66]. In this work, we leverage tensor decomposition for radiance field modeling. We directly apply CP decomposition and also introduce a new vector-matrix decomposition, which can be seen as a special BTD.

Scene Representations and Radiance Fields. Various scene representations, including meshes [18,60], point clouds [46], volumes [22,47], implicit functions [35,45], have been extensively studied in recent years. Many neural representations [4,10,33,52,70] are proposed for high-quality rendering or natural signal representation [29,51,55]. NeRF [37] introduces radiance fields to address novel view synthesis and achieves photo-realistic quality. This representation has been quickly extended and applied in diverse graphics and vision applications, including generative models [9,40], appearance acquisition [3,5], surface reconstruction [41,61], fast rendering [17,20,48,67], appearance editing [32,63], dynamic capture [28,43] and generative model [8,40]. While leading to realistic rendering and a compact model, NeRF with its pure MLP-based representation has known limitations in slow reconstruction and rendering. Recent methods [20,31,67] have leveraged a voxel grid of features in radiance field modeling, achieving fast rendering. However, these grid-based methods still require long reconstruction time and even lead to high memory costs, sacrificing the compactness of NeRF. Based on feature grids, we present a novel tensorial scene representation, leveraging tensor factorization techniques, leading to fast reconstruction and compact modeling.

Other methods design generalizable network modules trained across scenes to achieve image-dependent radiance field rendering [12,56,62,68] and fast reconstruction [11,64]. Our approach focuses on radiance field representation and only considers per-scene optimization (like NeRF). We show that our representation can already lead to highly efficient radiance field reconstruction without any across-scene generalization. We leave the extensions to generalizable settings as future work.

Concurrent Work. The field of radiance field modeling is moving very fast and many concurrent works have appeared on arXiv as preprints over the last three months. DVGO [54] and Plenoxels [49] also optimize voxel grids of (neural or SH) features for fast radiance field reconstruction. However, they still optimize per-voxel features directly like previous voxel-based methods, thus requiring large memory. Our approach instead factorizes the feature grid into compact

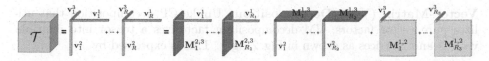

Fig. 2. Tensor factorization. Left: CP decomposition (Eq. 1), which factorizes a tensor as a sum of vector outer products. Right: our vector-matrix decomposition (Eq. 3), which factorizes a tensor as a sum of vector-matrix outer products.

components and leads to significantly higher memory efficiency. Instant-NGP [38] uses multi-resolution hashing for efficient encoding and also leads to high compactness. This technique is orthogonal to our factorization-based technique; potentially, each of our vector/matrix factor can be encoded with this hashing technique and we leave such combination as future work.

3 CP and VM Decomposition

We factorize radiance fields into compact components for scene modeling. To do so, we apply both the classic CP decomposition and a new vector-matrix (VM) decomposition; both are illustrated in Fig. 2. We now discuss both decompositions with an example of a 3D (3rd-order) tensor. We will introduce how to apply tensor factorization in radiance field modeling (with a 4D tensor) in Sect. 4.

CP Decomposition. Given a 3D tensor $\mathcal{T} \in \mathbb{R}^{I \times J \times K}$, CP decomposition factorizes it into a sum of outer products of vectors (shown in Fig. 2):

$$\mathcal{T} = \sum_{r=1}^{R} \mathbf{v}_r^1 \circ \mathbf{v}_r^2 \circ \mathbf{v}_r^3 \qquad (1)$$

where $\mathbf{v}_r^1 \circ \mathbf{v}_r^2 \circ \mathbf{v}_r^3$ corresponds to a rank-one tensor component, and $\mathbf{v}_r^1 \in \mathbb{R}^I$, $\mathbf{v}_r^2 \in \mathbb{R}^J$, and $\mathbf{v}_r^3 \in \mathbb{R}^K$ are factorized vectors of the three modes for the rth component. Superscripts denote the modes of each factor; $\circ$ represents the outer product. Hence, each tensor element $\mathcal{T}_{ijk}$ is a sum of scalar products:

$$\mathcal{T}_{ijk} = \sum_{r=1}^{R} \mathbf{v}_{r,i}^1 \mathbf{v}_{r,j}^2 \mathbf{v}_{r,k}^3 \qquad (2)$$

where i, j, k denote the indices of the three modes.

CP decomposition factorizes a tensor into multiple vectors, expressing multiple compact rank-one components. CP can be directly applied in our tensorial radiance field modeling and generate high-quality results (see Table 1). However, because of too high compactness, CP decomposition can require many components to model complex scenes, leading to high computational costs in radiance field reconstruction. Inspired by block term decomposition (BTD), we present a new VM decomposition, leading to more efficient radiance field reconstruction.

Vector-Matrix (VM) Decomposition. Unlike CP decomposition that utilizes pure vector factors, VM decomposition factorizes a tensor into multiple vectors and matrices as shown in Fig. 2 right. This is expressed by

$$
\mathcal{T} = \sum_{r=1}^{R_1} \mathbf{v}_r^1 \circ \mathbf{M}_r^{2,3} + \sum_{r=1}^{R_2} \mathbf{v}_r^2 \circ \mathbf{M}_r^{1,3} + \sum_{r=1}^{R_3} \mathbf{v}_r^3 \circ \mathbf{M}_r^{1,2} \tag{3}
$$

where $\mathbf{M}_r^{2,3} \subset \mathbb{R}^{J \times K}$, $\mathbf{M}_r^{1,3} \in \mathbb{R}^{I \times K}$, $\mathbf{M}_r^{1,2} \in \mathbb{R}^{I \times J}$ are matrix factors for two (denoted by superscripts) of the three modes. For each component, we relax its two mode ranks to be arbitrarily large, while restricting the third mode to be rank-one; e.g., for component tensor $\mathbf{v}_r^1 \circ \mathbf{M}_r^{2,3}$, its mode-1 rank is 1, and its mode-2 and mode-3 ranks can be arbitrary, depending on the rank of the matrix $\mathbf{M}_r^{2,3}$. In general, instead of using separate vectors in CP, we combine every two modes and represent them by matrices, allowing each mode to be adequately parametrized with a smaller number of components. R_1, R_2, R_3 can be set differently and should be chosen depending on the complexity of each mode. Our VM decomposition can be seen as a special case of general BTD.

Note that, each of our component tensors has more parameters than a component in CP decomposition. While this leads to lower compactness, a VM component tensor can express more complex high-dimensional data than a CP component, thus reducing the required number of components when modeling the same complex function. On the other hand, VM decomposition is still of very high compactness, reducing memory complexity from $\mathcal{O}(N^3)$ to $\mathcal{O}(N^2)$, compared to dense grid representations.

Tensor for Scene Modeling. In this work, we focus on the task of modeling and reconstructing radiance fields. In this case, the three tensor modes correspond to XYZ axes, and we thus directly denote the modes with XYZ to make it intuitive. Meanwhile, in the context of 3D scene representation, we consider $R_1 = R_2 = R_3 = R$ for most of scenes, reflecting the fact that a scene can distribute and appear equally complex along its three axes. Therefore, Eq. 3 can be re-written as

$$
\mathcal{T} = \sum_{r=1}^{R} \mathbf{v}_r^X \circ \mathbf{M}_r^{Y,Z} + \mathbf{v}_r^Y \circ \mathbf{M}_r^{X,Z} + \mathbf{v}_r^Z \circ \mathbf{M}_r^{X,Y} \tag{4}
$$

In addition, to simplify notation and the following discussion in later sections, we also denote the three types of component tensors as $\mathcal{A}_r^X = \mathbf{v}_r^X \circ \mathbf{M}_r^{YZ}$, $\mathcal{A}_r^Y = \mathbf{v}_r^Y \circ \mathbf{M}_r^{XZ}$, and $\mathcal{A}_r^Z = \mathbf{v}_r^Z \circ \mathbf{M}_r^{XY}$; here the superscripts XYZ of $\mathcal{A}$ indicate different types of components. With this, a tensor element $\mathcal{T}_{ijk}$ is expressed as

$$
\mathcal{T}_{ijk} = \sum_{r=1}^{R} \sum_{m} \mathcal{A}_{r,ijk}^m \tag{5}
$$

where $m \in XYZ$, $\mathcal{A}_{r,ijk}^X = \mathbf{v}_{r,i}^X \mathbf{M}_{r,jk}^{YZ}$, $\mathcal{A}_{r,ijk}^Y = \mathbf{v}_{r,j}^Y \mathbf{M}_{r,ik}^{XZ}$, and $\mathcal{A}_{r,ijk}^Z = \mathbf{v}_{r,k}^Z \mathbf{M}_{r,ij}^{XY}$. Similarly, we can also denote a CP component as $\mathcal{A}^\gamma = \mathbf{v}_r^X \circ \mathbf{v}_r^Y \circ \mathbf{v}_r^Z$, and Eq. 5 can also express CP decomposition by considering $m = \gamma$, where the summation over m can be removed.

4 Tensorial Radiance Field Representation

We now present our Tensorial Radiance Field Representation (TensoRF). For simplicity, we focus on presenting TensoRF with our VM decomposition. CP decomposition is simpler and its decomposition equations can be directly applied with minimal modification (like Eq. 5).

4.1 Feature Grids and Radiance Field

Our goal is to model a radiance field, which is essentially a function that maps any 3D location $\mathbf{x}$ and viewing direction d to its volume density σ and view-dependent color c, supporting differentiable ray marching for volume rendering. We leverage a regular 3D grid $\mathcal{G}$ with per-voxel multi-channel features to model such a function. We split it (by feature channels) into a geometry grid $\mathcal{G}_\sigma$ and an appearance grid $\mathcal{G}_c$, separately modelling the volume density σ and view-dependent color c.

Our approach supports various types of appearance features in $\mathcal{G}_c$, depending on a pre-selected function S that coverts an appearance feature vector and a viewing direction d to color c. For example, S can be a small MLP or spherical harmonics (SH) functions, where $\mathcal{G}_c$ contains neural features and SH coefficients respectively. We show that both MLP and SH functions work well with our model (see Table 1). On the other hand, we consider a single-channel grid $\mathcal{G}_\sigma$, whose values represent volume density directly, without requiring an extra converting function. The continuous grid-based radiance field can be written as

$$\sigma, c = \mathcal{G}_\sigma(\mathbf{x}), S(\mathcal{G}_c(\mathbf{x}), d) \qquad (6)$$

where $\mathcal{G}_\sigma(\mathbf{x})$, $\mathcal{G}_c(\mathbf{x})$ represent the trilinearly interpolated features from the two grids at location $\mathbf{x}$. We model $\mathcal{G}_\sigma$ and $\mathcal{G}_c$ as factorized tensors.

4.2 Factorizing Radiance Fields

While $\mathcal{G}_\sigma \in \mathbb{R}^{I \times J \times K}$ is a 3D tensor, $\mathcal{G}_c \in \mathbb{R}^{I \times J \times K \times P}$ is a 4D tensor. Here I, J, K correspond to the resolutions of the feature grid along the X, Y, Z axes, and P is the number of appearance feature channels.

We factorize these radiance field tensors to compact components. In particular, with the VM decomposition. the 3D geometry tensor $\mathcal{G}_\sigma$ is factorized as

$$\mathcal{G}_\sigma = \sum_{r=1}^{R_\sigma} \mathbf{v}_{\sigma,r}^X \circ \mathbf{M}_{\sigma,r}^{YZ} + \mathbf{v}_{\sigma,r}^Y \circ \mathbf{M}_{\sigma,r}^{XZ} + \mathbf{v}_{\sigma,r}^Z \circ \mathbf{M}_{\sigma,r}^{XY} = \sum_{r=1}^{R_\sigma} \sum_{m \in XYZ} \mathcal{A}_{\sigma,r}^m \qquad (7)$$

The appearance tensor $\mathcal{G}_c$ has an additional mode corresponding to the feature channel dimension. Note that, compared to the XYZ modes, this mode is often of lower dimension, leading to a lower rank. Therefore, we do not combine this mode with other modes in matrix factors and instead only use vectors,

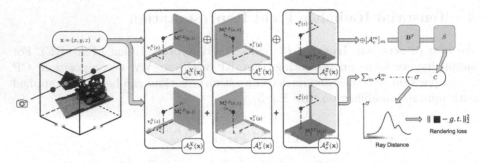

Fig. 3. TensoRF (VM) reconstruction and rendering. We model radiance fields as tensors using a set of vectors ($\mathbf{v}$) and matrices ($\mathbf{M}$), which describe the scene along their corresponding (XYZ) axes and are used for computing volume density σ and view-dependent color c in differentiable ray marching. For each shading location $\mathbf{x} = (x, y, z)$, we use linearly/bilinearly sampled values from the vector/matrix factors to efficiently compute the corresponding trilinearly interpolated values ($\mathcal{A}(\mathbf{x})$) of the tensor components. The density component values ($\mathcal{A}_\sigma(\mathbf{x})$) are summed to get the volume density (σ) directly. The appearance values ($\mathcal{A}_c(\mathbf{x})$) are concatenated into a vector ($\oplus[\mathcal{A}_c^m(x)]_m$) that is then multiplied by an appearance matrix $\mathbf{B}$ and sent to the decoding function S for RGB color (c) regression.

denoted by $\mathbf{b}_r$, for this mode in the factorization. Specifically, $\mathcal{G}_c$ is factorized as

$$
\mathcal{G}_c = \sum_{r=1}^{R_c} \mathbf{v}_{c,r}^X \circ \mathbf{M}_{c,r}^{YZ} \circ \mathbf{b}_{3r-2} + \mathbf{v}_{c,r}^Y \circ \mathbf{M}_{c,r}^{XZ} \circ \mathbf{b}_{3r-1} + \mathbf{v}_{c,r}^Z \circ \mathbf{M}_{c,r}^{XY} \circ \mathbf{b}_{3r}
$$

$$
= \sum_{r=1}^{R_c} \mathcal{A}_{c,r}^X \circ \mathbf{b}_{3r-2} + \mathcal{A}_{c,r}^Y \circ \mathbf{b}_{3r-1} + \mathcal{A}_{c,r}^Z \circ \mathbf{b}_{3r} \tag{8}
$$

Note that, we have $3R_c$ vectors $\mathbf{b}_r$ to match the total number of components.

Overall, we factorize the entire tensorial radiance field into $3R_\sigma + 3R_c$ matrices ($\mathbf{M}_{\sigma,r}^{YZ},...,\mathbf{M}_{c,r}^{YZ},...$) and $3R_\sigma + 6R_c$ vectors ($\mathbf{v}_{\sigma,r}^X,...,\mathbf{v}_{c,r}^X,...,\mathbf{b}_r$). In general, we adopt $R_\sigma \ll I, J, K$ and $R_c \ll I, J, K$, leading to a highly compact representation that can encode a high-resolution dense grid. In essence, the XYZ-mode vector and matrix factors, $\mathbf{v}_{\sigma,r}^X$, $\mathbf{M}_{\sigma,r}^{YZ}$, $\mathbf{v}_{c,r}^X$, $\mathbf{M}_{c,r}^{YZ}$, ..., describe the spatial distributions of the scene geometry and appearance along their corresponding axes. On the other hand, the appearance feature-mode vectors $\mathbf{b}_r$ express the global appearance correlations. By stacking all $\mathbf{b}_r$ as columns together, we have a $P \times 3R_c$ matrix $\mathbf{B}$; this matrix $\mathbf{B}$ can also be seen as a global appearance dictionary that abstracts the appearance commonalities across the entire scene.

4.3 Efficient Feature Evaluation

Our factorization-based model can compute each voxel's feature vector at low costs, only requiring one value per XYZ-mode vector/matrix factor. We also enable efficient trilinear interpolation for our model, leading to a continuous field.

Direct Evaluation. With VM factorization, a density value $\mathcal{G}_{\sigma,ijk}$ of a single voxel at indices ijk can be directly and efficiently evaluated by following Eq. 5:

$$\mathcal{G}_{\sigma,ijk} = \sum_{r=1}^{R_\sigma} \sum_{m\in XYZ} \mathcal{A}_{\sigma,r,ijk}^m \tag{9}$$

Here, computing each $\mathcal{A}_{\sigma,r,ijk}^m$ only requires indexing and multiplying two values from its corresponding vector and matrix factors.

As for the appearance grid $\mathcal{G}_c$, we always need to compute a full P-channel feature vector, which the shading function S requires as input, corresponding to a 1D slice of $\mathcal{G}_c$ at fixed XYZ indices ijk:

$$\mathcal{G}_{c,ijk} = \sum_{r=1}^{R_c} \mathcal{A}_{c,r,ijk}^X \mathbf{b}_{3r-2} + \mathcal{A}_{c,r,ijk}^Y \mathbf{b}_{3r-1} + \mathcal{A}_{c,r,ijk}^Z \mathbf{b}_{3r} \tag{10}$$

Here, there's no additional indexing for the feature mode, since we compute a full vector. We further simplify Eq. 10 by re-ordering the computation. For this, we denote $\oplus[\mathcal{A}_{c,ijk}^m]_{m,r}$ as the vector that stacks all $\mathcal{A}_{c,r,ijk}^m$ values for $m = X, Y, Z$ and $r = 1, ..., R_c$, which is a vector of $3R_c$ dimensions; $\oplus$ can also be considered as the concatenation operator that concatenates all scalar values (1-channel vectors) into a $3R_c$-channel vector in practice. Using matrix $\mathbf{B}$ (introduced in Sect. 4.1) that stacks all $\mathbf{b}_r$, Eq. 10 is equivalent to a matrix vector product:

$$\mathcal{G}_{c,ijk} = \mathbf{B}(\oplus[\mathcal{A}_{c,ijk}^m]_{m,r}) \tag{11}$$

Note that, Eq. 11 is not only formally simpler but also leads to a simpler implementation in practice. Specifically, when computing a large number of voxels in parallel, we first compute and concatenate $\mathcal{A}_{c,r,ijk}^m$ for all voxels as column vectors in a matrix and then multiply the shared matrix $\mathbf{B}$ once.

Trilinear Interpolation. We apply trilinear interpolation to model a continuous field. Naïvely achieving trilinear interpolation is costly, as it requires evaluation of 8 tensor values and interpolating them, increasing computation by a factor of 8 compared to computing a single tensor element. However, we find that trilinearly interpolating a component tensor is naturally equivalent to interpolating its vector/matrix factors linearly/bilinearly for the corresponding modes, thanks to the beauty of linearity of the trilinear interpolation and the outer product.

For example, given a component tensor $\mathcal{A}_r^X = \mathbf{v}_r^X \circ \mathbf{M}_r^{YZ}$ with its each tensor element $\mathcal{A}_{r,ijk} = \mathbf{v}_{r,i}^X \mathbf{M}_{r,jk}^{YZ}$, we can compute its interpolated values as:

$$\mathcal{A}_r^X(\mathbf{x}) = \mathbf{v}_r^X(x)\mathbf{M}_r^{YZ}(y,z) \tag{12}$$

where $\mathcal{A}_r^X(\mathbf{x})$ is $\mathcal{A}_r$'s trilinearly interpolated value at location $\mathbf{x} = (x, y, z)$ in the 3D space, $\mathbf{v}_r^X(x)$ is $\mathbf{v}_r^X$'s linearly interpolated value at x along X axis, and $\mathbf{M}_r^{YZ}(y,z)$ is $\mathbf{M}_r^{YZ}$'s bilinearly interpolated value at (y, z) in the YZ plane. Similarly, we have $\mathcal{A}_r^Y(\mathbf{x}) = \mathbf{v}_r^Y(y)\mathbf{M}_r^{XZ}(x,z)$ and $\mathcal{A}_r^Z(\mathbf{x}) = \mathbf{v}_r^Z(z)\mathbf{M}_r^{XY}(x,y)$ (for

CP decomposition $\mathcal{A}_r^\gamma(\mathbf{x}) = \mathbf{v}_r^X(x)\mathbf{v}_r^Y(y)\mathbf{v}_r^Z(z)$ is also valid). Thus, trilinearly interpolating the two grids is expressed as

$$\mathcal{G}_\sigma(\mathbf{x}) = \sum_r \sum_m \mathcal{A}_{\sigma,r}^m(\mathbf{x}) \tag{13}$$

$$\mathcal{G}_c(\mathbf{x}) = \mathbf{B}(\oplus[\mathcal{A}_{c,r}^m(\mathbf{x})]_{m,r}) \tag{14}$$

These equations are very similar to Eqs. 9 and 11, simply replacing the tensor elements with interpolated values. We avoid recovering 8 individual tensor elements for trilinear interpolation and instead directly recover the interpolated value, leading to low computation and memory costs at run time.

4.4   Rendering and Reconstruction

Equations 6, 12–14 describe the core components of our model. By combining Eqs. 6,13,14, our factorized tensorial radiance field can be expressed as

$$\sigma, c = \sum_r \sum_m \mathcal{A}_{\sigma,r}^m(\mathbf{x}) \, , \, S(\mathbf{B}(\oplus[\mathcal{A}_{c,r}^m(\mathbf{x})]_{m,r}), d) \tag{15}$$

i.e., we obtain continuous volume density and view-dependent color given any 3D location and viewing direction. This allows for high-quality radiance field reconstruction and rendering. Note that, this equation is general and describes TensoRF with both CP and VM decomposition. Our full pipeline of radiance field reconstruction and rendering with VM decomposition is illustrated in Fig. 3.

Volume Rendering. To render images, we use differentiable volume rendering, following NeRF [37]. Specifically, for each pixel, we march along a ray, sampling Q shading points along the ray and computing the pixel color by

$$C = \sum_{q=1}^Q \tau_q(1 - \exp(-\sigma_q \Delta_q))c_q, \ \tau_q = \exp(-\sum_{p=1}^{q-1} \sigma_p \Delta_p) \tag{16}$$

Here, σ_q, c_q are the corresponding density and color computed by our model at their sampled locations $\mathbf{x}_q$; Δ_q is the ray step size and τ_q represents transmittance.

Reconstruction. Given a set of multi-view input images with known camera poses, our tensorial radiance field is optimized per scene via gradient descent, minimizing an L2 rendering loss, using only the ground truth pixel colors as supervision. Our radiance field is explained by tensor factorization and modeled by a set of global vectors and matrices as basis factors that correlate and regularize the entire field in the optimization. However, this can sometimes lead to overfitting and local minima issues in gradient descent, leading to outliers or noises in regions with fewer observations. We utilize standard regularization terms that are commonly used in compressive sensing, including an L1 norm loss and a TV (total variation) loss on our vector and matrix factors, which effectively address these issues. We find that only applying the L1 sparsity loss is adequate for most datasets. However, for real datasets that have very few input images (like LLFF [36]) or imperfect capture conditions (like Tanks and Temples [26,31] that has varying exposure and inconsistent masks), a TV loss is more efficient than the L1 norm loss.

To further improve quality and avoid local minima, we apply coarse-to-fine reconstruction. Unlike previous coarse-to-fine techniques that require unique subdivisions on their sparse chosen sets of voxels, our coarse-to-fine reconstruction is simply achieved by linearly and bilinearly upsampling our XYZ-mode vector and matrix factors.

5   Implementation Details

We briefly discuss our implementation; please refer to the appendix for more details. We implement our TensoRF using PyTorch [44], without customized CUDA kernels. We implement the feature decoding function S as either an MLP or SH function and use $P = 27$ features for both. For SH, this corresponds to 3rd-order SH coefficients with RGB channels. For neural features, we use a small MLP with two FC layers (with 128-channel hidden layers) and ReLU activation.

We use the Adam optimizer [25] with initial learning rates of 0.02 for tensor factors and (when using neural features) 0.001 for the MLP decoder. We optimize our model for T steps with a batch size of 4096 pixel rays on a single Tesla V100 GPU (16GB). We apply a feature grid with a total number of N^3 voxels; the actual resolution of each dimension is computed based on the shape of the bounding box. To achieve coarse-to-fine reconstruction, we start from an initial low-resolution grid with N_0^3 voxels with $N_0 = 128$; we then upsample the vectors and matrices linearly and bilinearly at steps 2000, 3000, 4000, 5500, 7000 with the numbers of voxels interpolated between N_0^3 and N^3 linearly in logarithmic space. Please refer to Sect. 6 for the analysis on different total steps (T), different resolutions (N), and different number of total components ($3R_\sigma + 3R_c$).

6   Experiments

We now present an extensive evaluation of our tensorial radiance fields. We first analyze our decomposition techniques, the number of components, grid resolutions, and optimization steps. We then compare our approach with previous and concurrent works on both 360° objects and forward-facing datasets.

Analysis of Different TensoRF Models. We evaluate our TensoRF on the Synthetic NeRF dataset [37] using both CP and VM decompositions with different numbers of components and different numbers of grid voxels. Table 2 shows the averaged rendering PSNRs, reconstruction time, and model size for each model. We use the same MLP decoding function (as described in Sect. 5) for all variants and optimize each model for 30k steps with a batch size of 4096.

Note that both TensoRF-CP and TensoRF-VM achieve consistently better rendering quality with more components or higher grid resolutions. TensoRF-CP achieves super compact modeling; even the largest model with 384 components and 500^3 voxels requires less than 4MB. This CP model also achieves the best rendering quality in all of our CP variants, leading to a high PSNR of 31.56, which even outperforms vanilla NeRF (see Table 1).

On the other hand, because it compresses more parameters in each component, TensoRF-VM achieves significantly better rendering quality than TensoRF-CP; even the smallest TensoRF-VM model with only 48 components and 200^3 voxels is able to outperform the best CP model that uses many more components and voxels. Remarkably, the PSNR of 31.81 from this smallest VM model (which only takes 8.6 MB) is already higher than the PSNRs of NeRF and many other previous and concurrent techniques (see Table 1). In addition, 192 components are generally adequate for TensoRF-VM; doubling the number to 384 only leads to marginal improvement. TensoRF-VM with 300^3 voxels can already lead to high PSNRs close to or greater than 33, while retaining compact model sizes (<72MB). Increasing the resolution further leads to improved quality, but also larger model size.

Also note that all of our TensoRF models can achieve very fast reconstruction. Except for the largest VM model, all models finish reconstruction in less than 30 min, significantly faster than NeRF and many previous methods (see Table 1).

Optimization Steps. We further evaluate our approach with different optimization steps for our best CP model and the VM models with 300^3 voxels. PSNRs and reconstruction time are shown in Table 3. All of our models consistently achieve better rendering quality with more steps. Our compact CP-384 model (3.9MB) can even achieve a PSNR greater than 32 after 60k steps, higher than the PSNRs of all previous methods in Table 1. On the other hand, our VM models can quickly achieve high rendering quality in very few steps. With only 15k steps, many models achieve high PSNRs that are already state-of-the-art.

Comparisons on 360° Scenes. We compare our approach with state-of-the-art novel view synthesis methods, including previous works (SRN [53], NeRF [37], NSVF [31], SNeRG [20], PlenOctrees [67]) and concurrent works (Plenoxels [49], DVGO [54]). In particular, we compare with them using our best CP model and our VM models (300^3 voxels) with 48 and 192 components. We also show a 192-component VM model with spherical harmonics shading function. Table 1 shows the quantitative results (PSNRs and SSIMs) of ours and comparison methods on three challenging datasets, where we also show the corresponding batch size, optimization steps, time, and final output model size for each model, to compare all methods from multiple perspectives. Note that all of our CP and VM models can outperform NeRF on all three datasets while taking substantially less optimization time and fewer steps. Our best VM-192 model can even achieve the best PSNRs and SSIMs on all datasets, significantly outperforming the comparison methods. Our approach can also achieve qualitatively better renderings with more appearance and geometry details and less outliers, as shown in Fig. 4.

Our models are highly efficient, which all require less than 75MB space and can be reconstructed in less than 30 min. This corresponds to more than 70x

Table 1. We compare our method with previous and concurrent novel view synthesis methods on three datasets. All scores of the baseline methods are directly taken from their papers whenever available. We also report the averaged reconstruction time and model size for the Synthetic-NeRF dataset. NVSF requires 8 GPUs for optimization (marked by a star), while others run on a single GPU. DVGO's 30k steps correspond to 10k for coarse and 20k for fine reconstruction.

Method	Synthetic-NeRF						NSVF		TanksTemples	
	BatchSize	Steps	Time ↓	Size(MB)↓	PSNR↑	SSIM↑	PSNR↑	SSIM↑	PSNR↑	SSIM↑
SRN [53]	–	–	>10 h	–	22.26	0.846	24.33	0.882	24.10	0.847
NSVF [31]	8192	150k	>48* h	–	31.75	0.953	35.18	0.979	28.48	0.901
NeRF [37]	4096	300k	~35 h	5.00	31.01	0.947	30.81	0.952	25.78	0.864
SNeRG [20]	8192	250k	~15 h	1771.5	30.38	0.950	–	–	–	–
PlenOctrees [67]	1024	200k	~15 h	1976.3	31.71	0.958	–	–	27.99	0.917
Plenoxels [49]	5000	128k	11.4 m	778.1	31.71	0.958	–	–	27.43	0.906
DVGO [54]	5000	30k	15.0 m	612.1	31.95	0.957	35.08	0.975.	28.41	0.911
Ours-CP-384	4096	30k	25.2 m	3.9	31.56	0.949	34.48	0.971	27.59	0.897
Our-VM-192-SH	4096	30k	16.8 m	71.9	32.00	0.955	35.30	0.977	27.81	0.907
Ours-VM-48	4096	30k	13.8 m	18.9	32.39	0.957	35.34	0.976	28.06	0.909
Ours-VM-192	4096	15k	8.1 m	71.8	32.52	0.959	35.59	0.978	28.07	0.913
Ours-VM-192	4096	30k	17.4 m	71.8	33.14	0.963	36.52	0.982	28.56	0.920

Table 2. We compare the averaged PSNRs/optimization time (mm:ss)/model sizes (MB) of CP and VM TensoRF models on Synthetic NeRF dataset [37] with different numbers of components and grid resolutions, optimized for 30k steps.

	#Comp	200^3	300^3	500^3
TensoRF-CP	48	27.98/09:29/0.74	28.24/11:45/1.09	28.38/14:20/1.85
	96	28.50/09:57/0.88	28.83/12:12/1.29	29.06/15:27/2.18
	192	29.50/11:09/1.08	29.99/13:41/1.59	30.33/18:03/2.66
	384	30.47/14:41/1.59	31.08/18:09/2.33	31.56/25:11/3.93
TensoRF-VM	48	31.81/11:29/08.6	32.39/13:51/23.5	32.63/18:17/55.8
	96	32.33/11:54/16.5	32.86/14:08/37.3	33.06/20:11/105
	192	32.63/13:26/32.3	33.14/17:36/76.7	33.31/27:18/204
	384	32.69/17:24/63.4	33.21/25:14/143	33.39/43:19/397

Table 3. PSNRs and time of CP and VM models with different training steps on the Synthetic-NeRF dataset [37].

	5k	15k	30k	60k	5k	15k	30k	60k
CP-384	28.37	30.80	31.56	32.03	03:03	11:30	25:11	51:47
VM-48	29.28	31.80	32.39	32.68	01:57	06:21	13:51	27:20
VM-96	29.65	32.26	32.86	33.17	02:01	06:41	14:08	28:57
VM-192	29.86	32.52	33.14	33.44	02:16	08:08	17:37	35:50
VM-384	29.95	32.62	33.21	33.52	02:51	11:30	25:14	52:50

Table 4. Quantitative comparisons of our method with NeRF and Plenoxels on forward-facing scenes [36].

Method	Time ↓	Size	PSNR↑	SSIM↑
NeRF [37]	36 h	5.00M	26.50	0.811
Plenoxels [49]	24:00 m	2.59G	26.29	0.829
Ours-VM-48	19:44 m	90.4M	26.51	0.832
Ours-VM-96	25.43 m	179.7M	26.73	0.839

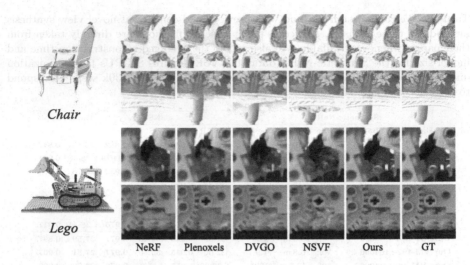

Fig. 4. Qualitative results of our VM-192–30k model and comparison methods (NeRF [37], plenoxels [49], DVGO [54], NSVF [31]) on two Synthetic NeRF scenes.

speed up compared to NeRF that requires about 1.5 d for optimization. Our CP model is even more compact than NeRF. Moreover, SNeRG and PlenOctrees require pre-training a NeRF-like MLP, requiring long reconstruction time too. DVGO and Plenoxels are concurrent works, which can also achieve fast reconstruction in less than 15 min. However, as both are voxel-based methods and directly optimize voxel values, they lead to huge model sizes similar to previous voxel-based methods like SNeRG and PlenOctrees. In contrast, we factorize feature grids and model them with compact vectors and matrices, leading to substantially smaller model sizes. Meanwhile, our VM-192 can even reconstruct faster than DVGO and Plenoxels, taking only 15k steps, and achieving better quality in most cases. In fact, Plenoxels' fast reconstruction relies on quickly optimizing significantly more steps (> 4 times our steps) with their CUDA implementation. Our models are implemented with standard PyTorch modules and already achieve much better rendering quality with fewer steps taking comparable and even less reconstruction time than Plenoxels. Note that our SH model essentially represents the same underlying feature grid as Plenoxels but can still lead to more compact modeling and better quality with fewer steps, showing the advantages of our factorization based modeling. In general, our approach enables fast reconstruction, compact modeling, and photo-realistic rendering simultaneously.

Forward-Facing Scenes. Our approach can also achieve efficient and high-quality radiance field reconstruction for forward-facing scenes. We show quantitative results of our two VM models on the LLFF dataset [36] and compare with NeRF and Plenoxels in Table 4. Our models outperform the previous state-of-the-art NeRF and take significantly less reconstruction time. Compared with Plenoxels [49], our approach leads to comparable or faster reconstruction speed, better quality, and substantially smaller model sizes.

7 Conclusion

We have presented a novel approach for high-quality scene reconstruction and rendering. We propose a novel scene representation – TensoRF which leverages tensor decomposition techniques to model and reconstruct radiance fields compactly as factorized low-rank tensor components. We hope our findings in tensorized low-rank feature modeling can inspire other modeling and reconstruction tasks.

References

1. Ballester-Ripoll, R., Pajarola, R.: Tensor decomposition methods in visual computing. IEEE Vis. Tutorials **3** (2016)
2. Ben-Younes, H., Cadene, R., Thome, N., Cord, M.: BLOCK: bilinear superdiagonal fusion for visual question answering and visual relationship detection. In: Proceedings of the AAAI Conference on Artificial Intelligence, vol. 33, pp. 8102–8109 (2019)
3. Bi, S., Xu, Z., et al.: Neural reflectance fields for appearance acquisition. arXiv preprint arXiv:2008.03824 (2020)
4. Bi, S., Xu, Z., et al.: Deep reflectance volumes: relightable reconstructions from multi-view photometric images. In: Proceedings ECCV, pp. 294–311 (2020)
5. Boss, M., Braun, R., Jampani, V., Barron, J.T., Liu, C., Lensch, H.: NeRD: neural reflectance decomposition from image collections. In: Proceedings of the IEEE/CVF International Conference on Computer Vision, pp. 12684–12694 (2021)
6. Candes, E.J., Plan, Y.: Matrix completion with noise. Proc. IEEE **98**(6), 925–936 (2010)
7. Carroll, J.D., Chang, J.J.: Analysis of individual differences in multidimensional scaling via an n-way generalization of "ckart-young" decomposition. Psychometrika **35**(3), 283–319 (1970)
8. Chan, E.R., et al.: Efficient geometry-aware 3D generative adversarial networks. In: CVPR, pp. 16123–16133 (2022)
9. Chan, E.R., Monteiro, M., Kellnhofer, P., Wu, J., Wetzstein, G.: pi-GAN: periodic implicit generative adversarial networks for 3D-aware image synthesis. In: Proceedings of the IEEE/CVF Conference on Computer Vision and Pattern Recognition, pp. 5799–5809 (2021)
10. Chen, A.: Deep surface light fields. Proc. ACM Comput. Graph. Interact. Tech. **1**(1), 1–17 (2018)
11. Chen, A., et al.: MVSNeRF: fast generalizable radiance field reconstruction from multi-view stereo. In: Proceedings of the IEEE/CVF International Conference on Computer Vision, pp. 14124–14133 (2021)
12. Chibane, J., Bansal, A., Lazova, V., Pons-Moll, G.: Stereo radiance fields (SRF): learning view synthesis from sparse views of novel scenes. In: IEEE Conference on Computer Vision and Pattern Recognition (CVPR), pp. 7911–7920. IEEE (2021)

13. De Lathauwer, L.: Decompositions of a higher-order tensor in block terms-part ii: definitions and uniqueness. SIAM J. Matrix Anal. Appl. **30**(3), 1033–1066 (2008)
14. Deng, H.: Constant-cost spatio-angular prefiltering of glinty appearance using tensor decomposition. ACM Trans. Graph. (TOG) **41**(2), 1–17 (2022)
15. Dong, W., Shi, G., Li, X., Ma, Y., Huang, F.: Compressive sensing via nonlocal low-rank regularization. IEEE Trans. Image Process. **23**(8), 3618–3632 (2014)
16. Gandy, S., Recht, B., Yamada, I.: Tensor completion and low-n-rank tensor recovery via convex optimization. Inverse Prob. **27**(2), 025010 (2011)
17. Garbin, S.J., Kowalski, M., Johnson, M., Shotton, J., Valentin, J.: FastNeRF: high-fidelity neural rendering at 200FPS. In: Proceedings of the IEEE/CVF International Conference on Computer Vision, pp. 14346–14355 (2021)
18. Groueix, T., Fisher, M., Kim, V.G., Russell, B.C., Aubry, M.: A papier-mâché approach to learning 3D surface generation. In: Proceedings of the IEEE Conference on Computer Vision and Pattern Recognition, pp. 216–224 (2018)
19. Harshman, R.A., et al.: Foundations of the PARAFAC procedure: models and conditions for an "explanatory" multimodal factor analysis (1970)
20. Hedman, P., Srinivasan, P.P., Mildenhall, B., Barron, J.T., Debevec, P.: Baking neural radiance fields for real-time view synthesis. arXiv preprint arXiv:2103.14645 (2021)
21. Ji, H., Liu, C., Shen, Z., Xu, Y.: Robust video denoising using low rank matrix completion. In: 2010 IEEE Computer Society Conference on Computer Vision and Pattern Recognition, pp. 1791–1798. IEEE (2010)
22. Ji, M., Gall, J., Zheng, H., Liu, Y., Fang, L.: SurfaceNet: an end-to-end 3D neural network for multiview stereopsis. In: Proceedings ICCV, pp. 2307–2315 (2017)
23. Ji, Y., Wang, Q., Li, X., Liu, J.: A survey on tensor techniques and applications in machine learning. IEEE Access **7**, 162950–162990 (2019)
24. Kamal, M.H., Heshmat, B., Raskar, R., Vandergheynst, P., Wetzstein, G.: Tensor low-rank and sparse light field photography. Comput. Vis. Image Underst. **145**, 172–181 (2016)
25. Kingma, D.P., Ba, J.: Adam: a method for stochastic optimization. arXiv preprint arXiv:1412.6980 (2014)
26. Knapitsch, A., Park, J., Zhou, Q.Y., Koltun, V.: Tanks and temples: benchmarking large-scale scene reconstruction. ACM Trans. Graph. **36**(4), 1–13 (2017)
27. Kolda, T.G., Bader, B.W.: Tensor decompositions and applications. SIAM Rev. **51**(3), 455–500 (2009)
28. Li, Z., Niklaus, S., Snavely, N., Wang, O.: Neural scene flow fields for space-time view synthesis of dynamic scenes. In: Proceedings of the IEEE/CVF Conference on Computer Vision and Pattern Recognition, pp. 6498–6508 (2021)
29. Liang, R., Sun, H., Vijaykumar, N.: CoordX: accelerating implicit neural representation with a split MLP architecture. arXiv preprint arXiv:2201.12425 (2022)
30. Liu, J., Musialski, P., Wonka, P., Ye, J.: Tensor completion for estimating missing values in visual data. IEEE Trans. Pattern Anal. Mach. Intell. **35**(1), 208–220 (2012)
31. Liu, L., Gu, J., Lin, K.Z., Chua, T.S., Theobalt, C.: Neural sparse voxel fields. NeurIPS **33**, 15651–15663 (2020)
32. Liu, S., Zhang, X., Zhang, Z., Zhang, R., Zhu, J.Y., Russell, B.: Editing conditional radiance fields. arXiv preprint arXiv:2105.06466 (2021)
33. Lombardi, S., Simon, T., Saragih, J., Schwartz, G., Lehrmann, A., Sheikh, Y.: Neural volumes: learning dynamic renderable volumes from images. ACM Trans. Graph. **38**, 1–14 (2019)

34. Martin-Brualla, R., Radwan, N., Sajjadi, M.S., Barron, J.T., Dosovitskiy, A., Duckworth, D.: NeRF in the wild: neural radiance fields for unconstrained photo collections. In: Proceedings of the IEEE/CVF Conference on Computer Vision and Pattern Recognition, pp. 7210–7219 (2021)

35. Mescheder, L., Oechsle, M., Niemeyer, M., Nowozin, S., Geiger, A.: Occupancy networks: learning 3D reconstruction in function space. In: Proceedings CVPR, pp. 4460–4470 (2019)

36. Mildenhall, B., et al.: Local light field fusion: practical view synthesis with prescriptive sampling guidelines. ACM Trans. Graph. (TOG) **38**(4), 1–14 (2019)

37. Mildenhall, B., Srinivasan, P.P., Tancik, M., Barron, J.T., Ramamoorthi, R., Ng, R.: NeRF: representing scenes as neural radiance fields for view synthesis. In: Vedaldi, A., Bischof, H., Brox, T., Frahm, J.-M. (eds.) ECCV 2020. LNCS, vol. 12346, pp. 405–421. Springer, Cham (2020). https://doi.org/10.1007/978-3-030-58452-8_24

38. Müller, T., Evans, A., Schied, C., Keller, A.: Instant neural graphics primitives with a multiresolution hash encoding. ACM Trans. Graph. **41**(4), 102:1-102:15 (2022)

39. Nam, G., Lee, J.H., Gutierrez, D., Kim, M.H.: Practical SVBRDF acquisition of 3D objects with unstructured flash photography. ACM Trans. Graph. (TOG) **37**(6), 1–12 (2018)

40. Niemeyer, M., Geiger, A.: GIRAFFE: representing scenes as compositional generative neural feature fields. In: Proceedings of the IEEE/CVF Conference on Computer Vision and Pattern Recognition, pp. 11453–11464 (2021)

41. Oechsle, M., Peng, S., Geiger, A.: UNISURF: unifying neural implicit surfaces and radiance fields for multi-view reconstruction. In: International Conference on Computer Vision (ICCV), pp. 5589–5599 (2021)

42. Panagakis, Y.: Tensor methods in computer vision and deep learning. Proc. IEEE **109**(5), 863–890 (2021)

43. Park, K., et al.: HyperNeRF: a higher-dimensional representation for topologically varying neural radiance fields. ACM Trans. Graph. **40**(6), 1–12 (2021)

44. Paszke, A., et al.: PyTorch: an imperative style, high-performance deep learning library. In: Advances in Neural Information Processing Systems 32 (2019)

45. Peng, S., Niemeyer, M., Mescheder, L., Pollefeys, M., Geiger, A.: Convolutional occupancy networks. In: Vedaldi, A., Bischof, H., Brox, T., Frahm, J.-M. (eds.) ECCV 2020. LNCS, vol. 12348, pp. 523–540. Springer, Cham (2020). https://doi.org/10.1007/978-3-030-58580-8_31

46. Qi, C.R., Su, H., Mo, K., Guibas, L.J.: PointNet: deep learning on point sets for 3D classification and segmentation. In: Proceedings CVPR, pp. 652–660 (2017)

47. Qi, C.R., Su, H., Nießner, M., Dai, A., Yan, M., Guibas, L.J.: Volumetric and multi-view CNNs for object classification on 3D data. In: Proceedings CVPR, pp. 5648–5656 (2016)

48. Reiser, C., Peng, S., Liao, Y., Geiger, A.: KiloNeRF: speeding up neural radiance fields with thousands of tiny MLPs. In: International Conference on Computer Vision (ICCV), pp. 14335–14345 (2021)

49. Sara, F.K., Alex, Yu., Tancik, M., Chen, Q., Recht, B., Kanazawa, A.: Plenoxels: radiance fields without neural networks. In: CVPR, pp. 5501–5510 (2022)

50. Schwarz, K., Liao, Y., Niemeyer, M., Geiger, A.: GRAF: generative radiance fields for 3D-aware image synthesis. In: Advances in Neural Information Processing Systems (NeurIPS), pp. 20154–20166 (2020)

51. Sitzmann, V., Martel, J., Bergman, A., Lindell, D., Wetzstein, G.: Implicit neural representations with periodic activation functions. Adv. Neural. Inf. Process. Syst. **33**, 7462–7473 (2020)
52. Sitzmann, V., Thies, J., Heide, F., Nießner, M., Wetzstein, G., Zollhofer, M.: Deep-Voxels: learning persistent 3D feature embeddings. In: Proceedings CVPR, pp. 2437–2446 (2019)
53. Sitzmann, V., Zollhöfer, M., Wetzstein, G.: Scene representation networks: continuous 3D-structure-aware neural scene representations. In: Advances in Neural Information Processing Systems (2019)
54. Sun, C., Sun, M., Chen, H.T.: Direct voxel grid optimization: super-fast convergence for radiance fields reconstruction. arXiv preprint arXiv:2111.11215 (2021)
55. Tancik, M., et al.: Fourier features let networks learn high frequency functions in low dimensional domains. NeurIPS **33**, 7537–7547 (2020)
56. Trevithick, A., Yang, B.: GRF: learning a general radiance field for 3D scene representation and rendering. In: arXiv:2010.04595 (2020)
57. Tucker, L.R.: Some mathematical notes on three-mode factor analysis. Psychometrika **31**(3), 279–311 (1966)
58. Vasilescu, M.A.O., Terzopoulos, D.: TensorTextures: multilinear image-based rendering. In: ACM SIGGRAPH 2004 Papers, pp. 336–342 (2004)
59. Wang, J., Dong, Y., Tong, X., Lin, Z., Guo, B.: Kernel nyström method for light transport. In: ACM SIGGRAPH 2009 papers, pp. 1–10 (2009)
60. Wang, N., Zhang, Y., Li, Z., Fu, Y., Liu, W., Jiang, Y.G.: Pixel2Mesh: generating 3D mesh models from single RGB images. In: Proceedings ECCV, pp. 52–67 (2018). https://doi.org/10.1007/978-3-030-01252-6_4
61. Wang, P., Liu, L., Liu, Y., Theobalt, C., Komura, T., Wang, W.: NeuS: learning neural implicit surfaces by volume rendering for multi-view reconstruction. In: NeurIPS (2021)
62. Wang, Q., et al: Learning multi-view image-based rendering. In: CVPR, pp. 4690–4699 (2021)
63. Xiang, F., Xu, Z., Hasan, M., Hold-Geoffroy, Y., Sunkavalli, K., Su, H.: NeuTex: neural texture mapping for volumetric neural rendering. In: Proceedings of the IEEE/CVF Conference on Computer Vision and Pattern Recognition, pp. 7119–7128 (2021)
64. Xu, Q., Xu, Z., Philip, J., Bi, S., Shu, Z., Sunkavalli, K., Neumann, U.: Point-NeRF: point-based neural radiance fields. In: Proceedings of the IEEE/CVF Conference on Computer Vision and Pattern Recognition, pp. 5438–5448 (2022)
65. Ye, J., Li, G., Chen, D., Yang, H., Zhe, S., Xu, Z.: Block-term tensor neural networks. Neural Netw. **130**, 11–21 (2020)
66. Ye, J., et al.: Learning compact recurrent neural networks with block-term tensor decomposition. In: Proceedings of the IEEE Conference on Computer Vision and Pattern Recognition, pp. 9378–9387 (2018)
67. Yu, A., Li, R., Tancik, M., Li, H., Ng, R., Kanazawa, A.: PlenOctrees for real-time rendering of neural radiance fields. arXiv preprint arXiv:2103.14024 (2021)
68. Yu, A., Ye, V., Tancik, M., Kanazawa, A.: PixelNeRF: neural radiance fields from one or few images. In: CVPR, pp. 4578–4587 (2021)
69. Zhang, K., Riegler, G., Snavely, N., Koltun, V.: NeRF++: analyzing and improving neural radiance fields. arXiv preprint arXiv:2010.07492 (2020)
70. Zhou, T., Tucker, R., Flynn, J., Fyffe, G., Snavely, N.: Stereo magnification: learning view synthesis using multiplane images. ACM Trans. Graph. **37**(4), 1–12 (2018)
71. Zhou, Z.: Sparse-as-possible SVBRDF acquisition. ACM Trans. Graph. (TOG) **35**(6), 1–12 (2016)

NeFSAC: Neurally Filtered Minimal Samples

Luca Cavalli[1]([✉]) [iD], Marc Pollefeys[1,2] [iD], and Daniel Barath[1] [iD]

[1] Department of Computer Science, ETH Zurich, Zurich, Switzerland
luca.cavalli@inf.ethz.ch
[2] Microsoft Mixed Reality and AI Zurich Lab, Zurich, Switzerland

Abstract. Since RANSAC, a great deal of research has been devoted to improving both its accuracy and run-time. Still, only a few methods aim at recognizing invalid minimal samples early, before the often expensive model estimation and quality calculation are done. To this end, we propose NeFSAC, an efficient algorithm for neural filtering of motion-inconsistent and poorly-conditioned minimal samples. We train NeFSAC to predict the probability of a minimal sample leading to an accurate relative pose, only based on the pixel coordinates of the image correspondences. Our neural filtering model learns typical motion patterns of samples which lead to unstable poses, and regularities in the possible motions to favour well-conditioned and likely-correct samples. The novel lightweight architecture implements the main invariants of minimal samples for pose estimation, and a novel training scheme addresses the problem of extreme class imbalance. NeFSAC can be plugged into any existing RANSAC-based pipeline. We integrate it into USAC and show that it consistently provides strong speed-ups even under extreme train-test domain gaps – for example, the model trained for the autonomous driving scenario works on PhotoTourism too. We tested NeFSAC on more than 100 k image pairs from three publicly available real-world datasets and found that it leads to *one order of magnitude* speed-up, while often finding more accurate results than USAC alone. The source code is available at https://github.com/cavalli1234/NeFSAC.

Keywords: RANSAC · Epipolar geometry estimation · Minimal samples · Machine learning · Motion prior · Autonomous driving

1 Introduction

Robust model estimation is a cardinal problem in Computer Vision. RANSAC [17] has been a very successful and widely applied approach to robust model estimation since the early days of Computer Vision, and a great research effort has been devoted to improving it. While initial efforts [11,12,14,15,17,23] and some recent works [2,5,10,28] are aimed at improving its accuracy, run-time,

Supplementary Information The online version contains supplementary material available at https://doi.org/10.1007/978-3-031-19824-3_21.

(a) With outliers   (b) Poorly conditioned   (c) Well conditioned

Fig. 1. Minimal sample filtering. We show three example minimal samples for Essential matrix estimation, with Sampson error E_s in pixels (maximum Sampson error of correspondences with respect to the ground truth Essential matrix), pose error (maximum of rotation and translation error) E_p in degrees, and our model's predicted quality score. *(a)*: a minimal sample encoding unlikely depth and motion due to outliers, easily recognized by NeFSAC only using the pixel's coordinates; *(b)*: an all-inlier sample but with two very close correspondences that lead to estimating a poorly conditioned model and, thus, high pose error; *(c)* a minimal sample with widely spaced correspondences. It leads to accurate pose estimation and is strongly preferred by NeFSAC.

and robustness attacking well-understood challenges with hand-engineered techniques, more recently we see substantial advancements in augmenting RANSAC for robust model estimation with learning-based techniques [8,25,29,30,38] that derive implicit models directly from data. Since one of the biggest challenges in RANSAC is handling large outlier ratios, most of the existing learning-based works are framed as an outlier rejection problem. This task is naturally good for learning, since in real scenes correct correspondences are strongly correlated, thus the global set of correspondences can be used to predict which subset is likely to be correct. However, we argue that there is more to be learned from real scenes than recognizing individual outliers. Another important challenge in RANSAC comes with degenerate and ill-conditioned minimal samples, such as in Fig. 1b. These configurations often occur in real scenes, e.g., in case of short baseline or when the epipole falls inside the image, when observing close-to-planar scenes or small textured areas leading to localized groups of inlier correspondences. This is problematic in RANSAC since it means that the often *expensive* model estimation and quality calculation is done unnecessarily on many samples which inherently lead to inaccurate models. Also, such models tend to have lots of inliers [15,21], thus misleading the quality calculation. Ideally, the perfect minimal sample filter would be able to recognize and avoid such samples to directly examine well-conditioned ones like the one in Fig. 1c.

Besides having inherently invalid samples, real-life images tend to follow certain motion patterns that can be also learned and used to further accelerate the robust estimation by rejecting incorrect minimal samples early. For example, in the autonomous driving scenario when the camera is mounted to a moving vehicle, it follows a distinctive motion pattern that significantly restricts the space of valid minimal sample configurations. Even without having such a strong assumption, e.g., when reconstructing internet images, people tend to take pictures approximately aligned with the gravity direction [16] that, again, gives a probabilistic constraint on the space of valid samples.

Learning a motion prior on minimal samples would allow RANSAC to find the ones that likely lead to the sought model early, spending fewer iterations on unlikely or impossible motions. For this purpose, we propose NeFSAC, which learns to filter invalid and motion-inconsistent minimal samples in RANSAC. NeFSAC can be straightforwardly integrated in any RANSAC variant, e.g. in USAC [28], and provide an important speed-up while *improving* accuracy of the estimation. We train an extremely lightweight neural network to score minimal samples prior to model estimation, thus being able to screen out thousands of minimal samples with negligible compute time. In the worst-case scenario, when the domain gap is too huge, NeFSAC degrades back to random filtering, which has no effect on the RANSAC run-time nor on the accuracy. Still, training in new domains requires only the collection of new image pairs with quasi-ground truth poses obtained from any existing pose estimation method. We integrated our approach into USAC, and measured a reduction of run-time of *one order of magnitude* with significant improvements in the estimation accuracy.

In summary, our contributions are as follows: (i) We propose NeFSAC, a novel framework to augment RANSAC by learning to efficiently distinguish good minimal samples. Our approach can be seamlessly integrated into any existing RANSAC-based pipeline. (ii) We propose a novel neural architecture for the task, and a novel training scheme for effectively learning the sample quality. (iii) We show that NeFSAC provides impressive speed-ups in RANSAC even without the need for strong motion constraints, while at the same time *improving* the accuracy. In the worst-case scenario, it degenerates to the baseline RANSAC with negligible run-time overhead and no drop in accuracy.

2 Related Works

Since RANSAC [17], great efforts from the research community have been concentrated into improving its components. Many works aim at improving the model scoring technique by modeling inlier and outlier distributions and using likelihood scores instead of the original inlier counting score [24, 32, 34, 35]. Similarly, MAGSAC++ [3–5] proposes to marginalize the inlier counting score over a range of possible thresholds, reducing the sensitivity of the scores to the choice of a specific noise scale. LO-RANSAC [14] proposes to perform local optimization of promising models during the search, with later improvements on the cost function and inlier selection [22] and with graph-cut masking of outliers [2]. Many of these improvements were combined in USAC [28] and VSAC [21] to achieve state-of-the-art performance.

Closer to our work, another line of research proposes improvements on the sampling scheme to increase the likelihood of detecting an all-inlier sample early. The most widely used approach is the PROSAC [12] algorithm, where the sampling is biased by prior-established likelihoods (e.g., from ratio-test). DSAC [9] first enabled learning through a RANSAC component, followed by Neural-guided RANSAC [8] and Deep MAGSAC++ [33] which learn inlier sampling likelihoods. Other works use spatial techniques to correlate the inlier likelihoods of individual correspondences by preferring neighboring correspondences [36] or by grouping similar ones [26]. Such methods combined with early termination techniques [11,23] can lead to significant improvements in robustness and run-time. However, none of these works can identify unlikely motions or depth configurations in minimal samples, nor can detect degeneracy of minimal samples. Moreover, we consider our work to be orthogonal to these, since it can be used on top of *any* of these approaches.

The cheirality test [37] is widely used to discard some impossible depth configurations. This test discards minimal samples which imply negative depths for some triangulated points. Unfortunately, while it is possible to perform the cheirality test directly on the minimal sample for homographies, it requires expensive epipolar geometry estimation in the cases of Essential matrix or Fundamental matrix estimation.

Even an all-inlier minimal sample can be in a degenerate configuration and lead to unstable relative poses, e.g. when observing a close-to-planar scene. This problem has been recognized and addressed by DEGENSAC [15] that checks for degeneracy and planar configurations of point samples *after* estimating the related epipolar geometry by the plane-and-parallax algorithm [20]. Moreover, QDEGSAC [18] identifies quasi-degenerate solutions in RANSAC and searches for the missing constraints in the outlier set. Differently from these works, we aim to detect such cases *prior to* the expensive epipolar geometry estimation, providing a consistent speed up to the whole procedure.

Outlier filtering techniques aim to filter the set of putative correspondences to increase the inlier rate prior to robust model estimation. These techniques look for spatial patterns in correspondences and perform explicit spatial verification [6,10] or learn a spatial verification model [25,38] optionally conditioned on descriptor information to perform matching altogether [30]. Since our approach does not score individual correspondences, but rather joint minimal samples, we consider our contribution to be orthogonal to outlier filtering techniques.

Despite the enormous research devoted to improving robust model estimation with RANSAC, the early selection of minimal samples is still under-explored. Particularly, to the best of our knowledge, no existing work provides a unique solution to embed general motion and depth priors to accelerate RANSAC. Existing techniques require expensive epipolar geometry estimation to handle degeneracy. In this paper, we show that a lightweight neural network can learn such a filter sufficiently well to provide important savings in run-time *and* improvements in terms of accuracy.

3   Neural Filtering of Minimal Samples

In robust model estimation, a set of data points $D = \{x \in \mathbb{R}^c\}$, optionally contaminated by outliers, is used to fit a model $M \in \mathbb{R}^q$ that minimizes the fitting cost $C = \sum_{x \in D} \mathcal{L}(E(M, x))$ where $E : \mathbb{R}^q \times \mathbb{R}^c \mapsto \mathbb{R}$ is a function that computes the fit error of a data point x with respect to model M, and $\mathcal{L} : \mathbb{R} \mapsto \mathbb{R}$ is a robust loss function that generally has small or zero gradients for large errors to minimize the influence of outlier data points.

Most of the real instances of the robust estimation problem are highly nonlinear, thus the approach proposed by RANSAC [17] is to discretely explore model hypotheses by successively sampling minimal sets of data points D_{min}^i such that they consist of the minimum number m of data points x that can fit exactly a finite set of models. The search is then stopped as soon as a satisfactory model has been found according to some termination criterion, and the final model is usually optimized locally to account for all of its inlier data points. The reason for using minimal sets stems from the RANSAC termination criterion where the required number of iterations depends exponentially on the sample size to provide probabilistic guarantees of finding the sought model.

In this work, we aim to drastically reduce the computational expense of such procedure by learning to pre-filter minimal samples before they are used for model estimation or compared to the rest of the data points. Notice how this is essentially different from previous works on outlier rejection, that, instead, filter out single data points with the objective of increasing the inlier ratio. While our formulation can be applied in general, in the following we will focus on the problems of Essential matrix estimation and Fundamental matrix estimation, where data points are image correspondences ($c = 4$), and minimal samples are constituted by, respectively, $m = 5$ and $m = 7$ correspondences.

In this section, we propose solutions for several challenges that come with the task of learning minimal sample filtering: how to design a lightweight neural architecture that respects all the invariants of minimal samples; how to supervise it in a context of extreme class imbalance; and how to efficiently apply it within RANSAC with the guarantee that, in the worst-case scenario of having a random filter, our method would not cause any degradation of accuracy.

3.1   Minimal Sample Filtering Network

We aim to learn a function $\mathcal{F} : \mathbb{R}^{c \times m} \mapsto [0, 1]$ to score minimal samples, where c is the dimensionality of a data point and m is the minimum number of data points required to fit a finite set of models. Particularly we are interested in Essential matrix estimation ($c = 4, m = 5$) and Fundamental matrix estimation ($c = 4, m = 7$). Note that we disregard information about the global configuration of correspondences across the two images: this simplification leads to a faster

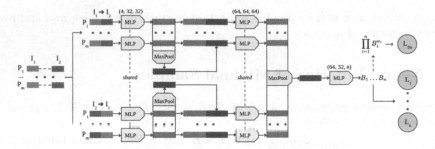

Fig. 2. NeFSAC's network architecture for minimal samples filtering. We predict the probability of a minimal sample leading to a good pose only taking its coordinates as input. We implement the main invariants of minimal samples with shared MLPs and channel-wise max pooling aggregation. The last MLP outputs n partial scores used during training, whose power-weighted product is the final score for use in RANSAC. The circular nodes represent the binary cross-entropy loss terms with their respective label. We do not propagate gradients across the dashed arrow.

and smaller model with very little capacity for overfitting. Particularly, since our primary objective is to reduce the computational load in RANSAC, our model of function $\mathcal{F}$ needs to be extremely lightweight. Moreover, our input is structured and the model needs to respect two main invariants: it should be invariant to the ordering of correspondences, and it should be invariant to swapping of the two images. We take inspiration from PointNet [27] and frame our main backbone encoder with shared MLPs that embed each correspondence independently in the same feature space, and then correlate them with channel-wise max pooling, thus preserving permutation invariance. Since our second invariant covers only two combinations, we run our backbone encoder with both alternatives and then max pool its features, before going through a final MLP classifier. We keep the network shallow and thin to keep its run-time negligible with respect to the subsequent RANSAC loop. An overall scheme of our network architecture is represented in Fig. 2. Note that our final MLP does not output a single score, but several partial scores whose power-weighted product is the final predicted score. This is to contrast the extreme class imbalance that is encountered with random minimal samples with a novel technique that we detail in Sect. 3.2.

3.2 Data Preprocessing and Network Supervision

We wish to supervise our network to predict a score for each minimal sample, such that higher scores are given to minimal samples which are more likely to lead to a good model estimation. Given a dataset with image correspondences and ground truth poses, the trivial approach would be to solve for the pose of each minimal sample, label them as positive or negative class based on the maximum between rotation and translation angular error, and train a classifier with binary cross-entropy. While extremely simple, we found that in practice this approach suffers from the extreme class imbalance. First, this is due to the fact that with an inlier ratio of r a minimal sample consisting of m data points has an exponentially lower inlier ratio of r^m. Second, not every all-inlier minimal sample leads to accurate or even meaningful models, as shown in Fig. 1b. Depending on the demanded accuracy to define a positive sample, this problem can lead to imbalance rates in the order of the *hundreds* in real datasets, making traditional techniques for unbalanced classification insufficient. Our observation aligns well with the common intuition of how many RANSAC iterations are required in practice to ensure a meaningful estimation of relative pose. We tackle this challenge by proposing to split the prediction of our network into multiple branches: one branch B_1 predicts if the minimal sample is constituted of all inliers (labeled on the maximum Sampson error of its correspondences with respect to the ground truth model), and a second branch B_2 predicts if the minimal sample leads to a good estimation of the pose, *given that* it is constituted of only inliers. In this setting, the first branch learns to score down minimal samples of impossible or unlikely motions, without suffering from the extra imbalance and complexity coming from ill-conditioned samples. The second branch, trained only on full-inlier samples, learns to score down the ill-conditioned configurations leading to noisy models. We underline the importance of this second branch, since such configurations are not only common in practical scenarios, but even detrimental for RANSAC, since they can collect a large consensus over the image [15, 21] and lead to erroneous early termination. For this reason, our approach not only can improve run-time, but it can also improve accuracy and robustness of the RANSAC pipeline it is used into.

In some scenarios, the possible real motions can be partly constrained with expert knowledge which could be useful as a prior to our network. For example, in an autonomous driving context we can *usually* assume that both rotation and translation only happen around the vertical axis. We propose to integrate expert knowledge into the minimal sample filter by the use of additional branches $B_3 \ldots B_n$, where each branch is tasked with predicting the adherence of a minimal sample to the analytical model defined by the expert. This extra supervision biases the feature extraction network to find features that can be discriminative also for the expert guidance, thus helping every branch with generalization. We detail the expert models used for the autonomous driving application and for PhotoTourism in the supplementary materials.

Finally, since a good sample is composed of all inliers, leads to a good final pose and is conform to expert models, we predict the final score as the product of all the partial scores. Since the different predictive power of each term is not known a-priori, we weight the product of the branches $B_1 \ldots B_n$ with weights $w_1 \ldots w_n$ at the exponents (i.e., we make a linear combination in log space) and supervise it to predict samples which are both inliers and lead to accurate models. Moreover, we do not propagate gradients to the branch scores $B_1 \ldots B_n$ to avoid unstable gradients from the power terms, therefore the branch terms are learned independently of the aggregate score. Overall, our loss function is:

$$\sum_i \mathcal{X}\left(B_i, \ l_i\right) + \mathcal{X}\left(\prod_i B_i^{w_i}, \ l_1 l_2\right) \tag{1}$$

where B_i are the output branches with respective assigned labels l_i and learned branch weights w_i, and $\mathcal{X}$ is the class-weighted cross-entropy loss. Note that, in Eq. 1, index $i = 1$ refers to the supervision on Sampson error, and index $i - 2$ refers to the supervision on pose error which is only applied to branch B_2 when the minimal sample is outlier-free. The calculation of assigned labels l_i is detailed in the supplementary materials. We did not experiment with tuning different weights for the losses of every branch.

3.3 Filtering Minimal Samples in RANSAC

Since our model learns to score minimal samples by the probability that they will lead to a successful pose estimate, in RANSAC we are interested in exploring high-scoring minimal samples first, and have a termination criterion to stop iterating when an accurate model is found. We iteratively take N minimal samples, sort them according to the score predicted by the network, and only process in RANSAC the first $k \ll N$, after which a new batch of N minimal samples is taken only if necessary – as controlled by the RANSAC termination criterion. This procedure guarantees that even in the worst case, when the actual motion does not conform with the learned one and the model degrades back to a random filter, RANSAC still finds the sought model eventually.

We found experimentally that good values are $N = 10000$ and $k = 500$, leading to aggressive filtering, but much lower values ($N = 128$, $k = 12$) also work reasonably well for compute-constrained applications. Processing one full batch takes $1.5ms$ on a RTX2080 GPU, or $20ms$ on an i7 7700K CPU. For simplicity we did not experiment adaptive strategies.

The proposed filtering can be straightforwardly combined with the state-of-the-art pre-emptive model verification strategies and samplers. We use the ones proposed in USAC [28], i.e., Sequential Probability Ratio Test [13], PROSAC sampling [12] and, also, LO-RANSAC [14] to find accurate results.

4   Experiments

In this Section we provide experimental insights into NeFSAC and its impact when integrated into a state-of-the-art RANSAC. We first investigate the quality of its filtering on a pool of random minimal samples, and show that it can improve its average precision (as defined in Sect. 4.1) by over two times in photo collection scenarios (PhotoTourism [31]) and by over one order of magnitude in strongly motion-constrained scenarios (KITTI [19]). Moreover, the filtering quality generalizes well across extremely different domains. Second, we validate the performance of NeFSAC when integrated in USAC [28], and observe *one order of magnitude* speed-up in practice, together with a *significant improvement* in estimation accuracy.

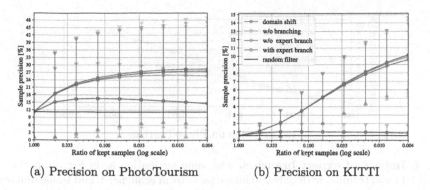

(a) Precision on PhotoTourism   (b) Precision on KITTI

Fig. 3. Precision of neural filtering. From a pool of minimal samples for E estimation, we keep the highest-scoring minimal samples according to our model and measure the precision of the kept set, i.e. the rate of samples with less than $10°$ of rotation and angular translation error, and less than 2 pixels of Sampson error. The distribution of results across images is represented with solid lines for the average and vertical lines for the two middle quartiles. Our method improves the precision of the minimal sample pool by **over one order of magnitude** in the autonomous driving scenario, and over two-fold on PhotoTourism.

4.1   Filtering Accuracy and Ablation Study

In this section, we compare several variations of our filtering network on the quality of the ordering they induce on minimal samples. In practice, for each tested baseline and for each test image, we take a pool of $N = 2^{16}$ random minimal samples, and sort them according to the predicted model score to have the best samples first. We then select the first k minimal samples for filtering rates $r \in \{1, 2, 4, 8, 16, 32, 64, 128, 256\}$ where $k = N/r$, and measure its precision, defined as the rate of samples leading to models with less than $10°$ of rotation and angular translation error, and less than 2 pixels of Sampson error. We test on a motion-constrained autonomous driving dataset and on a weakly-constrained image collection dataset. We use KITTI [19] for the motion-constrained scenario, and use sequences 0 to 4 for training, sequence 5 for validation and early stopping, and sequences 6 to 10 for testing. We train and validate using random frame differences between 1 and 7, and test with random frame differences between 1 and 5. In KITTI, we mostly see forward and turning motions with limited speed, thus a strong motion prior can be learned. For the weakly-constrained scenario, we use the PhotoTourism [31] data from the 2020 CVPR RANSAC Tutorial [1], with the suggested train-validation-test split. This dataset does not consist of image sequences but rather of crowd-sourced image collections of famous landmarks, therefore the motion prior that this data can exhibit is very limited. However, there are still distinctive motion patterns originating, e.g., from the fact that people usually align their photos with the gravity direction and, also, the range of translations along the vertical axis is limited.

We compare the following alternatives: (i) **w/o expert branch**: NeFSAC is trained only with branches B_1 and B_2 with Sampson error and pose error, as

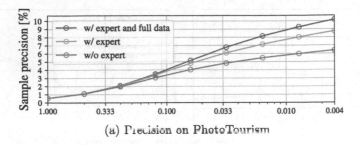

(a) Precision on PhotoTourism

Fig. 4. Impact of expert branches. The same evaluation as in Fig. 3b, performed on KITTI and training with only 250 image pairs from sequence 0 and frame difference 4. The expert branch significantly helps preserving the filtering accuracy in data-scarce conditions. We show only averages for clarity.

described in Sect. 3.2. (ii) **with expert branch**: NeFSAC, in addition to B_1 and B_2, is trained with a further branch B_3 with the expert supervision defined in the supplementary material. (iii) **w/o branching**: NeFSAC is directly trained to infer the complete label $l_1 l_2$ indicating low Sampson error and low pose error. Note that this is the same metric we use for testing, therefore this baseline has an intrinsic advantage in the testing process. Nonetheless, we show that branching leads to superior performance. (iv) **domain shift**: NeFSAC has been trained on a significantly different dataset from the one at test. We use the model trained on KITTI for the test on PhotoTourism, and the model trained on PhotoTourism for the test on KITTI. We use no expert branch for this baseline.

In Fig. 3a, we show results on 4000 image pairs from the PhotoTourism validation set. Our neural filtering model without any expert branch improves precision (as defined above) by 2.5 times on average at peak filtering rates compared to the original minimal sample pool. Expert knowledge, being inaccurate and hard to formulate in this context, has a slightly detrimental influence. The baseline without any branching, even though it is the only one trained end-to-end to optimize the test metric, does not keep up with the branched alternatives on higher filtering rates. Even with an extreme domain gap, the model trained on KITTI still manages to improve the quality of the original sample pool, showing that NeFSAC is very robust to distribution shifts. We attribute this robustness to the limited information that the neural filtering has at inference time, since our model never observes the global configuration of correspondences.

In Fig. 3b, we show results on 4000 image pairs from the KITTI sequences 6 to 10. The strong motion statistics on this dataset allow NeFSAC to improve the precision of the minimal sample pool **by over one order of magnitude** (18x) at peak filtering rates. Filtering is close-to-perfect up until 25% keep rate. On this dataset, we do not observe significant differences between the three main variants, likely due to the presence of a very simple and discriminative motion model that is well learned by all the baselines trained on KITTI. However, we can observe that the model with expert branch performs the best on this domain, where the expert supervision is more adherent to the real dataset statistics.

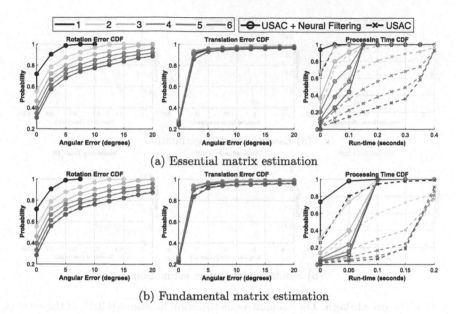

(a) Essential matrix estimation

(b) Fundamental matrix estimation

Fig. 5. CDF on KITTI. The cumulative distribution functions (CDF) of the rotation and translation errors (degrees) and run-time (seconds) of epipolar geometry estimation by USAC with and without the proposed neural sample filtering on 47700 image pairs from sequences 6–10 from the KITTI dataset [19]. Colors indicate the frame difference, e.g. the red curve uses a frame difference of 5. The corresponding mean values are in Table 1.

Interestingly, we found that the learned weight w_3 on the expert branch of this model is close to zero: this branch is not playing a significant role in the final prediction of the network, even though it still had a positive impact as a prior in learning good features for the other branches during training. The model trained on PhotoTourism, not taking advantage of the restricted motion statistics of this test set, still improves the precision of the original minimal sample pool by a factor up to 2, very close to its original performance on the PhotoTourism test.

Finally, in Fig. 4a, we test the influence of our expert branch in conditions of data scarcity. We keep the same evaluation protocol and test set as in Fig. 3b, but we train NeFSAC only on 250 image pairs from KITTI, all taken from sequence 0 and fixed frame difference of 4. We also report the baseline NeFSAC trained on the full training set for comparability. We observe that the impact of the expert branch is very significant when little training data is available, halving the gap to the baseline filtering accuracy. This scenario can be very important when training NeFSAC in a new domain with limited data.

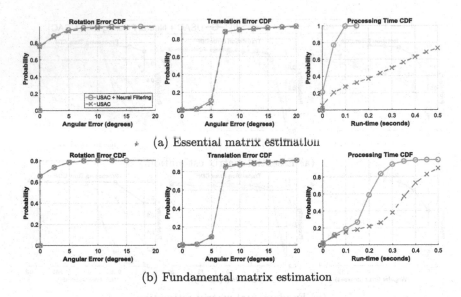

(a) Essential matrix estimation

(b) Fundamental matrix estimation

Fig. 6. CDF on Malaga. The cumulative distribution functions (CDF) of the rotation and translation errors (degrees) and run-time (seconds) of epipolar geometry estimation by USAC [28] with and without the proposed neural minimal sample filtering on 27147 image pairs from the Malaga dataset [7]. The corresponding mean values are in Table 1.

4.2   Comparative Experiments Within RANSAC

The interaction between several components in RANSAC is non-trivial: having observed an improvement of ten times in the average precision of a pool of random minimal samples does not necessarily translate into the equivalent speed-up of ten times in any RANSAC. In this section, we examine the effect of NeFSAC on a representative RANSAC variant with state-of-the-art components. We choose USAC [28] with cheirality tests, PROSAC sampling [12], LO-RANSAC [14], and SPRT [13] as preemptive verification. While there might be variants leading to better accuracy, e.g. MAGSAC++ [3], their low run-times still come from SPRT and PROSAC, therefore similar speed-ups are expected. We show additional experiments in the supplementary material.

In the following, we compare the rotation error ϵ_R, translation error ϵ_t and run-time t of USAC with and without NeFSAC filtering for the case of autonomous driving and for the case of unstructured image collections.

Autonomous Driving. We train NeFSAC on KITTI [19] on sequences 0 to 4 with random frame differences between 1 and 7, and use sequence 5 for validation. We train separate models for Essential matrix estimation and Fundamental matrix estimation. We then test such models on the KITTI sequences 6 to 10 as well as on the Malaga [7] dataset to test for generalization. We report results in Figs. 5 and 6 and Table 1. On KITTI, NeFSAC+USAC is over three times

Table 1. Results on KITTI and Malaga. The average rotation and translation errors (degrees), the run-time (milliseconds), and the number of models tested inside USAC [28] on the KITTI [19] and Malaga [7] datasets for essential (**E**) and fundamental matrix (**F**) estimation. NeFSAC provides great speed-ups while improving accuracy as well. The corresponding CDFs are in Figs. 5 and 6.

USAC	KITTI (47700 pairs)				Malaga (27147 pairs)			
	ϵ_R (°)	ϵ_t (°)	t (ms)	# models	ϵ_R (°)	ϵ_t (°)	t (ms)	# models
w/o NF (E)	4.3	2.5	234.8	941	3.3	8.9	350.0	3225
w/ NF (E)	4.3	2.3	69.7	260	1.9	8.7	34.0	753
w/o NF (F)	4.2	2.7	213.4	1974	1.4	9.0	380.2	3837
w/ NF (F)	4.2	2.3	85.9	357	1.4	8.6	77.1	467

Table 2. Results on PhotoTourism. The median rotation and translation errors (degrees), the average run-time (milliseconds), and the number of models tested inside USAC [28] on the PhotoTourism [31] (from [1]; 52200 image pairs) dataset. NF* is trained on KITTI [19]. NeFSAC provides great speed-ups while improving accuracy as well. The corresponding CDFs are in Fig. 7.

USAC	Essential matrix				Fundamental matrix			
	ϵ_R (°)	ϵ_t (°)	t (ms)	# models	ϵ_R (°)	ϵ_t (°)	t (ms)	# models
w/o NF	2.7	7.9	805.1	4550	4.8	22.5	154.6	5559
w/ NF	2.1	6.1	76.5	364	3.9	17.9	61.7	764
w/ NF*	2.6	7.8	103.0	660	4.8	22.3	61.2	740

faster on E estimation and more than twice as fast on F estimation compared to USAC, with slightly better accuracy. On Malaga, NeFSAC achieves a **ten-fold** speed-up and reduces the average rotation error by 1.4 °C on E estimation, and a five-fold speed-up on F estimation, **despite being trained on KITTI**.

PhotoTourism. We train NeFSAC on the PhotoTourism [31] data provided by the 2020 CVPR RANSAC Tutorial [1]. We use the standard split for training, validation and test. Results are reported in Fig. 7 and Table 2. NeFSAC improves run-time **again by one order of magnitude** on E estimation and two-fold on F estimation, while providing an **important improvement of accuracy** on both. Our aggressive filtering setup, tuned for challenging image pairs, causes a small overhead on the easy tail of the distribution, suggesting the use of adaptive strategies. We further perform an extreme generalization test training NeFSAC on KITTI (reported as NF* in Table 2). While the model trained on Photo-Tourism is superior, NeFSAC still manages to bring a very significant speed-up and some improvement in accuracy even under such extreme domain shift. This motivates us to claim that our model is partly learning very general knowledge on the task, and can robustly stay well above the worst-case scenario where it degenerates to the baseline RANSAC.

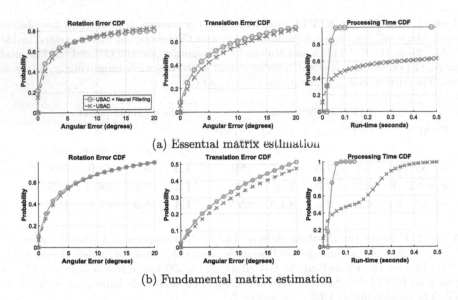

(a) Essential matrix estimation

(b) Fundamental matrix estimation

Fig. 7. CDF on PhotoTourism. The cumulative distribution functions (CDF) of the rotation and translation errors (in degrees) and run-time (in seconds) of epipolar geometry estimation by USAC [28] with and without the proposed neural minimal sample filtering on a total of 52200 image pairs from the PhotoTourism dataset as used in [1]. The corresponding mean values are in Table 2.

5   Conclusions

In this paper we proposed NeFSAC, a novel framework for Neural Filtering of minimal samples in RANSAC that can be seamlessly integrated into any existing RANSAC pipeline. NeFSAC learns to predict the quality of minimal samples by their crude pixel coordinates to filter out the ones consistent with unlikely or impossible motions and common poorly-conditioned configurations. We showed that NeFSAC can learn stronger filters when a constrained motion is present in the training data, but can be very discriminative even in datasets without a strong motion prior, like in general image collections, while being very robust to domain shifts. We showed that, in practice, NeFSAC can reduce the run-time by **one order of magnitude** in modern state-of-the-art RANSAC variants on Essential and Fundamental matrix estimation while often significantly *improving* estimation accuracy.

Acknowledgments. This work was supported by the ETH Zurich Postdoctoral Fellowship and the Google Focused Research Award.

References

1. Barath, D., Chin, T.J., Chum, O., Mishkin, D., Ranftl, R., Matas, J.: RANSAC in 2020 tutorial. In: CVPR (2020). http://cmp.felk.cvut.cz/cvpr2020-ransac-tutorial/
2. Barath, D., Matas, J.: Graph-cut RANSAC. In: CVPR, pp. 6733–6741 (2018)
3. Barath, D., Noskova, J., Ivashechkin, M., Matas, J.: MAGSAC++, a fast, reliable and accurate robust estimator. In: CVPR, pp. 1304–1312 (2020)
4. Barath, D., Noskova, J., Matas, J.: MAGSAC: marginalizing sample consensus. In: CVPR, pp. 10197–10205 (2019). https://github.com/danini/magsac
5. Barath, D., Noskova, J., Matas, J.: Marginalizing sample consensus. IEEE Trans. Pattern Anal. Mach. Intell. **44**(11), 8420–8432 (2021)
6. Bian, J., Lin, W.Y., Matsushita, Y., Yeung, S.K., Nguyen, T.D., Cheng, M.M.: GMS: grid-based motion statistics for fast, ultra-robust feature correspondence. In: CVPR, pp. 4181–4190 (2017)
7. Blanco-Claraco, J.L., Moreno-Duenas, F.A., González-Jiménez, J.: The Málaga urban dataset: high-rate stereo and LiDAR in a realistic urban scenario. Int. J. Robot. Res. **33**(2), 207–214 (2014)
8. Brachmann, E., Rother, C.: Neural-guided RANSAC: learning where to sample model hypotheses. In: CVPR, pp. 4322–4331 (2019)
9. Brachmann, E., et al.: DSAC-differentiable RANSAC for camera localization. In: Proceedings of the IEEE Conference on Computer Vision and Pattern Recognition, pp. 6684–6692 (2017)
10. Cavalli, L., Larsson, V., Oswald, M.R., Sattler, T., Pollefeys, M.: Handcrafted outlier detection revisited. In: Vedaldi, A., Bischof, H., Brox, T., Frahm, J.-M. (eds.) ECCV 2020. LNCS, vol. 12364, pp. 770–787. Springer, Cham (2020). https://doi.org/10.1007/978-3-030-58529-7_45
11. Chum, O., Matas, J.: Randomized RANSAC with tdd test. In: BMVC, vol. 2, pp. 448–457 (2002)
12. Chum, O., Matas, J.: Matching with PROSAC-progressive sample consensus. In: CVPR, vol. 1, pp. 220–226. IEEE (2005)
13. Chum, O., Matas, J.: Optimal randomized RANSAC. IEEE Trans. Pattern Anal. Mach. Intell. **30**(8), 1472–1482 (2008)
14. Chum, O., Matas, J., Kittler, J.: Locally optimized RANSAC. In: Michaelis, B., Krell, G. (eds.) DAGM 2003. LNCS, vol. 2781, pp. 236–243. Springer, Heidelberg (2003). https://doi.org/10.1007/978-3-540-45243-0_31
15. Chum, O., Werner, T., Matas, J.: Two-view geometry estimation unaffected by a dominant plane. In: CVPR, vol. 1, pp. 772–779. IEEE (2005)
16. Ding, Y., Barath, D., Kukelova, Z.: Minimal solutions for panoramic stitching given gravity prior. In: Proceedings of the IEEE/CVF International Conference on Computer Vision, pp. 5579–5588 (2021)
17. Fischler, M.A., Bolles, R.C.: Random sample consensus: a paradigm for model fitting with applications to image analysis and automated cartography. Commun. ACM **24**(6), 381–395 (1981)
18. Frahm, J.M., Pollefeys, M.: RANSAC for (quasi-)degenerate data (QDEGSAC). In: CVPR, vol. 1, pp. 453–460. IEEE (2006)
19. Geiger, A., Lenz, P., Urtasun, R.: Are we ready for autonomous driving? The KITTI vision benchmark suite. In: CVPR, pp. 3354–3361. IEEE (2012)
20. Hartley, R., Zisserman, A.: Multiple View Geometry in Computer Vision. Cambridge University Press, Cambridge (2003)

21. Ivashechkin, M., Barath, D., Matas, J.: VSAC: efficient and accurate estimator for H and F. ICCV, pp. 15243–15252 (2021)
22. Lebeda, K., Matas, J., Chum, O.: Fixing the locally optimized RANSAC. In: BMVC. Citeseer (2012)
23. Matas, J., Chum, O.: Randomized RANSAC with sequential probability ratio test. In: ICCV, vol. 2, pp. 1727–1732. IEEE (2005)
24. Moisan, L., Moulon, P., Monasse, P.: Automatic homographic registration of a pair of images, with a contrario elimination of outliers. Image Process. On Line **2**, 56–73 (2012)
25. Moo Yi, K., Trulls, E., Ono, Y., Lepetit, V., Salzmann, M., Fua, P.: Learning to find good correspondences. In: CVPR, pp. 2666–2674 (2018)
26. Ni, K., Jin, H., Dellaert, F.: GroupSAC: efficient consensus in the presence of groupings. In: ICCV, pp. 2193–2200. IEEE (2009)
27. Qi, C.R., Su, H., Mo, K., Guibas, L.J.: PointNet: deep learning on point sets for 3D classification and segmentation. In: CVPR, pp. 652–660 (2017)
28. Raguram, R., Chum, O., Pollefeys, M., Matas, J., Frahm, J.M.: USAC: a universal framework for random sample consensus. IEEE Trans. Pattern Anal. Mach. Intell. **35**(8), 2022–2038 (2013)
29. Ranftl, R., Koltun, V.: Deep fundamental matrix estimation. In: ECCV, pp. 284–299 (2018)
30. Sarlin, P.E., DeTone, D., Malisiewicz, T., Rabinovich, A.: SuperGlue: learning feature matching with graph neural networks. In: CVPR, pp. 4938–4947 (2020)
31. Snavely, N., Seitz, S.M., Szeliski, R.: Photo tourism: exploring photo collections in 3D. In: ACM siggraph 2006 papers, pp. 835–846 (2006)
32. Stewart, C.V.: MINPRAN: a new robust estimator for computer vision. IEEE Trans. Pattern Anal. Mach. Intell. **17**(10), 925–938 (1995)
33. Tong, W., Matas, J., Barath, D.: Deep MAGSAC++. arXiv preprint arXiv:2111.14093 (2021)
34. Torr, P.H.S.: Bayesian model estimation and selection for epipolar geometry and generic manifold fitting. Int. J. Comput. Vis. **50**, 35–61 (2002). https://doi.org/10.1023/A:1020224303087
35. Torr, P.H.S., Zisserman, A.: MLESAC: a new robust estimator with application to estimating image geometry. Comput. Vis. Image Underst. **78**(1), 138–156 (2000)
36. Torr, P.H., Nasuto, S.J., Bishop, J.M.: Napsac: high noise, high dimensional robust estimation-it's in the bag. In: BMVC, vol. 2, p. 3 (2002)
37. Werner, T., Pajdla, T.: Cheirality in epipolar geometry. In: ICCV, vol. 1, pp. 548–553. IEEE (2001)
38. Zhang, J., et al.: Learning two-view correspondences and geometry using order-aware network. In: CVPR, pp. 5845–5854 (2019)

SNeS: Learning Probably Symmetric Neural Surfaces from Incomplete Data

Eldar Insafutdinov, Dylan Campbell[(✉)], João F. Henriques,
and Andrea Vedaldi

University of Oxford, Oxford OX1 3PJ, UK
{eldar,dylan,joao,vedaldi}@robots.ox.ac.uk

Abstract. We present a method for the accurate 3D reconstruction of partly-symmetric objects. We build on the strengths of recent advances in neural reconstruction and rendering such as Neural Radiance Fields (NeRF). A major shortcoming of such approaches is that they fail to reconstruct any part of the object which is not clearly visible in the training image, which is often the case for in-the-wild images and videos. When evidence is lacking, structural priors such as symmetry can be used to complete the missing information. However, exploiting such priors in neural rendering is highly non-trivial: while geometry and non-reflective materials may be symmetric, shadows and reflections from the ambient scene are not symmetric in general. To address this, we apply a soft symmetry constraint to the 3D geometry and material properties, having factored appearance into lighting, albedo colour and reflectivity. We evaluate our method on the recently introduced CO3D dataset, focusing on the car category due to the challenge of reconstructing highly-reflective materials. We show that it can reconstruct unobserved regions with high fidelity and render high-quality novel view images.

Keywords: 3D reconstruction · Novel view synthesis · Neural rendering

1 Introduction

Photogrammetry has made substantial progress with recent advances in neural rendering [29]. Given a collection of posed images of an object, we can now use techniques such as COLMAP [25] and NeRF [18] to learn photo-realistic models of the object from which novel views can be generated. Extensions such as NeuS [32] and VolSDF [38] can also accurately recover the 3D shape of the object. Many of these advances arise from using neural networks to represent the complex functions that describe the geometry and reflectance of the object.

E. Insafutdinov and D. Campbell—Both authors contributed equally to this research.

Supplementary Information The online version contains supplementary material available at https://doi.org/10.1007/978-3-031-19824-3_22.

Seen (NeuS [32])   Seen (Ours)   Unseen (NeuS)   Unseen (Ours)

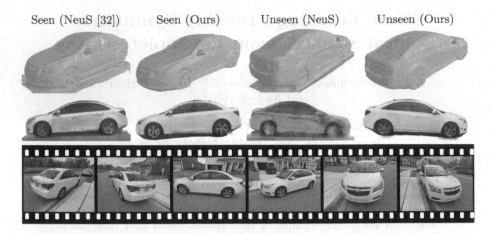

Fig. 1. From a sequence of frames that view a car in passing, our Symmetric Neural Surfaces (SNeS) model simultaneously learns the parameters of a symmetry transformation from the data and applies the symmetry as a soft constraint to reconstruct the model, despite the significantly different view densities between the seen and unseen sides. The learned symmetry allows SNeS to share information across the model, resulting in more accurate reconstructions and higher-fidelity novel synthesised views.

Despite such successes, significant practical limitations remain. While networks often have excellent generalisation capabilities, in methods such as NeRF and NeuS they are overfitted to individual scenes, such as a single 3D object. As a result, such networks generalise poorly and are unable to predict the parts of the object that are not visible in the training images; instead, they require a large number of views capturing uniformly on all sides of the object. This prevents applications in many realistic scenarios where only a limited and biased set of views is available, such as egocentric video or self-driving vehicles (Fig. 1).

Bilateral symmetry is a strong geometric prior that applies approximately to many man-made and natural objects, and can be used to extrapolate beyond the field of view. Unfortunately, symmetry is not directly applicable to current neural renderers, because they entangle potentially symmetric parts of the model (geometry, material) with ambient illumination and view-dependent effects (shadows, specularity, and reflections), which are not symmetric. Our proposed approach, named *Symmetric Neural Surfaces* (SNeS), decomposes a neural renderer's colour model into several components: material albedo (absorption), reflectivity, diffuse lighting, and reflected lighting. These components are combined linearly, inspired by Phong shading [23], and are modelled by neural networks with different input constraints to ensure that they factorise correctly. For example, albedo only depends on the position and not on the viewpoint. During training, we encourage symmetry for only a subset of these components, albedo and reflectivity, which are material-dependent. We also apply symmetry to the geometry model, which is a neural surface model based on a signed distance function (SDF) [39]. Given the emphasis on bilateral symmetry and highly-reflective materials, our experiments are focused on vehicle reconstruction, which presents these unique challenges. Our contributions are:

- an algorithm for reconstructing objects with arbitrary learned symmetries of a pre-defined type from incomplete observations;
- a technique for disentangling symmetric and asymmetric appearance; and
- a prior for handling violations of geometry and material symmetry.

We demonstrate high fidelity of reconstruction, both in visual appearance and in the accuracy of surface geometry, for parts of the objects that are unseen during training. Our method achieves state-of-the-art results on the CO3D dataset [24], improving the geometry estimates considerably compared to the baselines, especially on sequences where the view density between sides is unbalanced.

2   Related Work

The field of neural volume rendering has expanded rapidly in the last two years, with increasing photo-realism and reconstruction quality. We focus on the closest works, and refer readers to recent review papers for a complete account [28,29].

Neural Volume Rendering and Reconstruction. Neural Radiance Fields (NeRF) [18] and related approaches [3,15,16,33,40,41] generate images via a physically-based rendering process, where a ray is traced into the volume and neural network estimates of colour and density at sample points are integrated to render the pixel colour. With careful network design or regularisation, such a model will be able to accurately reconstruct the scene's geometry as well as modelling view-dependent effects. NeRF also introduced positional encoding, allowing MLPs to represent high frequency signals without increasing network capacity. Our rendering pipeline is similar, but extended to model symmetries.

Many works investigate more sophisticated lighting models that reason about the transport and scattering of light through the volume, allowing relighting and material editing [4–6,27,31,43]. For example, NeRFactor [43] converts a pre-trained NeRF model into a surface model, and optimises MLPs to represent light source visibility, surface normals, albedo, and the BRDF at any point on the surface, in addition to environment lighting, factoring appearance into material and lighting. Ref-NeRF [31], in contrast, trains a NeRF-like model from scratch, but replaces its parametrisation of outgoing radiance with one of reflected radiance to better model light transport, and estimates surface roughness to interpolate between blurry and sharp reflections. Our model also decomposes appearance into material properties and lighting, using a Phong colour model [23] and a loss that encourages the diffusely-lit albedo of a surface point to match the ground truth on average, integrating over viewing directions. Unlike existing work, this is motivated by symmetry learning, rather than editing applications, since lighting is typically asymmetric and impedes symmetry learning if ignored.

Many volume rendering approaches [3,18,41] attempt to concentrate their samples near surfaces, e.g., by using stratified sampling. Hybrid surface–volume representations [2,20,32,38,39] take this further by modelling surfaces directly, albeit implicitly, using occupancy [17] or signed distance function (SDF) [21] networks, combined with volume rendering for modelling view-dependent appearance. This was motivated by the observation that NeRF, while able to handle sudden depth changes, is unable to learn high-fidelity surfaces from its implicit representation. IDR [39] represents the geometry as an SDF and uses a NeRF-like view-dependent head to estimate colour, which also receives the surface normal to better disentangle geometry and appearance. However, the appearance network only receives one point per ray, at the first surface, which can cause the model to get stuck in local optima. UNISURF [20] relaxes this by using hierarchical sampling with root-finding in an occupancy field, allowing it to spread the gradient over multiple points, which nonetheless concentrate at the surface as training progresses. A similar approach is taken by NeuS [32] and VolSDF [38], which represent surfaces as the zero-level set of an SDF and explore approaches for mapping signed distances to opacities. Our work is a hybrid surface–volume approach of this type, since our aim is to reconstruct high-quality symmetric surfaces. However, unlike previous work, we exploit additional structure in the data by learning symmetries and use them to share information between views.

Symmetry in 3D Reconstruction. Symmetry cues have been used extensively in reconstruction, with shape-from-symmetry enabling single-view reconstruction by using the reflected image as another view [7,8,10,11,13,19,22,26, 30]. Symmetry detection has also been investigated [9,26]. Of particular relevance is the approach of Wu et al. [35–37], who use reflective and rotational symmetries to recover shape, material properties and lighting from single images. They enforce mirror symmetry by flipping internal representations of depth and albedo in image space, and estimate a confidence mask to allow asymmetries. Our work is inspired by this use of symmetry for reconstruction, and by the observation that asymmetric lighting must be removed to reason about appearance symmetries. However, we target the task of multi-view reconstruction, apply a soft symmetry constraint in 3D directly rather than in 2D, and learn the symmetry parameters to obviate the need for fronto-parallel images.

3   Disentangled Neural Rendering

In this section, we outline our disentangled neural rendering model that takes a collection of posed images and produces a signed distance function (SDF) of the geometry and an appearance model that can be queried from novel viewpoints. In the subsequent section, we show how this baseline model can be used to learn symmetric neural surfaces. A flowchart of our full model is shown in Fig. 2.

3.1   Disentangling Geometry and Appearance

Since the release of the NeRF model [18], there has been considerable research into improving the noisy surface reconstructions it obtains [20,32,39]. These

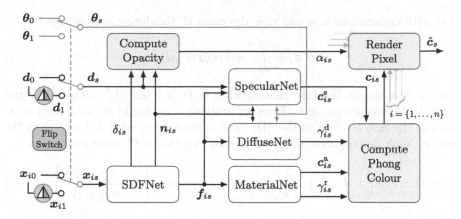

Fig. 2. The Symmetric Neural Surfaces (SNeS) model. For an input 3D point x_i and direction vector d, the model estimates the geometry with an SDF network that generates a signed distance δ_i, a normal vector n_i, and a feature vector f_i. The first two are used to compute the opacity α_i according to Eq. (3), which assigns high opacity to points near surfaces. The feature vector is passed to the appearance networks to compute the material properties of albedo colour c_i^a and reflectivity γ_i^r, and the lighting properties of diffuse shading γ_i^d and specular colour c_i^s. Lastly, the Phong model is used to compute the colour of the 3D point, and each sample along the ray is combined to render the pixel with colour $\hat{c}$. The subscript s indicates whether the geometry, material and lighting components were computed with inputs that had undergone a symmetry transformation (1) or not (0), denoted by the triangular symbol. In each case, the lighting networks take different parameters θ, since lighting is typically asymmetric.

have focused on replacing NeRF's density estimation network with a regularised SDF [32,39] or occupancy [20] network. We use NeuS [32] as our baseline, since it effectively disentangles geometry and appearance, and is able to model fine structures. For completeness, we recap the NeuS model now.

Given a set of images $\{I_\ell\}$ with associated camera poses and intrinsic matrices, the task is to reconstruct the geometry and view-dependent appearance of the object or scene. The geometry is represented implicitly as a signed distance function with zero-level set $\{x_i \in \mathbb{R}^3 \mid \phi_{\mathrm{SDF}}(x_i) = 0\}$ that coincides with opaque surfaces in the scene. The map $\phi_{\mathrm{SDF}} : \mathbb{R}^3 \to \mathbb{R}$, which converts a 3D point $x_i \in \mathbb{R}^3$ to a signed distance δ_i, is estimated with a fully-connected neural network. The view-dependent appearance is also estimated by fully-connected neural network layers, parametrising the function $\phi_{\mathrm{colour}} : \mathbb{R}^3 \times \mathbb{S}^3 \to \mathbb{R}^3$, which maps a 3D point and view direction d to a colour $c_i \in [0,1]^3$. Unlike NeuS, in this work the colour is estimated by a composition of functions to disentangle material and lighting properties, as shall be detailed in Sect. 3.2.

To learn these functions from images, physically-based rendering accumulates colours along a pixel ray. The ray is parametrised as $\{x(t) = o + td \mid t > 0\}$ for a ray with camera centre o and view direction d. Rendering is performed by

$$\hat{c}(o, d) = \int_0^\infty w(t)\, c(x(t), d)\, \mathrm{d}t, \tag{1}$$

where w is a weight function that satisfies $w(t) \geqslant 0$ and $\int_0^\infty w(t)\mathrm{d}t = 1$, and should be high near opaque surfaces. In particular, w should attain a local maximum at the zero-level set of the SDF, and should decay with distance from the camera. NeuS derives an appropriate weight function with these properties,

$$w(t) = \exp\left(-\int_0^t \rho(u)\, \mathrm{d}u\right) \rho(t), \text{ with } \rho(t) = \max\left\{0, \frac{-\frac{\mathrm{d}\sigma_\tau}{\mathrm{d}t}(\delta(t))}{\sigma_\tau(\delta(t))}\right\}, \tag{2}$$

where $\rho(t)$ is the opaque density function and $\sigma_\tau(x) = (1 + \exp(-\tau x))^{-1}$ is the sigmoid function parametrised by a learned scalar $\tau > 0$. As can be seen, NeuS does not predict the volume density directly like NeRF, but rather computes the density using the predicted signed distances in closed form. The learned scalar τ is proportional to the inverse standard deviation of the weight function (approximately a logistic density distribution), and controls the spread of the density about the zero-level crossing. It adapts to the data during training, resulting in a more concentrated distribution over time. This has two effects: colours of points near surfaces are assigned an increasingly high weight, and points are sampled increasingly close to surfaces, via an importance-sampling strategy. We refer the reader to Wang et al. [32] for a detailed derivation.

A discrete approximation of the weight function follows from the quadrature technique used in NeRF [18]. For n sampled points $\{x_i = o + t_i d \mid i = 1, \ldots, n;\ t_i < t_{i+1}\}$ along the ray, their weights are given by

$$w_i = \alpha_i \prod_{j=1}^{i-1}(1 - \alpha_j), \text{ with } \alpha_i = \max\left\{0, \frac{\sigma_\tau(\delta(t_i)) - \sigma_\tau(\delta(t_{i+1}))}{\sigma_\tau(\delta(t_i))}\right\}, \tag{3}$$

where the product term is the accumulated transmittance, and α_i is the discrete opacity. Note that to obtain the signed distance $\delta(t_i)$, the model uses the gradient (normal) vector to adjust the value of the nearest sampled signed distance. The final colour is then rendered as $\hat{c} = \sum_{i=1}^n w_i c_i$.

3.2   Disentangling Material and Lighting Properties

It is well-known that the NeRF colour formation model under-constrains the geometry, exhibiting a shape–radiance ambiguity where the training images can be perfectly explained by arbitrary geometry [41]. To impose a more realistic inductive bias on colour formation, without losing the flexibility and representation power of the unconstrained model, we disentangle the material and lighting properties using a Phong model [23]. As we shall show, this is also a necessary requirement for learning symmetric geometries from the data.

We separate the apparent colour into material and lighting properties. Specifically, albedo colour and reflectivity (or inverse roughness) represent material, and diffuse shading (assuming a white diffuse illuminant) and specular colour represent lighting. Here, we define the albedo as the average colour of a 3D point across viewpoints, under the scene lighting. Our colour formation model is

$$c_i = f_{\text{Phong}}\left(\gamma_i^{\text{d}}, c_i^{\text{a}}, \gamma_i^{\text{r}}, c_i^{\text{s}}\right) = \gamma_i^{\text{d}}(\boldsymbol{x}_i, \boldsymbol{n}_i)\, c_i^{\text{a}}(\boldsymbol{x}_i) + \gamma_i^{\text{r}}(\boldsymbol{x}_i)\, c_i^{\text{s}}(\boldsymbol{x}_i, \boldsymbol{n}_i, \boldsymbol{d}_i), \qquad (4)$$

where $c_i \in [0,1]^3$ is the estimated colour of the 3D point $\boldsymbol{x}_i$, $\gamma_i^{\text{d}} \in [0,2]$ is the diffuse lighting coefficient, $c_i^{\text{a}} \in [0,1]^3$ is the lighting-invariant albedo colour of the material, $\gamma_i^{\text{r}} \in [0,1]$ is the material reflectivity, and $c_i^{\text{s}} \in [0,1]^3$ is the specular colour of the reflected light. We see that the material properties depend on the geometry only, while the lighting depends additionally on the normal vector (diffuse lighting with self-shadows) and the viewing direction (specular colour). A more constrained parametrisation would learn the specular colour from the viewing ray reflected about the surface normal [31]. However, we found that this significantly over-smoothed the SDF model. While this colour model has the capacity to disentangle material and lighting properties, it needs to be regularised in order to do so. However, some objects, such as cars, are highly specular, making it undesirable to regularise the reflectivity. We instead encourage the diffusely-lit colour $\gamma_i^{\text{d}} c_i^{\text{a}}$, rendered along the ray, to match the ground-truth colour, as we shall detail in the next section. This acts to average the colour of a surface location across all viewing directions. In practice, the appearance networks also depend on a feature vector from the SDF network, encoding the geometric context of the 3D point [39].

4   Symmetric Neural Surfaces

The model described thus far is unable to take advantage of known or suspected symmetries. We define a symmetry as an arbitrary coordinate transformation, especially an affine transformation such as a reflection, rotation, translation, or scaling, that confers an invariance. To share information across symmetries, we explicitly model and optimise the transformation parameters and use the map induced by the symmetry to aggregate information in 3D. However, not all information is symmetric. Cars, for example, tend to have a bilateral symmetry in their geometry and material properties, but the lighting of the scene is rarely symmetric. There are also exceptions that break the geometric and material symmetry, such as asymmetrically-positioned spare tyres (geometric) and stickers (material colour), as shown in Fig. 3 (c). Due to these real-world partial symmetries, it is best implemented as a soft constraint mediated by loss functions, rather than a hard constraint. Our framework has the flexibility to handle multiple arbitrary and localised symmetries. Spatially-restricted symmetries can be useful for modelling parts of an object or scene that are locally-symmetric, like the wheels of a car. In this work we focus on the common case of reflection (bilateral) symmetry, and localise the predicted symmetry to the unit sphere, to avoid symmetrising the background. A diagram of our approach is shown in

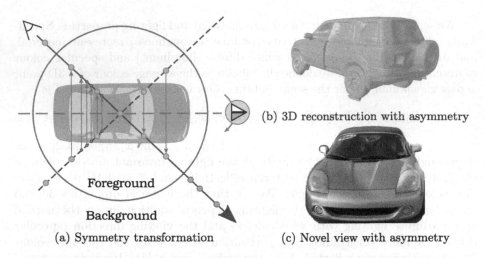

(b) 3D reconstruction with asymmetry

(a) Symmetry transformation

(c) Novel view with asymmetry

Fig. 3. (a) Applying a symmetry transformation for physically-based rendering. The SNeS algorithm scales the object of interest to fit inside the unit sphere, where it is modelled by an SDF network with appearance heads, while the region outside the sphere is represented by a NeRF++ background model [41]. Here, yellow dots denote points sampled coarsely along the ray, small blue dots denote points importance-sampled near dominant surfaces, green dots denote points inversely-sampled in the background, and the horizontal dashed line denotes the plane of (reflection) symmetry. The symmetry induces a transformation on the point samples inside the sphere, and the transformed points are used to compute the geometry and material properties. These components are combined with the diffuse and specular lighting estimates from the source ray to form a colour estimate. If the symmetry holds, and is accurately estimated, the resulting colour should match the source colour. (b) SNeS reconstruction showing that geometry asymmetries (spare tire, slightly-open door) are conserved. (c) SNeS novel view showing that appearance asymmetries (windshield sticker, lighting) are conserved. (Color figure online)

Fig. 3. In the following, we denote the original ray, and everything computed with respect to it, as "source", and the symmetry-transformed ray as "transformed".

4.1 Parametrising Symmetry

We parametrise a symmetry as a coordinate transformation with form $T_c^{-1} S T_c$, where $T_c = \begin{pmatrix} R_c & t_c \\ 0 & 1 \end{pmatrix}$ is the learned rigid transformation matrix from world coordinates to the canonical coordinates of the symmetry, defining its plane or axis, and S is the symmetry transformation in canonical coordinates. In this work, we consider a single bilateral reflection symmetry about the XZ plane in canonical coordinates, and so the symmetry transformation matrix is given by $S = I - 2e_2 e_2^T$, where e_i is the ith 4D unit basis vector. We apply the transformation to the source points x_0^h in homogeneous coordinates. The direction vectors d_0^h also undergo a symmetry transformation, although they are translation-invariant. This is implemented by the homogeneous coordinates, since directions are points at infinity with final coordinate equal to 0. Thus we obtain

$$\boldsymbol{x}_{i1}^{\mathrm{h}} = T_c^{-1} S T_c \boldsymbol{x}_{i0}^{\mathrm{h}} \tag{5}$$

$$\boldsymbol{d}_{i1}^{\mathrm{h}} = T_c^{-1} S T_c \boldsymbol{d}_{i0}^{\mathrm{h}}. \tag{6}$$

4.2 Learning Symmetric Geometry and Material

To encourage symmetric points to have the same geometry and material properties, we compute these quantities at both the source and transformed points, and compose them with predictions from the corresponding lighting model. Thus, for each point, we obtain the source colour $\boldsymbol{c}_{i00} = \gamma_{i0}^{\mathrm{d}} \boldsymbol{c}_{i0}^{\mathrm{a}} + \gamma_{i0}^{\mathrm{r}} \boldsymbol{c}_{i0}^{\mathrm{s}}$ and the symmetry-transformed colour $\boldsymbol{c}_{i11} = \gamma_{i1}^{\mathrm{d}} \boldsymbol{c}_{i1}^{\mathrm{a}} + \gamma_{i1}^{\mathrm{r}} \boldsymbol{c}_{i1}^{\mathrm{s}}$. The lighting models for the source and symmetry-transformed paths do not share weights, since lighting is rarely symmetric. The resulting point colours are rendered along the ray, and compared to the ground-truth source pixel colour. If symmetry is valid at that pixel, and is accurately estimated, the error should be low. However, most objects and scenes are not perfectly symmetric, and so symmetry should not be enforced when better visual evidence is available. Therefore, we penalise the error of the symmetry-transformed colour at a discount compared to the source colour.

We also mix the source and the transformed components, generating hybrid colours. This acts to supervise the transformed lighting network to emulate the source lighting network, up to the symmetry transformation. Without these terms, the lighting networks may diverge, allowing the network to explain away deviations from symmetry as fake perturbations in lighting. Specifically, we form the hybrid point-wise colours $\boldsymbol{c}_{i01} = \gamma_{i1}^{\mathrm{d}} \boldsymbol{c}_{i0}^{\mathrm{a}} + \gamma_{i0}^{\mathrm{r}} \boldsymbol{c}_{i1}^{\mathrm{s}}$ and $\boldsymbol{c}_{i10} = \gamma_{i0}^{\mathrm{d}} \boldsymbol{c}_{i1}^{\mathrm{a}} + \gamma_{i1}^{\mathrm{r}} \boldsymbol{c}_{i0}^{\mathrm{s}}$, render these along the ray, and compute the colour error as before.

It is important to disentangle the material and lighting, since the former is usually asymmetric. This means that simply applying symmetry to the NeRF colour model would not work, since the colour is entangled with a systematic nuisance variable. Another strategy to help estimate the symmetry parameters is to learn the ground plane simultaneously and enforce orthogonality between the ground plane and the symmetry plane. To do so, we model the foreground as a joint SDF, which consists of the minimum of the object's SDF and a ground plane SDF (an infinite plane). This allows the SDF network to spend more capacity on the object, and enables ground removal without post-processing.

4.3 Loss Functions

To fit our model, we minimise the error between the rendered and ground-truth pixels while regularising the SDF. No 3D supervision is used, beyond the known camera poses. We optimise the network parameters, symmetry transformation parameters, and the scalar τ that controls the variance of the density near surfaces. The per-pixel colour loss is given by

$$\mathcal{L}_{jk}^{\mathrm{colour}} = \tfrac{1}{3} \|\hat{\boldsymbol{c}}_{jk} - \boldsymbol{c}\|_1, \tag{7}$$

where c is the ground-truth colour and $\hat{c}_{jk}$ is the predicted colour. The indices jk indicate whether the colour prediction uses the source or symmetry-transformed geometry and material properties (j), and lighting (k). This is the mechanism by which symmetry is encouraged in regions with visual evidence to the contrary.

We also use two additional losses with the same form as Eq. (7). The first is a diffuse colour loss $\mathcal{L}_{jk}^{\text{diffuse}}$ where the predicted colour is rendered without the specular components, that is, the pixel colour is rendered from point colours $c_i^{\text{diffuse}} = \gamma_i^d c_i^a$. This encourages the network to disentangle the diffuse and specular components, setting the diffuse colour of a given surface location to the average colour across all viewing directions. This is important for symmetry, since the specular colour is usually not symmetric, so assisting the network to disentangle it can speed up convergence. The second is a symmetric lighting loss $\mathcal{L}_{jk}^{\text{lighting}}$ that applies a weak prior to the model to prefer symmetric lighting in the absence of contrary evidence. It applies the same colour loss as Eq. (7), but with the source lighting networks receiving symmetry-transformed inputs. This acts to apply symmetric lighting, which is generally incorrect, except at midday. Nonetheless, in the absence of image evidence, this prior provides a more naturalistic appearance. However, this loss should not be applied for quantitative analysis of unseen sides, because applying the symmetric lighting model is likely to be more detrimental than applying a baseline lighting model. For example, it may apply direct sunlight and specular reflections on the shadowed side of the object, which may look qualitatively convincing, but will be quantitatively poor.

Finally, we regularise the SDF network by applying an Eikonal loss [12] at the n sampled points along the ray, which encourages a unit gradient SDF:

$$\mathcal{L}_j^{\text{eikonal}} = \frac{1}{n} \sum_i^n (\|\nabla\phi_{\text{SDF}}(x_{ij})\|_2 - 1)^2. \tag{8}$$

The total per-pixel loss is given by

$$\mathcal{L} = \sum_{j,k}(1 + (\mathcal{X} - 1)j)\left(\mathcal{L}_{jk}^{\text{colour}} + \lambda^d\mathcal{L}_{jk}^{\text{diffuse}} + \lambda^l\mathcal{L}_{jk}^{\text{lighting}} + \lambda^e\mathcal{L}_j^{\text{eikonal}}\right), \tag{9}$$

where $\mathcal{X} \in [0,1]$ is the symmetricity factor that determines a prior on how symmetric an object or scene is expected to be, and the other λ factors denote the weights assigned to the remaining losses.

5   Results

5.1   Experimental Setup

Dataset. We evaluate our method on the cars subset of the recent Common Objects in 3D (CO3D) dataset [24], released under the BSD License. CO3D is a large-scale multi-view image dataset with ground-truth camera pose, intrinsics, depth map, object mask, and 3D point cloud annotations, collected in-the-wild by outdoor video capture. This real-world dataset is particularly challenging for reconstruction algorithms, having highly reflective (non-Lambertian) and low-textured surfaces, such as mirrors, dark windows, and metallic paint. Moreover, only 64% of the test sequences circumnavigate the object, with many seeing only one side of the car. This incomplete data motivates the use of symmetry for completing the reconstruction of partially-symmetric objects. Additional nuisance factors include significant motion blur from the handheld cameras, auto-exposure, and adverse weather, including fog and rain. One of the consequences of this challenging data is that the ground-truth point clouds and depth maps are sparse, very noisy, and contain many outliers, and 8% of test object masks entirely miss the object. This makes evaluating the reconstructed geometry, especially fine details, quite difficult. For the task of single-scene 3D reconstruction and novel view synthesis, the 'car' category has 22 test scenes with 102 frames each. We present results on other partly-symmetric categories in the appendix.

Metrics. We report five metrics to measure visual and geometric quality: the peak signal-to-noise ratio (PSNR), the mean squared colour error (MSE), and the perceptual LPIPS distance [42] between the masked predicted and ground-truth novel-view images; the mean absolute error (MAE) between the masked predicted and ground-truth depth maps; and the intersection-over-union (IoU) between the predicted and ground-truth object masks.

Baselines. We compare with two state-of-the-art baselines for novel-view synthesis and 3D reconstruction in unbounded, real-world scenes: NeRF++ [41] and NeuS [32]. We do not compare with the state-of-the-art classical multi-view stereo algorithm COLMAP [25], because the dataset's ground-truth point clouds and depth maps were obtained using this algorithm and are extremely noisy and sparse for this reflective and low-texture category. We focus on two strong and well-regarded baselines to avoid the evaluation becoming prohibitively expensive (each baseline trains for at least 24h on a single GPU).

Implementation Details. Following prior art [32,39], we implement the SDF network ϕ_{SDF} as an 8-layer MLP with hidden dimension 256, position-encoded inputs (6 frequencies) [18], and geometric initialisation for the network weights [1]. The material, diffuse, and specular networks are also implemented as MLPs with 4/2/4 hidden layers, with a 4-frequency positional encoding on the normal and view directions. NeRF++ [41] is used as the background model. We follow the hierarchical sampling strategy of NeuS [32] with 64 coarse, 64 fine, and 32 background samples per ray, with 1024 rays sampled per batch. We optimise the network with Adam [14] and an initial learning rate of 5e-4 and train for 300K iterations on a single GPU. Unless otherwise stated, we use the hyperparameters $[\lambda, \lambda^{\text{d}}, \lambda^{\text{l}}, \lambda^{\text{e}}] = [0.1, 0.01, 0.001, 0.1]$. Complete implementation details are reported in the appendix, and code is available at https://github.com/eldar/snes.

Table 1. Results on the random and structured test splits of the CO3D cars dataset [24]. We report the peak signal-to-noise ratio (PSNR), mean squared error (MSE), and LPIPS distance between the estimated and ground-truth masked images, the mean absolute error (MAE) between the estimated and ground-truth masked depth maps, and the intersection-over-union (IoU) of the estimated and ground-truth masks.

	Random split (overlapping views)					Structured split (biased views)				
	PSNR	MSE	LPIPS	MAE	IoU	PSNR	MSE	LPIPS	MAE	IoU
	RGB	RGB	RGB	Depth	Mask	RGB	RGB	RGB	Depth	Mask
Method	↑	↓	↓	↓	↑	↑	↓	↓	↓	↑
NeRF++ [41]	21.4	0.007	0.407	0.222	–	13.9	0.041	0.581	0.177	–
NeuS [32]	**23.3**	**0.005**	0.355	0.108	0.523	13.4	0.046	0.556	0.105	0.566
SNeS (ours)	**23.3**	**0.005**	**0.348**	**0.086**	**0.787**	**14.1**	**0.039**	**0.503**	**0.077**	**0.906**

5.2   Random Test Split

For this experiment, we use the train–test split provided by the dataset for single scene experiments ("test_known" and "test_unseen") [24], assigned at random

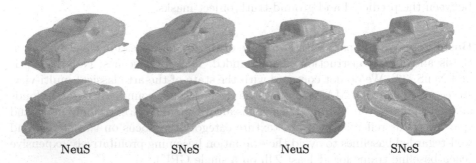

NeuS   SNeS   NeuS   SNeS

Fig. 4. Qualitative results on the structured test split of the CO3D cars dataset [24].

Fig. 5. Novel view renderings of the partly-observed (left) and fully-observed (right) sides. Top row: NeuS. Middle row: SNeS. Bottom row: SNeS albedo maps.

from the frames of the video. This evaluates the model's ability to interpolate between a dense set of views. This is the standard mode for evaluating novel view synthesis algorithms. Note that only 64% (14) of the video sequences entirely encircle the object of interest, with the remainder having coverage of as little as 135°. Our method is able to reconstruct the unseen sides, though we are unable to evaluate this as the requisite ground-truth is not present in the dataset. The results are shown in Table 1, and indicate that applying symmetry does not harm the performance of the baseline model, and indeed improves the geometry. This suggests that the model is able to learn the symmetry and integrate information from both sides of the object to improve the geometry estimate.

5.3   Structured Test Split

We propose a new train–test split that simulates the common situation where one side of an object is observed more thoroughly than the other. This tests the model's ability to handle variable view densities and incomplete information. To do so, we select the 14 test scenes where the camera circumnavigates the object, and define a test split that sets aside all camera poses within a 130° sector emanating from the object's centre, approximately perpendicular to the plane of bilateral symmetry. Thus, one side of the car is only seen obliquely. From the set aside poses, we systematically sample 8 test frames. This setting makes it possible for existing methods to reconstruct both sides of the object, but tests how well they are able to reconstruct the side that is viewed less fully. The results are shown in Table 1. Our method consistently outperforms the

Table 2. Ablation study on a random subset of our structured test split of the CO3D cars dataset [24]. We report the peak signal-to-noise ratio (PSNR), mean squared error (MSE), and LPIPS distance between the estimated and ground-truth masked images, the mean absolute error (MAE) between the estimated and ground-truth masked depth maps, and the intersection-over-union (IoU) of the estimated and ground-truth masks.

Method	PSNR RGB ↑	MSE RGB ↓	LPIPS RGB ↓	MAE Depth ↓	IoU Mask ↑
SNeS (ours)	**14.3**	**0.0372**	**0.564**	0.0706	0.894
$+\mathcal{L}^{\text{lighting}}$	13.7	0.0425	0.585	**0.0685**	0.914
$-\mathcal{L}^{\text{diffuse}}$	**14.3**	**0.0372**	0.566	0.0722	**0.917**
$-\mathcal{L}^{\text{col}}$	13.7	0.0422	0.576	0.0782	0.906

Ground-truth   Ours $+\mathcal{L}^{\text{lighting}}$ $-\mathcal{L}^{\text{diffuse}}$ $-\mathcal{L}^{\text{col}}$

Fig. 6. Qualitative ablation study. Novel view renderings of the unseen side.

NeuS baseline on the novel view synthesis metrics and significantly improves the depth accuracy on the unseen side, validating the effectiveness of our approach. Qualitative comparisons are shown in Figs. 4 and 5, demonstrating high-fidelity reconstructions and synthesised views on the unseen side. We include additional high-resolution qualitative results in the supplementary material, including a comparison of the different appearance components (material and lighting).

5.4   Ablation Study

To investigate the effect of different components, we ablate our model's performance on 4 randomly selected scenes from our structured test split of the CO3D cars dataset, as shown in Table 2 and Fig. 6. We ablate with respect to the model without the lighting loss (ours), since this loss is designed to produce qualitatively convincing renders in the absence of image evidence, but is unlikely to be quantitatively accurate in those areas. We indeed see that the symmetric lighting loss has a detrimental effect on the image-based results, predominantly in situations where direct sunlight is applied to the shadowed side of the car and vice versa. However, the resulting renders are qualitatively preferable, as shown at high resolution in the appendix. We verify that removing the diffuse colour loss harms the geometry, since it helps decouple the symmetric and asymmetric properties facilitating symmetry learning. Finally, we show that removing the symmetry loss $\mathcal{L}^{col}$ significantly reduces the visual and geometric quality.

6   Discussion and Limitations

One limitation of the approach is that it is only beneficial for objects or scenes with significant symmetries. However, this is not as restrictive as it might seem. While the natural world rarely has large-scale symmetries, they abound in the human environment, in architecture and object design. For example, out of the CO3D dataset, 90% of the categories have at least one major symmetry, such as ball, baseball bat, bench, bicycle, book, bottle, and bowl. More significant limitations of the approach, then, are that the type and number of symmetries must be specified in advance, that the symmetry has to be significant enough to be learnable from the data, and that the initialisation of the symmetry plane or axis must be good enough to avoid the network getting trapped in a local optimum. An alternative approach, such as multiple initialisations, may be necessary to prevent the latter in some cases. Another limitation of the approach is that it requires a significant number of views, even with the reductions facilitated by the symmetry. This is because it can be difficult to optimise the symmetry parameters, such as finding the reflection plane, without reasonable view coverage. This could be mitigated by learning about symmetries from a collection of scenes, such that a single view may be enough to partially constrain the symmetry plane parameters [44]. Our approach also relies on good camera estimates. While this requirement can be relaxed [34], additional unknown variables are likely to make the symmetry parameters more difficult to estimate. Finally, our approach does not explicitly handle symmetries that are present at different scales or resolutions. For example, a decorated cake or a pizza is symmetric at one scale, but may violate that symmetry when considering the finer details.

7   Conclusion

We have presented a 3D reconstruction and novel-view synthesis method for partly-symmetric objects, which learns symmetry parameters from a collection of posed images and uses the learned symmetry to share information across the model. This reduces the need for dense multi-view coverage of the object, making it suitable for use on in-the-wild data like the CO3D dataset. We demonstrated our algorithm on objects that exhibit bilateral symmetry at most locations— cars—and show that it can reconstruct unobserved regions with high fidelity.

Acknowledgements. We are grateful for support from Continental AG (E.I., D.C.), the European Research Council Starting Grant (IDIU 638009, E.I., D.C.), and the Royal Academy of Engineering (RF/201819/18/163, J.H.).

References

1. Atzmon, M., Lipman, Y.: SAL: sign agnostic learning of shapes from raw data. In: Proceedings of the IEEE Conference on Computer Vision and Pattern Recognition, pp. 2565–2574 (2020)
2. Azinović, D., Martin-Brualla, R., Goldman, D.B., Nießner, M., Thies, J.: Neural RGB-D surface reconstruction. In: Proceedings of the IEEE Conference on Computer Vision and Pattern Recognition, pp. 6290–6301 (2022)
3. Barron, J.T., Mildenhall, B., Tancik, M., Hedman, P., Martin-Brualla, R., Srinivasan, P.P.: Mip-NeRF: a multiscale representation for anti-aliasing neural radiance fields. In: Proceedings of the International Conference on Computer Vision, pp. 5855–5864 (2021)
4. Bi, S., et al.: Neural reflectance fields for appearance acquisition. arXiv preprint arXiv:2008.03824 (2020)
5. Boss, M., Braun, R., Jampani, V., Barron, J.T., Liu, C., Lensch, H.: NeRD: neural reflectance decomposition from image collections. In: Proceedings of the International Conference on Computer Vision, pp. 12684–12694 (2021)
6. Chen, W., et al.: DIB-R++: learning to predict lighting and material with a hybrid differentiable renderer. Adv. Neural. Inf. Process. Syst. **34**, 22834–22848 (2021)
7. Chen, X., et al.: AutoSweep: recovering 3D editable objects from a single photograph. IEEE Trans. Visual Comput. Graphics **26**(3), 1466–1475 (2018)
8. Fawcett, R., Zisserman, A., Brady, J.M.: Extracting structure from an affine view of a 3D point set with one or two bilateral symmetries. Image Vis. Comput. **12**(9), 615–622 (1994)
9. Forsyth, D.A., Mundy, J.L., Zisserman, A., Rothwell, C.A.: Recognising rotationally symmetric surfaces from their outlines. In: Sandini, G. (ed.) ECCV 1992. LNCS, vol. 588, pp. 639–647. Springer, Heidelberg (1992). https://doi.org/10.1007/3-540-55426-2_68
10. François, A.R., Medioni, G.G., Waupotitsch, R.: Mirror symmetry → 2-view stereo geometry. Image Vis. Comput. **21**(2), 137–143 (2003)

11. Gordon, G.G.: Shape from symmetry. In: Intelligent Robots and Computer Vision VIII: Algorithms and Techniques, vol. 1192, pp. 297–308. SPIE (1990)
12. Gropp, A., Yariv, L., Haim, N., Atzmon, M., Lipman, Y.: Implicit geometric regularization for learning shapes. In: Proceedings of the International Conference on Machine Learning, pp. 3569–3579 (2020)
13. Huynh, D.: Affine reconstruction from monocular vision in the presence of a symmetry plane. In: Proceedings of the 7th International Conference on Computer Vision, Kerkyra, Greece (1999)
14. Kingma, D.P., Ba, J.: Adam: a method for stochastic optimization. arXiv preprint arXiv:1412.6980 (2014)
15. Lombardi, S., Simon, T., Saragih, J., Schwartz, G., Lehrmann, A., Sheikh, Y.: Neural volumes: learning dynamic renderable volumes from images. ACM Trans. Graph. **38**(4), 1–14 (2019)
16. Martin-Brualla, R., Radwan, N., Sajjadi, M.S., Barron, J.T., Dosovitskiy, A., Duckworth, D.: NeRF in the wild: neural radiance fields for unconstrained photo collections. In: Proceedings of the IEEE Conference on Computer Vision and Pattern Recognition, pp. 7210–7219 (2021)
17. Mescheder, L., Oechsle, M., Niemeyer, M., Nowozin, S., Geiger, A.: Occupancy networks: learning 3D reconstruction in function space. In: Proceedings of the IEEE Conference on Computer Vision and Pattern Recognition, pp. 4460–4470 (2019)
18. Mildenhall, B., Srinivasan, P.P., Tancik, M., Barron, J.T., Ramamoorthi, R., Ng, R.: NeRF: representing scenes as neural radiance fields for view synthesis. In: Proceedings of the European Conference on Computer Vision, pp. 405–421. Springer (2020)
19. Mukherjee, D.P., Zisserman, A., Brady, J.M.: Shape from symmetry - detecting and exploiting symmetry in affine images. Philos. Trans. R. Soc. Lond. **351**, 77–106 (1995)
20. Oechsle, M., Peng, S., Geiger, A.: UNISURF: unifying neural implicit surfaces and radiance fields for multi-view reconstruction. In: Proceedings of the International Conference on Computer Vision, pp. 5589–5599 (2021)
21. Park, J.J., Florence, P., Straub, J., Newcombe, R., Lovegrove, S.: DeepSDF: learning continuous signed distance functions for shape representation. In: Proceedings of the IEEE Conference on Computer Vision and Pattern Recognition, pp. 165–174 (2019)
22. Phillips, C.J., Lecce, M., Daniilidis, K.: Seeing glassware: from edge detection to pose estimation and shape recovery. In: Robotics: Science and Systems, vol. 3, p. 3 (2016)
23. Phong, B.T.: Illumination for computer generated pictures. Commun. ACM **18**(6), 311–317 (1975)
24. Reizenstein, J., Shapovalov, R., Henzler, P., Sbordone, L., Labatut, P., Novotny, D.: Common objects in 3D: large-scale learning and evaluation of real-life 3D category reconstruction. In: Proceedings of the International Conference on Computer Vision, pp. 10901–10911 (2021)
25. Schönberger, J.L., Frahm, J.M.: Structure-from-motion revisited. In: Proceedings of the IEEE Conference on Computer Vision and Pattern Recognition, pp. 4104–4113 (2016)
26. Sinha, S.N., Ramnath, K., Szeliski, R.: Detecting and reconstructing 3D mirror symmetric objects. In: Fitzgibbon, A., Lazebnik, S., Perona, P., Sato, Y., Schmid, C. (eds.) ECCV 2012. LNCS, vol. 7573, pp. 586–600. Springer, Heidelberg (2012). https://doi.org/10.1007/978-3-642-33709-3_42

27. Srinivasan, P.P., Deng, B., Zhang, X., Tancik, M., Mildenhall, B., Barron, J.T.: NeRV: neural reflectance and visibility fields for relighting and view synthesis. In: Proceedings of the IEEE Conference on Computer Vision and Pattern Recognition, pp. 7495–7504 (2021)
28. Tewari, A., et al.: State of the art on neural rendering. In: Computer Graphics Forum, vol. 39, pp. 701–727. Wiley Online Library (2020)
29. Tewari, A., et al.: Advances in neural rendering. In: Computer Graphics Forum, vol. 41, pp. 703–735. Wiley Online Library (2022)
30. Thrun, S., Wegbreit, B.: Shape from symmetry. In: Proceedings of the International Conference on Computer Vision, vol. 2, pp. 1824–1831. IEEE (2005)
31. Verbin, D., Hedman, P., Mildenhall, B., Zickler, T., Barron, J.T., Srinivasan, P.P.: Ref-NeRF: structured view-dependent appearance for neural radiance fields. In: 2022 IEEE/CVF Conference on Computer Vision and Pattern Recognition (CVPR), pp. 5481–5490. IEEE (2022)
32. Wang, P., Liu, L., Liu, Y., Theobalt, C., Komura, T., Wang, W.: NeuS: learning neural implicit surfaces by volume rendering for multi-view reconstruction. In: Advances in Neural Information Processing Systems (2021)
33. Wang, Q., et al.: IBRNet: learning multi-view image-based rendering. In: Proceedings of the IEEE Conference on Computer Vision and Pattern Recognition, pp. 4690–4699 (2021)
34. Wang, Z., Wu, S., Xie, W., Chen, M., Prisacariu, V.A.: NeRF−: neural radiance fields without known camera parameters. arXiv preprint arXiv:2102.07064 (2021)
35. Wu, S., Makadia, A., Wu, J., Snavely, N., Tucker, R., Kanazawa, A.: De-rendering the world's revolutionary artefacts. In: Proceedings of the IEEE Conference on Computer Vision and Pattern Recognition, pp. 6338–6347 (2021)
36. Wu, S., Rupprecht, C., Vedaldi, A.: Unsupervised learning of probably symmetric deformable 3D objects from images in the wild. In: Proceedings of the IEEE Conference on Computer Vision and Pattern Recognition, pp. 1–10 (2020)
37. Wu, S., Rupprecht, C., Vedaldi, A.: Unsupervised learning of probably symmetric deformable 3D objects from images in the wild. IEEE Trans. Pattern Anal. Mach. Intell. (2021). https://doi.org/10.1109/TPAMI.2021.3076536
38. Yariv, L., Gu, J., Kasten, Y., Lipman, Y.: Volume rendering of neural implicit surfaces. Adv. Neural. Inf. Process. Syst. **34**, 4805–4815 (2021)
39. Yariv, L., et al.: Multiview neural surface reconstruction by disentangling geometry and appearance. In: Advances in Neural Information Processing Systems, vol. 33, pp. 2492–2502 (2020). https://nips.cc/Conferences/2020/
40. Yu, A., Ye, V., Tancik, M., Kanazawa, A.: PixelNeRF: neural radiance fields from one or few images. In: Proceedings of the IEEE Conference on Computer Vision and Pattern Recognition, pp. 4578–4587 (2021)
41. Zhang, K., Riegler, G., Snavely, N., Koltun, V.: NeRF++: analyzing and improving neural radiance fields. arXiv preprint arXiv:2010.07492 (2020)
42. Zhang, R., Isola, P., Efros, A.A., Shechtman, E., Wang, O.: The unreasonable effectiveness of deep features as a perceptual metric. In: Proceedings of the IEEE Conference on Computer Vision and Pattern Recognition, pp. 586–595 (2018)
43. Zhang, X., Srinivasan, P.P., Deng, B., Debevec, P., Freeman, W.T., Barron, J.T.: NeRFactor: neural factorization of shape and reflectance under an unknown illumination. ACM Trans. Graph. **40**(6), 1–18 (2021)
44. Zhou, Y., Liu, S., Ma, Y.: NeRD: neural 3D reflection symmetry detector. In: Proceedings of the IEEE Conference on Computer Vision and Pattern Recognition, pp. 15940–15949 (2021)

HDR-Plenoxels: Self-Calibrating High Dynamic Range Radiance Fields

Kim Jun-Seong[1], Kim Yu-Ji[2], Moon Ye-Bin[1], and Tae-Hyun Oh[1,2(✉)]

[1] Department of Electrical Engineering, Pohang University of Science and Technology (POSTECH), Pohang, South Korea
{junseong.kim,ybmoon,taehyun}@postech.ac.kr
[2] Graduate School of AI, Pohang University of Science and Technology (POSTECH), Pohang, South Korea
ugkim@postech.ac.kr
https://github.com/postech-ami/HDR-Plenoxels

Abstract. We propose high dynamic range (HDR) radiance fields, HDR-Plenoxels, that learn a plenoptic function of 3D HDR radiance fields, geometry information, and varying camera settings inherent in 2D low dynamic range (LDR) images. Our voxel-based volume rendering pipeline reconstructs HDR radiance fields with only multi-view LDR images taken from varying camera settings in an end-to-end manner and has a fast convergence speed. To deal with various cameras in real-world scenario, we introduce a tone mapping module that models the digital in-camera imaging pipeline (ISP) and disentangles radiometric settings. Our tone mapping module allows us to render by controlling the radiometric settings of each novel view. Finally, we build a multi-view dataset with varying camera conditions, which fits our problem setting. Our experiments show that HDR-Plenoxels can express detail and high-quality HDR novel views from only LDR images with various cameras.

Keywords: High dynamic range (HDR) · Novel view synthesis · Plenoptic function · Voxel-based volume rendering · Neural rendering

1 Introduction

The human eyes can respond to a wide range of brightness in the real-world scene, from very bright to very dark, *i.e.*, high dynamic range (HDR). Human can see an object with its color and texture even in dark and dim conditions. However, standard digital cameras capture a limited range of scenes due to the low dynamic range (LDR) limits of the sensors. HDR imaging and display techniques have been developed to overcome the sensors' limits and to share the beauty of the world as humans see.

J.-S. Kim and Y.-J. Kim—Authors contributed equally to this work.
T.-H. Oh—Joint affiliated with Yonsei University, Korea.

Supplementary Information The online version contains supplementary material available at https://doi.org/10.1007/978-3-031-19824-3_23.

S. Avidan et al. (Eds.): ECCV 2022, LNCS 13692, pp. 384–401, 2022.
https://doi.org/10.1007/978-3-031-19824-3_23

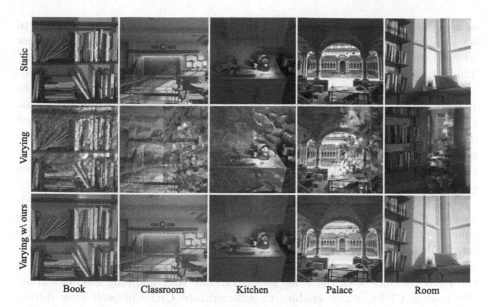

Static

Varying

Varying w\ ours

Book   Classroom   Kitchen   Palace   Room

Fig. 1. Qualitative results of static and varying camera settings. The static and varying mean camera conditions include exposure, white balance, and CRF. The static camera condition is a controlled environmental setting, *i.e.*, all views of the scene have the same components of exposure, white balance, and CRF. The varying camera condition is alternated environmental settings, *i.e.*, all views of the scene have different components. Each row represents camera conditions, and each column represents the class of synthetic datasets.

Existing studies on HDR recovery [4,19,31,34] have been mainly focused on a static view HDR from a monocular perspective or HDR video recovery. HDR images are typically reconstructed by merging multi-exposure LDR images in a fixed camera pose. To recover an HDR image from LDR images taken from various viewpoints, the prior work [3,34] suggests accumulating images after alignment. However, the HDR reconstruction results of the prior work are still limited to a given view. To overcome the limitations, we propose a method of restoring HDR radiance fields with only multi-view LDR images. The LDR images taken from varying cameras are used, where various radiometric conditions exist, including different exposure, white balance, and camera response functions (CRFs).

The novel view synthesis requires additional information to reconstruct and synthesize unseen views, given a sparse set of images. Previous arts inject prior knowledge by voxel-based [13,43,44], mesh-based [2,4,37,41], multi-plane [40], and volume rendering [15,22] to cope with the problem. Recently, Plenoxels [43] have shown outstanding efficiency of the voxel-based method by assigning spherical harmonics to each voxel corners. While maintaining comparable qualitative results, the Plenoxels achieve two orders of magnitude faster rendering speed than the Neural Radiance Fields (NeRF) [22], which utilizes the implicit neural functions to conduct volume rendering.

In this work, we extend Plenoxels by proposing HDR-Plenoxels that can restore HDR radiance fields with LDR images under diverse camera conditions in an end-to-end manner. Although many saturated regions are appeared due to a wide dynamic range of a scene during training, our HDR-Plenoxels are robust to saturated regions and represents accurate geometry and color at rendering. This is achieved by proposing a tone mapping module that approximates the in-camera pipeline, camera image signal processings (ISPs), from HDR radiance to LDR intensity, allowing flexible modeling of various radiometric and non-linear camera conditions. The tone mapping parameters are spontaneously learned during training. In addition, once 3D HDR radiance fields and the CRFs are fitted, our tone-mapping module can be freely controlled to synthesize different radiometric conditions of rendering in any view. Our tone mapping module can easily be attached to most volume rendering model variants as well.

Our HDR-Plenoxels mainly consist of two parts: 1) HDR radiance fields modeled by Plenoxels followed by 2) the tone mapping module. The differentiable tone mapping module renders HDR radiance values composited from Plenoxels into LDR intensity, which allows to back-propagate gradients to the voxel grid so that spherical harmonics (SH) coefficients and opacity are learned to span the HDR radiance with the scene geometry. The tone mapping module explicitly models CRFs, which enables to self-calibrate CRFs of each view during training. In addition, thereby, we can easily edit the rendering property by just controlling the radiometric curves of each novel view by virtue of the disentangled parameterization of the module. Our experiments show that our method achieves preferable performance on novel view synthesis with varying radiometric conditions of input. Our main contributions are summarized as follows:

- We propose an end-to-end HDR radiance field learning method, HDR-Plenoxels, that allow learning 3D HDR radiance fields from only multi-view and varying radiometric conditioned LDR images as input.
- We model the tone mapping module based on a physical camera imaging pipeline that maps HDR to LDR with explicit radiometric functions.
- We build a multi-view dataset containing varying camera conditions. The dataset includes synthetic and real scenes with various camera settings such as white balance, exposure, and CRF.

2   Related Work

The scope of our work contains HDR imaging, voxel-based volume rendering, and its calibration. We overview the prior work in each perspective in this section.

HDR Imaging. A standard HDR recovery [4] directly accumulates multi-exposure LDR images taken from a fixed camera pose, which are prone to ghosting artifacts in dynamic scenes. To cope with the limitation, several studies [3,34] suggest a method to recover an HDR image from LDR images taken from moving cameras by using image alignment methods, such as image warping or optical flows. However, they still suffer from large camera motion and occlusion due to the imperfect warping model in the alignment step. In contrast, our work exploits multi-view geometric information, which enables to obtain radiometrically calibrated HDR radiance of an entire 3D scene and to be robust even with large camera motion and occlusion.

Typical digital cameras can only deal with LDR due to the limited dynamic range and the inherent nonlinear components, which represent the real-world scene irradiance inferiorly in pixel values and cause discrepancy to the real scene during the image processing [4]. To obtain an accurate HDR, we have to understand an inherent nonlinear relationship of the camera, *i.e.*, the radiometric properties of camera ISPs. Traditional radiometric calibration models the components of physical pipelines of cameras, including white balance and CRF, and optimizes to reconstruct HDR from only given LDR images [4] or HDR-LDR image pairs [11]. The latest learning-based approaches [5,6,17] suggest an implicit model-based method but require ground truth HDR images paired with LDR images for training. Liu *et al.* [14] replace an implicit function with an explicit physical camera model, enhancing the HDR image reconstruction quality. Our method shares the same advantages by adopting the explicit tone-mapping module. Note that our HDR-Plenoxels learn HDR radiances up to scale, given only LDR images but without ground truth HDR images and camera parameters.

Volume Rendering. Volume rendering is the method of understanding the 3D information inherited in two-dimensional images to render images at unseen views, called novel views. Existing methods [22,35] show high performance in complex geometric shapes but require high memory for high expressiveness.

The recent volume rendering methods utilize multi-layer perceptron (MLP) based implicit neural function to predict the signed distance fields [7,24,42] and occupancy [20,26,32], and demonstrate the high expressiveness with high compression power. In particular, Neural Radiance Fields (NeRF) [22] shows fine-detailed rendering performance unprecedently. However, the NeRF-related studies [18,25,27,39] have a limitation of high training and rendering time complexity due to the forward process in every sampling point. Several studies [8,23,30,36] try to modify the neural network to reduce the computation at each sampling point to reduce the time cost.

Octree structure-based methods [13,43,44] are efficient methods that reduce rendering time by virtue of their structure. Plenoxels [43] optimize the octree structure with spherical harmonics instantaneously, requiring only tens of minutes of training time to achieve detailed rendering results comparable to NeRF. Our method uses Plenoxels as a volume rendering backbone for efficient rendering, and further expands the expression power of Plenoxels to 3D HDR radiance fields with negligible computational cost.

Calibrated Volume Rendering. Several methods [9,18,21,29] are proposed for better performance with relaxed assumptions in volume rendering. NeRF in the Wild (NeRF-W) [18] uses web images in the wild setting for reconstruction, which deals with varying camera conditions and occluded objects by introducing a handling mechanism by appearance and transient embeddings.

ADOP [29] is a point-based HDR neural rendering pipeline that consists of a differentiable and physically-based tone mapping. Due to the differentiable property, all the varying camera conditions can be optimized. However, ADOP requires dense COLMAP structure-from-motion package [33] results as input,

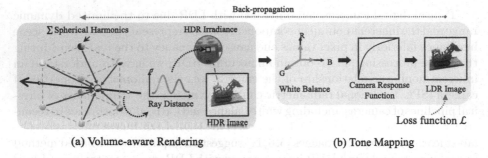

(a) Volume-aware Rendering   (b) Tone Mapping

Fig. 2. Overall pipeline of HDR-Plenoxels. 1) Plenoxels synthesize an HDR image from HDR radiance by ray-marching, then 2) the differentiable tone-mapping function maps from HDR to LDR in an end-to-end manner. The self-calibration is done by minimizing the residual between the synthesized LDR image and the captured one with regularizations.

which have expensive time costs. Also, the method itself has expensive time and memory costs during training due to the point-based method. Distinctive from ADOP, our method is cost efficient by utilizing an octree-based structure and camera poses without dense COLMAP.

Recently, HDR-NeRF [9] tackles a similar HDR radiance field problem with ours by NeRF, which is concurrent work with us. The work requires known exposure information, and does not take into account white balance parameters, in contrast to ours.

3   HDR Radiance Fields from Multi-view LDR Images

Our work aims to reconstruct HDR radiance fields of a visual scene from multi-view LDR input images. In this section, we first present the overall pipeline of our method (Fig. 2), which is composed of two parts, 1) volume-aware HDR image rendering (Sect. 3.1), and 2) synthesis of LDR images through the tone mapping module (Sect. 3.2). We then explain the details of optimization (Sect. 3.3).

3.1   Volume-Aware Rendering to HDR Images

To reconstruct the HDR irradiance fields from the multi-view LDR images, we parameterize HDR radiance fields by voxel grid with spherical harmonics (SH) called Plenoxels [43]. A bounded three-dimensional space of interest is represented as a sparse voxel grid, each of which has opacity and SH coefficients. The volume rendering method adopts a coarse-to-fine training scheme similar to NSVF [13]. The learning process starts with a broad and uniformly divided sparse voxel grid, and the voxels are upsampled to make a denser grid as learning progresses. The voxels are pruned according to the occupancy threshold to reduce the computational cost, as training iterations go. Upsampling and pruning are applied simultaneously during training and repeated several times.

As SH can compactly represent any functions on a sphere well with a few SH bases [1,44], it has been vastly used in graphics for HDR environmental lighting [28] and glossy representation [16], which motivates our HDR radiance representation. Furthermore, recent work has adopted SH in volume contents and has demonstrated its effectiveness in implicitly expressing the non-Lambertian effects [12,40]. Our HDR irradiance field modeling by SH based volume-aware rendering exploits these advantages.

The SH in each voxel grid is used for view representation. All the colors over every direction of a sphere are spanned by a weighted sum of pre-defined spherical basis functions and coefficients corresponding to each function. Therefore, the corresponding color can be defined for each specific angle. Each vertex of the voxel grid stores 28-dimensional vectors: 27 for SH coefficients (9 coefficients per color channels) and 1 for voxel opacity σ. Empirically, the values of the SH coefficients change significantly during training which makes the training unstable. To mitigate this, we initialize the color to grey by adding offset color 0.5 and the voxel opacity value to 0.1.

The HDR volume rendering part determines the color of a rendered HDR image pixel $\hat{C}(\mathbf{r})$ by ray-marching the color and opacity of points sampled along a ray in a bounded three-dimensional voxel grid volume. At any 3D point $(\mathbf{x}, \mathbf{y}, \mathbf{z})$ and normalized viewing angle $(\mathbf{v_x}, \mathbf{v_y}, \mathbf{v_z})$ inside the voxel grid of Plenoxels, the color and opacity of the point are trilinearly-interpolated from eight nearby voxel vertices. For a camera center $\mathbf{o}$ and given an image pixel grid, we can define the ray $\mathbf{r} = \mathbf{o} + t\mathbf{d}$ starting from $\mathbf{o}$ to each pixel in the camera along the direction $\mathbf{d}$. After that, N sampling points are sampled over the ray at regular intervals $\delta_i = t_{i+1} - t_i$. The color and opacity of each sampled point are denoted as $\mathbf{c_i}$ and σ_i, respectively, and T_i is the accumulated transmittance value up to the i-th point. The ray-marching proceeds as follows:

$$\hat{C}(\mathbf{r}) = \sum_{i=1}^{N} T_i \left(1 - \exp\left(-\sigma_i \delta_i\right)\right) \mathbf{c_i}, \text{ where } T_i = \exp\left(-\sum_{j=1}^{i-1} \sigma_j \delta_j\right). \quad (1)$$

The ray sampling randomly selects rays among the set of rays toward all pixels of an image for efficient training.

3.2 Tone Mapping

The tone mapping stage converts an HDR image into a LDR image. We denote a pixel value of an HDR image and a LDR image as I_h and I_l, respectively. The output of volume rendering is HDR radiance fields, and we obtain I_h as output by ray marching HDR radiance fields. We represent our explicit tone mapping module as a function $\mathcal{T}$ with radiometric parameters θ, i.e., $I_l = \mathcal{T}(I_h, \theta)$.

The tone mapping function $\mathcal{T}$ consists of two stages. Each stage is parameterized by the physical property of its components and represented as separate functions: white balance function w and camera response function (CRF) g. Note that we regard the white balance scale parameters are merged with the exposure value and learn at once. Two sub functions are applied sequentially as $I_l = \mathcal{T}(I_h) = g \circ (w(I_h))$ which follows the image acquisition process of common digital cameras.

Specifically, first, for a specific ray $\mathbf{r}$, the pixel color of an HDR image $C_h(\mathbf{r})$ is calculated through ray-marching. The white balance function $w(\cdot)$ is applied to $C_h(\mathbf{r})$ with $\theta_w = [w_r, w_g, w_b]^\top \in \mathbb{R}^3$, and the function output is a pixel of white balance calibrated image I_w. That is, given each channel components of $C_h(\mathbf{r}) = [c_h^r, c_h^g, c_h^h] \in \mathbb{R}^3$,

$$
I_w = w(C_h(\mathbf{r}), \theta_w) = C_h(\mathbf{r}) \odot \theta_w = \begin{bmatrix} c_h^r \\ c_h^g \\ c_h^b \end{bmatrix} \odot \begin{bmatrix} w_r \\ w_g \\ w_b \end{bmatrix} = \begin{bmatrix} w_r c_h^r \\ w_g c_h^g \\ w_b c_h^b \end{bmatrix}, \tag{2}
$$

where the operator $\odot$ stands for an element-wise product. To make white balance physically proper, we regularize θ_w to be a positive value.

The CRF g is applied to I_w. We paramterize non-linear CRFs with an approximated discrete piece-wise linear function. The function $g(\cdot)$ is divided into 256 intervals which are allocated for uniformly sampled points in $[0,1]$, and parameterized by 256 control points. The pixel value of white balance corrected image I_w is mapped to I_l by interpolating corresponding CRF values of nearby control points in domain. To make the CRF $g(\cdot)$ differentiable, we adapt 1D grid-sampling used in [10]. According to Debevec et al. [4], the CRF is enforced to follow the following boundary condition: $I_l = g(I_w; \theta_g)$, $g(0) = 0$, $g(1) = 1$. A range beyond the dynamic range $[0,1]$ is thresholded when applying the CRF g. To propagate a loss on the saturation region of the rendered images during training HDR radiance fields, we apply the leaky-thresholding method:

$$
g_{leaky}(x) = \begin{cases} \alpha x, & x < 0 \\ g(x), & 0 \leq x \leq 1 \\ -\frac{\alpha}{\sqrt{x}} + \alpha + 1, & 1 < x, \end{cases} \tag{3}
$$

where α is the thresholding coefficient.

3.3 Optimization

Leaky Saturation Mask. When taking a scene with a wide dynamic range, the LDR image may contain over- and under-saturation. In the saturated region, no cue exists to guess correct geometric and photometric information due to missing texture. This acts as outliers when taking into account it in the loss computation during optimization. To suppress the impact of saturation regions and prevent our recovery from being biased, we use saturation masking in the loss computation (Fig. 3). We define our leaky saturation mask as follows:

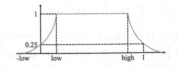

Fig. 3. Leaky saturation mask.

$$\text{mask}(x) = \begin{cases} \left(\frac{x+\text{low}}{2\text{low}}\right)^2 & x < \text{low}, \\ 1, & \text{low} \leq x \leq \text{high}, \\ \left(\frac{2-x}{2(1-\text{high})}\right)^2 & x > \text{high}, \end{cases} \tag{4}$$

We empirically set $\text{low} = 0.15$ and $\text{high} = 0.9$ for the experiment.

White Balance Initialization. There exists inherent ambiguity in the camera imaging pipeline, which occurs due to the inherent entangled relationship across model components in the pipeline, e.g., for an image of a view, if we increase its exposure time twice while reducing the white balance of the view by half, the resulting image appears same with the original setting of exposure time; i.e., there are multiple solutions that can produce the same LDR images.

We avoid such cumbersome ambiguity between exposure and white balance in our method. We use only the white balance module w to express both exposure as a scale and white balance ratio following the study [11] to workaround the scale ambiguity between exposure and white balance. However, with this representation, the overall scale of the white balance is trained extremely small or large. Therefore, we calculate the averaged color of all inputs $(r_a, g_a, b_a) \in \mathbb{R}^3$, select a reference image which has the closest value of (r_a, g_a, b_a), and fix the white balance of the reference image $(r_{ref}, g_{ref}, b_{ref}) \in \mathbb{R}^3$. This acts as regularization. This helps white balance be learned on the proper scale, which also means we have a suitable exposure value.

However, still there exists a similar ambiguity between *SH coefficients* and *white balance*. We observe that when the exposure differences are significantly dynamic among neighborhood views, observed LDR intensity differences by exposure times are misunderstood as the cause of the high-frequency reflectance[1] of the scene and different white balances. This tends to produce wrong geometry as the rays have reached different parts of the scene. We also found that the more abrupt the intensity changes among neighborhood views are, the more dominant the coefficients corresponding to high-frequency SH components become.

As a simple workaround, we use white balance information for each camera as a prior to resolve the ambiguity in the SH side. We introduce white balance initialization for each camera that guides initial solutions to physically plausible solutions; thereby, the optimization process becomes more stable and faster to converge to desirable solutions, and robust to such harsh input conditions. We estimate a reference color ratio by comparing per-image averaged pixel values to averaging each rgb value from the entire image set S. Then the initial white balances $wb_{c,i}$ for each camera, where $c \in \{r, g, b\}$ of each image I_i are initialized as $wb_{c,i} = \frac{\text{mean}_{k \in I_i}(c_k)}{\text{mean}_{j \in S}(c_j)}$.

---

[1] The high-frequency reflectance refers to the case that a subtle view direction change results in drastic reflectance ratio changes, such as glossy materials.

Spherical Harmonics Regularization. In the harsh input condition case, where LDR images obtained from neighborhood views have significantly dynamic exposure differences, the above initialization stabilizes early optimization steps. If the optimization speed of the white balance does not match that of the SH coefficients, the ambiguity may arise again in later optimization steps. In order to regularize this, we introduce SH coefficient masking that allows scheduling to learn from diffuse reflectance property (view direction invariant radiance) first to view direction sensitive ones, i.e., low frequency order SH to high frequency ones. We apply SH masking to the coefficient of SH of degrees 2 and 3. We decrease the rate of SH masking by 1/5 per epoch during the early five epochs for gradual learning. After the early five epochs, we update SH of all degrees with full rate, i.e., no SH masking. This scheduling notably stabilizes the optimization for the harsh condition input case.

Loss Functions. We optimize our pipeline w.r.t. voxel opacity, SH coefficients, white balance and CRF, given multi-view LDR images as input, with the following objective function:

$$\mathcal{L} = \mathcal{L}_{recon} + \lambda_{TV}\mathcal{L}_{TV} + \lambda_{smooth}\mathcal{L}_{smooth}, \qquad (5)$$

where each term is defined as follows. The LDR reconstruction loss for i-th image is defined as:

$$\mathcal{L}_{recon} = \frac{1}{|\mathcal{R}|} \sum_{\mathbf{r} \in \mathcal{R}} M_i(\mathbf{r}) \| I_i\left(\Pi_i(\mathbf{r})\right) - \mathcal{T}\left(\hat{C}(\mathbf{r})\right) \|_2^2, \qquad (6)$$

where $\Pi_i(\cdot)$ denotes the camera projection operator from a ray to the 2D pixel coordinate of the i-th LDR image, and $M_i(\mathbf{r}) = \mathtt{mask}(I_i(\Pi_i(\mathbf{r})))$ denotes the saturation mask computed from input LDR images. We randomly sample rays $\mathbf{r}_{sampled}$ among the possible set of rays $\mathcal{R}$ from $\mathcal{N}$ images. The loss is calculated through a color difference between the rendered results and the ground truth LDR values along each ray $\mathbf{r}_{sampled}$ considering the saturation masking $M_i(\mathbf{r})$. The total loss is applied by normalizing the number of ray sampled. The other two terms are for regularization. The total variation loss is defined as:

$$\mathcal{L}_{TV} = \frac{1}{|\mathcal{V}|} \sum_{\mathbf{v} \in \mathcal{V}, d \in [D]} \sqrt{\Delta_x^2(\mathbf{v}, d) + \Delta_y^2(\mathbf{v}, d) + \Delta_z^2(\mathbf{v}, d) + \epsilon}, \qquad (7)$$

where the differences Δ. are calculated between successive voxels along each respective (x, y, z)-axis, e.g., the d-th voxel value at (x, y, z) and the d-th voxel value at $(x + 1, y, z)$ for x-axis. The total variation loss is applied for opacity σ and SH coefficients separately. This encourages spatial and color consistency in the voxel space. In implementation, we use different weighting for SH coefficients $\lambda_{TV,SH}$ and opacity $\lambda_{TV,\sigma}$.

The smoothness loss is for obtaining a physically appropriate CRF [4] such that CRFs increase smoothly, which is defined as:

$$\mathcal{L}_{smooth} = \sum_{i=1}^{N} \sum_{e \in [0,1]} g_i''(e)^2, \qquad (8)$$

where $g''(e)$ denotes the second order derivative of CRFs *w.r.t.* the domain of CRFs. We set $\lambda_{TV,\sigma} = 5 \cdot 10^{-4}$, $\lambda_{TV,SH} = 1 \cdot 10^{-2}$ and $\lambda_{smooth} = 1 \cdot 10^{-3}$.

4   Experiments

We compare the qualitative and quantitative results of our HDR-Plenoxels from three perspectives: LDR image rendering accuracy, HDR irradiance image, and 3D structure reconstruction quality. We also conduct an ablation study on our tone-mapping components to demonstrate that our tone mapping components efficiently understand camera settings.

Fig. 4. **Qualitative novel view results in real scenes with various camera conditions.** Each row represents different real scenes, and the column represents HDR novel view rendering, LDR novel view rendering, LDR GT (*i.e.*, inputs of training), and RGB histograms of LDR novel view and LDR GT in order. Histograms of RGB are clipped from 0 to 150 at RGB radiance and from 0 to 10^4 at the number of RGB radiance for visual better visibility.

4.1   Experimental Settings

Due to the lack of open datasets proper to our experiment setting, *i.e.*, images under varying camera conditions, we collect synthetic and real data that fits our experimental settings: images with various exposure, white balance, and vignetting taken from the same camera poses. The details of the synthetic and real datasets are explained in the supplementary material.

Baseline and Counterparts. We compare our proposed method against the following three models: original Plenoxels (baseline) [43], NeRF-A [18], and Approximate Differentiable One-Pixel Point Rendering (ADOP) [29]. We conduct experiments for two environmental settings: the varying camera, which has various environments that are exposure, white balance, and CRF, and the static camera, which has controlled environments. Plenoxels with inputs of the static camera are assumed to be an upper bound of the task performance.

Evaluation. HDR-Plenoxels can learn the 3D HDR radiance fields and freely control the appearance of a novel view, *i.e.*, unseen viewpoint, according to camera conditions. We compute the similarity between the LDR image synthesized in the novel view and the ground truth LDR image to measure the performance for the novel view synthesis tasks. For quantitative evaluation, we use three metrics, PSNR, SSIM [38], and LPIPS [45]. Our method and NeRF-A need to learn tone mapping function and appearance embedding parameters separately at each image. We cannot predict the tone mapping parameters at novel views; thus, we use the left half of the test image (*i.e.*, unseen view) at training and evaluate the performance of the right half with learned parameters.

Table 1. Quatitative results of novel view synthesis on synthetic data. Values are average of the results for the test data of each scene. For evaluation, ADOP exploits all the input images as it needs dense reconstruction. For the other models, the left half of the image was included in the learning data and learned, and tested on the unseen right half of the image. Our model shows overall high performance compared to other models. $\mathcal{S}$ denote the static and $\mathcal{V}$ is the varying datasets. The blue and red color stand for the **best** and the second best, respectively.

Type	Method	Book PSNR↑	Book SSIM↑	Book LPIPS↓	Classroom PSNR↑	Classroom SSIM↑	Classroom LPIPS↓	Monk PSNR↑	Monk SSIM↑	Monk LPIPS↓	Room PSNR↑	Room SSIM↑	Room LPIPS↓	Kitchen PSNR↑	Kitchen SSIM↑	Kitchen LPIPS↓
$\mathcal{S}$	Baseline	22.53	0.796	0.293	28.71	0.902	0.261	27.15	0.848	0.281	30.70	0.912	0.183	33.43	0.957	0.138
$\mathcal{V}$	Baseline	11.92	0.454	0.597	12.83	0.542	0.660	15.81	0.535	0.542	13.28	0.599	0.643	18.24	0.718	0.496
	ADOP	22.15	0.824	**0.291**	21.04	0.800	0.345	21.92	0.764	0.392	19.25	0.834	0.329	20.13	0.827	0.280
	NeRF-A	**28.44**	**0.873**	0.310	29.30	0.895	0.295	27.33	0.793	0.398	**30.32**	0.891	**0.234**	31.30	0.928	0.233
	Ours	27.49	0.837	0.292	**29.87**	**0.908**	**0.284**	**28.27**	**0.852**	**0.297**	28.70	**0.900**	0.291	**31.53**	**0.936**	**0.156**

4.2 High Dynamic Range Radiance Fields

We evaluate the effectiveness of our HDR-Plenoxels by comparison against the counterpart models, which handle images with varying appearances.

Comparison. Our HDR-Plenoxels learn HDR radiance fields from LDR input images with various camera conditions at real scenes. The results in Fig. 4 represent the novel view synthesis of HDR images and tone mapping from HDR to LDR images in real datasets. Compared to previous work focusing on single perspective HDR [4], our method can reconstruct HDR radiance fields from varying camera LDR images with several multi-view. We can render novel LDR views from reconstructed HDR radiance fields with an explicitly controllable tone mapping module.

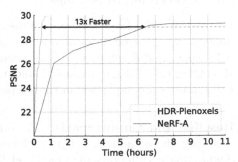

Fig. 5. Computation time.

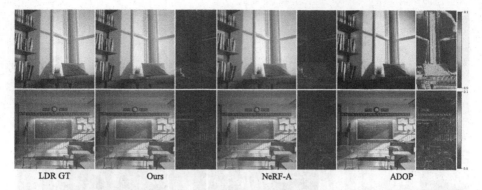

Fig. 6. Comparison in synthetic scenes with varying camera conditions. The left half of an image is used for training the tone mapping module T, and the right half is for the test. By applying the trained T at left half, we can synthesize the novel view images. MSE maps of each result are on the right of the corresponding render results.

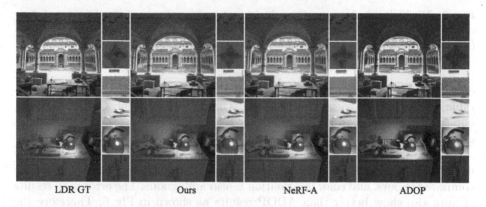

Fig. 7. Qualitative results from the experiments between other counterparts. Our result represents fine-grained and proper color rendering results. All experiments are trained with various radiometric conditions. The left half of an image is used in training, and the right half is only used to measure quantitative results.

Quantitative results are summarized in Table 1. NeRF-A [18] shows comparable novel view synthesis results. However, it cannot explicitly decompose each camera condition, such as exposure, white balance, and CRF, because those information is implicitly entangled in the embedding; thus, it cannot predict *radiance* in contrast to ours. NeRF-A also needs considerable training time compared to our neural networks free method as shown in Fig. 5. To reach PSNR 29, our method takes 30 min, but NeRF-A takes 6 h and 30 min, which is 13 times larger. We use RTX 3090 for training.

The qualitative results of rendered novel LDR views on our synthetic dataset are shown in Fig. 6 and Fig. 7. ADOP tends to incorrectly estimate the camera components such as white balance, vignetting, and CRF, leading to inaccurate

LDR GT   HDR novel view   HDR GT

Fig. 8. High dynamic range rendering at saturation points. Our novel view rendering results show robustness to under-saturation (1st row) and over-saturation (2nd row) points because we train the HDR radiance fields.

color-mapped rendering results. The rendering result of NeRF-A shows comparable quality to ours overall, but the details tend to be deficient. On the contrary, our HDR-Plenoxels can render relatively accurate LDR images in both aspects of color and geometry.

ADOP [29] shows deficient novel view rendering results compared to our method. In the Fig. 7, they cannot reconstruct fine-grained geometry structure compared to ours, and color information is also ambiguous. The error map results of ours also show better than ADOP results as shown in Fig. 6. Therefore the visual quality of the novel view results of ADOP is not satisfying, and we outperform quantitative results with PSNR metrics at Table 1.

To verify that our model can restore HDR radiance field robust to under- or over- saturated points, we qualitatively compared HDR details on saturation points as shown in Fig. 8. There are severe dark or bright points, so some regions are saturated and cannot distinguish color or geometry. We train with these saturated LDR input images at our HDR-Plenoxels. They can render high-quality HDR novel views, which means we can handle wide dynamic ranges and render non-saturated novel HDR views.

We also compare our HDR-Plenoxels and original Plenoxels [43] with images of different camera settings in Fig. 1. The novel view synthesis results of the Plenoxels with static camera condition are considered as our upper bound performance and represent fine-detailed rendering results with clear color estimation. With the varying camera setting, the Plenoxels fail to reconstruct proper 3D geometry, especially in the right-half of images unseen view during training. These results imply that previous volume rendering methods such as Plenoxels are prone to degrade at varying camera conditions due to their static photometric assumption, which needs to be compensated with additional regularization. With our tone mapping module, the quality of novel view synthesis improves considerably by showing comparable details to original Plenoxels trained with static LDR images. This demonstrates that our tone mapping module precisely disentangles varying cameras and properly reconstructs informative HDR radiance fields.

Ablation Studies. To verify the effectiveness of our tone mapping module components, we conduct an ablation study by removing each component as in Table 2. We report the averaged results of five synthetic datasets. Comparing (A) with (B), the considerable performance improvement by the white balance module means that disentanglement of exposure and white balance helps to learn accurate geometry and color.

Table 2. Effect of tone mapping components on novel view synthesis. **WB** stands for white balance, **VIG** for vignetting, and **CRF** for camera response function. (A) is the baseline. (D) is the performance of ours.

	WB	VIG	CRF	PSNR↑	SSIM↑	LPIPS↓
(A)				14.42	0.569	0.587
(B)	✓			23.03	0.811	0.355
(C)	✓	✓		21.12	0.799	0.352
(D)	✓		✓	**29.34**	**0.876**	**0.294**
(E)	✓	✓	✓	26.73	0.878	0.264

The performance degradation from (B) to (C) and from (D) to (E) implies that decomposing the vignetting effect of images is inconducive. According to the characteristics of our tone mapping module, which trains quickly according to the learning speed of SH, the vignetting function significantly increases the complexity of the model and hinders training. The result in (D) demonstrates that all components of our tone mapping module are essential.

To confirm whether the CRF expression is suitable for defining camera non-linearity we proceed an ablation study by replacing CRF function. Our method adopt a piece-wise linear CRF model that considers the mapping relationship of the pixel value. NeRF-W and HDR-NeRF [9] suggest that an implicit function can represent CRF. We compare the performance between our explicit piece-wise linear function and implicit function such as

Fig. 9. Implicit CRF. GT (left), MLP (middle), and ours (right).

multi-layer perceptrons (MLPs). Following the concurrent work, HDR-NeRF, we replace our CRF with three MLPs to predict each color channel. As shown in Fig. 9, rendering results are degraded with MLP-based CRF. The averaged PSNR of all synthetic datasets with ours is 28.18, and the MLP-based method is 26.11. We verify that our physically-based explicit tone mapping module outperforms than MLP-based method since our CRF satisfies real-world physical conditions and can disentangle non-linear components correctly.

5   Conclusion

We present an HDR-Plenoxels, which learn to synthesize 3D HDR radiance field from multi-view LDR images of the varying camera by self-calibrating radiometric characteristics. Distinctive from conventional HDR reconstruction methods, ours can get a novel view, depth, and 3D HDR radiance fields simultaneously in an end-to-end manner. We investigate that the white balance and CRF functions are critical factors among the in camera components and find an effective representation of the CRF function. With these observations, we present a simple and straightforward physical-based tone-mapping module, which can be easily attached to various volume rendering models extending one's usability. Using the tone mapping module, we can take fine-grained HDR rendering results as well as LDR images of varying cameras, *e.g.*, exposure, white balance, and CRF. The HDR radiance fields represent real-world scenes more realistically with a wide dynamic range similar to the way human sees. Our work could improve the experiences of many HDR-based applications, such as movie post-production. Since we focus on covering HDR radiance fields of static scenes, it has room to improve in dealing with dynamic objects as future work.

Acknowledgment. This work was partly supported by the National Research Foundation of Korea (NRF) grant funded by the Korea government (MSIT) (No. NRF-2021R1C1C1006799), Institute of Information & communications Technology Planning & Evaluation (IITP) grant funded by the Korea government (MSIT) (No. 2022-0-00290, Visual Intelligence for Space-Time Understanding and Generation based on Multilayered Visual Common Sense; and No. 2019-0-01906, Artificial Intelligence Graduate School Program(POSTECH)).

References

1. Basri, R., Jacobs, D.: Lambertian reflectance and linear subspaces. IEEE Trans. Pattern Anal. Mach. Intell. **25**(2), 218–233 (2003)
2. Buehler, C., Bosse, M., McMillan, L., Gortler, S., Cohen, M.: Unstructured lumigraph rendering. In: ACM Transactions on Graphics (SIGGRAPH) (2001)
3. Chen, G., Chen, C., Guo, S., Liang, Z., Wong, K.Y.K., Zhang, L.: HDR video reconstruction: a coarse-to-fine network and a real-world benchmark dataset. In: IEEE International Conference on Computer Vision (ICCV), pp. 2502–2511 (2021)
4. Debevec, P.E., Taylor, C.J., Malik, J.: Modeling and rendering architecture from photographs: a hybrid geometry- and image-based approach. In: ACM Transactions on Graphics (SIGGRAPH) (1996)
5. Eilertsen, G., Kronander, J., Denes, G., Mantiuk, R.K., Unger, J.: HDR image reconstruction from a single exposure using deep CNNs. ACM Trans. Graph. **36**(6), 1–15 (2017)
6. Endo, Y., Kanamori, Y., Mitani, J.: Deep reverse tone mapping. ACM Trans. Graph. **36**(6), 1–10 (2017)
7. Gropp, A., Yariv, L., Haim, N., Atzmon, M., Lipman, Y.: Implicit geometric regularization for learning shapes. In: International Conference on Machine Learning (ICML) (2020)

8. Hedman, P., Srinivasan, P.P., Mildenhall, B., Barron, J.T., Debevec, P.: Baking neural radiance fields for real-time view synthesis. In: IEEE International Conference on Computer Vision (ICCV), pp. 5875–5884 (2021)

9. Huang, X., Zhang, Q., Feng, Y., Li, H., Wang, X., Wang, Q.: HDR-NeRF: high dynamic range neural radiance fields. In: IEEE Conference on Computer Vision and Pattern Recognition (CVPR), pp. 18398–18408 (2022)

10. Jaderberg, M., Simonyan, K., Zisserman, A., Kavukcuoglu, K.: Spatial transformer networks. Adv. Neural Inf. Process. Syst. **28** (2016)

11. Kim, S.J., Lin, H.T., Lu, Z., Süsstrunk, S., Lin, S., Brown, M.S.: A new in-camera imaging model for color computer vision and its application. IEEE Trans. Pattern Anal. Mach. Intell. **34**(12), 2289–2302 (2012)

12. Kuang, Z., Olszewski, K., Chai, M., Huang, Z., Achlioptas, P., Tulyakov, S.: NeROIC: neural object capture and rendering from online image collections. Comput. Res. Repository (CoRR) (2022)

13. Liu, L., Gu, J., Lin, K.Z., Chua, T.S., Theobalt, C.: Neural sparse voxel fields. Adv. Neural. Inf. Process. Syst. **33**, 15651–15663 (2021)

14. Liu, Y.L., et al.: Single-image HDR reconstruction by learning to reverse the camera pipeline. In: IEEE Conference on Computer Vision and Pattern Recognition (CVPR), pp. 1651–1660 (2020)

15. Lombardi, S., Simon, T., Saragih, J., Schwartz, G., Lehrmann, A., Sheikh, Y.: Neural volumes: learning dynamic renderable volumes from images. ACM Trans. Graph. **38**(4) (2019)

16. Mahajan, D., Ramamoorthi, R., Curless, B.: A theory of frequency domain invariants: spherical harmonic identities for BRDF/lighting transfer and image consistency. IEEE Trans. Pattern Anal. Mach. Intell. **30**(2), 197–213 (2008)

17. Marnerides, D., Bashford-Rogers, T., Hatchett, J., Debattista, K.: ExpandNet: a deep convolutional neural network for high dynamic range expansion from low dynamic range content. In: European Association for Computer Graphics (Eurographics) (2019)

18. Martin-Brualla, R., Radwan, N., Sajjadi, M.S.M., Barron, J.T., Dosovitskiy, A., Duckworth, D.: NeRF in the wild: neural radiance fields for unconstrained photo collections. In: IEEE Conference on Computer Vision and Pattern Recognition (CVPR), pp. 7210–7219 (2021)

19. Mertens, T., Kautz, J., Van Reeth, F.: Exposure fusion. In: 15th Pacific Conference on Computer Graphics and Applications (PG 2007), pp. 382–390. IEEE (2007)

20. Mescheder, L., Oechsle, M., Niemeyer, M., Nowozin, S., Geiger, A.: Occupancy networks: learning 3D reconstruction in function space. In: IEEE Conference on Computer Vision and Pattern Recognition (CVPR), pp. 4460–4470 (2019)

21. Mildenhall, B., Hedman, P., Martin-Brualla, R., Srinivasan, P., Barron, J.T.: NeRF in the dark: high dynamic range view synthesis from noisy raw images. In: IEEE Conference on Computer Vision and Pattern Recognition (CVPR), pp. 16190–16199 (2022)

22. Mildenhall, B., Srinivasan, P.P., Tancik, M., Barron, J.T., Ramamoorthi, R., Ng, R.: NeRF: representing scenes as neural radiance fields for view synthesis. In: European Conference on Computer Vision (ECCV) (2020)

23. Neff, T., et al.: DONeRF: towards real-time rendering of compact neural radiance fields using depth oracle networks. Comput. Graph. Forum **40**(4), 45–59 (2021)

24. Park, J.J., Florence, P., Straub, J., Newcombe, R., Lovegrove, S.: DeepSDF: learning continuous signed distance functions for shape representation. In: IEEE Conference on Computer Vision and Pattern Recognition (CVPR), pp. 165–174 (2019)

25. Park, K., et al.: Nerfies: deformable neural radiance fields. In: IEEE International Conference on Computer Vision (ICCV), pp. 5865–5874 (2021)
26. Peng, S., Niemeyer, M., Mescheder, L., Pollefeys, M., Geiger, A.: Convolutional occupancy networks. In: Vedaldi, A., Bischof, H., Brox, T., Frahm, J.-M. (eds.) ECCV 2020. LNCS, vol. 12348, pp. 523–540. Springer, Cham (2020). https://doi.org/10.1007/978-3-030-58580-8_31
27. Pumarola, A., Corona, E., Pons-Moll, G., Moreno-Noguer, F.: D-NeRF: neural radiance fields for dynamic scenes. In: IEEE Conference on Computer Vision and Pattern Recognition (CVPR), pp. 10318–10327 (2020)
28. Ramamoorthi, R., Hanrahan, P.: An efficient representation for irradiance environment maps. In: Proceedings of the 28th Annual Conference on Computer Graphics and Interactive Techniques, pp. 497–500 (2001)
29. Rückert, D., Franke, L., Stamminger, M.: ADOP: approximate differentiable one-pixel point rendering. ACM Trans. Graph. **41**(4), 1–14 (2022)
30. Reiser, C., Peng, S., Liao, Y., Geiger, A.: KiloNeRF: speeding up neural radiance fields with thousands of tiny MLPs. In: IEEE International Conference on Computer Vision (ICCV), pp. 14335–14345 (2021)
31. Robertson, M.A., Borman, S., Stevenson, R.L.: Dynamic range improvement through multiple exposures. In: Proceedings 1999 International Conference on Image Processing (Cat. 99CH36348), vol. 3, pp. 159–163. IEEE (1999)
32. Saito, S., Huang, Z., Natsume, R., Morishima, S., Kanazawa, A., Li, H.: PIFu: pixel-aligned implicit function for high-resolution clothed human digitization. IEEE International Conference on Computer Vision (ICCV), pp. 2304–2314 (2019)
33. Schonberger, J.L., Frahm, J.M.: Structure-from-motion revisited. In: CVPR, pp. 4104–4113 (2016)
34. Sen, P., Kalantari, N.K., Yaesoubi, M., Darabi, S., Goldman, D.B., Shechtman, E.: Robust patch-based HDR reconstruction of dynamic scenes. ACM Trans. Graph. **31**(6), 1–11 (2012)
35. Sitzmann, V., Zollhöfer, M., Wetzstein, G.: Scene representation networks: continuous 3D-structure-aware neural scene representations. Adv. Neural Inf. Process. Syst. **32** (2020)
36. Song, W., et al.: AutoInt: automatic feature interaction learning via self-attentive neural networks. In: Proceedings of the 28th ACM International Conference on Information and Knowledge Management, pp. 1161–1170 (2019)
37. Waechter, M., Moehrle, N., Goesele, M.: Let there be color! Large-scale texturing of 3D reconstructions. In: Fleet, D., Pajdla, T., Schiele, B., Tuytelaars, T. (eds.) ECCV 2014. LNCS, vol. 8693, pp. 836–850. Springer, Cham (2014). https://doi.org/10.1007/978-3-319-10602-1_54
38. Wang, Z., Simoncelli, E., Bovik, A.: Multiscale structural similarity for image quality assessment. In: Asilomar Conference on Signals, Systems & Computers, vol. 2, pp. 1398–1402. IEEE (2003)
39. Wang, Z., Wu, S., Xie, W., Chen, M., Prisacariu, V.A.: NeRF-: neural radiance fields without known camera parameters. arXiv preprint arXiv:2102.07064 (2021)
40. Wizadwongsa, S., Phongthawee, P., Yenphraphai, J., Suwajanakorn, S.: NeX: real-time view synthesis with neural basis expansion. In: IEEE Conference on Computer Vision and Pattern Recognition (CVPR), pp. 8534–8543 (2021)
41. Wood, D.N., et al.: Surface light fields for 3D photography. ACM Trans. Graph. (2000)
42. Yariv, L., et al.: Multiview neural surface reconstruction by disentangling geometry and appearance. Adv. Neural. Inf. Process. Syst. **33**, 2492–2502 (2020)

43. Yu, A., Fridovich-Keil, S., Tancik, M., Chen, Q., Recht, B., Kanazawa, A.: Plenoxels: radiance fields without neural networks. In: IEEE Conference on Computer Vision and Pattern Recognition (CVPR), pp. 5501–5510 (2022)
44. Yu, A., Li, R., Tancik, M., Li, H., Ng, R., Kanazawa, A.: PlenOctrees for real-time rendering of neural radiance fields. In: IEEE International Conference on Computer Vision (ICCV), pp. 5752–5761 (2021)
45. Zhang, R., Isola, P., Efros, A.A., Shechtman, E., Wang, O.: The unreasonable effectiveness of deep features as a perceptual metric. In: CVPR, pp. 586–595 (2018)

NeuMan: Neural Human Radiance Field from a Single Video

Wei Jiang[1,2]([✉]), Kwang Moo Yi[1,2], Golnoosh Samei[1], Oncel Tuzel[1], and Anurag Ranjan[1]

[1] Apple, Cupertino, USA
{golnoosh,otuzel,anuragr}@apple.com
[2] The University of British Columbia, Vancouver, Canada
{jw221,kmyi}@cs.ubc.ca

Abstract. Photorealistic rendering and reposing of humans is important for enabling augmented reality experiences. We propose a novel framework to reconstruct the human and the scene that can be rendered with novel human poses and views from just a single in-the-wild video. Given a video captured by a moving camera, we train two NeRF models: a human NeRF model and a scene NeRF model. To train these models, we rely on existing methods to estimate the rough geometry of the human and the scene. Those rough geometry estimates allow us to create a warping field from the observation space to the canonical pose-independent space, where we train the human model in. Our method is able to learn subject specific details, including cloth wrinkles and accessories, from just a 10 s video clip, and to provide high quality renderings of the human under novel poses, from novel views, together with the background. Code will be available at https://github.com/apple/ml-neuman.

1 Introduction

The quality of novel view synthesis has been dramatically improved since the introduction of Neural Radiance Fields (NeRF) [26]. While originally proposed to reconstruct a static scene with a set of posed images, it has since been quickly extended to dynamic scenes [15, 28, 29] and uncalibrated scenes [17, 44]. Recent efforts also focus on animation of these radiance field models [12, 19, 31, 32, 39] of human, with the aid of large controlled datasets, further extending the application domain of radiance-field-based modeling to enable augmented reality experiences.

In this work, we are interested in the scenario where only one single video is provided, and our goal is to reconstruct the human model and the static scene model, and enable novel pose rendering of the human, without any expensive multi-cameras setups or manual annotations. However, even with the recent advancements in NeRF methods, this is far from being trivial. Existing methods [19, 32] require multi-cameras setup, consistent lighting and exposure, clean

---

W. Jiang—Work done while interning at Apple.

Supplementary Information The online version contains supplementary material available at https://doi.org/10.1007/978-3-031-19824-3_24.

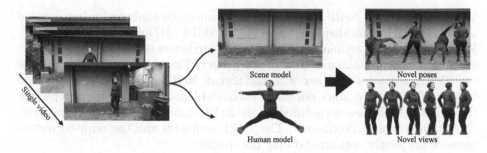

Fig. 1. Teaser – We train neural human and scene radiance fields from a single in-the-wild video to enable rendering with novel human poses and novel views.

Table 1. Method capacity comparison – We illustrate the capabilities of existing methods. Compared to other methods, ours is the only one with the ability to render both the scene and the reposed human from a single video.

	Scene background	Novel poses	Single video	Compositionality
HyperNeRF [29]	✔	✗	✔	✗
ST-NeRF [12]	✔	✗	✗	✔
Neural Actor [19]	✗	✔	✗	✗
HumanNeRF [46]	✗	✗	✔	✗
Vid2Actor [45]	✗	✔	✔	✗
Ours	✔	✔	✔	✔

backgrounds, and accurate human geometry to train the NeRF models. As shown in Table 1, HyperNeRF [29] models a dynamic scene based on a single video, but cannot be driven by human poses. ST-NeRF [12] reconstructs each individual with a time dependent NeRF model from multiple cameras, but the editing is limited to the transformation of the bounding box. Neural Actor [19] can generate novel poses of a human but requires multiple videos. HumanNeRF [46] builds a human model based on a single video with manually annotated masks, but doesn't show generalization to novel poses. Vid2Actor [45] generates novel poses of a human with a model trained on a single video but cannot model the background. We address these problems by introducing *NeuMan*, that reconstructs both the human and the scene with the ability to render novel human poses and novel views, from a single in-the-wild video.

NeuMan is a novel framework for training NeRF models for both the human and the scene, which allows high-quality pose-driven rendering as shown in Fig. 1. Given a video captured by a moving camera, we first estimate the human pose, human shape, human masks, as well as the camera poses, sparse scene model, and depth maps using conventional off-the-shelf methods [3,8,10,24,37,41].

We then train two NeRF models, one for the human and one for the scene guided by the segmentation masks estimated from Mask-RCNN [10]. Additionally, we regularize the scene NeRF model by fusing together depth estimates from both multi-view reconstruction [37] and monocular depth regression [24].

We train the human NeRF model in a pose independent canonical volume guided by a statistical human shape and pose model, SMPL [21] following Liu et al. [19]. We refine the SMPL estimates from ROMP [41] to better serve the training. However, these refined estimates are still not perfect. Therefore, we jointly optimize the SMPL estimates together with the human NeRF model in an end-to-end fashion. Furthermore, since our static canonical human NeRF cannot represent the dynamics that is not captured by the SMPL model, we introduce an error-correction network to counter it. The SMPL estimates and the error-correction network are jointly optimized during the training.

In summary,

- we propose a framework for neural rendering of a human and a scene from a single video without any extra devices or annotations;
- we show that our method allows high quality rendering of human under novel poses, from novel views, together with the scene;
- we introduce an end-to-end SMPL optimization and an error-correction network to enable training with erroneous estimates of the human geometry;
- our approach allows for the composition of the human and the scene NeRF models enabling applications such as telegathering.

2   Related Work

As our work is mainly based on neural radiance fields, we first review works on NeRF with a focus on works that aim to control and condition the radiance fields—a necessity for rendering a human in the scene in the context of creating visual and immersive experiences [19,32]. We also briefly review works that aim to reanimate and perform novel view synthesis of provided scenes.

Neural Radiance Fields (NeRF). Since its first introduction [26], NeRF has become a popular way [5] to model scenes and render them from novel views thanks to its high quality rendering. Representing a scene as a radiance field has the advantage that *by-construction* you will be able to render the scene from any supported views through volume rendering. Efforts have been made to adapt NeRF to dynamic scenes [15,28,29], and to even edit and compose scenes with various NeRF models [9,49], widening their potential application. While these methods have shown interesting and exciting results, they often require separate training of editable instances [9] or careful curation of training data [32]. In this work, we are interested in an *in-the-wild* setup.

Particularly related to our task of interest, various efforts have been made towards NeRF models conditioned by explicit human models, such as SMPL [21] or 3D skeleton [12,19,31,32,39]. Neural Body [32] associates a latent code to each SMPL vertex, and use sparse convolution to diffuse the latent code into the volume in observation space. Neural Actor [19] learns the human in the canonical space by a volume warping based on the SMPL [21] mesh transformation, it also utilize a texture map to improve the final rendering quality. Animatable NeRF [31] learns a blending weight field in both observation space and canonical space, and optimize for a new blending weight field for novel poses. ST-NeRF [12] separates the human into each 3D bounding box, and learns the dynamic human within each bounding box. It doesn't require to estimate the precise human geometry, but it cannot extrapolate to unseen poses since it is dependent on time(frame). However, all these methods require an expensive multi-cameras setup to obtain the ground truth bounding boxes, 3D poses or SMPL estimates. In other words, they cannot be used for our purpose of reconstructing and neural rendering of human from a *single* video, *without* extra devices or annotations, and *with* potential pose estimation errors.

HumanNeRF [46], a concurrent work, aims to create free-viewpoint rendering of human from a single video. While similar to our work, there are two main differences between HumanNeRF [46] and ours. First, HumanNeRF [46] relies on manual mask annotation to separate the human from the background, while our method learns the decomposition of the human and the scene with the help of modern detectors. Second, HumanNeRF [46] represents motion as a combination of the skeletal and the non-rigid transformations, causing ambiguous or unknown transformations under novel poses, while ours mitigates the ambiguity by using explicit human mesh. Another similar work is Vid2Actor [45], which builds animatable human from a single video by learning a voxelized canonical volume and skinning weights jointly. Although with similar goals, our method is able to reconstruct sharp human geometry with less than 40 images, comparing to thousands frames are required for Vid2Actor, our method is data-efficient.

Neural Rendering of Humans. Majority of the literature [1,20,22,27,35] only consider the problem of reposing a human from a source image to a target image without changing the viewing angle which is essential for enabling new immersive experiences. Grigorev et al. [7] tackled a similar problem to ours, namely resynthesizing a human image with a novel pose view given a single input image. They divide the problem into estimating the full texture map of the human body surface from partial texture observations and synthesizing a novel view given the estimated texture map from the first step. They employ two convolutional neural networks (CNN) for each of these steps. With the second one responsible for generating the novel pose consuming the output of the first CNN. This method does not explicitly model the source and target pose, so it is unclear how well it would perform for a novel pose. Sarkar et al. [36] additionally consider re-rendering in a novel view as well as novel pose from a single input image. They use a parametric 3D human mesh to recover body pose and shape and a high dimensional UV feature map to encode appearance.

2.1   Preliminary: Neural Radiance Fields (NeRF)

For completeness, we quickly review the standard NeRF model [26]. We denote the NeRF network as $\mathcal{F}_\Theta$ with parameters Θ, that estimates the RGB color $\mathbf{c}$ and density σ of a given a 3D location $\mathbf{x}$ and a viewing direction $\mathbf{d}$ as

$$\mathbf{c}, \sigma = \mathcal{F}_\Theta\left(\mathbf{x}, \mathbf{d}\right) . \tag{1}$$

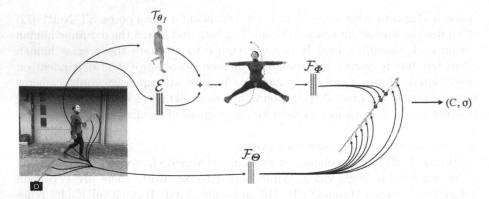

Fig. 2. Overview – The blue samples are for the scene branch, and the red samples for the human branch. The human samples are warped to canonical space based on the estimated SMPL mesh and the error-correction network. After the RGB and opacity are evaluated, the two sets of samples are merged for the final integral to obtain the pixel color. See Sect. 3.2 for more details. (Color figure online)

The radiance field function $\mathcal{F}_\Theta$ is often implemented with multi-layer perceptrons (MLPs) with positional encodings [26,42] and periodic activations [2]. The pixel color is then obtained by integrating a discretized ray $\mathbf{r}$ that consists of N samples from the camera in the view direction $\mathbf{d}$ through the volume given by

$$\mathbf{C}\left(\mathbf{r}\right) = \sum_{i=1}^{N} w_i \mathbf{c}_i; \quad \text{where,} \ w_i = \exp\left(-\sum_{j=1}^{i-1} \sigma_j \delta_j\right)\left(1 - \exp\left(-\sigma_i \delta_i\right)\right), \quad (2)$$

and δ_i is the distance between two adjacent samples. Here, the accumulated alpha value of a pixel, which represents transparency, can be obtained by $\alpha\left(\mathbf{r}\right) = \sum_{i=1}^{N} w_i$.

3   Method

An overview of our framework is shown in Fig. 2. Our framework is composed mainly of two NeRF networks[1]: the *human* NeRF that encodes the appearance and geometry of the human in the scene, conditioned on the human pose; and the *scene* NeRF that encodes how the background looks like. We train the scene NeRF first, then train the human NeRF conditioned on the trained scene NeRF.

3.1   The Scene NeRF Model

The scene NeRF model is analogous to the background model in traditional motion detection work [6,16,40], except it's a NeRF. For the scene NeRF model,

---

[1] In our work, we assume a single human being in the scene, but this can be trivially extended.

we construct a NeRF model and train it with only the pixels that are deemed to be from the background.

For a ray $\mathbf{r}$, given the human segmentation mask as $\mathcal{M}(\mathbf{r})$ where $\mathcal{M}(\mathbf{r}) = 1$ if the ray corresponds to the human and $\mathcal{M}(\mathbf{r}) = 0$ corresponding the background, we formulate the reconstruction loss for the scene NeRF model as

$$\mathcal{L}_{s,rgb}(\mathbf{r}) = (1 - \mathcal{M}(\mathbf{r})) \left\| \mathbf{C}_s(\mathbf{r}) - \hat{\mathbf{C}}(\mathbf{r}) \right\| , \qquad (3)$$

where $\hat{\mathbf{C}}(\mathbf{r})$ corresponds to the ground-truth RGB color value and $\mathbf{C}_s(\mathbf{r})$ corresponds to rendered color value from the scene NeRF model.

As in Video-NeRF [48], simply minimizing Eq. 3 leads to 'hazy' objects floating in the scene. Therefore, following Video-NeRF [48], we resolve this by adding a regularizer on the estimated density, and forcing it to be zero for space that should be empty—the space between the camera and the scene. For each ray $\mathbf{r}$, we sample the terminating depth value $\hat{z}_{\mathbf{r}} = \mathbf{D}_{fuse}(\mathbf{r})$ and minimize

$$\mathcal{L}_{s,empty}(\mathbf{r}) = \int_{t_n}^{\alpha \hat{z}_{\mathbf{r}}} \sigma_s(\mathbf{r}(t)) \, dt , \qquad (4)$$

where $\alpha = 0.8$ is a slack margin to avoid strong regularization when the depth estimates are inaccurate. The final loss that we use to train our scene NeRF is

$$\mathcal{L}_s = \mathcal{L}_{s,rgb}(\mathbf{r}) + \lambda_{empty} \mathcal{L}_{s,empty}(\mathbf{r}) , \qquad (5)$$

where $\lambda_{empty} = 0.1$ is a hyper parameter controlling the emptiness regularizer in all our experiments.

Preprocessing. Given a video sequence, we use COLMAP [37,38] to obtain the camera poses, sparse scene model, and multi-view-stereo (MVS) depth maps. Typically, MVS depth maps $\mathbf{D}_{mvs}$ contain holes, which we fill with the help of dense monocular depth maps $\mathbf{D}_{mono}$ using Miangoleh et al. [24]. We fuse $\mathbf{D}_{mvs}$ and $\mathbf{D}_{mono}$ together to obtain a fused depth map $\mathbf{D}_{fuse}$ with consistent scale. In more detail, we find a linear mapping between the two depth maps using the pixels that have both estimates. We then transform the values of $\mathbf{D}_{mono}$ with this mapping to match the depth scale in $\mathbf{D}_{mvs}$ to obtain a fused depth map $\mathbf{D}_{fuse}$ by filling in the holes. For retrieving human segmentation maps we apply Mask-RCNN [10]. We further dilate the human masks by 4% to ensure the human is completely masked out. With the estimated camera poses and the background masks, we train the scene NeRF model only over the background.

3.2   The Human NeRF Model

To build a human model that can be pose-driven, we require the model to be pose independent. Therefore, we define a canonical space based on the 大 -pose (Da-pose) SMPL [21] mesh, similar to [19,31]. In comparison to the traditional T-pose, Da-pose avoids volume collision when warping from observation space to canonical space for the legs.

To render a pixel of a human in the observation space with this model, we transform the points along that ray into the canonical space. The difficulty in doing so is how one expands the transformation of SMPL meshes into the entire observation space to allow this ray tracing in canonical space. Similar to Liu et al. [19], we use a simple strategy to extend the mesh skinning into a volume warping field.

In each frame f, given a 3D point $\mathbf{x}_f = \mathbf{r}_f(t)$ in observation space and the corresponding estimated SMPL mesh $\boldsymbol{\theta}_f$ obtained from preprocessing 3.2, we transform it into the canonical space by following the rigid transformation of its closest point on the mesh; see Fig. 2. We denote this mesh-based transform as $\mathcal{T}$ such that $\mathbf{x}'_f = \mathcal{T}_{\boldsymbol{\theta}_f}(\mathbf{x}_f)$. This transformation, however, relies completely on the accuracy of $\boldsymbol{\theta}_f$, which is not reliable even with the recent state of the art. To mitigate the misalignment between the SMPL estimates and the underlying human, we propose to jointly optimize $\boldsymbol{\theta}_f$ together with the neural radiance field while training. In Fig. 3, we show the effect of online optimization on correcting the estimates. Furthermore, to account for the details that can not be expressed by the SMPL model, we introduce the error-correction network $\mathcal{E}$, an MLP that corrects for the errors in the warping field. Finally, the mapping between the points in the observation space to the corrected points in the canonical space $\mathbf{x}_f \rightarrow \tilde{\mathbf{x}}'_f$ is obtained as

$$\tilde{\mathbf{x}}'_f = \mathcal{T}_{\boldsymbol{\theta}_f}(\mathbf{x}_f) + \mathcal{E}(\mathbf{x}_f, f) \ . \tag{6}$$

The error-correction net is only used during training, and is discarded for rendering with validation and novel poses. Since a single canonical space is used to explain all poses, the error-correction network naturally overfits to each frame and makes the canonical volume more generalized.

Due to the nature of the warping field, a straight line in the observation space is curved in the canonical space after warping. Therefore, we recompute the viewing angles by taking into account how the light rays *actually* travel in the canonical space by looking at where the previous sample is,

$$\mathbf{d}(t_i)'_f = \frac{\tilde{\mathbf{x}}'_f(t_i) - \tilde{\mathbf{x}}'_f(t_{i-1})}{\left\| \tilde{\mathbf{x}}'_f(t_i) - \tilde{\mathbf{x}}'_f(t_{i-1}) \right\|} \ , \tag{7}$$

where $\tilde{\mathbf{x}}'_f(t_i)$ and $\mathbf{d}(t_i)'_f$ are the coordinate and viewing angel of the i-th sample along the curved ray in canonical space. Finally, with the canonical space coordinates $\tilde{\mathbf{x}}'_f$ and the corrected viewing angles $\mathbf{d}'_f$ the radiance field values for the human model is obtained by

$$\mathbf{c}_h, \sigma_h = \mathcal{F}_{\boldsymbol{\Phi}}(\tilde{\mathbf{x}}'_f, \mathbf{d}'_f) \ , \tag{8}$$

where $\boldsymbol{\Phi}$ are the parameters of the human NeRF $\mathcal{F}_{\boldsymbol{\Phi}}$.

To render a pixel, we shoot two rays, one for the human NeRF, and the other for the scene NeRF. We evaluate the colors and densities for the two sets of samples along the rays. We then sort the colors and the densities in the ascending order based on their depth values, similar to ST-NeRF [12]. Finally, we integrate over these values to obtain the pixel using Eq. (2).

Training. To train the human radiance field, we sample rays on the regions covered by the human mask and minimize

$$\mathcal{L}_{h,rgb}(\mathbf{r}) = \mathcal{M}(\mathbf{r}) \left\| \mathbf{C}_h(\mathbf{r}) - \hat{\mathbf{C}}(\mathbf{r}) \right\|, \tag{9}$$

where $\mathbf{C}_h(\mathbf{r})$ is the rendered color from the human NeRF model. Similar to HumanNeRF [46], we also use LPIPS [50] as an additional loss term $\mathcal{L}_{lpips}$ by sampling a 32×32 patch. We use $\mathcal{L}_{mask}$ to enforce the accumulated alpha map from the human NeRF to be similar to the detected human mask.

$$\mathcal{L}_{mask}(\mathbf{r}) = \mathcal{M}(\mathbf{r}) \left\| 1 - \alpha_h(\mathbf{r}) \right\|, \tag{10}$$

where α_h corresponds to accumulated density over the ray as defined in Sect. 2.1.

To avoid blobs in the canonical space and semi-transparent canonical human, we enforce the volume inside the canonical SMPL mesh to be solid, while enforcing the volume outside the canonical SMPL mesh to be empty, given by

$$\mathcal{L}_{smpl}(\hat{\mathbf{x}}_f', \sigma_h) = \begin{cases} \left\| 1 - \sigma_h \right\|, & \text{if } \hat{\mathbf{x}}_f' \text{ inside SMPL mesh} \\ |\sigma_h|, & \text{otherwise} \end{cases}, \tag{11}$$

Moreover, we utilize hard surface loss $\mathcal{L}_{hard}$ [34] to mitigate the halo around the canonical human. To be specific, we encourage the weight of each sample to be either 1 or 0 given by,

$$\mathcal{L}_{hard} = -\log(e^{-|w|} + e^{-|1-w|}) \tag{12}$$

where w refers to the transparency where the ray terminates as defined in Sect. 2.1. However, this penalty alone is not enough to obtain a sharp canonical shape, we also add a canonical edge loss, $\mathcal{L}_{edge}$. By rendering a random straight ray in the canonical volume, we encourage the accumulated alpha values to be either 1 or 0. This is given by,

$$\mathcal{L}_{edge} = -\log(e^{-|\alpha_c|} + e^{-|1-\alpha_c|}) \tag{13}$$

where α_c is the accumulated alpha value obtained from a random straight ray in canonical space. Thus, the final loss is given by,

$$\begin{aligned} \mathcal{L} = \mathcal{L}_{h,rgb} + \lambda_{lpips}\mathcal{L}_{lpips} + \lambda_{mask}\mathcal{L}_{mask} \\ + \lambda_{smpl}\mathcal{L}_{smpl} + \lambda_{hard}\mathcal{L}_{hard} + \lambda_{edge}\mathcal{L}_{edge}. \end{aligned} \tag{14}$$

To train, we jointly optimize $\boldsymbol{\theta}_f$, $\mathcal{E}$, and $\mathcal{F}_\Phi$ by minimizing this loss. We set $\lambda_{lpips} = 0.01$, $\lambda_{mask} = 0.01$, $\lambda_{smpl} = 1.0$, $\lambda_{hard} = 0.1$, and $\lambda_{edge} = 0.1$. Since the detected masks are inaccurate, we linearly decay λ_{mask} to 0 through the training.

Preprocessing. We utilize ROMP [41] to estimate the SMPL [21] parameters of the human in the videos. However, the estimated SMPL parameters are not accurate. Therefore, we refine the SMPL estimates by optimizing the SMPL parameters using silhouette estimated from [8,47], and 2D joints estimated from [3,4] as detailed in the supplementary material. We then align the SMPL estimates in the scene coordinates.

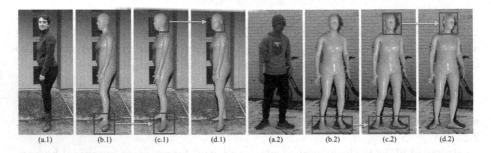

(a.1)   (b.1)   (c.1)   (d.1)   (a.2)   (b.2)   (c.2)   (d.2)

Fig. 3. Pose optimization examples – Our proposed preprosceeing and end-to-end optimization over SMPL parameters effectively produce better fits to the human, see the bounding boxes. (a) Original image. (b) ROMP estimates. (c) Preprocessed SMPL. (d) End-to-end optimized SMPL.

Fig. 4. Visualization of SMPL and scene alignment – We show sampled video frames (first row), and the estimated SMPL meshes overlaying on top of the scene point cloud (second row). The human is in the scene with a correct scale as the foot is touching the ground plane. SMPL meshes are colored based on time. (Color figure online)

Scene-SMPL Alignment. To compose a scene with a human in novel view and pose, and to train the two NeRF models, we align the coordinate systems in which the two NeRF models lie. This is, in fact, a non-trivial problem, as human body pose estimators [13,18,41] operate in their own camera systems with often near-orthographic camera models. To deal with this issue, we first solve the Perspective-n-Point (PnP) problem [14] between the estimated 3D joints and the projected 2D joints with the camera intrinsics from COLMAP.

This solves the alignment up to an arbitrary scale. We then assume that the human is standing on a ground at least in one frame, and solve for the scale ambiguity by finding the scale that allows the feet meshes of the SMPL model to touch the ground plan. We obtain the ground plane by applying RANSAC. We show the results of the aligned SMPL estimates in the scene in Fig. 4.

Once the two NeRF models are properly aligned we can render the pixel by shooting two rays, one for the human NeRF model, and the other for the scene NeRF model, as describe above. For the near and far planes to generate samples in Eq. 2, we use the estimated scene point cloud to determine them for scene NeRF, and use the estimated SMPL mesh to determine them for the human NeRF, following the strategy in Liu et al. [19].

4   Experiments

We introduce our dataset, show qualitative and quantitative results of our method and provide ablation studies. Our method is the first method that can render a human together with a scene with novel human poses and novel views from a single video. We show the importance of our geometry correction and novel loss terms in order to obtain a realistic and sharp human NeRF model.

4.1   Dataset

Existing human motion datasets are not suitable for our experiments. Generally, motion capture data [11,32] is captured with a static multi-cameras system in a controlled environment which defeats the purpose of reconstructing from a single video. Other video datasets [25,33] have multiple humans and crowded scenes

Fig. 5. Scene NeRF examples – We show the training samples (left), together with the renderings from validation views. Our scene models are able to remove the human in the scene effectively, and to produce high quality novel view renderings of the background even with limited coverage of the scene.

that are not suitable for our case. Therefore, we introduce NeuMan dataset, a collection of 6 videos about 10 to 20 s long each, where a single person performs a walking sequence captured using a mobile phone. Moreover, the camera reasonably pans through the scene to enable multi-view reconstruction. The sequences are named – Seattle, Citron, Parking, Bike, Jogging and Lab. For each video sequence, we first subsample the frames from the video and use them to train our NeRF models. We split frames into 80% training frames, 10% validation frames, and 10% test frames. We provide the details in supplementary material.

4.2 Qualitative Results

Scene NeRF Reconstructions. Figure 5 shows the novel view renderings of our scene NeRF models. By reconstructing the background pixels only, our model learns the consistent geometry of the scene, and effectively removes the dynamic human.

Human NeRF Reconstructions. Our framework learns an animatable human model with realistic details. It captures not only the texture details such as the pattern on the cloth, but also the subject specific geometric details, such as the sleeves, collar, even zipper. Notice that these geometric details are beyond the expressiveness of SMPL model. The learned human models can be reposed to novel driving motions, and produce high quality rendering of the human under

Fig. 6. Human NeRF model examples – We show front and side view of the reconstructed canonical human (left), novel human poses and views renderings with the reconstructed human model (middle), and composition of both the human and scene model with novel human poses (right).

novel poses from novel views. Although, the training sequence is as simple as walking, the model can perform stunning cartwheeling motion, which shows the ability to extrapolate to unseen poses. By simple composition, we can render both the human and the scene realistically; see Fig. 6.

Telegathering. The ability to render reposed human together with the scene further allows us to, for example, create telegathering of multiple individuals as in Fig. 7. The results show that our framework can facilitate combining human NeRF models in the same scene without any additional training.

4.3   Novel View Synthesis

To compare our method to existing solutions that can do similar tasks, we train NeRF with time(NeRF-T) [15] using the same training data as ours but without the empty space penalty. As HyperNeRF [29] requires a smoothly changing video, we provide it with densely sampled frames from the videos. NeRF-T and

Fig. 7. Telegathering – Our method is able to provide telegathering for multiple individuals: (left) is the SMPL meshes and scene point cloud overlay, others are the rendering results from novel views.

| NeRF-T | HyperNeRF | Ours | Ground Truth |

Fig. 8. Qualitative comparisons – We show the qualitative comparisons among NeRF-T, HyperNeRF and ours. NeRF-T and HyperNeRF failed to reconstruct the drastically dynamic scenes and to interpolate across space and time, while our method faithfully reconstructed both the human and the scene with high rendering quality.

Table 2. Novel view synthesis comparison – We report the quantitative results on test views. Our method achieves the best rendering quality across all scenes and all metrics by a large margin. Notice that the numbers for ours method depends on the estimated human pose.

	Seattle			Citron			Parking		
	PSNR↑	SSIM↑	LPIPS↓	PSNR↑	SSIM↑	LPIPS↓	PSNR↑	SSIM↑	LPIPS↓
NeRF-T	21.84	0.69	0.37	12.33	0.49	0.65	21.98	0.69	0.46
HyperNeRF	16.43	0.43	0.40	16.81	0.41	0.56	16.04	0.00	0.62
Ours	**23.98**	**0.77**	**0.26**	**24.71**	**0.80**	**0.26**	**25.43**	**0.79**	**0.31**

	Bike			Jogging			Lab		
	PSNR↑	SSIM↑	LPIPS↓	PSNR↑	SSIM↑	LPIPS↓	PSNR↑	SSIM↑	LPIPS↓
NeRF-T	21.16	0.71	0.36	20.63	0.53	0.49	20.52	0.75	0.39
HyperNeRF	17.64	0.42	0.43	18.52	0.39	0.52	16.75	0.51	0.23
Ours	**25.52**	**0.82**	**0.23**	**22.68**	**0.67**	**0.32**	**24.93**	**0.85**	**0.21**

HyperNeRF [29] do not perform well at reconstruction of drastically dynamic scenes with humans, while our method is able to do so even with less than 40 training images. We evaluate methods on the test views, and measure PSNR, SSIM [43], and LPIPS [50]. The results are shown in Table 2 and Fig. 8. Our method outperforms across all scenes and metrics. Notice that, unlike Hyper-NeRF, our method depends on the estimated human pose, and we discard the offset network when rendering validation or test views. Therefore, our reported numbers also reflect the errors in the estimated human pose.

4.4 Ablation Studies

Effect of Geometry Correction. Our method has 3 components to correct the estimated geometry of the human: the offline SMPL optimization in the preprocessing, the online end-to-end SMPL optimization during the training, and the error-correction network which accounts for the warping errors. Without any geometry corrections components(Ours-GC), the canonical volume overfits to each observations causing averaged color and shape instead of sharp details of the human. However, with geometry correction enabled, the human NeRF model can learn both the textural and geometric details of the human. We show the comparison between Ours-Full and Ours-GC in Fig. 9.

Effect of $\mathcal{L}_{smpl}$ When $\mathcal{L}_{smpl}$ is disabled, fog appears in the canonical volume around the human, and causes a halo in the final renderings, see Ours-$\mathcal{L}_{smpl}$ in Fig. 9. By encouraging the volume outside the canonical SMPL mesh to be empty, $\mathcal{L}_{smpl}$ effectively removes the fog and suppresses the halos.

Fig. 9. Ablation studies – We show the canonical (first row) and test view (second row) renderings of our full model, ours without any geometry corrections, and ours without $\mathcal{L}_{smpl}$. Geometry correction allows us to reconstruct the human with details, and $\mathcal{L}_{smpl}$ encourages a clean canonical volume and suppresses halo in the final renderings.

5   Conclusions

We have proposed a novel framework to reconstruct the human and the scene NeRF models that can be rendered with novel human poses and views from a single in-the-wild video. To do so, we use off-the-shelf methods to estimate either 2D or 3D geometry of the scene and the human to provide initialization. Our human NeRF model is able to learn texture details such as patterns on cloth, and geometric details such as sleeves, collar even zipper from less than 40 images.

Limitations and Future Work. One major limitation is that the dynamics beyond SMPL cannot be modeled with our static NeRF, those dynamics will degenerate to average shape or color. This is most evident in the hands when the gestures are changing over frames, see Fig. 6. We hope to apply more expressive body models to model hand gestures [30], even garment dynamics [23], to mitigate this problem.

Additionally, our warping function is a simple extension of the SMPL mesh skinning, it could cause volume collision in some extreme cases. A collision-aware volume warping method or a learned one is required to improve the generalization under extreme poses.

Finally, we assume that the human always has at least one contact point with the ground to estimate the scale relative to the scene. To apply our method to videos with jumping or uneven ground, we need smarter geometric reasoning.

Acknowledgement. We thank Ashish Shrivastava, Russ Webb and Miguel Angel Bautista Martin for providing insightful review feedback.

References

1. Balakrishnan, G., Zhao, A., Dalca, A.V., Durand, F., Guttag, J.: Synthesizing images of humans in unseen poses. In: Proceedings of the IEEE Conference on Computer Vision and Pattern Recognition. pp. 8340–8348 (2018)

2. Chan, E.R., Monteiro, M., Kellnhofer, P., Wu, J., Wetzstein, G.: pi-gan: Periodic implicit generative adversarial networks for 3d-aware image synthesis. In: Proceedings of the IEEE/CVF Conference on Computer Vision and Pattern Recognition. pp. 5799–5809 (2021)
3. Cheng, B., Xiao, B., Wang, J., Shi, H., Huang, T.S., Zhang, L.: HigherHRNet: scale-aware representation learning for bottom-up human pose estimation. In: CVPR (2020)
4. Contributors, M.: OpenMMLab Pose Estimation Toolbox and Benchmark (2020). https://github.com/open-mmlab/mmpose
5. Dellaert, F., Yen-Chen, L.: Neural Volume Rendering: NeRF And Beyond (2021)
6. Elgammal, A., Harwood, D., Davis, L.: Non-parametric model for background subtraction. In: Vernon, D. (ed.) ECCV 2000. LNCS, vol. 1843, pp. 751–767. Springer, Heidelberg (2000). https://doi.org/10.1007/3-540-45053-X_48
7. Grigorev, A., Sevastopolsky, A., Vakhitov, A., Lempitsky, V.: Coordinate-based texture inpainting for pose-guided human image generation. In: Proceedings of the IEEE/CVF Conference on Computer Vision and Pattern Recognition, pp. 12135–12144 (2019)
8. Güler, R.A., Neverova, N., Kokkinos, I.: DensePose: dense human pose estimation in the wild. In: Proceedings of the IEEE Conference on Computer Vision and Pattern Recognition, pp. 7297–7306 (2018)
9. Guo, M., Fathi, A., Wu, J., Funkhouser, T.: Object-Centric Neural Scene Rendering (2020). https://arxiv.org/abs/2012.08503
10. He, K., Gkioxari, G., Dollár, P., Girshick, R.: Mask R-CNN. In: Proceedings of the IEEE International Conference on Computer Vision, pp. 2961–2969 (2017)
11. Ionescu, C., Papava, D., Olaru, V., Sminchisescu, C.: Human3.6M: large scale datasets and predictive methods for 3d human sensing in natural environments. IEEE Trans. Pattern Anal. Mach. Intell. **36**(7), 1325–1339 (2014)
12. Jiakai, Z., et al.: Editable free-viewpoint video using a layered neural representation. In: ACM SIGGRAPH (2021)
13. Kocabas, M., Athanasiou, N., Black, M.J.: Vibe: video inference for human body pose and shape estimation. In: Proceedings of the IEEE/CVF Conference on Computer Vision and Pattern Recognition, pp. 5253–5263 (2020)
14. Lepetit, V., Moreno-Noguer, F., Fua, P.: EPNP: an accurate o(n) solution to the PNP problem. Int. J. Comput. Vision **81**, 155–166 (2009)
15. Li, Z., Niklaus, S., Snavely, N., Wang, O.: Neural scene flow fields for space-time view synthesis of dynamic scenes. In: Proceedings of the IEEE/CVF Conference on Computer Vision and Pattern Recognition, pp. 6498–6508 (2021)
16. Lim, L.A., Keles, H.Y.: Foreground segmentation using convolutional neural networks for multiscale feature encoding. Pattern Recogn. Lett. **112**, 256–262 (2018)
17. Lin, C.H., Ma, W.C., Torralba, A., Lucey, S.: BARF: bundle-adjusting neural radiance fields. In: ICCV (2021)
18. Lin, K., Wang, L., Liu, Z.: End-to-end human pose and mesh reconstruction with transformers. In: Proceedings of the IEEE/CVF Conference on Computer Vision and Pattern Recognition, pp. 1954–1963 (2021)
19. Liu, L., Habermann, M., Rudnev, V., Sarkar, K., Gu, J., Theobalt, C.: Neural actor: neural free-view synthesis of human actors with pose control. arXiv preprint arXiv:2106.02019 (2021)
20. Liu, W., Piao, Z., Min, J., Luo, W., Ma, L., Gao, S.: Liquid warping GAN: a unified framework for human motion imitation, appearance transfer and novel view synthesis. In: Proceedings of the IEEE/CVF International Conference on Computer Vision, pp. 5904–5913 (2019)

21. Loper, M., Mahmood, N., Romero, J., Pons-Moll, G., Black, M.J.: SMPL: a skinned multi-person linear model. ACM Trans. Graph. (TOG) **34**(6), 1–16 (2015)
22. Ma, L., Sun, Q., Georgoulis, S., Van Gool, L., Schiele, B., Fritz, M.: Disentangled person image generation. In: Proceedings of the IEEE Conference on Computer Vision and Pattern Recognition, pp. 99–108 (2018)
23. Ma, Q., et al.: Learning to dress 3d people in generative clothing. In: Proceedings of the IEEE/CVF Conference on Computer Vision and Pattern Recognition, pp. 6469–6478 (2020)
24. Miangoleh, S.M.H., Dille, S., Mai, L., Paris, S., Aksoy, Y.: Boosting monocular depth estimation models to high-resolution via content-adaptive multi-resolution merging. In: CVPR (2021)
25. Milan, A., Leal-Taixé, L., Reid, I., Roth, S., Schindler, K.: Mot16: a benchmark for multi-object tracking. arXiv preprint arXiv:1603.00831 (2016)
26. Mildenhall, B., Srinivasan, P.P., Tancik, M., Barron, J.T., Ramamoorthi, R., Ng, R.: NeRF: representing scenes as neural radiance fields for view synthesis. In: Vedaldi, A., Bischof, H., Brox, T., Frahm, J.-M. (eds.) ECCV 2020. LNCS, vol. 12346, pp. 405–421. Springer, Cham (2020). https://doi.org/10.1007/978-3-030-58452-8_24
27. Neverova, N., Alp Güler, R., Kokkinos, I.: Dense pose transfer. In: Ferrari, V., Hebert, M., Sminchisescu, C., Weiss, Y. (eds.) ECCV 2018. LNCS, vol. 11207, pp. 128–143. Springer, Cham (2018). https://doi.org/10.1007/978-3-030-01219-9_8
28. Park, K., et al.: Nerfies: deformable neural radiance fields. In: ICCV (2021)
29. Park, K., et al.: HyperNeRF: A Higher-Dimensional Representation for Topologically Varying Neural Radiance Fields. arXiv preprint arXiv:2106.13228 (2021)
30. Pavlakos, G., et al.: Expressive body capture: 3D hands, face, and body from a single image. In: Proceedings IEEE Conference on Computer Vision and Pattern Recognition (CVPR), pp. 10975–10985 (2019)
31. Peng, S., et al.: Animatable neural radiance fields for modeling dynamic human bodies. In: ICCV (2021)
32. Peng, S., Zhang, Y., Xu, Y., Wang, Q., Shuai, Q., Bao, H., Zhou, X.: Neural body: implicit neural representations with structured latent codes for novel view synthesis of dynamic humans. In: Proceedings of the IEEE/CVF Conference on Computer Vision and Pattern Recognition, pp. 9054–9063 (2021)
33. Ranjan, A., Hoffmann, D.T., Tzionas, D., Tang, S., Romero, J., Black, M.J.: Learning multi-human optical flow. Int. J. Comput. Vision **128**(4), 873–890 (2020)
34. Rebain, D., Matthews, M., Yi, K.M., Lagun, D., Tagliasacchi, A.: LOLNeRF: Learn from One Look. arXiv preprint arXiv:2111.09996 (2022)
35. Sanyal, S., et al.: Learning realistic human reposing using cyclic self-supervision with 3d shape, pose, and appearance consistency. In: Proceedings of the IEEE/CVF International Conference on Computer Vision, pp. 11138–11147 (2021)
36. Sarkar, K., Mehta, D., Xu, W., Golyanik, V., Theobalt, C.: Neural re-rendering of humans from a single image. In: Vedaldi, A., Bischof, H., Brox, T., Frahm, J.-M. (eds.) ECCV 2020. LNCS, vol. 12356, pp. 596–613. Springer, Cham (2020). https://doi.org/10.1007/978-3-030-58621-8_35
37. Schönberger, J.L., Frahm, J.M.: Structure-from-motion revisited. In: CVPR (2016)
38. Schönberger, J.L., Zheng, E., Frahm, J.-M., Pollefeys, M.: Pixelwise view selection for unstructured multi-view stereo. In: Leibe, B., Matas, J., Sebe, N., Welling, M. (eds.) ECCV 2016. LNCS, vol. 9907, pp. 501–518. Springer, Cham (2016). https://doi.org/10.1007/978-3-319-46487-9_31
39. Su, S.Y., Yu, F., Zollhoefer, M., Rhodin, H.: A-NeRF: Surface-free Human 3D Pose Refinement via Neural Rendering. https://arxiv.org/abs/2102.06199 (2021)

40. Sun, D., Sudderth, E.B., Black, M.J.: Layered segmentation and optical flow estimation over time. In: 2012 IEEE Conference on Computer Vision and Pattern Recognition, pp. 1768–1775. IEEE (2012)
41. Sun, Y., Bao, Q., Liu, W., Fu, Y., Michael J.B., Mei, T.: Monocular, One-stage, Regression of Multiple 3D People. In: ICCV, October 2021
42. Tancik, M., et al.: Fourier features let networks learn high frequency functions in low dimensional domains. arXiv preprint arXiv:2006.10739 (2020)
43. Wang, Z., Bovik, A.C., Sheikh, H.R., Simoncelli, E.P.: Image Quality Assessment: From Error Visibility to Structural Similarity. IEEE TIP **10**, 600 612 (2004)
44. Wang, Z., Wu, S., Xie, W., Chen, M., Prisacariu, V.A.: NeRF−: Neural Radiance Fields Without Known Camera Parameters. arXiv preprint arXiv:2102.07064 (2021)
45. Weng, C.Y., Curless, B., Kemelmacher-Shlizerman, I.: Vid2Actor: Free-viewpoint Animatable Person Synthesis from Video in the Wild. arXiv preprint arXiv:2012.12884 (2020)
46. Weng, C.Y., Curless, B., Srinivasan, P.P., Barron, J.T., Kemelmacher-Shlizerman, I.: HumanNeRF: Free-viewpoint Rendering of Moving People from Monocular Video. arXiv preprint arXiv:2201.04127 (2022)
47. Wu, Y., Kirillov, A., Massa, F., Lo, W.Y., Girshick, R.: Detectron2 (2019). https://github.com/facebookresearch/detectron2
48. Xian, W., Huang, J.B., Kopf, J., Kim, C.: Space-time neural irradiance fields for free-viewpoint video. In: Proceedings of the IEEE/CVF Conference on Computer Vision and Pattern Recognition (CVPR), pp. 9421–9431 (2021)
49. Yang, B., et al.: Learning Object-Compositional Neural Radiance Field for Editable Scene Rendering. In: ICCV, October 2021
50. Zhang, R., Isola, P., Efros, A.A., Shechtman, E., Wang, O.: The unreasonable effectiveness of deep features as a perceptual metric. In: CVPR (2018)

TAVA: Template-free Animatable Volumetric Actors

Ruilong Li[1,3($\boxtimes$)], Julian Tanke[2,3], Minh Vo[3], Michael Zollhöfer[3], Jürgen Gall[2], Angjoo Kanazawa[1], and Christoph Lassner[3]

[1] UC Berkeley, Berkeley, USA
ruilongli@berkeley.edu
[2] University of Bonn, Bonn, Germany
[3] Meta Reality Labs Research, Sausalito, USA

Abstract. Coordinate-based volumetric representations have the potential to generate photo-realistic virtual avatars from images. However, virtual avatars need to be controllable and be rendered in novel poses that may not have been observed. Traditional techniques, such as LBS, provide such a controlling function; yet it usually requires a hand-designed body template, 3D scan data, and surface-based appearance models. On the other hand, neural representations have been shown to be powerful in representing visual details, but are under-explored in dynamic and articulated settings. In this paper, we propose *TAVA*, a method to create *T*emplate-free *A*nimatable *V*olumetric *A*ctors, based on neural representations. We rely solely on multi-view data and a tracked skeleton to create a volumetric model of an actor, which can be animated at test time given novel poses. Since TAVA does not require a body template, it is applicable to humans as well as other creatures such as animals. Furthermore, TAVA is designed such that it can recover accurate dense correspondences, making it amenable to content-creation and editing tasks. Through extensive experiments, we demonstrate that the proposed method generalizes well to novel poses as well as unseen views and showcase basic editing capabilities. The code is available at https://github.com/facebookresearch/tava.

1 Introduction

Ever since the first 3D vector graphics games in the 1980s, we are striving to build better representations of 3D objects and humans. With increasing processing power, we can afford to capture, reconstruct and encode increasingly realistic representations. This makes exploring neural representations for graphical objects particularly appealing—it is a representation that has proven powerful [19,27,37,48,49], even though still being in its infancy. Recent methods for

---

Work done partially while Ruilong and Julian were at Meta Reality Labs Research.

Supplementary Information The online version contains supplementary material available at https://doi.org/10.1007/978-3-031-19824-3_25.

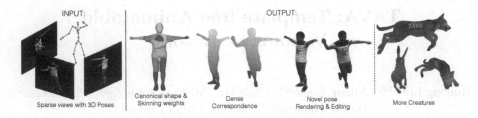

Fig. 1. *Method Overview.* **Left:** TAVA creates a virtual actor from multiple sparse video views as well as 3D poses. The same skeleton can later be used for animation. **Center:** TAVA uses this information to create a canonical shape and a pose-dependent skinning function and establishes correspondences across poses. The resulting model can be used for rendering and posing the virtual character as well as editing it. **Right:** the method can directly used for other creatures as long as a 3D skeleton can be defined.

neural 3D representations go beyond capturing surfaces and textures by modeling radiance fields [2,3,27], achieving more realistic results than rasterization-based approaches [20,23,38,50]. However, it is unclear how their representational power can be used to not only capture *static*, but also *dynamic* scenes that can be animated in a meaningful way, making the representations useful for capturing actors that can be "driven" post-capture. Also, due to the high-dimensional nature of pose configurations, it is generally neither possible nor practical to capture all pose variations in one capture. This poses a new problem absent in static settings: *generalization* to out-of-distribution (OOD) poses.

In this paper, we propose TAVA, a novel approach for **T**emplate-free **A**nimatable **V**olumetric **A**vatars (illustrated in Fig. 1). We propose to use coordinate-based radiance fields to capture appearance, leading to high quality, faithful renderings. We extend the radiance capture with a carefully designed deformation model: while it requires solely 3D skeleton information at training time, it captures non-linear pose-dependent deformations and exhibits stable generalization behavior to unseen poses thanks to being anchored in an LBS formulation. The radiance field and deformation model are optimized jointly and end-to-end, leading to a simple-to-use and powerful representation: creating it requires only a tracked skeleton and multi-view photometric data, **no** template mesh or artist-designed rigging; the appearance and the deformation model can complement each other for highest quality results. These properties make TAVA suitable for content creation and editing as well as correspondence-based matching.

In our experiments, we demonstrate that the proposed approach outperforms state-of-the art approaches for animating and rendering human actors on the ZJU motion capture dataset [35]. Thanks to being template-free, our approach is not limited to capturing humans: we present a detailed evaluation and ablation study on two synthetically rendered animals. This demonstrates the flexibility of the proposed approach and allows us to show additional applications in content-creation and editing.

2   Related Work

Deformable Neural Scene Representations: Coordinate-based neural scene representations produce impressive results in encoding shape [8,26,31] and appearance [24,27,40]. These methods train a coordinate-based neural network to model various properties of a scene, e.g., occupancy [26], distance to the closest surface [31], or density and color [27]. However, making implicit scene representations deformable and animatable remains a challenging research problem. Nerfies [32] and Neural 3D Video Synthesis [21] handle changes in the scene by optimizing a deformation field and a latent code for each frame. HyperNeRF [33] extends this by additionally creating a hyper-space which allows topology changes of the scene. Non-Rigid Neural Radiance Fields [43] optimize a rigidity model in addition to a deformation field. While these methods produce impressive results on dynamic scenes, they are designed to only memorize the scene and cannot control the scene beyond interpolations.

Animatable Neural Radiance Fields: Recently, many approaches for controllable animatable NeRFs have been proposed. Neural Actor [22] uses a pose-dependent radiance field by warping rays into the canonical space of a template body model while using 2D texture maps to model fine detail. NeuralBody [35] anchors latent codes on the vertices of a deformable mesh controlled by LBS. The follow-up work Animatable-NeRF [34] establishes a transformation between view and canonical space through optimizing the inverse deformation field. Other works like NARF and A-NeRF [29,42] predict the radiance field at a given 3D location based on its relative coordinates to the bones. Most recently, the concurrent work HumanNeRF [45] produces a free-viewpoint rendering of a human by modeling the inverse deformation as a mixture of affine fields [24]. Yet many of these methods [29,42] do *not* have a 3D canonical space that preserves correspondences across different poses, which is required for content-creation or editing. Some [22,34,35,45] are built on top of the SMPL [25] body template, which prohibits them to be applied to creatures beyond humans. Moreover, most of the aforementioned methods either introduce latent codes to better memorize the seen poses [34,35,42], or represent the deformation in the inverse direction from view space to the canonical space [29,34,42,45]. Thus, they do not generalize well to the unseen poses because the existence of pose-conditioned MLPs. In contrast, our approach is template-free, enables editing, and is designed to be robust to unseen poses. We provide an overview of the comparison between our method and those previous works in Table 1.

Animatable Shapes: Non-rigid shape reconstruction often utilizes a canonical space that is fixed across frames, with a deformation model to create a mapping between the canonical and the deformed space. Traditionally, this has been achieved by extracting a low dimensional articulated mesh [1,4–6,9,10,12,17,18,41,44,46], such as SMPL [25], or by extracting a rigged mesh via post-processing. Several methods [13,13,15,16,25,30,47,51] have been proposed to optimize blend weights and rigs from data. ARCH [14] deforms an estimated implicit representation to fit to a clothed human using a single image. Recent

Table 1. *Design differences.* TAVA's use of a forward deformation model without using per-frame latent codes ensures robustness to out-of-distribution poses. Being template-free extends its use to creatures beyond humans. TAVA also allows for content-creation and editing by using a 3D canonical space. †Note that NeuralBody's canonical space consists of the body template *without* clothing.

Methods	Template-free	No Per-frame Latent Code	3D Canonical Space	Deformation
NARF [29]	✓	✓	✗	Inverse
A-NeRF [42]	✓	✗	✗	Inverse
Animatable-NeRF [34]	✗	✗	✓	Inverse
HumanNeRF [45]	✗	✓	✓	Inverse
NeuralBody [35]	✗	✗	✓†	Forward
Ours (TAVA)	✓	✓	✓	Forward

approaches model inverse deformation fields [11,28,32,36,39], which map points from pose-dependent global space to pose-independent canonical space where the surface is represented. For example, SCANimate [39] regularizes the inverse skinning by using a cycle consistency loss. The main drawback of these inverse deformation approaches is that the inverse transformation is pose dependent and may not generalize well to previously unseen poses. SNARF [7] addresses this by learning a forward deformation field instead, mapping points from canonical to pose-dependent deformed space. However, unlike our approach, these methods require 3D geometry supervision and most do not optimize for appearance.

3   Method

Our goal is to create an animatable neural actor from multi-view images with known 3D skeleton information without requiring a body template. Similar to a traditional personalized body rig, we want to build a representation that not only represents the shape and appearance of the actor but also allows to animate it while maintaining correspondences among different poses and views. *TAVA* is designed to achieve the above goals with three components: (1) a canonical representation of the actor in neutral pose, (2) deformation modeling based on forward skinning, and (3) volumetric neural rendering with pose-dependent shading. Figure 2 illustrates an overview of our method. To employ volumetric neural rendering in the view space, our method first deforms the samples along a ray back to the canonical space through inverting the forward skinning via root-finding, then queries their colors and densities in the canonical space, as well as the pose-dependent effects. Below, we first establish preliminaries, then discuss each of the components.

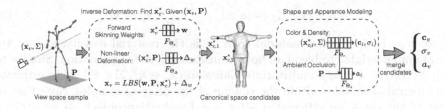

Fig. 2. *TAVA Overview.* We use volumetric rendering techniques to create the actor representation. For each sampled point, we use an LBS-based non-linear deformation combined with a blending weight model for which we identify the root in the canonical space. In this space, we use a color, density, and ambient occlusion model to parameterize the appearance. (Color figure online)

3.1 Preliminary: Rendering Neural Radiance Fields

NeRF [27] is a seminal technique for novel view synthesis of a *static* scene. It models the geometry and view-dependent appearance of the scene by using a multi-layer perceptron (MLP). Given a 3D coordinate $\mathbf{x} = (x, y, z)$ and the corresponding viewing direction (θ, ϕ), NeRF queries the emitted color $\mathbf{c} = (r, g, b)$ and material density σ at that location using the MLP. A pixel color $C(\mathbf{r})$ can then be computed by accumulating the view-dependent colors along the ray $\mathbf{r}$, weighted by their densities:

$$C(\mathbf{r}) = \sum_{i=1}^{N} T_i(1 - \exp(\sigma_i \delta_i))\mathbf{c}_i, \quad \text{where } T_i = \exp(-\sum_{j=1}^{i-1} \sigma_j \delta_j) , \qquad (1)$$

where δ_i denotes the distances between the sample points along the ray. To further take the size of the pixels into consideration, Mip-NeRF [2] extends NeRF to represent each ray $\mathbf{r}$ that passes through a pixel as a cone, and the samples $\mathbf{x}$ along the ray as conical frusta, which can be modeled by multivariate Gaussians $(\boldsymbol{\mu}, \boldsymbol{\Sigma})$. Thus, the density σ and view-dependent emitted color $\mathbf{c}$ for a sample on the ray are given by $F_\Theta : (\boldsymbol{\mu}, \boldsymbol{\Sigma}, \theta, \phi) \rightarrow (\mathbf{c}, \sigma)$, where $\boldsymbol{\mu} = (x, y, z)$ is the center of the Gaussian and $\boldsymbol{\Sigma} \in \mathbb{R}^{3\times 3}$ is its covariance matrix. The loss for optimizing the network parameters Θ of the neural radiance field is applied between the rendered pixel color $C(\mathbf{r})$ and the ground-truth $\hat{C}(\mathbf{r})$:

$$\mathcal{L}_{im} = ||C(\mathbf{r}) - \hat{C}(\mathbf{r})||_2^2 . \qquad (2)$$

Please refer to the original papers [2,27] for more details.

3.2 Canonical Neural Actor Representation

We represent an articulated subject as a volumetric neural actor in its canonical space. The representation includes a *Lambertian* neural radiance field F_{Θ_r} to represent the geometry and appearance of this actor, and a neural blend skinning function F_{Θ_s}, which describes how to animate the actor:

$$F_{\Theta_r} : (\mathbf{x}_c, \boldsymbol{\Sigma}) \to (\mathbf{c}, \sigma), \qquad F_{\Theta_s} : \mathbf{x}_c \to \mathbf{w}, \tag{3}$$

where $\mathbf{c} = (r, g, b)$ is the material color, σ is the material density, and $\mathbf{w}$ are the skinning weights to blend all bone transformations for animation. Similar to Mip-NeRF [2], we use a multivariate Gaussian ($\mathbf{x}_c \in \mathbb{R}^3, \boldsymbol{\Sigma} \in \mathbb{R}^{3\times 3}$) to estimate the integral of samples within the volume of the discrete samples. Note that in most of the cases, an articulated actor is a Lambertian object, so we exclude view directions from the input of F_{Θ_r}.

Discussion. This formulation not only models the *canonical* geometry and appearance of an avatar, but also describes its *dynamic* attributes through the skinning weights $\mathbf{w}$. Unlike previous works, such as SNARF [7], which models a pose-dependent geometry in the canonical space, and NARF [29] and A-NeRF [42], which entirely skip canonical space modeling, our method is based on a canonical representation that fully eliminates *any* effects of pose on the geometry and appearance. Moreover, the skinning weights learnt in the canonical space remain valid for a large range of poses, meaning that the actor is ready to be animated in novel poses outside of the training distribution (see Sect. 4.2 for validation of its robustness to out-of-distribution novel poses). Last but not least, our representation eases the correspondence finding problem across different poses and views, because the matching can be done in the pose-independent canonical space (see Sect. 4.2 for results).

3.3   Skinning-based Deformation

Forward Skinning. With the skinning weights $\mathbf{w} = (w_1, w_2, ..., w_B, w_{bg}) \in \mathbb{R}^{B+1}$ defined in the canonical space, and given a pose $\mathbf{P} = \{\mathbf{T}_1, \mathbf{T}_2, ..., \mathbf{T}_B\} \in \mathbb{R}^{B\times 4\times 4}$, we use forward LBS to define the deformation of a point $\mathbf{x}_c$ in the canonical space to $\mathbf{x}_v$ in the view space:

$$\mathbf{x}_v = LBS(\mathbf{w}(\mathbf{x}_c; \Theta_s), \mathbf{P}, \mathbf{x}_c) = \left[\sum_{j=1}^{B} w_j(\mathbf{x}_c; \Theta_s) \cdot \mathbf{T}_j + w_{bg} \cdot \mathbf{I_d} \right] \mathbf{x}_c, \tag{4}$$

where $\mathbf{I}_d \in \mathbb{R}^{4\times 4}$ is an identity matrix. Similar to [45], we extend the classic LBS defined only on the surface geometry of an object to the entire 3D space by introducing an additional term $w_{bg} \cdot \mathbf{I_d}$. This term allows the points in the background and empty space to *not* follow the skeleton when it is deformed. However, LBS is not sufficient for capturing some of the non-linear deformations, such as muscles and clothing dynamics [25]. Thus, we introduce an additional term $F_{\Theta_\Delta} : (\mathbf{x}_c, \mathbf{P}) \to \Delta_w \in \mathbb{R}^3$ on top of the learned LBS to model these deformations:

$$\mathbf{x}_v = LBS(\mathbf{w}(\mathbf{x}_c; \Theta_s), \mathbf{P}, \mathbf{x}_c) + \Delta_w(\mathbf{x}_c, \mathbf{P}; \Theta_\Delta). \tag{5}$$

Inverse Skinning. To render this model, we need to query color and density in the view space. Hence, it is required to find the the correspondence $\mathbf{x}_c$ in the canonical space for each $\mathbf{x}_v$ in the view space. As our forward skinning in Eq. 5

is defined through neural networks, there is no analytical form for the inverse skinning. Similar to SNARF [7], we pose this as a root finding problem:

$$\text{Find } \mathbf{x}_c^*, \quad \text{s.t. } f(\mathbf{x}_c^*) = LBS(\mathbf{w}(\mathbf{x}_c^*; \Theta_s), \mathbf{P}, \mathbf{x}_c^*) + \Delta_w(\mathbf{x}_c^*, \mathbf{P}; \Theta_\Delta) - \mathbf{x}_v = \mathbf{0} \quad (6)$$

and solve it numerically using Newton's method:

$$\mathbf{x}_c^{(k+1)} = \mathbf{x}_c^{(k)} - (\mathbf{J}^{(k)})^{-1} f(\mathbf{x}_c^{(k)}), \quad (7)$$

where $\mathbf{J}^{(k)} \in \mathbb{R}^{3 \times 3}$ is the Jacobian of $f(\mathbf{x}_c^{(k)})$ at the k-th step. Since the inverse skinning might be a one-to-many mapping when there is contact happening between body parts, we initialize Newton's method with multiple candidates using the inverse rigid transformation $\{\mathbf{x}_{c,i}^{(0)}\} = \{\mathbf{T}_i^{-1} \cdot \mathbf{x}_v\}$. However, simply applying all $B + 1$ transformations to initialize the Newton's method would lead to $B + 1$ canonical candidates to be processed, making it impractical for volumetric rendering as the complexity grows linearly in B. As points are less likely to be affected by bones further away, we only use the transformations of its $K = 5$ nearest bones by measuring the Euclidean distance between the point and the bones in the view space. This dramatically reduces the computational burden of the root finding process and the following canonical querying, making the formulation applicable for neural rendering. With that, our inverse skinning leads to multiple correspondences for a point in the view space through root finding (r.f.):

$$\mathbf{x}_v \xrightarrow{\text{r.f.}} \{\mathbf{x}_{c,1}^*, \mathbf{x}_{c,2}^*, ..., \mathbf{x}_{c,K}^*\} \quad (8)$$

The gradients of the network parameters Θ_s and Θ_Δ can be analytically computed for the inverse skinning [7]:

$$\frac{\partial \mathbf{x}_{c,i}^*}{\partial \Theta_s} = -\left[\frac{\partial \mathbf{x}_v}{\partial \mathbf{x}_{c,i}^*}\right]^{-1}\left[\frac{\partial \mathbf{x}_v}{\partial \Theta_s}\right], \quad \frac{\partial \mathbf{x}_{c,i}^*}{\partial \Theta_\Delta} = -\left[\frac{\partial \mathbf{x}_v}{\partial \mathbf{x}_{c,i}^*}\right]^{-1}\left[\frac{\partial \mathbf{x}_v}{\partial \Theta_\Delta}\right]. \quad (9)$$

Please refer to the supplemental material for the derivations of these terms.

3.4   Deformation-Based Neural Rendering

Similar to Mip-NeRF [2], we render the color of a pixel by accumulating the samples $(\mathbf{x}_v, \mathbf{\Sigma})$ along each pixel ray, using Eq. 1. Instead of directly querying the color and density of $\mathbf{x}_v$ in the view space, we first find the point's canonical correspondence candidates using the inverse skinning $\mathbf{x}_v \xrightarrow{\text{r.f.}} \{\mathbf{x}_{c,1}^*, \mathbf{x}_{c,2}^*, ..., \mathbf{x}_{c,K}^*\}$, and then query the colors and densities for all those candidates in the canonical space.

$$F_{\Theta_r} : (\mathbf{x}_{c,i}^*, \mathbf{\Sigma}) \to (\mathbf{c}_i^*, \sigma_i^*). \quad (10)$$

However, for a dynamic object, the shading on the surface may change depending on pose due to self-occlusion. This can lead to colors in the view space being darker than the colors in the canonical space, providing inconsistent supervision signals. However, it is non-trivial to accurately model this self-occlusion without ray tracing (including secondary rays) and known global illumination. A simple but effective estimator, widely used in modern rendering engines like Unreal and Blender is ambient occlusion, in which the shading caused by occlusion is modeled by *a scaling factor* multiplied with the color values, where the value is calculated by the percentage of view directions being occluded around each point on the surface. Since it is an attribute defined at each coordinate that depends on the global geometry of the actor, we model this shading effect use a coordinate based MLP F_{Θ_a} conditioned on the pose $\mathbf{P}$ of the actor:

$$F_{\Theta_r} : (\mathbf{x}_{c,i}^*, \Sigma) \to \mathbf{h} \to (\mathbf{c}_i^*, \sigma_i^*), \qquad F_{\Theta_a} : (\mathbf{h}, \mathbf{P}) \to a_i^*, \qquad (11)$$

where $\mathbf{h}$ is an intermediate activation from F_{Θ_r}, and a_i^* is the ambient occlusion at this location under pose $\mathbf{P}$. Note that only the ambient occlusion a_i^* is pose-conditioned, which makes sure the actor (geometry and appearance) is represented in a canonical space that is pose-independent, as described in Sect. 3.2.

With $(\mathbf{c}_i^*, \sigma_i^*, a_i^*)_{i=1,\ldots,K}$ queried in the canonical space, we then need to merge the K candidates to get the final attributes $(\mathbf{c}_v, \alpha_v, a_v)$ for the sample $(\mathbf{x}_v, \Sigma)$ in the view space. In the case of articulated objects, where multiple canonical point may originate from the same location, the one with the maximum density would dominate that location. Similar to previous works [7,11], we choose the attributes of $\mathbf{x}_v$ from all canonical candidates based on their density:

$$\mathbf{c}_v = \mathbf{c}_{c,t}^* \quad \sigma_v = \sigma_{c,t}^* \quad a_v = a_{c,t}^* \qquad \text{where } t = \operatorname{argmax}_i(\{\sigma_{c,i}^*\}), \qquad (12)$$

then we use $(\mathbf{c} = a_v * \mathbf{c}_v, \sigma = \sigma_v)$ as the final emitted color and density in the view space, for the volumetric rendering in Eq. 1.

Note that in general there is no way to guarantee that the inverse root finding converges. In practice, root finding fails for 1% to 8% of the points in the view space, making it impossible to query their attributes. For these points, an option is to just simply set their densities to zero, which would only be problematic if the points are close to the surface. A slightly better way is to estimate the color and density for those points by interpolating the attributes from their nearest valid neighbors along the ray. We conduct experiments on both strategies in supplemental material, which results in slightly better performance. We choose the second strategy in our full model.

3.5 Establishing Correspondences

As our method is endowed with a 3D canonical space, we have the ability to trace surface correspondences across different views and poses. When rendering an image using Eq. 1, besides accumulating colors $\{\mathbf{c}_m\}$ of the samples $\{\mathbf{x}_{v,m}\}$ along the ray $\mathbf{r}$, we also accumulate the corresponding canonical coordinates $\{\mathbf{x}_{c,m}\}$:

$$X(\mathbf{r}) = \sum_{m=1}^{N} T_m(1 - \exp(\sigma_m \delta_m)) \mathbf{x}_{c,m}, \qquad (13)$$

where $X(\mathbf{r}) \in \mathbb{R}^3$ is the coordinate in the canonical space that corresponds to the pixel of the ray. With that, for images under different poses/views, we can compute their *dense* pixel-to-pixel correspondences by matching $X(\mathbf{r})$ in the canonical space using the nearest neighbor algorithm.

3.6   Training Loss

Besides the image loss $\mathcal{L}_{im}$ defined in Eq. 2, we also employ two auxiliary losses that help the training. Due to the fact that all the points along a bone should have the same transformation, we encourage the skinning weights $\mathbf{w}$ of samples $\bar{\mathbf{x}}_c$ on the bones to be one-hot vectors $\hat{\mathbf{w}}$ (noted as $\mathcal{L}_w$). We also encourage the non-linear deformations $\boldsymbol{\Delta}_v$ of those samples to be zero given any pose $\mathbf{P}$ (noted as $\mathcal{L}_\Delta$). We use MSE to calculate both, $\mathcal{L}_w = ||\mathbf{w}(\bar{\mathbf{x}}_c) - \hat{\mathbf{w}})||_2^2$ and $\mathcal{L}_\Delta = ||\Delta_w(\bar{\mathbf{x}}_c, \mathbf{P}) - \mathbf{0})||_2^2$. Our final loss is: $\mathcal{L} = \mathcal{L}_{im} + \lambda\mathcal{L}_w + \beta\mathcal{L}_\Delta$, where λ is set to 1.0 and β is set to 0.1 in all our experiments.

4   Experiments

4.1   Datasets

We conduct experiments on 1) four human subjects (313, 315, 377, 386) in the ZJU-Mocap dataset [35], a public multi-view video dataset for human motion, and 2) two synthetic animal subjects (Hare, Wolf) introduced in this paper, rendered from multiple views using Blender.

Data Splits. Prior works [34,35] create the *train* and *val* sets on the ZJU-Mocap dataset by simply splitting each video with $500 \sim 2200$ frames into two splits, where the *training* set has $60 \sim 300$ frames and the *validation* set has $300 \sim 1000$ frames. This is not an ideal split to evaluate pose synthesis performance because 1) a training set with 60 consecutive frames in a 30fps video does not sufficiently cover pose variation to learn from, and 2) due to the repetitive motion of the actors, quite often similar poses are in both the *training* and *validation* sets, which should be avoided for evaluating a method on pose generalization. Therefore, we establish a new protocol to split the dataset by clustering the frames based on pose similarity. Specifically, for each subject, we first randomly withhold a chunk of consecutive frames to be the *test* set, for the purpose of the final evaluation. Then, we use the K-Medoids algorithm on the remaining frames to cluster them into $K = 10$ clusters, based on pose similarity measured by the V2V Euclidean distance using ground-truth mesh. The most different cluster is selected as the $\text{val}_{\text{pose}}^{\text{ood}}$ set, in which the frames are all considered to contain the *out-of-distribution* poses. For the remaining 9 clusters, we randomly split each cluster $2:1$ to form *train* and $\text{val}_{\text{pose}}^{\text{ind}}$ sets, where the frames in $\text{val}_{\text{pose}}^{\text{ind}}$ still contains new poses which are considered to be *in the distribution* of the training set. For the view splits, we follow the protocol from [34,35] for ZJU-Mocap, where 4 views are used for training and 17 views for testing. The animal subjects have 10 random views for training and 10 for testing. We denote val_{view} as our novel-view synthesis evaluation set, which contains all the training poses but rendered from different viewpoints. Please see the supplemental material for more details.

Table 2. *Comparisons on the animal subjects.* P2P is pixel-to-pixel error, for measuring image correspondences across different poses.

	Novel-view		Novel-pose (ind)			Novel-pose (ood)		
	PSNR ↑	SSIM ↑	PSNR ↑	SSIM ↑	P2P ↓	PSNR ↑	SSIM ↑	P2P ↓
Pose-NeRF	23.40	0.974	21.93	0.941	197.11	16.62	0.925	88.85
A-NeRF [42]	31.26	0.976	31.22	0.977	31.52	25.66	0.967	19.04
NARF [29]	36.55	0.988	36.65	0.988	9.28	30.92	0.982	8.46
Ours	**37.30**	**0.991**	**37.45**	**0.991**	**4.30**	**35.77**	**0.990**	**3.38**

Table 3. *Comparisons on the ZJU Mocap subjects.* We compare with both, template-free and template-based methods.

	Novel-view		Novel-pose (ind)		Novel-pose (ood)	
	PSNR ↑	SSIM ↑	PSNR ↑	SSIM ↑	PSNR ↑	SSIM ↑
SMPL-based Methods						
Animatable-NeRF [34]	30.75	0.971	29.34	0.966	28.67	0.961
NeuralBody [35]	**33.91**	**0.983**	**33.43**	**0.984**	**30.33**	**0.969**
Template-free Methods						
Pose-NeRF	31.88	0.975	32.09	0.976	28.43	0.954
A-NeRF [42]	32.45	0.978	32.65	0.978	30.41	0.967
NARF [29]	32.94	0.980	33.21	0.980	30.60	0.968
Ours	**33.11**	**0.981**	**33.35**	**0.981**	**30.69**	**0.969**

4.2   Evaluation and Comparison

Baselines. We compare our work with two types of previous methods: 1) Template-free methods, including NARF [29] and A-NeRF [42], as well as 2) SMPL-based methods, including Animatable-NeRF [34] and NeuralBody [35]. As our baseline, we use Pose-NeRF: we slightly modify Mip-NeRF [2] to learn the density and color conditioned on pose. We conduct experiments for all the methods above on ZJU-Mocap, but exclude Animatable-NeRF and NeuralBody for the animal subjects (they require a template 3D model). Although code is available for each method, we noticed that each is using a different set of hyper-parameters for neural rendering (e.g., number of MLP layers, number of samples, near and far planes) and different training schedules, all of which are not related to method design but can greatly affect the performance. To make as-fair-as-possible comparisons, we integrated the template-free methods, NARF and A-NeRF, into our code base, which shares the same set of hyper-parameters[1]. For Animatable-NeRF and NeuralBody, we use the original implementations since their designs are based on the SMPL body template.

---

[1] For NARF, our re-implementation achieves better performance than it's official implementation. Please refer to the supplmental material for further details.

Novel-view Synthesis. In this task, we conduct experiments on both, the ZJU-Mocap dataset and the two animal subjects Hare and Wolf, using val_{view} set. As shown in Table 2 and Table 3, our method outperforms other template-free methods measured by PSNR and SSIM. On the ZJU-Mocap dataset, our method achieves comparable performance with two template-based methods, Animatable-NeRF and NeuralBody, which greatly benefit from the SMPL body template, but do not work on other creatures like animals. See Fig. 3 for a qualitative comparison.

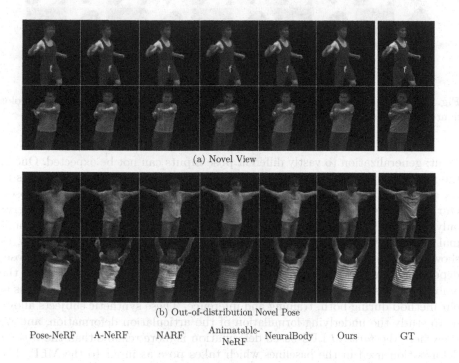

(a) Novel View

(b) Out-of-distribution Novel Pose

Pose-NeRF   A-NeRF   NARF   Animatable-NeRF   NeuralBody   Ours   GT

Fig. 3. *Rendering quality comparison with all baseline methods on the ZJU-Mocap Dataset.* Note that Animatable-NeRF and NeuralBody rely on the SMPL body model, and the other approaches do not. (Color figure online)

Novel-Pose Synthesis. Due to the high interdependency of appearance changes caused by pose and motion, novel-pose synthesis is a more challenging task than novel-view synthesis, especially for poses that are out of the training distribution. To carefully study this problem, we conduct experiments on both, in-distribution (InD) novel poses, using the $\text{val}_{\text{pose}}^{\text{ind}}$ set, and out-of-distribution(OOD) novel poses, using the $\text{val}_{\text{pose}}^{\text{ood}}$ set. Our experiments reveal that for InD poses, the performance of nearly all the methods are consistent with their performance on the novel-view task, as shown in Tables 2, 3. However, there is a huge drop in performance from InD poses to OOD pose (0.67 db~ 2.66 db on ZJU-Mocap; 1.68 db~ 5.73 db on animals). This is not surprising if the method contains neural networks that directly infer appearance information from pose

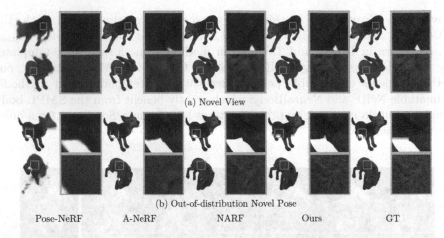

(a) Novel View

(b) Out-of-distribution Novel Pose

Pose-NeRF   A-NeRF   NARF   Ours   GT

Fig. 4. Comparison with template-free methods on the Hare and Wolf subjects. (Color figure online)

input: generalization to vastly different pose inputs can not be expected. One of the main goals in this paper is to reduce this reliance of the neural networks to the pose input, for improving the robustness of the method to the OOD poses. Our method benefits from explicitly incorporating the *forward* LBS. We observe only an 1.68db performance drop comparing InD to OOD poses on the animal subjects, whereas other methods suffer from $\sim$ 5db performance drops, as shown in Table 2. Since these two synthetic subjects are not rendered with pose-dependent shading, and do not have "clothing" deformations, we disabled the ambient occlusion a (set to 1.) and non-linear deformation Δ_v (set to 0.) terms in our method during both, training and inference. These synthetic subjects allows us to study the underlying formulation of the articulation deformation, and we show here the *forward* LBS-based deformation is more reliable than the *inverse* deformation used in the baselines which takes pose as input to the MLP. The results on the ZJU-Mocap dataset in Table 3 show that our method outperforms both, the template-free and template-based methods, on the OOD poses. All the methods are prone to nearly the same drop in performance on the ZJU-Mocap dataset comparing InD to OOD poses. This is, because currently all of these methods, including ours, are still implicitly modeling pose-dependent shading effects (e.g., self-occlusion) as either a neural network or a latent code during training, which does not generalize well to OOD poses. Our method, though, provides a possibility to factor out the shading effects during inference and reveal the albedo color of the actor, which yields better generalization but is not suitable for evaluation comparing to the ground-truth, as shown in supplemental material. See Figs. 3, 4 for qualitative comparisons.

Pixel-to-Pixel Correspondences. We quantitatively evaluate correspondence on the animal subjects against Pose-NeRF, A-NeRF [42] and NARF [29]. We show qualitative results on ZJU-Mocap since no ground-truth correspondences are available (see Fig. 5). Even though neither of the baseline methods demonstrate that they can establish correspondences, we still tried our best to create a valid comparison[2]. For quantitative evaluation, we randomly sample 2000 image pairs (A, B) in val_{pose}^{ood} set, and use the ground truth mesh to establish ground-truth pixel-to-pixel correspondences $(\chi_A \rightarrow \chi_B)$ for every pair of images $(A \rightarrow B)$, where χ_A and χ_B are the corresponding image coordinates. Then, we use each method to render this pair of images, and find the correspondences of χ_A in B as χ_B^*. The pixel-to-pixel error (P2P) is then calculated as the average distance between χ_B and χ_B^*: P2P $= \|\chi_B - \chi_B^*\|_2^2$. As shown in Table 2 and Fig. 6, our method achieves over 2x more accurate correspondences (3.38px v.s. 8.46px error in a 800×800 image) compared to the baselines. We visualize the extracted dense correspondences of our method in Fig. 5, which shows that correspondences across different subjects can be established as long as they share the same canonical pose (T-pose in ZJU-Mocap). Further more, we demonstrate that accurate correspondences can be used for content editing in Fig. 7.

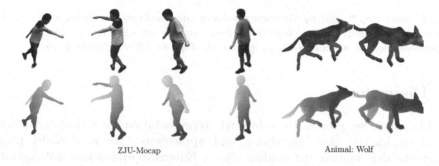

ZJU-Mocap   Animal: Wolf

Fig. 5. *Rendering with Dense Correspondence.* We show results of our novel-view rendering with dense correspondences. On the ZJU Mocap dataset, correspondences across different subjects can also be built because they share the same canonical pose.

---

[2] Pose-NeRF, A-NeRF and NARF all query the color and density of $(\mathbf{x}_v, \mathbf{P})$ in a higher dimensional (> 3) space, where we do the nearest neighbor matching for them using our approach as described in Sect. 3.5. Please refer to the supp.mat. for further details.

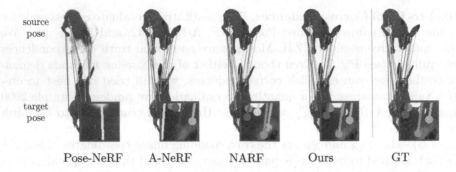

| Pose-NeRF | A-NeRF | NARF | Ours | GT |

Fig. 6. *Correspondence comparison on Hare.* We find the correspondence for the same set of pixels in the source image in the target image. Both source and target are rendered in novel poses.

Fig. 7. *Rendering & Editing.* We show results of our novel-pose rendering with content editing. We manually attach a logo to the image on the left, then use our pixel-to-pixel correspondences to automatically propagate the logo to different poses & views.

5   Discussion

In this paper, we proposed a volumetric representation for articulated actors based on learned skinning, shape, and appearance. We also model pose-dependent deformation and shading effects. Extensive evaluations demonstrate that our approach consistently outperforms previous methods when generalizing to out-of-distribution unseen poses. Our approach can recover much more accurate dense correspondences across different poses and views than prior works, enabling content editing applications. Moreover, it does not require any body templates, enabling applications for creatures beyond humans. While our approach has clear advantages, there are few limitations. First, our method trains much slower (5 to 8 times) than the baselines, due to the nature of the root finding process for inverse deformation. A future direction could be to use invertible neural networks to avoid the root finding process. Second, even though our forward LBS ensures generalization to unseen poses, pose-dependent *non-linear* deformation and shading effects are still challenging to estimate correctly for unseen poses. Such effects are fundamentally challenging to model, particularly for lighting-dependent shading. An interesting future direction could be to model these effects across multiple subjects so that information from all subjects can be used to improve non-linear deformation model performance.

Acknowledgements. Ruilong Li's work at UC Berkeley is partly supported by the CONIX Research Center, a Semiconductor Research Corporation (SRC) program sponsored by DARPA.

References

1. Anguelov, D., Srinivasan, P., Koller, D., Thrun, S., Rodgers, J., Davis, J.: Scape: shape completion and animation of people. In: ACM SIGGRAPH 2005 Papers, pp. 408–416 (2005)
2. Barron, J.T., Mildenhall, B., Tancik, M., Hedman, P., Martin-Brualla, R., Srinivasan, P.P.: Mip-nerf: a multiscale representation for anti-aliasing neural radiance fields. In: International Conference on Computer Vision (2021)
3. Barron, J.T., Mildenhall, B., Verbin, D., Srinivasan, P.P., Hedman, P.: Mip-nerf 360: Unbounded anti-aliased neural radiance fields. In: CVPR (2022)
4. Borshukov, G., Piponi, D., Larsen, O., Lewis, J.P., Tempelaar-Lietz, C.: Universal capture-image-based facial animation for "the matrix reloaded". In: SIGGRAPH 2005 Courses (2005)
5. Carranza, J., Theobalt, C., Magnor, M.A., Seidel, H.P.: Free-viewpoint video of human actors. Trans. Graphics **22**, 569–577 (2003)
6. Casas, D., Volino, M., Collomosse, J., Hilton, A.: 4D video textures for interactive character appearance. In: Computer Graphics Forum (2014)
7. Chen, X., Zheng, Y., Black, M.J., Hilliges, O., Geiger, A.: Snarf: Differentiable forward skinning for animating non-rigid neural implicit shapes. In: Proceedings of the IEEE/CVF International Conference on Computer Vision, pp. 11594–11604 (2021)
8. Chen, Z., Zhang, H.: Learning implicit fields for generative shape modeling. In: Conference on Computer Vision and Pattern Recognition (2019)
9. Collet, A., et al.: High-quality streamable free-viewpoint video. Trans. Graphics **34**, 1–13 (2015)
10. De Aguiar, E., Stoll, C., Theobalt, C., Ahmed, N., Seidel, H.P., Thrun, S.: Performance capture from sparse multi-view video. In: ACM SIGGRAPH 2008 papers, pp. 1–10 (2008)
11. Deng, B., et al.: NASA neural articulated shape approximation. In: Vedaldi, A., Bischof, H., Brox, T., Frahm, J.-M. (eds.) ECCV 2020. LNCS, vol. 12352, pp. 612–628. Springer, Cham (2020). https://doi.org/10.1007/978-3-030-58571-6_36
12. Guo, K., et al.: The relightables: volumetric performance capture of humans with realistic relighting. ACM Trans. Graphics (ToG) **38**(6), 1–19 (2019)
13. Hasler, N., Thormählen, T., Rosenhahn, B., Seidel, H.P.: Learning skeletons for shape and pose. In: SIGGRAPH Symposium on Interactive 3D Graphics and Games (2010)
14. Huang, Z., Xu, Y., Lassner, C., Li, H., Tung, T.: Arch: animatable reconstruction of clothed humans. In: Proceedings of the IEEE/CVF Conference on Computer Vision and Pattern Recognition, pp. 3093–3102 (2020)
15. James, D.L., Twigg, C.D.: Skinning mesh animations. Trans. Graphics **24**, 399–407 (2005)

16. Jiang, B., Zhang, J., Cai, J., Zheng, J.: Disentangled human body embedding based on deep hierarchical neural network. Trans. Visual. Comput. Graphics **26**, 2560–2575 (2020)
17. Li, H., et al.: Temporally coherent completion of dynamic shapes. ACM Trans. Graphics (TOG) **31**(1), 1–11 (2012)
18. Li, K., et al.: SPA: sparse photorealistic animation using a single RGB-D camera. Trans. Circuits Syst. Video Technol. **27**, 771–783 (2016)
19. Li, R., et al.: Learning formation of physically-based face attributes. In: Proceedings of the IEEE/CVF Conference on Computer Vision and Pattern Recognition, pp. 3410–3419 (2020)
20. Li, R., Xiu, Y., Saito, S., Huang, Z., Olszewski, K., Li, H.: Monocular real-time volumetric performance capture. In: Vedaldi, A., Bischof, H., Brox, T., Frahm, J.-M. (eds.) ECCV 2020. LNCS, vol. 12368, pp. 49–67. Springer, Cham (2020). https://doi.org/10.1007/978-3-030-58592-1_4
21. Li, Z., Niklaus, S., Snavely, N., Wang, O.: Neural scene flow fields for space-time view synthesis of dynamic scenes. In: Conference on Computer Vision and Pattern Recognition (2021)
22. Liu, L., Habermann, M., Rudnev, V., Sarkar, K., Gu, J., Theobalt, C.: Neural actor: neural free-view synthesis of human actors with pose control. ACM Trans. Graphics (TOG) **40**(6), 1–16 (2021)
23. Liu, S., Li, T., Chen, W., Li, H.: A general differentiable mesh renderer for image-based 3D reasoning. IEEE Trans. Pattern Anal. Mach. Intell. **44**, 50–62 (2020)
24. Lombardi, S., Simon, T., Saragih, J., Schwartz, G., Lehrmann, A., Sheikh, Y.: Neural volumes: Learning dynamic renderable volumes from images. ACM Trans. Graph. **38**(4), 65:1-65:14 (2019)
25. Loper, M., Mahmood, N., Romero, J., Pons-Moll, G., Black, M.J.: SMPL: a skinned multi-person linear model. Trans. Graphics **34**, 1–16 (2015)
26. Mescheder, L., Oechsle, M., Niemeyer, M., Nowozin, S., Geiger, A.: Occupancy networks: learning 3D reconstruction in function space. In: Conference on Computer Vision and Pattern Recognition (2019)
27. Mildenhall, B., Srinivasan, P.P., Tancik, M., Barron, J.T., Ramamoorthi, R., Ng, R.: NeRF: representing scenes as neural radiance fields for view synthesis. In: Vedaldi, A., Bischof, H., Brox, T., Frahm, J.-M. (eds.) ECCV 2020. LNCS, vol. 12346, pp. 405–421. Springer, Cham (2020). https://doi.org/10.1007/978-3-030-58452-8_24
28. Niemeyer, M., Mescheder, L., Oechsle, M., Geiger, A.: Occupancy flow: 4D reconstruction by learning particle dynamics. In: International Conference on Computer Vision (2019)
29. Noguchi, A., Sun, X., Lin, S., Harada, T.: Neural articulated radiance field. In: Proceedings of the IEEE/CVF International Conference on Computer Vision, pp. 5762–5772 (2021)
30. Osman, A.A.A., Bolkart, T., Black, M.J.: STAR: sparse trained articulated human body regressor. In: Vedaldi, A., Bischof, H., Brox, T., Frahm, J.-M. (eds.) ECCV 2020. LNCS, vol. 12351, pp. 598–613. Springer, Cham (2020). https://doi.org/10.1007/978-3-030-58539-6_36
31. Park, J.J., Florence, P., Straub, J., Newcombe, R., Lovegrove, S.: Deepsdf: learning continuous signed distance functions for shape representation. In: Conference on Computer Vision and Pattern Recognition (2019)
32. Park, K., et al.: Nerfies: deformable neural radiance fields. In: International Conference on Computer Vision (2021)

33. Park, K., et al.: Hypernerf: a higher-dimensional representation for topologically varying neural radiance fields. ACM Trans. Graph. **40**(6) (2021)
34. Peng, S., et al.: Animatable neural radiance fields for modeling dynamic human bodies. In: International Conference on Computer Vision (2021)
35. Peng, S., et al.: Neural body: Implicit neural representations with structured latent codes for novel view synthesis of dynamic humans. In: Proceedings of the IEEE/CVF Conference on Computer Vision and Pattern Recognition, pp. 9054–9063 (2021)
36. Pumarola, A., Corona, E., Pons-Moll, G., Moreno-Noguer, F.: D-nerf: neural radiance fields for dynamic scenes. In: Conference on Computer Vision and Pattern Recognition (2021)
37. Raj, A., Tanke, J., Hays, J., Vo, M., Stoll, C., Lassner, C.: ANR: articulated neural rendering for virtual avatars. In: Proceedings of the IEEE/CVF Conference on Computer Vision and Pattern Recognition, pp. 3722–3731 (2021)
38. Saito, S., Huang, Z., Natsume, R., Morishima, S., Kanazawa, A., Li, H.: PIFU: pixel-aligned implicit function for high-resolution clothed human digitization. In: Proceedings of the IEEE/CVF International Conference on Computer Vision, pp. 2304–2314 (2019)
39. Saito, S., Yang, J., Ma, Q., Black, M.J.: Scanimate: weakly supervised learning of skinned clothed avatar networks. In: Conference on Computer Vision and Pattern Recognition (2021)
40. Sitzmann, V., Zollhöfer, M., Wetzstein, G.: Scene representation networks: continuous 3d-structure-aware neural scene representations. In: Advances in Neural Information Processing Systems (2019)
41. Starck, J., Hilton, A.: Surface capture for performance-based animation. IEEE Comput. Graphics Appl. **27**(3), 21–31 (2007)
42. Su, S.Y., Yu, F., Zollhöfer, M., Rhodin, H.: A-nerf: articulated neural radiance fields for learning human shape, appearance, and pose. In: Advances in Neural Information Processing Systems, vol. 34 (2021)
43. Tretschk, E., Tewari, A., Golyanik, V., Zollhöfer, M., Lassner, C., Theobalt, C.: Non-rigid neural radiance fields: Reconstruction and novel view synthesis of a dynamic scene from monocular video. In: International Conference on Computer Vision. IEEE (2021)
44. Volino, M., Casas, D., Collomosse, J.P., Hilton, A.: Optimal representation of multi-view video. In: British Machine Vision Conference (2014)
45. Weng, C.Y., Curless, B., Srinivasan, P.P., Barron, J.T., Kemelmacher-Shlizerman, I.: Humannerf: free-viewpoint rendering of moving people from monocular video. In: CVPR (2022)
46. Xu, F., et al.: Video-based characters: creating new human performances from a multi-view video database. In: ACM SIGGRAPH 2011 papers (2011)
47. Xu, Z., Zhou, Y., Kalogerakis, E., Landreth, C., Singh, K.: RigNet: neural rigging for articulated characters. Trans. Graphics (2020)
48. Yu, A., Fridovich-Keil, S., Tancik, M., Chen, Q., Recht, B., Kanazawa, A.: Plenoxels: radiance fields without neural networks. In: Conference on Computer Vision and Pattern Recognition (2022)
49. Yu, A., Li, R., Tancik, M., Li, H., Ng, R., Kanazawa, A.: Plenoctrees for real-time rendering of neural radiance fields. In: Proceedings of the IEEE/CVF International Conference on Computer Vision, pp. 5752–5761 (2021)

50. Zhi, T., Lassner, C., Tung, T., Stoll, C., Narasimhan, S.G., Vo, M.: TexMesh: reconstructing detailed human texture and geometry from RGB-D video. In: Vedaldi, A., Bischof, H., Brox, T., Frahm, J.-M. (eds.) ECCV 2020. LNCS, vol. 12355, pp. 492–509. Springer, Cham (2020). https://doi.org/10.1007/978-3-030-58607-2_29

51. Zhou, K., Bhatnagar, B.L., Pons-Moll, G.: Unsupervised shape and pose disentanglement for 3D meshes. In: Vedaldi, A., Bischof, H., Brox, T., Frahm, J.-M. (eds.) ECCV 2020. LNCS, vol. 12367, pp. 341–357. Springer, Cham (2020). https://doi.org/10.1007/978-3-030-58542-6_21

EASNet: Searching Elastic and Accurate Network Architecture for Stereo Matching

Qiang Wang[1,2,3], Shaohuai Shi[4], Kaiyong Zhao[3,5], and Xiaowen Chu[3,4,6(✉)]

[1] Harbin Institute of Technology (Shenzhen), Shenzhen, China
qiang.wang@hit.edu.cn
[2] Guangdong Provincial Key Laboratory of Novel Security Intelligence Technologies, Shenzhen, China
[3] Hong Kong Baptist University, Hong Kong SAR, China
{qiangwang,chxw,kyzhao}@comp.hkbu.edu.hk
[4] The Hong Kong University of Science and Technology, Hong Kong SAR, China
shaohuais@cse.ust.hk
[5] XGRIDS, xgrids.com, Shenzhen, China
kyzhao@xgrids.com
[6] The Hong Kong University of Science and Technology (Guangzhou), Guangzhou, China
xwchu@ust.hk

Abstract. Recent advanced studies have spent considerable human efforts on optimizing network architectures for stereo matching but hardly achieved both high accuracy and fast inference speed. To ease the workload in network design, neural architecture search (NAS) has been applied with great success to various sparse prediction tasks, such as image classification and object detection. However, existing NAS studies on the dense prediction task, especially stereo matching, still cannot be efficiently and effectively deployed on devices of different computing capability. To this end, we propose to train an elastic and accurate network for stereo matching (EASNet) that supports various 3D architectural settings on devices with different compute capability. Given the deployment latency constraint on the target device, we can quickly extract a sub-network from the full EASNet without additional training while the accuracy of the sub-network can still be maintained. Extensive experiments show that our EASNet outperforms both state-of-the-art human-designed and NAS-based architectures on Scene Flow and MPI Sintel datasets in terms of model accuracy and inference speed. Particularly, deployed on an inference GPU, EASNet achieves a new SOTA 0.73 EPE on the Scene Flow dataset with 100 ms, which is 4.5× faster than LEAStereo with a better quality model. The codes of EASNet are available at: https://github.com/HKBU-HPML/EASNet.git.

Keywords: Stereo matching · Neural architecture search

© The Author(s), under exclusive license to Springer Nature Switzerland AG 2022
S. Avidan et al. (Eds.): ECCV 2022, LNCS 13692, pp. 437–453, 2022.
https://doi.org/10.1007/978-3-031-19824-3_26

1 Introduction

Stereo matching, also called disparity estimation, is a conventional but important technique widely applied to various computer vision tasks, such as 3D perception, 3D reconstruction and autonomous driving. Stereo matching aims to find dense correspondences between a pair of rectified stereo images. As traditional stereo matching algorithms with manual feature extraction and matching cost aggregation fail on those textureless and repetitive regions in the images due to lack of their prior information, deep neural network (DNN) based methods avoid this failure by efficiently learning the data distribution and have achieved state-of-the-art (SOTA) performance in many public benchmarks [2,15,29,30] in recent years. However, DNN networks for stereo matching should also be well designed to achieve good performance. Existing human-designed stereo networks can be divided into two main classes, the U-shape network with 2D convolution (U-Conv2D) and cost volume aggregation with 3D convolution (CVA-Conv3D).

The U-Conv2D methods leverage the U-shape encoder-decoder structure with 2D convolution layers to directly predict the disparity map. The representative networks are the DispNet/FlowNet series [12,21,22,29] as well as their variants [33,42]. This category of networks enjoys computing efficiency of 2D convolution. However, recent studies [10] raise some concerns about the generalization ability of the U-Conv2D methods. In contrast, the CVA-Conv3D methods exploit the concept of semi-global matching [19] and construct a 4D feature volume by aggregating features from each disparity-shift to enhance the generalization ability. In CVA-Conv3D, it firstly constructs cost volumes by concatenating left feature maps with their corresponding right counterparts across each disparity candidate [8,24,45]. The cost volumes are then automatically aggregated and regressed by 3D convolution layers to produce the disparity map. This branch of methods nowadays achieves SOTA estimation quality and dominates the leaderboard of several public benchmarks [15,30]. However, due to the expensive computing cost of 3D operations, they typically run very slowly and are difficult for real-time deployment even on the modern powerful AI accelerators (e.g., GPUs).

On the other hand, AutoML [18] techniques (e.g., neural architecture search (NAS) [14]) recently become very popular to relieve AI practitioners from manual trial-and-error effort by automating network design. Recent years have witnessed tremendous successes of NAS in various computer vision tasks (e.g., classification [34,46], object detection [40], and semantic segmentation [26,31]). However, existing applications of NAS are mainly used on sparse prediction problems like classification and object detection. It would become very challenging to apply NAS to dense prediction problems like stereo matching because of the following two reasons. 1) In general, NAS needs to search through a humongous set of possible architectures to determine the network components, which requires extensive computational costs (e.g., thousands of GPU hours). 2) The memory footprint and the model computation workload of stereo matching networks are much larger than those of sparse prediction networks. Taking an example of two architectures, GANet [45] and ResNet-50 [17], on stereo matching problems and image classification problems, respectively. To process one sample on an Nvidia

Tesla V100 GPU, GANet requires nearly 29 GB of GPU memory and 1.9 s inference time (on the Scene Flow [29] dataset), while ResNet-50 only requires 1.5 GB and 0.02 s (on the ImageNet [11] dataset). Therefore, directly applying the strategies of sparse prediction in NAS to stereo matching can lead to prohibitive workloads due to the explosion of computational resource demands.

To avoid such a problem, Saikia et al. [36] propose AutoDispNet that searches the architecture based on the U-Conv2D methods, and it limits its search space on three different cell structures rather than the full architecture. Although AutoDispNet saves search time, it still cannot surpass the existing SOTA CVA-Conv3D methods (e.g. AANet [43]) in both model accuracy and inference speed. Later, Cheng [10] leveraged task-specific human knowledge in the search space design to reduce the demands of computational resources in searching architectures, and proposed an end-to-end hierarchical NAS network named LEAStereo, which achieved the SOTA accuracy among the existing CVA-3D methods. However, LEAStereo takes 0.3 s of model inference even on a high-end Nvidia Tesla V100 GPU, which is far away from the requirement of real-time applications. Moreover, both AutoDispNet and LEAStereo attempt to find a specialized network architecture, and train it from scratch, thus cannot be scaled to different devices. Notice that the deployment of stereo matching applications can have diverse computing resource constraints, from high-end cloud servers to low-end edge devices or robotics embedded devices. To meet the latency requirement of a new given device, the above two methods need to re-search and re-train the model, which requires large labor. The recent proposed once-for-all (OFA) network [5] tries to support diverse architectural settings, but it only explores the sparse prediction problem like image classification. In summary, existing stereo matching methods including human-designed architectures and searched architectures cannot well fulfill real-world deployment requirements which need to consider model accuracy, inference speed, and training cost.

To this end, we propose to train an elastic and accurate stereo matching network, EAS-Net, which enables model deployment on devices of different computing capability to guarantee the inference speed without additional training while the model accuracy can be maintained. Furthermore, our EASNet does not need to re-train or re-search the architecture for deployment on any new devices. In this paper, we make three-fold contributions:

- Based on the pipeline of the CVA-3D methods, we propose an end-to-end stereo matching network named EASNet that contains four function modules. We allow the network to search for both the layer level and the network level structures in a huge network candidate space.
- To efficiently train EASNet, we develop a multiple-stage training scheme for EASNet to reduce the model size across diverse dimensions of network architecture parameters including depth, width, kernel size and scale. Our training strategy can significantly improve the prediction accuracy of sub-networks sampled from the largest full EASNet structure, which enables flexible deployment according to the target device computing capability and latency requirement without any additional model training.

- We conduct extensive experiments to evaluate the effectiveness of EASNet on several popular stereo datasets among three GPUs of different computing power levels. Under all deployment scenarios, EASNet outperforms both the human-designed and NAS-based networks in terms of model accuracy and inference speed.

2   Related Work

2.1   Manual DNN Design for Stereo Matching

In recent years, many deep learning methods have been proposed for stereo matching by extracting effective features from a pair of stereo images and estimating their correspondence cost, which can be classified into 2D with the U-shape network (U-Conv2D) and 3D with cost volume aggregation (CVA-Conv3D) methods.

On the one hand, in the U-Conv2D networks, the U-shape network architecture mainly utilizes 2D convolution layers [29,33] to estimate disparity, which takes a pair of rectified stereo images as input and generates the disparity by direct regression. However, the pure 2D CNN architectures are difficult to capture the matching features such that the estimation results are not good. On the other hand, the 3D methods with cost volume aggregation, named CVA-Conv3D, are further proposed to improve the estimation performance [8,24,32,44,45], which apply 3D convolutions to cost volume aggregation. The cost volume is mainly constructed by concatenating left feature maps with their corresponding right counterparts across each disparity level [8,24], and the features of the generated cost volumes can be learned by 3D convolution layers. Nowadays the top-tier CVA-Conv3D methods [10,43,45] have achieved very good accuracy on various public benchmarks. However, the key limitation of CVA-Conv3D is its high computation resource requirements, which makes them be difficult for real-world deployment. For example, GANet [45] and LEAStereo [10] take 1.9 s and 0.3 s respectively on predicting the disparity map of a stereo pair of 960×540 even using a very powerful Nvidia Tesla V100 GPU. Though they achieve good accuracy, it is difficult to deploy them for real-time inference.

2.2   NAS-Based Stereo Matching

To lessen the effort dedicated to designing network architectures, AutoML [18], especially NAS [4,14,28,34,46], has become an increasingly active research area over the past few years. While most of the early studies [1,3,27,28,35,37] have proven the effectiveness of NAS in many sparse prediction tasks, the extension to dense prediction tasks, such as semantic segmentation [9,31] and stereo matching [10,36], is still at an early stage. AutoDispNet is the first work that adopts the DARTS NAS method to search the efficient basic cell structure for the U-Conv2D method. However, to reduce the prohibitive search space, it only searches partially three different cell structures rather than the full architecture methods, and thus achieves limited model accuracy and generalization. In contrast, LEAStereo [10] leveraged the domain knowledge of stereo matching and designed a hierarchy end-to-end pipeline, which allows the network to automatically select the optimal structures. However, LEAStereo is still difficult to be deployed on modern AI processors due to the high computational cost. Furthermore, to meet the latency requirement on the new target device, LEAStereo needs to tune the network search space accordingly, followed by re-searching and re-training the model, where the expensive network specialization is unavoidable.

Recent studies [4,6,16,20,23,25,39] take the hardware capability into account to search the network. As one of the existing SOTA studies, the once-for-all (OFA) network allows direct deployment under various computing devices and constraints by selecting only a part of the original full one without additional model training. However, they only discuss the case for image classification, while the domain knowledge and processing pipeline of stereo matching are much different from the sparse prediction task of OFA. In this paper, we propose a novel network named EASNet to search elastic and accurate stereo matching networks, and design a specialized network search space according to the prior geometric knowledge of stereo matching. Our EASNet covers a wide range of search dimensions (kernel size, width, depth, and scale). With negligible accuracy loss and without any extra model fine-tuning, our EASNet can be directly deployed on different scenarios of computing power and resource constraint, which refers to its "elastic" and "accurate" characteristics.

3   Our Method: EASNet

In this section, we present our proposed elastic network structure for stereo matching, EASNet, that covers four function modules in the search and training pipeline. We support up to four search dimensions for different modules in EASNet. We firstly describe the architecture search space of each function module, including their basic unit and supported search dimensions. Then we introduce the training approach across four search dimensions to maximizing the average model accuracy of all the derived sub-networks in EASNet.

3.1   The Architecture Space of EASNet

In this subsection, we introduce the overview structure of EASNet. As illustrated in Fig. 1, EASNet is composed of four modules: feature pyramid construction, cost volume, cost aggregation, and disparity regression and refinement. The functions of these modules are benefited from prior human knowledge in stereo matching and success of previous hand-crafted network architecture design. EASNet enables its flexibility and effectiveness by providing different levels of support of neural architecture search for these four modules.

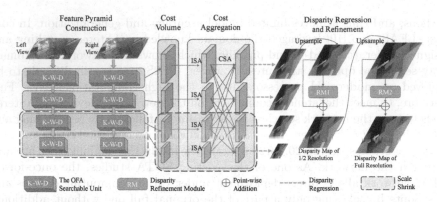

Fig. 1. The model structure of our proposed EASNet. It contains four modules with different functions derived from the domain knowledge of stereo matching. The OFA searchable unit applies the similar methodology in [5]. The parts covered by the shallow yellow dotted blocks can be alternatively skipped when applying scale shrinking. (Color figure online)

Feature Extraction. In feature extraction, we need to extract multi-scale features from the input left and right images and construct a feature pyramid for the latter cost volume stage. Thus, we design a sequence of searchable units (similar to [5]) that cover three important dimensions of CNNs, i.e., depth, width, and kernel size. The ith unit produces features maps of $1/(3 \times 2^{i-1})$ resolution by setting stride $= 2$ for the first convolution layer and stride $= 1$ for the rest in it. For example, in our experimental setting, there are totally four units providing different resolutions of feature maps from $1/3$ to $1/24$. We also enable each unit to use arbitrary numbers of layers (denoted as elastic depth) as that of OFA [5]. Then we allow each layer to use arbitrary numbers of channels (denoted as elastic width) and arbitrary kernel sizes (denoted as elastic kernel size). In our experimental setting, the depth of each unit is chosen from $\{2, 3, 4\}$; the width expansion ratio in each layer is chosen from $\{2, 4, 6, 8\}$; the kernel size is chosen from $\{3, 5, 7\}$. Therefore, with 4 units, we have roughly $((3 \times 4)^2 + (3 \times 4)^3 + (3 \times 4)^4)^4 \approx 10^{13}$ different architectures. Since all of these sub-networks share the same weights, we only require 5M parameters to store all of them. Without sharing, the total model size will be extremely large, which is impractical.

We further introduce one more dimension of the network search space, the total scale of the feature pyramid (denoted as elastic scale) to EASNet. As proved by existing studies [10], the number of scales in a feature pyramid can significantly affect the model accuracy of disparity prediction. Deeper feature pyramids typically provide better prediction accuracy but require more computational efforts. Thus, we allow our EASNet to skip some high levels of feature maps and fine-tune the low levels. Take an example shown in Fig. 1, the part covered by the shallow golden dotted blocks can be alternatively skipped during model fine-tune and inference. The scale of feature pyramid is chosen from $\{2, 3, 4\}$ in our experiments.

Cost Volume. After the feature pyramids of the left and right images are constructed, we then establish the multi-scale 3D cost volume by correlating left and right image features at corresponding scales with the point-wise multiplication operation, which is similar to AANet [43].

$$\mathbf{C}(d, h, w) = \frac{1}{N} \langle \mathbf{F}_l^s(h, w), \mathbf{F}_r^s(h, w - d) \rangle, \tag{1}$$

where $\langle \cdot, \cdot \rangle$ denotes the inner product of two feature vectors and N is the channel number of extracted features. $\mathbf{F}_l^s$ denotes the feature maps of the scale s extracted from the left view, and $\mathbf{F}_r^s$ refers to the ones from the right view. $\mathbf{C}(d, h, w)$ is the matching cost at location (h, w) for disparity candidate d. Thus, S scales of feature pyramid produce S 3D cost volume. The raw cost volume in this module will be then fed into the cost aggregation module. In the cost volume module, we also support elastic scale which can be chosen from [2–4]. The chosen scale is naturally consistent with the scale number of feature pyramid.

Cost Aggregation. The cost aggregation module is used to compute and aggregate matching costs from the concatenated cost volumes. We apply the stacked Adaptive Aggregation Modules (AAModules) for flexible and efficient cost aggregation, as it can simultaneously estimate the matching cost in the views of intrascale and cross-scale. An AAModule consists of S adaptive Intra-Scale Aggregation (ISA) modules and an adaptive Cross-Scale Aggregation (CSA) module for S pyramid levels.

For each scale of the cost volume, ISA can address the popular edge-fattening problem in object boundaries and thin structures by enabling sparse adaptive location sampling. In [43], ISA is implemented by dilated convolution. In particular, we use the same implementation of ISA in [43], which is a stack of three layers (i.e., 1×1 convolution, 3×3 deformable convolution and 1×1 convolution) and a residual connection.

Assume that the resulting cost volume after ISA is $\tilde{C}^s$, we apply the CSA module to explore the correspondence among different scales of $\tilde{C}^s$. To estimate the cross-scale cost aggregation of the scale s, we adopt

$$\hat{C}^s = \sum_{k=1}^{S} f_k(\tilde{C}^s), s = 1, 2, ..., S \tag{2}$$

where f_k is a function to adaptively combine the cost volumes from different scales. We adopt the same definition of f_k as HRNet [38], which is defined as

$$f_k = \begin{cases} \mathcal{I}, k = s, \\ (s - k) \ 3 \times 3 \text{ convs with stride} = 2, k < s, \\ \text{unsampling} \ \oplus 1 \times 1 \text{ conv}, k > s. \end{cases} \tag{3}$$

where $\mathcal{I}$ denotes the identity function and $\oplus$ indicates bilinear up-sampling to the same resolution followed by a 1×1 convolution to align the number of channels. In f_k, when $k < s$, $(s - k)$ 3×3 convolutions with stride $= 2$ are used for $2^{(s-k)}$ times down-sampling to make the resolution consistent.

In the cost aggregation module, we also support elastic scale which can be chosen from [2–4]. The chosen scale is naturally consistent with the scale number of feature pyramid. Notice that for S scales of cost volumes, the total number of combinations is $S^2/2$. Removing some scales can considerably reduce the computational efforts of cost aggregation.

Disparity Regression and Refinement. For each scale of the aggregated cost volumes, we use disparity regression as proposed in [24] to produce the estimated disparity map. The probability of each disparity d is calculated from the predicted cost C_s^d via the softmax operation $\sigma(\cdot)$. The estimated disparity $\hat{d}$ is calculated as the sum of each disparity candidate d weighted by its probability.

$$\hat{d} = \sum_{d=0}^{D_{\max}-1} d \times \sigma(c_d) \qquad (4)$$

where $D_{\max}$ is the maximum disparity range, $\sigma(\cdot)$ is the softmax function, and c_d is the aggregated matching cost for disparity candidate d. As discussed in [24], this regression has been proved to be more robust than using a convolution layer to directly produce the one-channel disparity map. In our EASNet, it will predict S scales of disparity maps of different resolutions, from $1/3$ to $1/(3\times2^{S-1})$.

Notice that the largest regressed disparity map is only $1/3$ of the original resolution. To produce the full resolution of disparity, we apply the same two refinement modules in StereoDRNet [7] to hierarchically upsample and refine the predicted $1/3$ disparity. The two refinement modules upsample the predicted disparity map from $1/3$ to $1/2$ and then $1/2$ to full resolution, respectively.

3.2   Training EASNet

As discussed in [5], directly finetuning the network from scratch leads to prohibitive training cost and interference of model quality among different sub-networks. To efficiently train EASNet, we extend the progressive shrinking (PS) strategy of OFA to support our specialized search space of stereo matching. We first start with training the largest neural network (denoted as the full EASNet) with the maximum kernel size (K = 7), depth (D = 4), width (W = 8) and scale (S = 4). Then we perform four stages to finetune EASNet to support different dimensions of elastic factors.

Elastic Kernel Size, Depth and Width. To search networks of different kernel sizes (K), depths (D) and widths (W), we apply the progressive shrinking strategy in [5], which is an effective and efficient training method to prevent interference among different sub-networks. First, we support elastic kernel size which can choose from $\{3, 5, 7\}$ at each layer, while the depth and width remain the maximum values. This is achieved by introducing kernel transformation matrices which share the kernel weights. For each layer, we have one 25×25 matrix and one 9×9 matrix that are shared among different channels, to transform the largest 7×7 kernels. Second, we support elastic depth. For a specific D, we keep the first D layers and skip the last $(N - D)$ layers (N is the original number of layers), which results that one depth setting only corresponds to one combination of layers. Third, we support elastic width. We introduce a channel sorting operation to support partial widths, which reorganizes the channels according to their importance (i.e., L1 norm of weights). Until now, we have finished three stages of model finetune.

Elastic Scale. The scale search covers all four function modules in EASNet, and can be chosen from $\{2, 3, 4\}$. Take an example of choosing the scale S for the largest scale N. Starting from feature pyramid construction, we keep the first S scales of feature maps and skip the rest, which forms a S-level of feature pyramid. Then for the cost volume, $N - S$ cost volumes are naturally removed. Next for the cost aggregation, we only need to process $S^2/2$ combinations instead of $N^2/2$. Finally, the last $N - S$ scales of disparity maps are also skipped. In our experiments, this scale shrinking operation not only preserves the accuracy of larger sub-networks but also significantly reduces the network inference time.

Loss Function. Given a pair of rectified stereo RGB images, our EASNet takes them as inputs and produces $S + 2$ disparity maps of different scales, where the first S scales (denoted by $\hat{d}_s^i$) are generated by the AAModules and the rest two are generated by the refinement modules. We denote $\hat{d}_h^i$ as the first refinement result and $\hat{d}_f^i$ as the second one. Assume that the input image size is $H \times W$. For each predicted $\hat{d}_i$, it is first bilinearly upsampled to the full resolution. Then we adopt the pixel-wise smooth L1 loss to calculate the error between the predicted disparity map $\hat{d}_i$ and the ground truth d_i,

$$L_s(d_s, \hat{d}_s) = \frac{1}{N} \sum_{i=1}^{N} smooth_{L_1}(d_s^i - \hat{d}_s^i), s \in [1, ..., S] \tag{5}$$

where N is the number of pixels of the disparity map, d_s^i is the ith element of $d_s \in \mathcal{R}^N$ and

$$smooth_{L_1}(x) = \begin{cases} 0.5x^2, & \text{if } |x| < 1 \\ |x| - 0.5, & \text{otherwise.} \end{cases} \tag{6}$$

The predicted refinement results $\hat{d}_h$ and $\hat{d}_f$ also follow the same smooth L1 loss calculation, denoted by L_h and L_f respectively. The final loss function is a weighted summation of losses over all disparity predictions as

$$L = \sum_{s=1}^{S} w_s L_s(d_s, \hat{d}_s) + w_h L_h(d_h, \hat{d}_h) + w_f L_f(d_f, \hat{d}_f). \tag{7}$$

In our experimental setting, the loss weights for the two lowest scale in (7) are set to $1/3$ and $2/3$, while the rest are all set to 1.0.

4   Evaluation

4.1   Experimental Settings

We conduct extensive experiments on four popular stereo datasets: Scene Flow [29], MPI Sintel [2], KITTI 2012 [15] and KITTI 2015 [30]. We use the training

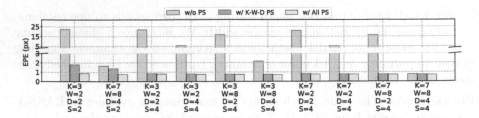

Fig. 2. Scene Flow EPE (px) performance of sub-networks extracted from the full EASNet. K: kernel size, W: width, D: depth, S: Scale.

set of 35,454 samples of Scene Flow to train our EASNet, and then evaluate it on the test set of Scene Flow. For Scene Flow and MPI Sintel, we use end-point error (EPE) to measure the accuracy of the methods, where EPE is the mean disparity error in pixels. For KITTI 2012 and KITTI 2015, we report EPE and official metrics (e.g., D1-all) in the online leader board.

We implement our EASNet using PyTorch 1.8. First, we train the full network for 64 epochs with an initial learning rate of 1×10^{-3}. Then we follow the schedule described in Sect. 3.2 to further fine-tune the full network, which contains five 25-epoch stages. The initial learning rate of each stage is set to 5×10^{-4}, which is decayed by half every 10 epochs.

To compete for the methods in the online official leader board, we also fine-tune our EASNet on two KITTI datasets. We use a crop size of 336×960, and first fine-tune the pre-trained Scene Flow model on mixed KITTI 2012 and 2015 training sets for 1000 epochs. The initial learning rate is 1×10^{-3} and it is decreased by half every 300 epochs. Then another 1000 epochs are trained on the separate KITTI 2012/2015 training set for benchmarking, with an initial learning rate of 1×10^{-4} and the same learning rate schedule as before.

As for data pre-processing, we follow the steps in [43], including color normalization and random cropping. For all the stages, we use the Adam ($\beta_1 = 0.9, \beta_2 = 0.999$) optimizer to train EASNet. The network is trained with a batch size of 16 on 8 V100 GPUs. The entire architecture search optimization takes about 48 GPU days. Although AutoDispNet and LEAStereo only take 42 and 10 GPU days, the training cost of model re-searching and re-training can be prohibitive when they are applied to new computing devices.

To validate the deployment flexibility and efficiency, we benchmark our EASNet on three Nvidia GPUs with different computing levels, including the server-level Tesla V100, the desktop-level GTX 2070, and the inference-level Tesla P40.

4.2 Experimental Results

Results of Different Sub-networks. Fig. 2 reports the Scene Flow EPEs of sub-networks derived from the full EASNet of different training schemes. Due to space limits, we take 10 sub-networks for comparison, and each of them is denoted as "(K = k, W = w, D = d, S = s)". It represents a sub-network that has

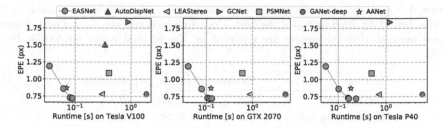

Fig. 3. Our proposed method, EASNet, sets a new state-of-the-art on the Scene Flow *test* dataset with much fewer parameters and much lower inference time. The data points on the EASNet line indicate different sub-networks sampled from its largest full network structure.

d layers for all units in the feature extraction module with the expansion ratio and kernel size set to w and k for all layers, and s scales throughout all the function modules in EASNet. "w/o PS" indicates that we only train the largest full EASNet without model finetune, while "w/ K-W-D PS" and "w/ All PS" indicate that the full EASNet is fine-tuned using progressive shrinking (PS) of the first three stages (kernel size, width, and depth) and the complete five stages, respectively. Without PS, the model accuracy is significantly degraded while shrinking width and depth (seen from the last four sub-networks.). After performing PS for K-W-D, the accuracy of all the sub-networks can be improved by a significant margin. Moreover, our proposed shrinking scheme on scale (S) and refinement (R) can further reduce nearly 50% of the estimation error (seen from the first two sub-networks). Specifically, without architecture optimization, our complete PS scheme can still achieve 0.86 of average EPE using only 0.78 M parameters under the architecture setting ($K = 3$, $W = 2$, $D = 2$, $S = 2$), which is on par with AANet (EPE: 0.87, 3.9 M parameters). In contrast, without the additional PS for scale and refinement, it only achieves 1.8, which is 0.94 worse.

EASNet under Different Hardware Computing Capability. Figure 3 summarizes the results of different sub-networks extracted from EASNet under three GPUs. We also plot the results of other existing SOTA methods for comparison. First, EASNet outperforms all the other methods with Pareto optimality of both model accuracy and inference time. Take the desktop GPU GTX 2070 as an example. EASNet achieves a new SOTA 0.73 EPE with the runtime of 0.12 s, being 0.14 lower EPE than AANet that has similar inference performance. To achieve similar accuracy of AANet, EASNet performs 0.08 s on GTX 2070, which is 33.3% lower than AANet. Second, since our EASNet only needs one time of training and does not need any further fine-tuning efforts when being deployed on devices of different computing capability, we can directly choose the sub-network from the full EASNet according to the latency requirement, while other methods cannot. For example, if we set the inference latency goal to 100 ms, for both the existing human-designed and NAS methods, only AANet on Tesla V100 can satisfy the requirement. However, our EASNet can provide a sub-network of competitive accuracy on all the three devices, i.e., 0.72 EPE with 0.09 s on Tesla

448   Q. Wang et al.

Table 1. Quantitative results on Scene Flow dataset. The runtime is measured on Nvidia Tesla P40. Bold indicates the best. Underline indicates the second best. Parentheses indicate that the results are reported by the original paper on Nvidia Tesla V100.

Method	Params [M]	EPE [px]	Runtime [s]
PSMNet [8]	5.22	1.09	0.5
GANet-deep [45]	6.58	0.78	5.5
AANet [43]	3.9	0.87	0.18
AutoDispNet-CSS [36]	37	1.51	(0.34)
LEAStereo [10]	<u>1.81</u>	0.78	0.71
DeepPruner (best) [13]	7.1	0.86	0.18
DeepPruner (fast) [13]	7.1	0.97	**0.06**
EASNet-L	5.07	**0.72**	0.24
EASNet-M	3.03	<u>0.73</u>	0.16
EASNet-S	**0.78**	0.86	<u>0.10</u>

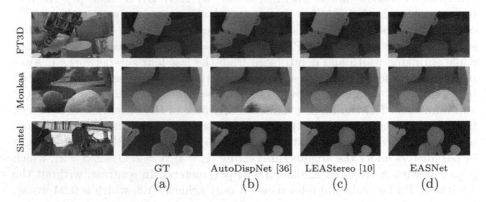

Fig. 4. Disparity predictions for the testing data of FlyingThings3D (FT3D), Monkaa and MPI Sintel. The leftest column shows the left images of the stereo pairs. The rest four columns respectively show the disparity maps estimated by (a) ground truth, (b) AutoDispNet [36], (c) LEAStereo [10], and (d) our EASNet.

V100, 0.73 EPE with 0.1 s on GTX 2070, and 0.86 EPE with 0.1 s on Tesla P40. This proves the flexibility and efficiency of our EASNet.

Benchmark Results on Scene Flow. For the rest of experiments, we pick three sub-networks from the full EASNet, EASNet-L ($K=7$, $W=8$, $D=4$, $S=4$), EASNet-M ($K=7$, $W=8$, $D=2$, $S=4$), and EASNet-S ($K=3$, $W=2$, $D=2$, $S=2$).

We compare our EASNet networks with five SOTA methods, including three hand-crafted and two NAS-based networks on Scene Flow [29] test set with 192 disparity level. In Table 1, we can observe that EASNet-M achieves the

Table 2. Quantitative results on other stereo datasets. Entries enclosed by parentheses indicate if they were tested on the target dataset without model finetuning. "DN-CSS" is short for DispNet-CSS. "ADN-CSS" is short for AutoDispNet-CSS. The time is measured on Nvidia Tesla V100 for KITTI resolution.

Method	Sintel (clean)	KITTI (2012)		KITTI (2015)		Time [s]
	EPE train	EPE train	Out-noc test	EPE train	D1-all test	
ADN-CSS [36]	(2.14)	(**0.93**)	1.70%	(**1.14**)	2.18%	0.34
GCNet [24]	–	–	1.77%	–	2.87%	0.9
GANet [45]	–	–	1.19%	–	1.81%	1.9
AANet [43]	–	–	1.91%	–	2.55%	0.07
LEAStereo [10]	–	–	**1.13%**	–	**1.65%**	0.3
DeepPruner (best) [13]	–	–	–	–	2.15%	0.18
≤ 100 ms						
DN-CSS [22]	(2.33)	(1.40)	1.82%	(1.37)	2.19%	0.08
DeepPruner (fast) [13]	–	–	–	–	2.59%	0.06
MADNet [41]	–	–	–	–	4.66%	**0.02**
EASNet-L	(**1.58**)	(1.91)	1.89%	(1.90)	2.70%	0.09
EASNet-M	(1.59)	(1.91)	1.96%	(2.18)	2.89%	0.08
EASNet-S	(1.95)	(2.44)	2.57%	(2.32)	3.43%	0.06

AANet [43]   LEAStereo [10]   EASNet

Fig. 5. Disparity predictions for KITTI 2012 and 2015 testing data. The leftest column shows the left images of the stereo pairs. The rest three columns show the disparity maps estimated by existing methods and our EASNet.

best performance using only near half of parameters in comparison to the SOTA hand-crafted methods (e.g., GANet [45]). Furthermore, the previous SOTA NAS-based method AutoDispNet [36] has 10× more parameters than our EASNet-M. Our smallest sub-network EASNet-S can still achieve much better accuracy than AutoDispNet and comparable accuracy to AANet with much fewer parameters and faster inference speed. As for the model runtime, EASNet-L outperforms the accuracy SOTA, GANet [45] and LEAStereo [10] by 3× and 22× respectively. EASNet-M achieves Pareto optimality in both accuracy and speed among all the methods. We show some of the qualitative results in Fig. 4. Our EASNet outperforms AutoDispNet in terms of estimation quality and achieves competitive accuracy to LEAStereo with only one third of inference time on P40.

Benchmark Results on Sintel and KITTI. We evaluate the model generalization of EASNet on the other two datasets, MPI Sintel and KITTI. Table 2 shows the results. Sintel is tested without any model finetune. EASNet-L achieves a much lower EPE than DispNet-CSS and AutoDispNet-CSS. Besides, after being finetuned on the KITTI training data, EASNet still shows satisfying accuracy with the state of the art on the common public benchmarks. EASNet-L achieves the best or second best accuracy among the methods of less than 100 ms. EASNet-S also achieves competitive accuracy with much lower latency. We show some of the qualitative results in Fig. 5. Our EASNet is able to capture the disparity information of those thin objects, such as street light and road fence.

4.3 Discussion

There are several hints from the experiments. 1. The scale of the feature extraction module does not need to be large to achieve a good performance, due to the fact that the sub-network of $(S = 2)$ has similar accuracy to that of $(S = 4)$ with our training strategy; 2. The inference time drop of EASNet-S mainly comes from shrinking the feature extraction units and the whole scale (nearly 58%);

5   Conclusion and Future Work

In this paper, we proposed EASNet, an elastic and accurate stereo matching network that leverages the domain knowledge of the CVM-Conv3D methods to design a specialized search space covering enormous architecture settings. To efficiently train EASNet with the target of maximizing the accuracy of all the sub-networks, we use the progressive shrinking strategy to support the specialized network search space of four dimensions, including depth, width, kernel size, and scale. Superior to the previous studies that design and train a neural network for each deployment scenario, our EASNet can quickly generate the sub-networks that satisfy the deployment requirement of accuracy and latency. Validated on public benchmarks among three devices of different computing capability, our EASNet achieves Pareto optimality in terms of model accuracy and inference speed among all state-of-the-art CVA-3D deep stereo matching architectures (human designed and NAS searched).

In the future, we plan to apply NAS to search the units of cost aggregation and disparity refinement, which owns great potential for deriving smaller sub-networks with consistent accuracy. Furthermore, how to combine the network search strategies of DARTS (for operator and cell link) and OFA (for cell/layer/block hyper-parameter) is also an interesting and potential direction of searching an efficient and effective network structure for stereo matching.

Acknowledgements. This work was supported in part by the Hong Kong RGC GRF grant under the contract HKBU 12200418, grant RMGS2019_1_23 and grant

RMGS21EG01 from Hong Kong Research Matching Grant Scheme, the NVIDIA Academic Hardware Grant, and Guangdong Provincial Key Laboratory of Novel Security Intelligence Technologies (2022B1212010005).

References

1. Bello, I., Zoph, B., Vasudevan, V., Le, Q.V.: Neural optimizer search with reinforcement learning. In: Proceedings of the 34th International Conference on Machine Learning. Proceedings of Machine Learning Research, vol. 70, pp. 459–468, 06–11 August 2017
2. Butler, D.J., Wulff, J., Stanley, G.B., Black, M.J.: A naturalistic open source movie for optical flow evaluation. In: Fitzgibbon, A., Lazebnik, S., Perona, P., Sato, Y., Schmid, C. (eds.) ECCV 2012. LNCS, vol. 7577, pp. 611–625. Springer, Heidelberg (2012). https://doi.org/10.1007/978-3-642-33783-3_44
3. Cai, H., Chen, T., Zhang, W., Yu, Y., Wang, J.: Reinforcement learning for architecture search by network transformation. Proceedings of the AAAI Conference on Artificial Intelligence 4 (2017)
4. Cai, H., Chen, T., Zhang, W., Yu, Y., Wang, J.: Efficient architecture search by network transformation. In: Proceedings of the AAAI Conference on Artificial Intelligence 32(1), April 2018
5. Cai, H., Gan, C., Wang, T., Zhang, Z., Han, S.: Once for all: train one network and specialize it for efficient deployment. In: International Conference on Learning Representations (2020)
6. Cai, H., Zhu, L., Han, S.: Proxylessnas: Direct neural architecture search on target task and hardware (2018)
7. Chabra, R., Straub, J., Sweeney, C., Newcombe, R., Fuchs, H.: Stereodrnet: dilated residual stereonet. In: Proceedings of the IEEE/CVF Conference on Computer Vision and Pattern Recognition (CVPR) (June 2019)
8. Chang, J.R., Chen, Y.S.: Pyramid stereo matching network. In: The IEEE Conference on Computer Vision and Pattern Recognition (CVPR), June 2018
9. Chen, W., Gong, X., Liu, X., Zhang, Q., Li, Y., Wang, Z.: Fasterseg: searching for faster real-time semantic segmentation (2019)
10. Cheng, X., et al.: Hierarchical neural architecture search for deep stereo matching. In: Advances in Neural Information Processing Systems, vol. 33 (2020)
11. Deng, J., Dong, W., Socher, R., Li, L.J., Li, K., Fei-Fei, L.: ImageNet: A large-scale hierarchical image database. In: IEEE Conference on Computer Vision and Pattern Recognition, 2009. CVPR 2009, pp. 248–255. IEEE (2009)
12. Dosovitskiy, A., et al.: Flownet: learning optical flow with convolutional networks. In: The IEEE International Conference on Computer Vision (ICCV), December 2015
13. Duggal, S., Wang, S., Ma, W.C., Hu, R., Urtasun, R.: Deeppruner: Learning efficient stereo matching via differentiable patchmatch. In: 2019 IEEE/CVF International Conference on Computer Vision (ICCV). pp. 4383–4392 (2019)
14. Elsken, T., Metzen, J.H., Hutter, F.: Neural architecture search: a survey. J. Mach. Learn. Res. 20(1), 1997–2017 (2019)
15. Geiger, A., Lenz, P., Urtasun, R.: Are we ready for autonomous driving? the kitti vision benchmark suite. In: 2012 IEEE Conference on Computer Vision and Pattern Recognition, pp. 3354–3361. IEEE (2012)

16. Hao, C., Zhang, X., Li, Y., Huang, S., Xiong, J., Rupnow, K., Hwu, W., Chen, D.: Fpga/dnn co-design: An efficient design methodology for 1ot intelligence on the edge. In: 2019 56th ACM/IEEE Design Automation Conference (DAC), pp. 1–6 (2019)

17. He, K., Zhang, X., Ren, S., Sun, J.: Deep residual learning for image recognition. In: The IEEE Conference on Computer Vision and Pattern Recognition (CVPR), June 2016

18. He, X., Zhao, K., Chu, X.: Automl: a survey of the state-of-the-art. Knowle.-Based Syst. **212**, 106622 (2021)

19. Hirschmuller, H.: Stereo processing by semiglobal matching and mutual information. IEEE Trans. Pattern Anal. Mach. Intell. **30**(2), 328–341 (2007)

20. Huang, G., Chen, D., Li, T., Wu, F., van der Maaten, L., Weinberger, K.Q.: Multi-scale dense networks for resource efficient image classification (2017)

21. Ilg, E., Mayer, N., Saikia, T., Keuper, M., Dosovitskiy, A., Brox, T.: Flownet 2.0: evolution of optical flow estimation with deep networks. In: The IEEE Conference on Computer Vision and Pattern Recognition (CVPR), July 2017

22. Ilg, E., Saikia, T., Keuper, M., Brox, T.: Occlusions, motion and depth boundaries with a generic network for disparity, optical flow or scene flow estimation. In: Ferrari, V., Hebert, M., Sminchisescu, C., Weiss, Y. (eds.) ECCV 2018. LNCS, vol. 11216, pp. 626–643. Springer, Cham (2018). https://doi.org/10.1007/978-3-030-01258-8_38

23. Jiang, W., Zhang, X., Sha, E.H.M., Yang, L., Zhuge, Q., Shi, Y., Hu, J.: Accuracy vs. efficiency: Achieving both through fpga-implementation aware neural architecture search. In: Proceedings of the 56th Annual Design Automation Conference 2019. DAC 2019 (2019)

24. Kendall, A., et al.: End-to-end learning of geometry and context for deep stereo regression. In: Proceedings of the IEEE International Conference on Computer Vision, pp. 66–75 (2017)

25. Lin, J., Rao, Y., Lu, J., Zhou, J.: Runtime neural pruning. In: Proceedings of the 31st International Conference on Neural Information Processing Systems, pp. 2178–2188 (2017)

26. Liu, C., Chen, L.C., Schroff, F., Adam, H., Hua, W., Yuille, A.L., Fei-Fei, L.: Auto-deeplab: Hierarchical neural architecture search for semantic image segmentation. In: Proceedings of the IEEE/CVF Conference on Computer Vision and Pattern Recognition (CVPR), June 2019

27. Liu, H., Simonyan, K., Vinyals, O., Fernando, C., Kavukcuoglu, K.: Hierarchical representations for efficient architecture search (2017)

28. Liu, H., Simonyan, K., Yang, Y.: Darts: Differentiable architecture search (2018)

29. Mayer, N., et al.: A large dataset to train convolutional networks for disparity, optical flow, and scene flow estimation. In: Proceedings of the IEEE Conference on Computer Vision and Pattern Recognition, pp. 4040–4048 (2016)

30. Menze, M., Heipke, C., Geiger, A.: Joint 3d estimation of vehicles and scene flow. In: ISPRS Workshop on Image Sequence Analysis (ISA) (2015)

31. Nekrasov, V., Chen, H., Shen, C., Reid, I.: Fast neural architecture search of compact semantic segmentation models via auxiliary cells. In: Proceedings of the IEEE/CVF Conference on Computer Vision and Pattern Recognition (CVPR), June 2019

32. Nie, G.Y., et al.: Multi-level context ultra-aggregation for stereo matching. In: Proceedings of the IEEE Conference on Computer Vision and Pattern Recognition, pp. 3283–3291 (2019)

33. Pang, J., Sun, W., Ren, J.S., Yang, C., Yan, Q.: Cascade residual learning: a two-stage convolutional neural network for stereo matching. In: The IEEE International Conference on Computer Vision (ICCV) Workshops, October 2017

34. Real, E., Aggarwal, A., Huang, Y., Le, Q.V.: Regularized evolution for image classifier architecture search. In: Proceedings of the AAAI Conference on Artificial Intelligence **33**(01), 4780–4789 (2019)

35. Real, E., et al.: Large-scale evolution of image classifiers. In: Proceedings of the 34th International Conference on Machine Learning. Proceedings of Machine Learning Research, vol. 70, pp. 2902–2911 06–11 August 2017

36. Saikia, T., Marrakchi, Y., Zela, A., Hutter, F., Brox, T.: Autodispnet: improving disparity estimation with automl. In: The IEEE International Conference on Computer Vision (ICCV) (October 2019)

37. Stanley, K.O., Miikkulainen, R.: Evolving Neural Networks through Augmenting Topologies. Evol. Comput. **10**(2), 99–127 (2002)

38. Sun, K., Xiao, B., Liu, D., Wang, J.: Deep high-resolution representation learning for human pose estimation. In: Proceedings of the IEEE/CVF Conference on Computer Vision and Pattern Recognition (CVPR), June 2019

39. Tan, M., et al.: Mnasnet: Platform-aware neural architecture search for mobile. In: Proceedings of the IEEE/CVF Conference on Computer Vision and Pattern Recognition (CVPR), June 2019

40. Tan, M., Pang, R., Le, Q.V.: Efficientdet: Scalable and efficient object detection. In: Proceedings of the IEEE/CVF Conference on Computer Vision and Pattern Recognition (CVPR), June 2020

41. Tonioni, A., Tosi, F., Poggi, M., Mattoccia, S., Stefano, L.D.: Real-time self-adaptive deep stereo. In: 2019 IEEE/CVF Conference on Computer Vision and Pattern Recognition (CVPR), pp. 195–204 (2019)

42. Wang, Q., Shi, S., Zheng, S., Zhao, K., Chu, X.: FADNet: a fast and accurate network for disparity estimation. In: 2020 IEEE International Conference on Robotics and Automation (ICRA 2020), pp. 101–107 (2020)

43. Xu, H., Zhang, J.: Aanet: Adaptive aggregation network for efficient stereo matching. In: Proceedings of the IEEE/CVF Conference on Computer Vision and Pattern Recognition, pp. 1959–1968 (2020)

44. Zbontar, J., LeCun, Y., et al.: Stereo matching by training a convolutional neural network to compare image patches. J. Mach. Learn. Res. **17**(1–32), 2 (2016)

45. Zhang, F., Prisacariu, V., Yang, R., Torr, P.H.: Ga-net: Guided aggregation net for end-to-end stereo matching. In: The IEEE Conference on Computer Vision and Pattern Recognition (CVPR), June 2019

46. Zoph, B., Vasudevan, V., Shlens, J., Le, Q.V.: Learning transferable architectures for scalable image recognition. In: Proceedings of the IEEE Conference on Computer Vision and Pattern Recognition (CVPR), June 2018

Relative Pose from SIFT Features

Daniel Barath[1]([✉]) and Zuzana Kukelova[2]

[1] ETH Zurich, Computer Vision and Geometry Group, Zürich, Switzerland
danielbela.barath@inf.ethz.ch
[2] Visual Recognition Group, Faculty of Electrical Engineering, Czech Technical University in Prague, Prague, Czechia
kukelzuz@fel.cvut.cz

Abstract. This paper derives the geometric relationship of epipolar geometry and orientation- and scale-covariant, e.g., SIFT, features. We derive a new linear constraint relating the unknown elements of the fundamental matrix and the orientation and scale. This equation can be used together with the well-known epipolar constraint to, e.g., estimate the fundamental matrix from four SIFT correspondences, essential matrix from three, and to solve the semi-calibrated case from three correspondences. Requiring fewer correspondences than the well-known point-based approaches (e.g., 5PT, 6PT and 7PT solvers) for epipolar geometry estimation makes RANSAC-like randomized robust estimation significantly faster. The proposed constraint is tested on a number of problems in a synthetic environment and on publicly available real-world datasets on more than 800 00 image pairs. It is superior to the state-of-the-art in terms of processing time while often leading more accurate results. The solvers are included in GC-RANSAC at https://github.com/danini/graph-cut-ransac.

Keywords: Epipolar geometry · Covariant features · Minimal solver · RANSAC

1 Introduction

This paper addresses the problem of interpreting orientation- and scale-covariant features, *e.g.* SIFT [23] or SURF [13], w.r.t. the epipolar geometry characterized either by a fundamental or an essential matrix. The derived relationship is then exploited to design minimal relative pose solvers that allow significantly faster robust estimation than by using the traditional point-based solvers.

Nowadays, a number of algorithms exist for estimating or approximating geometric models, *e.g.*, homographies, using fully affine-covariant features. Some methods [31,36] approximate the epipolar geometry from one or two affine correspondences by converting them to point pairs. Bentolila et al. [14] proposed a solution for estimating the fundamental matrix using three affine features. Raposo et al. [34,35] and Barath et al. [9] showed that two correspondences are enough for estimating the relative pose when having calibrated cameras. Moreover, two correspondences are enough for solving the semi-calibrated case, *i.e.*, when the objective is to find the essential matrix and

---

Supplementary Information The online version contains supplementary material available at https://doi.org/10.1007/978-3-031-19824-3_27.

(a) Sacre Coeur   (b) St. Peter's Square   (c) KITTI

Fig. 1. Example image pairs from the PhotoTourism [3] and KITTI [15] datasets where the proposed SIFT-based solver estimates the (a) fundamental and (b) essential matrix and (c) solves the semi-calibrated case (*i.e.*, unknown focal length). A hundred random inliers are drawn.

a common unknown focal length [6]. Guan et al. [16] proposed ways of estimating the generalized pose from affine correspondences. Also, homographies can be estimated from two affine correspondences as shown in the dissertation of Kevin Koser [19], and, in the case of known epipolar geometry, from a single correspondence [4]. There is a one-to-one relationship between local affine transformations and surface normals [11,19]. Pritts et al. [32,33] showed that the lens distortion parameters can be retrieved using affine features. The ways of using such solvers in practice are discussed in [12].

Affine correspondences encode higher-order information about the underlying the scene geometry. This is why the previously mentioned methods solve geometric estimation problems (*e.g.*, homographies and epipolar geometry) using only a few correspondences – significantly fewer than what point-based methods need. However, requiring affine features implies their major drawback. Detectors for obtaining accurate affine correspondences, for example, Affine-SIFT [29], Hessian-Affine or Harris-Affine [24], MODS [26], HesAffNet [27], are slow compared to other detectors. Therefore, they are not applicable in time-sensitive applications, where real-time performance is required.

In this paper, the objective is to bridge this problem by exploiting partially affine covariant features. The typically used detectors (*e.g.*, SIFT and ORB) obtain more information than simply the coordinates of the feature points, for example, the orientation and scale. Even though this information is actually available "for free", it is ignored in point-based solvers. We focus on exploiting this already available information without requiring additional computations, *e.g.*, to extract expensive affine features.

Using partially affine covariant features for model estimation is a known approach with a number of papers published in the recent years. In [25], the feature orientations are used to estimate the essential matrix. In [1], the fundamental matrix is assumed to be a priori known and an algorithm is proposed for approximating a homography exploiting the rotations and scales of two SIFT correspondences. The approximative nature comes from the assumption that the scales along the axes are equal to the SIFT scale

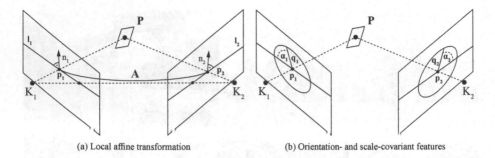

(a) Local affine transformation   (b) Orientation- and scale-covariant features

Fig. 2. (a) The geometric interpretation of the relationship of a local affine transformations and the epipolar geometry (Eq. (6); proposed in [6]). Given the projection p_i of point P in the ith camera K_i, $i \in \{1, 2\}$. The normal n_1 of epipolar line l_1 is mapped by affinity $A \in \mathbb{R}^{2 \times 2}$ into the normal n_2 of epipolar line l_2. (b) Visualization of the orientation- and scale-covariant features. Point P and the surrounding patch projected into cameras K_1 and K_2. The rotation of the feature in the ith image is $\alpha_i \in [0, 2\pi)$ and the size is $q_i \in \mathbb{R}$. The scaling from the 1st to the 2nd image is calculated as $q = q_2/q_1$ and the rotation as $\alpha = \alpha_2 - \alpha_1$.

and the shear is zero. In general, these assumptions do not hold. The method of Barath et al. [7] approximates the fundamental matrix by enforcing the geometric constraints of affine correspondences on the epipolar lines. Nevertheless, due to using the same affine model as in [1], the estimated epipolar geometry is solely an approximation.

In [2], a two-step procedure is proposed for estimating the epipolar geometry. First, a homography is obtained from three oriented features. Finally, the fundamental matrix is retrieved from the homography and two additional correspondences. Even though this technique considers the scales and shear as unknowns, thus estimating the epipolar geometry instead of approximating it, the proposed decomposition of the affine matrix is not justified theoretically. Therefore, the geometric interpretation of the feature rotations is not provably valid. Barath et al. [8] proposes a way of recovering affine correspondences from the feature rotation, scale, and the fundamental matrix. In [10], a method is proposed to estimate the homography from two SIFT correspondences and a theoretically justifiable affine decomposition and general constraints on the homography are provided. Even though having a number of methods estimating geometric entities from SIFT features, there are *no solvers* that directly exploit the feature orientations and scales for estimating the epipolar geometry in the general case. The reason is that the constraints derived in [10] does not allow directly solving for the pose since each new correspondence yields two equations and, also, two additional unknowns – no constraint is gained on epipolar geometry from considering the orientation and scale.

The contributions of the paper are: (i) We introduce new constraints relating the oriented circles centered on the observed point locations. These constraints relate the SIFT orientations and scales in two images with the elements of affine correspondence A. As such, we show that constraints relating A and the parameters of a SIFT correspondence derived in [10] do not describe the full geometric relationship and, therefore, are not sufficient for estimating the epipolar geometry. (ii) Exploiting the new constraints that relate A and the SIFT correspondence, we derive the geometric relationship between orientation and scale-covariant features and epipolar geometry. The new SIFT-based constraint is a linear equation that can be straightforwardly used together with the well-known epipolar constraint to efficiently solve relative pose problems. (iii) Finally, we exploit the new constraint in minimal solvers for estimating epipolar geometry of uncalibrated, calibrated and partially-calibrated cameras with unknown focal length. The new solvers require four SIFT correspondences for estimating the fundamental matrix and three for finding the essential matrix both in the fully and in the partially calibrated cases. The reduced sample size accelerates randomized robust estimation by a large margin on a number of real-world datasets while often leading to better accuracy. Example image pairs are shown in Fig. 1.

2   Theoretical Background

Affine correspondence $(\mathbf{p}_1, \mathbf{p}_2, \mathbf{A})$ is a triplet, where $\mathbf{p}_1 = [u_1 \ v_1 \ 1]^T$ and $\mathbf{p}_2 = [u_2 \ v_2 \ 1]^T$ are a corresponding homogeneous point pair in two images and $\mathbf{A}$ is a 2×2 linear transformation which is called *local affine transformation*. Its elements in a row-major order are: a_1, a_2, a_3, and a_4. To define $\mathbf{A}$, we use the definition provided in [28] as it is given as the first-order Taylor-approximation of the 3D $\to$ 2D projection functions. For perspective cameras, the formula for $\mathbf{A}$ is the first-order approximation of the related *homography* matrix as:

$$
\begin{aligned}
a_1 &= \frac{\partial \mathbf{u}_2}{\partial u_1} = \frac{h_1 - h_7 u_2}{s}, \quad a_2 = \frac{\partial \mathbf{u}_2}{\partial v_1} = \frac{h_2 - h_8 u_2}{s}, \\
a_3 &= \frac{\partial \mathbf{v}_2}{\partial u_1} = \frac{h_4 - h_7 v_2}{s}, \quad a_4 = \frac{\partial \mathbf{v}_2}{\partial v_1} = \frac{h_5 - h_8 v_2}{s},
\end{aligned}
\tag{1}
$$

where $\mathbf{u}_i$ and $\mathbf{v}_i$ are coordinate functions given the projection function in the ith image $(i \in \{1, 2\})$ and $s = u_1 h_7 + v_1 h_8 + h_9$ is the projective depth. The elements of homography $\mathbf{H}$ in a row-major order are written as h_1, h_2, ..., h_9.

The relationship of an affine correspondence and a homography is described by six linear equations [4]. First, since an affine correspondence contains a point pair, the well-known equations (from $\alpha \mathbf{H} \mathbf{p}_1 = \mathbf{p}_2$, $\alpha \in \mathbb{R}$) relating the point coordinates hold [18]. The resulting two linearly independent equations are written as follows:

$$
\begin{aligned}
u_1 h_1 + v_1 h_2 + h_3 - u_1 u_2 h_7 - v_1 u_2 h_8 - u_2 h_9 &= 0, \\
u_1 h_4 + v_1 h_5 + h_6 - u_1 v_2 h_7 - v_1 v_2 h_8 - v_2 h_9 &= 0.
\end{aligned}
\tag{2}
$$

Second, after re-arranging Eq. (1), 4 linear constraints are obtained from $\mathbf{A}$ as

$$
h_1 - (u_2 + a_1 u_1) h_7 - a_1 v_1 h_8 - a_1 h_9 = 0, \quad h_2 - (u_2 + a_2 v_1) h_8 - a_2 u_1 h_7 - a_2 h_9 = 0,
$$
$$
h_4 - (v_2 + a_3 u_1) h_7 - a_3 v_1 h_8 - a_3 h_9 = 0, \quad h_5 - (v_2 + a_4 v_1) h_8 - a_4 u_1 h_7 - a_4 h_9 = 0.
$$

Consequently, an affine correspondence provides six linear equations in total, for the elements of the related homography matrix.

Fundamental matrix $\mathbf{F}$ relating two images of a rigid scene is a 3×3 projective transformation ensuring the so-called epipolar constraint

$$
\mathbf{p}_2^T \mathbf{F} \mathbf{p}_1 = 0.
\tag{3}
$$

Since its scale is arbitrary and $\det(\mathbf{F}) = 0$, matrix $\mathbf{F}$ has 7 degrees-of-freedom (DoF).

The relationship of the epipolar geometry (either a fundamental or essential matrix) and affine correspondences are described in [6] through the effect of $\mathbf{A}$ on the corresponding epipolar lines. Suppose that fundamental matrix $\mathbf{F}$, point pair $\mathbf{p}$, $\mathbf{p}'$, and the related affinity $\mathbf{A}$ are given. It can be proven that $\mathbf{A}$ transforms $\mathbf{v}$ to $\mathbf{v}'$, where $\mathbf{v}$ and $\mathbf{v}'$ are the directions of the epipolar lines $(\mathbf{v}, \mathbf{v}' \in \mathbb{R}^2$ s.t. $\|*\| \mathbf{v}_2 = \|*\| \mathbf{v}'_2 = 1)$ in the first and second images [14], respectively. It can be seen that transforming the infinitesimally close vicinity of $\mathbf{p}$ to that of $\mathbf{p}'$, $\mathbf{A}$ has to map the lines going through the points. Therefore, constraint $\mathbf{A}\mathbf{v} \parallel \mathbf{v}'$ holds.

As it is well-known [40], formula $\mathbf{A}\mathbf{v} \parallel \mathbf{v}'$ can be reformulated as follows:

$$\mathbf{A}^{-T}\mathbf{n} - \beta\mathbf{n}', \qquad (4)$$

where $\mathbf{n}$ and $\mathbf{n}'$ are the normals of the epipolar lines $(\mathbf{n}, \mathbf{n}' \in \mathbb{R}^2$ s.t. $\mathbf{n} \perp \mathbf{v}$, $\mathbf{n}' \perp \mathbf{v}')$. Scalar β denotes the scale between the transformed and the original vectors if $\|*\| \mathbf{n}_2 = \|*\| \mathbf{n}'_2 = 1$. The normals are calculated as the first two coordinates of epipolar lines

$$\mathbf{l} = \mathbf{F}^T\mathbf{p}' = [a\ b\ c]^T, \quad \mathbf{l}' = \mathbf{F}\mathbf{p} = [a'\ b'\ c']^T. \qquad (5)$$

Since the common scale of normals $\mathbf{n} = \mathbf{l}_{[1:2]} = [a\ b]^T$ and $\mathbf{n}' = \mathbf{l}'_{[1:2]} = [a'\ b']^T$ comes from the fundamental matrix, Eq. (4) is modified as follows:

$$\mathbf{A}^{-T}\mathbf{n} = -\mathbf{n}'. \qquad (6)$$

Formulas (5) and (6) yield two equations which are linear in the parameters of the fundamental matrix as:

$$(u' + a_1 u)f_1 + a_1 v f_2 + a_1 f_3 + (v' + a_3 u)f_4 + a_3 v f_5 + a_3 f_6 + f_7 = 0, \qquad (7)$$
$$a_2 u f_1 + (u' + a_2 v)f_2 + a_2 f_3 + a_4 u f_4 + (v' + a_4 v)f_5 + a_4 f_6 + f_8 = 0. \qquad (8)$$

Points (u_1, v_1) and (u_2, v_2) are the points in the first and second image, respectively.

In summary, *the linear part* of a local affine transformation *gives two linear equations*, Eqs. (7) and (8), for epipolar geometry estimation. A point correspondence yields a third one, Eq. (3), through the epipolar constraint. Thus, an affine correspondence yields three linear constraints. As the fundamental matrix has seven DoF, three affine correspondences are enough for estimating $\mathbf{F}$ [12].[1] Essential matrix $\mathbf{E}$ has five DoF and, thus, two affine correspondences are enough for the estimation [9].

3   Epipolar Geometry and SIFT Features

In this section, we show the relationship of epipolar geometry and orientation and scale-covariant features. Even though we will use SIFT as an alias for this kind of features, the derived formulas hold for all of them. First, the affine transformation model is described in order to interpret the SIFT angles and scales. This model is substituted into the relationship of affine transformations and epipolar geometry. Combining the derived constraint using elimination ideals [20], we finally propose a linear equation characterizing the epipolar consistency of the orientation and scale part of the SIFT features.

---

[1] Precisely, fundamental matrix $\mathbf{F}$ can be estimated from two affine and a point correspondence.

3.1 Interpretation of SIFT Features

Reflecting the fact that we are given a scale $q_i \in \mathbb{R}^+$ and rotation $\alpha_i \in [0, 2\pi)$ independently in each image ($i \in \{1, 2\}$; see Fig. 2b), the objective is to define affine correspondence $\mathbf{A}$ as a function of them. Such an interpretation was proposed in [10]. In this section, we simplify the formulas in [10] in order to reduce the number of unknowns in the system. To understand the orientation and scale part of SIFT features, we exploit the definition of affine correspondences proposed by Barath et al. [11]. In [11], $\mathbf{A}$ is defined as the multiplication of the Jacobians of the projection functions w.r.t. the image directions in the two images as follows:

$$\mathbf{A} = \mathbf{J}_2 \mathbf{J}_1^{-1}, \tag{9}$$

where $\mathbf{J}_1$ and $\mathbf{J}_2$ are the Jacobians of the 3D $\rightarrow$ 2D projection functions. Proof is in [10]. For the ith Jacobian, we use the following decomposition:

$$\mathbf{J}_i = \mathbf{R}_i \mathbf{U}_i = \begin{bmatrix} \cos(\alpha_i) & -\sin(\alpha_i) \\ \sin(\alpha_i) & \cos(\alpha_i) \end{bmatrix} \begin{bmatrix} q_{u,i} & w_i \\ 0 & q_{v,i} \end{bmatrix}, \tag{10}$$

where angle α_i is the rotation in the ith image, $q_{u,i}$ and $q_{v,i}$ are the scales along axes u and v, and w_i is the shear. Plugging Eq. (10) into Eq. (9) leads to $\mathbf{A} = \mathbf{R}_2 \mathbf{U}_2 (\mathbf{R}_1 \mathbf{U}_1)^{-1} = \mathbf{R}_2 \mathbf{U}_2 \mathbf{U}_1^{-1} \mathbf{R}_1^{\mathsf{T}}$, where $\mathbf{U}_1$ and $\mathbf{U}_2$ contain the unknown scales and shears in the two images. Since we are not interested in finding them separately, we replace $\mathbf{U}_2 \mathbf{U}_1^{-1}$ by upper-triangular matrix $\mathbf{U} = \mathbf{U}_2 \mathbf{U}_1^{-1}$ simplifying the formula to

$$\mathbf{A} = \mathbf{R}_2 \mathbf{U} \mathbf{R}_1^{\mathsf{T}} = \begin{bmatrix} \cos(\alpha_2) & -\sin(\alpha_2) \\ \sin(\alpha_2) & \cos(\alpha_2) \end{bmatrix} \begin{bmatrix} q_u & w \\ 0 & q_v \end{bmatrix} \begin{bmatrix} \cos(\alpha_1) & \sin(\alpha_1) \\ -\sin(\alpha_1) & \cos(\alpha_1) \end{bmatrix}.$$

Angles α_1 and α_2 are known from the SIFT features. Let us use the notation $c_i = \cos(\alpha_i)$ and $s_i = \sin(\alpha_i)$. The equations after the matrix multiplication become

$$\mathbf{A} = \begin{bmatrix} a_1 & a_2 \\ a_3 & a_4 \end{bmatrix} = \begin{bmatrix} c_2(c_1 q_u - s_1 w) + s_2 s_1 q_v & c_2(s_1 q_u + c_1 w) - s_2 c_1 q_v \\ s_2(c_1 q_u - s_1 w) - c_2 s_1 q_v & s_2(s_1 q_u + c_1 w) + c_2 c_1 q_v \end{bmatrix}.$$

After simplifying the equations, we get the following linear system

$$\begin{aligned} a_1 &= c_2 c_1 q_u - c_2 s_1 w + s_2 s_1 q_v, & a_2 &= c_2 s_1 q_u + c_2 c_1 w - s_2 c_1 q_v, \\ a_3 &= s_2 c_1 q_u - s_2 s_1 w - c_2 s_1 q_v, & a_4 &= s_2 s_1 q_u + s_2 c_1 w + c_2 c_1 q_v, \end{aligned} \tag{11}$$

where the unknowns are the affine parameters a_1, a_2, a_3, a_4, scales q_u, q_v and shear w.

In addition to the previously described constraints, we are given two additional ones. First, it can be seen that the uniform scales of the SIFT features are proportional to the area of the underlying image region and, therefore, the scale change provides constraint

$$\det \mathbf{A} = \det \left(\mathbf{R}_2 \mathbf{U} \mathbf{R}_1^{\mathsf{T}} \right) = \det \mathbf{U} = q_u q_v = \frac{q_2^2}{q_1^2}, \tag{12}$$

where q_1 and q_2 are the SIFT scales in the two images. Second, the SIFT orientations and scales in the two images provide an additional constraint as

$$q_1 \mathbf{A} \begin{bmatrix} \cos(\alpha_1) \\ \sin(\alpha_1) \end{bmatrix} = q_2 \begin{bmatrix} \cos(\alpha_2) \\ \sin(\alpha_2) \end{bmatrix} \tag{13}$$

relating the oriented circles centered on the point correspondence. Next, we show how these constraints can be used to derive the constraint relating the SIFT orientation and scale with the epipolar geometry.

3.2 SIFT Epipolar Constraint

Our goal is to derive constraints that relate epipolar geometry and orientation- and scale-covariant features. To do this, we consider the constraints that relate the elements of Λ and the measured orientations α_i and scales q_i of the features in the images. In [10], such constraints were derived by eliminating q_u, q_v and w from the ideal generated by (11), (12) and trigonometric identities $c_i^2 + s_i^2 = 1$ for $i \in \{1, 2\}$, using the elimination ideal technique [20]. This method resulted into two constraints, $i.e.$, the generators of the elimination ideal, one of which is directly (12) and the second one is of form

$$c_1 s_2 a_1 + s_1 s_2 a_2 - c_1 c_2 a_3 - c_2 s_1 a_4 = 0. \tag{14}$$

Here, we will show that once the constraints (13) are added to the ideal, and we ensure $q_1 \neq 0$ and $q_2 \neq 0$ by saturating the ideal with q_1 and q_2, then the elimination ideal is generated directly by constraints (12) and (13). This means that for the derivation of the constraints that relate the elements of matrix $\mathbf{A}$ and the measured orientations α_i and scales q_i, equations (11) are not necessary. These new constraints are as follows:

$$a_2 a_3 - a_1 a_4 + q^2 = 0, \tag{15}$$

$$a_3 c_1 + a_4 s_1 - s_2 q = 0, \tag{16}$$

$$a_1 c_1 + a_2 s_1 - c_2 q = 0, \tag{17}$$

where $q = \frac{q_2}{q_1}$. Moreover, thanks to constraints (13) relating the oriented circles centered on the points, which were not used in [10], we have three constraints, compared to the two polynomials derived in [10][2]. This will help us to derive a new constraint relating epipolar geometry and covariant features that was not possible to derive using only the two constraints proposed in [10]. For this purpose, we create an ideal J generated by polynomials (15)–(17), (7) and (8). Then the unknown elements of the affine transformation $\mathbf{A}$ are eliminated from the generators of J. We do this by computing the generators of the elimination ideal $J_1 = J \cap \mathbb{C}[f_1, \ldots, f_9, u_1, v_1, u_2, v_2, q, s_1, c_1, s_2, c_2]$. The elimination ideal J_1 is generated by the polynomial

$$c_2 q f_1 u_1 + s_2 q f_4 u_1 + c_2 q f_2 v_1 + s_2 q f_5 v_1 + c_2 q f_3 + s_2 q f_6 + \tag{18}$$
$$c_1 f_1 u_2 + s_1 f_2 u_2 + c_1 f_4 v_2 + s_1 f_5 v_2 + c_1 f_7 + s_1 f_8 = 0.$$

Note that (18) is linear in the elements of $\mathbf{F}$ and, as such, it can be straightforwardly used together with the well-known epipolar constraint for point correspondences to estimate the epipolar geometry.

---

[2] Note that the constraint (14) derived in [10] is a linear combination of constraints (16) and (17) and can be obtained by eliminating q from these two equations.

3.3   Solvers for Epipolar Geometry

In this section, we will describe different solvers for estimating epipolar geometry using orientation- and scale-covariant features (*e.g.*, SIFT correspondences). In Sect. 3.2, we showed that each SIFT correspondence gives us two linear constraints on the elements of the fundamental (or essential) matrix. One constraint is the well-known epipolar constraint (3) for point correspondences and one is the new derived SIFT-based constraint (18). As such, we can directly transform *all* existing point-based solvers for estimating epipolar geometry to solvers working with SIFT features. The only difference will be that for solvers that estimate the geometry from n point correspondences, we will use $\lceil \frac{n}{2} \rceil$ SIFT ones, and in the solver we will replace $\lfloor \frac{n}{2} \rfloor$ epipolar constraints (3) from point correspondences with $\lfloor \frac{n}{2} \rfloor$ SIFT constraints of the form (18). This will affect only some coefficients in coefficient matrices used in these solvers and not the structure of the solver. Moreover, for problems where n, which in this case corresponds to the DoF of the problem, is not a multiple of two, we can use all $\lceil \frac{n}{2} \rceil$ available constraints of the form (18) to simplify the solver. Next, we will describe solutions to three important relative pose problems, *i.e.* for uncalibrated, calibrated, and partially calibrated perspective cameras with unknown focal length. However, note, that our method is not only applicable to these problems and presented solvers, but can be directly applied to all existing point-based solvers for estimating epipolar geometry.

Fundamental Matrix. This is a 7 DoF problem, which means that we need four SIFT correspondences $(\mathbf{p}_1^i, \mathbf{p}_2^i, \alpha_1^i, \alpha_2^i, q)$, $i \in \{1, 2, 3, 4\}$ to solve it. For the ith correspondence, the epipolar constraint (3) and the proposed SIFT-based constraint (18) can be written as $\mathbf{C}_i \mathbf{f} = 0$, where matrix $\mathbf{C}_i \in \mathbb{R}^{2 \times 9}$ is the coefficient matrix consisting of two rows and vector $\mathbf{f} = [f_1, f_2, f_3, f_4, f_5, f_6, f_7, f_8, f_9]^T$ consists of the unknown elements of the fundamental matrix. As mentioned above, in this case, we can either use all four constraints of the form (18) and simplify the solver by not using the $\det \mathbf{F} = 0$ constraint[3], or we can use just three equations of the form (18) and solve the obtained cubic polynomial implied by the constraint $\det \mathbf{F} = 0$. In our experiments, we decided to test the second solver, which corresponds to the well-known seven-point solver [18] and which leads to more accurate results.

Essential Matrix. The relative pose problem for calibrated cameras is a 5 DoF problem and we need three SIFT correspondences $(\mathbf{p}_1^i, \mathbf{p}_2^i, \alpha_1^i, \alpha_2^i, q)$, $i \in \{1, 2, 3\}$ to solve it. Similarly to the uncalibrated case, for the ith correspondence, the epipolar constraint and the new SIFT-based one can be written as $\mathbf{C}_i \mathbf{e} = 0$, where $\mathbf{e} = [e_1, \ldots, e_9]^T$ is the vector of the unknown elements of the essential matrix. Matrix $\mathbf{C}_i \in \mathbb{R}^{2 \times 9}$ is the coefficient matrix consisting of two rows, the first one containing coefficients from the epipolar constraint and the second one from the SIFT-based one (18). Considering the three feature case, $\mathbf{C}$ is of size 6×9 as $\mathbf{C} = [\mathbf{C}_1^T, \mathbf{C}_2^T, \mathbf{C}_3^T]^T$. While using the top 5×9 sub-matrix of $\mathbf{C}$ would allow using the well-known solvers for solving the five-point problem [17,21,30], having 6 rows in $\mathbf{C}$ allows to use simpler solvers. We, thus, adopt the solver from [9] proposed, originally, for estimating from affine correspondences.

First, the 3-dimensional null-space of $\mathbf{C}$ is obtained by, *e.g.*, LU decomposition as it is significantly faster than the SVD and Eigen decompositions. The solution is

---

[3] This solver corresponds to the well-known eight-point solver [18].

given by a linear combination of the three null-space basis vectors $\mathbf{n}_1$, $\mathbf{n}_2$, and $\mathbf{n}_3$ as $\mathbf{e} = \alpha\mathbf{n}_1 + \beta\mathbf{n}_2 + \gamma\mathbf{n}_3$, where parameters α, β, and γ are unknown non-zero scalars. These scalars are defined up to a common scale, therefore, one of them can be set to an arbitrary value. In the proposed algorithm, $\gamma = 1$.

By substituting this expression for $\mathbf{e}$ to the determinant constraint $\det \mathbf{E} = 0$ and the trace constraint, $i.e.$, $\mathbf{E}\mathbf{E}^T\mathbf{E} - \frac{1}{2}\text{trace}(\mathbf{E}\mathbf{E}^T)\mathbf{E} = 0$, ten polynomial equations in two unknowns α and β are obtained. They can be formed as $\mathbf{Q}\mathbf{y} = \mathbf{b}$, where $\mathbf{Q}$ and $\mathbf{b}$ are the coefficient matrix and the inhomogeneous part (i.e., coefficients of monomial 1), respectively. Vector $\mathbf{y} = [\alpha^3, \beta^3, \alpha^2\beta, \alpha\beta^2, \alpha^2, \beta^2, \alpha\beta, \alpha, \beta]^T$ consists of nine monomials of the system and $\mathbf{Q}$ is a 10×9 coefficient matrix. Not considering dependencies of monomials in $\mathbf{y}$, we can consider this an over-determined system of ten linear equations in nine unknowns. Its optimal solution in least squares sense is given by $\mathbf{y} = \mathbf{Q}^\dagger\mathbf{b}$, where matrix $\mathbf{Q}^\dagger$ is the Moore-Penrose pseudo-inverse of matrix $\mathbf{Q}$. The solver has only a single solution which is beneficial for the robust estimation.

The elements of the solution vector $\mathbf{y}$ are dependent. Thus α and β can be obtained in multiple ways, $e.g.$, as $\alpha_1 = y_8$, $\beta_1 = y_9$ or $\alpha_2 = \sqrt[3]{y_1}$, $\beta_2 = \sqrt[3]{y_2}$. To choose the best candidates, we paired every possible α and β and selected the one minimizing the trace constraint $\mathbf{E}\mathbf{E}^T\mathbf{E} - \frac{1}{2}\text{trace}(\mathbf{E}\mathbf{E}^T)\mathbf{E} = 0$.

Fundamental Matrix and Focal Length. Assuming the unknown common focal length in both cameras, the relative pose problem has 6 DoF. As such, it can be solved from three SIFT correspondences $(\mathbf{p}_1^i, \mathbf{p}_2^i, \alpha_1^i, \alpha_2^i, q)$, $i \in \{1, 2, 3\}$. In this case, three SIFT correspondences generate exactly the minimal case. We can apply one of the standard 6PT solvers [17,20,22,37]. We choose the method from [20] that uses elimination ideals to eliminate the unknown focal length and generates a smaller elimination template matrix than the original Gröbner basis solver [37].

4 Experiments

In this section, we test the proposed SIFT-based solvers in a fully controlled synthetic environment and on a number of publicly available real-world datasets.

4.1 Synthetic Experiments

To test the accuracy of the relative pose obtained by exploiting the proposed SIFT constraint, first, we created a synthetic scene consisting of two cameras represented by their 3×4 projection matrices $\mathbf{P}_1$ and $\mathbf{P}_2$. They were located randomly on a center-aligned sphere with its radius selected uniformly randomly from range $[0.1, 10]$. Two planes with random normals were generated at most one unit far from the origin. For each plane, ten random points, lying on the plane, were projected into both cameras. Note that we need the correspondences to originate from at least two planes in order to avoid having a degenerate situation for fundamental matrix estimation. To get the ground truth affine transformation for a correspondence originating from the jth plane, $j \in \{1, 2\}$, we calculated homography $\mathbf{H}_j$ by projecting four random points from the plane to the cameras and applying the normalized DLT [18] algorithm. The local affine

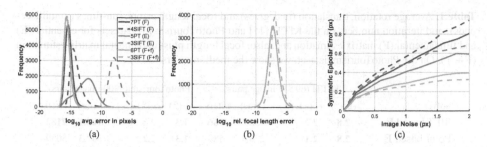

Fig. 3. *Synthetic experiments.* (a) The frequencies (100 000 runs; vertical axis) of $\log_{10}$ sym. epipolar errors (horizontal; in pixels) in the essential and fundamental matrices estimated by point and SIFT-based solvers. (b) The frequencies of $\log_{10}$ relative focal length errors (horizontal) estimated by point and SIFT-based solvers. (c) The symmetric epipolar error plotted as a function of the image noise in pixels.

transformation of each correspondence was computed from the ground truth homography by (1). Note that $\mathbf{H}$ could have been calculated directly from the plane parameters. However, using four points promised an indirect but geometrically interpretable way of noising the affine parameters: adding noise to the coordinates of the four points initializing $\mathbf{H}$. To simulate the SIFT orientations and scales, $\mathbf{A}$ was decomposed to $\mathbf{J}_1, \mathbf{J}_2$. Since the decomposition is ambiguous, α_1, $q_{u,1}$, $q_{v,1}$, w_1 were set to random values. $\mathbf{J}_1$ was calculated from them. Finally, $\mathbf{J}_2$ was calculated as $\mathbf{J}_2 = \mathbf{A}\mathbf{J}_1$. Zero-mean Gaussian-noise was added to the point coordinates, and, also, to the coordinates which were used to estimate the affine transformations.

Figure 3a reports the numerical stability of the methods in the noise-free case. The frequencies (vertical axis), *i.e.*, the number of occurrences in 100 000 runs, are plotted as the function of the $\log_{10}$ average symmetric epipolar error (in pixels; horizontal) computed from the estimated model and the unused correspondences. All methods on all problems lead to stable solutions. While the 3SIFT essential matrix solver seems the least stable, it is important to note that the horizontal axis is in pixels and, therefore, having $\approx 10^{-5}$ pixel maximum error can be considered stable. Figure 3b reports the numerical stability of the estimated focal lengths in the semi-calibrated case. The horizontal axis is the $\log_{10}$ relative focal length error calculated as $\epsilon_f = |f_{est} - f_{gt}|/f_{gt}$. Both methods lead to stable solutions.

In Fig. 3c, the average symmetric epipolar (over 10 000 runs; in pixels) errors are plotted as the function of the image noise added both to the point coordinates and affine parameters (indirectly, via contaminating the initializing homography). The error is calculated on correspondences not used for the estimation. The SIFT-based solvers are slightly more sensitive to the noise than the point-based one. This is expected since the image noise has a larger impact on the affine parameters, due to their localized nature, than on the point coordinates [12]. Interestingly, this is not the case when solving the semi-calibrated case, where the SIFT-based solver leads to the most accurate relative poses. Still, the main message from Fig. 3c is that the solvers behave reasonably well against increasing image noise. In the next section, we will show that, due to the reduced

Table 1. Average rotation, translation (in degrees) and focal length errors, run-times (in milliseconds), and iteration numbers on the KITTI [15] and PhotoTourism [3] datasets for essential ($\mathbf{E}$) and fundamental ($\mathbf{F}$) matrix estimation and, also, focal length plus fundamental matrix estimation ($\mathbf{F} + f$). On the PhotoTourism dataset, we show the median errors.

	KITTI (69 537 image pairs)					PhotoTourism (9900 image pairs)				
Solver	ϵ_R (°)	ϵ_t (°)	ϵ_f	t (ms)	# iters	ϵ_R (°)	ϵ_t (°)	ϵ_f	t (ms)	# iters
SIFT-based $\mathbf{E}$	2.8	2.2	–	53.6	166	1.3	2.3	–	108.1	2182
Point-based $\mathbf{E}$	2.8	2.1	–	276.4	389	1.3	2.2	–	847.3	5059
SIFT-based $\mathbf{F}$	2.7	2.2	–	67.3	304	2.1	6.7	–	48.8	4189
Point-based $\mathbf{F}$	2.7	2.3	–	154.4	1860	2.3	7.8	–	127.3	7145
SIFT-based $\mathbf{F} + f$	2.8	2.2	0.77	61.5	100	1.5	2.6	0.61	290.7	2386
Point-based $\mathbf{F} + f$	2.8	2.2	0.80	225.8	731	2.6	4.5	0.62	743.0	6423

combinatorics of the problem, the SIFT-based methods often yield more accurate solutions than their point-based counterparts inside RANSAC.

4.2 Real-World Experiments

For testing the methods, we use the KITTI benchmark [15] and the datasets from CVPR tutorial *RANSAC in 2020* [3]. Considering that the orientation and scale of local features are noisier than their point coordinates, we chose to use a locally optimized RANSAC, *i.e.*, GC-RANSAC [5], as the robust estimator, where the local optimization is applied to only the point coordinates, similarly as in [10, 12]. The required confidence is set to 0.99 and the maximum iteration number to 5000.

In GC-RANSAC (and other RANSAC-like methods), two different solvers are used: (a) one for fitting to a minimal sample and (b) one for fitting to a non-minimal sample when doing model polishing on all inliers or in the local optimization step. For (a), the main objective is to solve the problem using as few points as possible since the run-time depends exponentially on the number of points required for the model estimation. The proposed and compared solvers were included in this part of the robust estimator.

The KITTI odometry benchmark consists of 22 stereo sequences. Only 11 sequences (00–10) are provided with ground truth trajectories for training. We use these 11 sequences to evaluate the compared solvers. Each image is of resolution 1241×376. We ran the methods on image pairs formed such that the frame distance is 1, 2 or 4. For example, frame distance 2 means that we form pairs from images I_i and I_{i+2}, where $i \in [1, n]$ and $n \in \mathbb{N}^+$ is the number of images in a sequence. In total, the algorithms were tested on 69 537 pairs. To form tentative correspondences, we detected 8000 SIFT keypoints in both images to have a reasonably dense point cloud reconstruction and precise camera poses [39]. We combined mutual nearest neighbor check with standard distance ratio test [23] to establish tentative correspondences, as recommended in [39].

The RANSAC tutorial dataset comes from the train and validation sets of the CVPR IMW 2020 PhotoTourism challenge. We use the two scenes, each consisting of 4950

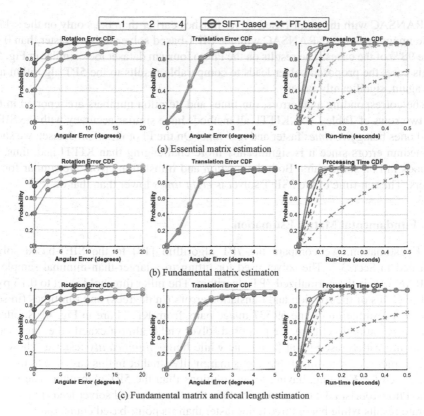

Fig. 4. The cumulative distribution functions of the rotation and translation errors ($^\circ$) and run-times (secs) of epipolar geometry estimation by GC-RANSAC [5] combined with point-based and the proposed SIFT-based minimal solvers on 69 537 image pairs from the KITTI dataset [15]. The frame difference is denoted by color, *e.g.*, pairs (I_i, I_{i+2}) are considered for the green curve.

image pairs, provided for validation purposes to test the proposed SIFT-based and the traditional point-based solvers.

4.3 Essential Matrix Estimation

For essential matrix estimation, we compare the 5PT algorithm (implemented in the Theia library [38]) to the SIFT-based solver described in Sect. 3.3. The solver used for fitting to a larger-than-minimal sample in GC-RANSAC is the 5PT algorithm. The inlier-outlier threshold is set to 0.75 pixels and is normalized by the focal lengths.

The cumulative distribution functions (CDF) of the rotation and translation errors (in degrees) and run-times (in seconds) of $\mathbf{E}$ estimation on the 69 537 image pairs from the KITTI dataset are in Fig. 4a. The frame difference is denoted by color, *e.g.*, image pairs (I_i, I_{i+2}) are considered for the green curve. The proposed solver yields almost exactly the same accuracy as the widely used point-based one while being *significantly* faster as shown in the right plot. For example, when the frame distance is 4,

GC-RANSAC with the point-based solver finishes earlier than 0.1 s only on the ≈17% of the images pairs. GC-RANSAC with the SIFT-based solver finishes faster than 0.1 s in the 98% of the cases. The results on the PhotoTourism dataset look similar in Fig. 5a. In this case, the proposed solver leads to comparable results to the 5PT algorithm and it is, again, significantly faster.

The corresponding avg. errors, run-times and iteration numbers are reported in the first two rows of Table 1. On KITTI, all methods have similar accuracy with the SIFT-based ones being *five times* faster and *real-time*. On the PhotoTourism dataset, we show the median errors since it is significantly more challenging than KITTI and, thus, all methods fail on some pairs. Both the rotation and translation errors are similar for all solvers. The run-time of the 3SIFT solver is *eight times* lower than that of 5PT.

4.4 Fundamental Matrix Estimation

For F estimation, we compare the 7PT algorithm [18] to the SIFT-based solver described in Sect. 3.3. The solver used for fitting to a larger-than-minimal sample in GC-RANSAC is the normalized 8PT algorithm. The inlier threshold is set to 0.75 px.

The CDFs of the rotation and translation errors (in degrees) and run-times (in seconds) of F estimation on the 69 537 image pairs from KITTI are in Fig. 4b. Similarly as in the E estimation figure, the proposed solver yields almost exactly the same accuracy as the widely used point-based one while being *significantly* faster as shown in the right plot. The run-time difference is marginally smaller in this case due to the 7PT solver, used for F fitting, having fewer solutions than the 5PT algorithm. The results on the PhotoTourism dataset in Fig. 5b show that the proposed solver leads to the most accurate results while being three times faster than its point-based counterpart.

The corresponding average errors, run-times and iteration numbers are reported in the second two rows of Table 1. On KITTI, all methods have similar accuracy while the SIFT-based solver is almost *three times* faster than the point-based one. On the PhotoTourism dataset, the SIFT-based solver leads to results superior to the point-based one both in terms of relative pose accuracy and run-time. Additional experiments are in the supplementary material.

4.5 Fundamental Matrix and Focal Length Estimation

For F with focal length estimation, we compare the 6PT algorithm of [20] to the SIFT-based solver described in Sect. 3.3. The inlier-outlier threshold is set to 0.75 pixels. The CDFs of the rotation and translation errors (in degrees) and run-times (in seconds) on the 69 537 image pairs from the KITTI dataset are in Fig. 4c. Similarly as in the previous experiments, the proposed solver leads to almost exactly the same accuracy as the widely used point-based one while being *significantly* faster as shown in the right plot. The results on the PhotoTourism dataset in Fig. 5c show that the proposed solver leads to increased accuracy compared to the 6PT solver while, also, being notably faster. Note that, in order to use this solver, we used only those image pairs from the PhotoTourism dataset where the focal lengths are similar.

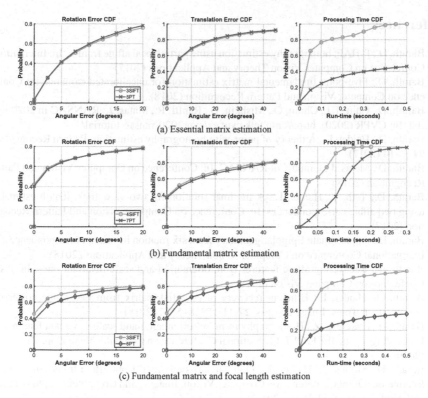

(a) Essential matrix estimation

(b) Fundamental matrix estimation

(c) Fundamental matrix and focal length estimation

Fig. 5. The cumulative distribution functions of the rotation and translation errors (°) and run-times (secs) of epipolar geometry estimation by GC-RANSAC [5] combined with point-based and the proposed SIFT-based minimal solvers on 9900 image pairs from the PhotoTourism dataset [3].

The corresponding average errors, run-times and iteration numbers are reported in the last two rows of Table 1. The proposed solvers lead to the most accurate results while being the fastest by a large margin on both datasets.

5   Conclusion

We derive the general relationship of the epipolar geometry of perspective cameras and orientation and scale-covariant features. It is characterized by two linear equations, one from the point correspondence and one from the orientations and scales. These constraints can be used within *all* existing relative pose solvers to halve the number of correspondences required for the estimation. This leads to either similar or better accuracy while significantly accelerating the robust estimation – by 4.3 times, on average, on the tested popular computer vision problems.

Acknowledgments. This work was supported by the ETH Zurich Postdoctoral Fellowship, by the OP VVV funded project CZ.02.1.01/0.0/0.0/16_019/0000765 "Research Center for Informatics", and the ERC-CZ grant MSMT LL1901.

References

1. Barath, D.: P-HAF: homography estimation using partial local affine frames. In: International Conference on Computer Vision Theory and Applications (2017)
2. Barath, D.: Five-point fundamental matrix estimation for uncalibrated cameras. In: Conference on Computer Vision and Pattern Recognition (2018)
3. Barath, D., Chin, T.J., Chum, O., Mishkin, D., Ranftl, R., Matas, J.: RANSAC in 2020 tutorial. In: CVPR (2020). http://cmp.felk.cvut.cz/cvpr2020-ransac-tutorial/
4. Barath, D., Hajder, L.: A theory of point-wise homography estimation. Pattern Recogn. Lett. **94**, 7–14 (2017)
5. Barath, D., Matas, J.: Graph-Cut RANSAC. In: Conference on Computer Vision and Pattern Recognition (2018)
6. Barath, D., Toth, T., Hajder, L.: A minimal solution for two-view focal-length estimation using two affine correspondences. In: Conference on Computer Vision and Pattern Recognition (2017)
7. Barath, D.: Approximate Epipolar geometry from six rotation invariant correspondences. In: International Conference on Computer Vision Theory and Applications (2018)
8. Barath, D.: Recovering affine features from orientation-and scale-invariant ones. In: Asian Conference on Computer Vision (2018)
9. Barath, D., Hajder, L.: Efficient recovery of essential matrix from two affine correspondences. IEEE Trans. Image Process. **27**(11), 5328–5337 (2018)
10. Barath, D., Kukelova, Z.: Homography from two orientation-and scale-covariant features. In: Proceedings of the IEEE/CVF International Conference on Computer Vision, pp. 1091–1099 (2019)
11. Barath, D., Molnar, J., Hajder, L.: Optimal surface normal from affine transformation. In: International Joint Conference on Computer Vision, Imaging and Computer Graphics Theory and Applications. SciTePress (2015)
12. Barath, D., Polic, M., Förstner, W., Sattler, T., Pajdla, T., Kukelova, Z.: Making affine correspondences work in camera geometry computation. In: Vedaldi, A., Bischof, H., Brox, T., Frahm, J.-M. (eds.) ECCV 2020. LNCS, vol. 12356, pp. 723–740. Springer, Cham (2020). https://doi.org/10.1007/978-3-030-58621-8_42
13. Bay, H., Tuytelaars, T., Van Gool, L.: SURF: speeded up robust features. In: Leonardis, A., Bischof, H., Pinz, A. (eds.) ECCV 2006. LNCS, vol. 3951, pp. 404–417. Springer, Heidelberg (2006). https://doi.org/10.1007/11744023_32
14. Bentolila, J., Francos, J.M.: Conic epipolar constraints from affine correspondences. In: Computer Vision and Image Understanding (2014)
15. Geiger, A., Lenz, P., Urtasun, R.: Are we ready for autonomous driving? the KITTI vision benchmark suite. In: Conference on Computer Vision and Pattern Recognition (CVPR) (2012)
16. Guan, B., Zhao, J., Barath, D., Fraundorfer, F.: Relative pose estimation for multi-camera systems from affine correspondences. In: International Conference on Computer Vision. IEEE (2021)
17. Hartley, R., Li, H.: An efficient hidden variable approach to minimal-case camera motion estimation. Pattern Anal. Mach. Intell. **34**, 2303–2314 (2012)
18. Hartley, R., Zisserman, A.: Multiple View Geometry in Computer Vision. Cambridge University Press, Cambridge (2003)
19. Köser, K.: Geometric Estimation with Local Affine Frames and Free-form Surfaces. Shaker (2009)
20. Kukelova, Z., Kileel, J., Sturmfels, B., Pajdla, T.: A clever elimination strategy for efficient minimal solvers. In: Conference on Computer Vision and Pattern Recognition (2017). http://arxiv.org/abs/1703.05289

21. Li, H., Hartley, R.: Five-point motion estimation made easy. In: International Conference on Pattern Recognition (2006)
22. Li, H.: A simple solution to the six-point two-view focal-length problem. In: Leonardis, A., Bischof, H., Pinz, A. (eds.) ECCV 2006. LNCS, vol. 3954, pp. 200–213. Springer, Heidelberg (2006). https://doi.org/10.1007/11744085_16
23. Lowe, D.G.: Object recognition from local scale-invariant features. In: International Conference on Computer Vision (1999)
24. Mikolajczyk, K., et al.: A comparison of affine region detectors. Int. J. Comput. Vision 65(1–2), 43–72 (2005)
25. Mills, S.: Four-and seven-point relative camera pose from oriented features. In: International Conference on 3D Vision, pp. 218–227. IEEE (2018)
26. Mishkin, D., Matas, J., Perdoch, M.: MODS: fast and robust method for two-view matching. Comput. Vis. Image Underst. 141, 81–93 (2015)
27. Mishkin, D., Radenović, F., Matas, J.: Repeatability is not enough: learning affine regions via discriminability. In: Ferrari, V., Hebert, M., Sminchisescu, C., Weiss, Y. (eds.) ECCV 2018. LNCS, vol. 11213, pp. 287–304. Springer, Cham (2018). https://doi.org/10.1007/978-3-030-01240-3_18
28. Molnár, J., Chetverikov, D.: Quadratic transformation for planar mapping of implicit surfaces. J. Math. Imaging Vision 48, 176–184 (2014)
29. Morel, J.M., Yu, G.: ASIFT: a new framework for fully affine invariant image comparison. SIAM J. Imag. Sci. 2(2), 438–469 (2009)
30. Nistér, D.: An efficient solution to the five-point relative pose problem. Pattern Anal. Mach. Intell. 26, 756–770 (2004)
31. Perdoch, M., Matas, J., Chum, O.: Epipolar geometry from two correspondences. In: International Conference on Pattern Recognition (2006)
32. Pritts, J., Kukelova, Z., Larsson, V., Chum, O.: Radially-distorted conjugate translations. In: Conference on Computer Vision and Pattern Recognition (2018)
33. Pritts, J., Kukelova, Z., Larsson, V., Chum, O.: Rectification from radially-distorted scales. In: Jawahar, C.V., Li, H., Mori, G., Schindler, K. (eds.) ACCV 2018. LNCS, vol. 11365, pp. 36–52. Springer, Cham (2019). https://doi.org/10.1007/978-3-030-20873-8_3
34. Raposo, C., Barreto, J.P.: Theory and practice of structure-from-motion using affine correspondences. In: Computer Vision and Pattern Recognition (2016)
35. Raposo, C., Barreto, J.P.: π match: monocular vSLAM and piecewise planar reconstruction using fast plane correspondences. In: Leibe, B., Matas, J., Sebe, N., Welling, M. (eds.) ECCV 2016. LNCS, vol. 9912, pp. 380–395. Springer, Cham (2016). https://doi.org/10.1007/978-3-319-46484-8_23
36. Riggi, F., Toews, M., Arbel, T.: Fundamental matrix estimation via tip-transfer of invariant parameters. In: International Conference on Pattern Recognition, vol. 2, pp. 21–24. IEEE (2006)
37. Stewénius, H., Nistér, D., Kahl, F., Schaffalitzky, F.: A minimal solution for relative pose with unknown focal length. Image Vis. Comput. 26(7), 871–877 (2008)
38. Sweeney, C., Hollerer, T., Turk, M.: Theia: a fast and scalable structure-from-motion library. In: Proceedings of the 23rd ACM International Conference on Multimedia, pp. 693–696 (2015)
39. Trulls, E., Jun, Y., Yi, K., Mishkin, D., Matas, J., Fua, P.: Image matching challenge. In: CVPR (2020). http://cmp.felk.cvut.cz/cvpr2020-ransac-tutorial/
40. Turkowski, K.: Transformations of surface normal vectors. In: Technical report 22, Apple Computer (1990)

Selection and Cross Similarity
for Event-Image Deep Stereo

Hoonhee Cho [ID] and Kuk-Jin Yoon[✉][ID]

Korea Advanced Institute of Science and Technology, Daejeon, South Korea
{gnsgnsgml,kjyoon}@kaist.ac.kr

Abstract. Standard frame-based cameras have shortcomings of low
dynamic range and motion blur in real applications. On the other hand,
event cameras, which are bio-inspired sensors, asynchronously output
the polarity values of pixel-level log intensity changes and report continuous stream data even under fast motion with a high dynamic range.
Therefore, event cameras are effective in stereo depth estimation under
challenging illumination conditions and/or fast motion. To estimate the
disparity map with events, existing state-of-the-art event-based stereo
models use the image together with past events that occurred up to
the current image acquisition time. However, not all events equally contribute to the disparity estimation of the current frame since past events
occur at different times under different movements with different disparity values. Therefore, events need to be carefully selected for accurate
event-guided disparity estimation. In this paper, we aim to effectively
deal with events that continuously occur with different disparity values
in the scene depending on the camera's movement. To this end, we first
propose the differentiable event selection network to select the most relevant events for current depth estimation. Furthermore, we effectively
use feature-like events triggered around the boundary of objects, leading them to serve as ideal guides in disparity estimation. To this end,
we propose a neighbor cross similarity feature (NCSF) that considers
the similarity between different modalities. Finally, our experiments on
various datasets demonstrate the superiority of our method to estimate
the depth using images and event data together. Our project code is
available at: https://github.com/Chohoonhee/SCSNet.

Keywords: Event cameras · Stereo depth · Multi-modal fusion

1 Introduction

Estimating depth from a stereo image pair has been an important problem in the
field of computer vision [17,28]. Stereo-based depth estimation methods generally
find correspondences for all pixels in the stereo pair image (*i.e.*, stereo matching)
and estimate the depth through triangulation using camera parameters. It plays

Supplementary Information The online version contains supplementary material
available at https://doi.org/10.1007/978-3-031-19824-3_28.

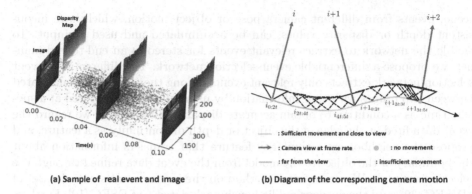

(a) Sample of real event and image   (b) Diagram of the corresponding camera motion

Fig. 1. Visualization of real-world events and images of indoor flying 1 in MVSEC datasets for stereo. For the disparity estimation of an image, the most recent events from the time that the image was acquired are used. (b) is a schematic diagram of the camera motion corresponding to (a). Here, i is the index of the frame, and t corresponds to 0.01 s in (a). Therefore, the time interval between the two frames corresponds to $5t$.

an important role in autonomous driving and augmented reality, which require 3D information of the scene.

Most of recent stereo matching algorithms are learning-based and perform well on various large-scale public benchmarks [6,7,12,13,32,34]. However, there still exist some challenges in stereo matching because of the limitations of frame-based RGB sensors (*e.g.*, difficulty in operation in blurred or low dynamic range) and algorithmic incompletion [28] (*e.g.*, edge-fattening at depth discontinuities).

The event camera [4,19], a novel bio-inspired sensor, has provided a satisfactory solution to the limitations of frame-based RGB sensors in poor lighting or motion conditions. The event cameras asynchronously report the per-pixel changes of intensity in the form of a stream, called events. Event cameras have very low latency and cover a high dynamic range, making them intrinsically immune to motion blur and suitable for extreme lighting scenes. Therefore, the event camera can enrich the missing information as a complementary source for the shortcomings of the RGB sensor.

However, although event cameras can be a breakthrough to overcome the shortcoming of frame-based cameras, they require a significant transition in approach for real applications. Besides the new stereo matching algorithms for events, it is also essential to find optimal ways to represent the event data and put it into a depth estimation network, which has been a trend in event stereo research. In general, to estimate the depth map at a specific time using event cameras, the most recent events are used (see (a) of Fig. 1). Recently some stereo methods accumulate all events between two frames [2,29] or specify the number of recent events to stack [22]. However, these methods should make an assumption that the events corresponding to the same 3D scene point have the same disparity in the stack, which is not true in dynamic situations. In fact, the depth or disparity values of events can vary with time based on the movement of the camera and the scene. Therefore, depending on the motion of the camera or the scene, events from different camera pose or object motion, which have inconsistent depth or disparity values, can be accumulated and used as input. To enable the network to extract relevant events for stereo in an end-to-end manner, we propose a differentiable event selection network. The differentiable event selection network extracts only relevant events among the all events accumulated between two frames with time information by using the image captured at a specific time as a condition to obtain accurate disparity. In addition, we regard the event data fired at the edge of the object or depth discontinuity as a feature, and propose the neighbor cross similarity feature that transfers information about the boundary of the object to the model from the event data refined through the selection network. We evaluate our method on the indoor event stereo dataset of MVSEC [39], and the outdoor public benchmark dataset of DSEC [10]. Furthermore, we present qualitative and quantitative comparisons for comparing with the state-of-the-art event stereo methods.

2   Related Works

2.1   Stereo Depth Estimation Using Images

The most successful methods of early studies using conventional RGB images have adopted end-to-end deep learning networks [6,12,18,30,32–35,37]. The networks generally comprise embedding, matching, and regularization modules. They outperform traditional methods by a large margin on public benchmarks (e.g., Scene Flow [20] and KITTI [21]). However, the effects of motion blur and lightning on depth estimation remains a problem in terms of application.

2.2   Stereo Depth Estimation Using Events

With the rising of event cameras, attempts have been made to perform stereo depth estimation using temporally dense events. Using an event camera in the algorithm can solve the limitations of the RGB sensor, but finding a match between event pairs in the form of asynchronous streams is a remained issue. Early attempts utilized the hand-crafted method to determine corresponding events [5,8,15,24–27,38,41,42]. Their primary approach used window- or patch-based method defining the neighborhoods, and they succeeded in generating a depth map using spatial-temporal sparse event cameras. However, the characteristics of the event that do not follow the predefined pattern led to the inability to extract detailed and dense depth, and the performance was inferior to that of the learning-based method.

Recent methods improved the accuracy by adopting a learning-based approach capable of estimating dense depth with a sparse event. A new embedding of a 4D queue including both temporal and spatial information of event data for deep learning was proposed in [29], and the later study [2] improved the accuracy using various techniques. The state-of-the-art event stereo network [22] complemented spatially sparse events by using images together. They integrate events

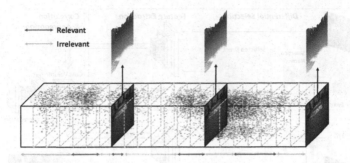

Fig. 2. Sample images and events from the MVSEC dataset [39]. The *relevant* event is generated by semantically related motion to the scene and is sufficient to estimate disparity. On the other hand, the *irrelevant* event corresponds to a view far from the scene of disparity to be obtained or contains insufficient information comprising real-world noise.

and images through a recycling structure. Their method shows better performance than the setting that uses only an event or image data. However, they followed the existing event representation [9,31] used in the image reconstruction, and embedding for event-image disparity network has been less studied. Unlike high frame-rate image reconstruction, which requires only the most recent accumulated events for a short-time, in stereo matching, different threshold sensitivities between event camera pairs must be considered, and an event at an appropriate point in time according to motion and scene is required. In this paper, to tackle this problem, we explore a novel event embedding method for stereo depth estimation using events with images together.

3 Motivation

Existing event representation techniques that transform stream form of events to a machine-interpretable representation can be broadly classified into two categories: number- and time-based stacking. Number-based stacking methods [9,22,31] accumulate a certain number of events predefined by the user and put them into the network in the form of images. If a conservative amount of events is specified, insufficient events lead to ambiguity for matching, and conversely, too much amount gets rid of details and sharp edges. Also, even in the same dataset, the number of fired events varies depending on the scene. Because the number to be specified varies according to the distribution of the dataset, it is necessary to be able to access the dataset in advance, which may limit the application. The time-based stacking method [2,29,40] generally discretizes the event between two frames of an image along the time axis. Then, it converts it into a 3D or 4D image tensor for input to neural network architecture. The strength of this approach is that it is independent of the number of events triggered depending on the scene or motion. However, all events between two frames are not informative to obtain the disparity synchronized with the image. As depicted in Fig. 2.,

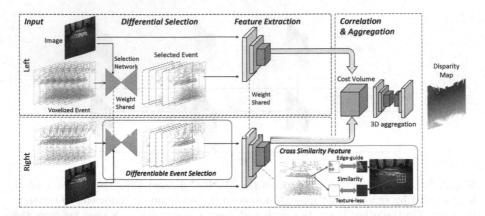

Fig. 3. The overview of architecture. In *differential selection*, we select the most relevant event series from a voxelized event stack using a selection network (Sect. 4.1). We transform two inputs (events and images) of different modalities into a unified fused feature by using *feature extraction* that considers cross similarity features (Sect. 4.2). By utilizing *correlation* and *aggregation* (Sect. 4.3), we generate the final dense disparity output.

spatial-temporally sparse events cannot be preprocessed with a statically unified pattern.

The proposed event-image deep stereo algorithm is motivated by observations. First, all events between two frames are not required to estimate the time-synchronized depth with the image. Second, each pair of stereo event cameras has different threshold sensitivity. Even the stereo camera seeing the same view, the aspect of the event in each camera is other depending on the motion. Therefore, we propose a differentiable event selection network that selects relevant events to deal with a scene and motion variant issue.

4   Proposed Methods

Event Preparation. We represent the stream format of events in the voxel grid format, considering both spatial and temporal coordinates. First, we collect events between two consecutive images. Then, following [40], we scale the timestamps to the range $[0, B-1]$ for inserting events into the discretized volume with the size of $w \times h \times B$ using a linearly weighted accumulation. Then, we can use the convolutional layer for the event data.

The overall framework of the proposed end-to-end depth estimation network is illustrated in Fig. 3. It consists of four sub-networks: differentiable event selection network, neighbor cross similarity feature extraction, correlation, and aggregation. Given a rectified image pair I_l, I_r and voxelized events E_l, E_r from stereo pairs of event cameras, using the differentiable event selection network, we extract the selected events S_l, S_r that are most relevant to the scene of disparity to be estimated. Next, the image and selected event are unified as a fused

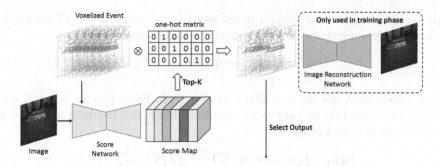

Fig. 4. Structures of the differentiable event selection network. Given a pair of images and events, the score network creates a score map to extract relevant events using images as conditions. Then, the selected event is inserted into the image reconstruction sub-network to restore the image and used for disparity estimation.

feature F_l, F_r through feature extraction. Then, 3D cost volume is constructed by correlating left fused feature F_l and right fused feature F_r. Finally, through the 3D aggregation network, we can obtain the dense disparity map.

4.1 Differentiable Event Selection Network

For the unity of denotation, we describe the left camera E_l, I_l as an example. The score network predicts a relevance score for each time region of the voxelized events concerning the image as the condition. The score map M is a grid with a size of $1 \times 1 \times B$ as $M \in \mathbb{R}^B$, and each grid has a degree of relevance with the image. Given score map, we select the K most relevant event grids by creating a one-hot matrix $H \in \{0,1\}^{B \times K}$. The one-hot matrix H consists of K number of one-hot vectors with a B dimension as $H = [h_1, h_2, \cdots, h_K]$. Then, selected events can be extracted using a matrix multiplication as $S_l = E_l H$. Although these selected events can be directly used for depth estimation, we utilize an image reconstruction network to encourage the selection network to extract higher-quality events (see Fig. 4). The image reconstruction network is solely used during training to save computation time in inference without significantly increasing the memory footprint. The optimization of event selection network can be represented as a linear program of the form

$$\arg\max_{\boldsymbol{y} \in \mathcal{C}} \langle \boldsymbol{y}, M\boldsymbol{1}^\top \rangle, \tag{1}$$

where $M\boldsymbol{1}^\top \in \mathbb{R}^{B \times K}$ is score matrix obtained by multiplication, $\boldsymbol{y}$ is optimization variable, and $\mathcal{C}$ is a convex polytope set. However, one-hot operations from Top-K algorithms is non-differentiable, so we adopt the perturbed maximum method [3].

   To define the gradients, add to input M a sampled random noise vector εZ, where $\varepsilon > 0$ is a hyper-parameter and Z has differentiable density $d\mu(z) \propto$

$\exp(-\nu(z))\mathrm{d}z$. Given the random perturbed inputs, expectations of results for each of n independent samples leads to smoothed versions as:

$$\boldsymbol{y}_\varepsilon = \mathbb{E}[\arg\max_{\boldsymbol{y}\in\mathcal{C}}\langle \boldsymbol{y}, M\boldsymbol{1}^\top + \varepsilon Z\rangle]. \qquad (2)$$

In our experiment, we set $n = 200$ and $\varepsilon = 0.05$. From [1], for noise Z with $\mathrm{d}\mu(z) \propto \exp(-\nu(z))\mathrm{d}z$ and any twice differentiable ν, the Jacobian matrix of $\boldsymbol{y}_\varepsilon$ at M can be obtained as follows:

$$J_M\boldsymbol{y}_\varepsilon = \mathbb{E}[\arg\max_{\boldsymbol{y}\in\mathcal{C}}\langle \boldsymbol{y}, M\boldsymbol{1}^\top + \varepsilon Z\rangle\nabla_z\nu(Z)^\top/\varepsilon]. \qquad (3)$$

Being able to compute the perturbed maximizer and its Jacobian allows optimizing functions that depend on M through $\boldsymbol{y}_\varepsilon$. Other distributions can be used in Z, but we use the Gumbel distribution [11] which is well-known in machine learning tasks. More details of the implementation for score network and image reconstruction network are provided in the supplementary material. This selection module applies equally to the right camera.

4.2   Neighbor Cross Similarity Feature Extraction

For the finding correspondences between left and right feature map, we should integrate the selected event S_l and image I_l into one feature F_l (For the right camera, this corresponds to S_r, I_r and F_r). Early study using events and images together for estimating depth in stereo setup [22] utilize the *recycling network*, which recurrently stacks events and images. Their method shows better performance than the settings when using only events or images. However, because of the difference in modality between events and images, it is not practical to simply concatenate on the channel dimension or add in the entire feature dimension. Instead, we focus on the characteristic of events mainly fired at object edges as intensity changes usually happen. This characteristic can make the events ideal guidance to allow sharp depth values in boundaries, which is a challenging issue in image data. On the other hand, images have spatially dense characteristics, which can hand over the information about the entire scene to sparse and noisy events. According to this intuition, events and images can complement each other. To this end, we design feature extraction, including the Neighbor Cross Similarity Feature (NCSF) module, to extract representations that effectively include these correlations.

Our proposed feature extraction is demonstrated in details in Fig. 5. Feature extraction consists of cascaded Neighbor Cross Similarity Feature (NCSF) modules that contains the similarity between the two modalities. The NCSF module computes a similarity map using the cosine similarity between events and image features. Even if the image and the event are pixel-wise aligned, since the event changes temporally, unlike a static image, we consider the surrounding neighborhood together. Assuming that the size of the kernel considering the neighborhood is specified as $w \times h$, the event feature in the kernel is represented as $\{e_1, e_2, \cdots, e_{w\times h}\}$ and the image feature corresponding to the pair

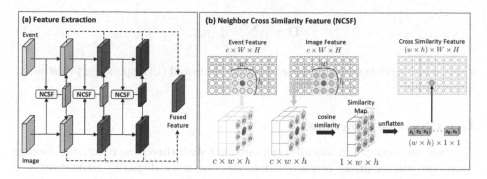

Fig. 5. The detailed structure of feature extraction. Feature extraction extracts the fused feature from an event and image pair from the identical camera. For correlating between two modalities, feature extraction consists of several cascaded Neighbor Cross Similarity Feature (NCSF) modules. NCSF modules generate cross similarity features by computing a similarity map between event and image features.

is represented as $\{i_1, i_2, \cdots, i_{w \times h}\}$. Then, similarity map can be represented as $\{s_1, s_2, \cdots, s_{w \times h}\}$ and element of similarity map s_k can be obtained as follows:

$$\underset{k \in \{1, \cdots, w \times h\}}{s_k} = \left(\frac{e_k}{\|e_k\|_2}\right)^T \cdot \left(\frac{i_k}{\|i_k\|_2}\right) \tag{4}$$

Then, s_k is used as k-th channnel element in the cross similarity feature. In practice, we compute the cross similarity feature of every pair of pixels in the image and the event feature. To combine cross similarity features and event (or image) features, we design a fusion module for each modality consisting of a 1×1 convolution layer followed by BatchNorm and ReLU layers. In addition, we utilize this fusion module to extract the final fused features F_l. We concatenate all image and event features generated in the intermediate stage and apply the fusion module. In our experiments, we set the $w = h = 3$.

4.3 Correlation and Aggregation Network

For depth estimation, we need to correlate between the fused features pair F_l and F_r. By our proposed feature extraction, fused features contain much information, such as structure, boundary, and texture-less region. We adopt the group-wise correlation proposed in [12] to reduce information loss when obtaining the correlation between these two fused features. We set the number of groups N_g as 40. Besides, we utilize the stacked hourglass architecture proposed in [12]. They modified the stacked hourglass architecture proposed in [6]. There are four output modules for training, and only the last output module is adopted for inference. In each output module, the probability volume with a size of $D_{max} \times H \times W \times 1$ is generated using two 3D convolutions with upsampling and softmax function. The estimated disparity $\widetilde{D}$ of each pixel can be obtained as follows:

$$\widetilde{\mathbf{D}} = \sum_{d=0}^{D_{max}-1} d \cdot p_d, \tag{5}$$

where d and p_d denote the possible disparity value and corresponding probability, respectively.

4.4 Objective Functions

We train our network in an end-to-end manner with three loss functions. Among them, two are for image reconstruction, and one is for disparity estimation.

Image Reconstruction Loss. In addition to the disparity estimation loss, we use the learned perceptual similarity loss (LPIPS) [36] and the L_1 loss as image reconstruction losses to train the differentiable event selection network more robustly. Through back-propagation in supervised learning with disparity ground-truth, although the selection network can be trained to some extent, we also utilize the image reconstruction, which has a much higher degree of relation to events than disparity estimation. As demonstrated in [36], the combination of these two losses encourage the sharp structural details. For LPIPS, we use variants of AlexNet [16]. We use the conv1-conv5 layers from [36].

Disparity Estimation Loss. We adopt the smooth L_1 loss function to train the proposed model. Smooth L_1 can be obtained as:

$$\text{smooth}_{L_1}(x) = \begin{cases} 0.5x^2, & \text{if } |x| < 1 \\ |x| - 0.5, & \text{otherwise} \end{cases} \tag{6}$$

The predicted disparity maps from the four output modules are denoted as $\widetilde{\mathbf{D}}_0$, $\widetilde{\mathbf{D}}_1$, $\widetilde{\mathbf{D}}_2$, $\widetilde{\mathbf{D}}_3$. Then,

$$\mathcal{L}_{disp} = \sum_{i=0}^{i=3} \Lambda_i \cdot \text{smooth}_{L_1} \left(\widetilde{\mathbf{D}}_i - \mathbf{D}^* \right), \tag{7}$$

where $\mathbf{D}^*$ denotes the ground-truth for the dense disparity map.

Our final loss ($\mathcal{L}$) is obtained by combining the image reconstruction losses ($\mathcal{L}_{L_1}, \mathcal{L}_{LPIPS}$) and the disparity estimation loss ($\mathcal{L}_{disp}$) as

$$\mathcal{L} = \mathcal{L}_{disp} + \lambda_1 \mathcal{L}_{L_1} + \lambda_2 \mathcal{L}_{LPIPS}. \tag{8}$$

5 Experiment

5.1 Datasets

We use two publicly available stereo real event camera datasets, the Multi-Vehicle Stereo Event Camera Dataset (MVSEC) [39] for indoor environments and the stereo event camera dataset for driving scenarios (DSEC) [10] for outdoor environments.

MVSEC has a stereo setup with two DAVIS [4] cameras that can provide the images and pixel-wise aligned events with a resolution of 346 × 260 pixels. Following [2,22,29], we also use the *Indoor Flying* dataset from MVSEC, which is captured from a drone flying in a room with various objects, and partition them into three splits. We also do not evaluate the *split* 2 quantitatively due to the difference in dynamic characteristics in the training and testing events, as mentioned in [2,29]. For a fair comparison, we use the *mean depth error*, *mean disparity error* and *one-pixel-accuracy* used in [2,22,29] as the metrics.

DSEC provides high-resolution stereo event cameras captured in large-scale outdoor driving scenes. It contains 53 driving scenarios taken in various lighting conditions. However, DSEC does not provide an event aligned with the image; the event and the image are captured by different devices and have different resolutions and baselines. The image cameras with resolutions of 1440 × 1080 have a baseline of 4.5 cm with the event cameras with resolutions of 640 × 480, which leads to a disparity between pixels of events and images. Therefore, we approximately warp the image to the event location, which is not precisely aligned but can be used for evaluation. Since the ground-truth of the disparity map for the DSEC test set has not been publicly available, we evaluate the performance on the benchmark website. We use the *one-pixel error* (1PE), *two-pixel error* (2PE), *mean absolute error* (MAE), and *root-mean-square error* (RMSE) as the metrics.

5.2 Experimental Setup

We set the coefficients of Eq. 7 as $\Lambda_0 = 0.5$, $\Lambda_1 = 0.5$, $\Lambda_2 = 0.7$, and $\Lambda_3 = 1.0$, and the coefficients of Eq. 8 as $\lambda_1 = 1$ and $\lambda_2 = 1$. Our network is implemented with PyTorch [23]. We use the Adam [14] optimizer with $\beta_1 = 0.9$, $\beta_2 = 0.999$. We set the voxelized event capacity B as 5 and the number of selections K as 3 in all experiments.

For MVSEC datasets, we train the our network for 30 epochs with a batch size of 2. The initial learning rate is set to 0.0001 without down-scale.

For DSEC datasets, we train the stereo networks for 120 epochs with a batch size of 8. The learning rate is set to 0.001 and down-scaled by 10 at 20, 40, and 60 epochs. The input voxelized event is randomly cropped with a size of 384 × 256 and vertical flip is applied for data augmentation. The input image is also cropped in proportion to the voxelized event size.

5.3 Quantitative Results

For quantitative analysis, we compare the results of our proposed model with the state-of-the-art method. There was no case of comparing with the frame-based methods on the MVSEC *indoor flying* dataset. Therefore, we train the frame-based model [6,12] using intensity images (APS) from the MVSEC dataset

Table 1. Results obtained for disparity estimation on MVSEC datasets. I indicates that the intensity image is adopted as the model modality, and E implies that the event data are adopted as the input. E + I means both conditions are adopted. The best and the second best scores are **highlighted** and underlined.

Model	Using Modality	Mean disparity error[pix] ↓		One-pixel accuracy [%] ↑		Mean depth error [cm] ↓	
		Split 1	Split 3	Split 1	Split 3	Split 1	Split 3
PSMNet [6]	I	0.57	0.68	88.6	83.1	15.9	18.3
GwcNet-gc [12]	I	0.50	0.61	89.9	85.8	15.0	17.4
PSN [29]	E	0.59	0.94	89.8	82.5	16.6	23.5
Ahmed et al. [2]	E	0.55	0.75	92.1	89.6	14.2	19.4
EIS [22]	E+I	–	–	89.0	88.1	13.7	22.4
Ours	E+I	**0.38**	**0.39**	**94.7**	**94.0**	**11.4**	**13.5**

Table 2. Results obtained for disparity estimation on DSEC datasets. (E) implies that the event data are adopted as the input, and (E+I) means both event and image are adopted. We report the results for each sequence in three different areas (Interlaken, Thun, and Zurich City) as well as the results of all sequences averages. The best and the second best scores are **highlighted** and underlined.

Model	1PE ↓				2PE ↓				MAE ↓				RMSE ↓			
	Inter	Thun	City	All	Inter	Thun	City	All	Inter	Thun	City	All	Inter	Thun	City	All
PSN (E) [29]	10.67	10.85	11.18	10.92	3.13	3.23	2.59	2.91	0.57	0.63	0.56	0.58	1.36	1.63	1.33	1.38
EIS (E+I) [22]	**4.77**	**5.15**	7.07	5.81	0.91	1.31	1.14	1.06	0.36	0.40	0.43	0.40	0.83	1.08	0.94	0.91
Ours (E+I)	4.86	5.30	**6.62**	**5.67**	**0.87**	**1.24**	**1.05**	**0.99**	0.36	0.40	0.41	0.39	**0.79**	**1.02**	**0.87**	**0.85**

and select the models with the best performance in the validation until convergence. Table 1 presents a comparison of the proposed method with previous single modality methods (only-events [2,29] or only-images [6,12]) and events-images fusion methods [22]. Our proposed modality fusion stereo network outperforms the earlier approaches by large margins in all evaluation metrics.

Furthermore, we also evaluate the proposed model on the DSEC dataset. Since DSEC's test dataset is not publicly accessible for the ground-truth disparity, we evaluate the network performance through the benchmark website. As presented in Table 2, we report the results for each sequence in different areas and the total average as well. Analytically, our method shows better performance on the overall sequence average than both the existing DSEC event-only baseline [29] and the state-of-the-arts [22] that use image and event fusion. Furthermore, especially in the Zurich City sequences that contain a lot of challenging illumination, such as Fig. 7, we show quantitatively better performance than the existing method through cross-modality similarity features between relevant events and images.

5.4   Qualitative Results

As shown in in Fig. 6, we qualitatively compare our results with previous works on MVSEC dataset. For comparison, we borrow the results of event-based approach [29] and event-image fusion method [22] from the original papers, respec-

(a) Intensity Image (APS)   (b) Ground Truth   (c) Proposed Methods   (d) DDES

(a) Intensity Image (APS)   (b) Ground Truth   (c) Proposed Methods   (e) EIS

Fig. 6. Qualitative comparison of the proposed method with the previous methods from the MVSEC dataset. For comparison, we select frames similar to the ones used in [22,29]. Note that the results of DDES [29] and EIS [22] are borrowed from the original papers, respectively. (Color figure online)

tively. In addition, we try our best to match the different color codings to those papers. As can be seen in the top row of Fig. 6 showing the comparison with the event-only method, our method using both modalities together allows for less noisy depth estimation. In addition, the bottom row shows the comparison with the event-image fusion method. Both our method and EIS use the same input of two types, different modalities. Still, our approach uses the event refined by the selection network and considers the correlation between modalities, estimating the artifact-free and much sharper results. In addition, we show the results of driving scene in challenging illumination conditions, which remains an open problem in stereo depth estimation, samples from the DSEC dataset. As can be seen in the highlighted region of Fig. 7, event data can capture an object with a high range covering an area that cannot be seen in the image. However, the event data also becomes noisier in situations such as night than in a general scene, and for this part, we supplement the context information from the image. Our strategy uses both event and image modalities to detect the depth of objects even under challenging illumination, which can be a breakthrough of direction that can solve the issues that remain in the conventional stereo matching from an application perspective.

482   H. Cho and K.-J. Yoon

Table 3. Ablation studies of the proposed components on the depth estimation.

Ablation Settings	Mean disparity error[pix] ↓		One-pixel accuracy [%] ↑		Mean depth error [cm] ↓	
	Split 1	Split 3	Split 1	Split 3	Split 1	Split 3
Baseline (GwcNet-g [12])	0.4020	0.4358	93.8809	91.7874	12.8391	16.5391
+ Differentiable Event Selection (DES)	0.4111	0.4153	94.1659	93.7863	12.3184	14.3000
+ Neighbor Cross Similarity Feature (NCSF)	0.3909	0.4095	94.1027	93.0166	11.6721	13.7153
Proposed (+ DES + NCSF)	**0.3776**	**0.3895**	**94.7201**	**94.0321**	**11.3645**	**13.4750**

(a) Proposed Method   (b) Overlay the event on the image   (c) Event   (d) Image

Fig. 7. Qualitative results of our proposed method from the challenging illumination scene on the DSEC dataset.

5.5   Ablation Studies

We perform ablation studies to confirm the effectiveness of the proposed methods using MVSEC dataset. Starting from the baseline, we add each sub-network to evaluate the performance. Since we adopt the 3D correlation network and aggregation network from [12], we use GwcNet-g as the baseline. In baseline, to combine the two modalities, event and image, we use a concatenation operation followed by a convolution layer. In Table 3, all of the proposed methods effectively improve the performance significantly.

5.6   Impact of the Differentiable Event Selection

Results for the selection module are shown in Fig. 8. Unlike the method that fully accumulates between two frames, our method extracts the event most related to the boundary in the scene. Events refined by our differential event selection network, which is properly matched to object edges, can resolve discontinuous boundaries and be an ideal tool for estimating the sharp depth value. As mentioned in [29], in stereo depth estimation, spatial context is more reliable than temporal information, so our method that considers spatial correlation with images in continuous events leads to better depth results.

Furthermore, we analyze the effectiveness of the number of selection K and the voxel capacity B on the results of depth estimation in Table 4. When $B = K = 5$, it means using the entire voxel, and we analyze while reducing the K event

Table 4. Impact of the voxelized event capacity B and the number of selection K on performance. The table shows the *one-pixel-accuracy* for *split* 1 test set in MVSEC dataset.

	The number of selection K				
voxel capacity B	1	2	3	4	5
5	91.6541	93.2581	**94.7201**	94.2207	94.1027
voxel capacity B	2	4	6	8	
10	92.6156	92.8351	<u>94.2313</u>	93.8791	

Fig. 8. The example of overlapping selected events and images. Selected events are shown in red. Except for the noise, most events are aligned to the object's boundary. Red: the selected events, green: the ignored events. (Color figure online)

select value. As the number of select decreases, the performance tends to improve, but when less than 3, the performance decreases. The reason for decreasing is that the amount of events is not sufficient to represent the overall scene, so it is challenging to obtain correspondence. In addition, when we increase the voxel capacity B to 10 and increase the number of selections K in proportion to B, the number of permutation cases increases significantly, and overall performance decreases. Still, it performs better than using the entire discritized voxel.

6   Conclusions

In this paper, we present the novel stereo depth estimation network using both modalities of events and images together. Specifically, we propose the differentiable event selection (DES) network to extract the events relevant to the scenes. Furthermore, we also propose a neighbor cross similarity feature (NCSF) that considers the similarity between different modalities. Finally, we evaluate our method with two real-world datasets, DSEC and MVSEC, and show the superiorness of our method in both quantitative and qualitative analyses. Our approach is effective for networks that use events and images together and can be generalized to other tasks.

Acknowledgements. This work was supported by the National Research Foundation of Korea(NRF) grant funded by the Korea government (MSIT) (NRF-2022R1A2B5B03002636).

References

1. Abernethy, J., Lee, C., Tewari, A.: Perturbation techniques in online learning and optimization. Perturbations, Optimization, and Statistics, p. 223 (2016)
2. Ahmed, S.H., Jang, H.W., Uddin, S.N., Jung, Y.J.: Deep event stereo leveraged by event-to-image translation. In: Proceedings of the AAAI Conference on Artificial Intelligence, vol. 35, pp. 882–890 (2021)
3. Berthet, Q., Blondel, M., Teboul, O., Cuturi, M., Vert, J.P., Bach, F.: Learning with differentiable pertubed optimizers. Adv. Neural. Inf. Process. Syst. **33**, 9508–9519 (2020)
4. Brandli, C., Berner, R., Yang, M., Liu, S.C., Delbruck, T.: A 240 × 180 130 db 3 μs latency global shutter spatiotemporal vision sensor. IEEE J. Solid-State Cir. **49**, 2333–2341 (2014)
5. Camunas-Mesa, L.A., Serrano-Gotarredona, T., Ieng, S.H., Benosman, R.B., Linares-Barranco, B.: On the use of orientation filters for 3D reconstruction in event-driven stereo vision. Front. Neurosci. **8**, 48 (2014)
6. Chang, J.R., Chen, Y.S.: Pyramid stereo matching network. 2018 IEEE/CVF Conference on Computer Vision and Pattern Recognition, pp. 5410–5418 (2018)
7. Cheng, X., et al.: Hierarchical neural architecture search for deep stereo matching. arXiv abs/2010.13501 (2020)
8. Cho, H., Jeong, J., Yoon, K.J.: EOMVS: event-based omnidirectional multi-view stereo. IEEE Robot. Autom. Lett. **6**(4), 6709–6716 (2021). https://doi.org/10.1109/LRA.2021.3096161
9. Choi, J., et al.: Learning to super resolve intensity images from events. In: Proceedings of the IEEE/CVF Conference on Computer Vision and Pattern Recognition, pp. 2768–2776 (2020)
10. Gehrig, M., Aarents, W., Gehrig, D., Scaramuzza, D.: DSEC: a stereo event camera dataset for driving scenarios. IEEE Robot. Autom. Lett. **6**(3), 4947–4954 (2021)
11. Gumbel, E.J.: Statistical theory of extreme values and some practical applications: a series of lectures, vol. 33. US Government Printing Office (1954)
12. Guo, X., Yang, K., Yang, W., Wang, X., Li, H.: Group-wise correlation stereo network. In: 2019 IEEE/CVF Conference on Computer Vision and Pattern Recognition (CVPR), pp. 3268–3277 (2019)
13. Kendall, A., Martirosyan, H., Dasgupta, S., Henry, P.: End-to-end learning of geometry and context for deep stereo regression. In: 2017 IEEE International Conference on Computer Vision (ICCV), pp. 66–75 (2017)
14. Kingma, D.P., Ba, J.: Adam: a method for stochastic optimization. arXiv preprint arXiv:1412.6980 (2014)
15. Kogler, J., Humenberger, M., Sulzbachner, C.: Event-based stereo matching approaches for frameless address event stereo data. In: International Symposium on Visual Computing, pp. 674–685. Springer (2011)
16. Krizhevsky, A., Sutskever, I., Hinton, G.E.: ImageNet classification with deep convolutional neural networks. In: Advances in Neural Information Processing Systems 25 (2012)
17. Laga, H., Jospin, L.V., Boussaïd, F., Bennamoun: a survey on deep learning techniques for stereo-based depth estimation. In: IEEE Transactions on Pattern Analysis and Machine Intelligence (2020)
18. Liang, Z., et al.: Learning for disparity estimation through feature constancy. In: Proceedings of the IEEE Conference on Computer Vision and Pattern Recognition, pp. 2811–2820 (2018)

19. Lichtsteiner, P., Posch, C., Delbrück, T.: A 128 × 128 120 db 15 µs latency asynchronous temporal contrast vision sensor. IEEE J. Solid-State Circ. **43**, 566–576 (2008)
20. Mayer, N., et al.: A large dataset to train convolutional networks for disparity, optical flow, and scene flow estimation. In: Proceedings of the IEEE Conference on Computer Vision and Pattern Recognition, pp. 4040–4048 (2016)
21. Menze, M., Geiger, A.: Object scene flow for autonomous vehicles. In: Proceedings of the IEEE Conference on Computer Vision and Pattern Recognition, pp. 3061–3070 (2015)
22. Mostafavi, M., Yoon, K.J., Choi, J.: Event-intensity stereo: estimating depth by the best of both worlds. In: Proceedings of the IEEE/CVF International Conference on Computer Vision, pp. 4258–4267 (2021)
23. Paszke, A., et al.: PyTorch: an imperative style, high-performance deep learning library. In: Advances in Neural Information Processing Systems 32 (2019)
24. Piatkowska, E., Belbachir, A., Gelautz, M.: Asynchronous stereo vision for event-driven dynamic stereo sensor using an adaptive cooperative approach. In: Proceedings of the IEEE International Conference on Computer Vision Workshops, pp. 45–50 (2013)
25. Piatkowska, E., Kogler, J., Belbachir, N., Gelautz, M.: Improved cooperative stereo matching for dynamic vision sensors with ground truth evaluation. In: Proceedings of the IEEE Conference on Computer Vision and Pattern Recognition Workshops, pp. 53–60 (2017)
26. Rebecq, H., Gallego, G., Mueggler, E., Scaramuzza, D.: EMVS: event-based multi-view stereo-3D reconstruction with an event camera in real-time. Int. J. Comput. Vision **126**, 1394–1414 (2017)
27. Rogister, P., Benosman, R., Ieng, S.H., Lichtsteiner, P., Delbruck, T.: Asynchronous event-based binocular stereo matching. IEEE Trans. Neural Netw. Learn. Syst. **23**(2), 347–353 (2011)
28. Scharstein, D., Szeliski, R.: A taxonomy and evaluation of dense two-frame stereo correspondence algorithms. Int. J. Comput. Vision **47**, 7–42 (2004)
29. Tulyakov, S., Fleuret, F., Kiefel, M., Gehler, P., Hirsch, M.: Learning an event sequence embedding for dense event-based deep stereo. In: Proceedings of the IEEE/CVF International Conference on Computer Vision, pp. 1527–1537 (2019)
30. Tulyakov, S., Ivanov, A., Fleuret, F.: Practical deep stereo (pds): toward applications-friendly deep stereo matching. arXiv preprint arXiv:1806.01677 (2018)
31. Wang, L., et al.: Event-based high dynamic range image and very high frame rate video generation using conditional generative adversarial networks. In: Proceedings of the IEEE/CVF Conference on Computer Vision and Pattern Recognition, pp. 10081–10090 (2019)
32. Xu, H., Zhang, J.: AANet: adaptive aggregation network for efficient stereo matching. 2020 IEEE/CVF Conference on Computer Vision and Pattern Recognition (CVPR), pp. 1956–1965 (2020)
33. Yang, G., Zhao, H., Shi, J., Deng, Z., Jia, J.: SegStereo: exploiting semantic information for disparity estimation. In: Ferrari, V., Hebert, M., Sminchisescu, C., Weiss, Y. (eds.) ECCV 2018. LNCS, vol. 11211, pp. 660–676. Springer, Cham (2018). https://doi.org/10.1007/978-3-030-01234-2_39
34. Zhang, F., Prisacariu, V.A., Yang, R., Torr, P.H.S.: GA-Net: guided aggregation net for end-to-end stereo matching. In: 2019 IEEE/CVF Conference on Computer Vision and Pattern Recognition (CVPR), pp. 185–194 (2019)

35. Zhang, F., Qi, X., Yang, R., Prisacariu, V., Wah, B., Torr, P.: Domain-invariant stereo matching networks. In: Vedaldi, A., Bischof, H., Brox, T., Frahm, J.-M. (eds.) ECCV 2020. LNCS, vol. 12347, pp. 420–439. Springer, Cham (2020). https://doi.org/10.1007/978-3-030-58536-5_25
36. Zhang, R., Isola, P., Efros, A.A., Shechtman, E., Wang, O.: The unreasonable effectiveness of deep features as a perceptual metric. In: Proceedings of the IEEE Conference on Computer Vision and Pattern Recognition, pp. 586–595 (2018)
37. Zhong, Y., Dai, Y., Li, H.: Self-supervised learning for stereo matching with self-improving ability. arXiv preprint arXiv:1709.00930 (2017)
38. Zhu, A.Z., Chen, Y., Daniilidis, K.: Realtime time synchronized event-based stereo. In: Ferrari, V., Hebert, M., Sminchisescu, C., Weiss, Y. (eds.) ECCV 2018. LNCS, vol. 11210, pp. 438–452. Springer, Cham (2018). https://doi.org/10.1007/978-3-030-01231-1_27
39. Zhu, A.Z., Thakur, D., Özaslan, T., Pfrommer, B., Kumar, V., Daniilidis, K.: The multivehicle stereo event camera dataset: an event camera dataset for 3D perception. IEEE Robot. Autom. Lett. **3**(3), 2032–2039 (2018)
40. Zhu, A.Z., Yuan, L., Chaney, K., Daniilidis, K.: Unsupervised event-based learning of optical flow, depth, and egomotion. In: Proceedings of the IEEE/CVF Conference on Computer Vision and Pattern Recognition, pp. 989–997 (2019)
41. Zou, D., et al.: Context-aware event-driven stereo matching. In: 2016 IEEE International Conference on Image Processing (ICIP), pp. 1076–1080. IEEE (2016)
42. Zou, D., et al.: Robust dense depth map estimation from sparse DVS stereos. In: British British Machine Vision Conference (BMVC), vol. 1 (2017)

D³Net: A Unified Speaker-Listener Architecture for 3D Dense Captioning and Visual Grounding

Dave Zhenyu Chen[1(✉)], Qirui Wu[2], Matthias Nießner[1], and Angel X. Chang[2]

[1] Technical University of Munich, Munich, Germany
zhenyu.chen@tum.de
[2] Simon Fraser University, Burnaby, Canada
https://daveredrum.github.io/D3Net/

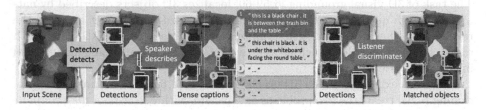

Fig. 1. We introduce D³Net, an end-to-end neural speaker-listener architecture that can **d**etect, **d**escribe and **d**iscriminate. D³Net also enables semi-supervised training on ScanNet data with partially annotated descriptions.

Abstract. Recent work on dense captioning and visual grounding in 3D have achieved impressive results. Despite developments in both areas, the limited amount of available 3D vision-language data causes overfitting issues for 3D visual grounding and 3D dense captioning methods. Also, how to discriminatively describe objects in complex 3D environments is not fully studied yet. To address these challenges, we present D³Net, an end-to-end neural speaker-listener architecture that can **d**etect, **d**escribe and **d**iscriminate. Our D³Net unifies dense captioning and visual grounding in 3D in a self-critical manner. This self-critical property of D³Net encourages generation of discriminative object captions and enables semi-supervised training on scan data with partially annotated descriptions. Our method outperforms SOTA methods in both tasks on the Scan-Refer dataset, surpassing the SOTA 3D dense captioning method by a significant margin.

1 Introduction

Recently, there has been increasing interest in bridging 3D visual scene understanding [5,11,18,19,22,41,46] and natural language processing [4,13,34,48,55].

Supplementary Information The online version contains supplementary material available at https://doi.org/10.1007/978-3-031-19824-3_29.

S. Avidan et al. (Eds.): ECCV 2022, LNCS 13692, pp. 487–505, 2022.
https://doi.org/10.1007/978-3-031-19824-3_29

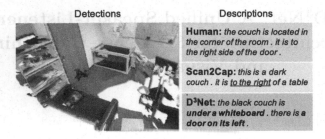

Detections   Descriptions

Fig. 2. Prior work [7] struggle to produce discriminative object captions. Also, captions often appear to be template-based. In contrast, our D³Net generates discriminative object captions.

The task of 3D visual grounding [6,59,60] localizes 3D objects described by natural language queries. 3D dense captioning proposed by Chen et al. [7] is the reverse task where we generate descriptions for 3D objects in RGB-D scans. Both tasks enable applications such as assistive robots and natural language control in AR/VR systems.

However, existing work on 3D visual grounding [1,6,23,59,60] and dense captioning [7,58] treats the two problems as separate, with *detect-then-dis-criminate* or *detect-then-describe* being the common strategies for tackling the two tasks. Separating the two complementary tasks hinders holistic 3D scene understanding where the ultimate goal is to create models that can infer: 1) what are the objects; 2) how to describe each object; 3) what object is being referred to through natural language. The disadvantages of having separated strategies are twofold. First, the detect-then-describe strategy often struggles to describe target objects in a discriminative way. In Fig. 2, the generated descriptions from Scan2Cap [7] fail to uniquely describe the target objects, especially in scenes with several similar objects. Second, existing 3D visual grounding methods [6,60] in the detect-then-discriminate strategy suffer from severe overfitting issue, partly due to the small amount of 3D vision-language data [1,6] which is limited compared to counterpart 2D datasets such as MSCOCO [32].

To address these issues, we propose an end-to-end self-critical solution, D³Net, to enable discriminability in dense caption generation and utilize the generated captions improve localization. Relevant work in image captioning [33,36] tackles similar issues where the generated captions are indiscriminative and repetitive by explicitly reinforcing discriminative caption generation with an image retrieval loss. Inspired by this scheme, we introduce a speaker-listener strategy, where the captioning module "speaks" about the 3D objects, while the localization module "listens" and finds the targets. Our proposed speaker-listener architecture can **d**etect, **d**escribe and **d**iscriminate, as illustrated in Fig. 1. The key idea is to reinforce the speaker to generate discriminative descriptions so that the listener can better localize the described targets given those descriptions.

This approach brings another benefit. Since the speaker-listener architecture self-critically generates and discriminates descriptions, we can train on scenes without any object descriptions. We see further improvements in 3D dense captioning and 3D visual grounding performance when using this additional data alongside annotated scenes. This can allow for semi-supervised training on RGB-D scans beyond the ScanNet dataset. To summarize, our contributions are:

- We introduce a unified speaker-listener architecture to generate discriminative object descriptions in RGB-D scans. Our architecture allows for a semi-supervised training scheme that can alleviate data shortage in the 3D vision-language field.
- We study how the different components impact performance and find that having a strong detector is essential, and that by jointly optimizing the detector, speaker, and listener we can improve detection as well as 3D dense captioning and visual grounding.
- We show that our method outperforms the state-of-the-art for both 3D dense captioning and 3D visual grounding method by a significant margin.

2   Related Work

Vision and Language in 3D. Recently, there has been growing interest in grounding language to 3D data [1,2,6,8,44,47,52]. Chen et al. [6] and Achlioptas et al. [1] introduce two complementary datasets consisting of descriptions of real-world 3D objects from ScanNet [11] reconstructions, named ScanRefer and ReferIt3D, respectively. ScanRefer proposes the joint task of detecting and localizing objects in a 3D scan based on a textual description, while ReferIt3D is focused on distinguishing 3D objects from the same semantic class given ground-truth bounding boxes. Yuan et al. [59] localize objects by decomposing input queries into fine-grained aspects, and use PointGroup [25] as their visual backbone. However, the frozen detection backbone is not fine-tuned together with the localization module. Zhao et al. [60] propose a transformer-based architecture with a VoteNet [41] backbone to handle multimodal contexts during localization. Despite the improved matching module, their work still suffers from poor quality detections due to the weak 3D detector. We show that fine-tuning an improved 3D detector is essential to getting good predictions and good localization performance. Chen et al. [7] introduce the task of densely detecting and captioning objects in RGB-D scans. Recently, Yuan et al. [58] aggregate the 2D features to point cloud to generate faithful object descriptions. Although their methods can effectively detect objects and generate captions w.r.t. their attributes, the quality of the bounding boxes and the discriminability of the captions are inadequate. Our method explicitly handles the discriminability of the generated captions through a self-critical speaker-listener architecture, resulting in the state-of-the-art performance in both 3D dense captioning and 3D visual grounding tasks.

Generating Captions in Images. Image captioning has attracted a great deal of interest [3,14,26,28,35,43,45,50,53]. Recent work [33,36] suggest that traditional encoder-decoder-based image captioning methods suffer from the discriminability issues. Luo et al. [36] propose an additional image retrieval branch to reinforce discriminative caption generation. Liu et al. [33] propose a reinforcement learning method to train not only on annotated web images, but also images without any paired captions. In contrast to generating captions for the entire image, in the dense captioning task we densely generate captions for each detected object in the input image [27,30,54]. Although such methods are effective for generating captions in 2D images, directly applying such training techniques on 3D dense captioning can lead to unsatisfactory results, since the captions involve 3D geometric relationships. In contrast, we work directly on 3D scene input dealing with object attributes as well as 3D spatial relationships.

Grounding Referential Expressions in Images. There has been tremendous progress in the task of grounding referential expressions in images, also known as visual grounding [20,21,29,38,40,56]. Given an image and a natural language text query as input, the target object is either localized by a bounding box [21,56], or a segmentation mask [20]. These methods have achieved great success in the image domain. However, they are not designed to deal with 3D geometry inputs and handle complex 3D spatial relationships. Our proposed method directly decomposes the 3D input data with a sparse convolutional detection backbone, which produces accurate object proposals as well as semantically rich features.

Speaker-Listener Models for Grounding. The speaker-listener model is a popular architecture for pragmatic language understanding, where a line of research explores how the context and communicative goals affect the linguistics [10,16]. Recent work use neural speaker-listener architectures to tackle referring expression generation [37,38,57], vision-language navigation [15], and shape differentiation [2]. Mao et al. [38] construct a CNN-LSTM architecture optimized by a softmax loss to directly discriminate the generated referential expressions. There is no separate neural listener module compared with our method. Luo and Shakhnarovich [37] and Yu et al. [57] introduce a LSTM-based neural listener in the speaker-listener pipeline, but generating the referential expression is not directly supervised via the listener model, but rather trained via a proxy objective. In contrast, our method directly optimizes the Transformer-based neural listener for the visual grounding task by discriminating the generated object captions without any proxy training objective. Similarly, Achlioptas et al. [2] includes a pretrained and frozen listener in the training objective, while ours enables joint end-to-end optimization for both the speaker and listener via policy gradient algorithm. We experimentally show our method to be effective for semi-supervised learning in the two 3D vision-language tasks.

3   Method

D^3Net has three components: a 3D object detector, the speaker (captioning) module, and the listener (localization) module. Figure 3 shows the overall architecture and training flow. The point clouds are fed into the detector to predict object proposals. The speaker takes object proposals as input to produce

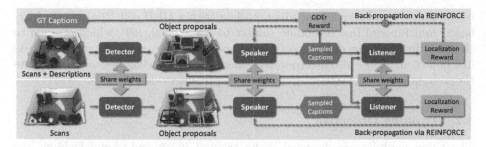

Fig. 3. D³Net architecture. We input point clouds into the *detector* to predict object proposals. Then, those proposals are fed into the speaker to generate captions that *describes* each object. To *discriminate* the object described by each caption, the listener matches the generated captions with object proposals. The captioning and localization results are back-propagated via REINFORCE [51] as rewards through the dashed lines. D³Net also enables end-to-end training on point clouds with no GT object descriptions (bottom blue block). (Color figure online)

captions. To increase caption discriminability, we match these captions with object proposals via the listener. Caption quality is measured by the CIDEr [49] scores and the listener loss, which are back-propagated via REINFORCE [51] as rewards to the speaker. Our architecture can handle scenes without ground-truth (GT) object descriptions by reinforcing the speaker with the listener loss only.

3.1 Modules

Detector. We use PointGroup [25] as our detector module. PointGroup is a relatively simple model for 3D instance segmentation that achieves competitive performance on the ScanNet benchmark. We use ENet to augment the point clouds with multi-view features, following Dai and Nießner [12]. PointGroup uses a U-Net architecture with a SparseConvNet backbone to encode point features, cluster the points, and uses ScoreNet, another U-Net structure, to score each cluster. We take the cluster features after ScoreNet as the encoded object features. We refer readers to the original paper [25] for more details. The object bounding boxes are determined by taking the minimum and maximum points in the point clusters, and are produced as final outputs of our detector module.

Speaker. We base our speaker on the dense captioning method introduced by Chen et al. [7]. Our speaker module has two submodules: 1) a relational graph module, which is responsible for learning object-to-object spatial location relationships; 2) a context-aware attention captioning module, which attentively generates descriptive tokens with respect to the object attributes as well as the object-to-object spatial relationships.

Listener. For the listener, we follow the architecture introduced by Chen et al. [6] but replace the multi-modal fusion module with the transformer-based multi-modal fusion module of Zhao et al. [60]. Our listener module has two submodules: 1) a language encoding module with a GRU cell; 2) a transformer-based multi-modal fusion module similar to Zhao et al. [60], which attends to elements in the input query descriptions and the detected object proposals. As in Chen et al. [6], we also incorporate a language object classifier to discriminate the semantics of the target objects in the input query descriptions.

3.2 Training Objective

The three modules are designed to be trained in an end-to-end fashion (see Fig. 3). In this section, we describe the loss for each module, and how they are combined for the overall loss.

Detection Loss. We use the instance segmentation loss introduced in Point-Group [25] to train the 3D backbone. The detection loss is composed of four parts: $L_{det} = L_{sem} + L_{o\_reg} + L_{o\_dir} + L_{c\_score}$. L_{sem} is a cross-entropy loss supervising semantic label prediction for each point. L_{o_reg} is a L_1 regression loss constraining the learned point offsets belonging to the same cluster. L_{o_dir} constrains the direction of predicted offset vectors, defined as the means of minus cosine similarities. It helps regress precise offsets, particularly for boundary points of large-size objects, since these points are relatively far from the instance centroids. L_{c_score} is another binary cross-entropy loss supervising the predicted objectness scores.

Listener Loss. The listener loss is composed of a localization loss L_{loc} and a language-based object classification loss $L_{lobjcls}$. To obtain the localization loss L_{loc}, we first require a target bounding box. We use the detected bounding box with the highest IoU with the GT bounding box as the target bounding box. Then, a cross-entropy loss L_{loc} is applied to supervise the matching score prediction. In the end-to-end training scenario, the detected bounding boxes associated with the generated descriptions from the speaker are treated as the target bounding boxes. The language object classification loss is a cross-entropy loss $L_{lobjcls}$ to supervise the classification based on the input description. The target classes are consistent with the ScanNet 18 classes, excluding structural objects such as "floor" and "wall".

Speaker Loss Using MLE Training Objective. The speaker loss is a standard captioning loss from maximum likelihood estimation (MLE). During training, provided with a pair of GT bounding box and the associated GT description, we optimize the description associated with the predicted bounding box which has the highest IoU score with the current GT bounding box. We first treat the description generation task as a sequence prediction task, factorized as: $L_{spk-XE}(\theta) = -\sum_{t=1}^{T} \log p(\hat{c}_t | \hat{c}_1, ..., c_{t-1}; I, \theta)$, where $\hat{c}_t$ denotes the generated token at step t; I and θ represent the visual signal and model parameter, respectively. The token $\hat{c}_t$ is sampled from the probability distribution over the pre-defined vocabulary. The generation process is performed by greedy decoding or beam search in an autoregressive manner, and we use the argmax function to sample each token.

Joint Loss Using REINFORCE Training Objective. We use REIN-FORCE to train the detector-speaker-listener jointly. We first describe the enhanced speaker-loss, $L_{\text{spk-R}}$ that is trained using reinforcement learning to produce discriminative captions. We then describe the overall loss used in end-to-end training. Following prior work [17,33,36,42,43,57], generating descriptions is treated as a reinforcement learning task. In the setting of reinforcement learning, the speaker module is treated as the "agent", while the previously generated words and the input visual signal I are the "environment". At step t, generating word $\hat{c}_t$ by the speaker module is deemed as the "action" taken with the policy p_θ, which is defined by the speaker module parameters θ. Specifically, with the generated description $\hat{C} = \{c_1, ..., c_T\}$, the objective is to maximize the reward function $R(\hat{C}, I)$. We apply the "REINFORCE with baseline" algorithm following Rennie et al. [43] to reduce the variance of this loss function, where a baseline reward $R(C^*, I)$ of the description C^* independent of $\hat{C}$ is introduced. We apply beam search to sample descriptions and choose the greedily decoded descriptions as the baseline. The simplified policy gradient is:

$$L_{\text{spk-R}}(\theta) \approx -(R(\hat{C}, I) - R(C^*, I)) \sum_{t=1}^{T} \log p(\hat{c}_t | I, \theta) \tag{1}$$

Rewards. As the word-level sampling through the argmax function is non-differentiable, the subsequent listener loss cannot be directly back-propagated through the speaker module. A workaround is to use the gumbel softmax reparametrization trick [24]. Following the training scheme of Liu et al. [33] and Luo et al. [36], the listener loss can be inserted into the REINFORCE reward function to increase the discriminability of generated referential descriptions. Specifically, given the localization loss L_{loc} and the language object classification loss L_{lobjcls}, the reward function $R(\hat{C})$ is the weighted sum of the CIDEr score of the sampled description and the listener-related losses:

$$R(\hat{C}, I) = R^{\text{CIDEr}}(\hat{C}, I) - \alpha[L_{\text{loc}}(\hat{C}) + \beta L_{\text{lobjcls}}(\hat{C})] \tag{2}$$

where α and β are the weights balancing the CIDEr reward and the listener rewards. We empirically set them to 0.1 and 1 in our experiments, respectively. To stabilize the training, the reward related to the baseline description $R(C^*)$ should be formulated analogously. Note that there should be no gradient calculation and back-propagation for the baseline C^*. For scenes with no GT descriptions provided, the CIDEr reward is cancelled in the reward function, which in this case becomes $R(\hat{C}, I) = -\alpha[L_{\text{loc}}(\hat{C}) + \beta L_{\text{lobjcls}}(\hat{C})]$.

Relative Orientation Loss. Following Chen et al. [7], we adopt the relative orientation loss on the message passing module as a proxy loss. The object-to-object relative orientations ranging from 0° to 180° are discretized into 6 classes. We apply a simple cross-entropy loss L_{ori} to supervise the relative orientation predictions.

Overall Loss. We combine loss terms in our end-to-end joint training objective as: $L = L_{\text{det}} + L_{\text{spk-R}} + 0.3L_{\text{ori}}$.

3.3   Training

We use a stage-wise training strategy for stable training. We first pretrain the detector backbone on all training scans in ScanNet via the detector loss L_{det}. We then train the dense captioning pipeline with the pretrained detector and a newly initialized speaker end-to-end via the detector loss and the speaker MLE loss $L_{\text{spk-XE}}$. After the speaker MLE loss converges, we train the visual grounding pipeline with the fine-tuned frozen detector and the listener via the listener loss L_{loc}. Finally, we fine-tune the entire speaker-listener architecture with the overall loss L.

3.4   Inference

During inference, we use the detector and the speaker to do 3D dense captioning and the listener to do visual grounding. The detector first produces object proposals, and the speaker generates a description for each object proposal. We take the minimum and maximum coordinates in the predicted object instance masks to construct the bounding boxes. For the object proposals that are assigned to the same ground truth, we keep only the one with the highest IoU with the GT bounding box. When evaluating the detector itself, the non-maximum suppression is applied.

4   Experiments

4.1   Dataset

We use the ScanRefer [6] dataset consisting of around 51k descriptions for over 11k objects in 800 ScanNet [11] scans. The descriptions include information about the appearance of the objects, as well as the object-to-object spatial relationships. We follow the official split from the ScanRefer benchmark for training and validation. We report our visual grounding results on the validation split and benchmark results on the hidden test set[1]. Our dense captioning results are on the validation split due to the lack of the test grounding truth. We also conduct experiments on the ReferIt3D dataset [1] (please see the supplemental).

4.2   Semi-supervised Training with Extra Data

As the scans in ScanRefer dataset are only a subset of scans in ScanNet, we extend the training set by including all re-scans of the same scenes for semi-supervised training. Unlike the scans in ScanRefer, these re-scans do not have per object descriptions. We can control how much extra data to use by randomly

---

[1] http://kaldir.vc.in.tum.de/scanrefer_benchmark.

Table 1. Quantitative results on 3D dense captioning and object detection. As in Chen et al. [7], we average the conventional captioning evaluation metrics with the percentage of the predicted bounding boxes whose IoU with the GTs are higher than 0.5. Our speaker model outperforms the baseline Scan2Cap without training via REINFORCE, while training with CIDEr reward further boosts the dense captioning performance. We also showcase the effectiveness of training with additional scans with no description annotations. Our speaker-listener architecture trained with 1x extra data achieves the best performance.

	C@0.5IoU	B-4@0.5IoU	M@0.5IoU	R@0.5IoU	mAP@0.5
Scan2Cap [7]	39.08	23.32	21.97	44.78	32.21
X-Trans2Cap [58]	43.87	25.05	22.46	44.97	35.31
Ours (MLE)	46.07	30.29	24.35	51.67	50.93
Ours (CIDEr)	57.88	32.64	24.86	52.26	51.01
Ours (CIDEr+fixed loc.)	58.93	33.36	25.12	52.62	51.04
Ours (CIDEr+loc.)	61.30	34.50	25.25	52.80	52.07
Ours (CIDEr+loc.+lobjcls.)	61.50	35.05	25.48	53.31	52.58
Ours (w/ 0.1x extra data)	61.91	35.03	25.38	53.25	52.64
Ours (w/ 0.5x extra data)	62.36	35.54	25.43	53.67	53.17
Ours (w/ 1x extra data)	**62.64**	**35.68**	**25.72**	**53.90**	**53.95**

sampling (with replacement) from the set of re-scans. We experiment with augmenting our data with 0.1 to 1 times the amount of annotated data as extra data. During training, we randomly select detected objects in the sampled extra scans for subsequent dense captioning and visual grounding. For the complete 'extra' scenario, we use a comparable amount (1x) of extra data as the annotated data in ScanRefer.

4.3   Implementation Details

We implement the PointGroup backbone using the Minkowski Engine [9] (see supplement). For the backbone, we train using Adam [31] with a learning rate of 2e-3, on the ScanNet train split with batch size 4 for 140k iterations, until convergence. For data augmentation, we follow Jiang et al. [25], randomly applying jitter, mirroring about the YZ-plane, and rotation about the Z axis (up-axis) to each point cloud scene. We then use the Adam optimizer with learning rate 1e-3 to train the detector and the listener on the ScanRefer dataset with batch size 4 for 60k iterations, until convergence. Each scan is paired with 8 descriptions (i.e. 4 scans and 32 descriptions per batch iteration). Then, we combine the trained detector with the newly initialized speaker on the ScanRefer dataset for the 3D dense captioning task, where the weights of the detector are frozen. We again use Adam with learning rate 1e-3, with the training process converging within 14k iterations. All our experiments are conducted on a RTX 3090, and all neural modules are implemented using PyTorch [39].

Table 2. Quantitative results on 3D visual grounding. We adapt the evaluation setting as in Chen et al. [6]. "Unique" means there is only one object belongs to a specific class in the scene, while "multiple" represents the cases where more than one object from a specific class can be found in the scene. Clearly, our base visual grounding network outperforms all baselines even before being put into the speaker-listener architecture. After the speaker-listener fine-tuning, our method achieves the state-of-the-art performance on the ScanRefer validation set and the public benchmark. Note that 3DVG-Trans+ is an unpublished extension of 3DVG-Trans [60] which appears only on the public benchmark.

	Val Acc@0.5IoU			Test Acc@0.5IoU		
	Unique	Multiple	Overall	Unique	Multiple	Overall
ScanRefer [6]	53.51	21.11	27.40	43.53	20.97	26.03
TGNN [23]	56.80	23.18	29.70	58.90	25.30	32.80
InstanceRefer [59]	66.83	24.77	32.93	66.69	26.88	35.80
3DVG-Trans [60]	60.64	28.42	34.67	55.15	29.33	35.12
3DVG-Trans+ [60]	–	–	–	57.87	**31.02**	37.04
Ours (w/o fine-tuning)	70.35	27.11	35.58	65.79	27.26	35.90
Ours	**72.04**	**30.05**	**37.87**	**68.43**	30.74	**39.19**

4.4 Quantitative Results

3D Dense Captioning and Detection. Table 1 compares our 3D dense captioning and object detection results against the baseline methods Scan2Cap [7] and X-Trans2Cap [58]. Leveraging the improved PointGroup based detector, our speaker model trained with the conventional MLE objective (Ours (MLE)) outperforms Scan2Cap and X-Trans2Cap by a large margin in all metrics. As expected, training with the CIDEr reward (Ours (CIDEr)) significantly improves the CIDEr score. We note that other captioning metrics are also improved, but the detection mAP@0.5 remains similar. Training with object localization reward (Ours (CIDEr+loc.)) improves both captioning and detection further due to the improved discriminability during description generation. Note that if we use a frozen pretrained listener (Ours (CIDEr+fixed loc.)), the improvement is not as significant as when we allow the listener weights to be fine-tuned (Ours (CIDEr+loc.)). Our full model with the full listener reward incorporates an additional language object classification loss (Ours (CIDEr+loc.+lobjcls.)) and further improves the performance for both tasks.

Does Additional Data Help? As our method allow for training the listener with scans without language data, we investigate the effectiveness of training with additional ScanNet data that have not been annotated with descriptions. We vary the amount of extra scan data (without descriptions) from 0.1x to 1x of fully annotated data and train our full model with CIDEr and full listener reward (loc.+lobjcls.). Our results (last three rows of Table 1), show that our semi-supervised training strategy can leverage the extra data to improve both dense captioning and object detection.

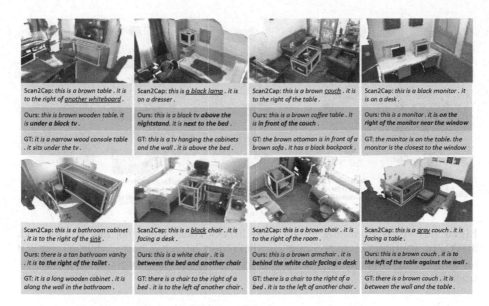

Fig. 4. Qualitative results in 3D dense captioning task from Scan2Cap [7] and our method. We underline the inaccurate words and mark the spatially discriminative phrases in bold. Our method qualitatively outperforms Scan2Cap in producing better object bounding boxes and more discriminative descriptions. (Color figure online)

3D Visual Grounding. Table 2 compares our results against prior 3D visual grounding methods ScanRefer [6], TGNN [23], InstanceRefer [59] and 3DVG-Transformer [60], and 3DVG-Trans+, an unpublished extension. Our method trained only with the detection loss and the listener loss ("Ours w/o fine-tuning"), i.e. without the speaker-listener setting, outperforms all the previous methods in the "Unique" and "Overall" scenarios. We find the improved fusion module together with the improved detector is sufficient to outperform 3DVG-Trans. Due to the improved detector, our method can distinguish objects in the "Unique" case, where the semantic labels play an important role. Meanwhile, 3DVG-Trans [60] still outperforms our base listener when discriminating objects from the same class ("Multiple" case). Our end-to-end speaker-listener (last row) outperforms all previous method including 3DVG-Trans.

4.5 Qualitative Analysis

3D Dense Captioning. Figure 4 compares our results with object captions from Scan2Cap [7]. Descriptions generated by Scan2Cap cannot uniquely identify the target object in the input scenes (see the yellow block on the bottom right). Also, Scan2Cap produces inaccurate object bounding boxes, which affects the quality of object captions (see the yellow block on the top left). Compared to captions from Scan2Cap, our method produces more discriminative object

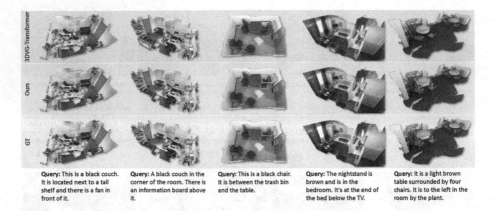

Query: This is a black couch. It is located next to a tall shelf and there is a fan in front of it.

Query: A black couch in the corner of the room. There is an information board above it.

Query: This is a black chair. It is between the trash bin and the table.

Query: The nightstand is brown and is in the bedroom. It's at the end of the bed below the TV.

Query: It is a light brown table surrounded by four chairs. It is to the left in the room by the plant.

Fig. 5. 3D visual grounding results using 3DVG-Transformer [60] and our method. 3DVG-Transformer fails to accurately predict object bounding boxes, while our method produces accurate bounding boxes and correctly distinguishes target objects from distractors.

captions that specifies more spatial relations (see bolded phrases in the blue blocks).

3D Visual Grounding. Figure 5 compares our results with 3DVG-Transformer [60]. Though 3DVG-Transformer is able to pick the correct object, it suffers from poor object detections and is constrained by the performance of the VoteNet-based detection backbone (see the first column). Our method is capable of selecting the queried objects while also predicting more accurate object bounding boxes.

4.6   Analysis and Ablation Studies

Does better detection backbone help? From Table 1, we see that using a better detector can significant improve performance. We further examine the effect of using different detection backbones (VoteNet and PointGroup) compared to GT bounding boxes in Table 3. For each detection backbone, we use four variants of our method: the models trained without the joint speaker-listener architecture, and the speaker-listener architecture trained with CIDEr reward, listener reward and extra ScanNet data. The results with GT boxes show the effectiveness of our speaker-listener architecture, when detections are perfect. The large improvement from VoteNet [41] to PointGroup [25] show the importance of a better detection backbone. The gap between GT and VoteNet/PointGroup shows there is room for further improvement.

Are the generated descriptions more discriminative? To check whether the speaker-listener architecture generates more discriminative descriptions, we conduct an automatic evaluation via a reverse task. In this task, we feed the

Table 3. Quantitative results on object detection, dense captioning and visual grounding in RGB-D scans. We train our method using different detection backbones as well as the ground truth bounding boxes. Our method trained with CIDEr and listener reward as well as the additional data outperforms the pretrained speaker and listener models.

Method	Detection	mAP@0.5	C@0.5IoU	B-4@0.5IoU	M@0.5IoU	R@0.5IoU	Unique Acc@0.5IoU	Multiple Acc@0.5IoU	Overall Acc@0.5IoU
Ours (MLE)	GT	100.00	71.41	42.95	29.67	64.93	88.45	36.46	46.03
Ours (CIDEr)	GT	100.00	94.80	47.92	30.80	**66.34**	–	–	–
Ours (CIDEr+lis.)	GT	100.00	95.62	47.65	**30.93**	66.31	89.76	36.85	47.14
Ours (CIDEr+lis.+extra)	GT	100.00	**96.31**	**48.20**	30.80	66.10	**89.86**	**40.66**	**48.17**
Ours (MLE)	VoteNet	32.21	39.08	23.32	21.97	**44.78**	56.41	21.11	27.95
Ours (CIDEr)	VoteNet	37.66	46.88	25.96	22.10	44.69	–	–	–
Ours (CIDEr+lis.)	VoteNet	38.03	47.32	24.76	21.66	43.62	57.90	20.73	28.03
Ours (CIDEr+lis.+extra)	VoteNet	**38.82**	**48.38**	**26.09**	**22.15**	44.74	**58.40**	21.66	**29.25**
Ours (MLE)	PointGroup	47.19	46.07	30.29	24.35	51.67	70.35	27.11	35.58
Ours (CIDEr)	PointGroup	52.44	57.88	32.64	24.86	52.26	–	–	–
Ours (CIDEr+lis.)	PointGroup	52.58	61.50	35.05	25.48	53.31	71.04	27.40	35.62
Ours (CIDEr+lis.+extra)	PointGroup	**53.95**	**62.64**	**35.68**	**25.72**	**53.90**	**72.04**	**30.05**	**37.87**

Table 4. We automatically evaluate the discriminability of the generated object descriptions. A pretrained neural listener similar to Zhao et al. [60] is fed with the GT object features and the descriptions generated by Scan2Cap [7] as well as our method. Higher grounding accuracy indicates better discriminability, especially in the "multiple" case. To alleviate noisy detections, the evaluation results on the descriptions generated from the GT object features are also presented. Our method generates more discriminative descriptions compared to Scan2Cap.

	Detection	Unique Acc@0.5IoU	Multiple Acc@0.5IoU	Overall Acc@0.5IoU
Scan2Cap [7]	VN [41]	80.52	29.95	39.08
Ours (w/ CIDEr & lis.)	PG [25]	81.16	30.22	41.62
Ours (w/ CIDEr & lis. & extra)	PG [25]	**81.27**	**30.33**	**41.73**
Ours (w/ CIDEr & lis.)	GT	89.76	38.53	48.07
Ours (w/ CIDEr & lis. & extra)	GT	**90.29**	**40.66**	**49.71**

generated descriptions and GT bounding boxes into a pretrained neural listener model similar to Zhao et al. [60]. The predicted visual grounding results are evaluated in the same way as in our 3D visual grounding experiments. Higher grounding accuracy indicates better discrimination, especially in the "Multiple" case. Results (Table 4) show that our speaker-listener architecture generates more discriminative descriptions compared to Scan2Cap [7]. The discrimination is further improved when training with extra ScanNet data. To disentangle the affect of imperfectly predicted bounding boxes, we also train and evaluate our method with GT boxes (see last two rows in Table 4). We see that our semi-supervised speaker-listener architecture generates more discriminative descriptions.

Does the listener help with captioning? The third to the sixth rows in Table 1 measure the benefit of training the speaker together with the listener

Table 5. Manual analysis of captions generated by Scan2Cap [7] and variants of our method. We measure accuracy in three different aspects: object categories, appearance attributes and spatial relations. Our method generates more accurate descriptions in all aspects, especially for describing spatial relations.

	Acc. (Category)	Acc. (Attribute)	Acc. (Relation)
Scan2Cap [7]	84.10	64.21	69.00
Ours (MLE)	88.00 (+3.84)	74.73 (+10.53)	69.00 (+0.00)
Ours (CIDEr)	88.89 (+4.73)	75.00 (+10.79)	68.00 (−1.00)
Ours (CIDEr+lis.)	90.91 (+6.75)	77.38 (+13.17)	75.00 (+6.00)
Ours (CIDEr+lis.+extra)	92.93 (**+8.77**)	80.95 (**+16.74**)	78.57 (**+9.57**)

(Ours (CIDEr+loc.) and Ours (CIDEr+loc.+lobjcls.)) rather than training the speaker alone (Ours (CIDEr)). Training with the listener improves all captioning metrics. Also, training jointly with an unfrozen listener (Ours (CIDEr+loc.) leads to a better performance when compared with the variant with a pretrained and frozen listener (Ours (CIDEr+fixed loc.), which is similar to Achlioptas et al. [2]. Additionally, as the detector is not only fine-tuned with the speaker but also with the listener, the additional supervision from the listener helps with the detection performance as well.

To analyze the quality of the generated object captions, we asked 5 students to perform a fine-grained manual analysis of the captions. Each student was presented with a batch of 100 randomly selected object captions with associated objects highlighted in the 3D scene. The student are then asked to indicate if the respective aspects were included and correctly described. The manual analysis results in Table 5 shows that our method generates more accurate descriptions compared to Scan2Cap. In particular, training with the listener and extra Scan-Net data produces more accurate spatial relations in the descriptions. The results of fine-grained manual analysis complements the automatic captioning evaluation metric. While metrics such as CIDEr captures the overall similarity of the generated sentences against the references, the accuracies in Table 5 measures the correctness of the decomposed visual attributes.

Does the speaker help with grounding? Table 2 compares grounding results between a pretrained listener (Ours w/o fine-tuning) and a fine-tuned speaker-listener model (Ours). Although the grounding performance drops in the "Unique" subset, the improvements in "Multiple" suggests better discriminability in tougher and ambiguous scenarios.

5 Conclusion

We present D³Net, an end-to-end speaker-listener architecture that can detect, describe and discriminate. Specifically, the speaker iteratively generates descriptive tokens given the object proposals detected by the detector, while the listener discriminates the object proposals in the scene with the generated captions. The self-discriminative property of D^{3}Net also enables semi-supervised training on ScanNet data without the annotated descriptions. Our method outperforms the previous SOTA methods in both tasks on ScanRefer, surpassing the previous SOTA 3D dense captioning method by a significant margin. Our architecture can serve as an initial step towards leveraging unannotated 3D data for language and 3D vision. Overall, we hope that our work will encourage more future research in 3D vision and language.

Acknowledgements. This work is funded by Google (AugmentedPerception), the ERC Starting Grant Scan2CAD (804724), and a Google Faculty Award. We would also like to thank the support of the TUM-IAS Rudolf Mößbauer and Hans Fischer Fellowships (Focus Group Visual Computing), as well as the the German Research Foundation (DFG) under the Grant *Making Machine Learning on Static and Dynamic 3D Data Practical*. This work is also supported in part by the Canada CIFAR AI Chair program and an NSERC Discovery Grant.

References

1. Achlioptas, P., Abdelreheem, A., Xia, F., Elhoseiny, M., Guibas, L.: ReferIt3D: neural listeners for fine-grained 3d object identification in real-world scenes. In: Vedaldi, A., Bischof, H., Brox, T., Frahm, J.-M. (eds.) ECCV 2020. LNCS, vol. 12346, pp. 422–440. Springer, Cham (2020). https://doi.org/10.1007/978-3-030-58452-8_25
2. Achlioptas, P., Fan, J., Hawkins, R., Goodman, N., Guibas, L.J.: ShapeGlot: learning language for shape differentiation. In: Proceedings of the IEEE International Conference on Computer Vision (2019)
3. Anderson, P., et al.: Bottom-up and top-down attention for image captioning and visual question answering. In: Proceedings of the IEEE Conference on Computer Vision and Pattern Recognition, pp. 6077–6086 (2018)
4. Brown, T.B., et al.: Language models are few-shot learners. arXiv preprint arXiv:2005.14165 (2020)
5. Chang, A., et al.: Matterport3D: learning from RGB-D data in indoor environments. In: Proceedings of the International Conference on 3D Vision, pp. 667–676, IEEE (2017)
6. Chen, D.Z., Chang, A.X., Nießner, M.: ScanRefer: 3d object localization in RGB-D scans using natural language. In: Vedaldi, A., Bischof, H., Brox, T., Frahm, J.-M. (eds.) ECCV 2020. LNCS, vol. 12365, pp. 202–221. Springer, Cham (2020). https://doi.org/10.1007/978-3-030-58565-5_13
7. Chen, D.Z., Gholami, A., Nießner, M., Chang, A.X.: Scan2Cap: context-aware dense captioning in RGB-D scans. In: Proceedings of the IEEE/CVF Conference on Computer Vision and Pattern Recognition, pp. 3193–3203 (2021)
8. Chen, K., Choy, C.B., Savva, M., Chang, A.X., Funkhouser, T., Savarese, S.: Text2Shape: generating shapes from natural language by learning joint embeddings. In: Jawahar, C.V., Li, H., Mori, G., Schindler, K. (eds.) ACCV 2018. LNCS, vol. 11363, pp. 100–116. Springer, Cham (2019). https://doi.org/10.1007/978-3-030-20893-6_7

9. Choy, C., Gwak, J., Savarese, S.: 4D spatio-temporal ConvNets: Minkowski convolutional neural networks. In: Proceedings of the IEEE Conference on Computer Vision and Pattern Recognition, pp. 3075–3084 (2019)
10. Cole, P., Morgan, J.L.: Syntax and semantics. volume 3: Speech acts. Tijdschrift Voor Filosofie **39**(3), 550-551 (1977)
11. Dai, A., Chang, A.X., Savva, M., Halber, M., Funkhouser, T., Nießner, M.: ScanNet: richly-annotated 3D reconstructions of indoor scenes. In: Proceedings of the IEEE Conference on Computer Vision and Pattern Recognition, pp. 5828–5839 (2017)
12. Dai, A., Nießner, M.: 3DMV: joint 3D-multi-view prediction for 3D semantic scene segmentation. In: Ferrari, V., Hebert, M., Sminchisescu, C., Weiss, Y. (eds.) ECCV 2018. LNCS, vol. 11214, pp. 458–474. Springer, Cham (2018). https://doi.org/10.1007/978-3-030-01249-6_28
13. Devlin, J., Chang, M.W., Lee, K., Toutanova, K.: BERT: pre-training of deep bidirectional transformers for language understanding. arXiv preprint arXiv:1810.04805 (2018)
14. Donahue, J., et al.: Long-term recurrent convolutional networks for visual recognition and description. In: Proceedings of the IEEE Conference on Computer Vision and Pattern Recognition, pp. 2625–2634 (2015)
15. Fried, D., et al.: Speaker-follower models for vision-and-language navigation. In: Advances in Neural Information Processing Systems (2018)
16. Golland, D., Liang, P., Klein, D.: A game-theoretic approach to generating spatial descriptions. In: Proceedings of the 2010 Conference on Empirical Methods in Natural Language Processing, pp. 410–419 (2010)
17. Hendricks, L.A., Akata, Z., Rohrbach, M., Donahue, J., Schiele, B., Darrell, T.: Generating visual explanations. In: Leibe, B., Matas, J., Sebe, N., Welling, M. (eds.) ECCV 2016. LNCS, vol. 9908, pp. 3–19. Springer, Cham (2016). https://doi.org/10.1007/978-3-319-46493-0_1
18. Hou, J., Dai, A., Nießner, M.: 3D-SIS: 3D semantic instance segmentation of RGB-D scans. In: Proceedings of the IEEE/CVF Conference on Computer Vision and Pattern Recognition, pp. 4421–4430 (2019)
19. Hou, J., Dai, A., Nießner, M.: RevealNet: seeing behind objects in RGB-D scans. In: Proceedings of the IEEE/CVF Conference on Computer Vision and Pattern Recognition, pp. 2098–2107 (2020)
20. Hu, R., Rohrbach, M., Darrell, T.: Segmentation from natural language expressions. In: Leibe, B., Matas, J., Sebe, N., Welling, M. (eds.) ECCV 2016. LNCS, vol. 9905, pp. 108–124. Springer, Cham (2016). https://doi.org/10.1007/978-3-319-46448-0_7
21. Hu, R., Xu, H., Rohrbach, M., Feng, J., Saenko, K., Darrell, T.: Natural language object retrieval. In: Proceedings of the IEEE Conference on Computer Vision and Pattern Recognition, pp. 4555–4564 (2016)
22. Hua, B.S., Pham, Q.H., Nguyen, D.T., Tran, M.K., Yu, L.F., Yeung, S.K.: SceneNN: a scene meshes dataset with annotations. In: 2016 Fourth International Conference on 3D Vision (3DV), pp. 92–101, IEEE (2016)
23. Huang, P.H., Lee, H.H., Chen, H.T., Liu, T.L.: Text-guided graph neural networks for referring 3D instance segmentation. In: Proceedings of the AAAI Conference on Artificial Intelligence (2021)
24. Jang, E., Gu, S., Poole, B.: Categorical reparameterization with gumbel-softmax. arXiv preprint arXiv:1611.01144 (2016)

25. Jiang, L., Zhao, H., Shi, S., Liu, S., Fu, C.W., Jia, J.: PointGroup: dual-set point grouping for 3D instance segmentation. In: Proceedings of the IEEE/CVF Conference on Computer Vision and Pattern Recognition, pp. 4867–4876 (2020)

26. Jiang, W., Ma, L., Jiang, Y.-G., Liu, W., Zhang, T.: Recurrent fusion network for image captioning. In: Ferrari, V., Hebert, M., Sminchisescu, C., Weiss, Y. (eds.) ECCV 2018. LNCS, vol. 11206, pp. 510–526. Springer, Cham (2018). https://doi.org/10.1007/978-3-030-01216-8_31

27. Johnson, J., Karpathy, A., Fei-Fei, L.: Densecap: fully convolutional localization networks for dense captioning. In: Proceedings of the IEEE Conference on Computer Vision and Pattern Recognition, pp. 4565–4574 (2016)

28. Karpathy, A., Fei-Fei, L.: Deep visual-semantic alignments for generating image descriptions. In: Proceedings of the IEEE Conference on Computer Vision and Pattern Recognition, pp. 3128–3137 (2015)

29. Kazemzadeh, S., Ordonez, V., Matten, M., Berg, T.: Referitgame: referring to objects in photographs of natural scenes. In: Proceedings of the 2014 Conference on Empirical Methods in Natural Language Processing (EMNLP), pp. 787–798 (2014)

30. Kim, D.J., Choi, J., Oh, T.H., Kweon, I.S.: Dense relational captioning: triple-stream networks for relationship-based captioning. In: Proceedings of the IEEE/CVF Conference on Computer Vision and Pattern Recognition, pp. 6271–6280 (2019)

31. Kingma, D.P., Ba, J.: Adam: a method for stochastic optimization. arXiv preprint arXiv:1412.6980 (2014)

32. Lin, T.-Y., et al.: Microsoft COCO: common objects in context. In: Fleet, D., Pajdla, T., Schiele, B., Tuytelaars, T. (eds.) ECCV 2014. LNCS, vol. 8693, pp. 740–755. Springer, Cham (2014). https://doi.org/10.1007/978-3-319-10602-1_48

33. Liu, X., Li, H., Shao, J., Chen, D., Wang, X.: Show, tell and discriminate: image captioning by self-retrieval with partially labeled data. In: Ferrari, V., Hebert, M., Sminchisescu, C., Weiss, Y. (eds.) ECCV 2018. LNCS, vol. 11219, pp. 353–369. Springer, Cham (2018). https://doi.org/10.1007/978-3-030-01267-0_21

34. Liu, Y., et al.: Roberta: a robustly optimized BERT pretraining approach. arXiv preprint arXiv:1907.11692 (2019)

35. Lu, J., Xiong, C., Parikh, D., Socher, R.: Knowing when to look: adaptive attention via a visual sentinel for image captioning. In: Proceedings of the IEEE Conference on Computer Vision and Pattern Recognition, pp. 375–383 (2017)

36. Luo, R., Price, B., Cohen, S., Shakhnarovich, G.: Discriminability objective for training descriptive captions. In: Proceedings of the IEEE Conference on Computer Vision and Pattern Recognition, pp. 6964–6974 (2018)

37. Luo, R., Shakhnarovich, G.: Comprehension-guided referring expressions. In: Proceedings of the IEEE Conference on Computer Vision and Pattern Recognition, pp. 7102–7111 (2017)

38. Mao, J., Huang, J., Toshev, A., Camburu, O., Yuille, A.L., Murphy, K.: Generation and comprehension of unambiguous object descriptions. In: Proceedings of the IEEE Conference on Computer Vision and Pattern Recognition, pp. 11–20 (2016)

39. Paszke, A., et al.: Pytorch: an imperative style, high-performance deep learning library. In: Wallach, H., Larochelle, H., Beygelzimer, A., d' Alché-Buc, F., Fox, E., Garnett, R. (eds.) Advances in Neural Information Processing Systems 32, pp. 8024–8035, Curran Associates, Inc. (2019)

40. Plummer, B.A., Wang, L., Cervantes, C.M., Caicedo, J.C., Hockenmaier, J., Lazebnik, S.: Flickr30k entities: collecting region-to-phrase correspondences for richer

image-to-sentence models. In: Proceedings of the IEEE International Conference on Computer Vision, pp. 2641–2649 (2015)

41. Qi, C.R., Litany, O., He, K., Guibas, L.J.: Deep Hough voting for 3D object detection in point clouds. In: Proceedings of the IEEE/CVF International Conference on Computer Vision, pp. 9277–9286 (2019)

42. Ranzato, M., Chopra, S., Auli, M., Zaremba, W.: Sequence level training with recurrent neural networks. arXiv preprint arXiv:1511.06732 (2015)

43. Rennie, S.J., Marcheret, E., Mroueh, Y., Ross, J., Goel, V.: Self-critical sequence training for image captioning. In: Proceedings of the IEEE Conference on Computer Vision and Pattern Recognition, pp. 7008–7024 (2017)

44. Roh, J., Desingh, K., Farhadi, A., Fox, D.: LanguageRefer: spatial-language model for 3D visual grounding. In: Proceedings of the Conference on Robot Learning (2021)

45. Sidorov, O., Hu, R., Rohrbach, M., Singh, A.: TextCaps: a dataset for image captioning with reading comprehension. In: Vedaldi, A., Bischof, H., Brox, T., Frahm, J.-M. (eds.) ECCV 2020. LNCS, vol. 12347, pp. 742–758. Springer, Cham (2020). https://doi.org/10.1007/978-3-030-58536-5_44

46. Song, S., Lichtenberg, S.P., Xiao, J.: SUN RGB-D: A RGB-D scene understanding benchmark suite. In: Proceedings of the IEEE Conference on Computer Vision and Pattern Recognition, pp. 567–576 (2015)

47. Thomason, J., Shridhar, M., Bisk, Y., Paxton, C., Zettlemoyer, L.: Language grounding with 3D objects. In: Proceedings of the Conference on Robot Learning (2021)

48. Vaswani, A., et al.: Attention is all you need. In: Advances in neural information processing systems, pp. 5998–6008 (2017)

49. Vedantam, R., Lawrence Zitnick, C., Parikh, D.: Cider: consensus-based image description evaluation. In: Proceedings of the IEEE Conference on Computer Vision and Pattern Recognition, pp. 4566–4575 (2015)

50. Vinyals, O., Toshev, A., Bengio, S., Erhan, D.: Show and tell: a neural image caption generator. In: Proceedings of the IEEE Conference on Computer Vision and Pattern Recognition, pp. 3156–3164 (2015)

51. Williams, R.J.: Simple statistical gradient-following algorithms for connectionist reinforcement learning. Mach. Learn. 8(3), 229–256 (1992)

52. Wu, X., Averbuch-Elor, H., Sun, J., Snavely, N.: Towers of babel: combining images, language, and 3D geometry for learning multimodal vision. In: Proceedings of the IEEE/CVF International Conference on Computer Vision (2021)

53. Xu, K., et al.: Show, attend and tell: neural image caption generation with visual attention. In: International conference on machine learning, pp. 2048–2057 (2015)

54. Yang, L., Tang, K., Yang, J., Li, L.J.: Dense captioning with joint inference and visual context. In: Proceedings of the IEEE Conference on Computer Vision and Pattern Recognition, pp. 2193–2202 (2017)

55. Yang, Z., Dai, Z., Yang, Y., Carbonell, J., Salakhutdinov, R.R., Le, Q.V.: XLNet: generalized autoregressive pretraining for language understanding. In: Advances in Neural Information Processing Systems 32 (2019)

56. Yu, L., et al.: MattNet: modular attention network for referring expression comprehension. In: Proceedings of the IEEE Conference on Computer Vision and Pattern Recognition, pp. 1307–1315 (2018)

57. Yu, L., Tan, H., Bansal, M., Berg, T.L.: A joint speaker-listener-reinforcer model for referring expressions. In: Proceedings of the IEEE Conference on Computer Vision and Pattern Recognition, pp. 7282–7290 (2017)

58. Yuan, Z., et al.: X-Trans2Cap: cross-modal knowledge transfer using transformer for 3D dense captioning (2022). arXiv:2203.00843
59. Yuan, Z., et al.: InstanceRefer: cooperative holistic understanding for visual grounding on point clouds through instance multi-level contextual referring. In: Proceedings of the IEEE/CVF International Conference on Computer Vision, pp. 1791–1800 (2021)
60. Zhao, L., Cai, D., Sheng, L., Xu, D.: 3DVG-Transformer: relation modeling for visual grounding on point clouds. In: Proceedings of the IEEE/CVF International Conference on Computer Vision, pp. 2928–2937 (2021)

CIRCLE: Convolutional Implicit Reconstruction and Completion for Large-Scale Indoor Scene

Han-Xiang Chen[ID], Jiahui Huang[ID], Tai-Jiang Mu[✉][ID], and Shi-Min Hu[ID]

BNRist, Department of Computer Science and Technology,
Tsinghua University, Beijing 100084, China
{chx20,huang-jh18}@mails.tsinghua.edu.cn,
{taijiang,shimin}@tsinghua.edu.cn

Abstract. We present CIRCLE, a framework for large-scale scene completion and geometric refinement based on local implicit signed distance functions. It is based on an end-to-end sparse convolutional network, CircNet, which jointly models local geometric details and global scene structural contexts, allowing it to preserve fine-grained object detail while recovering missing regions commonly arising in traditional 3D scene data. A novel differentiable rendering module further enables a test-time refinement for better reconstruction quality. Extensive experiments on both real-world and synthetic datasets show that our concise framework is effective, achieving better reconstruction quality while being significantly faster.

Keywords: Scene reconstruction · Scene completion · Differentiable rendering

1 Introduction

In recent years, 3D reconstruction from RGB-D camera data has been widely explored thanks to its ease of acquisition with many applications in robotic perception, virtual reality, games, *etc.*. It is well-accepted that an ideal reconstruction algorithm should be capable of simultaneously (i) restoring fine-grained geometric details in the target scene (ii) handling with large scenes efficiently, and (iii) completing the missing regions. Additionally, the underlying 3D representation should be flexible enough to allow further optimization of geometric quality.

However, traditional algorithms along with their accompanying representations fail to effectively fulfill the above requirements. For instance, methods using the *truncated signed distance function* (TSDF) [10,34] are hampered by limited voxel resolution and lack robustness to noisy data. Surfels [52] offer more flexibility by treating the 3D scene as unstructured points, but maintaining

---

Supplementary Information The online version contains supplementary material available at https://doi.org/10.1007/978-3-031-19824-3_30.

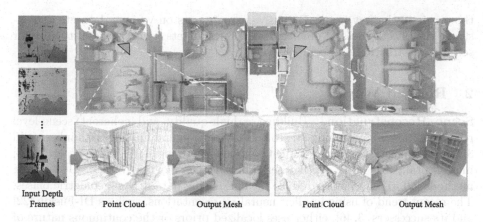

Input Depth Frames   Point Cloud   Output Mesh   Point Cloud   Output Mesh

Fig. 1. CIRCLE efficiently reconstructs and completes 3D scene from a given a sequence of posed depth images, commonly corrupted by noise and missing data: the inference time for this scene takes only 17 s, 10× faster than [39].

correct topology is challenging. Furthermore, these methods cannot fill in missing geometry in the scene, which is common in practice due to the sensor limitations, incomplete coverage of the scanning trajectory, or unreachable areas.

The recent introduction of deep implicit representations [7,32,38] has enabled a plethora of research directions for 2D and 3D data processing. Parameterized by a neural network, implicit functions are inherently continuous and differentiable. Notably, in the field of 3D reconstruction, various works [8,9,16,17,36,44] have already demonstrate their ability to learn *object-level* geometric priors from the shape repositories. However, when applied to large-scale scenes, the above methods are typically impractical. The reasons are three-fold. Firstly, the structure of a scene is substantially more complicated than that of a single object. A typical end-to-end, optimization-free, framework is weak at capturing the entangled geometric priors of cluttered regions. Secondly, though there exist other work [1,5,23,43,48] that overfits the scene geometry, to avoid the necessity of prior learning, it usually involves costly optimization procedures. Thirdly, some efforts [22,39,46,47] have been made to reconstruct scenes in real-time with deep implicit functions, but performed at a cost of low reconstruction quality.

To tackle these issues, we introduce the CIRCLE framework, as shown in Fig. 1. It employs a novel CircNet, short for fully-convolutional implicit network for reconstruction and completion of large-scale indoor 3D scenes from partial point clouds. It is capable of both preserving scene geometric details and completing missing regions of the scene in a semantically-meaningful way. Specifically, we adopt a local implicit grid to represent the local details of the whole scene, and learn the global contextual information for scene completion via a sparse U-Net. Our network is also efficient, in that it encodes and decodes the sparsity pattern of the scene geometry by learning, and only non-empty portions need to be evaluated. Furthermore, we provide a fast and novel differentiable rendering approach tailored for refining our output representation, which can greatly improve the geometric quality during inference to provide resilience to the errors in the raw input. Extensive experiments on various datasets demonstrate the effectiveness of our framework, which sets a new state-of-the-art for scene reconstruction and completion.

2 Related Work

Scene Reconstruction. Building a high-quality and coherent scene-level reconstruction is challenging due to noise, occlusion and missing data inherent in 3D data acquisition sensors. While traditional methods [4,13,30,34,37,41,52,53] incrementally fuse input depth observations using a moving average [10], learning methods [50,51] can further reduce the noise using data-driven geometric biases. The recent trend of using implicit neural representations, such as DI-Fusion [22] and its successors [3,46], either uses localized priors or the continuous nature of a globally-supported network function. In comparison, our method can not only accurately recover detailed scene geometry, but also rebuild missing parts via a global structural reasoning based on learning. We refer readers to [26] for a more comprehensive understanding on scene reconstruction.

Scene Completion. The main challenge in scene completion is to fill missing regions with data that are semantically coherent with the existing content. [45] casts the problem in terms of panoramic image completion but important geometric details are significantly missing. [14] first brings the aid of semantic segmentation to the completion problem in the 3D domain. Subsequent lines of work [12,15] tackle the problems of geometric sparsity and color generation. We note that many end-to-end frameworks [1,39] using implicit representations also provide decent scene extrapolation due to the continuous nature of networks, even though they are not specifically designed for this task.

Differentiable Rendering. The technique of differentiating the rendering process bridges the gap between 3D geometry and 2D observations of it by allowing for end-to-end optimization directly from the captured raw sensor data, which was first applied to triangular meshes [25,29] and later to implicit fields [24,28,35]. The prevalence of NeRF [33] motivates many studies to improve rendering efficiency and fitting speed, either through localized structures [27], level-of-detail rendering [48], caching [55], or multi-view stereo [42,54]. In conjunction with our novel local implicit representation, we devise a new differentiable rendering approach which can rapidly and effectively refine the geometric details of the reconstructed scene during inference.

3 CIRCLE: Convolutional Implicit Scene Reconstruction and Completion

Problem Formulation. The input to our method is a sequence of posed depth frames $\{\mathcal{D}_t, \mathbf{T}_t\}_{t=1}^T$, with $\mathcal{D}_t \in \mathbb{R}^{W \times H}$ and $\mathbf{T}_t \in \mathbb{SE}(3)$ being the depth image and the 6-DoF camera pose, respectively. Our goal is to build a high-quality and complete 3D reconstruction of the scene, represented using M a local sparse

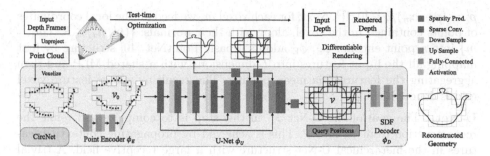

Fig. 2. Pipeline. We first voxelize the accumulated unprojected points from the input posed depth frames into a sparse grid. The feature volume is then fed to CircNet, which comprises 3 neural networks: ϕ_E, ϕ_U, and ϕ_D, and outputs an implicit completed surface. Inference-time refinement is enabled by our differentiable rendering, aiming at better and more complete reconstruction.

implicit voxel grid $\mathcal{V} = \{(\boldsymbol{c}_m, \boldsymbol{l}_m)\}_{m=1}^{M}$ that contain the surface of the scene geometry. Here, $\boldsymbol{c}_m \in \mathbb{R}^3$ is the voxel coordinate and $\boldsymbol{l}_m \in \mathbb{R}^L$ is the latent vector describing the local voxel grid's geometry, from which we can decode the signed distance values of the full scene and finally extract the mesh. The size of each voxel is $b \times b \times b$.

Overview. As Fig. 2 shows, we first unproject all the depths $\mathcal{D}_t$ under the given poses $\mathbf{T}_t$ to obtain an accumulated point cloud $\mathcal{P} = \{(\boldsymbol{p}_i, \boldsymbol{n}_i)\}_{i=1}^{N}$, where $\boldsymbol{p}_i \in \mathbb{R}^3$ and $\boldsymbol{n}_i \in \mathbb{R}^3$ are the point position and its estimated normal, using [34]. $\mathcal{P}$ is then voxelized into initial sparse 3D grid and processed by CircNet (see Sect. 3.1). Being aware of both global scene structure and local geometric details, CircNet simultaneously refines the voxelized points and adds additional points using a point encoder ϕ_E and a U-Net ϕ_U, and produces $\mathcal{V}$ defining the latent vector of local implicit geometry, which is then decoded to TSDF values by a multi-layer perceptron (MLP) ϕ_D. One can later extract the mesh using marching cubes [31] from these TSDF values. Moreover, the reconstructed geometry can be further optimized during inference-time via a novel differentiable rendering scheme described in Sect. 3.2, to refine both the scene geometry and the camera pose. Detailed loss functions for the training procedure and the inference-time refinement are discussed in Sect. 3.3.

3.1   CircNet Architecture

Given the unprojected point cloud $\mathcal{P}$ from the input views, CircNet sequentially applies three trainable components: a point encoder network ϕ_E, a U-Net ϕ_U, and an SDF decoder ϕ_D to produce an implicit representation of the underlying scene. We now describe these components in turn.

Point Encoder. We first split the input point cloud into voxels. For a point $\boldsymbol{p}_i$, the index of its belonging voxel m_i is determined by the m satisfying $\boldsymbol{p}_i \in [\boldsymbol{c}_m, \boldsymbol{c}_m + b)$. We define the local coordinate of $\boldsymbol{p}_i$ within its belonging voxel as

$p_i^l = (p_i - c_m)/b \in [0,1]^3$. Next, for each voxel m, we feed all the local coordinates of points contained in the voxel, along with their normals: $\{(p_i^l, n_i) \in \mathbb{R}^6 \mid m_i = m\}$ into a point encoder ϕ_E. ϕ_E adopts a basic PointNet [40] structure by first mapping all the input features into L-dimensions with a shared MLP and then aggregating the features via mean pooling. The resulting sparse feature voxel grid is denoted by $\mathcal{V}_0$.

U-Net. The goal of the U-Net ϕ_U in this step is to complete and refine the reconstruction from $\mathcal{V}_0$ into $\mathcal{V}$. This is achieved by propagating contextual features in the hierarchical U-Net structure with a large receptive field. A trivial implementation falls back to a dense convolution that generates a dense feature grid even if many voxels are actually empty. Due to the sparse nature of the geometry, we instead use submanifold sparse convolution [18] for our convolution layer. For the decoder branch, inspired by [49], we append a *sparsity prediction* module to each layer of the decoder. This module is instantiated with a shared MLP applied to each voxel and predicts the confidence of the current voxel containing the true surfaces; voxels with scores lower than 0.5 are pruned. Accordingly, usual skip connections are replaced by sparsity-guided skip connections: connections are only added for voxels predicted to be non-empty. Apart from the efficiency gain, this design also eases network training by obviating the need to model the full geometry of empty regions.

SDF Decoder. To recover the final scene geometry, we traverse all points p in the non-empty regions of $\mathcal{V}$ and learn the signed distance values using an implicit decoder instantiated with an MLP $\phi_D : (p^l, \hat{l}) \in \mathbb{R}^{3+L} \mapsto [-1, 1]$, where p^l is the local coordinate of p and $\hat{l}$ is the interpolated feature taken from $\mathcal{V}$. To smooth the geometric interpolation across voxel boundaries, we apply an additional $2 \times 2 \times 2$ convolution over $\mathcal{V}$ to propagate the features stored at voxel *centers* to voxel *corners*, obtaining $\{l_m'\}$. The input feature $\hat{l}$ can then be trilinearly interpolated $\psi(\cdot)$ from the features stored at its 8 nearest voxel corners: $\hat{l} = \psi(p^l, \{l_{(1)}', \ldots, l_{(8)}'\})$.

3.2 Differentiable Local Implicit Rendering

Despite the good-quality, end-to-end reconstruction provided by CircNet, some desired geometric details can be lost. The reasons are two-fold. Firstly, the real-world depth acquisition usually suffers from noisy pose and sensor limitations, resulting in erroneous reconstruction and severe missing regions. Secondly, a simple feed-forward network trained on large-scale datasets can underfit geometric features or generate excessive contents [32,38]. Being aware of these issues, we propose a novel differentiable renderer for our implicit representation, allowing for effective differentiation through both geometry and camera pose. Specifically, for each pixel to be rendered, we emit a ray with an origin o and a unit direction d, and compute the depth of the intersection z so that the intersection point is $p = o + zd$. The forward and backward passes are defined as follows:

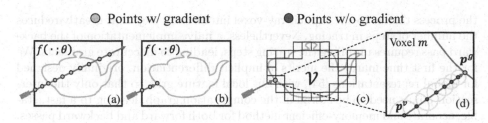

Fig. 3. Rendering strategies. Rendering a globally-supported implicit representation with (a) uniform query points [33] and (b) differentiable sphere tracing [28]. (c, d) Our approach with both sphere tracing and implicit differentiation, only computes gradients for on-surface points, thus being highly efficient.

Forward Pass. The forward pass is composed of two steps as shown in Fig. 3 (c–d):

1. **Voxel-level Intersection.** As the sparsity prediction modules from the different layers of our U-Net decoder naturally form an *octree* structure thanks to the upsampling operator, we can use any existing ray-octree intersection algorithm for this step. In our implementation, we choose the fast algorithm in [48] that generates a list of intersection pairs $\{(z^v, m^v)\}$, where z^v is the depth and m^v is the voxel index of the intersection.
2. **Geometry-level Intersection.** The sphere tracing algorithm [20] is applied for each intersecting voxel m^v, starting from $o + z^v d$ and ending at $p^g = o + z^g d$ that hits the surface. Note that only the smallest z^g among all the voxels is returned as the final depth z due to occlusion.

Backward Pass. For clarity, we abstract our full CircNet as an implicit network $f(p; \theta)$ whose inputs are the position p and the intermediate features or network parameters θ, and the output is the signed distance value. We wish to compute the first-order derivative of the depth z w.r.t. θ as well as the camera ray o and d for optimization. Inspired by [54], we employ the fact that $f(o + zd; \theta) \equiv 0$ and use implicit differentiation to obtain:

$$\frac{\partial z}{\partial \theta} = -\gamma \frac{\partial f}{\partial \theta}, \quad \frac{\partial z}{\partial o} = -\gamma \frac{\partial f}{\partial p}, \quad \frac{\partial z}{\partial d} = -\gamma z \frac{\partial f}{\partial p}, \tag{1}$$

where $\gamma = \langle d, \partial f / \partial p \rangle^{-1}$ is a scalar, $\langle \cdot, \cdot \rangle$ denotes the vector inner product, and other derivatives related to f can be efficiently evaluated using reverse-mode back-propagation. Empirically, we observe that full gradient-based optimization over all network parameters fails to converge. Hence we choose to only optimize the latent vectors in $\mathcal{V}$: $\theta = \{l_m\}$, and fix all other parts of the networks.

Discussion. A comparison between our method and previous approaches is shown in Fig. 3. Methods similar to, *e.g.*, NeRF [33] exhaustively query all points along the ray; most of the unnecessary computations far away from the surface can be saved with sphere tracing [20, 28]. Our use of *localized* grid further speed up the process thanks to the explicit ray-voxel intersection step that greatly reduces the number of steps in tracing. Nevertheless, a naive implementation of the backward pass requires unrolling the tracing steps, leading to inaccurate gradients. We for the first time marry the merits of implicit differentiation, originally designed for global representations [54], with our local feature grid, so that only the intersection points need to be stored in the computation graph, leading to a fast, stable, accurate and memory-efficient method for both forward and backward passes. Experiments verifying our design choices are shown in Sect. 4.3.

3.3 Loss Functions

CircNet Loss Function. The three networks ϕ_E, ϕ_U and ϕ_D are jointly trained in an end-to-end manner, using the following loss function:

$$\mathcal{L} = \mathcal{L}_{\text{sdf}} + \alpha \mathcal{L}_{\text{norm}} + \beta \mathcal{L}_{\text{struct}} + \delta \sum_{m=1}^{M} \|l_m\|, \tag{2}$$

where $\|\cdot\|$ is the vector norm. $\mathcal{L}_{\text{sdf}}$ is the data term defined as the L1 distance between the predicted signed distance from the decoder $\phi_D(p^l, \hat{l})$ and the ground-truth values $s^{\text{gt}}(p)$:

$$\mathcal{L}_{\text{sdf}} = \int_{\Omega_u \cup \Omega_n} |\phi_D(p^l, \hat{l}) - s^{\text{gt}}(p)| \, dp. \tag{3}$$

Here Ω_u denotes the occupied region of the voxels $\mathcal{V}$ while Ω_n is a narrow band region near the surface. The normal of the predicted geometry, computed as $\nabla_p \phi_D$, is constrained by the normal loss:

$$\mathcal{L}_{\text{norm}} = \int_{\Omega_u \cup \Omega_n} |\|\nabla_p \phi_D\| - 1| \, dp + \int_{\Omega_n} (1 - \langle \nabla_p \phi_D, n^{\text{gt}}(p) \rangle) \, dp, \tag{4}$$

where the first term enforces the eikonal equation of the signed distance field while the second term minimizes the angle between predicted normal and ground-truth normal n^{gt}.

$\mathcal{L}_{\text{struct}}$ uses cross-entropy loss to supervise the sparsity prediction module for each layer in the decoder branch of ϕ_U. Specifically, we obtain the ground-truth sparsity pattern of the target geometry at multiple resolutions in accordance with the output sparsity map from the U-Net, and directly supervise the predicted confidence score. During training, we use the ground-truth sparsity map instead of the predicted one for the skip-connections and pruning of the next layer.

Inference-Time Refinement. During inference, our differentiable rendering module is applied to refine the predicted geometry and the camera poses. For each depth image $\mathcal{D}_t$ and its pose $\mathbf{T}_t$, we can render a depth image as $\mathcal{D}'_t(\mathbf{T}_t, \theta) \in \mathbb{R}^{W \times H}$, whose values are the depths $\{z\}$ from Sect. 3.2. By minimizing the error between the rendered depth and the observed depth, we can jointly optimize the quality of geometry and input poses:

$$\min_{\theta, \{\delta \mathbf{T}_t\}} \sum_{t=1}^{T} |\mathcal{D}_t - \mathcal{D}'_t(\delta \mathbf{T}_t \mathbf{T}_t, \theta))|, \tag{5}$$

where we optimize an increment to pose $\delta \mathbf{T}_t$ instead of $\mathbf{T}_t$ itself, for better convergence.

4   Experiments

4.1   Datasets and Settings

Datasets.   The main dataset used to evaluate our framework is N-Matterport3D. Adapted from [6], this dataset contains 1,788 and 394 scans of rooms from 90 buildings for training/validation and testing, respectively, captured by a Matterport Pro Camera. We follow the self-supervised setting from [12] by randomly sampling 50% of the frames to generate an incomplete version of each room and supervise our method with a complete version reconstructed from all frames. To test the robustness of our model, we follow [50] and add synthetic noise to each individual depth frame (denoted by the prefix 'N-'), because raw MatterPort3D dataset have little noise. We additionally used the well-known ICL-NUIM [19] public benchmark containing 4 scan trajectories for testing only, to demonstrate the generalizability of our method. We also show qualitative results on ScanNetv2 [11] dataset to demonstrate how our network works under real-world noise. Due to the incomplete ground-truth meshes and inaccurate poses in ScanNetv2, it is not ideal for training. We hence directly apply our model trained on N-Matterport3D to this dataset.

Parameter Settings.   Our CircNet was trained and tested on a single Nvidia GeForce RTX 2080Ti GPU. The weights of the loss terms are empirically set to $\alpha = 0.1$, $\beta = 1$ and $\delta = 0.001$. We used the Adam optimizer with a learning rate of 0.001. For efficient training, we uniformly split the input point cloud $\mathcal{P}$ into patches of size $3.2\,\mathrm{m} \times 3.2\,\mathrm{m} \times 3.2\,\mathrm{m}$, although as a fully convolutional architecture, our pipeline could easily scale to the full scene during inference. ϕ_E, ϕ_U and ϕ_D have 4, 5, and 3 layers respectively. With the scale of indoor scenes, the voxel size b is set to 0.05m and the width of Ω_n is set to 2.5 mm. Further details of our network structure are given in the supplementary material.

Baseline.   Our method is compared to a full spectrum of methods, including those providing reconstruction from sequential depth frames, *i.e.*, RoutedFusion [50] (denoted as "R-Fusion") and DI-Fusion [22] using representations of either local implicit grid or a neural signed-distance volume. We further consider methods operating on fully-fused geometry, *i.e.*, the convolutional occupancy network [39] (denoted as "ConvON") is the state-of-art local implicit network for surface reconstruction considering global information, while SPSG [15] is the up-to-date scene completion approach that takes TSDF volumes as input. For methods that are cannot be trained on large-scale scenes, we used pre-trained weights obtained from synthetic datasets.

Metrics.   We use root mean square error (RMSE), chamfer distance (CD), surface precision, recall, and F-score during evaluation. RMSE, CD, and surface precision mainly measure the accuracy of the reconstruction, surface recall

Table 1. Quantitative results using the N-Matterport3D dataset.

	RMSE ↓ (×10⁻³)	CD ↓ (×10⁻³)	F-Score ↑ (%)	Precision ↑ (%)	Recall ↑ (%)
SPSG [15]	27.1	1.05	80.12	76.03	85.21
ConvON [39]	31.4	1.85	62.34	52.32	78.45
R-Fusion [50]	24.6	0.98	65.64	64.10	67.54
DI-Fusion [22]	20.9	1.14	82.36	82.31	82.68
Ours (w/o optim.)	16.5	0.47	89.11	88.93	89.11
Ours	**16.2**	**0.47**	**89.23**	**89.20**	**89.24**

↓ / ↑: Lower/higher is better. **Bold** numbers indicate the best and underlined numbers indicate the second best.

mainly assesses the degree of completeness, and F-score reflects both accuracy and completeness. All reconstruction results from different methods are converted to point clouds for fair comparisons. RMSE and CD are measured in meters, and for precision and recall, a predicted or ground truth point is accepted if its distance to the closest ground truth or predicted point is smaller than 0.02 m.

4.2   Comparisons to Other Methods

Table 1 shows that our proposed method performs the best in terms of all metrics, for the N-Matterport3D dataset. Qualitative results are presented in Fig. 4. The dense structure of ConvON makes it difficult to simultaneously capture the local and global information from real-world datasets. R-Fusion and DI-Fusion only learn local geometric priors from the synthetic datasets. Specifically, although DI-Fusion fits local details with local implicit functions and achieves competitive performance, its lack of global information prevents it from completing missing regions. SPSG shows a capability for scene completion; however, limited by the discrete TSDF representation, the precision of the reconstructed surface is unsatisfactory. Our method learns global contextual information from local implicit grid by the convolutional neural network ϕ_U, and thus can faithfully reconstruct local geometric details as well as recovering many missing regions. As highlighted with the red boxes in Fig. 4, our network effectively fills in the holes in the planar regions (*e.g.*, walls, floors, and ceilings). Some of the objects such as beds, tables, pillows, *etc..*, can also be completed in a semantically meaningful way.

We further evaluate the generalizability of all approaches using the ICL-NUIM dataset; quantitative results are given in Table 2. Remarkably, although our method is trained using panoramic scans as in [6], thanks to our effective learning scheme in 3D space, it generalizes well to hand-held trajectories whose geometric distributions are drastically different.

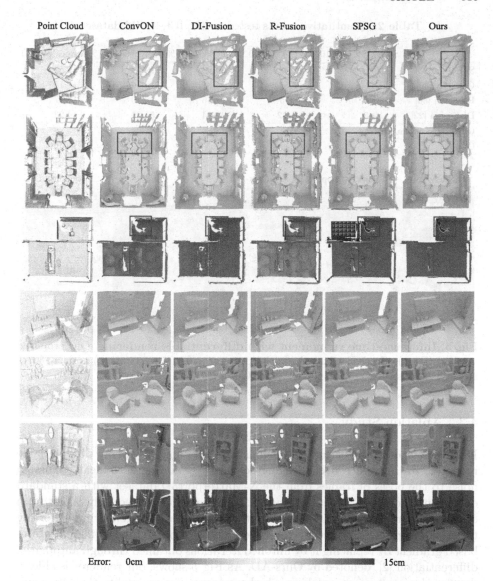

Point Cloud   ConvON   DI-Fusion   R-Fusion   SPSG   Ours

Error: 0cm ▬▬▬▬▬▬▬▬▬▬▬▬▬▬▬▬▬▬▬▬ 15cm

Fig. 4. Visual comparison using N-Matterport3D. Results show both global views (part 1, top three rows) and close-up views (part 2, bottom four rows). The last row in each part shows each method's per-point error, the distance between each reconstructed vertex and the corresponding closest ground truth point.

Table 2. Quantitative results tested on the ICL-NUIM dataset.

	RMSE ↓ ($\times 10^{-3}$)	CD ↓ ($\times 10^{-3}$)	F-Score ↑ (%)	Precision ↑ (%)	Recall ↑ (%)
SPSG [15]	36.6	2.07	20.29	29.70	15.62
ConvON [39]	42.3	3.55	13.81	18.46	11.15
R-Fusion [50]	40.9	2.75	14.56	22.20	11.07
DI-Fusion [22]	**19.5**	**1.32**	22.14	<u>51.21</u>	14.23
Ours (w/o optim.)	22.7	1.54	<u>23.89</u>	51.02	<u>15.78</u>
Ours	<u>22.1</u>	<u>1.46</u>	25.54	50.55	16.99

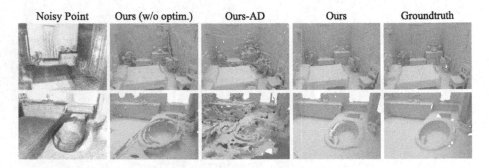

Fig. 5. Inference-time refinement with differentiable rendering. Our proposed method (Ours) effectively fixes the initial pose error (Ours w/o optim.) and produces a better reconstruction than the baseline (Ours-AD).

4.3   Ablation Study

Differentiable Rendering. To demonstrate the capability of our differentiable renderer, we introduce a challenging scenario by adding zero-mean Gaussian noise to the poses of frames from the N-Matterport3D dataset with a standard deviation of 3cm and 2° for the translation and rotation, respectively. Apart from direct comparisons with the version without differentiable rendering (referring to as "w/o optim."), we verify the effectiveness of our implicit-differentiation-based gradient by replacing it by unrolled iterations obtained through automatic-differentiation [2], denoted by Ours-AD. As Fig. 5 shows, our renderer is able to denoise the input poses, reaching a higher reconstruction quality than its counterparts, the refinements of which are non-trivial due to the discrete TSDF representation used. Moreover, compared to Ours-AD, our full gradient optimization is also more effective, thanks to the accuracy and stability provided by the closed-form derivative computation. Our method also saves a considerable amount of optimization time and memory by avoiding propagating gradients through all points along the ray. A detailed time and memory analysis of our differentiable rendering is given in the supplementary material.

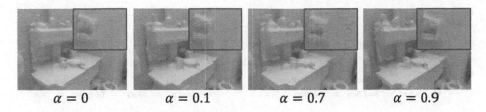

$$\alpha = 0 \qquad \alpha = 0.1 \qquad \alpha = 0.7 \qquad \alpha = 0.9$$

Fig. 6. Effect of normal loss. Reconstructions obtained by training with varying weights for $\mathcal{L}_{norm}$, *i.e.*, α. Red boxes highlight the differences. (Color figure online)

TSDF-Fusion   Ours(w/o optim.)   Ours

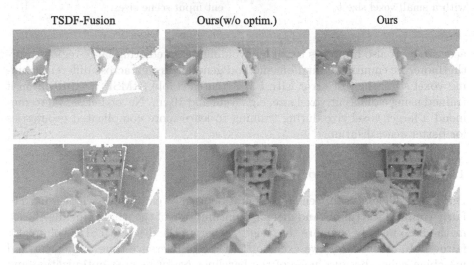

Fig. 7. Qualitative results using the ScanNetv2 dataset. Our method generalizes well in presence of real-world noise and occlusions.

Weight of $\mathcal{L}_{norm}$. After fixing the gauge freedom of the weights for $\mathcal{L}_{sdf}$ and $\mathcal{L}_{struct}$ to 1, we show the effect of changing $\mathcal{L}_{norm}$ in Fig. 6 by varying its weight $\alpha \in [0, 1]$. The addition of normal loss can effectively improve the precision of the reconstruction. However it only works when α is small, showing the importance of carefully choosing the weight parameter, especially in our setting with a small localized voxel size.

Depth Noise. We demonstrate results on the ScanNetv2 dataset in Fig. 7. Although our method is trained using synthetic depth noise, it generalizes well to real-world noise. Compared to the traditional TSDF fusion approach, our differentiable renderer fixes inaccurate poses and significantly sharpens the geometric features. The effect of synthetic noise level on reconstruction results is given in the supplementary material.

Voxel Size. Figure 8 shows how the reconstruction quality varies when trained and tested with the same voxel size b (using 5 cm, 7.5 cm and 10 cm). A smaller voxel size captures more details from the input and models the surface more

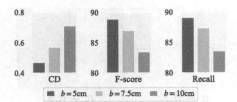

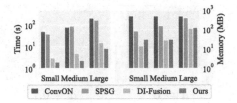

Fig. 8. Performance for varying voxel sizes. Our method works best with a small voxel size b.

Fig. 9 Run time and memory. Results for different methods and different input scene sizes.

accurately. It also improves recall by avoiding mis-predicting large regions. Furthermore, we empirically find our method generalizes well across different training voxel sizes: the test error with $b = 7.5$ cm is stable (RMSE ≈ 0.019) even if trained using a different voxel size, e.g., 5 cm and 10 cm. Nevertheless, we recommend a larger voxel size during training to learn more complicated geometries for better generalization.

4.4   Timing and Memory

Due to the differences in scene representation used by each approach, it is hard to fairly compare the timing and memory consumption of the whole pipeline of each method. So we only compare the time to generate the discrete TSDF volume for fairness. In other words, we exclude the time of inference-time refinement and marching cubes, because none of the baselines performs post-optimization and the implementation of marching cubes varies a lot from each other. Because the time comparison between online methods and offline methods is meaningless, we extend DI-Fusion to an offline version and do not consider R-Fusion in following experiment. Figure 9 compares the inference time and memory footprint of the baselines for different scene sizes. Thanks to the sparse feature volume, our method runs 10–50× faster than ConvON and SPSG, and is comparable in speed to DI-Fusion. However, as the scene gets larger, the time taken by DI-Fusion increases more rapidly than our method due to the difference in voxel interpolation strategy. As for memory cost, ConvON stays constant due to its sliding window inference scheme. SPSG maintains a dense discrete TSDF volume, so memory requirements grow drastically with scene size. Our method is memory-efficient due to its sparse representation and uses only marginally more memory than DI-Fusion while providing better reconstruction accuracy.

As for the time of inference-time refinement, our differentiable renderer could reach an average speed of 1M rays/s (the speed is illustrated in our supplementary material). In our experiments, we render 512×640 pixels for each room. Each room has an average of 44 frames, and we optimize for 20 epochs. In total, it takes ~440 s to optimize one room using PyTorch. This optimizing process can be further speeded up using Jittor [21], a new deep learning framework which is efficient for training neural networks, and we will also release code using Jittor.

4.5 Limitations and Discussion

Our approach has three main limitations. Firstly, our network makes no use of object-level priors, resulting in partially reconstructed objects even after completion. Training with semantic supervision may improve completion performance. Secondly, reconstruction quality relies on a small voxel size that limits further improvements in efficiency. This can be overcome with local implicit grid [23], which can learn local geometric priors from CAD models using large voxels with further optimization for real-world scenes. Thirdly, textures are not recovered by our method. Inspired by NeRF [33], training a neural radiance field together with SDF using differentiable rendering can incorporate texture information into our pipeline.

5 Conclusions

This paper has introduced CIRCLE, a framework for large-scale scene reconstruction and completion using local implicit signed distance functions. The key part of our method is a convolutional neural network that can learn global contextual information from local implicit grid, contributing to the completion of missing regions. Together with our novel differentiable rendering strategy, we are able to generate an accurate and detailed reconstruction, while being fast and memory-efficient. In the future, we hope to bridge the gap between large-scale geometric reconstruction and the use of object shape priors, as well as to incorporate color information into our pipeline, for better completion and reconstruction.

Acknowledgments. We would like to thank all the anonymous reviewers for their valuable suggestions. This work is supported by the National Key R&D Program of China (Grant No.: 2021ZD0112902) and the National Science Foundation of China (Grant No.: 61902210).

References

1. Azinović, D., Martin-Brualla, R., Goldman, D.B., Nießner, M., Thies, J.: Neural RGB-D surface reconstruction. In: IEEE CVPR, pp. 6290–6301 (2022)
2. Baydin, A.G., Pearlmutter, B.A., Radul, A.A., Siskind, J.M.: Automatic differentiation in machine learning: a survey. J. Mach. Learn. Res. (JMLR) **18**, 153:1–153:43 (2017)
3. Bozic, A., Palafox, P.R., Thies, J., Dai, A., Nießner, M.: Transformerfusion: monocular RGB scene reconstruction using transformers. In: NeurIPS, pp. 1403–1414 (2021)
4. Cao, Y.P., Kobbelt, L., Hu, S.M.: Real-time high-accuracy three-dimensional reconstruction with consumer RGB-D cameras. ACM Trans. Graph. (TOG) **37**(5), 171:1–171:16 (2018)
5. Chabra, R., et al.: Deep local shapes: learning local SDF priors for detailed 3D reconstruction. In: Vedaldi, A., Bischof, H., Brox, T., Frahm, J.-M. (eds.) ECCV 2020. LNCS, vol. 12374, pp. 608–625. Springer, Cham (2020). https://doi.org/10.1007/978-3-030-58526-6_36

6. Chang, A.X., et al.: Matterport3D: learning from RGB-D data in indoor environments. In: International Conference on 3D Vision (3DV), pp. 667–676 (2017)
7. Chen, Y., Liu, S., Wang, X.: Learning continuous image representation with local implicit image function. In: IEEE CVPR, pp. 8628–8638 (2021)
8. Chen, Z., Tagliasacchi, A., Zhang, H.: BSP-net: generating compact meshes via binary space partitioning. In: IEEE CVPR, pp. 42–51 (2020)
9. Chibane, J., Alldieck, T., Pons-Moll, G.: Implicit functions in feature space for 3D shape reconstruction and completion. In: IEEE CVPR, pp. 6968–6979 (2020)
10. Curless, B., Levoy, M.: A volumetric method for building complex models from range images. In: ACM SIGGRAPH, pp. 303–312 (1996)
11. Dai, A., Chang, A.X., Savva, M., Halber, M., Funkhouser, T.A., Nießner, M.: ScanNet: richly-annotated 3D reconstructions of indoor scenes. In: IEEE CVPR, pp. 2432–2443 (2017)
12. Dai, A., Diller, C., Nießner, M.: SG-NN: sparse generative neural networks for self-supervised scene completion of RGB-D scans. In: IEEE CVPR, pp. 846–855 (2020)
13. Dai, A., Nießner, M., Zollhöfer, M., Izadi, S., Theobalt, C.: Bundlefusion: real-time globally consistent 3D reconstruction using on-the-fly surface reintegration. ACM Trans. Graph. (TOG) 36(3), 24:1–24:18 (2017)
14. Dai, A., Ritchie, D., Bokeloh, M., Reed, S., Sturm, J., Nießner, M.: ScanComplete: large-scale scene completion and semantic segmentation for 3D scans. In: IEEE CVPR, pp. 4578–4587 (2018)
15. Dai, A., Siddiqui, Y., Thies, J., Valentin, J., Nießner, M.: SPSG: self-supervised photometric scene generation from RGB-D scans. In: IEEE CVPR, pp. 1747–1756 (2021)
16. Genova, K., Cole, F., Sud, A., Sarna, A., Funkhouser, T.A.: Local deep implicit functions for 3D shape. In: IEEE CVPR, pp. 4856–4865 (2020)
17. Genova, K., Cole, F., Vlasic, D., Sarna, A., Freeman, W.T., Funkhouser, T.A.: Learning shape templates with structured implicit functions. In: IEEE ICCV, pp. 7153–7163 (2019)
18. Graham, B., Engelcke, M., van der Maaten, L.: 3D semantic segmentation with submanifold sparse convolutional networks. In: IEEE CVPR, pp. 9224–9232 (2018)
19. Handa, A., Whelan, T., McDonald, J., Davison, A.J.: A benchmark for RGB-D visual odometry, 3D reconstruction and SLAM. In: IEEE International Conference on Robotics and Automation (ICRA), pp. 1524–1531 (2014)
20. Hart, J.C.: Sphere tracing: a geometric method for the antialiased ray tracing of implicit surfaces. Vis. Comput. 12(10), 527–545 (1996)
21. Hu, S.M., Liang, D., Yang, G.Y., Yang, G.W., Zhou, W.Y.: Jittor: a novel deep learning framework with meta-operators and unified graph execution. Sci. China Inf. Sci. 63(12), 222103 (2020)
22. Huang, J., Huang, S.S., Song, H., Hu, S.M.: Di-fusion: online implicit 3D reconstruction with deep priors. In: IEEE CVPR, pp. 8932–8941 (2021)
23. Jiang, C.M., Sud, A., Makadia, A., Huang, J., Nießner, M., Funkhouser, T.A.: Local implicit grid representations for 3D scenes. In: IEEE CVPR, pp. 6000–6009 (2020)
24. Jiang, Y., Ji, D., Han, Z., Zwicker, M.: SDFdiff: differentiable rendering of signed distance fields for 3D shape optimization. In: IEEE CVPR, pp. 1248–1258 (2020)
25. Kato, H., Ushiku, Y., Harada, T.: Neural 3D mesh renderer. In: IEEE CVPR, pp. 3907–3916 (2018)

26. Li, J., Gao, W., Wu, Y., Liu, Y., Shen, Y.: High-quality indoor scene 3D reconstruction with RGB-D cameras: a brief review. Comput. Vis. Media **8**(3), 369–393 (2022)
27. Liu, L., Gu, J., Lin, K.Z., Chua, T.S., Theobalt, C.: Neural sparse voxel fields. In: NeurIPS, pp. 15651–15663 (2020)
28. Liu, S., Zhang, Y., Peng, S., Shi, B., Pollefeys, M., Cui, Z.: DIST: rendering deep implicit signed distance function with differentiable sphere tracing. In: IEEE CVPR, pp. 2016–2025 (2020)
29. Liu, S., Chen, W., Li, T., Li, H.: Soft rasterizer: a differentiable renderer for image-based 3D reasoning. In: IEEE ICCV, pp. 7707–7716 (2019)
30. Liu, Z.N., Cao, Y.P., Kuang, Z.F., Kobbelt, L., Hu, S.M.: High-quality textured 3d shape reconstruction with cascaded fully convolutional networks. IEEE Trans. Visual. Comput. Graph. (TVCG) **27**(1), 83–97 (2021)
31. Lorensen, W.E., Cline, H.E.: Marching cubes: a high resolution 3D surface construction algorithm. In: ACM SIGGRAPH, pp. 163–169 (1987)
32. Mescheder, L.M., Oechsle, M., Niemeyer, M., Nowozin, S., Geiger, A.: Occupancy networks: learning 3D reconstruction in function space. In: IEEE CVPR, pp. 4460–4470 (2019)
33. Mildenhall, B., Srinivasan, P.P., Tancik, M., Barron, J.T., Ramamoorthi, R., Ng, R.: NERF: representing scenes as neural radiance fields for view synthesis. Commun. ACM **65**(1), 99–106 (2021)
34. Newcombe, R.A., et al.: KinectFusion: real-time dense surface mapping and tracking. In: IEEE International Symposium on Mixed and Augmented Reality (ISMAR), pp. 127–136 (2011)
35. Niemeyer, M., Mescheder, L.M., Oechsle, M., Geiger, A.: Differentiable volumetric rendering: learning implicit 3D representations without 3D supervision. In: IEEE CVPR, pp. 3501–3512 (2020)
36. Oechsle, M., Mescheder, L.M., Niemeyer, M., Strauss, T., Geiger, A.: Texture fields: learning texture representations in function space. In: IEEE ICCV, pp. 4530–4539 (2019)
37. Oleynikova, H., Taylor, Z., Fehr, M., Siegwart, R., Nieto, J.I.: Voxblox: incremental 3D Euclidean signed distance fields for on-board MAV planning. In: IEEE International Conference on Intelligent Robots and Systems (IROS), pp. 1366–1373 (2017)
38. Park, J.J., Florence, P., Straub, J., Newcombe, R.A., Lovegrove, S.: DeepSDF: learning continuous signed distance functions for shape representation. In: IEEE CVPR, pp. 165–174 (2019)
39. Peng, S., Niemeyer, M., Mescheder, L., Pollefeys, M., Geiger, A.: Convolutional occupancy networks. In: Vedaldi, A., Bischof, H., Brox, T., Frahm, J.-M. (eds.) ECCV 2020. LNCS, vol. 12348, pp. 523–540. Springer, Cham (2020). https://doi.org/10.1007/978-3-030-58580-8_31
40. Qi, C.R., Su, H., Mo, K., Guibas, L.J.: PointNet: deep learning on point sets for 3D classification and segmentation. In: IEEE CVPR, pp. 77–85 (2017)
41. Ren, B., Wu, J.C., Lv, Y.L., Cheng, M.M., Lu, S.P.: Geometry-aware ICP for scene reconstruction from RGB-D camera. J. Comput. Sci. Technol. (JCST) **34**(3), 581–593 (2019)
42. Rosu, R.A., Behnke, S.: NeuralMVS: bridging multi-view stereo and novel view synthesis. In: IEEE International Joint Conference on Neural Networks (IJCNN) (2022)

43. Sitzmann, V., Martel, J.N.P., Bergman, A.W., Lindell, D.B., Wetzstein, G.: Implicit neural representations with periodic activation functions. In: NeurIPS, pp. 7462–7473 (2020)
44. Song, H., Huang, J., Cao, Y.P., Mu, T.J.: HDR-net-fusion: real-time 3D dynamic scene reconstruction with a hierarchical deep reinforcement network. Comput. Vis. Media **7**(4), 419–435 (2021)
45. Song, S., Zeng, A., Chang, A.X., Savva, M., Savarese, S., Funkhouser, T.A.: Im?pann3D: extrapolating 360° structure and semantics beyond the field of view. In: IEEE CVPR, pp. 3847–3856 (2018)
46. Sucar, E., Liu, S., Ortiz, J., Davison, A.J.: iMap: implicit mapping and positioning in real-time. In: IEEE ICCV, pp. 6209–6218 (2021)
47. Sun, J., Xie, Y., Chen, L., Zhou, X., Bao, H.: NeuralRecon: real-time coherent 3D reconstruction from monocular video. In: IEEE CVPR, pp. 15598–15607 (2021)
48. Takikawa, T., et al.: Neural geometric level of detail: real-time rendering with implicit 3d shapes. In: IEEE CVPR, pp. 11358–11367 (2021)
49. Wang, P.S., Liu, Y., Tong, X.: Deep octree-based CNNs with output-guided skip connections for 3D shape and scene completion. In: IEEE CVPR Workshops, pp. 1074–1081 (2020)
50. Weder, S., Schönberger, J.L., Pollefeys, M., Oswald, M.R.: RoutedFusion: learning real-time depth map fusion. In: IEEE CVPR, pp. 4886–4896 (2020)
51. Weder, S., Schönberger, J.L., Pollefeys, M., Oswald, M.R.: NeuralFusion: online depth fusion in latent space. In: IEEE CVPR, pp. 3162–3172 (2021)
52. Whelan, T., Salas-Moreno, R.F., Glocker, B., Davison, A.J., Leutenegger, S.: ElasticFusion: real-time dense SLAM and light source estimation. Int. J. Robot. Res. (IJRR) **35**(14), 1697–1716 (2016)
53. Yang, S., et al.: Noise-resilient reconstruction of panoramas and 3D scenes using robot-mounted unsynchronized commodity RGB-D cameras. ACM Trans. Graph. (TOG) **39**(5), 152:1–152:15 (2020)
54. Yariv, L., et al.: Multiview neural surface reconstruction by disentangling geometry and appearance. In: NeurIPS, pp. 2492–2502 (2020)
55. Yu, A., Li, R., Tancik, M., Li, H., Ng, R., Kanazawa, A.: PlenocTrees for real-time rendering of neural radiance fields. In: IEEE ICCV, pp. 5732–5741 (2021)

ParticleSfM: Exploiting Dense Point Trajectories for Localizing Moving Cameras in the Wild

Wang Zhao[1,3], Shaohui Liu[2,3], Hengkai Guo[3], Wenping Wang[4], and Yong-Jin Liu[1(✉)]

[1] Tsinghua University, Beijing, China
liuyongjin@tsinghua.edu.cn
[2] ETH Zurich, Zurich, Switzerland
[3] ByteDance Inc., Beijing, China
[4] Texas A&M University, College Station, USA

Abstract. Estimating the pose of a moving camera from monocular video is a challenging problem, especially due to the presence of moving objects in dynamic environments, where the performance of existing camera pose estimation methods are susceptible to pixels that are not geometrically consistent. To tackle this challenge, we present a robust *dense indirect* structure-from-motion method for videos that is based on dense correspondence initialized from pairwise optical flow. Our key idea is to optimize long-range video correspondence as dense point trajectories and use it to learn robust estimation of motion segmentation. A novel neural network architecture is proposed for processing irregular point trajectory data. Camera poses are then estimated and optimized with global bundle adjustment over the portion of long-range point trajectories that are classified as static. Experiments on MPI Sintel dataset show that our system produces significantly more accurate camera trajectories compared to existing state-of-the-art methods. In addition, our method is able to retain reasonable accuracy of camera poses on fully static scenes, which consistently outperforms strong state-of-the-art dense correspondence based methods with end-to-end deep learning, demonstrating the potential of dense indirect methods based on optical flow and point trajectories. As the point trajectory representation is general, we further present results and comparisons on in-the-wild monocular videos with complex motion of dynamic objects. Code is available at https://github.com/bytedance/particle-sfm.

Keywords: Structure-from-motion · Motion segmentation · Video correspondence · Visual reconstruction

Supplementary Information The online version contains supplementary material available at https://doi.org/10.1007/978-3-031-19824-3_31.

Fig. 1. We present a dense indirect method that is able to recover reliable camera trajectories from in-the-wild videos with complex object motion in dynamic scenes. (See Fig. 6 for qualitative comparisons with COLMAP [61])

1   Introduction

Localizing moving cameras from monocular videos is a fundamental task in a variety of applications such as augmented reality and robotics. Many videos exhibit complex foreground motion from humans, vehicles and general moving objects, posing severe challenges for robust camera pose estimation. Traditional indirect SfM methods [21,34,46] are built on top of feature point detectors and descriptors. These methods rely on high-quality local features and perform non-linear optimization over the geometric reprojection error. Conversely, direct methods [19,20,47] track cameras by optimizing photometric error of the full image assuming consistent appearance across views. While both types of methods have produced compelling results, neither is robust against large object motion in dynamic environments, which is however ubiquitous in daily videos.

To mitigate the influence of moving objects, several existing monocular SLAM and SfM methods [5,82,86] attempt to focus on specific semantic classes of objects that are likely to move around, e.g. humans and cars. However, there are many general objects that can possibly move in the scene in practice (e.g. a chair carried by a human). And moreover, those "special" objects such as humans and cars are not necessarily moving in the videos, making these semantics-based methods limited. Recent methods employ end-to-end deep learning to implicitly deal with those complex motion patterns, placing focus on static parts with the aid of training data. However, the end-to-end learning on camera poses brings up limitation on the system generalization on in-the-wild daily videos.

We present a new *dense indirect* structure-from-motion system for videos that explicitly tackles the issues brought by general moving objects. Our method is based on dense correspondence initialized from pairwise optical flow. Inspired by the success of Particle video [59], our method exploits long-range video correspondence as dense point trajectories, which serves as an intermediate representation and provides abundant information for estimating motion segmentation and optimizing cross-view geometric consistency at global bundle adjustment.

Specifically, our method first connects and optimizes dense point trajectories using pairwise dense correspondence from optical flow. Then, we propose a specially designed network architecture to learn robust estimation of motion labels from point trajectories with variable lengths. Finally, we apply global bundle adjustment to estimate and optimize camera poses and maps over portions of each point trajectory that are classified as static. Since the point trajectories are high-level abstraction of the input monocular videos, training motion estimation solely on synthetic datasets such as FlyingThings3D [43] exhibits great generalization ability and enables our system to produce robust camera trajectories on general videos that contain complex and dense motion patterns (as shown in Fig. 1).

Experiments on MPI Sintel dataset [10] validate that our method significantly improves over state-of-the-art SfM pipelines on localizing moving cameras in dynamic scenes. In addition, on full static ScanNet dataset [13], our method is able to retain reasonable accuracy on the predicted camera trajectories, consistently outperforming strong dense correspondence based methods with end-to-end deep learning, such as DROID-SLAM [70]. We further present results and comparisons on in-the-wild monocular videos to demonstrate the improved robustness on dealing with complex object motion in dynamic environments.

2 Related Work

Dense Correspondence in Videos: Cross-image correspondences are conventionally built on local feature point detection and description [41,58], and recent methods employ deep neural networks to improve local features [15,18] and matching [60]. While the de-facto methods for localization and mapping operate on sparse feature points, dense pixel correspondences [23,57,65] have shown great potential especially on videos, thanks to the rapid developments of optical flow predictors. Early methods such as SIFT-Flow [39] achieve dense correspondences across different scenes, while recent advances [17,28,64] with deep learning regress the optical flow through differentiable warping and feature cost volumes. One notable recent work is RAFT [69] that introduces iterative recurrent refinement with strong cross-dataset generalization. While these optical flow methods have achieved remarkable performance on per-pixel accuracy, they intrinsically limit the correspondences to image pairs rather than the whole video data. Conversely, long-range video correspondence is early studied in Particle video [59] which first employs point trajectories to represent motion patterns in videos. However, the method is very computational expensive and practically not suitable for long videos. Sundaram et al. [67] further propose a fast parallel implementation of variational large displacement optical flow [9], and directly accumulate optical flow to get dense point trajectories. Inspired by these pioneer works, we present a method that sequentially tracks the optical flow and optimizes the pixel locations by exploiting path consistency to acquire reliable dense point trajectories.

Motion Segmentation: Motion segmentation aims to predict what is move for each image in a video sequence. Classical methods [63,73] estimate the motion mask based on optical flow analysis, with follow-up works [8,12] formulating joint optimization over optical flow and motion segmentation. Recent methods with deep neural networks [29,71,92] extract both appearance and optical flow features with a specially designed two-branch networks, or exploit semantic information [14] with optical flow based motion grouping. Self-supervised methods [79,83] are also proposed to overcome the requirement of labeling data. To better parse the object motion, relative camera motion is estimated and incorporated in [6,7,36,80]. However, these optical-flow based methods mostly suffer from temporal inconsistency and in-the-wild generalization to dynamic videos with different shapes and textures. On the other hand, point trajectories contain rich information for temporal object motion. There are a number of existing works [22,30,37,48,49,62] that cluster the tracked point trajectories into motion segments with hand-crafted features and measurements. However, all theses clustering-based methods rely on heavy optimization and hand-crafted design, making them less scalable and general on in-the-wild video sequences. In this work, we combine the best of both worlds and introduce a specially designed network architecture for predicting trajectory attributes, specifically motion labels from irregular data of dense point trajectories.

SfM and SLAM: Traditional structure-from-motion methods can be generally classified into indirect and direct methods. Indirect approaches [21,34,45,46,56, 61,77,85] rely on matched salient keypoints to determine geometric relationship for multi-view images. Conversely, direct methods [2,19,20,47,81] approximate gradients over dense photometric registration on the full image. While both trends of methods achieve great success in practice, they both suffer in dynamic scenes due to the large number of pixel outliers. Most related to us, recent literature attempts to exploits dense correspondences from optical flow. In particular, [55, 91] employ two-view geometric consistency check to detect moving objects, and visual odometry systems are built by triangulating optical flow correspondences in [87,91]. VOLDOR [44] employs a probabilistic graphical model over optical flow to recover camera poses as hidden states. In TartanVO [74], optical flow is fed into an end-to-end network to directly predict camera poses. R-CVD [35] jointly optimizes depth and pose with flexible deformations and geometry-aware filtering. DROID-SLAM [70] implicitly learns to exclude dynamic objects by training on synthetic data with dynamic objects and employing deep bundle adjustment over keyframes. While our method also benefits from dense correspondences from pairwise optical flow, we do not employ end-to-end deep learning to encourage better generalization. Instead, we explicitly model dense point trajectories and perform bundle adjustment over these video correspondences.

Localizing Cameras in Dynamic Scenes: Localizing cameras in dynamic scenes is challenging due to violation of rigid scene assumption in multi-view geometry. Classical SfM and SLAM methods reject moving pixels as outliers through robust cost function [34] and RANSAC [46,61], yet consistently fail under highly dynamic scenes with complex motion patterns. Beyond monocular SLAM, effective segmentation and tracking of dynamic objects can be achieved [1,4,27, 31,38,66,76] with auxiliary depth data from stereo, RGB-D and LiDAR, which, however, is not generally available for in-the-wild captured videos. Thanks to the rapid development of deep learning on visual recognition, many works [3,5,82, 86,90] tackle this problem by exploring the combination with object detection,

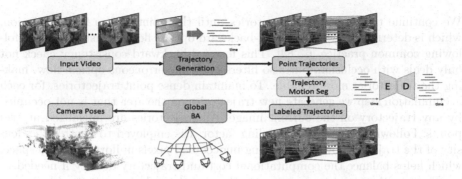

Fig. 2. Overview of our proposed system for localizing moving cameras. Given an input video, we first accumulate and optimize over pairwise optical flow to acquire high-quality dense point trajectories. Then, a specially designed network architecture is employed to process irregular point trajectory data to predict per-trajectory motion labels. Finally, the optimized dense point trajectories along with the motion labels are exploited for global bundle adjustment (BA) to optimize the final camera poses

semantic and instance segmentation. However, These methods are often restricted to pre-defined semantic classes. On the contrary, our method exploits the potential of long-range point trajectories in videos for robust motion label estimation.

3 Methods

The core idea of the proposed system is to exploit long-range video correspondences as dense point trajectories throughout the pipeline. Figure 2 shows an overview of the system. We first accumulate and optimize point trajectories sequentially in a sliding-window manner from optical flow. Then, those point trajectories are fed into the specially designed trajectory processing network to predict per-trajectory motion labels. Finally, we estimate initial camera poses, triangulate global maps from the portions of each trajectory that are classified as static, and perform bundle adjustment over those point tracks to optimize both camera poses and 3d points. As our method employs dense correspondence, the maps built from our system are denser and more complete than top sparse indirect methods such as COLMAP [61] with comparable running time needed.

3.1 Acquiring Dense Point Trajectories

We aim to acquire reliable point trajectories for motion estimation and global bundle adjustment. Following the practice of early literature [59,67] that focus on long-range video correspondence, we start from pairwise optical flow and sequentially accumulate them into point trajectories. We use RAFT [69] as the base optical flow predictor.

For accumulation of dense point trajectories, given the current pixel location p_0 on image 0 (sized $H \times W$) and the optical flow $F_{0\rightarrow 1} \in \mathbb{R}^{H \times W \times 2}$ from image 0 to image 1, the trajectory can be extended with: $p_1 = p_0 + F_{0\rightarrow 1}(p_0)$.

We continue tracking point trajectories until the point suffers from occlusion, which is determined by the forward-backward optical flow consistency check following common practice [67,84]. This forward-backward consistency check not only deals with occlusion, but also filters out some erroneous optical flow, making the trajectories more reliable. To maintain dense point trajectories, for each accumulation step we generate new trajectories on the area that is not occupied by any trajectory on the current image. All trajectories are initialized at grid points. Following [67], a sub-sampling factor λ is employed to control the density of the trajectory by sub-sampling unoccupied pixels uniformly on 2D space, which helps balance the computational cost and trajectory density if needed.

The resulting point trajectories are dense and roughly correct as video correspondences. However, small errors from the optical flow accumulates across time, incurring the tracked pixel locations to gradually drift away from the true ones. Similar drifting errors often occur for tracking-based methods [32,88] for accumulating sensor measurements. To fight against drifting, Particle video [59] attempts to perform a heavy optimization on pixel locations directly using appearance error on raw intensity images. Different from theirs, our method exploits path consistency that benefits from optical flow from non-adjacent image pairs.

Specifically, given consecutive frames I_0, I_1, I_2 and pairwise optical flows $F_{i \to j}$ from I_i to I_j, we first initialize the point trajectory p_1, p_2 on I_1 and I_2 sequentially with direct accumulation:

$$p_1' = p_0 + F_{0 \to 1}(p_0), \quad p_2' = p_1' + F_{1 \to 2}(p_1'). \tag{1}$$

Then, we compute stride-2 optical flow $F_{0 \to 2}$ and optimizes p_1 and p_2 with respect to the following objectives:

$$L = (p_1 - p_1')^2 + (p_2 - (p_0 + F_{0 \to 2}(p_0)))^2 \\ + (p_2 - (p_1 + F_{1 \to 2}(p_1)))^2 \tag{2}$$

Gradients are numerically tractable with interpolation on the optical flow map $F_{1 \to 2}$. Through the optimization we jointly adjust the pixel locations along the track to encourage consistency. The framework is easily extended for longer windows to exploit longer range of optical flow correspondences but we empirically find that adding a single stride-2 constraints already consistently improves the track quality by mitigating the drifting problem.

It is also worth noting that the success of path consistency formulation relies on the key assumption that the direct pairwise measurements are relatively more accurate than cumulative results when constructing point trajectories. This is generally true for accumulating sensor measurements for visual odometry, while in our case the assumption can be violated because if the pixel motion between two images is too significant the accuracy of the pairwise optical flow will degrade. Thus, it is relatively safe to keep a small window to avoid large degradation of the long-range optical flow. In practice, if $F_{0 \to 2}$ does not pass forward-backward consistency check, we skip the optimization at the timestamp and keep the initial accumulated positions. The point trajectory is sequentially extended and optimized until occlusion is detected.

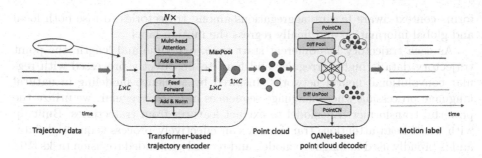

Fig. 3. Illustration of the trajectory-based motion segmentation network. To process irregular point trajectory data, we first employ a transformer-based encoder to extract features for each trajectory. Then, all trajectory features are considered as high-dimensional point cloud and fed into an OANet-based [89] decoder to predict per-trajectory motion labels. In practice, we split long-range point trajectories into segments and map the predicted motion labels for each segment back onto the pixels

3.2 Trajectory-Based Motion Segmentation

Moving objects, while being ubiquitous in daily videos, pose severe challenges for camera pose estimation as it violates geometric consistency across different timestamps, making it crucial to design strategies to filter out dynamic objects. One trend of commonly-used methods in dynamic SLAMs [5,82,86] is to utilize semantic segmentation model, e.g. Mask-RCNN [25] to get per-pixel semantic masks, and remove all potentially moving pixels according to its semantic labels, such as person, car, dog, etc. While these methods are effective under certain scenarios, they are intrinsically not general for segmenting moving objects, since it completely relies on pre-defined semantic classes and cannot distinguish moving or static objects within the same semantic category (e.g. moving and static cars). Conversely, another alternative is to use two-frame motion segmentation methods [71,92], which are recently powered with various convolutional neural network (CNN) models. These methods provide true motion labels instead of semantic candidates. However, two-frame based CNN models suffer from severe temporal inconsistency, degraded estimation when input flows are noisy, and exhibit limited out-of-domain generalization on in-the-wild videos.

We propose to exploit the dense point trajectories we acquired for estimating motion labels. Trajectory-based methods are generally more robust and consistent compared to two-frame flow models for motion segmentation. Unfortunately, traditional cluster-based trajectory segmentation methods rely on heavy optimization and hand-crafted features, and are hard to scale with dense trajectories. To deal with such issues, we propose a novel neural network for processing trajectory data for prediction, which enables fast, robust and accurate dense point trajectory based motion segmentation. As shown in Fig. 3, our proposed network employs a encoder-decoder architecture. Specifically, the encoder directly consumes irregular trajectory data and embeds into high-dimensional feature space. Then, all the encoded trajectories are together fed into the decoder, which performs context-aware feature aggregations among trajectories to fuse both local and global information and finally regress the motion label.

As each trajectory has different start time, end time and length, the point trajectory data is highly irregular and hard to be directly processed with regular convolutional neural networks. Inspired by sequence modeling in natural language processing where language sequences are also irregular, we utilize the powerful transformer [72] model to extract features from trajectories. Built up with multi-head attention, transformer can effectively process sequential data, and is broadly used in language model, and recently extended to vision tasks [16]. Our input data for transformer encoder is N trajectories, and each trajectory includes a set of normalized pixel coordinates (u_i, v_i). We first cut and pad all the trajectories to the temporal window size L. After that, all trajectories have the shape of $(L, 2)$ with masks indicating where the pixel coordinates are zero-padded. To better exploit motion information, we augment the trajectory data $\{(u_i, v_i), i \in [0, L)\}$ with consecutive motion $(\Delta u_i, \Delta v_i) = (u_{i+1} - u_i, v_{i+1} - v_i)$. Furthermore, since the moving objects are much easier to be classified in 3d space, we integrate relative depth information from MiDaS [54] to disambiguate the motion segmentation from pure 2d pixel movements. The estimated relative depth is normalized to $(0, 1)$ and used to back-project the 2d pixels into 3d camera coordinates (x_i, y_i, z_i). We also include the 3d motion data $(\Delta x_i, \Delta y_i, \Delta z_i) = (x_{i+1} - x_i, y_{i+1} - y_i, z_{i+1} - z_i)$ for the trajectory input. The final augmented trajectories have the shape of $(L, 10)$. This data is then embedded by two MLPs, resulting in intermediate features with shape (L, C), which is fed into the transformer module. The transformer consists of 4 blocks, each with multi-head attention and feed-forward layers to encode the temporal information of each trajectory. The output of the transformer module is encoded features also with shape (L, C). To get feature representation of the whole trajectory instead of each point, we further perform max-pooling over temporal dimension, resulting in $(1, C)$ feature vector for each trajectory.

To segment a trajectory as moving objects or static background, the model not only needs to extract motion pattern from each trajectory data, but also has to communicate and compare with other trajectories before making decisions, which is achieved by the decoder. All encoded trajectory features with shape (N, C) naturally forms a feature cloud in high-dimensional space. Thus, we build the decoder on top of carefully designed point cloud processing architectures.

Specifically, we choose OANet [89] as our backbone to benefit from its efficiency and well-designed local-global context mechanism. To capture the local feature context, the network first clusters input points by learning a soft assignment matrix (Diff Pool in Fig. 3). Then, the clusters are spatially correlated to explore the global feature context. Next, the detailed context features of each point are recovered from embedded clusters through differentiable unpooling. And finally, several PointCN layers are applied, followed by sigmoid activation to get the binary prediction mask. We refer the reader to [89] for more details about differentiable pooling, unpooling and PointCN layer.

Our proposed trajectory motion segmentation network is fast, robust and general. It could process tens of thousands trajectories within a few seconds. By only trained on synthetic dataset *FlyingThings3D* [43], the network generalizes well across various scenarios including indoor, outdoor, synthetic movies and daily videos. Furthermore, the proposed network can also be easily extended to predict other trajectory attributes that benefit video understanding.

3.3 Global Bundle Adjustment over Point Trajectories

The optimized dense point trajectories along with the predicted motion labels can be jointly used for localizing moving cameras for monocular videos. Specifically, given a video sequence, we first accumulate and optimize optical flow to get long-range point trajectories. Then, the trajectory motion segmentation network predicts trajectory motion labels in a sliding-window manner with window size L. These motion labels are mapped back onto each pixel to get final per-point motion segmentation. In the map construction and global bundle adjustment we only consider the portions of each trajectory that have static labels.

Since we have dense video correspondences, we can directly formulate non-linear geometric optimization over the point tracks. Inspired by [68,77], we build a global SfM pipeline with dense point trajectories. Specifically, relative camera poses for neighboring views are first solved [24] with sampled correspondences from pairs of static pixels from the point trajectories with its motion labels. Then, rotation averaging [11] and translation averaging [50] are performed to get the initial camera pose estimations. Finally, global bundle adjustment is applied over the constructed point tracks at triangulation stage. Note that the point tracks are consistent with the original dense point trajectories since it comes from dense correspondences sampled from it. Thus, we achieve final pose refinement by making use of the static pixels along the trajectories without considering outlier pixels that are classified as parts of moving objects. As the trajectory processing network is well generalized, our method can recover reliable camera trajectories on in-the-wild daily videos with complex foreground motion.

4 Experiments

4.1 Implementation Details

We use the pre-trained RAFT [69] model on *FlyingThings3D* dataset [9]. The sub-sampling factor λ of point trajectory is set to 2 for all the experiments to balance the reconstruction density and computation time. For trajectory motion segmentation network, we use 4 heads for multi-head attention and 64 dimension for feed-forward layer. As for OANet, we set the cluster number to 100 and the layer number to 8. We train the proposed network on the training split of *FlyingThings3D* dataset [43]. We implement the network in PyTorch [51] and train it using Adam optimizer [33] with learning rate 1e-4 for 30 epochs. At inference, we use a window size L of 10 by default.

We test our system on Sintel [10], ScanNet [13], and in the wild video sequences from DAVIS [52]. For ScanNet dataset, we evaluate our method on the first 20 scenes in the test split. Since the whole video sequence is very long and

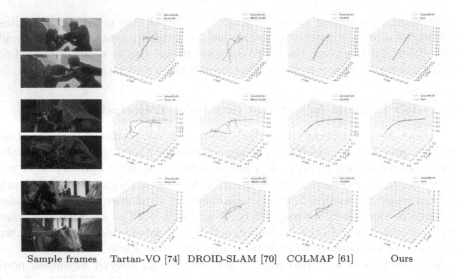

Sample frames   Tartan-VO [74]   DROID-SLAM [70]   COLMAP [61]   Ours

Fig. 4. Qualitative results of moving camera localization on MPI Sintel dataset [10]

not suitable for evaluating time-consuming offline methods like COLMAP [61], we only take the first 1500 frames and down-sample with stride 3 for each scene, resulting in a roughly 10 FPS video. Since all the methods use monocular video as input, we first scale and align all the output camera trajectories with respect to groundtruth, and then calculate commonly used pose metrics: RMSE of absolute trajectory error, translation and rotation part of relative pose error.

4.2 Evaluation on MPI Sintel Dataset

MPI Sintel dataset [10] contains 23 synthetic sequences of highly dynamic scenes. We remove sequences that are not valid to evaluate monocular camera pose (e.g. static cameras, perfectly straight line), resulting in a total of 14 sequences for comparison. We compare our system with both feature based indirect SfM method COLMAP [61] and state-of-the-art deep learning methods [35,70,74]. The results are summarized in Table 1. We also provide comparisons with representative SLAM methods ORB-SLAM [46] and DynaSLAM [5] in the supplementary materials. Since COLMAP fails in 5 of 14 sequences, we perform comparison on the subset of other 9 sequences. Furthermore, we set up baselines by extracting motion masks from state-of-the-art methods MAT [92] and Mask-RCNN [25] to augment COLMAP [61], where no feature points are extracted in the dynamic region. For Mask-RCNN [25], all the pixels that belong to potentially dynamic objects (person, vehicle, animals) are considered dynamic. As shown in Table 1, while explicit motion removal improves the performance, our method outperforms compared baselines by a largin margin thanks to the advantages of long-range point trajectories. For learning-based methods, Tartan-VO [74] and DROID-SLAM [70] are both trained on large-scale dataset TartanAir [75] and have demonstrated strong generalization ability across different

Table 1. Quantitative evaluation on MPI Sintel dataset [10]. COLMAP [61] is additionally compared on its successful subset. Metrics are averaged across sequences

	Methods	ATE (m)	RPE trans (m)	RPE rot (deg)
COLMAP subset	COLMAP [61]	0.145	0.035	0.550
	MAT [92] + [61]	0.069	0.024	0.726
	Mask-RCNN [25] + [61]	0.109	0.039	0.605
	Ours	**0.019**	**0.005**	**0.124**
Full set	COLMAP [61]	X	X	X
	R-CVD [35]	0.360	0.154	3.443
	Tartan-VO [74]	0.290	0.092	1.303
	DROID-SLAM [70]	0.175	0.084	1.912
	Ours	**0.129**	**0.031**	**0.535**

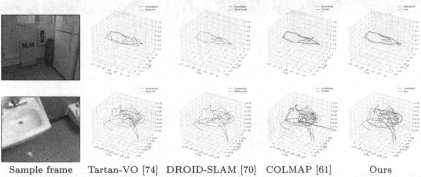

Sample frame   Tartan-VO [74]   DROID-SLAM [70]   COLMAP [61]   Ours

Fig. 5. Qualitative results of moving camera localization on ScanNet dataset [13]

datasets. However, they struggle on dynamic scenes and fail to predict reliable camera trajectories. Some qualitative examples are shown in Fig. 4, where our system produces accurate camera poses over highly dynamic sequences.

4.3 Evaluation on ScanNet

To study the generalization of the proposed dense indirect SfM system, we further test our method on fully static indoor dataset ScanNet [13]. Some sequences in ScanNet contain inf values in groundtruth poses and we exclude them from evaluation, resulting in out of 20 test sequences. The results are shown in Table 2. Our method consistently improve dense baselines and provide reasonable camera trajectories with complex camera motions, as shown in Fig. 5. As for feature based method, COLMAP fails in 3 sequences out of 17, while our dense indirect system succeeds on all 17 sequences. We further present comparisons on the successful subset of COLMAP. Our method is slightly behind on ATE, but better on RPEs. This is possibly due to the degraded quality of indoor optical flow and the missing loop closure in our global bundle adjustment.

534   W. Zhao et al.

Table 2. Quantitative evaluation on ScanNet [13]. COLMAP [61] is additionally compared on its successful subset. Metrics are averaged across sequences

	Methods	ATE (m)	RPE trans (m)	RPE rot (deg)
COLMAP subset	COLMAP [61]	**0.171**	0.064	2.900
	Ours	0.319	**0.017**	**0.632**
Full set	COLMAP [61]	X	X	X
	R-CVD [35]	0.408	0.065	7.626
	Tartan-VO [74]	0.353	0.045	2.620
	DROID-SLAM [70]	0.687	0.038	3.117
	Ours	**0.349**	**0.024**	**0.924**

Fig. 6. Top row: COLMAP [61]. **Bottom row:** Ours. Qualitative comparison on in-the-wild videos from DAVIS [52]. Our dense indirect system produces robust camera trajectory and denser maps for videos with complex foreground motion

4.4   Qualitative Evaluation on In-the-Wild Videos

As our system is general, we further present results and comparisons with COLMAP [61] on in-the-wild monocular videos with complex motion of dynamic objects in Fig. 6. Videos are taken from DAVIS [52]. While COLMAP sometimes fails to predict reasonable camera poses (see the first and second sample of Fig. 6), our method generalizes well in the wild, and is more robust to dynamic objects. Furthermore, our dense indirect solution is able to build significantly denser 3d reconstructions, which demonstrates the potential of indirect methods for recovering fine-grained 3D geometry.

4.5   Ablation Study

We ablate different components of our system on MPI Sintel dataset [10]. Table 3 shows the results. Without trajectory motion segmentation, all candidate correspondences, including those on moving objects, are used for map construction and global bundle adjustment. Results show that this leads to significantly

Table 3. Results of ablation studies on MPI Sintel dataset [10]. We report metrics for all methods on both the full set (left) and the successful subset for SIFT + Global BA (right). "Optim" denotes trajectory optimization and "Seg" denotes trajectory-based motion segmentation and its use for global bundle adjustment

Methods	ATE (m)	RPE trans (m)	RPE rot (deg)
SIFT + Global BA	X/0.060	X/0.042	X/0.635
SIFT + MAT [92] + Global BA	X/0.054	X/0.055	X/0.621
Traj + Global BA	X/0.071	X/0.041	X/0.969
Traj + Optim + Global BA	X/0.072	X/0.042	X/0.929
Traj + Seg + Global BA	0.146/0.046	0.039/0.015	0.567/0.212
Traj + Optim + Seg + Global BA	**0.129/0.042**	**0.031/0.013**	**0.535/0.199**

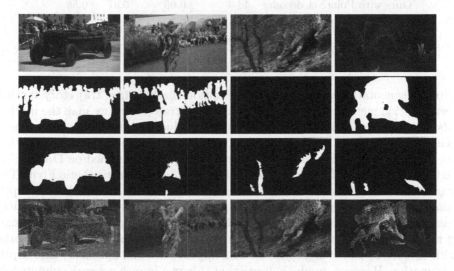

Fig. 7. Qualitative results on motion segmentation. **From top to bottom:** sample image, Mask-RCNN [25], MAT [92] and our trajectory-based motion segmentation

degraded accuracy of recovered poses, indicating the important of removing dynamic pixels. Moreover, by optimizing point trajectories with path consistency, the mean endpoint error of trajectories is reduced by around 10%, which consequently improves camera localization (the last two rows). To further validate the necessity of dense point trajectories, we introduce two feature-based baselines that are built on SIFT [41], where one is also integrated with MAT [92] for removing moving pixels. As shown in Table 3, these two methods sometimes fail on sequences, and are behind on accuracy when tested on their successful subset compared to our system, demonstrating the effectiveness of dense point trajectories.

To study the effects of different components in the trajectory motion segmentation network, we perform ablation studies on MPI Sintel dataset [10] by eval-

Table 4. Evaluation and ablation studies for motion segmentation on MPI Sintel dataset [10]. We compare our method with several state-of-the-arts and ablate different components in our design on trajectory-based motion segmentation

Methods	mIoU (%)	Precision	Recall	F1-score
MAT [92]	47.5	**0.82**	0.54	0.56
COS [42]	55.0	0.67	**0.77**	0.65
MotionGrouping [79]	10.2	0.64	0.10	0.25
AMD [40]	31.5	0.42	0.62	0.45
Two-branch CNN w/o depth	29.2	0.54	0.49	0.39
Two-branch CNN	33.7	0.62	0.50	0.44
Ours with MLP encoder	54.8	0.67	0.73	0.66
Ours with PointNet decoder	46.3	0.65	0.67	0.58
Ours w/o depth	54.6	0.72	0.70	0.65
Ours	**60.6**	0.79	0.74	**0.72**

uating segmentation w.r.t groundtruth motion masks. Since trajectory motion segmentation methods only offer predictions for trajectories, we map the motion labels into corresponding pixel locations and evaluate all methods only on these pixels. Table 4 shows the results. We compare our method with state-of-the-art supervised motion segmentation method [92] that is trained on DAVIS [52] and YouTube-VOS [78]. Our method, while only trained on synthetic FlyingThings3D dataset [43], achieves better motion segmentation even without depth information. Figure 7 shows some qualitative results, where our method predicts reliable motion masks for moving pixels. To further support the novel design of the network, we introduce a baseline that utilize two-branch CNN networks with ResNet-50 [26] to aggregate motion, appearance, and optionally also depth information. However, results indicate that this two-branch network exhibits low generalization ability when trained on FlyingThings3D dataset. Finally, we also ablate the architecture design by substituting the encoder with vanilla MLPs and the decoder with PointNet [53]. Results clearly show the advantages of using attention-based encoder and local-global context-aware decoder in our system.

Runtime Analysis. For a 50-frame video, our system runs within 690 s on average, including all the I/O time of each module. Specifically, optical flow extraction takes around 57 s, the acquisition of dense point trajectories takes 200 s, the trajectory motion segmentation takes around 65 s, and the final global BA takes 368 s. For comparison, COLMAP [61] takes 410 s on average. Note that it is computationally unaffordable to run COLMAP with dense correspondences from the acquired dense point trajectories, while our method achieves dense correspondence with reasonable overhead.

5 Conclusions

In this work, we present a general *dense indirect* system for localizing moving cameras from in-the-wild videos. The key to the success of our method is to optimize and exploit long-range dense video correspondences as point trajectories, which are used for motion analysis and global bundle adjustment. A specially designed trajectory-based motion segmentation network is proposed to process the irregular point trajectory data. Experimental results show that our method can recover reliable camera trajectories from in-the-wild videos with complex motion patterns. Possible future directions include advanced optimization for long-range point trajectories and integration of loop closure for pose optimization.

Acknowledgements. We thank anonymous reviewers for their valuable feedback. This work was supported by the Natural Science Foundation of China (61725204) and Tsinghua University Initiative Scientific Research Program.

References

1. Alcantarilla, P.F., Yebes, J.J., Almazán, J., Bergasa, L.M.: On combining visual SLAM and dense scene flow to increase the robustness of localization and mapping in dynamic environments. In: 2012 IEEE International Conference on Robotics and Automation, pp. 1290–1297. IEEE (2012)
2. Alismail, H., Browning, B., Lucey, S.: Photometric bundle adjustment for vision-based SLAM. In: Lai, S.-H., Lepetit, V., Nishino, K., Sato, Y. (eds.) ACCV 2016. LNCS, vol. 10114, pp. 324–341. Springer, Cham (2017). https://doi.org/10.1007/978-3-319-54190-7_20
3. Ballester, I., Fontan, A., Civera, J., Strobl, K.H., Triebel, R.: Dot: dynamic object tracking for visual slam. In: 2021 IEEE International Conference on Robotics and Automation (ICRA), pp. 11705–11711. IEEE (2021)
4. Bârsan, I.A., Liu, P., Pollefeys, M., Geiger, A.: Robust dense mapping for large-scale dynamic environments. In: 2018 IEEE International Conference on Robotics and Automation (ICRA), pp. 7510–7517. IEEE (2018)
5. Bescos, B., Fácil, J.M., Civera, J., Neira, J.: DynaSLAM: tracking, mapping, and inpainting in dynamic scenes. IEEE Robot. Autom. Lett. **3**(4), 4076–4083 (2018)
6. Bideau, P., Learned-Miller, E.: It's moving! A probabilistic model for causal motion segmentation in moving camera videos. In: Leibe, B., Matas, J., Sebe, N., Welling, M. (eds.) ECCV 2016. LNCS, vol. 9912, pp. 433–449. Springer, Cham (2016). https://doi.org/10.1007/978-3-319-46484-8_26
7. Bideau, P., Menon, R.R., Learned-Miller, E.: MoA-net: self-supervised motion segmentation. In: Leal-Taixé, L., Roth, S. (eds.) ECCV 2018. LNCS, vol. 11134, pp. 715–730. Springer, Cham (2019). https://doi.org/10.1007/978-3-030-11024-6_55
8. Brox, T., Bruhn, A., Weickert, J.: Variational motion segmentation with level sets. In: Leonardis, A., Bischof, H., Pinz, A. (eds.) ECCV 2006. LNCS, vol. 3951, pp. 471–483. Springer, Heidelberg (2006). https://doi.org/10.1007/11744023_37
9. Brox, T., Malik, J.: Large displacement optical flow: descriptor matching in variational motion estimation. IEEE Trans. Pattern Anal. Mach. Intell. **33**(3), 500–513 (2010)

10. Butler, D.J., Wulff, J., Stanley, G.B., Black, M.J.: A naturalistic open source movie for optical flow evaluation. In: Fitzgibbon, A., Lazebnik, S., Perona, P., Sato, Y., Schmid, C. (eds.) ECCV 2012. LNCS, vol. 7577, pp. 611–625. Springer, Heidelberg (2012). https://doi.org/10.1007/978-3-642-33783-3_44

11. Chatterjee, A., Govindu, V.M.: Efficient and robust large-scale rotation averaging. In: Proceedings of the IEEE International Conference on Computer Vision, pp. 521–528 (2013)

12. Cremers, D., Soatto, S.: Motion competition: a variational approach to piecewise parametric motion segmentation. Int. J. Comput. Vision 62(3), 249–265 (2005)

13. Dai, A., Chang, A.X., Savva, M., Halber, M., Funkhouser, T., Nießner, M.: ScanNet: richly-annotated 3D reconstructions of indoor scenes. In: Proceedings of the IEEE Conference on Computer Vision and Pattern Recognition, pp. 5828–5839 (2017)

14. Dave, A., Tokmakov, P., Ramanan, D.: Towards segmenting anything that moves. In: Proceedings of the IEEE/CVF International Conference on Computer Vision Workshops (2019)

15. DeTone, D., Malisiewicz, T., Rabinovich, A.: SuperPoint: self-supervised interest point detection and description. In: Proceedings of the IEEE Conference on Computer Vision and Pattern Recognition Workshops, pp. 224–236 (2018)

16. Dosovitskiy, A., et al.: An image is worth 16x16 words: transformers for image recognition at scale. arXiv preprint arXiv:2010.11929 (2020)

17. Dosovitskiy, A., et al.: FlowNet: learning optical flow with convolutional networks. In: Proceedings of the IEEE International Conference on Computer Vision, pp. 2758–2766 (2015)

18. Dusmanu, M., et al.: D2-net: a trainable CNN for joint description and detection of local features. In: Proceedings of the IEEE/CVF Conference on Computer Vision and Pattern Recognition, pp. 8092–8101 (2019)

19. Engel, J., Koltun, V., Cremers, D.: Direct sparse odometry. IEEE Trans. Pattern Anal. Mach. Intell. 40(3), 611–625 (2017)

20. Engel, J., Schöps, T., Cremers, D.: LSD-SLAM: large-scale direct monocular SLAM. In: Fleet, D., Pajdla, T., Schiele, B., Tuytelaars, T. (eds.) ECCV 2014. LNCS, vol. 8690, pp. 834–849. Springer, Cham (2014). https://doi.org/10.1007/978-3-319-10605-2_54

21. Forster, C., Pizzoli, M., Scaramuzza, D.: SVO: fast semi-direct monocular visual odometry. In: 2014 IEEE International Conference on Robotics and Automation (ICRA), pp. 15–22. IEEE (2014)

22. Fragkiadaki, K., Zhang, G., Shi, J.: Video segmentation by tracing discontinuities in a trajectory embedding. In: 2012 IEEE Conference on Computer Vision and Pattern Recognition, pp. 1846–1853. IEEE (2012)

23. Germain, H., Bourmaud, G., Lepetit, V.: S2DNet: learning image features for accurate sparse-to-dense matching. In: Vedaldi, A., Bischof, H., Brox, T., Frahm, J.-M. (eds.) ECCV 2020. LNCS, vol. 12348, pp. 626–643. Springer, Cham (2020). https://doi.org/10.1007/978-3-030-58580-8_37

24. Hartley, R.I.: In defense of the eight-point algorithm. IEEE Trans. Pattern Anal. Mach. Intell. 19(6), 580–593 (1997)

25. He, K., Gkioxari, G., Dollár, P., Girshick, R.: Mask R-CNN. In: Proceedings of the IEEE International Conference on Computer Vision, pp. 2961–2969 (2017)

26. He, K., Zhang, X., Ren, S., Sun, J.: Deep residual learning for image recognition. In: Proceedings of the IEEE Conference on Computer Vision and Pattern Recognition, pp. 770–778 (2016)

27. Huang, J., Yang, S., Mu, T.J., Hu, S.M.: ClusterVO: clustering moving instances and estimating visual odometry for self and surroundings. In: Proceedings of the IEEE/CVF Conference on Computer Vision and Pattern Recognition, pp. 2168–2177 (2020)
28. Ilg, E., Mayer, N., Saikia, T., Keuper, M., Dosovitskiy, A., Brox, T.: FlowNet 2.0: evolution of optical flow estimation with deep networks. In: Proceedings of the IEEE Conference on Computer Vision and Pattern Recognition, pp. 2462–2470 (2017)
29. Jain, S.D., Xiong, B., Grauman, K.: FusionSeg: learning to combine motion and appearance for fully automatic segmentation of generic objects in videos. In: 2017 IEEE Conference on Computer Vision and Pattern Recognition (CVPR), pp. 2117–2126. IEEE (2017)
30. Keuper, M., Andres, B., Brox, T.: Motion trajectory segmentation via minimum cost multicuts. In: Proceedings of the IEEE International Conference on Computer Vision, pp. 3271–3279 (2015)
31. Kim, D.H., Kim, J.H.: Effective background model-based RGB-D dense visual odometry in a dynamic environment. IEEE Trans. Rob. 32(6), 1565–1573 (2016)
32. Kim, P., Coltin, B., Kim, H.J.: Low-drift visual odometry in structured environments by decoupling rotational and translational motion. In: 2018 IEEE International Conference on Robotics and Automation (ICRA), pp. 7247–7253. IEEE (2018)
33. Kingma, D.P., Ba, J.: Adam: a method for stochastic optimization. arXiv preprint arXiv:1412.6980 (2014)
34. Klein, G., Murray, D.: Parallel tracking and mapping for small AR workspaces. In: 2007 6th IEEE and ACM International Symposium on Mixed and Augmented Reality, pp. 225–234. IEEE (2007)
35. Kopf, J., Rong, X., Huang, J.B.: Robust consistent video depth estimation. In: Proceedings of the IEEE/CVF Conference on Computer Vision and Pattern Recognition, pp. 1611–1621 (2021)
36. Lamdouar, H., Yang, C., Xie, W., Zisserman, A.: Betrayed by motion: camouflaged object discovery via motion segmentation. In: Proceedings of the Asian Conference on Computer Vision (2020)
37. Lezama, J., Alahari, K., Sivic, J., Laptev, I.: Track to the future: spatio-temporal video segmentation with long-range motion cues. In: CVPR 2011, pp. 3369–3376. IEEE (2011)
38. Li, S., Lee, D.: RGB-D SLAM in dynamic environments using static point weighting. IEEE Robot. Autom. Lett. 2(4), 2263–2270 (2017)
39. Liu, C., Yuen, J., Torralba, A.: Sift flow: dense correspondence across scenes and its applications. IEEE Trans. Pattern Anal. Mach. Intell. 33(5), 978–994 (2010)
40. Liu, R., Wu, Z., Yu, S., Lin, S.: The emergence of objectness: learning zero-shot segmentation from videos. In: NeurIPS (2021)
41. Lowe, D.G.: Distinctive image features from scale-invariant keypoints. Int. J. Comput. Vision 60(2), 91–110 (2004)
42. Lu, X., Wang, W., Shen, J., Crandall, D., Luo, J.: Zero-shot video object segmentation with co-attention Siamese networks. T-PAMI (2020)
43. Mayer, N., et al.: A large dataset to train convolutional networks for disparity, optical flow, and scene flow estimation. In: Proceedings of the IEEE Conference on Computer Vision and Pattern Recognition, pp. 4040–4048 (2016)
44. Min, Z., Yang, Y., Dunn, E.: Voldor: visual odometry from log-logistic dense optical flow residuals. In: Proceedings of the IEEE/CVF Conference on Computer Vision and Pattern Recognition, pp. 4898–4909 (2020)

45. Moulon, P., Monasse, P., Marlet, R.: Global fusion of relative motions for robust, accurate and scalable structure from motion. In: Proceedings of the IEEE International Conference on Computer Vision, pp. 3248–3255 (2013)
46. Mur-Artal, R., Montiel, J.M.M., Tardos, J.D.: ORB-SLAM: a versatile and accurate monocular slam system. IEEE Trans. Rob. **31**(5), 1147–1163 (2015)
47. Newcombe, R.A., Lovegrove, S.J., Davison, A.J.: DTAM: dense tracking and mapping in real-time. In: 2011 International Conference on Computer Vision, pp. 2320–2327. IEEE (2011)
48. Ochs, P., Brox, T.: Higher order motion models and spectral clustering. In: 2012 IEEE Conference on Computer Vision and Pattern Recognition, pp. 614–621. IEEE (2012)
49. Ochs, P., Malik, J., Brox, T.: Segmentation of moving objects by long term video analysis. IEEE Trans. Pattern Anal. Mach. Intell. **36**(6), 1187–1200 (2013)
50. Ozyesil, O., Singer, A.: Robust camera location estimation by convex programming. In: Proceedings of the IEEE Conference on Computer Vision and Pattern Recognition, pp. 2674–2683 (2015)
51. Paszke, A., et al.: Automatic differentiation in PyTorch (2017)
52. Perazzi, F., Pont-Tuset, J., McWilliams, B., Van Gool, L., Gross, M., Sorkine-Hornung, A.: A benchmark dataset and evaluation methodology for video object segmentation. In: Proceedings of the IEEE Conference on Computer Vision and Pattern Recognition, pp. 724–732 (2016)
53. Qi, C.R., Su, H., Mo, K., Guibas, L.J.: PointNet: deep learning on point sets for 3D classification and segmentation. In: Proceedings of the IEEE Conference on Computer Vision and Pattern Recognition, pp. 652–660 (2017)
54. Ranftl, R., Lasinger, K., Hafner, D., Schindler, K., Koltun, V.: Towards robust monocular depth estimation: mixing datasets for zero-shot cross-dataset transfer. arXiv preprint arXiv:1907.01341 (2019)
55. Ranjan, A., Jampani, V., Balles, L., Kim, K., Sun, D., Wulff, J., Black, M.J.: Competitive collaboration: joint unsupervised learning of depth, camera motion, optical flow and motion segmentation. In: Proceedings of the IEEE/CVF Conference on Computer Vision and Pattern Recognition, pp. 12240–12249 (2019)
56. Resch, B., Lensch, H., Wang, O., Pollefeys, M., Sorkine-Hornung, A.: Scalable structure from motion for densely sampled videos. In: Proceedings of the IEEE Conference on Computer Vision and Pattern Recognition, pp. 3936–3944 (2015)
57. Rocco, I., Cimpoi, M., Arandjelović, R., Torii, A., Pajdla, T., Sivic, J.: Neighbourhood consensus networks. In: Advances in Neural Information Processing Systems, vol. 31 (2018)
58. Rublee, E., Rabaud, V., Konolige, K., Bradski, G.: ORB: an efficient alternative to sift or surf. In: 2011 International Conference on Computer Vision, pp. 2564–2571. Ieee (2011)
59. Sand, P., Teller, S.: Particle video: long-range motion estimation using point trajectories. Int. J. Comput. Vision **80**(1), 72–91 (2008)
60. Sarlin, P.E., DeTone, D., Malisiewicz, T., Rabinovich, A.: Superglue: learning feature matching with graph neural networks. In: Proceedings of the IEEE/CVF Conference on Computer Vision and Pattern Recognition, pp. 4938–4947 (2020)
61. Schonberger, J.L., Frahm, J.M.: Structure-from-motion revisited. In: Proceedings of the IEEE Conference on Computer Vision and Pattern Recognition, pp. 4104–4113 (2016)
62. Sheikh, Y., Javed, O., Kanade, T.: Background subtraction for freely moving cameras. In: 2009 IEEE 12th International Conference on Computer Vision, pp. 1219–1225. IEEE (2009)

63. Shi, J., Malik, J.: Motion segmentation and tracking using normalized cuts. In: Sixth International Conference on Computer Vision (IEEE Cat. No. 98CH36271), pp. 1154–1160. IEEE (1998)
64. Sun, D., Yang, X., Liu, M.Y., Kautz, J.: PWC-Net: CNNs for optical flow using pyramid, warping, and cost volume. In: Proceedings of the IEEE Conference on Computer Vision and Pattern Recognition, pp. 8934–8943 (2018)
65. Sun, J., Shen, Z., Wang, Y., Bao, H., Zhou, X.: LoFTR: detector-free local feature matching with transformers. In: Proceedings of the IEEE/CVF Conference on Computer Vision and Pattern Recognition, pp. 8922–8931 (2021)
66. Sun, Y., Liu, M., Meng, M.Q.H.: Improving RGB-D slam in dynamic environments: a motion removal approach. Robot. Auton. Syst. **89**, 110–122 (2017)
67. Sundaram, N., Brox, T., Keutzer, K.: Dense point trajectories by GPU-accelerated large displacement optical flow. In: Daniilidis, K., Maragos, P., Paragios, N. (eds.) ECCV 2010. LNCS, vol. 6311, pp. 438–451. Springer, Heidelberg (2010). https://doi.org/10.1007/978-3-642-15549-9_32
68. Sweeney, C.: Theia multiview geometry library: tutorial & reference. http://theia-sfm.org
69. Teed, Z., Deng, J.: RAFT: recurrent all-pairs field transforms for optical flow. In: Vedaldi, A., Bischof, H., Brox, T., Frahm, J.-M. (eds.) ECCV 2020. LNCS, vol. 12347, pp. 402–419. Springer, Cham (2020). https://doi.org/10.1007/978-3-030-58536-5_24
70. Teed, Z., Deng, J.: DROID-SLAM: deep visual slam for monocular, stereo, and RGB-D cameras. In: Advances in Neural Information Processing Systems, vol. 34 (2021)
71. Tokmakov, P., Schmid, C., Alahari, K.: Learning to segment moving objects. Int. J. Comput. Vision **127**(3), 282–301 (2019)
72. Vaswani, A., et al.: Attention is all you need. In: Advances in Neural Information Processing Systems, vol. 30 (2017)
73. Wang, J.Y., Adelson, E.H.: Representing moving images with layers. IEEE Trans. Image Process. **3**(5), 625–638 (1994)
74. Wang, W., Hu, Y., Scherer, S.: TartanVO: a generalizable learning-based vo. arXiv preprint arXiv:2011.00359 (2020)
75. Wang, W., et al.: TartanAir: a dataset to push the limits of visual slam. In: 2020 IEEE/RSJ International Conference on Intelligent Robots and Systems (IROS), pp. 4909–4916. IEEE (2020)
76. Wang, Y., Huang, S.: Motion segmentation based robust RGB-D SLAM. In: Proceeding of the 11th World Congress on Intelligent Control and Automation, pp. 3122–3127. IEEE (2014)
77. Wilson, K., Snavely, N.: Robust global translations with 1DSfM. In: Fleet, D., Pajdla, T., Schiele, B., Tuytelaars, T. (eds.) ECCV 2014. LNCS, vol. 8691, pp. 61–75. Springer, Cham (2014). https://doi.org/10.1007/978-3-319-10578-9_5
78. Xu, N., et al.: YouTube-VOS: sequence-to-sequence video object segmentation. In: Ferrari, V., Hebert, M., Sminchisescu, C., Weiss, Y. (eds.) ECCV 2018. LNCS, vol. 11209, pp. 603–619. Springer, Cham (2018). https://doi.org/10.1007/978-3-030-01228-1_36
79. Yang, C., Lamdouar, H., Lu, E., Zisserman, A., Xie, W.: Self-supervised video object segmentation by motion grouping. In: Proceedings of the IEEE/CVF International Conference on Computer Vision, pp. 7177–7188 (2021)
80. Yang, G., Ramanan, D.: Learning to segment rigid motions from two frames. In: Proceedings of the IEEE/CVF Conference on Computer Vision and Pattern Recognition, pp. 1266–1275 (2021)

81. Yang, S., Scherer, S.: Direct monocular odometry using points and lines. In: 2017 IEEE International Conference on Robotics and Automation (ICRA), pp. 3871–3877. IEEE (2017)
82. Yang, S., Scherer, S.: CubeSLAM: monocular 3-D object SLAM. IEEE Trans. Rob. **35**(4), 925–938 (2019)
83. Yang, Y., Loquercio, A., Scaramuzza, D., Soatto, S.: Unsupervised moving object detection via contextual information separation. In: Proceedings of the IEEE/CVF Conference on Computer Vision and Pattern Recognition, pp. 879–888 (2019)
84. Yin, Z., Shi, J.: GeoNet: unsupervised learning of dense depth, optical flow and camera pose. In: Proceedings of the IEEE Conference on Computer Vision and Pattern Recognition, pp. 1983–1992 (2018)
85. Yokozuka, M., Oishi, S., Thompson, S., Banno, A.: Vitamin-e: visual tracking and mapping with extremely dense feature points. In: Proceedings of the IEEE/CVF Conference on Computer Vision and Pattern Recognition, pp. 9641–9650 (2019)
86. Yu, C., et al.: DS-SLAM: a semantic visual slam towards dynamic environments. In: 2018 IEEE/RSJ International Conference on Intelligent Robots and Systems (IROS), pp. 1168–1174. IEEE (2018)
87. Zhan, H., Weerasekera, C.S., Bian, J.W., Reid, I.: Visual odometry revisited: What should be learnt? In: 2020 IEEE International Conference on Robotics and Automation (ICRA), pp. 4203–4210. IEEE (2020)
88. Zhang, J., Singh, S.: Visual-lidar odometry and mapping: Low-drift, robust, and fast. In: 2015 IEEE International Conference on Robotics and Automation (ICRA), pp. 2174–2181. IEEE (2015)
89. Zhang, J., et al.: Learning two-view correspondences and geometry using order-aware network. In: Proceedings of the IEEE/CVF International Conference on Computer Vision, pp. 5845–5854 (2019)
90. Zhang, J., Henein, M., Mahony, R., Ila, V.: VDO-SLAM: a visual dynamic object-aware SLAM system. arXiv preprint arXiv:2005.11052 (2020)
91. Zhao, W., Liu, S., Shu, Y., Liu, Y.J.: Towards better generalization: joint depth-pose learning without posenet. In: Proceedings of the IEEE/CVF Conference on Computer Vision and Pattern Recognition, pp. 9151–9161 (2020)
92. Zhou, T., Wang, S., Zhou, Y., Yao, Y., Li, J., Shao, L.: Motion-attentive transition for zero-shot video object segmentation. In: Proceedings of the AAAI Conference on Artificial Intelligence, vol. 34, pp. 13066–13073 (2020)

4DContrast: Contrastive Learning with Dynamic Correspondences for 3D Scene Understanding

Yujin Chen$^{(\boxtimes)}$, Matthias Nießner, and Angela Dai

Technical University of Munich, Munich, Germany
{yujin.chen,niessner,angela.dai}@tum.de

Abstract. We present a new approach to instill 4D dynamic object priors into learned 3D representations by unsupervised pre-training. We observe that dynamic movement of an object through an environment provides important cues about its objectness, and thus propose to imbue learned 3D representations with such dynamic understanding, that can then be effectively transferred to improved performance in downstream 3D semantic scene understanding tasks. We propose a new data augmentation scheme leveraging synthetic 3D shapes moving in static 3D environments, and employ contrastive learning under 3D-4D constraints that encode 4D invariances into the learned 3D representations. Experiments demonstrate that our unsupervised representation learning results in improvement in downstream 3D semantic segmentation, object detection, and instance segmentation tasks, and moreover, notably improves performance in data-scarce scenarios. Our results show that our 4D pre-training method improves downstream tasks such as object detection mAP@0.5 by 5.5%/6.5% over training from scratch on ScanNet/SUN RGB-D while involving no additional run-time overhead at test time.

Keywords: 3D scene understanding · Point cloud recognition · 3D semantic segmentation · 3D instance segmentation · 3D object detection

1 Introduction

3D semantic scene understanding has seen remarkable progress in recent years, in large part driven by advances in deep learning as well as the introduction of large-scale, annotated datasets [1,7,10]. In particular, notable progress has been made to address core 3D scene understanding tasks such as 3D semantic segmentation, object detection, and instance segmentation, which are fundamental to many real-world computer vision applications such as robotics, mixed reality, or autonomous driving. Such approaches have developed various methods to learn on different 3D scene representations, such as sparse or dense volumetric

---

Supplementary Information The online version contains supplementary material available at https://doi.org/10.1007/978-3-031-19824-3_32.

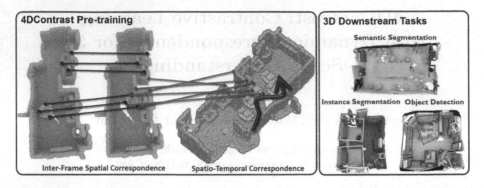

Fig. 1. We propose 4DContrast to imbue learned 3D representations with 4D priors. We introduce a data augmentation scheme to composite synthetic 3D objects with real-world 3D scans to create 4D sequence data with inherent correspondence information. We then leverage a combination of 3D-3D, 3D-4D, and 4D-4D constraints within a contrastive learning framework to learn 4D invariance in the 3D representations. The learned features can be transferred to improve performance in various downstream 3D scene understanding tasks.

grids [6,7,11], point clouds [29,30], meshes [19], or multi-view approaches [8,38]. Recently, driven by the success of unsupervised representation learning for transfer learning in 2D, 3D scene understanding methods have been augmented with unsupervised 3D pre-training to further improve performance to downstream 3D scene understanding tasks [17,20,43,46] (Fig. 1).

While such 3D representation learning has focused on feature representations learned from static 3D scenes, we observe that important notions of objectness are given by 4D dynamic observations – for instance, object segmentations can often be naturally intuited by observing objects moving around an environment without any annotations required, which can be more difficult in a static 3D observation. We thus propose to leverage this powerful 4D signal in unsupervised pre-training to imbue 4D object priors into learned 3D representations, that can then be effectively transferred to various downstream 3D scene understanding tasks for improved recognition performance.

In this work, we introduce 4DContrast to learn about objectness from both static 3D and dynamic 4D information in learned 3D representations. We leverage a combination of static 3D scanned scenes and a database of synthetic 3D shapes, and augment the scenes with moving synthetic shapes to generate 4D sequence data with inherent motion correspondence. We then employ a contrastive learning scheme under both 3D and 4D constraints, correlating local 3D point features with each other as well as with 4D sequence features, thus imbuing learned objectness from dynamic information into the 3D representation learning.

To demonstrate our approach, we pre-train on ScanNet [7] along with Model-Net [41] shapes for unsupervised 3D representation learning. Experiments on 3D semantic segmentation, object detection, and instance segmentation show that 4DContrast learns effective features that can be transferred to achieve improved performance in various downstream 3D scene understanding tasks. 4DContrast can also generalize from pre-training on ScanNet and ModelNet to improved performance on SUN RGB-D [36]. Additionally, we show that our learned representations remain robust in limited training data scenarios, consistently improving performance under a various amounts of training data available.

Our main contributions are summarized as follows:

- We propose the first method to leverage 4D sequence information and constraints for 3D representation learning, showing transferability of the learned features to the downstream 3D scene understanding tasks of 3D semantic segmentation, object detection, and instance segmentation.
- Our new unsupervised pre-training based on constructing 4D sequences from synthetic 3D shapes in real-world, static 3D scenes improves performance across a variety of downstream tasks and different datasets.

2   Related Work

3D Semantic Scene Understanding. Driven by rapid developments in deep learning and the introduction of several large-scale, annotated 3D datasets [1, 7,10], notable progress has been made in 3D semantic scene understanding, in particular the tasks of 3D semantic segmentation [6–8,11,18,19,24,30,32], 3D object detection [25–27,42,47], and 3D instance segmentation [9,13,16,21,45]. Many methods have been proposed, largely focusing on learning on various 3D representations, such as sparse or dense volumetric grids [6,7,11], point clouds [21,27,29,30], meshes [19,35], or multi-view hybrid representations [8,22]. In particular, approaches leveraging backbones built with sparse convolutions [6,11] have shown strong effectiveness across a variety of 3D scene understanding tasks and datasets. We propose a new unsupervised pre-training approach to learn 4D priors in learned 3D representations, leveraging sparse convolutional backbones for both 3D and 4D feature extraction.

3D Representation Learning. Inspired by the success of representation learning in 2D, particularly that leveraging instance discrimination with contrastive learning [2,3,15], recent works have explored unsupervised learning with 3D pretext tasks that can be leveraged for fine-tuning on downstream 3D scene understanding tasks [5,14,17,20,23,31,33,34,39,40,43,46]. For instance, [14,34] learn feature representations from point-based instance discrimination for object classification and segmentation, and [17,43,46] extend to more complex 3D scenes by generating correspondences from various different views of scene point clouds.

In particular, given the more scarce data availability of real-world 3D environments, Hou et al. [17] additionally demonstrate the efficacy of contrastive 3D pretraining for various 3D semantic scene understanding tasks under a variety of limited training data scenarios. In contrast to these methods that employ 3D-only pretext tasks for representation learning, we propose to learn from 4D sequence data to embed 4D priors into learned 3D representations for more effective transfer to downstream 3D tasks.

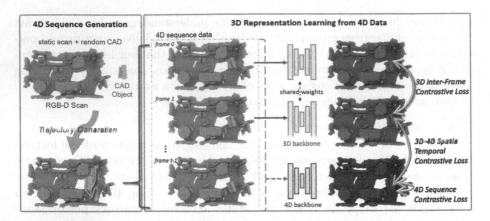

Fig. 2. Method overview. 4DContrast learns effective 3D feature representations imbued with 4D signal from moving object sequences. During pre-training, we augment static 3D scene data with a moving object from a synthetic shape dataset. We can then establish dynamic correspondences between the spatio-temporal features learned from the 4D sequence with 3D features of individual static frames. We employ contrastive learning under not only 3D geometric correspondence between individual frames, but also with their corresponding 4D counterpart, as well as 4D-4D constraints to anchor the 4D feature learning. This enables 4D-invariant representation learning, which we can apply to various downstream 3D scene understanding tasks.

Recently, Huang et al. [20] propose to learn from the inherent sequence data of RGB-D video to incorporate the notion of a temporal sequence. Constraints are established across pairs of frames in the sequence; however, the sequence data itself represents static scenes without any movement within the scene, limiting the temporal signal that can be learned. In contrast, we consider 4D sequence data containing object movement through the scene, which can provide additional semantic signal about objectness through an object's motion. Additionally, Rao et al. [31] propose to learn from 3D scenes that are synthetically generated by randomly placing synthetic CAD models on a rectangular layout. They employ object-level contrastive learning on object-level features, resulting in improved 3D object detection performance. We also leverage synthetic CAD models for data augmentation, but we compose them with real-world 3D scan data to generate 4D sequences of objects in motion, and exploit learned 4D features to enhance learned 3D representations, with performance improvement on various downstream 3D scene understanding tasks.

3   4D Invariant Representation Learning

4DContrast presents a new approach to 3D representation learning: our key idea is to employ 4D constraints during pre-training, in order to imbue learned features with 4D invariance from learned objectness from seeing an object in motion. We consider a dataset of 3D scans $\mathcal{S} = \{S_i\}$ as well as a dataset of synthetic

3D objects $\mathcal{O} = \{O_j\}$, and construct dynamic sequences with inherent correspondence information by moving a synthetic object O_j in a static 3D scan S_i. This enables us to establish 4D correspondences along with 3D-4D correspondence as constraints under a contrastive learning framework for unsupervised pre-training. An overview of our approach is shown in Fig. 2.

3.1 Revisiting SimSiam

We first revisit SimSiam [4], which introduced a simple yet powerful approach for contrastive 2D representation learning. Inspired by the effectiveness of SimSiam, we build an unsupervised contrastive learning scheme for embedding 4D priors into 3D representations.

SimSiam considers two augmented variants of an image I, I_1, and I_2, which are input to weight-shared encoder network Φ_{2D} (a 2D convolutional backbone followed by a projection MLP). Then a prediction MLP head P_{2D} transforms the output of one view as $p_1^{2D} = P_{2D}(\Phi_{2D}(I_1))$ to match to the another output $z_2^{2D} = \Phi_{2D}(I_2)$, with minimizing the negative cosine similarity [12]:

$$\mathcal{D}(p_1^{2D}, z_2^{2D}) = -\frac{p_1^{2D}}{||p_1^{2D}||_2} \cdot \frac{z_2^{2D}}{||z_2^{2D}||_2}. \tag{1}$$

SimSiam also uses a stop-gradient (SG) operation that treats z_2^{2D} as a constant during back-propagation, to prevent collapse during the training, thus modifying Eq. 1 as: $\mathcal{D}(p_1^{2D}, SG(z_2^{2D}))$. A symmetrized loss is defined for the two augmented inputs:

$$\mathcal{L}^{2D} = \frac{1}{2}\mathcal{D}(p_1^{2D}, SG(z_2^{2D})) + \frac{1}{2}\mathcal{D}(p_2^{2D}, SG(z_1^{2D})). \tag{2}$$

SimSiam has shown to be very effective at learning invariances under various image augmentations, without requiring negative samples or very large batches. We thus build from this contrastive framework for our 3D-4D constraints, as it allows for our high-dimensional pre-training design.

3.2 4D-Invariant Contrastive Learning

To imbue effective 4D priors into learned 3D features, we consider a static 3D scan S and a synthetic 3D object O as a train sample, and compose them together to form dynamic object movement in the scene $\{F_0, ..., F_{t-1}\}$ for t time steps (as described in Sect. 3.3). We then establish spatial correspondences between frames (3D-3D), spatio-temporal correspondences (3D-4D), and dynamic correspondences (4D-4D) as constraints. 3D features are extracted with a 3D encoder Φ_{3D} and 4D features with a 4D encoder Φ_{4D}, with respective prediction MLPs P_{3D} and P_{4D}.

Inter-Frame Spatial Correspondence. For each pair of frames (F_i, F_j) in a train sequence F, we consider their spatial correspondence across sequence frames in order to implicitly pose invariance over the dynamic sequence. That

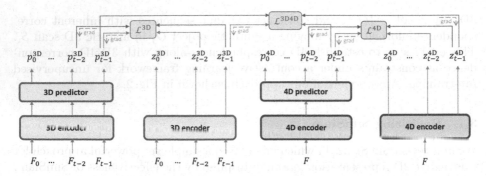

Fig. 3. 4DContrast pre-training. We visualize 3D-3D, 3D-4D, and 4D-4D losses across frame and spatio-temporal correspondence. Note that losses are established across all pairs of frames for $\mathcal{L}^{3D}$ $\mathcal{L}^{4D}$ and across all frames for $\mathcal{L}^{3D4D}$; for visualization we only show those associated with frames F_{t-2} and F_{t-1}, and only for F_{t-1} for $\mathcal{L}^{3D4D}$. Each loss only propagates back according to the gradient arrows due to stop-gradient operations for stable training. (Color figure online)

is, points that correspond to the same location in the original 3D scene S or original object O should also correspond in feature space. For the set of corresponding point locations $\mathcal{A}_{i,j}$ from frames (F_i, F_j), we consider each pair of point locations $(\mathbf{a}_i, \mathbf{b}_j) \in \mathcal{A}$, we obtain their 3D backbone features at the respective locations: $p_{i,a}^{3D} = P_{3D}(\Phi_{3D}(F_i))(\mathbf{a}_i)$ and $z_{j,b}^{3D} = \Phi_{3D}(F_j)(\mathbf{b}_j)$. We then compute a symmetrized negative cosine similarity loss between features of corresponding point locations:

$$\mathcal{L}_{\mathcal{A}_{i,j}}^{3D} = \sum_{(a,b)\in\mathcal{A}_{i,j}} \left(\frac{1}{2}\mathcal{D}(p_{i,a}^{3D}, SG(z_{j,b}^{3D})) + \frac{1}{2}\mathcal{D}(p_{j,b}^{3D}, SG(z_{i,a}^{3D})) \right). \quad (3)$$

In Fig. 3, we use green arrows to indicate constraints between frame F_{t-2} and frame F_{t-1}.

We compute Eq. 3 over each pair of frames in the whole sequence F:

$$\mathcal{L}^{3D} = \sum_{\substack{i=0 \\ i<j}}^{t-1} \sum_{j=0}^{t-1} \mathcal{L}_{\mathcal{A}_{i,j}}^{3D}. \quad (4)$$

By establishing constraints across 3D frames in a 4D sequence, we encode pose invariance of moving objects across varying background into the learned 3D features.

Spatio-Temporal Correspondence. In addition to implicitly encoding pose invariance of moving objects, we establish explicit 3D-4D correspondences to learn 4D priors, encouraging 4D-invariance in the learned features. For a train sequence $F = \{F_0, ..., F_{t-1}\}$, we use the 4D encoder Φ_{4D} and the 4D predictor P_{4D} to extract 4D features from the whole sequence. Then $z_{i,a}^{4D}$ indicates the 4D features output by the 4D encoder Φ_{4D} at point location $\mathbf{a}_i$ in frame i, and $p_{i,a}^{4D}$ denotes the 4D features output by the 4D predictor P_{4D}. Then for a frame F_i, we consider each 3D point $\mathbf{a}_i \in \mathcal{A}_i$ in this set of frame points F_i, and establish a constraint between its corresponding 3D feature extracted by 3D network (Φ_{3D} and P_{3D}) and its corresponding 4D feature extracted by 4D network (Φ_{4D} and P_{4D}):

$$\mathcal{L}_{\mathcal{A}_i}^{3D4D} = \sum_{a \in \mathcal{A}_i} \left(\frac{1}{2} \mathcal{D}(SG(p_{i,a}^{3D}), z_{i,a}^{4D}) + \frac{1}{2} \mathcal{D}(SG(p_{i,a}^{4D}), z_{i,a}^{3D}) \right). \tag{5}$$

As shown in Fig. 3, we use orange arrows to indicate constraints of frame F_{t-1}. For the entire input sequence F, we calculate Eq. 5 for every frame, and the 3D-4D contrastive loss $\mathcal{L}^{3D4D}$ is defined as:

$$\mathcal{L}^{3D4D} = \sum_{i=0}^{t-1} \mathcal{L}_{\mathcal{A}_i}^{3D4D}. \tag{6}$$

Additionally, in order to learn spatio-temporally consistent 4D representations, we employ 4D-4D correspondence constraints inherent to the 4D features within the same point cloud sequence. This is formulated analogously to Eq. 3, replacing the 3D features with the 4D features from different time steps that correspond spatially:

$$\mathcal{L}_{\mathcal{A}_{i,j}}^{4D} = \sum_{(a) \in \mathcal{A}_{i,j}} \left(\frac{1}{2} \mathcal{D}(p_{i,a}^{4D}, SG(z_{j,a}^{4D})) + \frac{1}{2} \mathcal{D}(p_{j,a}^{4D}, SG(z_{i,a}^{4D})) \right). \tag{7}$$

In Fig. 3, we use blue arrows to indicate 4D constraints between frame F_{t-2} and frame F_{t-1}. We evaluate Eq. 7 over every pair of frames in the entire input sequence F, with the 4D contrastive loss $\mathcal{L}^{4D}$ defined as:

$$\mathcal{L}^{4D} = \sum_{\substack{i=0 \\ i<j}}^{t-1} \sum_{j=1}^{t-1} \mathcal{L}_{\mathcal{A}_{i,j}}^{4D}. \tag{8}$$

Joint Learning. Our overall training loss $\mathcal{L}$ consists of three parts including 3D contrastive loss $\mathcal{L}^{3D}$, 3D-4D contrastive loss $\mathcal{L}^{3D4D}$, and 4D contrastive loss $\mathcal{L}^{4D}$:

$$\mathcal{L} = w_{3D} \mathcal{L}^{3D} + w_{3D4D} \mathcal{L}^{3D4D} + w_{4D} \mathcal{L}^{4D}, \tag{9}$$

where constant weights w_{3D}, w_{3D4D} and w_{4D} are used to balance the losses.

3.3   Generating 4D Correspondence via Scene-Object Augmentation

To learn from 4D sequence data to embed 4D priors into learned 3D representations, we leverage existing large-scale real-world 3D scan datasets in combination with synthetic 3D shape datasets. This enables generation of 4D correspondences without requiring any labels – by augmenting static 3D scenes with

Table 1. Summary of fine-tuning of 4DContrast for various downstream 3D scene understanding tasks and datasets. Our pre-training approach learns effective, transferable features, resulting in notable improvement over the baseline learning paradigm of training from scratch.

Datasets	Stats (#train/#val)	Task	Gain (from scratch)
ScanNetV2 [7]	1.2K/312 scenes	Sem. Seg.	+2.3% mIoU
		Ins. Seg.	+4.2% mAP@0.5
		Obj. Det.	+5.5% mAP@0.5
SUN RGB-D [36]	5.2K/5K frames	Obj. Det	+6.5% mAP@0.5

generated trajectories of a moving synthetic object within the scene, which provides inherent 4D correspondence knowledge across the object motion. Thus for pre-training, we consider pairs of reconstructed scans and an arbitrarily sampled synthetic 3D shape (S, O), and generate a 4D sequence $F = \{F_0, ..., F_{t-1}\}$ by moving the object through the scene.

Trajectory Generation. We first generate a trajectory for O in S. We voxelize S at 10 cm voxel resolution, and accumulate occupied surface voxels in the height dimension to acquire a 2D map of the scene geometry. Valid object locations are then identified as those in the 2D map with a voxel accumulation ≤ 1, with the max height of the accumulated voxels near to the ground floor (within 20 cm of the average floor height). For the object O, we consider all possible 2D locations, and if O does not exceed the valid region (based on its bounding sphere), then the location is taken as a candidate object position. A random position sampled from these candidate positions is taken as the starting point of the trajectory, we can randomly sample a step distance in $[30, 90]$ cm and step direction such that the angular change in trajectory is $<150°$, and then select the nearest valid candidate position as the second trajectory point. We repeat this process for t time steps in the sequence to obtain 4D scene-object augmentations for pre-training.

4D Sequence Generation. A sequence of point clouds are then generated based on the computed object trajectory for the scan, up to sequence length t, by compositing the object into the scene under its translation and rotation steps per frame. This provides inherent correspondence information between 3D scene locations and 4D object movement through the scene.

Scene Augmentation. We augment the 4D sequences by randomly sampling different points across the geometry in each individual frame. We also randomly remove cubic chunks of points in the background 3D scene for additional data variation, with the number of chunks removed randomly sampled from $[5, 15]$ and the size of the chunks randomly sampled in $[0.15, 0.45]$ as a proportion of the scene extent. We discard any sequences that do not have enough correspondences in its frames; that is, $\geq 30\%$ of the points in the original scan and $\geq 30\%$ of the points of the synthetic object should be consistently represented in each frame, and each frame must maintain at least 50% of its points through the augmentation process. Additionally, we further augment the static 3D frame interpretations of the sequence (but not the sequence) by applying random rotation, translation, and scaling to each individually considered 3D frame.

3.4 Network Architecture for Pre-training

During pre-training, we leverage correspondences induced by our 4D data generation, between encoded 3D frames as well as across the encoded 4D sequence. To this end, we employ 3D and 4D feature extractors as meta-architectures for 4D-invariant learning.

To extract per-point features from a 3D scene, we use a 3D encoder Φ_{3D} and a 3D predictor P_{3D}. Φ_{3D} is a U-Net architecture based on sparse 3D convolutions with residual block followed by a $1 \times 1 \times 1$ sparse convolutional projection layer, and P_{3D} is two $1 \times 1 \times 1$ sparse convolutional layers.

To extract spatio-temporal features from a 4D sequence, we use a 4D encoder Φ_{4D} and a 4D predictor P_{4D}. These are structured analogously to the 3D feature extraction, using sparse 4D convolutions instead. For more detailed architecture specifications, we refer to the supplemental material.

4 Experimental Setup

We demonstrate the effectiveness of our 4D-informed pre-training of learned 3D representations for a variety of downstream 3D scene understanding tasks.

Pre-training Setup. We use reconstructed 3D scans from ScanNet [7] and synthetic 3D shapes from ModelNet [41] to compose our 4D sequence data for pre-training. We use the official ScanNet train split with 1201 train scans, augmented with shapes from ModelNet from eight furniture categories: chair, desk, dresser, nightstand, sofa, table, bathtub, and toilet. For each 3D scan, we generate 20 trajectories of an object moving through the scan, following Sect. 3.3 with $t = 4$. For sequence generation we use 2 cm resolution for the scene and 1000 randomly sampled points from the synthetic object to compose together.

The 3D and 4D sparse U-Nets are implemented with MinkowskiEngine [6] using 2 cm voxel size for 3D and 5cm voxel size for 4D. For pre-training we consider only geometry information from the scene-object sequence augmentations. We use an SGD optimizer with initial learning rate 0.25 and a batch-size of 12. The learning rate is decreased by a factor of 0.99 every 1000 steps. We train for 50K steps until convergence.

Fine-Tuning on Downstream Tasks. We use the same pre-trained backbone network in the three 3D scene understanding tasks of semantic segmentation, instance segmentation, and object detection. For semantic segmentation, we directly use the U-Net architecture for dense label prediction, and for object detection and instance segmentation, we use VoteNet [27] and PointGroup [21] respectively, both with our pre-trained 3D U-Net backbone. All experiments,

Table 2. 3D object detection on ScanNet. Our 4DContrast pre-training leads to improved performance in comparison with state of the art object detection and 3D pretraining schemes.

Method	Input	mAP@0.5
DSS [37]	Geo + RGB	6.8
F-PointNet [28]	Geo + RGB	10.8
GSPN [44]	Geo + RGB	17.7
3D-SIS [16]	Geo + RGB	22.5
VoteNet [27]	Geo + Height	33.5
Scratch + VoteNet	Geo only	34.5
RandomRooms [31] + VoteNet	Geo only	36.2 (+1.7)
PointContrast [43] + VoteNet	Geo only	38.0 (+3.5)
CSC [17] + VoteNet	Geo only	39.3 (+4.8)
Ours + VoteNet	Geo only	**40.0** (+5.5)

including comparisons with state of the art, are trained with geometric information only, unless otherwise noted. Fine-tuning experiments on semantic segmentation are trained with a batch size of 48 for 10K steps, using an initial learning rate of 0.8 with polynomial decay with power 0.9. For instance segmentation, we use the same training setup as PointGroup, and use an initial learning rate of 0.1. For object detection, the network is trained for 500 epochs, and the learning rate is 0.001 and decayed by a factor of 0.5 at epochs 250, 350, and 450. We use a batch size of 6 on ScanNet and 16 on SUN RGB-D.

5   Results

We demonstrate that our learned features under 3D-4D constraints can effectively transfer well to a variety of downstream 3D scene understanding tasks. We consider both in-domain transfer to 3D scene understanding tasks on ScanNet [7] (Sect. 5.1), as well as out-of-domain transfer to SUN RGB-D [36] (Sect. 5.2); a summary is shown in Table 1. We also show data-efficient scene understanding (Sect. 5.3) and additional analysis (Sect. 5.4). Note that for all downstream experiments, we do not use the 4D backbone and thus use the same 3D U-Net architecture as PointContrast [43] and CSC [17].

All experiments, including our method and all baseline comparisons, are trained on geometric data only without any color information.

5.1   ScanNet

We first demonstrate our 4DContrast pre-training in fine-tuning for 3D object detection, semantic segmentation, and instance segmentation on ScanNet [7], showing the effectiveness of learning 3D features under 4D constraints. Tables 2,

3, and 4 evaluate performance on 3D object detection, semantic segmentation, and instance segmentation, respectively.

Table 2 shows 3D object detection results, for which our pretraining approach improves over baseline training from scratch (+5.5% mAP@0.5) as well as over the strong 3D-based pre-training methods of RandomRooms [31], PointContrast [43] and CSC [17].

In Tables 3 and 4, we evaluate semantic segmentation in comparison with state-of-the-art 3D pre-training approaches [17,43], as well as a baseline training paradigm from scratch. These pre-training approaches improve notably over training from scratch, and our 4DContrast approach leveraging learned representations under 4D constraints, leads to additional performance improvement over train from scratch (+2.3% mIoU for semantic segmentation and +4.2% mAP@0.5 for instance segmentation). We show qualitative results for semantic segmentation in Fig. 4.

5.2   SUN RGB-D

We additionally show that our 4DContrast learning scheme can produce transferable representations across datasets. We leverage our pre-trained weights from ScanNet + ModelNet, and explore downstream 3D object detection on the SUN RGB-D [36] dataset. SUN RGB-D is a dataset of RGB-D images, containing 10,335 frames captured with a variety of commodity RGB-D sensors. It contains 3D object bounding box annotations for 10 class categories. We follow the official train/test split of 5,285 train frames and 5,050 test frames.

Table 5 shows 3D object detection performance on SUN RGB-D, with qualitative results visualized in Fig. 5. We use the same pre-training as with ScanNet, with downstream fine-tuning on SUN RGB-D data. 4DContrast improves over training from scratch (+6.5% mAP@0.5), with our learned representations surpassing the 3D-based pre-training [17,31,43,46].

Table 3. Semantic segmentation on ScanNet. Our 4D-informed pre-training learns effective features that lead to improved performance boost over training from scratch as well as state-of-the-art 3D-based pre-training of CSC [17] and PointContrast [43].

Method	mIoU	mAcc
Scratch	70.0	78.1
CSC [17]	70.7 (+0.7)	78.8 (+0.7)
PointContrast [43]	71.3 (+1.3)	79.3 (+1.2)
Ours	**72.3** (+2.3)	**80.8** (+2.7)

554   Y. Chen et al.

Table 4. Instance segmentation on ScanNet. Our 4D-imbued pre-training leads to significantly improved results over training from scratch, as well as favorable performance over other 3D-only pretraining schemes.

Method	mAP@0.5	mIoU
Scratch	53.4	69.0
PointContrast [43]	55.8 (+2.4)	70.9 (+1.9)
CSC [17]	56.5 (+3.1)	71.1 (+2.1)
Ours	**57.6** (+4.2)	**71.4** (+2.4)

5.3 Data-Efficient 3D Scene Understanding

We evaluate our approach in the scenario of limited training data, as shown in Fig. 6. 4DContrast improves over baseline training from scratch as well as over state-of-the-art data-efficient scene understanding CSC [17] in semantic segmentation and object detection under various different percentages of ScanNet training data. With only 20% of the training data, we can recover 87% of the fine-tuned semantic segmentation performance training with 100% of the train data from scratch. In object detection, our pre-training enables improved performance for all percentage settings, notably in the very limited regime with +3.0/4.5% mAP@0.5 over CSC/training from scratch at 10% data, and +2.5/5.9% mAP@0.5 with 20% data.

5.4 Ablation Studies

Effect of 3D and 4D Data Augmentation. We consider a baseline variant of our approach that considers only the static 3D scene data without any

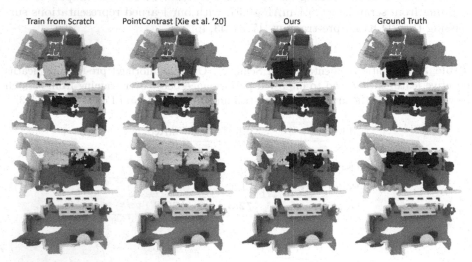

Fig. 4. Qualitative results on ScanNet semantic segmentation. Our 4DContrast pre-training to encode 4D priors enables more consistent segmentation results, in comparison to training from scratch as well as 3D-based PointContrast [43] pre-training.

Table 5. 3D object detection on SUN RGB-D. Our 4D-based pre-training learns effective 3D representations, improving performance over training from scratch and state-of-the-art 3D pre-training methods. *indicates that PointNet++ is used as a backbone instead of a 3D U-Net.

Method	Input	mAP@0.5
VoteNet [27]	Geo + Height	32.9
Scratch + VoteNet [27]	Geo	31.7
PointContrast [43] + VoteNet	Geo	34.8 (+3.1)
RandomRooms [31]* + VoteNet	Geo	35.4 (+3.7)
DeepContrast [46]* + VoteNet	Geo	35.5 (+3.8)
CSC [17] + VoteNet	Geo	36.4 (+4.7)
Ours + VoteNet	Geo	**38.2** (+6.5)

scene-object augmentations with 3D-3D constraints during pre-training in Table 6 (*Ours (3D data, 3D-3D only)*), which provides some improvement over training from scratch but is notably improved with our 4D pre-training formulation. We additionally consider using our 4D scene-object augmentation with only 3D-3D constraints between sequence frames during pre-training (*Ours (4D data, 3D-3D only)*) in Table 6, which helps to additionally improve performance with implicitly learned priors from 4D data. Both are further improved by our approach to explicitly learn 4D priors in 3D features.

Effect of 4D-Invariant Contrastive Priors. In Table 6, we see that learning 4D-invariant contrastive priors through our 3D-4D and 4D-4D constraints during pretraining improves upon data augmentation variants only. Additionally, Table 7 evaluates the 3D variant of our approach with our full 4D-based pre-training across a variety of downstream tasks, showing consistent improvements from learned 4D-based priors.

Effect of SimSiam Contrastive Learning. We also consider the effect of our SimSiam contrastive framework as PointContrast [43] leverages a PointInfoNCE contrastive loss. We note that the 3D variant of our approach (*Ours (3D data, 3D-3D only)*) reflects a PointContrast [43] setting using our scene augmentation and SimSiam architecture, which our 4D-based feature learning outperforms.

5.5 Discussion

While 4DContrast pre-training demonstrates the effectiveness of leveraging 4D priors for learned 3D representations, various limitations remain. In particular, 4D feature learning with sparse convolutions involves considerable memory during pre-training, so we use half-resolution for characterizing 4D features relative to 3D features and limited sequence durations. Additionally, we consider a subset of 4D motion when augmenting scenes with moving synthetic objects, and believe exploration of articulated motion or more complex dynamic object

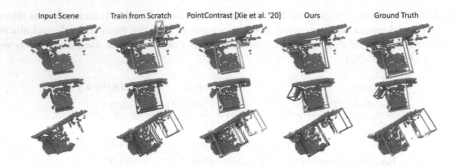

Fig. 5. Qualitative results on SUN RGB-D [36] object detection. Our 4DContrast pre-training to encode 4D priors enables more accurate detection results, in comparison to training from scratch as well as 3D-based PointContrast [43] pre-training. Different colors denote different objects.

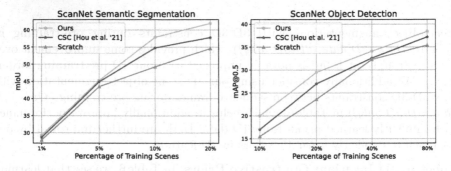

Fig. 6. Data-efficient learning on ScanNet semantic segmentation and object detection. Under limited data scenarios, our 4D-imbued pre-training effectively improves performance over training from scratch as well as the state-of-the-art CSC [17].

interactions would lead to additional insight and robustness of learned feature representations.

Memory and Speed. Our 4D-imbued pre-training results in consistent improvements across a variety of tasks and datasets, even with only using the learned 3D backbone for downstream training and inference. Thus, our method maintains the same memory and speed costs for inference as purely 3D-based pre-training approaches. For pre-training, our joint 3D-4D training uses additional parameters (33M for the 4D network in addition to the 38M for the 3D network), but due to jointly learning 4D priors with SimSiam, we do not require as large of a batch size to train as PointContrast [43] (12 vs their 48), nor as many iterations (up to 30K vs 60K), resulting in slightly less total memory use and pre-training time overall.

Table 6. Additionally ablation variants: compared to a baseline of using 3D-3D constraints on static 3D scene data only, leveraging augmented 4D sequence data improves feature learning even under 3D only constraints. Our final 4DContrast pre-training leveraging constraints with learned 4D features achieves the best performance.

Method/Data Augmentation	Pre-training Loss Term(s)	mIoU	mAcc
Scratch	-	70.0	78.1
Ours (3D data, 3D-3D only)	$\mathcal{L}^{3D}$(static scene)	71.5 (+1.5)	79.7 (+1.6)
Ours (4D data, 3D-3D only)	$\mathcal{L}^{3D}$(dynamic scene)	71.7 (+1.7)	80.0 (+1.9)
Ours	$\mathcal{L}^{3D},\mathcal{L}^{3D4D},\mathcal{L}^{4D}$(dynamic scene)	**72.3** (+2.3)	**80.5** (+2.4)

Table 7. Extended ablation of the 3d-only variant of our approach on ScanNet.

Task	Ours (3D data, 3D-3D only)	Ours
Ins. Seg. (mAP@0.5)	54.1	**57.6** (+3.5)
Obj. Det. (mAP@0.5)	38.7	**40.0** (+1.3)
Sem. Seg. 1% data (mIoU)	27.0	**28.2** (+1.2)
Sem. Seg. 5% data (mIoU)	44.4	**45.3** (+0.9)
Sem. Seg. 10% data (mIoU)	56.3	**57.9** (+1.6)
Sem. Seg. 20% data (mIoU)	60.6	**61.9** (+1.3)
Sem. Seg. 100% data (mIoU)	71.5	**72.3** (+0.8)

6   Conclusion

We have presented 4DContrast, a new approach for 3D representation learning that incorporates 4D priors into learned features during pre-training. We propose a data augmentation scheme to construct 4D sequences of moving synthetic objects in static 3D scenes, without requiring any semantic labels. This enables learning from 4D sequences, and we and establish contrastive constraints between learned 3D features and 4D features from the inherent correspondences given in the 4D sequence generation. Our experiments demonstrate that our 4D-imbued pre-training results in performance improvement across a variety of 3D downstream tasks and datasets. Additionally, our learned features effectively transfer to limited training data scenarios, significantly outperforming state of the art in the low training data regime. We hope that this will lead to additional insights in 3D representation learning and new possibilities in 3D scene understanding.

Acknowledgements. This project is funded by the Bavarian State Ministry of Science and the Arts and coordinated by the Bavarian Research Institute for Digital Transformation (bidt), the TUM Institute of Advanced Studies (TUM-IAS), the ERC Starting Grant Scan2CAD (804724), and the German Research Foundation (DFG) Grant Making Machine Learning on Static and Dynamic 3D Data Practical.

References

1. Chang, A., et al.: Matterport3D: learning from RGB-D data in indoor environments. In: International Conference on 3D Vision, pp. 667–676 (2017)
2. Chen, T., Kornblith, S., Norouzi, M., Hinton, G.: A simple framework for contrastive learning of visual representations. In: International Conference on Machine Learning, pp. 1597–1607 (2020)
3. Chen, X., Fan, H., Girshick, R., He, K.: Improved baselines with momentum contrastive learning. arXiv preprint arXiv:2003.04297 (2020)
4. Chen, X., He, K.: Exploring simple Siamese representation learning. In: Conference on Computer Vision and Pattern Recognition, pp. 15750–15758 (2021)
5. Chen, Y., et al.: Shape self-correction for unsupervised point cloud understanding. In: International Conference on Computer Vision, pp. 8382–8391 (2021)
6. Choy, C., Gwak, J., Savarese, S.: 4D spatio-temporal convnets: Minkowski convolutional neural networks. In: Conference on Computer Vision and Pattern Recognition, pp. 3075–3084 (2019)
7. Dai, A., Chang, A.X., Savva, M., Halber, M., Funkhouser, T., Nießner, M.: Scannet: richly-annotated 3d reconstructions of indoor scenes. In: Conference on Computer Vision and Pattern Recognition, pp. 5828–5839 (2017)
8. Dai, A., Nießner, M.: 3DMV: joint 3D-multi-view prediction for 3D semantic scene segmentation. In: Ferrari, V., Hebert, M., Sminchisescu, C., Weiss, Y. (eds.) ECCV 2018. LNCS, vol. 11214, pp. 458–474. Springer, Cham (2018). https://doi.org/10.1007/978-3-030-01249-6_28
9. Engelmann, F., Bokeloh, M., Fathi, A., Leibe, B., Nießner, M.: 3D-MPA: multi-proposal aggregation for 3D semantic instance segmentation. In: Conference on Computer Vision and Pattern Recognition, pp. 9031–9040 (2020)
10. Geiger, A., Lenz, P., Urtasun, R.: Are we ready for autonomous driving? The KITTI vision benchmark suite. In: Conference on Computer Vision and Pattern Recognition, pp. 3354–3361 (2012)
11. Graham, B., Engelcke, M., Van Der Maaten, L.: 3D semantic segmentation with submanifold sparse convolutional networks. In: Conference on Computer Vision and Pattern Recognition, pp. 9224–9232 (2018)
12. Grill, J.B., et al.: Bootstrap your own latent: a new approach to self-supervised learning. arXiv preprint arXiv:2006.07733 (2020)
13. Han, L., Zheng, T., Xu, L., Fang, L.: OccuSeg: occupancy-aware 3D instance segmentation. In: Conference on Computer Vision and Pattern Recognition, pp. 2940–2949 (2020)
14. Hassani, K., Haley, M.: Unsupervised multi-task feature learning on point clouds. In: International Conference on Computer Vision, pp. 8160–8171 (2019)
15. He, K., Fan, H., Wu, Y., Xie, S., Girshick, R.: Momentum contrast for unsupervised visual representation learning. In: Conference on Computer Vision and Pattern Recognition, pp. 9729–9738 (2020)
16. Hou, J., Dai, A., Nießner, M.: 3D-SIS: 3D semantic instance segmentation of RGB-D scans. In: Conference on Computer Vision and Pattern Recognition, pp. 4421–4430 (2019)
17. Hou, J., Graham, B., Nießner, M., Xie, S.: Exploring data-efficient 3D scene understanding with contrastive scene contexts. In: Conference on Computer Vision and Pattern Recognition, pp. 15587–15597 (2021)
18. Hu, W., Zhao, H., Jiang, L., Jia, J., Wong, T.T.: Bidirectional projection network for cross dimension scene understanding. In: Conference on Computer Vision and Pattern Recognition, pp. 14373–14382 (2021)

19. Huang, J., Zhang, H., Yi, L., Funkhouser, T., Nießner, M., Guibas, L.J.: TextureNet: consistent local parametrizations for learning from high-resolution signals on meshes. In: Conference on Computer Vision and Pattern Recognition, pp. 4440–4449 (2019)

20. Huang, S., Xie, Y., Zhu, S.C., Zhu, Y.: Spatio-temporal self-supervised representation learning for 3D point clouds. In: International Conference on Computer Vision, pp. 6535–6545 (2021)

21. Jiang, L., Zhao, H., Shi, S., Liu, S., Fu, C.W., Jia, J.: PointGroup: dual-set point grouping for 3D instance segmentation. In: Conference on Computer Vision and Pattern Recognition, pp. 4867–4876 (2020)

22. Kundu, A., et al.: Virtual multi-view fusion for 3D semantic segmentation. In: European Conference on Computer Vision, pp. 518–535 (2020)

23. Liang, H., et al.: Exploring geometry-aware contrast and clustering harmonization for self-supervised 3D object detection. In: International Conference on Computer Vision, pp. 3293–3302 (2021)

24. Nekrasov, A., Schult, J., Litany, O., Leibe, B., Engelmann, F.: Mix3D: out-of-context data augmentation for 3D scenes. In: 2021 International Conference on 3D Vision (3DV), pp. 116–125. IEEE (2021)

25. Nie, Y., Hou, J., Han, X., Nießner, M.: RFD-net: point scene understanding by semantic instance reconstruction. In: Conference on Computer Vision and Pattern Recognition, pp. 4608–4618 (2021)

26. Qi, C.R., Chen, X., Litany, O., Guibas, L.J.: ImvoteNet: boosting 3D object detection in point clouds with image votes. In: Conference on Computer Vision and Pattern Recognition, pp. 4404–4413 (2020)

27. Qi, C.R., Litany, O., He, K., Guibas, L.J.: Deep Hough voting for 3D object detection in point clouds. In: International Conference on Computer Vision, pp. 9277–9286 (2019)

28. Qi, C.R., Liu, W., Wu, C., Su, H., Guibas, L.J.: Frustum pointnets for 3D object detection from RGB-D data. In: Conference on Computer Vision and Pattern Recognition, pp. 918–927 (2018)

29. Qi, C.R., Su, H., Mo, K., Guibas, L.J.: PointNet: deep learning on point sets for 3D classification and segmentation. In: Conference on Computer Vision and Pattern Recognition, pp. 652–660 (2017)

30. Qi, C.R., Yi, L., Su, H., Guibas, L.J.: PointNet++: deep hierarchical feature learning on point sets in a metric space. In: Neural Information Processing Systems (2017)

31. Rao, Y., Liu, B., Wei, Y., Lu, J., Hsieh, C.J., Zhou, J.: RandomRooms: unsupervised pre-training from synthetic shapes and randomized layouts for 3D object detection. In: International Conference on Computer Vision, pp. 3283–3292 (2021)

32. Rozenberszki, D., Litany, O., Dai, A.: Language-grounded indoor 3D semantic segmentation in the wild. arXiv preprint arXiv:2204.07761 (2022)

33. Sanghi, A.: Info3D: representation learning on 3D objects using mutual information maximization and contrastive learning. In: Vedaldi, A., Bischof, H., Brox, T., Frahm, J.-M. (eds.) ECCV 2020. LNCS, vol. 12374, pp. 626–642. Springer, Cham (2020). https://doi.org/10.1007/978-3-030-58526-6_37

34. Sauder, J., Sievers, B.: Self-supervised deep learning on point clouds by reconstructing space. In: Neural Information Processing Systems (2019)

35. Schult, J., Engelmann, F., Kontogianni, T., Leibe, B.: DualconvMesh-net: joint geodesic and Euclidean convolutions on 3D meshes. In: Conference on Computer Vision and Pattern Recognition, pp. 8612–8622 (2020)

36. Song, S., Lichtenberg, S.P., Xiao, J.: Sun RGB-D: a RGB-D scene understanding benchmark suite. In: Conference on Computer Vision and Pattern Recognition, pp. 567–576 (2015)
37. Song, S., Xiao, J.: Deep sliding shapes for amodal 3D object detection in RGB-D images. In: Conference on Computer Vision and Pattern Recognition, pp. 808–816 (2016)
38. Su, H., Maji, S., Kalogerakis, E., Learned-Miller, E.: Multi-view convolutional neural networks for 3D shape recognition. In: International Conference on Computer Vision, pp. 945–953 (2015)
39. Wang, H., Liu, Q., Yue, X., Lasenby, J., Kusner, M.J.: Unsupervised point cloud pre-training via occlusion completion. In: International Conference on Computer Vision, pp. 9782–9792 (2021)
40. Wang, P.S., Yang, Y.Q., Zou, Q.F., Wu, Z., Liu, Y., Tong, X.: Unsupervised 3D learning for shape analysis via multiresolution instance discrimination, vol. 35, pp. 2773–2781 (2021)
41. Wu, Z., et al.: 3D shapenets: a deep representation for volumetric shapes. In: Conference on Computer Vision and Pattern Recognition, pp. 1912–1920 (2015)
42. Xie, Q., et al.: MlcvNet: multi-level context votenet for 3D object detection. In: Conference on Computer Vision and Pattern Recognition, pp. 10447–10456 (2020)
43. Xie, S., Gu, J., Guo, D., Qi, C.R., Guibas, L., Litany, O.: PointContrast: unsupervised pre-training for 3D point cloud understanding. In: Vedaldi, A., Bischof, H., Brox, T., Frahm, J.-M. (eds.) ECCV 2020. LNCS, vol. 12348, pp. 574–591. Springer, Cham (2020). https://doi.org/10.1007/978-3-030-58580-8_34
44. Yi, L., Zhao, W., Wang, H., Sung, M., Guibas, L.J.: GSPN: generative shape proposal network for 3D instance segmentation in point cloud. In: Conference on Computer Vision and Pattern Recognition, pp. 3947–3956 (2019)
45. Zhang, B., Wonka, P.: Point cloud instance segmentation using probabilistic embeddings. In: Conference on Computer Vision and Pattern Recognition, pp. 8883–8892 (2021)
46. Zhang, Z., Girdhar, R., Joulin, A., Misra, I.: Self-supervised pretraining of 3D features on any point-cloud. In: International Conference on Computer Vision, pp. 10252–10263 (2021)
47. Zhang, Z., Sun, B., Yang, H., Huang, Q.: H3DNet: 3D object detection using hybrid geometric primitives. In: Vedaldi, A., Bischof, H., Brox, T., Frahm, J.-M. (eds.) ECCV 2020. LNCS, vol. 12357, pp. 311–329. Springer, Cham (2020). https://doi.org/10.1007/978-3-030-58610-2_19

Few '*Zero Level Set*'-Shot Learning of Shape Signed Distance Functions in Feature Space

Amine Ouasfi and Adnane Boukhayma[(✉)]

Inria, Univ. Rennes, CNRS, IRISA, M2S, Rennes, France
adnane.boukhayma@gmail.com

Abstract. We explore a new idea for learning based shape reconstruction from a point cloud, based on the recently popularized implicit neural shape representations. We cast the problem as a few-shot learning of implicit neural signed distance functions in feature space, that we approach using gradient based meta-learning. We use a convolutional encoder to build a feature space given the input point cloud. An implicit decoder learns to predict signed distance values given points represented in this feature space. Setting the input point cloud, i.e. samples from the target shape function's zero level set, as the support (i.e. context) in few-shot learning terms, we train the decoder such that it can adapt its weights to the underlying shape of this context with a few (5) tuning steps. We thus combine two types of implicit neural network conditioning mechanisms simultaneously for the first time, namely feature encoding and meta-learning. Our numerical and qualitative evaluation shows that in the context of implicit reconstruction from a sparse point cloud, our proposed strategy, i.e. meta-learning in feature space, outperforms existing alternatives, namely standard supervised learning in feature space, and meta-learning in euclidean space, while still providing fast inference.

1 Introduction

One of the driving motives behind the ongoing research in 3D computer vision is enabling machines to reason about and understand 3D given limited observations in the same way we humans can evidently do. This ability is in turn crucial for most downstream 3D based computer vision and machine learning tasks. A popular instance of this ability is manifested in the problem of full 3D shape reconstruction from a sparse incomplete point cloud. The prominence of this problem is additionally due to the ubiquity of such partial inputs, either as acquired through the increasingly accessible 3D scanning technologies, or being an intermediate output of numerous classical computer vision algorithms such as Structure from Motion or Multi-View Stereo. Classical solutions to this problem

---

Supplementary Information The online version contains supplementary material available at https://doi.org/10.1007/978-3-031-19824-3_33.

such as Poisson surface reconstruction [31] still offer competitive reconstruction performances from dense point sets. However, as the inputs get sparser and less complete, learning based approaches become naturally more suitable to the task by virtue of their capacity to reason about shapes more globally and inpaint missing information based on previously seen examples.

A class of the these learning based approaches that emerged recently proposes to represent shapes in the form of an implicit function whose zero level set coincides with the surface, parameterised by a neural network. Compared to their traditional alternatives, these representations offer many advantages, most notably enabling modelling shapes with variable topology unlike point clouds and meshes, and operating virtually at infinite spatial resolution unlike voxel grids. In practice, these shape functions are typically multi layer perceptrons mapping the domain to the co-domain, i.e. 3D euclidean space to occupancies or signed distances. The zero level set of the inferred field can be rendered differentiably through e.g. variants of ray marching [27] and tessellated into explicit meshes with e.g. Marching Cubes [43]. Coupling these implicit neural functions with a conditioning mechanism allows generalization across multiple shapes. For instance, combining their inputs with features generated from an additional encoder network yields single forward pass inference models that can learn to reconstruct from various input modalities. In particular, recent models [13,52] obtaining state-of-the-art performances on reconstruction from point cloud benchmarks [10] use a convolutional encoder that builds a feature embedding for euclidean points given the input point cloud. The implicit neural shape function learns to map these points from that feature space to their occupancy or signed distance values. These models are trained using dense points sampled near the surface with corresponding ground-truth singed distance or occupancy values. Our aim here is to improve the performance of such models with negligible additional test-time computational cost.

As obtaining larger training data corpora remains prohibitive in 3D, most recent advances in this avenue focus on revamping the models, e.g. their architectures [58], input representations [13,52,64], training objectives [25,38], and training procedures [18], while remaining within the standard supervised learning paradigm. Conversely, we propose here to cast the problem of surface reconstruction from a point cloud, with an encoder endowed implicit neural function, as a few-shot learning problem.

Beyond merely using the input point cloud in a single encoding forward pass for inference, we observe that we can additionally further fine-tune the conditioned shape function using the point cloud elements as training samples [25], as they naturally belong to the surface and hence can be used to further overfit the shape signed distance function with their zero target values. To ensure this fine-tuning improves the initial result and that it is initialized from optimal shape function weights, we formalize it in a more principled learning strategy that is few-shot learning [21,61,69]. Each shape is represented by a support set: the points of the input point cloud, and a query set: the dense pre-sampled training points. For a given shape, the objective is to optimize predictions on the query set, i.e. adapt the shape function to the current shape, using the support set. We implement this strategy using gradient based meta-learning, namely the

MAML algorithm [21]. At every training step on a given shape, the adaptation consists in back-propagating the loss on the sparse support at the surface for a few iterations (5 steps). The main shape function's parameters are then updated by back-propagating the loss of the adapted shape function on the dense query set. Notice that by representing points in feature space during this process, we combine two types of implicit shape function conditioning through both the encoder and meta-learning for the first time.

Using standard test beds we show that our approach outperforms comparable baselines in various 3D shape reconstruction metrics, and we provide qualitative results that support this as well. Through our experiments, we show that using few-shot leaning in feature space improves on both standard supervised learning in feature space (IF-Nets [13]) and few-shot learning in euclidean space (MetaSDF [57]), both in single and multi-class shape setups for shape reconstruction from a sparse point cloud (less than 3k input points). The performance gap w.r.t. our standard supervised learning baseline increases even further with coarser inputs. We note that we follow the same experimental data setup as in our baselines IF-Nets and MetaSDF. We also point that while we use IF-Nets as our backbone model in this work, this idea could be extended to any convolutional encoder equipped implicit neural shape network.

2   Related Work

We review in this section work that we deemed most relevant to the context of our contribution.

Traditional Shape Representations.   Perhaps an intuitive way to categorize 3D shape representations within deep learning frameworks is into intrinsic and extrinsic representations. Intrinsic representations are efficient in that they are discretizations of the shape itself. however when represented explicitly, as in meshes [30,70] or point clouds [20], they are inherently limited to a fixed topology, which is unpractical for generating varying shape objects and classes. Other forms of intrinsic representations include combining 2D patches [17,26,73], 3D shape primitives such as cuboids [67,81], planes [39] and Gaussians [24]. However patches induce discontinuities, and the approximation quality of primitive shapes remains limited by their simplicity. Extrinsic representations on the other hand model the 3D space containing the shape of interest. The most adopted one to date has been voxel grids [75,76], being a natural extension of 2D pixels to 3D. Nonetheless, the cubic memory cost in voxel grid resolution limits the ability to represent details. Sparse voxel representations such as octrees [55,65,71] can help alleviate these memory efficiency issues albeit with complex implementations.

Implicit Neural Shape Representations.   Recent years have seen a surge in extrinsic implicit neural shape representations for modelling 3D objects and scenes. Thanks to their ability to continuously represent detailed shapes with arbitrary topologies in a memory-efficient way, these representations remedy many of the shortcomings of the aforementioned traditional alternatives, and are currently drawing increasing attention both in 3D shape and appearance modelling (e.g. [32,46,78]). Implicit neural shape models are typically parameterized with MLPs that map 3D space to occupancy [45], signed [50] or unsigned distances [14] relative to the shape. Different forms of training supervision have been proposed, the most common one being 3D points pre-sampled around the surface, with weaker forms of supervision such as 2D segmentation masks through a 2D based SDF lower bound [37], or color and depth images [32,48,78] through differentiable rendering [29,29,42]. Recent contributions in this area include learning octree scafolded implicit mooving least squares [41], representing shapes as an implicit template and an implicit warp [80], and implicit/explicit hybrid representations [11,16,79] based on differentiable space partitioning.

Conditioning Implicit Neural Shape Models.   Implicit shape models require conditioning mechanisms to represent more than a single shape. The mechanisms explored so far include concatenation, batch normalization, hypernetworks [58–60] and meta-learning [57]. Concatenation like conditioning was first introduced through a single latent code [12,45,50], and subsequently improved through the use of local features [13,23,28,52,62,66].

Current methods that meta-learn implicit 3D neural representations use gradient based meta-learning (e.g. MAML [21], Reptile [47]) to learn a meta-radiance field that can be adapted from images [22,63], or a meta-SDF that can be adapted from both zero level set and random domain samples [57]. In contrast to these methods, we propose here to combine encoder-based local feature concatenation conditioning and meta-learning conditioning in the same model, performing implicit reconstruction from a sparse point cloud. We note also that in the work by Sitzmann et al., the meta-learning conditioning requires many surface samples (10k new points sampled at each of the 5 MAML iterations = 50k pts). Differently, we extend this idea to a true few-shot reconstruction setup (300 or 3k fixed input points) and multi shape class for the first time, and show that it can only scale thusly in feature space.

Reconstruction from a Point Cloud.   Among classical solutions to this task, combinatorial approaches define shapes with a space partitioning based on the input points, using e.g. alpha shapes [4] Voronoi diagrams [1] or triangulation [8,40,54]. Alternatively, implicit function based approaches use the point samples to define a function whose zero level set approximates the surface, through fitting e.g. radial basis functions [7], Gaussian kernels [56], piece-wise polynomials [49], moving least-squares [34,41], or by solving a Poisson equation [31]. Closer to our scope, recent work proposes to obtain these implicit functions through deep learning. These include two families of work: supervised and unsupervised ones.

For the latter, a neural network is fitted to the raw input point cloud without any further supervision. Among contributions in this area, Gropp et al. [25] introduces a regularization on the function's spatial gradient based on the Eikonal equation. Atzmon et al. learns a signed distance function from unsigned distance supervision [2], and further supervises the spatial gradient of the function using point normals [3]. Ma et al. [44] supervises the training through expressing the nearest neighbor on the surface as a function of the neural signed distance and its

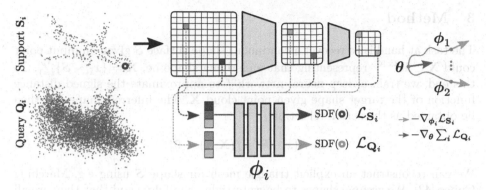

Fig. 1. Overview of our method. Our input is a sparse point cloud (Support $\mathbf{S}_i$) and our output is an implicit neural SDF f. f is a neural network comprised of a convolutional encoder (top in gray) and an MLP decoder (bottom in gray). The decoder predicts SDF values for 3D points (red/blue circles) through their spatially sampled features (squares in shades of red/blue) from the encoder's activation maps. Following a gradient-based few-shot learning algorithm (MAML [21]), we learn a meta-decoder in encoder feature space, parameterized with $\boldsymbol{\theta}$, that can quickly adapt to a new shape, i.e. new parameters ϕ_i, given its support. This is achieved by iterating per-shape 5-step adaptation gradient descent (orange arrow) using the support loss $\mathcal{L}_{\mathbf{S}_i}$, and one-step meta gradient-descent (green arrow) by back-propagating the Query set ($\mathbf{Q}_i$) loss $\mathcal{L}_{\mathbf{Q}_i}$ evaluated with the specialized parameters ϕ_i w.r.t. the meta-parameters $\boldsymbol{\theta}$. At test time, 5 fine-tuning iterations are performed similarly starting from the converged meta-model to evaluate f. (Color figure online)

spatial gradient. All of the aforementioned methods benefit from efficient gradient computation through back-propagation in the implicit neural function. [58] introduces periodic activations. [74] proposes to learn infinitely wide shallow ReLU networks as random feature kernels. Lipman [38] formalizes a loss ensuring the function converges to occupancy while its log transform converges to a distance function.

Supervised methods on the other hand assume a training dataset of shapes with ground-truth signed distance or occupancy values for dense space samples i.e. points. Auto-decoding based methods e.g. [9,28,50,66] require test time optimization to fit the implicit function's features to the observed point cloud, which can take several seconds for a simple object. Conversely, encoder-decoder based approaches enable faster single forward pass inference and superior generalization. For these approaches, pooling-based set encoders (e.g. PointNet [53]) were first proposed [12,19,23,45], but they have been shown to underfit for large and detailed inputs. More recently, convolutional encoders [13,41,52] enable access to more expressive local point features and incorporate inductive biases such as translational equivariance, thus enabling fine-grained implicit reconstruction. We propose here to extend such supervised convolutional encoder-decoder models to a few-shot setting to further improve their reconstruction abilities from a sparse point cloud input, while still offering fast inference unlike auto-decoding.

3   Method

The task at hand is to recover a continuous shape surface $\mathcal{S}$ given an input point could $\mathbf{X} \subset \mathbb{R}^{3 \times N_p}$ representing that underlying shape i.e. $\mathbf{X} = \{x_i \sim \mathcal{S}\}_{i=1}^{N_p}$. To this end, we train a deep neural network f to approximate the signed distance function of the target shape given point cloud $\mathbf{X}$. The inferred shape can then be obtained as the zero level set of f:

$$\hat{\mathcal{S}} = \{x \in \mathbb{R}^3 \mid f(\mathbf{X}, x) = 0\}. \tag{1}$$

We can reconstruct an explicit triangle mesh for shape $\hat{\mathcal{S}}$ using e.g. Marching Cubes [43]. We assume shapes to be watertight manifolds, and that they are all normalized into a domain $\Omega \subset \mathbb{R}^3$.

3.1   The Base Model

For our neural network f, we use an encoder-decoder architecture that follows the model introduced by Chibane et al. [13]. Such models (e.g. [13,52]) combining local features extracted with convolutional encoders with implicit decoders have been shown to yield superior performances in the class of single forward pass prediction methods for surface reconstruction. Differently from [13], we note that we learn signed distance instead of occupancy functions.

As illustrated in Fig. 1, The encoder takes as input point cloud $\mathbf{X}$ and produces spatial feature maps. In order to apply this 3D convolutional network to the point cloud, the latter is first voxelized into a discrete 3D grid in $\mathbb{R}^{N \times N \times N}$ (cf. Fig. 2), N being the input spatial resolution. It then passes through successive convolutional down-sampling blocks resulting in n multi-scale deep feature grids $\mathbf{F}_1, \ldots, \mathbf{F}_n$, where $\mathbf{F}_k \in \mathbb{R}^{C_k \times N_k \times N_k \times N_k}$. The feature map channels C_k increase with the encoder's depth while their resolution decreases $N_k = N/2^{k-1}$. The shallow features represent local details while the deeper ones account for more global shape variation. Given a 3D point $x \in \Omega$, we can extract its encoder generated features using trilinear interpolation. We define this process with a neural function $\Psi_{\mathbf{X}} : \Omega \to \mathbb{R}^{C_1} \times \cdots \times \mathbb{R}^{C_n}$ such that:

$$\Psi_{\mathbf{X}}(x) = (\mathbf{F}_1(x), \ldots, \mathbf{F}_n(x)). \tag{2}$$

The decoder is tasked with predicting the signed distance to the ground-truth shape $\mathcal{S}$ for a given 3D point x. It uses the features obtained with the encoder as input point representation. It consists of a MLP with ReLU non-linearities and a final Tanh activation, and we denote it as $\Phi : \mathbb{R}^{C_1} \times \cdots \times \mathbb{R}^{C_n} \to \mathbb{R}$. Hence we can express the approximated signed distance function given a point cloud $\mathbf{X}$ as follows:

$$f(\mathbf{X}, x) = \Phi \circ \Psi_{\mathbf{X}}(x). \tag{3}$$

In standard supervised learning, this network is trained by back-propagating the prediction loss over a set of training points $\mathbf{Y} \subset \Omega$ per training shape using their respective pre-computed ground-truth signed distance values. These dense point sets are typically built by sampling near the ground-truth surface $\mathcal{S}$, i.e. sampling points on the surface and offsetting them with normally distributed displacements:

$$\mathbf{Y} = \{x + n : x \sim \mathcal{S}, n \sim \mathcal{N}(0, \mathbf{\Sigma})\}, \tag{4}$$

where $\mathbf{\Sigma} = \text{diag}(\sigma) \in \mathbb{R}^{3 \times 3}$ is a diagonal covariance matrix. An illustrative example of such a set can be seen in the bottom left of Fig. 1.

3.2 Few-Shot Learning in Feature Space

We would like to build a model f that can learn to adapt to a new shape $\mathcal{S}$ given limited observations, namely the input point cloud $\mathbf{X}$. While the network is already conditioned to the input $\mathbf{X}$ through the encoder in the standard supervised learning regime e.g. [13,52], we seek here to adapt it even further to that input through meta-learning. Let us recall that for each training shape $\mathcal{S}_i$ we have two sets of points available: $\mathbf{X}_i$ the sparse input point cloud at the surface, and $\mathbf{Y}_i$ the dense point set sampled near the ground-truth surface. Corresponding ground-truth signed distances are available for both of these sets as well. However at test time, only $\mathbf{X}_i$ is available.

Support and Query Sets. We position ourselves in a meta-learning based few-shot learning setup [21,61,69]. Traditionally, a network is trained to adapt to a new task given limited training samples in this setup. A task is defined with a loss, a support (or context) set and a query set. These sets are input-target pairs for the given task. The model is trained to perform tasks on their query sets, after being adapted to them through e.g. metric learning [69] or gradient descent [21] on their respective limited support sets. We adopt the same strategy, where a task consists in learning the signed distance function f for a given shape $\mathcal{S}_i$. We define the support set as the pairs made of the points of the input point cloud and their corresponding ground-truth signed distances, as such a set is available at test time:

$$\mathbf{S}_i = \{(x, s) : x \in \mathbf{X}_i, s := \text{SDF}(x)\}. \tag{5}$$
$$= \{(x, 0) : x \in \mathbf{X}_i\}. \tag{6}$$

Since $\mathbf{X}_i$ contains exclusively points from the surface, i.e. the zero level set of the shape function, all ground-truth singed distances are null. We define the query set as the pairs made of the dense points pre-sampled around the surface and their corresponding ground-truth singed distance values:

$$\mathbf{Q}_i = \{(x, s) : x \in \mathbf{Y}_i, s := \text{SDF}(x)\}. \tag{7}$$

Meta-Learning in Feature Space. We apply gradient-based meta-learning to our supervised few-shot shape function learning, in particular the MAML algorithm by Finn et al. [21]. For a given shape $\mathcal{S}_i$, and assuming a pre-trained encoder Ψ, the signed distance function f is obtained through a specialization

Algorithm 1. The training procedure of our model.

Input: Dataset fo shapes $\mathcal{S}_i$, pre-trained encoder Ψ, meta-decoder learning rate β
Output: meta-decoder weights θ, decoder learning rates α
  initialize θ, α
  while not done **do**
    sample batch of shapes $\{\mathcal{S}_i\} := \{(\mathbf{X}_i, \mathbf{Q}_i)\}$
    initialize $\mathcal{L}_\mathbf{Q} \leftarrow 0$
    for $\mathcal{S}_i$ in $\{\mathcal{S}_i\}$ **do**
      initialize $\phi_i \leftarrow \theta$
      for K times **do**
        $\mathcal{L}_{\mathbf{S}_i} = \sum_{x \in \mathbf{X}_i} |\Phi_{\phi_i} \cup \Psi_{\mathbf{A}_i}(x)|$
        $\phi_i \leftarrow \phi_i - \alpha \odot \nabla_{\phi_i} \mathcal{L}_{\mathbf{S}_i}$
      end for
      $\mathcal{L}_\mathbf{Q} \leftarrow \mathcal{L}_\mathbf{Q} + \sum_{(x,s) \in \mathbf{Q}_i} |\Phi_{\phi_i} \circ \Psi_{\mathbf{X}_i}(x) - s|$
    end for
    $(\theta, \alpha) \leftarrow (\theta, \alpha) - \beta \nabla_{\theta, \alpha} \mathcal{L}_\mathbf{Q}$
  end while

---

denoted ϕ_i of the parameters θ of an underlying meta-decoder Φ_θ operating in feature space $\Psi_{\mathbf{X}_i}(\Omega)$:

$$f(\mathbf{X}_i, x) = \Phi_{\phi_i} \circ \Psi_{\mathbf{X}_i}(x). \tag{8}$$

For lower computational and memory costs and a less noisy meta-learning loss (cf. Sect. 4.4), we fix the convolutional encoder Ψ after pre-training it. This encoder is pre-trained by training the base model f in the standard supervised learning regime using the training dataset's query sets $\{\mathbf{Q}_i\}$ for supervision (i.e. standard supervised learning). As such, the meta-learning of model f consists in training the meta-decoder Φ_θ in feature space. Each training step in this process is two fold: First, a fixed number of inner training steps, i.e. adaptation of the meta-decoder Φ_θ into Φ_{ϕ_i}, followed by an outer training step, i.e. update of the meta-decoder Φ_θ. Similarly to Sitzmann et al. [57], we build on the Meta-SGD [35] MAML [21] variant proposed by Li et al., which advocates the use of per-parameter learning rates in the adaptation stage for improved flexibility.

Given a batch of training shapes $\{\mathcal{S}_i\}$, the inner training step of the decoder is performed for each shape $\mathcal{S}_i$ independently. The L_1 loss $\mathcal{L}_{\mathbf{S}_i}$ is computed using the current specialized decoder Φ_{ϕ_i} over the support set $\mathbf{S}_i$ (i.e. $\mathbf{X}_i$), and is back-propagated w.r.t. ϕ_i:

$$\mathcal{L}_{\mathbf{S}_i} = \sum_{x \in \mathbf{X}_i} |\Phi_{\phi_i} \circ \Psi_{\mathbf{X}_i}(x)|, \tag{9}$$

$$\phi_i \leftarrow \phi_i - \alpha \odot \nabla_{\phi_i} \mathcal{L}_{\mathbf{S}_i}, \tag{10}$$

where weights ϕ_i are initialized with the current meta-decoder weights θ for all the batch shapes. α contains the per parameter learning rates, which are learned as part of the outer training loop. $\odot$ symbolizes element-wise product. We note that while the support loss $\mathcal{L}_{\mathbf{S}_i}$ could include additional regularisation such as the Eikonal constraint [25], we keep it simple to limit the computational footprint of the meta-learning.

After K such shape specific adaptation steps, one outer training step is performed for the entire batch of shapes. The L_1 losses $\{\mathcal{L}_{\mathbf{Q}_i}\}$ are computed using

Fig. 2. Visualization of voxelizations at resolutions 32^3 and 128^3 of input point clouds with 300 and 3000 points.

the specialized decoders $\{\Phi_{\phi_i}\}$ over their respective query sets $\{Q_i\}$, and their average is back-propagated w.r.t. the meta-parameters θ and α accordingly:

$$\mathcal{L}_{Q_i} = \sum_{(x,s)\in Q_i} |\Phi_{\phi_i} \circ \Psi_{X_i}(x) - s|, \tag{11}$$

$$(\theta, \alpha) \leftarrow (\theta, \alpha) - \beta \nabla_{\theta,\alpha} \sum_i \mathcal{L}_{Q_i}, \tag{12}$$

where β is a scalar learning rate. For ease of understanding, Algorithm 1 provides a summary of this training procedure.

At test time, given an input X, the inference consists in a forward pass of the model f after a K-step adaptation of the converged meta-decoder Φ_θ. To produce mesh reconstructions, we use the model to predict signed distance values of a grid of points at a desired resolution, and then apply the Marching Cubes [43] algorithm on the inferred signed distance grid.

4   Results

We present in this section our experimental setup and showcase our results. We evaluate our method on both multi-class and single class setups in ShapeNet [10] on reconstruction from a sparse point cloud, and we also show results on the FAUST [5] dataset. We follow the noise-free benchmark in our baselines IF-Nets [13] and MetaSDF [57]. We experiment with two sizes of input point clouds $N_p = 3000$ and $N_p = 300$ similarly to [13], and two voxelization resolutions $N = 128$ and $N = 32$ (Fig. 2) of these point sets. Let us recall that inputs require voxelization due to the 3D convolutional encoder of our base model [13]. We evaluate numerically in terms of Intersection over Union (IoU), L1 ($CD_1 \times 10^{-1}$) and L2 ($CD_2 \times 10^{-3}$) Chamfer distance. We detail the expressions of these metrics in the supplementary material. In summary, our proposed approach outperforms all baselines including the same base model trained in standard supervised learning (IF-Nets [13]), and the decoder of the base model trained through meta-learning (MetaSDF [57]). Results show additionally that our approach is more resilient to coarser inputs compared to IF-Nets. Besides, the performance increase brought by our approach comes with minimal additional computational cost, as inference takes 150 ms for our model, and 60 ms for IF-Nets, on a RTX A4000.

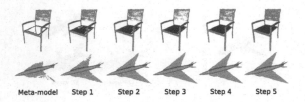

Fig. 3. Visualization of reconstructions from 3000 points throughout the $K = 5$ testing inner-loop iterations in the ShapeNet multi-class setup.

4.1   Implementation Details

The base model follows the architecture in [13], hence we use $n = 6$ feature maps with feature dimensions $C_1 = 1$, $C_2 = 16$, $C_3 = 32$, $C_4 = 64$, $C_5 = 128$ and $C_6 = 128$. Regarding the meta-learning, we use $K = 5$ steps in the inner training loop and we initialize the per-parameter learning rates α with 10^{-6}. In the outer loop, we set the meta-decoder learning rate to $\beta = 10^{-6}$. We train for 100 epochs with batches of 4 shapes, leveraging the N_p training points in the inner loop, and 50k training points in the outer loop per shape. To train the base model in the standard supervised learning mode, we perform a maximum of 50 epochs with a learning rate of 10^{-5}, using batches of 8 shapes with 50k training points per shape. All trainings use the Adam [33] solver on a RTX A4000 in the PyTorch [51] framework. All Marching Cubes reconstructions are done with a 256^3 sized grid.

4.2   Datasets

Similar to prior work we evaluate our method using the ShapeNet benchmark [10] which consists of various instances of 13 different object classes. Similarly to [13], we use the pre-processing by [77] to obtain watertight meshes which enables computing ground-truth signed distances. All meshes are subsequently normalized using their bounding boxes thus fitting inside the domain $\Omega = [-1, 1]^3$. We use the train/test split provided by [13], which is based on the original split of Choy et al. [15] minus 508 distorted shapes due to pre-processing failures. To create the input point cloud $\mathbf{X}$ for a given shape, N_p sized sets of points are randomly pre-sampled from the processed mesh. For the training points with ground-truth signed distances, we pre-sample 100k points near the surface with $\sigma = 0.1$ and $\sigma = 0.01$ (cf. Equ. 4). At training, 50k points are sampled equally from these pre-made two sets to make the per shape training points batch $\mathbf{Y}$. We also use the FAUST dataset [5] for testing. It consists of 100 registered meshes of 10 human body identities in 10 different poses.

4.3   Multiple Shape Class Evaluation

We evaluate here our work and the competition using the entire ShapeNet dataset, which counts 26834 training shapes and 7148 testing ones. For the input

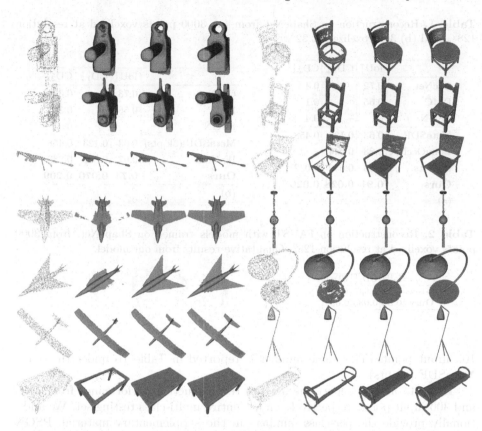

Fig. 4. Qualitative comparison of reconstructions from 3000 points on ShapeNet with our main baseline, i.e. same base model in standard supervised learning. (Input / IF-Nets [13] / **Ours** / Ground-truth).

point cloud size and voxelization resolution of our method, we consider here the two extreme cases for brevity: i.e. 3000 points at 128^3 resolution (Table 1a), and 300 points at 32^3 resolution (Table 1b). We refer the reader to a more detailed analysis in the ablative single class evaluation (Sect. 4.4). We relay the performances of OccNet [45], DMC [36], PSGN [20] as they were reported in [13]. We reproduced the performance of ConvOccNet [52] with 3000 input points in the noise-free benchmark of IF-Nets [13] and we obtained an IoU of 0.86, which is also confirmed by the results of other contemporary work [72]. The authors of ConvOccNet report higher numbers (0.88), where noise is added to the input point cloud. For fairness, we report ConvOccNet's higher numbers (i.e. 0.88 IoU). We train our own IF-Nets [13] model on signed distances and reproduce the same results in the main paper. MetaSDF here refers to our implementation of the work in [57] with 3000 input surface points, i.e. our model without an encoder trained for hundreds of epochs, from which we perform numerous evaluations and pick the best one. We note that original paper [57] only showed results for

Table 1. Reconstruction on ShapeNet from (a) 3000 points voxelized at resolution 128^3., and (b) 300 voxelized at 32^3.

	IoU↑	CD$_1$↓	CD$_2$↓
OccNet	0.72	–	0.4
DMC	0.65	–	0.1
PSGN	–	–	0.4
MetaSDF	0.63	0.123	0.458
ConvOccNet	0.88	0.044	–
IF-Nets	0.88	0.032	0.032
Ours	**0.91**	**0.028**	**0.026**

(a)

	IoU↑	CD$_1$↓	CD$_2$↓
OccNet	0.73	–	0.3
DMC	0.58	–	0.3
PSGN	–	–	0.4
MetaSDF (3k pts)	0.63	0.123	0.458
IF-Nets	0.67	0.091	0.232
Ours	**0.74**	**0.070**	**0.209**

(b)

Table 2. Reconstruction on FAUST with models trained on ShapeNet, from 3000 points voxelized at resolution 128^3. Qualitative results from our model.

	IoU↑	CD$_1$↓	CD$_2$↓
IF-Nets	0.82	0.037	0.060
Ours	**0.84**	**0.035**	**0.051**

10k input points. This same number is reported in Table 1b under the name MetaSDF (3k pts).

Tables 1a and 1b report the average reconstruction performance from 3000 and 300 input points respectively on the entire multi-class testing set. We additionally provide the per-class numbers in the supplementary material. PSGN generates point sets with competitive distances to the ground-truth but does not provide any connectivity (Hence the absence of IoU). DMC's performance is limited by its voxel grid resolution. OccNet performs strongly and almost similarly in the 300 and 3000 input cases, which suggests that pooling set encoders underfit the context. For both input situations and across all metrics, our method outperforms the competition, including convolutional encoder equipped implicit shape models (IF-Nets and ConvOccNet), and our encoder-free meta-learning baseline MetaSDF. We find the performance of the latter particularly underwhelming, which suggests that despite the encouraging single class reconstruction results in [57] from 10k input surface points, such strategy struggles to scale to more challenging settings with multiple classes of shape, sparser point clouds, and under relatively limited training time. When decreasing the input size and voxel resolution in Table 1b, both the encoders of our method and IF-Nets are exposed to very poor inputs (cf. Fig. 2). While the performance of IF-Nets is heavily affected by these coarser inputs, our method is more resilient thanks to the meta-learning addition. In fact, our IoU drops by 18% compared to 23% for the standard supervisedly learned baseline. We additionally show reconstruction results on the FAUST dataset from models trained on ShapeNet in Table 2, where out method outperforms IF-Nets. Note that neither models have seen human shapes nor articulated shapes for that matter in training.

The numerical superiority of our method w.r.t. our closest baseline (IF-Nets) is supported with qualitative comparisons in Fig. 4. We notice that our method manages to recover more thin structures and fine topological features, such as cylindrical holes in rifles, wings in planes, thin flat surfaces in tables, benches and chairs. In addition, we provide examples in Fig. 3 showing the evolution of the reconstruction at various iterations of our inference.

4.4 Single Shape Class Ablation

We show further quantitative evaluations in a single shape class setup on the largest class of ShapeNet, i.e. table, for ablative purposes and also for a more fair comparison to MetaSDF [57]. The table class counts 5364 training shapes and 1679 testing ones. We report numbers for MetaSDF and a pooling set encoder based implicit model (PoinNet enc.) from their paper [57] using 10k input points. We compare multiple variants of our approach. For our method (Ours), the meta-decoder is initialized from the weights of a pre-trained base model. For Ours w/o dec. pret., it is initiated with the standard PyTorch initialization instead. Finally Ours w/o meta learn. (i.e. IF-Nets) is again our base model trained in standard supervised learning.

Tables 3 and 4 show reconstruction results from 3000/300 points at 128^3 and 32^3 input voxel resolution respectively. Even under 10k input points, MetaSDF [57] can yet barely reach our performance on just 300 input points. Most notably, our method improves on the standard supervised learning baseline (Ours w/o meta learn. (i.e. IF-Nets)) across all input sizes and input voxel discretizations for all metrics. While the input point cloud size affects both our method and IF-Nets almost equally, decreasing the encoder's input resolution hinders IF-Nets's performance substantially more severely. In fact, when going from 128^3 to 32^3 resolution inputs, our IoU drops by roughly 14% vs. 20% for IF-Nets for 3000 points, and by 13% vs. 19% for IF-Nets when using 300 points.

Decoder Pre-training.   As witnessed by Tables 3 and 4, while initializing the meta-decoder can improve the performance slightly, it is not crucial for obtaining satisfactory results, which suggests that we learn a proper meta-decoder and not just a fine-tuned base-model.

Encoder Pre-training and Tuning.   As meta-learning both the encoder and decoder is computationally and memory expensive, we only meta-learn the decoder. We found that tuning the encoder during this meta-learning leads to noisy losses, without a clear improvement in the results. In fact, for reconstruction from 3000 points at resolution 128^3 in class table, whilst fixing the encoder yields an IoU of 0.87, tuning it gives a comparable performance (0.86) while requiring more time and memory for training. We found the resulting noisier loss makes it also harder to decide the convergence epoch in this case. Thus we fix the encoder after pre-training it. We pre-train the encoder by training the encoder-decoder in the standard supervised learning setup.

Table 3. Reconstruction on class table of ShapeNet from 3000 (left) and 300 (right) points voxelized at resolution 128^3.

	IoU↑		CD$_1$↓		CD$_2$↓	
PointNet enc. (10k pts)	0.66		–		0.69	
MetaSDF (10k pts)	0.75		–		0.32	
Ours w/o meta learn. (i.e. IF-Nets)	0.82	0.72	0.040	0.057	0.062	0.097
Ours w/o dec. pret	0.80	0.74	0.035	0.057	0.030	0.203
Ours	**0.87**	**0.76**	**0.033**	**0.051**	**0.030**	**0.082**

Table 4. Reconstruction on class table of ShapeNet from 3000 (left) and 300 (right) points voxelized at resolution 32^3.

	IoU↑		CD$_1$↓		CD$_2$↓	
Ours w/o meta learn. (i.e. IF-Nets)	0.65	0.58	0.071	0.092	0.089	0.169
Ours w/o dec. pret	0.73	0.61	0.057	0.083	0.082	0.169
Ours	**0.74**	**0.66**	**0.052**	**0.076**	**0.068**	**0.142**

5   Limitations

As SDFs can only represent closed surfaces, we will experiment next with other representations such as points [6,68] and unsigned distances [14]. Point cloud voxelization (cf. Fig. 2) hinders the expressiveness of the input, thus we will be considering different convolutional encoders subsequently. Furthermore, the MAML algorithm [21] requires computing second-order gradients which raises the memory complexity in training. Finally, we follow here the noise-free benchmarks in our baselines IF-Nets [13] and MetaSDF [57]. Considering noisy and real inputs (e.g. 2.5D, SFM, etc.) is part of our future work.

6   Conclusion

We proposed to perform 3D shape reconstruction from a sparse point cloud using a implicit neural model conditioned with both encoder generated local features and meta-learning simultaneously. Our results demonstrate numerically and qualitatively that this approach improves on its standard supervised learning counterpart with minimal additional test time computational cost, and this performance gap increases for coarser inputs. Future avenues of improvement include tackling more real world downstream tasks such as partial shape reconstruction, making use of normals, meta-learning of reconstruction from images and depth maps through differentiable rendering, and exploring other meta-learning techniques.

References

1. Amenta, N., Choi, S., Kolluri, R.K.: The power crust, unions of balls, and the medial axis transform. Comput. Geom. **19**, 127-153 (2001)
2. Atzmon, M., Lipman, Y.: SAL: Sign agnostic learning of shapes from raw data. In: CVPR (2020)
3. Atzmon, M., Lipman, Y.: SALD: Sign agnostic learning with derivatives. In: ICML (2020)
4. Bernardini, F., Mittleman, J., Rushmeier, H., Silva, C., Taubin, G.: The ball-pivoting algorithm for surface reconstruction. Trans. Vis. Comput. Graph. **5**, 349-359 (1999)
5. Bogo, F., Romero, J., Loper, M., Black, M.J.: FAUST: Dataset and evaluation for 3D mesh registration. In: CVPR (2014)
6. Cai, R., et al.: Learning gradient fields for shape generation. In: Vedaldi, A., Bischof, H., Brox, T., Frahm, J.-M. (eds.) ECCV 2020. LNCS, vol. 12348, pp. 364–381. Springer, Cham (2020). https://doi.org/10.1007/978-3-030-58580-8_22
7. Carr, J.C., et al.: Reconstruction and representation of 3d objects with radial basis functions. In: SIGGRAPH (2001)
8. Cazals, F., Giesen, J.: Effective Computational Geometry for Curves and Surfaces (2006)
9. Chabra, R., et al.: Deep local shapes: learning local SDF priors for detailed 3D reconstruction. In: Vedaldi, A., Bischof, H., Brox, T., Frahm, J.-M. (eds.) ECCV 2020. LNCS, vol. 12374, pp. 608–625. Springer, Cham (2020). https://doi.org/10.1007/978-3-030-58526-6_36
10. Chang, A.X., et al.: ShapeNet: An information-rich 3D model repository. arXiv preprint arXiv:1512.03012 (2015)
11. Chen, Z., Tagliasacchi, A., Zhang, H.: Bsp-net: Generating compact meshes via binary space partitioning. In: Proceedings of the IEEE/CVF Conference on Computer Vision and Pattern Recognition (2020)
12. Chen, Z., Zhang, H.: Learning implicit fields for generative shape modeling. In: CVPR (2019)
13. Chibane, J., Alldieck, T., Pons-Moll, G.: Implicit functions in feature space for 3d shape reconstruction and completion. In: CVPR (2020)
14. Chibane, J., Mir, A., Pons-Moll, G.: Neural unsigned distance fields for implicit function learning. In: NeurIPS (2020)
15. Choy, C.B., Xu, D., Gwak, J.Y., Chen, K., Savarese, S.: 3D-R2N2: a unified approach for single and multi-view 3D object reconstruction. In: Leibe, B., Matas, J., Sebe, N., Welling, M. (eds.) ECCV 2016. LNCS, vol. 9912, pp. 628–644. Springer, Cham (2016). https://doi.org/10.1007/978-3-319-46484-8_38
16. Deng, B., Genova, K., Yazdani, S., Bouaziz, S., Hinton, G., Tagliasacchi, A.: CvxNet: Learnable convex decomposition. In: CVPR (2020)
17. Deprelle, T., Groueix, T., Fisher, M., Kim, V.G., Russell, B.C., Aubry, M.: Learning elementary structures for 3D shape generation and matching. In: NeurIPS (2019)
18. Duan, Y., Zhu, H., Wang, H., Yi, L., Nevatia, R., Guibas, L.J.: Curriculum DeepSDF. In: Vedaldi, A., Bischof, H., Brox, T., Frahm, J.-M. (eds.) ECCV 2020. LNCS, vol. 12353, pp. 51–67. Springer, Cham (2020). https://doi.org/10.1007/978-3-030-58598-3_4
19. Erler, P., Guerrero, P., Ohrhallinger, S., Mitra, N.J., Wimmer, M.: POINTS2SURF learning implicit surfaces from point clouds. In: Vedaldi, A., Bischof, H., Brox, T.,

Frahm, J.-M. (eds.) ECCV 2020. LNCS, vol. 12350, pp. 108–124. Springer, Cham (2020). https://doi.org/10.1007/978-3-030-58558-7_7

20. Fan, H., Su, H., Guibas, L.J.: A point set generation network for 3D object reconstruction from a single image. In: CVPR (2017)
21. Finn, C., Abbeel, P., Levine, S.: Model-agnostic meta-learning for fast adaptation of deep networks. In: ICML (2017)
22. Gao, C., Shih, Y., Lai, W.S., Liang, C.K., Huang, J.B.: Portrait neural radiance fields from a single image. arXiv preprint arXiv:2012.05903 (2020)
23. Genova, K., Cole, F., Sud, A., Sarna, A., Funkhouser, T.: Local deep implicit functions for 3D shape. In: CVPR (2020)
24. Genova, K., Cole, F., Vlasic, D., Sarna, A., Freeman, W.T., Funkhouser, T.: Learning shape templates with structured implicit functions. In: ICCV (2019)
25. Gropp, A., Yariv, L., Haim, N., Atzmon, M., Lipman, Y.: Implicit geometric regularization for learning shapes. In: ICML (2020)
26. Groueix, T., Fisher, M., Kim, V.G., Russell, B.C., Aubry, M.: A papier-mâché approach to learning 3D surface generation. In: CVPR (2018)
27. Hart, J.C.: Sphere tracing: A geometric method for the antialiased ray tracing of implicit surfaces. Vis. Comput. **12**, (1996)
28. Jiang, C., Sud, A., Makadia, A., Huang, J., Nießner, M., Funkhouser, T., et al.: Local implicit grid representations for 3D scenes. In: CVPR (2020)
29. Jiang, Y., Ji, D., Han, Z., Zwicker, M.: SDFDiff: Differentiable rendering of signed distance fields for 3d shape optimization. In: CVPR (2020)
30. Kato, H., Ushiku, Y., Harada, T.: Neural 3D mesh renderer. In: CVPR (2018)
31. Kazhdan, M., Hoppe, H.: Screened poisson surface reconstruction. ACM Transa. Graph. **32**, 1–13 (2013)
32. Kellnhofer, P., Jebe, L.C., Jones, A., Spicer, R., Pulli, K., Wetzstein, G.: Neural lumigraph rendering. In: CVPR (2021)
33. Kingma, D.P., Ba, J.: Adam: A method for stochastic optimization. In: ICLR (2015)
34. Kolluri, R.: Provably good moving least squares. ACM Trans. Algorithm **4**, 1–25 (2008)
35. Li, Z., Zhou, F., Chen, F., Li, H.: Meta-SGD: Learning to learn quickly for few-shot learning. In: NeurIPS (2017)
36. Liao, Y., Donne, S., Geiger, A.: Deep marching cubes: Learning explicit surface representations. In: CVPR (2018)
37. Lin, C.H., Wang, C., Lucey, S.: SDF-SRN: Learning signed distance 3D object reconstruction from static images. In: NeurIPS (2020)
38. Lipman, Y.: Phase transitions, distance functions, and implicit neural representations. In: ICML (2021)
39. Liu, C., Yang, J., Ceylan, D., Yumer, E., Furukawa, Y.: PlaneNet: Piece-wise planar reconstruction from a single RGB image. In: CVPR (2018)
40. Liu, M., Zhang, X., Su, H.: Meshing point clouds with predicted intrinsic-extrinsic ratio guidance. In: Vedaldi, A., Bischof, H., Brox, T., Frahm, J.-M. (eds.) ECCV 2020. LNCS, vol. 12353, pp. 68–84. Springer, Cham (2020). https://doi.org/10.1007/978-3-030-58598-3_5
41. Liu, S.L., Guo, H.X., Pan, H., Wang, P.S., Tong, X., Liu, Y.: Deep implicit moving least-squares functions for 3D reconstruction. In: CVPR (2021)
42. Liu, S., Saito, S., Chen, W., Li, H.: Learning to infer implicit surfaces without 3D supervision. In: NeurIPS (2019)
43. Lorensen, W.E., Cline, H.E.: Marching cubes: A high resolution 3D surface construction algorithm. In: SIGGRAPH (1987)

44. Ma, B., Han, Z., Liu, Y.S., Zwicker, M.: Neural-pull: Learning signed distance functions from point clouds by learning to pull space onto surfaces. In: ICML (2021)
45. Mescheder, L., Oechsle, M., Niemeyer, M., Nowozin, S., Geiger, A.: Occupancy networks: Learning 3D reconstruction in function space. In: CVPR (2019)
46. Mildenhall, B., Srinivasan, P.P., Tancik, M., Barron, J.T., Ramamoorthi, R., Ng, R.: NeRF: representing scenes as neural radiance fields for view synthesis. In: Vedaldi, A., Bischof, H., Brox, T., Frahm, J.-M. (eds.) ECCV 2020. Nerf: Representing scenes as neural radiance fields for view synthesis, vol. 12346, pp. 405–421. Springer, Cham (2020). https://doi.org/10.1007/978-3-030-58452-8_24
47. Nichol, A., Achiam, J., Schulman, J.: On first-order meta-learning algorithms. arXiv preprint arXiv:1803.02999 (2018)
48. Niemeyer, M., Mescheder, L., Oechsle, M., Geiger, A.: Differentiable volumetric rendering: Learning implicit 3D representations without 3D supervision. In: CVPR (2020)
49. Ohtake, Y., Belyaev, A., Alexa, M.: Sparse low-degree implicit surfaces with applications to high quality rendering, feature extraction, and smoothing. In: SGP (2005)
50. Park, J.J., Florence, P., Straub, J., Newcombe, R., Lovegrove, S.: DeepSDF: Learning continuous signed distance functions for shape representation. In: CVPR (2019)
51. Paszke, A., et al.: PyTorch: An imperative style, high-performance deep learning library. In: NeurIPS (2019)
52. Peng, S., Niemeyer, M., Mescheder, L., Pollefeys, M., Geiger, A.: Convolutional occupancy networks. In: Vedaldi, A., Bischof, H., Brox, T., Frahm, J.-M. (eds.) ECCV 2020. LNCS, vol. 12348, pp. 523–540. Springer, Cham (2020). https://doi.org/10.1007/978-3-030-58580-8_31
53. Qi, C.R., Su, H., Mo, K., Guibas, L.J.: PointNet: Deep learning on point sets for 3D classification and segmentation. In: CVPR (2017)
54. Rakotosaona, M.J., Aigerman, N., Mitra, N., Ovsjanikov, M., Guerrero, P.: Differentiable surface triangulation. In: SIGGRAPH Asia (2021)
55. Riegler, G., Osman Ulusoy, A., Geiger, A.: Octnet: Learning deep 3D representations at high resolutions. In: CVPR (2017)
56. Schölkopf, B., Giesen, J., Spalinger, S.: Kernel methods for implicit surface modeling. In: NeurIPS (2004)
57. Sitzmann, V., Chan, E.R., Tucker, R., Snavely, N., Wetzstein, G.: MetaSDF: Meta-learning signed distance functions. In: NeurIPS (2020)
58. Sitzmann, V., Martel, J., Bergman, A., Lindell, D., Wetzstein, G.: Implicit neural representations with periodic activation functions. In: NeurIPS (2020)
59. Sitzmann, V., Rezchikov, S., Freeman, W.T., Tenenbaum, J.B., Durand, F.: Light field networks: Neural scene representations with single-evaluation rendering. In: NeurIPS (2021)
60. Sitzmann, V., Zollhoefer, M., Wetzstein, G.: Scene representation networks: Continuous 3D-structure-aware neural scene representations. In: NeurIPS (2019)
61. Snell, J., Swersky, K., Zemel, R.S.: Prototypical networks for few-shot learning. In: NeurIPS (2017)
62. Takikawa, T., et al.: Neural geometric level of detail: Real-time rendering with implicit 3D shapes. In: CVPR (2021)
63. Tancik, M., et al.: Learned initializations for optimizing coordinate-based neural representations. In: CVPR (2021)
64. Tancik, M., et al.: Fourier features let networks learn high frequency functions in low dimensional domains. In: NeurIPS (2020)

65. Tatarchenko, M., Dosovitskiy, A., Brox, T.: Octree generating networks: Efficient convolutional architectures for high-resolution 3D outputs. In: ICCV (2017)
66. Tretschk, E., Tewari, A., Golyanik, V., Zollhöfer, M., Stoll, C., Theobalt, C.: Patch-Nets: patch-based generalizable deep implicit 3d shape representations. In: Vedaldi, A., Bischof, H., Brox, T., Frahm, J.-M. (eds.) ECCV 2020. LNCS, vol. 12361, pp. 293–309. Springer, Cham (2020). https://doi.org/10.1007/978-3-030-58517-4_18
67. Tulsiani, S., Su, H., Guibas, L.J., Efros, A.A., Malik, J.: Learning shape abstractions by assembling volumetric primitives. In: CVPR (2017)
68. Venkatesh, R., et al.: Deep implicit surface point prediction networks. In: CVPR (2021)
69. Vinyals, O., Blundell, C., Lillicrap, T., Wierstra, D., et al.: Matching networks for one shot learning. In: NeurIPS (2016)
70. Wang, N., Zhang, Y., Li, Z., Fu, Y., Liu, W., Jiang, Y.-G.: Pixel2Mesh: generating 3D mesh models from single RGB images. In: Ferrari, V., Hebert, M., Sminchisescu, C., Weiss, Y. (eds.) ECCV 2018. LNCS, vol. 11215, pp. 55–71. Springer, Cham (2018). https://doi.org/10.1007/978-3-030-01252-6_4
71. Wang, P.S., Liu, Y., Guo, Y.X., Sun, C.Y., Tong, X.: O-CNN: Octree-based convolutional neural networks for 3D shape analysis. ACM Trans. Graph. **36**, 1–11 (2017)
72. Williams, F., et al.: Neural fields as learnable kernels for 3D reconstruction. In: CVPR (2022)
73. Williams, F., Schneider, T., Silva, C., Zorin, D., Bruna, J., Panozzo, D.: Deep geometric prior for surface reconstruction. In: CVPR (2019)
74. Williams, F., Trager, M., Bruna, J., Zorin, D.: Neural splines: Fitting 3D surfaces with infinitely-wide neural networks. In: CVPR (2021)
75. Wu, J., Zhang, C., Xue, T., Freeman, W.T., Tenenbaum, J.B.: Learning a probabilistic latent space of object shapes via 3D generative-adversarial modeling. In: NeurIPS (2016)
76. Wu, Z., et al.: 3D ShapeNets: a deep representation for volumetric shapes. In: CVPR (2015)
77. Xu, Q., Wang, W., Ceylan, D., Mech, R., Neumann, U.: DISN: Deep implicit surface network for high-quality single-view 3D reconstruction. In: NeurIPS (2019)
78. Yariv, L., et al.: Multiview neural surface reconstruction by disentangling geometry and appearance. In: NeurIPS (2020)
79. Yavartanoo, M., Chung, J., Neshatavar, R., Lee, K.M.: 3DIAS: 3D shape reconstruction with implicit algebraic surfaces. In: ICCV (2021)
80. Zheng, Z., Yu, T., Dai, Q., Liu, Y.: Deep implicit templates for 3D shape representation. In: CVPR (2021)
81. Zou, C., Yumer, E., Yang, J., Ceylan, D., Hoiem, D.: 3D-PRNN: Generating shape primitives with recurrent neural networks. In: CVPR (2017)

Solution Space Analysis of Essential Matrix Based on Algebraic Error Minimization

Gaku Nakano[✉][iD]

NEC Corporation, Kawasaki, Japan
g-nakano@nec.com

Abstract. This paper reports on a solution space analysis of the essential matrix based on algebraic error minimization. Although it has been known since 1988 that an essential matrix has at most 10 real solutions for five-point pairs, the number of solutions in the least-squares case has not been explored. We first derive that the Karush-Kuhn-Tucker conditions of algebraic errors satisfying the Demazure constraints can be represented by a system of polynomial equations without Lagrange multipliers. Then, using computer algebra software, we reveal that the simultaneous equation has at most 220 real solutions, which can be obtained by the Gauss-Newton method, Gröbner basis, and homotopy continuation. Through experiments on synthetic and real data, we quantitatively evaluate the convergence of the proposed and the existing methods to globally optimal solutions. Finally, we visualize a spatial distribution of the global and local minima in 3D space.

Keywords: Essential matrix · Two-view geometry · Structure-from-motion · System of polynomial equations · Gröbner basis · Homotopy continuation

1 Introduction

Two-view geometry is a fundamental problem in computer vision for reconstructing the 3D shape of objects and camera motions using two images [17]. It has been widely used in various applications such as V-SLAM [5,34], novel view synthesis [2,33], visual localization [42,47], city-scale Structure-from-Motion [1,49], and human interaction understanding [20]. Particularly, the most basic form shown in Fig. 1, finding the relative motion between two calibrated cameras, is called the essential matrix estimation. An essential matrix is a rank-deficient 3×3 matrix of which two singular values are equal. Because of this constraint, the essential matrix estimation has been studied for decades.

It has been well known since 1913 that an essential matrix can be obtained from at least five point correspondences [24][1]. In 1988, Demazure [10] proved that

---

[1] English translation: https://arxiv.org/abs/1801.01454.

S. Avidan et al. (Eds.): ECCV 2022, LNCS 13692, pp. 579–595, 2022.
https://doi.org/10.1007/978-3-031-19824-3_34

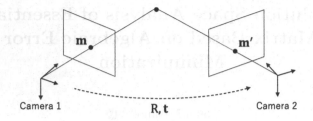

Fig. 1. Relative pose estimation problem.

there are at most 10 solutions in the five-point case. However, 6- [38,39], 7- [17], and 8-point [17] algorithms had been used until a practical 5-point algorithm was first developed by Nister [37] in 2004. The 5-point method was extended to various problems, *e.g.* 3-point with known gravity direction [13,21,36], 5-point with a small motion [44], 6- and 7-point for uncalibrated cameras [19,25, 28,40]. These methods, called minimal solvers, are usually incorporated with RANSAC [12] to remove outliers existing in the input point matches.

On the other hand, the essential matrix estimation for the least-squares case, where given more than five points, has been thought to be a more challenging problem than the minimal case due to the aforementioned constraints of the essential matrix. Many efforts have been extensively devoted to developing a method for solving the constrained least-squares, which can be classified into two categories: locally optimal methods [11,18,23,32] and globally optimal methods [4,7,16,48]. However, unlike the 5-point minimal case, the solution space of the least-square case has not been well investigated in the past. There are still open questions; *How many real solutions are there? Is a solution obtained by a local method the global optimum or a local minimum? Does a global method surely return the global optimum?*

To answer those questions, we analyze the solution space of the essential matrix estimation in the sense of the algebraic error minimization in this paper. We first derive the new KKT (Karush-Kuhn-Tucker) conditions as a system of polynomial equations without Lagrange multipliers. Utilizing an algebraic geometry software, we reveal the number of the solutions in the least-square case. Then, we propose three direct methods for solving the new KKT conditions. Finally, we conduct synthetic and real data evaluations to validate whether the proposed and existing methods provide globally optimal solutions or not.

2   Theoretical Background

The essential matrix E is a 3×3 matrix that gives a constraint on the relative motion and a pair of corresponding point between two images. Let $R \in SO(3)$ and t be the relative rotation matrix and the translation vector, respectively, and $\{m \leftrightarrow m'\}$ an image point correspondence in 3×1 homogeneous coordinates between two calibrated cameras. The essential matrix satisfies

$$m'^{\mathsf{T}} E m = 0, \tag{1}$$

where

$$E = [\mathbf{t}]_\times R, \quad [\mathbf{t}]_\times = \begin{bmatrix} 0 & -t_3 & t_2 \\ t_3 & 0 & -t_1 \\ -t_2 & t_1 & 0 \end{bmatrix}. \tag{2}$$

Since Eq. (1) holds up to any scale of $\mathbf{t}$, the essential matrix E has 5 DoF (Degrees of Freedom). This property is equivalent to that two of its singular values are equal, and the third is zero:

$$E = U \operatorname{diag}(1, 1, 0) \ V^\mathsf{T}. \tag{3}$$

Demazure [10] expressed the above constraint in a matrix form

$$2EE^\mathsf{T}E - \operatorname{tr}(EE^\mathsf{T})E = \mathbf{0}_{3\times 3}. \tag{4}$$

Given more than five point pairs, the essential matrix estimation can be formulated as a non-linear constrained problem

$$\min_E \quad \mathbf{e}^\mathsf{T} M \mathbf{e}$$
$$\text{s.t.} \ \ \|\mathbf{e}\|^2 = 1, \ 2EE^\mathsf{T}E - \operatorname{tr}(EE^\mathsf{T})E = \mathbf{0}_{3\times 3}, \tag{5}$$

where $M = \sum_i (\mathbf{m}'_i \otimes \mathbf{m}_i)(\mathbf{m}'_i \otimes \mathbf{m}_i)^\mathsf{T}$ and $\mathbf{e}$ is a 9-dimensional vector representation of E. The L2 norm constraint is required to avoid the trivial solution $\mathbf{e} = \mathbf{0}$.

The objective function of Eq. (5), $\mathbf{e}^\mathsf{T} M \mathbf{e}$, is called the algebraic error, which is not a geometrically meaningful metric but widely used in computer vision due to its simple form. In this paper, we focus on discussing approaches for finding the global optimum of the algebraic error minimization.

3   Previous Work

In this section, we briefly introduce the existing methods for estimating an essential matrix in the sense of least-squares.

Eight-Point DLT Solver [16]. Ignoring the Demazure constraint, we can reformulate Eq. (5) by a single constrained problem, *i.e.*

$$\min_E \mathbf{e}^\mathsf{T} M \mathbf{e}, \quad \text{s.t.} \ \|\mathbf{e}\|^2 = 1. \tag{6}$$

Using the method of Lagrange multiplier, the solution of the above equation can be written by a linear equation:

$$M \mathbf{e} = \lambda \mathbf{e}, \tag{7}$$

where λ is a Lagrange multiplier and also an eigenvalue of M. Since $\mathbf{e}^\mathsf{T} M \mathbf{e} = \lambda \mathbf{e}^\mathsf{T} \mathbf{e} = \lambda$, the optimal solution $\mathbf{e}$ can be obtained by an eigenvector corresponding to the smallest eigenvalue $\lambda_{\min}$. The optimum of Eq. (6) may not be an essential matrix due to the lack of the Demazure constraint. To ensure the constraint, the singular value correction

$$E \leftarrow U \operatorname{diag}(1, 1, 0) \ V^\mathsf{T} \tag{8}$$

is typically applied as a post-processing. The above procedure is called the DLT (Direct Linear Transform) method and has been regarded as the standard approach for decades because of its simpleness.

Local Parameterization Solver [18]. A straightforward way of satisfying the Demazure constraint is to parameterize an essential matrix by 5 DoF. Two orthogonal matrices U and V can be represented by the exponential map, *i.e.*

$$U = \exp([\mathbf{x}_1]_\times), \quad V = \exp([\mathbf{x}_2]_\times), \tag{9}$$

where $\mathbf{x}_1 = \frac{1}{\sqrt{2}}[x_1, x_2, \frac{x_3}{\sqrt{2}}]^\mathsf{T}$ and $\mathbf{x}_2 = \frac{1}{\sqrt{2}}[x_4, x_5, -\frac{x_3}{\sqrt{2}}]^\mathsf{T}$. Note that U and V share a common variable x_3. An essential matrix is parameterized by

$$E(\mathbf{x}_1, \mathbf{x}_2) = U(\mathbf{x}_1) \operatorname{diag}(1,1,0) V(\mathbf{x}_2)^\mathsf{T}. \tag{10}$$

Thus, Eq. (5) can be rewritten in an unconstrained problem

$$\min_{x_1,\ldots,x_5} \mathbf{e}(\mathbf{x}_1, \mathbf{x}_2)^\mathsf{T} M\, \mathbf{e}(\mathbf{x}_1, \mathbf{x}_2). \tag{11}$$

Eigenvalue Minimization Solver [23]. Another way to satisfy the Demazure constraint is to find a rotation that minimizes the smallest eigenvalue $\lambda_{\min}$. Using Eq. (2), the vector expression $\mathbf{e}$ can be written by

$$\mathbf{e} = A\mathbf{t}, \quad A = \begin{bmatrix} 0 & -r_3 & r_2 \\ r_3 & 0 & -r_1 \\ -r_2 & r_1 & 0 \end{bmatrix}, \tag{12}$$

where r_k denotes the k-th row of R. Equation (5) can be reformulated by

$$\min_{R,t} \quad \mathbf{t}^\mathsf{T} A^\mathsf{T} M A \mathbf{t} \\ \text{s.t. } \|\mathbf{t}\|^2 = 1, \quad R \in SO(3). \tag{13}$$

The optimal translation $\mathbf{t}$ can be given in the same way as the DLT method by the eigenvector associated with the smallest eigenvalue:

$$A^\mathsf{T} M A \mathbf{t} = \lambda_{\min} \mathbf{t}. \tag{14}$$

The 3×3 matrix $A^\mathsf{T} M A$ consists of unknown rotation of 3 DoF. Using the Cayley transform, $R(\mathbf{x}) = (I - [\mathbf{x}]_\times)(I + [\mathbf{x}]_\times)^{-1}$ with $\mathbf{x} = [x_1, x_2, x_3]^\mathsf{T}$, Eq. (13) can be further rewritten by an unconstrained problem

$$\min_{x_1,x_2,x_3} \lambda_{\min}(R(\mathbf{x})). \tag{15}$$

SDP-Relaxation Solver [48]. The above two solvers are locally optimal methods that require a good initial guess to converge to the global optimum. To avoid the convergence to a local minimum, a globally optimal solution was proposed using SDP (Semi-Definite Programming) relaxation. Using the orthogonality condition $R^\mathsf{T} R = I$, Eq. (5) can be rewritten by

$$\min_{e,t} \quad \mathbf{e}^\mathsf{T} M \mathbf{e} \\ \text{s.t. } EE^\mathsf{T} = [\mathbf{t}]_\times [\mathbf{t}]_\times^\mathsf{T}, \quad \|\mathbf{t}\|^2 = 1. \tag{16}$$

The objective and constraints are quadratic with respect to E and t, therefore, the above equation is a non-convex QCQP (Quadratically Constrained Quadratic Program). Letting $X = \begin{bmatrix} e \\ t \end{bmatrix} [e^T t^T]$, we can write the non-convex QCQP by

$$\min_X \quad \mathrm{tr}\left(\begin{bmatrix} M & \\ & 0_{3\times3} \end{bmatrix} X\right) \tag{17}$$
$$\text{s.t. } X \succeq 0, \ \mathrm{tr}(B_i X) = c_i, \ 1 \leq i \leq 7,$$

where $X \succeq 0$ represents that X is positive semi-definite, and B_i and c_i are coefficients corresponding to the quadratic constraints of Eq. (16). The rank constraint $\mathrm{rank}(X) = 1$ is dropped due to NP-hard in Eq. (17), which is called SDP-relaxation. Owing to the relaxation, Eq. (17) becomes a convex optimization that the global optimum can always be obtainable. It should be noted that E and t recovered from X do not strictly satisfy the original constraints in Eq. (16) because generally $\mathrm{rank}(X) > 1$ even for the global optimum of Eq. (17).

4 Analysis of Solution Space

In this section, we first formulate the new KKT conditions, or the first-order optimality conditions, without Lagrange multipliers. Our derivation is inspired by the optimal PnP method [35]. The new KKT conditions are represented as a system of polynomials in an essential matrix. Then, we reveal the number of the solutions of the polynomial system by using Gröbner basis. Finally, we introduce three direct methods for finding the solutions of the new KKT conditions.

4.1 New KKT Conditions

The Lagrangian function of Eq. (5) can be written by

$$L = \frac{1}{2}e^T M e + \frac{\mu}{2}\left(1 - \mathrm{tr}(EE^T)\right) + \mathrm{tr}\left(S\left(2EE^T E - \mathrm{tr}(EE^T)E\right)\right), \tag{18}$$

where μ and S are a Lagrange multiplier and a 3×3 matrix consisting of nine Lagrange multipliers, respectively. Note that $\mathrm{tr}(EE^T) = \|e\|^2$ and the multiplier $1/2$ is merely for convenience. The gradient of L with respect to E is given by

$$\frac{\partial L}{\partial E} = \mathrm{mat}(Me) - \mu E + 2S^T E^T E + 2ESE$$
$$+ 2EE^T S^T - \mathrm{tr}(EE^T)S^T - 2\,\mathrm{tr}(SE)E = 0_{3\times3}, \tag{19}$$

where $\mathrm{mat}(\,\cdot\,)$ is a linear operator converting a 9-dimensional vector to a 3×3 matrix: $\mathbb{R}^9 \to \mathbb{R}^{3\times3}$. Multiplying E^T from left and right to Eq. (19), we obtain the following two equations:

$$\mathbf{E}^\mathsf{T} \frac{\partial L}{\partial \mathbf{E}} = \mathbf{E}^\mathsf{T} \operatorname{mat}(\mathbf{Me}) - s\mathbf{E}^\mathsf{T}\mathbf{E} + 2\mathbf{E}^\mathsf{T}(\mathbf{S}^\mathsf{T}\mathbf{E}^\mathsf{T} + \mathbf{E}\mathbf{S})\mathbf{E}$$
$$+ (2\mathbf{E}\mathbf{E}^\mathsf{T}\mathbf{E} - \operatorname{tr}(\mathbf{E}\mathbf{E}^\mathsf{T})\mathbf{E})^\mathsf{T}\mathbf{S}^\mathsf{T} = \mathbf{0}_{3\times 3}, \tag{20a}$$

$$\frac{\partial L}{\partial \mathbf{E}}\mathbf{E}^\mathsf{T} = \operatorname{mat}(\mathbf{Me})\mathbf{E}^\mathsf{T} - s\mathbf{E}\mathbf{E}^\mathsf{T} + 2\mathbf{E}(\mathbf{S}\mathbf{E} + \mathbf{E}^\mathsf{T}\mathbf{S}^\mathsf{T})\mathbf{E}^\mathsf{T}$$
$$+ \mathbf{S}^\mathsf{T}(2\mathbf{E}\mathbf{E}^\mathsf{T}\mathbf{E} - \operatorname{tr}(\mathbf{E}\mathbf{E}^\mathsf{T})\mathbf{E})^\mathsf{T} = \mathbf{0}_{3\times 3}, \tag{20b}$$

where $s = \mu + 2\operatorname{tr}(\mathbf{SE})$. Using $2\mathbf{E}\mathbf{E}^\mathsf{T}\mathbf{E} - \operatorname{tr}(\mathbf{E}\mathbf{E}^\mathsf{T})\mathbf{E} = \mathbf{0}$, we can rewrite Eqs. (20a) and (20b) by

$$\mathbf{E}^\mathsf{T} \operatorname{mat}(\mathbf{Me}) = s\mathbf{E}^\mathsf{T}\mathbf{E} - 2\mathbf{E}^\mathsf{T}\left(\mathbf{S}^\mathsf{T}\mathbf{E}^\mathsf{T} + \mathbf{E}\mathbf{S}\right)\mathbf{E}$$
$$= \mathbf{E}^\mathsf{T}\left(s\mathbf{I} - 2(\mathbf{ES})^\mathsf{T} - 2\mathbf{ES}\right)\mathbf{E}, \tag{21a}$$

$$\operatorname{mat}(\mathbf{Me})\mathbf{E}^\mathsf{T} = s\mathbf{E}\mathbf{E}^\mathsf{T} - 2\mathbf{E}\left(\mathbf{SE} + \mathbf{E}^\mathsf{T}\mathbf{S}^\mathsf{T}\right)\mathbf{E}^\mathsf{T}$$
$$= \mathbf{E}\left(s\mathbf{I} - 2\mathbf{SE} - 2(\mathbf{SE})^\mathsf{T}\right)\mathbf{E}^\mathsf{T}. \tag{21b}$$

The right-hand side of Eqs. (21a) and (21b) is a 3×3 symmetric matrix. Thus, the left-hand side, $\mathbf{E}^\mathsf{T} \operatorname{mat}(\mathbf{Me})$ and $\operatorname{mat}(\mathbf{Me})\mathbf{E}^\mathsf{T}$, also must be a symmetric matrix. Defining $\mathbf{P} = \mathbf{E}^\mathsf{T} \operatorname{mat}(\mathbf{Me})$ and $\mathbf{Q} = \operatorname{mat}(\mathbf{Me})\mathbf{E}^\mathsf{T}$, we can formulate the symmetry constraint as the following six polynomial equations:

$$P_{12} - P_{21} = 0, \quad P_{13} - P_{31} = 0, \quad P_{32} - P_{23} = 0,$$
$$Q_{12} - Q_{21} = 0, \quad Q_{13} - Q_{31} = 0, \quad Q_{32} - Q_{23} = 0, \tag{22}$$

where P_{ij} and Q_{ij} denote the (i, j) elements of $\mathbf{P}$ and $\mathbf{Q}$, respectively. Finally, the new KKT conditions can be given by

$$P_{ij} - P_{ji} = 0, \ Q_{ij} - Q_{ji} = 0, \ \forall i, j \in \{1, 2, 3\},$$
$$\operatorname{tr}(\mathbf{E}\mathbf{E}^\mathsf{T}) = 1, \ 2\mathbf{E}\mathbf{E}^\mathsf{T}\mathbf{E} - \operatorname{tr}(\mathbf{E}\mathbf{E}^\mathsf{T})\mathbf{E} = \mathbf{0}_{3\times 3}. \tag{23}$$

Equation (23) is a polynomial system in 16 equations with nine variables of $\mathbf{E}$.

4.2   Solution Space

We can use an algebraic geometry software Macaulay2 [15][2] to analyze the solution space of Eq. (23). Macaulay2 computes the Gröbner basis of a polynomial system in a finite prime field, and we have found that Eq. (23) have 440 solutions. Due to the L2 norm constraint, $\operatorname{tr}(\mathbf{E}\mathbf{E}^\mathsf{T}) = 1$, there is a 2-fold ambiguity in the 440 solutions. In other words, $\mathbf{E}$ and $-\mathbf{E}$ are exactly the same solutions. To remove the ambiguity, we can set one of $\mathbf{E}$ as a scalar instead of $\operatorname{tr}(\mathbf{E}\mathbf{E}^\mathsf{T}) = 1$. For example, $E_{13} = 1$ leads to 220 solutions. Readers may refer to [26] for more details of how to use Macaulay2 for geometric problems in computer vision.

---

[2] http://www.math.uiuc.edu/Macaulay2/.

```
%  m1, m2: 3xN set of homogeneous 2D points
%  E_ini : Initial guess of essential matrix
%  E_opt : Optimized essential matrix
1  function E_opt = Emat_KKTGN(m1, m2, E_ini)
2      M    = [m2(1,:)'.*m1', m2(2,:)'.*m1', m2(3,:)'.*m1'];
3      E_opt = fsolve(@(x)KKTeqs(x,M'*M), E_ini);
4  end
5  function eqs = KKTeqs(E, M)
6      e    = reshape(E',9,1);
7      matMe = reshape(M*e, 3, 3)';
8      P    = E'*matMe;
9      Q    = matMe*E';
10     ceq1  = trace(E*E') - 1;
11     ceq2  = 2*(E*E')*E - E;
12     eqs   = [P(1,2)-P(2,1); P(1,3)-P(3,1); P(2,3)-P(3,2);
13             Q(1,2)-Q(2,1); Q(1,3)-Q(3,1); Q(2,3)-Q(3,2);
14             ceq1; ceq2(:)];
15 end
```

Fig. 2. 15-line MATLAB code for solving Eq. (23) by the Gauss-Newton method.

4.3   Direct Least-Squares Solvers

We propose three solvers to directly find an essential matrix that satisfies Eq. (23).

Gauss-Newton Solver. A typical approach to finding a single solution to a polynomial system is to apply the Gauss-Newton method with an initial guess. The Gauss-Newton method is easy to implement and is often already built-in as a subroutine in optimization libraries. Figure 2 shows a MATLAB example with `fsolve` function written in 15-lines of code. Note that a single solution satisfying the KKT conditions is a local minimum, which is not guaranteed to be the global optimum.

Gröbner Basis Solver. As a method for finding all solutions of multivariate polynomials, Gröbner basis method has been widely used in computer vision for the last decade [27,29]. We applied an automatic generator [29] on Eq. (23) with replacing $\mathrm{tr}(\mathbf{E}\mathbf{E}^\mathsf{T}) = 1$ by $E_{13} = 1$ and obtained a Gröbner basis solver that returns 220 solutions. Unfortunately, the generated solver is not numerically stable due to a large elimination template of size 5149×5369. We have found that the solver does not return meaningful solutions that satisfy Eq. (23).

Homotopy Continuation Solver. Another approach for obtaining all solutions is to use a homotopy continuation method, a classical but useful tool widely known in numerical algebraic geometry [30]. Several software packages are publicly available, such as Bertini [3][3], PHCPack [45][4], Hom4PS [6][5]. We will use Bertini for experiments in Sect. 5 because it is the fastest among the three software for solving Eq. (23).

---

[3] https://bertini.nd.edu/.

[4] https://github.com/janverschelde/PHCpack.

[5] http://www.hom4ps3.org/.

5   Experiment

We report experimental results on both synthetic and real data in this section. All experiments were conducted on a PC with Core i7-7920X.

5.1   Implementation

We have implemented the existing methods (Sect. 3) and the new direct methods (Sect. 4.3) in MATLAB. The details are as follows:

DLT. The standard eight-point DLT algorithm [17] shown in Eqs. (6) and (8).

Expm-GN. Local parameterization method, Eq. (11), using the exponential map with a Gauss-Newton optimization. Readers may refer to Sect. 4 in [18] for the implementation details.

minEig. Eigenvalue minimization method [23] implemented in OpenGV [22][6], a C++ library for camera pose estimation problems. The Jacobian of Eq. (15) is supplied using numerical differentiation to avoid complex arithmetic (See Sect. 3.1 in [23]). We selected a rotation matrix from the initial $\mathbf{E}$ by checking the orientation of the projective depth to be positive [9].

QCQP. SDP-relaxation method for a non-convex QCQP [48] shown in Eq. (17). We have rewritten the original C++ code[7] in MATLAB using SDPA-M 7.3.9 [46], a MATLAB wrapper for an SDP solver, SDPA[8].

Bertini. Direct method for obtaining all real roots of Eq. (23) using Bertini 1.6 [3], a software for solving polynomial systems based on homotopy continuation. Since $P_{ij} - P_{ji} = 0$ and $Q_{ij} - Q_{ji} = 0$ in Eq. (23) hold up to scale, we set $E_{13} = 1$ instead of $\mathrm{tr}(\mathbf{E}\mathbf{E}^{\mathsf{T}}) = 1$. Moreover, a random 3×3 rotation was multiplied to the point correspondences to avoid a numerical degeneracy, $E_{13} = 0$. We selected the global optimum from all real solutions that gives the smallest algebraic error, $\mathbf{e}^{\mathsf{T}}\mathbf{M}\mathbf{e}$.

KKT-GN. Gauss-Newton-based method for solving Eq. (23). A code example is shown in Fig. 2, but we used a simple Gauss-Newton implementation with the analytic Jacobian for efficiency instead of `fsolve` function.

BA. Bundle adjustment minimizing reprojection error [43]. In addition to a rotation matrix and a translation vector, 3D points are jointly optimized. This is the only one method minimizing a geometrically meaningful error in this experiment.

For quantitative evaluations, we measured three criteria: rotation error E_{R}, translation error E_{t}, and the first-order optimality E_{KKT}. The three metrics were computed by

$$E_{\mathsf{R}} = \frac{180°}{\pi} \cos^{-1}\left(\frac{\mathrm{tr}(\mathbf{R}_{\mathrm{gt}}^{\mathsf{T}}\mathbf{R}_{\mathrm{est}}) - 1}{2} \right), \quad E_{\mathsf{t}} = \frac{180°}{\pi} \cos^{-1}\left(\frac{\mathbf{t}_{\mathrm{gt}}^{\mathsf{T}}\mathbf{t}_{\mathrm{est}}}{\|\mathbf{t}_{\mathrm{gt}}\|\,\|\mathbf{t}_{\mathrm{est}}\|} \right),$$

$$E_{\mathrm{KKT}} = \frac{\max(|P_{12} - P_{21}|, \dots, |Q_{32} - Q_{23}|)}{\|\mathbf{M}\|_F \,\|\mathbf{E}\|_F}, \tag{24}$$

---

[6] http://laurentkneip.github.io/opengv.
[7] https://github.com/jizhaox/npt-pose.
[8] http://sdpa.sourceforge.net/.

where $\|\cdot\|_F$ represents the Frobenius norm of a matrix. E_{KKT} represents a convergence to a local minimum under 5 DoF; an estimated E having a sufficiently low E_{KKT} is a valid local minimum that can be decomposed into R and t.

5.2 Synthetic Data

We generated synthetic scenes to quantitatively compare the methods. We set the first camera as the origin of the world coordinates, *i.e.* the rotation matrix as an 3×3 identity matrix and the translation as a zero vector. The second camera was randomly positioned within $[\pm 1, \pm 1, \pm 2.5]$. The rotation matrix of the second camera was given by random Euler angles in the range of $[10°, \pm 60°, \pm 90°]$. The image resolution is 640×480, and both cameras have a focal length of 800 pixels and the optical center at $[320, 240]$. To generate 3D points, we first uniformly determined 2D points in the normalized image plane of the first camera and then randomly set their depth from 5 to 10. We projected the 3D points onto the two cameras and obtained 2D point correspondences. DLT was used as the initial guess for the iterative methods, *i.e.* Expm-GN, minEig, KKT-GN, and BA.

Accuracy w.r.t. Image Noise. We evaluated the robustness against image noise. The number of the 2D points was fixed to 100, and zero-mean Gaussian noise was added to the points with the standard deviation $0.5 \leq \sigma \leq 5$ pixels. Figure 3 summarizes the average estimation error of 1000 independent trials for each noise level. Bertini gives the best performance among the algebraic error minimization methods. This result shows that we can obtain the global optimum by solving Eq. (23). Expm-GN and minEig are comparable each other. QCQP gives almost the same accuracy with DLT for rotation estimation. KKT-GN performs well for small noise levels $\sigma \leq 3$ but becomes worse than DLT as the noise increases whereas KKT-GN is initialized by DLT. According to the result of E_{KKT}, KKT-GN and QCQP get trapped by a bad local minimum specially for high noise levels. Feature points are generally detected on subpixel accuracy, *e.g.* $\sigma \leq 2$, therefore, Expm-GN, minEig, and KKT-GN are expected to have a similar performance in practice.

Accuracy w.r.t. Number of Points. We compared the methods by varying the number of the points from 10 to 100. The noise level was fixed to $\sigma = 2$. The average error over 1000 independent trials is shown in Fig. 4. Expm-GN and minEig have similar performance with Bertini, which provides the global optimum close to BA, while E_{KKT} of minEig is 10^{-8} that does not reach to the machine epsilon like Expm-GN and Bertini. This observation suggests that $E_{\mathrm{KKT}} < 10^{-8}$ is sufficiently low to obtain a local minimum with preserving the decomposability of an essential matrix. For ≤ 25 points, QCQP and KKT-GN are less accurate than the other methods even though their E_{KKT} is less than 10^{-8}. It is inferred that KKT-GN and QCQP converge to a bad local minimum for few point correspondences. QCQP is slightly inferior to KKT-GN in terms of E_{R} even for > 25 points, therefore, KKT-GN can be comparable to Expm-GN and minEig if many points are available.

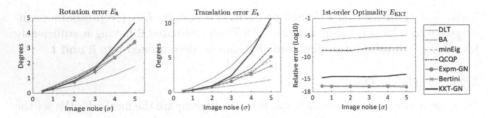

Fig. 3. Mean estimation error w.r.t. the image noise level over 1000 independent trials for each noise level.

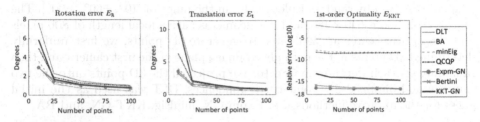

Fig. 4. Mean estimation error w.r.t. the number of point correspondences over 1000 independent trials for each point.

Computational Time. Figure 5 shows the computational time up to 1000 points with $\sigma = 2$. Expm-GN, minEig, and KTT-GN spend only 1 milliseconds for 1000 points, which is fast enough for real-time applications such as V-SLAM. Moreover, Expm-GN and KTT-GN are written in MATLAB, therefore, they can be further accelerated if implemented in C++. QCQP is much slower by orders of magnitude than the runtime reported in [48]. In fact, we had confirmed that the original QCQP written in C++ runs in 4 milliseconds. The main cause is that the Windows binary of SDPA-M is not well optimized due to a cross-compilation on Debian. This observation indicates that QCQP requires a highly-optimized SDP library whereas Expm-GN/KTT-GN does not. However, the conclusion still remains that QCQP suffers from high noise levels even run on C++. Bertini requires more than 1 min, which is difficult to use for real-time applications.

Number of Real Solutions. We counted the number of real solutions obtained by Bertini in two scenarios: varying the number of the points from 6 to 1000 with $\sigma = 2$, and varying the noise level up to $\sigma = 5$ with 100 points. We ran 100 independent trials for each point and noise level. As shown in Fig. 6, the number of real solutions ranges between 25 to 40 regardless of the number of the points and an image noise level. One point pair leads to a rank-1 update to the coefficient matrix M up to $\text{rank}(M) = 9$; however, no statistical significance was found from 6 to 1000 points. This is an interesting result that neither many points nor low noise level does not reduce the number of real solutions.

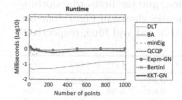
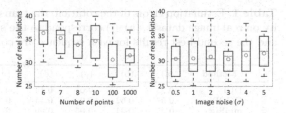

Fig. 5. Computational time w.r.t. the number of point correspondences. The result of Bertini, > 1 minute, is not displayed.

Fig. 6. The number of real solutions obtained by Bertini. Circles and bars in orange show the mean and the median values, respectively. (Color figure online)

(a) Castle-P19: 18, rotational. (b) Entry-P10: 9, sideways. (c) Fountain-P11: 10, orbital. (d) Herz-Jesu-P8: 7, sideways. (e) Corridor: 10, forward.

(f) ModelHouse: 9, orbital. (g) 00: 454, forward. (h) 01: 110, forward. (i) 02: 466, forward.

Fig. 7. Images used in the real data evaluation. Each subcaption describes its sequence name followed by the number of image pairs and the camera motion. (a)–(d): Strecha, (c)–(d): VGG, (g)–(i): KITTI.

5.3 Real Data

We evaluated the methods for various conditions of scenes and camera motions in publicly available dataset: four sequences from Strecha *et al.*'s dense MVS dataset [41][9], twos from VGG multi-view dataset[10], threes from KITTI visual odometry dataset [14][11]. The details of the sequences are shown in Fig. 7.

Quantitative Evaluation. We conducted quantitative evaluations as follows. First we obtained initial point correspondences between two consecutive frames by using SIFT [31] in OpenCV 4.5[12]. We picked every 10th and 11th frames for KITTI because a single sequence of KITTI consists of more than 1000 frames.

---

[9] https://www.epfl.ch/labs/cvlab/data/.
[10] https://www.robots.ox.ac.uk/~vgg/data/mview/.
[11] http://www.cvlibs.net/datasets/kitti/eval_odometry.php.
[12] https://github.com/opencv/opencv/.

Table 1. Estimation errors of the rotation, the translation, and the first-order optimality on real image dataset. (a)–(i) correspond to the sequences shown in Fig. 7. The best and the second-best results for each sequence are colored in red and blue, respectively.

	Method	(a)	(b)	(c)	(d)	(e)	(f)	(g)	(h)	(i)
E_R [degrees]	DLT	0.23	0.32	0.07	0.14	0.20	0.81	0.14	0.37	0.12
	QCQP	0.37	0.62	0.04	0.14	0.17	0.64	0.09	0.17	0.08
	minEig	0.25	0.24	0.05	0.09	0.15	0.60	0.08	0.17	0.07
	Expm-GN	0.25	0.24	0.05	0.09	0.16	0.58	0.08	0.18	0.07
	KKT-GN	0.25	0.22	0.05	0.10	0.17	0.59	0.09	0.18	0.07
	Bertini	0.25	0.22	0.05	0.09	0.16	0.58	0.08	0.17	0.07
	BA	0.24	0.18	0.05	0.10	0.14	0.58	0.08	0.15	0.06
E_t [degrees]	DLT	1.40	1.89	0.54	0.82	3.10	3.95	2.45	2.25	1.48
	QCQP	1.69	4.78	0.19	0.76	2.84	2.84	2.28	2.19	1.34
	minEig	1.07	1.27	0.25	0.42	2.71	1.85	2.09	2.21	1.29
	Expm-GN	1.05	1.21	0.23	0.39	2.84	1.85	2.08	2.23	1.29
	KKT-GN	1.05	1.15	0.23	0.43	2.93	1.88	2.15	2.27	1.27
	Bertini	1.05	1.15	0.23	0.39	2.84	1.85	2.08	2.23	1.27
	BA	1.00	1.00	0.25	0.43	2.40	1.81	2.32	2.31	1.26
E_{KKT} ($\log_{10}$)	DLT	−3.17	−3.52	−3.79	−3.51	−4.73	−2.82	−4.32	−3.47	−4.49
	QCQP	−8.19	−7.84	−8.14	−7.91	−8.78	−7.82	−8.56	−8.53	−8.60
	minEig	−8.20	−8.74	−8.74	−8.78	−9.28	−7.25	−8.46	−8.39	−9.67
	Expm-GN	−16.08	−16.42	−16.41	−16.29	−15.85	−15.82	−16.18	−15.91	−16.30
	KKT-GN	−12.24	−12.35	−12.19	−12.16	−9.33	−12.23	−9.95	−9.27	−12.34
	Bertini	−16.32	−16.21	−15.91	−15.70	−16.41	−16.28	−15.85	−15.59	−15.56
	BA	−6.23	−6.47	−6.79	−6.62	−5.10	−6.10	−5.25	−5.09	−5.33

Then we perform LO-RANSAC [8] with the five-point method [37] as a hypothesis generator and each least-squares method as a local optimizer. Since Bertini is not efficient for RANSAC scenarios, we ran Bertini for the final refinement over inliers obtained by the Expm-GN local optimizer. LO-RANSAC was configured to have a threshold by 3-pixels, a confidence by 0.995, the maximum number of iterations by 10000, and the inner loops of an LO step by five. We conducted 100 independent trials for each sequence and fixed a random seed in each trial so that LO-RANSAC draws exactly the same samples for all methods.

Table 1 shows the average values of the three criteria, E_R, E_t, E_{KKT}, for each sequence. First of all, we can observe that three locally optimal methods, *i.e.* minEig, Expm-GN, and KKT-GN, have similar performance comparable to the globally optimal method, Bertini. Therefore, the three methods can be almost considered as globally optimal solvers in practice. On the other hand, QCQP is slightly worse than the three local methods in half of the sequences. Considering the two motion errors and E_{KKT}, we can say that the numerical accuracy of E_{KKT} is practically enough at 10^{-8} to 10^{-10}. These results are consistent with the synthetic data evaluation in Sect. 5.2.

Table 2 summarizes the RANSAC iterations and computational time. There are no significant differences on the number of RANSAC iterations. Since the same random seed was set for a single trial of all methods, this result suggests that each method obtains almost the same inliers at an LO step. DLT is the fastest due to its simpleness, followed by mingEig, Expm-GN, and KKT-GN.

Table 2. The number of RANSAC iterations and computational time on the sequences (a)–(i) shown in Fig. 7. The runtime of Bertini is omitted here because it takes several minutes for a single trial. The best and the second-best results for each sequence are colored in red and blue, respectively. The last row denotes the average of the number of real solutions with one standard deviation, which were obtained by Bertini.

	Method	(a)	(b)	(c)	(d)	(e)	(f)	(g)	(h)	(i)
# of iters.	DLT	1049	63	30	95	11	77	52	36	53
	QCQP	951	60	29	89	11	70	52	35	53
	minEig	1002	60	29	88	11	70	52	35	53
	Expm-GN	1002	60	29	88	11	68	52	34	53
	KKT-GN	1003	60	29	88	11	68	52	34	53
	BA	1001	60	29	88	11	68	52	34	53
Time [msec]	DLT	880	112	40	95	9	55	45	28	50
	QCQP	3067	1864	1581	1975	1229	1767	1340	1417	1379
	minEig	766	96	38	83	16	63	46	39	53
	Expm-GN	853	114	45	99	17	64	54	35	58
	KKT-GN	858	115	45	99	21	63	56	38	60
	BA	1348	510	367	441	222	373	352	299	383
# of real sols.		29 ± 7	30 ± 5	32 ± 9	33 ± 6	29 ± 6	30 ± 8	28 ± 7	33 ± 7	32 ± 5

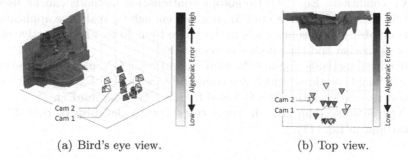

(a) Bird's eye view.   (b) Top view.

Fig. 8. 3D visualization of real solutions obtained by Bertini. The first camera (the world origin) is depicted in blue. The second camera (the global optimum) and the others (local minima) are colored based on their algebraic error. (Color figure online)

However, the difference between the three methods is slight. Expm-GN and KKT-GN can be potentially faster than minEig if implemented in C++.

Finally, we report the number of real solutions in each sequence. We constructed the coefficient matrix M from the inliers detected by LO-RANSAC with Expm-GN and solved Eq. (23) by Bertini. The last row of Table 2 indicates an interesting result, as in Sect. 5.2, that the number of real solutions is in the range of 20 to 40 in almost all cases irrespective of scenes and camera motions.

Qualitative Evaluation. We visualized the distribution of local minima, which are real solutions computed by Bertini. Figure 6 shows a 3D scene of Fountain-P11, which was reconstructed using the 5th and 6th frames of the sequence. We colored the first camera (the 5th frame, the world origin) in blue and the second cameras (the 6th frame, local minima) based on their algebraic error. The global

optimum of the second camera is colored in white. For ease of viewing, we display
only 17 s-cameras facing the direction of the fountain.

There is a local minimum in orange near the global optimum in white. Iterative methods may fall into the local minimum, not the global one, if an initial
guess is closer to the local minimum than the global optimum. Moreover, there
are many local minima having various error values behind the first camera. If
an optimization scheme starts around them, it is difficult to escape the valley of
the local minima.

As shown in the example above, we can visually validate the difficulty of a
sequence by calculating all real solutions. The solution space visualization tells
us why and how an estimation method successes or fails.

6   Discussion

As the results of the experiments in Sect. 5, we obtained the following findings.

- The global optimum of the algebraic error can be obtained by solving the new
  KKT conditions, Eq. (23). Homotopy continuation methods can be used to
  obtain the global optimum but are not fast enough for real-time applications.
- The number of real solutions is in the range from 20 to 40 irrespective of the
  camera motion and the number of the points.
- Three local methods, Expm-GN, minEig, and KKT-GN, provide almost globally optimal solutions, which are comparable with BA. Expm-GN gives the
  lowest first-order optimality, followed by KKT-GN and minEig.
- QCQP is worse than DLT in some cases due to the drop of rank(X) = 1
  constraint in Eq. (17).

7   Conclusions

In this paper, we analyzed the solution space of the essential matrix estimation and revealed that there are at most 220 solutions in the algebraic error
minimization. This is the first theoretical contribution in the three decades
since Demazure gave the number of the solutions for the five-point minimal
case in 1988. Exhaustive experiments showed that three locally optimal methods compute almost globally optimal solutions in effect. The proposed theory
can be used to stabilize essential matrix estimation in real applications, e.g.
reliable scene graph construction in Structure-from-Motion, motion analysis in
near-degenerate situations, and so on. For future work in this research field, we
pointed out the limitations of the current direct solvers based on Gröbner basis
or homotopy continuation, namely the need to improve stability and efficiency
for solving large polynomial systems such as the proposed KKT conditions. The
mathematical condition also needs to be analyzed to clarify what determines
the number of real solutions and their spatial distribution. Furthermore, our
mathematical derivation contributes to explore the future development of globally optimal methods for multi-view geometry, especially for two-view geometry
with both or either unknown focal length and unknown lens distortions.

References

1. Agarwal, S., et al.: Building Rome in a day. Commun. ACM **54**(10), 105–112 (2011)
2. Avidan, S., Shashua, A.: Novel view synthesis in tensor space. In: Proceedings of IEEE Computer Society Conference on Computer Vision and Pattern Recognition, pp. 1034–1040. IEEE (1997)
3. Bates, D.J., Hauenstein, J.D., Sommese, A.J., Wampler, C.W.: Bertini: software for numerical algebraic geometry. https://bertini.nd.edu/
4. Briales, J., Kneip, L., Gonzalez-Jimenez, J.: A certifiably globally optimal solution to the non-minimal relative pose problem. In: Proceedings of the IEEE Conference on Computer Vision and Pattern Recognition, pp. 145–154 (2018)
5. Cadena, C., et al.: Past, present, and future of simultaneous localization and mapping: toward the robust-perception age. IEEE Trans. Robot. **32**(6), 1309–1332 (2016)
6. Chen, T., Lee, T.L., Li, T.Y.: Hom4PS-3: a parallel numerical solver for systems of polynomial equations based on polyhedral homotopy continuation methods. In: International Congress on Mathematical Software, pp. 183–190. Springer (2014). https://doi.org/10.1007/978-3-662-44199-2_30
7. Chesi, G.: Camera displacement via constrained minimization of the algebraic error. IEEE Trans. Pattern Anal. Mach. Intell. **31**(2), 370–375 (2008)
8. Chum, O., Matas, J., Kittler, J.: Locally optimized RANSAC. In: Joint Pattern Recognition Symposium, pp. 236–243. Springer (2003). https://doi.org/10.1007/978-3-540-45243-0_31
9. Chum, O., Werner, T., Matas, J.: Epipolar geometry estimation via RANSAC benefits from the oriented epipolar constraint. In: Proceedings of the 17th International Conference on Pattern Recognition, 2004. ICPR 2004, vol. 1, pp. 112–115. IEEE (2004)
10. Demazure, M.: Sur deux problemes de reconstruction. Technical report RR-0882, INRIA, July 1988. https://hal.inria.fr/inria-00075672
11. Fathy, M.E., Rotkowitz, M.C.: Essential matrix estimation using adaptive penalty formulations. J. Comput. Vis. **74**(2), 117–136 (2007)
12. Fischler, M.A., Bolles, R.C.: Random sample consensus: a paradigm for model fitting with applications to image analysis and automated cartography. Commun. ACM **24**(6), 381–395 (1981)
13. Fraundorfer, F., Tanskanen, P., Pollefeys, M.: A minimal case solution to the calibrated relative pose problem for the case of two known orientation angles. In: European Conference on Computer Vision, pp. 269–282. Springer (2010). https://doi.org/10.1007/978-3-642-15561-1_20
14. Geiger, A., Lenz, P., Urtasun, R.: Are we ready for autonomous driving? The kitti vision benchmark suite. In: Conference on Computer Vision and Pattern Recognition (CVPR) (2012)
15. Grayson, D.R., Stillman, M.E.: Macaulay2, a software system for research in algebraic geometry. http://www.math.uiuc.edu/Macaulay2/
16. Hartley, R.I., Kahl, F.: Global optimization through rotation space search. Int. J. Comput. Vis. **82**(1), 64–79 (2009)
17. Hartley, R.I., Zisserman, A.: Multiple View Geometry in Computer Vision. Cambridge University Press, ISBN: 0521540518, second edn. (2004)
18. Helmke, U., Hüper, K., Lee, P.Y., Moore, J.: Essential matrix estimation using gauss-newton iterations on a manifold. Int. J. Comput. Vis. **74**(2), 117–136 (2007)

594   G. Nakano

19. Jiang, F., Kuang, Y., Solem, J.E., Åström, K.: A minimal solution to relative pose with unknown focal length and radial distortion. In: Asian Conference on Computer Vision, pp. 443–456. Springer (2014). https://doi.org/10.1007/978-3-319-16808-1_30
20. Joo, H., et al.: Panoptic studio: a massively multiview system for social interaction capture. IEEE Trans. Pattern Anal. Mach. Intell. **41**(1), 190–204 (2019). https://doi.org/10.1109/TPAMI.2017.2782743
21. Kalantari, M., Hashemi, A., Jung, F., Guédon, J.P.: A new solution to the relative orientation problem using only 3 points and the vertical direction. J. Math. Imaging Vis. **39**(3), 259–268 (2011)
22. Kneip, L., Furgale, P.: OpenGV: a unified and generalized approach to real-time calibrated geometric vision. In: 2014 IEEE International Conference on Robotics and Automation (ICRA), pp. 1–8. IEEE (2014)
23. Kneip, L., Lynen, S.: Direct optimization of frame-to-frame rotation. In: Proceedings of the IEEE International Conference on Computer Vision, pp. 2352–2359 (2013)
24. Kruppa, E.: Zur ermittlung eines objektes aus zwei perspektiven mit innerer orientierung. Sitzungsberichte der Mathematisch-Naturwissenschaftlichen Kaiserlichen Akademie der Wissenschaften, pp. 1939–1948 (1913)
25. Kuang, Y., Solem, J.E., Kahl, F., Astrom, K.: Minimal solvers for relative pose with a single unknown radial distortion. In: Proceedings of the IEEE Conference on Computer Vision and Pattern Recognition, pp. 33–40 (2014)
26. Kukelova, Z.: Algebraic methods in computer vision. Ph.D. thesis, Czech Technical University in Prage (2013)
27. Kukelova, Z., Bujnak, M., Pajdla, T.: Automatic generator of minimal problem solvers. In: European Conference on Computer Vision, pp. 302–315. Springer (2008). https://doi.org/10.1007/978-3-540-88690-7_23
28. Kukelova, Z., Bujnak, M., Pajdla, T.: Polynomial Eigenvalue solutions to minimal problems in computer vision. IEEE Trans. Pattern Anal. Mach. Intell. **34**(7), 1381–1393 (2011)
29. Larsson, V., Astrom, K., Oskarsson, M.: Efficient solvers for minimal problems by syzygy-based reduction. In: Proceedings of the IEEE Conference on Computer Vision and Pattern Recognition, pp. 820–829 (2017)
30. Leykin, A.: Numerical algebraic geometry. J. Softw. Algebra Geometr. **3**(1), 5–10 (2011)
31. Lowe, D.G.: Distinctive image features from scale-invariant keypoints. Int. J. Comput. Vis. **60**(2), 91–110 (2004)
32. Ma, Y., Košecká, J., Sastry, S.: Optimization criteria and geometric algorithms for motion and structure estimation. Int. J. Comput. Vis. **44**(3), 219–249 (2001)
33. Mildenhall, B., Srinivasan, P.P., Tancik, M., Barron, J.T., Ramamoorthi, R., Ng, R.: Nerf: Representing scenes as neural radiance fields for view synthesis. In: European Conference on Computer Vision, pp. 405–421. Springer (2020)
34. Mur-Artal, R., Montiel, J.M.M., Tardos, J.D.: ORB-SLAM: a versatile and accurate monocular slam system. IEEE Trans. Rob. **31**(5), 1147–1163 (2015)
35. Nakano, G.: Globally optimal DLS method for PnP problem with Cayley parameterization. In: Proceedings of the British Machine Vision Conference (BMVC), pp. 78.1–78.11 (2015)
36. Nakano, G., Takada, J.: A robust least squares solution to the calibrated two-view geometry with two known orientation angles. In: International Conference on Computer Vision, Imaging and Computer Graphics, pp. 132–145. Springer (2013). https://doi.org/10.1007/978-3-662-44911-0_9

37. Nistér, D.: An efficient solution to the five-point relative pose problem. IEEE Trans. Pattern Anal. Mach. Intell. **26**(6), 756–770 (2004)
38. Philip, J.: Critical point configurations of the 5-, 6-, 7-, and 8-point algorithms for relative orientation. Technical report TRITA-MAT-1998-MA-13, Department of Mathematics, Royal Institute of Technology (1998)
39. Pizarro, O., Eustice, R.M., Singh, H.: Relative pose estimation for instrumented, calibrated imaging platforms. In: DICTA, pp. 601–612, Sydney, Australia (2003)
40. Stewénius, H., Nistér, D., Kahl, F., Schaffalitzky, F.: A minimal solution for relative pose with unknown focal length. Image Vis. Comput. **26**(7), 871–877 (2008)
41. Strecha, C., Von Hansen, W., Van Gool, L., Fua, P., Thoennessen, U.: On benchmarking camera calibration and multi-view stereo for high resolution imagery. In: 2008 IEEE Conference on Computer Vision and Pattern Recognition, pp. 1–8. IEEE (2008)
42. Taira, H., et al.: InLoc: indoor visual localization with dense matching and view synthesis. In: Proceedings of the IEEE Conference on Computer Vision and Pattern Recognition, pp. 7199–7209 (2018)
43. Triggs, B., McLauchlan, P.F., Hartley, R.I., Fitzgibbon, A.W.: Bundle adjustment — a modern synthesis. In: Triggs, B., Zisserman, A., Szeliski, R. (eds.) IWVA 1999. LNCS, vol. 1883, pp. 298–372. Springer, Heidelberg (2000). https://doi.org/10.1007/3-540-44480-7_21
44. Ventura, J., Arth, C., Lepetit, V.: Approximated relative pose solvers for efficient camera motion estimation. In: European Conference on Computer Vision, pp. 180–193. Springer (2014). https://doi.org/10.1007/978-3-319-16178-5_12
45. Verschelde, J.: Algorithm 795: PHCpack: a general-purpose solver for polynomial systems by homotopy continuation. ACM Trans. Math. Softw. **25**(2), 251–276 (1999). https://doi.org/10.1145/317275.317286
46. Yamashita, M., Fujisawa, K., Fukuda, M., Kobayashi, K., Nakata, K., Nakata, M.: Latest developments in the SDPA family for solving large-scale SDPS. In: Handbook on Semidefinite, Conic and Polynomial Optimization, pp. 687–713. Springer (2012). https://doi.org/10.1007/978-1-4614-0769-0_24
47. Zeisl, B., Sattler, T., Pollefeys, M.: Camera pose voting for large-scale image-based localization. In: Proceedings of the IEEE International Conference on Computer Vision, pp. 2704–2712 (2015)
48. Zhao, J.: An efficient solution to non-minimal case essential matrix estimation. IEEE Trans. Patt. Anal. Mach. Intell. **44**(4), 1777–1792 (2020). https://doi.org/10.1109/TPAMI.2020.3030161
49. Zhu, S., et al.: Very large-scale global SFM by distributed motion averaging. In: Proceedings of the IEEE Conference on Computer Vision and Pattern Recognition, pp. 4568–4577 (2018)

Approximate Differentiable Rendering
with Algebraic Surfaces

Leonid Keselman[✉] and Martial Hebert

Carnegie Mellon University, Pittsburgh, PA, USA
{lkeselma,hebert}@cs.cmu.edu

Abstract. Differentiable renderers provide a direct mathematical link between an object's 3D representation and images of that object. In this work, we develop an approximate differentiable renderer for a compact, interpretable representation, which we call Fuzzy Metaballs. Our approximate renderer focuses on rendering shapes via depth maps and silhouettes. It sacrifices fidelity for utility, producing fast runtimes and high-quality gradient information that can be used to solve vision tasks. Compared to mesh-based differentiable renderers, our method has forward passes that are 5x faster and backwards passes that are 30x faster. The depth maps and silhouette images generated by our method are smooth and defined everywhere. In our evaluation of differentiable renderers for pose estimation, we show that our method is the only one comparable to classic techniques. In shape from silhouette, our method performs well using only gradient descent and a per-pixel loss, without any surrogate losses or regularization. These reconstructions work well even on natural video sequences with segmentation artifacts. Project page: https://leonidk.github.io/fuzzy-metaballs

Keywords: Differentiable rendering · Metaballs · Implicit surfaces · Pose estimation · Shape from silhouette · Gaussian mixture models

1 Introduction

Rendering can be seen as the inverse of computer vision: turning 3D scene descriptions into plausible images. There are countless classic rendering methods, spanning from the extremely fast (as used in video games) to the extremely realistic (as used in film and animation). Common to all of these methods is that the rendering process for opaque objects is discontinuous; rays that hit no objects have no relationship to scene geometry and when intersections do occur, they typically only interact with the front-most component of geometry.

Differentiable Rendering is a recent development, designing techniques (often sub-gradients) that enable a more direct mathematical relationship between an image and the scene or camera parameters that generated it. The easy access

---

Supplementary Information The online version contains supplementary material available at https://doi.org/10.1007/978-3-031-19824-3_35.

| Components | Depth | Alpha | Normals | Phong |

Fig. 1. Our differentiable renderer producing images of Stanford bunny, using a representation with 400 parameters. From left to right: the 40 components at one standard deviation, followed by our differentiable renderer generating depth, alpha, surface normals and a shaded image.

to derivatives allows for statistical optimization and natural integration with gradient-based learning techniques. There exist several recent differentiable renderers which produce images comparable in fidelity to classic, non-differentiable, photorealistic rendering methods [33,46,49,75] (Fig. 1).

Our paper presents a different approach: a differentiable renderer focused on utility for computer vision tasks. We are interested in the quality and computability of gradients, not on matching the exact image formation task. We willingly sacrifice fidelity for computational simplicity (and hence speed). Our method focuses on a rendering-like process for shapes which generates good gradients that rapidly lead to viable solutions for classic vision problems. Other methods may produce more pleasing images, but we care about the quality of our local minima and our ability to easily find those minima. Our experiments show how, compared to classic methods, differentiable renderers can be used to solve classic vision problems using only gradient descent, enabling a high degree of robustness to noise such as under-segmented masks or depth sensor artifacts.

Our approach is built on a specific 3D representation. Existing representations often have undesirable properties for rendering or optimization. Point clouds require splatting or calculating precise point sizes [74]. Meshes explicitly represent the object surface, making changes of genus difficult. Other representations require optimization or numerical estimation of ray-shape intersections [6,46]. Our proposed method is formulated with independent rays, represents object surfaces implicitly and computes ray termination in closed form.

Most existing differentiable renders focus on GPU performance. However, GPUs are not always available. Many robotics platforms do not have a GPU [64] or find it occupied running object detection [73], optical flow [61] or a SLAM method [47]. While a single method may claim to be real-time on a dedicated GPU [62], an autonomous system requires a sharing of resources. To run in parallel with the countless GPU-friendly techniques of today, CPU-friendly methods are desirable. Thus, while our method is implemented in JAX [8], supporting CPU and GPU backends, our focus is typically on CPU runtimes.

Lastly, in the era of deep learning, techniques which support gradient-based optimization are desirable. Since our objects have an explicit algebraic form, gradients are simple and easy to compute. Importantly, every pixel has a non-zero (if very slight) relationship with each piece of geometry in the scene (even those behind the camera!). This allows for gradient flow (up to machine precision), even when objects start far from their initialization. While this can also true of large over-parmaterized implicit surfaces (such as NeRF [46]), our representation is extremely compact and each parameter has approximate geometric meaning.

2 Related Work

Early work in 3D shape representation focused on building volumes from partial observations [3] but most modern methods instead focus on surface representation. Meshes, point clouds and surfels [51] focus on representing the exterior of an object. In contrast, our method works by representing volumes, and obtaining surface samples is implicit; similar to recent work on implicit neural surfaces [46].

In using low-fidelity representations, our work is hardly unique. Often learning-based methods settle for pseudorendering [37] or even treating images as layers of planar objects [67]. Settling for low fidelity contrasts sharply with a wide array of differentiable renderers focused on accurate light transport, which are slower but can simulate subtle phenomena [4,75]. High-quality results can also be obtained by using learning methods and dense voxel grids [39].

Differentiable Rendering has many recent works. OpenDR [40] demonstrated pose updates for meshes representing humans. Neural Mesh Renderer [28] developed approximate gradients and used a differentiable renderer for a wide array of tasks. SoftRasterizer [38] developed a subgradient function for meshes with greatly improved gradient quality. Modular Primitives [33] demonstrated fast, GPU-based differentiable rendering for meshes with texture mapping. Differentiable Surface Splatting [74] developed a differentiable renderer for point clouds by building upon existing rendering techniques [79]. Conversion of point clouds to volumes is also differentiable [26]. Pulsar [34] uses spheres as the primary primitive and focuses on GPU performance. PyTorch3D [52] implements several of these techniques for mesh and point cloud rendering. Some methods exploit sampling to be generic across object representation [12]. Many methods integrate with neural networks for specific tasks, such as obtaining better descriptors [36] or predicting 3D object shape from a single images [10,63].

The use of an algebraic surface representation, which came to be known as *metaballs* can be attributed to Blinn [6]. These algebraic representations were well studied in the 1980s and 1990s. These include the development of ray-tracing approximations [22,70,71] and building metaball representations of depth images [48]. Non-differentiable rendering metaballs has many methods, involving splatting [2], data structures [20,59] or even a neural network [24].

Metaballs, especially in our treatment of them, are related to the use of Gaussian Mixture Models (GMMs) for surface representation. Our method could be considered a *differentiable renderer for GMMs*. Gaussian Mixture Models as a shape representation has some appeal to roboticists [50,60]. Methods developed to render GMMs include search-based methods [57] and projection for occupancy maps [50]. Projection methods for GMMs have also found application in robot pose estimation [25]. In the vision community, GMMs have been studied as a shape representation [16] and used for pose estimation [14,15]. In the visual learning space, GMMs [23], or their approximations [19] have also been used.

Concurrent work also uses Gaussians for rendering. VoGE [68] uses existing volume rendering techniques [44,46]. Others use a DGT to build screen-space Gaussians for point clouds [1]. In contrast, our contribution is the development of an approximate differentiable renderer that produces fast & robust results.

3   Fuzzy Metaballs

Our proposed object representation, dubbed Fuzzy Metaballs, is an algebraic, implicit surface representation. Implicit surfaces are an object representations where the surface is represented as

$$F(x, y, z) = 0. \tag{1}$$

While some methods parameterize F with neural networks [46], Blinn's algebraic surfaces [6], also known as blobby models or metaballs, are defined by

$$F(x, y, z) = \sum_i \lambda_i P(x, y, z) - T, \tag{2}$$

where $P(x, y, z)$ is some geometric component and T is a threshold for sufficient density. While Blinn used isotropic Gaussians (hence balls), in our case, we use general multidimensional Gaussians that form ellipsoids:

$$P(\vec{x}) = |\Sigma|^{-\frac{1}{2}} \exp\left(-\frac{1}{2}(\vec{x} - \mu)^T \Sigma^{-1}(\vec{x} - \mu)\right). \tag{3}$$

To obtain Fuzzy Metaballs, we relax the restriction on T being a hard threshold set by the user and instead develop a ray-tracing formulation for Gaussians. To achieve this, we develop two components: a way of defining intersections between Gaussians and rays (Sect. 4.1), and a way of combining intersections across all Gaussians (Sect. 4.2). In our definition, all rays always intersect all Gaussians, leading to smooth gradients.

Our implementation is in JAX [8], enabling CPU and GPU acceleration as well as automatic backpropagation. The rendering function that takes camera pose, camera rays and geometry is 60 lines of code. To enable constraint-free backpropagation, we parameterize Σ^{-1} with its Cholesky decomposition: a lower triangular matrix with positive diagonal components. We ensure that the diagonal elements are positive and at least 10^{-6}. The determinant is directly computed from a product of the diagonal of L. When analyzing ray intersections, one can omit the $|\Sigma|^{-\frac{1}{2}}$ term as maximizing requires only the quadratic form. For example, $\vec{x}$ is replaced with a ray intersection of $\vec{v}t$ with $\vec{v} \in \mathbf{R}^3$ and $t \in \mathbf{R}$:

$$s(vt) = (vt - \mu)^T \Sigma^{-1}(vt - \mu), \tag{4}$$

giving a Mahlanobis distnace [42] that is invariant to object scale and allows us to use constant hyperparameters, irrespective of object distance. Using probabilities would be scale-sensitive as equivalent Gaussians that are further are also larger and would have smaller likelihoods at the same points.

To produce an alpha-mask, we simply have two hyperparameters for scale and offset and use a standard sigmoid function:

$$\alpha = \sigma \left(\beta_4 \left[\sum_i \lambda_i \exp(-\frac{1}{2} s(vt)) \right] + \beta_5 \right). \tag{5}$$

4 Approximate Differentiable Rendering

Instead of using existing rendering methods, we develop an approximate renderer that produces smooth, high-quality gradients. While inexact, our formulation enables fast and robust differentiable rendering usable in an analysis by synthesis pipeline [5]. We split the process into two steps: intersecting each component independently in Sect. 4.1 and combining those results smoothly in Sect. 4.2.

4.1 Intersecting Gaussians

What does it mean to have a particular intersection of a ray with a Gaussian? We propose three methods. The *linear* method is where the ray intersects the Gaussian at the point of highest probability. Maximizing Eq. (4) is solved by

$$t = \frac{\mu^T \Sigma^{-1} v}{v^T \Sigma^{-1} v}. \tag{6}$$

An alternative view is a volume model, intersecting at the maximum magnitude of the gradient of the Gaussian:

$$||p(tv)||^2 = P(tv)^2 (tv - \mu)^T \Sigma^{-1} \Sigma^{-1} (tv - \mu). \tag{7}$$

Obtaining the gradient of Eq. (7) and setting it equal to zero leads to a cubic equation, hence the *cubic* method. Defining $m = \Sigma \mu$ and $r = \Sigma v$ leads to:

$$0 = -t^3 (r^T r)(v^T r)$$
$$+ t^2 \left[(m^T r + r^T m)(v^T r) + (r^T r)(v^T m) \right]$$
$$- t \left[(m^T m)(v^T r) + (m^T r + r^T m)(v^T m) - r^T r \right]$$
$$+ (m^T m)(v^T m) - r^T m.$$

While standard formulas exist for the cubic, the higher order polynomial all-but-ensures that numerical issues will arise. We implement a numerically stable solver for the cubic [7]. However, even the numerically stable version produces problematic pixels in 32bit floating point. Errors at a rate of about 1 in 1,000 produce NaNs and make backpropagation impossible.

The *quadratic* method approximates the cubic by intersecting the Gaussian at the one standard deviation ellipsoid. Clipping the inside of square roots to be non-negative leads to reasonable results when the ray misses the ellipsoid.

$$t^2 v^T \Sigma^{-1} v - 2tv^T \Sigma^{-1} \mu + \mu^T \Sigma^{-1} \mu = 1$$

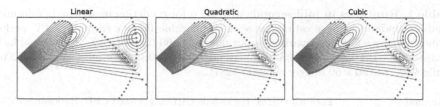

Fig. 2. Two dimensional version of our approximate renderer with camera rays cast from the center left. Three components are shown by their contour maps and their intersections with dots. The blended results are shown with red rays. (Color figure online)

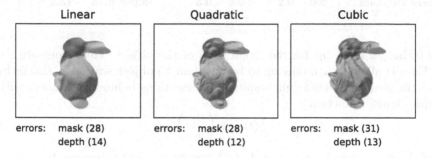

| errors: | mask (28) | errors: | mask (28) | errors: | mask (31) |
| | depth (14) | | depth (12) | | depth (13) |

Fig. 3. Visual examples of normal maps from different methods of ray intersection, along with the respective mask and depth errors. See Sect. 4.1 for details

$$a = v^T \Sigma^{-1} v \qquad b = -2v^T \Sigma^{-1} \mu \qquad c = \mu^T \Sigma^{-1} \mu - 1$$

Figures 2 and 3 illustrate all three methods. The linear method produces smooth surfaces and the quadratic surface shows the individual ellipsoids protruding from the surface of the object and the cubic shows artifacts.

In 3D evaluation on objects, for a forward pass, the linear method is the fastest, the quadratic method takes 50% longer and the cubic method takes twice as long as the linear method. The quadratic method has the lowest errors in depth and mask errors. However, due to its stability, in all evaluation outside this section, we use the linear method.

4.2 Blending Intersections

We present a particular solution to the hidden-surface problem [58]. Our method is related to prior work on *Order Independent Transparency (OIT)* [17,45] but extended to 3D objects with opaque surfaces. We combine each pixel's ray-Gaussian intersections with a weighted average

$$t_f = \frac{1}{\sum_i w_i} \sum_i w_i t_i. \tag{8}$$

The weights are an exponential function with two hyperparameters β_1 and β_2 balancing high-quality hits versus hits closer closer to the camera:

$$w_i = \exp\left(\beta_1 s(vt_i) h(t_i) - \frac{\beta_2}{\eta} t_i\right). \tag{9}$$

Table 1. Runtimes in milliseconds with $\mu \pm \sigma$ for rendering images and performing gradient updates in pose estimation with comparable fidelity (Sect. 6). CPU performance may be a fairer comparison as our method is 60 lines of JAX [8] code and lacks a custom CUDA kernel. CUDA numbers use 160×120 images on a Quadro P2000, while CPU use 80×60 images on an i5-7287U.

Method	Forward CUDA	Backwards CUDA	Forward CPU	Backwards CPU
Point Cloud [52]	12.1 ± 0.5	23.4 ± 0.5	18.0 ± 1.0	23.8 ± 4.0
Pulsar [34]	7.8 ± 0.3	11.2 ± 0.4	16.4 ± 1.4	63.6 ± 7.9
SoftRas Mesh [38,52]	17.0 ± 0.4	27.2 ± 0.5	21.5 ± 2.0	384.7 ± 93.8
Fuzzy Metaballs	$\mathbf{3.0 \pm 0.2}$	$\mathbf{9.6 \pm 0.5}$	$\mathbf{3.0 \pm 0.15}$	$\mathbf{13.2 \pm 1.4}$

We include a term (η) for the rough scale of the object. This, along with use of Eq. (4) allows our rendering to be invariant to object scale. We also include an extra term to down-weight results of intersections behind the camera with a simple sigmoid function:

$$h(t) = \sigma \left(\frac{\beta_3}{\eta} t \right). \tag{10}$$

Our blending solution requires only $O(N)$ evaluations of Gaussians for each ray.

4.3 Obtaining Fuzzy Metaballs

A representation can be limited in utility by how easily one can convert to it. We propose that, unlike classic Metaballs, Fuzzy Metaballs have reasonably straightforward methods for conversion from other formats.

Since we've developed a differentiable renderer, one can optimize a Fuzzy Metaball representation from a set of images. One could use several different losses, but experiments with silhouettes are described in Sect. 7.2.

If one has a mesh, the mathematical relationship of Fuzzy Metaballs and Gaussian Mixture Models can be exploited by fitting a GMM with Expectation-Maximization [13]. With Fuzzy Metaballs being between a surface and volume representation, there are two forms of GMM one could fit. The first is a surface GMM (sGMM) as used by many authors [16,30,60], where a GMM is fit to points sampled from the surface of the object. The second is to build a volumetric GMM (vGMM). To build a vGMM, one takes a watertight mesh [29], and samples points from the interior of the object. Fitting a GMM to these interior points is what we call a volumetric GMM. Both representations can then further be optimized using the differentiable renderer. Our experiments show that both forms of GMM initialization work well, but we use vGMMs in our experiments.

Extraction is also straightforward. Point clouds can easily be sampled from our proper probability distributions. Extracting a mesh is possible by running marching cubes [41] with an optimized iso-surface level. The details of these experiments can be found in the supplementary material.

5   Data

We use ten models for evaluation: five from the Stanford Model Repository [35] (arma, buddha, dragon, lucy, bunny), three from Thingi10K [78] (gear, eiffel, rebel) and two from prior rendering literature (yoga, plane). All ten are used for reconstruction, and seven are used for pose estimation. We selected objects with different scales, genus, and variety in features. We choose 40 component FMs based on prior literature suggesting 20 to 60 GMMs for object representation [14].

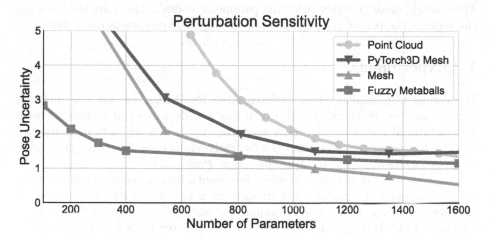

Fig. 4. Perturbation sensitivity is the average error in pose when registration is performed with ground truth pose as initialization. See Sect. 6 for details. The underlying ground truth is a decimated mesh, so only the mesh representation approaches exactly zero error while other asymptote at a higher mark.

6   Comparing Representations

Fairly comparing object representations requires some notion of what to hold constant. As the parameter counts of each representation increase, so do their representational ability. It would be unfair to compare a million point pointcloud against a 100 face triangle mesh. Since our goal is utility in vision tasks, our definition of fidelity will also be task-centric.

In this case, our metric of fidelity will be a representation's *perturbation sensitivity*. We define this as the pose error obtained when optimizing an object's camera pose given a depth map, when the optimization process was initialized with ground truth camera pose. The given depth map is of the full representation object, but the methods are evaluated using lower fidelity versions, leading to perturbations of optimal pose and our fidelity metric. Pose errors are reported using the geometric mean of rotation error and translation error.

Results of our fidelity experiments can be seen in Fig. 4. We evaluate point clouds and meshes using a standard Iterative Closest Point (ICP) method [77], with the point clouds randomly subsampled and the meshes undergoing decimation [18]. We also use PyTorch3D [52], a differential mesh renderer, and obtain its perturbation curve. These experiments are conditional on an experimental setup and methods used, and thus these results may change under different conditions.

In our experiments, a 40 component Fuzzy Metaball (the size we throughout across this paper) produces a pose uncertainty equivalent to a 470 point point cloud (roughly triple the parameter count of a fuzzy metaball) and 85 vertex, 170 triangle mesh (roughly twice the parameter count). These are the sizes use throughout the rest of the paper, in our attempt to keep comparisons fair.

7 Experiments

For comparison against other Differentiable Renderers, we use the methods implemented in PyTorch3D [52], which has a wide variety of techniques with well-optimized routines. The mesh rendering method is an implementation of the *SoftRasterizer* [38]. For point clouds, PyTorch3D cites *Direct Surface Splatting* [74], while also implementing the recent *Pulsar* [34].

With the fidelity of different object representations normalized out (Sect. 6), we can compare the runtime performance in a fair way, with times shown in in Table 1. On the CPU, where comparisons are more equal (due to lacking a custom CUDA kernel), our renderer is 5 times faster for a forward pass, and significantly faster (30x) for a backwards pass compared to the mesh rendering methods. The point cloud renderer is more comparable in runtime to ours but need a pre-specified point size, often producing images with lots of holes (when points are too small) or a poor silhouette (when points are too big).

To the demonstrate the ability our differentiable renderer to solve classic computer vision tasks, we look at pose estimation (Sect. 7.1) and 3D reconstruction from silhouettes (Sect. 7.2). Our renderer is a function that takes camera pose and geometry, and produces images. It seems natural to take images and evaluate how well either camera pose or geometry can be reconstructed, when the other is given. All five hyperparameters for our rendering algorithm ($\beta_{1,2,3,4,5}$) were held constant throughout all experiments.

Since pose estimation and shape from silhouette (SFS) are classic computer vision problems, there are countless methods for both tasks. We do not claim to be the best solution to these problems, as there are many methods specifically designed for these tasks under a variety of conditions. Instead, we seek to demonstrate how our approximate differentiable renderer is comparable in quality to typical solutions, using only gradient descent, without any regularization.

Table 2. Pose Estimation Results. Pose Errors are reported with a geometric mean of rotation and translation error. The reported numbers are mean ± IQR. We report results clean data and data with simulated depth and silhouette noise.

	Parameters	Noise-free error	Noisy error
Initialization		20.2 ± 18	20.2 ± 18
Pulsar [34]	1,200	20.2 ± 18	20.2 ± 18
Point Cloud [52]	1,200	18.5 ± 16	18.4 ± 16
SoftRas Mesh [38]	750	14.9 ± 15	17.0 + 17
Equal Fidelity ICP (Plane) [77]	1,200	10.8 ± 12	8.2 ± 3.3
Equal Fidelity ICP (Point) [77]	1,200	7.6 ± 9.9	8.7 ± 6.6
High Fidelity ICP (Plane) [77]	120,000	8.2 ± 0.8	8.0 ± 3.6
High Fidelity ICP (Point) [77]	120,000	6.2 ± 3.7	6.8 ± 3.3
Fuzzy Metaballs	400	**4.0 ± 1.5**	**4.2 ± 2.1**

7.1 Pose Estimation

Many differential renderers show qualitative results of pose estimation [38, 74]. We instead perform quantitative results over our library of models rendered from random viewpoints. Methods are given a perturbed camera pose (±45° rotation and a random translation up to 50% of model scale) and the ground truth depth image from the original pose. The methods are evaluated by their ability to recover the original pose from minimizing image-based errors. The resulting pose is evaluated for rotation error and translation error. We quantify the score for a model as the geometric mean of the two errors. All methods are tested on the same random viewpoints and with the same random perturbations.

For Fuzzy Metaballs, we establish projective correspondence [54] and optimize silhouette cross-entropy loss averaged over all pixels:

$$CE(\alpha, \hat{\alpha}) = \alpha \log(\hat{\alpha}) + (1 - \alpha) \log(1 - \hat{\alpha}). \tag{11}$$

Estimated alpha is clipped to $[10^{-6}, 1 - 10^{-6}]$ to avoid infinite error. We also evaluate with an additional depth loss of $MSE(z, \hat{z})$ where $|z|$ normalizes the errors to be invariant to object scale and comparable in magnitude to $CE(\alpha, \hat{\alpha})$.

$$MSE(z, \hat{z}) = \left\| \frac{(z - \hat{z})}{|z|} \right\|_2 \tag{12}$$

There is a subtle caveat in the gradients of Fuzzy Metaballs. The gradient of the translation scales by the inverse of model scale.. We correct for this by scaling the gradients by η^2. Alternatively one could scale the input data to always be of some canonical scale [72]. To maintain scale invariance, we limit our use of adaptive learning rate methods to SGD with Momentum.

We provide point cloud ICP results for point-to-point and point-to-plane methods [54] as implemented by Open3D [77]. For the differentiable rendering experiments, we use PyTorch3D [52] and tune its settings (see supplementary). All differentiable rendering methods use the same loss, learning rate decay criteria and are run until the loss stops reliably decreasing.

Pose Estimation Results. Overall results are found in Table 2 and a more detailed breakdown in Fig. 5. All methods sometimes struggle to find the correct local minima in this testing setup. Prior differentiable renderers significantly under-performed classic baselines like ICP, while our approximate renderer even outperforms the ICP baselines under realistic settings with synthetic noise.

ICP on noise-free data had bimodal results: it typically either recovered the correct pose to near machine precision or it fell into the wrong local minima. Despite having a higher mean error, ICP's median errors on noise-free data were $\frac{1}{10}$ of Fuzzy Metaballs (FMs). With noisy data, this bimodal distribution disappears and Fuzzy Metaballs outperform on all tested statistical measures. FMs even outperformed ICP with high-fidelity point clouds, suggesting a difference in method not just fidelity. This may be due to our inclusion of a silhouette loss, the benefits of projective correspondence over the nearest neighbors used by this ICP variant [77] or the strengths of visual loss over geometric loss [65].

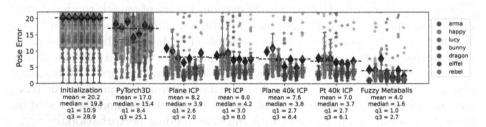

Fig. 5. Noisy Pose Estimation Dashed lines are averages for the method, while the black diamonds show the average for that method and model. Here Fuzzy Metaballs win in all statistical measures, typically by a factor of $\approx$ 2.

7.2   3D Reconstruction

Reconstruction experiments are common in the differential rendering literature [34,74]. However, instead of optimizing with annotations of color [33] or normals [74], we instead only optimize only over silhouettes, as in the classic Shape From Silhouette (SFS) [11]. Unlike many prior examples in the literature, which require fine-tuning of several regularization losses [52,74], we use no regularization in our experiments and can keep constant settings for all objects.

We initialize with a sphere (isosphere for meshes, an isotropic Gaussian of points for point clouds and a small blobby sphere for Fuzzy Metaballs). Given a set of silhouette images and their camera poses, we then optimize silhouette loss for the object. In our experiments, we use 64 × 64 pixel images and have 32 views. For these experiments, we resize all models to a canonical scale and use the Adam [32] optimizer. For baseline hyperparameters, we use the PyTorch3D settings with minimal modification. For SoftRas, we use a twice subdivided icosphere. For NeRF [46], we use a two layer MLP with 30 harmonic function embedding with 128 hidden dimension and the same early exit strategy as FMs.

Inspired by artifacts seen in real videos (Fig. 9), we produce a noisy silhouette dataset where training data had $\frac{1}{8}$ of each silhouette under-segmented (Fig. 8) in 16 of 32 images by clustering silhouette coordinates [56] and removing a cluster.

Fig. 6. Shape from Silhouette (SFS) reconstructions. On the left is a 40 component Fuzzy Metaball result and the right is the mesh ground-truth of about 2,500 faces, both colored by depth maps.

Table 3. Shape from Silhouette reconstruction fidelity as measured by cross-entropy silhouette loss on 32 novel viewpoints for each of 10 sample models. Runtimes were the average per model and performed on CPU. Results show $\mu \pm \sigma$.

	Time (s)	Noise-free recon. error	Noisy recon. error
Voxel carving [43,77]	82	0.31 ± 0.100	1.119 ± 0.367
PyTorch3D point [52]	185	0.075 ± 0.066	0.100 ± 0.079
PyTorch3D mesh [38]	3008	0.062 ± 0.049	0.072 ± 0.051
NeRF [46]	7406	$\mathbf{0.032 \pm 0.022}$	0.062 ± 0.063
Fuzzy Metaballs	**68**	0.040 ± 0.015	$\mathbf{0.055 \pm 0.016}$

Shape from Silhouette Results. We show qualitative reconstructions from Fuzzy Metaballs (Fig. 6), along with quantitative results against baselines (Table 3) and some example reconstructions from all methods (Fig. 8).

Overall, we found that our method was significantly faster than the other differentiable renderers, while producing the best results in the case of noisy reconstructions. Classic voxel carving [43] with a 384^3 volume was reasonably fast, but the 32 views of low resolution images didn't produce extremely sharp contours (see supplementary). With under-segmentation noise, voxel carving fails completely while the differentiable renderers reasonably reconstruct all models.

Among the differentiable renders, we can see how the mesh-based approach struggles to change genus from a sphere to the Eiffel tower. The point cloud renderer lacks the correct gradients to successfully pull spurious points into the model. NeRF [46] performs reasonably well in shape from silhouette, even with spurious masks. In fact, it was the best performer for noise-free data, and in a majority of the reconstructions in noisy data (its mean performance was hurt by results on `eiffel` and `lucy` with long thin surfaces). NeRF is a sophisticated model with many settings, and it may have a configuration where it successfully reconstructs all the models, but due to its dense volumetric rendering and use of an MLP, it is 100x slower than our low degree of freedom representation (Fig. 7).

Fig. 7. Shape from Silhouette steps Top row shows synthetic data with reconstructed depth. Bottom row shows reconstructed masks for a CO3D video [53].

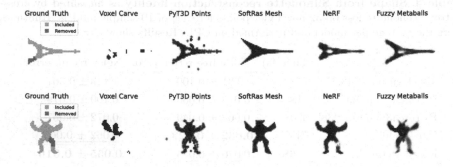

Fig. 8. Shape from Silhouette Results with simulated under-segmentation.

8   Discussion

The focus of our approximate differentiable rendering method has been on shape. While it is possible to add per-component colors to Fuzzy Metaballs (see supplementary), that has not been the focus of our experiments. Focusing on shape allows us to circumvent modeling high-frequency color textures, as well as ignoring lighting computations. This shape-based approach can use data from modern segmentation methods [21] and depth sensors [31]. Low-degree of freedom models have a natural robustness and implicit regularization that allows for recovery from significant artifacts present in real systems. For example, Fig. 9 shows robust recovery from real over/under-segmentation artifacts in video sequences.

Our approximate approach to rendering by using OIT-like methods creates a trade-off. The downside is that small artifacts can be observed since the method coarsely approximates correct image formation. The benefits are good gradients, speed & robustness, all of which produce utility in vision tasks.

Compared to prior work [34, 38], our results do not focus on the same areas of differentiable rendering. Unlike other work, we do not perform GPU-centric optimizations [33]. Additionally, prior work focuses on producing high-fidelity color images (and using them for optimization). Unlike prior work, we benchmark our method across a family of objects and report quantitative results against classic baselines. Unlike some popular implicit surface methods such as the NeRF [46] family, our object representation is low degree of freedom, quick to optimize from scratch, and all the parameters are interpretable with geometric meaning.

While our experiments focus on classic computer vision tasks such as pose estimation or shape from silhouette, the value of efficiently rendering interpretable, low degree of freedom models may have the biggest impact outside of classic com-

FM SFS Depth   FM SFS Mask   Mask-RCNN Mask

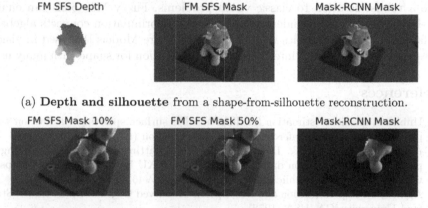

(a) **Depth and silhouette** from a shape-from-silhouette reconstruction.

FM SFS Mask 10%   FM SFS Mask 50%   Mask-RCNN Mask

(b) **Recovering from undersegmentation in the ground truth masks.** While a 50% threshold does a good job recovering the head, better recovery can be shown with a 10% threshold, also recovering the leg.

FM SFS Mask 10%   FM SFS Mask 50%   Mask-RCNN Mask

(c) **Recovering from oversegmentation in ground truth masks.** Even the $\alpha = 10\%$ threshold only leads to minor over-segmentation in the mask, suggesting a setting that be appropriate in general.

Fig. 9. Shape from silhouette reconstruction on natural images from a hand-held cell phone video, using COLMAP [55] and Mask RCNN [21] for automatic camera poses and silhouettes. The low degree of freedom leads to natural regularization and recovery from errors in ground truth.

puter vision contexts. For example, in scientific imaging it is often impossible to obtain high-quality observations since the sensors are limited. For example, in non-light-of-sight imaging [66], sonar reconstruction [69], lightcurve inversion [27] and CryoEM [9,76]. In all these contexts, getting good imaging information is extremely hard and low degree of freedom models could be desirable.

9   Conclusion

Approximate differentiable rendering with algebraic surfaces enables fast analysis-by-synthesis pipelines for vision tasks which focus on shapes, such as pose estimation and shape from silhouette. For both tasks, we show results with realistic, simulated noise. The robustness of our approach enables it to runs naturally on silhouettes extracted from real video sequences without any regularization. Whereas classic methods can struggle once noise is introduced, differentiable renderers naturally recovery by using stochastic optimization techniques. By using gradient-based optimization, differentiable rendering techniques provide a robust solution to classic vision problems. Fuzzy Metaballs can enable low-latency differential rendering on CPUs. Our formulation connects algebraic surfaces [6] used in graphics with Gaussian Mixture Models [16] used in vision. These provide a compact, interpretable representation for shape with many uses.

References

1. Unbiased gradient estimation for differentiable surface splatting via Poisson sampling. In: European Conference on Computer Vision (ECCV) (2022)
2. Adams, B., Lenaert, T., Dutré, P.: Particle splatting: interactive rendering of particle-based simulation data. Report CW 453, KU Leuven, July 2006. https://www.cs.kuleuven.be/publicaties/rapporten/cw/CW453.abs.html
3. Agin, G.J.: Representation and Description of Curved Objects. Ph.D. thesis, Stanford University, CA, USA (1972)
4. Bangaru, S., Li, T.M., Durand, F.: Unbiased warped-area sampling for differentiable rendering. ACM Trans. Graph. **39**(6), 245:1–245:18 (2020)
5. Bell, C.G., Fujisaki, H., Heinz, J.M., Stevens, K.N., House, A.S.: Reduction of speech spectra by analysis-by-synthesis techniques. J. Acoust. Soc. Am. **33**(12), 1725–1736 (1961). https://doi.org/10.1121/1.1908556
6. Blinn, J.F.: A generalization of algebraic surface drawing. ACM Trans. Graph. **1**(3), 235–256 (1982). https://doi.org/10.1145/357306.357310
7. Blinn, J.F.: How to solve a cubic equation, part 5: back to numerics. IEEE Comput. Graph. Appl. **27**(3), 78–89 (2007). https://doi.org/10.1109/MCG.2007.60
8. Bradbury, J., et al.: JAX: composable transformations of Python+NumPy programs (2018). https://github.com/google/jax
9. Brubaker, M., Punjani, A., Fleet, D.: Building proteins in a day. CVPR (2015). https://doi.org/10.1109/cvpr.2015.7298929
10. Chen, W., et al.: Learning to predict 3D objects with an interpolation-based differentiable renderer. Adv. Neural Inf. Process. Syst. **32** (2019)
11. Cheung, K.M.G., Baker, S., Kanade, T.: Shape-from-silhouette across time part I: theory and algorithms. Int. J. Comput. Vis. **62**(3), 221–247 (2005). https://doi.org/10.1007/s11263-005-4881-5

12. Cole, F., Genova, K., Sud, A., Vlasic, D., Zhang, Z.: Differentiable surface rendering via non-differentiable sampling (2021)
13. Dempster, A., Laird, N., Rubin, D.B.: Maximum likelihood from incomplete data via the EM algorithm. J. Royal Stat. Soc. (B) **39**(1), 1–38 (1977). https://doi.org/ 10.2307/2984875
14. Eckart, B., Kim, K., Kautz, J.: HGMR: hierarchical gaussian mixtures for adaptive 3D registration. In: ECCV 2018, pp. 730–746 (2018)
15. Eckart, B., Kim, K., Troccoli, A., Kelly, A., Kautz, J.: MLMD: maximum likelihood mixture decoupling for fast and accurate point cloud registration. In: 3DV, pp. 241–249 (2015). https://doi.org/10.1109/3DV.2015.34
16. Eckart, B., Kim, K., Troccoli, A., Kelly, A., Kautz, J.: Accelerated generative models for 3D point cloud data. In: CVPR, pp. 5497–5505 (2016). https://doi. org/10.1109/CVPR.2016.593
17. Enderton, E., Sintorn, E., Shirley, P., Luebke, D.: Stochastic transparency. In: I3D 2010: Proceedings of the 2010 Symposium on Interactive 3D Graphics and Games, pp. 157–164. New York, NY, USA (2010)
18. Garland, M., Heckbert, P.S.: Surface simplification using quadric error metrics. In: SIGGRAPH, pp. 209–216 (1997). https://doi.org/10.1145/258734.258849
19. Genova, K., Cole, F., Sud, A., Sarna, A., Funkhouser, T.: Local deep implicit functions for 3D shape (2020)
20. Gourmel, O., Pajot, A., Paulin, M., Barthe, L., Poulin, P.: Fitted BVH for fast raytracing of metaballs. Comput. Graph. Forum **3**, 7–288 (2010)
21. He, K., Gkioxari, G., Dollár, P., Girshick, R.B.: Mask R-CNN. In: 2017 IEEE International Conference on Computer Vision (ICCV), pp. 2980–2988 (2017)
22. Heckbert, P.S.: Fun with gaussians. In: SIGGRAPH 1986 Advanced Image Processing Seminar Notes (1986)
23. Hertz, A., Hanocka, R., Giryes, R., Cohen-Or, D.: PointGMM: a neural GMM network for point clouds. In: Proceedings of the IEEE Conference on Computer Vision and Pattern Recognition (2020)
24. Horvath, R.: Image-Space Metaballs Using Deep Learning. Master's thesis, Faculty of Informatics, TU Wien, July 2019. https://www.cg.tuwien.ac.at/research/ publications/2019/horvath-2018-ism/
25. Huang, H., Ye, H., Sun, Y., Liu, M.: GMMLoc: structure consistent visual localization with gaussian mixture models. IEEE Robot. Autom. Lett. **5**(4), 5043–5050 (2020). https://doi.org/10.1109/LRA.2020.3005130
26. Insafutdinov, E., Dosovitskiy, A.: Unsupervised learning of shape and pose with differentiable point clouds (2018)
27. Kaasalainen, M., Torppa, J.: Optimization methods for asteroid lightcurve inversion. Icarus **153**(1), 24–36 (2001)
28. Kato, H., Ushiku, Y., Harada, T.: Neural 3D mesh renderer (2017)
29. Kazhdan, M., Bolitho, M., Hoppe, H.: Poisson surface reconstruction. In: Sheffer, A., Polthier, K. (eds.) Symposium on Geometry Processing. The Eurographics Association (2006). https://doi.org/10.2312/SGP/SGP06/061-070
30. Keselman, L., Hebert, M.: Direct fitting of gaussian mixture models. In: 2019 16th Conference on Computer and Robot Vision (CRV), pp. 25–32 (2019). https://doi. org/10.1109/CRV.2019.00012
31. Keselman, L., Woodfill, J.I., Grunnet-Jepsen, A., Bhowmik, A.: Intel realsense stereoscopic depth cameras. CoRR abs/1705.05548 (2017). arxiv:1705.05548
32. Kingma, D.P., Ba, J.: Adam: a method for stochastic optimization. In: ICLR (Poster) (2015). arxiv:1412.6980

33. Laine, S., Hellsten, J., Karras, T., Seol, Y., Lehtinen, J., Aila, T.: Modular primitives for high-performance differentiable rendering. ACM Trans. Graph. **39**(6), 1–14 (2020)
34. Lassner, C., Zollhöfer, M.: Pulsar: efficient sphere-based neural rendering. arXiv:2004.07484 (2020)
35. Levoy, M., Gerth, J., Curless, B., Pull, K.: The Stanford 3D scanning repository 5(10) (2005). https://graphics.stanford.edu/data/3Dscanrep/
36. Li, L., Zhu, S., Fu, H., Tan, P., Tai, C.L.: End-to-end learning local multi-view descriptors for 3D point clouds (2020)
37. Lin, C.H., Kong, C., Lucey, S.: Learning efficient point cloud generation for dense 3D object reconstruction. In: AAAI Conference on Artificial Intelligence (AAAI) (2018)
38. Liu, S., Li, T., Chen, W., Li, H.: Soft rasterizer: a differentiable renderer for image-based 3D reasoning. In: Proceedings of the IEEE/CVF International Conference on Computer Vision (ICCV), October 2019
39. Lombardi, S., Simon, T., Saragih, J., Schwartz, G., Lehrmann, A., Sheikh, Y.: Neural volumes: learning dynamic renderable volumes from images. ACM Trans. Graph. **38**(4), 65:1–65:14 (2019)
40. Loper, M.M., Black, M.J.: OpenDR: an approximate differentiable renderer. In: Fleet, D., Pajdla, T., Schiele, B., Tuytelaars, T. (eds.) ECCV 2014. LNCS, vol. 8695, pp. 154–169. Springer, Cham (2014). https://doi.org/10.1007/978-3-319-10584-0_11
41. Lorensen, W.E., Cline, H.E.: Marching cubes: a high resolution 3D surface construction algorithm. ACM SIGGRAPH Comput. Graph. **21**(4), 163–169 (1987)
42. Mahalanobis, P.C.: On the generalized distance in statistics. In: Proceedings of the National Institute of Sciences (Calcutta), pp. 49–55 (1936)
43. Martin, W.N., Aggarwal, J.K.: Volumetric descriptions of objects from multiple views. IEEE Trans. Patt. Anal. Mach. Intell. PAMI-**5**(2), 150–158 (1983). https://doi.org/10.1109/TPAMI.1983.4767367
44. Max, N.: Optical models for direct volume rendering. IEEE Trans. Visual. Comput. Graph. **1**(2), 99–108 (1995). https://doi.org/10.1109/2945.468400
45. McGuire, M., Bavoil, L.: Weighted blended order-independent transparency. J. Comput. Graph. Tech. (JCGT) **2**(2), 122–141 (2013). https://jcgt.org/published/0002/02/09/
46. Mildenhall, B., Srinivasan, P.P., Tancik, M., Barron, J.T., Ramamoorthi, R., Ng, R.: NERF: representing scenes as neural radiance fields for view synthesis. In: Vedaldi, A., Bischof, H., Brox, T., Frahm, J.M. (eds.) Computer Vision - ECCV 2020, pp. 405–421. Springer International Publishing, Cham (2020). https://doi.org/10.1007/978-3-030-58452-8_24
47. Miller, I.D., et al.: Mine tunnel exploration using multiple quadrupedal robots (2020)
48. Muraki, S.: Volumetric shape description of range data using "blobby model". In: Proceedings of the 18th Annual Conference on Computer Graphics and Interactive Techniques, pp. 227–235. SIGGRAPH 1991. Association for Computing Machinery, New York, NY, USA (1991). https://doi.org/10.1145/122718.122743
49. Nimier-David, M., Vicini, D., Zeltner, T., Jakob, W.: Mitsuba 2: a retargetable forward and inverse renderer. ACM Trans. Graph. **38**(6) (2019). https://doi.org/10.1145/3355089.3356498
50. O'Meadhra, C., Tabib, W., Michael, N.: Variable resolution occupancy mapping using Gaussian mixture models. IEEE Robot. Autom. Lett. **4**(2), 2015–2022 (2019). https://doi.org/10.1109/LRA.2018.2889348

51. Pfister, H., Zwicker, M., van Baar, J., Gross, M.: Surfels: surface elements as rendering primitives. In: Proceedings of the 27th Annual Conference on Computer Graphics and Interactive Techniques, pp. 335–342. SIGGRAPH 2000. ACM Press/Addison-Wesley Publishing Co., USA (2000). https://doi.org/10.1145/344779.344936

52. Ravi, N., et al.: Accelerating 3D deep learning with pytorch3d. arXiv:2007.08501 (2020)

53. Reizenstein, J., Shapovalov, R., Henzler, P., Sbordone, L., Labatut, P., Novotny, D.: Common objects in 3D: large-scale learning and evaluation of real-life 3D category reconstruction. In: International Conference on Computer Vision (2021)

54. Rusinkiewicz, S., Levoy, M.: Efficient variants of the ICP algorithm. In: Proceedings Third International Conference on 3D Digital Imaging & Modeling, pp. 145–152 (2001). https://doi.org/10.1109/IM.2001.924423

55. Schönberger, J.L., Zheng, E., Pollefeys, M., Frahm, J.M.: Pixelwise view selection for unstructured multi-view stereo. In: European Conference on Computer Vision (ECCV) (2016). https://doi.org/10.1007/978-3-319-46487-9_31

56. Sculley, D.: Web-scale k-means clustering. In: Proceedings of the 19th International Conference on World Wide Web, pp. 1177–1178. WWW 2010. Association for Computing Machinery, New York, NY, USA (2010). https://doi.org/10.1145/1772690.1772862

57. Shankar, K.S., Michael, N.: MRFMap: online probabilistic 3D mapping using forward ray sensor models. In: Robotics: Science and Systems (2020)

58. Sutherland, I.E., Sproull, R.F., Schumacker, R.A.: A characterization of ten hidden-surface algorithms. ACM Comput. Surv. **6**(1), 1–55 (1974). https://doi.org/10.1145/356625.356626

59. Szécsi, L., Illés, D.: Real-time metaball ray casting with fragment lists. In: Eurographics (2012)

60. Tabib, W., O'Meadhra, C., Michael, N.: On-manifold GMM registration. IEEE Robot. Autom. Lett. **3**(4), 3805–3812 (2018). https://doi.org/10.1109/LRA.2018.2856279

61. Teed, Z., Deng, J.: RAFT: recurrent all-pairs field transforms for optical flow. In: 16th European Conference on Computer Vision, pp. 402–419, Germany (2020). https://doi.org/10.1007/978-3-030-58536-5_24

62. Teed, Z., Deng, J.: Droid-SLAM: deep visual SLAM for monocular, stereo, and RGB-D cameras (2021)

63. Tewari, A., et al.: MoFA: model-based deep convolutional face autoencoder for unsupervised monocular reconstruction. In: 2017 IEEE International Conference on Computer Vision (ICCV), pp. 3735–3744 (2017). https://doi.org/10.1109/ICCV.2017.401

64. Tomic, T., et al.: Toward a fully autonomous UAV: research platform for indoor and outdoor urban search and rescue. IEEE Robot. Autom. Mag. **19**(3), 46–56 (2012). https://doi.org/10.1109/MRA.2012.2206473

65. Triggs, B., McLauchlan, P.F., Hartley, R.I., Fitzgibbon, A.W.: Bundle adjustment – a modern synthesis. In: Triggs, B., Zisserman, A., Szeliski, R. (eds.) Vision Algorithms: Theory and Practice, pp. 298–372. Springer, Berlin, Heidelberg (2000). https://doi.org/10.1007/3-540-44480-7_21

66. Tsai, C., Sankaranarayanan, A., Gkioulekas, I.: Beyond volumetric albedo. In: CVPR, June 2019

67. Tucker, R., Snavely, N.: Single-view view synthesis with multiplane images. In: Proceedings of the IEEE/CVF Conference on Computer Vision and Pattern Recognition, pp. 551–560 (2020)

68. Wang, A., Wang, P., Sun, J., Kortylewski, A., Yuille, A.: VoGE: a differentiable volume renderer using gaussian ellipsoids for analysis-by-synthesis. arXiv preprint arXiv:2205.15401 (2022)
69. Westman, E., Gkioulekas, I., Kaess, M.: Volumetric albedo framework for 3D imaging sonar. In: ICRA (2020)
70. Wyvill, G., McPheeters, C., Wyvill, B.: Data structure forsoft objects. Vis. Comput. **2**(4), 227–234 (1986). https://doi.org/10.1007/BF01900346
71. Wyvill, G., Trotman, A.: Ray-tracing soft objects. In: Chua, T.S., Kunii, T.L. (eds.) CG International, pp. 469–476. Springer Japan, Tokyo (1990). https://doi.org/10.1007/978-4-431-68123-6_27
72. Yang, J., Li, H., Jia, Y.: Go-ICP: solving 3D registration efficiently and globally optimally. In: 2013 IEEE International Conference on Computer Vision, pp. 1457–1464 (2013). https://doi.org/10.1109/ICCV.2013.184
73. Yang, S., Scherer, S.: CubeSLAM: Monocular 3-D object slam. IEEE Trans. Rob. **35**(4), 925–938 (2019). https://doi.org/10.1109/TRO.2019.2909168
74. Yifan, W., Serena, F., Wu, S., Öztireli, C., Sorkine-Hornung, O.: Differentiable surface splatting for point-based geometry processing. ACM Trans. Graph. **38**(6), 1–14 (2019). https://doi.org/10.1145/3355089.3356513
75. Zhang, C., Miller, B., Yan, K., Gkioulekas, I., Zhao, S.: Path-space differentiable rendering. ACM Trans. Graph. **39**(4), 143:1–143:19 (2020). https://doi.org/10.1145/3386569.3392383
76. Zhong, E.D., Lerer, A., Davis, J.H., Berger, B.: CryoDRGN2: Ab initio neural reconstruction of 3D protein structures from real cryo-EM images. In: Proceedings of the IEEE/CVF International Conference on Computer Vision (ICCV), pp. 4066–4075, October 2021
77. Zhou, Q.Y., Park, J., Koltun, V.: Open3D: a modern library for 3D data processing. arXiv:1801.09847 (2018)
78. Zhou, Q., Jacobson, A.: Thingi10k: a dataset of 10, 000 3D-printing models. CoRR abs/1605.04797 (2016). arxiv:1605.04797
79. Zwicker, M., Pfister, H., van Baar, J., Gross, M.: Surface splatting. In: Proceedings of the 28th Annual Conference on Computer Graphics and Interactive Techniques, pp. 371–378. SIGGRAPH 2001 (2001). https://doi.org/10.1145/383259.383300

CoVisPose: Co-visibility Pose Transformer for Wide-Baseline Relative Pose Estimation in 360° Indoor Panoramas

Will Hutchcroft[1]($\boxtimes$), Yuguang Li[1], Ivaylo Boyadzhiev[1], Zhiqiang Wan[1], Haiyan Wang[2], and Sing Bing Kang[1]

[1] Zillow Group, Seattle, USA
{willhu,yuguangl,ivaylob,zhiqiangw,singbingk}@zillow.com
[2] The City College of New York, New York, USA
hwang005@citymail.cuny.edu

Abstract. We present *CoVisPose*, a new end-to-end supervised learning method for relative camera pose estimation in wide baseline 360° indoor panoramas. To address the challenges of occlusion, perspective changes, and textureless or repetitive regions, we generate rich representations for direct pose regression by jointly learning dense *bidirectional* visual overlap, correspondence, and layout geometry. We estimate three image column-wise quantities: *co-visibility* (the probability that a given column's image content is seen in the other panorama), *angular correspondence* (angular matching of columns across panoramas), and *floor layout* (the vertical floor-wall boundary angle). We learn these dense outputs by applying a transformer over the image-column feature sequences, which cover the full 360° field-of-view (FoV) from both panoramas. The resultant rich representation supports learning robust relative poses with an efficient 1D convolutional decoder. In addition to learned direct pose regression with scale, our network also supports pose estimation through a RANSAC-based rigid registration of the predicted corresponding layout boundary points. Our method is robust to extremely wide baselines with very low visual overlap, as well as significant occlusions. We improve upon the SOTA by a large margin, as demonstrated on a large-scale dataset of real homes, ZInD.

Keywords: Indoor · 360° Panorama · Indoor · Pose estimation · Camera localization · Structure-from-motion · Layout

1 Introduction

With the increasing affordability of 360° capture devices, omnidirectional imagery has become an important capture modality for indoor environments[1]. The large-

---

[1] https://www.ricoh360.com/tours/.

Supplementary Information The online version contains supplementary material available at https://doi.org/10.1007/978-3-031-19824-3_36.

S. Avidan et al. (Eds.): ECCV 2022, LNCS 13692, pp. 615–633, 2022.
https://doi.org/10.1007/978-3-031-19824-3_36

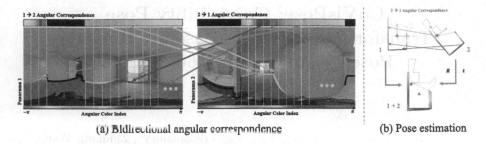

(a) Bidirectional angular correspondence   (b) Pose estimation

Fig. 1. Our system (a) establishes bidirectional column-wise (angular) correspondence while computing (b) pose estimation between two panoramas that visually overlap.

FoV provides an immersive experience as well as comprehensive context for indoor scene understanding; this enables applications such as AR/VR, autonomous navigation, virtual tours, room layout estimation, and floor plan reconstruction. The omnidirectional information allows sparser capture while maintaining geometric context. Concurrent with the rise of deep learning, these advantages have inspired a rapid increase in research focused on the spherical domain, including layout estimation [36,45,46,54,55,58], depth estimation [46,53,58], semantic segmentation [19,59], object detection [30], and network design [29,44].

Commercially, for practical and economic reasons, panoramic captures for virtual tours and floor plan reconstruction typically result in sparse coverage, with wide baselines between panoramas [12,37,43]. In particular, the indoor environments of real homes in ZInD [12] have extensive featureless regions and strong visual similarity between rooms, which present challenges to classical feature-based Structure-from-Motion (SfM) approaches. To alleviate that, other methods require denser RGB [1,6] or RGB-D [8,38] captures. However, those are at the expense of more time (to capture) or investment in specialized hardware.

In this paper, we propose a new method to estimate relative pose for a pair of 360° indoor panoramas under a wide range of baselines *(small to extreme)*. To address the challenges associated with operating in the spherical domain, we take inspiration from the horizontal (1D column-wise) representation for layout estimation [45,46]. We jointly learn to regress relative pose alongside estimation of image-column-wise representations of visual overlap (co-visibility), correspondence, and layout geometry. To learn the highly non-local associative tasks of co-visibility and correspondence, we apply a transformer to image-column feature sequences, allowing the network to attend globally across the full 360° context from both panoramas. Further, jointly learning to estimate layout geometry provides the network with a strong prior for the indoor environment. By providing dense supervision, we reduce ambiguity and guide the transformer to learn rich representations for robust pose regression, even in the presence of minimal visual overlap and wide baselines.

Our contributions are:

- Novel representation for relative pose estimation between two upright 360° cameras, which factors the auxiliary tasks of visual overlap, correspondence, and layout estimation as image-column-wise quantities.

- Transformer-based architecture that operates over the image-column feature sequences across both panoramas, applying inter and intra-image column attention.
- Support for both end-to-end direct pose regression as well as a post-processing step using iterative robust model fitting, e.g., RANSAC [61], enabled through the densely predicted corresponding layout boundary points.
- Co-visibility score generated by our co-visibility representation, which gives a strong measure of trust in a given predicted relative pose. Using this measure, we demonstrate strong pose precision and recall performance for pose estimation in unordered panoramas.
- Direct estimation of two-view SfM with scale. To our knowledge, this is the first end-to-end learning approach to estimate the pose of upright panoramas with respect to predicted layout geometry.
- SOTA performance on a challenging real world dataset [12]. We achieve a 78% and 85% decrease in median rotation and translation error, respectively, over a SOTA deep feature matching approach, while at the same time successfully estimating a pose for 35% more panorama pairs.

2   Related Work

In this section, we briefly review representative methods in the related areas of pose estimation and room layout estimation.

Two-View Pose Estimation. Classical methods for relative pose estimation (RPE) first extract and match image features like SIFT [31], which are then used to derive the relative camera motion by estimating the fundamental or essential matrix, for uncalibrated or calibrated cameras, respectively [62]. These methods are generally well behaved and robust when the camera motions are small and the scene texture is amenable to extraction and matching of features; however, common failure modes include repetitive or limited texture, as well as large camera motion between views. Recent works have attempted to address these challenges using deep learning. Many works have focused on modeling those components of the classical pipeline which are especially susceptible to failure, such as feature detection [14,18], correspondence estimation [40,47,57], and model fitting [4,39].

Of the recent works for deep feature detection, description, and correspondence estimation, a combination of [14] and [40] has proven particularly effective for relative pose estimation. The system of [14] replaces hand-crafted interest-point detection and descriptors with learned counterparts by attaching two separate decoder branches to a shared CNN encoder. The method of [40] accepts two detection sets and learns the feature matching step with a Graph Neural Network (GNN). Its attentional GNN variant combines both inter- and intra-image attention in order to reason about both appearance and spatial cues. However, there is no feedback from matching; correspondence estimation is subject to the input detection quality with no global reasoning.

LoFTR [47] learns to perform both steps in a detector-free approach and directly outputs dense correspondences. Their system also leverage inter- and intra-image attention with a transformer applied in a coarse-to-fine approach. This global reasoning improves matching for regions with limited texture or repetitive patterns. This method sets a new state-of-the-art on multiple benchmarks, including indoor relative pose estimation in the perspective imagery of ScanNet. Nevertheless, this method only focuses on one portion of the SfM pipeline, and may still be subject to difficulties with model fitting.

In contrast, other techniques directly learn the mapping function between images and pose [9,32,50], demonstrating improved performance for classically challenging cases, including wide baselines. Similar to our work, many techniques [9,20,32] first apply a feature extractor in a Siamese configuration, sharing weights across the input pair. Melekhov et al. [32] use the extracted feature representations directly as input to two fully-connected layers to regress the relative pose. En et al. [20] propose multiple variants, including relative pose computation from two absolute pose estimates, with a similar fully-connected regressor displaying the best overall performance. Notably, they estimate the full translation vector and report errors in meters. Chen et al. [9] formulate a directional parameterization of the relative pose. They stack multiple decoder blocks on top of a Siamese encoder and estimate discrete distributions over the sphere. Their best performing archite-cture follows a two-stage approach which first derotates the image before estimating the translation component, making it robust to wide baselines.

Such direct regression methods have also been proposed for the task of absolute pose estimation (APE), with the aim of learning the camera-to-scene transformation directly [5,25,26,52]. One subproblem of APE is the visual relocali-zation task, which aims to localize one or more target images against scene images of known pose. This problem may be framed as retrieval-then-RPE, wherein nearest neighbors are retrieved, with the scene pose subsequently determined through RPE. Such methods have demonstrated strong ability to generalize [2,28] as the pose regressor is not tied to a scene-specific coordinate frame. Laskar et al. [28] first train a Siamese architecture to regress relative pose, and then use the learned feature representation for database retrieval of neighboring panoramas. Balntas et al.'s work [2] is in a similar spirit with ours in that they estimate a camera frustum overlap, analogous to our co-visibility. From the same feature embeddings, they additionally regress the relative pose, which strengthens the retrieval performance while serving to localize to scene coordinates.

Two-view pose estimation with given priors (e.g., gravity-aligned vertical direction [16,17,27]) or constrained motions (e.g., planar camera motion [1,11, 21]) is an active area of research. This has many practical applications such as robotics [34] and virtual walkthroughs [1,12], and are enabled by the availability and robust integration of low-cost IMU sensors [22] and improved algorithms for upright camera corrections [13,23,24]. In our work, we assume a planar motion model for the spherical cameras, i.e., all the cameras lie on the same plane with a fixed height and a gravity-aligned vertical direction. These practical constraints are used in commercial applications, e.g., application of Street View technology indoors [1]. Those assumptions reduce the general 6-DoF two-view spherical geometry [48] to a 3-DoF problem solved in the 2D plane [1].

Layout Estimation. HorizonNet [45] introduced the horizontal representation for layout estimation in 360° indoor panoramas, significantly improving SOTA by factoring layout into output vectors over the image columns. By applying an LSTM to the image column features produced through a height compression module (HCM), they estimate both the floor and ceiling boundary contours as well as the corner probability score. HorizonNet further exploits the upright camera assumption to post-process Manhattan layouts. HoHoNet [46] improves the HCM efficiency, and demonstrates the ability to predict per-pixel modalities by applying an inverse discrete cosine transform to decompress the latent feature representation.

Our work is inspired by the success of the horizontal representation in the indoor domain. To learn rich pose representations, we frame correspondence and visual overlap estimation as column-wise prediction, and additionally estimate the layout contour from both views, to provide a strong prior for the indoor environment. Similar to [47], we leverage a transformer to attend to inter and intra-image relationships; however, our transformer is applied over image column feature sequences, analogous to sequence processing in NLP, to efficiently aggregate the full 360° range. Moreover, we do not require full depth maps for training; only the sparse wall layout geometry is necessary. As has been demonstrated in the perspective domain [9], direct pose regression provides advantages for wide-baselines, occlusion, textureless regions, and other classically challenging cases. The rich representations learned by our CoVis transformer bring these benefits, for the first time, to the spherical domain.

3 Overview

Our CoVisPose architecture is shown in Fig. 2(a). The inputs to our system are a pair of 360° panoramas in equirectangular projection, captured in an indoor space. We assume the camera is upright, with a fixed height for each home. The orientation with the gravity vector is imposed via straightening as a pre-processing step [60]. Each panorama may or may not have visual overlap with neighboring panoramas. Further, we assume Atlanta world layouts [42], where the walls are upright and orthogonal to the floor. As seen in Fig. 2(a), we adopt the feature extractor from HorizonNet [45] in a Siamese configuration, with shared weights between the branches. Each branch consists of a ResNet50 backbone followed by an HCM to produce a feature sequence over the image columns. The feature sequences from each image are then summed with fixed positional encodings and per-image segment embeddings with learnable weights, concatenated length-wise, and passed as input sequence to the CoVis transformer. The output embedding sequence from the transformer is then passed as input to two decoders which are trained jointly.

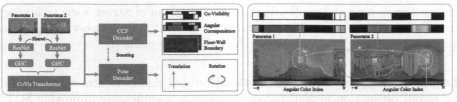

(a) Architecture of CoVisPose Network   (b) Illustration of CCF Decoder's output

Fig. 2. CoVisPose system.(a) The architecture consists of CoVis transformer, the Co-visibility, angular Correspondence and Floor-wall boundary (CCF) decoder, and pose decoder. (b) An example to illustrate the CCF decoder's outputs.

The Co-visibility, angular Correspondence and Floor-wall boundary (CCF) decoder is a single fully connected layer which maps the transformer embedding space to the per-column outputs. In Fig. 2(b), we illustrate the CCF decoder's output representation for an example image pair. In the predicted co-visibility probability vector, note the large gap in estimated co-visibility in panorama 1's view of the interior of the room, spanning from the right edge of the window to the doorway. This represents the section of floor-wall boundary not being visible to panorama 2. We highlight two particular angular correspondences. The highlighted correspondence from panorama 1 estimates that the center of the window is visible at location $\approx 90°$ in panorama 2, while the correspondence from panorama 2 estimates that the banister is visible at location $\approx 180°$ in panorama 1.

Our pose decoder consists of a simple 6 layer 1D CNN, applied separately to the output transformer embedding sequence from each image. The outputs are then once again concatenated and passed to a fully-connected layer to regress the relative pose. In addition to this direct pose regression, we also demonstrate recovery of relative pose through a RANSAC procedure applied directly to the correspondence network's outputs. Projected into the floor plane, the floor-wall boundary contours form a pair of 2D point sets. For those boundary points with predicted co-visibility, the correspondence angles then suggest corresponding point pairs between the two sets. The pose may subsequently be recovered by rigid registration, which we estimate with a RANSAC iteration.

4   Method

In this section, we provide details on the components of CoVisPose, how training is done, and how RANSAC is used for relative pose estimation. We also describe how ZInD [12] is processed for evaluation. We first define the architecture outputs: relative pose, co-visibility, angular correspondence, and floor-wall boundary.

Relative Pose. Given an equirectangular image pair, $(I_1, I_2) \in \mathbb{R}^{3 \times H \times W}$, we estimate the relative pose $\mathbf{P}_{2,1}$ of panorama I_2 w.r.t. the local coordinate system of I_1 centered at the origin. Under the upright camera, camera-axis-aligned walls, and orthogonal floor orientation assumptions, the camera pose may be simplified to planar motion with a single rotation angle about the camera axis, i.e., a translation vector $\mathbf{t} \in \mathbb{R}^2$ and a rotation matrix $R \in SO(2)$. Therefore, the pose $\mathbf{P}_{2,1} \in SE(2)$. For direct regression, we represent the pose by five parameters, estimating the unit rotation and translation vectors $\mathbf{r}$ and $\mathbf{t}$, as well as the translation scale s. The network is trained to estimate the translation scale normalized by the camera height. This decoupled representation allows both rotation and translation to be framed as directional estimation.

Co-visibility, Angular Correspondence, and Floor-Wall Boundary. Under the wall-floor geometry assumptions, wall geometry may be represented by a 1D contour, the position of which is defined for a given image column i as a vertical angle $\phi_i \in [0, \pi/2]$ as in [45,47]. For relative pose estimation, we extend this column-wise vector representation to two additional quantities: (1) The co-visibility vector, i.e., a binary value $p_{c,i}$ with value 1 if column i's floor-wall boundary is visible to the other panorama and 0 otherwise, and (2) the angular correspondence, i.e., the horizontal angle $\alpha_i \in [-\pi, \pi]$ at which column i's floor-wall boundary is visible in the other panorama's FoV (defined only if $p_{c,i} = 1$). For a given panorama pair, these quantities are defined bidirectionally.

4.1 CoVisPose Network Architecture

Our architecture consists of the feature extractor, CoVis transformer, Co-Visibility, Angular Correspondence, Floor-Wall Boundary (CCF) decoder, and pose decoder.

Feature Extractor. We leverage the single image feature extractor from [45], a ResNet50 backbone followed by an HCM. For each panorama, this produces a feature sequence over the (downsampled) column-space. For an input image $I_k \in \mathbb{R}^{3 \times 512 \times 1024}$, we obtain the features $f_k \in \mathbb{R}^{256 \times 1024}$.

CoVis Transformer. While LSTM and CNN architectures have been applied successfully for per-column prediction of layout [45,47], the local inductive biases of these architectures [3,56] makes them ill-suited for the inherently non-local tasks of co-visibility and correspondence estimation across pairs of 360° panoramas. On the contrary, transformers [51] update embeddings globally and in parallel.

Inspired by [15,51], we add fixed sinusoidal positional encodings and learnable per-image segment embeddings. Both are crucial for the angular correspondence task; they provide the permutation invariant transformer the necessary information to distinguish both relative position of image columns and image membership while attending globally to both intra and inter-image column relationships. We then concatenate the updated column-wise feature sequences length-wise to form the input to the transformer, $F_{in} = (\hat{f}_1, \hat{f}_2) \in \mathbb{R}^{512 \times 1024}$. Our transformer consists of 6 encoder layers, each with 8 heads of internal self-attention, followed by a feed-forward layer of dimension 2048. The output embeddings are of the same dimensionality as the input, $F_{tr} \in \mathbb{R}^{512 \times 1024}$. Those serve as input to two decoders, to estimate the per-column outputs, and regress the relative pose.

Co-visibility, Angular Correspondence, and Floor-Wall Boundary Decoder. We apply a single fully connected layer to map the transformer embeddings F_{tr} to the column-wise outputs $F_{out} \in \mathbb{R}^{512 \times 12}$. Each vector of the output sequence predicts the values for 4 image columns, and thus may be reshaped to three column-wise vectors for each image, $[\phi^k, \alpha^k, \mathbf{p}^k] \in \mathbb{R}^{1024}$, $k \in [1, 2]$.

Pose Decoder. To regress the relative pose from the rich column-wise co-visibility, correspondence, and wall depth information embedded in F_{tr}, we separately apply a 6-layer 1-D CNN to each image's embedding sequence. Each layer consists of a convolution with kernel size 3, followed by batch normalization and a ReLU non-linearity. Each conv layer reduces the feature dimension by half. We then once again concatenate the feature sequences, before flattening the sequence and applying a fully-connected layer to map to the five-dimensional pose output representation, $(\mathbf{r}, \mathbf{t}, s)$. The scale parameter is made non-negative by applying a ReLU.

4.2   Training

The model is implemented in PyTorch; we train in mixed precision on 4 NVIDIA Tesla V100 for 30 epochs with a learning rate of .0001. We select the best model by the lowest validation loss sum. During training we apply random rotational augmentation, as well as randomly swapping the panorama pair order, inverting the relative pose for regression.

Loss Functions. We apply the L1 loss for the angular floor-wall boundary and correspondence outputs, and the binary cross entropy (BCE) loss for the co-visibility probability. Being both angular quantities in radians, the floor-wall boundary and correspondence losses are naturally of similar magnitude. To equilibrate the magnitude of the BCE loss, we apply a scaling parameter β_c. The total column-wise output loss is

$$L_{covis} = ||\phi^k - \hat{\phi}^k||_1 + ||\alpha^k - \hat{\alpha}^k||_1 + \beta_c \cdot BCE(\mathbf{p}_c^k, \hat{\mathbf{p}}_c^k), k \in [1, 2]. \quad (1)$$

For regressing the relative pose, we normalize the estimated rotation and translation direction to be unit vectors, and multiply the translation direction by the estimated scale, s, to produce the final estimated translation $\mathbf{t}_s$. To learn the pose parameters we minimize mean-squared error over both vectors. We similarly scale the magnitude of both the rotation and translation loss functions as we find these losses to have an overall stronger effect than the per-column loss functions above:

$$L_{pose} = \beta_r \cdot ||\mathbf{r} - \hat{\mathbf{r}}||_2^2 + \beta_t \cdot ||\mathbf{t}_s - \hat{\mathbf{t}}_s||_2^2. \tag{2}$$

We did not carefully tune the loss scaling parameters as we did not find the optimization to be particularly sensitive to these values. In our experiments, we used $\beta_c = .25, \beta_r = 3 \times 10^{-3}, \beta_t = 6 \times 10^{-2}$.

Positive/Negative Sampling. For constructing the dataset for training and testing, we form "positive" training examples by retaining all panorama pairs from ZInD which have $>= 10\%$ co-visibility score. We further sample "negative" examples with zero co-visibility with a probability of .1. These settings result in an overall ratio of positives to negatives of approximately 2.5.

4.3   Relative Pose Estimation by RANSAC

In addition to learning direct pose regression, the CCF decoder outputs support alignment by rigid registration. Projected into the floor plane using the assumptions of upright camera and orthogonal floor plane, the floor-wall boundary points from both images form two 2D point sets. For those boundary points whose co-visibility probability is high, the predicted correspondence angle can be used to sample a point on the neighboring panoramas floor-wall boundary contour. In this way, a set of corresponding points can be determined bidirectionally using the predictions from both images in the pair. Figure 2(a) illustrates bidirectional correspondence estimation, while (b) illustrates the resultant connectivity between floor-wall boundary points generated by the estimated correspondence, which can then be used to obtain pose by rigid registration.

It is possible to directly solve for the rotation and translation using singular value decomposition on the corresponding point sets [49]; however, this method is sensitive to noise. To compensate, we instead apply RANSAC. At each iteration, we randomly select two pairs of corresponding points from the set predicted by the model. A candidate rotation and translation is then determined from the point pair by a 2-point minimal solver. A Hungarian algorithm-based assignment to determine inliers can be used; however, given the quality of the correspondences predicted by the model, we find greedy assignment to be faster with minimal performance loss. After the RANSAC loop, given the alignment candidate with the highest number of inliers, we use the inlier assignment to do an SVD refit in order to determine the final rotation and translation.

4.4   ZInD Pre-processing

ZInD's complete geometry allows computation of visual overlap and floor-wall boundary angular correspondence by comparing points on the visible wall layout for panorama pairs that share the same space; however, with no signal on whether the doors are open or closed, these quantities cannot be confidently extended across doorways. To allow extension of our method to whole floors without the burden of fully labeling all doors, a sample of 5K doors were labeled. We then bootstrap off of these annotations by training a classification network consisting of one convolutional and one fully connected classification layer, stacked on top of pretrained mid-level depth, normal, and room layout features from [41]. This classifier was then used to label the remainder of the dataset in a semi-supervised manner. See the supplementary for more details and examples of this step.

5   Results

In this section, we describe how ZInD is used for evaluation, the evaluation metrics, and comparisons with a few baselines. We also describe results of our ablation study.

5.1   Dataset

We split out dataset with mined positives and negatives into train, test, and validation sets according to the publicly released ZInD split. We evaluate our method on the test set; the statistics on number of examples by visual overlap and baseline distance can be found in the supplementary. Our dataset contains a wide range of co-visibility, with a large fraction of examples subject to extremely low visual overlap; 32% of positive examples have less than 25% co-visibility. Further, our dataset contains extremely wide baselines between panoramas; 36% of positive pairs have a baseline distance of more than 4 m.

5.2   Baselines

We compare our method to multiple baselines for relative pose estimation.

SIFT+OpenMVG. We run 2-view SfM from OpenMVG [33] with the three-point upright relative pose solver [35] on the full panorama image pair. It assumes an upright camera and solves for the horizontal rotation and 3 DoF translation. Note that the recovered translation is not up-to-scale with the predicted room layout geometry from CoVisPose.

LoFTR+OpenMVG. We split each panorama image into perspective crops with a combination of horizontal angle at [0°, 60°, 120°, 180°, 240°, 300°] and vertical angle [−30°, 0°, 30°]. The crops are projected with a 90° horizontal field-of-view, and a resolution of 640 by 640 pixels. We use the LoFTR [47] feature matcher as trained in the original paper, exhaustively run on combinations of crops from a panorama pair, and project putative feature matches back to spherical space. Then we solve relative camera pose using openMVG with settings similar to the SIFT+OpenMVG baseline.

LayoutLoc. We run LayoutLoc [12] on panorama pairs; it applies a semantic-based camera alignment based on predicted room layout and wall features. It solves the panorama relative poses with the same scale as predicted room layout geometry. The success of a localization is determined by thresholding the estimated camera pose confidence score.

DirectionNet. DirectionNet [10] is a recent supervised learning approach, achieving SOTA performance on the challenging task of wide-baseline relative pose estimation for perspective, limited FoV cameras in indoor scenes. Direction-Net is a representative of the line of work focused on end-to-end camera pose estimation without explicit feature correspondences. We adapted and re-trained their released code-base[2] on our domain (pairs of 360° spherical cameras) using the same training set and data augmentations as described above. More details on the training protocol are provided in the supplementary.

5.3   Evaluation Metrics

For relative pose error, we report the absolute error in the predicted rotation and translation angles for all methods. For those methods which produce scale, we additionally report the translation error in meters. For all of these quantities, we report the mean and median errors in Table 1. For rotation and translation angle errors, we also report % of total samples which have error less than 2.5°, and for translation errors, % of total samples with error less than 5 m.

As optimization-based models may fail given insufficient input correspondences, or lack of consistency in the set, to better understand this, we report the success rate in %. Further, as many direct regression methods may not come with a measure of confidence in a given pose, to demonstrate the strength of our co-visibility output, we compute true positive/false positive rate curves as function of a threshold applied to a method-specific measure of confidence. For the methods which solve for the essential matrix given correspondences, we use the number of inliers of the fit. For CoVisPose, we use a threshold on the estimated co-visibility score [12,55] between the pair. For LayoutLoc we use the pose confidence score.

5.4   Relative Pose Estimation Accuracy

We report error metrics stratified by the GT co-visibility score in Table 1. First, we observe that our CoVisPose achieves the best performance in almost all cases across the range of visual overlap, for both rotation and translation errors. Similar to [7,9], our empirical studies suggest that feature-based approaches, e.g., classic methods like SIFT [31] and learned ones like LoFTR [47], are competitive in the high-overlap regime, where point features can be matched robustly. However, those become less reliable as the visual overlap decreases. LayoutLoc [12] can be seen as a learned, semantic feature-based approach, which outperforms

---

[2] https://arthurchen0518.github.io/DirectionNet.

626 W. Hutchcroft et al.

Table 1. Relative pose statistics by co-visibility. We report the mean ("Mn") and median ("Med") angular rotation and translation errors in degrees, as well as the fraction of test set pairs for which the angular error was less than 2.5°. In addition, as our method additionally estimates two-view scale, we report the mean and median translation distance error in meters, as well as the fraction of pairs for which the translation error was less than .5 m. Highlights: 1st, 2nd and 3rd best results.

Co-Vis.%	Method	Success (% ↑)	Rotation			Translation angle			Translation vector		
			Mn(°↓)	Med(°↓)	2.5°(% ↑)	Mn(°↓)	Med(°↓)	2.5°(% ↑)	Mn(m.↓)	Med(m.↓)	.5m.(% ↑)
75–100	SIFT-OpenMVG [31]	69.17%	12.50	0.58	53.10	17.31	1.62	41.00	–	–	–
	LoFTR-OpenMVG [47]	89.12%	15.71	0.90	60.71	19.25	2.29	46.53	–	–	–
	DirectionNet [10]	100.00%	16.35	1.48	69.28	18.43	5.53	25.12	–	–	–
	LayoutLoc [12]	78.69%	13.13	0.00	70.19	14.86	1.46	51.12	0.64	0.11	63.96
	CoVisPose-Ransac	99.73%	1.20	0.53	96.51	2.86	0.91	84.09	0.10	0.07	98.51
	CoVisPose-Direct	100.00%	1.27	0.56	97.87	3.38	1.15	78.50	0.12	0.09	98.87
50–75	SIFT-OpenMVG [31]	47.88%	22.01	0.83	31.79	25.01	2.22	25.23	–	–	–
	LoFTR-OpenMVG [47]	71.36%	24.54	1.84	38.25	26.53	4.13	27.93	–	–	–
	DirectionNet [10]	100.00%	27.44	2.02	57.52	24.06	6.46	22.18	–	–	–
	LayoutLoc [12]	60.84%	41.64	0.00	40.17	38.57	4.26	26.18	1.86	0.53	30.13
	CoVisPose-Ransac	99.22%	1.45	0.67	92.36	1.92	0.89	83.46	0.16	0.08	94.93
	CoVisPose-Direct	100.00%	1.48	0.73	94.71	2.13	1.09	81.55	0.16	0.10	96.93
25–50	SIFT-OpenMVG [31]	26.58%	41.51	7.94	11.05	45.18	14.68	8.13	–	–	–
	LoFTR-OpenMVG [47]	52.26%	40.58	12.86	16.36	43.07	18.25	12.18	–	–	–
	DirectionNet [10]	100.00%	38.38	2.75	47.58	29.88	9.04	17.56	–	–	–
	LayoutLoc [12]	49.85%	77.39	90.00	18.57	63.40	50.52	8.27	3.56	3.15	8.94
	CoVisPose-Ransac	96.42%	2.51	0.98	80.02	2.19	1.00	77.49	0.24	0.12	88.06
	CoVisPose-Direct	100.00%	3.47	1.03	83.89	3.00	1.24	75.57	0.28	0.14	92.45
10–25	SIFT-OpenMVG [31]	16.55%	68.70	61.78	2.46	72.02	64.10	1.63	–	–	–
	LoFTR-OpenMVG [47]	39.76%	59.32	37.75	5.16	63.71	50.83	3.95	–	–	–
	DirectionNet [10]	100.00%	53.37	5.97	37.85	42.47	18.94	9.53	–	–	–
	LayoutLoc [12]	46.59%	91.30	90.00	11.85	77.21	70.11	2.19	5.04	4.71	1.64
	CoVisPose-Ransac	88.46%	6.18	1.78	54.36	4.82	1.59	57.66	0.56	0.22	67.64
	CoVisPose-Direct	100.00%	8.90	2.10	55.87	6.79	2.13	56.15	0.72	0.27	73.56

the point-based base-lines (SIFT and LoFTR) in this modality. Similar to them, its performance quickly drops for wide to extreme baselines. Note that LayoutLoc achieves 0° median rotation error for high visual overlap cases. This is due to rooms in ZInD being aligned by the computed vanishing angle which LayoutLoc aligns with as a final step. This results in zero rotation error when the geometric alignment is successful. Similar to the trends reported in Chen et al. [9], DirectionNet (that we trained end-to-end) performs substantially better than the feature-based approaches in the mid-to-low overlap regimes.

CoVisPose RANSAC shows a small advantage over CoVisPose Direct; when accurate correspondences are available, a robust iterative fitting is often capable of finding a more accurate pose. However, CoVisPose Direct inference only requires 50 ms, whereas RANSAC iteration and inlier assignment typically requires 5–30 secs to fully exploit the dense correspondences. Moreover, direct regression, like DirectionNet, returns a valid pose 100% of the time. Under very low visual overlap this may be an advantage as a fitting algorithm may have few available correspondences as input. This 100% success rate is potentially both a positive and negative; without a reliable measure of confidence it is difficult to know whether or not a directly regressed pose should be trusted. CoVisPose's

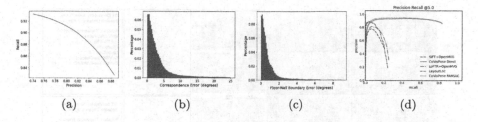

(a)   (b)   (c)   (d)

Fig. 3. (a) Precision and recall of per-column co-visibility. (b) Histogram of angular correspondence error, in degrees. (c) Histogram of floor-wall boundary error, in degrees. (d) Relative pose precision and recall curves for CoVisPose and baseline methods. True positives defined by maximum of rotation and translation errors less than 5°.

Table 2. Ablation study on direct pose regression performance by removing dense column-wise outputs.

Method	Rotation			Translation angle			Translation vector		
	Mn(° ↓)	Med(° ↓)	2.5°(% ↑)	Mn(° ↓)	Med(° ↓)	2.5°(% ↑)	Mn(m.↓)	Med(m.↓)	.5m.(% ↑)
CoVisPose Boundary	16.35	6.07	24.84	14.15	5.76	26.02	1.01	.48	51.89
CoVisPose Boundary+CoVis	4.94	1.24	74.34	4.83	1.57	66.45	.41	.16	86.13
CoVisPose Boundary+CoVis+AC	**4.33**	**.97**	**80.17**	**4.14**	**1.39**	**71.13**	**.36**	**.14**	**88.72**

co-visibility vector provides such a measure, allowing the method to be run in an unordered set of panoramas, without a separate retrieval module.

Precision and Recall. We demonstrate the estimated co-visibility as a measure of pose confidence by computing precision and recall over the entire test set, including negative examples with no visual overlap, in Fig. 3(d). CoVisPose demonstrates strong precision and recall, with similarly high accuracy for both direct regression and RANSAC poses, correctly rejecting negative examples through accurate estimated co-visibility (see Fig. 3(a)(b)(c) for an in-depth analysis). For computing the curves, true positives are defined as poses with the maximum of rotation and translation angle errors less than 5°. Returning a confident pose for a pair with zero visual overlap is considered a false positive for this analysis.

5.5 Per-column Prediction Accuracy Analysis

We report per-column prediction errors for co-visibility, angular correspondence and floor-wall boundary estimation over all image columns from test images in Fig. 3(a)(b)(c). We see that CoVisPose produces less than 5° of error in angular correspondence for more than 73.1% of all image columns and less than 2.5° error in the floor-wall boundary position for more than 83.1% of all columns.

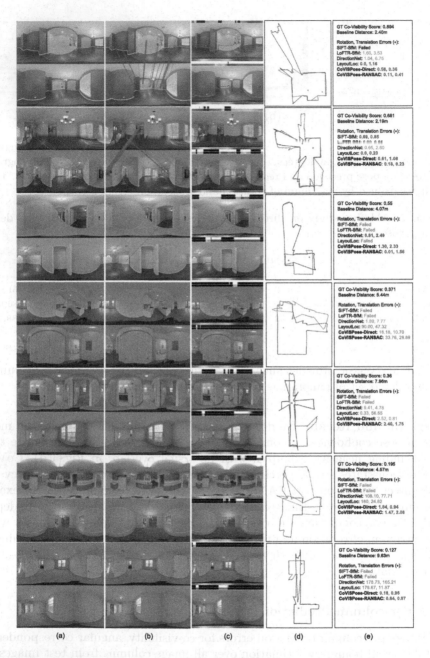

Fig. 4. Qualitative evaluation on ZInD. (a) SIFT feature point inliers generated by 2-view SfM with OpenMVG, (b) LoFTR feature point inliers generated by the same solver as (a), (c) CoViSPose prediction, (d) predicted floor-wall boundaries for **Panorama 1** and **Panorama 2** aligned by CoViSPose direct regression. (e) Pose errors for each method. Color scheme corresponds to maximum of rotation and translation errors: Failure to recover pose or error $> 10°$, error in $[2.5°, 10°]$, error $< 2.5°$.

5.6 Qualitative Results

Figure 4 shows results from CoVisPose and baseline methods on ZInD panoramas. We arrange result rows by ground truth (GT) co-visibility score, in decreasing order. Common sources of baseline failure include lack of texture for feature matching, wide-baselines, and low visual overlap. (Failure examples are in the supplemental.) On the contrary, we see that CoVisPose produces accurate poses for the vast majority of cases, including for panorama pairs with wide to extreme baselines. In column (c), we further see the high spatial precision in geometry estimation and alignment; in most cases the predicted room contours align well. In row 4 we show a case where the competing direct regression method, DirectionNet, shows better performance. We further examine limitations and failure cases in the supplementary.

5.7 Ablation Study

We demonstrate the impact of jointly training our pose decoder alongside dense column-wise outputs by training three CoVisPose variants. We found it difficult to tune the model to converge without *any* column-wise outputs. When compared with just the boundary output, we find that the performance increases dramatically when adding the co-visibility mask (CoVis), and increases further with addition of the angular correspondence (AC). While the boundary information offers a strong geometry prior, we hypothesize that co-visibility increases performance by providing a strong signal on inter-view association, which the angular correspondence further refines. We also note that the gap between the training and validation errors is markedly reduced as column-wise outputs are added, indicating increased generalization. Details can be found in the supplementary.

6 Conclusion

We present a novel end-to-end learning approach for relative pose estimation in wide baseline 360° indoor panoramas. We have shown how jointly learning dense column-wise representations of visual overlap, correspondence, and layout geometry increases the feasibility and accuracy of direct pose regression. This representation yields accurate poses through a RANSAC-based approach applied to the densely predicted corresponding boundary points. Further, our co-visibility vector provides a strong measure of pose confidence. We set a new SOTA for this task, improving upon existing methods, including classical SfM, deep feature matching-based SfM, and direct pose regression.

References

1. Aly, M., Bouguet, J.Y.: Street view goes indoors: automatic pose estimation from uncalibrated unordered spherical panoramas. In: 2012 IEEE Workshop on the Applications of Computer Vision (WACV), pp. 1–8. IEEE (2012)

2. Balntas, V., Li, S., Prisacariu, V.: RelocNet: continuous metric learning relocalisation using neural nets. In: Proceedings of the European Conference on Computer Vision (ECCV), September 2018

3. Bello, I., Zoph, B., Vaswani, A., Shlens, J., Le, Q.V.: Attention augmented convolutional networks. In: Proceedings of the IEEE/CVF International Conference on Computer Vision (ICCV), October 2019

4. Brachmann, E., et al.: DSAC - differentiable RANSAC for camera localization. In: 2017 IEEE Conference on Computer Vision and Pattern Recognition (CVPR), pp. 2492–2500 (2017). https://doi.org/10.1109/CVPR.2017.267

5. Brahmbhatt, S., Gu, J., Kim, K., Hays, J., Kautz, J.: MapNet: geometry-aware learning of maps for camera localization. CoRR abs/1712.03342 (2017). arxiv:1712.03342

6. Cabral, R., Furukawa, Y.: Piecewise planar and compact floorplan reconstruction from images. In: 2014 IEEE Conference on Computer Vision and Pattern Recognition, pp. 628–635. IEEE (2014)

7. Cai, R., Hariharan, B., Snavely, N., Averbuch-Elor, H.: Extreme rotation estimation using dense correlation volumes. In: IEEE/CVF Conference on Computer Vision and Pattern Recognition (CVPR) (2021)

8. Chang, A., et al.: Matterport3D: learning from RGB-d data in indoor environments. arXiv preprint arXiv:1709.06158 (2017)

9. Chen, K., Snavely, N., Makadia, A.: Wide-baseline relative camera pose estimation with directional learning. In: Proceedings of the IEEE/CVF Conference on Computer Vision and Pattern Recognition (CVPR), pp. 3258–3268, June 2021

10. Chen, K., Snavely, N., Makadia, A.: Wide-baseline relative camera pose estimation with directional learning. In: Proceedings of the IEEE/CVF Conference on Computer Vision and Pattern Recognition, pp. 3258–3268 (2021)

11. Choi, S., Kim, J.H.: Fast and reliable minimal relative pose estimation under planar motion. Image Vis. Comput. **69**, 103–112 (2018)

12. Cruz, S., Hutchcroft, W., Li, Y., Khosravan, N., Boyadzhiev, I., Kang, S.B.: Zillow indoor dataset: annotated floor plans with 360deg panoramas and 3D room layouts. In: Proceedings of the IEEE/CVF Conference on Computer Vision and Pattern Recognition (CVPR), pp. 2133–2143, June 2021

13. Davidson, B., Alvi, M.S., Henriques, J.F.: 360 camera alignment via segmentation. In: European Conference on Computer Vision, pp. 579–595. Springer (2020). https://doi.org/10.1007/978-3-030-58604-1_35

14. DeTone, D., Malisiewicz, T., Rabinovich, A.: SuperPoint: self-supervised interest point detection and description. CoRR abs/1712.07629 (2017). arxiv:1712.07629

15. Devlin, J., Chang, M.W., Lee, K., Toutanova, K.: BERT: pre-training of deep bidirectional transformers for language understanding. In: Proceedings of the 2019 Conference of the North American Chapter of the Association for Computational Linguistics: Human Language Technologies, Volume 1 (Long and Short Papers), pp. 4171–4186. Association for Computational Linguistics, Minneapolis, Minnesota, June 2019. https://doi.org/10.18653/v1/N19-1423, https://www.aclanthology.org/N19-1423

16. Ding, Y., Barath, D., Kukelova, Z.: Homography-based egomotion estimation using gravity and sift features. In: Proceedings of the Asian Conference on Computer Vision (2020)

17. Ding, Y., Barath, D., Yang, J., Kong, H., Kukelova, Z.: Globally optimal relative pose estimation with gravity prior. In: Proceedings of the IEEE/CVF Conference on Computer Vision and Pattern Recognition, pp. 394–403 (2021)

18. Dusmanu, M., et al.: D2-net: a trainable CNN for joint description and detection of local features. In: Proceedings of the IEEE/CVF Conference on Computer Vision and Pattern Recognition (CVPR), June 2019

19. Eder, M., Shvets, M., Lim, J., Frahm, J.M.: Tangent images for mitigating spherical distortion. In: IEEE/CVF Conference on Computer Vision and Pattern Recognition (CVPR), June 2020

20. En, S., Lechervy, A., Jurie, F.: RPNet: an end-to-end network for relative camera pose estimation. In: ECCV Workshops (2018)

21. Guan, B., Zhao, J., Li, Z., Sun, F., Fraundorfer, F.: Minimal solutions for relative pose with a single affine correspondence. In: Proceedings of the IEEE/CVF Conference on Computer Vision and Pattern Recognition (CVPR), June 2020

22. Herath, S., Yan, H., Furukawa, Y.: RoNIN: robust neural inertial navigation in the wild: benchmark, evaluations, & new methods. In: 2020 IEEE International Conference on Robotics and Automation (ICRA), pp. 3146–3152. IEEE (2020)

23. Jung, J., Lee, J.Y., Kim, B., Lee, S.: Upright adjustment of 360 spherical panoramas. In: 2017 IEEE Virtual Reality (VR), pp. 251–252. IEEE (2017)

24. Jung, R., Lee, A.S.J., Ashtari, A., Bazin, J.C.: Deep360Up: a deep learning-based approach for automatic VR image upright adjustment. In: 2019 IEEE Conference on Virtual Reality and 3D User Interfaces (VR), pp. 1–8. IEEE (2019)

25. Kendall, A., Cipolla, R.: Geometric loss functions for camera pose regression with deep learning. CoRR abs/1704.00390 (2017). arxiv:1704.00390

26. Kendall, A., Grimes, M.K., Cipolla, R.: PoseNet: a convolutional network for real-time 6-DOF camera relocalization. In: 2015 IEEE International Conference on Computer Vision (ICCV), pp. 2938–2946 (2015)

27. Kukelova, Z., Bujnak, M., Pajdla, T.: Closed-form solutions to minimal absolute pose problems with known vertical direction. In: Asian Conference on Computer Vision, pp. 216–229. Springer (2010). https://doi.org/10.1007/978-3-642-19309-5_17

28. Laskar, Z., Melekhov, I., Kalia, S., Kannala, J.: Camera relocalization by computing pairwise relative poses using convolutional neural network. CoRR abs/1707.09733 (2017). arxiv:1707.09733

29. Lee, Y., Jeong, J., Yun, J., Cho, W., Yoon, K.J.: SpherePHD: applying CNNs on a spherical polyhedron representation of 360deg images. In: Proceedings of the IEEE/CVF Conference on Computer Vision and Pattern Recognition (CVPR), June 2019

30. Li, J., Su, J., Xia, C., Tian, Y.: Distortion-adaptive salient object detection in 360° omnidirectional images. IEEE J. Sel. Top. Sign. Process. **14**(1), 38–48 (2020). https://doi.org/10.1109/JSTSP.2019.2957982

31. Lowe, D.G.: Distinctive image features from scale-invariant keypoints. Int. J. Comput. Vis. **60**(2), 91–110 (2004)

32. Melekhov, I., Kannala, J., Rahtu, E.: Relative camera pose estimation using convolutional neural networks. CoRR abs/1702.01381 (2017). arxiv:1702.01381. https://doi.org/10.1007/978-3-319-70353-4_57

33. Moulon, P., Monasse, P., Perrot, R., Marlet, R.: OpenMVG: open multiple view geometry. In: International Workshop on Reproducible Research in Pattern Recognition, pp. 60–74. Springer (2016). https://doi.org/10.1007/978-3-319-56414-2_5

34. Ortin, D., Montiel, J.M.M.: Indoor robot motion based on monocular images. Robotica **19**(3), 331–342 (2001)

35. Oskarsson, M.: Two-view orthographic epipolar geometry: minimal and optimal solvers. J. Math. Imaging Vis. **60**(2), 163–173 (2018). https://doi.org/10.1007/s10851-017-0753-1

632   W. Hutchcroft et al.

36. Pintore, G., Agus, M., Gobbetti, E.: AtlantaNet: Inferring the 3D indoor layout from a single 360 image beyond the Manhattan world assumption. In: Proceedings of the ECCV, August 2020. https://vic.crs4.it/vic/cgi-bin/bib-page.cgi?id=Pintore:2020:AI3. https://doi.org/10.1007/978-3-030-58598-3_26
37. Pintore, G., Ganovelli, F., Pintus, R., Scopigno, R., Gobbetti, E.: 3D floor plan recovery from overlapping spherical images. Comput. Vis. Media **4**(4), 367–383 (2018). https://doi.org/10.1007/s41095-018-0125-9
38. Ramakrishnan, S.K., et al.: Habitat-matterport 3D dataset (HM3d): 1000 large-scale 3D environments for embodied AI. In: Thirty-fifth Conference on Neural Information Processing Systems Datasets and Benchmarks Track (Round 2) (2021). https://openreview.net/forum?id=-v4OuqNs5P
39. Ranftl, R., Koltun, V.: Deep fundamental matrix estimation. In: Proceedings of the European Conference on Computer Vision (ECCV) (September 2018)
40. Sarlin, P.E., DeTone, D., Malisiewicz, T., Rabinovich, A.: SuperGlue: learning feature matching with graph neural networks. In: IEEE/CVF Conference on Computer Vision and Pattern Recognition (CVPR), June 2020
41. Sax, A., Emi, B., Zamir, A.R., Guibas, L.J., Savarese, S., Malik, J.: Mid-level visual representations improve generalization and sample efficiency for learning visuomotor policies (2018)
42. Schindler, G., Dellaert, F.: Atlanta world: an expectation maximization framework for simultaneous low-level edge grouping and camera calibration in complex man-made environments. In: Proceedings of the 2004 IEEE Computer Society Conference on Computer Vision and Pattern Recognition 2004. CVPR 2004, vol. 1, p. I. IEEE (2004)
43. Shabani, M.A., Song, W., Odamaki, M., Fujiki, H., Furukawa, Y.: Extreme structure from motion for indoor panoramas without visual overlaps. In: Proceedings of the IEEE/CVF International Conference on Computer Vision (ICCV), pp. 5703–5711, October 2021
44. Su, Y.C., Grauman, K.: Learning spherical convolution for fast features from 360° imagery. In: Guyon, I., Luxburg, U.V., Bengio, S., Wallach, H., Fergus, R., Vishwanathan, S., Garnett, R. (eds.) Advances in Neural Information Processing Systems, vol. 30. Curran Associates, Inc. (2017). https://proceedings.neurips.cc/paper/2017/file/0c74b7f78409a4022a2c4c5a5ca3ee19-Paper.pdf
45. Sun, C., Hsiao, C.W., Sun, M., Chen, H.T.: HorizonNet: learning room layout with 1d representation and Pano stretch data augmentation. In: Proceedings of the IEEE/CVF Conference on Computer Vision and Pattern Recognition (CVPR), June 2019
46. Sun, C., Sun, M., Chen, H.T.: HoHoNet: 360 indoor holistic understanding with latent horizontal features. In: Proceedings of the IEEE/CVF Conference on Computer Vision and Pattern Recognition (CVPR), pp. 2573–2582, June 2021
47. Sun, J., Shen, Z., Wang, Y., Bao, H., Zhou, X.: LoFTR: detector-free local feature matching with transformers. In: Proceedings of the IEEE/CVF Conference on Computer Vision and Pattern Recognition (CVPR), pp. 8922–8931, June 2021
48. Torii, A., Imiya, A., Ohnishi, N.: Two-and three-view geometry for spherical cameras. In: Proceedings of the Sixth Workshop on Omnidirectional Vision, Camera Networks and Non-classical Cameras, pp. 81–88. Citeseer (2005)
49. Umeyama, S.: Least-squares estimation of transformation parameters between two point patterns. IEEE Trans. Patt. Anal. Mach. Intell. **13**(04), 376–380 (1991). https://doi.org/10.1109/34.88573

50. Ummenhofer, B., et al.: Demon: depth and motion network for learning monocular stereo. In: CVPR, pp. 5622–5631. IEEE Computer Society (2017). https://dblp. uni-trier.de/db/conf/cvpr/cvpr2017.html#UmmenhoferZUMID17

51. Vaswani, A., et al.: Attention is all you need. In: Guyon, I., Luxburg, U.V., Bengio, S., Wallach, H., Fergus, R., Vishwanathan, S., Garnett, R. (eds.) Advances in Neural Information Processing Systems, vol. 30. Curran Associates, Inc. (2017). https://proceedings.neurips.cc/paper/2017/file/ 3f5ee243547dee91fbd053c1c4a845aa-Paper.pdf

52. Walch, F., Hazirbas, C., Leal-Taixé, L., Sattler, T., Hilsenbeck, S., Cremers, D.: Image-based localization using LSTMs for structured feature correlation. In: 2017 IEEE International Conference on Computer Vision (ICCV), pp. 627–637 (2017)

53. Wang, F.E., Yeh, Y.H., Sun, M., Chiu, W.C., Tsai, Y.H.: BiFuse: monocular 360 depth estimation via bi-projection fusion. In: Proceedings of the IEEE/CVF Conference on Computer Vision and Pattern Recognition (CVPR), June 2020

54. Wang, F.E., Yeh, Y.H., Sun, M., Chiu, W.C., Tsai, Y.H.: LED2-Net: monocular 360deg layout estimation via differentiable depth rendering. In: Proceedings of the IEEE/CVF Conference on Computer Vision and Pattern Recognition (CVPR), pp. 12956–12965, June 2021

55. Wang, H., Hutchcroft, W., Li, Y., Wan, Z., Boyadzhiev, I., Kang, S.B.: PSMNET: position-aware stereo merging network for room layout estimation (in press). In: Proceedings of the IEEE/CVF Conference on Computer Vision and Pattern Recognition (CVPR) (2022)

56. Wang, X., Girshick, R., Gupta, A., He, K.: Non-local neural networks. In: 2018 IEEE/CVF Conference on Computer Vision and Pattern Recognition, pp. 7794–7803 (2018). https://doi.org/10.1109/CVPR.2018.00813

57. Yi, K.M., Trulls, E., Ono, Y., Lepetit, V., Salzmann, M., Fua, P.: Learning to find good correspondences. In: Proceedings of the IEEE Conference on Computer Vision and Pattern Recognition (CVPR), June 2018

58. Zeng, W., Karaoglu, S., Gevers, T.: Joint 3D layout and depth prediction from a single indoor panorama image. In: Vedaldi, A., Bischof, H., Brox, T., Frahm, J.-M. (eds.) ECCV 2020. LNCS, vol. 12361, pp. 666–682. Springer, Cham (2020). https://doi.org/10.1007/978-3-030-58517-4_39

59. Zhang, C., Liwicki, S., Smith, W., Cipolla, R.: Orientation-aware semantic segmentation on icosahedron spheres. In: Proceedings of the IEEE/CVF International Conference on Computer Vision (ICCV), October 2019

60. Zhang, Y., Song, S., Tan, P., Xiao, J.: PanoContext: a whole-room 3D context model for panoramic scene understanding. In: Fleet, D., Pajdla, T., Schiele, B., Tuytelaars, T. (eds.) ECCV 2014. LNCS, vol. 8694, pp. 668–686. Springer, Cham (2014). https://doi.org/10.1007/978-3-319-10599-4_43

61. Zhang, Z., Deriche, R., Faugeras, O., Luong, Q.T.: A robust technique for matching two uncalibrated images through the recovery of the unknown epipolar geometry. Artif. Intell. **78**(1–2), 87–119 (1995)

62. Özyeşil, O., Voroninski, V., Basri, R., Singer, A.: A survey of structure from motion. Acta Numerica **26**, 305–364 (2017). https://doi.org/10.1017/S096249291700006X

Affine Correspondences Between Multi-camera Systems for 6DOF Relative Pose Estimation

Banglei Guan[1] and Ji Zhao[2]([✉])

[1] National University of Defense Technology, Changsha 410073, China
guanbanglei12@nudt.edu.cn
[2] Beijing, China
zhaoji84@gmail.com

Abstract. We present a novel method to compute the 6DOF relative pose of multi-camera systems using two affine correspondences (ACs). Existing solutions to the multi-camera relative pose estimation are either restricted to special cases of motion, have too high computational complexity, or require too many point correspondences (PCs). Thus, these solvers impede an efficient or accurate relative pose estimation when applying RANSAC as a robust estimator. This paper shows that the relative pose estimation problem using ACs permits a feasible minimal solution, when exploiting the geometric constraints between ACs and multi-camera systems using a special parameterization. We present a problem formulation based on two ACs that encompass two common types of ACs across two views, *i.e.*, inter-camera and intra-camera. Experiments on both virtual and real multi-camera systems prove that the proposed solvers are more efficient than the state-of-the-art algorithms, while resulting in a better relative pose accuracy. Source code is available at https://github.com/jizhaox/relpose-mcs-depth.

Keywords: Relative pose estimation · Multi-camera system · Affine correspondence · Minimal solver

1 Introduction

Estimating the relative poses of a monocular camera, or a multi-camera system is a key problem in computer vision, which plays an important role in structure from motion (SfM), simultaneous localization and mapping (SLAM), and augmented reality (AR) [20,22,26,39,42,43,45]. A multi-camera system refers to a system of individual cameras that are rigidly fixed onto a single body, and it can be set in a configuration that maximizes the field-of-view. Motivated by the fact that multi-camera systems are an interesting choice in the context of robotics applications such as autonomous drones and vehicles, relative pose estimation for multi-camera systems has started to receive attention lately [1,18,20,22,35].

Supplementary Information The online version contains supplementary material available at https://doi.org/10.1007/978-3-031-19824-3_37.

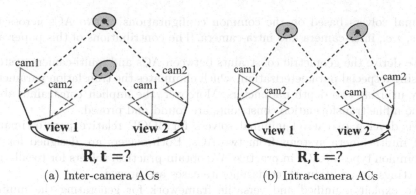

(a) Inter-camera ACs   (b) Intra-camera ACs

Fig. 1. Relative pose estimation from two ACs for a multi-camera system. Red triangle represents a single camera, and gray ellipse represents a spatial patch which relates to an AC. Specifically, inter-camera ACs refer to correspondences which are seen by different cameras over two consecutive views. Intra-camera ACs refer to correspondences which are seen by the same camera over two consecutive views.

Different from monocular cameras which are modeled by the perspective camera model, the multi-camera systems can be modeled by the generalized camera model [16,37,46]. The generalized camera model does not have a single center of projection. The light rays that pass through the multi-camera system do not intersect in a single center of projection, *i.e.*, non-central projection [40]. Thus, the relative pose estimation problem of multi-camera systems [45] is different from the monocular cameras [39], which results in different equations. In addition, since feature correspondences established by feature matching inevitably contain outliers, the relative pose estimation algorithms are typically employed inside a robust estimation framework such as the Random Sample Consensus (RANSAC) [13]. The computational complexity of the RANSAC estimator increases exponentially with respect to the number of feature correspondences needed. Thus, minimal solvers for relative pose estimation are very desirable for RANSAC schemes, which maximizes the probability of picking an all-inlier sample and reduces the number of necessary iterations [24,27,31,33,45,48].

The development of minimal solvers for relative pose estimation of multi-camera systems ranges back to the method of Stewénius *et al.* with six point correspondences (PCs) [45]. Later, some methods have been subsequently proposed, such as the linear method with seventeen PCs [31], iterative optimization method [26] and global optimization method [50]. In recent years, a number of solvers use affine correspondences (ACs), instead of PCs, to estimate the relative pose, which reduces the number of required correspondences [1,4,5,11,18,19,41]. Because an AC carries more information than a PC. However, existing AC-based solvers to the 6DOF relative pose estimation for multi-camera systems are either restricted to pose priors [17] or require at least six ACs [1]. It is desirable to find an AC-based minimal solver for 6DOF relative pose estimation of multi-camera systems, whose efficiency and accuracy are both satisfactory. This allows us to reduce the computational complexity of the RANSAC procedure.

In this paper, we focus on the 6DOF relative pose estimation problem of multi-camera systems from a minimal number of two ACs, see Fig. 1. We propose minimal solvers based on the common configurations of two ACs across two views, *i.e.*, inter-camera and intra-camera. The contributions of this paper are:

- We derive the geometric constraints between ACs and multi-camera systems using a special parameterization, which eliminates the translation parameters by utilizing two depth parameters. Moreover, the implicit constraints about the affine transformation constraints are found and proved.
- We develop two novel minimal solvers for 6DOF relative pose estimation of multi-camera systems from two ACs. Both solvers are designed for two common types of ACs in practice. We obtain practical solvers for totally new settings. In addition, three degenerate cases are proved.
- We exploit a unified and versatile framework for generating the minimal solvers, which uses the hidden variable technique to eliminate the depth parameters. This framework can be extended to solve various relative pose estimation problems, *e.g.*, relative pose estimation for a monocular camera.

2   Related Work

Stewénius *et al.* proposed the first minimal solver based on algebraic geometry, and this solver requires 6 PCs in order to come up with 64 solutions [45]. Kim *et al.* later presented alternative solvers for relative pose estimation with non-overlapping multi-camera systems using second-order cone programming [23] or branch-and-bound technique over the space of all rotations [24]. Clipp *et al.* also derived a solver using 6 PCs for non-overlapping multi-camera systems [9]. Lim *et al.* presented antipodal epipolar constraints on the relative pose by exploiting the geometry of antipodal points, which are available in large field-of-view cameras [33]. Li *et al.* used 17 PCs to solve the relative pose of multi-camera systems linearly, which ignores side-constraints on the generalized essential matrix and the contained essential and rotation matrices [31]. Kneip and Li proposed an iterative approach for the relative pose estimation with an efficient eigenvalue minimization strategy [26]. The above mentioned works are designed for 6DOF relative pose estimation of multi-camera systems.

A number of methods estimate the relative pose of multi-camera systems with a prior. Typically, the priors include multi-camera movement prior and known vertical direction prior, which reduce the DOF of the relative pose problem. Lee *et al.* [29] used a minimum of 2 PCs to recover the 2DOF relative pose, while the multi-camera system is mounted on ground robots and the movement follows the Ackermann motion model. In addition, when the vertical direction of the multi-camera system is obtained by vanishing point estimation or sensor fusion with an IMU, Sweeney *et al.* [47], Lee *et al.* [30] and Liu *et al.* [34] proposed several minimal solvers with 4 PCs to solve 4DOF relative pose.

Recently, using ACs to estimate the relative pose of multi-camera systems has drawn much attention. Alyousefi and Ventura [1] proposed a linear solver to recover the 6DOF relative pose using 6 ACs, which generalizes the 17 PCs solver proposed by Li *et al.* [31]. Guan *et al.* [17] used a first-order approximation to relative rotation to estimate the 6DOF relative pose, which generalizes the 6 PCs solver proposed by Ventura *et al.* [48]. They assume that the relative rotation of the multi-camera systems between two consecutive views is small. Furthermore, Guan *et al.* [18] estimated the 3DOF relative pose under planar motion with a single AC and estimated the 4DOF relative pose with known vertical direction with 2 ACs. In this paper, we focus on using a minimal number of 2 ACs to estimate the 6DOF relative pose of multi-camera systems, which does not rely on any motion constraints or pose priors.

3   Relative Pose Estimation for Multi-Camera Systems

In this section, we assume that both the intrinsic and extrinsic parameters of multi-camera systems are known. Aiming at the common configurations of two ACs across two views in Fig. 1, our purpose is to find the minimal solvers for inter-camera ACs and intra-camera ACs. The proposed solvers are the most common ones in practice for multi-camera systems.

3.1   Parameterization

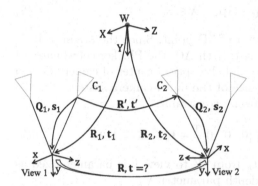

Fig. 2. Relative pose estimation for multi-camera systems.

We first formulate and parameterize the relative pose estimation problem for a multi-camera system. As shown in Fig. 2, the multi-camera system is composed of multiple perspective cameras. The extrinsic parameters of C_i are denoted as $\{\mathbf{Q}_i, \mathbf{s}_i\}$, where $\mathbf{Q}_i$ and $\mathbf{s}_i$ represent relative rotation and translation to the reference of the multi-camera system. Denote the relative pose of multi-camera systems as $\{\mathbf{R}, \mathbf{t}\}$, which represents the relative rotation and translation from view 1 to view 2 of the multi-camera system.

In order to eliminate the translation parameters, we use a special parameterization to formulate the relative pose estimation problem [45]. Take an AC seen by the different cameras for an example. The j-th AC relates the camera C_1 and C_2 across two views, see Fig. 2. Let us denote the j-th AC as $(\mathbf{x}_j, \mathbf{x}'_j, \mathbf{A}_j)$, where $\mathbf{x}_j$ and $\mathbf{x}'_j$ are the normalized homogeneous image coordinates of feature points in the view 1 and view 2, respectively. $\mathbf{A}_j$ is a 2×2 local affine transformation, which relates the infinitesimal patches around $\mathbf{x}_j$ and $\mathbf{x}'_j$ [2,41]. Suppose the j-th AC is chosen to define a world reference system W. The origin of W is set to the position of the j-th AC in 3D space and the orientation of W is consistent with the reference of the multi-camera system in view 1. Denote the relative rotation and translation from reference W to view 1 as $\{\mathbf{R}_1, \mathbf{t}_1\}$. Denote the relative rotation and translation from reference W to view 2 as $\{\mathbf{R}_2, \mathbf{t}_2\}$. It can be seen that $\mathbf{R}_1 = \mathbf{I}$, $\mathbf{R}_2 = \mathbf{R}$.

In this paper, the Cayley parameterization is used to parametrized the relative rotation $\mathbf{R}$:

$$\mathbf{R} = \frac{1}{1 + q_x^2 + q_y^2 + q_z^2} \begin{bmatrix} 1 + q_x^2 - q_y^2 - q_z^2 & 2q_xq_y - 2q_z & 2q_y + 2q_xq_z \\ 2q_xq_y + 2q_z & 1 - q_x^2 + q_y^2 - q_z^2 & 2q_yq_z - 2q_x \\ 2q_xq_z - 2q_y & 2q_x + 2q_yq_z & 1 - q_x^2 - q_y^2 + q_z^2 \end{bmatrix},$$

$$(1)$$

where $[1, q_x, q_y, q_z]^T$ is a homogeneous quaternion vector. Note that the Cayley parameterization introduces a degeneracy for 180° rotations, but this is a rare case for consecutive views in the robotics applications [26,44,49,51].

Next, we show that the translation parameters $\mathbf{t}_1$ and $\mathbf{t}_2$ can be removed by using two depth parameters. For a calibrated multi-camera system, each image point corresponds to a unique line in the reference of the multi-camera system. This line in 3D can be represented as a Plücker vector $\mathbf{L} = [\mathbf{p}^T, \mathbf{q}^T]^T$, where the 3D vectors $\mathbf{p}$ and $\mathbf{q}$ represent the unit direction vector and the moment vector, respectively [40]. They satisfy the constraint $\mathbf{p} \cdot \mathbf{q} = 0$. Thus, the set of points $\mathbf{X}(\lambda)$ on the 3D line can be parameterized as

$$\mathbf{X}(\lambda) = \mathbf{q} \times \mathbf{p} + \lambda\mathbf{p}, \quad \lambda \in \mathbb{R}. \tag{2}$$

where λ is the unknown depth parameter of 3D point. Since the origin of W is set to the 3D position $\mathbf{X}_j$ corresponding to j-th AC, the Plücker coordinates of the line connecting the 3D position $\mathbf{X}_j$ and the optical center of camera C_i can be described as $[\mathbf{p}_{ij}^T, \mathbf{q}_{ij}^T]^T$ in the reference of the multi-camera system. The 3D position $\mathbf{X}_j$ in view k satisfies the following constraint:

$$\mathbf{q}_{ij} \times \mathbf{p}_{ij} + \lambda_{jk}\mathbf{p}_{ij} = \mathbf{R}_k \begin{bmatrix} 0, & 0, & 0 \end{bmatrix}^T + \mathbf{t}_k, \quad k = 1, 2. \tag{3}$$

Based on Eq. (3), the translation $\mathbf{t}_k$ from W to view k is parameterized as the linear expression in the unknown depth parameter λ_{jk}

$$\mathbf{t}_k = \mathbf{q}_{ij} \times \mathbf{p}_{ij} + \lambda_{jk}\mathbf{p}_{ij}, \quad k = 1, 2. \tag{4}$$

where k represents the index of the views, i represents the index of the cameras, and j represents the index of the ACs. It can be seen that λ_{j1} and λ_{j2} are the depth parameters of the origin of W in views 1 and 2, respectively.

Through the above special parameterization, the 6DOF relative pose of multi-camera systems can be described by five unknowns, which consist of three rotation parameters $\{q_x, q_y, q_z\}$ and two depth parameters $\{\lambda_{j1}, \lambda_{j2}\}$.

3.2 Geometric Constraints

It has been shown in Fig. 2 that each AC relates two perspective cameras in view 1 and view 2. The relative pose between two cameras $[\mathbf{R}', \mathbf{t}']$ is determined by the composition of four transformations: (i) from one perspective camera to view 1, (ii) from view 1 to W, (iii) from W to view 2, (iv) from view 2 to the other perspective camera. Among these four transformations, the part (i) and (iv) are determined by known extrinsic parameters. In the part (ii) and (iii), there are unknowns $\mathbf{R}$, $\mathbf{t}_1$ and $\mathbf{t}_2$ which are parameterized as $\{q_x, q_y, q_z, \lambda_{j1}, \lambda_{j2}\}$. Formally, the relative pose $[\mathbf{R}', \mathbf{t}']$ is represented as:

$$
\begin{bmatrix} \mathbf{R}' & \mathbf{t}' \\ \mathbf{0} & 1 \end{bmatrix} = \begin{bmatrix} \mathbf{Q}_2 & \mathbf{s}_2 \\ \mathbf{0} & 1 \end{bmatrix}^{-1} \begin{bmatrix} \mathbf{R} & \mathbf{t}_2 \\ \mathbf{0} & 1 \end{bmatrix} \begin{bmatrix} \mathbf{I} & \mathbf{t}_1 \\ \mathbf{0} & 1 \end{bmatrix}^{-1} \begin{bmatrix} \mathbf{Q}_1 & \mathbf{s}_1 \\ \mathbf{0} & 1 \end{bmatrix}
$$

$$
= \begin{bmatrix} \mathbf{Q}_2^{\mathrm{T}} \mathbf{R} \mathbf{Q}_1 & \mathbf{Q}_2^{\mathrm{T}} (\mathbf{R}\mathbf{s}_1 - \mathbf{R}\mathbf{t}_1 + \mathbf{t}_2 - \mathbf{s}_2) \\ \mathbf{0} & 1 \end{bmatrix}. \tag{5}
$$

Once the relative pose $[\mathbf{R}', \mathbf{t}']$ between two perspective cameras for each AC is expressed, the essential matrix $\mathbf{E}' = [\mathbf{t}']_\times \mathbf{R}'$ can be represented as:

$$
\mathbf{E}' = \mathbf{Q}_2^{\mathrm{T}} \left(\mathbf{R}[\mathbf{s}_1 - \mathbf{t}_1]_\times + [\mathbf{t}_2 - \mathbf{s}_2]_\times \mathbf{R} \right) \mathbf{Q}_1. \tag{6}
$$

By substituting Eq. (4) into Eq. (6), we obtain:

$$
\mathbf{E}' = -\lambda_{j1} \mathbf{Q}_2^{\mathrm{T}} \mathbf{R} [\mathbf{p}_{ij}]_\times \mathbf{Q}_1 + \lambda_{j2} \mathbf{Q}_2^{\mathrm{T}} [\mathbf{p}'_{ij}]_\times \mathbf{R} \mathbf{Q}_1
$$

$$
+ \mathbf{Q}_2^{\mathrm{T}} \left(\mathbf{R}[\mathbf{s}_1 - \mathbf{q}_{ij} \times \mathbf{p}_{ij}]_\times + [\mathbf{q}'_{ij} \times \mathbf{p}'_{ij} - \mathbf{s}_2]_\times \mathbf{R} \right) \mathbf{Q}_1. \tag{7}
$$

It can be verified that each entry in the essential matrix $\mathbf{E}'$ is linear with $\{\lambda_{j1}, \lambda_{j2}\}$. Generally speaking, one AC $(\mathbf{x}_j, \mathbf{x}'_j, \mathbf{A}_j)$ yields three independent constraints on the relative pose estimation of a multi-camera system, which consist of one epipolar constraint derived from PC $(\mathbf{x}_j, \mathbf{x}'_j)$ and two affine transformation constraints derived from local affine transformation $\mathbf{A}_j$. With known intrinsic camera parameters, the epipolar constraint of PC between view 1 and view 2 is given as follows [21]:

$$
\mathbf{x}'^{\mathrm{T}}_j \mathbf{E}' \mathbf{x}_j = 0, \tag{8}
$$

The affine transformation constraints which describe the relationship of essential matrix $\mathbf{E}'$ and local affine transformation $\mathbf{A}_j$ is formulated as follows [2,41]:

$$
(\mathbf{E}'^{\mathrm{T}} \mathbf{x}'_j)_{(1:2)} = -\mathbf{A}_j^{\mathrm{T}} (\mathbf{E}' \mathbf{x}_j)_{(1:2)}, \tag{9}
$$

where the subscript (1:2) represents the first two equations.

Even though the perspective cameras are assumed, the geometric constraints can straightforwardly be generalized to generalized camera models as long as local image patches across views are obtained equivalently by arbitrary central camera models [2,12]. Based on Eqs. (8) and (9), two ACs provide six independent constraints. Considering that the relative pose estimation problem of multi-cameras systems has 6DOF, the number of constraints is equal to the number of unknowns. Thus, we explore the minimal solvers using two ACs.

3.3   Equation System Construction

Note that the special parameterization has been adopted by choosing one AC as the origin of world reference system in the Subsect. 3.1, we found the PC derived from the chosen AC cannot contribute one constraint since the coefficients of the resulting equation are zero. Thus, when j-th AC is chosen to build up the world reference system W, five equations can be provided by two ACs. Specifically, j-th AC provides two equations based on Eq. (9) and the other AC provides three equations based on Eqs. (8) and (9). By substituting Eq. (7) into Eqs. (8) and (9) and using the hidden variable technique [10], the five equations provided by two ACs can be written as:

$$\underbrace{\mathbf{F}_j(q_x, q_y, q_z)}_{5\times 3} \begin{bmatrix} \lambda_{j1} \\ \lambda_{j2} \\ 1 \end{bmatrix} = \mathbf{0}. \tag{10}$$

The entries in $\mathbf{F}_j$ are quadratic in unknowns q_x, q_y, and q_z. Since Eq. (10) has non-trivial solutions, the rank of $\mathbf{F}_j$ satisfies $\mathrm{rank}(\mathbf{F}_j) \leq 2$. Thus, all the 3×3 sub-determinants of $\mathbf{F}_j$ must be zero. This gives 10 equations about three unknowns $\{q_x, q_y, q_z\}$. Moreover, we can choose the other AC to build up the world reference system, and its orientation is also consistent with the reference of the multi-camera system in view 1. Suppose the j'-th AC is chosen, we build a new equation system about the same rotation parameters $\{q_x, q_y, q_z\}$, which is similar to Eq. (10):

$$\underbrace{\mathbf{F}_{j'}(q_x, q_y, q_z)}_{5\times 3} \begin{bmatrix} \lambda_{j'1} \\ \lambda_{j'2} \\ 1 \end{bmatrix} = \mathbf{0}. \tag{11}$$

Note that Eq. (11) provides new constraints which is different from Eq. (10). We use the computer algebra system `Macaulay 2` [15] to find that there are one dimensional families of extraneous roots if only Eq. (10) or Eq. (11) is used. This phenomenon has also been observed in [35,45]. Based on Eqs. (10) and (11), we have 20 equations with three unknowns $\{q_x, q_y, q_z\}$:

$$\det(\mathbf{N}(q_x, q_y, q_z)) = 0,$$
$$\mathbf{N} \in \{3 \times 3 \text{ submatrices of } \mathbf{F}_j\} \cup \{3 \times 3 \text{ submatrices of } \mathbf{F}_{j'}\}. \tag{12}$$

These equations have a degree of 6, *i.e.*, the highest of the degrees of the monomials with non-zero coefficients is 6.

Moreover, we derive extra implicit constraints in our problem, *i.e.*, the rank of $(\mathbf{F}_j)_{(1:2,1:3)}$ is 1. The proof is provided as follows:

Theorem 1. *When j-th AC is chosen to build up the world reference system, the corresponding affine transformation constraints satisfy* $\mathrm{rank}((\mathbf{F}_j)_{(1:2,1:3)}) = 1$.

Proof. To achieve this goal, we need to prove that $(\mathbf{F}_j)_{(1:2,1:3)}$ has two linearly independent null space vectors $\mathbf{v}_1$ and $\mathbf{v}_2$. Based on Eq. (10), $\mathbf{v}_1 = [\lambda_{j1}, \lambda_{j2}, 1]^{\mathrm{T}}$ is obviously a null space vector. Then we suppose that the second null space vector can be expressed as $\mathbf{v}_2 = [\lambda_{z1}, \lambda_{z2}, 0]^{\mathrm{T}}$, where λ_{z1} and λ_{z2} are two unknown depth parameters of the origin of world reference system W in camera 1 (view 1) and camera 2 (view 2), respectively.

For the multi-camera system in Fig. 2, we parameterize the transformation of cameras with respect to the world reference system W. Denote the transformation between camera 1 in view 1 and W as $[\mathbf{Q}_1^T, \lambda_{z1}\mathbf{Q}_1^T\mathbf{p}_{ij}]$, and the transformation between camera 2 in view 2 and W as $[\mathbf{Q}_2^T\mathbf{R}, \lambda_{z2}\mathbf{Q}_2^T\mathbf{p}'_{ij}]$. The transformation between camera 1 in view 1 and camera 2 in view 2 $\{\tilde{\mathbf{R}}, \tilde{\mathbf{t}}\}$ can be computed. Thus, the corresponding essential matrix $\tilde{\mathbf{E}} = [\tilde{\mathbf{t}}]_\times \tilde{\mathbf{R}}$ is represented as

$$\tilde{\mathbf{E}} = -\lambda_{z1}\mathbf{Q}_2^T\mathbf{R}[\mathbf{p}_{ij}]_\times\mathbf{Q}_1 + \lambda_{z2}\mathbf{Q}_2^T[\mathbf{p}'_{ij}]_\times\mathbf{R}\mathbf{Q}_1. \tag{13}$$

Note that the coefficients of the unknowns λ_{z1} and λ_{z2} in Eq. (13) are the same as the coefficients of the unknowns λ_{j1} and λ_{j2} in Eq. (7). Based on the Eq. (9), the affine transformation constraints can be written as follows

$$(\mathbf{G}_j)_{(1:2,1:2)} \begin{bmatrix} \lambda_{z1} \\ \lambda_{z2} \end{bmatrix} = \mathbf{0}. \tag{14}$$

In comparison with Eq. (10), $(\mathbf{G}_j)_{(1:2,1:2)}$ is the first 2×2 sub-matrix of $(\mathbf{F}_j)_{(1:2,1:3)}$. We can see that the null space vector $\mathbf{v}_2 = [\lambda_{z1}, \lambda_{z2}, 0]^T$ is also the null space vector of $(\mathbf{F}_j)_{(1:2,1:3)}$. Thus, the rank of $(\mathbf{F}_j)_{(1:2,1:3)}$ is 1.

Based on Theorem 1, the affine transformation constraints provide extra equations for our problem. Only if j-th AC is chosen to build up the world reference system W, two affine transformation constraints of j-th AC are used in the equation system construction. Similarly, when we choose the j'-th AC to build up the world reference, the extra equations of the corresponding affine transformation constraints can also be provided. Thus, there are 6 extra equations for the relative pose estimation using ACs:

$$\det(\mathbf{M}(q_x, q_y, q_z)) = 0,$$

$$\mathbf{M} \in \{2 \times 2 \text{ submatrices of } (\mathbf{F}_j)_{(1:2,1:3)}\} \cup \{2 \times 2 \text{ submatrices of } (\mathbf{F}_{j'})_{(1:2,1:3)}\}. \tag{15}$$

These extra equations have a degree of 4. Note that the extra implicit constraints Eq. (15) are independent of Eqs. (10) and (11). For geometric explanation, the extra constraints encode that the affine transformation constraints come from a perspective camera of two viewpoints. As we will see later, using the extra constraints from Theorem 1 reduces the number of solutions.

3.4 Polynomial System Solving

We propose two minimal solvers based on the common configurations of two ACs in multi-camera systems, including an inter-camera solver and an intra-camera solver. The inter-camera solver uses inter-camera ACs which are seen by different cameras over two consecutive views. It is suitable for multi-camera systems with large overlapping of views. The intra-camera solver uses intra-camera ACs which are seen by the same camera over two consecutive views. It is suitable for multi-camera systems with non-overlapping or small-overlapping of views.

A suitable way to find algebraic solutions to the polynomial equation system Eqs. (12) and (15) is to use the Gröbner basis technique. To keep numerical stability and avoid large number arithmetic during the calculation of Gröbner basis, a random instance of the original equation system is constructed in a finite prime field $\mathbb{Z}_p$ [32]. The relations between all observations are appropriately preserved. Then, we use Macaulay 2 [15] to calculate Gröbner basis. Finally, the solver is found with the automatic Gröbner basis solver [28]. We denote these polynomial equations in Eq. (12) and Eq. (15) as $\mathcal{E}_1$ and $\mathcal{E}_2$, respectively. Note that the polynomial equations $\mathcal{E}_1$ and $\mathcal{E}_2$ can be extended to solve various relative pose estimation problems, such as with known rotation angle and unknown focal lengths. In this paper, $\mathcal{E}_1$ is sufficient to solve the relative pose with inter-camera ACs. For intra-camera ACs, there are one-dimensional families of extraneous roots if only $\mathcal{E}_1$ is used. Moreover, using both $\mathcal{E}_1$ and $\mathcal{E}_2$ can reduce the number of solutions in the inter-camera case.

Table 1 shows the resulting inter-camera and intra-camera solvers. We have the following observations. (1) If $\mathcal{E}_1$ is used, the inter-camera solver maximally has 56 complex solutions and the elimination template of size 56×120. But the intra-camera case has one-dimensional families of extraneous roots. (2) If both $\mathcal{E}_1$ and $\mathcal{E}_2$ are used, the number of complex solutions obtained by the inter-camera solver can be reduced to 48. The number of complex solutions obtained by the intra-camera solver is also 48. The elimination template of the inter-camera solver and intra-camera solver is 64×120 and 72×120, respectively. (3) For the inter-camera case, using equations from $\mathcal{E}_1$ results in smaller eliminate templates than using $\mathcal{E}_1 + \mathcal{E}_2$. Meanwhile, the solver resulting from $\mathcal{E}_1$ has better numerical stability than the solver resulting from $\mathcal{E}_1 + \mathcal{E}_2$. This phenomenon has also been observed in previous literature [7], which shows that the number of basis might affect the numerical stability.

Table 1. Minimal solvers for the multi-camera systems. #sol indicates the number of solutions. 1-dim indicates one dimensional families of extraneous roots.

AC type	$\mathcal{E}_1$		$\mathcal{E}_1 + \mathcal{E}_2$	
	#sol	Template	#sol	Template
Inter-camera	56	56×120	48	64×120
Intra-camera	1-dim	—	48	72×120

Once the rotation parameters $\{q_x, q_y, q_z\}$ are obtained, $\mathbf{R}$ can be obtained immediately. Then $\{\lambda_{jk}\}_{k=1,2}$ and $\{\lambda_{j'k}\}_{k=1,2}$ are determined by finding the null space of $\mathbf{F}_j$ and $\mathbf{F}_{j'}$, respectively. Note that the translations estimated by $\{\lambda_{jk}\}$ and $\{\lambda_{j'k}\}$ are theoretically the same in minimal problems. Take the translation estimation using $\{\lambda_{jk}\}$ for an example. We can calculate $\mathbf{t}_1$ and $\mathbf{t}_2$ by Eq. (4). Finally we calculate the relative pose by compositing the transformations $[\mathbf{R}_1, \mathbf{t}_1]$ and $[\mathbf{R}_2, \mathbf{t}_2]$. Moreover, our minimal solver generation framework can be easily extended to recover the relative pose of a monocular camera. See supplementary material for details.

3.5 Degenerated Configurations

We prove three cases of critical motions for relative pose estimation from ACs.

Proposition 1. *For inter-camera ACs, if a multi-camera system undergoes pure translation and the baseline of two camera is parallel with the translation direction, the metric scale of translation cannot be recovered.*

Proposition 2. *For intra-camera ACs, when a multi-camera system undergoes pure translation or constant rotation rate, both cases are degenerate motions. Specifically, the metric scale of translation cannot be recovered.*

Due to space limitations, the proof of degenerate cases and the methods to overcome the degenerate cases are provided in the supplementary material.

4   Experiments

The performance of our solvers is validated using both synthetic and real-world data. The proposed 2AC method are referred to as 2AC-inter for inter-camera ACs, and 2AC-intra for intra-camera ACs. To further distinguish two solvers for inter-camera ACs, 2AC-inter-56 and 2AC-inter-48 are used to refer the solvers resulting from $\mathcal{E}_1$ and $\mathcal{E}_1 + \mathcal{E}_2$, respectively. The proposed solvers are implemented in C++. The 2AC-inter solver and the 2AC-intra solver are compared with state-of-the-art methods including 17PC-Li [31], 8PC-Kneip [26], 6PC-Stewénius [45] and 6AC-Ventura [1]. The methods which estimate the relative pose with a prior are not compared in this paper [17,18,47,48]. All the solvers are integrated into RANSAC in order to remove outlier matches of the feature correspondences. The relative pose which produces the most inliers is used to measure the relative pose error. This also allows us to select the best candidate from multiple solutions by counting their inliers.

The relative rotation and translation of the multi-camera systems are compared separately in the experiments. The rotation error compares the angular difference between the ground truth rotation and the estimated rotation: $\varepsilon_{\mathbf{R}} = \arccos((\text{trace}(\mathbf{R}_{gt}\mathbf{R}^{T})-1)/2)$, where $\mathbf{R}_{gt}$ and $\mathbf{R}$ denote the ground truth rotation and the corresponding estimated rotation, respectively. We evaluate the translation error by following the definition in [30]: $\varepsilon_{\mathbf{t}} = 2\,\|(\mathbf{t}_{gt} - \mathbf{t})\|\,/(\|\mathbf{t}_{gt}\| + \|\mathbf{t}\|)$, where $\mathbf{t}_{gt}$ and $\mathbf{t}$ denote the ground truth translation and the corresponding estimated translation, respectively. $\varepsilon_{\mathbf{t}}$ denotes both the metric scale error and the direction error of the translation. The translation direction error is also evaluated separately by comparing the angular difference between the ground truth translation and the estimated translation: $\varepsilon_{\mathbf{t},\text{dir}} = \arccos((\mathbf{t}_{gt}^{T}\mathbf{t})/(\|\mathbf{t}_{gt}\| \cdot \|\mathbf{t}\|))$.

4.1   Experiments on Synthetic Data

A simulated multi-camera system is made to evaluate the inter-camera and intra-camera solvers simultaneously [17,18]. The baseline length between two simulated cameras is set to 1 m, and the movement length of the multi-camera system is set to 3 m. The resolution of cameras is 640×480 pixels with a focal length of 400 pixels. The principal points are set to the image center (320, 240).

Table 2. Runtime comparison of relative pose estimation solvers (unit: μs).

Methods	17PC-Li [31]	8PC-Kneip [26]	6PC-Stew. [45]	6AC-Vent. [1]	2AC-inter-56	2AC-inter-48	2AC-intra
Runtime	43.3	102.0	3275.4	38.1	1084.8	842.3	871.6

We carry out a total of 1000 trials and assess the rotation and translation error by the median of errors in the synthetic experiment.

In each test, 100 ACs are generated randomly, including 50 ACs from a ground plane and 50 ACs from 50 random planes. The synthetic scene is randomly generated in a cubic region of size $[-5, 5] \times [-5, 5] \times [10, 20]$ meters. For each AC, the PC is obtained by reprojecting a random 3D point from a plane into two cameras. The associated affine transformation is obtained as follows: First, four additional image points are chosen as the vertices of a square in view 1, where its center is the PC of AC. The side length of the square is set to 30 or 40 pixels. A larger side length means the larger support regions for generating the ACs, which causes smaller noise of affine transformation. The support region is used for AC noise simulation only. Second, the ground truth homography is used to calculate the four corresponding image points in view 2. Third, Gaussian noise is added to the coordinates of four sampled image point pairs. Fourth, the noisy affine transformation is calculated from the first-order approximation of the noisy homography, which is estimated by using four noise image point pairs. This procedure promises an indirect but geometrically interpretable way of noising the affine transformation [3]. The Gaussian noise with a standard deviation is added to the PCs, and, also, to the sampled image point pairs which are used to estimate the affine transformations. In the experiments, the required ACs are selected randomly for the solvers within the RANSAC scheme. For the PC-based solvers, only the PCs derived from the ACs are used.

Efficiency Comparison and Numerical Stability. The proposed solvers are evaluated on an Intel(R) Core(TM) i7-7800X 3.50 GHz. All comparison solvers are implemented in C++. The 17PC-Li, 8PC-Kneip and 6PC-Stewénius are provided by OpenGV library [25]. The 6AC-Ventura is publicly available from the code of [1]. Table 2 shows the average processing times of the solvers over 10,000 runs. The methods 17PC-Li and 6AC-Ventura have low runtime, because they solve for the multi-camera motion linearly. Among the minimal solvers, all the proposed solvers 2AC-inter-56, 2AC-inter-48 and 2AC-intra are significantly more efficient than the 6PC-Stewénius solver.

Figure 3 reports the numerical stability comparison of all the solvers in noise-free cases. We repeat the procedure 10,000 times and plot the empirical probability density functions as the function of the $\log_{10}$ estimated errors. Numerical stability represents the round-off error of solvers in noise-free cases. The solvers 17PC-Li and 6AC-Ventura have the best numerical stability, because the linear solvers with smaller computation burden have less round-off error. Since the 8PC-Kneip solver uses the iterative optimization, it is susceptible to falling into local minima. Among the minimal solvers, all the proposed solvers

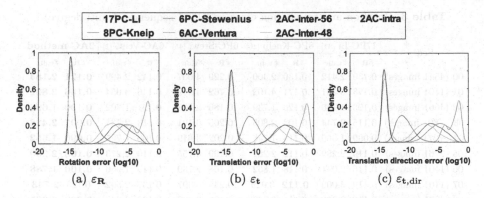

Fig. 3. Probability density functions over relative pose estimation errors on noise-free observations for multi-camera systems. The horizontal axis represents the $\log_{10}$ errors, and the vertical axis represents the density.

2AC-inter-56, 2AC-inter-48 and 2AC-intra have better numerical stability than the 6PC-Stewénius solver. Moreover, 2AC-inter-56 has better numerical stability than 2AC-inter-48, which shows that adding the extra equations $\mathcal{E}_2$ is not helpful in improving the numerical stability of the 2AC-inter solver. Even though 2AC-inter-48 produces the less solutions, we prefer to perform 2AC-inter-56 for the sake of numerical accuracy in the follow-up experiments. In addition to efficiency and numerical stability, another important factor for a solver is the minimal number of needed feature correspondences between two views. Since the proposed solvers require only two ACs, the number of RANSAC iterations is obviously lower than PC-based methods. Thus, our solvers have an advantage in detecting the outlier and estimating the initial motion efficiently when integrating them into the RANSAC framework. See supplementary material for details. Due to space limitations, the performance of the proposed solvers with different image noise is also shown in the supplementary material. As we will see later, the proposed solvers have better overall efficiency than the comparative solvers in the experiments on real-world data.

4.2   Experiments on Real Data

We evaluate the performance of the proposed solvers on three public datasets in popular modern robot applications. Specifically, the KITTI dataset [14] and nuScenes dataset [8] are collected on an autonomous driving environment. The EuRoc MAV dataset [6] is collected on an unmanned aerial vehicle environment. These datasets provide challenging image pairs, such as large motion and highly dynamic scenes. We compare the proposed solvers against state-of-the-art 6DOF relative pose estimation techniques. The rotation error $\varepsilon_{\mathbf{R}}$ and the translation direction error $\varepsilon_{\mathbf{t},\mathrm{dir}}$ are used to evaluate the accuracy of the proposed solvers [1, 26,34]. We tested on a total of 30,000 image pairs. Our solvers focus on relative pose estimation, $i.e.$, integrating the minimal solver with RANSAC. To ensure

Table 3. Rotation and translation error on KITTI sequences (unit: degree).

Seq.	17PC-Li [31]		8PC-Kneip [26]		6PC-Stew. [45]		6AC-Vent. [1]		2AC method	
	ε_R	$\varepsilon_{t,dir}$	ε_R	$\varepsilon_{t,dir}$	ε_R	$\varepsilon_{t,dir}$	ε_R	$\varepsilon_{t,dir}$	ε_R	$\varepsilon_{t,dir}$
00 (4541 images)	0.139	2.412	0.130	2.400	0.229	4.007	0.142	2.499	**0.121**	**2.184**
01 (1101 images)	0.158	5.231	0.171	4.102	0.762	41.19	0.146	3.654	**0.136**	**2.821**
02 (4661 images)	0.123	1.740	0.126	1.739	0.186	2.508	0.121	1.702	**0.120**	**1.696**
03 (801 images)	0.115	2.744	0.108	2.805	0.265	6.191	0.113	2.731	**0.097**	**2.428**
04 (271 images)	0.099	1.560	0.110	1.746	0.202	3.619	0.100	1.725	**0.090**	**1.552**
05 (2761 images)	0.119	2.289	0.112	2.281	0.199	4.155	0.116	2.273	**0.103**	**2.239**
06 (1101 images)	0.116	2.071	0.118	1.862	0.168	2.739	0.115	1.956	**0.106**	**1.788**
07 (1101 images)	0.119	3.002	**0.112**	3.029	0.245	6.397	0.137	2.892	0.123	**2.743**
08 (4071 images)	0.116	2.386	0.111	2.349	0.196	3.909	0.108	2.344	**0.089**	**2.235**
09 (1591 images)	0.133	1.977	0.125	1.806	0.179	2.592	0.124	1.876	**0.116**	**1.644**
10 (1201 images)	0.127	1.889	**0.115**	1.893	0.201	2.781	0.203	2.057	0.184	**1.687**

Table 4. Runtime of RANSAC averaged over KITTI sequences (unit: s).

Methods	17PC-Li [31]	8PC-Kneip [26]	6PC-Stew. [45]	6AC-Vent. [1]	**2AC method**
Mean time	52.82	10.36	79.76	6.83	4.87
Standard deviation	2.62	1.59	4.52	0.61	0.35

the fairness of the experiments, the PCs derived from the ACs are used in the PC-based solvers. Due to space limitations, the experiment results on the EuRoc MAV dataset are shown in the supplementary material.

Experiments on KITTI Dataset All the solvers are evaluated on KITTI dataset [14] collected on outdoor autonomous vehicles with a forward facing stereo camera. We treat it as a general multi-camera system by ignoring the overlap in their fields of view. The 2AC-intra solver is tested on all the available 11 sequences, which consist of 23000 image pairs in total. The ground truth is directly given by the output of the GPS/IMU localization unit [14]. For consecutive views in each camera, the ASIFT [38] is used to establish the ACs. There are also strategies to speed up the extraction of ACs, such as MSER [36], GPU acceleration, or approximating ACs from SIFT features [18]. To deal with outlier matches, all the solvers are integrated into a RANSAC framework. To select the right solution from multiple solutions, we counted their inliers in a RANSAC-like procedure and the solution with the most inliers is chosen.

Table 3 shows the rotation and translation error of the proposed 2AC method for KITTI sequences. The median error is used to evaluate the performance. It is seen that the overall performance of the 2AC method outperforms the comparative methods in almost all cases. Moreover, to compare the advantage of computation efficiency, the RANSAC runtime averaged over all the KITTI sequences for the solvers is shown in Table 4. The reported runtimes represent the relative pose estimation by RANSAC combined with a minimal solver, which mainly includes

Table 5. Rotation and translation error on nuScenes sequences (unit: degree).

Part	17PC-Li [31]		8PC-Kneip [26]		6PC-Stew. [45]		6AC-Vent. [1]		2AC method	
	ε_R	$\varepsilon_{t,dir}$	ε_R	$\varepsilon_{t,dir}$	ε_R	$\varepsilon_{t,dir}$	ε_R	$\varepsilon_{t,dir}$	ε_R	$\varepsilon_{t,dir}$
01 (3376 images)	0.161	2.680	0.156	2.407	0.203	2.764	0.143	2.366	**0.114**	**2.017**

hypothesis generation and best candidate selection from multiple solutions by counting their inliers. Even though some solvers are faster than the proposed 2AC method in Table 2, our method has better overall efficiency than all the comparative methods when integrating them into the RANSAC framework. The detailed analysis is presented in the supplementary material.

Experiments on NuScenes Dataset The performance of the solvers is also tested on the nuScenes dataset [8], which consists of consecutive keyframes from 6 cameras. This multi-camera system provides full 360° field of view. We utilize all the keyframes of Part 1 for the evaluation, and there are 3376 images in total. The ground truth is given by a lidar map-based localization scheme. Similar to the experiments on KITTI dataset, the ASIFT detector is used to establish the ACs between consecutive views in six cameras. The proposed 2AC method is compared with state-of-the-art methods including 17PC-Li [31], 8PC-Kneip [26], 6PC-Stewénius [45] and 6AC-Ventura [1]. All the solvers are integrated into RANSAC in order to remove outlier matches of the feature correspondences.

Table 5 shows the rotation and translation error of the proposed 2AC method for the Part1 of nuScenes dataset. The median error is used to evaluate the estimation accuracy. It is demonstrated that the proposed 2AC method offers the best performance among all the methods. In comparison with experiments on KITTI dataset, this experiment also demonstrates that our 2AC method can be directly used to the relative pose estimation for the systems with more cameras.

5 Conclusion

By exploiting the geometric constraints using a special parameterization, we estimate the 6DOF relative pose of a multi-camera system using a minimal number of two ACs. The extra implicit constraints about the affine transformation constraints are found and proved. Two minimal solvers are designed for two common types of ACs across two views, *i.e.*, inter-camera and intra-camera. Moreover, three degenerate cases are proved. The framework for generating the minimal solvers is unified and versatile, and can be extended to solve various problems, *e.g.*, relative pose estimation for a monocular camera. Compared with existing minimal solvers, our solvers require fewer feature correspondences and are not restricted to special cases of multi-camera motion. Based on a series of experiments on synthetic data and three real-world image datasets, we demonstrate that our solvers can be used efficiently for ego-motion estimation and outperform the state-of-the-art methods in both accuracy and efficiency.

Acknowledgment. This work has been partially funded by the National Natural Science Foundation of China (Grant Nos. 11902349 and 11727804).

References

1. Alyousefi, K., Ventura, J.: Multi-camera motion estimation with affine correspondences. In: International Conference on Image Analysis and Recognition, pp. 417–431 (2020)
2. Barath, D., Hajder, L.: Efficient recovery of essential matrix from two affine correspondences. IEEE Trans. Image Process. **27**(11), 5328–5337 (2018)
3. Barath, D., Kukelova, Z.: Homography from two orientation-and scale-covariant features. In: IEEE International Conference on Computer Vision, pp. 1091–1099 (2019)
4. Barath, D., Polic, M., Förstner, W., Sattler, T., Pajdla, T., Kukelova, Z.: Making affine correspondences work in camera geometry computation. In: Vedaldi, A., Bischof, H., Brox, T., Frahm, J.-M. (eds.) ECCV 2020. LNCS, vol. 12356, pp. 723–740. Springer, Cham (2020). https://doi.org/10.1007/978-3-030-58621-8_42
5. Bentolila, J., Francos, J.M.: Conic epipolar constraints from affine correspondences. Comput. Vis. Image Underst. **122**, 105–114 (2014)
6. Burri, M., et al.: The EuRoC micro aerial vehicle datasets. Int. J. Robot. Res. **35**(10), 1157–1163 (2016)
7. Byröd, M., Josephson, K., Astrṏm, K.: Fast and stable polynomial equation solving and its application to computer vision. Int. J. Comput. Vision **84**(3), 237–256 (2009)
8. Caesar, H., et al.: nuScenes: a multimodal dataset for autonomous driving. In: IEEE Conference on Computer Vision and Pattern Recognition, pp. 11621–11631 (2020)
9. Clipp, B., Kim, J.H., Frahm, J.M., Pollefeys, M., Hartley, R.: Robust 6dof motion estimation for non-overlapping, multi-camera systems. In: IEEE Workshop on Applications of Computer Vision, pp. 1–8. IEEE (2008)
10. Cox, D.A., Little, J., O'Shea, D.: Using algebraic geometry. Springer Science & Business Media (2006)
11. Eichhardt, I., Barath, D.: Relative pose from deep learned depth and a single affine correspondence. In: Vedaldi, A., Bischof, H., Brox, T., Frahm, J.-M. (eds.) ECCV 2020. LNCS, vol. 12357, pp. 627–644. Springer, Cham (2020). https://doi.org/10.1007/978-3-030-58610-2_37
12. Eichhardt, I., Chetverikov, D.: Affine correspondences between central cameras for rapid relative pose estimation. In: Ferrari, V., Hebert, M., Sminchisescu, C., Weiss, Y. (eds.) ECCV 2018. LNCS, vol. 11210, pp. 488–503. Springer, Cham (2018). https://doi.org/10.1007/978-3-030-01231-1_30
13. Fischler, M.A., Bolles, R.C.: Random sample consensus: a paradigm for model fitting with applications to image analysis and automated cartography. Commun. ACM **24**(6), 381–395 (1981)
14. Geiger, A., Lenz, P., Stiller, C., Urtasun, R.: Vision meets robotics: the KITTI dataset. Int. J. Robot. Res. **32**(11), 1231–1237 (2013)
15. Grayson, D.R., Stillman, M.E.: Macaulay 2, a software system for research in algebraic geometry (2002). https://faculty.math.illinois.edu/Macaulay2/
16. Grossberg, M.D., Nayar, S.K.: A general imaging model and a method for finding its parameters. In: IEEE International Conference on Computer Vision, vol. 2, pp. 108–115. IEEE (2001)

17. Guan, B., Zhao, J., Barath, D., Fraundorfer, F.: Efficient recovery of multi-camera motion from two affine correspondences. In: IEEE International Conference on Robotics and Automation, pp. 1305–1311 (2021)
18. Guan, B., Zhao, J., Barath, D., Fraundorfer, F.: Minimal cases for computing the generalized relative pose using affine correspondences. In: IEEE International Conference on Computer Vision, pp. 6068–6077 (2021)
19. Hajder, L., Barath, D.: Relative planar motion for vehicle-mounted cameras from a single affine correspondence. In: IEEE International Conference on Robotics and Automation, pp. 8651–8657 (2020)
20. Häne, C., et al.: 3D visual perception for self-driving cars using a multi-camera system: calibration, mapping, localization, and obstacle detection. Image Vis. Comput. **68**, 14–27 (2017)
21. Hartley, R., Zisserman, A.: Multiple view geometry in computer vision. Cambridge University Press (2003)
22. Heng, L., et al.: Project AutoVision: localization and 3D scene perception for an autonomous vehicle with a multi-camera system. In: IEEE International Conference on Robotics and Automation, pp. 4695–4702 (2019)
23. Kim, J.H., Hartley, R., Frahm, J.M., Pollefeys, M.: Visual odometry for non-overlapping views using second-order cone programming. In: Asian Conference on Computer Vision. pp. 353–362 (2007)
24. Kim, J.H., Li, H., Hartley, R.: Motion estimation for nonoverlapping multicamera rigs: Linear algebraic and L_∞ geometric solutions. IEEE Trans. Pattern Anal. Mach. Intell. **32**(6), 1044–1059 (2009)
25. Kneip, L., Furgale, P.: OpenGV: A unified and generalized approach to real-time calibrated geometric vision. In: IEEE International Conference on Robotics and Automation, pp. 12034–12043 (2014)
26. Kneip, L., Li, H.: Efficient computation of relative pose for multi-camera systems. In: IEEE Conference on Computer Vision and Pattern Recognition, pp. 446–453 (2014)
27. Kneip, L., Sweeney, C., Hartley, R.: The generalized relative pose and scale problem: View-graph fusion via 2D–2D registration. In: IEEE Winter Conference on Applications of Computer Vision, pp. 1–9 (2016)
28. Larsson, V., Aström, K., Oskarsson, M.: Efficient solvers for minimal problems by syzygy-based reduction. In: IEEE Conference on Computer Vision and Pattern Recognition, pp. 820–828 (2017)
29. Lee, G.H., Faundorfer, F., Pollefeys, M.: Motion estimation for self-driving cars with a generalized camera. In: IEEE Conference on Computer Vision and Pattern Recognition, pp. 2746–2753 (2013)
30. Lee, G.H., Pollefeys, M., Fraundorfer, F.: Relative pose estimation for a multi-camera system with known vertical direction. In: IEEE Conference on Computer Vision and Pattern Recognition, pp. 540–547 (2014)
31. Li, H., Hartley, R., Kim, J.H.: A linear approach to motion estimation using generalized camera models. In: IEEE Conference on Computer Vision and Pattern Recognition, pp. 1–8 (2008)
32. Lidl, R., Niederreiter, H.: Finite Fields. Cambridge University Press (1997)
33. Lim, J., Barnes, N., Li, H.: Estimating relative camera motion from the antipodal-epipolar constraint. IEEE Trans. Pattern Anal. Mach. Intell. **32**(10), 1907–1914 (2010)
34. Liu, L., Li, H., Dai, Y., Pan, Q.: Robust and efficient relative pose with a multi-camera system for autonomous driving in highly dynamic environments. IEEE Trans. Intell. Transp. Syst. **19**(8), 2432–2444 (2017)

35. Martyushev, E., Li, B.: Efficient relative pose estimation for cameras and generalized cameras in case of known relative rotation angle. J. Math. Imaging Vis. **62**, 1076–1086 (2020)
36. Matas, J., Chum, O., Urban, M., Pajdla, T.: Robust wide-baseline stereo from maximally stable extremal regions. Image Vis. Comput. **22**(10), 761–767 (2004)
37. Miraldo, P., Araujo, H., Queiró, J.: Point-based calibration using a parametric representation of the general imaging model. In: IEEE International Conference on Computer Vision, pp. 2304–2311. IEEE (2011)
38. Morel, J.M., Yu, G.: ASIFT. a new framework for fully affine invariant image comparison. SIAM J. Imag. Sci. **2**(2), 438–469 (2009)
39. Nistér, D.: An efficient solution to the five-point relative pose problem. IEEE Trans. Pattern Anal. Mach. Intell. **26**(6), 756–777 (2004)
40. Pless, R.: Using many cameras as one. In: IEEE Conference on Computer Vision and Pattern Recognition, pp. 1–7 (2003)
41. Raposo, C., Barreto, J.P.: Theory and practice of structure-from-motion using affine correspondences. In: IEEE Conference on Computer Vision and Pattern Recognition, pp. 5470–5478 (2016)
42. Scaramuzza, D., Fraundorfer, F.: Visual odometry: the first 30 years and fundamentals. IEEE Robot. Autom. Mag. **18**(4), 80–92 (2011)
43. Schönberger, J.L., Frahm, J.M.: Structure-from-motion revisited. In: IEEE Conference on Computer Vision and Pattern Recognition, pp. 4104–4113 (2016)
44. Stewénius, H., Nistér, D., Kahl, F., Schaffalitzky, F.: A minimal solution for relative pose with unknown focal length. In: IEEE Conference on Computer Vision and Pattern Recognition, pp. 789–794 (2005)
45. Stewénius, H., Oskarsson, M., Aström, K., Nistér, D.: Solutions to minimal generalized relative pose problems. In: Workshop on Omnidirectional Vision in conjunction with ICCV, pp. 1–8 (2005)
46. Sturm, P., Ramalingam, S.: A generic concept for camera calibration. In: Pajdla, T., Matas, J. (eds.) ECCV 2004. LNCS, vol. 3022, pp. 1–13. Springer, Heidelberg (2004). https://doi.org/10.1007/978-3-540-24671-8_1
47. Sweeney, C., Flynn, J., Turk, M.: Solving for relative pose with a partially known rotation is a quadratic eigenvalue problem. In: International Conference on 3D Vision, pp. 483–490 (2014)
48. Ventura, J., Arth, C., Lepetit, V.: An efficient minimal solution for multi-camera motion. In: IEEE International Conference on Computer Vision, pp. 747–755 (2015)
49. Zhao, J., Kneip, L., He, Y., Ma, J.: Minimal case relative pose computation using ray-point-ray features. IEEE Trans. Pattern Anal. Mach. Intell. **42**(5), 1176–1190 (2020)
50. Zhao, J., Xu, W., Kneip, L.: A certifiably globally optimal solution to generalized essential matrix estimation. In: IEEE Conference on Computer Vision and Pattern Recognition, pp. 12034–12043 (2020)
51. Zheng, E., Wu, C.: Structure from motion using structure-less resection. In: IEEE International Conference on Computer Vision, pp. 2075–2083 (2015)

GraphFit: Learning Multi-scale Graph-Convolutional Representation for Point Cloud Normal Estimation

Keqiang Li[1,3], Mingyang Zhao[1,2], Huaiyu Wu[1(✉)], Dong-Ming Yan[1,3],
Zhen Shen[1], Fei-Yue Wang[1], and Gang Xiong[1]

[1] SKLMCCS/NLPR, Institute of Automation, Chinese Academy of Sciences,
Beijing, China
{likeqiang2020,huaiyu.wu,zhen.shen,feiyue.wang,gang.xiong}@ia.ac.cn,
myzhao@baai.ac.cn
[2] Beijing Academy of Artificial Intelligence, Beijing, China
[3] School of Artificial Intelligence, University of Chinese Academy of Sciences,
Beijing, China

Abstract. We propose a precise and efficient normal estimation method that can deal with noise and nonuniform density for unstructured 3D point clouds. Unlike existing approaches that directly take patches and ignore the local neighborhood relationships, which make them susceptible to challenging regions such as sharp edges, we propose to learn *graph convolutional feature representation* for normal estimation, which emphasizes more local neighborhood geometry and effectively encodes intrinsic relationships. Additionally, we design a novel adaptive module based on the *attention mechanism* to integrate point features with their neighboring features, hence further enhancing the robustness of the proposed normal estimator against point density variations. To make it more distinguishable, we introduce a *multi-scale architecture* in the graph block to learn richer geometric features. Our method outperforms competitors with the *state-of-the-art* accuracy on various benchmark datasets, and is quite robust against noise, outliers, as well as the density variations. The code is available at https://github.com/UestcJay/GraphFit.

Keywords: Normal estimation · Unstructured 3D point clouds · Graph convolution · Multi-scale

1 Introduction

The normal estimation of point clouds is a fundamental problem in 3D computer vision and computer graphics, which has a wide variety of applications in practice. Commonly, the scanned point clouds only contain spatial locations along

K. Li and M. Zhao—The authors contribute equally in this work.

Supplementary Information The online version contains supplementary material available at https://doi.org/10.1007/978-3-031-19824-3_38.

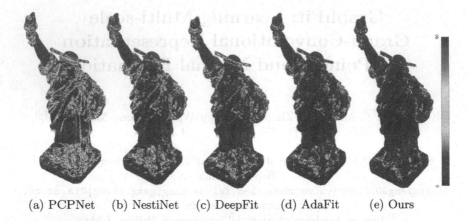

<table>
(a) PCPNet   (b) NestiNet   (c) DeepFit   (d) AdaFit   (e) Ours
</table>

Fig. 1. Comparison of the normal estimation error (colored by the heat map) of learning-based methods PCPNet [17], NestiNet [5], DeepFit [3], AdaFit [45] and the proposed method, where our method shows higher estimation accuracy, especially on complex regions.

with sampling density, noise, outliers or textures, while lacking local surface geometry, like point normals. High-quality normals can facilitate a large number of downstream tasks, such as point cloud denoising [28,29], surface reconstruction [14,23] and model segmentation [10].

Normal estimation is essential and has been studied for a long time, yet not well-solved. Traditional methods [6,9,20,27] usually adopt *principle component analysis* (PCA) and *singular value decomposition* (SVD) for normal estimation. They attain satisfactory results for simple and clean data but suffer from noise, outliers, and complex shapes. Moreover, their performance heavily depends on the parameter tuning. Recently, several learning-based methods [5,17,18,40,44] have been proposed to directly regress normals and have exhibited promising performance. Nevertheless, as pointed out in [45], direct regression brings in finite generalization and stability, especially for laser scanned real-world point clouds.

Different from the previous brute-force regression, a more accurate paradigm is to combine traditional methods involving geometry information with learning-based models for normal estimation, which typically specifies a fixed neighborhood around each point and then fits a local surface such as a plane to infer the normal. However, when point clouds are contaminated by noise or outliers, the estimated normals tend to be erroneous. To mitigate this problem, the *weighted least-squares* (WLS) fitting is invoked [3,26,43,45], in which point-wise weights are predicted. Despite that the improvements of accuracy and robustness, precise normal estimation in complex regions are still difficult, as illustrated in Fig. 1. In principle, point normals are local geometric properties, and are significantly affected by the geometric relations among the local neighborhood. However, previous methods directly adopt patches for normal estimation, and usually ignore the *intrinsic relationship* between points in the same patch, which empirically enables richer features and higher accuracy.

Motivated by this observation, in this paper, we present a novel method using graph-convolutional layers for robust and accurate normal estimation. Benefiting from the graph structure, we not only extract features but also encode local geometric relationship between points in the same patch. To enhance the feature integration capability and generate richer geometric information, we further utilize the adaptive module based on a attention mechanism to integrate point features with its neighboring features. Additionally, we design a novel multi-scale representation to learn more accurate and expressive local information, as well as reducing the influence of noise and outliers. In contrast to the cascaded scale aggregation layer used in previous approaches, which directly takes the global features of varying patches, our proposed multi-scale representation fuses local information from two different scales in the feature space, and casts more attention on the local features. We compare the proposed method with representative state-of-the-art approaches on popular benchmark datasets. Results demonstrate that our method outperforms competitors with higher accuracy, and it is quite robust against noise, outliers and density variations. We further verify the advantages of our method by applying it to surface reconstruction and point cloud denoising in the supplemental material. To summarize, our main contributions are threefold as follows:

- We propose a new method for accurate and robust normal estimation via the graph-convolutional feature learning, which effectively integrates local features and their relationships among the same point cloud patch.
- We design an adaptive module using the attention mechanism to fuse the point features with its neighboring features, which brings high-quality feature integration.
- We introduce a multi-scale representation module to extract more expressive features, bringing higher robustness against noise and varying point density.

2   Related Work

2.1   Classical Methods

The most popular and simplest way for normal estimation is based on the principal component analysis [20], in which the normal of a query point is calculated as the eigenvector corresponding to the smallest eigenvalue of a covariance matrix. Although this method is simple, it usually suffers from the choice of the neighboring size, noise, and outliers. Later, many variants such as *moving least squares* (MLS) [27], *truncated Taylor expansion* (n-jet) [9], and fitting local spherical surfaces [16] have been proposed. These approaches usually select a large-scale neighborhood to improve the robustness against noise and outliers, meanwhile trying to keep a correct normal estimation for sharp features. Particularly, Mitra et al. [31] delicately analyze the influence of the neighboring size, the curvature, sampling density, and noise to find an optimal neighbor radius. To attain more features, some methods utilize *Voronoi diagram* [1,2,12,30] to estimate the structure of the underlying surface, while others adopt *Hough Transform* (HT) [6] to achieve analogous effects. Nevertheless, HT-based methods typically require high computational complexity and fine tuning of hyper-parameters. Recent works have also been designed to robustly estimate normals for point clouds contaminated by outliers [24,33] or noise [15] with an adaptive neighboring size [8,11,32].

2.2 Learning-Based Approaches

Recently, with the marvelous success of deep learning in a wide variety of domains [13,19,34–37,39,41,42], some learning-based attempts have been made to estimate normals of point clouds, which can be generally categorized into two types: *regression-based* and *geometry-guided* methods.

Regression-Based Methods. Due to the estimation of surface normals from patches and the use of fully connected layers, regression-based methods are commonly simple. For instance, Lu et al. [28] transform point cloud patches into 2D height maps by computing the distances between points and a plane, while Ben-Shabat et al. [4] modify the *Fisher Vector* to describe points with their deviations from a *Gaussian Mixture Model* (GMM). HoughCNN [7] projects points into a Hough space via the Hough transform and then uses a 2D CNN to regress the normal vector. Another line of studies focus on the direct regression for unstructured point clouds. Inspired by the high efficiency of PointNet [35], [17] proposes a deep multi-scale PointNet for normal estimation (PCPNet), but requires a set of scale values. Hashimoto et al. [18] also use PointNet to extract the local features such as neighboring points while extract spatial representation by the voxel network 3DCNN. Nesti-Net [5] introduces a new normal estimation method for irregular 3D point clouds based on the mixture of experts and scale prediction, which yields high accuracy but suffers from high computational complexity.

Geometry-Guided Methods. Despite that regression-based methods are direct and simple, they usually produce weak generalization and unstable prediction results. To circumvent these limitations, most recent works combine deep learning with classical geometric methods. IterNet [26] and DeepFit [3] employ a deep neural network to learn point-wise weights for weighted-least-squares fitting to estimate the normals, leading to good normal estimation quality and have been extended to estimate other geometrical properties such as principal curvatures. Zhang et al. [43] propose a geometry-guided network for robust surface normal estimation, which improves the learning performance and the interpretability of the weights. A more recent work, AdaFit [45] incorporates a *Cascaded Scale Aggregation* (CSA) layer to aggregate features from multiple neighborhood sizes and adds additional offsets to enable the output normals more robust and accurate. Different from previous approaches, in this paper, we propose to use graph-convolutional layers for feature learning and normal estimation, and incorporate a multi-scale architecture that emphasizes richer local geometric features to generate more accurate normal estimation results.

3 Methodology

Problem Definition. Given a 3D point cloud $\mathcal{P} = \left\{ \mathbf{p}_i \in \mathbb{R}^3 \right\}_{i=1}^N$ and a query point $\mathbf{p}_i \in \mathcal{P}$, our target is to solve for the normal of each point in $\mathcal{P}$. We first

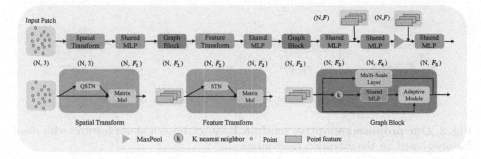

Fig. 2. Overview of our proposed network architecture. Graph block is utilized to encode the relationship between neighbor points, which contains an adaptive model to effectively integrate point features with the local neighbor features. A multi-scale layer is employed to extract richer local features. Given an input patch, our network predicts a point-wise weight and offset to fit a surface for normal estimation.

extract a local patch $N_k(\mathbf{p}_i) = \{\mathbf{p}_i \in \mathbb{R}^3 \mid i = 1, 2, \ldots, N_p\} \subset \mathcal{P}$, N_p is the size of $N_k(\mathbf{p}_i)$, then we employ the truncated Taylor expansion (n-jet) for surface fitting [9] to represent any regular embedded smooth surface, as the graph of a bi-variate *height function* with respect to any z direction does not belong to the tangent space. An n-order Taylor expansion of the *height function* is defined as

$$z = f(x, y) = J_{\beta, n}(x, y) = \sum_{k=0}^{n} \sum_{j=0}^{k} \beta_{k-j, j} x^{k-j} y^j, \tag{1}$$

where $\beta = \{\beta_{k-j,j} \mid j = 0, 1, \cdots, k; k = 0, 1, \cdots, n\}$ are the coefficients of the jet that consists of $N_n = (n+1)(n+2)/2$ terms. The goal is to fit a surface to $N_k(\mathbf{p}_i)$. We define the *Vandermonde matrix* $\mathbf{M} = \left(1, x_i, y_i, \ldots, x_i y_i^{n-1}, y_i^n\right)_{i=1,\ldots,N_p} \in \mathbb{R}^{N_p \times N_n}$ and the height function vector $\mathbf{z} = \left(z_1, z_2, \ldots, z_{N_p}\right) \in \mathbb{R}^{N_p}$. The sampled points in Eq. (1) can be expressed as

$$\mathbf{M}\beta = \mathbf{z}. \tag{2}$$

To enhance the robustness of the fitting method against noise and outliers, like [3], we adopt the weighted least-squares fitting of polynomial surfaces here, which can also relieve the problem of over-fitting or under-fitting [45]. Then our objective is to predict the point-wise weight w_i and offset $(\Delta x_i, \Delta y_i, \Delta z_i)$ to adjust the point distribution. The optimization problem becomes:

$$\hat{\beta} = \operatorname*{argmin}_{\beta} \sum_{i}^{N_p} w_i \left\| J_{\beta, n}(x_i + \Delta x_i, y_i + \Delta y_i) - (z_i + \Delta z_i) \right\|^2. \tag{3}$$

The solution to Eq. (3) can be expressed in a closed-form:

$$\hat{\beta} = \left(\mathbf{M}^\top \mathbf{W} \mathbf{M}\right)^{-1} \left(\mathbf{M}^\top \mathbf{W} \mathbf{z}\right), \tag{4}$$

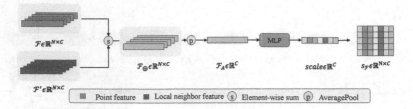

Fig. 3. Our proposed adaptive module. It integrates neighbour features with point features based on the attention mechanism.

where $\mathbf{W}$ is a diagonal weight matrix $\mathbf{W} = \text{diag}\left(w_1, w_2, \ldots, w_{N_p}\right) \in \mathbb{R}^{N_p \times N_p}$, in which the diagonal element w_i is the weight of the point $\mathbf{p}_i$. Once getting the jet coefficients β, the estimated normal $\hat{\mathbf{n}}_i$ of the point $\mathbf{p}_i$ is

$$\hat{\mathbf{n}}_i = \frac{(-\beta_1, -\beta_2, 1)}{\|(-\beta_1, -\beta_2, 1)\|_2}, \tag{5}$$

where we define $\beta_1 = \beta_{1,0}, \beta_2 = \beta_{0,1}$. Then the normals of neighboring points of the query point can be calculated by transforming n-jet to the implicit surface form, e.g., $F(x, y, z) = 0$:

$$\hat{\mathbf{n}}_j = \frac{\nabla F}{\|\nabla F\|}\bigg|_{p_{i,j}} = \frac{\left(-\beta \frac{\partial \mathbf{M}^T}{\partial x}, \beta \frac{\partial \mathbf{M}^T}{\partial y}, 1\right)}{\|\nabla F\|}\bigg|_{p_{i,j}}. \tag{6}$$

Motivation. The point normal on the surface is a locally geometric property, which is significantly affected by their mutual relations. To investigate this characteristic, we utilize the local neighbor information of the points in the same patch to achieve more accurate surface fitting. An overview of the proposed network architecture is presented in Fig. 2. The first block is composed of two point convolutions that gradually transform the 3D spatial points into a higher feature space. Then a cascade of two *graph blocks* is used, with several *skip connections* to enhance the feature expression ability. These representations are then concatenated and fed into *Multi-layer Perceptrons* (MLP) to predict weights and offsets for all points. We present detailed descriptions of the designed network architecture in the following.

Graph Block. The core of the proposed network in our method is the graph block. *Graph convolution*, as a generalization of the ordinary convolution to point data, represents point clouds with graph structures. Suppose the features $\mathcal{F} = \{f_i \mid i = 1, 2, \ldots, N\} \in \mathbb{R}^{N \times C}$ correspond to the input point cloud $\mathcal{P} \in \mathbb{R}^{N \times 3}$. Then we construct a graph by selecting the *k-nearest neighbors* (k-NN) of each point with respect to the Euclidean distance in the feature space. We attain the local neighborhood information using a feature mapping function $\phi_c(\cdot)$ over the point features (f_i, f_j):

$$g_{ijc} = \phi_c\left(\Delta f_{ij}\right), j \in N(i), \tag{7}$$

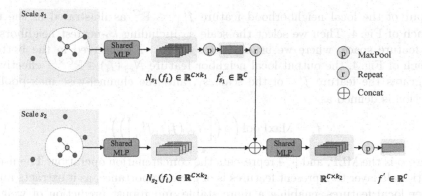

Fig. 4. Overview of the proposed multi-scale layer. It is employed to extract richer local features.

where $c = 1, 2, \cdots, C$. $\phi_c(\cdot)$ can be implemented as a *shared MLP*, and $N(i)$ denotes the neighborhood of the feature f_i. In order to combine the global shape structure and the local neighborhood information [39], we define $\Delta f_{ij} = [f_j - f_i, f_i]$ as the input of $\phi_c(\cdot)$, where $[\cdot, \cdot]$ represents the *concatenation operation*. Then we stack g_{ijc} of each channel to yield the local information feature $g_{ij} = [g_{ij1}, g_{ij2}, \ldots, g_{ijC}] \in \mathbb{R}^C$. Finally, we output the local neighborhood information for each input feature f_i:

$$f_i' = \max_{j \in N(i)} g_{ij}. \tag{8}$$

Moreover, we design an adaptive module to integrate the local patch information and the point feature. Inspired by the high efficiency of SENet [21] with simple and lightweight channel attention mechanism, we design an adaptive module based on the attention mechanism between the point feature $\mathcal{F} = \{f_i \mid i = 1, 2, \ldots, N\} \in \mathbb{R}^{N \times C}$ and the local neighborhood information $\mathcal{F}' = \{f_i' \mid i = 1, 2, \ldots, N\} \in \mathbb{R}^{N \times C}$. The adaptive module is presented in Fig. 3, in which the scale is

$$\mathbf{s}_{\mathcal{F}} = \text{Sigmoid}\left(\phi\left(\text{AvgPool}\left(\mathcal{F}' + \mathcal{F}\right)\right)\right), \tag{9}$$

where $+$ is *element-wise sum operation*, and $\phi(\cdot)$ represents the feature mapping function implemented by the MLP. Finally, we attain the output adaptive feature $\bar{\mathcal{F}}$ as

$$\bar{\mathcal{F}} = \mathbf{s}_{\mathcal{F}} \odot \mathcal{F} + \mathbf{s}_{\mathcal{F}'} \odot \mathcal{F}', \tag{10}$$

where $\mathbf{s}_{\mathcal{F}'} = (1 - \mathbf{s}_{\mathcal{F}})$, and $\odot$ is the *Hadamard product*.

Multi-scale Representation. To extract more distinguishable local features, we also introduce a novel layer to enhance the multi-scale representation ability of the designed network. As shown in Fig. 4, for a central feature $f_i \in \mathbb{R}^C$, we first construct a graph by selecting the k_1-nearest neighbors in the feature space, which indicates the scale s_1. After the operation mentioned above, we get the output of the local neighborhood feature $f'_{i_{s_1}} \in \mathbb{R}^C$ as illustrated in the top branch of Fig. 4. Then we select the scale s_2 including k_2-nearest neighbors in the feature space, where we usually set $s_2 < s_1$. As observed in the bottom branch of Fig. 4, the output local neighbor feature $N_{s_2}(f_i) \in \mathbb{R}^{C \times k_2}$ effectively integrates the feature $f'_{i_{s_1}}$ of the scale s_1, and the channel-wise max-pooling function is defined as

$$f'_i = \text{MaxPool}\left(\phi\left(\left[N_{s_2}(f_i), f'_{i_{s_1}}\right]\right)\right), \tag{11}$$

where ϕ is the MLP, and $[\cdot, \cdot]$ represents the concatenation operation. The use of multi-scale layer to represent features is of great importance, as it extracts much richer local features, enabling a more stable and robust prediction of weights and offsets.

Loss Functions. Similar to [3], we use the *angle loss* and the *consistency loss* to train our proposed network. The angle loss measures the deviations of the ground truth normals and the estimated ones, while the consistency loss targets to constrain points that locate on the fitting surface. Furthermore, we regularize the transformation matrix for much easier optimization. Our objective function is defined as

$$\mathcal{L}_{\text{tol}} = |\mathbf{n}_{gt} \times \hat{\mathbf{n}}| + \mathcal{L}_{\text{con}} + \lambda_3 \mathcal{L}_{\text{reg}}, \tag{12}$$

where λ_1, λ_2 and λ_3 are the weights to trade off different losses, and

$$\mathcal{L}_{\text{con}} = \frac{1}{N_{p_i}}\left[-\lambda_1 \sum_{j=1}^{N_{p_i}} \log(w_j) + \lambda_2 \sum_{j=1}^{N_{p_i}} w_j |\mathbf{n}_{gt,j} \times \hat{\mathbf{n}}_j|\right], \quad \mathcal{L}_{\text{reg}} = |I - AA^T|. \tag{13}$$

4   Experimental Evaluation

Implementation Details. We train our proposed network on the benchmark PCPNet dataset [17] including eight models: four CAD objects and four high-quality scanning figurines, whereas the test set has 19 different models. More details of the used models are provided in the supplemental material. To be fair, we adopt the same training and evaluation setup as PCPNet. Our network is trained on 32,768 (1,024 samples by 32 shapes) random subsets of the 3.2 M training samples at each epoch. The training process is implemented with PyTorch on Nvidia Tesla V100 GPU, using the Adam optimizer [25] with the batch size and the learning rate equal to 256 and 1e−3, respectively. We run the training for 600 epochs totally. The polynomial order n for the surface fitting is 3.

Evaluation Criteria. To assess the performance of the proposed method, we compare it with two types of representative state-of-the-art approaches: 1) the geometric methods PCA [20] and n-jets [9]; 2) deep-learning-based methods including PCPNet [17], Nesti-Net [5], IterNet [26], DeepFit [3], and AdaFit [45].

Table 1. RMSE comparison for unoriented normal estimation to traditional (PCA [20] and Jet [9]) and learning-based methods on the PCPNet dataset.

Aug.	Ours	AdaFit	DeepFit	IterNet	Nesti-Net	PCPNet	Jet	PCA
w/o Noise	**4.45**	5.19	6.51	6.72	6.99	9.62	12.25	12.29
$\sigma = 0.125\%$	**8.74**	9.05	9.21	9.95	10.11	11.37	12.84	12.87
$\sigma = 0.6\%$	**16.05**	16.44	16.72	17.18	17.63	18.87	18.33	18.38
$\sigma = 1.2\%$	**21.64**	21.94	23.12	21.96	22.28	23.28	27.68	27.5
Gradient	**5.22**	5.90	7.31	7.73	9.00	11.70	13.13	12.81
Striped	**5.48**	6.01	7.92	7.51	8.47	11.16	13.39	13.66
Average	**10.26**	10.76	11.80	11.84	12.41	14.34	16.29	16.25

For Nesti-Net [5], the mixture of experts model is used to obtain normals. Suppose the estimated normal set of the point cloud $\mathcal{P}$ is $\mathcal{N}(\mathcal{P}) = \{\hat{\mathbf{n}}_i \in \mathbb{R}^3\}_{i=1}^{N_\mathcal{P}}$, then we use the *root-mean-squared error* (RMSE) of angles between the predicted and the ground truth normals $\hat{\mathbf{n}}_i$ and $\mathbf{n}_i$ to evaluate the performance:

$$\mathrm{RMSE}(\mathcal{N}(\mathcal{P})) = \sqrt{\frac{1}{N_\mathcal{P}} \sum_{i=1}^{N_\mathcal{P}} \arccos^2\left(\hat{\mathbf{n}}_i, \mathbf{n}_i\right)}, \tag{14}$$

where $(\cdot, \cdot)$ is the inner product of two vectors. Additionally, we use the metric of the percentage of good points $\mathrm{PGP}(\alpha)$ with an angle tolerance equal to α to report more detailed evaluation:

$$\mathrm{PGP}(\alpha) = \frac{1}{N_\mathcal{P}} \sum_{i=1}^{N_\mathcal{P}} \mathcal{I}\left(\arccos\left(\hat{\mathbf{n}}_i, \mathbf{n}_i\right) < \alpha\right), \tag{15}$$

where $\mathcal{I}$ is an *indicator function*.

Synthetic Test. We conduct a series of quantitative experiments to compare the performance of all methods on the PCPNet dataset [17], in which the point clouds are contaminated by different noise levels with varying standard deviation σ. Besides, we perform experiments on two different types of point density to simulate the effects of distance from the sensor (Gradient) and the local occlusions (Striped). The results are reported in Table 1. As observed, the proposed method attains the highest accuracy under different noise levels and varying point density, demonstrating the effectiveness of our proposed graph-structure-based normal estimation. AdaFit shows satisfactory results but it is relatively sensitive to density variations. Compared with learning-based approaches, traditional methods including Jet and PCA show more deviations.

We further evaluate the normal estimation performance on the PCPNet using the percentage of good points ($PGP\alpha$) metric. The results are reported in Fig. 5. It can be noted that the proposed method has the overall best performance under different test settings, meaning that it achieves more accurate normal

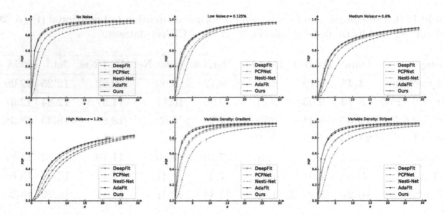

Fig. 5. Comparison of the proposed method with state-of-the-art learning-based approaches regarding the percentage of good points ($PGP\alpha$).

Table 2. Statistics of the angle RMSE on the real-world SceneNN dataset [22].

Method	Ours	AdaFit	DeepFit	PCPNet
Average	**21.33**	22.61	24.59	27.27

estimation. The normal prediction results of our method is visualized in the left panel of Fig. 6. The right panel of Fig. 6 exhibits the angular error in each test point cloud for all methods, where it can be seen that our proposed method obtains lower RMSE. Besides, it is quite robust against challenging regions, such as sharp edges and corners.

Real-World Test. We also assess the effectiveness of our method on real-world datasets to demonstrate its generalization and stability. We adopt the NYU Depth V2 dataset [38] for test. It contains 1,449 aligned and preprocessed RGBD frames, which are transformed to point clouds before applying our method. Note that all compared methods are only trained once on the PCPNet dataset. Compared with synthetic data, normal estimation of real-world scanning data are more challenging due to the occlusion and varying noise patterns. In particular, the noise often has the same magnitude as some of the features. Like most real datasets, there is no ground truth for each point.

As shown in Fig. 7, our proposed method is comparable to AdaFit on preserving fine details, meanwhile its performance is better than other compared approaches that typically result in over-smoothing results. However, to a certain extent, this also leads to the sharp extraction of scanning artifacts, as seen on the walls of the scanned room and the refrigerator surface in Fig. 7.

We further validate the proposed model on the SceneNN dataset [22], which contains 76 scenes re-annotated with 40 NYU-D v2 classes collected by a *depth*

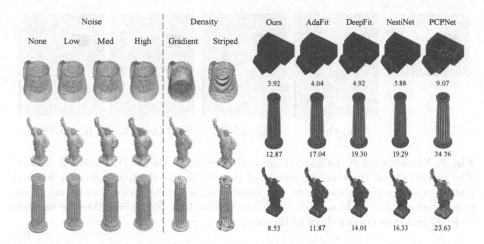

Fig. 6. Left: Normal estimation under four different noise levels (Columns one–four), and varying point density (Columns five–six). We map the normals to RGB for easy visualization. Right: Illustration of the normal estimation errors for three different point clouds. The errors are mapped to a heatmap ranging from 0° to 60°. Quantities under the point clouds are the corresponding RMSE.

Table 3. Complexity comparison of learning-based normal estimators.

Aug.	Params (M)	Model size (MB)	Avg. error
PCPNet	21.30	85.41	14.56
Nesti-Net	170.10	2,010.00	12.41
DeepFit	**3.36**	**13.53**	11.80
AdaFit	4.36	18.74	10.76
Ours	4.06	16.38	**10.26**

camera with ground-truth reconstructed meshes. We obtain the sampled point clouds and compute ground-truth normals from the meshes. The statistical angle RMSE of all methods are reported in Table 2. Thanks to the integration of more local neighbor features, our method significantly outperforms all competitors and achieves the state-of-the-art performance. We visualize the normal error of a random scene in Fig. 8.

Computational Complexity. We further compare the complexity of our model with state-of-the-art approaches, where the number of parameters of each method, their model size, and the average RMSE are reported. Table 3 indicates that DeepFit has the smallest computational complexity, but its RMSE is relatively large. Instead, the proposed method has the lowest average error along with comparable complexity of DeepFit, thereby it achieves a good balance between accuracy and complexity.

(a) Ours   (b) AdaFit   (c) DeepFit   (d) PCPNet

Fig. 7. Visualization of the normal estimation result on the NYU Depth V2 dataset. The second row is the zoom-in images of the red box in the first row. Our method embraces better generalization to this dataset while retains more details and sharp edges than others, yet the scanning artifacts are also kept and visible. We map normals to RGB and then project them to the image.

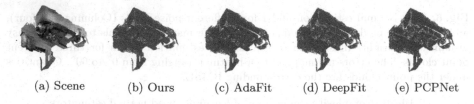

(a) Scene   (b) Ours   (c) AdaFit   (d) DeepFit   (e) PCPNet

Fig. 8. Normal estimation for a real-world scene. The errors are mapped to a heatmap ranging from $0°$ to $60°$. For (b)–(e), the normal errors are **26.03**, 27.08, 28.86 and 30.83, respectively.

Comparison with DGCNN. We compare our network with the baseline backbone DGCNN [39], which can be seen as a standard graph convolution version of our proposed method. To be fair, we train DGCNN on the PCPNet dataset to predict point-wise weights and offsets. The neighborhood size and the jet order of the two methods are the same and equal to 256 and 3, respectively. The left panel of Table 4 summarizes the comparison results, where our method outperforms DGCNN in various settings, such as different noise levels and varying point density, demonstrating the overall advantages of our designed network.

Robustness Against the Jet Orders. We also investigate the influence of the Jet order for normal estimation in our method. To this end, we set $n = 1, 2, 3, 4$, and the neighborhood size is fixed as 256 points. Table 5 shows the RMSE on the PCPNet dataset. As observed, with Jet order increasing, our method gradually produces more accurate normal estimation. Even under lower Jet order, the estimated normals are still comparable to DeepFit [3] and AdaFit [45] as reported in Table 1, which shows our method is quite robust against Jet orders. Table 5 also records the ablation study results of our proposed multi-scale layer, from which we conclude that the multi-scale layer effectively fuses richer geometric features hence assures more accurate normal estimation.

Table 4. Left: RMSE comparison of the proposed method with DGCNN [39] on the PCPNet dataset. Right: Effect of the adaptive module.

Aug.	Ours	DGCNN
w/o Noise	**4.49**	5.47
$\sigma = 0.125\%$	**8.80**	8.90
$\sigma = 0.6\%$	**16.54**	16.57
$\sigma = 1.2\%$	**22.69**	22.85
Gradient	**5.15**	6.19
Striped	**5.28**	6.52
Average	**10.49**	11.08

Aug.	Graph-block	
with adaptive module		✓
w/o Noise	4.87	**4.56**
$\sigma = 0.125\%$	8.94	**8.87**
$\sigma = 0.6\%$	16.58	**16.57**
$\sigma = 1.2\%$	22.83	**22.77**
Gradient	5.60	**5.33**
Striped	5.77	**5.38**
Average	10.74	**10.58**

Table 5. RMSE comparison with different Jet order n on the PCPNet dataset.

Aug.	$n = 1$		$n = 2$		$n = 3$		$n = 4$	
Graph-block	✓	✓	✓	✓	✓	✓	✓	✓
Multi-scale		✓		✓		✓		✓
w/o Noise	5.02	4.60	5.26	4.40	4.56	4.49	4.80	4.34
$\sigma = 0.125\%$	9.15	8.97	9.08	8.76	8.87	8.80	9.00	8.85
$\sigma = 0.6\%$	16.65	16.59	16.60	16.54	16.57	16.54	16.61	16.48
$\sigma = 1.2\%$	22.75	22.74	22.88	22.73	22.77	22.69	22.87	22.69
Gradient	5.85	5.36	5.74	5.23	5.33	5.15	5.60	5.06
Striped	5.93	5.49	5.95	5.36	5.38	5.28	5.59	5.22
Average	10.91	**10.63**	10.92	**10.50**	10.58	**10.49**	10.75	**10.44**

Table 6. Investigation on the neighbor size k on normal estimation.

Aug.	$k = 256$		$k = 500$		$k = 700$	
Graph-block	✓	✓	✓	✓	✓	✓
Multi-scale		✓		✓		✓
w/o Noise	4.56	4.49	4.80	4.45	4.78	4.83
$\sigma = 0.125\%$	8.87	8.80	8.90	8.74	8.77	8.70
$\sigma = 0.6\%$	16.57	16.54	16.16	16.05	15.99	16.04
$\sigma = 1.2\%$	22.77	22.69	21.80	21.64	21.45	21.36
Gradient	5.33	5.15	5.45	5.22	5.50	5.51
Striped	5.38	5.28	5.90	5.48	5.78	5.61
Average	10.58	**10.49**	10.50	**10.26**	10.38	**10.34**

Robustness Against the Neighborhood Size. We also conduct experiments on the PCPNet dataset to test the robustness of the proposed method against the neighborhood size $k = 256, 500, 700$. The default Jet order $n = 3$ is used. From Table 6, we see that the average RMSE is relatively stable and changes around

10.50. There is no significant fluctuation even under different noise levels and varying point density. Hence we can use $k = 256$ for general normal estimation tasks. Note that AdaFit [45] uses a fixed large patch size ($k = 700$) for training, which usually consumes more time and computing resource. The ablation study of the multi-scale layer in Table 6 again evidences its advantages.

Effect of the Proposed Adaptive Module. The designed adaptive module on the basis of attention mechanism can effectively improve the normal estimation precision. We implement ablation study to verify this and the results are reported in the right panel of Table 4, in which the neighborhood size is set as 256 and the jet order is equal to 3. It can be seen that by adding an adaptive module, the network returns more accurate normals, particularly, it effectively reduces the influence of the uneven point density, which can be concluded from the cases of Gradient and Striped.

5   Conclusion

We presented an accurate and robust pipeline for normal estimation of unstructured 3D point clouds, which achieves state-of-the-art performance compared with competing approaches. Our contribution is highlighting the local neighborhood relationships for normal estimation which are usually neglected by previous methods, meanwhile, we invoke graph convolutional learning to efficiently encode such situation. Moreover, based on the attention mechanism, we introduce an adaptive module on top of the graph block, to effectively combine the point features with their local neighbor features. As demonstrated, this operation significantly improves the network's robustness against point density variations. Together, we leverage the multi-scale layer to extract richer geometric features and consequently enhance the normal estimation precision.

Extensive experiments are conducted on a wide variety of datasets from synthetic to real-world data. Results demonstrate that our method achieves the state-of-the-art performance in accuracy and robustness on the benchmark PCP-Net dataset, and shows quite stable generalization ability on the real-world NYU Depth V2 scenes, which suggests its potential as a fast normal estimation technique. In the future, we will customize the proposed method for CAD models, especially for surface reconstruction and denosing from scanned point clouds.

Acknowledgement. This work was supported in part by National Natural Science Foundation of China under Grants 62172415, 61872365, U1909204, U19B2029; Chinese Guangdong's S&T project under Grant 2019B1515120030, 2021B1515140034; Ministry of Industry and Information Technology Project (TC200802B). CAS Key Technology Talent Program (Zhen Shen), the Tencent AI Laboratory Rhino-Bird Focused Research Program under Grant JR202127 (Dong-Ming Yan), and the Alibaba Group through Alibaba Innovative Research Program.

References

1. Alliez, P., Cohen-Steiner, D., Tong, Y., Desbrun, M.: Voronoi-based variational reconstruction of unoriented point sets. In: Proceedings of the 5th Eurographics Symposium on Geometry Processing, pp. 39–48 (2007)
2. Amenta, N., Bern, M.: Surface reconstruction by voronoi filtering. Discrete Comput. Geom. **22**(4), 481–504 (1999)
3. Ben-Shabat, Y., Gould, S.: DeepFit: 3D surface fitting via neural network weighted least squares. In: Proceedings of the European Conference on Computer Vision, pp. 20–34 (2020)
4. Ben-Shabat, Y., Lindenbaum, M., Fischer, A.: 3DMFV: three-dimensional point cloud classification in real-time using convolutional neural networks. IEEE Robot. Autom. Lett. **3**(4), 3145–3152 (2018)
5. Ben-Shabat, Y., Lindenbaum, M., Fischer, A.: Nesti-Net: Normal estimation for unstructured 3D point clouds using convolutional neural networks. In: Proceedings of the IEEE/CVF Conference on Computer Vision and Pattern Recognition, pp. 10112–10120 (2019)
6. Boulch, A., Marlet, R.: Fast and robust normal estimation for point clouds with sharp features. Comput. Graph. Forum. **31**(5), 1765–1774 (2012)
7. Boulch, A., Marlet, R.: Deep learning for robust normal estimation in unstructured point clouds. Comput. Graph. Forum **35**(5), 281–290 (2016)
8. Castillo, E., Liang, J., Zhao, H.: Point cloud segmentation and denoising via constrained nonlinear least squares normal estimates, pp. 283–299 (2013)
9. Cazals, F., Pouget, M.: Estimating differential quantities using polynomial fitting of osculating jets. Comput. Aided Geom. Des. **22**(2), 121–146 (2005)
10. Che, E., Olsen, M.J.: Multi-scan segmentation of terrestrial laser scanning data based on normal variation analysis. ISPRS J. Photogramm. Remote. Sens. **143**, 233–248 (2018)
11. Comino, M., Andujar, C., Chica, A., Brunet, P.: Sensor-aware normal estimation for point clouds from 3D range scans. Comput. Graph. Forum **37**(5), 233–243 (2018)
12. Dey, T.K., Goswami, S.: Provable surface reconstruction from noisy samples. Comput. Geom. **35**(1–2), 124–141 (2006)
13. Fan, S., Dong, Q., Zhu, F., Lv, Y., Ye, P., Wang, F.Y.: SCF-Net: learning spatial contextual features for large-scale point cloud segmentation. In: Proceedings of the IEEE/CVF Conference on Computer Vision and Pattern Recognition, pp. 14504–14513 (2021)
14. Fleishman, S., Cohen-Or, D., Silva, C.T.: Robust moving least-squares fitting with sharp features. ACM Trans. Graph. **24**(3), 544–552 (2005)
15. Giraudot, S., Cohen-Steiner, D., Alliez, P.: Noise-adaptive shape reconstruction from raw point sets. Comput. Graph. Forum **32**(5), 229–238 (2013)
16. Guennebaud, G., Gross, M.: Algebraic point set surfaces. ACM Trans. Graph. **26**, 23-es (2007)
17. Guerrero, P., Kleiman, Y., Ovsjanikov, M., Mitra, N.J.: Pcpnet learning local shape properties from raw point clouds. Comput. Graph. Forum. **37**(2), 75–85 (2018)
18. Hashimoto, T., Saito, M.: Normal estimation for accurate 3D mesh reconstruction with point cloud model incorporating spatial structure. In: Proceedings of the IEEE/CVF Conference on Computer Vision and Pattern Recognition Workshops, pp. 54–63 (2019)

19. Hermosilla, P., Ritschel, T., Ropinski, T.: Total denoising: Unsupervised learning of 3D point cloud cleaning. In: Proceedings of the IEEE/CVF International Conference on Computer Vision, pp. 52–60 (2019)
20. Hoppe, H., DeRose, T., Duchamp, T., McDonald, J., Stuetzle, W.: Surface reconstruction from unorganized points. In: Proceedings of the 19th Annual Conference on Computer Graphics and Interactive Techniques, pp. 71–78 (1992)
21. Hu, J., Shen, L., Sun, G.: Squeeze-and-Excitation networks. In: Proceedings of the IEEE/CVF Conference on Computer Vision and Pattern Recognition, pp. 7132–7141 (2018)
22. Hua, B.S., Tran, M.K., Yeung, S.K.: Pointwise convolutional neural networks. In: Proceedings of the IEEE/CVF conference on Computer Vision and Pattern Recognition, pp. 984–993 (2018)
23. Kazhdan, M., Bolitho, M., Hoppe, H.: Poisson surface reconstruction. In: Proceedings of the 4th Eurographics Symposium on Geometry Processing, vol. 7 (2006)
24. Khaloo, A., Lattanzi, D.: Robust normal estimation and region growing segmentation of infrastructure 3D point cloud models. Adv. Eng. Inform. **34**, 1–16 (2017)
25. Kingma, D.P., Ba, J.: Adam: a method for stochastic optimization. In: Proceedings of the International Conference on Learning Representations (2015)
26. Lenssen, J.E., Osendorfer, C., Masci, J.: Deep iterative surface normal estimation. In: Proceedings of the IEEE/CVF Conference on Computer Vision and Pattern Recognition, pp. 11247–11256 (2020)
27. Levin, D.: The approximation power of moving least-squares. Math. Comput. **67**(224), 1517–1531 (1998)
28. Lu, D., Lu, X., Sun, Y., Wang, J.: Deep feature-preserving normal estimation for point cloud filtering. Comput. Aided Des. **125**, 102860 (2020)
29. Lu, X., Schaefer, S., Luo, J., Ma, L., He, Y.: Low rank matrix approximation for 3D geometry filtering. IEEE Trans. Visual Comput. Graphics **28**(04), 1835–1847 (2022)
30. Mérigot, Q., Ovsjanikov, M., Guibas, L.J.: Voronoi-based curvature and feature estimation from point clouds. IEEE Trans. Visual Comput. Graphics **17**(6), 743–756 (2010)
31. Mitra, N.J., Nguyen, A.: Estimating surface normals in noisy point cloud data. In: Proceedings of the 19th Annual Symposium on Computational Geometry, pp. 322–328 (2003)
32. Nurunnabi, A., Belton, D., West, G.: Robust statistical approaches for local planar surface fitting in 3D laser scanning data. ISPRS J. Photogramm. Remote. Sens. **96**, 106–122 (2014)
33. Nurunnabi, A., West, G., Belton, D.: Outlier detection and robust normal-curvature estimation in mobile laser scanning 3D point cloud data. Pattern Recogn. **48**(4), 1404–1419 (2015)
34. Pistilli, F., Fracastoro, G., Valsesia, D., Magli, E.: Learning graph-convolutional representations for point cloud denoising. In: Proceedings of the European Conference on Computer Vision, pp. 103–118 (2020)
35. Qi, C.R., Su, H., Mo, K., Guibas, L.J.: PointNet: Deep learning on point sets for 3D classification and segmentation. In: Proceedings of the IEEE/CVF Conference on Computer Vision and Pattern Recognition, pp. 652–660 (2017)
36. Qi, C.R., Yi, L., Su, H., Guibas, L.J.: PointNet++: deep hierarchical feature learning on point sets in a metric space, pp. 5100–5109 (2017)
37. Rakotosaona, M.J., La Barbera, V., Guerrero, P., Mitra, N.J., Ovsjanikov, M.: PointCleanNet: learning to denoise and remove outliers from dense point clouds. Comput. Graph. Forum. **39**(1), 185–203 (2020)

38. Silberman, N., Hoiem, D., Kohli, P., Fergus, R.: Indoor segmentation and support inference from rgbd images. In: Proceedings of the European Conference on Computer Vision, pp. 746–760 (2012)
39. Wang, Y., Sun, Y., Liu, Z., Sarma, S.E., Bronstein, M.M., Solomon, J.M.: Dynamic graph CNN for learning on point clouds. ACM Trans. Graph. **38**(5), 1–12 (2019)
40. Wang, Z., Prisacariu, V.A.: Neighbourhood-insensitive point cloud normal estimation network (2020)
41. Yu, L., Li, X., Fu, C.-W., Cohen-Or, D., Heng, P.-A.: EC-net: an edge-aware point set consolidation network. In: Ferrari, V., Hebert, M., Sminchisescu, C., Weiss, Y. (eds.) ECCV 2018. LNCS, vol. 11211, pp. 398–414. Springer, Cham (2018). https://doi.org/10.1007/978-3-030-01234-2_24
42. Zhang, D., Lu, X., Qin, H., He, Y.: PointFilter: point cloud filtering via encoder-decoder modeling. IEEE Trans. Visual Comput. Graphics **27**(3), 2015–2027 (2020)
43. Zhang, J., Cao, J.J., Zhu, H.R., Yan, D.M., Liu, X.P.: Geometry guided deep surface normal estimation. Comput. Aided Des. **142**, 103119 (2022)
44. Zhou, H., et al.: Geometry and learning co-supported normal estimation for unstructured point cloud. In: Proceedings of the IEEE/CVF Conference on Computer Vision and Pattern Recognition, pp. 13238–13247 (2020)
45. Zhu, R., Liu, Y., Dong, Z., Wang, Y., Jiang, T., Wang, W., Yang, B.: AdaFit: rethinking learning-based normal estimation on point clouds. In: Proceedings of the IEEE/CVF International Conference on Computer Vision, pp. 6118–6127 (2021)

IS-MVSNet: Importance Sampling-Based MVSNet

Likang Wang[1]([✉]) [ID], Yue Gong[2] [ID], Xinjun Ma[2] [ID], Qirui Wang[2] [ID],
Kaixuan Zhou[3,4] [ID], and Lei Chen[1] [ID]

[1] Department of Computer Science and Engineering, Hong Kong University
of Science and Technology, Clear Water Bay, Hong Kong
{lwangcg,leichen}@ust.hk
[2] Distributed and Parallel Software Lab, Huawei Technologies, Shenzhen, China
{gongyue1,maxinjun1,wangqirui1}@huawei.com
[3] Riemann Lab, Huawei Technologies, Shenzhen, China
[4] Fundamental Software Innovation Lab, Huawei Technologies, Shenzhen, China
zhoukaixuan2@huawei.com

Abstract. This paper presents a novel coarse-to-fine multi-view stereo (MVS) algorithm called importance-sampling-based MVSNet (IS-
MVSNet) to address a crucial problem of limited depth resolution
adopted by current learning-based MVS methods. We proposed an
importance-sampling module for sampling candidate depth, effectively
achieving higher depth resolution and yielding better point-cloud results
while introducing no additional cost. Furthermore, we proposed an unsupervised error distribution estimation method for adjusting the density variation of the importance-sampling module. Notably, the proposed sampling module does not require any additional training and
works reasonably well with the pre-trained weights of the baseline
model. Our proposed method leads to up to 20× promotion on the
most refined depth resolution, thus significantly benefiting most scenarios and excellently superior on fine details. As a result, IS-MVSNet
**outperforms all the published papers on TNT's intermedi-
ate benchmark** with an F-score of 62.82%. Code is available at
github.com/NoOneUST/IS-MVSNet.

Keywords: 3D reconstruction · Multi-view stereo · Importance
sampling

1 Introduction

Multi-view stereo (MVS) is one of the most fundamental computer vision challenges. MVS aims to reconstruct the 3D structure of scenes from multiple 2D
image slots taken at different angles and positions. Most existing MVS algorithms formulate the reconstruction task as a problem of maximizing the geometric consistency among views. Inspired by the great successes of deep learning in visual perception [7,11,17], MVSNet [26] introduced convolutional neural
networks (CNNs) for better reconstruction quality. While these learning-based
methods are proven effective, they encountered difficulties handling large-scale

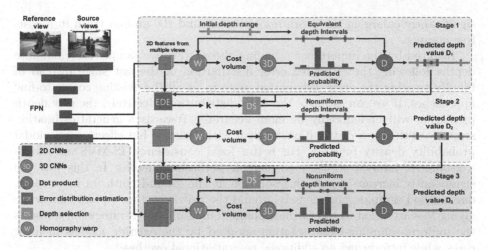

Fig. 1. Model structure of IS-MVSNet. At stage $s = 1$, we uniformly sample depth candidates. At each stage $s > 1$, we first estimate the former error distribution on the whole dataset, then we sample depth candidates according to the former prediction and error distribution. Next, we establish a cost volume at the sampled depths. Afterward, we adopt a 3D CNN to estimate the probability of each sampled depth to be true. The depth prediction (purple point) is calculated as the dot product of the sampled depths and the corresponding probability estimations. (Color figure online)

scenes due to the heavy computational overhead. For example, the maximum resolution of MVSNet is limited to $1152 \times 864 \times 192$ (width, height, depth) given a GPU with 11GB graphics memory [3]. Follow-up works [6,28] partially eased the resolution constraints via predicting the depth maps in a coarse-to-fine manner. Specifically, these papers start from a low-resolution depth prediction, then gradually enlarge the resolution while shrinking the depth range and reducing the candidate depth number. In the end, we can obtain a depth prediction with a higher resolution. The basic assumption behind these coarse-to-fine algorithms is that the coarse prediction is a reliable ground truth estimation.

Even with the coarse-to-fine strategy, the depth resolution is still a crucial factor preventing us from high accuracy and efficiency at the same time [4]. We argue that the existing coarse-to-fine algorithms [6,25,28] did not fully use the reliable former prediction assumption because these methods equally treat each candidate within the depth range. In this paper, instead, we put more effort into the most promising candidates. Then, the new problem is to distinguish which depths are the most trustworthy. Although the coarse prediction is assumed to be close to the actual depth, it is not 100% accurate. Thus, towards a more precise localization of the ground truth, it becomes crucial to estimate the error distribution of the coarse prediction.

Based on such considerations, we propose a novel MVS algorithm named importance-sampling-based MVSNet (IS-MVSNet), introducing an effective candidate depth sampling strategy to conduct a more precise depth prediction via significantly enlarging the depth resolution around the ground truth in a cost-free manner.

Inspired by the importance sampling theory [12], we sample the candidate depths following the estimated error distribution of the last stage instead of blindly treating the error distribution uniform as all the existing coarse-to-fine approaches. If we can estimate the error distribution effectively, the new depth prediction will undoubtedly be more accurate. Towards a general estimation strategy of the error distribution, we fit it with a simple but effective uni-modal probability density function. For better local consistency, IS-MVSNet adopts a geometric interval sequence to place hypothesized depths. In this way, we significantly increase the depth resolution at the ground truth. In most cases, our method samples more densely around the previous stage's prediction while giving less attention to the furthest points. Our sampling strategy outperforms the uniform-sampling-based solution adopted by the existing models in most cases while introducing no additional computational overhead.

Besides the importance-sampling-based strategy, we propose an unsupervised algorithm to estimate the error distribution based on photometric consistency. In this way, our model becomes adaptive to new datasets. With these properties, IS-MVSNet generalizes very well on various unseen scenarios.

Finally, our extensive experiments on the most popular MVS datasets, including Tanks & Temples [10] (TNT), ETH3D [19], and DTU [1], demonstrate IS-MVSNet's superiority over current SOTAs. With an F-score of 62.82%, IS-MVSNet surpasses all the published MVS algorithms on TNT's intermediate benchmark by a clear margin.

2   Related Work

Multi-view stereo has been studied for decades as a fundamental computer vision task. Before the prosperity of deep learning, there had been various hand-crafted methods [5,18,21]. Despite the traditional solutions' success, learning-based algorithms provide better semantic insights and are more robust in illumination and parallax.

As the first learning-based MVS algorithm, SurfaceNet [8] suffers significant GPU memory overhead and applicable restricted scenarios due to the divide-and-conquer framework and the adopted 3D CNNs. Most modern models inherit the main framework proposed by MVSNet [26] to ease the constraints above. MVSNet separates the depth map prediction from the point cloud fusion and establishes a differentiable end-to-end depth prediction network containing four sequential sub-steps: representation learning for input views, geometric-consistency-based scoring at hypothesized depths, scoring refinement, and depth regression. Although MVSNet demonstrates a practical and universal pipeline, its performance is intensively restricted by the image resolution and depth sampling. Specifically, MVSNet can only achieve an F-score of 43.48% on a GPU with 11GB of graphics memory.

For the sake of high-quality, large-scale 3D reconstruction, the follow-up papers generally ease MVSNet's resolution barrier in two ways: RNN-based [24,24] and CNN-based [4,6,25]. The RNN-based methods utilize GRU or LSTM instead of CNN to regularize the cost volume. While the RNN-based models trade temporal overheads for spatial advantages, the CNN-based models generally inherit the coarse-to-fine framework proposed in [16].

CasMVSNet [6] first sparsely samples hypothesized depths from a wide range and generates a rough depth estimation, then repeatedly shrinks the depth range and refines the depth prediction. CVP-MVSNet [25] tunes the depth range based on the image resolution. UCSNet [4] decides the depth range according to the former stage's confidence. However, its depth resolution may be lower than other fixed-depth-range methods because of its unstable depth range determining strategy [14].

In this paper, we inherit both the learning-based framework and the hierarchical pipeline. However, we promote the depth resolution around the ground truth via non-uniformly sampling of the candidate depths. Specifically, inspired by the importance sampling theory, we first unsupervisedly estimate the previous stage's error distribution, then based on which, we sample the current stage's candidate depths. Compared to CasMVSNet, we retain both the depth range and the depth number while sampling at different locations. Compared to CVP-MVSNet and UCSNet, we aim to find better candidates within an arbitrary depth range while not caring about the depth range or the depth number itself. There are also non-MVS methods considering candidate selection. For example, AdaBins [2] assumes the model can learn how to tune the bin density with an additional sub-network. UASNet [14] and NeRF [15] first infer an initial prediction, then sample based on it. We argue these methods generalize worse on unseen datasets because a) UASNet, UCSNet, and NeRF estimate distributions for every pixel individually, which is difficult. We estimate the distribution of the whole dataset, which is statistically more stable and accurate; b) we can unsupervisedly adjust the sampling strategy on unseen datasets, but UASNet and UCSNet cannot, thus are easy to overfit.

3 Methodology

In this section, we first present the main structure of IS-MVSNet and then provide a comprehensive introduction to the model's details. Following Cas-MVSNet [6] and VisMVSNet [28], IS-MVSNet inherits a coarse-to-fine network structure. The overall framework of our model is shown in Fig. 1. Firstly, IS-MVSNet adopts a feature pyramid network [13] (FPN) to extract the hierarchical representations for both the reference and source images. The FPN allows IS-MVSNet to capture both the global contexts and the local pixel-wise details. Then, a group of hypothesized depths is sampled for further evaluation.

For the coarsest stage $s = 1$, we uniformly sample hypothesized depths within the pre-defined depth range. For stages $s > 1$, we propose an importance-sampling-based hypothesized depth selection strategy, which is formally described in Sect. 3.1. This strategy provides IS-MVSNet with much higher sampling effectiveness without sacrificing efficiency. In Sect. 3.2, we propose an unsupervised method to estimate appropriate hyper-parameters for importance sampling.

After this, we project the source feature maps to the reference view at the chosen hypothesized depths and calculate the inter-view matching cost at each hypothesized depth to form a cost volume. Next, we adopt a 3D CNN to regularize the cost volume and predict the probability of each hypothesized depth as the ground truth. Finally, the current stage's depth prediction is calculated as the inner product of the depth samples and the corresponding probability predictions.

3.1   Importance-Sampling Based Hypothesized Depth Selection

As a coarse-to-fine algorithm, IS-MVSNet gradually refines the depth prediction. Given stage $s > 1$, although the former prediction D_p^{s-1} is generally close to the actual depth d_{gt}, there is still a gap between them. Suppose we can estimate each pixel's depth prediction error and further sample hypothesized depth around the ground truth with greater resolution. In that case, the model's capability of capturing fine details can be immensely enhanced.

Although it is difficult and impractical to estimate the error for each pixel, we propose to estimate the error distribution for the whole dataset and adjust the hypothesized depth sampling accordingly. While all the existing MVS algorithms did not consider the error estimation and blindly treated the prediction error as a uniform random variable. In IS-MVSNet, we propose a method to find out n_s promising candidate depth values $\{d_i^s\}_{i=1}^{n_s}$ for each pixel at stage $s > 1$, based on both the former stage's depth prediction D_p^{s-1} and the probability density function (PDF) $f_e^{s-1}(\delta)$ of the depth prediction error $\delta \sim \Delta_p^{s-1} = d_{gt} - D_p^{s-1}$, where d_{gt} denotes the pixel's real depth, estimated on all the pixels within the dataset. Then, we sample at $\{d_i^s\}_{i=1}^{n_s}$ to generate a more precise depth prediction $D_p^s = \sum_{i=1}^{n_s} d_i^s \cdot p(d_i^s)$, where $p(d_i^s)$ denotes the probability that the candidate depth $d_i^s \in \{d_j^s\}_{j=1}^{n_s}$ is the nearest neighbor of d_{gt}.

In this way, we can locate the most promising candidate depths more precisely and then allocate more attention to them. The result is that depth precision gets promoted due to the finest depth resolution increment around the ground truth.

Error Formulation. The first problem is how to formulate the error distribution. We argue it is reasonable to approximate the error PDF as a uni-modal function for three reasons. Firstly, since many factors influence the prediction error, the central limit theorem [9] suggests that the error tends to follow a zero-mean uni-modal distribution. Secondly, the coarse prediction is generated via uniform sampling, which leads to unbiased estimation [12]. Thirdly, our experiments on various real datasets verify that the error indeed follows a uni-modal distribution with a mean close to zero. Notably, we do not require the former stage to give a uni-modal probability prediction for a given pixel's hypothesized depths. Instead, we prefer the distance from the actual depth to the depth prediction calculated from all the hypothesized depths to follow a uni-modal distribution.

Suppose most pixels' depths are correctly estimated in the former stage, it is clear that our method outperforms uniform sampling. In Fig. 4d, our experiments on real datasets show that sampling following zero-mean Gaussian distribution indeed significantly surpasses uniform distribution. Moreover, even in extreme cases where most pixels' depths are wrongly estimated in the former stage, sampling following Gaussian distribution benefits the majority of pixels by providing a higher sampling density at these pixels' actual depths. Even if we do not estimate the mean and sample following a zero-mean Gaussian distribution, our method still benefits more pixels than uniform sampling. Our sampling method is better or comparable to uniform sampling even in the regions containing the most wrong former predictions, e.g., repetitive and textureless regions, small and thin objects distant from backgrounds.

Discrete Interval. Compared to sampling from a continuous PDF, discretized intervals have two advantages. First, given a limited depth number, e.g., 8, discretized intervals lead to a sampling density more stable and closer to the actual error distribution than i.i.d. sampling. Second, discretized intervals benefit the convolutions because the neighboring pixels have similar sampled depths, and the spatial correlation is crucial for convolution.

We further propose to sample the candidate depths following a pre-defined interval sequence unevenly based on such considerations. Precisely, the error PDF should control the depth interval: in positions with larger PDF, the interval should be smaller; otherwise, it should be larger. Let μ_e^{s-1} denote the mean error at stage $s-1$, then the depth interval close to $D_p^{s-1} + \mu_e^{s-1}$ should be smaller, otherwise larger. We adopt a simple and typical geometric sequence to fit the interval pattern to satisfy the requirement. Note that other sequences with similar trends are also acceptable as if they have similar properties with a Gaussian distribution $N(\mu_e^{s-1}, \sigma_e^{s-1})$, i.e., both have only one single mode at μ_e^{s-1} and the sequence has a parameter with similar effect as σ_e^{s-1} of $N(\mu_e^{s-1}, \sigma_e^{s-1})$. In addition, it is unnecessary to strictly force the interval sequence to converge to $N(\mu_e^{s-1}, \sigma_e^{s-1})$ when the number of intervals $\to \infty$. For example, the arithmetic sequence also works well. In this way, we sample the depths following the error distribution while preserving the local consistency. Our detailed importance sampling algorithm is described below.

Detailed Algorithm. We use discretized intervals to put depth hypotheses in the depth range rather than directly sampling depths from a continuous PDF. In the first stage, we divide the whole depth range R_1 into $n_1 - 1$ equivalent intervals of size R_1/n_1-1 because there is no prior unbiased depth estimation given at stage $s = 1$. In the following stages $s \in \{2, 3, \ldots\}$, we adopt a trivial geometric progression for generating the depth hypothesis with promoted sampling density in the central area. The discretized intervals are parameterized by k_s, a hyperparameter determining the shape of the intervals. As illustrated in Fig. 2, the minimum interval is reduced to $\frac{1}{k_s}$ and the change velocity of interval lengths is c_s, which is controlled by k_s. A larger k_s means to sample more densely near the rectified former prediction $D_p^{s-1} + \mu_e^{s-1}$. When $k_s > 1$, the central hypothesized

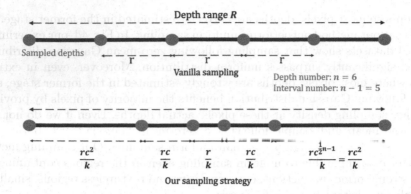

Fig. 2. The illustration of depth selection given a depth number of 6. In our sampling strategy, the depth range is retained the same. The minimum depth interval is reduced to $\frac{1}{k_s}$ and the interval lengths are increasing at the ratio of c_s, which is uniquely controlled by k_s following Eq. 1. A greater k_s leads to a smaller minimum interval, a greater c_s, and a higher changing velocity of the interval lengths.

depths have intervals reduced to $1/k_s$, while the fringing depths have intervals enlarged. In other words, the central interval r_s/k_s gets smaller than the uniform sampling interval r_s by a factor of $1/k_s$. When $k_s = 1$, our importance sampling down-grades to uniform sampling. When $0 < k_s < 1$, our method can deal with the case that most former predictions are wrong.

To be specific, the depth intervals form a symmetric geometric progressions $T = [\frac{1}{k_s}r_s c_s^{\frac{n_s}{2}-1}, \cdots, \frac{1}{k_s}r_s c_s^2, \frac{1}{k_s}r_s c_s, \frac{1}{k_s}r_s, \frac{1}{k_s}r_s c_s, \frac{1}{k_s}r_s c_s^2, \cdots, \frac{1}{k_s}r_s c_s^{\frac{n_s}{2}-1}]$, where $t_j = \frac{1}{k_s}r_s c_s^{|\frac{n_s}{2}-j|}$ is the jth interval, $r_s = \frac{R_s}{n_s-1}$ is the depth interval in uniform sampling, and c_s is the common ratio between adjacent intervals. Since we want to keep IS-MVSNet's depth range and the number of hypothesized depths the same as those of the baseline model, i.e., $\sum_{i=1}^{n_s-1} t_i = R_s$, c_s is uniquely controlled by k_s, r_s, and n_s according to Eq. (1). In practice, c_s is numerically calculated as the root of Eq. (1).

$$c_s^{\frac{n_s}{2}} - 1 = \frac{1}{2}(k_s n_s - k_s + 1)(c_s - 1) \tag{1}$$

The depth candidates are defined uniquely for each pixel. To be specific, first, each pixel has its own set of discrete depth candidates defined by the interval sequence; second, the intervals between depth candidates and the depth range R (i.e., the sum of intervals) are consistent among all the pixels in terms of sizes; third, the center position of the depth range R along the depth axis is set to each pixel's previous depth estimate D_p^{s-1}. As a result, each pixel has a unique set of depth candidates whose intervals are but the same among pixels; fourth, if the mean error μ_e^{s-1} is estimated, the position of the range is further "rectified" to $D_p^{s-1} + \mu_e^{s-1}$.

3.2 Unsupervised Error Distribution Estimation

In IS-MVSNet, we introduce two new hyper-parameters k_s and μ_s, to adjust the sampling function $g^s(x)$'s shape in stages $s > 1$. In practice, the depth estimation error concentratedly distributes around zero. Thus, in default, we treat the mean error $\mu_s = 0$ and only estimate k_s. However, the k_s estimation solution proposed in this section is also applicable to μ_s. If we want to estimate both k_s and μ_s, we first fix k_s and estimate μ_s, then fix μ_s and estimate k_s.

As analyzed in Sect. 3.1, the optimal k_s can be uniquely determined by minimizing the sampling function $g^s(x)$'s difference to the actual error distribution with the true depths known. However, we do not know the actual depth in real scenarios, and the scale, illumination, and camera intrinsics are distinct in different datasets. Thus, it is necessary to estimate a k_s for each dataset. We treat the matching costs as cues for the actual depths and demonstrate that estimating the error distribution is equivalent to minimizing the matching costs, which is always obtainable. This section proposes a general unsupervised hyper-parameter k_s selection strategy, making the importance-based sampling module hyper-parameter-free in all scenarios.

Recall that in MVS, the input 2D images and the camera parameters are always obtainable, and photometric consistency exists among different views.

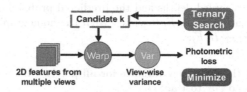

Fig. 3. The illustration of the error distribution estimation module. We evaluate k with the photometric loss and apply a ternary search to find the optimal k following Algorithm 1 and Algorithm 2.

Algorithm 1: Unsupervised k selection

Data: k_l: the minimum hypothesis k,
       k_r: the maximum hypothesis k
Result: k_e^*: the estimated optimal k
1 **while** *within the allowed iterations* **do**
2    $k_{mid} \leftarrow \frac{k_l+k_r}{2}$, $k_{midmid} \leftarrow \frac{k_{mid}+k_r}{2}$;
3   Measure the photometric cost $C_l, C_r, C_{mid}, C_{midmid}$ with Algorithm 2;
4   **if** $C_{mid} < C_{midmid}$ **then**
5 | $k_r \leftarrow k_{midmid}$;
6   **else**
7 | $k_l \leftarrow k_{mid}$;
8   **end**
9 **end**
10 $k_e^* \leftarrow \arg\min_k (C_l, C_r, C_{mid}, C_{midmid})$ % the minimum C must be in the four;

Given a 3D point P with the depth d_r and projection P_r in the reference view, then, P's projection in the vth source view P_v's coordinate can be computed as $P_v = H_v(d_r)P_r$, where $H_v(d_r) = K_v(R_v - \frac{1}{d_r}t_v a_r{}^T)K_v{}^{-1}$ is a homography matrix, a_r denotes the reference view's principal axis, and K_v, R_v, t_v denote the vth camera's intrinsics, relative rotations, and translations, separately.

Algorithm 2: Photometric cost calculation

Data: k: the sampling hyper-parameter,
   F_i: representation for the ith view,
   V: number of views,
   q: number of selected reference views,
   D_p^{s-1}: the former stage's depth prediction
Result: C_k: the photometric cost
1 **for** *each scene in the dataset* **do**
2   Randomly select q views as the reference views ;
3   **for** *each reference view i* **do**
4   **for** *each source view j* **do**
5   Sample hypothesized depths according to k and the former stage's depth prediction D_p^{s-1} following Sect. 3.1;
6   Infer each hypothesized depth's probability with the trained model;
7   Calculate the depth prediction D_p^s for each pixel as the dot product of the sampled depths and the predicted probabilities;
8   Map each pixel in F_j to view i with the homography matrix H_j at D_p^s: $F_j \leftarrow H_j F_j$;
9   **end**
10   Calculate the inter-view variance for all pixels: $var \leftarrow \frac{\sum F_j{}^2}{V} - \left(\frac{\sum F_j}{V}\right)^2$, then append var to $VarSet$
11   **end**
12 **end**
13 $C_k \leftarrow \overline{Varset}$

Suppose the depth estimation D_p^s is correct, then $P_v^s = H_v(D_p^s)P_r^s$ should represent the same 3D point as P_r^s, saying that P_r^s's feature $F_r^s = F_v^s$. Since multiple views are given, we use the variance $Var[F_v^s]$ to measure their similarity. Thus, the best depth estimation $D_p^* = \underset{d_e}{\arg\min} \, Var[F_v^s]$.

As mentioned in Sect. 3.1, k determines the estimated error distribution's PDF. Specifically, a larger k refers to an error distribution with a smaller variance. When $k = 1$, the importance sampling performs the same as the uniform sampling; only one candidate has the chance to be sampled when $k = \infty$. Clearly, $k = \{1, \infty\}$ both lead to a non-minimum difference between the estimation and the actual PDF. Thus, as shown in Fig. 4a, when k increases starting from 1, the model's performance first gets promoted, then gradually decreases. We use a uni-modal function to approximate the performance-k curve. Based on such consideration, we proposed a ternary-search-based unsupervised hyper-parameter k

selection algorithm as described in Algorithm 1, Algorithm 2 and Fig. 3. Since the ternary search reduces the search range by a constant ratio in each iteration, it converges very fast. Generally, 3 to 5 iterations are enough to find a satisfying k. Our experiments in Fig. 4c show that randomly picking two reference views from each scan is enough for k's determination.

4   Experiment

Our experiments adopt the most popular MVS datasets: Tanks & Temples (TNT), ETH3D, DTU, and BlendedMVS [27]. We summarize their properties in Table 1. We compare IS-MVSNet to the SOTA learning-based algorithms, e.g., VisMVSNet [28], CasMVSNet, CVP-MVSNet, UCS-MVSNet, Patch-matchNet [20], and traditional algorithms, e.g., COLMAP [18], ACMM [21], ACMP [22]. On Tanks & Temples and ETH3D datasets, the metric is F-score, while on the DTU dataset, the metric is the overall distance. Our model only requires the number of stages $S > 1$. In our experiments, we set $S = 3$ following most existing models [6,28] for two reasons. First, in this way, we can conduct more fair comparisons to the mainstream models. Second, $S = 3$ provides satisfying precision while maintaining high efficiency. Note that for a fair comparison, we use the same hypothesized depth number (even) as Vis-MVSNet. Thus, D_p^{s-1} is not sampled to make the sampling symmetric. It is reasonable to adopt any progression with increasing intervals. Here we choose the geometric progression T to approximate the error distribution instead of other sequences for the following two reasons. The first reason is that it is both trivial and easy to implement. The second reason is that compared with the arithmetic sequence, the interval in the geometric progression increases much faster and thus can mimic the Gaussian-like noise more accurately.

Table 1. Adopted datasets

Dataset	Indoor scenes	Outdoor scenes	High resolution
TNT [10]	✔	✔	✔
BlendedMVS [27]	✔	✔	✔
ETH3D [19]	✔	✔	✔
DTU [1]	✔	✘	✘

Training Setting. Following VisMVSNet, we train IS-MVSNet on two datasets: BlendedMVS and DTU. When the model is evaluated on the DTU's testing set, we train IS-MVSNet on DTU's training set; otherwise, we train it on the BlendedMVS's training set. While training, the image resolution is fixed at 640 × 512, the number of source views is three, and the total number of stages is three. We sample 32 hypothesized depths with equivalent intervals in the first stage. While in the second and third stages, the depth intervals are determined following our novel sampling strategy described in Sect. 3.1, and the numbers of hypothesized depths are 16 and 8, respectively. We use an Adam optimizer to train the model for ten epochs. The batch size is four, and the initial learning rate is 10^{-3}. The learning rate is decayed by a factor of 0.5 in epochs 6, 8, and 9, respectively.

Evaluation Setting. We evaluate IS-MVSNet on three datasets: Tanks & Temples, ETH3D, and DTU, without fine-tuning. When synthesizing the point clouds, we adopt the dynamic consistency checking approach [24].

Tanks and Temples Dataset. When predicting the depth maps, the number of source views is seven, the minimum consistency among views is four, the input image size is 1920×1056, and the estimated $k^* = 10$. Thus, the finest depth resolution is $10\times$ promoted. As shown in Table 2, IS-MVSNet surpasses all published methods on the intermediate benchmark. Note that IS-MVSNet is superior to the SOTA method Vis-MVSNet in nearly all scenes. At the same time, IS-MVSNet also achieves a higher F-score than nearly all published learning-based methods on the advanced dataset. Although ACMP [22] achieves a higher F-score on the advanced dataset, it does not hurt our importance sampling's superiority. This is because ACMP's advantage comes from its use of planar information, which does not conflict with our sampling strategy. Without the planar information, ACMP degrades to ACMM [21], which performs worse than our method on both datasets. The point cloud generated by our algorithm is of high reconstruction quality and precise details.

Table 2. F-score (higher is better) results on the Tanks & Temples [10].

Method	Intermediate set %									Advanced set %						
	Mean	Fam	Franc	Horse	Light	M60	Pan	Play	Train	Mean	Audi	Ballr	Courtr	Museum	Palace	Temple
COLMAP [18]	42.14	50.41	22.25	25.63	56.43	44.83	46.97	48.53	42.04	27.24	16.02	25.23	34.70	41.51	18.05	27.94
CVP-MVSNet [25]	54.03	76.50	47.74	36.34	55.12	57.28	54.28	57.43	47.54	-	-	-	-	-	-	-
CasMVSNet [6]	56.84	76.37	58.45	46.26	55.81	56.11	54.06	58.18	49.51	31.12	19.81	38.46	29.10	43.87	27.36	28.11
UCSNet [4]	54.83	76.09	53.16	43.03	54.00	55.60	51.49	57.38	47.89	-	-	-	-	-	-	-
Vis-MVSNet [28]	60.03	77.40	60.23	47.07	63.44	62.21	57.28	60.54	52.07	-	-	-	-	-	-	-
ACMM [21]	57.27	69.24	51.45	46.97	63.20	55.07	57.64	60.08	54.48	34.02	23.41	32.91	41.17	48.13	23.87	34.60
ACMP [22]	58.41	70.31	54.06	**54.11**	61.65	54.16	57.60	58.12	**57.25**	**37.44**	**30.12**	34.68	**44.58**	**50.64**	27.20	37.43
PatchmatchNet [20]	53.15	66.99	52.64	43.24	54.87	52.87	49.54	54.21	50.81	32.31	23.69	37.73	30.04	41.80	28.31	32.29
Ours	**62.82**	**79.92**	**62.05**	52.54	62.68	**63.65**	**62.57**	**62.94**	56.21	34.87	20.54	**39.88**	33.07	47.73	**30.12**	**37.91**

ETH3D Dataset. The number of source views is seven, the minimum consistency among views is four, the input image size is 3072×2048, and the estimated $k^* = 6$. Thus, the finest depth resolution is $6\times$ promoted. As shown in Table 3, IS-MVSNet offers significant advantages over the learning-based SOTAs PVSNet [23] and PatchmatchNet [20]. Although ACMP shows a higher F-score on the training set, our method performs better on the testing set, which is obviously more important than the training set.

Table 3. F-score ↑ on the ETH3D high-res set at evaluation threshold 2cm.

Method	Training set (%)	Testing set (%)
Gipuma [5]	36.48	45.18
COLMAP [18]	67.66	73.01
PVSNet [23]	67.48	72.08
PatchmatchNet [20]	64.21	73.12
ACMP [22]	**79.79**	81.51
Ours	73.33	**83.15**

Table 4. Overall distance (mm), accuracy distance (mm), and completeness distance (mm) on the DTU testing set. All three metrics are preferred to be smaller.

Method	Overall distance	Accuracy distance	Completeness distance
COLMAP [18]	0.532	0.400	0.664
MVSNet [26]	0.462	0.396	0.527
VisMVSNet [28]	0.365	0.369	0.361
UCSNet [4]	**0.344**	0.338	**0.349**
CasMVSNet [6]	0.355	**0.325**	0.385
Ours	0.355	0.351	0.359

DTU Dataset. The number of source views is four, the minimum consistency among views is five, the input image size is 1152×864, and the estimated $k^* = 20$. Thus, the finest depth resolution is 20× promoted. The 20× promotion is compared to the finest stage of Vis-MVSNet (a typical uniform-sampling-based method). For example, Vis-MVSNet's finest depth resolution on DTU is 2.65 mm, while our method is 0.13 mm. It is hard to quantitatively compare to UCSNet and UASNet because their resolutions rely on network predictions. Still, we generalize better and are more stable, as stated in Sect. 2.

Following Vis-MVSNet, we predict depth maps of half sizes, while other mentioned methods are in full sizes. Since objects in DTU are pretty small, the depth maps require higher plane resolution. In consequence, our improvements on TNT are more significant than on DTU. As shown in Table 4, our method outperforms Vis-MVSNet, where all the improvements come from our sampling strategy. Although UCSNet shows a better overall distance, its advantage relies on the depth range determination strategy, which does not conflict with our depth-range-agnostic sampling algorithm.

5 Ablation Study

5.1 Error Distribution

Without adopting the importance sampling strategy, we measure the coarse stage's error distributions on BlendedMVS and DTU and find out the distribution is indeed uni-modal. We calculate the per-pixel error as the predicted depth's difference to the ground truth: $\delta = d_{gt} - d_p$. Moreover, the error distribution concentrates around 0. Thus, it is reasonable to trust the last stage's prediction and sample more densely around it.

5.2 The Effectiveness of k

To analyze k's impact on the model's performance, we test IS-MVSNet with different k. The performance to k curve is shown in Fig. 4a and Fig. 4b. When $k = 1$, the importance sampling is equivalent to the uniform sampling. As k increases, the performance first gets better, then gradually decreases. It can be observed that an extensive range of k brings about significant improvement.

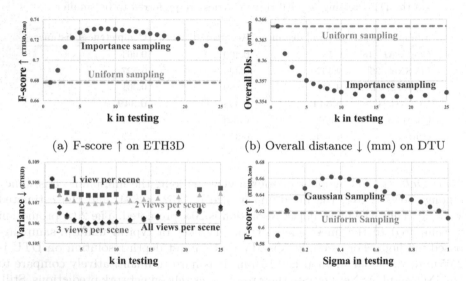

(a) F-score ↑ on ETH3D   (b) Overall distance ↓ (mm) on DTU

(c) Variance ↓ estimation with varying k (d) F-score ↑ with varying σ (Gaussian)

Fig. 4. Ablation studies. (a) and (b) demonstrate that importance sampling is superior to uniform sampling under a wide range of k. (c) reveals that two to three samples per scene are enough to estimate k accurately. (d) shows that importance sampling does not rely on the probability approximation function because continuous Gaussian sampling also outperforms uniform sampling.

Reliability of Coarse Prediction. On the ETH3D training set, the F-score at threshold 50 cm is as high as 0.96, 0.97, and 0.98 at stages $1 \rightarrow 3$, respectively; on DTU, the overall distance is as low as 0.73, 0.41, and 0.35 mm at stages $1 \rightarrow 3$, respectively. Regarding the 2 cm F-score measured on the ETH3D training set, uniform sampling achieves 0.14, 0.32, and 0.44 at stages $1 \rightarrow 3$, respectively, while our sampling strategy achieves 0.14, 0.41, and 0.58 at stages $1 \rightarrow 3$, respectively. These facts suggest that the coarse prediction on real datasets is reliable, and our method works well in reality.

5.3 The Necessity of Interval Sequence Sampling

Although i.i.d. sampling is straightforward, it suffers from the local consistency problem mentioned in Sect. 3.1. Empirically, converting the i.i.d uniform sampling to identical interval sampling leads to 6.4% F-score improvement on the ETH3D high-res training set. Moreover, as shown in Fig. 4d, i.i.d. sampling following Gaussian distribution with a proper variance σ significantly outperforms uniform distribution. These facts suggest that sampling following an increasing interval sequence is beneficial and necessary.

5.4 Unsupervised k Selection

To validate the effectiveness of our unsupervised k selection algorithm, we fix the weights and use different k to generate the point clouds. It can be observed in Fig. 4a and Fig. 4c that the variance curve matches very well with the F-score curve. The minimum variance on the whole ETH3D dataset occurs when $k = 6$, exactly where the highest F-score is achieved according to Fig. 4a. Moreover, in Fig. 4c, we show that randomly evaluating two reference images from each scene is enough for variance estimation. Thus, our hyper-parameter selection algorithm is lightweight.

6 Conclusion

This paper presents an effective importance-sampling-based multi-view stereo network and the corresponding hyper-parameter estimation algorithm. Both theoretical analysis and extensive experiments strongly prove our method's superiority. Although, like other coarse-to-fine models, our model is limited to corner cases, in which the coarse prediction is too far from the ground truth. Our depth sampling and hyper-parameter estimation techniques could benefit most coarse-to-fine solutions.

Acknowledgments. We gratefully acknowledge the support from MindSpore.

References

1. Aanæs, H., Jensen, R.R., Vogiatzis, G., Tola, E., Dahl, A.B.: Large-scale data for multiple-view stereopsis. Int. J. Comput. Vision **120**(2), 153–168 (2016)
2. Bhat, S.F., Alhashim, I., Wonka, P.: Adabins: depth estimation using adaptive bins. In: Proceedings of the IEEE/CVF Conference on Computer Vision and Pattern Recognition, pp. 4009–4018 (2021)
3. Chen, R., Han, S., Xu, J., Su, H.: Point-based multi-view stereo network. In: Proceedings of the IEEE/CVF International Conference on Computer Vision, pp. 1538–1547 (2019)
4. Cheng, S., et al.: Deep stereo using adaptive thin volume representation with uncertainty awareness. In: Proceedings of the IEEE/CVF Conference on Computer Vision and Pattern Recognition, pp. 2524–2534 (2020)

5. Galliani, S., Lasinger, K., Schindler, K.: Massively parallel multiview stereopsis by surface normal diffusion. In: Proceedings of the IEEE International Conference on Computer Vision, pp. 873–881 (2015)
6. Gu, X., Fan, Z., Zhu, S., Dai, Z., Tan, F., Tan, P.: Cascade cost volume for high-resolution multi-view stereo and stereo matching. In: Proceedings of the IEEE/CVF Conference on Computer Vision and Pattern Recognition, pp. 2495–2504 (2020)
7. He, K., Zhang, X., Ren, S., Sun, J.: Deep residual learning for image recognition. In: Proceedings of the IEEE Conference on Computer Vision and Pattern Recognition, pp. 770–778 (2016)
8. Ji, M., Gall, J., Zheng, H., Liu, Y., Fang, L.: Surfacenet: an end-to-end 3d neural network for multiview stereopsis. In: Proceedings of the IEEE International Conference on Computer Vision, pp. 2307–2315 (2017)
9. Kallenberg, O., Kallenberg, O.: Foundations of Modern Probability, vol. 2. Springer (1997)
10. Knapitsch, A., Park, J., Zhou, Q.Y., Koltun, V.: Tanks and temples: benchmarking large-scale scene reconstruction. ACM Trans. Graph. (ToG) **36**(4), 1–13 (2017)
11. Krizhevsky, A., Sutskever, I., Hinton, G.E.: Imagenet classification with deep convolutional neural networks. Adv. Neural. Inf. Process. Syst. **25**, 1097–1105 (2012)
12. Li, D.: Statistical Computing. Higher Education Press (2017)
13. Lin, T.Y., Dollár, P., Girshick, R., He, K., Hariharan, B., Belongie, S.: Feature pyramid networks for object detection. In: Proceedings of the IEEE Conference on Computer Vision and Pattern Recognition, pp. 2117–2125 (2017)
14. Mao, Y., et al.: Uasnet: uncertainty adaptive sampling network for deep stereo matching. In: Proceedings of the IEEE/CVF International Conference on Computer Vision, pp. 6311–6319 (2021)
15. Mildenhall, B., Srinivasan, P.P., Tancik, M., Barron, J.T., Ramamoorthi, R., Ng, R.: NeRF: representing scenes as neural radiance fields for view synthesis. In: Vedaldi, A., Bischof, H., Brox, T., Frahm, J.-M. (eds.) ECCV 2020. LNCS, vol. 12346, pp. 405–421. Springer, Cham (2020). https://doi.org/10.1007/978-3-030-58452-8_24
16. Okutomi, M., Kanade, T.: A multiple-baseline stereo. IEEE Trans. Pattern Anal. Mach. Intell. **15**(4), 353–363 (1993)
17. Ren, S., He, K., Girshick, R., Sun, J.: Faster R-CNN: towards real-time object detection with region proposal networks. IEEE Trans. Pattern Anal. Mach. Intell. **39**(6), 1137–1149 (2016)
18. Schönberger, J.L., Zheng, E., Frahm, J.-M., Pollefeys, M.: Pixelwise view selection for unstructured multi-view stereo. In: Leibe, B., Matas, J., Sebe, N., Welling, M. (eds.) ECCV 2016. LNCS, vol. 9907, pp. 501–518. Springer, Cham (2016). https://doi.org/10.1007/978-3-319-46487-9_31
19. Schöps, T., et al.: A multi-view stereo benchmark with high-resolution images and multi-camera videos. In: Conference on Computer Vision and Pattern Recognition (CVPR) (2017)
20. Wang, F., Galliani, S., Vogel, C., Speciale, P., Pollefeys, M.: Patchmatchnet: learned multi-view patchmatch stereo. In: IEEE Conference on Computer Vision and Pattern Recognition, CVPR 2021, virtual, June 19–25, 2021, pp. 14194–14203. Computer Vision Foundation/IEEE (2021)
21. Xu, Q., Tao, W.: Multi-scale geometric consistency guided multi-view stereo. In: Proceedings of the IEEE/CVF Conference on Computer Vision and Pattern Recognition, pp. 5483–5492 (2019)

22. Xu, Q., Tao, W.: Planar prior assisted patchmatch multi-view stereo. In: The Thirty-Fourth AAAI Conference on Artificial Intelligence, AAAI 2020, The Thirty-Second Innovative Applications of Artificial Intelligence Conference, IAAI 2020, The Tenth AAAI Symposium on Educational Advances in Artificial Intelligence, EAAI 2020, New York, NY, USA, 7–12 February, 2020, pp. 12516–12523. AAAI Press (2020)
23. Xu, Q., Tao, W.: Pvsnet: pixelwise visibility-aware multi-view stereo network. arXiv preprint arXiv:2007.07714 (2020)
24. Yan, J., et al.: Dense hybrid recurrent multi-view stereo net with dynamic consistency checking. In: Vedaldi, A., Bischof, H., Brox, T., Frahm, J.-M. (eds.) ECCV 2020. LNCS, vol. 12349, pp. 674–689. Springer, Cham (2020). https://doi.org/10.1007/978-3-030-58548-8_39
25. Yang, J., Mao, W., Alvarez, J.M., Liu, M.: Cost volume pyramid based depth inference for multi-view stereo. In: Proceedings of the IEEE/CVF Conference on Computer Vision and Pattern Recognition, pp. 4877–4886 (2020)
26. Yao, Y., Luo, Z., Li, S., Fang, T., Quan, L.: MVSNet: depth inference for unstructured multi-view stereo. In: Ferrari, V., Hebert, M., Sminchisescu, C., Weiss, Y. (eds.) ECCV 2018. LNCS, vol. 11212, pp. 785–801. Springer, Cham (2018). https://doi.org/10.1007/978-3-030-01237-3_47
27. Yao, Y., et al.: Blendedmvs: a large-scale dataset for generalized multi-view stereo networks. In: Proceedings of the IEEE/CVF Conference on Computer Vision and Pattern Recognition, pp. 1790–1799 (2020)
28. Zhang, J., Yao, Y., Li, S., Luo, Z., Fang, T.: Visibility-aware multi-view stereo network. In: 31st British Machine Vision Conference 2020, BMVC 2020, Virtual Event, UK, 7–10 September, 2020. BMVA Press (2020)

Point Scene Understanding via Disentangled Instance Mesh Reconstruction

Jiaxiang Tang[1]([✉]), Xiaokang Chen[1], Jingbo Wang[2], and Gang Zeng[1]

[1] Key Laboratory of Perception (MoE), School of AI,
Peking University, Beijing, China
{tjx,pkucxk,zeng}@pku.edu.cn
[2] Chinese University of Hong Kong, Hong Kong, China
wj020@ie.cuhk.edu.hk

Abstract. Semantic scene reconstruction from point cloud is an essential and challenging task for 3D scene understanding. This task requires not only to recognize each instance in the scene, but also to recover their geometries based on the partial observed point cloud. Existing methods usually attempt to directly predict occupancy values of the complete object based on incomplete point cloud proposals from a detection-based backbone. However, this framework always fails to reconstruct high fidelity mesh due to the obstruction of various detected false positive object proposals and the ambiguity of incomplete point observations for learning occupancy values of complete objects. To circumvent the hurdle, we propose a Disentangled Instance Mesh Reconstruction (DIMR) framework for effective point scene understanding. A segmentation-based backbone is applied to reduce false positive object proposals, which further benefits our exploration on the relationship between recognition and reconstruction. Based on the accurate proposals, we leverage a mesh-aware latent code space to disentangle the processes of shape completion and mesh generation, relieving the ambiguity caused by the incomplete point observations. Furthermore, with access to the CAD model pool at test time, our model can also be used to improve the reconstruction quality by performing mesh retrieval without extra training. We thoroughly evaluate the reconstructed mesh quality with multiple metrics, and demonstrate the superiority of our method on the challenging Scan-Net dataset. Code is available at https://github.com/ashawkey/dimr.

Keywords: Point scene understanding · Mesh generation and retrieval · Point instance completion

1 Introduction

Semantic scene reconstruction can facilitate numerous real-world applications, such as robot navigation, AR/VR and interior design. This task aims to understand the semantic information of each object and recover their geometries from

---

Supplementary Information The online version contains supplementary material available at https://doi.org/10.1007/978-3-031-19824-3_40.

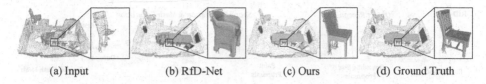

| (a) Input | (b) RfD-Net | (c) Ours | (d) Ground Truth |

Fig. 1. Point scene instance mesh reconstruction. With an incomplete point cloud scene as input, our method learns to recognize each object instance and reconstruct a complete mesh that matches the input observation well.

partial observations (*e.g.* point cloud from 3D scans). Several previous methods only focus on object recognition in the scene [6,13,29,32,33,37,63] by semantic and instance segmentation, or the completion of the partial observed point cloud [16,17,19,28,35,55]. In order to further explore both semantic and geometry information, in this paper, we aim to jointly complete these two different tasks in one framework.

Recently, researchers begin to explore the relationship of semantic and geometry information for scene understanding. Semantic Scene Completion [7,24,43, 57] reconstructs occluded geometry by performing semantic segmentation for both visible and occluded space in dense voxel grids. Similarly, RevealNet [31] performs instance segmentation in dense voxel grids. Due to the demanding memory requirement, these works are typically limited by the low-resolution dense voxel grids and can not reconstruct high fidelity objects in the scene. RfD-Net [49] first proposes to work directly on sparse point clouds, which can recognize and reconstruct objects in high-resolution mesh representation. However, as shown in Fig. 1(b), this Reconstruction-from-Detection pipeline always fails to reconstruct high fidelity objects. In general, the reason can be mainly categorized into two aspects. The first one is the numerous false positive proposals from the detection module. These false positive proposals cause the mismatch between the incomplete point clouds and the complete mesh, thus obstructing training an effective shape completion network. The second one is the structure ambiguity caused by incomplete point observations for directly learning occupancy values of complete objects. Therefore, to further explore this problem, we should answer the following two questions for this task: *i*) Does the accurate foreground object proposals improve the reconstruction quality? *ii*) How to mitigate the structure ambiguity of incomplete point cloud for mesh reconstruction?

In this paper, we propose our Disentangled Instance Mesh Reconstruction framework to answer these two questions. Our pipeline contains two stages, namely instance segmentation and instance mesh reconstruction. Comparing against state-of-the-art point cloud detection approaches [44,53,68], we observe that instance segmentation framework [6,37] can reduce the false positive rate of object proposal significantly. Therefore, we generate the object proposal for object completion based on instance segmentation. With the proposals from the instance segmentation framework, the quality of completed objects is improved consequentially. For the second question, we propose a disentangled instance mesh reconstruction approach to recover high fidelity mesh of each incomplete object. Different from directly learning occupancy values of complete objects

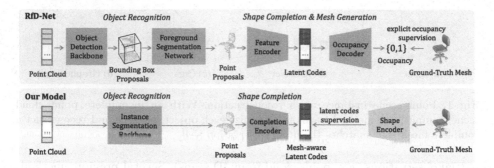

Fig. 2. A comparison of the training process between our method and RfD-Net. For object recognition, RfD-Net uses a detection-based backbone to predict bounding boxes, then extracts the foreground points with a segmentation network, while we apply a straight-forward instance segmentation backbone. Furthermore, we disentangle shape completion and mesh generation by adopting a pre-trained mesh autoencoder and supervise shape completion by latent codes. The mesh generation part is only used during inference (not shown in the figure), mitigating the issue of difficult explicit occupancy supervision in RfD-Net. Without harming the end-to-end training of object recognition and shape completion, our method significantly improves the quality of generated meshes.

based on incomplete point observations [49], we propose to disentangle the shape completion and mesh generation for mesh reconstruction. The shape completion module aims to recover the necessary structure information of incomplete objects to mitigate the ambiguity for high-fidelity mesh reconstruction, which is the goal of the mesh generation module. Especially, our shape completion module does not focus on direct completion of mesh, due to the noisy information from input point observations. More effectively, we propose the mesh-aware latent code as the supervision for our shape completion module. The target latent code is encoded from the complete point cloud by a pre-trained encoder, and can be used for mesh reconstruction by a pre-trained decoder, namely the mesh generator. Therefore, the structure information of the complete point cloud for mesh reconstruction is encoded into our mesh-aware latent code, and our shape completion module can learn this structure information directly. After training, the structure information of incomplete point observations can be recovered by this module and mitigate the ambiguity for mesh reconstruction. With the pre-trained mesh generator, our method can generate high-quality meshes consistent with the point observations as shown in Fig. 1 (c). Furthermore, if we have access to the CAD model pool, our model can be used to search the nearest neighbors in the latent code space to perform mesh retrieval or assist mesh generation, without the need of extra training.

To summarize, the contributions of this paper are as follows:

– We analyze the weaknesses of the previous detection based framework and propose a new pipeline for point scene instance mesh reconstruction, which first performs instance segmentation on incomplete point scenes and then completes each object instance with a mesh that matches the observed points.

– We design a disentangled instance mesh reconstruction strategy to mitigate the ambiguity of learning complete shapes from incomplete point cloud observations, by leveraging a mesh-aware latent code space. Furthermore, it can also be used for mesh retrieval with the access to a provided model pool.
– We studied multiple metrics to measure the performance in mesh completion quality, and proposed a new metric to measure point-to-mesh mapping quality. Results show that our method performs better than previous state-of-the-arts on the challenging ScanNet dataset, especially on complex structures such as chairs and tables.

2   Related Work

2.1   Point Scene Instance Segmentation

Instance segmentation has been an important topic for point scene understanding with the availability of large-scale point cloud scene datasets. Current methods can be categorized into detection-based and segmentation-based methods. Detection-based methods [20,30,70] first regress 3D bounding boxes and then mask out background points inside each box to get the final instance segmentation. However, the two-step pipeline is not straightforward and usually inefficient. Instead, segmentation-based methods [6,26,29,37,40,42,52,64,73] directly predict semantic segmentation and then cluster points into instance proposals. For example, PointGroup [37] uses sparse 3D CNNs [23,45,59,69] to extract point cloud features, and propose a dual-set clustering algorithm to better distinguish the void space between object instances. Later works [6,29] mainly focuses on more efficient and concise instance clustering algorithms such as dynamic convolution and hierarchical aggregation. We choose the segmentation-based backbone for its simplicity, and bridge instance segmentation to mesh reconstruction in end-to-end training.

2.2   3D Shape Completion

Object Completion. This line of research mainly focuses on shape completion of single objects. Many works [50,61,65,71] focus on the completion of point cloud shapes, with incomplete point clouds as the input and completed point clouds as the output. However, these methods usually complete up to a limited number of points which is not enough to represent high resolution shapes due to the sampling problem. Other works choose dense voxel grids [18,27,58] or implicit functions [11,12] to perform shape completion. Many works [11,41,47, 51,67] adopt an autoencoder architecture to learn a compact latent code for each shape. BSP-Net [9,10] proposes to approximate shapes with a Binary Space Partitioning (BSP) tree, which shows good results on mesh reconstruction from dense voxel grids and single view images.

688   J. Tang et al.

Scene Completion. Instead of focusing on single objects, scene completion aims to complete all objects from a partial observation such as a 3D scan. Early works usually start from volumetric representations and the completion task can be viewed as a dense labeling task on voxel grids. Semantic Scene Completion [7,8,17,24,43,57,60] voxelizes the point cloud into dense voxel grids and predicts semantic labels of all voxels in both visible and occluded regions. Reveal-Net [31] proposes semantic instance completion, which performs object detection on voxel grids and then completes each instance within the cropped voxel grids. Other works focus on mesh representations. Total 3D understanding [21,40,72] performs object detection and mesh reconstruction on RGB images. RfD-Net [49] first performs semantic instance completion on point clouds directly and generates completed instance meshes. It adopts a detection-based backbone and uses implicit functions for mesh reconstruction, demonstrating that these two tasks are complementary. Assuming the availability of a CAD model pool, CAD retrieval aims to find the best-fitting CAD models and align them to the point scenes [2,3,14,22,25], images [39], or videos [46], optionally allowing for deformation of single objects [36,62]. Our method follows this line of research, with point clouds as the direct input and reconstructed instance meshes as the output. Differently, we separate shape completion and mesh generation tasks to ease the training process with the proposed latent instance mesh reconstruction.

3   Method

We introduce our pipeline as illustrated in Fig. 3. Overall, the pipeline consists of two training stages: point-wise learning and proposal-wise learning. The first stage (Sect. 3.1) takes a sparse 3D CNN backbone to perform point-wise predictions including semantic labels, instance center offsets, and rotation angles. In the second stage (Sect. 3.2), another sparse 3D CNN is used to predict proposal-wise results including residual bounding boxes, confidence scores, and the latent distributions of complete meshes. Only in inference, the latent codes sampled from these distributions are decoded to generate compact meshes (Sect. 3.3), which are transformed back to the world coordinate system with the refined bounding boxes to compose the final reconstructed scene.

3.1   Learning Point-Wise Features

In this stage, we focus on learning point-wise features including the semantic labels for semantic segmentation, offsets from the instance center for instance segmentation, and instance rotation angles for bounding box regression. We follow [37] and use a sparse 3D U-Net [23,54] as the backbone to extract features. The input to the network is a point set $\mathbb{P} = \{\mathbf{p}_1, \mathbf{p}_2, \cdots, \mathbf{p}_N\}$, where each point is described by its coordinate $\mathbf{p}_i = (x_i, y_i, z_i), i \in [1, N]$. These points are voxelized before being fed to the backbone. To obtain the per-point feature, we map the voxel feature from the backbone back to the point and get $\mathbf{F}_{\text{point}} \in \mathbb{R}^{N \times D_{\text{point}}}$, where D_{point} is the feature dimension. Then, three Multi-Layer Perceptrons

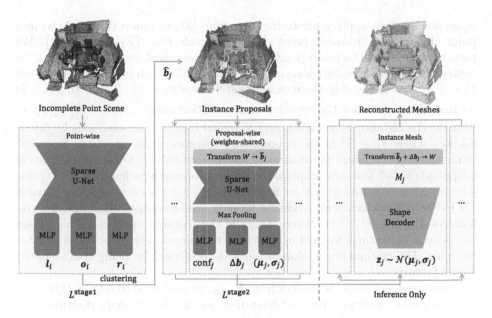

Fig. 3. Overview of the network architecture. The network first learns point-wise features including semantic labels $\mathbf{l}_i$, instance offsets $\mathbf{o}_i$ and instance rotations $\mathbf{r}_i$. Then, instance proposals are clustered and fed to the second stage for learning proposal-wise features including confidence scores conf_j, residual bounding boxes $\Delta\mathbf{b}_j$, and latent shape distributions $\mathcal{N}(\boldsymbol{\mu}_j, \boldsymbol{\sigma}_j)$. During inference, instance meshes are generated by decoding the mesh-aware latent codes sampled from the latent shape distributions.

(MLPs) are applied to regress three point-wise targets respectively. For the semantic label, the prediction is the classification logits $\mathbf{l}_i \in \mathbb{R}^C$, where C is the total number of classes. For the instance offset, the prediction is the offset $\mathbf{o}_i = (\Delta x_i, \Delta y_i, \Delta z_i)$ from the current point to the instance center it belongs to. In addition to these two regular heads for instance segmentation [6,37], we use a third head to predict the orientation of the instance that covers the current point to build an approximate oriented bounding box. We only predict the rotation angle $r_i \in [-\pi, \pi)$ along the z-axis following [49], since the rotation along x, y-axes for most instances can be ignored.

To optimize the afore-mentioned objectives, we use the cross-entropy loss $L_{\mathrm{cls}}^{\mathrm{semantic}}$ for semantic segmentation, the L1 Loss $L_{\mathrm{reg}}^{\mathrm{offset}}$ for instance offset regression, and follow [34,49] to disentangle the angle loss into a hybrid of classification and regression loss $\mathcal{L}_{\mathrm{cls}}^{\mathrm{angle}} + \mathcal{L}_{\mathrm{reg}}^{\mathrm{angle}}$. So far, the loss function for the first stage $\mathcal{L}^{\mathrm{stage1}}$ can be concluded as the sum of these four parts.

3.2 Learning Proposal-Wise Features

The second stage handles proposal-wise predictions that bridge instance segmentation to instance mesh reconstruction. Given the point-wise predictions from stage one, we first apply a clustering algorithm [37] to group the whole scene's point cloud into L instance point cloud proposals $\mathcal{P} = \{P_1, P_2, \cdots, P_L\}$. We then transform each instance point cloud to its canonical coordinate system for better proposal-wise feature learning [56]. Specifically, each instance point cloud $P_j \in \mathcal{P}$ is: 1) recentered at the mean instance center $\bar{\mathbf{c}}_j = \frac{1}{|P_j|} \sum_{i \in P_j} (\mathbf{p}_i + \mathbf{o}_i)$; 2) rotated along z-axis for the negative mean rotation angle $-\bar{r}_j = -\frac{1}{|P_j|} \sum_{i \in P_j} r_i$ to make the instance front-facing; and 3) scaled into $[0, 1]$ on each axis by dividing $\mathbf{s}_j$, where $\mathbf{s}_j \subset \mathbb{R}^3$ is the approximate instance scale calculated from the minimum and maximum coordinates of the rotated points. Another voxelization is applied on each instance proposal to extract proposal-wise features. The transformed instance points with their features $\mathbf{F}_{\text{point}}$ are fed into the second sparse 3D U-Net, after which a max-pooling layer is used to output the proposal-wise features $\mathbf{F}_{\text{prop}} \in \mathbb{R}^{L \times D_{\text{prop}}}$, where D_{prop} is the feature dimension. This allows the point-wise features learned in stage one to be smoothly propagated to later modules. The original scale information $\mathbf{s}_j$ is preserved by being concatenated to the features.

To reconstruct instance meshes from $\mathbf{F}_{\text{prop}}$, we still need to regress three targets: proposal confidence, residual bounding box and latent shape distributions.

Proposal Confidence. An MLP followed by a sigmoid function is applied to regress the confidence value $\text{conf}_j \in [0, 1]$ for proposal P_j. The ground truth for the confidence is decided by the largest point Intersection over Union (IoU) between the proposal and ground-truth instances following [37].

Residual Bounding Box. From the first stage, we already have an initial 7 Degree-of-Freedom (DoF) oriented bounding box $\hat{\mathbf{b}}_j = \{\bar{r}_j, \bar{\mathbf{c}}_j, \mathbf{s}_j\}$. However, this bounding box is inaccurate due to partial observation and occlusion, especially for the instance scale (*e.g.*, missing of chair legs leads to underestimated scale on the z-axis). We therefore use an MLP to predict a residual bounding box $\Delta\mathbf{b}_j$ to refine this initial bounding box, and the final bounding box is given by $\mathbf{b}_j = \hat{\mathbf{b}}_j + \Delta\mathbf{b}_j$.

Latent Shape Distributions. To address the ambiguity problem in shape completion, a probabilistic generative model is usually adopted [1,49,66]. We take a similar way by assuming that the complete shape is sampled from a latent Gaussian distribution, and learn it through the reparameterization trick [38]. An MLP is used to regress the mean and standard deviation $\boldsymbol{\mu}_j, \boldsymbol{\sigma}_j \in \mathbb{R}^{D_{\text{shape}}}$, where D_{shape} is the latent shape code dimension. To allow supervised learning, we need to know the ground-truth latent distribution $(\boldsymbol{\mu}_j^{\text{gt}}, \boldsymbol{\sigma}_j^{\text{gt}})$ of ground-truth meshes, which will be described in Sect. 3.3.

The loss function for the second stage $\mathcal{L}^{\text{stage2}}$ further adds three regression terms on the basis of $\mathcal{L}^{\text{stage1}}$, *i.e.*, the confidence loss $\mathcal{L}_{\text{reg}}^{\text{conf}}$, the bounding box loss $\mathcal{L}_{\text{reg}}^{\text{bbox}}$, and the latent distribution loss $\mathcal{L}_{\text{reg}}^{\text{latent}}$, all using the weighted smooth L1 loss to alleviate the class imbalance in object proposals.

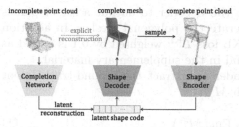
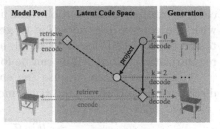

(a) Disentangled Instance Mesh Reconstruction   (b) Mesh Retrieval and Generation

Fig. 4. (a) Instead of explicitly predicting a complete mesh in 3D space, we leverage a mesh-aware latent code space to disentangle shape completion and mesh generation. (b) The gray circle is the predicted latent code from the observed partial point cloud. We can directly use it to generate a mesh via the decoder (green right arrow with $k = 0$). With access to the CAD meshes or their latent codes (yellow diamonds) from the model pool, we can further perform model retrieval (yellow left arrows) or assisted generation by projecting the latent code to the nearest k neighbors (green right arrows with $k > 0$). (Color figure online)

3.3   Disentangled Instance Mesh Reconstruction

Instance mesh reconstruction from a partially observed point cloud is a challenging task, requiring both shape completion and mesh generation. Previous methods perform these two tasks as a whole, but fail to generate high fidelity meshes that match the observation. The problems are two-fold: 1) The difficulty of optimizing a conditioned mesh generator with the detection network, where lots of false positive proposals are used as inputs. 2) The ambiguity of learning complete shapes from incomplete point cloud observations. To handle these problems, we propose a disentangled mesh reconstruction approach as illustrated in Fig. 4a. The core idea here is to disentangle shape completion and mesh generation into two stages. First, we pre-train a mesh Variational Autoencoder (VAE) to encode 3D meshes into a latent code space, which can be viewed as a mesh generator. Note that this mesh generator is trained with complete GT meshes, and there is no ambiguity in shape learning since no completion happens here. For shape completion, we can simply train another encoder that maps incomplete instance proposals into the same latent code space. This completion encoder is supervised with these low-dimension latent codes as described in Sect. 3.2, which are much easier to optimize compared to high-dimension conditioned occupancy values. Thus, the mesh generation part is detached from the training process of object recognition and shape completion.

We adopt BSP-Net [9,10], which proposes an efficient approach to approximate low-poly meshes by learning convex decomposition, as the autoencoder model. Specifically, we adopt a Conditional VAE (CVAE) variant for better generation quality. Following [9], we sample complete point clouds from the CAD models and voxelize them as the input to the encoder, which outputs a latent distribution $\mathcal{N}(\boldsymbol{\mu}, \boldsymbol{\sigma})$ that characterizes the shape. Then, we sample a latent

692   J. Tang et al.

code $\mathbf{z}$ from this distribution, and use the decoder to output a set of planes with the convex decomposition to generate the polygonal meshes. In addition to the original BSP loss $\mathcal{L}^{\mathrm{bsp}}$ in [9], a KL loss $\mathcal{L}^{\mathrm{KL}}$ weighted by 0.1 is added as regularization. More details can be found in the supplementary material.

After convergence, we use the encoder to extract the ground-truth latent distribution for each ground-truth mesh M_j^{gt}:

$$\boldsymbol{\mu}_j^{\mathrm{gt}}, \boldsymbol{\sigma}_j^{\mathrm{gt}} = \mathrm{Enc}(M_j^{\mathrm{gt}}) \tag{1}$$

Therefore, to reconstruct mesh M_j from a partially observed point instance, we only need to regress the latent distribution and sample a latent code $\mathbf{z}_j \sim \mathcal{N}(\boldsymbol{\mu}_j, \boldsymbol{\sigma}_j)$, then decode it through:

$$M_j = \mathrm{Dec}(\mathbf{z}_j) \tag{2}$$

Optional post-processing like the Iterative Closest Point (ICP) algorithm can be used to further fine-tune the mesh location. By default, we use the expectation as the latent code so $\mathbf{z}_j = \boldsymbol{\mu}_j$, but we can also sample different latent codes for different explanations of the partial point observation to address the ambiguity problem. Furthermore, if we have access to the model pool $\mathcal{M}$ at test time, our model can also perform CAD retrieval task without any further training, by searching the nearest mesh from the model pool in the latent space:

$$M_j^{\mathrm{retr}} = \arg\min_{m \in \mathcal{M}} \|\mathbf{z}_m - \mathbf{z}_j\|_2 \tag{3}$$

where $\mathbf{z}_m$ is the latent code of CAD model m. However, maintaining the whole model pool requires extra storage (about 238 MB for the 2238 models used in Scan2CAD). Another option is to only maintain the latent codes $\{\mathbf{z}_m | m \in \mathcal{M}\}$, which is a 256-d vector for each mesh (about 2.2 MB for the same models). These latent codes can serve as priors to assist the mesh generation, by projecting the predicted latent code to the hyperplane spanned by the nearest k latent codes $\{\mathbf{z}_{n1}, \mathbf{z}_{n2}, \cdots, \mathbf{z}_{nk}\}$ from the model pool:

$$M_j^{\mathrm{proj}} = \mathrm{Dec}(\mathrm{proj}_{\mathrm{span}\{\mathbf{z}_{n1}, \mathbf{z}_{n2}, \cdots, \mathbf{z}_{nk}\}}(\mathbf{z}_j)) \tag{4}$$

Figure 4b illustrates the relationship between these methods.

4   Experiment

4.1   Experimental Settings

Datasets. Three datasets are involved in our experiments: ScanNet v2 [15], ShapeNet [4], and Scan2CAD [2]. The ScanNet dataset consists of 1,513 real world indoor scene scans. Inline with [31,49], The official data split is used in all experiments. Only the incomplete point clouds are used as the input data, with the semantic and instance labels as the point-level supervision. The Scan2CAD

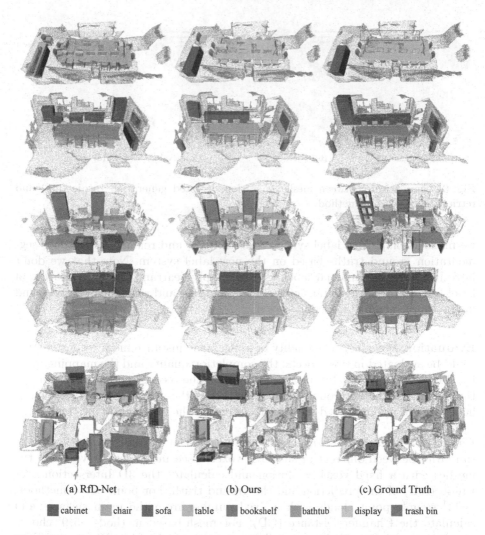

(a) RfD-Net   (b) Ours   (c) Ground Truth

■ cabinet   ■ chair   ■ sofa   ■ table   ■ bookshelf   ■ bathtub   ■ display   ■ trash bin

Fig. 5. Qualitative Comparison on the ScanNet dataset. Please zoom in to see details. We only visualize meshes with confidence larger than 0.5 for RfD-Net as in [49], and 0.3 for Ours. Red-dash boxes show missing or incorrect human annotations in the ground truth, *e.g.*, missing chairs, incorrectly scaled table and cabinet. More visualizations can be found in the supplementary material. (Color figure online)

dataset provides the alignment of CAD models in ShapeNet to scenes in ScanNet. We use the aligned CAD models as the proposal-level supervision.

It's worth noting that the semantic and instance labels of ScanNet point clouds are inconsistent with Scan2CAD meshes. The point cloud instance segmentation literature [6,29,37] usually adopts a 20-class label system, with 2 stuff categories and 18 object categories. However, the instance mesh reconstruction literature [49] only uses 8 object categories. To bridge between these two tasks,

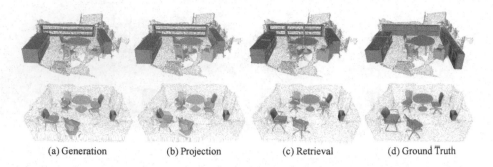

(a) Generation   (b) Projection   (c) Retrieval   (d) Ground Truth

Fig. 6. Comparison between mesh generation, assisted generation (projection) and retrieval mode of our method.

we make a compatible label system to both tasks and relabel the instance segmentation ground truths based on the new label system. Note that we don't introduce any new manual labeling, but simply rearrange the two sources of label information. The details of the label mapping and relabeling can be found in the supplementary material.

Evaluation Metrics. The quality of point scene instance mesh reconstruction could be evaluated in two aspects: the completion quality and the mapping quality. The completion quality measures how well the reconstructed meshes match the human-annotated ground-truth meshes, and the mapping quality measures how well the reconstructed mesh surfaces match the observed point clouds.

Completion Quality. Several approaches have been proposed to measure the similarity between different meshes. For voxel-based methods, [49] voxelizes the meshes with a fixed voxel resolution and calculates the 3D Intersection over Union (IoU) of the prediction and the ground truth. For point-based methods, [9,11] sample point clouds with a fixed number from the mesh surfaces and calculate the Chamfer Distance (CD). For mesh-based methods, [5,9] choose to render multi-view 2D images and calculate the Light Field Distance (LFD). All of these metrics can only partially represent the underlying mesh similarity. For example, 3D IoU requires the predicted mesh to occupy the exact voxels as the ground-truth mesh, CD measures the distance between mesh surfaces, and LFD compares more on visual appearance. Previous works [31,49] only adopt 3D IoU as the metric, but we argue that 3D IoU at a coarse voxel resolution fails to reflect the quality of mesh surface and visual appearance, which are also important for measuring mesh similarity. For a thorough comparison, we adopt all the three metrics with different thresholds to determine whether a predicted mesh can match a ground-truth mesh, and report the 3D detection mean AP over all classes.

Mapping Quality. As shown in Fig. 1, the human-annotated ground-truth meshes may not be the only plausible reconstruction due to the ambiguity of input.

Therefore, only using the completion quality may lead to biased evaluation. To alleviate this problem, we use mapping quality to measure how well the reconstructed mesh surfaces match the observed point clouds. Specifically, we propose the Point Coverage Ratio (PCR), which computes the nearest distance from each observed instance point to the corresponding mesh surface, and uses a threshold to determine whether this point belongs to the reconstructed surface:

$$\text{PCR} = \frac{1}{|\mathcal{P}|} \sum_{\mathbf{p} \in \mathcal{P}} \mathbb{1}_{\{\text{dist}(\mathbf{p}, \mathcal{M}) < \omega\}} \tag{5}$$

where $\mathbf{p}$ is a point from the observed ground-truth instance point cloud $\mathcal{P}$, $\mathbb{1}$ means the indicator function, $\mathcal{M}$ is the reconstructed mesh, $\text{dist}(\mathbf{p}, \mathcal{M})$ is the Euclidean distance from the point to the mesh surface, and ω is the distance threshold. A larger PCR means more observed points are located near the mesh surface, and thus better mapping quality. Similarly, we report the 3D detection mean AP over all classes using PCR as the metric.

Baselines. We mainly compare our results with the current state-of-the-art RfD-Net [49], which is the first work that generates high-resolution mesh for point scene instance reconstruction. The officially released model is used to generate results for evaluation and comparison. Also, we investigate different variants of our method including direct mesh generation, assisted mesh generation by latent code projection and mesh retrieval with different levels of access to the CAD model pool. All methods in our experiments are trained on the same dataset split, and evaluated with the same hyper-parameters.

Implementation Details. We set the voxel size as 0.02 m for point-wise sparse U-Net, and 0.05m for proposal-wise sparse U-Net. We use $D_{\text{point}} = 32$, $D_{\text{prop}} = 64$, and $D_{\text{shape}} = 128$. We train 256 epochs for the first stage, and 256 epochs for the second stage with a batch size of 8 on a single Nvidia Tesla V100 GPU. The Adam optimizer is used with an initial learning rate of 0.001 for the first stage and 0.0001 for the second stage. In training, we set the clustering radius as 0.03 m following PointGroup [37]. The weight for each loss term defaults to 1.0. In evaluation, we use a multi-scale clustering method at $\{0.01, 0.03, 0.05\}$m to spot more proposals. The nearest neighbour count k is set to 1 for the projection model. The voxel size for 3D IoU calculation and the threshold ω for PCR calculation are both set to 0.047 m following [49]. The proposal confidence threshold is set to 0.09, and each proposal should have at least 100 points.

4.2 Comparisons

Quantitative Comparisons. Table 1 shows the quantitative comparisons of completion quality. Our method outperforms state-of-the-art on five out of six evaluation settings in terms of mAP. This benefits from the proposed pipeline

Table 1. Comparisons on mesh completion quality. We report mean AP for different metric@threshold. For IoU, higher threshold is more difficult. For CD and LFD, smaller thresholds are more difficult. Better results are in bold. We don't compare with projection and retrieval models since they use extra information.

	IoU@0.25	IoU@0.5	CD@0.1	CD@0.047	LFD@5000	LFD@2500
RfD-Net [49]	42.52	**14.35**	46.37	19.09	28.59	7.80
Ours	**46.34**	12.54	**52.39**	**25.71**	**29.47**	**8.55**
Ours + proj	46.50	12.59	52.06	24.84	29.95	9.67
Ours + retr	47.20	12.83	51.77	25.10	30.80	10.12

Table 2. Comparisons on point-to-mesh mapping quality. The AP scores are measured with PCR@0.5.

	table	chair	bookshelf	sofa	trash bin	cabinet	display	bathtub	mean
Scan2CAD [2]	36.60	69.31	**65.03**	28.92	56.93	**41.82**	70.81	45.07	45.07
RfD-Net [49]	32.54	76.54	30.66	22.91	40.54	24.37	67.64	52.69	43.49
Ours	**49.78**	**78.64**	29.25	**60.33**	**65.30**	18.75	**76.56**	**75.51**	**56.76**
Ours + proj	60.57	78.88	28.93	61.00	65.61	18.45	78.02	72.79	58.03
Ours + retr	62.28	75.57	45.23	52.60	65.27	17.14	76.61	73.81	58.82

Table 3. Object Recognition Precision. We report the precision of object recognition at different IoU thresholds. Our method greatly reduces the number of false positive proposals.

	Prec.@0.25	Prec.@0.5
RfD-Net [49]	22.99	7.92
Ours	**43.70**	**15.09**

that reduces false positive proposals (Table 3) and enhances the quality of generated meshes through the disentangled mesh reconstruction approach. A reason for the lower 3D IoU with 0.5 as the threshold might be that 3D IoU with a high threshold discourages meshes with thin structures, since a small displacement can result in huge drop in the metric value, even if the shape is of good quality (*e.g.* the chair in Fig. 1). With the access of an external model pool, the projection and retrieval models (denoted as Ours + proj. and Ours + retr.) produce more robust meshes. In particular, the retrieval model achieves a better LFD score, since the retrieved meshes are guaranteed to be rational.

Table 2 shows the quantitative comparisons of mapping quality. We achieve significant improvement in mAP and surpass the human-annotated Scan2CAD dataset. This is to be expected. Since the ShapeNet dataset is synthetic and has a finite number of models, the human-annotated CAD models may not perfectly match the point cloud observations. Interestingly, the results also partially reveal the capability of the CAD model pool. For example, retrieved meshes show better performance on bookshelf, but perform worse on sofa, which means there may

Table 4. Ablation study of proposed modules.

ResBox	MSC	ICP	IoU@0.25	CD@0.1	LFD@5000
	✓	✓	41.76	46.51	27.55
✓		✓	43.57	48.26	28.91
✓	✓		42.33	52.19	29.11
✓	✓	✓	**46.34**	**52.39**	**29.47**

be fewer suitable sofa CAD models that fit real world ScanNet data. In such cases, generated meshes can be potentially better.

Qualitative Comparisons. Figure 5 shows the qualitative comparisons. The meshes generated by our method have better visual appearance and more accurate locations. Besides, we show that when the human-annotated ground truths conflict with the observed point clouds, our model can still successfully detect these instances and output plausible meshes. In Fig. 6, we also show the results of the projection and retrieval models. With extra information from the model pool, the model can produce more robust meshes.

4.3 Ablation Study

We conducted ablation studies to verify the influence of proposed modules in Table 4. 'ResBox' means we learn a residual bounding box $\Delta \mathbf{b}_j$ to refine the empirical bounding box deduced from observed point clouds. 'MSC' means we use multiple clustering radii to find more proposals at test time. 'ICP' means we apply the ICP algorithm to post-process the reconstructed meshes. The results indicate that the combination of these three modules achieves overall the best performance. In particular, the proposed residual bounding box learning refines the object location and improves all metrics, while ICP post-processing mainly affects the IoU metric.

5 Conclusion

In this paper, we introduce a Disentangled Instance Mesh Reconstruction pipeline for point scene understanding. Our method first performs instance segmentation to generate accurate object proposals, then applies a disentangled instance mesh reconstruction strategy to mitigate the ambiguity of learning complete shapes from incomplete point observations. We evaluate the experimental results on the challenging ScanNet dataset from the perspectives of completion quality and mapping quality, and demonstrate the superior performance of our method.

Acknowledgements. This work is supported by the National Key Research and Development Program of China (2020YFB1708002), National Natural Science Foundation of China (61632003, 61375022, 61403005), Beijing Advanced Innovation Center for Intelligent Robots and Systems (2018IRS11), and PEK-SenseTime Joint Laboratory of Machine Vision.

References

1. Achlioptas, P., Diamanti, O., Mitliagkas, I., Guibas, L.: Learning representations and generative models for 3d point clouds. In: ICML. pp. 40–49. PMLR (2018)
2. Avetisyan, A., Dahnert, M., Dai, A., Savva, M., Chang, A.X., Nießner, M.: Scan2cad: Learning cad model alignment in rgb-d scans. In: CVPR. pp. 2614–2623 (2019)
3. Avetisyan, A., Khanova, T., Choy, C., Dash, D., Dai, A., Nießner, M.: Scenecad: Predicting object alignments and layouts in rgb-d scans. arXiv preprint arXiv:2003.12622 (2020)
4. Chang, A.X., Funkhouser, T., Guibas, L., Hanrahan, P., Huang, Q., Li, Z., Savarese, S., Savva, M., Song, S., Su, H., et al.: Shapenet: An information-rich 3d model repository. arXiv preprint arXiv:1512.03012 (2015)
5. Chen, D.Y., Tian, X.P., Shen, Y.T., Ouhyoung, M.: On visual similarity based 3d model retrieval. In: Computer graphics forum. vol. 22, pp. 223–232. Wiley Online Library (2003)
6. Chen, S., Fang, J., Zhang, Q., Liu, W., Wang, X.: Hierarchical aggregation for 3d instance segmentation. arXiv preprint arXiv:2108.02350 (2021)
7. Chen, X., Lin, K.Y., Qian, C., Zeng, G., Li, H.: 3D sketch-aware semantic scene completion via semi-supervised structure prior. In: CVPR, pp. 4193–4202 (2020)
8. Chen, X., Xing, Y., Zeng, G.: Real-time semantic scene completion via feature aggregation and conditioned prediction. In: ICIP, pp. 2830–2834. IEEE (2020)
9. Chen, Z., Tagliasacchi, A., Zhang, H.: BSP-Net: generating compact meshes via binary space partitioning. In: CVPR (2020)
10. Chen, Z., Tagliasacchi, A., Zhang, H.: Learning mesh representations via binary space partitioning tree networks. TPAMI, 1 (2021). https://doi.org/10.1109/TPAMI.2021.3093440
11. Chen, Z., Zhang, H.: Learning implicit fields for generative shape modeling. In: CVPR, pp. 5939–5948 (2019)
12. Chibane, J., Alldieck, T., Pons-Moll, G.: Implicit functions in feature space for 3D shape reconstruction and completion. In: CVPR, pp. 6970–6981 (2020)
13. Choy, C., Gwak, J., Savarese, S.: 4D spatio-temporal convnets: Minkowski convolutional neural networks. In: CVPR, pp. 3075–3084 (2019)
14. Dahnert, M., Dai, A., Guibas, L.J., Nießner, M.: Joint embedding of 3D scan and cad objects. In: ICCV, pp. 8749–8758 (2019)
15. Dai, A., Chang, A.X., Savva, M., Halber, M., Funkhouser, T., Nießner, M.: ScanNet: richly-annotated 3d reconstructions of indoor scenes. In: CVPR, pp. 5828–5839 (2017)
16. Dai, A., Diller, C., Nießner, M.: SG-NN: sparse generative neural networks for self-supervised scene completion of RGB-D scans. In: CVPR, pp. 849–858 (2020)
17. Dai, A., Ritchie, D., Bokeloh, M., Reed, S., Sturm, J., Nießner, M.: ScanComplete: large-scale scene completion and semantic segmentation for 3D scans. In: CVPR, pp. 4578–4587 (2018)

18. Dai, A., Ruizhongtai Qi, C., Nießner, M.: Shape completion using 3D-encoder-predictor CNNs and shape synthesis. In: CVPR, pp. 5868–5877 (2017)
19. Dai, A., Siddiqui, Y., Thies, J., Valentin, J., Nießner, M.: SPSG: self-supervised photometric scene generation from RGB-D scans. In: CVPR, pp. 1747–1756 (2021)
20. Engelmann, F., Bokeloh, M., Fathi, A., Leibe, B., Nießner, M.: 3D-MPA: multi-proposal aggregation for 3D semantic instance segmentation. In: CVPR, pp. 9031–9040 (2020)
21. Engelmann, F., Rematas, K., Leibe, B., Ferrari, V.: From points to multi-object 3D reconstruction. In: CVPR, pp. 4588–4597 (2021)
22. Grabner, A., Roth, P.M., Lepetit, V.: 3D pose estimation and 3D model retrieval for objects in the wild. In: CVPR, pp. 3022–3031 (2018)
23. Graham, B., van der Maaten, L.: Submanifold sparse convolutional networks. arXiv preprint arXiv:1706.01307 (2017)
24. Guo, Y.X., Tong, X.: View-volume network for semantic scene completion from a single depth image. ArXiv abs/1806.05361 (2018)
25. Hampali, S., Stekovic, S., Sarkar, S.D., Kumar, C.S., Fraundorfer, F., Lepetit, V.: Monte carlo scene search for 3D scene understanding. In: CVPR, pp. 13804–13813 (2021)
26. Han, L., Zheng, T., Xu, L., Fang, L.: OccuSeg: occupancy-aware 3D instance segmentation. In: CVPR, pp. 2940–2949 (2020)
27. Han, X., Li, Z., Huang, H., Kalogerakis, E., Yu, Y.: High-resolution shape completion using deep neural networks for global structure and local geometry inference. In: ICCV, pp. 85–93 (2017)
28. Han, X., et al.: Deep reinforcement learning of volume-guided progressive view inpainting for 3D point scene completion from a single depth image. In: CVPR, pp. 234–243 (2019)
29. , He, T., Shen, C., van den Hengel, A.: DyCo3D: robust instance segmentation of 3D point clouds through dynamic convolution. In: CVPR, pp. 354–363 (2021)
30. Hou, J., Dai, A., Nießner, M.: 3D-SIS: 3D semantic instance segmentation of RGB-D scans. In: CVPR, pp. 4421–4430 (2019)
31. Hou, J., Dai, A., Nießner, M.: RevealNet: seeing behind objects in RGB-D scans. In: CVPR, pp. 2098–2107 (2020)
32. Hu, W., Zhao, H., Jiang, L., Jia, J., Wong, T.T.: Bidirectional projection network for cross dimension scene understanding. In: CVPR, pp. 14373–14382 (2021)
33. Hu, Z., et al.: VMNet: voxel-mesh network for geodesic-aware 3D semantic segmentation. In: ICCV, pp. 15488–15498 (2021)
34. Huang, S., Qi, S., Xiao, Y., Zhu, Y., Wu, Y.N., Zhu, S.C.: Cooperative holistic scene understanding: unifying 3D object, layout, and camera pose estimation. In: NeurIPS, pp. 207–218 (2018)
35. Huang, Y.K., Wu, T.H., Liu, Y.C., Hsu, W.H.: Indoor depth completion with boundary consistency and self-attention. In: ICCV Workshops (2019)
36. Ishimtsev, V., et al.: Cad-deform: deformable fitting of cad models to 3D scans. arXiv preprint arXiv:2007.11965 (2020)
37. Jiang, L., Zhao, H., Shi, S., Liu, S., Fu, C.W., Jia, J.: PointGroup: dual-set point grouping for 3D instance segmentation. In: CVPR, pp. 4867–4876 (2020)
38. Kingma, D.P., Welling, M.: Auto-encoding variational bayes. arXiv preprint arXiv:1312.6114 (2013)
39. Kuo, Weicheng, Angelova, Anelia, Lin, Tsung-Yi., Dai, Angela: Mask2CAD: 3D shape prediction by learning to segment and retrieve. In: Vedaldi, Andrea, Bischof, Horst, Brox, Thomas, Frahm, Jan-Michael. (eds.) ECCV 2020. LNCS, vol. 12348,

pp. 260–277. Springer, Cham (2020). https://doi.org/10.1007/978-3-030-58580-8_16

40. Lahoud, J., Ghanem, B., Pollefeys, M., Oswald, M.R.: 3D instance segmentation via multi-task metric learning. In: ICCV, pp. 9256–9266 (2019)

41. Li, J., Xu, K., Chaudhuri, S., Yumer, E., Zhang, H., Guibas, L.: Grass: generative recursive autoencoders for shape structures. TOG 36(4), 1–14 (2017)

42. Liang, Z., Li, Z., Xu, S., Tan, M., Jia, K.: Instance segmentation in 3D scenes using semantic superpoint tree networks. arXiv preprint arXiv:2108.07478 (2021)

43. Liu, S., et al.: See and think: disentangling semantic scene completion. In: NeurIPS, pp. 261–272 (2018)

44. Liu, Z., Zhang, Z., Cao, Y., Hu, H., Tong, X.: Group-free 3D object detection via transformers. In: ICCV, pp. 2949–2958 (2021)

45. Liu, Z., Tang, H., Lin, Y., Han, S.: Point-voxel CNN for efficient 3D deep learning. In: NeurIPS, vol. 32, pp. 965–975 (2019)

46. Maninis, K.K., Popov, S., Nießner, M., Ferrari, V.: Vid2CAD: CAD model alignment using multi-view constraints from videos. arXiv preprint arXiv:2012.04641 (2020)

47. Mo, K., et al.: StructureNet: hierarchical graph networks for 3D shape generation. arXiv preprint arXiv:1908.00575 (2019)

48. Nie, Y., Han, X., Guo, S., Zheng, Y., Chang, J., Zhang, J.J.: Total3DUnderstanding: joint layout, object pose and mesh reconstruction for indoor scenes from a single image. In: CVPR, pp. 55–64 (2020)

49. Nie, Y., Hou, J., Han, X., Niessner, M.: RfD-Net: point scene understanding by semantic instance reconstruction. In: CVPR. pp. 4608–4618, June 2021

50. Nie, Y., et al.: Skeleton-bridged point completion: from global inference to local adjustment. arXiv preprint arXiv:2010.07428 (2020)

51. Paschalidou, D., Katharopoulos, A., Geiger, A., Fidler, S.: Neural parts: learning expressive 3D shape abstractions with invertible neural networks. In: CVPR, pp. 3204–3215 (2021)

52. Pham, Q.H., Nguyen, T., Hua, B.S., Roig, G., Yeung, S.K.: JSIS3D: joint semantic-instance segmentation of 3D point clouds with multi-task pointwise networks and multi-value conditional random fields. In: CVPR, pp. 8827–8836 (2019)

53. Qi, C.R., Litany, O., He, K., Guibas, L.J.: Deep hough voting for 3D object detection in point clouds. In: ICCV, pp. 9277–9286 (2019)

54. Ronneberger, O., P. Fischer, Brox, T.: U-net: Convolutional networks for biomedical image segmentation. In: MICCAI. LNCS, vol. 9351, pp. 234–241. Springer (2015), http://lmb.informatik.uni-freiburg.de/Publications/2015/RFB15a, (available on arXiv:1505.04597 [cs.CV])

55. Senushkin, D., Belikov, I., Konushin, A.: Decoder modulation for indoor depth completion. arXiv preprint arXiv:2005.08607 (2020)

56. Shi, S., Wang, X., Li, H.: PointRCNN: 3D object proposal generation and detection from point cloud. In: CVPR, pp. 770–779 (2019)

57. Song, S., Yu, F., Zeng, A., Chang, A.X., Savva, M., Funkhouser, T.: Semantic scene completion from a single depth image. In: CVPR, pp. 1746–1754 (2017)

58. Stutz, D., Geiger, A.: Learning 3D shape completion from laser scan data with weak supervision. In: CVPR, pp. 1955–1964 (2018)

59. Tang, H., et al.: Searching efficient 3D architectures with sparse point-voxel convolution. In: Vedaldi, Andrea, Bischof, Horst, Brox, Thomas, Frahm, Jan-Michael. (eds.) ECCV 2020. LNCS, vol. 12373, pp. 685–702. Springer, Cham (2020). https://doi.org/10.1007/978-3-030-58604-1_41

60. Tang, J., Chen, X., Wang, J., Zeng, G.: Not all voxels are equal: semantic scene completion from the point-voxel perspective. arXiv preprint arXiv:2112.12925 (2021)
61. Tchapmi, L.P., Kosaraju, V., Rezatofighi, H., Reid, I., Savarese, S.: TopNet: structural point cloud decoder. In: CVPR, pp. 383–392 (2019)
62. Uy, M.A., Kim, V.G., Sung, M., Aigerman, N., Chaudhuri, S., Guibas, L.J.: Joint learning of 3D shape retrieval and deformation. In: CVPR, pp. 11713–11722 (2021)
63. Wang, P.S., Liu, Y., Guo, Y.X., Sun, C.Y., Tong, X.: O-CNN: octree-based convolutional neural networks for 3D shape analysis. TOG 36(4), 1–11 (2017)
64. Wang, W., Yu, R., Huang, Q., Neumann, U.: SGPN: similarity group proposal network for 3D point cloud instance segmentation. In: CVPR, pp. 2569–2578 (2018)
65. Wang, X., Ang Jr, M.H., Lee, G.H.: Cascaded refinement network for point cloud completion. In: CVPR, pp. 790–799 (2020)
66. Wu, J., Zhang, C., Xue, T., Freeman, B., Tenenbaum, J.: Learning a probabilistic latent space of object shapes via 3D generative-adversarial modeling. In: NeurIPS, pp. 82–90 (2016)
67. Wu, R., Zhuang, Y., Xu, K., Zhang, H., Chen, B.: PQ-NET: a generative part Seq2Seq network for 3D shapes. In: CVPR, pp. 829–838 (2020)
68. Xie, Q., et al.: MLCVNet: multi-level context VoteNet for 3D object detection. In: CVPR, pp. 10447–10456 (2020)
69. Yan, Y., Mao, Y., Li, B.: Second: sparsely embedded convolutional detection. Sensors 18(10), 3337 (2018)
70. Yang, B., et al.: Learning object bounding boxes for 3D instance segmentation on point clouds. arXiv preprint arXiv:1906.01140 (2019)
71. Yuan, W., Khot, T., Held, D., Mertz, C., Hebert, M.: PCN: point completion network. In: 3DV, pp. 728–737. IEEE (2018)
72. Zhang, C., Cui, Z., Zhang, Y., Zeng, B., Pollefeys, M., Liu, S.: Holistic 3D scene understanding from a single image with implicit representation. In: CVPR, pp. 8833–8842 (2021)
73. Zhong, M., Chen, X., Chen, X., Zeng, G., Wang, Y.: MaskGroup: hierarchical point grouping and masking for 3D instance segmentation. In: ICME (2022)

DiffuStereo: High Quality Human Reconstruction via Diffusion-Based Stereo Using Sparse Cameras

Ruizhi Shao⑩, Zerong Zheng⑩, Hongwen Zhang⑩, Jingxiang Sun⑩, and Yebin Liu$^{(\boxtimes)}$⑩

Tsinghua University, Beijing, China
liuyebin@mail.tsinghua.edu.cn

Abstract. We propose DiffuStereo, a novel system using only sparse cameras (8 in this work) for high-quality 3D human reconstruction. At its core is a novel diffusion-based stereo module, which introduces diffusion models, a type of powerful generative models, into the iterative stereo matching network. To this end, we design a new diffusion kernel and additional stereo constraints to facilitate stereo matching and depth estimation in the network. We further present a multi-level stereo network architecture to handle high-resolution (up to 4k) inputs without requiring unaffordable memory footprint. Given a set of sparse-view color images of a human, the proposed multi-level diffusion-based stereo network can produce highly accurate depth maps, which are then converted into a high-quality 3D human model through an efficient multi-view fusion strategy. Overall, our method enables automatic reconstruction of human models with quality on par to high-end dense-view camera rigs, and this is achieved using a much more light-weight hardware setup. Experiments show that our method outperforms state-of-the-art methods by a large margin both qualitatively and quantitatively.

Keywords: 3d human reconstruction · Diffusion model · Multiview

1 Introduction

High quality 3D human reconstruction is essential to large number of applications ranging from telecommunications, education, entertainment, and so on. High-end systems [1,2,8,13,14,44] based on dense camera rigs (up to 100 cameras [11,30]) and custom-designed lighting conditions [19,57] can achieve high-quality reconstruction, but the sophisticated setup limits their deployment in practice. Recently, researchers have proposed to employ neural implicit functions as a learning approach to reconstruct 3D humans from single-view RGB [49,50], sparse-view RGB [27,70] or sparse-view RGBD inputs [64]. Benifiting from the representation power of deep implicit functions, these works demonstrated visually pleasing results and inspired many follow-up works [22,28,36,72].

Supplementary Information The online version contains supplementary material available at https://doi.org/10.1007/978-3-031-19824-3_41.

Fig. 1. Our DiffuStereo system can reconstruct high accurate 3D human models with sharp geometric details using only 8 RGB cameras. Such results can only be achieved using nearly hundred of cameras before. See Supp. video for more video results.

Despite the significant progresses, reconstructing *highly accurate* 3D human models from sparse-view (<10) passive RGB cameras is still far from a solved problem: the afore-mentioned learning-based approaches are still unable to reconstruct very high accurate results as even fed with dense inputs. The underlying reason is that these two types of methods take different cues to reconstruct 3D models. Current learning-based sparse-view methods mainly rely on the appearance cues and high-level semantics in each individual image to "guess" the geometry, neglecting the cross-view correspondence relationship. In contrast, dense-view systems explicitly perform stereo matching to establish dense correspondences across different views for analytical depth calculation, thus they can produce more accurate models without any data-driven prior. Therefore, we believe accurate stereo matching is the key to bring the sparse-view reconstruction quality to the next level, and we seek to provide a solution in this paper.

However, this is not an easy task considering the variations of 3D humans and the potential occlusions under sparse camera settings. Current state-of-the-art stereo methods, either for general purpose [37] or for human reconstruction [26], typically assume close viewpoints and operate in a low resolution. Besides, their result quality is also limited by the discrete nature of pixel-wise cost volumes, failing to achieve sub-pixel accuracy. To address these challenges, we introduce a novel stereo formulation based on diffusion models [24,52]. Diffusion models are a class of generative models designed for synthesizing data via modeling the gradient of data distribution. They can synthesize photo-realistic images and even beat GANs in terms of image quality [12]. The generative power of these models mainly owes to a natural fit to the inductive biases of image data when equipping a UNet as the network backbone [45]. As mentioned in [54], the diffusion process can be regarded as learning to solve a continuous stochastic differential equations, which, interestingly, coincides with traditional stereo methods based on a continuous variational formulation [38]. Such similarity inspires us to propose *diffusion-based human stereo*, a novel stereo method that combines the continuity of diffusion models with existing learning-based iterative stereo to achieve high-quality human depth estimation. To the best of our knowledge, our method is the first one that link the separate research threads of diffusion models and stereo in a synergistic architecture. As shown in the experiments, our diffusion-based stereo can produce high-quality human depth at the same accuracy level as traditional dense systems, while taking much less images as input.

Taking our diffusion-based human stereo as the core, we further present DiffuStereo, a novel system for high-quality human volumetric reconstruction from sparse views. The key idea of our system is to utilize diffusion-based stereo to iteratively refine the geometry reconstructed by existing implicit representation-based methods, and this is done in a 2D flow domain. In particular, we first adopt DoubleField [51] to reconstruct a coarse human mesh and render the coarse depth maps from multiple viewpoints. Then we transform them into disparity flows and compute the masks to identify possible occlusions. To deal with the challenge of stereo for sparse views and achieve sub-pixel accuracy for high-resolution inputs, we make two key designs as follows. Firstly, we condition the diffusion network with several features to ensure stereo consistency and add epipolar constraints to the predicted flow. Secondly, we design a two-level network structure to tackle with the memory issues for high-resolution images. The global level extracts human semantic features from the downsampled images, while the diffusion level introduces the global feature into our diffusion stereo network and iteratively refines the disparity flow. This two-level structure allows us to train the network in a patch-based manner and thus resolves the memory bottleneck caused by high-resolution inputs. To fuse the depth maps from different viewpoints into a 3D model, we propose a light-weight hybrid fusion strategy, which gracefully deals with calibration error on real-world data and completes the occluded region. This fusion step firstly aligns the refined depth point clouds and the coarse human model through non-rigid ICP. Then we select the points from the coarse mesh to complete the invisible regions and reconstruct the final model.

Overall, our method requires only 8 passive cameras and can reconstruct high-quality human models at a level of detail that was never thought to be possible before. The quality of our geometry reconstruction in visible regions is even competitive with the ground truth on THuman2.0 dataset [64]. In summary, our contributions in this work are:

1) We propose DiffuStereo, a light-weight and high-quality system for human volumetric reconstruction under sparse multi-view cameras.
2) To the best of our knowledge, we present the first method to introduce diffusion models into stereo and human reconstruction. We extend the vanilla diffusion model by carefully designing a new diffusion kernel and introducing additional stereo constraints into the diffusion conditions.
3) We propose a novel multi-level diffusion stereo network to achieve accurate and high-quality human depth estimation. Our network can gracefully handle high-resolution (up to 4k) images without suffering from memory overload.

2   Related Work

Stereo matching aims at computing the disparity between two camera views. The classical pipelines typically consist of two stages, namely matching and filtering. In the literature, much attention has been paid to designing better matching cost [21,66] and better filter algorithms [6,23,33]. With the advent of deep learning era, convolutional neural networks (CNNs) were introduced to improve pixel matching in the stereo pipeline [40,74]. To fully realize the potential of deep networks, researchers proposed many end-to-end stereo architectures [9,20,23,32,62,67–69]. At the core is a 3D cost volume constructed over 2D feature maps, followed by 3D convolutional layers for correspondence filtering. However, such architectures come at a high computational cost and limits the possible operating resolution. Recently, RAFT-stereo [37] proposed a memory-efficient stereo method by replacing 3D convolutions with 2D ones and predicting disparity in an iterative manner. Other methods [35,58,60] formulating stereo matching in an iterative process further improve the geometry accuracy and generalization ability. Although these methods achieve impressive results on datasets such as KITTI [17,41] and DTU [29], we fount that they cannot work well in our sparse-view, high-resolution setting. Therefore, we design a novel diffusion-based stereo method for sparse-view human reconstruction.

Traditional 3D human reconstruction methods rely on multi-view images [39,55,57,61] or RGB(D) image sequences [3,4,7,13,14,63–65,71] to reconstruct the geometric model. Extremely high-quality reconstruction results have also been demonstrated with a large amount of cameras [11,19]. The most essential part in these pipelines is the depth point cloud obtained using classical stereo matching, and researchers have adopted various technologies to further improve the accuracy of depth estimation, such as photometric stereo under different illuminations [57] or deep learning on active stereo patterns [15]. Variational formulation was also proposed for the purpose of continuous depth computation and excels at detail capture [38], but solving such a variational energy easily falls into local minimals, resulting into poor robustness. We overcome this problem by employing diffusion models, which solves the problem of variational depth estimation with data-driven knowledge and demonstrates robust performance.

Learning-based 3D human reconstruction are recently proposed in order to reduce the difficulty in system setup. They learn a data-driven prior from high-quality 3D human database and reconstruct 3D humans from sparse camera views [18,27,51] or even single-view images [5,16,22,28,36,42,49,50,59,72,73]. For example, PIFu [49] and PIFuHD [50] proposed to regress a deep implicit function using pixel-aligned image features and is able to reconstruct high-resolution results. DoubleField [65] combined the merits of implicit geometric representations and radiance fields for high-fidelity human reconstruction and rendering. In spite of the progress in these works, challenges still remain in reconstructing highly accurate human models from sparse views, and we identify accurate, high-resolution stereo matching for sparse views as the key to this problem.

Diffusion Models are a class of generative models based on a Markov chain [24,52,53]. They convert samples from a standard Gaussian distribution into ones from an empirical data distribution through an iterative denoising process. The denoising process can be extended for the purpose of conditional generation by adding other signals as the condition [10]. When implementing the network backbone as a UNet, diffusion models are well suited for image-like data and achieved state-of-the-art results in image generation [12,43,45], super-resolution [25,34,48], image-to-image translation [47] and so on. In this paper, we show that diffusion models, with some slight modifications, can also be used in sparse-view stereo matching for human reconstruction.

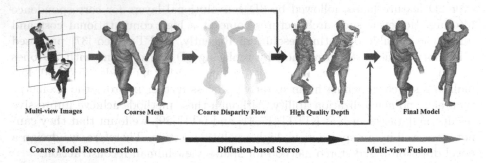

Multi-view Images   Coarse Mesh   Coarse Disparity Flow   High Quality Depth   Final Model

Coarse Model Reconstruction   Diffusion-based Stereo   Multi-view Fusion

Fig. 2. Overview of the DiffuStereo system. Our system consists of three key steps to reconstruct high-quality human models from sparse-view inputs: i) An initial human mesh is predicted by DoubleField [51], and rendered as the coarse disparity flow (Sect. 3.1); ii) The coarse disparity maps are refined in the diffusion-based stereo to obtain the high-quality depth maps (Sect. 3.2); iii) The initial human mesh and high-quality depth maps are fused as the final high-quality human mesh (Sect. 3.3).

3 Method

As shown in Fig. 2, our system DiffuStereo can reconstruct high-quality human models from sparse (as few as 8) cameras. All cameras evenly distribute on a ring surrounding the target human.

Such a sparse setting poses huge challenges to high-quality reconstruction as the angle between two neighboring views can be large as 45°. DiffuStereo tackles the challenges with the joint efforts of an off-the-shelf reconstruction method DoubleField [51], a diffusion-based stereo network, and a light-weight multiview fusion module. Overall, DiffuStereo consists of three key steps to reconstruct high-quality human models from sparse-view inputs:

i) An initial human mesh is predicted by DoubleField [51], and rendered as the coarse disparity maps (Sect. 3.1); In DoubleField, one of the most recent state-of-the-art human reconstruction methods, the surface and radiance fields are bridged to leverage human geometry priors and multi-view appearances, providing a good initialization of mesh given sparse-view inputs.

ii) For each two neighboring views, the coarse disparity maps are refined in the diffusion-based stereo network to obtain the high-quality depth maps (Sect. 3.2); The diffusion-based stereo network has a strong capability to improve the disparity maps for each input views, where a diffusion process is employed for continuous disparity refinements.

iii) The initial human mesh and high-quality depth maps are fused into the final high-quality human mesh (Sect. 3.3), where a light-weight multiview fusion module takes the initial mesh as the anchor position and effectively assembles the partial refined depth maps.

3.1 Mesh, Depth, Disparity Initialization

Given a set of N-view images $\{\mathbf{I}^1, \ldots, \mathbf{I}^N\}$, an initial human mesh $\mathbf{m}_c$ is predicted by DoubleField [51] and rendered as the coarse depth maps $\{\mathbf{D}_c^1, \ldots, \mathbf{D}_c^N\}$ for N input viewpoints. These depth maps are further transformed into the disparity maps as they are necessary for stereo matching. Without loss of generality, let m and n be the index of two neighboring views. To obtain the coarse disparity map $\mathbf{x}_c$ from the view m to its neighboring view n, we take the depth map $\mathbf{D}_c^m$ of the view m and compute disparity at the pixel position $o = (i, j)$ as following:

$$\mathbf{x}_c(o) = \pi^n \left((\pi^m)^{-1} \left([o, \mathbf{D}_c^m(o)]^{\mathrm{T}} \right) \right) - o \tag{1}$$

where $(\pi^m)^{-1}$ transforms the points from the depth map $\mathbf{D}_c^m$ to the world coordinate system and π^n projects the points in the world coordinate system to the image coordinate system.

Since the initial disparity maps are calculated from a coarse human mesh, the large displacement and occlusion region issues can be largely alleviated. As will be presented shortly, these disparity maps are further refined by a Diffusion-based Stereo to obtain high-quality depth maps for each input viewpoint.

3.2 Diffusion-based Stereo for Disparity Refinement

Existing stereo methods [9,20,23,32,62,67–69] adopt 3D/4D cost volumes to predict disparity map in a discrete manner, which is difficult to achieve sub-pixel level flow estimation. To overcome this limitation, we propose a diffusion-based stereo such that the stereo network can learn a continuous flow during the iterative process. Specifically, our diffusion-based stereo contains a forward process and a reverse process to obtain the final high-quality disparity map. In the forward process, the initial disparity maps are diffused to the maps with noise distribution. In the reverse process, the high-quality disparity maps will be recovered from the noisy maps with the condition of several stereo-related features. In the following, we give a brief introduction of generic diffusion models and then introduce our solution to combine the continuity of diffusion models and the learning-based iterative stereo. Moreover, we also present a multi-level network structure to resolve the memory issues for high-resolution images input.

3.2.1 Generic Diffusion Model

The standard T-step diffusion model [24] contains a forward process and a reverse process. The forward process is about gradually adding Gaussian noise to the original input $\mathbf{y}_0$ in each step t such that they are turned into the pure noise $\mathbf{y}_T$ at step T. The reverse process is about recovering $\mathbf{y}_0$ from the noise $\mathbf{y}_T$ iteratively, which can be regarded as denoising. More formally, the diffusion model can be written as two Markov Chains:

$$q(\mathbf{y}_{1:T}|\mathbf{y}_0) = \prod_{t=1}^{T} q(\mathbf{y}_t|\mathbf{y}_{t-1}), \tag{2}$$

$$q(\mathbf{y}_t|\mathbf{y}_{t-1}) = \mathcal{N}(\sqrt{1-\beta_t}\mathbf{y}_{t-1}, \beta_t I) \tag{3}$$

$$p_\theta(\mathbf{y}_{0:T}|\mathbf{s}) = p(\mathbf{y}_T) \prod_{t=1}^{T} p_\theta(\mathbf{y}_{t-1}|\mathbf{y}_t, \mathbf{s}), \tag{4}$$

where $q(\mathbf{y}_{1:T}|\mathbf{y}_0)$ is the forward function, $q(\mathbf{y}_t|\mathbf{y}_{t-1})$ is the diffusion kernel representing the way to add noise, $\mathcal{N}$ the normal distribution, $\mathbf{I}$ the identical matrix, $p_\theta()$ the reverse function which adopts a denoising network $\mathcal{F}_\theta$ to denoise $\mathbf{y}_T$ and $\mathbf{s}$ the additional condition. When $T \to \infty$, the forward and the reverse process can be seen as a continuous process or stochastic differential equations [54], which is a natural form for continuous flow estimation. As validated in previous work [54], injecting Gaussian noise into the parameter updates makes the iterative process more continuous and can avoid collapses into local minimal. In this work, we will show that, such a powerful generative tool can be also leveraged to produce continuous flows for the human-centric stereo task.

Compared with the generic diffusion models, two task-specific designs are adopted in our diffusion-based stereo: i) a new diffusion kernel is used in consideration that the stereo flow estimation is not purely a generative task; ii) stereo-related features and supervisions are involved in the reverse process to ensure the color consistency and epipolar constraints.

3.2.2 Disparity Forward Process

In diffusion-based stereo, the forward process gradually transforms the distribution of disparity flows to the noisy distribution. Specifically, the input $\mathbf{y}_0$ of the diffusion model in our case is the residual disparity $\hat{\mathbf{y}}_0$ between the ground truth disparity maps $\hat{\mathbf{x}}$ and the coarse disparity maps $\mathbf{x}_c$, i.e., $\hat{\mathbf{y}}_0 = \hat{\mathbf{x}} - \mathbf{x}_c$. Different from existing generative diffusion model for image synthesis which utilizes $\sqrt{1-\beta_t}$ to gradually reduce the scale of $\mathbf{y}_{t-1}$, we design a diffusion kernel to preserve the scale of $\mathbf{y}_{t-1}$ and linearly drifts $\mathbf{y}_0$ to $\mathbf{y}_t$, i.e., Eqn. (3) is rewritten as:

$$q(\mathbf{y}_t|\mathbf{y}_{t-1}) = \mathcal{N}(\mathbf{y}_t|\mathbf{y}_{t-1} - \alpha_t\mathbf{y}_0, \alpha_t\mathbf{I}), \tag{5}$$

where α_t is the parameter to scale the noise. Based on this new diffusion kernel, the disparity forward process gradually adds noise to the ground truth residual disparity $\hat{\mathbf{y}}_0$ using Eq. (2) and (5). In our experiments, we find our diffusion kernel makes the reverse process more stable and efficiently reduces the needed number of iterative steps at inference. Derivation of the forward process under our new kernel is similar with [24] and can be found in Supp.Mat.

3.2.3 Stereo-Conditioned Reverse Process

The reverse process of diffusion-based stereo aims at recovering the residual disparity $\hat{\mathbf{y}}_0$ from the noise $\mathbf{y}_T$ using Eq. (4). In this process, a diffusion stereo

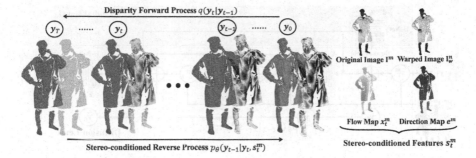

Fig. 3. Illustration of the forward process and the reverse process in our diffusion-based stereo. In the forward process, the initial residual disparity maps $\mathbf{y}_T$ are diffused to the noisy maps $\mathbf{y}_0$. In the reverse process, the high-quality residual disparity maps will be recovered from the noisy maps with the condition of several stereo-related features $\mathbf{s}_t^m$.

network acts as the denoising network $\mathcal{F}_\theta$ in Eq. (4) by taking $\mathbf{y}_t$ and $\mathbf{s}$ as inputs and predict $\tilde{\mathbf{y}}_0$.

As the diffusion kernel also influences the reverse process, the denoising process of our network is different from the generic one under our new kernel. Given the kernel in Eq. (5), the formulation of each step in the reverse process can be written as:

$$p_\theta(\mathbf{y}_{t-1}|\mathbf{y}_t,\mathbf{s}) = \mathcal{N}(\mathbf{y}_{t-1}|\mu_\theta(\mathbf{y}_t,\gamma_t,\mathbf{s}),\sigma_t^2\mathbf{I}), \qquad (6)$$

where $\gamma_t = \sum_{i=1}^t \alpha_i$, $\sigma_t^2 = \frac{\alpha_t\gamma_{t-1}}{\gamma_t}$, and $\mu_\theta()$ is the prediction process of the denoising network $\mathcal{F}_\theta$. Moreover, we substitute the predicted $\tilde{\mathbf{y}}_0$ into the posterior distribution of $q(\mathbf{y}_{t-1}|\mathbf{y}_t,\mathbf{y}_0)$ to represent the mean of $p_\theta(\mathbf{y}_{t-1}|\mathbf{y}_t)$:

$$\mu_\theta(\mathbf{y}_t,\gamma_t,\mathbf{s}) = \frac{\alpha_t}{\gamma_t}\tilde{\mathbf{y}}_0 + \frac{\gamma_{t-1}}{\gamma_t}\mathbf{y}_t. \qquad (7)$$

In this way, the whole reverse process can be formulated as:

$$\mathbf{y}_{t-1} \leftarrow \frac{\alpha_t}{\gamma_t}\tilde{\mathbf{y}}_0 + \frac{\gamma_{t-1}}{\gamma_t}\mathbf{y}_t + \frac{\alpha_t\gamma_{t-1}}{\gamma_t}\epsilon_t, \epsilon_t \sim \mathcal{N}(\mathbf{0},\mathbf{1}). \qquad (8)$$

Since the disparity refinement is not a fully generative process, the diffusion stereo network $\mathcal{F}_\theta$ takes additional conditions as inputs to recover the high quality disparity flows. In our solution, four types of stereo-related maps (Fig. 3 Right) act as the additional conditions $\mathbf{s}$ in Eq. (4) to ensure the color consistency and epipolar constraints at each step of the reverse process:

1) The original image $\mathbf{I}^m$ of the view m;

2) The warped image $\mathbf{I}_w^n$ of view n, which is obtained by transforming pixels of $\mathbf{I}^n$ using current flow $\mathbf{x}_t^m = \mathbf{x}^m + \mathbf{y}_t$:

$$\mathbf{I}_w^n(\mathbf{o}) = \mathbf{I}^n(\mathbf{x}_t^m(\mathbf{o}) + \mathbf{o}). \qquad (9)$$

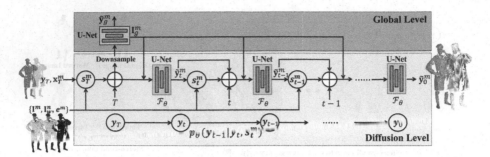

Fig. 4. The proposed multi-level stereo network structure. A global network $\mathcal{F}_g$ is combined with the diffusion stereo network $\mathcal{F}_\theta$ so that our method can leverage information at both global and diffusion levels to predict high-quality depths.

3) The current flow map $\mathbf{x}_t^m$;

4) The direction map $\mathbf{e}^m$ of epipolar line, which is computed as:

$$\mathbf{e}^m = (\dot{\mathbf{x}}_c^m - \mathbf{x}_c^m)/\|\dot{\mathbf{x}}_c^m - \mathbf{x}_c^m\|_2, \tag{10}$$

where $\dot{\mathbf{x}}_c^m$ is the shifted flow map transformed based on the coarse depth map $\mathbf{D}_c^m$ and a fixed shift β:

$$\dot{\mathbf{x}}_c^m(\boldsymbol{o}) = \pi^n((\pi^m)^{-1}([\boldsymbol{o}, \mathbf{D}_c^m(\boldsymbol{o}) + \beta]^T)) - \boldsymbol{o}. \tag{11}$$

Among the above four conditions, $\mathbf{I}^m$ and $\mathbf{I}_w^n$ encourage the network to be aware of color consistency, while $\mathbf{x}_t^m$ and $\mathbf{e}^m$ provide the hints about the flow movement to network for better predictions. We condition the network by concatenating the above stereo-related maps as $\boldsymbol{s}_t^m = \bigoplus(\mathbf{I}^m, \mathbf{I}_w^n, \mathbf{x}_t^m, \mathbf{e}^m)$. The conditions $\boldsymbol{s}_t^m$ are further concatenated with $(\mathbf{y}_t^m, t)$ and fed into the diffusion stereo network. Additionally, we also constrain the network output map $\boldsymbol{R}$ to only one channel such that the predicted residual flow $\widetilde{\mathbf{y}}_t = \mathbf{e}^m \cdot \boldsymbol{R}$ is forced to move along the epipolar line.

When the reverse process is finished, the final flow $\mathbf{x}^m + \widetilde{\mathbf{y}}_0^m$ will be transformed back to the refined depth map $\mathbf{D}_f^m$ of the view m using the inverse formulation of Eq. (1).

3.2.4   Multi-level Network Structure

For high quality human reconstruction, it is essential to leverage high-resolution input images. When applying the above diffusion stereo network, the memory issues arise when high-resolution images (4K in our experiments) are taken as inputs. Inspired by PIFuHD [50], we tackle this issue using a multi-level network structure, in which a global network $\mathcal{F}_g$ is combined with the diffusion stereo network $\mathcal{F}_\theta$. In this way, $\mathcal{F}_g$ and $\mathcal{F}_\theta$ can produce the disparity flow at the global level and the diffusion level, respectively.

As shown in Fig. 4, at the global level, both the coarse initial flow $\mathbf{x}_c^m$ and the conditional stereo features $\boldsymbol{s}^m$ are downsampled to the resolution of 512×512 and then fed into the global network $\mathcal{F}_g$. which directly predicts a low-resolution residual flow $\widetilde{\mathbf{y}}_g^m$. Note that the flow estimation at the global level is not a diffusion process but it learns global features which contains human semantic information. At the diffusion level, we adopt the last image features $\mathbf{I}_g^m$ from the global network as an additional condition for the diffusion stereo network. Thus, the stereo-related features in the local-level network is modified to $\mathbf{s}_t^m = \bigoplus(\mathbf{I}^m, \mathbf{I}_w^n, \mathbf{x}_t^m, \mathbf{e}^m, \mathbf{I}_g^m)$. Benefiting from the multi-level structure, the memory issues can be largely overcomed as the diffusion stereo network can be trained in a patch-based manner. Moreover, with the guidance of the global feature $\mathbf{I}_g^m$, our diffusion stereo network can focus more on the recovery of fine details.

3.2.5   Training of Diffusion-based Stereo

Global Level. We downsample the ground truth residual flow to the resolution of 512 and train the global network $\mathcal{F}_g$ with the global loss $\mathcal{L}_g$:

$$\mathcal{L}_g = \frac{1}{HW} \sum_{i=1}^{H} \sum_{j=1}^{W} \|\widetilde{\mathbf{y}}_g(i,j) - \mathbf{y}_0(i,j)\|^2, \tag{12}$$

The global loss encourages the network to learn human semantic features for the flow estimation.

Diffusion Level. Following [10], we generate training samples by randomly selecting a time step t and diffusing the ground truth residual flow $\mathbf{y}_0$ to $\mathbf{y}_t$ using:

$$q(\mathbf{y}_t|\mathbf{y}_0) = \mathcal{N}(\mathbf{y}_t|(1-\gamma_t)\mathbf{y}_0, \gamma_t \mathbf{I}). \tag{13}$$

Then we adopt diffusion loss $\mathcal{L}_d$ to train our diffusion stereo network $\mathcal{F}_\theta$ at the t-th step:

$$\mathcal{L}_d = \frac{1}{HW} \sum_{i=1}^{H} \sum_{j=1}^{W} \|(\mathcal{F}_\theta(\mathbf{y}_t, \mathbf{s}_t, t))(i,j) - \mathbf{y}_0(i,j)\|_2^2. \tag{14}$$

3.3   Light-Weight Multi-view Fusion

In this section, we propose a light-weight multi-view hybrid fusion to fuse the refined depth maps $\mathbf{D}_f^1, ..., \mathbf{D}_f^n$ and the coarse human mesh $\mathbf{m}_c$ to reconstruct the final model. Before fusion, we first remove the depth boundaries using an erosion kernel and transform each refined depth map $\mathbf{D}_f^i$ to a point cloud $\mathbf{p}^i = (\pi^i)^{-1}(\mathbf{D}_f^i)$. Since calibration error is inevitable in real-world data, the refined depth maps estimated from multi-view may not be accurately aligned. To handle this issue, we utilize non-rigid ICP to align the depth point cloud $\mathbf{p}^i$ and the point cloud $\mathbf{p}^c$ of the coarse mesh, where the coarse point cloud serves as the anchor model for subsequent alignment. In our non-rigid ICP, the optimization objectives $\mathcal{L}_{icp} = \mathcal{L}_d + \mathcal{L}_s$ consist of the data term $\mathcal{L}_d$ and the smooth term $\mathcal{L}_s$, which are defined as following:

$$\mathcal{L}_d = \sum_{i=1}^{n} \sum_{j=i+1}^{n} \sum_{(a,b)\in\tilde{\mathbf{N}}^{i,j}} \|\tilde{\mathbf{p}}_a^i - \tilde{\mathbf{p}}_b^j\|^2 + \lambda_d \sum_{i=1}^{n} \sum_{(a,b)\in\tilde{\mathbf{N}}_c^i} \|\tilde{\mathbf{p}}_a^i - \mathbf{p}_b^c\|^2 \qquad (15)$$

$$\mathcal{L}_s = \lambda_s \sum_{i=1}^{n} \sum_{(a,b)\in\mathbf{N_i}} \|\tilde{\mathbf{d}}_a^i - \tilde{\mathbf{d}}_h^i\|^2 / \|\mathbf{p}_a^i - \mathbf{n}_b^i\|^2 , \qquad (16)$$

where $\mathbf{d}^i$ is the displacement of the depth point cloud $\mathbf{p}^i$, $\mathbf{N}$ is the set of the searched neighborhood correspondence. We adopt the nearest neighbour algorithm to search correspondence and the threshold of search radius is 2 mm.

After optimization, the final point cloud $\mathbf{p}^f$ is the union of optimized depth point cloud $\tilde{\mathbf{p}}^i$ and the coarse point cloud $\mathbf{p}^c$, while the final mesh can be reconstructed from the final point cloud $\mathbf{p}^f$ using Poisson Reconstruction [31].

Table 1. Qualitative comparisons of stereo matching on the THuman2.0 dataset.

Method	AvgErr			1/2pix (%)			1pix (%)			3pix (%)		
	20°	30°	45°	20°	30°	45°	20°	30°	45°	20°	30°	45°
Stereo-PIFu [26]	12.03	14.57	17.92	–	–	–	–	–	–	–	–	–
Raft-Stereo [37]	11.79	13.95	15.42	–	–	–	–	–	–	–	–	–
Stereo-PIFu(w. $\mathbf{D}_c$)	1.052	1.411	2.248	45.6	32.8	18.6	68.1	56.1	35.4	92.2	87.9	77.2
Raft-Stereo (w. $\mathbf{D}_c$)	0.812	1.020	1.567	54.0	44.1	26.1	74.9	68.6	48.0	95.1	93.4	89.7
Our method(w./o. diff.)	0.799	0.933	1.448	56.2	47.2	28.2	76.9	71.6	51.1	95.4	94.4	89.4
Our method(Origin. diff.)	0.618	0.704	0.881	62.5	57.8	52.9	85.2	81.5	77.2	97.5	96.7	94.8
Our method	**0.483**	**0.515**	**0.632**	**71.3**	**70.0**	**67.6**	**90.6**	**89.0**	**85.9**	**98.6**	**97.9**	**96.6**

4   Experiment

4.1   Implementation Details

In our implementation, we adopt a U-Net [46] model which is similar with [12] as the structure of the global network $\mathcal{F}_g$ and the diffusion network $\mathcal{F}_\theta$. The T in our diffusion model is 30 which is much less than the original model in image generation tasks. For the other diffusion parameters including α_t, γ_t and more implementation details, please refer to the Supplementary Material.

Training Data Preparation. We collect 300 models from Twindom [56] and render images pairs for training. We first render images and depth maps with 4K resolution densely from 360° angles. We then run DoubleField [51] on the images of 8 even-distributed views to predict the SDF volume with a resolution of 512^3 and further retrieve the coarse human mesh using marching cube. During the training of our diffusion-based stereo network, we randomly select two views from the rendered images of the same model and constrain their angle in the interval of $[20, 50]$. We also compute occlusion regions between two views and filter out bad parts to avoid unstable training.

Evaluation Data Preparation. We randomly pick 300 models from the THUman2.0 [64] dataset for evaluation. Person images and depth maps with 4K resolution are rendered from 360 angles.

4.2 Comparisons on Stereo

We quantitatively and qualitatively compare our diffusion-based stereo network with the state-of-the-art stereo method RAFT-Stereo [37] and the stereo matching network in StereoPIFu [26] based on 3D convolution. For each synthetic human model, we select 4 pairs of views with the view angle randomly chosen from $(20°, 30°, 45°)$ and evaluate the performance of stereo. We also prepare the initial disparity flow based on the coarse mesh predicted by DoubleField [51] for RAFT-Stereo and StereoPIFu. For quantitative comparisons, we follow RAFT-Stereo [37] to adopt the same metrics, i.e., the average error in pixels and the ratio of pixel error in three levels (1/2 pix, 1 pix and 3 pix). As shown in Tab. 1, our method significantly beats the other two methods in all metrics and achieves the best performance especially at the sub-pixel level. There are 71.3, 70.0, and 67.6 percent of our disparity estimation results within 1/2 pixel error for view angles of $20°$, $30°$, and $45°$, respectively. More importantly, when two views become sparser, the sub-pixel level performance of our method remains very strong (only a decrease of 3.7%) compared with the other two methods (decrease of 27% and 27.9%), which validates the efficiency of our diffusion stereo network and the powerful ability of diffusion model for continuous disparity flow estimation. We also compare our method with the original RAFT-Stereo and StereoPIFu without initial value $\mathbf{D}_c$. However, they all fail to estimate disparity flow with sparse-view inputs and result in large average errors (≥ 10 pixel). Hence, we only report the average error in pixels for StereoPIFu and RAFT-Stereo under this setting. We also report qualitative results on THuman2.0 dataset in Fig. 5 and the Supp.Doc. Compared with StereoPIFu and RAFT-Stereo, our method recovers more geometry details and the quality of depth is even competitive to the ground truth. Such a high-quality depth estimation is also benefited from our diffusion-based stereo and the design of multi-level network structure, as demonstrated in our ablation study.

Table 2. Quantitative human geometry reconstruction results.

Method	THuman2.0 (8 views)				
	Chamfer	P2S	1 mm(%)	2 mm(%)	5 mm(%)
PIFuHD [50]	3.018	2.509	21.0	58.9	90.0
StereoPIFu [26]	2.629	2.251	26.0	64.7	91.7
DoubleField [51]	2.879	2.389	23.2	61.6	90.8
Our method	**1.198**	**1.258**	**68.1**	**91.9**	**96.6**

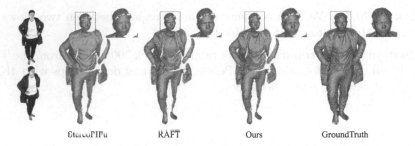

| StereoPIFu | RAFT | Ours | GroundTruth |

Fig. 5. Comparison in terms of depth estimation quality. Compared to state-of-the-art method, ours can produce more geometric details, which is important for subsequent mesh reconstruction.

4.3 Comparisons on Human Reconstruction

We also compare our method with the state-of-the-art implicit-based human reconstruction methods, including DoubleField [51], PIFuHD [50], and StereoPIFu [26]. Since PIFuHD focuses on single-view reconstruction and StereoPIFu is mainly proposed for binocular stereo in their original papers, we extend them by adopting the attention mechanism in DeepMultiCap [70] to fuse multi-view inputs. We train each method on the same Twindom dataset with the same learning setup. We select 8 views with the view angle of 45° as inputs and quantitatively evaluate the geometry reconstruction using the Chamfer distance and P2S metrics (mm). To fully demonstrate the high-quality reconstruction performances of our method, we also report the ratio of points in the reconstructed model with different error thresholds (1 mm, 2 mm, and 5 mm). As shown in Table 2, our method achieves the best reconstruction quality again. For high-

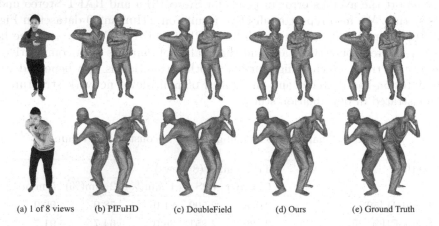

| (a) 1 of 8 views | (b) PIFuHD | (c) DoubleField | (d) Ours | (e) Ground Truth |

Fig. 6. Comparison in terms of reconstruction quality. The human model reconstructed by our method shows significantly higher quality than those reconstructed by the baseline methods.

precise reconstruction areas (i.e., within ≤ 1 mm), our method outperforms the previous methods by more than 42%, Compared with the coarse human model provided by DoubleField, our method reduces the Chamfer distance and P2S by 54.4% and 44.1%, respectively, which proves the efficiency of our conditional stereo network in preserving the color consistency and epipolar constraint under the sparse-view setting. Moreover, for the reconstruction areas with larger errors (≤ 5mm), our method also has the best performance since the reconstruction of occlusion regions are improved by our light-weight multi-view fusion. We also show the qualitative results in Fig. 6, where our method achieves much higher quality of reconstruction in comparison with other methods.

4.4 Ablation Study

Different Coarse Model. Our method relies on the coarse human model for diffusion-based stereo. Since the reverse process manually adds noises to the coarse model, our method can handle small errors in the initial depth. As shown in Fig. 7(b), even using the visual hull (VH) from 8 views as the initial coarse model, our method can still recover details in visible region.

Diffusion Model. To validate the key components of our multi-level diffusion stereo network, we remove the diffusion model from the stereo network. Such a modified network can be regarded as an iterative refinement model which is similar with Raft-Stereo [37]. Table 1 reports the quantitative results and shows that the modified network can only achieve the performances competitive to Raft-Stereo [37], which validates that the diffusion model is one of the key components in our diffusion-based stereo.

| Original
1000 Steps | Ours
10 Steps | Ours
30 Steps | Ours
50 Steps |
| (a) |

Visual Hull   PIFu

PIFuHD   (b)   DoubleField

Fig. 7. (a) Ablation study of diffusion kernel and steps. The left image shows the unstable noisy result obtained by using the original diffusion kernel in some cases. The right images show the results based on our diffusion kernel in different number of reverse step. **(b) Results using different coarse model as the initial value.** In each image group, the left shows the coarse model and the right illustrates the diffusion results.

Diffusion Kernel and Step. As mentioned in Sect. 3.2.2, we adopt a different diffusion kernel for faster and more accurate disparity flow estimation. To validate our new kernel, we report results under the different kernels in Table 1. For the method using the original diffusion kernel, we adopt a 1000-steps diffusion model and the same learning setup to train the network. As shown in Table 1, the stereo network based on the original diffusion kernel is not as accurate as ours. In addition, we found that the original diffusion kernel is not stable for stereo matching in our experiments. As shown in Fig. 7, it generates noisy depth maps in some cases. We also ablate our diffusion model with different steps and illustrate results in Fig. 7. Our method is more efficient in the reverse process and can recover details in only 10 steps. For time cost, our method takes about 50 ms in one forward step and predicts the depth maps of 8 views in 12s with 30 diffusion steps, which is much faster than the original 1000-step diffusion model.

5   Discussion

Conclusion. We introduced DiffuStereo, a novel system for reconstructing high-quality 3D human models from sparse-view RGB images. With an initial estimate of the human model, our system leverages a novel iterative stereo network based on diffusion models to produce highly accurate depth maps from every two neighboring views. This diffusion-based stereo network is carefully designed to handle sparse-view, high-resolution inputs. The high-quality depth maps can be assembled to generate the final 3D model. Compared to existing methods, ours can reconstruct sharper geometrical details and achieve higher accuracy.

Limitation. The main limitation of our method is the dependence on DoubleField to estimate an initial human model. In addition, our method cannot reconstruct the geometric details in invisible regions due to the lack of observation in our sparse-view setting.

Acknowledgements. This paper is supported by National Key R&D Program of China (2021ZD0113501) and the NSFC project No. 62125107 and No. 61827805.

References

1. 4DViews. http://www.4dviews.com/
2. 8i. https://8i.com/
3. Alldieck, T., Magnor, M., Xu, W., Theobalt, C., Pons-Moll, G.: Detailed human avatars from monocular video. In: 3DV, September 2018
4. Alldieck, T., Magnor, M., Xu, W., Theobalt, C., Pons-Moll, G.: Video based reconstruction of 3D people models. In: CVPR, June 2018
5. Alldieck, T., Pons-Moll, G., Theobalt, C., Magnor, M.: Tex2Shape: detailed full human body geometry from a single image. In: ICCV, pp. 2293–2303 (2019)
6. Barnes, C., Shechtman, E., Finkelstein, A., Goldman, D.B.: PatchMatch: a randomized correspondence algorithm for structural image editing. ACM TOG **28**, 24 (2009)

7. Bogo, F., Black, M.J., Loper, M., Romero, J.: Detailed full-body reconstructions of moving people from monocular RGB-D sequences. In: ICCV, pp. 2300–2308 (2015)
8. Bradley, D., Popa, T., Sheffer, A., Heidrich, W., Boubekeur, T.: Markerless garment capture. ACM TOG **27**(3), 1–9 (2008)
9. Chang, J.R., Chen, Y.S.: Pyramid stereo matching network. In: CVPR, pp. 5410–5418 (2018)
10. Chen, N., Zhang, Y., Zen, H., Weiss, R.J., Norouzi, M., Chan, W.: WaveGrad: estimating gradients for waveform generation. In: ICLR (2021)
11. Collet, A., et al.: High-quality streamable free-viewpoint video. ACM TOG **34**(4), 69 (2015)
12. Dhariwal, P., Nichol, A.: Diffusion models beat GANs on image synthesis. In: NeurIPS, vol. 34 (2021)
13. Dou, M., et al.: Motion2Fusion: real-time volumetric performance capture. ACM TOG **36**(6), 246:1–246:16 (2017)
14. Dou, M., et al.: Fusion4D: real-time performance capture of challenging scenes. ACM TOG **35**(4), 1–13 (2016)
15. Fanello, S.R., et al.: UltraStereo: efficient learning-based matching for active stereo systems. In: CVPR, pp. 6535–6544 (2017)
16. Gabeur, V., Franco, J.S., Martin, X., Schmid, C., Rogez, G.: Moulding humans: non-parametric 3D human shape estimation from single images. In: ICCV, pp. 2232–2241 (2019)
17. Geiger, A., Lenz, P., Urtasun, R.: Are we ready for autonomous driving? the kitti vision benchmark suite. In: CVPR (2012)
18. Gilbert, A., Volino, M., Collomosse, J., Hilton, A.: Volumetric performance capture from minimal camera viewpoints. In: Ferrari, V., Hebert, M., Sminchisescu, C., Weiss, Y. (eds.) ECCV 2018. LNCS, vol. 11215, pp. 591–607. Springer, Cham (2018). https://doi.org/10.1007/978-3-030-01252-6_35
19. Guo, K., et al.: The relightables: volumetric performance capture of humans with realistic relighting. ACM TOG **38**(6), 1–19 (2019)
20. Guo, X., Yang, K., Yang, W., Wang, X., Li, H.: Group-wise correlation stereo network. In: CVPR, pp. 3273–3282 (2019)
21. Hannah, M.J.: Computer Matching of Areas in Stereo Images. Stanford University (1974)
22. He, T., Xu, Y., Saito, S., Soatto, S., Tung, T.: Arch++: animation-ready clothed human reconstruction revisited. In: ICCV, pp. 11046–11056 (2021)
23. Hirschmuller, H.: Stereo processing by semiglobal matching and mutual information. IEEE TPAMI **30**(2), 328–341 (2008)
24. Ho, J., Jain, A., Abbeel, P.: Denoising diffusion probabilistic models. In: NeurIPS, vol. 33, pp. 6840–6851 (2020)
25. Ho, J., Saharia, C., Chan, W., Fleet, D.J., Norouzi, M., Salimans, T.: Cascaded diffusion models for high fidelity image generation. arXiv preprint arXiv:2106.15282 (2021)
26. Hong, Y., Zhang, J., Jiang, B., Guo, Y., Liu, L., Bao, H.: StereoPIFu: depth aware clothed human digitization via stereo vision. In: CVPR (2021)
27. Huang, Z., et al.: Deep volumetric video from very sparse multi-view performance capture. In: Ferrari, V., Hebert, M., Sminchisescu, C., Weiss, Y. (eds.) ECCV 2018. LNCS, vol. 11220, pp. 351–369. Springer, Cham (2018). https://doi.org/10.1007/978-3-030-01270-0_21
28. Huang, Z., Xu, Y., Lassner, C., Li, H., Tung, T.: Arch: animatable reconstruction of clothed humans. In: CVPR (2020)

29. Jensen, R., Dahl, A., Vogiatzis, G., Tola, E., Aanæs, H.: Large scale multi-view stereopsis evaluation. In: 2014 IEEE Conference on Computer Vision and Pattern Recognition, pp. 406–413. IEEE (2014)
30. Joo, H., et al.: Panoptic studio: a massively multiview system for social motion capture. In: ICCV (2015)
31. Kazhdan, M., Bolitho, M., Hoppe, H.: Poisson surface reconstruction. In: ESGP, vol. 7 (2006)
32. Kendall, A., et al.: End-to-end learning of geometry and context for deep stereo regression. In: ICCV, pp. 66–75 (2017)
33. Kolmogorov, V.: Convergent tree-reweighted message passing for energy minimization. IEEE TPAMI 28(10), 1568–1583 (2006)
34. Li, H., et al.: SRDiff: single image super-resolution with diffusion probabilistic models. Neurocomputing 479, 47–59 (2022)
35. Li, J., et al.: Practical stereo matching via cascaded recurrent network with adaptive correlation. In: Proceedings of the IEEE/CVF Conference on Computer Vision and Pattern Recognition, pp. 16263–16272 (2022)
36. Li, Z., Yu, T., Zheng, Z., Guo, K., Liu, Y.: POSEFusion: pose-guided selective fusion for single-view human volumetric capture. In: CVPR (2021)
37. Lipson, L., Teed, Z., Deng, J.: Raft-stereo: multilevel recurrent field transforms for stereo matching. In: 3DV, pp. 218–227 (2021)
38. Liu, Y., Cao, X., Dai, Q., Xu, W.: Continuous depth estimation for multi-view stereo. In: CVPR, pp. 2121–2128 (2009)
39. Liu, Y., Dai, Q., Xu, W.: A point-cloud-based multiview stereo algorithm for free-viewpoint video. IEEE TVCG 16(3), 407–418 (2009)
40. Mayer, N., et al.: A large dataset to train convolutional networks for disparity, optical flow, and scene flow estimation. In: CVPR, pp. 4040–4048 (2016)
41. Menze, M., Geiger, A.: Object scene flow for autonomous vehicles. In: CVPR (2015)
42. Natsume, R., et al.: SiCloPe: silhouette-based clothed people. In: CVPR. pp. 4480–4490 (2019)
43. Nichol, A.Q., Dhariwal, P.: Improved denoising diffusion probabilistic models. In: ICML, pp. 8162–8171 (2021)
44. Pons-Moll, G., Pujades, S., Hu, S., Black, M.J.: ClothCap: seamless 4D clothing capture and retargeting. ACM TOG 36(4), 1–15 (2017)
45. Rombach, R., Blattmann, A., Lorenz, D., Esser, P., Ommer, B.: High-resolution image synthesis with latent diffusion models. arXiv preprint arXiv:2112.10752 (2021)
46. Ronneberger, O., Fischer, P., Brox, T.: U-Net: convolutional networks for biomedical image segmentation. In: Navab, N., Hornegger, J., Wells, W.M., Frangi, A.F. (eds.) MICCAI 2015. LNCS, vol. 9351, pp. 234–241. Springer, Cham (2015). https://doi.org/10.1007/978-3-319-24574-4_28
47. Saharia, C., et al.: Palette: image-to-image diffusion models. In: NeurIPS Workshop (2021)
48. Saharia, C., Ho, J., Chan, W., Salimans, T., Fleet, D.J., Norouzi, M.: Image super-resolution via iterative refinement. arXiv:2104.07636 (2021)
49. Saito, S., Huang, Z., Natsume, R., Morishima, S., Kanazawa, A., Li, H.: PIFu: pixel-aligned implicit function for high-resolution clothed human digitization. In: ICCV, pp. 2304–2314 (2019)
50. Saito, S., Simon, T., Saragih, J., Joo, H.: PIFuHD: multi-level pixel-aligned implicit function for high-resolution 3D human digitization. In: CVPR, pp. 84–93 (2020)
51. Shao, R., et al.: DoubleField: bridging the neural surface and radiance fields for high-fidelity human reconstruction and rendering. In: CVPR (2022)

52. Sohl-Dickstein, J., Weiss, E., Maheswaranathan, N., Ganguli, S.: Deep unsupervised learning using nonequilibrium thermodynamics. In: ICML, pp. 2256–2265 (2015)
53. Song, J., Meng, C., Ermon, S.: Denoising diffusion implicit models. In: International Conference on Learning Representations, ICLR (2021)
54. Song, Y., Sohl-Dickstein, J., Kingma, D.P., Kumar, A., Ermon, S., Poole, B.: Score-based generative modeling through stochastic differential equations. In: International Conference on Learning Representations, ICLR (2021)
55. Starck, J., Hilton, A.: Surface capture for performance-based animation. IEEE Comput. Graphics Appl. **27**(3), 21–31 (2007)
56. Twindom (2020). https://web.twindom.com
57. Vlasic, D., et al.: Dynamic shape capture using multi-view photometric stereo. ACM TOG **28**(5), 174:1–174:11 (2009)
58. Wang, F., Galliani, S., Vogel, C., Pollefeys, M.: IterMVS: iterative probability estimation for efficient multi-view stereo. In: Proceedings of the IEEE/CVF Conference on Computer Vision and Pattern Recognition, pp. 8606–8615 (2022)
59. Wang, L., Zhao, X., Yu, T., Wang, S., Liu, Y.: NormalGAN: learning detailed 3D human from a single RGB-D image. In: Vedaldi, A., Bischof, H., Brox, T., Frahm, J.-M. (eds.) ECCV 2020. LNCS, vol. 12365, pp. 430–446. Springer, Cham (2020). https://doi.org/10.1007/978-3-030-58565-5_26
60. Wang, S., Li, B., Dai, Y.: Efficient multi-view stereo by iterative dynamic cost volume. In: Proceedings of the IEEE/CVF Conference on Computer Vision and Pattern Recognition, pp. 8655–8664 (2022)
61. Wu, C., Varanasi, K., Liu, Y., Seidel, H., Theobalt, C.: Shading-based dynamic shape refinement from multi-view video under general illumination. In: ICCV, pp. 1108–1115 (2011)
62. Yao, Y., Luo, Z., Li, S., Fang, T., Quan, L.: MVSNet: depth inference for unstructured multi-view stereo. In: Ferrari, V., Hebert, M., Sminchisescu, C., Weiss, Y. (eds.) ECCV 2018. LNCS, vol. 11212, pp. 785–801. Springer, Cham (2018). https://doi.org/10.1007/978-3-030-01237-3_47
63. Yu, T., et al.: BodyFusion: real-time capture of human motion and surface geometry using a single depth camera. In: ICCV, pp. 910–919. IEEE (2017)
64. Yu, T., Zheng, Z., Guo, K., Liu, P., Dai, Q., Liu, Y.: Function4D: real-time human volumetric capture from very sparse consumer RGBD sensors. In: CVPR, pp. 5746–5756 (2021)
65. Yu, T., et al.: DoubleFusion: real-time capture of human performances with inner body shapes from a single depth sensor. In: CVPR, pp. 7287–7296. IEEE (2018)
66. Zabih, R., Woodfill, J.: Non-parametric local transforms for computing visual correspondence. In: Eklundh, J.-O. (ed.) ECCV 1994. LNCS, vol. 801, pp. 151–158. Springer, Heidelberg (1994). https://doi.org/10.1007/BFb0028345
67. Zhang, F., Prisacariu, V., Yang, R., Torr, P.H.: GA-Net: guided aggregation net for end-to-end stereo matching. In: CVPR, pp. 185–194 (2019)
68. Zhang, F., Qi, X., Yang, R., Prisacariu, V., Wah, B., Torr, P.: Domain-invariant stereo matching networks. In: Vedaldi, A., Bischof, H., Brox, T., Frahm, J.-M. (eds.) ECCV 2020. LNCS, vol. 12347, pp. 420–439. Springer, Cham (2020). https://doi.org/10.1007/978-3-030-58536-5_25
69. Zhang, Y., et al.: Adaptive unimodal cost volume filtering for deep stereo matching. In: AAAI, vol. 34, pp. 12926–12934 (2020)
70. Zheng, Y., et al.: DeepMultiCap: performance capture of multiple characters using sparse multiview cameras. In: ICCV (2021)

71. Zheng, Z.: HybridFusion: real-time performance capture using a single depth sensor and sparse IMUs. In: Ferrari, V., Hebert, M., Sminchisescu, C., Weiss, Y. (eds.) ECCV 2018. LNCS, vol. 11213, pp. 389–406. Springer, Cham (2018). https://doi.org/10.1007/978-3-030-01240-3_24

72. Zheng, Z., Yu, T., Liu, Y., Dai, Q.: PaMIR: parametric model-conditioned implicit representation for image-based human reconstruction. IEEE TPAMI **44**(6), 3170–3184 (2021)

73. Zhu, H., Zuo, X., Wang, S., Cao, X., Yang, R.: Detailed human shape estimation from a single image by hierarchical mesh deformation. In: CVPR, pp. 4491–4500 (2019)

74. Žbontar, J., LeCun, Y.: Computing the stereo matching cost with a convolutional neural network. In: CVPR, pp. 1592–1599 (2015)

Space-Partitioning RANSAC

Daniel Barath[1]([⊠]) and Gábor Valasek[2]

[1] Computer Vision and Geometry Group, ETH Zürich, Zürich, Switzerland
danielbela.barath@inf.ethz.ch
[2] Eötvös Loránd University, Budapest, Hungary
valasek@inf.elte.hu

Abstract. A new algorithm is proposed to accelerate the RANSAC model quality calculations. The method is based on partitioning the joint correspondence space, e.g., 2D-2D point correspondences, into a pair of regular grids. The grid cells are mapped by minimal sample models, estimated within RANSAC, to reject correspondences that are inconsistent with the model parameters early. The proposed technique is general. It works with arbitrary transformations even if a point is mapped to a point set, e.g., as a fundamental matrix maps to epipolar lines. The method is tested on thousands of image pairs from publicly available datasets on fundamental and essential matrix, homography and radially distorted homography estimation. On average, the proposed space partitioning algorithm reduces the RANSAC run-time by 41% with provably no deterioration in the accuracy. When combined with SPRT, the run-time drops to its 30%. It can be straightforwardly plugged into any state-of-the-art RANSAC framework. The code is available at https://github.com/danini/graph-cut-ransac.

Keywords: RANSAC · Preemptive verification · Space partitioning

1 Introduction

Robust model estimation is a fundamental problem in computer vision, allowing the estimation of accurate geometric models, *e.g.* relative camera pose, from noisy input data. The RANdom SAmple Consensus (RANSAC) algorithm, proposed by Fischler and Bolles [19], has become one of the most prominent robust estimators with a number of real-world applications. For instance, it is used for building large-scale 3D reconstructions by running in state-of-the-art structure-from-motion [41,42] (SfM) or simultaneous localization and mapping [10,33] (SLAM) algorithms. It is used for pose-graph initialization in global SfMs [7], for wide baseline image matching [31,32,37], multi-model fitting [3,23,35,56], and image mosaicing [17,21].

While being one of the most successful robust estimators in vision, the RANSAC algorithm iterates three conceptually simple steps. First, it randomly selects a minimal sample of data points, *e.g.*, five 2D-2D point correspondences. Second, it estimates the model parameters, *e.g.*, essential matrix, from the minimal sample. Third, it measures the model quality as the cardinality of its support, *i.e.*, the number of points closer than

Supplementary Information The online version contains supplementary material available at https://doi.org/10.1007/978-3-031-19824-3_42.

(a) Homography Verification   (b) Epipolar Geometry Verification   (c) Radial Homography Verification

Fig. 1. Examples of the proposed space partitioning-based model quality calculation. For a cell (red rectangle) in the top image, only those correspondences are checked where the point is in the rectangle and its corresponding pair falls inside a green rectangle in the bottom image. (Color figure online)

a manually set inlier-outlier threshold. Even though several improvements have been proposed throughout the years, the basic structure of the algorithm remained the same. In this paper, we focus on speeding up the model quality calculation via partitioning the correspondences into pairs of n-dimensional cells, and we select the potential inliers extremely efficiently before computing the quality of each candidate model.

Many recent variants of RANSAC focus on improving the accuracy by locally optimizing each so-far-the-best model [2,4,5,16,28]. This local optimization can be, *e.g.*, an iteratively re-weighted least-squares procedure [4,5], or an inner RANSAC [16,28] that exploits additional global information, *e.g.*, spatial structures in the data [2]. Some algorithms aim at achieving higher accuracy by learning [6] or better modelling [4,5,46,47] the noise in the input data. Also, several methods have been proposed in the recent years including deep learning in the RANSAC procedure as an inlier probability predictor [8,39,43,44,52,54,55] that helps filtering outliers. As it is shown in [25], such methods are essential to have state-of-the-art accuracy on real world data.

There have also been a lot of papers published aiming to accelerate the robust estimation procedure. Most commonly, researchers focus on improving the sampling process to increase the probability of finding a good sample early and, thus, a model that triggers the termination criterion. The NAPSAC [45] sampler assumes that inliers are spatially coherent. The first point in the sample is selected randomly. The others are from a hyper-sphere centered on the first location-defining one. The GroupSAC algorithm [34] is built on the assumption that the inliers of a model have "similar" properties and, therefore, can be separated into groups prior to the estimation. The PROSAC [14] algorithm exploits a predicted inlier probability rank of each point. It starts the sampling from the most promising ones and then progressively increases the sampling pool.

Progressive NAPSAC [4] combines the advantages of local and global sampling by drawing samples from a gradually growing hyper-sphere. Recently, papers also focus on rejecting likely ill-conditioned or degenerate minimal samples early [6, 12] to avoid estimating the model parameter unnecessarily.

Another way of making the procedure more efficient is to avoid unnecessary calculations when computing the quality of a candidate model. In most robust estimators, the quality calculation is done for every estimated model by computing *all* point-to-model residuals. This procedure is generally of $\mathcal{O}(NK)$ complexity, where N is the number of input data points and K is the number of models generated inside RANSAC. In the case of having thousands of input data points or a low inlier ratio, the quality calculation dominates the run-time of the robust estimation. To tackle this issue, preemptive model verification strategies have been proposed to recognize incorrect models early during the model quality calculation. The $T_{D,D}$ test [13] runs the model verification on $D \in \mathbb{N}^+$ points selected at random (where $D \ll N$). The rest of the data points are checked only if the evaluated D points are all inliers. The method was extended by the bail-out test [11] that calculates the inlier ratio on a subset of the data points. If the ratio on the subset is significantly lower than the so-far-the-best one, the probability of the current model being better than the previous best is small and thus, the model is rejected early. In [15, 30], Wald's Sequential Probability Ratio Test (SPRT) [50] is used to develop an optimal model verification method. The SPRT algorithm solves a constrained optimization problem, where the user supplies acceptable probabilities for errors in rejecting a good model and accepting a bad one. The resulting optimal test is a trade-off between the time spent before a decision and the errors committed.

These methods, however, do not exploit that in computer vision the estimated model is usually an $\mathbb{R}^n \rightarrow \mathbb{R}^m$ mapping defined on geometrically interpretable data points, such as 2D-2D point correspondences. This property allows us to partition the input points by bounding structures, *e.g.* n-dimensional axis-aligned boxes (AABB), and to define the sought model as a mapping between the bounded domains. This is an extremely efficient way of selecting candidate inliers without calculating the point-to-model residuals of the rejected points. The benefit is two-fold: first, significantly fewer points are needed to be tested when calculating the model quality. Second, it allows an early model rejection if the number of selected candidate inliers is lower than that of the so-far-the-best model. Moreover, the proposed algorithm is *general*. It works for all kinds of models used in computer vision, *e.g.*, rigid motion, homography, epipolar geometry. It can be straightforwardly included in state-of-the-art frameworks, *e.g.* VSAC [24], and be combined with its "bells and whistles", *e.g.*, the SPRT test [15, 30].

2   Background and Problem Formulation

Recent robust model fitting algorithms [2, 4, 5, 9, 24, 27, 38] spend a considerable amount of time calculating the point-to-model residuals when selecting the inliers of each verified model. The objective of this paper is to speed up the quality metric calculation by conservatively filtering out correspondences that are guaranteed to be outliers.

For simplicity, we explain the idea through a simple example before formalizing it in a general way. Assume that we are given a homography, estimated from four point correspondences between two images, and the objective is to calculate the support of

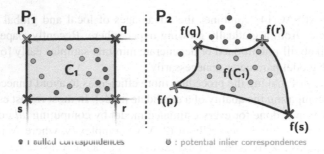

Fig. 2. Cell C_1 in image plane P_1 and its projection $f(C_1)$ by model f to P_2. A correspondence (p, q) with q in P_2 falling outside $f(C_1)$ is rejected (red dots). The potential inliers (green dots) of f are the ones where p falls inside C_1 and q in its image $f(C_1)$. (Color figure online)

the model, *i.e.*, the number of inliers. As a preliminary step, we partition the points in each image to a regular grid, *i.e.*, we have two grids in total. To determine the number of inliers, we process each cell of the first grid. Each cell stores a set of (p, q) correspondences between the two images. We keep all (p, q) pairs for which q is inside the projected image of the cell under the homography. More precisely, only those (p, q) correspondences are kept as candidate inliers, where q is in a cell in the second image which overlaps with the projection (by the homography) of the cell in which p falls. See Figs. 1, 2 for examples.

Our formal description incorporates classes of models that map sets of points to points, so that we may address problem such as epipolar geometry estimation, where epipolar lines are mapped to points [22]. This comes at the expense of notational complexity but it also demonstrates the generality of our method.

General Formulation. Let $\mathcal{S} = \{(p_i, q_i) \in \mathbb{R}^n \times \mathbb{R}^m \mid i = 1, .., N\}$ be a set of correspondences. Points from the domain, or first image, are denoted by $p_i \in \mathbb{R}^n$ and points in the range, *i.e.* from the second image, are written as $q_i \in \mathbb{R}^m$. Set $\mathcal{S}$ may consist of 2D-2D point pairs ($n = m = 2$) found in two images and then used for estimating a homography or the epipolar geometry [22], 2D-3D correspondences ($n = 2, m = 3$) used to solve the perspective-n-point problem [53], or 3D-3D ones ($n = m = 3$) for point cloud registration [36]. Let us assume that these correspondences stem from a $g : \mathbb{R}^n \rightarrow \mathcal{P}(\mathbb{R}^m)$ ground truth mapping, where $\mathcal{P}(\mathbb{R}^m)$ denotes the power set of $\mathbb{R}^m$, *i.e.*, the set of all possible subsets of $\mathbb{R}^m$. Usually, the range sets consist of a single point or posses a simple structure. For example, they form lines in the second image, such as in the case of estimating epipolar geometry where a point is mapped to an epipolar line [22]. Due to various sources of error, *e.g.* measurement and quantization, only $q_i \approx g(p_i)$ holds.

Our objective is to find an $f : \mathbb{R}^n \rightarrow \mathcal{P}(\mathbb{R}^m)$ *model mapping* from the (p_i, q_i) correspondences that best approximates g in the sense that it produces a maximal inlier set for a given $\epsilon > 0$ inlier threshold. That is, we seek the largest cardinality of the set

$$\mathcal{I}_f = \{(p_i, q_i) \in \mathcal{S} \mid \exists q \in f(p_i) : |q - q_i| < \epsilon\}, \tag{1}$$

where norm $|\cdot| : \mathbb{R}^m \rightarrow \mathbb{R}$ is some distance function defined on the points, *e.g.*, reprojection error for homographies. This is the robust model fitting problem. Note that

---

Algorithm 1. Inlier prefiltering with conservative rejection

1: **Input:** model $f : \mathbb{R}^n \to \mathcal{P}(\mathbb{R}^m)$; inlier threshold ϵ; $\mathcal{C}_1, \mathcal{C}_2$ partitionings in images P_1, P_2.
2: **Output:** potential inliers $\mathcal{I}$
3: $\mathcal{I} \leftarrow \varnothing$
4: **for** $\forall C_1 \in \mathcal{C}_1$ **do**   ▷ Iterate through the 2D cells in P_1. Section 3.1.
5: $\quad B \leftarrow \text{Bound}(f(C_1), \epsilon)$ ▷ Bounding structure of $f(C_1)$ in P_2. Section 3.2.
6: $\quad$ **for** $\forall C_2 \in \mathcal{C}_2$ **do**
7: $\quad\quad$ **if** $C_2 \cap B \neq \varnothing$ **then**   ▷ Cells that intersect with B in P_2.
8: $\quad\quad\quad$ **for** $\forall (p_i, q_i) \in (C_1, C_2)$ **do** ▷ Correspondences falling inside cells (C_1, C_2).
9: $\quad\quad\quad\quad \mathcal{I} \leftarrow \mathcal{I} \cup \{(p_i, q_i)\}$

---

while our model quality function maximizes the inlier number, it is straightforward to use our proposed method with state-of-the-art functionals as well, such as the truncated quadratic loss of MSAC [47] or that of MAGSAC [5] and MAGSAC++ [4] marginalizing over a range of noise scale.

3   Correspondence Culling

Let $\mathcal{P}_1 \subset \mathbb{R}^n$ denote the domain of the $f : \mathbb{R}^n \to \mathcal{P}(\mathbb{R}^m)$ model mappings and $\mathcal{P}_2 \subset \mathbb{R}^m$ the range. Our proposed method partitions the correspondences based on a spatial subdivision of $\mathcal{P}_1$ into cells, for example into a regular grid. We show that the image of such regions may be conservatively bounded for a wide range of model mappings in the sense that it is guaranteed that no point of the cell may map outside of this bound. A (p_i, q_i) correspondence is culled if $q_i \in \mathcal{P}_2$ is outside of the bounded image of the cell containing $p_i \in \mathcal{P}_1$. The resulting set of nD-mD point correspondences is further processed by computing the exact inlier count or model score.

Algorithm 1 summarizes our approach. For the sake of simplicity, we will describe each step assuming that we are given 2D-2D point correspondences. Nevertheless, the algorithm is general and, thus, also works with other data types. In Step 4, we iterate through the cells in $\mathcal{C}_1$, *i.e.*, the partitioning in domain $\mathcal{P}_1$ (*i.e.*, the first image). Next, we calculate the bounding structure $B(f(C_1), \epsilon)$ in domain $\mathcal{P}_2$ (*i.e.*, the second image) of the current cell C_1. In Steps 6 and 7, we iterate through all cells in $\mathcal{C}_2$ and select those which intersect with $B(f(C_1), \epsilon)$. Assuming that $\mathcal{C}_2$ consists of axis-aligned boxes (*e.g.*, it is a uniform grid or a quad-tree) and $B(f(C_1), \epsilon)$ is an axis-align bounding box, this step simply calculates the intersection of two axis-aligned rectangles that has negligible time demand. In Step 8, we iterate through all (p_i, q_i) correspondences where p_i falls inside C_1 and q_i is in C_2. Note that this step does not require checking all correspondences. Point correspondence (p_i, q_i) can be considered as a 4D point s_i in the concatenated space $\mathbb{R}^{n+m}$, where $n = m = 2$. Cell correspondence (C_1, C_2) is basically a 4D box C_{12} and, thus, the containment test degrades to checking if s_i falls inside C_{12}. When using hash maps and suitable hashing functions this step has $\mathcal{O}(1)$ complexity.

3.1 Correspondence Partitioning

Let us partition $\mathcal{P}_1$ into a disjoint set of $C_j \in \mathcal{C}$ cells ($j \in \mathbb{N}_{>0}$) and store the correspondences based on these, *i.e.* let $\mathcal{S}_j = \{(p_i, q_i) \in \mathcal{S} \mid p_i \in C_j\}$. Set $\mathcal{S}_j$ consists of the correspondences where the first point falls inside cell C_j in $\mathcal{P}_1$. In our particular case, we use a regular grid of equally sized axis-aligned rectangular cells for the subdivision. Partitioning is a pre-processing step with $\mathcal{O}(N)$ complexity and it only needs to be computed once, for example, upon reading the point correspondences. Decomposing $\mathcal{S}$ into the $\mathcal{S}_j$ partitions is not strictly necessary, however, it is an important component of efficient culling.

Note that the proposed method can be also used with more advanced space partitioning structures, such as quad-trees. We, however, empirically found that the required computational overhead is too large for the typical computer vision problems consisting of, at most, a few thousands of data points. This overhead stems from the tree construction and the increased number of cells to be projected by the proposed algorithm.

3.2 Culling by Images of Cells

Suppose that we are given a model $f : \mathcal{P}_1 \to \mathcal{P}_2$ estimated, for example, from a minimal sample. The image of a $C_j \subset \mathcal{P}_1$ cell depends on the current model f and cannot be pre-computed. Consequently, we have to devise efficient means to compute or estimate this image, as it is calculated at every RANSAC iteration.

Depending on the algebraic properties of the model mapping, there are two cases to consider. If f is invertible, we cull $(p_i, q_i), p_i \in C_j$ if f^{-1} does not map q_i into C_j, that is, if $f^{-1}(q_i) \notin C_j$. If f is not invertible, we bound the image of the C_j cell under f with some $B \subset \mathcal{P}_2$ and reject (p_i, q_i) if $q_i \notin B$ holds. This is further decomposed into two cases: B may be either an approximate or a conservative bound.

Invertible Case. Let us define the image of cell C_j as the image of all points in C_j, *i.e.*

$$f(C_j) = \{y \in \mathbb{R}^m \mid \exists x \in C_j : y \in f(x)\}. \tag{2}$$

Note that x and y denote arbitrary points in $\mathbb{R}^n$ and $\mathbb{R}^m$, respectively, and not necessarily the input correspondences.

Let us assume that there exists an f^{-1} inverse of the model map. The $f^{-1}(q_i) \in C_j$ containment is trivially resolved if we have a regular grid in $\mathcal{P}_1$. In the general case, let us assume that C_j is written as the intersection of a finite number of

$$Q_{kj} = \{x \in \mathcal{P}_1 \mid q_{kj}(x) \le 0\} \tag{3}$$

volumes, *i.e.* $C_j = \cap_k Q_{kj}$, where $q_{kj} : \mathcal{P}_1 \to \mathbb{R}$ is the implicit representation of the j-th boundary volume. This intersection contains all points inside and on the boundary of C_j. For example, a 2D rectangular cell may be written as the intersection of four half-planes of the form $a_k x + b_k y + c_k \le 0, k \in \{1, 2, 3, 4\}$. Recalling that the intersection of implicitly defined volumes may be written as a maximum operation [40], a $(x, y) \in \mathcal{S}_j$ correspondence is culled, if and only if $\max\{q_{kj}(f^{-1}(y))\}_k > 0$. Thus, the containment test in the transformed space $\mathcal{P}_2$ is reduced to a test in $\mathcal{P}_1$.

Although closed-form inversion is a strict restriction, all non-singular projective transformations possess this property. While no speed-up is achieved by transforming all points inside a cell in this way, the definitions will later be important to efficiently cull against AABBs of the cell boundaries.

General Case. If no closed-form inverse is available for f, we may bound the image of cell C_j by using polynomial approximations of the transformed boundaries. We propose to use Lagrange interpolation at Chebyshev nodes to obtain these approximations. Once these polynomial approximations are obtained, we convert them to Bernstein basis and use the resulting Bézier control points to form an AABB bound of the cell image. This bounding characteristic follows from the fact that Bézier curves possess the convex hull property [18], that is, the entire image of the cell under the approximations should lie within the convex hull of the control points, and in turn, within their AABB.

In terms of specifics to achieve the above, let us assume that the boundaries of the transformed cell, $f(C_j)$, are the images of the cell boundaries in C_j as $f(\{x \in \mathcal{P}_1 \mid q_{kj}(x) = 0\})$. This merely simplifies the identification of the boundary curves of $f(C_j)$. This is straightforward for models that map points to points as the polynomial approximations are traditional two or three dimensional Bézier curves. Models that map points to sets of points, *e.g.* epipolar geometry, can be embedded into this framework by assuming that there is a simple set of basis functions in which the image sets may be represented. For example, let us assume that the image sets are one parameter families and there exists a function basis that spans all sets. Formally, this means that, for all $x \in \mathcal{P}_1$, we assume the existence of a $p_x : \mathbb{R} \to \mathcal{P}_2$ parametric mapping such that

$$f(x) = \{y \in \mathcal{P}_2 \mid \exists t \in \mathbb{R} : y = p_x(t)\} . \tag{4}$$

Let $\{e_i(t) : \mathbb{R} \to \mathbb{R}\}_{i=1}^k$ denote the basis that spans the images, *i.e.*, $\forall x \in \mathcal{P}_1 : \forall i \in \{1, \ldots, k\} : \exists a_{x,i} \in \mathcal{P}_2$:

$$p_x(t) = \sum_{i=1}^k a_{x,i} e_i(t) . \tag{5}$$

For example, lines in $\mathcal{P}_2$ may be represented in the $\{1, t\}$ basis as $p_x(t) = p_{x,0} + t v_x$. The polynomial approximation of the boundary is reduced to the construction of a higher dimensional Bézier curve that maps from $\mathbb{R}$ to $\mathbb{R}^{mk}$, *i.e.* the Bézier curve is used to approximate the $a_{x,i}$ coefficients. As shown in the example of epipolar geometry estimation, this can be made simpler for a particular problem.

Conservative Bounds. The polynomial approximations shown above can be made conservative by applying the Lagrange interpolation error term to them.

If an arbitrary boundary curve of cell C_j is parametrized over an interval $[a, b]$ by some $q_{kj} : [a, b] \to \mathcal{P}_1$ ($k \in \{1, 2, 3, 4\}$) mapping, then interpolating $f \circ q$ at k Chebyshev nodes $f(q_{kj}(x_l))$, where

$$x_l = \frac{a+b}{2} + \frac{b-a}{2} \cos \frac{2l-1}{2k} \pi, l = 1, \ldots, k \tag{6}$$

yields a polynomial that is within

$$\frac{1}{2^{k-1} k!} \left(\frac{b-a}{2} \right)^k \cdot \max_{\xi \in [a,b]} \|(f \circ q)^{(k+1)}(\xi)\|_\infty \tag{7}$$

Algorithm 2. Bound($f(C_j), \epsilon$) with AABB

    Input: current candidate mapping $f : \mathbb{R}^2 \to \mathcal{P}(\mathbb{R}^2)$;
    approximation degree k; C_j cell; $\epsilon > 0$

1: $x_{min,j}, y_{min,j} \leftarrow +\infty$
2: $x_{max,j}, y_{max,j} \leftarrow -\infty$
3: **for** $\forall e$ edge of C_j **do**
4:     $a, b \leftarrow$ the endpoints of edge e
5:     $\{x_l \leftarrow a + t_l(b - a)\}_{l=1}^{k}$; t_l are Chebyshev nodes
6:     $c(t) \leftarrow$ polynomial interpolating $\{f(x_l)\}_{l=1}^{k}$
7:     $b_0, \ldots, b_{k+1} \leftarrow$ Bézier control points of $c(t)$
8:     $x_{min,j} \leftarrow \min\left\{x_{min,j}, \min_{i=0}^{k+1}\{[1,0] \cdot b_i\}\right\}$
9:     $y_{min,j} \leftarrow \min\left\{y_{min,j}, \min_{i=0}^{k+1}\{[0,1] \cdot b_i\}\right\}$
10:    $x_{max,j} \leftarrow \max\left\{x_{min,j}, \max_{i=0}^{k+1}\{[1,0] \cdot b_i\}\right\}$
11:    $y_{max,j} \leftarrow \max\left\{y_{min,j}, \max_{i=0}^{k+1}\{[0,1] \cdot b_i\}\right\}$
12: $M \leftarrow$ bound on $\|f^{(k+1)}(a + t(b - a))\|_\infty, t \in [0,1]$
13: $C \leftarrow \max_x \Pi_{j=0}^{k}|x - t_j| = \frac{1}{2^{2k-1}k!}$
14: $\delta \leftarrow \epsilon + \|b - a\|_\infty \cdot M + C$
15: **return** $\left(\begin{bmatrix} x_{min,j} - \delta \\ y_{min,j} - \delta \end{bmatrix}, \begin{bmatrix} x_{max,j} + \delta \\ y_{max,j} + \delta \end{bmatrix}\right)$

---

of a $(k + 1)$ times continuously differentiable $f \circ q$ mapping [48]. Thus, offsetting the AABB of the Bézier control points by this value ensures that no points in C_j may map outside the AABB bounding the image $f(C_j)$ of cell C_j. Moreover, to account for the inlier-outlier threshold of the robust estimation procedure set, the AABB should additionally be offsetted by the threshold.

The simplest case is when the cells are axis-aligned rectangles and the q_{kj} boundaries are linear interpolations between the vertices of the edges. Algorithm 2 summarizes the construction of conservative bounds to the images in such a configuration. This has to be run once for each cell. For each edge of the cell, it requires k evaluations of f. Steps 6 and 7 can be carried out simultaneously by a multiplication of a $(k-1) \times (k+1)$ matrix with a $(k + 1) \times 2$ matrix. Step 12 depends on the candidate mapping family. In the case when no closed-form solutions are available for the bound, one has to estimate it by numerical means. The bound on the image can be made tighter by using the second grid on $\mathcal{P}_2$ and select the cells that intersect the convex hull of the control points.

Note that when using regular grids, the proposed algorithm can be significantly sped up by projecting the boundaries shared by multiple cells only once.

3.3 Early Model Rejection

The proposed approach provides all cell correspondences that might contain inliers of the currently estimated model. Besides being extremely useful for the verification, it also helps in rejecting models early without calculating their quality. The total number of data points stored in the selected cells is basically an upper bound on the inlier number. In the case this bound does not exceed the inlier number of the previous so-far-the-best model, the current model can be immediately rejected as it will not have more inliers than the best model so far. Therefore, a model θ is rejected if $\epsilon_r|\mathcal{I}^*| > |\mathcal{I}_\theta|$, where $\mathcal{I}^*$ and $\mathcal{I}_\theta$ are, respectively, the inlier sets of the so-far-the-best and the currently tested models. Parameter $\epsilon_r = 1$ provably leads to no accuracy change. However, in practice, ϵ_r can be set marginally higher as we will show in the experiments.

Note that this approach works for all quality functions where the model quality is calculated from points closer than a manually set threshold, *e.g.*, as in RANSAC, MSAC or even in MAGSAC++ which uses a maximum threshold.

4 Model Estimation Problems

We show how the described general algorithm can be used in computer vision tasks.

4.1 Homography Estimation

Given homography $\mathbf{H} \in \mathbb{R}^{3 \times 3}$, the implied relationship of the points in the two images is written as $\alpha \mathbf{H} x_1 = x_2$, where α is a scaling that is inverse proportional to the homogeneous coordinate. The implied mapping is as

$$f_{\text{hom}}(x) = \begin{bmatrix} f_u(x) \\ f_v(x) \end{bmatrix} = \begin{bmatrix} h_1^\mathsf{T} x / h_3^\mathsf{T} x \\ h_2^\mathsf{T} x / h_3^\mathsf{T} x \end{bmatrix},$$

where $h_1, h_2, h_3 \in \mathbb{R}^3$ are the rows of $\mathbf{H}$, and $f_u(x)$, $f_v(x)$ are coordinate functions. Since $\mathbf{H}$ maps lines to lines and we use a regular grid, the culling algorithm can be simplified to using the AABB of the cell corners projected by f_{hom}. This is a degree-one polynomial approximation that is also exact.

4.2 Epipolar Geometry Estimation

Given fundamental matrix $\mathbf{F}$, the implied relationship of the points in the two images is written as $x_2^\mathsf{T} \mathbf{F} x_1 = 0$, meaning that point x_2 in the second image must fall on the corresponding epipolar line $l_2 = \begin{bmatrix} a_2 & b_2 & c_2 \end{bmatrix}^\mathsf{T} = \mathbf{F} x_1$. To bound the problem, we can assume that our model maps to the angle of the epipolar line as follows:

$$f_{\text{epi}}(x) = \tan^{-1} \frac{b_2(x)}{a_2(x)}, \quad f_{\text{epi}}^{-1}(x) = \tan^{-1} \frac{b_1(x)}{a_1(x)},$$

where $l_i(x) = \begin{bmatrix} a_i(x) & b_i(x) & c_i(x) \end{bmatrix}$ is the epipolar line implied by x in the ith image. Given cell C_j containing the epipolar angles, it can be straightforwardly seen that

$$f_{\text{epi}}(C_j) : [\min\{\alpha \in C_j\}, \max\{\alpha \in C_j\}] \to [\min\{\alpha \in f_{\text{epi}}(C_j)\}, \max\{\alpha \in f_{\text{epi}}(C_j)\}].$$

Due to the convexity of the problem and the used regular grid, it can be decomposed into two sub-problems. First, the min and max operations are performed only on the intersections of the boundaries, *i.e.*, the cell corners. Therefore, a cell is not culled if at least one epipolar angle implied by its corners fall inside interval $[\min\{\alpha \in f_{\text{epi}}(C_j)\}, \max\{\alpha \in f_{\text{epi}}(C_j)\}]$. Second, a cell is not culled if one of its boundary lines intersects with the epipolar lines implied by angles $\min\{\alpha \in f_{\text{epi}}(C_j)\}$ and $\max\{\alpha \in f_{\text{epi}}(C_j)\}$. This is a more efficient formulation of the problem than considering epipolar lines as point sets.

4.3 Radial Homography Estimation

We use the one-parameter division model [20], for modeling radial distortion, is of form $g(x, \lambda) = [u, v, 1 + \lambda(x^2 + y^2)]^T$, where $x = [u, v]^T$ is an image point. Given homography $\mathbf{H} = [h_1, h_2, h_3]^T$ with rows $h_1, h_2, h_3 \in \mathbb{R}^3$, the points in the images are related as $\lambda_2 g(x_2, \lambda_2) = \mathbf{H}g(x_1, \lambda_1)$, where x_i and λ_i are, respectively, the point and the distortion parameter in the ith image, $i \in [1, 2]$. This implies the following mapping function $f_{\text{rad}}(x) = [f_u(x), f_v(x)]^T$, where $f_u, f_v : \mathbb{R} \to \mathbb{R}$ are coordinate functions as follows:

$$f_u(x) = \frac{h_1^T g(x)}{h_3^T g(x)}, \quad f_v(x) = \frac{h_2^T g(x)}{h_3^T g(x)}. \tag{8}$$

The conservative bounds described in the previous sections are calculated from (8).

5 Experiments

We compare the proposed space partitioning-based model verification technique to the traditional one and to the SPRT [15] algorithm, *i.e.*, the state-of-the-art preemptive model verification technique. Besides comparing to SPRT, we also show that combining the two methods is highly beneficial. For robust estimation, we use LO-RANSAC [16] with PROSAC [14] sampling. We do not report model accuracy since the proposed technique leads to exactly the same number of inliers as verifying all points.

Homography Estimation. For testing the methods on homography estimation, we used the datasets from CVPR tutorial *RANSAC in 2020* [1]. We used the inlier-outlier threshold for RANSAC tuned in [1]. We ran the method only on scene Sacre Coeur consisting of 4950 image pairs. To form tentative correspondences, we detect 8000 SIFT keypoints in both images, and use mutual nearest neighbor check with SNN ratio test [29] as suggested in [49]. The average inlier ratio of the tested dataset is 14% for E/F and 6% for H estimation ranging from 0.9% to 68%.

In Fig. 3c, the relative run-time is plotted as the function of the $\log_{10}$ iteration number that was used as a fixed iteration number for RANSAC. Early rejection was turned off. Each curve shows the results of using a regular grid with different number of cells shown in brackets. The proposed approach leads to a speed-up with all tested cell numbers. In this case, 256 cells (each image is divided into 4×4 cells) lead to the fastest procedure. The run-time drops to its 50% when doing 10 000 iterations.

Figure 5a shows the cumulative distribution functions (CDF) of the run-times (in ms) of SPRT, the proposed and traditional algorithms, and the proposed method with SPRT. For these experiments, we ran RANSAC with its confidence set to 0.99 and max. iteration number to 5000. This max. iteration number is a strict upper bound, preventing RANSAC to run longer. We set early rejection threshold ϵ_r to 1.6. The proposed technique with SPRT runs, on avg. for 31.2 ms, while the avg. time of SPRT is 39.3 ms.

Fundamental Matrix Estimation. Same data is used as before. In Fig. 3a, the relative run-time (*i.e.*, ratio of the time of the proposed and traditional approaches), the number of points verified in total and the processing time (in seconds) are plotted as the function

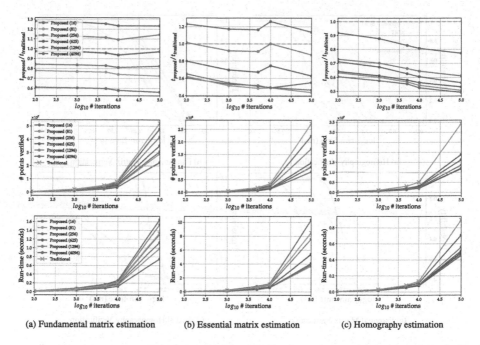

(a) Fundamental matrix estimation   (b) Essential matrix estimation   (c) Homography estimation

Fig. 3. The ratio of times of the proposed and traditional methods (top row; vertical axis), the number of points verified within the RANSAC loop (middle) and the run-time in seconds (bottom) are plotted as a function of $\log_{10}$ iteration number (horizontal). The number of 2D-2D cell pairs used in the proposed algorithm is written in brackets. For example, if the cell number is $2^4 = 16$, both images were divided into 2 pieces along each axis. We tested 2^4, 3^4, 4^4, 5^4, 6^4, and 8^4 subdivisions running the algorithm on a wide range of cell sizes.

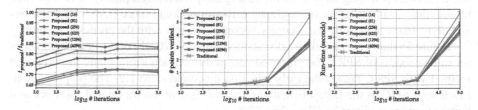

Fig. 4. The ratio of the run-times of the proposed and traditional methods, the number of points verified (middle) and the actual run-time (bottom) are plotted as a function of $\log_{10}$ iteration number for radial homography estimation on 16k image pairs from the Sun360 dataset.

of the $\log_{10}$ iteration number – used as a fixed iteration number for RANSAC. The proposed early rejection was turned off. Each curve shows the results of using a regular grid with different number of cells shown in brackets. For example, $16(= 2^4)$ means that each image axis is divided into 2 parts, thus, having 16 2D-2D cells in total. For **F** estimation, 16 cells lead to the fastest calculation with almost halving the run-time of the traditional approach. The time increases proportionally with the cell number. This is due to the fact that while having more cells provides a tighter approximation of the inlier

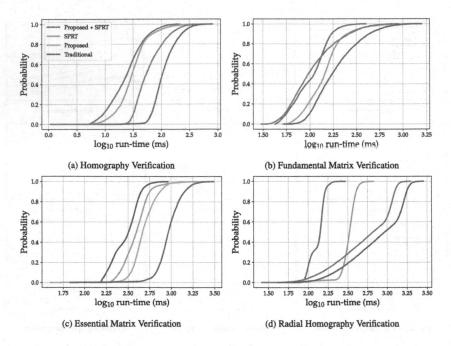

Fig. 5. Cumulative distribution functions (CDF) of the times (ms) of the proposed and traditional algorithms, SPRT [15] and that of SPRT combined with the proposed method on homography, fundamental and essential matrix estimation on 4950 image pairs, and radial homography estimation on 16056 pairs. Being fast is indicated by a curve close to the top-left corner.

set, it requires bounding more cells increasing the problem complexity. It is important to note that, similarly as for homography estimation, doing more RANSAC iterations and, thus, likely increasing the accuracy becomes cheaper with the proposed method.

Figure 5b shows the cumulative distribution functions (CDF) of the processing times (in milliseconds) of SPRT, the proposed and traditional algorithms, and the proposed method with SPRT. We set the early rejection threshold ϵ_r to 1.2. The proposed approach with SPRT is the fastest by halving the run-time of the traditional approach and being, on average, faster by 50 ms than SPRT.

Essential Matrix Estimation. For essential matrix estimation, we used the same data as for fundamental matrices. In Fig. 3b, the relative run-time, the number of verified points and the actual run-time are plotted as the function of the $\log_{10}$ iteration number that was used as a fixed iteration number for RANSAC. Early rejection was turned off. Each curve shows the results of using a regular grid with different number of cells. Similarly as for fundamental matrix estimation, 16 cells lead to the fastest quality calculation. The speed-up is now even bigger: the run-time drops to its 40% when doing 10 000 iterations. This is caused by the fact that the five-point solver returns a maximum of 10 candidate solutions – the same number of RANSAC iterations requires more models to be verified than for fundamental matrix estimation.

Figure 5c shows the cumulative distribution functions (CDF) of the processing times (in milliseconds) of SPRT, the proposed and traditional algorithms, and the proposed method with SPRT. We set early rejection threshold ϵ_r to 1.2. It can be seen that the proposed approach causes a quite significant speed-up. The proposed technique with SPRT runs, on average, for 317.1 ms, while the average time of SPRT is 416.2 ms.

Radial Homography Estimation. To test the proposed techniques on real-world data, we chose the Sun360 [51] panorama dataset. The purpose of the Sun360 database is to provide academic researchers a comprehensive collection of annotated panoramas covering 360×180-degree full view for a large variety of environmental scenes, places and the objects within. To build the core of the dataset, high-resolution panorama images were downloaded and grouped into different place categories. To obtain radially distorted image pairs from each $360°$ panoramic scene, we cut out images simulating a $80°$ FOV camera with a step size of $10°$ as done in [17]. Thus, the rotation around the vertical axis between two consecutive images is always $10°$. Finally, image pairs were formed by pairing the consecutive images in each scene. In total, 16056 image pairs were generated. For estimating radial distortion homographies from minimal samples, we use the solvers from [26]. See Fig. 6 for an example image stitching results using a radial homography on an image pair from the Sun360 dataset.

The effect of the grid density is shown in Fig. 4. The proposed approach accelerates the robust radial homography estimation on the tested wide range of cell numbers. The best run-times are achieved by partitioning the images into 3 pieces along each axis and, thus, having 81 cell correspondences in total.

Figure 5d shows the cumulative distribution functions (CDF) of the processing times (in milliseconds) of SPRT, the proposed and traditional algorithms, and the proposed method with SPRT. We set early rejection threshold ϵ_r to 1.2. The proposed technique with SPRT runs, on average, for 134.7 ms, while the average time of SPRT is 331.3 ms which is almost three times higher than when using the proposed space partitioning.

Timing Breakdown. We show the times spent on each steps of the robust estimation with and without SPRT when using the proposed space partitioning-based verification. The times and, also, the accuracy are shown in Table 1 on homography, essential and fundamental matrix estimation. The same datasets are used as in the previous sections. The cell rejection t_r has negligible time demand compared to the verification t_v. The verification time, when using the proposed approach, is significantly reduced. The AUC@10 scores are the same without SPRT and similar with SPRT.

Early Rejection. In the left plot of Fig. 6, the change in the run-time and the final inlier number is plotted as the function of the early rejection threshold ϵ_r. The results are divided by the result of the $\epsilon_r = 1$ case that provably does not lead to deterioration in the accuracy. The vertical lines are placed so the rejection threshold leads to lower than 1% drop in the inlier number. The green, orange and red lines overlap. For homographies, $\epsilon_r = 1.6$ leads to negligible accuracy drop while further decreasing the run-time by approximately 20%. For all other tested problems, setting ϵ_r to 1.2 is a reasonable choice decreasing the processing time by 22% and 9%, respectively.

Table 1. The avg. (over all image pairs) time spent on cell rejection (t_r), model verification using the kept cells (t_v), in the traditional verification (t_v^{trad}) in ms; and the AUC@10 score of the max. of the rotation and translation errors, decomposed from homographies (**H**) fundamental (**F**) and essential matrices (**E**), when using the proposed and traditional approaches.

Problem	SPRT	t_r	t_v	t_v^{trad}	AUC@10	AUC@10^{trad}
H	No	0.6	40.0	88.8	0.54	0.54
	Yes	0.4	3.8	6.8	0.53	0.53
F	No	0.9	50.3	113.7	0.39	0.39
	Yes	1.1	22.5	53.2	0.38	0.37
E	No	5.4	251.2	537.6	0.65	0.65
	Yes	4.8	29.4	79.7	0.63	0.61

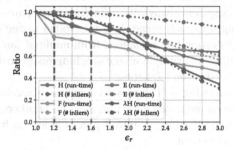

Fig. 6. (Left) Cumulative distribution functions (CDF) of the times (in ms) of the proposed and traditional techniques on homography (H), fundamental (F) and essential matrix (E) estimation on 4950 image pairs, and radial homography estimation (λH) on 16056 pairs. Being fast is indicated by a curve close to the top-left corner. **(Right)** Radial homography in the Sun360 dataset [51].

6 Conclusion

We propose a new general algorithm for accelerating the RANSAC model quality calculation. The method is based on partitioning the joint correspondence space to a pair of regular grids. Cells of the grids are then projected by each minimal sample model, before calculating its quality, to efficiently reject all correspondences that are inconsistent with the model. Besides speeding up the quality calculation significantly, it also allows us to reject models early if the upper bound of their inlier number does not exceed the inlier number of the so-far-the-best model. We found that dividing the domain, *e.g.* images, into only a few cells is a good trade-off between getting a tight-enough approximation of the inlier set without significantly increasing the problem complexity.

The proposed technique reduces the RANSAC run-time by 41% on average on a wide range of problems and datasets. When it is combined with the SPRT test, it leads to an approximately 3.4 times speed-up compared to the traditional algorithm and, also, reduces the SPRT time to its 66%. It can be straightforwardly inserted into any state-of-the-art robust estimator, *e.g.*, VSAC [24] or MAGSAC++ [4], to accelerate them, provably, without any negative side-effect.

Acknowledgments. This work was supported by the ETH Zurich Postdoctoral Fellowship.

References

1. Barath, D., Chin, T.J., Chum, O., Mishkin, D., Ranftl, R., Matas, J.: RANSAC in 2020 tutorial. In: CVPR (2020). https://github.com/ducha-aiki/ransac-tutorial-2020-data
2. Barath, D., Matas, J.: Graph-cut RANSAC. In: CVPR, pp. 6733–6741 (2018)
3. Barath, D., Matas, J.: Progressive-X: efficient, anytime, multi-model fitting algorithm. In: ICCV, pp. 3780–3788 (2019)
4. Barath, D., Noskova, J., Ivashechkin, M., Matas, J.: MAGSAC++, a fast, reliable and accurate robust estimator. In: CVPR (2020)
5. Barath, D., Noskova, J., Matas, J.: MAGSAC: marginalizing sample consensus. In: CVPR (2019). https://github.com/danini/magsac
6. Barath, D., Cavalli, L., Pollefeys, M.: Learning to find good models in RANSAC. In: Proceedings of the IEEE/CVF Conference on Computer Vision and Pattern Recognition, pp. 15744–15753 (2022)
7. Barath, D., Mishkin, D., Eichhardt, I., Shipachev, I., Matas, J.: Efficient initial pose-graph generation for global SFM. In: Proceedings of the IEEE/CVF Conference on Computer Vision and Pattern Recognition, pp. 14546–14555 (2021)
8. Brachmann, E., Rother, C.: Neural-guided RANSAC: learning where to sample model hypotheses. In: ICCV (2019)
9. Cai, Z., Chin, T.J., Koltun, V.: Consensus maximization tree search revisited. In: ICCV, pp. 1637–1645 (2019)
10. Campos, C., Elvira, R., Rodríguez, J.J.G., Montiel, J.M., Tardós, J.D.: ORB-SLAM3: an accurate open-source library for visual, visual-inertial, and multimap slam. IEEE Trans. Rob. **37**(6), 1874–1890 (2021)
11. Capel, D.P.: An effective bail-out test for RANSAC consensus scoring. In: BMVC (2005)
12. Cavalli, L., Pollefeys, M., Barath, D.: NeFSAC: neurally filtered minimal samples. In: Farinella, T. (ed.) ECCV 2022, LNCS 13692, pp. 351–366 (2022)
13. Chum, O., Matas, J.: Randomized RANSAC with TDD test. In: BMVC, vol. 2, pp. 448–457 (2002)
14. Chum, O., Matas, J.: Matching with PROSAC-progressive sample consensus. In: CVPR. IEEE (2005)
15. Chum, O., Matas, J.: Optimal randomized RANSAC. TPAMI **30**(8), 1472–1482 (2008)
16. Chum, O., Matas, J., Kittler, J.: Locally optimized RANSAC. In: Michaelis, B., Krell, G. (eds.) DAGM 2003. LNCS, vol. 2781, pp. 236–243. Springer, Heidelberg (2003). https://doi.org/10.1007/978-3-540-45243-0_31
17. Ding, Y., Barath, D., Kukelova, Z.: Minimal solutions for panoramic stitching given gravity prior. In: Proceedings of the IEEE/CVF International Conference on Computer Vision, pp. 5579–5588, October 2021
18. Farin, G.: Curves and Surfaces for Computer Aided Geometric Design: A Practical Guide, 3rd edn. Academic Press Professional Inc., San Diego (1993)
19. Fischler, M.A., Bolles, R.C.: Random sample consensus: a paradigm for model fitting with applications to image analysis and automated cartography. Commun. ACM **24**(6), 381–395 (1981)

20. Fitzgibbon, A.W.: Simultaneous linear estimation of multiple view geometry and lens distortion. In: CVPR, vol. 1, p. I. IEEE (2001)
21. Ghosh, D., Kaabouch, N.: A survey on image mosaicking techniques. J. Vis. Commun. Image Represent. **34**, 1–11 (2016)
22. Hartley, R., Zisserman, A.: Multiple View Geometry in Computer Vision. Cambridge University Press, Cambridge (2003)
23. Isack, H., Boykov, Y.: Energy-based geometric multi-model fitting. IJCV **97**(2), 123–147 (2012)
24. Ivashechkin, M., Barath, D., Matas, J.: VSAC: efficient and accurate estimator for H and F (2021)
25. Jin, Y., et al.: Image matching across wide baselines: from paper to practice. IJCV **129**(2), 517–547 (2021)
26. Kukelova, Z., Heller, J., Bujnak, M., Pajdla, T.: Radial distortion homography. In: CVPR, pp. 639–647 (2015)
27. Le, H.M., Chin, T.J., Eriksson, A., Do, T.T., Suter, D.: Deterministic approximate methods for maximum consensus robust fitting. TPAMI **43**(3), 842–857 (2019)
28. Lebeda, K., Matas, J., Chum, O.: Fixing the locally optimized RANSAC. In: BMVC. Citeseer (2012)
29. Lowe, D.G.: Object recognition from local scale-invariant features. In: ICCV. IEEE (1999)
30. Matas, J., Chum, O.: Randomized RANSAC with sequential probability ratio test. In: ICCV, vol. 2, pp. 1727–1732. IEEE (2005)
31. Matas, J., Chum, O., Urban, M., Pajdla, T.: Robust wide-baseline stereo from maximally stable extremal regions. IVC **43**(3), 842–857 (2004)
32. Mishkin, D., Matas, J., Perdoch, M.: MODS: fast and robust method for two-view matching. CVIU **43**(3), 842–857 (2015)
33. Mur-Artal, R., Tardós, J.D.: ORB-SLAM2: an open-source slam system for monocular, stereo, and RGB-D cameras. IEEE Trans. Rob. **33**(5), 1255–1262 (2017)
34. Ni, K., Jin, H., Dellaert, F.: GroupSAC: efficient consensus in the presence of groupings. In: ICCV, pp. 2193–2200. IEEE (2009)
35. Pham, T.T., Chin, T.J., Schindler, K., Suter, D.: Interacting geometric priors for robust multimodel fitting. TIP **23**(10), 4601–4610 (2014)
36. Pomerleau, F., Colas, F., Siegwart, R.: A review of point cloud registration algorithms for mobile robotics. Found. Trends Robot. **4**(1), 1–104 (2015)
37. Pritchett, P., Zisserman, A.: Wide baseline stereo matching. In: ICCV. IEEE (1998)
38. Raguram, R., Chum, O., Pollefeys, M., Matas, J., Frahm, J.M.: USAC: a universal framework for random sample consensus. TPAMI (2013). https://www.cs.unc.edu/~rraguram/usac
39. Ranftl, R., Koltun, V.: Deep fundamental matrix estimation. In: Ferrari, V., Hebert, M., Sminchisescu, C., Weiss, Y. (eds.) ECCV 2018. LNCS, vol. 11205, pp. 292–309. Springer, Cham (2018). https://doi.org/10.1007/978-3-030-01246-5_18
40. Ricci, A.: A constructive geometry for computer graphics. Comput. J. **16**(2), 157–160 (1973). https://doi.org/10.1093/comjnl/16.2.157
41. Schönberger, J.L., Zheng, E., Frahm, J.-M., Pollefeys, M.: Pixelwise view selection for unstructured multi-view stereo. In: Leibe, B., Matas, J., Sebe, N., Welling, M. (eds.) ECCV 2016. LNCS, vol. 9907, pp. 501–518. Springer, Cham (2016). https://doi.org/10.1007/978-3-319-46487-9_31
42. Schönberger, J.L., Frahm, J.M.: Structure-from-motion revisited. In: CVPR (2016)
43. Sun, W., Jiang, W., Tagliasacchi, A., Trulls, E., Yi, K.M.: Attentive context normalization for robust permutation-equivariant learning. In: CVPR (2020)
44. Tong, W., Matas, J., Barath, D.: Deep MAGSAC++. arXiv preprint arXiv:2111.14093 (2021)
45. Torr, P.H., Nasuto, S.J., Bishop, J.M.: NAPSAC: high noise, high dimensional robust estimation-it's in the bag (2002)

46. Torr, P.H.S.: Bayesian model estimation and selection for epipolar geometry and generic manifold fitting. IJCV **50**(1), 35–61 (2002)
47. Torr, P.H.S., Zisserman, A.: MLESAC: a new robust estimator with application to estimating image geometry. CVIU **78**(1), 138–156 (2000)
48. Trefethen, L.N.: Approximation Theory and Approximation Practice. SIAM, Philadelphia (2012)
49. Trulls, E., Jun, Y., Yi, K., Mishkin, D., Matas, J., Fua, P.: Image matching challenge. In: CVPR (2020). https://cmp.felk.cvut.cz/cvpr2020-ransac-tutorial/
50. Wald, A.: Sequential Analysis. Courier Corporation, North Chelmsford (2004)
51. Xiao, J., Ehinger, K.A., Oliva, A., Torralba, A.: Recognizing scene viewpoint using panoramic place representation. In: CVPR (2012). https://3dvision.princeton.edu/projects/2012/SUN360
52. Yi, K.M., Trulls, E., Ono, Y., Lepetit, V., Salzmann, M., Fua, P.: Learning to find good correspondences. In: CVPR (2018)
53. Yuan, J.S.C.: A general photogrammetric method for determining object position and orientation. Trans. Robot. Autom. **5**(2), 129–142 (1989)
54. Zhang, J., et al.: Learning two-view correspondences and geometry using order-aware network. In: ICCV (2019)
55. Zhao, C., Ge, Y., Zhu, F., Zhao, R., Li, H., Salzmann, M.: Progressive correspondence pruning by consensus learning. In: ICCV (2021)
56. Zuliani, M., Kenney, C.S., Manjunath, B.S.: The multiRANSAC algorithm and its application to detect planar homographies. In: ICIP. IEEE (2005)

Author Index

Printed in the United States
by Baker & Taylor Publisher Services

Printed in the United States
by Baker & Taylor Publisher Services